This new study by Igor Nebolsin covers, in remarkable detail, a number of forgotten and overlooked armoured engagements on the Eastern Front during the final year of the war, based firmly on Soviet and German archival records.

After defeating German Group Army Centre in Belorussia (Operation Bagration) in the first days of August 1944 the Red Army rapidly approached East Prussia. Here, near the borders of the Third Reich in the area of Wiłkowyszki heavy tank combats broke out. German Panzer-Grenadier Division *Großdeutschland* engaged the Soviet 33rd Army, reinforced by the 2nd Guards Tank Corps and separate Anti-tank artillery brigades and regiments, in fierce and extensive combat. Based on the archival documents from both sides and other sources Igor Nebolsin provides a meticulous analysis of this battle and challenges myths created by some German authors.

By mid-October 1944 the Soviet 3rd Belorussian Front was ready to invade East Prussia. 2nd Guards Tank Corps was committed to the main axis of attack, and developed an operational breakthrough in the direction of Gumbinnen, soon capturing an important crossing over the Angerapp River at Nemmersdorf. For two days Soviet units were engaged in severe fighting against *Fallschirm-Panzer-Division Hermann Göring*, 5th *Panzer* Division and the *Führer-Begleit-Brigade*. Combat in East Prussia were notable, even by Eastern Front standards, for their severity, mercilessness and heavy losses in personnel and material for both sides.

In January 1945 the Red Army managed to break the strong German defence in East Prussia and swiftly reached the Baltic, cutting off East Prussia from Germany. 5th Guards Tank Army played a decisive role in this breakthrough. At the final stage of this operation the Army contained a desperate attempt of the German 4th Army to escape from East Prussia to Germany in tank engagements at Wormditt and Frauenburg.

This book also covers tank battles near Kielce, Poland in January 1945 where *XXIV Panzer Korps* (16th *Panzer* Division, 17th *Panzer* Division, 20th *Panzer-Grenadier* Division, 424th *Schwere-Panzer-Abteilung*) was engaged in an engagement lasting three days against forces of the Soviet 4th Guards Tank Army.

The day-by-day coverage of events, honest views of the Soviet and German commanders, statistical data from both Russian and German viewpoints, and the 'human element' based on the exciting first-hand reminiscences of Soviet tank officers all make this study an incredibly valuable source of information. The text is fully supported by specially-commissioned color maps and an extensive selection of photographs.

Igor Nebolsin is the author of six documentary monographs and other publications on military history. He was born in the Soviet Union in 1976. He graduated with honors from the Academy of the National Economy under the Government of the Russian Federation in Moscow in 1998 and earned a Masters degree at the University of Warwick (UK) where he successfully completed his dissertation in 2010. The history of the Second World War has been his passion from an early age. His grandfather and father were both Soviet tank forces officers. Igor Nebolsin's research focuses on Eastern front armored battles of 1943-1945. His monographs on the combat history of the Soviet Guards tank armies are strictly based on the analysis of archival documents from both the Russian and German viewpoints, and materials provided by the Russian Second World War Veterans' Councils including the United Council of the Soviet Tank and Mechanized Forces, and Guards Tank Armies' museums. Igor is an active participant of international military forums. He is married and has two sons.

TANK BATTLES IN EAST PRUSSIA AND POLAND, 1944-1945

Igor Nebolsin

Chief Consultant: Iurii Gavrilovich Zavizion,
Lieutenant General of Tank Forces

Edited by I.V. Lebedeva

Translated by Stuart Britton

Helion & Company

Publisher's Note. The reader should bear in mind that much of the text within this book quotes directly, or is taken from, wartime Soviet documentation, and may not accurately reflect correct German terminology, or unit assignations and designations.

Helion & Company Limited
Unit 8 Amherst Business Centre
Budbrooke Road
Warwick
CV34 5WE
England
Tel. 01926 499 619
Email: info@helion.co.uk
Website: www.helion.co.uk
Twitter: @helionbooks
Visit our blog http://blog.helion.co.uk/

Published by Helion & Company 2019. Reprinted in paperback 2021
Designed and typeset by Mach 3 Solutions Ltd (www.mach3solutions.co.uk)
Cover designed by Paul Hewitt, Battlefield Design (www.battlefield-design.co.uk)

Text © Igor Nebol'sin 2019. English edition translated and edited by Stuart Britton, © Helion & Company Limited 2019.
Images © see Bibliography
Maps drawn by George Anderson © Helion & Company 2019

Every reasonable effort has been made to trace copyright holders and to obtain their permission for the use of copyright material. The author and publisher apologize for any errors or omissions in this work, and would be grateful if notified of any corrections that should be incorporated in future reprints or editions of this book.

ISBN 978-1-914059-61-2

British Library Cataloguing-in-Publication Data.
A catalogue record for this book is available from the British Library.

All rights reserved. No part of this publication may be reproduced, stored in a retrieval system, or transmitted, in any form, or by any means, electronic, mechanical, photocopying, recording or otherwise, without the express written consent of Helion & Company Limited.

For details of other military history titles published by Helion & Company Limited contact the above address, or visit our website: http://www.helion.co.uk.

We always welcome receiving book proposals from prospective authors.

Contents

List of Maps		iv
German glossary of terms and abbreviations in Chapter 4's tables		vi
Introduction		vii
1	The Tank Battle in the Wiłkowyszki [Vilkaviškis] Area	9
2	In East Prussia	114
3	The Kielce – Łysów Tank Battle	216
4	Combat operations of the 5th Guards Tank Army in East Prussia (14 January–28 February 1945)	300
Bibliography		507
Index		511

List of Maps

1 Operational map of the German Third Panzer Army as of evening, 3 August 1944. — i
2 Operational map of the German Third Panzer Army as of evening, 9 August 1944. — ii
3 Soviet 2nd Guards Tank Corps position as of 12.00, 6 August 1944. — iii
4 Battle for Wiłkowyszki, 9 August 1944 – Soviet operational map. — iv
5 Soviet map with location of the captured and knocked-out German panzers and SP guns in the area of Wiłkowyszki, August 1944. — v
6 Soviet operational map of the 26th Guards Tank Brigade of the 2nd GTC combat actions as of 19 October 1944, East Prussia. — vi
7 Soviet operational map of the 26th Guards Tank Brigade's combat actions as of 20 October 1944, East Prussia. — vii
8 Soviet operational map of the 25th Guards Tank Brigade's combat actions as of 21 October 1944, East Prussia. — viii
9 Soviet operational map of the 4th Guards Tank Brigade's combat actions as of 22 October 1944, East Prussia. — ix
10 Soviet operational map of the 4th Guards Motorized Rifle Brigade's combat actions as of 22 October 1944, East Prussia. — x
11 Soviet operational map of the 4th Guards Tank Brigade's combat actions as of 23 October 1944, East Prussia. — xi
12 Soviet operational map of the 2nd Guards Tank Corps combat actions as of 20–22 October, Gumbinnen area, East Prussia. — xii
13 Soviet operational map of the 2nd Guards Tank Corps combat actions as of 23–25 October, Tanennberg area, East Prussia. — xiii
14 Soviet operational map of the 10th Guards Tank Corps as of morning of 13 January 1945. — xiv
15 Soviet operational map of the 10th Guards Tank Corps combat actions as of evening of 13 January 1945, Battle for Lisow. — xv
16 Soviet operational map of the 10th Guards Tank Corps combat actions as of 14–15 January 1945. — xvi
17 Soviet operational map of the 4th Tank Army in the area of Kielce, Lisow, 13–15 January 1945. — xvii
18 Combat actions of the Soviet 5th Guards Tank Army in East Prussia, January–February 1945. — xviii
19 Soviet operational map of the 5th Guards Tank Army as of 18–19 January 1945. — xix
20 Soviet operational map of the 5th Guards Tank Army as of 20 January 1945. — xx
21 Soviet operational map of the 5th Guards Tank Army as of 22 January 1945. — xxi
22 Soviet operational map of the 5th Guards Tank Army as of 21 January 1945. — xxii
23 Soviet operational map of the 5th Guards Tank Army as of 23–25 January 1945, Elbing area, East Prussia. — xxiii
24 Soviet operational map of the 5th Guards Tank Army as of 21 January 1945, Tannenberg area, East Prussia. — xxiv

XXX	Infantry Corps
XXIV Pz	Panzer Corps
61	Rifle Division
217	Infantry Division
7 Pz	Panzer Division
A	Army
Art	Artillery
Abt	Battalion
B	Brigade
Bn	Battalion
C	Corps
CC	Cavalry Corps
G	Guard
HSPR	Heavy Self-Propelled Regiment
HTR	Heavy Tank Regiment
JB	Jaeger Brigade
MRB	Motorised Rifle Brigade
Mo	Mortar
Mech	Mechanised
Mcl	Motorcycle
M	Motorised
Pa	Parachute
pln	Platoon
PzGrD	Panzer Grenadier Division
PzD	Panzer Division
RD	Rifle Division
R	Rifle
s	Heavy
S.201	Security
S	Shock
SPR	Self Propelled Gun Regiment
SMG	sub machine gunners
T	Tank
TC	Tank Corps
TB	Tank Brigade
TR	Tank Regiment

German glossary of terms and abbreviations in Chapter 4's tables

Chapter 4 contains tables that include German documents, captured German documents that were converted into Russian, and Russian documents that refer to German formations and units. I decided to standardize the German for the convenience of the reader, so I offer below a list of the German abbreviations and terms used.

Abt. – *Abteilung* – German unit of battalion size, applied to panzers and artillery
AOK – *Armeeoberkommando* – Army headquarters
Artillerie Gesch. – *Artillerie geschützen* (artillery guns)
Arko – *Artilleriekommandeur* – Artillery commander
Armee – Army
Aufklärung (or Aufklär.) – Reconnaissance
Aufklär. Lehr-Abt. – Reconnaissance training battalion
Bat. – *Batterie* (Artillery battery)
Bef. – *Befehl* (Command, as used in *Befehlspanzer*, or command tank)
Fallschirm (or Fsch.) – Parachute
Fest. Pak-Kp. – (*Festung Panzerabwehrkanone Kompanie*), or Fortress Antitank Company.
Gruppe – Group
Höhe-Arko – Senior artillery commander – General Staff officer in charge of coordinating Army-level artillery or an army-level numbered headquarters used to control artillery assets.
Infanterie – Infantry
Jg.Pz. – *Jagdpanzer* (tank destroyer)
Jäger – Light infantry
K – *Kannone* (cannon)
Kampfgruppe (or KG) – Combat group

Kavallerie – Cavalry
Korps – Corps
Kp. – Kompanie (company)
Lage der panzerbrechenden Waffen – Distribution of armor-piercing weapons
Lehr – Training
(mot. Z) – Motorized tow
Pak – *Panzerabwehrkanone* (Anti-tank gun)
PzSp Wg – *Panzerspähwagen* (armored car)
Pionier – Engineer
Pz.Jg. — *Panzerjäger* – Antitank
Radfahr-Jäger – Bicycle mounted light infantry
s – *schwere* (heavy)
Sfl – *Selbstfahrlafette* (Self-propelled carriage, usually referring to a self-propelled gun)
Sicherungs – Security
sPz.Jg – schwere Panzerjäger (Heavy tank hunter)
sPak – Heavy anti-tank guns
sPanzerjäger – Heavy tank hunter
sPanzer – Heavy Tank
Stab – Headquarters
SPW – *Schützenpanzerwagen* (armored personnel carrier), or armored halftrack
StuG – *Sturmgeschütz* (Assault gun)
Sturm – Assault
Verb – *Verband* (formation)
Volksgrenadier – People's grenadier

Introduction

The subject of this book is the little-known – both in Russian and the West – armor battles in the concluding stage of the war: in Lithuania – in the area of Wiłkowiszki (1-11 August 1944), in East Prussia (16-25 October 1944 and 17 January to 28 February 1945), and in Poland (12-18 January 1945).

The first chapter discusses a rather large tank battle around the Lithuanian town of Wiłkowiszki on the approaches to East Prussia, which took place in August 1944 with the participation on the German side of the Wehrmacht's elite Panzergrenadier Division *Grossdeutschland* and other units, and on the Soviet side – formations and units of the 33rd Army, reinforced with separate destroyer antitank artillery brigades and regiments, as well as the 2nd Guards Tank Corps, which had been weakened in the preceding fighting. This operation can be considered as the prelude to the start of the fighting in East Prussia.

In the second chapter, the fighting of the 2nd Guards Tank Corps in the areas of Gumbinnen and Nemmersdorf in the course of the first East Prussian operation is analyzed in some detail. Here the tank corps at first broke through the German strong defenses and seized an important bridge across the Angerapp River, and then in the following two days repulsed the counterattacks by a strong enemy panzer grouping consisting of the Fallschirm. Panzerkorps [Parachute-Panzer Corps] *Hermann Göring*, the 5th Panzer Division, and the Führer Grenadier Brigade.

In the third chapter, the subject of discussion is the meeting battle in the Kielce and Lisow area in January 1945 between major armored forces, when units of Colonel General of Tank Forces D.D. Leliushenko's 4th Tank Army crushed General Walter Nehring's XXIV Panzerkorp, consisting of the 16th and 17th Panzer Divisions, the 20th Panzergrenadier Division, and the *Schwere Panzer Abteilung* [Heavy Panzer Battalion] 424 (previously 501), which was equipped with Tiger tanks.

The final, fourth chapter discusses the combat employment of the 5th Guards Tank Army in the January-February 1945 fighting to destroy the German grouping in East Prussia. This is an outstanding example of breaking through a deeply-echeloned enemy defense, saturated with fortifications and artillery. In the conclusive stage of the operation, the little-known tank battles in the Wormditt – Frauenburg area, which took place in the period between 27 January and 10 February 1945, and which included on the German side units of the 18th Panzergrenadier Division, Kampgruppe von Einem of the 24th Panzer Division, and several infantry divisions, reinforced with StuG [*Sturmgeschütz* (Assault Gun)] Battalions 209 and 904. On the Soviet side were the formations and units of the 5th Guards Tank Army and the 8th Mechanized Corps, reinforced with rifle divisions.

Thus, the book analyzes four army-level operations. In one of them, the German Panzer Division *Grossdeutschland* was on the attacking side, which faced overcoming a powerful antitank defense. In two operations, the Soviet 2nd Guards Tank Corps and 5th Guards Tank Army are the attacking sides, which had to overcome a powerful German antitank defense in East Prussia, before repulsing a strong German counterblow. In the final chapter both sides, German and Soviet, clashed in a major meeting tank battle.

I hope the book will be read with interest both by professional scholars and by lovers of military history.

1

The Tank Battle in the Wiłkowyszki [Vilkaviškis] Area

(1-11 August 1944)

The forces of the 3rd Belorussian Front, which had gone over to the offensive on 23 June 1944, by 1 August 1944 had fought its way forward approximately 620 kilometers and were approaching the border of East Prussia. Here, on the approaches to the Third Reich, they became tied up in heavy fighting. Falling back to the west, the enemy sought to prevent the Soviet forces from entering East Prussia and were hastily throwing up defensive lines. Attaching great significance to the major road hub of Wiłkowyszki [alternatively referred to as Wilkowischken, Volkovyshki, Vilkovyshki, Wiłkowyszki and Wolfsburg in wartime documents], the Germans attempted to create a strongpoint here. On three sides, the town was protected by two, and in separate sectors three lines of full-profile trenches, linked by a dense network of communication trenches. Cement wells, intended to serve as fighting positions, were being built 50-60 meters apart from one another, both 10-15 meters in front of each trench and behind the trenches. However, the Soviet advance was so swift, that the Germans didn't manage to complete the lay-out of the lines of defense.

In certain sectors the enemy had time to throw up barbed wire obstacles in front of the trenches. Intending to construct a continuous perimeter of barbed wire covering the approaches to Wiłkowyszki, the enemy had brought up a large amount of barbed wire to the town. The city was also surrounded on three sides by an antitank ditch, which was half-filled with water.

German work on the defenses showing the cement fighting pits in the process of construction.

Panorama of Wiłkowyszki.

Russian Orthodox church of Wiłkowyszki.

On the basis of a directive from the Commander-in-Chief of the 3rd Belorussian Front General of the Army I.D. Cherniakhovsky, the 2nd Guards "Tatsinskaia" Tank Corps under the command of Major General A.S. Burdeinyi became operationally subordinate to the 33rd Army on 27 July 1944, and at 2200 on 27 July set out to the Poswiecie, Wazatkiemie, Rudupie Nowe, woods north of Nowalki area (all on the western bank of the Neman River). By 0400 on 28 July, the corps reached its staging area for crossing the Neman River. Observing strict discipline and the masking of lights while on the march, the corps' units moved out along their designated routes and by the morning of 28 July had crossed the Neman River and assembled in the Rudupie area with the 25th Guards Tank Brigade, 79th Motorcycle Battalion and 4th Guards Motorized Rifle Brigade. The 4th Guards Tank Brigade, in view of the collapse of the bridge in the Dukiszki area, didn't cross the river and had to wait until 0500 on 28 July, when it began to cross the Neman using a pontoon bridge. By the sunrise on 28 July, only one of its tank battalions had made it across the river. With the fall of żkness on 28 July, the 26th Guards Tank Brigade and 4th Guards Tank Brigade had fully crossed the river and were assembled in their jumping-off area.

Table 1.1: Status of the tanks and self-propelled guns of the 2nd Guards Tank Corps on 27 July 1944

	Operational			Minor repairs	Moderate repairs	Major repairs	Requires evacuation
	T-34	SU-85	SU-76				
4 Guards Tank Brigade	36	-	-	-	4	4	-
25 Guards Tank Brigade	25	-	-	4	7	-	-
26 Guards Tank Brigade	30	-	-	-	12	1	1
79 Motorcycle Battalion	7	-	-	1	1	-	-
1 Guards Signal Battalion	4	-	-	-	1	-	-
1500 S-P Artillery Regiment	-	-	11	-	1	5	-
401 Guards S-P Artillery Regiment	-	17	-	-	1	-	-
Total	102	17	11	5	25/2	5/5	1

Commander of the 2nd Guards Tank Corps Major General of Tank Forces A.S. Burdeinyi
Corps chief of staff Guards Colonel Karavan

By 2400 on 29 July the corps' units had reached the jumping-off area for the offensive: Moczuny, Nowe Rudupie, Stara Huta, Dumiszki. At 0500 on 30 July, the 2nd Guards Tank Corps was introduced into the fighting in the direction of Marijampolė, entering the breakthrough in two columns: the right-hand column (4th Guards Tank Brigade, 401st Self-propelled Artillery Regiment, a battery of the 1695th Anti-aircraft Artillery Regiment, and the 26th Guards Tank Brigade) along the Moczuny, Michalin, Płutyszki, Szymaki, Debowa Buda, Kozłowa Ruda route; the left-hand column (25th Guards Tank Brigade, a battery of the 1695th Anti-Aircraft Artillery Regiment, the 4th Guards Motorized Rifle Brigade, the 1500th Self-propelled Artillery Regiment and the 273rd Mortar Regiment) along the Stara Huta, Jesiotraki, Szara Buda, Gabowa, Vysoka route. The corps with an energetic attack broke through to the Kozlowa Ruda, Pilwycski area, cut the Kaunas – Marijampolė road, and over the day advanced 35-40 kilometers with fighting as the crow flies.

By this, a turning point in the course of the fighting on the approaches to Kaunas has been achieved. The rapid maneuver of the 2nd Guards Tank Corps facilitated the success of the 33rd Army, which advanced 25-30 kilometers over 24 hours. As a result, the threat of encirclement faced the enemy grouping that was defending the Kaunas area, which was completely mopped up of the enemy by the end of 31 July.

General Characteristics of the Terrain

Out in front was a water obstacle – the Neman River. The river was 80 meters wide with a depth of 2-4 meters. The terrain was wooded and cut by creeks and streams. The soil was sandy, which in certain places made the movement of wheeled vehicles difficult. There was an abundant network of village and side roads, narrow, but adequate for all types of transportation. There were no fords across the Neman River. The terrain on our side of the river was visible to the enemy out to a range of 5-10 kilometers. There were concealed approaches to the enemy.

Excerpt from Combat Report No. 039 of the headquarters of the 2nd Guards Tank Corps, 29 July 1944, 1900

The corps' formations and units are in their jumping-off areas in readiness to carry out their assignments: 4th Guards Tank Brigade and the 401st Self-propelled Artillery Regiment together with one battery of the 1695th Anti-aircraft Artillery Regiment – Poswiecie and the woods to the southeast; 26th Guards Tank Brigade and one battery of the 1695th Anti-aircraft Artillery Regiment – eastern fringe of the woods west of Kempiszki; 25th Guards Tank Brigade and one battery of the 1695th Antitank Artillery Regiment – Rudupie; 4th Guards Motorized Rifle Brigade and the 1500th Self-propelled Artillery Regiment with the 273rd Mortar Regiment – Rudupie; 79th Motorcycle Battalion – woods 1 km south of Powsiecie; 28th Separate Guards Mortar Battalion – woods north of Kowalki. Throughout the day the brigades reconnoitered in their directions. At 1900 on 29 July 1944, the brigade's forward detachments are located: 4th Guards Tank Brigade's forward detachment – on the road 1 km north of Moczuny; 25th Guards Tank Brigade's forward detachment – 1 km east of Stara Huta. The corps' reconnaissance unit (79th Motorcycle Battalion) is scouting to the north, west and south.

In their jumping-off areas, the brigades have the following number of tanks and self-propelled guns: 4th Guards Tank Brigade – 37 T-34; 25th Guards Tank Brigade – 28 T-34; 26th Guards Tank Brigade: 29 T-34; 79th Motorcycle Battalion – 8 T-34; 1st Guards Separate Signals Battalion – 5 T-34; 401st Guards Self-propelled Artillery Regiment – 18 SU-85; 1500th Self-propelled Artillery Regiment: 10 SU-76.

Commander of the 2nd Guards Tank Corps
Guards Major General of Tank Forces A.S. BURDEINYI
Corps chief of staff Guards Colonel KARAVAN

The enemy with units of the 6th Panzer Division and the 52nd and 221st Security Divisions and attached units of reinforcement throughout the day of 31 July 1944 were falling back in the western and southwestern directions, covered by rearguard detachments strengthened by tanks, self-propelled guns and artillery. The enemy air force was bombing the combat formations of our forces in groups of 10-15 aircraft. Up to 40 aircraft sorties were noted.

The corps commander Major General of Tank Forces A.S. Burdeinyi decided from the morning of 30 July 1944 to continue pursuing the retreating enemy to the west with a forced march along two directions. By 0100 on 30 July 1944, the corps' units were fully assembled in their jumping-off areas, and from the morning of 30 July went on the attack along two axes: 4th Guards Tank Brigade and 26th Guards Tank Brigade – in the Moczuny, Chlebiszki, Płutyszki, Kupry, Sulima Buda, Sosnowo hamlet direction; 25th Guards Tank Brigade and 4th Guards Motorized Rifle Brigade – in the Stara Huta, Jesiotraki, Gabowo, Sosnowo village direction.

The 4th Guards Tank Brigade with its forward detachment by 0500 on 30 July took Chlebiszki with fighting, while its 3rd Tank Battalion at 0630 on 30 July captured Polwandupe. Developing the offensive and overcoming opposition by enemy tanks and self-propelled artillery, the brigade by 1030 on this day took Szymaki and Kupry, before conducting a reinforced reconnaissance in the northern and northwestern directions and capturing Sulima Buda and the road intersection to the west of there from the march. Here it encountered an enemy column of artillery, vehicles and wagons that was retreating from Kaunas toward Marijampolė. The enemy in panic fled along roads to the east and northeast, abandoning equipment and various loads together with their vehicles and wagons, striving to save as many troops and weapons as possible while covering the retreat with tanks and self-propelled guns.

The 4th Guards Tank Brigade's 2nd Tank Battalion, operating at the forefront of the brigade, reached the main Kaunas – Marijampolė road, where it intercepted the enemy's retreating column, and not allowing the enemy's tank and artillery to deploy into combat formations, with energetic actions attacked the column, destroying the enemy with fire and tracks, and reached the bend in the road in the direction of Kaunas, thereby fulfilling its immediate task. As a result of the battle on the road in the Debowa Buda area, 5 enemy tanks were destroyed and 3 tanks were knocked out; up to 300 vehicles and around 300 wagons were destroyed or captured together with their horses and loads; and up to 300 Nazis were wiped out and 200 prisoners were taken. In the process, the 4th Guards Tank Brigade's 2nd Tank Battalion lost only 2 T-34 tanks, 5 dead and 10 wounded.

The 4th Guards Tank Brigade's 1st Tank Battalion together with a motorized battalion of submachine gunners, operating along a forest road branching off the main Kaunas – Marijampolė road toward Kozłowa Ruda, along with the 3rd Tank Battalion operating along a railroad leading from Bobroliszki to the north by 1500 on 30 July captured Kozłowa Ruda. As a result of the combat for this village the 1st Tank Battalion captured a steam engine and train that was carrying enemy troops; as the Germans spilled out of the train, they were either killed or captured. In addition, the tank battalion captured 100 vehicles loaded with combat gear and ammunition. By 1900 on 30 July, the 4th Guards Tank Brigade was assembled in the area of Kozłowa Ruda with the assignment to prevent an enemy retreat to the west or southwest.

The 26th Guards Tank Brigade, moving behind the 4th Guards Tank Brigade, by 1430 on 30 July reached the Kozliszki, Oszkiszki area. A forward detachment consisting of its 1st Tank Battalion had been sent out of the Grejzbuda area toward Gustajcie and Wejwery, with the task to cut the German path of retreat from Kaunas to the southwest. At 1200, having destroyed up to a battalion of Germans and engaged in stubborn fighting with enemy tanks and infantry, at 1300 it cut the Kaunas – Marijampolė highway in the vicinity of Skrawdzie while exchanging fire with the enemy on the southern outskirts of Wejwery. Lengthy enemy columns of vehicles and tanks, being cut-off, made several attempts to break out to the west, but suffering heavy losses from the fire of tanks in ambush positions, were compelled to retreat to the northwest through wooded and swampy terrain, abandoning weapons and transport.

After fighting through the night, the forward detachment of the 26th Guards Tank Brigade by 0830 the next morning took full possession of Wejwery, where it took up a defense, having deprived the enemy of the last paths of retreat out of Kaunas. Thus as a result of energetic actions in the direction toward Wejwery, the 26th Guards Tank Brigade cut off the enemy's Kaunas grouping and deprived it of its last paths of retreat to the west, thereby hastening the capture of Kaunas by our units that were attacking from the north and northwest.

The 25th Guards Tank Brigade, operating on the corps' left-hand route, throughout the day of 30 July encountered the fire of an enemy rearguard detachments consisting of panzergrenadiers and 20 tanks in the Huta, Jesiotraki, Wysoka sector. By 1300 of this day, it cut the road and railroad artery in the Sosnowo, Surgucie area, and by 1430 forced a crossing of the Szeszupa River and reached the Kozliszki, Tursucie area, having fulfilled its immediate task.

A reinforced mobile group was sent out by the 25th Guards Tank Brigade, consisting of a submachine gun company, one 76mm gun and a company of tanks with the order to take Pilwiszki. At 1800 on 30 July 1944 it moved out to the northwest and with a bold and decisive dash, not allowing the enemy to bring his scattered columns of vehicles loaded with ammunition, cargo and towing artillery back into order, smashed an enemy column of vehicles and wagons on the approaches to Pilwiszki, inflicting great damage to the enemy in men and equipment. Then with a decisive attack, it hurled the enemy back to the west, captured Pilwiszki and the bridges across the Szeszupa River in the area that were of important tactical significance of the further advance of our forces, and continued to defend the town until the arrival of the main forces.

The 4th Guards Motorized Rifle Brigade, advancing in the wake of the 25th Guards Tank Brigade, by 1500 on 30 July reached the Surgucie area, operating with a forward detachment along the highway and railroad artery toward Marijampolė. At 1700 on this same day it burst into Rudziszki railroad station and captured an enemy troop train consisting of 8 railcars loaded with infantry, that was moving toward Kaunas toward the front. The enemy troops were either killed or captured. The forward detachment of the 4th Guards Motorized Rifle Brigade, together with self-propelled guns of the 1500th Self-propelled Artillery Regiment, with rapid actions unexpectedly for the enemy broke into Marijampolė from the northeast, where it became tied up in combat on many streets. However, by midnight on 30 July 1944, the town of Marijampolė was completely cleared of the enemy.

Thus, by the end of 30 July 1944 the 2nd Guards Tank Corps fulfilled its immediate task and with its main forces reached the Bobroliszki, Kozliszki, Tursucie, Sosnowo, Sulima Buda area and had cut the highway and railroad artery, thereby by cutting the enemy's path of retreat out of Kaunas. The rifle units had lagged behind the tanks, and the tank corps was vulnerable to Germans retreating from the Kaunas direction and in the woods northeast of Kozłowa Ruda.

As a result of the fighting on the day of 30 July alone, the 2nd Guards Tank Corps killed up to 1,300 enemy soldiers and officers, and destroyed 17 tanks, 325 trucks and cars, 2 steam engines, 15 railcars loaded with a variety of military goods, up to 600 wagons together with their horses, and 3 artillery batteries. In the process the corps suffered insignificant losses in men and materiel – 4 tanks were destroyed.

Excerpt from Operational Summary No. 0197 from the headquarters of the 2nd Guards Tank Corps, 31 July 1944, 0600

At 20.00 on 30 July 1944, the situation of the corps' units was as follows: 4th Guards Tank Brigade – Kozłowa Ruda, Point 64.2; 25th Guards Tank Brigade with its main forces – Kozliszki, Tursucie, and a reinforced tank company – Pilwiszki; 4th Guards Motorized Rifle Brigade – Surgucie, forward detachment – Skrawdzie.

As a result of the day's fighting, the corps killed up to 1,090 enemy soldiers and officers and destroyed the following materiel: 15 tanks, 5 tractors, 325 vehicles, 2 steam engines, 3 railcars with a variety of military goods, up to 600 wagons, and 3 artillery batteries. It captured 30 vehicles loaded with a variety of military items, 100 horses, 144 enemy soldiers and officers, 1 steam engine and 33 railcars. In the process, the corps suffered the following losses: 18 men killed, 30 wounded; 6 T-34 and 4 vehicles destroyed.

Status of combat materiel: Operational T-34 tanks: 4th Guards Tank Brigade – 30, 25th Guards Tank Brigade – 26, 26th Guards Tank Brigade – 28, 79th Guards T-34 tanks – 8, 1st Guards Separate Signals Battalion – 5, for a total of 97 operational T-34. The 1500th Self-propelled Artillery Regiment – 10 SU-76; 401st Guards Self-propelled Artillery Regiment – 17 SU-85. Supplies: fuel – 1.5 refills; KB-70 high-octane fuel – 1.7 refills; diesel fuel – 2.3 refills; MK grease – 1.3 refills; ammunition – 1.6 standard combat loads; food – 3 days of rations.

Corps chief of staff Guards Colonel KARAVAN
Corps chief of operations Guards Lieutenant Colonel REPIN

Excerpts from the combat journals of the 2nd Guards Tank Corps' brigades

4th Guards Tank Brigade having 37 operational T-34 tanks, together with the 401st Guards Self-propelled Artillery Regiment, a battery of the 1695th Anti-aircraft Artillery Regiment and attached units, pursuant to a combat order from the corps headquarters, on 30 July 1944 set out from the wooded area west of Moczuny, having the task to attack in the Szawliszki, Chlebiszki,

Michalin, Sulima-Buda direction with the immediate task to take Pletiszki, to emerge subsequently in the Bormaliszki, Brastas area, and having cut the railroad leading to Marijampolė by reaching the Brastas area, to take Kozłowa Ruda from the south. At the signal "555", given over the radio by the corps headquarters, the brigade launched the offensive, and by 0630 the lead battalion, overcoming enemy fire resistance, captured Polowan Ducze. Developing the offensive and overcoming the enemy's resistance using tanks and self-propelled artillery, the brigade by 1030 on 30 July 1944 took Szymaki and Kruty, after which, conducting reinforced reconnaissance in the northern and northwestern directions, the brigade's units from the march captured Sulima Buda and the road junction lying west of there. Having reached the Sulima-Buda area, the brigade encountered a large enemy column consisting of vehicles, artillery and supply trains that was retreating from Kaunas toward Marijampolė. In the area of Dembowa Buda, the 2nd Tank Battalion destroyed up to 200 vehicles, 300 horse-drawn wagons and 9 tanks.

By 1300 the brigade carried out its subsequent task, reaching: 2nd Tank Battalion – bend in the highway north of Dembowa Buda with a front to the northeast; 3rd Tank Battalion – on the northern and northwestern outskirts of Bobroliszki; 1st Tank Battalion – Sulima-Buda as a reserve. At 1430 on 30 July 1944, the 1st Tank Battalion together with the motorized rifle battalion moved out to carry out the order to take Kozłowa Ruda and by 1500 took it with fighting. A steam engine and 4 railcars were captured, and 150 Nazis were killed. The 3rd Tank Battalion in the area of Bobroliszki and to the north destroyed up to 100 vehicles with various loads and ammunition. As a result of the fighting on 30 July 1944, the brigade lost 2 tanks destroyed, 6 men killed and 13 wounded. By the end of the day, the brigade had 44 T-34 tanks, 32 of which were operational.

The **4th Guards Tank Brigad**e and its attached units was positioned south of Kozłowa Ruda. At 0815 on 31 July 1944 it received a combat order from the corps headquarters, according to which the brigade was to be in readiness to take Point 83.6 and the northeastern outskirts of Wejwery, while simultaneously scouting in the direction of Wiłkowyszki and Buda. At 20.20 the brigade's forward column reached the area of Pilwiszki and the bridge across the Schirwindt River; the bridge had been demolished by enemy aircraft. After crossing the Schirwindt River, according to an order from the corps commander, the brigade's units were halted until 0400 along the Solovoj road – intersection of the turnpike and the road 4 km west of Pilwiszki. By the end of the day, the brigade had 30 operational T-34 tanks.

26th Guards Tank Brigade: On 30 July 1944, having reached Grejzbuda, the brigade sent out a forward detachment consisting of the 1st Tank Battalion in the direction of Gustajcie and Wejwery with the assignment to cut the Kaunas – Marijampolė highway, having taken Wejwery and the Kaunas – Kozłowa Ruda railroad and with one platoon the Skrawdzie siding, and to prevent the enemy's retreat to the north and northwest. The 1st Tank Battalion, operating in the direction of Wejwery, at 1320 on 30 July 1944 cut the Kaunas – Marijampolė highway in the Skrawdzie – Wejwery sector, where it became tied up in fighting with enemy tanks and infantry on the southwestern outskirts of Wejwery. At 1705 the 1st Tank Battalion took the Sdrawdzie railroad siding. At 1845 the enemy, in strength of up to two battalions of motorized infantry and up to 15 tanks, drove the 1st Tank Battalion out of Wejwery and dug in on the southwestern outskirts. Engaged in combat with superior enemy forces, the 1st Tank Battalion fell back to the southwest and dug in, having taken up a defense in the sector between the Skrawdzie railroad siding and the southeastern slopes of Hill 91.1, saddling the railroad and highway. A brigade reconnaissance force consisting of a platoon of T-34 tanks, with an outflanking maneuver to the right in the Pokiewliszki, Szurupie, Mazuryszki, Wejwery direction, reached Maurucie. Advancing on Wejwery along the highway from the northeast, it lost 2 tanks burned-out and one man killed (the platoon commander), and fell back to the southwestern outskirts of Maurucie.

As a result of the fighting, the 1st Tank Battalion in the Wejwery area killed up to 100 enemy soldiers and officers; destroyed 1 tank, 1 tractor, 2 transports with ammunition, 2 steam engines,

20 railcars holding various cargo, up to 50 vehicles, 1 antitank gun; and took 5 soldiers prisoner. Over the same period of time the 26th Guards Tank Brigade lost 2 T-34 burned-out, 1 man killed and 3 wounded. By the end of the day 30 July, the brigade had 28 operational T-34/85 tanks (one of which was malfunctioning), 3 M3A1 halftracks, 1 BA-64 armored car, 3 76mm antitank guns, 3 37mm anti-aircraft guns, and 1 DShK machine gun. In addition, the brigade had 1 T-34 tank undergoing capital repair and 10 T-34 tanks undergoing moderate repairs. Ten T-34 and another two tanks required evacuation from a swamp and have to be repaired.

26th Guards Tank Brigade: 1st Tank Battalion on the night of 30-31 July 1944 attacked in the direction of Wejwery and by 0330 reached the southwestern outskirts of this point, where it engaged in combat with enemy tanks and infantry that were falling back to the north. As a result of the combat, the 1st Tank Battalion by 0830 on 31 July took Wejwery, where it took up a defense. At 1800 on 31 July, on the basis of an order from the corps commander, the brigade's units moved out from their occupied areas with the task to reach the Podziszki area and to take Schirwindt and Naumiestis. By 24.00 31 July 1944, the brigade's forward detachment reached Olksniany and continued to carry out its assignment in the direction of Dydwiże [Dydryžiai]. En route the brigade scouted the enemy in the direction of the hamlet of Szelwy [Selviai] and Giedriai [just north-northwest of Wiłkowyszki]. During the reconnaissance, the brigade had losses from enemy artillery and mortar fire, and from enemy aircraft: 2 T-34 tanks destroyed, one BA-64 armored car knocked out, as well as 2 men killed and 13 wounded. In its area of combat operations, the 26th Guards Tank Brigade had 23 operational T-34 tanks; another 3 T-34 tanks lagged behind due to mechanical problems.

25th Guards Tank Brigade at 20.00 31 July 1944 received a combat order from the 2nd Guards Tank Corps headquarters with the task to take Wiłkowyszki. At 20.10 the brigade set out along its route and at 23.15 the brigade's units reached the area of the village of Szelwy [as opposed to the nearby hamlet with the same name], where they became tied up in fighting with enemy tanks, self-propelled guns and artillery. By 24.00, they took Szelwy, where they took up jumping-off positions for the attack toward Wiłkowyszki.

From the Combat Path of the 2nd Guards Tank Corps:

On 30 July 1944 the units of the 2nd Guards Tank Corps, smashing through enemy rearguard detachments, emerged in the enemy rear and cut the Kaunas – Marijampolė highway and railroad, thereby blocking the enemy's path of retreat out of Kaunas, which contributed to the defeat of the enemy's Kaunas grouping and the liberation of Lithuania's capital, Kaunas.

The Guardsmen's forward detachments swiftly moved on toward Marijampolė. Guards Lieutenant Boiko's destroyer antitank gun battery broke into a railroad way-station where a German military train was standing. With accurate fire from their guns, the artillerymen knocked out the steam engine, killed more than 100 enemy soldiers and officers, and captured 10 railcars with military cargo. At 20.30 30 July 1944 units of Colonel Antipin's 4th Guards Motorized Rifle Brigade, pursuant to an order from the corps commander General Burdeinyi, broke into Marijampolė, where it became tied up in bitter street fighting. The motorized rifle companies, supported by tanks, mopped up the enemy from building after building, street after street.

The machine gunners of Lieutenant Andreiuk's platoon, quickly alternating positions, cut down enemy soldiers with machine-gun fire from windows, rooftops and cellars, sowing panic among the Nazis. The adversary resisted for three and a half hours with tenacious stubbornness, but was eventually destroyed. By 2400 the town of Marijampolė was completely mopped up of its defenders.

On this same day of 30 July, the Guardsmen of Colonel Losik's 4th Guards Tank Brigade captured an important communications hub – Pilwiszki [Pilviskiai]. On 31 July 1944, at an order from the Supreme Commander-in-Chief, it was announced: "Forces of the 3rd Belorussian Front, going on the offensive, forced a crossing of the Neman River and over three days of offensive fighting advanced up to 50 kilometers into the depth, having expanded the breach in the front up to 230 kilometers. In the course of the offensive, the Front's troops took the city and important railroad station of Marijampolė, and the important communications hub of Pilwiszki." The order indicated that in the fighting when forcing a crossing of the Neman River and breaking through the Germans' defenses, Major General of Tank Forces Burdeinyi's tankers distinguished themselves.

The Fighting for Wiłkowyszki

The enemy with units of the 6th Panzer Division, artillery and infantry, defending the Wiłkowyszki area, was putting up stubborn resistance. By 1 August 1944 his firing means were positioned in the area of Hill 61.4, Hill 60.6 and Hill 50.2 on the southern outskirts of Wiłkowyszki; an antitank ditch and three lines of full-profile trenches and bunkers ran along the town's eastern side.

The 25th Guards Tank Brigade, pursuant to its combat order, at 2245 on 31 July had reached the village of Nowiniki with a forward detachment consisting of the 1st Tank Battalion, where it became engaged in combat with enemy artillery, tanks and infantry. As a result of the forward detachment's energetic and decisive actions, the enemy was forced out of the Nowiniki area and shoved back to the area of the village of Szelwy; at 2315 the forward detachment took Szelwy, where it took up jumping-off positions for an attack toward Wiłkowyszki. At 0400 on 1 August 1944, the brigade's units moved out on the attack toward Wiłkowyszki, with the tank battalions out of the Szelwy area, and the motorized rifle battalion of submachine gunners out of the Nowiniki area. The motorized rifle battalion supported by a tank company reached the Wiłkowyszki Station area, where it ran into heavy enemy resistance in strength of up to a regiment of infantry backed by artillery and tanks. Bitter fighting erupted. The tanks were engaged in stubborn fighting in the Wyszczokajmie area. Having broken the enemy's stubborn resistance, at 1330 on 1 August the tanks of the 25th Guards Tank Brigade unexpectedly for the enemy burst into the northern outskirts of Wiłkowyszki at high speed. The enemy, offering tough resistance with fire, repeatedly launched counterattacks, striving to thrown the brigade's units back to their jumping-off positions.

Meanwhile the 4th Guards Motorized Rifle Brigade was attacking toward Wiłkowyszki from the east. At 0430 its 3rd Motorized Rifle Battalion drove the enemy out of the three trench lines, captured them, and broke into the eastern outskirts of Wiłkowyszki with one company. At 1240 on 1 August the tanks of the 25th Guards Tank Brigade, stubbornly fighting their way forward, reached the center of the town, where at 1300 they linked up with the infantry units of the 4th Guards Motorized Rifle Brigade. Tough street fighting broke out for the southern outskirts of the town. By 1800 1 August, the tanks of the 25th Guards Tank Brigade had battled their way forward to the Szejmena River, which runs through the southern section of Wiłkowyszki, where they took up fixed firing positions in order to support the operations of the 4th Guards Motorized Rifle Brigade's units to take the town's southern outskirts. By the end of day 1 August 1944, after day-long street fighting, Wiłkowyszki was completely mopped up of the enemy.

At 1510 on 1 August 1944, General Burdeinyi sent the following message to the commanders of the 33rd Army, the 33rd Army's armored and mechanized forces and the 3rd Belorussian Front's armored and mechanized forces:

Through reconnaissance, prisoner interrogation, local residents and a German deserter, it was established at 1000 on 1 August 1944 that the enemy had previously prepared a defensive line running from Sklawcze through Sudava and Giedriai to Wołkowyszki. The defenses were constructed by local residents and German troops; the defensive line has 3-4 full-profile trenches in the Sudava, Wiłkowyszki area and an antitank ditch that was 4 meters wide and up to 3 meters deep. Prisoners captured in the Wiłkowyszki area belong to the 1st (East Prussia) Infantry Division, which had arrived in this sector from Tilsit on 29 July 1944. The remaining units are on the approach. A prisoner saw up to 20 Tiger tanks in the Wiłkowyszki area. A prisoner from the 3rd Infantry Division's Infantry Regiment 246, captured north of Wiłkowyszki, arrived in this area from Germany on 31 July 1944. The remaining units are on the approach. The 1st Infantry Division and 3rd Infantry Division have reformed and have up to 150 men in their companies. Prisoners have also been taken from the Grenadier Regiment 1072 in the Wiłkowyszki area.

The enemy is defending actively on the entire front, periodically launching counterattacks with infantry and tanks, supported by artillery and mortar fire. Enemy aircraft in groups of 10-50 are bombing our combat formations. At 1000 on 1 August 1944, the corps' units were engaged in combat: 26th Guards Tank Brigade – to take Sudava in the direction of Pracapol and Naumiestis. Meeting organized enemy resistance including artillery and tanks, the 25th Guards Tank Brigade and 4th Guards Tank Brigade are engaged in combat to take Wiłkowyszki, repulsing incessant attacks by enemy infantry and tanks supported by artillery. The antitank ditch in the Wiłkowyszki area has been filled with water. The 4th Guards Tank Brigade is in reserve in the Olksniany area. The corps' losses: 3 tanks destroyed and 4 tanks knocked-out. The tank has killed 300 enemy soldiers and officers and destroyed 10 tanks and self-propelled guns. I am located 2 km northwest of Olksniany.

Burdeinyi
1 August 1944

Excerpts from the combat diaries of the 2nd Guards Tank Corps' brigades

4th Guards Tank Brigade: Together with the 401st Guards Self-propelled Artillery Regiment, according to an order from the corps commander, by 04.00 1 August 1944 was halted before dawn with the forward column at the intersection of the road and railroad in the Jurksze area; resuming the march, the brigade by 05.30 was assembled in Olksniany. By 16.45 the brigade's units reached a jumping-off area, having the mission to attack to the west and to take the Zielenka road hub, and subsequently to operate in the direction of Verszbolowo. The brigade's further advance was halted by strong enemy fire. At 1900 on 1 August 1944 the brigade's units took up a defense on the Dydviże, Gałakausze line with the task to hold the passages across the antitank ditch and to repel possible enemy counterattacks until the arrival of the rifle units. By the end of the day the brigade had 29 operational T-34, 8 T-34 under moderate repair, and 4 T-34 requiring factory repairs.

At 9.30 1 August 1944 the **26th Guards Tank Brigade's** 2nd Tank Battalion and motorized rifle battalion, with supporting fire from the 1st Tank Battalion, launched an attack in the Dydviże, Sudawa direction, overcoming heavy enemy fire. As a result of offensive actions, the 26th Guards Tank Brigade and 28th Separate Guards Mortar Battalion captured Sterki, Dydviże, Kausze and Łujsze. The 1st and 2nd Tank Battalions and the motorized rifle battalion reached the northwestern and western outskirts of Dydviże, while a tank platoon and submachine gun company crossed the antitank ditch in the Sudawa area and took up a defense. The brigade's remaining units remained in their previous occupied areas of dispositions. As a result of combat actions, the brigade killed up to 100 enemy soldiers and officers and destroyed 5 antitank guns,

2 tanks, 5 vehicles and 15 machine guns. In the area of its combat operations, the 26th Guards Tank Brigade had 16 operational T-34 tanks, 3 76mm antitank guns, 3 37mm anti-aircraft guns and 6 DShK machine guns.

In the course of the day of 1 August 1944, the **25th Guards Tank Brigade's** units engaged in heavy offensive fighting against enemy tanks, self-propelled guns and artillery, while being subjected to a large enemy airstrike conducted by 30-40 aircraft. As a result of impetuous offensive fighting, the brigade's units by 12.40 1 August 1944 had broken into the center of Wiłkowyszki, where it became tied up in street fighting and at 13.00 linked up with the 4th Guards Motorized Rifle Brigade; wicontinuing to mop up the town of the enemy, at 17.50 they reached the Szejmena River, where they took up a defense while supporting with fire from fixed positions the 4th Guards Motorized Rifle Brigade's actions to take the southern outskirts of the town. Over the day of fighting the 25th Guards Tank Brigade destroyed 6 tanks, 4 self-propelled guns, 15 guns of various calibers, 80 vehicles, 5 prime movers and killed up to 800 enemy soldiers and officers. At Wiłkowyszki Station a train was captured that was loaded with food, uniforms and various military gear. Over this same period of time, the brigade lost 6 T-34 tanks destroyed and 7 knocked out, 8 vehicles, and had 82 casualties, including 12 men killed, 61 wounded and 9 missing in action. By the end of day 1 August 1944, the 25th Guards Tank Brigade had 11 operational T-34 tanks; 6 T-34 tanks were undergoing minor repairs, and another 6 T-34 were undergoing moderate repairs.

The **25th Guards Tank Brigade** up until 23.00 1 August 1944 was engaged in combat to mop of Wiłkowyszki of enemy infantry. At this time, a combat order arrived from the 2nd Guards Tank Corps headquarters, according to which the brigade received the task to hold the occupied area and conduct reconnaissance, while simultaneously operating with the 4th Guards Motorized Rifle Brigade to reinforce the latter's defense on the villages of Szelwy – Wiłkowyszki line with tanks. Carrying out this order, the brigade's units took up a defense on the following line: 1st Tank Battalion – center and western outskirts of Wiłkowyszki; motorized rifle battalion – northwestern outskirts of Wiłkowyszki. The brigade had 13 T-34 operational, 2 T-34 undergoing minor repairs, 10 T-34 undergoing moderate repairs, 2 T-34 requiring factory repair, and one more tank requiring evacuation.

From the Combat Path of the 2nd Guards Tank Corps

Continuing their rapid advance, units of the 2nd Guards Tank Corps 1 August 1944 broke into the town of Wiłkowyszki. The 8th Motorized Rifle Company commanded by Senior Lieutenant Sabir Iuldashev drove the German units out of a strongpoint northeast of the town, cleared three trench lines, and was the first to enter the town. Iuldashev's company in this action killed 180 enemy soldiers and officers and captured 80 Nazis. In a hand-to-hand clash for one of the buildings, the company commander fell heroically on the battlefield.

Heavy street fighting, consisting of hundreds of isolated combats, continued … Guards Private Gornostaev was belly crawling across a bridge. A heavy antitank rifle was hindering his progress. However, the target was close, and the soldiers' strength increases manifold. Behind the corner of a building, an enemy tank was standing, firing its cannon at the windows of a building that was occupied by our company. Gornostaev fires at the tank from point-blank range and forces it to fall silent.

Guards Senior Lieutenant Kvaratskhvely's platoon and Guards Lieutenant Leliavin's platoon killed more than 50 enemy soldiers and officers. They unexpectedly and swiftly charged four German tanks upon which German soldiers were mounted. Using grenades, the Guardsmen severed the tracks of the German tanks, killed the tank riders, before pouring gasoline all over the tanks and igniting it with burning straw bundles. German tankers were killed as they clambered out of their burning tanks. Having repulsed numerous enemy counterattacks and having broken the enemy resistance, the "tankers" of the 2nd Guards Tank Corps by 21.30 1 August 1944 had fully mopped up Wiłkowyszki of the enemy.

At this time the tankers learned that Moscow was once again saluting the troops of the 3rd Belorussian Front, including General Burdeinyi's Guardsmen, for the capture of Kaunas. The corps' whirlwind attacks through the German rear areas helped the rifle units take this city.

The tanks bearing a white arrow on their turrets resumed the advance toward East Prussia. However, it became more and more difficult to make progress. Hitler's command had previously prepared a line of defense west of Wiłkowyszki extending right up to Germany's border. In heavy and stubborn fighting, General Burdeinyi's tankers were laying down a path to East Prussia.

Excerpts from the Operational Summary of the German Third Panzer Army (Pz AOK 3) to the headquarters of Army Group Center No. 851/44; 1 August 1944. Daily operational report:

On the day of 1 August 1944, major enemy forces of tanks and infantry broke through our defense in the Wiłkowyszki area and to the north of there. In addition, the Russians began to envelop the army's northern flank.

The 561st Volksgrenadier Division from late evening on 31 July was engaged in heavy fighting with superior enemy forces at Wiłkowyszki and to the north. In the course of the first half of the day the army's units succeeded in driving the Russians out of Wiłkowyszki. However, on the evening of 1 August Wiłkowyszki was again lost by us. The combat in this sector was made difficult by the fact that the hastily-formed 561st Volksgrenadier Division didn't have enough weapons (just 3-5 machine guns per battalion). Moreover, the remaining units, which were operating as covering screens, proved to have low capabilities and became intermingled with each other.

Northwest of Wiłkowyszki Station, a 4-kilometer-wide breach arose at the boundary with Grupp Knebel, into which enemy units infiltrated throughout the entire evening. North of the Szeszupa River, groups of enemy tanks with tank riders aboard knocked aside our weak covering screen, which didn't have enough antitank weapons, and broke through in the direction of the Naumiestis – Szaki road.

The 6th Panzer Division ended its process of assembling and went on the attack out of the Gryszkabuda area to the southeast, having left behind a covering force in front of the western fringe of the large wooded area. In the first half of the day, reconnaissance north of Pilwiszki detected only insignificant enemy forces and advanced as far as the wooded fringes and forest firebreaks without making contact with the enemy; however, in the middle of the day the enemy rapidly strengthened his defenses in the Pilwiszki area and simultaneously launched an attack to the north. Strong enemy resistance didn't permit the expansion of the bridgehead north of Pilwiszki and to bring up the panzers through this sector.

The offensive toward Pilwiszki with the subsequent task to launch an attack out of Pilwiszki to the west had to be called off, because all of the 6th Panzer Division's units had been drawn into combat with the enemy's vanguard forces. Stubborn fighting with these vanguard forces developed on a general line [extending from] 3 km east of the Pilwiszki – Gryszkabuda road to north of this road. Thus, it was already impossible to go to the relief of the units fighting in the Wiłkowyszki area …

On 2 August, the enemy with units of the 6th Panzer Division, 1st Infantry Division, 3rd Infantry Division and Panzergrenadier Regiments 1068 and 1072 was holding its previous line of defense:

Romantyszki, Sudawa, Giedriai, Kilyszki. In the course of the day, the Germans repeatedly went on the counterattack in the Sudawa sector in strength of up to a regiment of infantry with the support of tanks and self-propelled guns. The enemy air force in groups of 10-15 aircraft bombed the corps' forward edge of defense. Altogether up to 120 individual aircraft sorties were registered.

Units of the 2nd Guards Tank Corps throughout the day of 2 August stubbornly held their occupied line of defense: 26th Guards Tank Brigade – northwestern outskirts of Dydwiże; 4th Guards Tank Brigade – west of Glakausze, 25th Guards Tank Brigade – along the western and northern outskirts of Wiłkowyszki, and together with the 4th Guards Motorized Brigade, continued to hold the town.

The corps' units throughout the day repulsed counterattacks by small groups of enemy and reconnoitered in the northwestern and western directions. At 1820 2 August, up to a regiment of infantry, supported by self-propelled guns and tanks, counterattacked northwest of Wiłkowyszki. As a result of the fighting, the enemy lost up to 200 soldiers and officers killed and 20 vehicles destroyed; the fire of three mortar batters was silenced. In the process, the corps suffered the following losses: the commander of the 1500th Self-propelled Artillery was wounded and the deputy commander killed; two T-34 tanks were destroyed and one tank was knocked out. By the end of 2 August, the 2nd Guards Tank Corps had 73 T-34, 16 SU-85 and 5 SU-76 still operational.

Excerpts from the combat diaries of the brigades of the 2nd Guards Tank Corps

4th Guards Tank Brigade and the 401st Guards Self-propelled Artillery Regiment throughout the day of 2 August 1944 conducted no combat operations, holding in readiness to operate in the direction of the 25th and 26th Guards Tank Brigades. At 7.30 a reconnaissance patrol consisting of a platoon of tanks was sent out in Majoryski, village of Szelwy, Semeneliszki estate direction along the railroad leading toward Kibarty, with the task to scout the enemy and the bridges across the Schirwindt River. At 1430 the patrol reached Semeneliszki, where it was shelled by enemy artillery firing from the western bank of the Schirwindt River. At 1930 enemy tanks counterattacked the tank patrol, as a result of which the patrol fell back to the area of Wiłkowyszki Station. The brigade has 33 operational T-34 tanks.

26th Guards Tank Brigade in the course of the day continued to defend Wiłkowyszki from the northern and northwestern directions, in readiness to repulse enemy counterattacks. At 1500 on 2 August 1944, a scouting party consisting of a squad of scouts was sent out in the direction of the Wyszczokajmie and Semeneliszki estates with the task to establish the composition and grouping of the enemy west and northwest of Wiłkowyszki. At 1600 2 August 1944 the patrol reached the area west of Wyszczokajmie, where it detected enemy infantry reinforced with two artillery batteries and one mortar battery in the Semeneliszki area. At 1840 another patrol consisting of halftracks and a reconnaissance platoon was sent out in the direction of the Wiłkowyszki railroad station with the task to establish the enemy's composition, strength, and direction of actions. Through the actions of the reconnaissance patrol it was established that 300 meters north of the railroad station, the Germans were counterattacking in the direction of the station in strength of a battalion of infantry and 7 self-propelled guns, supported by artillery. Until the arrival of the brigade's tanks, the enemy counterattack was being held off by three 76mm guns of the destroyer antitank battalion, which were occupying firing positions in this area. As a result of the fighting, two of the antitank guns were destroyed. At 1930 four tanks of the 1st Tank Battalion, which were sent out to reinforce the antitank artillery battalion, drove back the German counterattack. In the process, 1 enemy self-propelled gun, 1 cannon and 2 vehicles were destroyed, and up to 70 Nazis killed.

In order to secure the defense of the Wiłkowyszki railroad station, a tank ambush was set up, directed toward the northern and northwestern directions. By the end of day, the 25th Guards Tank Brigade had 16 operational T-34 tanks, 6 T-34 tanks undergoing minor repairs, 2 T-34 undergoing moderate repairs, and 2 T-34 requiring factory repair. The increase in combat-ready tanks resulted from the return to service of repaired tanks of the 2nd Tank Battalion.

Excerpt from the operational summary of the headquarters of the Third Panzer Army (Pz AOK 3) to the headquarters of Army Group Center, 2 August 1944; daily operational summary:

In the sector of the 561st Volksgrenadier Division with its cut-off position at Wiłkowyszki, the enemy units that had broken through to Semenelyszki were successfully counterattacked by our reserves. On the left-hand sector of the division's front, units of Grupp Knebel with assault guns advanced in the direction of Wiłkowyszki, attacking from the northwest. In the process the enemy lost 70 men killed, 25 men captured, 3 tanks, 1 armored car and 4 antitank guns.

Enemy units again advanced further to the west on the northern flank of the panzer army, which was bent back to the rear and shortened in order to free up forces for the fighting on the deep front.

At sunrise, major forces of Russian infantry, with the support of up to 50 tanks, went on the offensive on the entire front of the 6th Panzer Division. The direction of the main attack runs northeast of Bardża [Brydzie?] and at Gryszkabuda. The enemy was trying to envelop the division's southern flank in the area north of Pilwiszki, while simultaneously attacking the northern flank.

The division, which was defending a broad front that had been breached by the enemy in many places, launched several counterattacks that inflicted heavy losses on the enemy; however, it was nevertheless forced to withdraw to the forward East Prussian line. The first attacks by enemy infantry together with several tanks against this line, which began that evening southwest and northwest of Gryszkabuda, were driven back. The Luksze – Tilsit road was cut by the vanguards of major enemy forces, attacking from the southeast.

In this sector first and foremost there is inadequate strength for the rapid construction of the forward edge of defense, thus the threat exists of an enemy breakthrough to the Neman River.

At combat readiness:
6th Panzer Division – 12 Pz.kpfw. IV tanks;
I/Panzer Regiment *Grossdeutschland* – 10 Pz.kpfw. V tanks;
Heavy Panzer Battalion 510 – 10 Pz.kpfw. VI tanks;
StuG Battalion 277 – 15 StuG.

Enemy losses: 6th Panzer Division knocked out 15 enemy tanks and destroyed or captured 22 antitank guns (of which 9 guns on 1 August). The enemy left 1000 – 1100 dead on the battlefield. Motorized Brigade von Werthern on 1 August destroyed 1 tank and 5 heavy antitank guns. IX Corps destroyed 9 enemy tanks. Grupp Knebel: *Wachtmeister* Flegel on 1 August in the course of 12 hours knocked out 6 enemy tanks.

Having lost the defensive line in the Wiłkowyszki area, which according to the intentions of the German command was supposed be a solid barrier, blocking the Soviet forces' path to East Prussia, the enemy was feverishly attempting to regain the lost positions in this area and incessantly counterattacked the attacking units of the 33rd Army's 19th Rifle Corps and of the 2nd Guards Tank Corps. Both sides were suffering heavy losses in men and equipment in this fighting.

In the course of the day 3 August the corps was stubbornly holding its occupied lines of defense. At a directive from the commander of the 33rd Army, the corps' units and formations turned over their areas of defense to rifle units and with the onset of darkness moved into jumping-off positions in readiness to initiate actions at 0600 4 August 1944 in the western direction with the task to reach the border of East Prussia in the Stanajcie area and to take Eydtkuhnen [known as Eydtkau between 1938 and 1945]. By the end of the day of 3 August, the 2nd Guards Tank Corps had the following operational T-34 tanks: 33 in the 4th Guards Tank Brigade, 16 in the 25th Guards Tank Brigade, 17 in the 26th Guards Tank Brigade; as well as 16 operational SU-85 and 4 operational SU-76. The tank corps had 1 refill of fuel and lubricants and 1.3 standard combat loads of ammunition.

Excerpts from the combat diaries of the brigades of the 2nd Guards Tank Corps

4th Guards Tank Brigade and the 401st Guards Self-propelled Artillery Regiment was located in the area southeast of Dydwiże; in the course of 3 August 1944 it conducted no combat operations, while scouting in the western and southwestern directions. At 19.30 the brigade's units moved out from the area southeast of Dydwiże and by 23.30 3 August was assembled in the jumping-off area for the offensive 1 km southeast of Wiłkowyszki Station, having 35 operational T-34 tanks.

26th Guards Tank Brigade in the course of 3 august 1944 stubbornly held its occupied area of defense, fighting to repulse enemy attacks. On the night of 3-4 August, the men of the brigade's motorized rifle battalion did field work to improve the line of defense. Constant observation over the enemy's activity was organized. In execution of a combat order from the corps headquarters, received at 17.00, with the onset of darkness on 3 August the brigade's units were removed from the occupied line of defense in the Dydwiże area and by 24.00 had assembled in Naszyszki. The brigade had 22 operational T-34, of which 5 were in the area of Bastūnai Station. The brigade had 19 T-34 tanks in the area of assembly, of which 2 tanks were in need of maintenance.

Units of the **25th Guards Tank Brigade** until 16.00 on 3 August 1944 was defending Wiłkowyszki. At 16.00, pursuant to a verbal order from the commander of the 2nd Guards Tank Corps, the brigade's units were removed from the defense of Wiłkowyszki and by 19.00 had taken up jumping-off positions for the offensive: 1st Tank Battalion – 300 meters southwest of Nowiniki; 2nd Tank Battalion – Nowiniki; motorized rifle battalion – with the tank battalions.

At 19.00 3 August 1944 a written combat order was received from the corps headquarters, according to which the 25th Guards Tank Brigade had the task from the morning of 4 August 1944 to enter a breakthrough as part of the corps, attacking in the second echelon along the route Nowiniki, village of Szelwy, Semeneliszki, Bobławka, Uszkurajcie, Szykszniewo, Szmilgen, from where with an attack from the northwest it was to take Eydtkuhnen.

In the course of the day 3 August 1944 the men of the day brought their tanks and weapons into order, topped up with ammunition, and prepared for combat operations from the morning of 4 August 1944.

Excerpt from Operational Summary No. 859/44 from the headquarters of the Third Panzer Army (Pz AOK 3) to the headquarters of Army Group Center, 3 August 1944; Daily operational report:

The situation on the panzer army's southern flank in the area of Wiłkowyszki remains as before unchanged. At the same time in the sector of the 6th Panzer Division, as expected, the enemy launched a major offensive in the second half of the day. However, in this sector the Russians initially sent only solitary tanks into the battle. The main bulk of the tanks was assembled in jumping-off positions. In all sectors the enemy was thrown back with heavy losses for him.

On the front of the 561st Volksgrenadier Division, the enlivened activity of enemy reconnaissance groups and patrols was noted. Enemy movement north of Wiłkowyszki was noted, and the appearance of 4 tanks was spotted. In the second half of the day the fire of enemy artillery increased, while at the same time the registration of heavy artillery fire on the central sector of the division's defensive front was noted. In the morning hours, the 6th Panzer Division liquidated the local penetration achieved by the enemy on 2 August, and also repulsed a reconnaissance-in-force conducted by up to a battalion of infantry with the support of solitary tanks …

The panzer group of the 7th Panzer Division on 2 August attacked the enemy in the Žaiginys area, eliminating enemy infantry and antitank guns, before continuing the attack toward Šiluva, where it destroyed up to a regiment of infantry, heavy weapons and artillery.

The 5th Panzer Division together with its operationally subordinate 52nd Security Division became subordinate to the headquarters of Third Panzer Army. The headquarters of XXXX Panzer Corps at 18.00 on 3 August took command over the arriving units of Panzergrenadier Division *Grossdeutschland*, and at 21.00 – over the 561st Volksgrenadier Division. Communications with the 5th Panzer Division has been interrupted at the present time.

Kampfgruppe Mäder in the vicinity of Schaulen [Šiauliai] has become subordinate to the headquarters of Gruppe von Rotkirch. The 1st Battery of StuG Brigade 276 has been made subordinate to 6th Panzer Division.

Arrived: Panzerjäger Battalion 1054 (in Insterburg; an order has been issued to reload the panzerjägers again for transport to Eydtkuhnen); three trains of the 1st Mortar Brigade; four trains of the Panzergrenadier Division *Grossdeutschland* (carrying the division headquarters, elements of the 1st Battalion of the motorized regiment, elements of the reconnaissance battalion, and one sapper company). The II/Security Regiment 75 has joined with Gruppe von Rotkirch.

At combat readiness:
6th Panzer Division – 11 Pz.kpfw. IV tanks;
I/Panzer Regiment *Grossdeutschland* – 11 Pz.kpfw. V tanks;
7th Panzer Division – 30 Pz.kpfw. V tanks, 5 StuG;
Heavy Panzer Battalion 510 – 10 Pz.kpfw. VI tanks;
Heavy Panzerjäger Battalion 519 – 4 Nashorn self-propelled guns;
Heavy Panzerjäger Battalion 731 – 13 Hetzer self-propelled guns;
StuG Brigade 232 – 27 StuG;
StuG Brigade 277 – 13 StuG;
Motorized Brigade von Wethern – 1 Pz.kpfw. IV tank;
StuG Brigade 203 (minus one battery) – 20 StuG.

Enemy losses: 561st Volksgrenadier Division has captured 6 heavy machine guns; 6th Panzer Division has destroyed 1 tank and 8 antitank guns; Motorized Brigade von Wethern has destroyed 1 tank and taken 15 prisoners; 7th Panzer Division has destroyed or captured: 14 guns, 3 self-propelled antitank guns, 12 medium antitank guns, 2 heavy mortars, 3 antitank rifles, 11 machine guns, and 7 submachine guns.

As noted by Gerd Niepold, on 4 August 1944, the staff of XXXX Panzer Corps arrived from Romania on the southern wing of the Third Panzer Army and took command of the 561st Grenadier Division, the 52nd Security Division and the 5th Panzer Division. Across the entire front, a significant battle erupted on the nearest approaches to East Prussia.

Command Staff of the 3rd Belorussian Front, 33rd Army and 2nd Guards Tank Corps, summer-autumn 1944

General A.G. Rodin.

General A.P. Pokrovsky.

General I.D. Cherniakhovsky.

S.I. Morozov.

A.P. Penchevsky.

D.I. Samarsky.

Ia.S. Vorob'ev.

P.K. Bodganovich.

V.S. Bodrov.

S.A. Akhtiamov.

G.P. Khavanov.

A.K. Kudianov.

M.A. Enshin.

S.A. Krasnovsky.

A.S. Burdeinyi (2nd GTC).

A.F. Karavan.

S.K. Nesterov.

O.A. Losik.

Guards Colonel S.M. Bulygin.

Guards Colonel M.S. Antipin.

Guards Colonel V.K. Shanin.

P.D. Govorunenko.

E.A. Bikbov.

B.V. Ovchinnikov.

L.A. Olovin (Operations Dept.).

Guards Colonel D.L. Margulis.

P. Savchuk.

P. Cheplov.

Sh.L. Gamtsemlidze.

Iu.N. Malakhov.

D.G. Frolikov.

N.I. Kolychev.

E.V. Anisimov.

Command Staff of the 33rd Army

Army commander – Lieutenant General S.I. Morozov
Military Council member – Major General R.N. Babiichuk
Chief of staff – Major General A.P. Penchevsky
Commander of the armored and mechanized forces: Colonel Vakhrushev
Commander of artillery – Lieutenant General V.S. Bodrov
Chief of staff of the armored and mechanized forces: Guards Lieutenant Colonel Ivanov
Chief of staff of artillery – Colonel Iablochkin

62nd Rifle Corps: Commander – Major General Ia.S. Vorob'ev
70th Rifle Division: Commander – Colonel S.A. Krasnovsky
49th Rifle Division: Commander – Major General P.K. Bogdanovich
344th Rifle Division: Commander – Colonel G.I. Druzhinin

19th Rifle Corps: Commander – Major General D.I. Samarsky
32nd Rifle Division: Commander – Colonel A.S. Belov

222nd Rifle Division: Commander – Colonel G.P. Savchuk
362nd Rifle Division: Commander – Major General M.A. Enshin
43rd Destroyer Antitank Artillery Brigade: Commander – Colonel I.I. Kii
47th Destroyer Antitank Artillery Brigade: Commander – Colonel D.L. Margulis

2nd Guards Tank Corps (as of 20 July 1944)
Commander – Guards Major General of Tank Forces Aleksei Burdeinyi
Deputy commander for personnel – Major General Petr Govorunenko (replaced by Colonel Stepan Nesterov)
Deputy commander for political affairs – Guards Colonel Ivan Chernyshov
Deputy commander for rear services – Guards Colonel Grigorii Gavrilov
Assistant corps commander (engineer services) – Guards Engineer-Lieutenant Colonel Ivan Shapkin
Commander of artillery – Guards Colonel Boris Dubman
Chief of staff – Guards Colonel Aleksandr Karavan
Chief of operations, deputy chief of staff – Guards Lieutenant Colonel Nikolai Repin
Chief of intelligence – Guards Lieutenant Colonel Viktor Kuznetsov
Chief of communications – Guards Lieutenant Colonel Boris Geller
Corps engineer – Lieutenant Colonel Nikifor Sveshnikov

4th Guards Tank Brigade
Commander – Guards Lieutenant Colonel Oleg Losik
Deputy commander for personnel – Guards Lieutenant Colonel Aleksandr Kryzhanovsky
Assistant commander for technical matters – Guards Captain Fedor Stoianov
Assistant commander for rear services – Guards Major Konstantin Lupindin
Chief of staff – Guards Lieutenant Colonel Pavel Chepkov
Chief of communications – Guards Captain Vasilii Perevalov

25th Guards "El'nia" Tank Brigade
Commander – Guards Colonel Semen Bulygin
Deputy commander for political affairs – Guards Lieutenant Colonel Petr Slepov
Deputy commander for personnel – Guards Lieutenant Colonel Grigorii Titov
Assistant commander for technical matters – Guards Engineer-Major Aleksandr Kremnev
Assistant commander for rear services – Guards Captain Serafim Kolokolov
Chief of staff – Guards Lieutenant Colonel Petr Davydov
Deputy chief of staff for operations – Guards Captain Ivan Zhukov
Chief of engineer services – Guards Captain Il'ia Burukov
Chief of communications – Guards Captain Nikolai Severin

26th Guards "El'nia" Tank Brigade
Commander – Guards Colonel Stepan Nesterov (replaced by Nikolai Burmistrov)
Deputy commander for political affairs – Guards Colonel Afanasii Getman
Deputy commander for personnel – Guards Lieutenant Colonel Ivan Timofeev (replaced by Viktor Shanin)
Assistant commander for technical matters – Engineer-Lieutenant Colonel Vasilii Efremov
Assistant commander for rear services – Guards Major Ivan Gusikhin
Chief of staff – Guards Lieutenant Colonel Gennadii Ibriaev
Deputy chief of staff for operations – Guards Major Nikolai Iakovlev
Chief of engineer services – Guards Captain Emanuil Shteiman
Chief of communications – Guards Captain Aleksandr Katanov

4th Guards "Smolensk" Motorized Rifle Brigade
Commander – Guards Lieutenant Colonel Mikhail Antipin
Deputy commander for political affairs – Guards Lieutenant Colonel Konstantin Romakin
Deputy commander for personnel – Guards Lieutenant Colonel Fedor Aksenov
Assistant commander for technical matters – Guards Major Dmitrii Malakhov
Assistant commander for rear services – Guards Lieutenant Colonel Aleksei Novikov
Chief of staff – Guards Colonel Mikhail Prokopenko
Deputy chief of staff for operations – Guards Major Aleksandr Sivopliasov
Chief of engineer services – Guards Major Boris Martynov
Chief of communications – Guards Major Ivan Vernyi

401st Guards Red Banner Self-propelled Artillery Regiment
Commander – Guards Major Iurii Stepanov (replaced by Guards Major Timofei Kotliarov)
Deputy commander for political affairs – Guards Major Nikolai Vasil'ev
Deputy commander for personnel – Guards Captain Fedor Bushuev
Assistant commander for technical matters – Guards Engineer-Captain Pavel Prokhorenko
Assistant commander for supplies – Guards Captain Aleksandr Potashnikov (replaced by Guards Captain Aleksei Atenko)
Chief of staff – Guards Captain Fedor Tel'nov
Deputy chief of staff for operations – Guards Senior Lieutenant Nikolai Eremin
Chief of communications – Guards Captain Vladimir Sorokin

1500th Self-propelled Artillery Regiment
Commander – Major Tikhon Zotov
Deputy commander for political affairs – Guards Major Ivan D'iachenko
Deputy commander for personnel – Captain Nikita Dakhno
Assistant commander for technical matters – Captain Vasilii Tregub
Assistant commander for supplies – Senior Lieutenant Ivan Karelin
Chief of staff – Major Aleksandr Loginov

73rd Mortar Regiment
Commander – Lieutenant Colonel Aleksandr Pytalev
Deputy commander for political affairs – Major Dmitrii Stoliarov
Deputy commander for personnel – Major Boris Khuldonov
Assistant commander for technical matters – Senior Technician-Lieutenant Vladimir Adoevtsev
Assistant commander for supplies – Guards Major Pavel Shemchuk
Chief of staff – Guards Major Iakov Veselov

1695th Anti-aircraft Artillery Regiment
Commander – Major Nikolai Sereda
Deputy commander for political affairs – Major Nikolai Bogoliubov
Deputy commander for personnel – Major Iakov Mirotol'sky
Chief of staff – Captain Ivan Bushuev
Assistant commander for material and technical equipping – Captain of Quartermaster Service Gennadii Rysakov
Chief of communications – Captain Andrei Saksonov

28th Guards Mortar Battalion
Commander – Guards Major Konstantin Mikhailov

Deputy commander for political affairs – Guards Major Nikolai Iadrennikov
Assistant commander for technical matters – Guards Captain Viktor Volodin
Chief of staff – Guards Major Stepan Shilov
Chief of communications – Guards Lieutenant Petr Zapara

79th Separate Motorcycle Battalion
Commander – Major Trofim Kaverov
Deputy commander for political affairs – Captain Nikolai Andreenkov
Deputy commander for personnel – Captain Aleksandr Kukushkin
Assistant commander for technical matters – Captain Fedor Dotsenko
Senior adjutant – Captain Aleksandr Skrylev

1st Separate Guards Signals Battalion
Commander – Guards Major Leon Sharshun
Deputy commander for personnel – Guards Major Aleksei Karavaev
Assistant commander for supplies – Guards Captain Mikhail Kaliverda
Chief of staff – Guards Captain Vitalii Kotov

51st Separate Engineer Battalion
Commander – Guards Major Akim Mel'nikov
Deputy commander for political affairs – Major Pavel Iurkovets
Senior Adjutant – Captain Perfilov

159th Medical-Sanitation Battalion
Commander – Guards Major of Medical Services Vasilii Malyshko
Deputy commander for political affairs – Captain Abbas Shafiev
Senior adjutant – Guards Captain Konstantin Puzakin

Defensive fighting in the Zielonka – Wiłkowyszki area

The occupation of Wiłkowyszki by our units meant for the enemy the loss of an intermediate line that had been previously prepared for a defense on the immediate approaches to the East Prussian borders. The enemy's efforts were directed toward regaining the lost positions. The first days of August 1944 were characterized by intensified enemy aerial activity and frequent counterattacks with the support of a large quantity of tanks and self-propelled guns.

At an order from the commander of the 33rd Army, the units of the 2nd Guards Tank Corps in the course of 3 August turned over their areas of defense and by the end of the day the corps received the order to launch an attack to the west on the morning of 4 August with the task to reach the East Prussian border in the Stanajcie area and to take Eydtkuhnen.

At 2200 on 3 August, the corps' units began to move out to their jumping-off areas and by 0200 4 August they had fully reassembled without any losses in their jumping-off areas: 4th Guards Tank Brigade (18 combat-ready T-34 tanks) – 1 kilometer east of Wiłkowyszki Station; 25th Guards Tank Brigade (12 combat-ready T-34 tanks) – in the area of Point 58.7; 26th Guards Tank Brigade (18 combat-ready tanks) – in the area of Hill 65.9; 4th Guards Motorized Rifle Brigade – in the area 600 meters southeast of Wiłkowyszki. The corps' units were at readiness for actions in the western direction and were organizing constant observation over the enemy.

The enemy with infantry, tanks, self-propelled guns and artillery with repeated counterattacks from the flanks in the course of 4 August strove to disrupt the offensive of the Soviet forces, bringing up reserves from the depth. Up to 30 tanks and self-propelled guns were operating opposite the 2nd Guards Tank Corps' front. At 1800 on 4 August, reconnaissance established the approach of a large column of tanks, artillery and motorized infantry from the Wielkupie and Kręgżdie areas, and a column of infantry and artillery moving to the northeast from the Uszkurajcie area. Enemy air groups were bombing the combat positions and rear areas of our troops.

At 0930 4 August the corps' units stepped off to carry out their assignment. By 1200 on 4 August, overcoming heavy enemy fire, the corps' units reached the following line: 4th Guards Tank Brigade with two tank battalions – the road hub 1 kilometer north of Bobławka, and with one tank battalion – 1 kilometer west of Semeneliszki; the 4th Guards Motorized Rifle Brigade – saddling the railroad 1 kilometer north of Bobławka; 26th Guards Tank Brigade – Semeneliszki; 1st Tank Battalion – the road fork 1.5 kilometers from Žwangučiai, motorized rifle battalion – woods 500 meters southwest of Gudele; 25th Guards Tank Brigade – 500 meters southwest of Semeneliszki. On the achieved lines, the corps' units repulsed repeated enemy counterattacks from the directions of Zielonka, Leopoldowo and Maldehne while being subjected to artillery and mortar fire. As a result of the fighting, up to 400 enemy soldiers and officers were killed, and 13 tanks, 11 firing positions, 15 cannons and 20 vehicles were destroyed. In return, the corps' losses amounted to 12 destroyed T-34 and 4 knocked out T-34 in the 4th Guards Tank Brigade; 6 destroyed T-34 in the 25th Guards Tank Brigade; and 1 destroyed tank in the 26th Guards Tank Brigade. In addition, the 401st Guards Self-propelled Artillery Regiment lost 6 SU-85 self-propelled guns destroyed, and 3 knocked out. The corps' losses in men amounted to 49 killed and 123 wounded.

Continuing to carry out their assigned task, the corps' units were engaged in combat with units of the East Prussian Grenadier Division, which had been reinforced by a group of 45-50 tanks and self-propelled guns. By the morning of 5 August they dislodged the enemy and drove the Germans back to the western bank of the Szyrwinta River on the front stretching from Hill 50.6 and Bobławka, thereby reaching the western bank of the river themselves: 26th Guards Tank Brigade with 14 T-34 tanks in the area of Hill 50.6; 4th Guards Tank Brigade and the 401st Guards Self-propelled Artillery Regiment, in cooperation with the 4th Guards Motorized Rifle Brigade – in the area of the crossroads 1 km north of Bobławka; 25th Guards Tank Brigade – in the area of Patwiecie (east of the Szyrwinta River) in reserve of the 33rd Army commander; seven of its tanks began to advance to the west, while its 2nd Tank Battalion with 5 tanks was operating in the direction of Szukle and Point 44.4.

By the end of 4 August 1944, the 2nd Guards Tank Corps had the following tanks and self-propelled guns and supplies: 4th Guards Tank Brigade had 18 operational T-34; the 25th Guards Tank Brigade had 12 operational T-34; the 26th Guards Tank Brigade – 18 operational T-34; and the two self-propelled artillery regiments had 7 SU-85 and 4 SU-76; the corps had 1.2 refills of fuel and lubricants and 1.5 standard combat loads of ammunition.

Excerpts from the combat diaries of the brigades of the 2nd Guards Tank Corps

The **4th Guards Tank Brigade** together with the 401st Guards Self-propelled Artillery Regiment was operating in two columns in the course of 4 August 1944 after taking Semeneliszki and Lewki, and emerged on the western bank of the Szyrwinta River in the Bobławka area. As a result of the day's combat, the brigade destroyed 7 tanks and 3 self-propelled guns of the enemy's, 8 vehicles together with their loads, and 3 artillery batteries. It killed up to 150 Nazis. In return the brigade lost 13 T-34 tanks destroyed and 4 tanks knocked out, as well as 17 men killed and 42 wounded. The brigade has 18 operational T-34 tanks.

At 00.30 on 4 August 1944, the units of the **26th Guards Tank Brigade** moved out of Naszyszki and by 01.30 they were assembled in the jumping-off positions in the woods west of Grenszej. In this area the tanks were dispersed and camouflaged, and all-round security was organized. The men were allowed to rest and with the dawning of the new day, given hot breakfasts. At 11.10 on 4 August 1944, the brigade set out from its jumping-off area in the vicinity of the hamlet of Szelwy, and by 12.30 it crossed to the western bank of the Szejmena River in the Wyszczokajmie area with the forces of the 1st Tank Battalion, 2nd Tank Battalion and motorized rifle battalion. There they were met by heavy artillery and mortar fire, as well as fire from enemy tanks. At 16.30 of this same day, the enemy in strength of up to a battalion of infantry and 7 self-propelled guns, supported by artillery fire, counterattacked the brigade's units from out of the areas of Budziszki and Hill 58.5. In the resulting battle the brigade killed up to 100 Nazis and destroyed 3 antitank guns and 2 vehicles, while knocking out one self-propelled gun. The enemy counterattack was repulsed. Continuing to carry out their assigned task in the face of stubborn enemy resistance, the units of the 26th Guards Tank Brigade by midnight captured the Gużele estate, Bocianowo, Budziszki and Hill 52.3, where they dug in and took up a defense. Over the day of fighting the brigade lost one T-34 tank destroyed, 1 antitank gun and 23 men, including 4 killed and 19 wounded. In its area of combat operations, the brigade had 18 T-34 tanks, of which 3 were non-serviceable.

At 11.00 on 4 August 1944, the **25th Guards Tank Brigade**, at a signal from the corps commander, set out on the march in the wake of the 4th Guards Tank Brigade; by 14.00 it was crossing the Szeymena River in the area of Wyszczokajmie. By 1500, the brigade had fully crossed to the western bank of the river. At 16.00 the entire brigade moved out in the direction of Szelgajcie and Żwangucie with the task to envelop the enemy from the left. At 16.30, having reached an isolated cottage northeast of Szelgajcie, the brigade ran into resistance from enemy tanks and artillery and became tied up in stubborn fighting. Fighting its way forward, by 17.30 it reached an area 300 meters north of Szelgajcie. At 19.30, after reconnoitering, the brigade attacked in two directions: 1st Tank Battalion – Szelgajcie and northwest of Žvangučiai; 2nd Tank Battalion – from behind the right flank of the 1st Tank Battalion attacked Žvangučiai from the northwest; the motorized rifle battalion followed behind the combat formations of the tank brigade.

The **401st Guards Self-propelled Artillery Regiment**, occupying a defense of Dydwiże, by the end of 2 August 1944 had placed some of its SU-85 subordinate to the commander of the 4th Guards Tank Brigade in support of the 25th Guards Tank Brigade in the area of Wiłkowyszki Station, with the task to guard it from the west and screen the brigade's flank.

On 3 August 1944 the regiment received the mission to support the actions of the 4th Guards Tank Brigade to take Szykszniewo and in the future capture Bilderweitschen (East Prussia). By 2.00 on 4 August 1944 the regiment, having completed its march, was assembled in jumping-off positions in Korale. By 12.00 the regiment, together with the tank brigade, took Semeneliszki with fighting, having first forced a crossing of the Szejmena River and having driven the enemy from his line along the Szejmena River. A counterattack undertaken by the enemy toward Semeneliszki with major forces of infantry, supported by tanks and assault guns, was driven back by the fire from the regiment's SU-85s. At mid-day on 4 August 1944, the regiment was shifted to the area of the bridges across the Szywinta River at Bobławka with orders to hold the bridge and the occupied line.

In the fighting on 4 August 1944, the regiment suffered heavy losses: 3 SU-85 destroyed and 7 SU-85 knocked out, as well as 18 casualties – 1 officer and 5 sergeants and privates killed, and 5 officers and 7 sergeants and privates wounded. On the same day, the regiment inflicted damage to the enemy: 1 self-propelled gun and 2 field guns destroyed, and up to 200 soldiers and officers killed. The regiment's heavy losses are explained primarily by the fact that the self-propelled guns were used like tanks, receiving and implementing independent tasks just like a tank unit.

34 TANK BATTLES IN EAST PRUSSIA AND POLAND, 1944-1945

Excerpt from Operational Summary No. 863/44 from the headquarters of the Third Panzer Army (Pz AOK 3) to the headquarters of Army Group Center, 4 August 1944. Daily operational report.

Today as we expected, the Russians went over to a large attack on almost the entire front of the panzer army. However, the heroic resistance of our units didn't allow the Russians to break through to East Prussia. The enemy was attacking with massed artillery fire, ground attack aircraft and large tank forces. The direction of the main attacks came in the areas northwest of Kalwarja [Kalvarija] and northwest and west of Wiłkowyszki. The enemy that penetrated into our defense was stopped or thrown back with counterattacks by our forces. Approximately 40 enemy tanks alone attacked north of the Wirballen [Virbalis] – Wiłkowyszki railroad, followed by infantry. In this sector, it has been planned on 5 August to launch an attack with one reinforced regiment of the *Grossdeutschland* Division in order to restore the situation.

In the course of 4 August, 115 enemy tanks were destroyed in the area of the panzer army's operations, and another 5 enemy tanks were knocked out. Our air force was effectively supporting the defensive fighting.

Panzerjäger Battalion 1064 has become subordinate to XXXX Panzer Corps. Arrived: units of Artillery Regiment 1561, Panzerjäger Battalion 1065; from Panzergrenadier Division *Grossdeutschland*: motorized regiment (minus the 13th Company), the artillery regiment's II Battalion, and 12 Pz.kpfw. VI tanks. II Battalion of Security Regiment 603 and I Battalion of Security Regiment 609 have joined Gruppe von Rotkirch. The command post of Panzergrenadier Division *Grossdeutschland*: Vištytis.

Table 1.2: Status of the panzers, SPW and self-propelled guns of the German III Panzer Army at day's end on 4 August 1944

Units	Tanks, halftracks and self-propelled guns	Combat-ready	In repair	
			Short-term	Long-term
5.Panzer Division	Pz-IV	5	-	-
	Pz-V	11	-	-
6.Panzer Division	Pz-IV	12	48	3
	SPW	-	1	-
I/Panzer Rgt. *Grossdeutschland*	Pz-V	8	39	3
	SPW	-	5	-
7.Panzer Division	Pz-V	27	-	-
	Assault guns	5	-	-
sPanzer Abt. 510	Pz-VI	12	3	-
sPanzerjäger Abt. 519	Nashhorn	6	-	-
	Hummel	1	-	-
	Assault guns	1	-	-
sPanzerjäger Abt. 731	Hetzer	11	-	-
StuG Brigade 232	StuG	25	-	-
StuG Brigade 277	StuG	14	-	-
Brigade Von Werthern	Pz-IV	1	-	-
StuG Brigade 203	StuG	25	-	-
StuG Brigade 276	StuG	15		

Having resumed the offensive from the morning of 5 August and having broken the enemy resistance, the 2nd Guards Tank Corps with its forward detachment – the 26th Guards Tank Brigade's 1st Tank Battalion – reached the Leopoldowo, Skordupiany area, while with its main forces reached the line of the Szyrwinta River in the Andrykajmie, Drebulinė area. Thus, the enemy's previously prepared line of defense on the approaches to the East Prussian border had been breached.

Combat Report No. 033 from the headquarters of the 2nd Guards Tank Corps, 5 August 1944, 2400

To the commander-in-chief of the 3rd Belorussian Front General of the Army Cherniakhovsky
To the commander of the 3rd Belorussian Front's armored and mechanized forces Colonel General Rodin
To the commander of the 33rd Army Lieutenant General Morozov
To the commander of the 33rd Army's armored and mechanized forces Colonel Vakhrushev

I am reporting on the brigade's combat operations for 5 August 1944

1. Units of the East Prussian Grenadier Division, reinforced by a group of 45-50 tanks and self-propelled guns, with stubborn fighting over the day of 5 August 1944 was thrown back to the western bank of the Szyrwinta River on the front: Point 50.6, Bobławka.
2. The corps' units with fighting by the morning of 5 August 1944 emerged on the western bank of the Szyrwinta River: a) 26th Guards Tank Brigade with 14 tanks in the area of Point 50.6; b) 4th Guards Tank Brigade and the 401st Guards Self-propelled Artillery Regiment in cooperation with the 4th Guards Motorized Rifle Brigade – crossroads 1 km northwest of Bobławka; c) the 25th Guards Tank Brigade – reached the area of Patwiecie in the reserve of the 33rd Army; d) 4th Guards Motorized Rifle Brigade, cooperating with the 4th Guards Tank Brigade, in the tank combat formations.
3. Combat operations of the corps' units for the day of 5 August 1944:
   a) 26th Guards tank Brigade from the morning with a forward detachment of 7 tanks began to advance to the west; the 2nd Tank Battalion numbering 5 tanks was operating in the direction of Szukle and Point 44.4;
   b) 4th Guards Tank Brigade, in cooperation with the 4th Guards Motorized Rifle Brigade, was attacking toward Kregżdzie and Skordupiany;

The 1st Tank Battalion of the 26th Guards Tank Brigade by 10.00 5 August 1944 took Leopoldowo, and brushing aside small enemy detachments, reached the Naumiestis – Kibarty road at Point 49.3 with 4 tanks, while 3 tanks remained behind in Leopoldowo. There was no infantry with the tanks. The enemy at this time launched a counterattack in strength of up to 40 tanks, self-propelled guns and infantry from the north, west and south. The forward reconnaissance of the 26th Guards Tank Brigade, seeing the enemy's superiority, fell back to Leopoldowo and linked up with the battalion.

In the course of the day 5 August 1944 the enemy launched 6 counterattacks with the support of groups of 15-30 aircraft. The tanks of the 26th Guards Tank Brigade, stubbornly fighting against superior enemy forces, repulsed all the counterattacks on its direction, but suffered heavy losses in the process. Almost all of the tanks of the 26th Guards Tank Brigade were destroyed by the enemy on the western bank of the Szyrwinta River. Of the 14 tanks located on the western bank, 11 tanks were left burned-out, and one tank was knocked out. Of the tanks that were lost, 8 were destroyed by the fire of enemy aircraft, and 1 was knocked out. The remaining 3 destroyed tanks were struck by the fire of tanks and artillery. The remaining two tanks of the battalion commanders were withdrawn by the brigade commander to the eastern bank of the Szyrwinta River in order to keep possession of the bridge in the area of Point 39.7; the 4th Guards Tank Brigade in cooperation with the 4th Guards Motorized Rifle Brigade also repulsed all of the enemy counterattacks, while also taking heavy losses in the process. Over the day of combat on 5 August 1944, it lost 4 T-34 and 2 SU-76 destroyed by enemy aircraft, and 2 tanks destroyed by artillery fire.

By the end of day, the brigade's remaining tanks were occupying an advantageous line on the western bank of the Szyrwinta River in the vicinity of Point 49.7. The brigade is continuing to hold this bridgehead.

1. Our losses over the day of combat: 17 tanks destroyed and 1 tank knocked out; 2 SU-76 destroyed and 1 knocked out; one T-34 tank was destroyed by the fire of our own ground attack aircraft. Twenty vehicles were smashed. The corps lost 184 men, including 57 killed and 127 wounded. Enemy losses: up to 900 soldiers and officers killed, and 19 tanks and self-propelled guns either destroyed or knocked out.
2. **Conclusion:** The enemy, sensing the threat of a breakthrough by our units to the German border, brought up major reserves and with incessant counterattacks and aircraft attempted to hurl our units back to the western bank of the Szyrwinta River. The enemy aircraft were particularly active JU-87 dive bombers set ablaze a lot of tanks and knocked out many guns. I believe there is no basis to put the officers of the 26th Guards Tank Brigade on trial. The brigade commander had been given an admonition, given the brigade's limited strength, not to allow the forward reconnaissance and the forward units to become widely separate.

Commander of the 2nd Guards Tatsinskaia Tank Corps
Guards Major General of Tank Forces BURDEINYI
Corps chief of staff Guards Colonel KARAVAN

By the end of 5 August 1944, the 2nd Guards Tank Corps had operational 41 T-34 and 4 SU-85. The situation with supplies: 1.2 refills of fuel and lubricants, 1.9 standard combat loads of ammunition, and 2 days of food. The weather is dry and warm. The roads are passable for all types of transport.

Excerpts from the combat diaries of the brigades of the 2nd Guards Tank Corps

4th Guards Tank Brigade with the 401st Guards Self-propelled Artillery Regiment, in cooperation with the 4th Guards Motorized Rifle Brigade, throughout the day of 5 August 1944 was holding the bridgehead across the Szyrwinta River, repulsing enemy counterattacks using tanks, self-propelled artillery and infantry. At 10.30 7 enemy tanks and 3 self-propelled guns with up to a battalion of infantry attacked from the Leopoldowo direction; up to 10 tanks and a battalion of infantry launched a counterattack along the road from Skordupiany. The brigade's tanks, together with the motorized riflemen of the 4th Guards Motorized Rifle Brigade, with fire from fixed positions and out of ambush positions fought for two hours with the enemy's counterattacking tanks and infantry. As a result of the tanks' intensive fire, the counterattack was beaten back. As a result of the combat the brigade destroyed 3 self-propelled guns and 1 tank; knocked out 4 tanks; destroyed up to two infantry companies; and suppressed the fire of two artillery batteries.

In return the brigade lost 6 T-34 tanks destroyed and 2 knocked out, and had 7 men killed and 23 wounded. By the end of the day, the brigade had 15 T-34 tanks operational.

From the morning of 5 August 1944 the enemy in strength of up to a regiment of infantry, with the support of 20 tanks and self-propelled guns and supporting artillery fire and airstrikes, incessantly counterattacked the units of the **26th Guards Tank Brigade** from the west, northwest and southwest, as a result of which the enemy managed to shove the brigade's units back and to reach the western bank of the Szyrwinta River. The brigade for one and a half hours exchanged fire with the enemy, while being constantly under enemy bomber attacks and having no support on either flank from the units that hadn't reached the brigade's line by this time. The 26th Guards Tank Brigade's 1st Tank Battalion, under the influence of superior enemy forces that were enveloping it on the right and left, was forced to fall back with fighting from its occupied area and to dig in on the Hill 49.5 – Kregzdzė line; the 2nd Tank Battalion and motorized rifle battalion continued to hold their occupied line. The infantry of the 49th Rifle Division, which had been occupying a line between Szukle and Hill 50.6, withdrew to the eastern bank of the Szyrwinta River.

Subsequently throughout the rest of the day, the enemy constantly attacked the brigade's combat positions with tanks and infantry from the west and southwest, supported by powerful artillery and mortar fire and airstrikes. The units of the 26th Guards Tank Brigade stubbornly exchanged fire with the enemy tanks and infantry, suffering heavy losses in men and tanks, primarily from enemy aircraft and artillery fire. Having no supporting infantry or artillery, and also lacking sufficient air cover, the remaining 3 T-34 tanks, 2 76mm antitank guns, 3 82mm mortars and up to 30 vehicles were forced to fall back to the eastern bank of the Szyrwinta River, and by 19.00 on 5 August 1944 took up a defense at the crossroads southeast of the Szyrwinta.

At the decision of the brigade commander, the remaining combat-ready T-34 tanks were merged into a single battalion. The remaining men of the submachine gun companies and tank riding companies of the motorized rifle battalion were merged into a single submachine gun company.

Throughout the night of 5-6 August 1944, the men of the brigade's units topped up the remaining tanks with fuel and ammunition. From the number of T-34 tanks repaired at Bastunė Station, 6 T-34 tanks arrived in the brigade's occupied area. One more T-34 tank containing an RS radio set was received from corps headquarters. With the fall of darkness, knocked out and disabled combat and wheeled materiel were evacuated from the battlefield.

As a result of the combat, the brigade had losses from enemy artillery fire and aircraft: 11 T-34 tanks burned out and 2 tanks knocked out, and one T-34 tank bogged down in a swamp; one antitank gun and one mortar were smashed, and two 37mm anti-aircraft guns were damaged along with 1 DShK machine gun; 10 wheeled vehicles were destroyed and 5 damaged. In return, the brigade killed up to 300 enemy soldiers and officers, and destroyed 4 antitank guns, 3 mortar batteries and 10 vehicles.

In the 26th Guards Tank Brigade's defensive area, there are 10 operational T-34 tanks, 2 76mm antitank guns, 3 anti-aircraft cannons, 5 DShK machine guns, and 3 82mm mortars. In the attached units, there are 3 37mm anti-aircraft cannons (a battery of the 1695th Anti-Aircraft Regiment) and 1 DShK machine gun.

Units of the **25th Guards Tank Brigade** throughout the day of 5 August 1944 continued to hold their occupied line of defense. A set-up ambush with T-34 tanks northwest of Patwiecie destroyed 1 self-propelled gun, 4 vehicles and up to a platoon of Nazis. In the sector of the 4th Guards Tank Brigade, the enemy went over to repeated counterattacks with tanks and infantry, which were all repulsed. As a result of enemy artillery and mortar fire, the 25th Guards Tank Brigade lost 4 men killed and 6 wounded. One T-34 tank was destroyed. By the end of day 5 August 1944, the 25th Guards Tank Brigade had 10 operational T-34 tanks, 6 T-34 tanks undergoing moderate repairs, and 3 tanks requiring factory repair.

The actions of the 1500th Self-propelled Artillery Regiment

By the end of 4 August 1944, the regiment had set out from its staging area and had taken up firing positions on the southwestern outskirts of Semeneliszki, and by the morning of 5 August 1944 was in the area 1.5 km north of Bobławka, guarding the bridge across the Szyrwinta River with the assignment to block enemy counterattacks from the southern and southwestern directions.

In the course of 5 August 1944, the regiment repulsed repeated enemy attacks, while in the process destroying 1 medium tank, 1 antitank gun, 15 machine guns, and killing 120 enemy soldiers and officers. Over the day, the regiment lost 1 SU-76 self-propelled gun destroyed and 1 knocked out. By the end of 5 August 1944, at an order from the corps' artillery commander, the regiment was withdrawn from combat in order to make repairs and bring the self-propelled guns, weapons, motor transport and men back to order.

All of the artillery units handled their assignments well. The operations of the 401st Guards Self-propelled Artillery Regiment were particularly indicative. As a result of the arising situation, the need arose to use the self-propelled guns like tanks, having given them an independent task.

The mission was executed by the regiment, and the incurred losses proved to be completely justified. The experience of the recent fighting showed that it is necessary to mount machine guns on the self-propelled guns in the conditions of close combat with enemy infantry. Considering the excessive wear on both the engines and rolling assemblies of the self-propelled guns, the latter can be used effectively only on the defense, and in offensive operations – only given insignificant marches.

Excerpt from Operational Summary No. 867/44 from the headquarters of the Third Panzer Army to the headquarters of Army Group Center, 5 August 1944. Daily operational report:

On 5 August 1944 the enemy with major infantry forces supported by a large quantity of tanks once again attempted to break through our defense. The directions of the enemy's main attacks came from the same directions as they did on 4 August. South of the Neman River, the Russians didn't manage to breach the front line, and with a counterattack by units of the Panzergrenadier Division *Grossdeutschland* the enemy was thrown back to their jumping-off positions. Nevertheless, the situation on this sector of the front remains tense, because our units are defending an excessively broad front.

In the sector of the 561st Volksgrenadier Division, the enemy launched two attacks with minor forces along both sides of Wiłkowyszki, neither of which had success. Units of the *Grossdeutschland* Division, which were operating in the sector of the enemy's penetration north of the railroad, attacked out of the area northeast of Virbalis, and after stubborn fighting with major enemy tank forces took Drebulinė on the afternoon of 5 August.

Attacking units of the Division *Grossdeutschland* are continuing to push to the north with the task to destroy the enemy forces that reached Szukle. Up to the present time 9 enemy tanks and 27 antitank guns have been destroyed. In the latter half of the day, the enemy shoved back Gruppe Knebel by 1-2 km to the west.

In the sector of the 6th Panzer Division, after our successful attack on 4 August, the enemy launched a counterattack on the afternoon of 5 August. This counterattack, plainly conducted in haste, was in general repulsed. The enemy didn't manage to break through to Naumiestis. On our front that runs along the eastern outskirts of Žvirgždaičiai [north of Wiłkawyszki], there is no solid line of defense; only strongpoints are defending here. Through the maneuvering actions of the panzer group, the enemy's further advance to the west was stopped.

Subordination: I/Mortar Regiment 57 is subordinate to XXXX Panzer Corps. The II/Fusilier Regiment *Grossdeutschland* and two batteries are temporarily subordinate to 5th Panzer Division. The reconnaissance training battalion is subordinate to XXV Army Corps for operations as part of the 69th Infantry Division.

Arrived: From Panzergrenadier Division *Grossdeutschland*, the signals battalion, the rest of the motorized regiment, fresh units of the panzer division's fusilier regiment and the panzer division's artillery regiment; 10th and 11th Companies of the panzer regiment (up to present, 17 Pz.kpfw. VI tanks have arrived); the headquarters and one battery of a StuG Brigade (to the present point, 5 assault guns have arrived); a battalion of Flak artillery; and III Battalion and elements of II Battalion of Mortar Regiment 57. I Battalion of Security Regiment 51 has arrived at Gruppe von Rotkirch.

Table 1.3: Status of the panzers, SPW and self-propelled guns of the German Third Panzer Army by day's end of 5 August 1944

Units	Tanks, halftracks and self-propelled guns	Combat-ready	In repair	
			Short-term	Long-term
5.Panzer Division	Pz-IV	15	13	-
	Pz-V	18	2	11
6.Panzer Division	Pz-IV	18	37	16
	SPW	-	-	-
I/Panzer Rgt. *Grossdeutschland*	Pz-V	7	30	-
	SPW	-	-	-
Korps Gruppe "D"	A-T gun on self-propelled carriage	1	-	-
sPanzer Abt. 510	Pz-VI	11	24	-
sPanzerjäger Abt. 519	Nashorn	6	-	-
	Hummel	1	-	-
	Assault guns	1	-	-
sPanzerjäger Abt. 731	Hetzer	11	-	-
StuG Brigade 232	StuG	19	7	-
StuG Brigade 277	StuG	9	11	-
Brigade Von Werthern	Pz-IV	-	1	-
StuG Brigade 203	StuG	26	1	4
StuG Brigade 276	StuG	10	10	8

Information found on a map of the dispositions of the 2nd Guards Tank Corps' units

1. 4th Guards Motorized Rifle Brigade is occupying a defense on the western bank of the Szyrwinta River behind the road; from the river, its right flank is west of Drebulinė, while its left flank is saddling the railroad. The 401st Guards Self-propelled Artillery Regiment with the motorized rifle brigade has 8 serviceable SU-85, of which 3 SU-85 are on the western bank behind the combat positions of the infantry, and 5 SU-85 are on the eastern bank of the river.
2. 4th Guards Tank Brigade has 19 operational T-34 tanks, of which 7 T-34 of the 3rd Tank Battalion are on the western bank, and 6 T-34 of the 1st Tank Battalion are on the eastern bank. The 2nd Tank Battalion with 6 operational T-34 is in the corps' reserve.

3. 26th Guards Tank Brigade had 3 operational T-34; 5 more T-34 are on the approach. The brigade is occupying a defense on the eastern bank of the river on the northwest outskirts of Wejliszki and to the north.
4. 25th Guards Tank Brigade has 12 operational T-34 in the Patwiecie area.
5. For the convenience of observation and command, the commander of the 2nd Guards Tank Corps is located together with the corps' operational command group.

Assistant chief of staff of the 33rd Army's armored and mechanized forces
Captain Bogoslavsky
6 August 1944

As outlined by Gerd Niepold in *Panzer Operationen "Doppelkopf" und "Cäsar"* on 5.8 and 6.8.44 the Soviets were thrown back at Wiłkowyszki by units of the Panzer Grenadier Division Gross Deutschland. But, the situation remained very tense. The bulk of the Gross Deutschland Division was concentrated in the area northeast of the Vystitis Lake. In the afternoon of 7 August Field Marshal Model visited the commander of the 3rd Panzer Army, Colonel-General Reinhardt, at Schlossberg. He stated that he anticipated launching an offensive with several divisions on his left wing. Although he did not mention it, the long-expected attack on Army Group North would soon begin.

As noted by Kurt Dieckert and Horst Grossman in their book *Der Kampf um Ostpreussen*, on 4 August 1944 the Soviets launched attacks toward Bilderweitschen and Schirwindt that almost reached the border. Reserves were rushed up, including Panzergrenadier Division Grossdeutschland, which made a substantial contribution to the defense. The defense of the Wiłkowyszki – Wirballen – Eydtkuhnen – Ebenrode transportation artery was important. After both the northern flank and the arterial road were held, on 5 and 6 August a Grossdeutschland kampfgruppe launched an attack at Hill 51 northeast of Skordupiany and stopped the enemy's further advance in heavy fighting.

Excerpt from Intelligence Summary No. 105 from the headquarters of the 3rd Belorussian Front, 6 August 1944

Gumbinnen direction
The enemy on 6 August was driven out of the villages of Žynie, Rumaki, Pracapol, Iszkarty, Zielonka (all points 7-11 km southeast of Naumiestis), and out of the area of Leopoldowo (9 km south of Naumiestis). The enemy, with the forces of up to a battalion of infantry and 11 tanks, supported by artillery and mortar fire and airstrikes, attacked to the east. The fighting is ongoing. Out of the areas west of Mercze (5 km southeast of Naumiestis), Bobławka, (8 kilometers northwest of Wiłkawyszki), Degucie (14 km west of Mariampol) and Lubow, the enemy in strength between a company and a battalion of infantry, with the support of 8-15 tanks, 3-5 self-propelled guns and artillery and mortar fire launched 8 unsuccessful attacks. Throughout the day, 34 artillery and 15 mortar batteries, 4 rocket launchers and up to 100 tanks and self-propelled guns were supporting the infantry's actions.

On 5 August 1944 the commander of a combat group of the 256th Infantry Division, Major Walter Rixecker, was taken prisoner in the Modajcie area; he revealed under interrogation that tanks from the *Grossdeutschland* Panzer Division's panzer regiment were operating in the sector of the 69th Infantry Division. The troops defending in this sector have the overall task of delaying the Russians' advance for as long as possible on intermediary lines, in order to gain time for completing the construction of fortifications along the border of East Prussia.

The 33rd Army in the course of the day of 6 August fought off repeated enemy counterattacks, and overcoming his stubborn resistance, made an advance of 3 km with its right flank. By end of day 6 August, it was engaged in fighting on the following line: 62nd Rifle Corps: 70th Rifle Division – Mercze, crossroads 1 km west of Zielonka, crossroads 1 km southeast of Szukle, further along the eastern bank of the Szyrwinta River as far as the road west of the map label "Drebulinė"; 344th Rifle Division – crossroads 1 km north of Bobławka, eastern outskirts of Bobławka, southwestern outskirts of Žvangučiai. The 19th Rifle Corps in the course of the day was engaged in intense fighting with counterattacking enemy units and repulsed 6 counterattacks in strength of two infantry companies each together with 3-4 tanks and self-propelled guns. By 22.00 the corps' units had made no advance and were still engaged in combat on their previously occupied lines. The casualties of the 33rd Army for 5 August 1944 amounted to 130 men killed and 369 wounded. Eight guns of various calibers were knocked out of action. For 6 August 1944, up to 500 enemy soldiers and officers have been killed, and 2 self-propelled guns, 7 tanks, 2 field guns, 3 mortars, 16 machine guns and 8 vehicles have been knocked out by the army. Captured: 36 prisoners, 1 tank, 1 halftrack, 4 guns, 9 machine guns, and 46 rifles and submachine guns.

Heroes of the 2nd Guards Tank Corps, August 1944

Guards Lieutenant Fedor Andreiuk – commander of a machine-gun platoon of the 2nd Motorized Rifle Battalion of the 2nd Guards Tank Corps' 4th Guards Motorized Rifle Brigade. On 30 July 1944 during the attack toward Mariampol, he led his platoon courageously; with his platoon he wiped out up to two platoons of enemy infantry, two machine-gun nests, and one antitank gun. On 1 August 1944 during the attack toward Wiłkowyszki he spotted a group of Germans in up to company strength moving from the rear in the direction of the battalion headquarters. Andreiuk allowed them to close within short range and then opened fire with his platoon from 10 machine guns and killed up to 50 Germans, and took 26 men prisoner. When his unit was crossing the Šesna River [sic], the enemy counterattacked them, but Andreiuk, allowing the enemy to close within short range, opened point-blank fire at them, inflicting enormous casualties on the enemy. He was awarded the Order of the Red Banner.

Guards Sergeant Ivan Slepov – a squad commander in the 3rd Motorized Rifle Battalion of the 2nd Guards Tank Corps' 4th Guards Motorized Rifle Brigade. In the combat in the Wiłkowyszki area on 31 July 1944, he demonstrated exceptional valor and bravery. While on reconnaissance on the northern outskirts of the town, he reported accurate information about the enemy, revealed all the enemy firing positions, and when the company attacked the town on the morning of 1 August 1944, Smelov spotted a German firing position – an anti-aircraft machine gun that was firing at the attackers, and with the cry of "Uraa!", he charged the machine gun, captured it, and turned it in the opposite direction and began to shoot down the fleeing Nazis. When the platoon commander was knocked out of action, he assumed command of the platoon. He was awarded the Order of the Patriotic War 2nd Class.

Guards Senior Lieutenant Mikhail Petrov – the commander of a mortar battery in the 1st Motorized Rifle Battalion of the 2nd Guards Tank Corps' 4th Guards Motorized Rifle Brigade. In the fighting for Wiłkowyszki on 1 August 1944, at a moment when the battalion was threatened with encirclement, his mortar battery showed great skill in eliminating Germans. In this action the battery killed up to 50 enemy soldiers and officers. He's been awarded the Order of the Patriotic War 1st Class.

Guards Lieutenant Nikolai Gavrilov – the commander of a rifle platoon in the 2nd Motorized Rifle Battalion of the 2nd Guards Tank Corps' 4th Guards Motorized Rifle Brigade. During the attack toward Wiłkowyszki on 1 August 1944, his platoon quickly overcame an enemy trench line and an antitank ditch and was the first to enter the town's outskirts. In the fighting, his platoon killed up to 50 Nazi soldiers, captured 10 enemy soldiers and officers, and seized 3 functioning light machine guns and 1 heavy machine gun. While fighting in the town, where a firing position was hindering the company's advance, he attacked and destroyed it, thereby permitting the company to move forward. In the fighting, when the company commander was wounded, he assumed command of the company and by his personal example, located out in front of the attacking company, he led the soldiers on the attack. He's been awarded the Order of the Patriotic War 2nd Class.

Guards Sergeant Ivan Andriushin – the commander of an antitank rifle squad in the 3rd Motorized Rifle Battalion of the 2nd Guards Tank Corps' 4th Guards Motorized Rifle Brigade. During the attack toward Wiłkowyszki on 1 August 1944 his platoon commander was wounded. Andriushin bravely assumed command and throughout the entire operation skillfully commanded the platoon. In this action Andriushin's platoon destroyed 7 enemy firing positions and killed 10 Nazis. He was awarded the Order of the Red Star.

Guards Lieutenant Ivan Leliavin – commander of an antitank rifle company in the 2nd Guards Tank Corps' 4th Guards Motorized Rifle Brigade. In the course of 5 and 6 August, the enemy in numerically superior forces repeatedly counterattacked in the Bobławka area. Leliavin's antitank rifle company courageously fought off the German onslaught. On 5 August, having repulsed 6 powerful counterattacks, the company knocked out 1 tank, conducted volley fire at the attacking tanks and suppressed the fire coming from 4 firing positions, killing more than 30 Nazis. On 6 August, when German tanks suddenly emerged on the right flank, the company conducted volley fire from its antitank rifles, and when three tanks were disabled, Leliavin raised the company on the attack, charged the tanks, and having covered them with straw, set fire to the tanks. Recommended for the Order of the Red Banner; awarded the Order of the Patriotic War 2nd Class.

Guards Junior Lieutenant Zakhar Roslik – commander of a machine-gun platoon of the 2nd Guards Tank Corps' 4th Guards Motorized Rifle Brigade. In the course of 5 and 6 August 1944, the enemy repeatedly launched counterattacks with numerically superior forces. On 5 August Roslik's platoon tenaciously repulsed 6 enemy counterattacks with infantry and tanks, killing up to 70 Germans in the fighting. On 6 August in the Bobławka area, when enemy tanks suddenly emerged on the right flank, Roslik and his platoon separated the German infantry from the tanks, and when three tanks were disabled, Roslik issued an order to attack the tanks. His soldiers helped cover the tanks with straw and set them ablaze. Wounded, Roslik refused to leave the battlefield and continued to conduct fire at the enemy. He's been awarded the Order of the Patriotic War 2nd Class.

Guards Sergeant Vasilii Gorelov – commander of a squad in the reconnaissance company of the 2nd Guards Tank Corps' 4th Guards Motorized Rifle Brigade. In the fighting he showed himself to be a bold scout and a valorous and aggressive squad commander. Over the period of fighting between 26 July and 8 August 1944, he repeatedly took part in attempts to snatch prisoners while scouting the directions and brought back valuable information about the enemy. His squad killed several dozen Germans and took 20 Nazis prisoner. Gorelov personally killed 5 Nazis. On 6 August while on reconnaissance he acted boldly and decisively. Sticking with the lead attacking infantry and tanks, he pointed out targets for them. Being wounded, he refused to abandon his post. He was awarded the Order of the Patriotic War 2nd Class.

Starting from 6 August 1944, the enemy began to assemble major forces. The elite, fresh Panzergrenadier Division *Grossdeutschland*, fully staffed and well-equipped, under the command of General Hasso von Manteuffel, was transferred to the area south of Wiłkowyszki. The German command was preparing to launch a counterattack in this sector, calculating with an attack in the direction of Mariampol and further on toward Kaunas to cut off the salient in the lines that had been created here, in which the Soviet 33rd and 5th Armies were located, along with their attached assets, including Major General of Tank Forces A.S. Burdeinyi's 2nd Guards Tank Corps. Thereby, the Germans would eliminate the threat of a Soviet invasion into East Prussia.

The units of the 2nd Guards Tank Corps in the course of 6 August continued to defend their previously-occupied lines, repelling three counterattacks of the enemy, which was attempting to force a crossing of the Szyrwinta River, and exchanging fire on the following lines: 4th Guards Tank Brigade together with the 4th Guards Motorized Rifle Brigade on the western bank of the Szyrwinta River in the Point 49.7 – Bobławka area; 26th Guards Tank Brigade on the northwestern outskirts of Wejliszki, with one platoon of tanks on a nameless elevation 1.5 km northwest of Wejliszki; 25th Guards Tank Brigade in Patwiecie, having a combat security outpost in Andrykajmie and northeast of there. As a result of the day's fighting on 6 August, the corps destroyed 12 enemy tanks, of which 4 were Tiger tanks, 4 cannons, 5 vehicles and 8 machine guns, while killing 250 enemy soldiers and officers. One of the knocked-out Tigers was located in the dispositions of the 4th Guards Tank Brigade and might be put back into service after replacing the main gun. In the process, the corps suffered losses: 5 men killed and 10 wounded, and one burned-out T-34.

By the end of the day of 6 August, the 2nd Guards Tank Corps had 50 operational T-34. The operational command group is in Drebulinė; the corps headquarters is in Baziliškai.

Excerpts from the combat diaries of the brigades of the 2nd Guards Tank Corps

The **25th Guards Tank Brigade**'s units are continuing to occupy their present lines of defense. A deployed ambush using T-34 tanks northwest of Patwiecie in the course of 6 August destroyed 1 self-propelled gun, 4 vehicles and up to a platoon of Nazis. In the sector of the 4th Guards Tank Brigade and 26th Guards Tank Brigade, the enemy continued to counterattack with tanks and infantry. All of the counterattacks were repulsed. As a result of enemy artillery and mortar fire, the brigade lost 1 T-34 tank destroyed, and 4 men killed and 5 wounded. On the afternoon of 6 August, the enemy launched two counterattacks in strength of up to a battalion of infantry supported by artillery, tanks and self-propelled guns, but both were driven back by our units. The brigade continues to hold a defense on the line 400 meters west of Patwiecie in readiness to repulse enemy counterattacks and to carry out the task of firmly holding its occupied defensive area. By the end of the day, the brigade had 14 operational T-34, 2 T-34 undergoing moderate repairs, 2 tanks requiring factory repairs, and 1 tank that lagged behind due to a mechanical breakdown.

The **26th Guards Tank Brigade**: the brigade's task for 6 August was to hold its occupied line along the eastern bank of the Szyrwinta River and to defend against enemy attacks from the west and southwest. The enemy in the course of the day was massing infantry on the western bank of the Szyrwinta River under the cover of heavy artillery and mortar fire, as well as tanks. Reconnaissance and observation established: at 7.30 6 August 4 tanks and a company of infantry in the Szukle area; at 13.40 10 tanks and an aggregation of infantry in the vicinity of Hill 50.6; and the movement of 30 vehicles from Leopoldowo in the direction of Bobławka. With a series of unsuccessful attacks, the enemy in the course of 6 August attempted to force a crossing of the Szyrwinta River and to reach its eastern bank in the Hill 50.6 – Szukle area. The brigade, consisting of the 2nd Tank Battalion and the motorized rifle battalion, was occupying a defense in separate knots of resistance in the vicinity of the crossroads 800 meters southeast of Hill 39.7, with the task to defend against enemy attacks. Throughout the day of 6 August, the enemy in strength of up to a battalion of infantry with the support of tanks and artillery and mortar fire attacked our units three times, trying to force a crossing of the Szyrwinta River and to reach the eastern bank in the area of Szukle and Hill 50.6. With the fire from the tanks of the 2nd Tank Battalion and the motorized rifle battalion, the enemy was thrown back with heavy losses. The brigade's units were firmly holding their occupied position, while simultaneously scouting for the enemy along the eastern bank of the Szyrwinta to the north and south. On the night of 6-7 August, the tanks were topped up with fuel and ammunition.

As a result of the fighting to repulse the enemy, the following damage was inflicted to the enemy by the brigade: 2 tanks knocked out, 4 tanks destroyed and up to 100 enemy soldiers and officers killed. In return, the brigade lost 1 man wounded. By the end of day on 6 August the brigade had 14 T-34 tanks in the area of defense, of which 3 tanks required light repairs. In addition, one tank overturned on a collapsing bridge across the Szyrwinta River in the area of Point 50.6 and required evacuation. In the area of defense, the brigade had 1 refill of fuel and lubricants, 1 standard combat load of ammunition, and 1 day of rations. The brigade's command post is in Wejliszki.

The **4th Guards Motorized Rifle Brigade:** in the fighting on 6 August the brigade eliminated 66 enemy soldiers and officers while scattering or partially destroying up to a platoon of infantry; knocked out or destroyed 3 tanks and captured 1 tank; and destroyed 8 firing positions and suppressed the fire of a mortar battery. Our casualties for 6 August were 4 men killed and 4 wounded.

On this same day, a decree was received about awarding the brigade with the Order of the Red Banner for taking the city of Minsk. All the men greeted the joyful news with enormous happiness and inspiration. The artillery battalion fired a salvo at East Prussian territory.

Inspired by the high government honor, the soldiers and officers of the machine-gun company and antitank rifle company headed respectively by Guards Lieutenant Kvaratskhvely and Guards Lieutenant Leliavin captured four disabled German Tiger heavy tanks. The enemy tanks had been immobilized by the tankers of the 4th Guards Tank Brigade's 3rd Tank Battalion, but were continuing to fire from their positions. The men of the 3rd Motorized Rifle Battalion's antitank rifle company and machine-gun company demonstrated courage and heroism. Their commanders Guards Lieutenant Kvaratskhvely and Guards Lieutenant Leliavin at the head of their companies charged the tanks and wiped out the infantry that was covering them, and captured the tanks. Having covered three of the knocked-out Tiger tanks with straw, they set them alight. The fourth, operable Tiger was given to the tankers of the 4th Guards Tank Brigade. The tankers towed the tanks back to our lines. By end of day 6 August the brigade had 11 76mm guns, 9 57mm guns, 7 120mm mortars, 11 RPD machine guns, 34 antitank rifles, 5 halftracks and 3 armored cars still operational.

The **4th Guards Tank Brigade** consisting of 15 T-34 tanks together with the 8 SU-85 of the 401st Guards Self-propelled Artillery Regiment throughout the day of 6 August 1944 was holding its previous line of defense on the Szyrwinta River, fighting off enemy counterattacks with tanks and infantry. At 7.00 6 August 1944 the enemy in strength of up to two battalions of tanks (including heavy tanks) went on the counterattack. In the course of several minutes of combat, 4 Tiger tanks were knocked out by the fire of our tanks, and the German infantry was cut off by fire from the tanks and hurled back. One Tiger was evacuated to the brigade's immediate rear area. The other Tigers were set ablaze. The brigade destroyed one artillery battery and killed up to 100 enemy soldiers and officers. In the process the brigade lost 1 T-34 tank burned out from enemy tank fire, and 1 T-34 tank was towed away to a field repair shop due to mechanical problems. The brigade's casualties were 1 killed and 4 wounded. By day's end the brigade had 13 operational T-34 tanks and 8 operational SU-85; 2 T-34 tanks were undergoing moderate repairs.

The German perspective of these combats has been well described by Helmut Spaeter in his history of Panzerkorps Grossdeutschland.

Panzer-Grenadier Regiment GD alone lost one NCO and five men killed as well as 20 wounded.

Table 1.4: Status of the Third Panzer Army's tanks and self-propelled guns by end of day 6 August 1944

Units	Tanks and self-propelled guns, types	Combat-ready	In repair Short-term	Long-term
5.Panzer Division	Pz.IV	18	10	-
	Pz.V	15	5	11
	S-P Panzerjägers	4	-	-
6.Panzer Division	Pz.IV	20	35	10
I/Panzer Rgt. *Grossdeutchland*	Pz.V	11	33	4
7.Panzer Division	Pz.V	22	23	12
	StuG	5	-	-
	S-P Panzerjägers	17	-	-
sPanzer Abt. 510	Pz.VI	12	24	-
sPanzerjäger Abt. 519	Nashorn	6	-	-
	Hummel	1	-	-
	StuG	1	-	-
sPanzerjäger Abt. 731	Hetzer	7	19	11
	Two Hetzers irrecoverably lost			
StuG Brigade 203	StuG	22	6	1
StuG Brigade 232	StuG	18	6	-
StuG Brigade 276	StuG	14	5	-
StuG Br 277	StuG	10	8	2
Panzergrenadier Division *Grossdeutschland*	Pz.V	19	3	-
	6 Panthers irrecoverably lost over the day of 6 August			
	Pz.VI	22	9	1
	StuG	14	1	1

Excerpt from Operational Summary No. 871/44

Subordination: II/Security Regiment 603 has been subordinated to 7th Panzer Division. Von Wethern's motorized brigade is deployed in the area of Wodjgiry under the panzer army's command. Heavy Panzer Battalion 510 is deployed 8 km south of Gelgudyszki. SS Parachute Jäger Battalion 500 is deployed in the Slowiki area.

Arrived: from Panzergrenader Division *Grossdeutschland* – the main forces of the Fusilier Regiment, fresh units of the panzer regiment and elements of I/Panzer Regiment 26, fresh units of the panzer division's artillery regiment (regiment headquarters and headquarters battery of I Battalion, headquarters of IV Battalion, and the 3rd and 12th Batteries), a StuG brigade (3rd Battery), and the headquarters and 1st Company of a Pioneer Battalion. Also, remnants of the units of the 390th Security Division.

Excerpt from Intelligence Summary No. 106 of the headquarters of the 3rd Belorussian Front, 7 August 1944

Gumbinnen direction
The enemy on 7 August on the Słoboda – Szukle line (6-8 km southeast of Naumiestis) in strength of two companies up to two battalions of infantry, supported by 5-20 tanks, 5-7 self-propelled guns and artillery and mortar fire, undertook 11 counterattacks; on the Mackobudzie – Budweitschen line (6-11 km south of Wiłkowyszki), the enemy in strength of a company to a battalion of infantry together with 3-18 tanks launched 3 counterattacks. All the counterattacks were repulsed. In the course of 7 August, 35 artillery and 18 mortar batteries, 14 individual guns and mortars, and 5 rocket launchers were employed to support the attack.

33rd Army: Units of the 62nd Rifle Corps throughout the day of 7 August was engaged in intense combat with a regiment-sized enemy force supported by up to 45 tanks and self-propelled guns, which undertook repeated counterattacks from the Zalesie, Darženinkai, Jodupiany front and the woods north of Szukle in the directions of Žynie and Iszkarty. As a result of the counterattacks, the enemy managed to take Mercze. Altogether over the course of the day, 19 Nazi counterattacks were repulsed by the corps' units. The 19th Rifle Corps, fortifying its occupied positions, destroyed enemy equipment and personnel with its fire. The casualties of the 33rd Army over the day of 6 August 1944 amounted to 153 killed and 685 wounded. Over the day of 7 August, up to 670 enemy soldiers and officers were killed. In addition, 32 tanks and self-propelled guns were knocked out or destroyed (of which 11 by ground attack aircraft), as well as 8 vehicles, 6 machine guns and 2 mortars. One enemy aircraft was shot down by the fire of anti-aircraft artillery. Seven Germans were taken prisoner.

The 2nd Guards Tank Corps received a decree from the Presidium of the Supreme Soviet about awarding the corps with the Order of the Red Banner. Meetings were held in all the units in honor of the occasion.

On the basis of an order from the commander of the 33rd Army, the tank corps by 5.00 on 7 August 1944 was withdrawn into the army's second echelon in the Bocianowo, Budziszki, Gużele area in readiness to operate toward Podupliany, Leopoldowo and Molodony.

In the course of 7 August, the 2nd Guards Tank Corps was held out of combat.

From the combat path of the 2nd Guards Tank Corps

Finally at 1000 on 6 August 1944 the corps' artillery batteries fired their first salvo at East Prussia, and then on 7 August the corps was pulled out of combat and shifted to the right flank of the Front's attacking forces, where the enemy was preparing to launch a massive counterattack. Early on the morning of 8 August, the Guardsmen-tankers took up a defense on the right flank of the 33rd Army, where they camouflaged and dug all their tanks into the earth.

Excerpts from the combat diaries of the brigades of the 2nd Guards Tank Corps

The **4th Guards Tank Brigade** now numbering 13 operational T-34 tanks was withdrawn from combat at 5.00 7 August 1944, and by 6.30 was assembling in the Bocianowo area, with the task to defend against enemy attacks from the directions of Szukle, Skordupiany and Olwita [Alvitus]. Pursuant to an order from the commander of the 2nd Guards Tank Corps, the brigade set out from the Bocianowo area at 13.40, crossed the Szejmena River, and by 15.00 took up the following positions: 1st Tank Battalion – the southeastern outskirts of Zielonka and the ravine 700 meters from that point; 3rd Tank Battalion – road fork 1 km southeast of Zielonka; motorized rifle battalion

– crossroads 200 meters south of Point 55.3. According to a verbal order from the commander of the 2nd Guards Tank Corps, the 401st Guards Self-propelled Artillery Regiment was removed from operational subordination to the brigade and taken out of the system of the brigade's defense. Over 6-7 August 1944, the brigade lost 5 men killed and 5 wounded. By end of day, the brigade had 13 operational T-34 tanks, 5 tanks under factory repair, and 8 T-34 tanks under moderate repairs.

The **25th Guards Tank Brigade** in the course of the day of 7 August continued to occupy a defense in the area of the western outskirts of Semeneliszki with the mission to repulse possible enemy counterattacks. The enemy was continuing to occupy its previous line of defense. The enemy artillery was placing methodical fire on the combat positions of our units from out of the areas 1 km southeast of Bjorki, isolated cottages by the railroad at Jonajcie and Point 58.0. The condition of the tanks: 14 operational T-34, 2 under moderate repairs, 3 requiring factory repair.

The **26th Guards Tank Brigade**: on 7 August the enemy was defending the line: eastern outskirts of Darveniki, Hill 45.7, Hill 49.7, eastern fringe of the woods west of Zielonka. Throughout the day of 7 August, the staging of 3 to 5 tanks and 11 halftracks with infantry was observed in the area of the road junction 800 meters west of Hill 49.7, and the massing of tanks and infantry in the areas of Hill 44.7 and the "barn" west of Zielonka. Throughout the day of 7 August, the enemy showed no activity and conducted harassing artillery and mortar fire on the combat positions of our units and the firing positions of the artillery. The enemy air force showed no activity.

On the basis of a combat order from the commander of the 2nd Guards Tank Corps, at 4.00 the brigade together with the battery of the 1695th Anti-aircraft Artillery Regiment was removed from its defenses on the eastern bank of the Szyrwinta River in the area of the road intersection 800 meters east of Hill 50.6, and by 6.00 had assembled in the Pracapole – Patwiecie area. On the basis of a verbal order from the commander of the 2nd Guards Tank Corps, at 10.20 the brigade's units and the battery of the 1695th Anti-aircraft Artillery Regiment moved out of the Pracapole – Patwiecie area and by 12.00 took up a defense with the 2nd Tank Battalion in platoon-sized strongpoints on the Žynie – Iszkarty line; motorized rifle battalion east of Iszkarty, saddling the road running from Iszkarty to Zalesie and toward Hill 55.7, with the mission to block enemy counterattacks in the eastern direction; the brigade's anti-aircraft machine-gun company and the battery of the 1695th Anti-Aircraft Artillery Regiment were in firing positions with the assignment to cover the brigade's units from the air. In the course of the day, the enemy was scouted in the northwestern, western and southwestern directions. In order to repulse possible enemy counterattacks, communications were set up with the 70th Rifle Division and questions of cooperation were worked out for joint actions. In the area of defense the brigade had 12 operational T-34, 2 76mm antitank guns, 3 37mm anti-aircraft guns, 6 DShK machine guns and 3 82mm mortars. The 1695th Anti-Aircraft Artillery Regiment's battery had three 37mm anti-aircraft guns and one DShK machine gun.

The **4th Guards Motorized Rifle Brigade** by 7.00 on 7 August had turned over its defensive line on the western bank of the Szyrwinta River to the units of the 344th Rifle Division, and moved into the 33rd Army's second echelon. The brigade took up strongpoints in the following areas: 3rd Motorized Rifle Battalion – Patwiecie, in readiness to repel enemy counterattacks from Naumiestis; 2nd Motorized Rifle Battalion – Budziszki, in readiness to repel enemy counterattacks from the Leopoldowo – Skordupiany direction; 1st Tank Battalion – in Semeneliszki, in readiness to repel enemy counterattacks from the direction of Olwita. The artillery was in firing positions: the artillery battalion in Gużele; the mortar battery in the area east of Budziszki; the 273rd Mortar Regiment in the area southeast of Budziszki. The brigade's men camouflaged and dispersed their firing means in full readiness for combat operations. The enemy was firmly holding its previous lines and conducting artillery and mortar fire on the combat positions of the forward units, while periodically shelling the strongpoints of our battalions and the firing positions of the artillery and launching counterattacks with tanks and infantry from the Naumiestis direction. The brigade's casualties for the day of 7 August: 2 men wounded. The command post is 1 km southwest of Gużele.

The **401st Guards Self-propelled Artillery Regiment** by the end of 7 August 1944 had been withdrawn into the reserve of the corps' artillery commander and had taken up a defense in the woods west of Zielonka in readiness to repulse enemy counterattacks from the northwest and southwest. By the end of 8 August it had become known that the enemy had assembled up to 200 tanks in the area southwest of Wiłkowyszki. The regiment, together with the corps' units, received a new assignment and by the morning of 9 August was occupying firing positions on the western fringe of the woods south of Skraudze in readiness to repulse enemy tank attacks from the Budeziory, Sudawa direction.

The regiment in the course of 9-11 August 1944 was located in readiness to repulse enemy counterattacks, occupying firing positions on the southwestern fringes of Sterniszki, Matuliszki and Pogramdyszki.

Excerpt from Operational Summary No. 875/44 from the headquarters of the German Third Panzer Army (Pz AOK 3) to the headquarters of Army Group Center, 7 August 1944. Daily operational report.

On this day the panzer reconnaissance battalion of Panzergrenadier Division *Grossdeutschland* was shifted by railroad to Skaudwile and placed under the command of the panzer army. From Panzergrenadier Division *Grossdeutschland*, the artillery regiment's III Battalion and 12 Pz.kpfw. V tanks of Panzer Regiment 26 still haven't arrived.

Table 1.5: Status of the panzers and self-propelled guns of the German Third Panzer Army by end of day 7 August 1944

Units	Tanks and self-propelled guns, types	Combat-ready	In repair Short-term	Long-term
5.Panzer Division	Pz.IV	16	12	-
	Pz.V	18	2	-
	S-P Panzerjägers	3	-	-
6.Panzer Division	Pz.IV	11	34	13
	Pz.V	12	32	4
	4 Pz.IV tanks presumed irrecoverably lost			
I/Panzer Rgt. *Grossdeutschland*	Pz.V	19	20	17
7.Panzer Division	Guns on self-propelled carriages	18	-	-
	StuG	5	-	-
sPanzer Abt. 510	Pz.VI	10	26	-
sPanzerjäger Abt. 519	Nashorn	6	-	-
	Hummel	1	-	-
	StuG	1	-	-
sPanzerjäger Abt. 731	Hetzer	7	19	-
StuG Brigade 203	StuG	27	2	-
StuG Brigade 232	StuG	17	6	2
StuG Brigade 276	StuG	11	9	8
StuG Brigade 277	StuG	10	4	6
Brigade "von Werthern"	StuG	16	-	-
	Nashorn	3	-	-
Panzergrenadier Division *Grossdeutschland*	Pz.III	2	-	-
	Pz.IV	9	3	2
	Pz.V	62	14	2
	Pz.VI	27	6	8

Excerpt from Intelligence Summary No. 107 from the headquarters of the 3rd Belorussian Front, 8 August 1944

Gumbinnen direction

The enemy on 8 August was fortifying his occupied positions, while simultaneously bringing up tanks and infantry to the area of Wiłkowyszki from the areas of Brzezina and Jurgiszki (3-5 kilometers north of Lubow); groups of 30-40 submachine gunners conducted reconnaissance. The enemy artillery was shelling our troops' combat positions with occasional harassing fire.

In the course of the day of 8 August, 15 artillery batteries and 9 mortar batteries, along with 19 separate guns and mortars, were put into action.

33rd Army was digging in on its achieved line on 8 August, throwing up defensive works and exchanging fire with the enemy. The enemy showed no activity with infantry. Through observation between 19.30 and 20.00, the movement of enemy tanks and vehicles was spotted: from Szukle to the south – 18 tanks, 20 vehicles; from Wierzbołowo [Virbalis] to Mažucie – 60 tanks; from Olwita to Maldehne – up to 55 tanks and halftracks, of which 26 tanks were towing guns.

The losses of the 33rd Army for the day of 7 August: 142 killed and 523 wounded. Over the day of 8 August, up to 350 enemy soldiers and officers were killed; 11 machine guns were destroyed; and 6 tanks, 1 halftrack, 1 gun, 3 mortars and 2 vehicles were knocked out.

In execution of an order from the commander of the 33rd Army, on 8 August 1944 the units of the 2nd Guards Tank Corps took up a defense consisting of strongpoints that were echeloned in depth on the following lines: 26th Guards Tank Brigade, with 12 T-34 tanks, took up a defense in the Zynie, Iszkarty area, and the motorized rifle battalion was on the eastern outskirts of Iszkarty, saddling the road running from Iszkarty to Zalesie and Hill 55.7. Their mission was to thwart enemy counterattacks to the east. The corps settled questions of cooperation with the 33rd Army's 70th Rifle Division. The 4th Guards Tank Brigade was in the Zielonka area, where it was organizing two anti-tank hedgehogs together with the 551st Rifle Regiment. Its 1st Tank Battalion had reached the area of the southeastern outskirts of Zielonka, having the task to repulse possible enemy counterattacks in the southeastern direction; its 2nd Tank Battalion was at the road fork 1 km southeast of Zielonka; and its motorized rifle battalion of submachine gunners was at the road intersection 200 meters south of Point 55.3. The 4th Guards Motorized Rifle Brigade together with the 273rd Tank Regiment was in strong points in the following areas: 3rd Motorized Rifle Battalion – Patwiecie; 2nd Motorized Rifle Battalion – Budziszki; 1st Motorized Rifle Battalion – Semeneliszki. They were in readiness to repulse counterattacks from the directions of Naumiestis, Leopoldowo, Skordupiany and Olwita. The 25th Guards Tank Brigade was on the western outskirts of Semeneliszki.

Excerpts from the combat diaries of the brigades of the 2nd Guards Tank Corps, 8 August 1944

The **25th Guards Tank Brigade** throughout the day was not involved in combat and was occupying its current line of defense. The condition of the materiel is without changes.

The **26th Guards Tank Brigade** in the course of the day, in cooperation with the 70th Rifle Division, having the 11th Assault Battalion on the right and the 4th Guards Tank Brigade and 49th Rifle Division on the left, was occupying three defensive hedgehogs on tank-vulnerable directions on the line running from Hill 45.7 on the right and the road fork 700 meters west of Hill 49.7 on the left, with the assignment to defend against enemy attacks in the eastern and northeastern directions from out of Darženinkai and Jodupiany areas. The brigade's anti-aircraft machine-gun company and the battery from the 1695th Anti-Aircraft Artillery Regiment were in firing positions with the task to provide air cover for the brigade's units. Over 8 August 1944, the brigade had no losses in men or equipment. In its area of defense, the brigade had 15 operational T-34 tanks, 2 76mm antitank guns, 3 37mm anti-aircraft guns, 6 DShK machine guns and 3 82mm mortars. The 1695th Anti-Aircraft Artillery Regiment's battery had 3 37mm anti-aircraft guns and 1 DShK machine gun.

The **4th Guards Motorized Rifle Brigade** in the course of 8 August was not engaged in combat and was located in its previous areas of defense in readiness to repulse enemy counterattacks.

The **4th Guards Tank Brigade,** numbering 16 T-34 tanks, throughout the day of 8 August continued to occupy a defense in two antitank hedgehogs: the first consisting of the 1st Tank Battalion (8 T-34 tanks) with a company of the motorized rifle battalion in the area of Hill 49.7; the second consisting of the 3rd Tank Battalion (6 T-34 tanks) with the second submachine gun company from the motorized rifle battalion – road fork 1 km east of Zielonka, bend in the Sejmena River. Throughout the day of 8 August, the brigade conducted no combat operations. The men of the tank crews were studying the enemy's defenses. Status of the brigade's tanks: 16 operational T-34 tanks, 5 undergoing moderate repairs, and 5 requiring factory repair.

At 0930 on 8 August 1944, General Burdeinyi sent the following report to the commander of the 33rd Army, the commander of the 33rd Army's armored and mechanized forces, and to the commander of the 3rd Belorussian Front's armored and mechanized forces:

In execution of your order on the night of 7-8 August, the following was completed by the corps:

1. The corps units and formations fully completed setting up their areas of defense. The tanks and vehicles were dug into the earth and camouflaged. Each crew was given its task on the spot.
2. Reconnaissance of the probably directions to repulse the enemy's likely attacks was conducted.
3. Questions of cooperation were settled with the forward infantry and artillery.
4. The entire system of defense, depending on terrain conditions, was organized in strong points, echeloned in depth, with the availability of reserves.
5. Simultaneously I am reporting that the antitank artillery in the sector of the 26th Guards Tank Brigade is located not up among the tanks' combat positions, but significantly behind the tanks. This significantly weakens the defense. In the sector of the 4th Guards Tank Brigade, only several antitank guns have been deployed. Such an attitude toward the organization of an antitank defense on the part of the commanders of the divisions and regiments makes the defense vulnerable.

Excerpt from Operational Summary No. 879/44 from the headquarters of Third Panzer Army (Pz AOK 3) to the headquarters of Army Group Center, 8 August 1944. Daily operational report:

Panzergrenadier Division *Grossdeutschland*'s sector north of the railroad has once again been turned over to the 561st Volksgrenadier Division (Gruppe Schmidt). The main forces of *Grossdeutschland*'s motorized regiment has been replaced by the panzer army's assault battalion and II Battalion of the Parachute-Jäger Regiment.

Arrived: the combat echelons of the *Grossdeutschland* Division (except III/Heavy Mortar Regiment 1). The forward command post of XXXX Panzer Corps: Purwiniszki. The forward command post of the *Grossdeutschland* Division: 1 km northwest of Bajoraicie.

Combat strength of the 2nd Guards Tank Corps on 8 August 1944

By end of day on 8 August, the 2nd Guards Tank Corps had 57 T-34, 10 SU-85 and 3 SU-76 still operational. The artillery and mortar units of the 2nd Guards Tank Corps had the following in service: 401st Guards Self-propelled Artillery Regiment – 10 SU-85; 1500th Self-propelled Artillery Regiment – 0 SU-76; 273rd Mortar Regiment – 25 120mm mortars; 28th Separate Guards Mortar Regiment – 8 M-13 rocket launchers; 1695th Anti-aircraft Artillery Regiment – 12 37mm guns, 14 DShK machine guns. In the course of 8 August, the corps was not involved in combat and spent the day bringing the tanks and self-propelled guns, weapons and men back to order in readiness to carry out a combat task.

Table 1.6: Information on the roster strength of the 33rd Army's rifle divisions (information for 4 August 1944)

Units	Personnel				Number of replacements that arrived by the end of 4 August, but hadn't yet been assigned
	Officers	Sergeants	Rank and file	Total	
32 Rifle Division	641	1195	2795	4631	270
157 Rifle Division	634	1232	3140	5006	100
362 Rifle Division	693	899	2669	4271	350
145 Penal Company (with 362 RD)	8	9	137	154	-
70 Rifle Division	677	907	2509	4093	440
49 Rifle Division	759	1375	3781	5915	-
344 Rifle Division	631	971	2755	4357	200
147 Penal Company (with 344 RD)	10	15	157	182	-
222 Rifle Division	692	1191	2845	4728	200
Total:	6713	7794	20788	33337	1560

Senior assistant of the 3rd Department of Staffing Lieutenant SILKOV

Table 1.7: Status of Panzergrenadier Division *Grossdeutschland*'s panzers and self-propelled guns at end of day on 8 August 1944

Units	Tanks and self-propelled guns, types	Combat-ready	In repair	
			Short-term	Long-term
Panzergrenadier Division *Grossdeutschland*	Pz.III	2	-	-
	Pz.IV	10	-	-
	Pz.V	70	7	7
	Pz.VI	27	6	8
	StuG	15	-	1
	S-P Panzerjägers	4	-	-
Total:	Tanks and SP guns	128	13	16

Personnel: 17,381 men
Available halftracks, specialized machines and artillery:
SPW, PzSp Wg – 79, sPak (Sfl) – 4, sPak (mot. Z) – 29, Art Gesch – 60[a]

[a] Author's note: Information on personnel, specialized machines and artillery given for July 1944.

The troops of the 33rd Army were keeping constant observation over the enemy's preparations. Having correctly guessed his intentions, the army commander on the night of 8-9 August shifted two tank and one motorized rifle brigade of the 2nd Guards Tank Corps from the army's right flank to the area east of Wiłkowyszki. In addition, on the same night at the order of the 3rd

Belorussian Front's commander-in-chief General Cherniakhovsky, the 153rd Tank Brigade moved out of the Front's reserve in Mariampol toward Wiłkokwyszki with the mission to prevent an enemy breakthrough in the direction of Mariampol.

Table 1.8: Scheme of the 33rd Army's antitank artillery defense in the sector of the 32nd and 362nd Rifle Divisions, 8 August 1944

Division	Number of the anti-tank region	Composition	Chief of the anti-tank region	Anti-tank region with which it was assigned to cooperate	Anti-tank gun reserve
32 Rifle Division	16	45mm – 2 AT artillery[a] – 3 Divisional artillery – 4	A battery commander of 2/133 AR	Anti-tank Regions 17 and 18	5 divisional guns
	17	45mm – 4 AT artillery – 3 Divisional artillery – 4	A battery commander of 2/133 AR	Anti-tank Regions 16, 18 and 19	
	18	45mm – 4 Divisional artillery – 4	A battery commander of 2/133 AR	Anti-tank Regions 16 and 17	
	19	45mm – 4 AT artillery – 3 Divisional artillery – 4	A battery commander of 2/133 AR	Anti-tank Regions 17, 20 and 21	
	20	45mm – 3 Divisional artillery – 2	A battery commander of 2/133 AR	Anti-tank Regions 17, 19 and 21	
362 Rifle Division	21	45mm – 4 Anti-tank artillery – 6	A battery commander of 1/936 AR	Anti-tank Regions 19 and 22	6 divisional guns
	22	45mm – 4 Anti-tank artillery – 2 Divisional artillery – 3	A battery commander of 1/936 AR	Anti-tank Regions 21 and 24	
	23	45mm – 4 Divisional artillery – 2	A battery commander of 1/936 AR	Anti-tank Regions 21 and 23	
	24	45mm – 4 Anti-tank artillery – 4 Divisional artillery – 4	A battery commander of 3/936 AR	Anti-tank Regions 22 and 25	
	25	45mm – 5 Anti-tank artillery – 4 Divisional artillery – 4	A battery commander of 2/936 AR	Anti-tank Regions 22 and 24	
	25a	45mm – 4	A battery commander of 2/936 AR	Anti-tank Region 25	
	26	45mm – 4		Anti-tank Regions 24, 25 and 25[a]	

a Anti-tank artillery – anti-tank guns with a caliber of 57mm and 76mm

Excerpt from Operational Summary No. 99 from the headquarters of the 33rd Army's artillery, 8 August 1944, 20.00:

First: The army's troops throughout the day conducted no combat operations. The artillery units were regrouped to support the antitank defenses, and antitank strong points were built. Combat positions were set up that corresponded to a strict antitank and anti-infantry defense. The forward edge is the same as before.

Second: **The artillery of the rifle divisions**, pursuant to the latest order, have taken up positions in the following areas:

- 237th Artillery Regiment – in the area of Romantyszki (Quadrant 68-29);
- 31st Artillery Regiment – in the Bocianowo area (Quadrant 68-27) in indirect firing positions. Three cannon batteries have been set up in the division's antitank regions to fire over open sights;
- 913th Artillery Regiment – in the area of Quadrant 59-39, Gudele (Quadrant 58-34). A portion of the cannon artillery batteries have been set up to fire over open sights in the antitank regions;
- 666th Artillery Regiment – in the Suwalki (Quadrant 59-36), Wilkiszki (Quadrant 59-38), Sterniszki (Quadrant 59-39) area;
- 133rd Artillery Regiment – didn't change its combat position. It has 18 76mm guns in the antitank regions deployed to fire open sights and 6 guns in reserve;
- 936th Artillery Regiment – didn't change its combat position. It has 12 guns deployed to fire over open sights and 6 guns in reserve.

Third: **The Army's artillery and artillery assets:**

- **142nd Cannon Artillery Brigade** – is occupying combat positions in the Budziszki, Semeneliszki, Potomkiszki area (Quadrant 63-25);
- **873rd Destroyer Antitank Artillery Regiment** – is occupying combat positions in the Vitajcie (Quadrant 54-36), Merinyszki area and has 3 batteries in reserve (Quadrant 60-38);
- **538th Army Mortar Regiment** – is occupying combat positions in the area 300 meters east of Wejliszki (Quadrant 61-91);
- **43rd Destroyer Antitank Artillery Brigade** – by regiments and by battery is occupying combat positions in the area of the southwestern outskirts of Wiłkowyszki
- **47th Destroyer Antitank Artillery Brigade** – has become operationally subordinate to the army's artillery. It is occupying combat positions in the following areas:
  - **1025th Self-propelled Artillery Regiment** – 500 meters south of Sardaki (Quadrant 56-34);
  - **573rd Destroyer Antitank Artillery Regiment** – in the Lukszyszki area (Quadrant 65-47);
- **367th and 326th Guards Mortar Regiments** – in their previous areas;
- Army's artillery headquarters – in Sarmaczuny.

33rd Army's artillery chief of staff Colonel IABLOCHKIN
Chief of operations of the 33rd Army's artillery headquarters
Lieutenant Colonel ZAITSEV

Description of the combat with enemy tanks in the Wiłkowyszki area, 9 August 1944

Preparing for an offensive with major forces, the enemy had assembled one group of panzers and self-propelled guns in the wooded area southwest of Point 108.2, and a second group in the Galeryszki – Oszkobole area. Both groups were under the command of Panzergrenadier Division *Grossdeutschland*.

According to the testimony of Obergefreitor Hans Keller, who was taken prisoner on 9 August 1944 in the Antupie [Antupiai] area, the division had arrived in the given sector of the front from Romania, where it had been resting and replenishing. The division marched along the route from Romania through Hungary, Poland, West Prussia, East Prussia; on 4 August the division had arrived in Ebenrode, and up until 8 August it was assembled in the Wirballen area.

On 9 August the *Grossdeutschland* Division moved out on the attack in the Wolencie area and to the south of that point with the objective to cut the Wiłkowyszki – Mariampol road in the Antupie area, and having advanced 15 kilometers over the day, to straighten out the front lines, having cut off the Russian units defending the Wiłkowyszki area. It was then to take up a defense.

A prisoner of the 11th Company of the Panzergrenadier Regiment of the *Grossdeutschland* Panzer Division, who was captured on 9 August 2 km west of Wiłkowyszki, testified that the division had been located in Romania up until 1 August; on 5 August it had arrived in full strength at the East Prussian border, whereupon it was sent aboard trucks to the area south of Wiłkowyszki. The division includes a panzer regiment, a panzergrenadier regiment and a fusilier regiment. The panzergrenadier regiment has three battalions with 350 men in each. An artillery battalion of two-battalion composition each with five 105mm howitzers and one 150mm howitzer, 5-6 rocket launchers, and 20 75mm antitank guns support each regiment. The panzer regiment had 70 Tiger tanks, 50 Panther tanks, 30 Pz.kpfw. IV tanks, 30 self-propelled guns equipped with 88mm guns, and 20 halftracks. In the 13th Company are eight 120mm and four 81mm mortars, as well as four heavy machine guns. The division's commander is General Manteuffel.

According to the Intelligence Departments of the 3rd Belorussian Front and 33rd Army, the *Grossdeutschland* Division consisted of the following formations and units:

a) A panzer regiment consisting of four battalions; one battalion was equipped with heavy Tiger tanks, two panzer battalions equipped with Panther tanks, and one battalion equipped with Pz.kpfw. IV tanks. Altogether there was up to 250 tanks in the regiment;
b) An artillery regiment; the regiment had 54 105mm and 150mm howitzers;
c) A fusilier and a panzergrenadier regiment. The regiments had similar structures, each having four battalions: three battalions of infantry and one heavy battalion. The first battalion was equipped with halftracks (12 machines), while the second and third battalions were equipped with trucks. The 1st Battalion has 15 antitank guns, 2 75mm guns and 9 120mm mortars. The 2nd Battalion has 12 antitank guns, 4 75mm guns and 9 120mm mortars. The 3rd Battalion has 12 antitank guns, 3 75mm guns and 9 120mm mortars. The 4th (Heavy) Battalion has 6 antitank guns and 6 150mm howitzers. Altogether there are 45 antitank guns, 9 75mm guns, 6 150mm howitzers and 27 120mm mortars in the fusilier regiment. In the two regiments (fusilier and panzergrenadier): 90 antitank guns, 18 75mm guns, 12 150mm howitzers and 12 self-propelled guns. The numerical strength of the infantry companies is 120 active bayonets each. The 1st Battalion has up to 600 active bayonets; the 2nd Battalion has up to 800 active bayonets; the 3rd Battalion has up to 600 active bayonets; and the 4th Battalion has up to 400 active bayonets. The total for each regiment: up to 2600 active bayonets. In the two regiments: a combined strength of 5,200 active bayonets.
d) A battalion of up to 30 assault guns.

e) A heavy anti-aircraft battalion consisting of four batteries each with 4 88mm guns; altogether 16 88mm guns. On the day of the offensive, a Panther brigade was attached to the battalion. In addition, a fresh, newly arrived infantry division is operating in the given sector;
f) A reconnaissance battalion;
g) A communications battalion;
h) A pioneer battalion;
i) Battalions of rocket launchers and mortars.

The *Grossdeutschland* Division was commanded by Major General Manteuffel; the commander of the Fusilier Regiment was Colonel Nieman; the Panzergrenadier Regiment was commanded by Colonel Lorenz. The field post number for the Fusilier Regiment was 04765.

The combat strength of the Panzergrenadier Division *Grossdeutschland* in tanks and self-propelled guns has been given in Table 1.7.

The enemy was occupying a line from the eastern banks of Lake Pojeziory through Budjeziory and Pustopedzie, to Pieczuliszki and further on to the south. On the night of 8-9 August 1944, the rumble of engines was audible.

From the growing sound of the engines, which continued until dawn, it was determined that the enemy was bringing up tanks and self-propelled guns to the areas of the woods northeast of Wenczlawka, Wiżajdy, alcohol factory and Dekszniszki, preparing for an offensive. From the sounds of the engines, which merged into a general roar, it was impossible to determine the number of tanks.

With the break of dawn on 9 August, using concealed approaches as well as the fog (and heavy showers), which restricted visibility to no more than 500-600 meters, the enemy without any artillery preparation attacked the forward edge of the Soviet forces with two echelons of tanks and self-propelled guns, primarily out of the Wiżajdy, alcohol factory and Dekszniszki areas.

The tanks and self-propelled guns, having shoved back the rifle units of the 33rd Army, approached right up to the artillery positions of the 873rd Destroyer Antitank Artillery Regiment, the 578th Destroyer Antitank Artillery Regiment (of the 47th Destroyer Antitank Artillery Brigade), the 43rd Destroyer Antitank Artillery Brigade, and the 307th Guards Mortar Regiment.

A smoky haze blanketed the earth. The gardens around the buildings and patches of woods greatly hindered observation over the enemy's actions that had started. Intense machine-gun fire, the rumble of the engine of tanks and self-propelled guns, the glow of buildings that had been set ablaze by the enemy, the shrubby terrain and weather conditions (fog, heavy rain showers) were complicating the combat actions of the defending Soviet forces.

The German panzers were advancing slowly, setting fire to all the structures and haystacks standing in the fields that were in their path. Enemy submachine gunners and machine gunners were advancing in the intervals between the panzers, their weapons spewing continuous fire. With the exception of shots from the panzers and self-propelled guns, the enemy was conducting no artillery fire.

The enemy, with units of the 1st "East Prussian" Grenadier Division, the 201st and 52nd Security Divisions, the 272nd Grenadier Division and units of Panzergrenadier Division *Grossdeutschland*, which had replenished their tanks, from the morning of 9 August 1944 launched an offensive from the direction southeast of Wiłkowyszki in the direction of that town, and from the direction of Bardowskie [Bardauskai] in the direction of Antupie. The Luftwaffe was periodically bombing the combat positions of the 33rd Army's units in groups of 10-20 aircraft.

On the morning of 9 August, at an order from the commander of the 33rd Army, the 26th Guards Tank Brigade, 4th Guards Tank Brigade and 4th Guards Motorized Rifle Brigade moved out of their former occupied areas and by 0530 9 August were assembled in new areas: 4th Guards Tank Brigade – western fringe of the Skrandupie Woods; 26th Guards Tank Brigade – southwestern fringe of the woods west of Ruda; 4th Guards Motorized Rifle Brigade – southeastern fringe of the woods north of Ruda. The 25th Guards Tank Brigade remained in Semeneliszki.

The batteries of the 873rd Destroyer Antitank Artillery Regiment and of the 578th Destroyer Antitank Artillery Regiment in the Znaczki, Połukiszki area were the first to join combat with the German panzers. The 4th Battery of the 873rd Destroyer Antitank Artillery Regiment was occupying combat positions in the Połukiszki area. The artillerymen allowed the enemy tanks to close within 500 meters before opening fire with two guns, later joined by the rest of the guns. As a result, 3 German panzers were destroyed and 3 were knocked out. In return, the battery itself lost 2 guns, 2 Studebaker prime movers and up to 10 men killed or wounded as a result of the tanks' fire.

Having encountered the strong antitank defense on the part of the 4th Battery, the enemy tanks began to maneuver and made an attempt to outflank it from the left, where it ran into the firing positions of the 3rd Battery, which from short range destroyed five tanks. Having discovered the 3rd Battery's positions, the enemy tanks charged the guns at high speed and crushed one gun beneath their tracks, while disabling two other guns. The remaining gun of the 3rd Battery continued to fire, as a result of which one more enemy tank was knocked out of action.

The 1st Battery, located in reserve, received an order to move up to the highways in the Antupie area, deploy from the march, and take up combat positions with the task to prevent the enemy tanks' expansion to the east and northeast.

The Germans, having left behind a small tank screen (8-10 tanks) in the area of Antupie, hurried on toward the highway leading to Wiłkowyszki with the main forces. Individual tanks, which had been left behind in the screen, attempted to reach the intersection of the Antupie – Skrandupie road with the highway. Having encountered fire from the 1st Battery, they fell back to the intersection of the Wiżajdy road with the highway. In the process, the Germans left behind two knocked out tanks on the battlefield from the fire of the antitank guns. In total, over the day of combat the artillerymen of the 873rd and 578th Destroyer Antitank Artillery Regiments destroyed 16 enemy tanks.

The 47th Destroyer Antitank Artillery Brigade's 578th Destroyer Antitank Artillery Regiment was occupying firing positions in the vicinity of Znaczki. During the German panzer attack, it took on the main blow.

The **1025th Self-propelled Artillery Regiment** was occupying combat positions at the boundary between two rifle divisions of the 33rd Army, with the 157th Rifle Division on the right, north of the 222nd Rifle Division. Its antitank neighbor on the left was the 578th Destroyer Antitank Artillery Regiment. It had no antitank unit on its right. Knowing the situation, the men of the regiment were at full combat readiness. At 0530 on 9 August 1944, the enemy initiated the panzer attack in the Łukszyszki – Antupie sector, then in the area of the 578th Destroyer Antitank Artillery Regiment, having launched 70 tanks and self-propelled guns on the attack. The left-flank 1st Battery opened fire at the enemy tanks, which were striving to cut the highway and reach the regiment's firing positions. The 2nd Battery, situated to the right of the 1st Battery, helped repulse the initial enemy attack, having destroyed 4 tanks.

At 0700 60 enemy tanks and self-propelled guns, some moving at high speed, other moving slowly, resumed the attack while firing intensively from their guns, advancing toward Wiłkowyszki. Bitter fighting ensued at close range. Ten immobilized enemy tanks were already emitting plumes of dark smoke on the battlefield. The foe, striving to achieve the objective, threw another 15 tanks into the battle, trying to break through the battery's firing positions. A critical situation arose on the left flank. The Germans had numerical superiority.

The commander of the 47th Separate Destroyer Antitank Artillery Brigade Hero of the Soviet Union Guards Colonel David Margulis ordered the 4th Battery to go to the help of the 1st, 2nd and 3rd Batteries.

Under the heavy antitank fire coming from the four batteries, the enemy was forced to retreat back beyond the highway. In the fighting on the approaches to Wiłkowyszki, the regiment destroyed 10 tanks, 2 self-propelled guns, 2 vehicles and killed 170 enemy soldiers and officers.

The **578th Destroyer Antitank Artillery Regiment** was occupying combat positions in the area of Kružmorgi and south of Znaczki. On the morning of 9 August, the rumble of the engines of the enemy panzers that were approaching out of the Merkszyszki area carried to the combat positions. Along the road from Merkszyszki at Hill 63.4, 40 enemy tanks and self-propelled guns appeared out of the fog in front of the combat positions of the 4th, 5th and 6th Batteries. Under the cover of the fog, the panzers closed to a range of 600-700 meters to the 4th and 5th Batteries. Targeted fire was opened at the German tanks. During the combat, the distance between the batteries and tanks fell to 300 meters. The German panzers were flowing around the batteries' front and flanks. The gun crews stayed at their positions and fired intensively at the attacking panzers. Fifteen enemy tanks and self-propelled guns were knocked out by the batteries. Unable to withstand the storm of artillery fire, the remaining German panzers retreated. The combat with the German tanks lasted 90 minutes.

Under cover, conducting a regrouping of the forces and having replenished the first echelon with tanks and self-propelled guns, the enemy in strength of 80 tanks and self-propelled guns launched a second attack from out the directions of Merkszyszki and the Wiżajdy – Połukiszki area. This time, the Germans led with a large number of submachine gunners out in front of the tanks and employed their company mortars. Tough fighting flared up. Under the cover of the fire from their self-propelled guns and submachine gunners, the enemy panzers broke into the batteries' firing positions.

Firing at pointblank range, the artillerymen with from their batteries knocked out another 13 enemy tanks and self-propelled guns. As a result of the fighting, the regiment destroyed approximately 20 tanks, 5 self-propelled guns, 3 armored cars, 1 antitank gun, 1 mortar and 1 machine gun, and killed approximately 400 enemy soldiers and officers.

The men of the regiments of the 47th Destroyer Antitank Artillery Brigade demonstrated the ability to destroy all types of highly-praised German armored vehicles on the field of battle. In the bitter, close-range fighting with the enemy tanks, the 578th Destroyer Antitank Artillery Regiment lost 22 57mm antitank guns and 20 vehicles.

The artillery of the 33rd Army's rifle divisions were also firing to repulse the attacks by enemy tanks and men. As a result of the fighting, they claimed 6 knocked out and 4 destroyed German tanks, and the destruction of 4 machine guns, 2 vehicles with their loads, 2 antitank guns. In addition, they destroyed or dispersed up to a battalion of enemy infantry.

An examination of the knocked-out and burned-out German tanks established:

a) The majority of the tanks were knocked out by armor piercing and armor piercing discarding sabot shells. Among the burned-out and knocked-out tanks, the majority received their fatal hits from 57mm guns;
b) The armor piercing discarding sabot shells of the 57mm guns at a range of 1000 meters penetrates every part of the tank except the frontal armor; at a range of 600 meters, it penetrates even the frontal armor;
c) The armor piercing shell at a range of 200-300 meters penetrates the rolling assembly and flanks of the Tiger tank. The most vulnerable place on the Tiger tank is the rolling assembly. The majority of the knocked-out tanks were hit in the forward half of the rolling assembly;
d) Vulnerable locations on the Tiger tank for the ZiS-3 cannons from a direct shot at 600-700 meters are: the flanks, rear, the turret and the tracks. For the armor piercing shell, the most vulnerable locations are the rolling assembly, fuel tank and turret cupola of the machine;
e) The armor-piercing discarding sabot and hollow-charge shells penetrate even the frontal armor of the Tiger tank from a range of 300-400 meters. The armor piercing shell is ineffective

against the Tiger's frontal armor and leaves only 40-500mm dimples. The ZiS-3 cannon is capable of penetrating the frontal armor of the enemy's medium tanks from a direct-fire range.

The enemy in strength of up to 60 tanks and infantry, with artillery support and air support, at 0530 9 August went on the offensive and by 0900 9 August broke through the defenses and reached the Ruda – Kružmorgi line, where the Germans were met with heavy fire from the 4th and 26th Guards Tank Brigades and the 4th Guards Motorized Rifle Brigade and brought to a halt. Leaving behind a covering screen of up to 15 tanks in the Antupie area, the enemy turned toward Wiłkowyszki.

Meanwhile, south of Wiłkowyszki, the enemy, having assembled up to 200 tanks and self-propelled guns and more than two regiments of infantry south of Wiłkowyszki, , tlaunched a counteroffensive at sunrise on 9 August 1944 in the Bardowskie, Mackobudzie, Patineli [Pašeimeniai] sector.

The first attack undertaken by the Germans in the eastern direction was driven back by units of the 32nd Rifle Division. Having reinforced the attacking group with tanks, self-propelled guns and infantry, the enemy at 0900 again attack out of the Wyżajdy area, but this time to the north, having committed more than 100 tanks and self-propelled guns and up to two regiments of infantry.

Having breached the forward edge of defense and having cut the Mariampol – Wiłkowyszki highway, the enemy, suffering heavy losses, penetrated 2 km into the 33rd Army's defenses. However, north of the Mariampol – Wiłkowyszki highway, the enemy tanks had been met by the units of the 2nd Guards Tank Corps and the gunners of the 1025th Self-propelled Artillery Regiment. Suffering losses from aerial attacks, the direct fire of tankers and antitank gunners, as well as infantry fire, the Germans were unable to make any deeper penetration into the defenses of the 33rd Army and by 12.00 9 August had given up on their main task to develop the success in the northern direction. Instead, they re-directed their attack along the highway toward Wiłkowyszki. The German group of panzers, and behind them the infantry, managed to break into the town along the highway. Committing new units into the fighting, the enemy by 2400 had taken complete possession of the town.

Excerpt from Operational Summary No. 100 from the headquarters of the 33rd Army, 9 August 1944, 18.00:

First. The army's troops from 6.00 on 9 August in the sector between where the railroad intersects the highway, to the north of Antupie – Wiłkowyszki and, to a point on the highway 6 km southeast of Wiłkowyszki, was engaged in bitter fighting to repulse an enemy attack made with tanks and infantry. As a result of the fighting, by 18.00 they [the Germans] had reached a line and fighting was going on 500 meters south of Varpeninkai [an eastern suburb of Wiłkowyszki] . They emerged on a sector of the highway 2 km south of Bobrowszczyzna south of Znaczki, 400 meters from Pikszyszki.

The enemy at 6.00 9 August 1944, in strength of two regiments numbering up to 140 tanks and one self-propelled gun regiment, supported by up to four battalions of infantry, attacked the army's units and by 13.00 reached Wiłkowyszki.

Second. The artillery of the rifle divisions is firing to repel the attacks of enemy tanks and infantry. As a result of their fire, according to preliminary information, 6 enemy tanks were knocked out and 4 tanks were destroyed, as well as 4 machine guns, 2 vehicles with their loads and 2 antitank guns; up to a battalion of enemy infantry was destroyed and partially dispersed. The firing activity is being confirmed. Losses: 3 officers, 2 sergeants and 10 privates wounded.

Four 45mm guns and 4 76mm guns have been destroyed. The artillery of the 62nd Rifle Corps is occupying the previous combat positions.

The **142nd Cannon Artillery Brigade** is occupying it former combat position. It fired to repel enemy tank attacks and infantry. It set ablaze or knocked out 5 tanks; suppressed the fire of two 75mm artillery batteries; and destroyed or partially dispersed up to a company of infantry. There were no losses.

The **873rd Destroyer Antitank Artillery Regiment** is occupying a combat position in the area of Varpeninkai with two batteries and the Kraužmorgi area with two batteries. The remaining two batteries were struck by tank attacks, and according to preliminary information, these two batteries were destroyed by the enemy. The regiment set ablaze or knocked out 8 enemy tanks. Our own losses are being determined.

The **538th Mortar Regiment**: Combat position as before. It fired at aggregations of infantry and manpower. It destroyed 1 machine gun and 2 antitank guns. Our own losses are being determined.

The **47th Destroyer Antitank Artillery Brigade:**

The 578th Destroyer Antitank Artillery Regiment was in firing positions in the Znaczki area and during the enemy tank attack took on the main blow. As a result of the fighting it knocked out or destroyed 26 enemy tanks and self-propelled guns, and itself lost 22 57mm antitank guns and 20 vehicles in this action;

The 1025th Self-propelled Artillery Regiment is occupying combat positions in the Varpininkai area and fired to repulse enemy attacks. As a result of the combat, it knocked out 5 tanks and self-propelled guns. According to unverified information, the regiment itself lost 6 self-propelled guns. The losses of men and equipment is being determined.

The **43rd Destroyer Antitank Artillery Brigade** fired to repulse an enemy tank attack. According to unverified information, it set ablaze or knocked out up to 30 enemy tanks and self-propelled guns. Losses are being determined.

367th Guards Mortar Regiment fired to repulse the enemy tank attack and at aggregations of enemy personnel; it set 2 tanks on fire and dispersed up to a platoon of enemy infantry. The **83rd Guards Artillery Regiment** arrived under the operational subordination to the army's artillery and took up firing positions in the area west of Stefanyszki; it fired at the attacking enemy. No results of its combat activity have been reported.

The **41st Cannon Artillery Brigade** was in firing positions in the Budziszki, Gužele area and didn't conduct any fire.

Chief of staff of the 33rd Army's artillery Colonel IABLOCHKIN
Operations chief of the army's artillery headquarters Lieutenant Colonel Zaitsev

The command of a destroyer antitank artillery regiment.

Warriors of the 33rd Army who distinguished themselves in the fighting in August 1944

SAENKO Petr Rodionovich – commander of the 1964th [Antitank] Artillery Regiment of the 33rd Army's 43rd Destroyer Antitank Artillery Brigade.

On the morning of 9 August 1944 the enemy in strength of the single Panzer Division *Grossdeutschland* and several infantry units, with the support of aviation, launched a counteroffensive with the aim of cutting the Marijampolė – Wiłkowyszki highway and with an attack toward Augalai [north of Wiłkowyszki and on the road to Sudawa and Zynie] to cut off our units located northwest and west of Wiłkowyszki. At this time the regiment under the command of P.R. Saenko was occupying a line on the southern and southwestern outskirts of Wiłkowyszki. German tanks initially in small groups of up to 20 machines, and then in a column of 100-120 machines escorted by infantry and artillery attacked the combat positions of the batteries of the 1964th Destroyer Antitank Artillery Regiment, enveloping them from the north and northeast. Nevertheless, the regiment didn't waver, not a single gun crew abandoned its position, and allowing the tanks to close within several dozen meters, fired at them from pointblank range. However, the enemy managed to drive back the neighboring units, take the northern, eastern and southeastern sections of the city, and to encircle the artillery regiment. In the situation that had arisen, the regiment's men took up a hedgehog defense and didn't take a single step out of their combat positions.

The bloody fighting lasted for 18 hours, and of the 15 antitank guns, only 2 were left in working order; several crews perished bravely: everyone but a single man (Kurilov's platoon). The fighting went over to hand-to-hand struggles. The command post and regiment headquarters were surrounded by enemy submachine gunners in one of the city's buildings. Lieutenant Colonel Saenko personally organized an all-round defense, which served to secure the headquarters, regiment banner and uninterrupted command and control in the fighting. During the combat, a German halftrack and motorcycles were destroyed and up to 50 Nazis killed, and 8 of our prisoners were liberated. After all the regiment's guns were knocked out and ammunition was running out, at 4.00 on 10 August 1944 Lieutenant Colonel Saenko with the authorization of superior headquarters skillfully organized a breakout through the encircling Germans and led the regiment's survivors and banner out of encirclement.

In this multi-hour combat action, the artillerymen showed themselves to be models of bravery, tenacity and military skill, and their commander – a model of leadership and command of a regiment in the most difficult circumstances, as well as valor, courage and heroism. Throughout the fighting he didn't lose command over the regiment for a single minute, and even being badly wounded, continued to carry out his combat duties. As a result of the regiment's stand, the enemy incurred heavy losses: 27 tanks and 9 halftracks destroyed, and up to 500 Nazis wiped out. The enemy's counteroffensive was disrupted.

P.R. Saenko, a wartime and postwar photographs.

For his exemplary execution of a combat order and for the courage and heroism demonstrated while doing so, P.R. Saenko has been awarded the title Hero of the Soviet Union.

Excerpt from Order No. 0341 to the troops of the 33rd Army about awards to the personnel, 30 August 1944:

In the name of the Presidium of the Supreme Soviet of the USSR, for the exemplary fulfillment of orders from above and for the valor and courage demonstrated in the process, I am awarding Lieutenant Colonel Konstantin Ivanovich Serov, the commander of the 873rd Destroyer Antitank Artillery Regiment, with the Order of the Red Banner.

Commander of the 33rd Army
Guards Lieutenant General MOROZOV
Member of the 33rd Army's Military Council Major
General BABIICHUK
Member of the Military Council and 33rd Army's artillery commander
Lieutenant General of Artillery BODROV

Lieutenant Colonel K.I. Serov.

Excerpt from the list of commendations:

In the fighting against the German aggressors, Lieutenant Colonel Serov demonstrated exemplary courage, valor and skill to defeat the enemy. His regiment in offensive operations from 23 July to 15 August 1944 took active participation three times in breaking through German strongly fortified defenses …

On 9-10 August 1944 Serov, following an order to mop up the ensconced enemy on the eastern outskirts of Wiłkowyszki, carried it out with honor. His full-strength regiment, setting up their guns to fire over open sights, without the support of rifle units, took the eastern outskirts of Wiłkowyszki with an assault. Over the past operation, his regiment destroyed 28 tanks, 9 self-propelled guns, 8 artillery batteries, 7 halftracks, 152 vehicles and more than 2,000 enemy soldiers and officers. Over this same period of time, more than 250 privates, sergeants and officers were decorated with Orders and medals. Awarded the Order of the Red Banner.

Postwar photograph of K.I. Serov.

From the recollections of the Full Cavalier of the Order of Glory Guards Sergeant I. Mamykin:

At dawn on 9 August 1944, when the fog was beginning to swirl above the swamps and the scent of overripe rye became particularly sharp, someone in a low voice exclaimed "Germans!" In fact, fascist tanks were slowly crawling out of the patch of woods that stretched about a kilometer out in front of my gun. There was a lot of them, so many that Guards Senior Lieutenant Komarov, who'd been in various altercations with the Germans, gloomily said: "Eh, if only to withstand the first onslaught."

I was sharing my commander's concern. Three years' worth of wartime experience suggested that all it took was for the Germans to break through to the highway – and that would be the end of our regiment. The three days of rest after our forces crossed the Neman River had plainly been used by the German command to prepare a counteroffensive. Enormous armored strength had been brought together on a very narrow sector of the front, the shock fist of which were super-heavy Tiger tanks, assault guns and halftracks.

And now by the will of fate a field of rye, nestling up against a swamp, lay in the path of the German *Grossdeutschland* Panzer Division [sic]. Our destroyer antitank artillery regiment, which was now supposed to withstand the Germans' main attack, was concealed in the rye field.

Was that moment frightening? It is hard to say. Now it seems frightening, but back then, if you will, it wasn't. I'd grown accustomed to danger. A shell explodes nearby, and you don't pay any attention to it.

The wave of armor rolled alongside the swamp like a terrible steamroller, and the 2nd Battalion, in which I had a lot of friends, ceased to exist. The fighting was now going on somewhere behind me, but I wasn't firing. The enemy tanks were passing to one side and at such a range from us that they were invulnerable.

Just then, however, a German tank began to advance toward me at high speed. Fire! Fire! The shells ricocheted off the thick armor of the German tank like peas. One of the shells struck a track, and the tank began to pivot in place. In such cases we never missed. A shot – and it burst into flames.

Another tank began to loom out of the pre-dawn fog, spitting out lethal fire. Two of my crewmen were wounded, one was killed, but the remaining men took their places at the gun. The second tank was brought to a stop with a successful shot.

Suddenly quite nearby I caught the sound of guttural, foreign speech. The senior lieutenant shouted, "Guys, retreat!" I feverishly began to remove the panoramic sight. "Halt!" The Germans plainly wanted to take the artillerymen alive and didn't shoot.

There was nowhere to run. On one side a swamp, and on the other – German tanks and halftracks. I threw myself into some reeds. Deeper, deeper. The stinking water rose up to my throat. There was a chatter of submachine guns, chopping the reeds above my head. Then everything fell silent.

How I made it back to friendly lines, I don't recall. Later I found out that out of my gun crew, only the gunner survived, and by this time he was no longer in the picture. I had to get back to my gun – the thought pounded persistently in my brain.

Such a possibility soon presented itself. Our infantry had once again retaken the highway. Not far from the city of Wiłkowyszki, the German panzer avalanche had been stopped by Soviet tanks.

The gun was intact, and next to it lay a box of shells. Some soldiers helped me manhandle the gun to a hillock, and I began to fire at the enemy. My physical strength and nerves gave out. I fell from fatigue, and my arms and legs cramped up. The soldiers poured water over me, and I got up to resume fire. A hit – and a self-propelled gun burst into flames.

"Good man!" an infantry lieutenant joyfully shouted.

For this action I was bestowed my third Order of Glory, but this time 1st Class, and that's how I became a Full Cavalier of the Order of Glory.

Guards Sergeant Ivan Mamykin – commander of 76mm gun crew of the 33rd Army's 873rd Destroyer Antitank Artillery Regiment. Proved himself to be a bold commander. In the fighting on 9 August 1944 in the Antupie area, the enemy went on the attack with major forces of tanks and infantry. Up to 15 tanks and up to a company of German submachine gunners advanced on his gun crew. Disdaining the heavy fire coming from all types of weapons, risking his life he opened fire from his gun over open sights and shot 2 enemy tanks from pointblank range. Ignoring the heavy losses, the Nazis continued to charge at his crew. With several shots Mamykin knocked out an enemy self-propelled gun. His gun was crushed by a tank, but the valiant artilleryman didn't leave the battlefield, but continued to fight to repulse the attack using his personal sidearm, killing up to 30 enemy soldiers and officers in the process. For his exemplary fulfillment of orders from above, he's been awarded the Order of Glory 1st Class and has become a Full Cavalier of the Order of Glory.

Guards Sergeant Guseinaga Ramazanov – squad commander in a submachine gun company of the 157th Rifle Division's 384th Rifle Regiment of the 33rd Army. He distinguished himself in the fighting in the city of Wiłkowyszki on 9 August 1944. In the course of the fighting, when submachine gunners of the guard of the regimental banner were killed or wounded, Ramanazov remained alone, surrounded by the Germans. In savage fighting, he destroyed a machine gun and 7 enemy soldiers, holding out until the arrival of help. He carried the banner through the entire enemy-occupied city. When coming out of encirclement he tossed grenades into an enemy trench and delivered the banner to regiment headquarters. For his exemplary bravery, demonstrated when saving the regimental banner, he's been awarded the Order of the Red Banner.

Senior Sergeant Fedor Astaf'ev – deputy commander of a gun of the 3rd Battery of the 48th Anti-Aircraft Division's 213th Guards Anti-Aircraft Regiment. In the fighting on 9 August 1944 in the area of Wiłkowyszki, he engaged in a pitiless struggle with enemy submachine gunners that had broken through to the battery's area, preventing them from entering the firing positions. He was wounded in the fighting. Awarded the Medal "For Bravery".

Corporal Aleksei Voronkin – a mortar direction layer of the 3rd Battery of the 4th Guards Motorized Rifle Brigade's 273rd Mortar Regiment. In the fighting in the Wiłkowyszki area, thanks to Voronkin's accurate and precise work, two enemy machine guns together with their crews were destroyed, one halftrack was knocked out, and up to a company of infantry was wiped out by the fire of his mortar.

From the memoirs of Hero of the Soviet Union A. Maiorov of the 2nd Guards Red Banner Bomber Aviation Regiment:

Over the entire period of fighting at the East Prussian border in August 1944, the regiment operated in the first echelon and was based immediately behind the front lines, closely cooperating with the units of the 2nd Guards Tank Corps and the 33rd Army.

As an example of how the cooperation with the ground forces was arranged, I can offer the regiment's activity on 9 August 1944, when the situation at the front became complicated by a strong German counterattack. The enemy had been counterattacking in the Wiłkowyszki area already for several days. It was necessary to determine the assembly areas of the German tanks. At 0600 on the morning of 9 August, three pairs of LaGG-5 went on reconnaissance over the area southwest and northwest of Wiłkowyszki. Each pair received its own sector to scout. In the course of the reconnaissance flight, several motorized columns and an aggregation of enemy troops and vehicles was spotted.

Having regrouped on the night of 8-9 August, the enemy at sunrise on 9 August launched an attack 8-14 kilometers southeast of Wiłkowyszki with large forces, up to 60 tanks and infantry, and exploiting the initial success, began advancing toward Wiłkowyszki, enveloping the units of the Red Army that were located west and southwest of the city.

It was decided to send every available aircraft on this sector of the front into the struggle against the enemy tanks, including 8 LaGG-5, which were personally led into battle by the commander of the 2nd Guards Fighter Aviation Regiment, Guards Major Sobolev. In order to counter enemy aircraft over the breakthrough area, between 1030 and 1830 9 August 1944, LaGG-5 fighters of the 2nd Guards Fighter Aviation Regiment were on almost constant patrol.

Hero of the Soviet Union fighter pilot Captain A.I. Maiorov in the cockpit of his LaGG-5FN of a squadron of the 2nd Guards Fighter Regiment of the 322nd Fighter Aviation Division "Mongol Arat".

Simultaneously the fighters were scouting with the aim of establishing the actual location of enemy tanks in the breakthrough area and determining the routes of approach of German reserves. The scouts discovered the location of a group of up to 60 German tanks on the eastern outskirts of Wiłkowyszki, as well as the movement of motorized columns and individual machines along the roads to the south of Wiłkowyszki in the direction of the breakthrough. Quickly Il-2 ground attack aircraft were directed toward the revealed targets. In the skies above the breakthrough, the Guardsmen became involved in four dogfights, including one against 40 Ju-87 and 12 Fw-190, shooting down two of the German fighters. With strafing runs, the LaGG-5 destroyed 18 vehicles and one tank. Over the day, the regiment flew 15 group combat sorties.

Units of the German *Grossdeutschland* Division, July-August 1944

Tiger tanks of the *Grossdeutschland* Division on platform railcars in Gumbinnen at the end of July 1944.

Panzergrenadier Division *Grossdeutschland* on the attack in the Baltics, August 1944.

Combat operations of the 2nd Guards Tank Corps, Summer-Autumn 1944

Commander of the armored and mechanized forces Guards Lieutenant General A.I. Rodin (on the right) and the commander of the 2nd Guards Tank Corps Guards Major General of Tank Forces A.S. Burdeinyi discuss a situation.

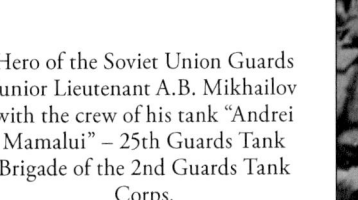

Hero of the Soviet Union Guards Junior Lieutenant A.B. Mikhailov with the crew of his tank "Andrei Mamalui" – 25th Guards Tank Brigade of the 2nd Guards Tank Corps.

Excerpt from Intelligence Summary No. 108 from the headquarters of the 3rd Belorussian Front, 9 August 1944:

Gumbinnen direction
The enemy with the forces of the *Grossdeutschland* Panzer Division [sic], supported from the air, on the morning of 9 August 1944 undertook an offensive out of the area south of Wiłkowyszki. With the forces of a battalion of infantry and 25 tanks, the enemy broke into Wiłkowyszki and by the end of day fighting was continuing in the city. In the course of 9 August, the enemy's actions were being supported by 27 artillery batteries, 10 mortar batteries, 15 separate guns, mortars, 8 rocket launchers and up to 200 tanks and self-propelled guns.

The units and formations of the 33rd Army on 9 August 1944 were engaged in tough fighting with the enemy's attacking tanks and infantry.

The **62nd Rifle Corps** in the period between 17.00 and 19.00 repulsed three enemy attacks: out of Mercze – a battalion of infantry with 10 tanks; out of the woods west of Zielonka – two companies with 10 tanks; and out of Banadinie – two companies with 12 tanks and self-propelled guns. By 21.00 9 August the corps' units were defending their previous lines.

The **19th Guards Rifle Corps**: 157th Rifle Division at 21.00 9 August with the forces of the 874th Rifle Regiment were holding the line: Point 61.4, Point 60.6. The 633rd Rifle Regiment, covering from the south, was engaged in combat in Wiłkowyszki with enemy tanks and infantry that have broken through to the city.

The 232nd Rifle Division from the morning of 9 August was engaged in combat with attacking enemy and by 12.00 had been shoved back to the Gudele, Bobrowszczyzna, Znaczki, Krużmorgi line. With decisive counterattacks supported by artillery and ground attack aircraft, by 15.00 the division had restored the situation and was occupying the Gudele, Point 54.8 and further along

A.B. Mikhailov.

I.Ia. Pan'kov.

A.A. Riabov.

A.P. Volkov.

Commander of the 2nd Guards Tank Corps General A.S. Burdeinyi attaching an Order to the brigade's banner.

Guards Colonel S.K. Nesterov kisses the Guards banner.

Commander of the 4th Guards "Minsk" Red Banner Order of Suvorov Tank Brigade Hero of the Soviet Union Oleg Losik (left) with his deputy and friend Guards Lieutenant Colonel Andrei Kryzhanovksy, 1944.

Officers of the 2nd Guards Tank Corps Captain N. Beletsky (left) and Major V.I. Flegentov.

The crew of the tank "Ivan Khomenko" of the 26th Guards Tank Brigade, summer 1944.

A T-34 tank with tank riders aboard on the approaches to East Prussia.

Guards Colonel Stepan Nesterov, commander of the 26th Guards Tank Brigade, stands on his T-34/85 tank and checks out a situation in the air, summer 1944.

T-34/85 tanks of the 4th Guards Tank Brigade (commanded by Guards Colonel Oleg Losik) of the 2nd Guards Tank Corps on the march, summer 1944.

A T-34/85 tank of the 2nd Guards Tank Corps' 25th Guards Tank Brigade, commanded by Guards Colonel Semen Bulygin, summer 1944.

A column of T-34/85 tanks of the 2nd Guards Tank Corps' 25th Guards Tank Brigade on the march, summer 1944.

Two crew members loading shells into a T-34/85 tank of the 2nd Guards Tank Corps' 4th Guards Tank Brigade, summer 1944.

the highway south to Antupie line with two regiments. The third regiment was assembled in reserve in the Suwałki, Znaczki area.

The 32nd Rifle Division with two regiments was engaged in fighting on the Nowiszki, Induryszki, Giejsztoryszki line. The third regiment was located in the corps' reserve on the Antupie – Powiłkowie line.

The 362nd Rifle Division is defending the previous line.

The **2nd Guards Tank Corps**, with forces of the 26th Guards Tank Brigade and 4th Guards Motorized Rifle Brigade by 21.00 on 9 August was engaged in fighting on the eastern and southeastern outskirts of Wiłkowyszki. The 25th Guards Tank Brigade – on the northeastern outskirts of Wiłkowyszki.

The 153rd Tank Brigade is on the northern outskirts of Wiłkowyszki.

The enemy shifted units of the Panzergrenadier Division *Grossdeutschland*, the 5th Panzer Division and the 1st East Prussian Division into the 33rd Army's sector, and having assembled up to 200 tanks, self-propelled guns and more than three regiments of infantry in the Iżencie – Nowa Wola sector, with the support of heavy artillery and mortar fire as well as bombers, in the course of 9 August engaged in bitter fighting, striving to break through in the northern direction.

At 6.00, in strength of up to two infantry battalions and 40 tanks and self-propelled guns, the enemy attacked out of the Jelekcie area in the direction of Merkszyszki. The German attack was driven back. At 7.20 of this same day, having reinforced the attacking group with tanks and infantry, the enemy attacked in the direction of Wiżajdy and Piłotyszki and by 11.00 had shoved the 232nd Rifle Division back beyond the Wiłkowyszki – Marijampolė highway and had reached the highway. At 12.55 50 tanks and two infantry battalions broke through to Wiłkowyszki from the east along the highway and by 21.00 was engaged in fighting on the southeastern, eastern and northeastern outskirts of the city. At 22.30 from out of the northern outskirts of Wiłkowyszki the enemy in strength of up to 150 men and 10 tanks broke through to the north and took the Wiłkowyszki railroad station.

As a result of the fighting on 9 August 1944, up to 1,100 soldiers were killed by the units and formations of the 33rd Army; in addition, 67 tanks and self-propelled guns were destroyed or knocked out, as well as 2 vehicles, 2 guns and 3 mortars. Four prisoners were taken, one of which belongs to the Panzer Division *Grossdeutschland*; the membership of the others is being determined. The army's command post is in Samarczuny.

The **1st Air Army** in the course of the day of 9 August, took part in repulsing enemy attacks, and with missions flown by bomber and ground attack aircraft destroyed his tanks, artillery and manpower in the areas west, south and southeast of Wiłkowyszki. Aerial reconnaissance was conducted out to the Tilsit, Insterburg, Lyck line. Altogether 816 individual aircraft sorties were flown. In aerial combats, 28 enemy aircraft were shot down. Individual enemy aircraft conducted reconnaissance to a depth of 20 km. Groups of up to 30 aircraft bombed our forces in the Wiłkowyszki area.

The weather on 9 August 1944: clouds at the altitude of 600 to 1500 meters, morning fog with a visibility of 0.5 to 2 km. Light winds out of the south. Temperature at night 8-14 degrees Celsius, in the daytime 25-27 degrees Celsius.

The **33rd Army**: Units of the 19th Rifle Corps from 6.00 on 9 August was engaged in stubborn fighting with the enemy's attacking tanks and infantry. 62nd Rifle Corps – on its former line. The enemy at 6.00 in strength of up to two regiments of infantry supported by 100 tanks and massed artillery fire, went on the offensive in the Bardowskie, Mackobudzie sector.

Excerpt from Combat Report No. 444 from the headquarters of the 3rd Belorussian Front, 9 August 1944, 21.00:

33rd Army: the 157th Rifle Division together with one regiment from the 153rd Tank Brigade and the 26th Guards Tank Brigade is engaged in stubborn fighting with enemy infantry and tanks in the northeastern and central sectors of the town of Wiłkowyszki. Two regiments of this division are holding the Kisieniszki, Point 60.6, Point 54.2 line. The 222nd Rifle Division is engaged in combat on the Gudele, Bobrowszczyzna, Znaczki, Antupie line. Separate elements of it have reached the Wiłkowyszki – Marijampolė highway. A prisoner from the Panzer Division *Grossdeutschland* was captured in the Gudele area.

The enemy at 13.00 and 17.00 twice attacked the left-flank units of the 344th Rifle Division in the direction of Žvangučiai with one to two companies of infantry and 12 tanks and self-propelled guns. At 14.00 the enemy in strength of two infantry battalions and 8 tanks attacked elements of the 32nd Rifle Division from the direction of Nowa Wola, west of Polajma. The attacks were repulsed. At 16.40 a column of vehicles and infantry was spotted moving out of Naumiestis, which subsequently assembled in the wooded area west of Zielonka.

POKROVSKY, IGOLKIN

From a report submitted by the commander of the 3rd Belorussian Front's armored and mechanized forces:

Having overrun our rifle units, enemy tanks by 9.00 9 August 1944 arrived at the Marijampolė – Wiłkowyszki highway and outflanked the destroyer antitank brigade that was being reinforced by the 1025th Self-propelled Artillery Regiment. In the course of a brief combat action, the enemy tanks cut the highway and began to expand to the northwest, where they were met by the fire coming from the tank ambushes set by the 2nd Guards Tank Corps, which had arrived by this time in the Sterniszki – Straudupie area …

Colonel General of Tank Forces A.G. Rodin

The commander of the 2nd Guards Tank Corps Major General of Tank Forces Aleksei Burdeinyi was to shift the 25th Guards Tank Brigade from the Semeneliszki area to the Gudele area; to send the 26th Guards Tank Brigade to the Wokszdny – Matuliszki area; and the 4th Guards Tank Brigade to the Znaczki – Point 63.4 area.

By 1630 9 August 1944 the 26th Guards Tank Brigade reached the indicated area, saddling the Wiłkowyszki – Marijampolė highway, where it became engaged in combat with enemy tanks. The 4th Guards Tank Brigade by 1630 9 August had fought its way forward to the Znaczki – Point 63.4 area. The 4th Guards Motorized Rifle Brigade by 1930 of this same day had reached the Pogramdyszki – Bobrowszczyzna line, where it took up a second echelon of defense in the rear of the corps' combat formations. At 2000 9 August the 2nd Guards Tank Corps' units were holding the occupied line and beating back enemy counterattacks. As a result of the day's combat, the corps' units killed up to 450 enemy soldiers and officers; and damaged or destroyed 7 medium tanks, 11 Tiger tanks and self-propelled guns, 16 vehicles, 5 guns of various calibers, and 2 halftracks. Four Pz.kpfw. IV tanks were captured.

The corps' own casualties for the day of 9 August 1944 amounted to 24 men killed or wounded. By day's end, the corps had 15 operational T-34 tanks in the 4th Guards Tank Brigade; 13 in the 25th Guards Tank Brigade; 14 in the 26th Guards Tank Brigade; 7 in the 79th Motorcycle Regiment; and an additional 3 T-34 tanks in attached units. The corps' self-propelled artillery regiment had 10 SU-85 and 3 SU-76.

Excerpts from the combat diaries of the brigades of the 2nd Guards Tank Corps

The **25th Guards Tank Brigade** had the task to saddle the Wiłkowyszki – Marijampolė highway completely. The enemy with units of the *Grossdeutschland* Division, remnants of the 1st, 2nd and 9th Reserve Battalions, and the Security Regiments 601 and 608 of the 201st Security Division after the offensive and counterattacks throughout the day of 9 August went over to a defense. The brigade by 20.30 on 9 August 1944 was completely blocking the Wiłkowyszki – Marijampolė highway in the area 1.5 kilometers north of Sardaki. The brigade throughout the night continued to defend its occupied lines of defense. The enemy showed no combat activity. At 22.30 9 August a reconnaissance patrol consisting of two submachine gun squads was sent out in the Wiłkowyszki, Budjeziory direction. The patrol established that enemy submachine gunners were in the city. In the southwestern direction, the enemy was defending the Sardaki line. In the course of the night of 9-10 August, there was the large movement of enemy tanks and vehicles to a bridge across the Szejmena River west of Wiłkowyszki. The condition of the brigade's tanks by the end of 9 August: 19 T-34 tanks on the list, 13 of which were operational, 2 were undergoing moderate repairs, 2 required factory repair, 1 had been knocked out and was being put back into service, and 1 tank was out of action with mechanical problems.

The **26th Guards Tank Brigade:** the enemy, having assembled a large quantity of tanks and motorized infantry in the Virbalis [Wirballen] area from the morning of 9 August initiated active offensive operations in the direction of Wiłkowyszki from the west and southwest. By 12.00 the Germans with a large number of tanks and the support of heavy artillery and mortar fire, managed to break through the defenses of the rifle units on the Antupie – Piłotyszki line, having cut on this line the Wiłkowyszki – Marijampolė highway, and as a result of offensive actions by 16.00 on 9 August to take Wiłkowyszki.

Having assembled up to 100 tanks and self-propelled guns as well as a large amount of infantry in Wiłkowyszki, the enemy attempted to break through the defense of our units in the northern and northeastern directions. Enemy aircraft were periodically bombing the combat positions of our units and constantly conducting aerial reconnaissance.

On the basis of a verbal order from the commander of the 2nd Guards Tank Corps General A.I. Burdeinyi, the brigade consisting of the 2nd Tank Battalion, motorized rifle battalion, a reconnaissance detachment, the anti-aircraft machine-gun company and the attached battery of the 1695th Anti-Aircraft Artillery Regiment at 2.00 on 9 August had been removed from its occupied Żynie – Iszkarty line of defense and had set out along the Dydwiże, Olksniany, Bałczuny, Budweitschen, Ruda route, and by 05.30 had taken up a defense with the task to block enemy counterattacks from the west, southwest and south. The 2nd Tank Platoon set up platoon-sized hedgehogs in the vicinity of Hill 65.9, north of the Wiłkowyszki – Marijampolė highway; the motorized rifle battalion was in the area of Hill 62.7, saddling the Wiłkowyszki – Marijampolė highway. In the occupied area of defense, the brigade had no contact with the enemy and was not engaged in combat, but it was being repeatedly attacked by our own ground attack and fighter aircraft, despite sending up signal flares indicating that our own forces were here. As a result of the attacks, the brigade had 2 men killed and 7 wounded, including the commander of the anti-aircraft machine-gun company.

At 13.30 on 9 August, on the basis of a verbal order from the commander of the 2nd Guards Tank Corps, the brigade was removed from its occupied defensive area and moved out along the Ruda, Sterniszki, Matuliszki route, and by 15.30 it was occupying a defense in readiness to block enemy counterattacks in the northern, northeastern and eastern directions. The 2nd Tank Battalion was occupying a line with one tank platoon at the intersection of two dirt roads 1 km west of Wokiszkiele, a second tank platoon on the southern outskirts of Matuliszki, saddling the Wiłkowyszki – Pilwiszki road, and a third tank platoon on the southern outskirts of Matuliszki with a front facing to the southwest; the motorized rifle battalion was on the southwestern outskirts of Matuliszki with a front to the southwest. Having taken up a defense, the brigade in the course of 9 August, with the support of ground attack aircraft but having no screening infantry out it front, repulsed counterattacks of the enemy, which attempted several times after taking Wiłkowyszki to break through the brigade's defenses to the north and northeast. Despite the repeated attacks of superior enemy forces, the brigade tenaciously held its occupied position. As a result of the fighting in the course of 9 August, the brigade's units killed up to 80 enemy soldiers and officers, and destroyed 2 tanks, 2 antitank guns and 4 vehicles. By the end of the day on 9 August, the brigade had 12 combat-capable T-34 tanks in the area of defense; 1 tank had been knocked out by the enemy, 2 tanks had been left behind en route due to mechanical breakdowns, and 1 tank out of service in the area of defense.

The **4th Guards Motorized Rifle Brigade**: On 9 August the enemy brought up a large quantity of tanks and infantry to the area west of Wiłkowyszki and was ready to go on the offensive toward Wiłkowyszki in order to regain his lost positions. At 3.00 on 9 August, according to a verbal order from the corps commanders, the brigade and the 273rd Mortar Regiment was removed from the occupied Patwiecie, Budzinski, Semeneliszki line, and having conducted a march on foot, by 7.00 on 9 August it was occupying a line of defense to repulse enemy tank and infantry attacks: the 1st Motorized Rifle Battalion southwest of the woods 1 km northeast of Ruda; 2nd Motorized Rifle Battalion was saddling the Wiłkowyszki – Marijampolė highway in the vicinity of an unnamed lake; 3rd Motorized Rifle Battalion on the southeastern fringe of woods lying 1 km northeast of Ruda; the artillery battalion and the 273rd Mortar Regiment were in firing positions in the Ruda area, with two guns of the artillery battalion in the vicinity of the nameless lake; a composite group of the rifle battalion's 57mm guns were in direct firing positions in the area west of Ruda (4 guns) and in the Draubolinie area (5 guns).

The main grouping of the German forces had managed to cut the highway in the Łukszyszki area. Leaving behind a covering screen of 15 tanks to guard its left flank, the main grouping then launched an attack toward Wiłkowyszki and captured it.

Our ground attack and fighter aircraft throughout the entire day of 9 August bombed and strafed the combat formations of the enemy tanks and infantry. Between 9.00 and 11.00 on 9 August, our ground attack aircraft and fighters mistakenly hit the positions of the 1st and 2nd Battalions and the firing positions of the artillery battalion and mortar battalion, thereby slowing the placement of fire on the enemy and inflicting casualties: the commander of the mortar battalion Guards Captain Samorodsky was wounded, and the senior adjutant of the mortar battalion Guards Senior Lieutenant Makhno was killed.

At 1800 on 9 August, according to a verbal order from the corps commander, the brigade and the 273rd Mortar Regiment were removed from their occupied line in the Ruda area, and by 2000 they had taken up a line with the 1st Motorized Rifle Battalion on the western outskirts of Matuliszki; the 2nd Motorized Rifle Battalion on the southwestern outskirts of Matuliszki; and the 3rd Motorized Rifle Battalion 500 meters east of Varpininkiai. The brigade's elements were in readiness to repulse the attacks of enemy infantry and tanks from the western and southwestern directions. The 2nd Motorized Rifle Battalion fired at German halftracks, and some of the crews were killed, the rest fled, and one halftrack was captured intact. The fire of the artillery battalion and mortar battalion dispersed and partially destroyed up to a platoon of infantry. The composite artillery battery under the command of Senior Lieutenant Moiseev destroyed four enemy vehicles together with their military cargo and personnel. The casualties of the 4th Guards Motorized Rifle Brigade over the day of combat on 9 August was 9 men killed and 1 wounded.

The **4th Guards Tank Brigade** consisting of 15 T-34 tanks at 2.30 on 9 August 1944, pursuant to a verbal order from the corps commander, was removed from its defenses in the Zielonka area, and by 5.00 on 9 August had reached the southwestern fringe of the woods northeast of Draubolinie.

According to a verbal directive from the corps commander, the brigade had the mission to operate along the highway running toward Wiłkowyszki, to take Znaczki and Hill 63.4, and subsequently to reach Sardaki, preventing the enemy's expansion to the north and northeast. At 11.45 9 August the brigade set out from the area of the southwestern fringe of the woods northeast of Draubolinie and Antupie, and by 16.30 it took Znaczki and Hill 63.4 with fighting, with the 3rd Tank Battalion on the western outskirts of Znaczki and the 1st Tank Battalion on the southwestern slopes of Hill 63.4. As a result of the fighting in the Znaczki area and east of Hill 63.4, the brigade destroyed one heavy Pz-VI tank and one self-propelled gun; southwest of Hill 63.4, it knocked out one heavy Pz-VI tank and 3 Pz-IV tanks, which were captured by the brigade. In addition, the brigade captured two tanks that had become bogged down in a swamp, and they were evacuated and sent to the rear in order for study by the personnel. In the course of the night of 9-10 August 1944, the brigade's units topped up their fuel and ammunition. The brigade has 15 operational T-34 tanks.

A conference; division commander General Hasso von Manteuffel (on the left), 1944.

According to Gerd Niepold the Germans believed that, despite their own heavy losses amongst Third Panzer Army's units, the Soviets were suffering even more damage, and that the main enemy threat would be overcome within a matter of days.

On 9 August the corps' artillery units, with the exception of the 1500th Self-propelled Artillery Regiment, which had been pulled out of combat back on 5 August, was supporting the actions of the corps' brigades. Over the day of combat operations on 9 August, the artillery units inflicted the following damage to the enemy: the **273rd Mortar Regiment,** located in firing positions in the area 300 meters east of Ruda, provided support to the 4th Guards Tank Brigade and helped repulse enemy attacks, and killed 60 enemy soldiers and officers and 2 heavy machine guns; the **28th Separate Guards Mortar Battalion**, located in the corps' reserve, helped repulse two counterattacks by enemy infantry out of the area of the woods northwest of Lukszszki, killed up to 200 enemy soldiers and officers and destroyed 3 guns and 4 heavy machine guns. The **401st Guards Self-propelled Artillery Regiment** and the **1695th Anti-aircraft Artillery Regiment** up until 19.00 on 9 August did not fire.

In the course of the day of 9 August, the artillery units of the 2nd Guards Tank Corps had no losses. By end of day on 9 August, the 401st Guards Self-propelled Artillery Regiment had 7 operational SU-85; the 1500th Self-propelled Artillery Regiment had no SU-76 left; the 28th Separate Guards Mortar Battalion had 8 M-13 rocket launchers; the 273rd Mortar Regiment had 25 120mm mortars; and the 1695th Anti-aircraft Artillery Regiment had 12 37mm anti-aircraft guns and 14 DShK machine guns.

Photographs of units of the Panzergrenadier Division *Grossdeutschland* in the Vilkaviškis (Wilkowischken), Marijampole Lithuania area, August 1944, taken by Kriegberichter Pfeiffer from the Propaganda-Kompanie, Division *Großdeutschland*.

Major Gerbener of the *Grossdeutschland* Division.

A Soviet soldier helps a comrade wounded in the battle. Judging from the camouflaged smocks, the soldiers in the photograph served in a front reconnaissance element probably from one of the Supreme High Command's assault-engineer units. Baltics, August 1944.

A Soviet heavy artillery battery shells German positions northwest of Marijampolė, Lithuania; August 1944.

Captain A.I. Kuzmin's guns of the 3rd Belorussian Front in their firing positions, summer 1944.

Men of one of the artillery crews of the 3rd Belorussian Front, including the gun commander Senior Sergeant V.G. Gureev and the gun layer Senior Sergeant A. Agibalov, summer 1944.

Men of a Soviet rifle division in combat on the approaches to the East Prussian border, August 1944.

Soviet submachine gunners advancing through a field toward the border with East Prussia, somewhere northwest of Marijampolė, Lithuania, August 1944.

Officers of the *Grossdeutschland* Division plan an operation.

Excerpt from Operational Summary No. 883/44 from the headquarters of the Third Panzer Army (Pz AOK 3) to the headquarters of Army Group Center, 9 August 1944; Daily Operational Report:

On the panzer army's southern flank Panzergrenadier Division *Grossdeutschland*, overcoming the enemy's strong antitank defense, after stubborn fighting with tanks and infantry, took Wiłkowyszki.

On the afternoon of 9 August, the division continued to attack to the north. All of the division's actions were significantly hampered by massed attacks of the enemy's ground attack aircraft, as a result of which our troops took heavy losses. A pinning attack by the enemy from the southeast and east had no success. It should be expected that the enemy will strengthen his attacks on the evening of 9 August and on 10 August. Our fighters shot down 29 enemy aircraft.

XXXX Panzer Corps: on the morning of 9 August the *Grossdeutschland* Division, attacking out of the Bardowskie area with two assault groups, fought its way through the enemy's antitank barrier and around 10.00 reached the southeastern sector of Wiłkowiszki.

According to intelligence from agents, the enemy was made aware of our offensive preparations from his own agents in our rear. Enemy resistance is increasing all the time. His aircraft are operating incessantly. The Russians' powerful antitank and tank defense forced the division to envelop Wiłkowyszki from the west.

By noontime, the town of Wiłkowyszki and the East Prussian forward line of defense on the eastern outskirts of Wiłkowyszki were in our possession. The further attack toward the north had to be halted temporarily, because elements of the Fusilier Regiment was forced once again to free the roads leading to Wiłkowyszki from the southwest of the enemy.

Despite heavy enemy resistance, our units that were attacking in the direction of the road's intersection with the railroad were making slow progress. When repulsing enemy counterattacks from the southeast and east, 4 tanks and 1 self-propelled gun were destroyed. The approach of enemy infantry and tanks from the southeast is being observed, and reports are coming in about new enemy jumping-off positions east of Wiłkowyszki. This forces us to anticipate a new powerful enemy attack.

The 561st Volksgrenadier Division with its right flank joined the offensive and re-took the East Prussian forward line of defense south of Wiłkowyszki. The area southwest of Wiłkowyszki and between the lake and the railroad is continuing to be mopped up of the enemy. Our offensive in the sector of Gruppe Schmidt was unable to penetrate the enemy's strong defenses.

On the corps' flanks, the enemy isn't undertaking any significant actions. Approximately 35 sorties by enemy aerial formations with a total of 375 aircraft has been noted. In addition, there have been approximately 400 individual sorties by enemy fighter-bombers (ground attack aircraft) and escorting fighter aircraft.

Arrived: StuG Battalions 1212 and 1241. The III/1st Heavy Mortar Regiment and III/Artillery Regiment *Grossdeutschland* have arrived in the Tauroggen area.

Table 1.9: Status of the Third Panzer Army's tanks and self-propelled guns by end of day 9 August 1944

Units	Tanks and self-propelled guns, types	Combat-ready	In repair Short-term	In repair Long-term
5.Panzer Division	Pz.IV	21	14	8
	Pz.V	20	11	10
	S-P Panzerjägers	4	-	-
	S-P guns on the chassis of Pz.IV tanks	17	6	3
6.Panzer Division	Pz.IV	17	30	15
I/Panzer Rgt. *Grossdeutschland*	Pz.V	16	26	6
7.Panzer Division	Pz.V	13	30	13
	One Pz.V tank lost irrecoverably			
	AT guns mounted on S-P carriages	17	-	-
	StuG	5	-	-
sPanzerjäger Abt. 519	Nashorn	2	1	3
	StuG	5	-	-
sPanzerjäger Abt. 731	Hetzer	4	21	9
StuG Brigade 203	StuG	23	-	-
StuG Brigade 232	StuG	22	4	-
StuG Brigade 276	StuG	17	6	-
StuG Brigade 277	StuG	13	8	-
SS Panzer Brigade "Gross"	Pz.V	4	-	-
	Pz.VI	1	-	-
Panzergrenadier Division *Grossdeutschland*	According to preliminary information, the division's losses amounted to 52 combat machines, including 24 lost irrecoverably			
sPanzer Abt. 510	A report well be sent in addition			
Brigade "von Werthern" (mot.)	A report will be sent in addition			

Enemy losses: the XXXX Panzer Corps has destroyed 4 tanks, 1 self-propelled gun, 11 antitank guns, and shot down 4 aircraft; 1 enemy aircraft had to make a forced landing and the pilot was captured. Our losses are also significant. Among the number of tanks and armored machines lost by the *Grossdeutschland* Division, 30 armored machines have been lost.

Both Spaeter and Jung claimed that Soviets had positioned entire Guards Corps (Jung stated that this Guards Corps comprised of elite regiments from three divisions) which was scattered, smashed and in some cases fled while fighting still raged in Wilkowischken. German authors claimed that Soviets lost 69 tanks plus 61 antitank guns.

Firstly, formations and units of the 33rd Army were operating in the Wiłkowyszki area; this was not considered an elite army, and its divisions and regiments were not Guards formations. Secondly, in fact the 2nd Guards Tatsiniskaia Tank Corps was operating in the Wiłkowyszki area, which could be called elite, however this tank corps didn't have "elite regiments from three divisions" on its roster, but instead consisted of three tank and one motorized rifle brigades. It had been located in constant fighting and on the eve of the fighting around Wiłkowyszki had only 57 T-34/85, 10 SU-85 and 3 SU-76 (as given on the evening of 8 August) against approximately 350 panzers, self-propelled guns and halftracks in the fresh, full-strength Panzergrenadier Division *Grossdeutschland*. Thirdly, neither in the German operational summaries of the Third Panzer Army and of the *Grossdeutschland* Division, nor in the operational documents of the 33rd Army and 3rd Belorussian Front, is there any mention of Soviet units fleeing from the battlefield. Fourthly, there are no signs that the 2nd Guards Tank Corps was destroyed in the fighting on 9-10 August 1944. According to the journal of combat operations, the tank corps lost no more than 11 tanks and self-propelled guns in this fighting (7 T-34 and 4 SU-85), and by the end of day 10 August still had 59 operational tanks and self-propelled guns (50 T-34, 6 SU-85 and 3 SU- 76). Fifthly, as is obvious from the archival documents presented by the author, in actual fact the Soviet units lost no more than 20 tanks and self-propelled guns and not more than 30 antitank guns in the fighting in the area of Wiłkowyszki on 9 and 10 August 1944. The German authors are only repeating the totally unconfirmed data from the operational summaries of the *Grossdeutschland* Division and of the Third Panzer Army, which tried to justify the heavy losses and present the fighting in the Wiłkowyszki area as a grand victory for propagandistic purposes. In reality, as the veteran of the *Grossdeutschland* Division Hans Heinz Refeld cited above testifies, "since the time of Operational Citadel's failure, we've never had such a defeat!" Indeed, despite the fact that the initial German attack east of Wiłkowyszki proved successful, subsequently the German assault grouping came under powerful artillery fire from the Soviet antitank artillery brigades of the 33rd Army, the Il-2 airstrikes, and the fire from the tanks of the 2nd Guards Tank Corps, and was unable to exploit the success on this axis. Finally, the losses of the elite German Panzergrenadier Division *Grossdeutschland* in tanks, self-propelled guns and armored halftracks in the course of the fighting in and around Wiłkowyszki exceeded the Soviet side's losses in tanks and self-propelled guns, and in particular, those of the 2nd Guards Tank Corps. That's how the myths and legends were created.

Excerpt from Intelligence Summary No. 109 from the headquarters of 3rd Belorussian Front, 10 August 1944:

Gumbinnen Direction
The enemy as a result of night fighting reached the line: Zalesie (8 km southeast of Naumiestis), west of Iszkarty, west of Zielonka, Szejmena River, Szelwy, eastern outskirts of Wiłkowyszki, Sardaki, west of Wiżajdy. Having suffered heavy losses in the fighting on 9 August, the enemy throughout the day of 10 August undertook no active operations and was digging in on the achieved lines. In the course of the day, the activity of 19 artillery and 7 artillery batteries, as well as 27 separate guns and mortars was noted.

From the morning of 10 August 1944, the units of the 2nd Guards Tank Corps were holding the following occupied line: 4th Guards Tank Brigade – Znaczki, Point 63.4; 26th Guards Tank Brigade – Wokiszkeli, Matuliszki, saddling the Wiłkowyszki – Pilwiszki road and the Wiłkowyszki – Szelwy road; 25th Guards Tank Brigade – 1.5 km north of Sardaki area, fully saddling the Wiłkowyszki – Marijampolė highway; 4th Guards Motorized Rifle Brigade – Matuliszki, Vernikiszki. At 0800 10 August, at the directive of the 33rd Army's commander, the 4th Guards Tank Brigade fought its way to the Sardaki area, having cut off the enemy's path of approach and retreat along the Jelekcie – Wiłkowyszki road. At 1430 the enemy with 10 tanks and 4 assault guns twice attacked the 26th Guards Tank Brigade out of Wiłkowyszki in the direction of Wokiszkeli. The attacks were thrown back.

By 2000 10 August the units of the 2nd Guards Tank Corps were holding a line: 26th Guards and 25th Guards Tank Brigades, 4th Guards Motorized Rifle Brigade – previous lines of defense. The 4th Guards Tank Brigade at 1330 was withdrawn from the defense in the Sardaki area and at 1530 was assembled on the southwestern fringe of the woods east of Bejraginie.

As a result of the day's fighting on 10 August, up to 80 enemy soldiers and officers were eliminated, as well as 5 tanks, 2 antitank guns and 3 vehicles; another 2 tanks were knocked out. Over this same period of time, the units of the 2nd Guards Tank Corps lost 5 men killed and 7 wounded, and 2 T-34 tanks left burned-out on the battlefield. By end of day 10 August, the 2nd Guards Tank Corps had 50 operational T-34 tanks, 6 SU-85 and 3 SU-76.

The **33rd Army** on the night of 9-10 August had conducted a regrouping. On the left flank and in the center, as a result of fierce fighting, the army had stopped the enemy's offensive and by 19.00 10 August was fighting on the line: the 62nd Corps' 70th Rifle Division – Zalesie, Žynie, Iszkarty; its 49th Rifle Division – Iszkarty, Zielonka, and further along the banks of the Szejmena River with its left flank 1 km northwest of Szelwy; its 344th Rifle Division – with one regiment together with a regiment of the 277th Rifle Division had taken the Wiłkowyszki railroad station, and with the other two regiments it was occupying a defense on the Tejbory, hamlet of Szelwy, Nowiniki line; its 277th Rifle Division with one regiment and the regiment from the 344th Rifle Division was occupying the Wiłkowyszki railroad station, while the other two regiments were holding the Szelwy, Karole, Matuliszki line. The 19th Rifle Corps was under the operational control of the 11th Army. Its 157th Rifle Division was on the eastern outskirts of Wiłkowyszki; its 222nd Rifle Division – on the southeastern outskirts of Wiłkowyszki and further to the south of the highway as far as Piłotyszki; its 32nd Rifle Regiment – Wiżajdy, Baczkiszki, Nowa Wola, Rostkowszczyzna; its 362nd Rifle Division – Kieturwłoki, eastern portion of Deguczy, Penkinele, Hill 119.5.

The **2nd Guards Tank Corps**' 26th Guards Tank Brigade was 2 km northeast of Wiłkowyszki; the 25th Guards Tank Brigade was 2 km southeast of Wiłkowyszki; the 4th Guards Tank Brigade was north of Sardaki; the 4th Guards Motorized Rifle Brigade was in the area of the crossroads north of Gudele. The 153rd Tank Brigade was on the eastern outskirts of Wiłkowyszki.

Then, on the night of 10-11 August 1944, the units of the 2nd Guards Tank Corps regrouped to respond to the situation that had arisen in the Wiłkowyszki area due to the German counteroffensive. Let's turn to their respective combat diaries to follow their movements:

Excerpts from the combat diaries of the brigades of the 2nd Guards Tank Corps:

The **25th Guards Tank Brigade** until 20.30 10 August 1944 was occupying a defense in the area 1 km south of Gudele, straddling the Wiłkowyszki – Marijampolė motorway with the task to prevent the enemy from advancing to the north and northwest. At 20.30 10 August 1944 the brigade was removed from its line of defense 1 km south of Gudele, and pursuant to a verbal order from the commander of the 2nd Guards Tank Corps, set out along the Gudele – Pogramdyszki – Nowiniki – Szelwy – Tejbery route, and by 2.00 11 August 1944 was occupying a defense along the Tejbery – Szelwy line, having deployed a tank platoon on the road in the Muck area, which is 1.5 km northwest of Tejbery. There the brigade topped up with fuel and ammunition. At 3.00 on 11 August, contact was made with the headquarters of the 244th Rifle Division. Status of the tanks: 10 operational T-34 tanks, with 3 tanks broken down in route with mechanical problems, 3 tanks undergoing moderate repairs, and 2 tanks requiring factory repairs; 1 tank has been turned over to the 26th Guards Tank Brigade. There are 8 T-34 tanks located in the area of defense.

The **26th Guards Tank Brigade**, pursuant to a verbal order from the commander of the 2nd Guards Tank Corps, was occupying a defense in front of the antitank ditch, with no infantry out in front of it, in three separate strong points on the line: isolated cottages north of the "Wokiszkiele" label, intersection of the dirt roads northeast of the "mekh" label, isolated cottages next to the swamp 800 meters east of the "mekh" label. The reserve of the brigade commander is in Korale. The tank crews, who's spent the last three days on the defense without any supporting infantry, were extremely exhausted and in need of rest. Throughout the day, questions of cooperation with the 277th Rifle Division were being settled; this division twice had an order to attack, but in fact didn't attack and at 19.00 was occupying a defense 1 km behind the tanks. Fighting to repulse enemy attacks, the brigade killed up to 50 enemy soldiers and officers; destroyed 2 heavy Tiger tanks; knocked out one self-propelled gun; and smashed 3 antitank guns and 10 vehicles. In return the brigade lost 4 men killed and 7 wounded, two T-34 tanks destroyed, one tank knocked out of action by mechanical problems, and one demolished wheeled vehicle. By the end of the day, the brigade had 11 operational T-34 tanks in the area of defense.

The **4th Guards Motorized Rifle Brigade** on 10 August together with the 273rd Mortar Regiment was not located in direct contact with the enemy. The brigade's elements were located in readiness to repulse enemy attacks from out of the Wiłkowyszki area and scouted out to the forward edge of the forward units, while keeping watch over the enemy's activity. The artillery fired at enemy firing points, infantry and tanks. The 1st Motorized Rifle Battalion is on the line of the intersection of country lanes north of Matuliszki; the 2nd Motorized Rifle Battalion is at the intersection of the country roads south of Matuliszki; the 3rd Motorized Rifle Battalion is in Massykwietyszki, with a front facing the southwest; the artillery battalion is in firing positions in the area east of Massykwietyszki; and the 273rd Mortar Regiment is in firing positions 1 km southwest of Dworkiele. The enemy is stubbornly defending Wiłkowyszki with self-propelled artillery and infantry. Throughout the day of 10 August, the enemy was placing heavy artillery and mortar fire on the combat positions of the forward units of the 222nd Rifle Division, on the lines of defense of our battalions, and on the artillery's firing positions. The enemy air force in one group of 13 Ju-87 dive bombers between 18.00 and 19.00 bombed the positions of the forward units. Our ground attack aircraft with escorting fighters in groups of 8 to 24 aircraft throughout the day was bombing the forward edge and depth of the enemy's defense. Over the day of 10 August, the brigade's elements destroyed 5 vehicles together with their cargo; dispersed or partially destroyed up to a company of infantry; and suppressed the fire of three mortar batteries and three artillery batteries. In return the brigade's losses amounted to 11 men killed or wounded, of which 2 men were killed and 6 wounded by the fire of our own aircraft.

The **4th Guards Tank Brigade** consisting of 16 T-34 tanks, saddling the highway leading into Wiłkowyszki north of Sardaki, had the task of also controlling the Islekcie – Wiłkowyszki road. At 01.30 on 10 August 1944, pursuant to a verbal order from the corps commander, the brigade's units were removed from the defense southwest of the fringe of woods east of Bejraginie and by 4.30 were assembled in the area of the hamlet of Szelwy [north of the village of Szelwy itself] with the task to repel enemy attacks from the northwest and west. Fifteen T-34 tanks arrived in the assembly area; one T-34 lagged behind due to a broken track. The personnel were busy with a technical inspection of the tanks and digging slit trenches. The condition of the tanks: 15 operational T-34 tanks. One tank was undergoing light repairs, 5 were undergoing moderate repairs, and 5 required factory overhauls.

The enemy throughout the day of 10 August 1944 continued to occupy their former positions, and had infantry massing in the antitank ditch. Enemy artillery was firing out of the Semeneliszki, Wyszczokajmie and Kisieniszki areas. According to the information from men that were coming out of encirclement, the Germans had up to 100 tanks in Wiłkowyszki. The staging of 10-18 tanks and self-propelled guns along the Szejmena River between Wiłkowyszki and the Wiłkowyszki railroad station was observed. The enemy twice attacked the brigade out of the area of the northern outskirts of Wiłkowyszki; both attacks were driven back by tank fire.

On 10 August 1944 the artillery units of the 2nd Guards Tank Corps, with the exception of the 1500th Self-propelled Artillery Regiment, were supporting the brigades' actions, and by 2200 on 10 August were positioned in the following areas: 401st Guards Self-propelled Artillery Regiment – Wiekierotyszki – Dworkiele; 1500th Self-propelled Artillery Regiment – 2 km east of Matuliszki;

28th Separate Guards Mortar Battalion – 260 meters south of Stefaniszki; 1695th Anti-aircraft Regiment – had a battery attached to each tank brigade; one battery and the DShK Company are covering the corps headquarters.

In the course of the day of 10 August, the corps' artillery units helped repulse enemy counterattacks and inflicted the following damage: 273rd Mortar Regiment, in support of the 4th Guards Tank Brigade, helped repulse the counterattacks of enemy tanks and infantry. In the process, it eliminated up to 400 Nazis, 6 vehicles together with their cargo, and 1 88mm gun; and silenced the fire of one mortar battery and one battery of antitank guns. The 401st Guards Self-propelled Artillery Regiment, the 28th Separate Guards Mortar Battalion and the 1695th Anti-aircraft Artillery Regiment remained unengaged throughout the day of 10 August.

The 273rd Mortar Regiment suffered losses: 5 men wounded and one vehicle demolished; one 120mm mortar malfunctioned and became disabled. By the end of the day of 10 August, the corps' artillery units had in service: 401st Guards Self-propelled Artillery Regiment – 6 SU-85; 1500th Self-propelled Artillery Regiment – 1 SU-76; 273rd Mortar Regiment – 24 120mm mortars; 28th Separate Guards Mortar Battalion – 8 M-13 rocket launchers; 1695th Anti-aircraft Artillery Regiment – 12 37mm anti-aircraft guns and 14 DShK machine guns.

On 10 August 1944, the following report was sent to the 3rd Belorussian Front's chief of operations by the chief of staff of the 2nd Guards Tank Corps:

1. The condition of the corps' units by end of day 10 August 1944:
    a) 4th Guards Motorized Rifle Brigade – 402 active bayonets;
    b) 4th Guards Tank Brigade – 16 combat-ready T-34 tanks;
    c) 25th Guards Tank Brigade – 11 combat-ready T-34 tanks;
    d) 26th Guards Tank Brigade – 12 combat-ready T-34 tanks;
    e) 79th Motorcycle Regiment – 7 combat-ready T-34 tanks;
    f) 401st Guards Self-propelled Artillery Regiment – 6 SU-85;
    g) 1500th Self-propelled Artillery Regiment – 3 SU-76;

2. Opposite the front of the 2nd Guards Tank Corps on 10 August 1944, the following enemy units were operating:
    a) Panzer Division *Grossdeutschland* [sic], which is confirmed by documents that were removed from knocked-out tanks in the following areas: 4 August 1944 – in the Bobławka area; 9 August 1944 – in the Ruda area; 10 August 1944 – in the vicinity of Point 63.4.
    b) East Prussian Volksgrenadier Division, which is confirmed by prisoners captured in the area of the western outskirts of Wiłkowyszki and in the Pracopol area. In the period between 1 and 5 August 1944, 10 prisoners were captured.
    c) Prisoners from the 201st and 52nd Security Divisions, as well as the 1072nd Grenadier Regiment, were captured in the Wiłkowyszki area. For the corps' positions at 20.00 10 August 1944 – see the attached map.

3. From the commander of the 3rd Belorussian Front's armored and mechanized forces, the corps received the task to assemble in the following area by the morning of 11 August in readiness to repulse enemy counterattacks from the Zynie and Wiłkowyszki directions: Garszwinie, Grenszej, Korale, Matuliszki. The brigades are arriving in the following areas: 4th Guards Tank Brigade – hamlet of Szelwy; 25th Guards Tank Brigade – Grenszej; 26th Guards Tank Brigade – Korale; 4th Guards Motorized Rifle Brigade – Matuliszki. The 25th Guards Tank Brigade set out to the indicated area at 22.30 10 August 1944. The remaining brigades will successively be assembling in the indicated areas.

4. Command and control have been organized:
   a) An operational group consisting of the corps commander, the deputies for personnel and political affairs, the artillery commander, the operations chief with officer couriers, the chief of intelligence and the signals chief.
   b) The command post – the chief of staff and all of the departments of the headquarters. The operational command group has wire, radio and officer couriers to connect with the brigades. With the headquarters it has wire and radio connections. The headquarters has contact with the units through wire, radio and couriers, and with the operational command group through wire and radio communications. Contact with the headquarters of the 33rd Army is by wire, radio and officer couriers; with the headquarters of the Front's armored and mechanized forces – by radio.

Chief of staff of the 2nd Guards Tatsinskaia Tank Corps
Guards Colonel KARAVAN

The enemy in the area of Wiłkowyszki showed no activity. On the right flank of the 33rd Army, the Germans attacked the units of the 70th Rifle Division three times out of the Darzeniki, Mercze area and the woods west of Zielonka with two battalions of infantry and 4-8 tanks. The attacks were driven back.

The casualties of the 33rd Army over the day of fighting on 9 August had amounted to 981 (226 men killed and 755 men wounded). It also lost 1 122mm gun, 15 76mm guns, 5 45mm guns and 6 120mm mortars, all destroyed.

Over the day of combat on 10 August, the army's formations and units eliminated up to 500 enemy soldiers and officers, and destroyed 1 gun, 2 mortars and 12 machine guns. Twenty-eight Germans were taken prisoner. The army's command post as before was in Samarczuny.

The **1st Air Army** with bombing missions and close support attacks destroyed enemy tanks and personnel in the area south and southwest of Wiłkowyszki, and also flew reconnaissance missions out to the Tilsit, Insterburg, Goldap line. Over the day it flew 371 individual sorties, 169 were bombing and close support missions. The enemy's aircraft in the course of the day of 10 August conducted reconnaissance over the battlefield and the rear areas out to a depth of 20 km. Up to 50 individual enemy aircraft sorties were spotted.

Excerpt from Combat Dispatch No. 447 of the headquarters of the 3rd Belorussian Front at 14.30 on 10 August 1944:

33rd Army: with part of its strength was attacking with the aim of regaining the positions in the Wiłkowyszki area. At 11.00 the 344th Rifle Division attacked the Wiłkowyszki railroad station with one regiment. According to preliminary information, at 11.40 the regiment was fighting on the northern outskirts of the station. 157th Rifle Division: one rifle regiment of the 157th Rifle Division and two rifle regiments of the 222nd Rifle Regiment, supported by tanks, launched an attack at 11.00 on 10 August toward Wiłkowyszki from the northeast, east and southeast. The enemy is putting up fierce fire resistance. At 11.40 south of Lake Pojeziory, an aggregation of an unestablished number of enemy vehicles and tanks was spotted.

Pokrovsky, Igol'kin

This message was followed by a later dispatch that updated the situation.

Excerpt from Combat Dispatch No. 448 from the headquarters of the 3rd Belorussian Front at 18.30 on 10 August 1944:

In the Front's center, the 33rd Army with part of its strength is continuing to fight to restore the situation in the Wiłkowyszki area. At 16.30 a regiment of the 344th Rifle Division and a regiment of the 277th Rifle Division were engaged in bitter fighting in the vicinity of the Wiłkowyszki railroad station. The enemy was putting up tough resistance to our units with the fire of artillery, mortars and tanks. At 17.30 out of the Darzeniki, Point 47.8 area, the enemy in strength of up to two battalions of infantry and 7 tanks attacked units of the 70th Rifle Division. The attack was repulsed.

Pokrovsky, Igol'kin

Excerpt from Combat Order No. 17 from the 33rd Army's artillery headquarters, 10 August 1944 at 13.00:

The enemy continues to hold the occupied line. Opposite the army's front, the following enemy units were identified: Kampfgruppe Knebel, Infantry Regiment 1 of the 1st East Prussian Infantry Division, a kampgruppe of the 6th Panzer Division, the Panzer Division *Grossdeutschland* [sic], the 1072nd Infantry Regiment and units of the 5th Panzer Division. Enemy reserves are located in the areas of Schirwindt, Naumiestis and Wirballen.

The army is temporarily going over to a strict defense on the Zalesie, Zielonka, Korale, Gudele, Baczkiszki, Bardowskie line in readiness to continue the offensive in the western direction.

62nd Rifle Corps (the 70th, 49th and 344th Rifle Divisions) together with the 535th Army Mortar Regiment is defending the Zalesie, Zielonka, Wiłkowyszki railroad station, hamlet of Szelwy, Dydwiże, Wola Skompska area.

The artillery's assignments:

1. Prevent the assembly of enemy tanks and infantry opposite the forward edge;
2. Prevent penetrations by tanks;
3. Prevent penetrations by infantry;
4. Organize an antitank defense built around antitank areas No. 1, No. 2, No. 3, No. 4, No. 5, No. 6, No. 7, No. 8, No. 9 and No. 10. The responsible zone of fire: on the right – the corps' boundary; on the left – Obszruty, Wiłkowyszki railroad station. Supplementary sector: On the left – Potomniszki, with one regiment. Area of firing positions: Romantyszki, Łujsze, hamlet of Szelwy together with the 83rd Guards Artillery Regiment.

The **277th Rifle Division** is defending the Wiłkowyszki railroad station, Wiłkowyszki – Pilwiszki turnpike, Zamszewo sector. The artillery's missions:

1. Prevent a breakthrough by enemy tanks and infantry along the railroad and along the turnpike toward Pilwiszki. Organize a strict antitank defense. Create antitank areas No. 11, No. 12, No. 13 and No. 14;
2. Responsible zone of fire: the division's sector. Supplementary sector on the left – Pojeziory with one battalion. Area of firing positions: Korale, Nowiniki, Szelwy.

The **232nd Rifle Division** is defending the Matuliszki, Sardaki, Sowalki sector. The artillery's missions:

1. Prevent the assembly of enemy tanks and infantry in front of the forward edge of defense;
2. Prevent penetrations by enemy tanks;
3. Thwart enemy infantry attacks;
4. Organize a strict antitank defense. Create antitank areas No. 15, No. 16, No. 17, No. 18 and No. 19. Sector of responsibility: On the right – the divisional boundary; on the left – Skrandupie, Sardaki, Olwita. Supplementary sector on the left – Budjeziory with one battalion. Area of firing positions: Bobrowszczyzna – Gudele.

The army's antitank group:

Group No. 1: 43rd Destroyer Antitank Artillery Brigade and 2nd Guards Destroyer Antitank Regiment. Group commander: the commander of the 43rd Destroyer Antitank Artillery Brigade. Task: Organize antitank areas No. 10, No. 12, No. 14. Do not allow a breakthrough by tanks in the sectors of the 49th Rifle Division and 277th Rifle Division. **Group No. 2: 47th Destroyer Antitank Artillery Brigade and the 873rd Destroyer Antitank Artillery Regiment.** Group commander: the commander of the 47th Destroyer Antitank Artillery Brigade. Task: Do not allow a breakthrough by tanks in the defensive sectors of the 277th and 222nd Rifle Divisions. Prepare antitank areas No. 15, No. 17 and No. 18.

The **General-Purpose Army Group**: the **4th Artillery Division and 142nd Cannon Artillery Brigade**, group commander – the commander of the 4th Artillery Division. Sector of responsibility: the army's right-hand boundary. Supplementary sector: on the right – Materny with one brigade; on the left – Saužbole with one brigade. Area of firing positions: Augulai, Łujsze, Gałakausze, Garszwinie, Pogramdyszki, Sterniszki, Stefaniszki. Missions:

1. Prevent the assembly of infantry and tanks in front of the forward edge of defense;
2. Prevent an attack by enemy tanks;
3. Prevent an attack by enemy infantry;
4. Silence the active enemy batteries in the areas: Podziszki, Szukle, Skordupiany, Rutkiszki, Maldehne, Powembry.

The Army Group of Guards Mortars: **7th Guards Mortar Division, 307th Guards Mortar Regiment** and **326th Guards Mortar Regiment**. Group commander – the commander of the 7th Guards Mortar Division. Mission: Reconnoiter routes leading into and out of firing positions in the area: Sklawcze – Sterki, Naszyszki, Obszruty, Sarmaczuny, Suwalki.

The army's antitank reserve: the 25th Destroyer Antitank Artillery Brigade. Assembly area: Mažucie, Obszruty. Mission: Reconnoiter routes leading into and out of firing positions in the Kausze, Poromaniszki and Obszruty directions.

Ready the artillery by the end of 11 August 1944.

Command post: Bamarczyny.

33rd Army's artillery commander Lieutenant General of Artillery BODROV
Chief of staff of the 33rd Army's artillery Colonel IABLOCHKIN

Excerpt from Operational Summary No. 101 from the 33rd Army's artillery headquarters, 10 August 1944 at 20.00:

First. In the course of the day, the army's forces with part of its strength was continuing to destroy the enemy that had broken through to Wiłkowyszki and along the road toward Szelwy. As a result of the fighting, the enemy suffered heavy losses in equipment. At 15.00 in the Zielonka – Mercze sector, the enemy undertook two attacks: one in the direction of Zielonka in strength of up to 200 men; the second toward Point 48.6 in strength of up to two platoons. Both attacks were driven back with heavy losses for the enemy.

Second. The rifle divisions' regiments have taken up the following combat positions:

> 70th Rifle Division's 227th Artillery Regiment – in the Romantyszki, Sudawa area;
> 49th Rifle Division's 31st Artillery Regiment – in the Pracapol area;
> 344th Rifle Division's 913th Artillery Regiment – in the Szelwy, Bazyliszki area;
> 277th Rifle Division's 346th Artillery Regiment – in the Pogramdyszki area;
> 157th Rifle Division's 422nd Artillery Regiment – in the Matuliszki area;
> 222nd Rifle Division's 666th Artillery Regiment – in the Antupie, Powiłkowie area;
> 32nd Rifle Division's 133rd Artillery Regiment – in the Dekszniszki area;
> 362nd Rifle Division's 936th Artillery Regiment – in the Beržyny area;

The artillery regiments were conducting fire to destroy the manpower and equipment of the enemy group that had broken through the lines and to destroy enemy counterattacks. As a result of the fire, 23 vehicles loaded with infantry, one 75mm gun, one prime mover, 12 heavy and 10 light machine guns, three 81mm mortar batteries and one antitank gun were destroyed; one enemy observation post was pulverized; and the fire of six artillery batteries and one self-propelled gun was silenced. According to updated information, over 9 and 10 August 1944, not 10 enemy tanks were knocked out or destroyed when repulsing tank attacks, but 47 tanks and 17 armored halftracks. Up to 700 enemy soldiers and officers were killed or wounded. In return our casualties amounted to 34 killed (11 officers, 7 sergeants and 16 enlisted men) and 92 wounded (15 officers, 34 sergeants and 43 enlisted men). In addition, 5 122mm howitzers, 6 120mm mortars, 6 76mm guns, 1 76mm antitank gun and 11 vehicles were knocked out or destroyed.

Third. The army's artillery and artillery reinforcements:

> 142nd Cannon Artillery Brigade is occupying combat positions in the Garszwinie area. It conducted fire to destroy the enemy grouping in the Wiłkowyszki area; took part in repulsing counterattacks; suppressed the fire of two 105mm batteries; and destroyed and partially dispersed up to a platoon of infantry. It had no losses.
> 873rd Destroyer Antitank Artillery Regiment is occupying combat positions in the Varpininki area, 500 meters north of Matuliszki. The regiment went into action and knocked out 2 tanks and 6 machine guns with its fire, and dispersed and partially destroyed up to a platoon of enemy infantry.
> The 538th Mortar Regiment is occupying combat positions in the Tejbery, Giedriai area. The regiment fired and destroyed 6 machine guns, 1 antitank gun and up to 40 enemy soldiers. It had no losses.
> The 43rd Destroyer Antitank Artillery Brigade is occupying combat positions: 1965th Destroyer Antitank Artillery Regiment – 1 km south of Bobrowszczyzna; 1966th Destroyer Antitank Artillery Regiment – in the Pobziory area. The regiment fired enemy tanks and personnel. The results of its combat activity have not been reported.
> The 47th Destroyer Antitank Artillery Brigade is occupying combat positions in the Kraužmorgi area. It fired at enemy tanks and personnel. The results of its combat activity haven't been reported.
> The 41st Cannon Artillery Brigade is occupying combat positions in the Stariszki area. It fired at counterattacking enemy tanks. It dispersed up to 20 tanks and a platoon of infantry. It had no losses.

The 83rd Guards Artillery Regiment is occupying combat positions in the Pogramdyszki area. With its fire, it dispersed and partially destroyed up to 150 enemy soldiers and officers and knocked out one tank. Losses: one private wounded.

The 367th Guards Mortar Regiment was supporting the 70th Rifle Division. It launched two battalion salvoes at enemy infantry and tanks in the Darzeniki, Bokisznele area and at the intersection of the railroad and paved roads. As a result of the fire, it suppressed the fire of one artillery and one mortar battery, set three tanks ablaze, and killed 30 soldiers. It had no losses.

The 326th Guards Mortar Regiment was supporting the 62nd Rifle Corps with one battalion and the 19th Rifle Corps with one battalion. It fired at attacking enemy tanks and infantry in the area of the hamlet of Szelwy and Zielonka. It dispersed and partially destroyed up to a company of infantry and knocked out one tank. Losses: 2 men killed, 2 wounded.

The 13th and 14th Cannon Artillery Brigades have arrived under the operational subordination to the army's artillery headquarters.

Fourth. From the morning, mists, by noon, cloudiness, and by the afternoon rain showers that intensified by evening. Visibility: 2 km.

Fifth. Trafficability of the roads has deteriorated as a consequence of the rain showers.

Sixth. Communication with the units by telephone, radio and officer couriers.

Seventh. The artillery headquarters is in Sarmaczuny.

Chief of staff of the 33rd Army's artillery headquarters
Colonel IABLOCHKIN
Chief of operations of the 33rd Army's artillery headquarters
Guards Lieutenant Colonel ZAITSEV

Excerpt from Operational Summary No. 887/44 from the headquarters of the Third Panzer Army (Pz AOK 3) to the headquarters of Army Group Center, 10 August 1944. Daily operational report:

In the Wiłkowyszki area Panzergrenadier Division *Grossdeutschland* successfully repulsed counterattacks by major enemy forces from the east and in the afternoon continued to attack in the northwestern direction. According to the latest dispatches, the division reached the river between the Wiłkowyszki railroad station and the southern outskirts of Žolasie, where it is constructing a new forward edge of defense. Enemy air formations again intervened in the course of the ground fighting, however the numerical strength of these formations fell in comparison with 9 August. The losses suffered by our forces on 9 August when overcoming the antitank obstacles and in the combat with enemy tanks were not in vain – our units achieved big successes. On 9 and 10 August in the Wiłkowyszki area, 69 tanks and self-propelled guns and 61 antitank guns were destroyed; the anti-aircraft artillery and infantry shot down 8 airplanes.

XXXX Panzer Corps: On the left flank the 5th Panzer Division repulsed two enemy attacks in strength of one or two companies. Observers spotted the movement of enemy trucks, some of which were towing guns, opposite the salient in the front west of Marijampolė, which testifies to the fact that the enemy is bringing up reinforcements to this sector.

Panzergrenadier Division *Grossdeutschland* on the morning of 10 August drove back several attacks by major forces of enemy infantry and tanks from the east and northeast; in the process the enemy suffered heavy losses in tanks. Fighting is continuing successfully to mop up the enemy from the southeastern section of Wiłkowyszki and the ground southwest of the city. The division conducted a regrouping and on the afternoon of 10 August again went on the offensive to the northwest with the objective to establish direct contact on the left with the 561st Volksgrenadier Division. Simultaneously with the *Grossdeutschland* Division's attack, the units of the 561st Volksgrenadier Division are attacking out of the area north of Alvitus [Olwita] to the north across the railway line.

In the area of Wiłkowyszki, 34 group airstrikes by Il-2 aircraft were counted, in which 276 machines took part, in addition to approximately 200 fighters. In the sector of the 6th Panzer Division, there's been no changes.

Table 1.10: Status of the Third Panzer Army's tanks and self-propelled guns by end of day of 10 August 1944

Units	Tanks and self-propelled guns, types	Combat-ready	In repair	
			Short-term	Long-term
5.Panzer Division	Pz.IV	22	13	1
	Pz.V.	19	15	10
	S-P Panzerjägers	4	-	-
	S-P guns mounted on chassis of Pz.IV	18	6	2
6.Panzer Division	Pz.IV	21	25	16
I/Panzer Rgt. *Grossdeutschland*	Pz.V	25	18	5
7.Panzer Division	Pz.V	26	24	13
	StuG	5	-	-
	AT guns on self-propelled carriage	19	-	-
Panzergrenadier Division *Grossdeutschland*	Pz.III	2	-	-
	Pz.IV	7	13	1
	Pz.V	42	15	15
	Pz.VI	12	-	11
	StuG	7	8	
	Irrecoverable losses of 9-10 August: 4 Pz.IV, 18 Pz.V and 5 Pz.VI			
sPanzer Abt. 510	Pz.VI	14	Will be reported in addition	
sPanzerjäger Abt. 519	Nashorn	2	1	3
	StuG	-	1	-
sPanzerjäger Abt. 731	Hetzer	15	10	9
StuG Brigade 203	StuG	20	9	-
StuG Brigade 232	StuG	22	4	-
StuG Brigade 276	StuG	15	7	5
StuG Brigade 277	StuG	16	7	-
Brigade "von Werthern"	StuG	4	5	9
	Pz.IV	2	1	4
StuG Abt. 1241	StuG	10	-	-

Excerpt from the combat diary of the German Third Panzer Army, 10 August 1944:

After successfully repulsing numerous and strong enemy attacks from the east in the area of Wiłkowyszki, the *Grossdeutschland*'s offensive was resumed in the northwestern direction. According to the latest dispatches, the offensive reached the course of the stream between the Wiłkowyszki railroad station and directly south of Žolesie. A new forward edge of defense is being built here. Numerous detachments of enemy aircraft were supporting the ground fighting; however, the number of aircraft was less than on the preceding day. Despite the heavy losses suffered when breaking through the enemy's antitank obstacles, in the course of 9 August we scored major successes. In the course of 9 and 10 August in the Wiłkowyszki area, 69 enemy tanks and self-propelled guns, as well as 61 antitank and infantry guns were destroyed. Our anti-aircraft artillery and ground units shot down 58 enemy aircraft.

The *Grossdeutschland* Division is engaged in combat with a tenaciously resisting enemy in the area where the railroad and highway intersects north of Wiłkowyszki. The enemy group that was defending in the southwestern portion of the city was destroyed by us in the course of the day.

In the course of the night in the sector of the 561st Volksgrenadier Division, the East Prussian Defensive Line was taken on both sides of Wiłkowyszki. In the course of the morning, the replacement of the *Grossdeutschland* Division by the Infantry Regiment 1142 continued. Enlivened activity by enemy aircraft reigned in the skies above the division's dispositions.

At 8.50 the commander of the Third Panzer Army reported to the Field Marshal over the telephone about the results of *Grossdeutschland*'s offensive. The forward attacking units made an advance in the area of the intersection of the railroad and highway. The Field Marshal is adhering to the view that if the forward attacking detachment continues to be located there, then the operation is a failure. If no success is achieved today, then he will issue an order for a withdrawal. The offensive can be continued in the course of the present day, but this evening it will be necessary to end it. The commander of Third Panzer Army responds that it is what he in fact assumed. The Field Marshal once again emphasizes that the main objective consists in strengthening the northern flank. For this, the units of the *Grossdeutschland* Division must be freed up as quickly as possible. The screening of the Rossiene – Kelmy area is most important.

Throughout the morning hours, the *Grossdeutschland* Division repulsed repeated strong attacks of enemy infantry and tanks from the eastern and northeastern directions. In the process a lot of enemy tanks were destroyed. The fighting to mop up the enemy from the southeastern section of Wiłkowyszki and southwest of the town continued successfully. In the morning the commander of the Third Panzer Army was located at the command post of the *Grossdeutschland* Division together with the commander of XXXX Panzer Corps.

Considering the losses suffered the day before and having seen the strength of the enemy's resistance, the division command considers it impossible to achieve all of the offensive's objectives if it isn't given another 24 hours. The corps commander fully shares this point of view. The commander of the Third Panzer Army emphasizes that only the afternoon of the present day has been granted in order to implement the offensive. To a proposal put forward to give help with the forces of 6th Panzer Division's panzer group, the commander of the Third Panzer Army responds that this group wouldn't be able to arrive in time. The withdrawal of the *Grossdeutschland* Division to the jumping-off line is rejected by the commander, since this would be a big mistake. The capture of Wiłkowyszki is a major tactical success.

At 11.25 the commander of Third Panzer Army decides that it is impossible to execute fully the large mission. The "East Prussian Defensive Line" must be occupied by our troops north of Wiłkowyszki as far as possible and strongly held. After this, the offensive should be continued in the northwestern direction with the aim of creating a defensive line along the course of the stream and making direct contact with Kampfgruppe Herzog.

Afterward the commander of the Third Panzer Army heads to the forward command post of the *Grossdeutschland* Division's commander in Wiłkowyszki. He explains the fresh task to the division commander and issues an order regarding the withdrawal of the first units by noon on 11 August. In the first place, the armored car battalion, artillery units and the pioneer battalion should be withdrawn. After conducting a regrouping, the *Grossdeutschland* Division in the afternoon goes on the attack in the northwestern direction with the aim of making contact on the left with the 561st Volksgrenadier Division. Simultaneously units of the 561st Division launches an attack north of Alvitus [Olwita] in the northern direction across the railroad line.

In the area of Wiłkowyszki, enemy aircraft conducted today 35 group airstrikes with Il-2s totaling 256 aircraft. Simultaneously up to 200 bombers with fighter escort flew missions. The units of the *Grossdeutschland* Division operating southeast and east of Wiłkowyszki will be replaced today by units of the 561st Volksgrenadier Division.

At 19.15 General Heidkämper issues an order over the telephone to the chief of staff of XXXX Panzer Corps to hasten the departure by all means. Colonel von Kahlden answers that the corresponding succinct orders have been timely issued. The *Grossdeutschland* Division repulsed a number of enemy attacks in the northern and northeastern sectors. The attack in the direction west of the Wiłkowyszki railroad station went successfully.

At 22.00 the commander of XXXX Panzer Corps reports over the telephone to the commander of the Third Panzer Army that the troops everywhere have reached the branch of the Szejmena River. The achieved area has been mopped up of the enemy. The panzer corps command is expecting an enemy attack tomorrow in the direction of the 5th Panzer Division's left flank. General von Knobelsdorff states that this would be extremely unpleasant, because the panzers of the 5th Panzer Division are badly worn out. The commander of the Third Panzer Army orders to defend with the available artillery and the mortar battalions. Simultaneously he indicated that according to evidence of intercepted radio messages, the enemy was intending to launch an attack toward Wiłkowyszki. The XVI Army Corps received an order to bring up reinforcements.

At 22.30 General Heidkämper has discussions with the chief of staff of Army Group Center and brings to his attention the expected enemy attack toward Wiłkowyszki. In connection with this, the units of the *Grossdeutschland* Division should remain there.

According to intelligence reports, it is possible to establish that the enemy has shifted from two to three Guards rifle divisions from out of the area west of Kalvarija and is using these formations in order to take Wiłkowyszki, having brought up 4 divisions and the 2nd Guards Tank Corps to there. One captured officer testified that an army that has arrived from the Far East and carries the title of "Breakthrough Army" has been assembling in the area 40-50 km east of Wiłkowyszki. Once the frontline formations reach the national boundary, this army will launch an attack into German territory. A telephone order is issued to shift the remaining units of StuG Brigade 277 to the southern bank of the Neman River. This same telegram contains an order to the IX Army Corps to move the units of one of the assault gun brigades to the sector of the 69th Infantry Division. General Heidkämper quickly issues this order in the name of the chief of staff of Army Group Center, which cancels the previous restrictions placed on using the *Grossdeutschland* Division's reconnaissance battalion. The enemy's advance must be halted by every means.

At 00.40 11 August the command is informed by telegraph by Rotkirch's division about an enemy attack in the direction of Užwentie. An order goes out to bring to bring the first East Prussian defensive line between the area 8 km northwest of Tauroggen and west of Plunge up to full combat readiness. The sectors adjacent to roads are to be the focal points of the defense. Reconnaissance must be conducted in the northeastern direction. It is additionally necessary to conduct reconnaissance with the forces of a panzer-reconnaissance company out of the Telsche area in the southwestern direction. Both attacking groups must prepare corresponding areas for deployment and assembly on the jumping-off lines. For this XXXX Panzer Corps by end of day

10 August must accelerate the freeing up of the *Grossdeutschland* Division and shift it to the area northeast of Skadwile. The enemy that has broken through in the Rossienie area must be attacked and the situation in this sector restored.

At 16.05 the command of the Third Panzer Army issues a telegraph order to free-up the main forces of the *Grossdeutschland* Division on the night of 10-11 August from its present operational area, and to assemble them in the Skadwile area and to the northeast. The assembly should be implemented under the direction of IX Army Corps, and from 13 August – under the leadership of XXXX Panzer Corps. Considering the fuel situation, it is necessary to use all the fuel tanks, including those of the wheeled transport. From the moment of abandoning command posts, all of the units of the *Grossdeutschland* Division are ordered to cease all radio communications. The 1st Mortar Brigade should remain in the present area of operations.

At 23.00 another telegraph order goes out about freeing-up all of the units of the *Grossdeutschland* Division, which must by 12 August be replaced by the lead regimental group of the arriving 549th Volksgrenadier Division. Upon the arrival of the rest of the 549th Volksgrenadier division's units, Kampfgruppe Herzog must be free-up. The final objective of the regrouping between the new, right-hand army boundary and the branch of the Szeszupa River on the left is the occupation of the southern sector by the 561st Volksgrenadier Division and the handling of the leadership in the northern sector by the 549th Volksgrenadier Division …

Excerpt from the operational summary of the Red Army's General Staff at 0800 on 10 August 1944:

3rd Belorussian Front. 33rd Army. The enemy, having brought up to the front the Panzer Division *Grossdeutschland*, the 5th Panzer Division and the 1st East Prussia Infantry Division, with the support of concentrated artillery fire and aircraft, from the morning of 9 August went on the offensive against the units of the 33rd Army. In the course of the day the enemy repeatedly attacked our units in the Wiłkowyszki area from the west and southeast in the total strength of more than three regiments of infantry and up to 200 tanks and self-propelled guns. Having focused the main efforts in the area southeast of Wiłkowyszki, the enemy by 12.00 in strength of two battalions of infantry and up to 50 tanks broke into Wiłkowyszki.

The **62nd Rifle Corps** in the period from 17.00 and 19.00 repulsed three enemy counterattacks in strength of up to a battalion of infantry and 15-20 tanks and self-propelled guns, and by 20.00 with part of its forces was engaged in intense combat with the enemy in the Szelwy area that had broken through north of Wiłkowyszki.

The **19th Rifle Corps'** 157th Rifle Division, occupying a line in the area of Point 61 (1 km southwest of Wiłkowyszki with one rifle regiment, and screening the southern direction with two rifle regiments, was engaged in combat to destroy the enemy infantry and tanks that had broken through to Wiłkowyszki. The 222nd Rifle Division was engaged in combat on the line: Gudele (2 km southeast of Wiłkowyszki), 2 km south of Kraužmorgi.

The **2nd Guards Tank Corps** by end of day was engaged in combat: the 26th Guards Tank Brigade, 4th Guards Tank Brigade and 4th Guards Motorized Rifle Brigade – eastern and southeastern outskirts of Wiłkowyszki; 25th Guards Tank Brigade – on the northeastern outskirts of Wiłkowyszki.

The Front's remaining armies were occupying their former positions, conducting reconnaissance and exchanging fire with the enemy. Over the day of fighting, the Front's forces killed 1,780 soldiers and officers, and destroyed up to 100 tanks and self-propelled guns, 4 guns, 6 mortars, 36 machine guns, 7 armored halftracks and 143 vehicles. The Front's air force, cooperating with the ground troops in repulsing enemy attacks, flew 816 individual aircraft sorties, which resulted in

25 aerial combats in which 24 enemy aircraft were shot down. The enemy's air forces with solitary aircraft was conducting reconnaissance to a depth of 20 km and in groups of up to 32 aircraft were bombing our forces in the Wiłkowyszki area, conducting 178 aircraft overflights. One enemy aircraft was shot down by our anti-aircraft artillery.

Chief of the Operations Department of the Red Army General Staff
Colonel General SHTEMENKO
Chief of the Information Section of the Operations Department of the Red Army General Staff
Major General PLATANOV

On 10 August 1944, the troops of the 3rd Belorussian Front managed to drive the Germans out of the Wiłkowyszki railroad station.

Combat Order No. 046 from the headquarters of the 2nd Guards Tank Corps, 10 August 1944:

1. The enemy continues to hold the occupied line. Kampfgruppe Knebel, the 1st East Prussia Infantry Division, the 3rd Infantry Division's Infantry Regiment 216, a kampfgruppe of the 6th Panzer Division, Kampfgruppe Schirmer, the Panzer Division *Grossdeutschland*, the 107th Infantry Regiment and units of the 5th Panzer Division are defending opposite the front of the 33rd Army. Enemy reserves are in the areas of Schirwindt, Naumiestis and Wirballen.
2. The 2nd Guards Tank Corps and the 153rd Tank Brigade are to go over to a defense on the Tejbery, Korale, Matuliszki, Varpininkai line, having one tank brigade between Majoryszki and Matuliszki, and one tank brigade in the Navininkai area.

The corps commander has ordered:
1. The 25th Guards Tank Brigade by 5.00 on 11 August 1944 is to shift to the Giedriai area, where it is to take up a defense together with the infantry with the task to repulse enemy counterattacks from the north and northwest;
2. The 26th Guards Tank Brigade is to remain in place and by 5.00 on 11 August 1944 is to take up a defense in the Korale area with the task to repulse enemy counterattacks from the west and southwest;
3. The 4th Guards Tank Brigade by 5.00 on 11 August 1944 is to move to the area of the hamlet of Szelwy, where it is to take up a defense and be ready to repulse enemy counterattacks;
4. The 431st Self-prepared Artillery Regiment by 5.00 is to reach the Tejbery area, where it is to take up a defense with the task together with the 25th Guards Tank Brigade to repulse enemy counterattacks from the north and northwest;
5. The 153rd Tank Brigade by 8.00 on 11 August 1944 is to move to the area of Point 61.0, where it is to take up a defense with the task to repulse enemy counterattacks from the west and southwest;
6. Dig the tanks and self-propelled guns into the ground and carefully camouflage them. Assign sectors of fire to each individual tank and tank crew.
7. Move out upon receipt of a special order.
8. The operational command group and the corps headquarters from 6.00 11 August 1944 will be in Smilgie. The corps headquarters command post – Budweitschen.

Chief of staff of the 2nd Guards Tatsinskaia Red Banner Tank Corps
Guards Colonel KARAVAN
Chief of operations
Lieutenant Colonel Repin

Excerpt from Intelligence Summary No. 110 from the headquarters of the 3rd Belorussian Front, 11 August 1944:

Gumbinnen Direction

The enemy on 11 August in the Wiłkowyszki area conducted a partial regrouping of forces and was assembling tanks in the area northwest of Wiłkowyszki. Out of the Mercze – woods west of Zielonka – Szelwy area, in strength of a company to a battalion of infantry supported by 3-11 tanks, the enemy undertook 6 unsuccessful attacks.

On the other sectors of the front, the Germans were fortifying their occupied positions. The enemy artillery was shelling our combat positions with rare methodical fire and brief barrages. Altogether, the enemy activated 18 artillery batteries and 10 mortar batteries, as well as 12 separate guns and mortars and 5 rocket launchers.

The 33rd Army throughout the day of 11 August was occupying its line of defense. The 62nd Rifle Corps' 70th Rifle Division – Zalesie, Zielonka; its 49th Rifle Division – Zielonka, Patwiecie, Wiłkowyszki railroad station; its 277th Rifle Division – Wiłkowyszki railroad station, Korale, isolated buildings 0.5 km north of the Wiłkowyszki map inscription; its 222nd Rifle Division – isolated buildings north of the Wiłkowyszki map inscription, Point 54.8, Sardaki; its 344th Rifle Division – in the second echelon in the Gałakausze, Garszwinie, Naszyszki area. The 19th Rifle Corps' 32nd Rifle Division – Wyżajdy, Jelekcie, Point 60.4; its 157th Rifle Division – in the Użbole, Pogramdyszki, Dworkiele area; its 362nd Rifle Division – in the Domejkiszki, Giże, Pogramdy area.

The 2nd Guards Tank Corps was assembled in the following areas: 25th Guards Tank Brigade – Giedriai; the 4th Guards Tank Brigade – hamlet of Szelwy; the 26th Guards Tank Brigade – Korale; and the 4th Guards Motorized Rifle Brigade was occupying the Gałakausze, Garszwinie, Nowiniki line. The 153rd Tank Brigade was 0.5 km north of Bejraginie.

The enemy in the center of the defensive front twice conducted combat reconnaissance out of the areas of Wokiszkiele (up to a battalion of infantry and 10 tanks) and the northeastern outskirts of Wiłkowyszki (up to 200 men and 8 tanks). Two of the German tanks were knocked out by antitank artillery fire and the infantry was dispersed. On other sectors of the front, the enemy conducted machine-gun fire and shelled the positions with artillery and mortars.

The army's casualties for 10 August 1944 was 51 killed and 263 wounded. Over the day of 11 August, up to 310 enemy soldiers and officers were killed, and 2 mortars and 2 machine guns were destroyed. Two Germans were taken prisoner.

At a directive from the commander of the 3rd Belorussian Front's armored and mechanized forces Colonel General of Tank Forces A.G. Rodin, at 5.00 on 11 August 1944 the 2nd Guards Tank Corps went over to a defense on the line: Tejbery, Korale, Matuliszki, Varpininkiai. The 25th Guards Tank Brigade was occupying the Tejbery – Szelwy sector; the 4th Guards Tank Brigade was in positions in the hamlet of Szelwy; the 26th Guards Tank Brigade was in strongpoints on the following line: 2nd Tank Battalion – 60 meters northwest of the "Korale" map inscription and the woods west of Majoryszki; the 1st and 3rd Tank Battalions – in Wokiszkiele. The brigades were located in readiness to repulse possible enemy counterattacks.

By end of day 11 August 1944, the units of the 2nd Guards Tank Corps had the following numbers of operational T-34 tanks: 4th Guards Tank Brigade – 16; 25th Guards Tank Brigade – 11; 26th Guards Tank Brigade – 12; 79th Motorcycle Battalion – 7; other units – 3; for a total of 48 operational T-34/85 tanks. The corps also had 4 operational SU-85.

Excerpts from the combat diaries of the brigades of the 2nd Guards Tank Corps, 11 August 1944:

The **4th Guards Motorized Rifle Brigade** and the 273rd Mortar Regiment, pursuant to a verbal order from the commander of the 2nd Guards Tank Corps, at 3.00 on 11 August 1944 was removed from its occupied line east of Wiłkowyszki, and having conducted a march on foot, took up a line of defense west of Garszwinie, center of the hamlet of Szelwy: 1st Motorized Rifle Battalion – 1 km northwest of Garszwinie; 2nd Motorized Rifle Battalion – 1.5 km west of Garszwinie; 3rd Motorized Rifle Battalion – central portion of the hamlet of Szelwy; mortar battery – in firing positions 800 meters southwest of Garszwinie; artillery battalion – in firing positions in the Szydziszki area; and the 273rd Mortar Regiment – in firing positions 1 km northeast of the hamlet of Szelwy. In the course of the day the brigade's elements and attached units remained at combat readiness to repulse counterattacks by enemy tanks and infantry from the west; conducted reconnaissance out in front of its line; established contact with the forward-operating units; and maintained observation over the enemy's actions.

The **4th Guards Tank Brigade** consisting of 16 T-34 tanks is occupying a line in the area of the hamlet of Szelwy with the assignment to repulse possible enemy attacks from the north, northwest and west. At 16.00 11 August 1944, a reconnoitering group of officers was sent out consisting of the battalion deputy commanders and adjutants. Lines for the deployment of tanks were determined: No. 1 – bridge 500 meters northwest of Romantyszki, isolated building 1 km south of Hill 50.8; No. 2 – 500 meters southwest of the "Rumaki" map inscription; No. 3 – western outskirts of Žynie; No. 4 – 1.5 km north of Romantyszki. In the course of the night, the brigade's men dug all their tanks and vehicles into the ground. The brigade has 16 operational T-34 tanks, 5 tanks undergoing moderate repairs, and 5 tanks undergoing factory repairs.

The **26th Guards Tank Brigade:** Throughout the day of 11 August 1944, the enemy attacked three times in the sector of the 277th Rifle Division in strength of up to 120 submachine gunners supported by 8-10 tanks. The enemy's attacks were driven back by the fire of artillery and rocket launchers. On the basis of a verbal order from the commander of the 2nd Guards Tank Corps, the units of the 26th Guards Tank Brigade were removed from the occupied line of defense and by 2.00 on 11 August 1944, had taken up a defense in the Korale area with a front facing to the west and southwest. The 2nd Tank Battalion was in strongpoints on the line: individual cottages lying 600 meters northwest of the "Korale" map inscription, woods west of the "Majoryszki" map inscription. There was no infantry in front of the tanks. The motorized rifle battalion was on the southwestern outskirts of Pogramdyszki.

The anti-aircraft-machine-gun company of the brigade and the attached battery of the 1695th Anti-aircraft Artillery Regiment had the task to cover the brigade's units from the air; they were in firing positions in the Užbole area. In case of necessity, they had the task to support the 2nd Tank Battalion and motorized rifle battalion with fire at ground targets.

With the arrival in the new area of defense, contact was established with the neighbors on the right (the 277th Rifle Division and 49th Rifle Division) and the neighbor on the left (the 157th Rifle Division). The 1st and 3rd Tank Battalions were positioned in the Oszkiszki area, where combat training exercises were conducted with the men. When conducting the march from the Matuliszki area to the Užbole area, one man was wounded by an artillery barrage. In the area of defense, the 26th Guard Tank Brigade had 13 operational T-34, one of which had mechanical problems; 1 76mm antitank gun; 3 37mm anti-aircraft guns and 5 DShK machine guns. The battery from the 1695th Anti-aircraft Artillery Regiment had three 37mm anti-aircraft guns and 1 DShK machine gun.

The **25th Guards Tank Brigade** throughout the day of 11 August 1944 continued to occupy a defense on the Tejbery – Szelwy line. At 23.00 on 11 August, a combat directive from the 2nd

Guards Tank Corps' commander was received, according to which it was ordered to dig-in the tanks and dig full-profile trenches for the men of the motorized rifle battalion. The movement of the men in daylight hours of the day had been banned. The anti-aircraft – machine-gun company is covering the brigade from the air. The status of the tanks and equipment is without changes.

Order No. 29 from the headquarters of the 33rd Army's armored and mechanized forces at 15.30 on 11 August 1944:

1. The 2nd Guards Tank Corps and the 343rd Heavy Self-propelled Artillery Regiment are to go over to a defense with the brigade's tanks dug into the earth as fixed firing positions in the following areas:
   a) 343rd Heavy Self-propelled Artillery Regiment – in Pracapol, subordinate to the 62nd Rifle Corps with the task, in cooperation with the 62nd Rifle Corps, to prevent an enemy breakthrough from the directions:
      i) Darzeniki, Sudawa;
      ii) Zielonka, Pracapol;
      iii) Žvanguciai, Patwiece;
      and to be in readiness to counterattack together with the units of the 344th Rifle Division in those same directions;
   b) the 25th Guards Tank Brigade – in the Tejbery, Giedriai area, subordinate to the commander of the 62nd Rifle Corps;
   c) the 26th Guards Tank Brigade in the Korale area cooperates with the 277th Rifle Division;
   d) the 401st Self-propelled Artillery Regiment 1 km southwest of Zamszewo cooperates with the 277th Rifle Division; the 4th Guards Tank Brigade – in the hamlet of Szelwy, Hill 65.9 area, in cooperation with the 62nd Rifle Corps, in readiness to counterattack in the directions: hamlet of Szelwy, Pracapol, along the railroad toward the Wiłkowyszki railroad station, Nowiniki, Suwalki, Sardaki.
2. The 4th Guards Motorized Rifle Brigade is in the second echelon behind the 25th Guards Tank Brigade.
3. By 10.00 on 12 August 1944, complete reconnoitering and work out questions of cooperation, both when repulsing attacks and when launching a counterattack with units of the 62nd Rifle Corps.

Commander of the 33rd Army's armored and mechanized forces
Colonel VAKHRUSHEV
Chief of staff of the 33rd Army's armored and mechanized forces
Guards Lieutenant Colonel IVANOV

From the Combat Path of the 2nd Guards Tank Corps:

The enemy on 9 August 1944 descended upon our combat positions with the forces of the 1st East Prussia Infantry Division, the 201st and 52nd Security Divisions, the 272nd Grenadier Regiment and the Panzer Division *Grossdeutschland*. "Not a step back!" – that was the order. So the Guardsmen stood firm, tightly hugging the ground, repelling attack after attack.

An enemy shell knocked out the entire crew of Guards Junior Lieutenant Andreianov's self-propelled gun. He, despite being severely wounded, continued to fire at the Nazis by himself. A second enemy shell set his machine ablaze. Andreianov was facing his own death. He lacked the strength to clamber out of the self-propelled gun. Guards Private Romanets, risking his life, under heavy enemy fire rushed to Andreianov's machine and saved the life of the severely wounded officer.

Guards Private Svetlyi saved the life of his own commander, Guards Senior Lieutenant Shedlonsky. In one of the fierce counterattacks, Shedlonsky was badly wounded. He fell about 50 meters out in front of our trenches, in no-man's land between our own trenches and the German trenches. Guardsmen Svetlyi, disregarding the intense machine-gun fire, crawled out to the wounded officer. However, two Nazis also crawled out of their trenches to meet the Soviet soldier. "They want to take me alive, the vermin" – flashed through his head, as he firmly held his submachine gun to his shoulder. Having allowed the adversaries to close to within short range, Private Svetlyi killed them with his accurate fire, and then carried his commander back to a place of safety.

Bitter fighting continued for more than a week; the enemy attacks were immediately followed by impetuous counterattacks by our tanks. In separate battalions there remained just two to three combat machines each. However, the assignment was carried out. Wherever the Guardsmen stood, the enemy did not pass.

Table 1.11: Damaged and destroyed German armored vehicles investigated on the battlefield

No. according to the scheme	Side number	Type	Direction of movement	Nature of damage
1	232	Halftrack	North	Struck by artillery fire; a side armor penetrated
2	None	Pz-IV	Northwest	Struck by artillery fire; 5 penetrations in the right-side armor plate. Burned out.
3	None	Pz-V	North	Struck by artillery fire; penetration of armor plate. Burned out.
4	322	SU-150 (on chassis of Pz-V)	Southeast	Struck by artillery fire; gun barrel smashed; left track damaged.
5	101	Pz-V	Northwest	Tank is serviceable; stuck in swamp.
6	None	Pz-IV	Northwest	Struck by artillery fire; 2 penetrations in side armor.
7	313	Pz-V	West	Struck by artillery fire; left side armor and engine penetrated. Burned out.
8	None	Halftrack	Southeast	Struck by artillery fire; penetrations in side armor in two places.
9	None	Pz-V	West	Struck by artillery fire; right side armor penetrated. Burned out.
10	A22	Pz-VI (Pz-IV in document)	West	Struck by artillery fire; penetration in turret. Burned out.
11	A03	Pz-IV	Northwest	Struck by artillery fire; frontal armor penetrated; impression in main gun.
12	11	Pz-V	Northwest	Struck by artillery fire; side armor penetrated. Burned out.
13	706	Pz-V	West	Struck by artillery fire; final drive damaged.
14	709	Pz-V	Northwest	Struck by artillery fire; penetration in right side armor. Burned out.
15	124	Pz-V	Northwest	Damaged by artillery fire; penetration in ride side armor. Burned out.
16	708	Pz-V	Northwest	Struck by artillery fire; engine compartment penetrated. Burned out.
17	A23	Pz-VI	West	Struck by artillery fire; penetration in left side armor. Burned out.

No. according to the scheme	Side number	Type	Direction of movement	Nature of damage
18	221	Pz-V	West	Knocked out by aircraft; turret blown off. Burned out.
19	None	Pz-V	West	Knocked out by artillery fire. Has a through and through penetration. Burned out.
20	201	Pz-V	West	Knocked out by aircraft; turret smashed and penetration in top armor plate.
21	612	Pz-IV	Southwest	Struck by artillery fire. Has multiple penetrations in side armor. Burned out.
22	None	Halftrack	West	Struck by artillery fire; burned out.
23	None	SU-75 (StuG)	Southwest	Struck by artillery fire; penetrations of side armor on both sides. Burned out.
24	None	Halftrack	Southwest	Struck by artillery fire.
25	None	Pz-VI	North	Struck by artillery fire. Has a penetration of the side armor and a damaged track.
26	None	Pz-V	North	Struck by artillery fire. Penetration of the side armor.

[a] By "artillery fire", the document means anti-tank artillery fire.

The enemy on the line stretching west from Zalesie through west of Žynie, Iszkarty, along the western bank of the Sjemena River, west of the railroad station to a point west of Wiłkowyszki in the course of 11 August shelled the forward units of the 70th Rifle Division and 49th Rifle Division and the areas of defense of our elements with mortars and artillery. According to information from the headquarters of the 33rd Army, the enemy had 40 tanks and infantry in the wooded area west of Zielonka.

Order No. 30 from the headquarters of the 33rd Army's armored and mechanized forces, 20.00, 11 August 1944:

The commander of the 33rd Army's armored and mechanized forces has ordered:

1. The 153rd Tank Brigade is to be removed from operational subordination to the 2nd Guards Tank Corps and is to be located in the army's reserve in the Matulyszki, Massykwieryszki, Point 61.6 area, with the assignment in cooperation with the 157th Rifle Division to be ready both to repulse enemy counterattacks and to launch an attack in the Matuliszki, Nowiniki, hamlet of Szelwy, Pracapol, Wiłkowyszki, Gudele, Sardaki and Antupie directions.
2. Dig all the tanks and vehicles into the ground and thoroughly camouflage them. Prepare firing positions on the probable directions of actions. Conduct reconnoitering with all the men and mark lines of deployment and lines of fire. Complete the digging in of the tanks and vehicles by 6.00 on 12 August 1944. Complete the reconnoitering, the compilation of range-cards and the resolution of questions of cooperation, both when fighting to repulse enemy attacks and when launching counterattacks, by 10.00 on 12 August 1944.
3. The headquarters of the army's armored and mechanized forces is in its previous location.
4. Report on the execution of this order, together with the presentation of maps, by 12.00 on 12 August 1944.

Chief of staff of the 33rd Army's armored and mechanized forces
Guards Lieutenant Colonel IVANOV

Order No. 070 to the troops of the 33rd Army, 11 August 1944:

1. On the basis of an order from the Deputy People's Commissar of Defense Marshal of the Soviet Union Vasilevsky – the chief of staff of the 33rd Army Major General A.P. Penchevsky is relieved of his occupied post and is placed under the direction of the chief of the 3rd Belorussian Front's Department of Cadres.
2. The army's deputy chief of staff and chief of operations Colonel G.N. Perventsev is relieved of his occupied post and assumes the duties of chief of staff of the 33rd Army's headquarters.
3. The senior assistant to the chief of the Operations Department Lieutenant Colonel I.A. Vinogradov is relieved of his occupied post and assumes the duties of 33rd Army's deputy chief of staff.

Commander of the 33rd Army Lieutenant General MOROZOV
Military Council Member Major General BABENCHUK

Excerpt from Operational Summary No. 102 from the 33rd Army's artillery headquarters, 20.00, 11 August 1944:

First. The army's troops throughout the day with part of their strength was engaged in fighting to strengthen their occupied line. The enemy over the past hours undertook no active operations. The enemy's artillery placed rare barrages on the forward edge of defense. The enemy's air force flew 4 individual aircraft reconnaissance sorties.

Second. The artillery of the rifle divisions fired at active enemy firing positions and aggregations of enemy troops. As a result of the fire, up to 240 enemy soldiers and officers were eliminated; 2 tanks were destroyed and 1 tank was knocked out; 9 vehicles were wrecked together with their loads; 14 machine guns were destroyed; the fire of 4 antitank guns and of two mortar batteries was silenced; and up to three companies of enemy infantry were dispersed. The artillery regiments of the rifle divisions lost 10 men wounded and one 45mm gun.

Third. The army's artillery and attached artillery assets:
142nd Cannon Artillery Brigade is occupying positions in the Garszwinie, Grenszej area. It placed fire on aggregations of enemy tanks and infantry in the areas of Budziszki and the intersection of the railroad and paved roads. It smashed one vehicle carrying ammunition, and dispersed up to 20 enemy tanks and two companies of infantry. It had no losses.
873rd Destroyer Antitank Artillery Regiment is occupying combat positions along the road in the area southeast of Wiłkowyszki. The regiment didn't fire and had no losses.
538th Mortar Regiment is occupying combat positions with the 1st Battalion on the eastern outskirts of Iszkarty and the 2nd Battalion on the eastern outskirts of Žynie. The regiment fired at and destroyed 9 machine guns; suppressed the fire of one antitank gun and one 81mm mortar battery; and dispersed up to platoon of infantry. It had no losses.
47th Guards Destroyer Antitank Artillery Brigade is occupying combat positions in the following areas: 339th Destroyer Antitank Artillery Regiment – 3 km northeast of Wiłkowyszki; 1478th Destroyer Antitank Artillery Regiment – 3 km southeast of Wiłkowyszki; 1025th Self-propelled Artillery Regiment – east of Gudele. The brigade didn't fire. On 9 and 10 August 1944, the 1025th Self-propelled Artillery Regiment fought to repulse enemy tank attacks; in addition to the casualties mentioned in the operational summary for 9 August, the regiment additionally lost 7 officers and 28 sergeants and privates killed; 4 officers, 3 sergeants and 12 privates wounded; and 10 sergeants and 12 privates missing in action. The casualties of the 578th Destroyer Antitank

Artillery Regiment are being determined, since the servicemen who went missing during a battle after losing their self-propelled gun are in the process of returning and showing up in infantry positions. The knocked-out self-propelled guns are being recovered and towed back to the rear, where they will be sorted and, as far as possible, repaired.

The **43rd Destroyer Antitank Artillery Brigade** is occupying combat positions in the following areas: 1966th Destroyer Antitank Artillery Regiment – in the Szelwy area; 1965th Destroyer Antitank Artillery Regiment – in the Korale area. The brigade didn't fire. The casualties over 9 and 10 August 1944: 3 officers, 7 sergeants and 9 privates killed, and 6 officers, 8 sergeants and 40 privates wounded; 2 officers, 29 sergeants and 30 privates are missing in action. Steps have been taken to search for them.

The **83rd Guards Artillery Regiment** is occupying combat positions in the Kumiałbole, Pogradyszki area. The regiment fired at aggregations of enemy infantry and dispersed up to a platoon of soldiers and officers, and silenced 4 machine guns. It had no losses.

The **4th Artillery Division** is occupying combat positions in the areas: 12th Brigade – Sterniszki; 13th Brigade – Gałakausze; 14th Brigade – east of Užbole. It fired at concentrations of enemy tanks and infantry in Wiłkowyszki. Losses: 2 killed, 1 wounded; 1 vehicle was wrecked.

The **307th Guards Mortar Regiment** fired salvoes. It killed 5 enemy soldiers. It had no losses.

The **326th Guards Mortar Regiment** fired salvoes at aggregations of infantry in the Mercze area and 900 meters west of Zielonka. It dispersed and partially destroyed up to a company of infantry and left 4 vehicles burning. It had no losses.

Chief of staff of the 33rd Army's artillery
Colonel IABLOCHKIN
Chief of operations of the 33rd Army's artillery headquarters
Guards Lieutenant Colonel ZAITSEV

On 11 and 12 August the 2nd Guards Tank Corps' artillery units were occupying a defense in readiness to repulse enemy attacks. As the fighting wound down, they didn't fire and had no losses. The status of the materiel was without changes.

Excerpt from Operational Summary No. 891/44 from the headquarters of the German Third Panzer Army (PZ AOK 3) to the headquarters of Army Group Center, 11 August 1944. Daily operational report:

On the entire front of the panzer army, there were no major combat operations on 11 August.

XXXX Panzer Corps: the enemy's antitank artillery and the artillery of the infantry conducted intense harassing fire on the left-hand sector of the 5th Panzer Division, and in separate cases conducted registration fire. Opposite this sector the enemy is shifting forces to the northwest, and observation spotted the 7 tanks.

On the front of the 561st Volksgrenadier Division, the enemy artillery conducted heavier fire on the right-hand sector of the division's defenses and on Wiłkowyszki. Enemy aircraft several times bombed the left-hand sector of the division's defenses. There were no changes in the sector of the 6th Panzer Division and on the front of the XXVI Army Corps.

The 561st Volksgrenadier Division took over the sector of the *Grossdeutschland* Division. All the units of the *Grossdeutschland* Division, with the exception of Panzer-Fusilier Regiments 2 and 3 and III/Panzergrenadier Regiment, one battery of assault guns, and IV/Panzer-Artillery Regiment were removed from the defense. Three echelons of the Panzergrenadier Regiment 13, remnants of I/Panzer Regiment 31 were sent away by railroad; from the roster of the *Grossdeutschland* Division: one battery of a Flak battalion, elements of the panzer regiment (15 Pz.kpfw. IV tanks), one echelon of II/Panzer-Artillery Regiment were also transported away by train.

Photographs from liberated Wiłkowyszki

Panorama of Wiłkowyszki.

Roman catholic church of Wiłkowyszki.

2nd Guards Tank Corps, 1944-1945

Left to right: A.S. Dmitriev; a sergeant of the 26th Guards Tank Brigade; A.I. Alekhin (1311th Destroyer Antitank Artillery Regiment); Guards Lieutenant Kotov (26th Guards Tank Brigade).

Left to right: G.G. Galka (401st Guards Self-propelled Artillery Regiment); Iu.M. Stepanov (401st Guards Self-propelled Artillery Regiment); A.P. Chuzhaikin (Political Department); P.A. Fadeev (4th Guards Tank Brigade)

Left to right: P.S. Chegodar' (4th Guards Tank Brigade); N.A. Fedchik (26th Guards Tank Brigade); D.Ia. Klinfel'd (25th Guards Tank Brigade); Shapkin (Corps' deputy commander for technical matters)

A.N. Gorodnichev (1311th Destroyer Antitank Artillery Regiment); V.G. Kreitor (401st Guards Self-propelled Artillery Regiment); E.I. Kuzin (1311th Destroyer Antitank Artillery Regiment); F.G. Stoianov (4th Guards Tank Brigade)

Tankers of the 2nd Guards Tank Corps, 1944-1945

The crew of Hero of the Soviet Union Guards Junior Lieutenant D.G. Frolikov's tank (4th Guards Tank Brigade). In the front row: Mechanic-driver I.A. Karpushev, tank platoon commander D.G. Frolikov, and gun layer V.F. Zotov; in the back row, loader V.M. Kosiakin, and machine-gunner – radio operator I.E. Kostiuk.

Tankers of the 26th Guards Tank Brigade (commanded by Guards Colonel Stepan Nesterov).

Conclusions regarding the operation

On 20 September 1944, the 3rd Belorussian Front's chief of operations Major General Igol'kin summarized the conclusions regarding the recently conducted operation in the following report:

In the course of the first ten days of August the enemy continued to strengthen his forces that were operating in the sector of the 3rd Belorussian Front by quickly bringing together shattered elements (which had been hastily brought up from the depth as the Front's troops approached East Prussia) into battle group units, and worked to set up command and control over them.

The German tanks were to drive a narrow gap into the defenses of the Soviet troops and swiftly emerge in the rear of the forces that were occupying narrow salient in the front. They were then to complete the encirclement of them before the arrival of our antitank reserves.

The enemy's operations on the whole are characterized by a stubborn resistance and frequent counterattacks. The retreat of the Germans was conducted in an organized fashion, striving to hold intermediate lines. In this fashion, the German command succeeded in reestablishing a continuous front and to get cooperation up and running between the units and with all means of reinforcement directly in front of East Prussia. The combat capabilities of the German forces once again rose to a rather high level. The enemy managed to achieve these results only thanks to moving up all possible reserves to the front, and by committing elements into battle without regard for their intended purpose. In essence, the German command was forced to conduct: by August, only separate units of those German forces that were responsible for holding the line of the Berezina River managed to become operational in the sector of the 3rd Belorussian Front. All the other units had been completely destroyed. The enemy actions in the course of August boiled down to delaying and wearing down our forces with stubborn fighting and counterattacks, and to gain time for preparing his main defensive lines.

The primary tactical forms of enemy resistance were resistance with fire and counterattacks. The resistance with fire was based on the cooperation of all means of fire. The artillery and mortars were used in massed fashion to bring down barrages of fire, as a rule with one to six battalions; the preponderant caliber of them was 75mm to 105mm. The German counterattacks struck narrow fronts, primarily against troops that had penetrated his defenses. The forces that took part in the counterattacks varied from a company to a battalion of infantry with 6 to 10 tanks and assault guns, up to one to two battalions of infantry with anywhere from 15 to 35 tanks and assault guns. The enemy launched particularly fierce counterattacks against our divisions of the 5th Army that had made the greatest advance toward the East Prussian border. In the period of the offensive operations by the 5th Army's 45th Rifle Corps and 72nd Rifle Corps between 4 and 18 August 1944, the enemy launched 56 counterattacks against these formations, in strength of a company to two battalions each, supported by groups of tanks that varied from 6-8 up to 25 armored fighting vehicles.

The enemy's losses testify to the bitterness of the fighting: over 20-21 August 1944 alone, in the sector of the 5th Army's 277th Rifle Division the Germans lost 37 tanks (of which 4 were Tigers and 33 were Panthers), 9 halftracks and more than 1,000 soldiers and officers killed or wounded. The Soviet losses in this sector amounted to 15 guns of various calibers and up to 500 men killed or wounded.

The enemy counterattack in the Wiłkowyszki area had the objective of liquidating our tactically-important salients in the front and to destroy the forces that were occupying them, as well as to take an important road hub. The enemy launched the attack toward Wiłkowyszki with the forces of the Panzergrenadier Division *Grossdeutschland*, and two infantry regiments of the 561st East Prussia Volksgrenadier Division. With the counterattack in the Wiłkowyszki area, the German command was also hoping to regain intact his permanent line of defense in front of the city, and to retake the sector of it that was occupied by Soviet forces. Operational maps of the Panzergrenadier Division *Grossdeutschland* that were captured by our troops gives the image of the enemy's intentions regarding the capture of Wiłkowyszki.

As is obvious from these maps, the command of Panzergrenadier Division *Grossdeutschland* was planning an attack from a short distance with the subsequent emergence in the rear of our grouping in the Wiłkowyszki area and the encirclement of our troops in places. The enemy tanks during the attack were to operate from south to north along roads, and in particular were to use the Wiłkowyszki – Naumiestis highway, which ran parallel to the front in the rear of our forces. A particular characteristic of the enemy in the fighting was the fact that the enemy, having initiated an attack, used tanks out in front of his infantry; moreover, the tanks operated in massed fashion, in large groups that seemingly led the way for the infantry. Such an arrangement of the combat formation was adopted, obviously, with respect to the shallow depth of the objectives given to the tanks, the unexpectedness of the attack, and the incomplete readiness of our antitank defenses. In repulsing the enemy's attacks and counterattacks, which employed tanks and assault guns everywhere, the destroyer antitank artillery played the main role, as well as the divisional artillery, which fired from open firing positions. Despite the enemy's massed, simultaneous use of his combat machines, this density [of artillery] proved sufficient and ensured the successful repulse of the enemy's attack with large losses for his side. The experience of these battles once again confirmed the need in all such cases to dig sufficiently deep and well-camouflaged shelters for the guns that are firing over open sights.

Our troops demonstrated great tenacity and military skill in the struggle with the attacking enemy tanks and infantry in the Wiłkowyszki area. The enemy's partial success was quickly localized by our counterattacks. The temporary abandonment of certain sectors of defense in the Wiłkowyszki area was conducted in an organized manner.

The German losses were quite high. For 9 August 1944 alone, the Nazis lost up to 50 tanks and self-propelled guns in the Wiłkowyszki area. The enemy suffered the main losses in tanks from antitank artillery and artillery fire, the latter firing over open sights. Certain of our batteries stood to the death, firing at the German tanks from pointblank range until the gun crews had been completely knocked out of action. For example, when examining the battlefield, in a radius of 200 meters around the firing positions of one of our batteries, 12 knocked-out Tiger and Panther tanks were standing, and one of the tanks was located just 35 meters from the battery, the guns of which had been crushed, while the men had fallen heroically in their firing positions.

Later, the forces of the 3rd Belorussian Front went on the offensive once again and not only fully regained the position in the Wiłkowyszki area, but also threw the Germans back to line of the national border in the Naumiestis area. When repulsing the enemy's massed tank attacks and counterattacks, the role of our infantry consisted primarily in forcing the German infantry to fall prone, to separate them from the tanks, and to protect the firing positions of the anti-tank artillery and divisional artillery from German submachine gunners that were approaching them. Simultaneously, tank hunters using antitank grenades and Molotov cocktails, as well as antitank rifle teams, fought against enemy tanks that had broken into their defensive sector.

The weak cooperation between rifle and tank units that was noted in certain divisions belong to the number of substantial shortcomings in the organization of combined-arms combat. When assembling our forces before an offensive, a lack of concern toward camouflage discipline and the violation of timetables when moving the infantry into jumping-off positions was observed. This at times led to the revealing of our intentions to the enemy and complicated the execution of combat assignments. The self-propelled artillery, in particular the corps' self-propelled artillery regiments, recommended themselves well as a powerful, maneuverable combat weapon. The self-propelled guns enjoy the great respect on the part of our infantry, and the commanders of rifle units persistently clamor for the attachment of self-propelled guns to them, both when on the defense and when on the attack.

Chief of operations of the 3rd Belorussian Front Major General Igolkin
20 September 1944

The commander of the 2nd Guards Tatsinskaia Tank Corps Guards Lieutenant General of Tank Forces A.S. Burdeinyi observed, "The combat operations of the corps in the Wiłkowyszki area when repulsing enemy counterattacks demonstrated that in the conditions of an inadequate organization of the defense of the combined-arms divisions, the maneuvering of tanks in the depth of the defense and their counterattacks against the enemy's attacking units are a basic means of repulsing these attacks and retaining possession of captured lines."

To the chief of staff of the 3rd Belorussian Front, 24 August 1944

I am presenting a map showing the positions of the enemy's knocked out armored vehicles. Appendix: a scheme on a 1:25000 map on four pages.

Temporarily acting chief of staff of the 5th Army
Colonel Putilin

Notes to the map showing the knocked-out German tanks in the Wiłkowyszki area:

In the area of Wiłkowyszki, scouts came upon 20 German tanks along both sides of the road [from Mariampol] and on the road itself. In the city of Wiłkowyszki on the western outskirts there is one Pz-V tank, and on the southeastern outskirts a 75mm self-propelled gun on the chassis of a Pz-III tank.

On the Wiłkowyszki – Veržbolowo highway 1-2 kilometers from the Wiłkowyszki railroad station before reaching Lake Pojeziory, there are one Pz-IV tank and one halftrack. There are two tanks in the Szelwy area: one Pz-V and one Pz-IV. The majority of the tanks were knocked out by antitank artillery fire, and only two tanks were disabled by aircraft. On the battlefield there are a lot of small craters from air bombs, which confirms the conjecture that the actions of our aircraft dispersed the formation of German tanks. The majority of the tanks located on the field of battle were burned out. Of the number of tanks suitable for repair, three tanks have been made operational again and turned over to the units. One Pz-V tank, in completely good working order, bogged down in a peat bog. According to the information brought back by the scouts, it has been established that the enemy managed to evacuate a significant portion of his knocked-out tanks, which is evident from the traces of the tanks' locations and the tracks left behind by the towing of them. Below is a table of the investigated tanks:

Table 1.12: Status of the panzers and self-propelled guns of the Panzergrenadier Division *Grossdeutschland* at end of day on 8 August 1944

	Type of tank or self-propelled gun	Combat-ready	Under repair		Total
			Short-term	Long-term	
Panzergrenadier Division *Grossdeutschland*	Pz-III	2	-	-	2
	Pz-IV	10	-	-	10
	Pz-V	70	7	7	84
	Pz.VI	27	6	8	41
	StuG	15	-	1	16
	Self-propelled Panzerjägers	4	-	-	4
Total:	Tanks and self-propelled guns	128	13	16	157

Chief of the 2nd Section of the 3rd Belorussian Front's 2nd Department of Captured Weapons
Engineer-Major GOFSHTEIN
21 August 1944

The German Army Group Center Commander Walter Model and Heinz Guderian, Chief of Staff of the Army, assessed the outcomes of the combat at Wiłkowyszki, 9 August, did not consider them as the success. Guderian stated total losses of 23 panzers in his report, but according to operational documents of the Third German Panzer Army "according to preliminary data the losses of Panzergrenadier Division Grossdeutschland amounted to 52 tank and SP guns including irrevocable losses of 24 tanks". 4 Tigers lost at Virbalis on 6 August and 6 Panthers lost the same day should be added to the total tank losses.

It is important to highlight not only the tactical outcomes of this operation but also its strategic implications. Tactically, the German re-capturing of Wiłkowyszki temporarily delayed the Soviet invasion into East Prussia but failed to encircle and destroy the Soviet 33rd Army and 2nd Guards Tank Corps and suffered significant losses, both in personnel and tanks, on the eve of the critical Operation "Doppelkopf". In order to justify high losses Panzergrenadier Grossdeutschland claimed that Soviet losses were considerably higher, which we have seen was not the case. Strategically, the combats at Wiłkowyszki significantly weakened

Panzergrenadier Grossdeutschland and resulted in its late arrival for "Doppelkopf". This was one of the reasons why Grossdeutschland Division failed to achieve its mission of retaking Šiauliai or cutting off the 6th Guards Army threatening Riga. Although Graf Strachwitz reached Sixteenth Army at Tukums and restored a front between Army Group North and Army Group Centre, the corridor between Third Panzer Army and Sixteenth Army was only 18 miles in width and more ambitious objectives for the operation were not achieved.

In the final analysis, Wiłkowyszki represent a good example that over-reliance on the German sources (e.g. Spaeter, Jung and operational reports of 3. AOK and GD) without cross-checking them with archival data from "the other side of the hill" often gives a distorted picture of the events and may overlook strategic implications.

North of Wiłkowyszki, the Soviet 5th Army at this time was repulsing an attack by the German 6th Panzer Division out of the Žvirgždajcie – Vale area. On 20 August the 5th Army launched a counteroffensive and took Žvirgždajcie and the surrounding places and hamlets. Forty-five knocked-out tanks and self-propelled guns of the German 6th Panzer Division fell into the hands of the Red Army.

When analyzing the losses of the Panzergrenadier Division *Grossdeutschland*, it is necessary to recall that on the eve of the offensive toward Wiłkowyszki on 8 August, the division had the following number of tanks and self-propelled guns:

Table 1.13: Status of the panzers and self-propelled guns of the Panzergrenadier Division *Grossdeutschland* on 16 August 1944

	Type	Combat-ready	Under repair (short- and long-term)	Total
Panzergrenadier Division *Grossdeutschland*	Pz-III	-	-	-
	Pz-IV	7	1	8
	Pz-V	41	13	54
	Pz-VI	29	8	37
	StuG	20	4	24
Total:	Tanks and self-propelled guns	97	26	123

Thus, over the period from 9 to 15 August 1944, the irreplaceable losses of the Panzergrenadier Division *Grossdeutschland* amounted to 38 panzers and self-propelled guns. If you examine the types of tanks, then you can see that the number of Pz.Kpfw. III tanks decreased by 2, the Pz.Kpfw. IV tanks by 2, the Pz.Kpfw. V tanks by 30, and the number of Pz.Kpfw. VI Tiger tanks by 4. In addition, 26 tanks and assault guns were undergoing repairs. It is fully possible that some of these were the combat machines knocked out in the fighting in and around Wiłkowyszki, which the Germans managed to evacuate from the battlefield because they were left behind friendly lines.

The Germans themselves according to a combat report from the Third Panzer Army assessed the division's losses as follows: "According to preliminary information, the losses of the

Captured, knocked-out German combat vehicles in the Wiłkowyszki area

A knocked-out Tiger of the *Grossdeutschland* Division (A22) that was disabled 2 km east of Wiłkowyszki.

This Tiger (A23) blundered into a nearby swamp without any means of evacuation.

Here, near where the above photo was taken near Piłotyszki, is an abandoned Hummel self-propelled howitzer. There is no evident damage to the machine.

A knocked-out Panther, abandoned by its crew in the Piłotyszki area: the unauthorized ladder for easing access into the tank on the machine's rear side is noticeable.

An entire group of Pz.Kpfw. V Panthers (in the background) knocked out in the area 1.5 km west of Znaczki.

A captured Sd.Kfz 251/9 "Stummel" ["Stump"] halftrack that mounted a 75mm L/24 low velocity gun in place of the standard machine gun. This *Schützenpanzerwagen* was knocked out near Łukszyszki and belonged to one of *Grossdeutschland*'s Panzer-Fusilier battalions.

A captured German 20mm automatic anti-aircraft gun mounted on the chassis of a halftracked vehicle on the eastern outskirts of Wiłkowyszki.

A StuG (345) of the *Grossdeutschland* Division, that was knocked out south of Gudele. The on-board ammunition load apparently detonated.

German Panthers, destroyed in the Wiłkowyszki area; August 1944.

Another knocked-out Panther in the Wiłkowyszki area; August 1944.

One more Panther tank that was also knocked-out in the Wiłkowyszki area; August 1944.

Another photo of a knocked-out Tiger of the *Grossdeutschland* Division (A22).

Another 88mm PAK-43 that fell into Soviet hands on the northern outskirts of the city after its towing vehicle was destroyed.

A German 88mm PAK-43 on the eastern outskirts of Wiłkowyszki.

This Tiger tank of the *Grossdeutschland* Division took repeated hits, one that apparently penetrated the thick armor and knocked out the tank; August 1944.

Grossdeutschland Division amounted to 52 combat machines, including 24 combat machines that were irrecoverably lost."

To this number, the 4 Tigers irrecoverably lost in the Wirballen area on 6 August 1944 should be added, as well as the 6 Panthers that were irrecoverably lost on the same day. As the report from the Third Panzer Army states, "Over the day of 6 August, 6 Pz.Kpfw. V tanks had to be written off."

In December 1943 Guards Colonel O.A. Losik was appointed as the commander of the 4th Guards Tank Brigade – one of the best units in the Red Army. This was a recognition of his tremendous service record. He justified his new appointment with honor.

In the summer of 1944 the Soviet forces conducted a massive operation to liberate Belorussia. Bypassing enemy strongpoints with the assistance of partisan guides, the troops of the 1st and 3rd Belorussian Frontsn made rapid progress toward Minsk. Losik's tank brigade, allowing the enemy no pause to rest or recover either day or night, was attacking in the lead echelon of the 2nd Guards Tatsinskaia Tank Corps. On the morning of 3 August, his tankers were the first to enter the city, where they became tied up in combat on its streets, driving the enemy toward the west.

In his later years, Hero of the Soviet Union Marshal of Tank Forces Oleg Losik remembered those heady days:

German tanks that have been knocked-out in one of the sectors of the 3rd Belorussian Front.

Oleg Losik in his senior years, proudly displaying his numerous decorations and the Gold Star of the Hero of the Soviet Union.

From the recollections of Hero of the Soviet Union Marshal of Tank Forces Oleg Losik:

When we began to move out from the jumping-off area (on 24 June 1944), there were 64 T-34/85 tanks in the brigade. It also had subordinate the 401st Guards Self-propelled Artillery Regiment equipped with 21 SU-85 self-propelled guns.

The Germans – infantry, tanks and artillery – were retreating, hurrying to take up a defense along the western banks of the Berezina River. Pursuing them, we were constantly advancing with combat – this was a parallel pursuit …

People can say whatever they want, but back then, our remembrace of the past and pride for the achievements of our people really gave us encouragement. The words of the Supreme Commander-in-Chief: "Let the courageous example of our great ancestors – Aleksandr Nevsky, Dmitri Donskoi, Kuzma Minin, Dmitry Pozharsky, Aleksandr Suvorov, Mikhail Putuzov – inspire you in this war!" – these were not just empty words …

The 4th Guards Tank Brigade, which I commanded, was in the center, advancing in front in the direction toward Minsk. It was anticipated that we would have to storm Minsk as a genuinely fortified fortress. Yet it would be very hard for the tanks, you understand, to operate on the streets of the fortified city. Moreover, we'd been marching almost the entire day and had advanced no less than 100 kilometers, and the crews were exhausted – consider, for days they hadn't slept, ever since the crossing of the Berezina. Fuel was running low, and some of the ammunition had already been expended … However, everyone recognized that Minsk was in front of us!

The Germans knew that we'd be arriving soon, but when we entered the city it was plainly a surprise for them, even though we had fighting on the approaches to the city – some small groups of tanks and artillery were saddling the road and set several of our machines ablaze, but we knocked them aside and kept advancing … and in the city, even though the Germans were indeed returning fire, I even saw some of them running away in their drawers.

The brigade commander is supposed to be in the lead battalion, and that's where I was located. The tanks weren't advancing in a single column, but by company, and even by platoon, even though the streets on the outskirts weren't as expansive as the streets in Moscow or even today in the city of Minsk itself. We had tank riders aboard the tanks – the brigade had a battalion of submachine gunners, and they were mounted on the tanks so that the tanks wouldn't be exposed. We were moving with bounding fire – there, wherever it was necessary to fire. Our advance started at 0300, and at 0500 we were already in Minsk … Of course, the Germans were firing back … even though I didn't notice their tanks, but there were Panzerfaust-equipped troops and antitank guns, while automatic weapons were blasting away at our infantry.

As soon as they caught sight of tanks bearing red stars, men and women would come running out of their farmouses and homes. Whenever we paused for a rest, they would run up to our tanks, some of them even bringing us gifts or something to eat or drink …

So, Losik's tank brigade was the first to enter the city on the morning of 3 July. They became tied up in heavy fighting on the streets, but soon other units arrived, and with the cooperation of the 4th Guards Tank Brigade, they fully liberated Minsk. On 17 July, long columns of German prisoners that had been captured in Belorussia were paraded under escort along the streets of Moscow.

For his role in the liberation of the capital of Belorussia, Oleg Aleksandrovich Losik was awarded the title Hero of the Soviet Union, and the 4th Guards Tank Brigade was given the honorific title of "Minsk" and was awarded the Order of the Red Banner. Many years later, the Marshal of Armored Forces said:

> There were T-34/85 tanks in my brigade – as I recall, there were 65 of them. This was a wonderful tank, most powerful and unequalled. In it we defeated both Panthers and Tigers, but only when we fired at the latter's flank … If you compare the characteristics of these machines – ours and the Germans' – they were pretty much similar. The heavy Tigers, incidentally, had the 88mm gun, while our T-34s had the 85mm gun. If you compare the medium tanks, then the T-34 was more compact than the Panther: it was shorter and lower, but had a superior gun and frontal armor – they had the 75mm gun.
>
> Primarily we encountered them (the Tigers and Panthers) already after Minsk, after passing the town of Ivenets [Iwieniec], which is 70 km west of Minsk. The corps commander

Hero of the Soviet Union Major General Aleksei Semenovich Burdeinyi assigned our brigade to serve as the forward detachment toward this town, and from there we next closed upon the administrative boundary with Lithuania, and in those places, one can say we didn't have any particular fighting for a relatively long period of time. We were surging ahead, and as it happened, the main fighting was already going on behind us, although we also had all sorts of encounters.

So, then I decided to use these knocked out German tanks for training our crews; it was a blessing that we had an adequate amount of ammunition and plenty of "practice targets". After all, our brigade, like many others, were back then constantly being replenished with young tankers that had arrived from the Urals, and who didn't have any combat experience or know their up from down. However, it was understandable, there was all sorts of talk: Well, would our T-34s take them out or not?

We were in a lager in a patch of woods, that looked out across expansive fields. We took several of the knocked-out Panthers and Tigers, towed them out into the fields, set them up and fired at them from a T-34 tank. It turned out very well … We were firing at 300 meters, at 200 meters – primarily from the side, at the flanks, and accordingly the shells penetrated. Then I decided to pass all of our tanks crews through gunnery training at these tanks, so that they could gain experience. I reported to Burdeinyi about what we were doing. He took an interest, came to visit us the very next day, and he even took a seat in the tank and fired at a Tiger …

In sum, I managed to give practice to all the crews: to fire at a "real" Tiger and a "real" Panther, so to say. This really helped our tankers in the following fighting – the men felt much more confident than before.

Losik's tank brigade operated as part of the 3rd Belorussian Front's 2nd Guards Tank Corps until the end of the war. In the second half of 1944, the Soviet forces continued their successful offensive. In all of the major battles, Colonel Losik's tank brigade was operating in the first echelon in the corps' combat formation. That's how it was in the Kaunas, Insterburg, and Königsberg operations. As was written in his next commendation: "Comrade Losik, commanding a tank brigade in the fighting on the

Recognition tactical emblems of the 2nd Guards Tank Corps

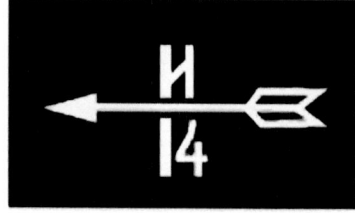

The recognition symbol was a white arrow pointing in the direction the tank was moving. The letter above the arrow represented the first letter of the brigade commander's surname. The machine's tactical number (as a rule, three digits for tank brigades and two digits for smaller units like the 79th Motorcycle Regiment or self-propelled gun regiments) was placed below the arrow. Numbers from 100 marked the 4th Guards Tank Brigade; from 200 – the 25th Guards Tank Brigade; and from 300 – the 26th Guards Tank Brigade.

Königsberg axis, was continuously up among the brigade's combat formations and showed himself to be a bold, capable and decisive officer."

Losik's actions were more than once highly evaluated by both the Front Commander-in-chief General of the Army Cherniakhovsky and the commander of the Front's armored and mechanized forces Colonel General Rodin. Marshal Losik talked about this:

> I recall how once the commander of the Front's armored and mechanized forces Hero of the Soviet Union Colonel General Aleksei Grigor'evich Rodin came to visit us. We were sitting in a dugout, drinking tea, and as was his custom, was patiently explaining to me: "You fought well, when you were commanding a separate tank regiment. But that regiment was an infantry support tank regiment, and you fought side by side with the infantry – this was one tank tactic, one means of operations. Now, however, you are in a brigade that is part of a tank corps. You are the Front's and army's mobile group – you must operate in the operational depth, in the enemy's rear. So, the enemy is in front of you, on your right and left, and behind you. You must advance boldly, with no fear for your flanks – forward, forward! Bypass enemy knots of resistance. Now you must have a different mindset, you must operate in a new way. Indeed, believe me, after such a conversation you have to do a lot of reconsidering and re-thinking …

After the war O.A. Losik climbed up almost all of the rungs on the career ladder: he commanded a mechanized division, a corps, and army, and finally a military district. In 1969 he became the chief of the Military Academy of Armored Forces. In this post he served 17 years, doing everything in order to implement the latest methods of training highly-qualified specialists, in order to cement the Academy's reputation as the main breeding ground for preparing command and engineer cadres for the armored forces. In 1972 he was awarded the title of Professor, and in 1975, was made a Marshal of Armored Forces. He is the author of many works on the theory and practice of armored forces. In August 2012, he was the last living USSS Marshal of Armored Forces.

2

In East Prussia

As a result of the Soviet 1944 summer offensive and the German defeat in Belorussia and Lithuania, the forces of the 3rd Belorussian Front arrived at borders of Germany in East Prussia. In early October 1944, the neighbor on the right – the 1st Baltic Front – launched an attack against the enemy on the Memel direction, having isolated a major German groupin in the Libau [Liepāja], Windau [Ventspils] area. Coordinating with the neighbor's offensive, the 3rd Belorussian Front between 6 and 12 October 1944 conducted the successful Tauroggen offensive with the forces of the 39th Army, as a result of which our forces reached the national boundary in a sector of the Neman River in the Naumiestis area.

The Front's remaining armies, situated on the defense, brought themselves back to order, replenished themselves with men and equipment, and scouted the enemy, in particular with thorough aerial reconnaissance photography of the border fortified areas and the depth of the German defenses all the way to Königsberg inclusively. Meanwhile, the neighbor on the left – the 2nd Belorussian Front – was engaged in intense offensive fighting to expand the bridgehead that had been established on the Narew River. By the middle of October 1944, the troops of the 3rd Belorussian Front were ready to launch a direct attack against the enemy forces in East Prussia.

The 2nd Guards Tank Corps' preparations for combat operations

Between 18 August and 15 October 1944, the 2nd Guards Tank Corps was occupying an assembly area in the Jura, Bogata, Kozłowa Ruda area in the reserve of the commander of the 3rd Belorussian Front's armored and mechanized forces. The corps was busy with combat preparations, bringing its number of tanks and self-propelled guns, weapons and men up to authorized strength, and getting ready for the pending combat operations. Over this period, new armored fighting vehicles and personnel arrived to bring the corps back up to strength, and by 10 October 1944 the process of equipping and staffing the corps was primarily finished.

On 10 October 1944, the corps had:

a) Personnel:

Table 2.1: Authorized personnel and personnel on the roster

	Authorized personnel	Personnel on the roster
Officers	1713	1720
Sergeants	3823	3845
Rank and file	6067	5536
Total:	11601	11101

b) Operational tanks and self-propelled guns:

Table 2.2: Operational tanks and self-propelled guns

Units	T-34/85	SU-85	SU-76
4 Guards Tank Brigade	65	-	-
25 Guards Tank Brigade	65	-	-
26 Guards Tank Brigade	65	-	-
79 Motorcycle Battalion	10	-	-
1 Guards Separate Signals Battalion	5	-	-
401 Guards Self-propelled Artillery Regiment	-	21	-
1500 Self-propelled Artillery Regiment	-	-	21

c) Supplies: 3.0 refills of diesel fuel, 3.0 refills of gasoline, 2.1 standard loads of ammunition, and 8 days' worth of food.

In parallel with the process of replenishing, tactical training exercises with the new armored fighting vehicles were conducted in all the corps' units in order to foster teamwork at the platoon, company and battalion levels, as well as individual and platoon live-fire exercises.

In the period between 24 August and 14 October 1944, the units of the **4th Guards Tank Brigade** were brought up to strength in tanks and men and conducting organizational training of the elements. The tanks for bringing the brigade back up to strength arrived in three groups: the first, numbering 30 T-34/85 tanks, arrived by rail at the Kozłowa Ruda railroad station on 24 August 1944; the second, numbering 20 T-34/85 tanks, was received on 2 October 1944. Finally, the third group numbering 15 T-34/85 tanks, arrived on 3 October 1944.

The batch of men for replenishing the brigade's motorized rifle battalion of submachine gunners arrived on 9 October. Thus, the forging of combat teamwork in the tank battalions, as well as in the companies of the motorized rifle battalion, and their preparations for combat operations took place in the period between 5 and 14 October after bringing them back up to full strength in combat materiel and personnel. The arriving replenishments for the brigade's units with respect to both tankers and submachine gunners had been satisfactorily prepared theoretically, but had insufficient practical training, particularly in tactics and gunnery, and in operating the tanks and in engaging in tank combat. In the course of ten days, tactical exercises in the tanks were conducted with the tankers in order to forge teamwork at the platoon, company and battalion level. The men also did live-fire training, both at the individual tank level and the level of the platoon, and also did combat rehearsals and studied the details of combat operations on East Prussian territory. All of the brigade's men were ready to engage in combat in the conditions of a strict enemy defense on enemy territory.

By 14 October 1944, the 4th Guards Tank Brigade had been brought back up to table strength with tanks and manpower: 65 combat-ready T-34/85 tanks; 285 officers, 654 non-commissioned officers and 557 men. As for supplies, it had 2.5 refills of diesel fuel and 4.4 refills of gasoline; 2.2 refills of MK lubricants; 12 days' worth of rations; and the following ammunition: 3.2 standard combat loads of 85mm shells, 2.0 standard combat loads of 76mm shells, 2.3 standard combat loads of 37mm anti-aircraft shells; 2.1 standard combat loads of 81mm mortar rounds; 2.2 standard combat loads of 12.7mm DShK rounds; 3.2 standard combat loads of rifle cartridges; and 1.9 standard combat loads of pistol ammunition. The brigade had 63 vehicles in order to load and transport the supplies, 216 metric tons of which were left behind in stockpiles on the calculation that 108 vehicles could deliver them in a single trip.

In the period between 21 August and 13 October 1944, the **25th Guards Tank Brigade** was re-forming in the area of Klein Trakischken, and by 14 October it had been fully brought back up to authorized strength in tanks with 65 combat-ready T-34/85 tanks. One tank was left behind in the training company. The brigade's men were intensively busy with combat preparations with a special emphasis on tactics, the equipment and gunnery practice, and by the resumption of combat operations they were satisfactorily prepared. In the process of training it was found that the personnel who had arrived to replenish the brigade had been poorly trained with respect to tactics and gunnery; they'd been insufficiently trained in actual firing and the tactics of tank combat. The principles of commanding a tank and a tank platoon hadn't been mastered.

The **26th Guards Tank Brigade** by the start of combat operations had been fully replenished with men, tanks, wheeled vehicles and weapons. With respect to materiel, it was back up to authorized strength. The men were busy with combat and political training, and the plan of preparing the brigade headquarters for combat operations had been fully implemented. The morale of the men was high, which was confirmed by the following combat operations. The command staff of the subordinate units with respect to their training was able to handle and command their subordinate elements. On 15 October 1944 the 26th Guards Tank Brigade had 1,386 men: 236 officers, 554 non-commissioned officers and 569 enlisted men. The tank brigade had the authorized 65 T-34/85 tanks and was fully-equipped with wheeled vehicles. By the start of combat operations, the brigade was combat-ready and could handle any tasks.

The **4th Guards Motorized Rifle Brigade** between 10 and 14 October 1944 was located in the area northeast of Pilwiszki and was engaged in preparatory work for the upcoming combat operations. All of the men were going through their final training exercises in overcoming artificial and natural obstacles, isolating and destroying bunkers and pillboxes, fighting in the trenches and along the communication trenches. The units were receiving replenishments in personnel and materiel; forging cohesion and teamwork; and bringing their weapons and vehicles up to full combat-readiness. The officers were reconnoitering and studying two routes of advance (a northern and a southern); the headquarters of the battalions and the brigade headquarters were making calculations regarding motorized transport, working up combat documents with respect to directing the troops, exerting command and control, and achieving cooperation with the air force.

Given the limited time available, the emphasis of the training was on marksmanship, tactical training and driving. Tactical exercises with aircraft were conducted between the corps headquarters and the headquarters of the subordinate brigades and battalions with respect to calling for air support and the means of communications with the aircraft. Particular attention was paid to preparing the officers staff at every level in the realm of command and control. Each officer diligently learned and knew his functional duties. Questions of cooperation were worked out. Exercises with artillery observers from the tanks and with air liaison officers from the air force formations were conducted. Meetings and conferences were held with the chiefs of staff the units and formations, as well as with the leaders of various service and support units. Meetings were also held with the radio operators and drivers. Staff officers and commanders systematically checked on the corps' process of replenishment and the forging of combat teamwork by traveling to the units and elements.

From the recollections of Lieutenant General of Tank Forces A.S. Burdeinyi:

In September and the first half of October 1944, the 2nd Guards Tank Corps was in the reserve of the 3rd Belorussian Front and was deployed in the area of Kozłowa Ruda. Throughout this period of time, the corps' units were being replenished with personnel, combat equipment, weapons and the necessary reserves of combat supplies. On the whole the corps regained its strength after the intense fighting to liberate Belorussia and Lithuania. We all understood full well that more heavy fighting was awaiting us, but now on the enemy's territory – in the adversary's lair, and therefore we were sensing a special responsibility, and sought to use each hour for studying the tanks and weapons, so as to make better use of them on the field of battle. A large batch of young, totally unseasoned soldiers, non-commissioned officers and officers had arrived, and thus once again particular attention was given to getting them up to speed with their particular branch of service, and not only to the competent use of their weapons, but also to the tight cooperation with all types of troops that would take part in the fighting. In contemporary battle, the adage "one on a battlefield is not a warrior" related to all arms of service, especially now, when the destruction of fascism in his own lair lay in front of us.

The foe had spent a long time preparing East Prussia for a defense, and considered it to be insurmountable. It would be required of us to overcome all these positions, lines, belts, and fortified areas in succession with the fewest number of losses for us, and as far as possible, in the shortest period of time. In connection with this, the main attention was given to questions of training the troops and hardening them. The commanders of the brigades and the separate units, as a rule, were experienced and had been hardened in the fighting, and regarded both the preparation of the individual soldier and the forging of teamwork among the elements and units on a whole particularly attentively.

The situation enabled each brigade and even a separate unit to have their own training fields, firing ranges, and even 2-3 training grounds which employed such objects as bunkers, armored turrets, tank mock-ups, minefields, antitank ditches and other particularly dangerous targets and obstacles for us, which might be encountered in combat. All of the training was conducted in the field.

For example, the commander of the 4th Guards Tank Brigade Guards Colonel Oleg Losik towed heavy Pz.kpfw. VI Tiger tanks, Pz.kpfw. V Panther tanks and self-propelled guns that had been knocked out in the fighting to his training ground in the area of Kozłowa Ruda, and all of the tank commanders (including the officers) and the turret gun commanders received training in firing armored-piercing and armored-piercing discarding sabot shells at these targets. The practice gunnery convinced them that "the devil wasn't as frightening as people made him out to be", and they confidently inflicting fatal damage to the tanks. Even a shell hit on the gun mantlet (where the thickest armor was located) was capable of knocking out the tank. This was the most important thing. Such training in practice convinced each gunner and commander in the capabilities of our tanks and made them completely confident in their ability to duel successfully with any enemy tank or self-propelled gun.

The same method was used to train accurate firing at such targets as the embrasures in bunkers and armored turrets. Ahead of the operation, assault groups were formed in the motorized rifle battalions, consisting of 2-3 tanks, a rifle platoon with machine guns, a sapper squad and means of communication with the battalion commander. The assault groups were used when attacking the most heavily-fortified objectives and were supported by the battalion's fire. As a rule, either the battalion commander or his deputy directed the actions of an assault group.

In the period of bringing up the brigades to strength, a reshuffling of the men in all the units was done so that each unit had experienced combatants and young Communists and Komsomol members. Therefore, great attention was constantly paid to the process of forming teamwork and cohesion of the units in their new composition, and at the same time to train the commander to competently and firmly command his unit. Without this teamwork and excellent training in every respect it was impossible to handle and direct a contemporary battle. The commanders at every level paid great attention to this matter, and so did in particular their chiefs of staff – A.V. Karavan, P.P. Chepkov, P.P. Davydov, G.V. Titov, G.K. Ibriaev, A.T. Sivopliasov and others, on whose shoulders the most difficult assignments in commanding the units were placed.

The commander of the 2nd Guards Tank Corps Guards Lieutenant General of Tank Forces A.S. Burdeinyi (seated second from the left in the first row) poses together with a group of officers.

In this period there occurred minor changes in the command staff of the corps and brigades as well. The corps' deputy commander Major General P.D. Govorunenko departed for a new service appointment, and an experienced veteran of our corps, the commander of the 26th Guards Tank Brigade Colonel S.K. Nesterov was promoted to take his place. Stepan Kuz'mich was well-known not only in the brigade, but also throughout the entire corps.

I will acquaint the reader with this remarkable commander, whose record and abilities were rivaled by his subordinates and many of the corps' officers. Stepan Kuz'mich was born in 1906 into a peasant family in the village of Talitsky Chamlyk (near Lipetsk). In 1928 he was called up into the army and since that time totally dedicated himself to service in it. He successfully completed a military school, received the officer's rank of lieutenant, and became a tank commander. He conscientiously studied the new at that time combat vehicle and the tactics of using it, and rose up the career ladder. He graduated from a military academy. In 1939 he took part in the war with Finland as the chief of staff of a tank battalion, before assuming command of the battalion.

In May of 1942 the young, but already combat-seasoned commander was appointed to take command of the Southern Front's 130th Tank Brigade. At the height of the fighting near Khar'kov, in June of this same year the 130th Tank Brigade became part of the 24th Tank Corps, and now as part of it participated in the fighting and operations. For its successful carrying out of assignments in the Tatsinskaia raid, the brigade was transformed into the 26th Guards Tank Brigade. In all the subsequent battles, the Guardsmen of this brigade always competently carried out the assignments given to them, for which the brigade was awarded with the Order of the Red Banner and the Order of Suvorov 2nd Class, whch were recognitions of the great service record of its commander as well.

Stepan Kuz'mich stood out among many officers by his level of organization, discipline and exacting standards for his subordinates. Even in the most difficult combat conditions, by nature he was always poised and self-restrained. He was a mature commander, who carried great responsibility for whatever task assigned to him. It was these performance and command qualities that enabled him to be promoted to the post of deputy commander of a tank corps. His former chief of staff Lieutenant Colonel V.K. Shanin, who was also a brigade veteran and an experienced and energetic officer, was appointed to take his place in command of the 26th Guards Tank Brigade.

We all exerted ourselves to prepare for the pending battles. Everyone understood well that here, on enemy soil, that we'd hardly be greeted with bouquets of flowers, or that locals would kiss the tracks left behind by Soviet tanks, or that we'd hardly be able to find a guide to help us find our way out of the labyrinth of convoluted roads. We would have to rely in everything on our own knowledge and strength. This circumstance placed particular responsibility on us for the morale and combat training of the soldiers, non-commissioned officers and officers.

List of the leading command group of the 2nd Guards Tatsinskaia Tank Corps and its subordinate brigades and units as of 13 October 1944

1. Corps commander – Guards Major General of Tank Forces Aleksei Burdeinyi
2. Deputy combat commander – Colonel Stepan Nesterov
3. Deputy political commander – Guards Colonel Ivan Chernyshov
4. Deputy commander for rear services – Guards Colonel Grigorii Gavrilov
5. Assistant corps commander (for engineering services) – Guards 6. Engineer-Colonel   Ivan Shapkin
6. Artillery commander – Guards Colonel Boris Lubman
7. Chief of staff – Guards Colonel Aleksandr Karavan
8. Artillery chief of staff – Guards Major Shtabe
9. Chief of operations – Guards Lieutenant Colonel Nikolai Repin
10. Chief of intelligence – Guards Lieutenant Colonel Viktor Kuznetsov
11. Chief of communications – Guards Lieutenant Colonel Boris Geller
12. Chief of chemical services – Guards Lieutenant Colonel Anton Shargorodsky
13. Corps engineer – Guards Colonel Nikifor Sveshnikov
14. Corps doctor – Guards Lieutenant Colonel of Medical Services Anatolii Grzhesiak
15. Chief of artillery supplies – Guards Lieutenant Colonel Anton Borovik
16. Chief of fuel and lubricant supplies – Guards Major Ivan Astashchenko
17. Corps intendant – Guards Major Pavel Shemchuk
18. Chief of personnel – Guards Major Fedor Nagai
19. Chief of the corps' 6th [Smersh – Death to spies] Department – Guards Captain Petr Iur'ev

4th Guards Tank Brigade
20. Brigade commander – Hero of the Soviet Union Guards Colonel Oleg Losik
21. Brigade chief of staff – Guards Lieutenant Colonel Pavel Chepkov

25th Guards "El'nia" Tank Brigade
22. Brigade commander – Guards Colonel Semen Bulygin
23. Brigade chief of staff – Guards Major Georgii Mokritsky

26th Guards "El'nia" Tank Brigade
24. Brigade commander – Guards Colonel Nikolai Burmistrov
25. Brigade chief of staff – Guards Lieutenant Colonel Gennadii Ib'riaev

4th Guards "Smolensk" Motorized Rifle Brigade
26. Brigade commander – Guards Lieutenant Colonel Mikhail Antipin
27. Brigade chief of staff – Guards Colonel Mikhail Prokopenko

401st Guards Red Banner Self-propelled Artillery Regiment
28. Regiment commander – Guards Major Timofei Kotliarov
29. Regiment chief of staff – Guards Captain Fedor Tel'nov

1500th Self-propelled Artillery Regiment
30. Regiment commander – Major Tikhon Zotov (on leave of absence due to illness; temporariliy acting regiment commander was the chief of staff Major Aleksandr Loginov)
31. Regiment chief of staff – Major Aleksandr Loginov

1695th Anti-aircraft Artillery Regiment
32. Regiment commander – Major Nikolai Sereda
33. Regiment chief of staff – Major Ivan Bushuev

273rd Mortar Regiment
34. Regiment commander – Lieutenant Colonel Aleksei Pytalev
35. Regiment chief of staff – Major Iakov Veselov

1311th Light Artillery Regiment
36. Regiment commander – Lieutenant Colonel Aleksei Gorodnichy
37. Regiment chief of staff – Major Vladimir Kamanin

79th Separate Motorcycle Battalion
38. Battalion commander – Major Trofim Kaverov
39. Battalion senior adjutant – Aleksandr Skrylev

51st Separate Sapper Battalion
40. Battalion commander – Guards Major Akim Mel'nikov
41. Battalion senior adjutant – Captain Aleksandr Perfilov

1st Separate Guards Signals Battalion
42. Battalion commander – Guards Major Leon Sharshun
43. Battalion chief of staff – Guards Captain Vitalii Kotov

159th Medical-Sanitation Battalion
44. Battalion commander – Guards Major of Medical Services Vasilii Malyshko
45. Battalion senior adjutant – Guards Captain Konstantin Puzakin

28th Guards Mortar Battalion
46. Battalion commander – Guards Major Stepan Shilov

Separate Air Signals Flight
47. Flight commander – Guards Lieutenant Aleksei Rasskazov

Chief of staff of the 2nd Guards Tank Corps
Guards Colonel KARAVAN

On the eve of the fighting in East Prussia, a questionnaire was circulated among the troops by the 2nd Guards Tank Corps' Political Department on the subject, "Why am I seeking revenge against the Germans?". Altogether, 5,949 men responded to the questionnaire. The results showed that 4,941 men stated that a family member or close relative (father, mother, brother, sister, children or

Troops of the 2nd Guards Tank Corps on the border with East Prussia. The sign reads: "Warriors of the Red Army! The lair of the fascist beast is in front of you."

One of the first inhabited places in East Prussia taken by units of the 2nd Guards Tank Corps. Autumn 1944.

other close relatives) had been killed by the Germans; 852 men stated that close relatives had been forcibly removed to Germany; 1,139 men stated that close relatives had been wounded or maimed by the Germans; 1,340 declared that the towns or villages in which they'd been living had been put to the torch; and 1,118 declared that their own homes had been burned down or demolished. All the responses were made known to the corps' personnel before the fighting in East Prussia.

Recollections of Lieutenant General of Tank Forces A.S. Burdeinyi:

In the period of our preparations for the upcoming fighting, on 2 October 1944 the commander-in-chief of the 3rd Belorussian Front General of the Army I.D. Cherniakhovsky arrived to visit us in the area of Kozłowa Ruda in order to bestow the corps with the Order of the Red Banner, which the corps had been awarded for its outstanding combat performance when liberating Belorussia. The Order was bestowed to us in a ceremony in front of an assembly of all the corps' men. All the men kneeled in front of the unfurled combat combat banners in order to give the oath of the Tatsinskaia Guardsmen. The soldiers swore to destroy the fascists proficiently and pitilessly in their own lair.

General of the Army I.D. Cherniakhovsky in his address to the troops congratulated the Guardsmen for their audacious and often heavy fighting when liberating Belorussia and expressed his firm belief that even now, in East Prussia, the Guardsmen would once again bring greater glory to their combat Guards banner in the upcoming battles, and would once again demonstrate their strength and might, and the courage and decisiveness of the Soviet soldier. Then the Front commander-in-chief chatted with the men in order to familiarize himself with their lives and daily routines, and checked the course of the combat training and combat readiness of individual units.

In conclusion, he asked the corps leadership to remain and in general outlines informed the officers about the forthcoming offensive by the forces of the 3rd Belorussian Front and the tasks of the tank corps. Without disclosing the plan of the entire operation, he stated that the Front's forces would have to carry out an important assignment, which consisted in completely destroying the enemy forces in East Prussia and thereby create favorable conditions for the further offensive of our forces on the Berlin direction.

First, we would have to smash through the enemy defenses on the approaches to East Prussia, then breach his defensive lines and fortified areas, where the enemy had prepared a lot of unexpected surprises for us, to which we would have to bring the attention of all the troops. Without thorough inspection, don't grab any loot and don't enter any homes.

The immediate objective would be to defeat the enemy in the Stallupönen, Gumbinnen and Insterburg areas and to reach the Insterburg – Darkehmen [Angerapp] – Goldap line. In this operation, the 2nd Guards Tank Corps would comprise the Front's mobile group, intended for exploiting a success by the all-arms armies after they breached the tactical zone of defense.

The ensuring of the corps' introduction into a breakthrough rested on the commander of the 5th Army Lieutenant General N.I. Krylov. The tank corps' immediate mission would consist, after entering the breach, in swiftly breaking out to the west, without getting tied up in combat for strongpoints and knots of resistance, and emerging in the rear of the enemy's Gumbinnen grouping and smashing the enemy reserves approaching from the west.

In conclusion, he wished us new successes in resoundly defeating the foe. In his short address, the Front commander-in-chief once again revealed to us his deep understanding of the nature of contemporary operations and the role of each branch of service in it. He left in our hearts the conviction that although young, a talented and wise leader would be directing us; and this was something very important for the troops …

East Prussia always occupied a special place in Germany's plans, but it acquired particularly important significance in the period of preparing for the Second World War, and in particular, when preparing the invasion of the Soviet Union. Its advantageous geographical location – proximity to countries of Eastern Europe – opened a path into the Baltic republics. To the north, the Baltic Sea covered East Prussia, which enabled the conducting of wide maneuvers of the German fleet and created resilient paths of suppy with everything necessary to both the population of this region, and to the German army.

The territory of East Prussia presents a flat topography with only low ridges of elevations and isolated hills, which is cut by a multitude of rivers, swampy streams, artificial canals, lakes and swamps, and blanketed by small forested areas – primarily of coniferous trees. The region had a well-developed network of airfields, roads and railroads, and a very well-developed irrigation and drainage system, which enable the residents to have constant stable harvests. In general, the terrain was extremely difficult for the maneuvering of troops, and especially for armored formations.

In the years of the war, the significance of East Prussia as a military-industrial region and a main source of food supply for Germany rose even higher. Major military, ship-building and machine-building enterprises operated here, which kept the German army supplied with arms and ammunition. The large strategic significance of East Prussia consisted in the fact that the foe in this area had major naval and sea-going fleets here, as well as major human and food reserves.

A significant portion of the East Prussian population consisted of the wealthy strata of the German bourgeouisie, burghers and Prussian Junkers (major landowners). Officers of the German Army who'd been discharged into the reserve settled here received land on attractive terms and were obliged to build up their domains according to a plan adopted by the military high command. As a rule, these structures fitted into a line of defense, equipped with necessary arsenals, and it required exerted efforts to break through them. The Prussian Junker class, which occupied the leading posts in the government apparatus and army was a hotbed of aggressive moods among the population.

These reactionary ideas had a great influence on all of Germany. Many of Germany's government and military actors, like Hermann Göring, Enrich Koch, Walter Weiß, Heinz Guderian and many others, who were natives of East Prussia, had expansive land holdings there, who actively propagandized and advocated the aggressive plans of German militarism, did everything to strengthen the military-economic standing of this region, and to prepare it as a staging area for implementing their aims, and first of all, for the invasion of the Soviet Union. Together with this, taking advantage of the favorable geographic, climactic and ecomonic conditions, they prepared East Prussia as an impenetrable region in case their aggressive plans failed.

Long before the First World War, Germany had built a large number of major fortresses here – Gumbinnen, Insterburg, Königsberg, as well as fortified areas and lines, and with Hitler's ascension to power, significantly expanded them and worked to strengthen the old ones. For example, three of the six large and well-prepared fortified areas stood in the path of our offensive. In the Heilsberg area alone, there were 911 concrete fortifications.

The most finished defensive works were in the sector of the 3rd Belorussian Front, north of the Masurian lakes, on the Gumbinnen – Insterburg axis. In the Lötzen area among the Masurian lakes, near to the city of Rastenburg, deep underground, was the *Wolfschanze*, the Führer's field headquarters in the East. In addition to the three indicated fortified areas, the city of Königsberg was located on this axis – a fortress city, or more accurately, a large fortified area centered on Königsberg, which was encircled by three fortified defensive belts, anchored on the north by the Kurisches Haff lagoon, and on the south by the Frisches Haff lagoon.

In the sector of the 3rd Belorussian Front, on the axis of the 5th Army's and 11th Guards Army's offensive, where it was intended to commit the 2nd Guards Tank Corps into the fighting, a strongly-fortified defensive system had been created, the depth of which extended to 150-200 kilometers. The defensive belt consisted of several battalion-sized areas of defense, each of which included company-sized or platoon-sized strongpoints. Thus, for example, the Stallupönnen center of resistance had several strongpoints – in Raudohnen, Williothen and Matzkutschen – which had 18 bunkers, 8 reinforced concrete shelters and 2 command-observation posts.

Each bunker consisted of a reinforced concrete blindage with two to five casemates for housing the soldiers, ammunition and food, wells, and protected steel turrets with embrasures for machine guns and guns. The thickness of the bunker's outer wall reached almost 2 meters, and the reinforced concrete overhead protection, more than 1.2 meters. Each bunker was covered by up to 50 centimeters of soil, overgrown with grass. Such a work had a depth of 6-8 meters. The bunker could withstand direct hits by 152mm shells.

As a rule, the centers of resistance and strongpoints were tied in with built-up areas, in which even the homes had been adapted for a general system of defense. On the axis of our offensive, such centers of resistance were Stallupönen, Gumbinnen, Goldap, Darkehmen [Angerapp], Insterburg and many others. The enemy had prepared forward defensive positions in front of the national border – a belt of defensive field works with a depth of 15-20 kilometers, which covered the approaches to the border from the east.

All of the adult and youth population were drawn into the defense of East Prussia. In each city, town and village, the people were assigned to specific points of defense. Striving to strengthen the morale of the troops and population, the Nazis employed extensive propaganda, trying to convince them that the entire population, from young to old, faced unavoidable death upon the entry of Soviet forces into East Prussia. In essence, everyone capable of carrying a gun was enrolled in the Volksturm. This entire frenzy was confirmed by Hitler's order, which emphasized: "Each bunker, each block of a German city, each German village must be turned into a fortress, upon which either the enemy will bleed to death, or the garrison of this fortress in hand-to-hand fighting will perish under its ruins …."

Here we faced completely new conditions – a previously prepared, deeply-echeloned defense with fortifications occupied by Hitler's soldiers and a population that was almost entirely hostile to us. All this demanded from the command staff at every level searches for new means and forms of conducting combat and operations, in order to achieve victory with the fewest losses. Of course, not all of us knew what we needed to know about the enemy's defenses. However, even that which was known compelled us to search for new forms of preparing the troops for operations and combats. We understood that there was no operational space here, in East Prussia, for a broad and deep maneuver, and that we would have to break through a defense to a deep depth through the joint efforts of the infantry, tanks and artillery, since each new defensive line in the enemy's operational depth might be the main one.

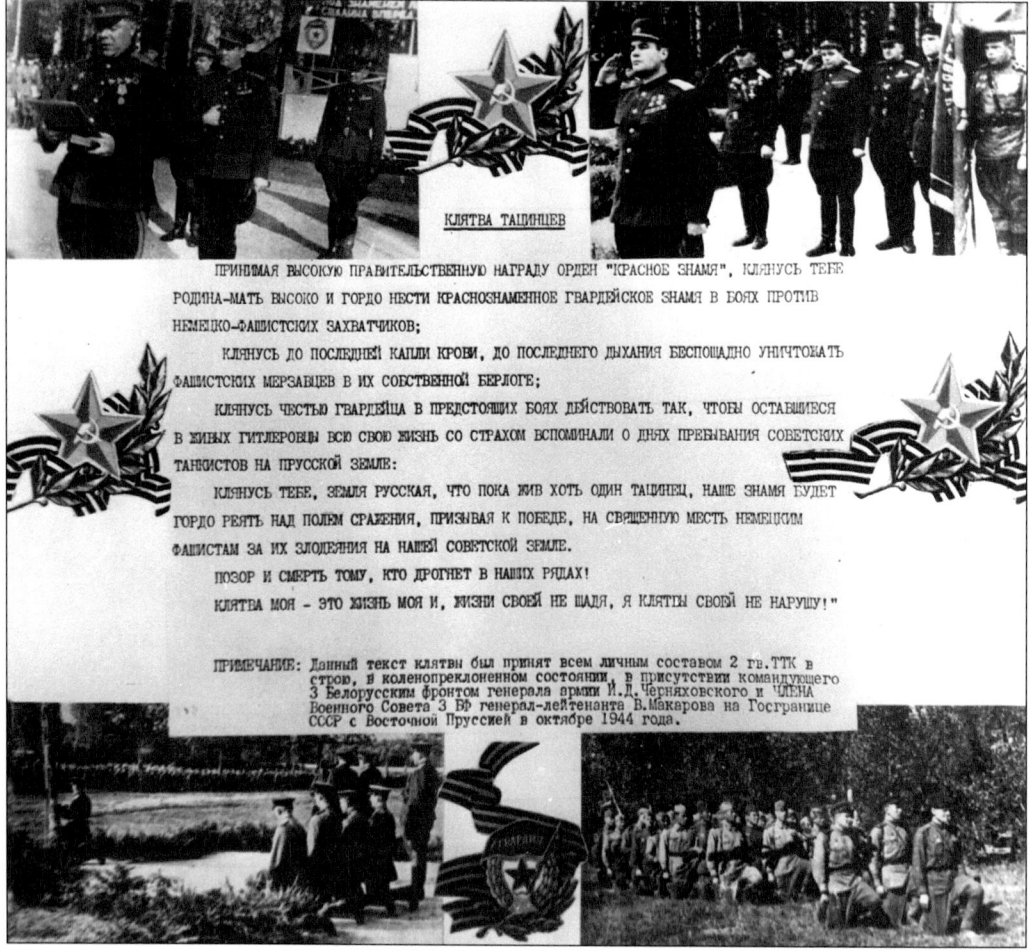

Men of the 2nd Guards Tank Corps taking their oath upon reception of the Order of the Red Banner. The oath reads: "Receiving the high government honor of the Order of the Red Banner, I swear to you, Mother Russia to carry the Red Banner Guards banner proudly and high in the fighting against the German-fascist aggressors; I swear upon the honor of a Guardsman to act in a way in the upcoming fighting so that the Hiterites that remain alive will recall with fear for the rest of their lives about the days when Soviet tankers appeared on Prussian soil; I swear to you, Russian earth, that as long as at least one Tatsinskaia Guardsman remains alive, our banner will proudly wave above the battlefield, summoning [us] to victory, to holy revenge on the German fascists for their evil deeds on our Soviet soil. Shame and death to the one who wavers in our ranks! My oath – is my life, and not sparing my life, I will not vioate my oath! Note: The given text of the oath was taken by all the personnel of the 2nd Guards Tatsinskaia Tank Corps in formation, kneeling in the presence of the commander-in-chief of the 3rd Belorussian Front General of the Army I.D. Cherniakhovsky and 3rd Belorussian Front Military Council member Lieutenant General Makarov at the national border of the USSR with East Prussia in October 1944.

Tankers and motorized riflemen of the 4th Guards Tank Brigade in their jumping-off positions, October 1944.

The bestowal of the Order of the Red Banner to the 2nd Guards Tank Corps for the liberation of Minsk. Commander-in-chief of the 3rd Belorussian Front General of the Army I.D. Cherniakhovsky, Military Council member Lieutenant General V.E. Makarov, and commander of the Front's armored and mechanized forces Colonel General A.G. Rodin, 2 October 1944.

The commander-in-chief of the 3rd Belorussian Front General of the Army I.D. Cherniakhovsky attaches the Order of the Red Banner to the combat banner of the 2nd Guards Tank Corps. In the photograph: In the center is the commander of the Front's armored and mechanized forces Colonel General A.G. Rodin, on the left, Front Military Council member Lieutenant General V.E. Makarov; October 1944.

The commander of the 2nd Guards Tank Corps Major General of Tank Forces A.S. Burdeinyi at the ceremony bestowing the Order of the Red Banner.

I.D. Cherniakhovsky addresses an assembly of men of the 2nd Guards Tank Corps. On the extreme right is the banner carrier, one of the best driver-mechanics of the 4th Guards Tank Brigade Sergeant Major Ivan Chmil'; October 1944.

The ceremony of the bestowal of the Order of the Red Banner to the 2nd Guards Tank Corps on 2 October 1944.

At the map of the commander of the 4th Guards Tank Brigade Hero of the Soviet Union Guards Colonel Oleg Losik.

The commander of the 4th Guards Tank Brigade Hero of the Soviet Union Guards Colonel Oleg Losik gives a combat order.

Officers of the 4th Guards Tank Brigade receive a combat assignment.

The deputy commander for political affairs of the 4th Guards Tank Brigade; October 1944.

Artillery in their firing positions.

Preparations for an attack.　　　　Interrogation of prisoners from the Herman Göring Division.

 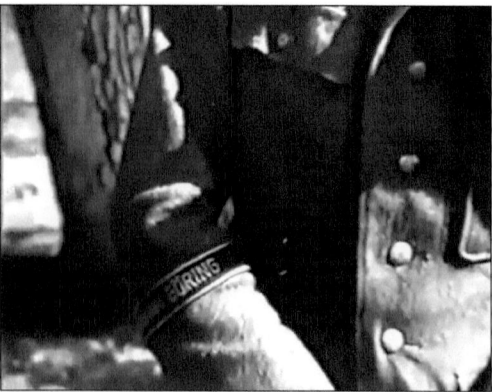

Interrogation of prisoners from the Herman Göring Division.

Motorized infantry of the 2nd Guards Tank Corps readies for combat.

East Prussia, October 1944.

Observation of the enemy's line.

On the eve of the offensive, tankers of the 4th Guards Tank Corps are loading shells into their T-34 tank.

German anti-tank obstacles on the border with East Prussia; October 1944.

Infantry cross the German border; East Prussia, October 1944.

Decision of the Front commander-in-chief

At the decision of the Front commander-in-chief, the main attack was planned on the front of the 5th and 11th Guards Armies. The 5th Army, having four rifle divisions in the first echelon and four rifle divisions in the second, would launch an attack on a frontage of 10 kilometers with the task to attack north of Gumbinnen in the general direction of Insterburg. The 11th Guards Army with four rifle divisions in the first echelon and four rifle divisions in the second would also attack on a sector of 10 kilometers with the task to attack in the direction of Darkehmen [Angerapp]. By the end of the fifth day of fighting, the troops of the Front's main forces had the task to reach a line west of Mallwischken, Gumbinnen, west of Groβ Rominten, Goldap, thereby having made an advance of 40-50 kilometers. The average daily rate of advance: 8-10 kilometers. Subsequently, they were to develop the offensive toward Insterberg and Darkehmen [Angerapp], having in view to reach the coast of the Baltic Sea south of Königsberg.

In order to exploit a success by the main grouping the Front had in reserve the 28th Army with three rifle divisions and the 2nd Guards Tank Corps. It was planned to introduce the 2nd Guards Tank Corps into a breakthrough in the sector of the 5th Army in order to help it carry out the objective of the first day of the offensive (an advance of 10 kilometers). Auxiliary attacks were to be delivered by portions of the 39th and 31st Armies.

Thus, the idea of the Front commander-in-chief General of the Army Ivan Cherniakovsky was to break through the enemy's defense with a powerful grouping consisting of 16 rifle divisions with reinforcements, then to fan out and widen the created breach by introducing strong second echelons of infantry and armor, to augment his strength in the course of the offensive and to overcome the enemy's numerous fortified lines and the East Prussian border fortified area from the march,

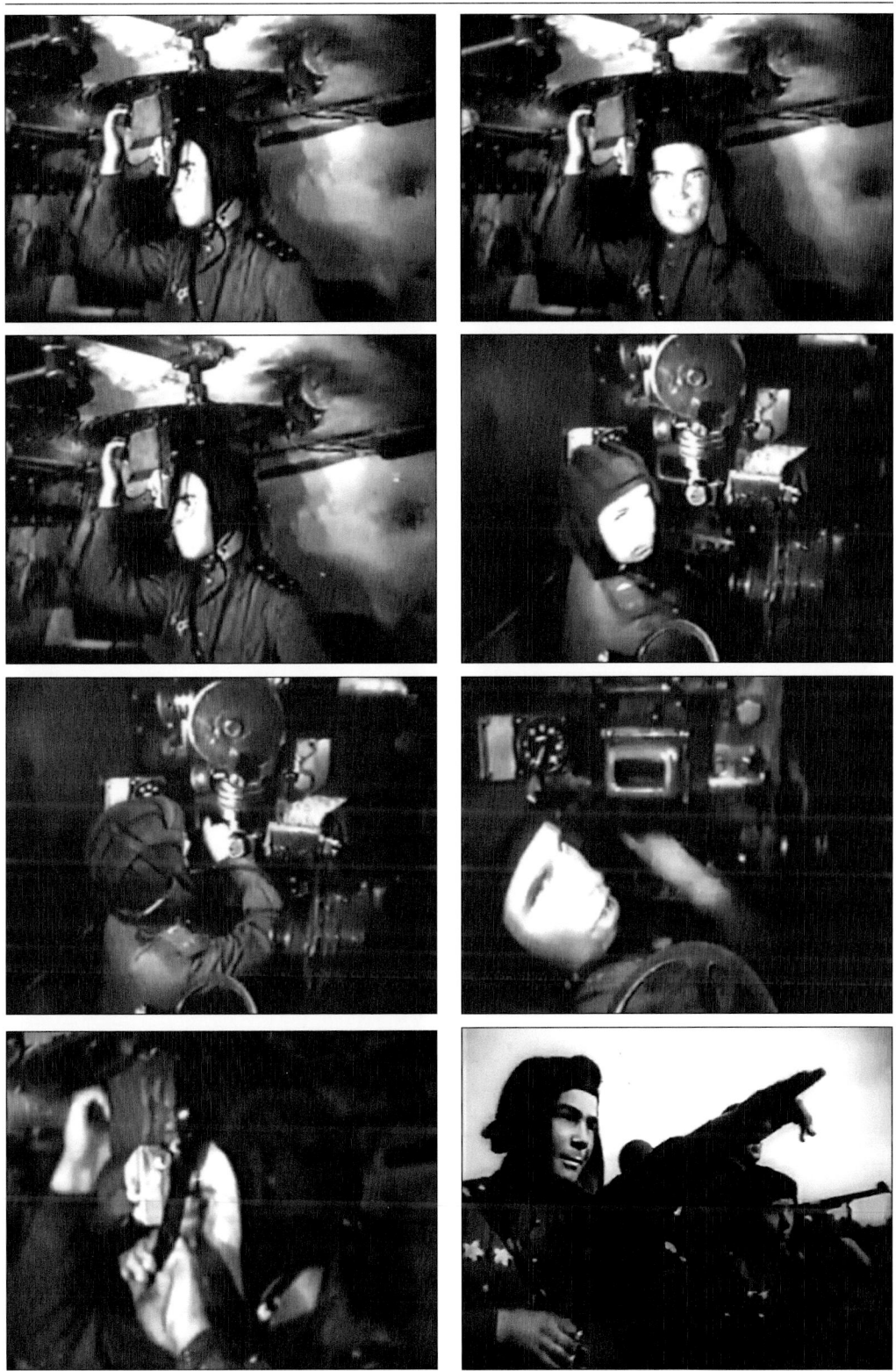
The crew of Guards Lieutenant Kosmodem'iansky in their SU-152 tank; East Prussia, October 1944.

not allowing the Germans the possibility to take up the lines that had been prepared for defense and to check our advance. The enemy's main forces were supposed to be destroyed in the fighting at the forward edge and in the tactical depth, and deprived of the possibility of withdrawing from one fortified position to the next.

From the point of view of the Front's direction of actions, the Front commander-in-chief's decision was based on using the main operational direction in East Prussia toward Gumbinnen and Insterberg, threatening to isolate the Königsberg, Tilsit area together with the German force grouping that was defending it from the rest of East Prussia.

By the end of 13 October 1944, the 2nd Guards Tank Corps was on the whole ready for combat operations. By 0800 15 October, the corps entered the sector of the 5th Army and was assembled in the Sarmorczuny, Ruda, Pojeziory area.

All the questions of cooperation before entering the breach, during the entry, and in the course of the offensive into the depth had been worked out by the commanders and headquarters in the period between 8 and 13 October. The 11th Guards Army was attacking on the left.

The 2nd Guards Tank Corps' combat task

On the basis of a verbal order from the commander-in-chief of the 3rd Belorussian Front, the 2nd Guards Tank Corps was given the mission to be ready for combat operations to take Gumbinnen according to two possible options:

Option 1: The 2nd Guards Tank Corps, supported by the 1st Guards Storm Aviation Division and the 303rd Fighter Aviation Division, having the assignment from its jumping-off area in the woods 6 km to the east of Wiłkowyszki to enter a breach in the 5th Army's sector and to operate in the overall direction toward the villages of Giedriai, Bobławka, Tutschen, Stannauschen, and by the end of the first day of fighting to reach the area of Jentkutkampen, Brakupönen and Trakehnen Station, and by the end of the second day to seize Gumbinnen, while reaching the western bank of the Angerapp River with forward attachments on the Wingeningken, Plimballen line, in readiness for operations in the western and southwestern directions.

Option 2: The 2nd Guards Tank Corps, supported by the 1st Guards Storm Aviation Division and the 303rd Fighter Aviation Division, having the assignment from its jumping-off area in the woods 6 km to the east of Wiłkowyszki, to enter a breach in the 11th Guards Army's sector and to operate in the overall direction toward Sterniszki, Budjeziory, Klauzupe, Kassuben and the Sodehnen and Nemmersdorf estates, and by the end of the first day of fighting is to reach the Gross Trakehnen, Kischken, Kassuben, Urbszen area with the main forces, having seized Ribbinnen, Budszedszen with the forward detachments of the brigades, and by the end of the second day, to take Gumbinnen, with forward detachments to emerge on the western bank of the Angerapp River on the Sabadszuhnen, Nemmersdorf line.

Since subsequently the corps was introduced according to Option 2, it makes sense to cite the decision of the 2nd Guards Tank Corps' commander Major General of Tank Forces A.S. Burdeinyi according to this option: to introduce the corps into the breach with two groups along two directions, having the main grouping on the right-hand axis of advance. The lead brigades were to have reinforced forward detachments.

The right-hand group would consist of a first echelon – the 26th Guards Tank Brigade, the 28th Separate Guards Mortar Battalion and the 1311th Light Artillery Regiment, and a second echelon – the 4th Guards Tank Brigade, the 4th Guards Motorized Rifle Brigade and the 401st

Guards Self-propelled Artillery Regiment. The direction of operations would be Sterniszki, Jelekcie, Skierpiejewo, Pillupönen, Kassuben, Kischken, Jodzuhnen, Marienthal Estate, Norgallen, Nemmersdorf.

In order to ensure the execution of the corps commander's decision, the corps' subordinate headquarters and units had fully completed the preparations for combat actions by 1500 on 13 October 1944, having reconnoitered the routes, terrain and the enemy, worked out cooperation with the lead rifle formations and supporting aviation formations, and with the attached artillery and engineer units. By the end of 13 October, the corps on the whole was ready for combat operations.

Situation opposite the Front on 15 October 1944
The nature of the enemy's actions before the corps' introduction

The enemy on the Gumbinnen axis was defending the occupied line in the first 10 days of October with forces of the Fourth Army (XXVI Korps and an unidentified army corps [XXVII Korps]), operating in small infantry groups that were conducting reconnaissance patrols and continuing to strengthen their positions on the forward edge of defense and in the depth. The artillery was supporting their reconnaissance probes and shelling the combat positions of our forces. The Luftwaffe limited its activity to conducting reconnaissance flights over the front.

Between 6 and 10 October 1944 the enemy conducted a regrouping of units with aim of bolstering the defense in the Kotowszina, Drebulinė sector.

By 15 October 1944 the enemy's grouping operating on the Gumbinnen axis had been identified: in the front line – four infantry divisions (the 1st East Prussia Infantry Division and the 547th, 549th and 561st Volksgrenadier Divisions), one separate regiment (a security regiment of Fallschirm. Panzerkorps *Hermann Göring*), two separate artillery regiments (Artillery Regiments 88 and 37), four separate battalions (505th, 557th, 796th and 659th), and five separate Panzerjäger [tank hunter] and Sturmgeschütz [StuG – assault gun] battalions (Panzerjäger Battalions 60, 1060, 1068 and 1065, and StuG Battalion 204). In tactical reserve were Infantry Regiments 43 and 1143, Fallschirmjäger Regiment 16, and the panzer battalion *Norge*. No operational reserves were noted.

Enemy airfields were located in Mückstein, Powunden, Königsberg, Insterburg, Gerdauen, and Lötzen, hosting fighter and bomber aircraft.

Three main defensive lines had been established on this direction. The main defensive line had a depth of 15 to 20 kilometers and consisted of an elaborate system of fortifications (full-profile trenches, mine fields, barbed wire obstacles, anti-tank ditches, dragon's teeth and anti-tank hedgehogs). The first line of defense ran from the strongly-fortified hub of resistance of Schirwindt along the western bank of the Szeszupa River: Mercze, Zielonka, Drebulinė, Pojeziory, Kamiec, Skierpiejewo, Užbole, Oszkobole. There were anti-tank ditches in the depth of the defense. The rear line of the main defensive belt ran from Pieragen through Wabbeln, Peschicken, Matzkutschen and Ackmonienen to Norbuden. The available lines could be occupied by units falling back from the first line of defense and the meager tactical reserves.

According to information from the Front's Intelligence Department, the enemy had no significant operational reserves with which to occupy the previously prepared lines. Over the recent days of the Front's offensive, the Third Panzer Army's grouping had been partially destroyed, and the Fourth Army's left flank had been crushed as well. In this situation the enemy, in the opinion of the Front's Intelligence Department, had no ability to shift significant reserves to cover the Fourth Army's left flank, nor to occupy the previously prepared defensive lines with fresh reserves.

General Characteristics of the Terrain

The terrain on the Gumbinnen axis was open, level, with no significant hills or valleys; the soil was sandy, and the ground was heavily cut by a multitude of small streams and a significant number of large rivers, which during the offensive would present serious obstacles. The Szeszupa, Szyrwinta, Rauszes, Pissa [Pisa], Rominte [Rominta] and Angerapp Rivers are among such.

The extent of visibility and observation is in the range of 1.5-2.0 kilometers. Natural camouflage is good. The ground is passable for tanks throughout the entire extent of the route. In order to support the corps' advance, it was necessary to attach sapper units to the lead brigades, and to strengthen them with ample tools and bridging equipment.

In order to force a crossing of the Pissa and Angerapp Rivers, it was necessary to have prepared wooden bridges and field expedient means in the units.

Position of the German units and formations on the eve of the offensive

By 16 October 1944 in the sector of the 3rd Belorussian Front, according to the information available to its Intelligence Department, the following enemy formations and units were defending:

- opposite the 39th Army: 56th and 349th Infantry Divisions with attached assets: Antitank Battalions 60, 1060 and 1965;
- opposite the 5th Army: 1st Infantry Division with Engineer Battalions 63 and 743;
- opposite the 11th Guards Army: the 549th and 561st Volksgrenadier Divisions with attached assets (Artillery Regiment 88 and Pioneer-Construction Battalion 558);
- opposite the 31st Army: the 547th and 558th Volksgrenadier Divisions, the 131st Infantry Division, Artillery Regiment 221, Panzerjäger Battalion 476, Mortar Battalion 1441, and Pioneer-Construction Battalion 419.

The enemy had no major reserves. In the tactical depth of his defenses, there were only a number of infantry and specialized battalions and Police Regiment 34.

Altogether opposite the 3rd Belorussian Front, the Germans were defending with nine infantry divisions, one separate regiment, one kampfgruppe, three separate artillery regiments, as well as a number of small elements and units of reinforcement. The German infantry divisions were almost fully staffed according to the new tables of organization (10,763 men), had a combat strength of up to 8,000 men, and were fully equipped with weapons and vehicles.

The personnel of the enemy divisions that were operating opposite the Front consisted in the overwhelming majority of Germans, residents of East Prussia. A significant percentage were volunteers. Most of the men had prior combat experience on the Eastern Front.

Discipline among the enemy troops stood at a high level. A significant portion of the soldiers, especially among the younger ones, were highly resolute, in the spirit of resisting to the last bullet. The 547th, 549th and 558th Volksgrenadier Divisions were divisions that had formed in the second half of 1944. Despite this, the personnel in the first two of these divisions had been selected from soldiers of units and formations that had previously been destroyed on the Eastern Front, as well as convalescent soldiers who had extensive combat experience. The men of the 558th Volksgrenadier Division sharply differed from the others, because this division had been formed during the most recent total mobilization and had not yet seen combat.

Table 2.3: Available tanks and self-propelled guns in the formations and units of the German Fourth Army on 16 October 1944

	Combat materiel				Out of service			Total in presence
	StuG	Tanks	Panzerjägers	Heavy AT guns	Short-term	Long-term	Irrecoverable	
LV Armee Korps								
28 Jäger Division	-	-	-	7	-	-	-	7
Pz.Jg. Kp. 1028	9	-	-	-	1	-	-	10
StuG Brigade 259	37	-	-	-	3	3	-	43
562.Volksgrenadier Div.	-	-	-	11	-	-	-	11
367.Infanterie Division	-	-	-	16	-	-	-	16
Pz.Jg. Kp. 1367	6	-	-	-	-	1	-	7
Fest. Pak Kp. 10	-	-	-	(5)a	-	-	-	(5)
Fest. Pak Kp. 17	-	-	-	(12)	-	-	-	(12)
Total for LV Korps:	52	-	-	34 (17)	4	4	-	94 (17)
VI Armee Korps								
203.Sicherungs Division	-	-	-	5	-	-	-	5
Panzer Abt. 118	9	-	-	-	-	-	-	9
50.Infanterie Division	-	-	-	15	-	1	-	16
Pz.Jg. Kp. 1150	9	-	-	-	-	1	-	10
IV/Lehr Brigade 920	7	-	-	-	1	1	-	9
Fest. Pak Kp. 19	-	-	-	(12)	(2)	-	-	(14)
Gruppe "Hannibal"	-	-	-	1	-	1	-	2
Total for VI Korps:	25	-	-	21 (12)	1 (2)	4	-	51 (14)
XXXXI Panzer Korps								
Kavallerie Brigade 4	-	3-II	-	-	1	-	-	4
Jagdpanzer Abt. 69	1	-	-	-	2	1	-	4
Jagdpanzer Abt. 70	11	-	-	-	-	-	-	11
Infantry Regiment 41	-	-	3	3	-	-	-	6
2 Kp./Jagdpanzer Abt. 70	8	-	-	-	2	-	-	10
Kavallerie Brigade 3	-	-	-	8	-	-	-	8
Jagdpanzer Abt. 69	15	-	-	-	2	2	-	19
(en route)	(9)	-	-	-	3	1	-	13
558.Volksgrenadier Div.	-	-	-	-	-	-	-	-
StuG Abt. 1558	7	-	-	-	-	2	-	9
170.Infanterie Division	-	-	-	13	1	-	-	14
Pz.Jg. Kp. 1240	10	-	-	-	-	-	-	10
Pz.Jg. Kp. 1057	-	-	-	13	-	-	-	13
Fest. Pak Kp. 2	-	-	-	(12)	-	-	-	(12)
Total for XXXXI Panzer Korps:	61	3	3	41 (12)	11	6	-	125 (12)
XXVII Armee Korps								
131.Infanterie Division								
547.Volksgrenadier Div.								
561.Volksgrenadier Div.								
549.Volksgrenadier Div.								

	Combat materiel				Out of service			Total in presence
	StuG	Tanks	Panzerjägers	Heavy AT guns	Short-term	Long-term	Irrecoverable	
StuG Brigade 276	7	-	-	-	-	-	-	7
StuG Brigade 203	20	-	-	-	-	-	-	20
Panzer Brigade 103	-	17	-	-	4	2	-	23
sPanzer Abt. 505	-	15	-	-	19	5	-	39
Fest. Pak Kp. 6	-	-	-	(12)	-	-	-	(12)
Fest. Pak Kp. 1	-	-	-	(12)	-	-	-	(12)
Fest. Pak Kp. 3	-	-	-	(11)	-	-	-	(11)
Fest. Pak Kp. 4	-	-	-	(12)	-	-	-	(12)
Fest. Pak Kp. 11	-	-	-	(12)	-	-	-	(12)
Total for XXVII Korps:	27	32	-	(59)	13	7	-	79 (59)
XXVI Armee Korps								
1.Infanterie Division	-	-	-	20	-	7	-	27
Aufklärung Abt. 1	-	-	2	-	2	-	-	4
Pz.Jg. Kp. 1001	7	-	-	-	3	-	-	10
Panzerjäger Abt. 1065	-	-	-	4	-	-	-	4
StuG Brigade 277	25	-	-	-	5	-	-	30
Pz. Abt. 118	14	-	-	-	2	-	-	16
349.Volksgrenadier Div.	-	-	-	6	-	1	-	7
56.Infanterie Division	-	-	-	11	3	-	-	14
Panzerjäger Kp. 1156								
Kampfgruppe Löwen								
StuG Abt. 290	21	-	-	-	-	-	-	21
Fest. Pak Kp. 5	-	-	-	(10)	(2)	-	-	(12)
Fest. Pak Kp. 9	-	-	-	(9)	-	-	-	(9)
Total for XXVI Korps:	67	-	2	51 (19)	15 (2)	8	-	143 (21)
Total for the Army:	232	3	5	147 (119)	31 (4)	22	-	440 (123)

a The numbers within parentheses indicate captured Soviet 76mm guns.

Table 2.4: Availability of artillery in the German Fourth Army on 16 October 1944

	Light field guns	Heavy field guns	Light field howitzers	Heavy field howitzers
LV Armee Korps	93	137	141	87
VI Armee Korps	84	135	105	101
XXXXI Panzer Korps	96	149	102	111
XXVII Armee Korps	85	119	106	99
XXVI Armee Korps	72	91	129	106

From the memoirs of General K.N. Galitsky, the commander of the 11th Guards Army:

Understanding that a successful offensive by Soviet forces at the boundary between Army Group North and Army Group Center might sharply and adversely affect the strategic situation on the entire northwestern sector of the Soviet – German front, the German command strove to block their further advance toward Tilsit and Königsberg.

In the first half of October 1944 the headquarters of the Fallschirm. Panzerkorps *Hermann Göring* and the 2nd Fallschirm. Panzergrenadier Division were hastily shifted from Germany to the Tilsit area, and from the Ninth Army – the 1st Panzer Division *Hermann Göring*, which was later renamed as the 1st Fallschirm. Panzer Division. The 349th Infantry Division and one regiment of the 367th Infantry Division (the main forces of which remained opposite the 2nd Belorussian Front in the Lomszki area) were introduced into the first line of defense in the Schillehnien area. Units of the 20th Panzer Division, which had been resting and refitting north of Johannisburg, were also moving up to this axis from out of the OKH Reserve. By 14 October, the 61st Infantry Division had arrived in the Gumbinnen area from Kurland and was busy building fortifications east of that town.

Including the Third Panzer Army, which had been passed to Army Group Center's control after being driven out of the Klaipeda area to the south, by 10 October the Army Group (commanded by Colonel-General H. Reinhardt) numbered four armies (Third Panzer, Fourth, Second and Ninth Armies) and 14 corps commands (controlling 48 divisions and brigades).

Forces of the Third Panzer Army (commanded by Colonel-General E. Raus), consisting of nine divisions and one brigade, were defending the northern and northeastern approaches to East Prussia – from Palangi (on the coast of the Baltic Sea) to Sudargi (8 kilometers southwest of Jurbarkasa). The operational density on this sector of the front amounted to one division per approximately 15 kilometers.

From Sudargi to Augustowa, opposite the 3rd Belorussian Front, were the units (nine infantry divisions, one panzer division and one cavalry brigade) of the left flank and center of the Fourth Army under the command of *General der Infanterie* F. Hoßbach. Here the operational density was the same as on the sector of the Third Panzer Army's front. The remaining divisions of the Fourth Army were in defensive positions opposite the 2nd Belorussian Front, covering the approaches to East Prussia from the southeast.

Striving to secure favorable conditions for future offensive operations toward Berlin and other vital centers of Germany, the *Stavka* VGK [Headquarters of the Supreme High Command] decided to invade East Prussia in order to weaken the German grouping on the central sector of the front by diverting reserves from there to the Königsberg direction. On 3 October 1944 the *Stavka*, based on the overall strategic plan, ordered the commander-in-chief of the 3rd Belorussian Front to prepare and conduct an offensive operation with the forces of three all-arms armies (the 5th, 11th Guards and 28th Armies), and in cooperation with the 1st Baltic Front, to destroy the German Tilsit – Insterburg grouping, before advancing another 170-180 kilometers to the west and taking Königsberg. The *Stavka* planned to launch the main attack with the adjacent flanks of the 5th and 11th Guards Army out of the Wiłkowyszki area in the general direction of Gumbinnen and further along the southern bank of the Preghel River.

The immediate task of the Front's troops was to take possession of the Insterburg – Darkehmen [Angerapp] – Goldap line no later than the 8-10th day of the operation. Subsequently pushing on in the direction of Allenburg and Pruess-Eylau, the Front was to have in mind detaching part of its strength for an attack against Königsberg from the south. It was recommended to keep the 28th Army in the second echelon behind the main grouping in order to augment the strength of the attack when exploiting a breakthrough.

Simultaneously, the *Stavka* proposed using the 39th Army after its arrival at the Neman River in order to augment the Front's shock grouping on the designated direction. This was essentially a secondary operation, but the Military Council of the 3rd Belorussian Front, as I subsequently learned from Military Council member Lieutenant General V.E. Makarov, who was present at the presentation of the operation's plan to I.V. Stalin, didn't know anything about this matter. The *Stavka* never revealed its master plan before the Front's troops had carried out their assigned tasks.

In the latter half of September 1944, even before receiving the *Stavka*'s directive, the 3rd Belorussian Front's commander-in-chief General of the Army I.D. Cherniakovsky had a verbal directive to work out a plan for an offensive into East Prussia. On 27 September, he reported this plan to the *Stavka*, which ordered some reworking of it and to make certain adjustments to it.

On the next day, the amended plan for the offensive was confirmed. The exploitation of a success by the forces of the main grouping rested on the 2nd Separate Guards Tank Corps. On 10 October 1944, the *Stavka* representative Marshal of the Soviet Union A.M. Vasilevsky and the Front commander-in-chief General of the Army Cherniakovsky visited the army. Their arrival delighted me. The opportunity appeared in a quasi-official situation to resolve a lot of questions connected with preparing and conducting the operation. In addition, whenever the senior chief was not in his office and not at his command post, but directly up among the troops, it was easier to appeal to him with requests, since he could immediately check the soundness of them and take steps to satisfy them.

On the afternoon of 15 October Marshal Vasilevsky again arrived at the command post. He listened to reports from deputy commanders who had just returned from the units, from the operations chief and intelligence chief, and from the chiefs of several services about the readiness for the offensive, and straightened out several questions. Late in the evening of 15 October, a telegram arrived from the Front headquarters, which set 0700 the next day as H-hour for the attack by forward battalions. The artillery preparation was to begin at 0930, and the army's general attack to begin at 1130.

The corps' movement into its jumping-off area and the situation of the troops prior to the corps' introduction into the breakthrough

At an order from the 3rd Belorussian Front's commander of armored and mechanized forces, the corps conducted a 25-30 km march along two routes and by 0800 15 October 1944 was assembled in its jumping-off area: Samarczuny, Sterniszki, Ruda, Pojeziory. In the jumping-off area the corps' units, having fully refueled, were ready for combat. The routes from the jumping-off area to the enemy's forward edge had been reconnoitered by the corps. Mobile command posts were dispatched to the sectors of the 5th and 11th Guards Armies, which kept watch over the actions of our units and those of the enemy. Officers from corps headquarters were constantly present at the headquarters of the 5th and 11th Guards Army.

By this time the enemy was defending the Naumiestis [Władisławow], Dierżiniki, Bobławka, Maldehne, woods southwest of Wiłkowyszki, Łankieliszki, Sodėnai, Šilbalai, Šeštinai line with units of the 1st Infantry Division and 549th Volkgrenadier Division, reinforced with assault guns and artillery. At 0930 16 October 1944, the artillery preparation began, and at 1100 the infantry went on the attack. By end of day 16 October, units of the 5th Army and 11th Guards Army had reached the line: Naumiestis, Kieturkowo, Wilkupie Szauduniszki, Ostankino.

The commander of the 2nd Guards Tank Corps decided to keep his units at full combat readiness for actions from the morning of 17 October 1944, while conducting reconnaissance with roving patrols behind the combat formations of the forward rifle divisions. The rifle units made a significant advance only at 1000 on 17 October. By this time the 5th Army had the greatest success by reaching the Naumiestis, Kibarty line, where separate units of the 5th Army arrived at the national border. In connection with this, at an order from the commander of the 3rd Belorussian Front's armored and mechanized forces, the 2nd Guards Tank Corps at full combat readiness conducted a 25-kilometer march and assembled in a new jumping-off area.

In order to support the corps' introduction in the sector of the 5th Army, reconnaissance was sent out toward Naumiestis and Stanajcie in order to make contact with the leading units; patrols established the presence of bridges across the Schirwindt River in the Naumiestis, Eydtkuhnen sector, and found passages through detected minefields.

In the course of 18 October 1944, the corps headquarters worked to settle questions of cooperation with the 5th Army's rifle units. Routes from its new jumping-off area to the enemy's forward edge were reconnoitered with all the personnel, while reconnaissance was conducted and minefields were cleared.

Units of the 5th Army and 11th Guards Army by the end of day 18 October, advancing against strong enemy fire resistance and a system of obstacles and minefields, reached the following line: 5th Army – Jodupönen, Kosakweitschen, Point 39.8, Wabbeln, Russen, Nickelnischken, Eydtkuhnen; 11th Guards Army – Lengwehnen, Pötschlauken, Groß Sodehnen, Gallkehmen, Point 141.6. Over the day the units of the 11th Guards Army appeared to make a clear breakthrough on the Kiberty, Wisztyniec line, where they partially crossed the national border and were continuing to push forward.

In connection with this, through an order from the commander-in-chief of the 3rd Belorussian Front General of the Army Cherniakovsky, the corps at 0020 on 19 October 1944 set out to a new jumping-off area: Pötschlauken, Groß Sodehnen, Kopsodzie, Matławka, and by 0700 19 October it was fully assembled in the indicated area, where it became operationally subordinate to the commander of the 11th Guards Army General Galitsky in readiness to operate in the sector of the 11th Guards Army. With its arrival in the new jumping-off area, reconnoitering of the routes of movement and enemy minefields was organized, and questions of cooperation with the rifle units operating out in front were resolved.

Through a verbal order from the commander of the 3rd Belorussian Front's armored and mechanized forces, the immediate objective given to the corps was to reach the Grünwietschen, Budszedszen, Kischken, Jodupen line. The next stage would be an attack from the southeast to take Gumbinnem and through the simultaneous actions of forward detachments in the western direction to seize bridges across the Angerapp in the Ischdaggen, Nemmersdorf, Szuskehmen sector.

The corps' combat formation was arranged in the following manner: The 2nd Guards Tank Corps had two groups, operating along two directions. The right-hand group consisted of the 26th Guards Tank Brigade in the lead, followed by an artillery group consisting of the 1311th Light Artillery Regiment and the 28th Separate Guards Mortar Battalion; trailing behind the artillery group in the second echelon were the 4th Guards Tank Brigade and the 401st Self-propelled Artillery Regiment – the corps' reserve. The left-hand group had the 25th Guards Tank Brigade in the lead, followed by an artillery group made up from the 273rd Mortar Regiment and the artillery of the 4th Guards Motorized Rifle Brigade; the 4th Guards Motorized Rifle Brigade itself and the 1500th Self-propelled Artillery Regiment brought up the rear.

Meanwhile, the units of the 11th Guards Army were making even better progress in the direction of Pillupönen. Units of the army reached the line of the Pissa River in the Kisseln, Egglenischken, Szuskehnen sector. The commander of the 11th Guards Army decided for the 2nd Guards Tank Corps to operate in Pillupönen, Podszohnen, Soginten direction, then subsequently according to the previously designated plan. At 1230 on 19 October, the corps' lead brigades – the 26th and 25th Guards Tank Brigades – went on the march to the Pillupönen jumping-off area at a signal from the corps commander Major General of Tank Forces A.S. Burdeinyi.

From the memoirs of Colonel General A.S. Burdeinyi:

On the morning of 16 October, after a lengthy artillery preparation, the troops of the 3rd Belorussian Front went on the offensive.

In the course of two and a half days, there'd been no success in breaking through the border defensive belt, and only by the end of 18 October was a success noted in the 11th Guards Army's sector. The Front commander-in-chief decided to exploit this success by subordinating his mobile group – the 2nd Guards Tank Corps – to the commander of the 11th Guards Army Colonel General K.N. Galitsky. Having summoned me to the telephone (at the time I was at the observation post of the 5th Army's commander), the Front commander-in-chief informed me of his decision to switch the tank corps to the sector of the 11th Guards Army's offensive, having first let me know that the corps' main task would remain as before: namely, to enter the breach in the 11th Guards Army's sector and to launch an attack in the direction of Walterkehmen, and bypassing knots of resistance and enemy strongpoints, to force a crossing of the Rominte River and to arrive in the area west of Gumbinnen, in order to cut off the Gumbinnen grouping and prevent approaching reserves from the west from reaching this area. With a portion of my strength, I was to seize a bridgehead on the western bank of the Angerapp River in the Nemmersdorf area. At the same time, he cautioned that a line of defense had been prepared along the western bank of the Angerapp, but enemy forces hadn't yet fully occupied it.

Further on he told me that since the corps was being made operationally subordinate to the commander of the 11th Guards Army, then all questions regarding the commitment of the tank corps into the breakthrough now rested on the commander of this army, to whom I must immediately go see and receive his concrete orders, as well as to agree upon all issues of cooperation with the rifle divisions that were operating in this direction.

Having received the new assignment, the corps on the night of 18-19 October in very difficult conditions – it rained all night and the dawn broke with dense fog – made a 50-60-kilometer march along the front from north to south, and by 0700 19 October was assembled in the Groß Sodehnen, Kopsodzie, Matławka area in the sector of the 11th Guards Army's attack.

The tankers arrived at the eastern border of Germany with elevated spirits and high combat morale. After all, we were to be among the first to cross the border of East Prussia and to begin to smash the foe on his own territory, about which we'd been dreaming of and speaking about even before the start of the Great Patriotic War. Now this moment had arrived.

At a meeting in the 26th Guards Tank Brigade, the commander of the 1st Tank Company of the 3rd Tank Battalion Senior Lieutenant I.M. Metel'sky declared: "We are worthy of the great honor to finish off the wounded fascist beast in his own lair. I assure the command that the tanks of my company will pitilessly destroy the foe even here, on Prussian soil. The Guardsmen will carry out their mission until the very end." The words of company commander I.M. Metel'sky reflected the thoughts and mood of all the corps' men.

On the night of 19 October, I and my operational command group, which included the chief of staff Colonel A.F. Karavan, the artillery commander Colonel V.V. Lubman, the operations chief Lieutenant Colonel N.R. Repin, the intelligence chief Lieutenant Colonel V.M. Kuznetsov, and the signals chief Lieutenant Colonel B.D. Geller, traveled to the headquarters of the 11th Guards Army in order to get a briefing on the situation facing the army, especially on the direction of the corps' introduction into the breakthrough.

In the center, on the main axis, the 16th Guards Rifle Corps was attacking with its two divisions, with the 31st Guards Rifle Division attacking in the first echelon. In the second echelon was the 1st Guards Rifle Division, reinforced with the 213th Tank Brigade, which comprised the army's mobile group.

During our work in the army's headquarters we found out how difficult and hard it had been to break through the enemy's defenses on the border. The foe had done everything to make East Prussia impenetrable for our forces. Having launched the offensive on 16 October, the 11th Guards Army over the first two days of the offensive had ground its way forward through the German defenses fronting the border and had only just arrived at the national boundary of East Prussia.

The enemy was continuing to offer stiff resistance. In addition to the 49th and 131st Infantry Divisions and the 561st and 547th Volksgrenadier Divisions, plus separate panzer battalions and anti-tank units that were operating opposite our offensive front, the enemy had deployed the 1st Parachute Panzer Division *Hermann Göring* and Panzer Brigade 102 on the main axis of the army's offensive. Altogether, the enemy had up to 250 tanks and self-propelled guns operating in the sector in front of the 11th Guards Army.

Our aerial reconnaissance was reporting that the enemy was bringing up major tank and motorized forces to the Gumbinnen area. The situation was becoming increasingly difficult, and the army headquarters believed it was necessary to augment the army's attack through the commitment of the Front's mobile group on the main axis.

In order to secure the tank corps' introduction into a breakthrough, the 11th Guards Army commander ordered the commander of the 16th Guards Rifle Corps to force a crossing of the Pissa River on the morning of 19 October and to seize a bridgehead; then, in close cooperation with the 2nd Guards Tank Corps, it was to attack in the Walterkehmen – Gumbinnen direction. The corps' commitment into battle was made difficult by the fact that a forced crossing of the Pissa River had to be made, and yet another fortified line on its western bank had to be breached.

Most vexing for us was the fact that the enemy had discovered the axis of the main attack and had begun to move up his panzer and mechanized forces to this direction. The panzer division of *Hermann Göring* had already appeared opposite the 11th Guards Army's front.

The tank corps had lost the element of surprise. Now we had to rely on the tight coordination of actions of all type of troops, and especially on the active work of both ground attack and bomber aviation.

Time was pressing, and even before dawn we (the corps' operational command group) drove out to the observation post of the commander of the 11th Guards Army on Hill 141.6, in the Gallkehmen area (already on the territory of East Prussia). Early on the morning of 19 October, having arrived at the observation post, we found there the commander of the Front's armored and mechanized forces Colonel General A.G. Rodin and the commander of the air army Colonel General T.T. Khriukin, who had already arrived. After exchanging brief greetings and ascertaining the dispositions of the rifle troops and the tank corps, the commander of the 11th Guards Army shared the latest information about the enemy and ended his presentation with a general conclusion. He stated: "The center of gravity in the development of the 3rd Belorussian Front's operation has shifted into the sector of the 11th Guards Army's offensive. The 2nd Guards Tank Corps will be moved up to here. In connection with the decision to commit the 2nd Guards Tank Corps in the offensive sector of our army, its tasks have changed somewhat. Now the army's forces must develop the success together with the Front's mobile group, and together with it, preempting the enemy, take Gumbinnen and simultaneously reach the line of the Angerapp River with an attack of the main forces in the northwestern direction."

Then, Colonel General K.N. Galitsky gave us our orders: "The 2nd Guards Tank Corps, in close cooperation with the 16th Guards Rifle Corps, is to enter a breakthrough on the western bank of the Pissa River in the Karklienen – Engelietken sector. The corps' immediate task is to destroy the opposing enemy, make an 18-20-kilometer penetration into his defenses, and reach the line of the Rominte River. Subsequently, screened by one brigade from the west on the line of the Angerapp River, be ready to attack Gumbinnen and to seize this important defensive hub. When exploiting toward Gumbinnen, the corps will be reinforced with the 11th Guards Rifle Division.

The commander has fixed the Pillupönen area as the jumping-off area prior to arriving at the line of introduction. The disposition of the brigades in the indicated area and the line of introduction must be coordinated with the commander of the 16th Guards Rifle Corps."

Then Galitsky added: "We consider progress by the divisions of the 16th Guards Rifle Corps on the army's main axis to be the main condition for the success of the Front's mobile group, both on the day of the tank corps' commitment and on following days. The attack by both corps must proceed in the closest cooperation, especially when the tanks approach Walterkehmen and Gumbinnen."

It must be said that the orders somewhat differed from the briefing I'd been given by the Front commander-in-chief, who believed that a tank corps could not take the fortified German town, and its task instead would be to bypass Gumbinnen as quickly as possible on its western side in order to isolate the Gumbinnen grouping and defeat the German reserves approaching from the west. In addition, the Front commander-in-chief believed that in favorable circumstances, it would be necessary not just "to screen the western direction with one brigade", but to seize a bridgehead on the western bank of the Angerapp River in the Nemmersdorf area and thereby create conditions for the subsequent development of the offensive. However, since the commander of the 3rd Belorussian Front's armored and mechanized forces Colonel General A.G. Rodin was present, I didn't think it was possible question these changes, assuming that the Front commander-in-chief had already made several changes in what he had previously told me. Moreover, it wasn't worth raising these questions, since the talk concerned the future task after forcing the Rominte River; I thought one way or another the subsequent operations would be clarified.

It encouraged me that we would be resolving our tasks jointly with the 16th Guards Rifle Corps, which had infantry and artillery, both its own and attached. In order to make requests for air support and direct it, the commander of the air army Colonel General T.T. Khriukin assigned a liaison officer with a radio set to me – Major Kapustin. The corps would receive material support – food, fuel and ammunition – from the Front's supply dumps and deliver it with its own transport.

I didn't make any changes in the arrangement of the combat formation – I left it as before: the 25th and 26th Guards Tank Brigades would advance in the first echelon, and in the second echelon, the 4th Guards Tank and 4th Guards Motorized Rifle Brigades. The brigades were assigned approach routes and a new jumping-off area.

At that point my chief of staff Colonel A.F. Karavan departed for the corps headquarters, in order to issue orders to the brigades to dispatching intelligence officers and observation posts to the combat positions of the 31st and 1st Guards Rifle Divisions, in the sector in which the corps would be introduced; and to send out detachments to support the brigade's movements along the approach routes, meet the brigades in the jumping-off areas, and to prepare locations for bridges across the Pissa River. We stipulated that the brigades would begin moving out to the jumping-off areas at my radio signal "333", and to the line of introduction – at the signal "444".

Together with the operational command group, I left to go see the commander of the 16th Guards Rifle Corps in order to agree upon all the matters connected with fulfilling the immediate task. Little time remained, and in such cases time passed inexorably quickly, so the trip had to be made very quickly and the discussion to coordinate had to be very brief, and only touch on questions that demanded a decision already in the nearest future.

From the memoirs of the commander of the 11th Guards Army General K.N. Galitsky:

Considering the situation that arose in the sector of the 3rd Belorussian Front's offensive, General of the Army Cherniakhovsky made the decision to introduce the 2nd Guards Tank Corps in the sector of the 11th Guards Army, which he announced to me over the telephone on the evening of

18 October. Simultaneously he ordered to report preliminary ideas about using the tank corps, stemming from the tasks that had been given to it.

Having assessed the prospects for developing the army's operation into the depth, I reported to Ivan Danilovich that it made sense to commit the tank corps into the breakthrough in the sector of the 16th Guards Rifle Corps, the divisions of which made the greatest progress. The tentative line of deployment for the introduction was on the western bank of the Pissa River, in the Susseitschen – Egglenischken sector, and to direct the corps' main effort toward Walterkehmen and further on toward Gumbinnen, as had been indicated in the Front's directive from 7 October. I also reported to the Front commander-in-chief that in the opinion of the army's Military Council, the most important thing in the use of the 2nd Guards Tank Corps should be the factor of surprise and the full concentration of its actions, so that by augmenting the attack from the depth to convert the tactical breakthrough achieved by the army into an operational one. Therefore, I asked the commander-in-chief to shift the corps from the sector of the 5th Army, where it had spent approximately five days, to the assembly area only under cover of darkness. In the opposite case, the German command, which attentively followed the movement of forces, would easily detect it. Throughout the morning of 19 October, I was continuing to report to the Front commander-in-chief that it would be necessary to reconnoiter the sector of the corps' commitment, to scout the directions of its operations, and to organize combat support and the cooperation of its brigades with the infantry and artillery.

General of the Army Cherniakhovsky confirmed my preliminary ideas. At the same time, he announced that the next morning, the commander of the Front's armored and mechanized forces Colonel General A.G. Rodin and the commander of the 1st Air Army Colonel General of Aviation T.T. Khriukin would arrive for a more detailed treatment of the questions regarding the commitment of the tank corps.

After reporting on the situation that had arisen in the army's sector and receiving instructions from the Front commander in chief about the operational subordination of the 2nd Guards Tank Corps to our army, I specified the tasks for the troops for the next day of combat.

In the first place the 16th Guards Corps was supposed to seize the line of the Pissa River and create a bridgehead on its western bank sufficient for the deployment and introduction into combat of the tank corps. Then it was to launch an attack to the west with the aim of taking a defensive line on the western bank of the Rominte River. Exploiting the success, together with the 2nd Guards Tank Corps, it was to capture Gumbinnen and to emerge in the rear of the enemy's Stallupönen grouping. At the same time, the rest of the army's forces, attacking to the west, were to seize a line on the Angerapp River.

On the morning of 19 October, the army's observation post was shifted into enemy territory in the Gallkehmen area to Hill 141.6. This event gave rise to a multitude of inexplicable feelings. It was seemingly nothing special – the change in location of the army's organ of command is a routine matter in a combat situation. However, this time it was not at all ordinary: the new location was on hostile soil.

We hadn't yet fully settled in the new place, when the Front's representatives arrived: Colonel General of Tank Forces A.G. Rodin and Colonel General of Aviation T.T. Khriukin. By this time the commander of the 2nd Guards Tank Corps Major General of Tank Forces A.S. Burdeinyi had been summoned to the observation post. We clarified the questions that had arisen in connection with the tank corps' commitment, based on my report to the Front commander-in-chief.

Then, having invited General Burdeinyi to approach the map, I issued the mission to the Guards tank corps: in cooperation with the 16th Guards Rifle Corps, to enter the breakthrough on the western bank of the Pissa River, in the Karklienen – Egglenischken sector in the direction toward Kassuben and Walterkehmen. The immediate task was to destroy the enemy, penetrate to a depth of 18-20 kilometers into his defenses, and to reach the line of the Rominte River. Subsequently, covered by one brigade from the west on the line of the Angerapp River, to be ready for an attack toward Gumbinnen and to take possession of this important hub of the German defenses. When developing the offensive toward Gumbinnen, I told Burdeinyi, his corps would be reinforced with the 11th Guards Rifle Division.

When drawing up the tank corps' offensive plan, we were anticipating that its combat operations in the depth of the enemy's defenses could unfold in a completely different operational-tactical direction. We believed the main condition of the success of the Front's mobile group, both on the day of the tank corps' commitment and on subsequent days was the progress made by the divisions of the 16th Rifle Corps on the army's main axis. Both corps' offensives should run in close cooperation, especially as the tanks approached Walterkehmen and Gumbinnen. Thus, it was intended to use the tank corps according to one of two options: either with the successful establishment of a bridgehead on the western bank of the Pissa, in which case it would be possible to develop an attack from the march directly from out of the staging area; or in the event that this didn't happen, the commitment would be possible only after thorough artillery preparation and air strikes. In the latter case, reinforced with infantry support tanks and the army's artillery, the rifle divisions were to penetrate the enemy's defense with a powerful frontal assault, to crush his resisting units, and to take the line of the Pissa River, where the tank corps would then deploy when committing it.

At the end of our conference, once all the tasks and the 2nd Guards Tank Corps' plan of actions had been made clear, as well as the measures to support it, especially with artillery and aviation, it was proposed to General A.S. Burdeinyi to prepare the corps' units for movement up to their jumping-off positions, first to an intermediary line in the Pillupönen area, then by the end of the day to the staging area on the western bank of the Pissa River for commitment into the breakthrough.

The weather on 19 October grounded all aircraft; from the morning, a light rain fell continuously. German aircraft made no appearance in the sky. The tank units could march with no concern about being observed by the enemy.

After the meeting General Burdeinyi, the army's chief of staff General Semenov, and the deputy commander of the 1st Air Army General Nikolaenko headed to the 16th Guards Rifle Corps in order to organize cooperation when committing the tank corps.

Thus, by 1600 the central grouping and the left flank of the 11th Guards Army had reached the Pissa River on a front of 16 kilometers, and having forced a crossing of it in several sectors, took possession of the enemy's strong defensive line. Here, favorable conditions for a successful development of the further offensive by means of committing supplementary forces into battle had been created.

Having reported on the situation from my observation post to the commander-in-chief of the 3rd Belorussian Front General of the Army I.D. Cherniakhovsky and having received authorization for committing the 2nd Guards Tank Corps, I issued an order to General A.S. Burdeinyi to move his corps out of the assembly area (Groß Sodehnen, Pillupönen, Wojdoty) to the sector of the 16th Guards Rifle Corps' offensive in order to move out in the wake of the combat formations of the 31st Guards Rifle Division's first echelon in the direction of Kassuben. At this time the corps had 210 T-34 tanks and 41 SU-85 and SU-76.

Thus, the situation at the army's front was characterized by the fact that the successful attacks, especially in the center of its order of battle, which is to say on the direction of the main attack, had created the possibility of introducing the 2nd Guards Tank Corps into the fighting. However, these successes complicated the situation on the army's flanking formations and created significant difficulties in achieving a further advance.

At this same time, as was established later, by the end of 19 October the enemy, having suffered a defeat in the struggle for the line of the Pissa River, began hastily reinforcing his grouping on the Gumbinnen axis through maneuvers along the front, shifting some units (3rd and 4th Cavalry Brigades, Assault Battalion 27, StuG Brigade 279 and others) from secondary sectors.

Simultaneously, the German command was shifting units of the 5th Panzer Division from the Tilsit area to the Gumbinnen area, and accelerating the assembly of the Parachute-Panzer Corps *Hermann Göring*. Back on the evening of 18 October, the commander-in-chief of Army Group Center, speaking over the telephone with the commander of the Third Panzer Army Colonel General Raus, had said that in addition to the Panzer Corps *Hermann Göring*, he was forced to demand the 5th Panzer Division as well. On the morning of 20 October, the chief of staff of Army Group Center announced, "… the commander-in-chief of the Army Group orders as soon as possible to send the 5th Panzer Division to the Gumbinnen area, where it is urgently needed."

The seizure of the bridgehead on the western bank of the Pissa River after three days of fighting plainly allowed the German command to determine the direction of our main attack and the subsequent course of its development rather accurately, and to create a plan of assembly and the direction of counterattacks against the 11th Guards Army's main grouping. One could assume that the German command, after assembling sufficient strength and means in the Gumbinnen area, would seek to execute a powerful flanking attack from the north against the units of the 11th Guards Army that had broken through, covered by the line of the Rominte River, and thereby halt their further advance.

In connection with the decision to commit the 2nd Guards Tank Corps in the sector of our army's offensive, our tasks became somewhat clearer. Now the army's forces were to exploit the success together with the Front's mobile group and together with it, getting a jump on the enemy, to take Gumbinnen with an attack to the northwest of the main forces while simultaneously reaching the line of the Angerapp River.

The successful actions of the 16th Guards Rifle Corps' divisions, and in particular, of its 31st Guards Rifle Division, secured the commitment of the tank corps according to the first option, which is to say, from the march, having deployed on a line west of the Pissa River.

The 2nd Guards Tank Corps made a forced march into the assembly area and by 1600 the lead 25th and 26th Guards Tank Brigades were approaching Pillupönen, and bit later arrived at the bridges on the Pissa River.

Table 2.5: Account on the status and losses of tanks, assault guns and self-propelled guns in the units of the German Fourth Army over the period between 15 and 18 October 1944

	On 15 October 1944				On 18 October 1944				Disabled				Total
	StuG	Tanks	Sf[a]	sPak[b]	StuG	Tanks	Sf	sPak	StuG	Tanks	Sf	sPak	(Written off)
	1	2	3	4	5	6	7	8	9	10	11	12	
LV Armee Korps													
28. Jäger Division	-	-	-	-	9	-	-	7	-	-	-	-	-
562.Volksgrenadier Div.	-	-	-	-	-	-	-	11	-	-	-	-	-
367.Infanterie Division	-	-	-	-	6	-	-	15	-	-	-	-	-
StuG Brigade 259	-	-	-	-	38	-	-	-	-	-	-	-	-
Total for LV Korps:	-	-	-	-	53	-	-	33	-	-	-	-	-
VI Armee Korps													
203.Sicherungs Division	-	-	-	-	-	-	-	5	-	-	-	-	-
50.Infanterie Division	-	-	-	-	9	-	-	15	-	-	-	-	-
3 Kp./Panzer Abt. 118	-	-	-	-	9	-	-	-	-	-	-	-	-
4 Bat./StuG Brigade 920	-	-	-	-	7	-	-	-	-	-	-	-	-

	On 15 October 1944				On 18 October 1944				Disabled				Total
	StuG	Tanks	Sf[a]	sPak[b]	StuG	Tanks	Sf	sPak	StuG	Tanks	Sf	sPak	(Written off)
	1	2	3	4	5	6	7	8	9	10	11	12	
3 Kp./Jagdpanzer Abt. 69	-	-	-	-	6	-	-	-	-	-	-	-	-
Total for VI Korps:	-	-	-	-	31	-	-	20	-	-	-	-	-
XXXXI Panzer Korps													
Kavallerie Brigade 4	-	-	-	4	-	-	-	4	-	-	-	-	-
Jagdpanzer Abt. 69	25	-	-	-	14	-	-	-	3 Co. transferred to VI AK				
558.Volksgrenadier Div.	7	-	-	-	7	-	-	-	-	-	-	-	-
170.Infanterie Division	9	-	-	13	9	-	-	13	-	-	-	-	-
131.Infanterie Division	-	-	-	-	3	-	-	14	5 (1)	-	-	-	2 (3)
Jagdpanzer Abt. 1057	-	-	-	13	-	-	-	13	-	-	-	-	-
Total for XXXXI Panzer Korps:	41	-	-	30	33	-	-	44	5 (1)	-	-	-	2 (3)
XXVII Armee Korps													
131.Infanterie Division	9	-	-	19	Transferred to XXXXI Panzer Korps								
547.Volksgrenadier Div.	7	-	-	4	2	-	-	2	5	-	-	2	-
561.Volksgrenadier Div.	-	-	-	9	-	-	-	2	-	-	-	-	8
549.Volksgrenadier Div.	10	-	-	13	Transferred to XXVI Armee Korps								
sJagdpanzer Abt. 663	-	-	-	24	-	-	-	6	-	-	-	18	-
StuG Brigade 279	32	-	-	-	17	-	-	-	6	-	-	-	9
StuG Brigade 203	29	-	-	-	17	-	-	-	3	-	-	-	9
StuG Brigade 276	25	-	-	-	Transferred to XXVI Armee Korps								
Panzer Brigade 103	-	36	-	-	-	17	-	-	-	19	-	-	-
sPanzer Abt. 505	-	13	-	-	-	15	-	-	-	24	-	-	1
Panzer Abt. 118 (- 3 Kp.)	-	-	-	-	20	-	-	-	12	-	-	-	-
Jagdpanzer Abt. 70	11	-	3	3	11	-	3	3	10	-	-	-	-
Korps *Hermann Göring*	-	-	-	-	-	56	-	-	-	-	-	-	-
Total for XXVII Korps:	123	49	3	72	67	88	3	13	362	432	-	202	27
XXVI Armee Korps													
549.Volksgrenadier Div.	-	-	-	-	5	-	-	4	5	-	-	12	-
1.Infanterie Division	7	-	4	27	9	-	4	4	-	-	-	-	23
349.Volksgrenadier Div.	6	-	-	6	-	-	-	6	-	-	-	-	-
56.Infanterie Division	10	-	-	11	9	-	-	11	1	-	-	-	-
Panzer Abt. 118 (- 3 Kp.)	15	-	-	-	Transferred to XXVII Armee Korps								
Panzer Brigade 102	-	-	-	-	-	8	-	-	-	15	-	-	-
Kampfgruppe Zahn	-	-	-	-	-	14	-	-	-	-	-	-	-
Jagdpanzer Abt. 42	-	-	-	-	-	2	2	3	-	-	-	-	-
Kampfgruppe Löwen	-	-	-	-	-	10	-	-	-	4	-	-	-
Jagdpanzer Abt. 92	-	-	-	-	8	-	-	-	13	-	-	-	-
sPanzerjäger Abt. 1065	-	-	-	23	-	-	-	6	-	-	-	1	16
StuG Brigade 276	-	-	-	-	10	-	-	-	15	-	-	-	-
StuG Brigade 277	27	-	-	-	20	-	-	-	7	-	-	-	-
Total for XXVI Korps:	65	-	4	67	61	18	20	34	41	19	-	13	39

	On 15 October 1944				On 18 October 1944				Disabled			Total
	StuG	Tanks	Sf[a]	sPak[b]	StuG	Tanks	Sf	sPak	StuG	Tanks	Sf	sPak (Written off)
	1	2	3	4	5	6	7	8	9	10	11	12
Grand Total:	229	49	7	169	224	106	23	144	82 (1)	62	-	33 68 (3)

a Sf – Selbstfahr (Self-propelled, not including Sturmgeschütz)

b sPak – schwere Panzerabwehrkanone (heavy anti-tank gun, 60-89mm)

Table 2.6: Report from the German Fourth Army [AOK 4] on the irreplaceable losses in materiel over the period between 16 and 18 October 1944[1]

Formation and unit	Assault Guns	Tanks	Anti-tank guns, including self-propelled guns
XXVII Armee Korps			
131.Infanterie Division	1	-	3
549.Volksgrenadier Division	8	-	12
561.Volksgrenadier Division	-	-	8
StuG Brigade 279	9	-	-
sPanzer Abt. 505	-	1	-
Total for XXVII Korps:	18	1	23
XXVI Armee Korps			
1.Infanterie Division	-	-	23
sPanzerjäger Abt. 1065	-	-	16
Total for XXVI Korps:	-	-	39
Grand Total:	18	1	62

1 Over this same time, in accordance with the reports from the units and formations of the German Fourth Army, 245 enemy tanks were destroyed.

Table 2.7: Status of the armored fighting vehicles of the German Fourth Army (AOK 4) by end of day of 19 October 1944

Formations and units	Type of tank or assault gun	Combat ready	Under repair	
			Short-term	Long-term
Panzerjäger Kp. 1028	StuG	9	1	-
Panzerjäger Kp. 1367	StuG	6	-	1
StuG Brigade 259	StuG	39	1	3
Panzerjäger. Kp. 1150	StuG	9	-	1
4 Bat., Lehr Brigade 920	StuG	7	1	1
Kavallerie Brigade 4 (mot.)	Pz II	3	1	-
	Pz IV	1	2	1
JagdPanzer Abt. 69	StuG and JagdPz. IV	17	4	3
StuG Abt. 1558	StuG	8	1	-
Panzerjäger Kp. 1240	StuG	10	-	-
Panzerjäger. Kp. 1131	StuG	4	3	2
StuG. Brigade 1547*	StuG	Information hasn't yet arrived		
StuG Brigade 279*	StuG	17	-	-
Panzerjäger Abt. 70*	StuG	11	-	-
	JagdPz. IV	3	-	-
StuG Brigade 203*	StuG	17	-	-

Formations and units	Type of tank or assault gun	Combat ready	Under repair Short-term	Long-term
Panzer Brigade 103*	Pz V, Bef, Flak Pz IV	17	-	-
sPanzer Abt. 505*	Pz VI	15	-	-
Korps *Hermann Göring*	Pz V	56	-	-
StuG Abt. 1549	StuG	4	2	1
KG von Lauchert, Panzer Brigade 102	Pz V	8	12	3
KG Löwen	Pz IV	10	1	3
Jagdpanzer Abt. 92	StuG	8	7	4
Panzer Rgt. 92	Pz IV	9	2	3
Jagdpanzer Kp. 1156	StuG	3	3	4
Panzer Abt. 118	StuG	29	5	8
StuG Brigade 276	StuG	15	7	-
Jagdpanzer Kp. 1001	StuG	6	4	-
StuG Brigade 277	StuG	17	2	10

German records also give the incomplete casualties of the units and formations of the German Fourth Army in the period between 16 and 20 October 1944:

50th Infantry Division: 26 killed, 94 wounded, 8 missing-in-action and 17 ill;
4th Cavalry Brigade: 2 officers killed, 2 officers wounded;
131st Infantry Division: 91 killed, 347 wounded, 12 missing-in-action;
549th Volksgrenadier Division: 2,000 men killed or missing-in-action;
1st (East Prussia) Infantry Division: 5 officers killed, 13 officers wounded, 3 officers missing-in-action and 2 officers not reporting for duty due to illness.

The actions of the 2nd Guards Tank Corps when crossing the Pissa River and its arrival at the Rominte River line

The enemy with units of the 131st Infantry Division, the 541st Volksgrenadier Division, one battalion of *Hermann Göring*'s panzer division, supported by the fire of five artillery batteries, was holding a defensive line from Kickweiden, through Kassuben to Wohren, and was placing artillery fire, tank fire and self-propelled gun fire on the crossing sites, while small groups of submachine gunners were putting pressure on them.

By 1600 19 October 1944, the lead brigades of the 2nd Guards Tank Corps approached the Pissa River in the following areas: 26th Guards Tank Brigade – Swainen; 25th Guards Tank Brigade – the Engelischken estate.

The **26th Guards Tank Brigade**, on the basis of a verbal order from the commander of the 2nd Guards Tank Corps, set out from its jumping-off positions (Pötschlauken, Plathen) in the following combat formation: forward detachment – 3rd Tank Battalion; main forces – 1st Tank Battalion, 2nd Tank Battalion, anti-aircraft machine-gun company, motorized rifle battalion, battery of the 1695th Anti-aircraft Regiment, and operating in the Rudszen, Pillupönen, Podszohnen, Swainen, Kassuben direction, at 1540 19 October crossed the Pissa River northeast of Swainen with its main forces. The forward detachment, operating in the direction of Kassuben, encountered the opposition of three enemy self-propelled guns in the areas of Hill 118.8 and the northern outskirts of Kassuben, and destroyed one self-propelled gun; the enemy abandoned another self-propelled gun. Continuing to pursue its orders, the brigade encountered strong enemy resistance of up to two artillery batteries and five tanks out of the Kickwieden area and the area of crossroads 700 meters west of Kickwieden. In addition, at the same time six enemy Ju-87 dive bombers struck the brigade's combat formations. At 1900 the enemy in strength of up to 15 tanks and a battalion of infantry counterattacked the brigade from the areas of Hill 94.2, Kickwieden and the crossroads 700 meters to the west of Kickwieden, with the support of up to a battalion of artillery and four six-barreled rocket launchers [Nebelwerfers].

With the onset of darkness on 19 October 1944, four German tanks and up to a company of submachine gunners emerged in the rear of the brigade out of the Karklienen area along the western bank of the Pissa River, threatening the 1st Tank Battalion and the brigade's wheeled vehicles, which were assembled at the bridges across the river in the Swainen area. As a result of two hours of combat the enemy reached the line: 400 meters north of Point 119.3, Point 118.8, Kassuben. The brigade, holding a line on the northern outskirts of Swainen and 400 meters east of Kassuben, throughout the night of 19-20 October fought to repel the counterattacks of enemy infantry and tanks. Over the day of combat on 19 October 1944, the 26th Guards Tank Brigade lost 11 T-34/85 tanks destroyed and 3 T-34/85 tanks knocked out. Manpower losses were 24 men killed, including the brigade's chief of staff and the commander of the 3rd Tank Battalion Captain Nikitin, and 40 men wounded. In return, the enemy lost up to 70 soldiers and officers, and 3 tanks, 1 self-propelled gun, 4 anti-tank guns and two bunkers destroyed. One enemy self-propelled gun and 3 villages were captured.

The **25th Guards Tank Brigade** at 2200 on 18 October 1944 set out on the march and by 0600 on 19 October reassembled in the Groß Sodehnen area with the assignment to attack to the west in close cooperation with the 1st "Moscow" Rifle Division, force a crossing of the Pissa River in the Semmetimmen, Wicknaweitschen area, and subsequently carry out the assigned order. At 1410 on 19 October, the brigade's units on the basis of a radio order from corps headquarters, set off along the Rudszen, Budweitschen, Pillupönen, Laukupönen route and at 1630 the brigade's forward detachment with a vigorous attack forced a crossing of the Pissa River in the Egglenischken area; continuing the attack, by 1800 it took Kassuben Station [south of Kassuben itself], having killed up to 30 soldiers and officers and having destroyed 4 antitank guns and a mortar battery in the process. At Kassuben Station, it captured a train carrying ammunition and communications equipment.

With the arrival of tanks on the northern outskirts of Kassuben, the brigade's units encountered enemy tanks, infantry and artillery, where they became tied up in tank combat. The brigade's forward detachment lost two T-34 tanks destroyed; the attack made no further progress and subsequently the forward detachment fought off repeated counterattacks by enemy tanks and infantry, inflicting losses in manpower and equipment to the Germans. At 1840 when repelling German counterattacks, two German Panther tanks were knocked out, and the fire of one 75mm artillery battery and one mortar battery was suppressed. The enemy air force in groups of 10-15 Ju-87 dive bombers bombed the brigade's combat formations, wounding 16 men.

Both brigades, having dug in on the achieved lines, spent the night of 19-20 October 1944 engaged in combat to repulse enemy counterattacks of tanks and infantry.

From the memoirs of Colonel General of Tank Forces A.S. Burdeinyi:

In the middle of the day on 19 October, the troops of the 1st and 31st Guards Rifle Divisions managed to drive the enemy from the eastern bank of the Pissa and to seize a lodgement on the western bank. The Pissa River is small, 5-8 meters wide and more than 1 meter deep, but it presented a serious obstacle to tanks. The river is bordered by high embankments. Without special work, they were very difficult to negotiate.

Having seized a bridgehead, the pioneers immediately set to work and created several fords, which allowed the tanks to begin to cross to the western bank. Tankers of the 25th and 26th Guards Tank Brigades, together with soldiers of the 31st Guards Rifle Division, attacked the enemy, destroyed nests of resistance, left several enemy tanks and self-propelled guns blazing, and crushed the enemy's antitank artillery.

The vigorous combined actions of the tankers and soldiers of the rifle division enabled the bridgehead to be greatly expanded right away. The enemy wasn't ready to repel this attack and was forced to yield significant territory.

The river crossing continued all night long. In fact, the line of the tank corps' introduction into the battle turned out to be the Pissa River. At this time the weather deteriorated – a fine rain was falling, the sky was covered with clouds, the ground became soft, and even for the tanks it was difficult to accelerate to a high speed. Enemy aircraft made no appearance in the sky. So, in fact bad weather shouldn't always be considered "bad". All this was very important for us as well because during the introduction into the breakthrough in the sector of the rifle troops, traffic became congested and the combat formations became bunched up, and it was just this sort of circumstances when the enemy aircraft might inflict heavy losses on us. Taking advantage of the advantageous weather conditions, by morning we had crossed to the western bank of the Pissa, and the corps' main forces, merging into the rifle combat formations, were ready to go on the offensive.

The night of 19-20 October went by for the men in hard toil, but the fighting didn't end – there was rifle and machine-gun fire, and the enemy was bringing down artillery and mortar fire on the crossing sites and supposed areas of troop concentrations. The enemy had good knowledge of the terrain. Our artillery was answering the enemy fire. In general, at night the front had its own combat life. Neither we nor the enemy got by without combat losses.

From the memoirs of the commander of the 11th Guards Army General K.N. Galitsky:

Having destroyed the small enemy groups that remained in our rear and the enemy's firing positions that had sprung to life, the brigades throughout the night were fording the Pissa River and by dawn on the following day were assembled east of Kassuben. The corps' 4th Guards Tank and 4th Guards Motorized Rifle Brigades, which comprised the second echelon, at this time also arrived in the area of the crossing sites. The tankers were crossing in rather difficult conditions: rain, which had started that morning, fell incessantly; the ground was soft and the brigades were negotiating the steep riverbanks in a nighttime gloom. However, the Guardsmen courageously and heroically pushed onward.

When crossing the river, the tankers destroyed 5 tanks and 8 assault guns and field guns of the enemy. The commander of the 2nd Guards Tank Corps with his operational command group was located in Karklienen, while the corps headquarters was in Laukupönen (3 kilometers southwest of Pillupönen). The offensive was supposed to have a good beginning. So, an order was issued to the commander of the 16th Guards Rifle Corps General S.S. Gur'ev and to the tank corps commander General A.S. Burdeinyi to get all of the units of the 11th Guards Army's divisions and of the tank corps across the river that night, so as to initiate active operations the next morning.

Over the day of fighting on 19 October 1944, the enemy suffered the following losses: up to 100 soldiers and officers killed, and 5 tanks, 1 self-propelled gun, 7 guns of various calibers and 2 bunkers destroyed. Two self-propelled guns and four villages were captured. In the process, the brigades of the 2nd Guards Tank Corps suffered losses: The 26th Guards Tank Brigade lost due to enemy artillery fire and airstrikes 11 T-34 destroyed and 3 T-34 knocked out, and 50 men dead or wounded, including the brigade chief of staff and the commander of the 3rd Tank Battalion who were both killed. The 25th Guards Tank Brigade lost 2 T-34 tanks and 15 men due to enemy artillery fire and airstrikes.

The brigades operating in the second echelon throughout the night crossed the river behind the lead brigades along their own directions of advance. The army's rifle units didn't push ahead any further than the western bank of the Pissa River.

On the morning of 20 October, the tank corps commander Major General of Tank Forces A.S. Burdeinyi received an order from the 11th Guards Army's commander:

> The 2nd Guards Tank Corps, in cooperation with the 16th Guards Rifle Corps, is to attack on the Karklienen – Leegen front, having the task to destroy the opposing enemy and to reach the Jodzuhnen, Budszedszen line, and subsequently be ready to attack and take Gumbinnen, covered by the forces of one brigade from the west on the line of the Angerapp River. During the offensive toward Gumbinnen, the 11th Rifle Division will be subordinate to the commander of the 2nd Guards Tank Corps. The army's artillery commander is to organize and secure the 2nd Guards Tank Corps' introduction into the breakthrough. Begin the artillery preparation at 1000 on 20 October 1944. Start the attack at 1030 20 October 1944.

On the basis of the combat order from the commander of the 11th Guards Army, the corps' units were issued the following combat directive:

> The enemy in his former grouping continues to offer stubborn resistance along the western bank of the Pissa River. The corps, in cooperation with the 16th Rifle Corps, on the morning of 20 October 1944 breaks through the enemy's defenses on the western bank of the Pissa and continues to carry out its previously assigned task. The 25th and 26th Guards Tank Brigades by 0900 20 October are to deploy into combat formations: 26th Guards Tank Brigade, in cooperation with the 11th Guards Rifle Divisoin – east of Kassuben and north of the railroad belt. The combat formation is to have two echelons, with two tank battalions in the first echelon and one tank battalion in the second echelon. Between 0800 and 1000 20 October, issue the tasks to the battalions and companies on the spot. Assign directions of attack to the tank platoons and separate tanks, and brief all the personnel and tank crews with the mission. Start of attack – 1100. Artillery preparation from 1040 to 1100. The start and cessation of the artillery preparation will be marked by a rocket salvo. The 4th Guards Tank Brigade constitutes the reserve of the corps commander and is to assemble in the area of Hill 119.3 and to be ready to exploit a success by the lead brigades. The 4th Motorized Rifle Brigade is to deploy into a combat formation and to advance behind the combat formations of the 25th Guards Tank Brigade.

At 1100 20 October, the corps' units, in cooperation with the 16th Rifle Corps, went on the offensive in the Kassuben, Leegend sector. In connection with the fact that the enemy was occupying a defense west of the Pissa and in order to continue to carry out the assignment, the corps' combat formation was arranged in the following manner: the two lead tank brigades in the jumping-off area were deployed into an arrowhead formation; the artillery was deployed behind it and with its fire was to support the tank brigades' attack to the depth of their advance.

The **26th Guards Tank Brigade** at 1100 following the artillery preparation, operating in the lead as part of the corps, attacked the enemy with the 2nd and 3rd Tank Battalions and two submachine gun companies of the motorized rifle battalion in the Kassuben, Bugdszen, Anderskehmen, Kischken, Karszamupchen direction and by 1400 on 20 October took Kischken, having in the process destroyed an enemy motorized column of up to 40 vehicles; after capturing Kischken, it was attacked by 10 enemy tanks out of the Kubillehn area along the highway and by 4 tanks advancing toward Anderskehmen. As a result of a 30-minute action, the enemy lost 3 tanks and retreated back to the north. Having left a screening tank platoon in the Kischken area, the brigade continued to carry out its assignment, and at 1500 the forward detachment cut the highway, took Karszamupchen, and smashed a motorized column of up to 60 vehicles, where it was counterattacked by 15 tanks from the northwest out of the direction of Mattischkehmen and 6 tanks from the northeast out of the direction of Ackmonienen. After an hour-long battle the enemy lost 6 tanks and up to 60 infantrymen and fell back to the north and northeast. The 1st Tank Battalion, attacking north of Kassuben, at 1500 bypassed the enemy from the left and, advancing behind the 25th Guards Tank Brigade, by 1700 on 20 October reached the Schiegseln area.

Continuing to carry out its assignment and engaging in combat with enemy rearguard units, the brigade at 1700 took the crossroads and Hill 78.6, where it destroyed three enemy self-propelled guns, and reached the line: 2nd Tank Battalion, 3rd Tank Battalion and motorized rifle battalion – Grünweitschen; 1st Tank Battalion – Schiegseln. At the decision of the brigade commander, having left a covering force of a tank platoon in the area of Hill 78.6, the brigade outflanked the enemy's defense from the left, and with an attack in the direction of Schmulken, Drutischen and Nestonkehmen, broke the German resistance and by 2200 on 20 October captured a bridge across the Rominte River.

As a result of the combat over the day of 20 October the 26th Guards Tank Brigade destroyed 13 enemy tanks and self-propelled guns, 8 cannons, two batteries of 88mm Flak guns and 70 vehicles with their loads, and killed up to 100 Nazis. Over the same time the 26th Guards Tank Brigade lost 11 T-34/85 destroyed and 2 T-34/85 knocked out. Casualties included 16 killed and 23 wounded. By the end of the day, the brigade had 38 operational T-34/85 tanks.

The **25th Guards Tank Brigade** up until 1000 on 20 October was firmly holding the Kassuben – Augusten line with its units, repulsing repeated enemy counterattacks, while simultaneously working out questions of cooperation with the 31st Guards Rifle Division. At 1125 following the artillery preparation, the brigade's units set out from the Kassuben area, and attacked in two echelons (first echelon: 3rd Tank Battalion and 2nd Tank Battalion; second echelon: 1st Tank Battalion and motorized rifle battalion) in the direction of Budszedszen, with the orders to seize Walterkehmen and take a bridge across the Rominte River in that area. As a result of the men's bold and decisive actions, the enemy was driven from the Bugdszen, Motzkuhnen, Martischken line; the Germans retreated to the west, covered by small groups of infantry, tanks and artillery.

Engaged in stubborn fighting, the brigade's units continued to fight their way to the west, and by 1230 20 October the leading 3rd Tank Battalion captured Sodehnem after a short battle. Exploiting the success, at 1330 the 3rd Tank Battalion then burst into the eastern outskirts of Budszedszen at high speed and after a 30-minute battle took the village and a bridge across the Swentischken River, having driven the Germans from the Budszedszen fortified line; in the process it destroyed 10 guns of various calibers, killed up to 60 soldiers and officers, and blew up an ammunition dump. Continuing the attack, at 1350 tanks of the 2nd and 3rd Tank Battalions reached the area southwest of Schmulken, where they became tied up in fighting for possession of a bridge across the Rominte River in the Walterkehmen area.

The enemy repeatedly launched counterattacks in strength of up to a battalion of infantry, supported by tanks and artillery, to the south from out of the Walterkehmen area and to the north from out of the Szurgupchen area. All the enemy counterattacks were repulsed.

Launching a decisive attack, at 2000 tanks of the 3rd Tank Battalion took Walterkehmen, having driven the Germans from this fortified area, and captured a bridge across the Rominte River. In the process 4 German tanks, 2 self-propelled guns, 10 vehicles, 3 antitank guns and 2 mortars were destroyed, and up to 20 German soldiers and officers were killed.

The losses of the 25th Guards Tank Brigade over the day of 20 October amounted to 3 tanks destroyed and 2 tanks knocked out. Casualties included 1 dead and 26 wounded, among which was the commander of the 2nd Tank Company Guards Captain Egorov.

Throughout the day the enemy air force repeatedly struck the brigade's combat formations in groups of 15-25 aircraft. As a result of the airstrikes, the brigade commander received a concussion; the commander of the 2nd Tank Battalion Guards Major Zhukov was wounded; the senior adjutant of the 1st Tank Battalion Guards Captain Orlov was concussed; the senior adjutant of the motorized submachine gun battalion Guards Captain Morozov was wounded; and the commander of the headquarters company's reconnaissance platoon Guards Senior Major Zav'alov was killed. Up until midnight on 20 October, the brigade's units were positioned in the Schmulken area, topping up with fuel and ammunition and inspecting their tanks, while the men were bringing themselves back to order. By day's end the brigade had 41 combat-ready T-34/85 tanks.

The **4th Guards Tank Brigade** throughout the night of 19-20 October engaged in combat with its 1st and 3rd Tank Battalions against enemy tanks and artillery on the western bank of the Pissa River in the Swainen area. On the morning of 20 October, the enemy launched a counterattack in strength of up to 16 tanks and 4 self-propelled guns with infantry in the direction of Kickwieden and Kinderlauken, supporting the attack with heavy artillery and mortar fire. With the fire of tanks from out of ambush positions, the 1st and 3rd Tank Battalions repulsed the German counterattack. In this action, two enemy self-propelled guns, 3 tanks, one artillery battery and up to two platoons of infantry were destroyed. The brigade lost 2 T-34/85 tanks destroyed by enemy tank fire (one tank of the 1st Tank Battalion and one tank of the 3rd Tank Battalion).

At 1100 on 20 October, after an artillery barrage by the corps artillery, the 4th Guards Tank Brigade resumed the advance, operating behind the 25th Guards Tank Brigade in the Motzkuhnen, Soginten, Budszedszden direction, and by 1400 on 20 October reached the Budszedszen area. Upon reaching Soginten, the brigade was subjected to heavy enemy artillery and tank fire out of the Anderskehmen area, as well as enemy airstrikes. In order to screen its right flank in the Anderskehmen area, the 401st Guards Self-propelled Artillery Regiment was left behind, while the rest of the brigade's units, refusing to get tied up in fighting with the enemy, continued to carry out the task, and by 1830 with fighting took a bridge across the Rominte River in the area of Praßlauken. Upon capturing the bridge by the 1st Tank Battalion, the brigade's main forces reached the western bank of the Rominte River, where it took up a position facing the north, west and southwest. The 2nd Tank Battalion was left behind on the eastern bank of the Rominte, where it took up a position facing to the south and southeast with the task to secure the brigade's actions against possible enemy counterattacks from the south or southeast. Following a reconnaissance conducted in the direction of Hill 103.9 and Schestoken, ambushes were set out on the highway running out of Walterkehmen to the south.

As a result of the day's combat on 20 October, the 4th Guards Tank Brigade lost 2 T-34/85 destroyed, 5 tanks knocked out, and 2 tanks rendered inoperable by mechanical failures. Casualties were 6 men killed and 23 wounded. At day's end on 20 October, the brigade had 55 combat-ready T-34/85 tanks.

The **4th Guards Motorized Rifle Battalion** at 1220 on 20 October, after a 30-minute artillery preparation, went on the attack behind the tanks of the 25th Guards Tank Brigade in the Walterkehmen Station, Buylien direction in the following combat formation: a forward detachment (consisting of the 1st Motorized Rifle Battalion and the 1500th Self-propelled Artillery Regiment), followed in turn by the 2nd and 3rd Motorized Rifle Battalions. Brushing aside rearguard detachments and overcoming enemy fire resistance, the brigade's battalions kept advancing successfully and by 1800 reached the line: 0.5 kilometers east of Walterkehmen, Tellitzkehmen Cemetery, Sodehnen; the artillery group was 1 kilometer west of Budszedszen. At 2000 the battalions forced a crossing of the Rominte River in the area of Walterkehmen Station and continued advancing to the west.

On the morning of 20 October, the **1500th Self-propelled Artillery Regiment** with its three batteries went on the march behind the 4th Guards Tank Brigade's 1st Motorized Rifle

Battalion in the direction of Budszedszen and Walterkehmen. When passing through the village of Martischken, the regiment's column came under an attack by enemy aircraft. Having spotted the movement of an enemy column along the road south of Kublischken, the regiment deployed. The 2nd Battery set ablaze two vehicles mounting anti-aircraft guns, while the guns of the 3rd Battery in the area northeast of the Tollmingkehmen railroad station destroyed a train hauling several railcars. When reaching some hamlet 1.5 kilometers southeast of Budszedszen, the regiment's column was again struck by enemy aircraft, which knocked out one SU-76 self-propelled gun. Soon, the regiment received an order from the corps commander to deploy into a combat formation and take up firing positions 1.5 kilometers northeast of Walterkehmen, with the task to be ready to operate to the northwest and west.

During the enemy airstrikes and at the observation post, smoke generators were used as a means of concealment, and this yielded positive results. The enemy aircraft couldn't spot the regiment's self-propelled guns in their firing positions in an open field; the vehicles weren't dug in and would have been otherwise easily observable from the air.

In the fighting on 20 October, the battery of Senior Lieutenant Kochetov (the 2nd Battery) and of Captain Bushuev (3rd Battery) distinguished themselves. At 1930 on 20 October the regiment together with the 4th Motorized Rifle Brigade's 1st Battalion launched an attack in the direction of Walterkehmen and Buylien, having the task to reach the area of bridges on the Angerapp River and to take Nemmersdorf, which should subsequently be held. In this nighttime advance, Senior Lieutenant Kochetov's 2nd Battery was marching at the head of the column and with direct fire at enemy concealed positions in Maygunischken and Buylien, secured the infantry's advance. With the fire of this same battery out of a concealed position on the road in the Karklienen area, a halftrack mounting a 75mm gun was knocked out, its crew was killed, and the gun was rendered inoperable. Out of this same ambush position, a car carrying an enemy major was blown apart at point-blank range.

When passing through Budweitschen, the regiment's column was subjected to an artillery barrage from defilade firing positions, and by artillery fire over open sights from the direction of a bend in the Angerapp River 1.5 kilometers west of Tutteln. Out of an area of hamlets lying 2.2 kilometers east of Nemmersdorf, the regiment deployed into a line by battery and began an advance toward Nemmersdorf. The lead battery was hit by flanking fire from enemy guns and tanks and engaged in combat with an enemy ambush concealed in isolated patches of brush and haystacks. The fire of the enemy guns was suppressed, and the enemy tanks fled. The regiment lost 3 SU-76 burned out and the commander of the 2nd Battery Senior Lieutenant Kochetov was killed; altogether, the regiment lost 10 men killed or wounded.

The enemy had hastily shifted units of Grenadier Regiment 76 and a group of up to 30 tanks and self-propelled guns from the 6th Panzer Division to the Samelucken – Walterkehmen line, preventing the corps from crossing the Rominte River in this sector. Simultaneously, the enemy had a strong group of tanks and self-propelled guns from the *Hermann Göring* Panzer Division in the Grünwietschen area, covering the direction to bridges in Augstupönen. Up to a battalion of heavy artillery was supporting this enemy group from the Pruszischken, Sadwietschen area [east of Gumbinnen].

The **26th Guards Tank Brigade** with a bypassing maneuver, taking advantage of the darkness, approached the Nestonkehmen bridge, and engaging in combat with an enemy tank grouping, reached the area southeast of Perkallen, which was being stubbornly held by the adversary and presented an enemy strongpoint that was covering the direction toward Gumbinnen. The tank brigade's further advance was checked.

The **25th Guards Tank Brigade**, engaged in stubborn fighting with the enemy in the Walterkehmen area, captured a bridge south of Walterkehmen and by 2400 20 October crossed the Rominte River, making good progress on its direction of advance.

A unit of the 2nd Guards Tank Corps rolls past a hotel in East Prussia, October 1944.

The **4th Guards Tank Brigade** and the 401st Guards Self-propelled Artillery Regiment, operating in the direction of Praβlauken, at 1830 on 20 October captured a bridge in the Praβlauken area with fighting, after which the brigade's main forces began crossing the Rominte River in this area.

The **4th Guards Motorized Rifle Brigade** was crossing the river in the wake of the 25th Guards Tank Brigade.

By 2400 20 October the corps' tank brigades had completed their crossing of the Rominte River and had reached the following areas: 25th Guards Tank Brigade – Budweitschen and the woods to the southeast; 26th Guards Tank Brigade – northeast of Perkallen; 4th Guards Tank Brigade – the road fork north of Praβlauken; 4th Guards Motorized Rifle Brigade – Buylien and the woods lying to the northwest. Over the day of fighting on 20 October 1944, the enemy had lost 14 tanks and self-propelled guns, 16 antitank guns, 25 vehicles, and 5 wagons loaded with ammunition, and suffered up to 300 soldiers and officers killed. According to incomplete data, at the same time the 2nd Guards Tank Corps lost in return 15 men killed, including the corps' deputy combat commander Guards Colonel Nesterov and the commander of the 26th Guards Tank Brigade's 2nd Tank Battalion Guards Captain Nikitin, and 70 wounded. Tank losses amounted to 17 tanks destroyed and 4 tanks knocked out. By day's end on 20 October 1944, the 2nd Guards Tank Corps had the following operational tanks: 4th Guards Tank Brigade – 57 T-34/85 tanks; 25th Guards Tank Brigade – 46 T-34/85 tanks; 26th Guards Tank Brigade – 40 T-34/85 tanks; 79th Motorcycle Battalion – 10 T-34/85 tanks; and the 1st Guards Separate Signals Battalion – 5 T-34/85 tanks, for a total of 154 T-34/85 tanks. In addition, 18 T-34/85 tanks were under repair (light repairs – 2; moderate repairs – 15; major overhaul – 1). The 401st Guards Separate Artillery Regiment had 19 SU-85 in service, and another 2 SU-85 undergoing moderate repair. The 1500th Self-propelled Artillery Regiment had 20 operational SU-76, and one more SU-76 under moderate repair. The corps' supply situation: 2 refills of fuel and lubricants, and 1.8 combat loads of ammunition.

The famous anti-fascist writer Il'ia Ehrenburg (second from the right), who was enrolled as an honorary tanker in one of the best tank crews of the 4th Guards Tank Brigade, once again called upon his Tatsinskaia Guardsmen and took an interest in their combat successes and the life at the front, East Prussia, October 1944.

Scenes of combat in East Prussia in October 1944: burning wreckage, surrendering Germans and knocked-out equipment.

Knocked out German tanks in East Prussia, October 1944.

A destroyed German gun (on the left) and a knocked out German tank with a dead German soldier lying next to it; East Prussia, October 1944.

Burning buildings in the German city of Stallupönen (Ebenrode).

Soviet artillery conducting fire in the area of Stallupönen.

The sign on the left marks the border with Germany; the one on the right reads "Warriors of the Red Army; in front of you is the lair of the fascist beast!"

Scenes of the fighting in East Prussia

Table 2.8: Status of the armored fighting vehicles of the German Fourth Army on 20 October 1944

Formations and units	Combat materiel				Knocked-out materiel			Total
	StuG	Tanks	Sf	sPak mot Z	Short-term	Long-term	Destroyed	
LV Armee Korps								
28.Jäger Division	-	-	-	7	-	-	-	7
Panzerjäger Kp. 1028	9	-	-	-	1	-	-	10
StuG Brigade 259	39	-	-	-	1	3	-	43
562.Volksgrenadier Division	-	-	-	9	-	-	-	9
Fest. Pak Kp. 10	-	-	-	(5)	-	-	-	(5)
Fest. Pak Kp. 17	-	-	-	(12)	-	-	-	(12)
Total for LV Korps:	48	-	-	16 (17)	2	3	-	69 (17)
VI Armee Korps								
203.Sicherungs Division	-	-	-	5	-	-	-	5
3 Kp./Panzer Abt. 118	8	-	-	-	1	-	-	9
50.Infanterie Division	-	-	-	15	1	-	-	16
Panzerjäger Kp. 1150	9	-	-	-	1	-	-	10
4 Bat., Lehr Brigade 920	8	-	-	-	-	1	-	9
Kampfgruppe Hannibal	-	-	-	1	1	-	-	2
3 Kp./JagdPanzer Abt. 69	7	-	-	2	-	-	-	9
Fest. Pak Kp.	-	-	-	(12)	(2)	-	-	(14)
Total for VI Korps:	32	-	-	21 (12)	6 (2)	1	-	60 (14)
XXXXI Panzer Korps								
Kavallerie Brigade 4 (mot.)	-	-	-	3	2	1	-	6
Jagdpanzer Abt. 69 (- 2 co.)	7	-	-	-	3	4	2	14
StuG Abt. 1558	8	-	-	-	1	-	-	9
170.Infanterie Division	-	-	-	12	2	-	-	14
Panzerjäger Kp. 1240	9	-	-	-	1	-	-	10
sPanzerjäger Abt. 1057	-	-	-	10	2	1	-	13
131.Infanterie Division	-	-	-	15	1	-	-	16
Panzerjäger Kp. 1131	4	-	-	-	2	2	1	8
367.Infanterie Division	-	-	-	15	1	-	-	16
Panzerjäger Kp. 1367	6	-	-	-	1	-	-	7
Fest. Pak Kp.	-	-	-	(12)	-	-	-	(12)
Total for XXXXI Panzer Korps	34	-	-	55 (12)	16	8	3	113 (12)
XXVI Armee Korps								
549.Volksgrenadier Division	-	-	-	5	-	-	-	5
StuG Abt. 1549	1	-	-	-	4	2	-	7
1 Bat., sPanzejäger. Abt. 665	-	-	-	3	-	-	2	3
3 Bat., StuG Brigade 203	6	-	-	-	1	1	-	8
Fest. Pak Kp.	-	-	-	3	-	-	-	3
349.Volksgrenadier Division	-	-	-	6	1	-	-	7
Panzerjäger Kp. 1349	10	-	-	-	-	-	-	10
Panzer Abt. 118 (- 3 Kp.)	12	-	-	-	10	11	-	33
Panzerjäger Kp. 1156	2	-	-	-	2	3	-	7
StuG Brigade 276	8	-	-	-	6	8	-	22
sPak Abt. 1065	-	-	-	6	1	-	-	7

Formations and units	Combat materiel				Knocked-out materiel			Total
	StuG	Tanks	Sf	sPak mot Z	Short-term	Long-term	Destroyed	
Jagdpanzer Abt. 92	6	-	-	-	10	4	-	20
4 Kp./Panzer Abt. 21	-	10 (IV)	-	-	1	3	-	14
sPanzer Abt. 302	17	-	-	-	5	8	-	30
Panzer Abt. 2101/Panzer Brigade 101	-	10 (V)	-	-	1	3	-	14
Jagdpanzer Kp. 42	-	-	16	3	-	-	-	11
1.Infanterie Division	-	-	-	2	1	1	-	4
Aufklärung Abt./1.Infanterie Division	-	-	1	-	2	1	-	4
Panzerjäger Kp. 1001	5	-	-	-	4	1	-	10
StuG Brigade 277	15	-	-	-	4	10	-	29
56.Infanterie Division	-	-	-	11	3	-	-	14
Panzerjäger Kp. 1156	3	-	-	-	-	-	-	3
Fest. Pak Kp. 6	-	-	-	(3)	-	-	(9)	(3)
Fest. Pak Kp. 11	-	-	-	(10)	-	-	(2)	(10)
Fest. Pak Kp. 5	-	-	-	(10)	-	-	-	(10)
Fest. Pak Kp. 9	-	-	-	(7)	-	-	-	(7)
Total for XXVI Korps:	85	20	17	39 (30)	56	53	2 (11)	280 (30)
The *Führer Grenadier* Brigade was en route								
Führer Grenadier Brigade	-	32 (V)	-	-	5	-	-	37
	-	5 (IV)	-	-	-	-	-	5
	12	-	-	-	-	-	-	12
	-	-	-	4	-	-	-	4
Total for the brigade:	12	37	-	4	-	-	-	53

Note: The parenthesized numbers represent captured Soviet 76mm guns. The "sPak mot Z" means schwere Panzerabwehrkanone motorisiert mit Zugmachine, or Heavy Anti-tank Gun motorized with towing vehicle.

From the recollections of Hero of the Soviet Union Colonel General of Tank Forces A.S. Burdeinyi:

We greeted the morning of 20 October in a blanket of dense fog; it was impossible to get the offensive underway. It was only around 1100 that the fog began to lift, and wishing to pre-empt the enemy, around 1200 our artillery preparation began, striking revealed targets. In the sky, gaps began to appear in the clouds, and the possibility appeared for our aircraft – bombers and fighters – to take off. The appearance in the sky of our aircraft not only boosted morale, but also somehow stirred everyone and prompted a desire not to let the moment miss when the enemy was forced to hug the ground by our air force, or had been chased by it into trench shelters. At 1230 the lead tank brigades and the Guardsmen of the 31st Guards Rifle Division went on the attack, joined by airstrikes by our ground attack aircraft.

We were all glad for the fact that we were getting air support, or to put it more accurately, our ground attack aircraft that were well known to us from the fighting in Belorussia – Colonel S.D. Prutkov's 1st Guards Assault Aviation Division – was attacking together with us. The pilots of this aviation division easily identified our tanks on the battlefield (which had a white circle on the turret, and a white arrow pointing in the direction of our offensive on both sides); taking guidance from them, they clearly knew that only the enemy could be out in front of us, and they courageously attacked targets. I'm not afraid of repeating myself and will say once again that such cooperation brought us general success.

The enemy was putting up fierce resistance on the territory of East Prussia. Each hamlet and farmstead had to be taken with fighting. The adversary left behind groups dressed in civilian clothing in our rear, which would suddenly open fire and inflicted a heavy cost to us. The offensive bogged down, and these groups, having carried out their duty, disappeared into previously prepared shelters. Of course, later they would be found and destroyed, but time was needed for this, and we didn't have time to spare. We literally had to wipe every building and structure we came across from the earth.

In the middle of the day, the 26th Guards Tank Brigade was moving in the direction of Kassuben. Its leading tank battalion, commanded by Major I.F. Lolenko, from the march broke into this village, destroyed several enemy tanks and self-propelled guns, crushed up to a battalion of field guns under their tank treads, killed a lot of Nazis, and seized this village of Kassuben that was so important to us.

Lolenko was an experienced and bold commander, with whom the reader has already become familiar from previous fighting described in this book, but he deserves particular mention once again. Ivan Fedorovich had recently arrived from a hospital, where he was being treated after being wounded near Minsk (he had already been hospitalized 13 times for wounds in the war), and re-assumed command of his own battalion. The battalion greeted him like a father, trusted him deeply, and obeyed his orders unquestioningly. This was already his fourteenth wounding in the war, but he had already led his brigade successfully, and he had been decorated several times with high government medals.

Here, too, separated from his brigade's main forces, he put up stubborn resistance to the counterattacking enemy. However, the enemy's superiority in force forced the battalion commander to abandon Kassuben. At this time the 25th Guards Tank Brigade, where the corps' deputy commander Colonel S.K. Nesterov was located, was attacking on the left. Having found out about the events around Kassuben and having received my go ahead, Nesterov pivoted the 25th Guards Tank Brigade to the north toward Kassuben, while he traveled to the 26th Guards Tank Brigade, which he had recently commanded, to organize cooperation between the two tank brigades on the spot (and also of course to assist the young brigade commander Lieutenant Colonel Shanin, who had recently taken over the brigade and unquestionably needed his assistance and advice).

The coordinated attack of these two brigades smashed this enemy grouping as well, and Kassuben was ours once again. On the battlefield the foe left behind 12 tanks burned out and just as many knocked out, as well as knocked out anti-tank guns and a large number of dead.

At the height of the fighting for Kassuben on 20 October, Stepan Kuz'mich Nesterov was mortally wounded by enemy submachine gunners. Having fallen bravely on the field of battle upon entering East Prussia, Guards Colonel S.K. Nesterov had carried out his duty to the end. For the courage and heroism he displayed in the fighting when breaking through the Germans' defense and for the invasion of East Prussia, Guards Colonel Stepan Kuz'mich Nesterov was posthumously awarded the title Hero of the Soviet Union.

Stepan Kuz'mich Nesterov had traveled a long and winding path in the war years. Commanding a brigade from May 1942, he took part in the Battle of Stalingrad (and had participated in the deep raid into the enemy rear toward Tatsinskaia) and in the liberation of eastern Ukraine, defeated the foe at Prokhorovka, and had participated in the fighting to liberate El'nia, Smolensk, Minsk and Kaunas. He'd been awarded the Orders of Lenin and of the Red Banner, two Orders of Suvorov, the Order of Aleksandr Nevsky, and many medals. As a mark of gratitude to the hero, the town of Stallupönen was renamed Nesterov, and a monument to him was erected in the center of the town.

The tank brigades swiftly advanced to the west. Naturally, the rifle units couldn't keep pace with the tanks and fell behind. The fighting in the Kassuben area delayed the tank brigades somewhat, so Colonel O.A. Losik's 4th Guards Tank Brigade was introduced into the fighting in order to maintain the pace of the advance and to expand its front, which would in turn make it possible to approach the river on a broad front, before forcing a crossing of it. The brigade received an order to exploit the success swiftly in the direction of Soginten and Praßlauken, to seize a bridge there, and then to establish a bridgehead on the western bank of the Rominte River.

Now three tank brigades were hurrying toward the Rominte. In reserve, the 4th Guards Motorized Brigade was moving in the center of the corps' advance. It had the task to be ready to move to whichever point where a more favorable situation had developed for crossing the Rominte. In essence, at this time (the end of day October 20), we had no contact with friendly forces on the right or the left. Destroying whatever disorganized enemy units they came across, by 1800-1900 the three tank brigades were closing on the Rominte River. The 26th Guards Tank Brigade emerged east of Druschken, the 25th Guards Tank Brigade – east of Walterkehmen, and the 4th Guards Tank Brigade – the Praßlauken area. The tank brigades were approaching the Rominte on a rather broad frontage of 8-10 kilometers. The 4th Guards Motorized Rifle Brigade was advancing in the center – in the second echelon. The 25th Guards Tank Brigade was the first to approach the Walterkehmen area. With the aim of hastening the crossing of the river, it was given one battalion of the motorized rifle brigade. The Rominte River presented a more serious obstacle than the Pissa River, but the rifle troops were nowhere nearby – they had lagged behind.

From the memoirs of the commander of the 11th Guards Army General K.N. Galitsky:

Early on the morning of 20 October, I arrived together with Generals Rodin and Nikolaenko at the observation post of the commander of the 16th Guards Rifle Corps. It was situated on a hill south of Kassuben (west of the Pissa River).

After the night of rain, the entire horizon was blanketed with fog; the weather was plainly grounding the aircraft. We'd have to wait a bit.

To wait … this meant to lose several hours. But there was the desire to launch the offensive the offensive sooner and thereby gain more daylight hours for the actions of the tank corps. However, it was also important to launch a powerful blow against the enemy with tanks, having laid down a path for them from the air with bombing runs and strikes by ground attack aircraft.

Now it was 1100. The weather began to clear. Visibility extended for 6-8 kilometers. General Nikolaenko was satisfied, and Gur'ev brightened up. I issue the order to begin. The signals are given. Instantly, the men somehow changed. Faces became concentrated, everyone was strained, and only concise, confident commands were heard in the observation post. The atmosphere was tense. All at once, the air shook from the powerful artillery salvoes.

The offensive began in the sector of the 16th Guards Rifle Corps after a powerful half-hour artillery preparation and airstrikes. The attack of the 31st Guards Rifle Division went successfully. From the observation post we watch as the forward lines of infantrymen, crouching low under the explosions of our own shells, burst into Padern, Motzkuhnen and Deeden, and after a short battle they took them. Then at this time the rising rumble of tank engines and the howl of bombers let it be known to us that the first echelon of General A.S Burdeinyi's tankers, Colonel G.A. Chuev's bombers and behind them Colonel S.D. Prutkov's ground attack aircraft were approaching the breakthrough sector. Soon, the tanks of the 25th and 26th Guards Tank Brigades, escorted in the air by ground attack aircraft, were passing through the combat ranks of the 31st Guards Rifle Division at high speed. Directed into the breach in the Anderskehmen – Soginten sector, the tankers overran elements of enemy infantry, knocked aside units of the *Hermann Göring* Panzer Division, and receded in the distance to the west.

Soon reports began to come in from the commanders of the 25th and 26th Guards Tank Brigades Colonels S.M. Bulygin and V.K. Shanin that their tanks were destroying artillery on the march and had smashed an enemy column of infantry and tanks. The enemy as a result of the suddenness of the attack had suffered heavy losses. The initial successes inspired the tankers even more, emboldened them, and gave them renewed strength.

The Guardsmen of the 31st Guards Rifle Division were lagging behind the tanks somewhat. The Germans decided to take advantage of this and to launch a counterattack, in order to isolate the tanks from the infantrymen, and to encircle and destroy them. However, this wasn't so easy to do. Having quickly assessed the situation, Burdeinyi and Gur'ev quickly committed the second echelons of the tank corps and of the 31st Guards Rifle Division, and not only repulsed the counterattack, but also drove the Nazis out of Anderskehmen, Ballupönen and other points, thereby expanding the breach up to 6 kilometers wide.

An attack made by the German Panzer Brigade 102, reinforced by units of the 1st Panzer Division [of *Hermann Göring*], out of the area southwest of Groß Trakehnen against the right flank of the 2nd Guards Tank Corps was also not crowned with success. The German command threw artillery, infantry and aircraft against the Soviet tankers. Groups of 20-30 German aircraft were constantly dive bombing the combat formations of the units of the corps' first echelon. At a critical moment of the counterattack, the deputy corps commander Colonel S.K. Nesterov, who was located up among the combat formations of the tanks, summoned fighter aircraft for assistance, deployed two tank battalions in the direction of the threatened flank, and ordered to screen the tanks with smoke pots. The first to deploy a smokescreen was tank commander Junior Lieutenant Akseniuk, and Sergeant Matveev got two billowing plumes of smoke going. The tanks wound up concealed from the enemy. His aircraft were unable to make targeted bomb runs and had to drop their bombs indiscriminately. Directing the battle, Stepan Kuz'mich Nesterov died as a hero, struck by a burst of machine-gun fire.

Having defeated the counterattacking enemy, the tankers together with the main forces of the 31st Guards Rifle Division continued to push on toward the line of the Rominte River. Having advanced approximately 20 kilometers, the lead 25th Guards Tank Brigade at 1800 closed on the major enemy strongpoint of Walterkehmen. By this time the enemy had taken up a defense on a previously prepared line along the western bank of the Rominte River, having assembled Panzergrenadier Regiment 76, more than 30 tanks, and two battalions of artillery in the Walterkehmen area. The 26th Guards Tank Brigade, which was attacking on the right together with one of the regiments of the 31st Guards Rifle Division, approached Schwiegseln, where it was suddenly attacked by two panzergrenadier battalions and 12 tanks. After a bitter hour-long battle, our tankers and infantrymen enveloped the counterattacking units from the flanks, pressed them back against the Schwentischeka River with its very boggy basin, and completely destroyed them. Units of the 4th Guards Tank Brigade, commanded by Hero of the Soviet Union Colonel O.A. Losik, arrived at the river in the Praßlauken area, 3 km southeast of Walterkehmen. By 2000 units of the 31st Guards Rifle Division were also closing on Walterkehmen.

In step with the advance made by the 2nd Guards Tank Corps and the rifle units that were cooperating with it into the interior of East Prussia, the bitterness and resistance of the foe grew.

The 2nd Guards Tank Corps attempts to take Gumbinnen

With the tank corps' arrival on the western bank of the Rominte River, the enemy's units (Panzergrenadier Regiment 76 and a group of tanks from the 6th Panzer Division) were continuing to occupy the Girnen, Ernstberg, Samelucken, Surminnen line, preventing the tank brigades of the 2nd Guards Tank Corps from operating to the north toward Gumbinnen and forcing the tank brigades to pivot to the southeast. Through the interrogation of prisoners, it was established that 20 enemy tanks and 70 vehicles loaded with infantry were on the move in the Gumbinnen area from the west, and the intensive movement of railroad trains in the Gumbinnen area was also noted. The positioning of the strong enemy grouping in the center of the corps' advance was blocking the 26th Guards Tank Brigade and 11th Guards Rifle Division, while simultaneously threatening the corps' lines of communication and rear areas.

The commander of the 2nd Guards Tank Corps Guards Major General of Tank Forces A.S. Burdeinyi decided to liquidate the enemy grouping in the Girnen, Surminnen, Ernstberg area with the forces of the 26th Guards Tank Brigade and 4th Guards Tank Brigade. The 26th Guards Tank Brigade and a regiment of the 11th Guards Rifle Division were ordered to take Perkallen.

The 4th Guards Tank Brigade was ordered to take Ernstberg with one tank battalion operating out of the Maygunischken area, and to take Plicken and Girnen with one tank battalion operating out of the Wilken area. The 25th Guards Tank Brigade and the 1st Battalion of the 4th Guards Motorized Rifle Brigade were ordered to reach the Nemmersdorf area in order to capture a bridge across the Angerapp River. The 11th Guards Rifle Division and the 16th Guards Rifle Corps, becoming operationally subordinate to the tank corps, by the morning of 21 October 1944 reached the eastern bank of the Rominte River in the Nestonkehmen – Walterkehmen sector, where they received an order to cross to the western bank and to operate toward Gumbinnen in cooperation with the 26th Guards Tank Brigade.

At 0920 on 21 October 1944, the corps' units set out to carry out the issued orders, and having destroyed a significant portion of the enemy grouping in the Perkallen area, by 1500 arrived at the following line: 26th Guards Tank Brigade – Gertschen; 4th Guards Tank Brigade and 4th Guards Motorized Rifle Brigade – Wilken and the road hub 1.5 kilometers northwest of there. On this line the 2nd Guards Tank Corps destroyed 100 vehicles, 12 tanks, 16 self-propelled guns, 40 guns of various calibers, 50 machine guns and 2 mortars, and killed more than 1,000 enemy soldiers and officers.

The enemy on this line had a previously prepared defensive line and offered stubborn resistance to the corps' further advance. The defensive line was occupied by enemy tanks, self-propelled guns, artillery and infantry.

Overcoming the resistance of German tanks and panzergrenadiers, the corps' units ground their way forward and by 1900 21 October reached a line running from southwest of Kailen to Stulgen. This line had been also previously prepared for a defense and had bunkers, full-profile trenches, barbed wire obstacles and anti-tank minefields. Groups of German tanks and self-propelled guns were covering the advantageous directions for actions toward Gumbinnen. By this time the Germans had been able to bring up fresh units of the *Hermann Göring* Panzer Division to the Gumbinnen area and southeast of there, and they were operating against the corps' units.

The **25th Guards Tank Brigade**, together with one battalion of the 4th Guards Motorized Rifle Brigade, continued to attack toward Nemmersdorf and with the forces of the 2nd Tank Battalion, in cooperation with the motorized rifle battalion, at 0930 on 21 October 1944 captured the village of Nemmersdorf and the reinforced concrete bridge across the Angerapp River there. In the process, they killed up to 60 enemy soldiers and officers and destroyed a retreating supply column carrying ammunition. Having mopped up Nemmersdorf of the remaining German infantry, the brigade's units took up an all-round defense in readiness to repulse possible enemy counterattacks.

The 3rd Tank Battalion from the northern fringe of woods lying south of Lutzicken at 0600 on 21 October launched an attack to the north toward Gumbinnen with the mission to cooperate with the units of the 4th Guards Tank Brigade and 26th Guards Tank Brigade in taking Gumbinnen by launching an attack from the left flank. Just an hour later in the Kallnen area, the 3rd Tank

Battalion caught up with a column of enemy that was retreating toward Gumbinnen and smashed it; in the process, it destroyed two 75mm guns, up to 10 carts, and killed up to 20 Nazis, while capturing a car and an ambulance. Continuing the offensive, at 0910 the 3rd Tank Battalion fought its way into Wilken and took it, destroying up to 10 loaded wagons and two transportation vehicles. They also captured 12 German soldiers, who were subsequently executed. Afterward, the 3rd Tank Battalion engaged in defensive fighting with enemy tanks, artillery and infantry, repelling repeated German counterattacks.

The 25th Guards Tank Brigade in the course of 21 October in the Nemmersdorf area fought off repeated enemy counterattacks of infantry and tanks, supported by artillery, out of the Hill 73.4, Krausehof area. In this sector, up to 20 German tanks and self-propelled guns and a panzergrenadier regiment from the *Hermann Göring* Parachute-Panzer Corps were operating in this sector.

The **26th Guards Tank Brigade**: From sunrise on 21 October, the enemy increased its pressure on the brigade. At 1100 up to two battalions of infantry supported by tanks and artillery counterattacked the brigade from out of the Gertschen area and the woods lying to the southwest of there. The brigade's tanks with fire out of ambush positions shot up the attacking infantry and tanks, and then the brigade counterattacked the enemy with the 3rd Tank Battalion and a battalion of infantry from the 11th Rifle Division. Destroying two self-propelled guns and up to a company of infantry, they took full possession of the intersection of roads 1 kilometer east of Gertschen, and consolidated their grip around it.

The brigade's 1st and 2nd Tank Battalions in the meantime attempted to take the road junction and German strongpoint of Perkallen, but had no success, because the enemy had thoroughly fortified the town and were holding it with infantry, antitank guns, artillery and up to six tanks. Artillery was needed to suppress them, but the brigade didn't have any, and there was no response to all their requests for help with artillery fire on Perkallen. At 1300 the 2nd Tank Battalion, bypassing Perkallen on its southeastern side, took the town with an attack from the south, having destroyed in the process 4 German self-propelled guns, 3 antitank guns and killed up to 60 Nazis. The 1st Tank Battalion, operating from the north and with fire from fixed positions, helped the 2nd Tank Battalion take Perkallen. Screened by the 2nd Tank Battalion from the southwest in the Perkallen area, with the rest its remaining forces the 26th Guards Tank Brigade went on the attack along the highway toward Gumbinnen together with a rifle regiment of the 11th Rifle Division, and at 1500 took a road junction lying 1 km northeast of Gertschen and the woods to the right of it, where it had run into heavy German fire from up to 10 tanks and 15 88mm Flak guns. The brigade suffered heavy casualties and a high loss of tanks while taking the woods. Screened on the achieved line by a tank platoon, and having brought up the 2nd Tank Battalion, the motorized rifle battalion and the rear services, which had broken through to the brigade, the tankers paused to top up with fuel and ammunition. Then the 26th Guards Tank Brigade outflanked the enemy from the left and with an attack along the railroad took Kailen and the western slopes of Hill 53.4 by 2200 on 21 October.

The **4th Guards Tank Brigade**: Developing the offensive, the brigade together with its attached units set out from the Praßlauken area in the direction of Schestocken, Buylien and Gumbinnen. By this time the enemy, taking advantage of the hilly, sharply cut terrain in the Giren, Marienthal area, had assembled up to 20 self-propelled guns, up to two battalions of halftracks, and up to three battalions of artillery, and was offering stiff resistance, striving to retain possession of its occupied center of resistance. The Germans were hitting the brigade with strong flanking fire from this area. In order to isolate and destroy the enemy grouping in the Giren – Marienthal area, the 1st Tank Battalion was sent from Praßlauken. Reaching the southern outskirts of Giren, for the rest of the day it was tying up the Germans and locked in bitter fighting to destroy the enemy. Simultaneously in order to secure the 2nd Guards Tank Corps' left flank, the 401st Guards Self-propelled Artillery set up battery-sized ambush positions in the Praßlauken, Maygunishcken and Buylien areas, with a front to the south and southwest.

By 1030 on 21 October, the 4th Guards Tank Brigade's 3rd Tank Battalion, 2nd Tank Battalion and motorized rifle battalion reached the northeastern fringe of the woods lying northwest of Buylien, and having shaken out into a combat formation with the 3rd Tank Battalion in the lead, it launched an attack toward Dauginten and Wilken. Upon reaching the Kallnen area, the lead battalion was met by strong enemy artillery fire and rifle and machine-gun fire from the direction of Wilken and the woods lying southwest of Plicken. The motorized battalion of submachine gunners was quickly brought up, and shaking out into a combat formation, with supporting fire from the tanks, attacked the German infantry on the northern fringe of the woods southwest of Plicken, and eliminated some of them, while driving the rest back in the direction of Plicken.

In order to support the 1st Tank Battalion that was operating toward Girnen, the 3rd Tank Battalion and the motorized rifle battalion were deployed in the northeastern direction and with active operations launched an attack in the direction of Plicken, Szameitschen and Gertschen, thereby encircling the enemy grouping in the Girnen, Marienthal area. Through energetic actions of the 1st Tank Battalion from the southeastern outskirts to the north in the direction of Girnen, and the 3rd Tank Battalion and motorized rifle battalion from the northwest toward Szameitschen and Gertschen, the enemy grouping was encircled and destroyed by the end of 21 October.

Elements of Germans that had broken out of the encirclement were trying to escape toward Gumbinnen; columns of them were destroyed on the Perkallen – Gumbinnen highway. Small enemy groups managed to escape the pocket; they scattered in various directions.

The 4th Guards Tank Brigade's battalions took Girnen, Perkallen Station, Gertschen, Szameitschen, Plicken and the commanding heights south and southeast of Plicken. Simultaneously the brigade's 2nd Tank Battalion conducted an attack toward Gumbinnen, and overcoming the strong German resistance of tanks and self-propelled artillery, by end of day 21 October took Wilken, Skardupchen, Kuttkuhnen and Stulgen.

In the fighting to destroy the encircled enemy grouping in the Girnen, Marienthal area and on the approaches to Gumbinnen, the 4th Guards Tank Brigade destroyed 13 German tanks and self-propelled guns, up to two companies of infantry, and up to a battalion of artillery. In return the brigade lost 10 T-34/85 tanks burned out or knocked out by the fire of enemy self-propelled guns and tanks.

In the fighting to destroy the encircled enemy grouping, tankers of the 4th Guards Tank Brigade's 1st Tank Battalion, 3rd Tank Battalion and motorized rifle battalion distinguished themselves. Among them was company commander Guards Senior Lieutenant Metel'sky, whose tank company was taking the lead in the Girnen area. When the enemy, having allowed a reconnaissance platoon to pass into the depth of their defenses, blocked approaches to the village with flanking fire. Metel'sky, instantly recognizing what the Germans were doing, outflanked the German ambush and with fire from the company's tanks destroyed two German tanks, one self-propelled gun and up to two platoons of infantry, thereby securing the battalion's successful actions to take Girnen.

Deputy brigade commander Guards Major Mastashev also stood out that day. Directly handling the battalion's tanks and correctly assessing the enemy strength in the depth of the German defenses, Mastashev organized the battalion's rapid-fire actions to destroy the pocketed enemy grouping and by his personal example and capable leadership led the battalion's tankers in the battle in terrain that was difficult for tanks and in the circumstances of a superior enemy force.

The submachine gun platoon commander of the motorized rifle battalion Guards Lieutenant Belenko in the combat for possession of the woods lying southwest of Plicken personally led his platoon on the attack and was the first to break into the enemy trenches, tossing grenades into it. All the platoon's soldiers followed his example and in a swift attack the German infantry was routed and took to flight. Belenko in this action personally killed 5 enemy soldiers and one officer.

A submachine gunner of the motorized rifle battalion Corporal Abronov when nearing an enemy trench in the Plicken area was the first to rise onto the attack, and with the cry "For the motherland! For Stalin!" swept the platoon's men along with him, as a result of which a large group of German infantry was wiped out.

According to a combat order from the corps headquarters, the 4th Guards Tank Brigade and 401st Guards Self-propelled Artillery Regiment, in cooperation with the 4th Guards Motorized Rifle Brigade, next had the task to move out of the Kuttkuhnen, Stulgen area toward Gumbinnen, with the first objective of cutting the railroad and highway running out of Gumbinnen to the west, and subsequently to take Stannaitschen with one battalion, while the main forces were to take the western outskirts of Gumbinnen.

By dawn on 22 October, the brigade's units had moved into jumping-off positions for the attack: the 3rd Tank Battalion and one battalion of the 4th Guards Motorized Rifle Brigade were in the Stulgen area; the 2nd Tank Battalion and a motorized rifle battalion were in the wooded area west of Stulgen; the 401st Self-propelled Artillery Regiment and one battalion of the 4th Guards Motorized Rifle Brigade were in the Hill 58.4, Kuttkuhnen area.

The **4th Guards Motorized Rifle Brigade**: In the course of 21 October the brigade's units, supported by artillery and breaking German resistance, successfully advanced to the north in the direction of Gumbinnen. The 3rd Battalion, a submachine gun company and an antitank rifle company were attacking toward the western outskirts of Gumbinnen; at 1600 they took the eastern outskirts of Kuttkuhnen and by 1900 reached a line 1.5 km to the north of Kuttkuhnen. In the fighting for the latter place and on the approaches to Gumbinnen, the 3rd Battalion inflicted significant damage to the enemy: four antitank guns, 12 vehicles and up to 90 soldiers and officers. Fifteen German soldiers were captured. In these actions, Guards Lieutenant Karpukhin's 7th Company particularly stood out.

The 1st Battalion and the 1500th Self-propelled Artillery Regiment were attacking on the 3rd Battalion's left; at 1600 they took the western outskirts of Kuttkuhnen and at 1900 captured Thuren, before pushing on to a line 400 meters north of Thuren. On its path of advance, the battalion met fierce enemy opposition, and the closer the soldiers and officers approached the railroad west of Gumbinnen, the tougher the German resistance.

In the vicinity of Stulgen a German aircraft appeared in the sky at an altitude of just 50-100 meters above the combat positions of the 1st Battalion, which was shot down by the battalion's soldiers. There were 5 Germans in the airplane, all of which perished in the crash.

The 4th Guards Motorized Rifle Brigade's 2nd Battalion attacked in the direction of Wilken, before deploying with a front to the west; continuing the attack toward Nemmersdorf, at 1400 on 21 October 1944 it forced a crossing of the Angerapp River and took possession of Nemmersdorf with fighting, thereby securing the crossing of the 25th Guards Tank Brigade's tanks.

At 1815 up to a battalion of enemy infantry and 20 tanks counterattacked the 2nd Battalion in the Nemmersdorf area from the direction of Hill 73.4 and the woods south of Budballen. The battalion successfully repulsed the counterattack, and in the process killed up to 120 German soldiers and destroyed 2 tanks, 2 self-propelled guns, 11 guns of various calibers and 8 halftracks; two German vehicles were captured.

The battalion's own losses were 1 man killed and 22 wounded. In addition, 1 truck and 1 57mm gun were destroyed. In this fighting Guards Lieutenant Gopt's 4th Company distinguished itself by knocking out 2 self-propelled guns and destroying or disabling 8 halftracks; the company also captured or destroyed 7 guns of various calibers. One soldier of the 4th Company Sergeant Saipushev was able to sneak right up to a self-propelled gun and set it ablaze.

Over the day of fighting on 21 October, the 4th Guards Motorized Rifle Brigade lost 19 killed and 57 wounded, as well as two vehicles, one armored transport, and one 57mm gun.

The **79th Motorcycle Battalion** conducted reconnaissance in three reconnaissance groups. Group No. 1 commanded by the motorcycle platoon commander Lieutenant Zolotorev consisted of 2 tanks, a radio-equipped halftrack and 6 motorcycles scouted in the operational sector of the 26th Guards Tank Brigade. Group No. 2, commanded by Lieutenant Poddubniak, consisting of 1 tank, a radio-equipped halftrack and 5 motorcycles, conducted reconnaissance in the operational sector of the 4th Guards Tank Brigade; Group No. 3, commanded by Guards Lieutenant Aleksashin, consisted of a radio-equipped halftrack and two motorcycles, and reconnoitered in the operational sector of the 25th Guards Tank Brigade.

By 1900 on 21 October, the battalion's nucleus was assembled at a point 1 kilometer southeast of Wilken. Over the day of combat, great damage was done to the enemy. In the process, the crew members of Guards Senior Lieutenant Bykovsky's tank of Reconnaissance Group No. 2, pursuant to a personal order from the corps commander Guards Major General of Tank Forces A.S. Burdeinyi, with machine-gun fire and their tracks destroyed a German infantry company in the Stulgen area that had been holding up the 4th Guards Motorized Rifle Brigade.

Captain Varaksin and the crew of his halftrack, operating under the direct command of the corps commander, with their bold and daring actions demonstrated models of courage and valor. A group of 40 German soldiers were spotted attempting to move from the woods in the Kallnen area to the Wandlanszen area. Carrying out an order from the corps commander to block the path of the retreating infantry, Varaksin and his crew cut the enemy off and with machine-gun fire killed 8 Nazis and captured 15 prisoners. Throughout the day of 21 October, the battalion had only one man wounded.

The **1500th Self-propelled Artillery Regiment** at 1300 on 21 October received an order to move out with three batteries to Wilken behind the 4th Guards Motorized Rifle Brigade's 1st Battalion, and to deploy into a combat formation northwest of Wilken with the task to attack in the Stulgen, Thuren direction, and further on to the southwestern outskirts of Gumbinnen. At 1400 21 October, having taken Stulgen, the batteries took up firing positions on its northern outskirts.

The 4th Guards Motorized Brigade's 1st Motorized Rifle Battalion and the regiment's batteries had no possibility to make any further progress on this day, since the enemy had a splendid view of the terrain and kept the infantry under intense artillery and mortar shelling and with direct antitank fire from a previously prepared line prevented any advance toward Thuren. One SU-76 was damaged by the artillery and mortar fire in an area 500 meters west of Hill 66.7; later that night it was successfully evacuated for repairs and subsequently returned to service.

Over the day of 21 October, the 2nd Guards Tank Corps inflicted the following damage to the enemy: 21 tanks and self-propelled guns, 23 pieces of artillery of various calibers, 1 aircraft, 13 vehicles, and up to 570 soldiers and officers. In return, the corps lost 30 men killed and 79 men wounded; 9 T-34/85 tanks and 3 SU-76 were destroyed, and 11 tanks were knocked out. By end of day on 21 October, the 2nd Guards Tank Corps had 138 operational T-34/85. In addition, 18 T-34/85 were under repair (2 light, 15 moderate, and 1 factory overhaul). The 401st Guards Self-propelled Artillery Regiment had 19 operational SU-85, while the 1500th Self-propelled Artillery Regiment had 14 operational SU-76. The corps' supply situation: 2 refills of fuel and lubricants; 1.5 standard combat loads of ammunition; and 6 days of rations.

Table 2.9 here: Status of the tanks and self-propelled guns of the German Fourth Army on 21 October 1944

Formations and units	Type of tank or self-propelled gun	Combat ready	In repair Short-term	In repair Long-term
Panzerjäger Kp. 1028	StuG	9	1	-
StuG Brigade 259	StuG	39	1	3
Panzerjäger Kp. 1150	StuG	9	1	-
4 Bat., StuG Brigade 920	StuG	8	-	1
Jagdpanzer Abt. 69 (minus 3 Kp.)	StuG	11	5	7
StuG Abt. 1158	StuG	3	-	-
Panzerjäger Kp. 1240	StuG	6	-	-
Panzerjäger Kp. 1131	StuG	4	2	2
Panzerjäger Kp. 1367	StuG	6	1	-
StuG Abt. 1547	StuG	3	-	-
StuG Brigade 279	StuG	10	4	5
Jagdpanzer Abt. 70	StuG	9	-	-
2 Kp., Jagdpanzer Abt. 69	Jg.Pz. IV	Information hasn't arrived		
StuG Brigade 203 (- 3 Kp.)	StuG	Information hasn't arrived		
Panzer Brigade 103	StuG	5	-	-
	Pz V	2	-	-
	Bef Wg, Flak Pz	Information hasn't arrived		
sPanzer Abt. 505	Pz VI	Information hasn't arrived		
Korps *Hermann Göring*	Pz V	47	-	-
	StuG	20	-	-
StuG Abt. 1549	StuG	2	2	3
3 Kp., StuG Brigade 203	StuG	6	2	1
Panzerjäger Kp. 1349	StuG	10	-	-
Panzer Abt. 118	StuG	20	10	11
Panzerjäger Kp. 1156	StuG	5	2	3
StuG Brigade 276	StuG	8	6	8
Jagdpanzer Abt. 92	Jg.Pz.	6	10	4
4 Kp., Panzer Abt. 21	Pz IV	10	1	3
Panzerjäger Kp. 1023	StuG	10	-	-
sPanzer Abt. 302	StuG	17	5	8
Panzer Abt. 2101, Panzer Brigade. 101	Pz V	10	1	-
Panzerjäger Kp. 1001	StuG	5	5	-
StuG Brigade 277	StuG	17	2	10
En route				
Panzer Brigade *Führer Grenadier*	Pz V	32	5	-
	Pz IV	5	-	-
	StuG	12	-	-
Total for the Fourth Army	Tanks and S-P Guns	366	66	72

Table 2.10: Losses of the *Fsch. Panzerkorps* (Parachute-Panzer Korps) *Hermann Göring* for 20-22 October 1944[1]

a)   Kampfgruppe Decker – Fsch. Gren. Div. 2 HG
b)   Fsch. Gren. Div. 1

Casualties	Officers	Non-commissioned officers	Rank and file	Total
Killed	6	10	44	60
Wounded	9	33	330	372
Missing in action	-	16	50	66
Total:	15	59	424	498

1 Over this same period of time, the corps reported the destruction of 176 tanks, 18 self-propelled guns, 24 anti-tank guns, 17 aircraft and more than 1,000 soldiers and officers of the enemy.

From the memoirs of Colonel General of Tank Forces A.S. Burdeinyi:

Obviously, not quite grasping the operational situation, the commander of the 11th Guards Army made a decision and on the evening of 20 October issued the following task to the tank corps:

> 2nd Guards Tank Corps and the 11th Guards Rifle Division at sunrise on 21 October are to continue a rapid offensive with the immediate objective of taking Gumbinnen. Secure the actions of the army's main grouping from the west with one tank brigade, which is to reach the Angerapp River, capture the bridges between Sabadszuhnen and Nemmersdorf [which lay 7 km apart] and establish a bridgehead on the river's western bank. The 16th Guards Rifle Corps (the 31st, 1st and 11th Guards Rifle Divisions) has been ordered from the morning to continue the offensive with units of the 31st Guards Rifle Division, in cooperation with the 2nd Guards Tank Corps, with the immediate task to force a crossing of the Rominte River and to make a subsequent advance to the southwest in the general direction toward Didziddern (9 kilometers southwest of Walterkehmen) and Darkehmen.

This order had the effect of splitting the 16th Guards Rifle Corps into two pieces: one portion (the 1st and 11th Guards Rifle Division) were drawn into the fighting in the Groß Trakehnen area (east of Gumbinnen), while the other portion (the 31st Guards Rifle Division) was directed to the southwest in the direction of Darkehmen. To the left along this axis of advance, the 36th Guards Rifle Corps was attacking. Essentially, this order excluded the possibility of joint operations with the 16th Guards Rifle Corps to take Gumbinnen, since its divisions were moving in divergent directions.

    Having received the order from the 11th Guards Army commander, we pondered it for a long while. The army's main forces – the 36th and 16th Guards Rifle Corps – had been directed not toward Gumbinnen (the operation's primary and immediate objective), but were moving off to the sides, as if opening a gate for someone. We came to the conclusion that apparently the 28th Army would be committed on this axis, and we would take Gumbinnen together with it. We could not explain the large gap in the combat formation of the 11th Guards Army in any other way.

    There was no time to waste, so we set out to carry out the assignment we'd been given – to seize a bridgehead on the western bank of the Rominte River and to prepare for an offensive toward Gumbinnen. By this time the chief of staff of the 25th Guards Tank Brigade Major G.A. Mokritsky reported that the Rominte River in places was just like the Pissa River, but that north and south of Walterkehmen there were fords, and in the center of the village we had captured an intact bridge. On the western bank, primarily in the Walterkehmen area, infantry units were defending, but seemingly no German tanks were in sight. The situation suggested that the enemy hadn't had time to bring up major forces to this sector and the Rominte River had to be crossed quickly, which meant that day, on the evening of 20 October. With regard for the existing situation, the brigades were given the following tasks: 25th Guards Tank Brigade together with the 2nd Battalion of the 4th Guards Motorized Rifle Brigade (which was following behind the 25th Guards Tank Brigade), supported by the 273rd Mortar Regiment and the motorized rifle brigade's artillery battalion, was to force a crossing of the Rominte River north and south of Walterkehmen using the available fords there, and seize the western bank; without getting tied up in fighting for Walterkehmen, it was to advance swiftly toward Nemmersdorf, and in favorable conditions seize a bridgehead there on the morning of 21 October on the western bank of the Angerapp River. The 4th Guards Motorized Rifle Brigade, in cooperation with the 25th Guards Tank Brigade, was to cross the Rominte, seize a bridgehead on its western bank, and mop up the enemy in Walterkehmen. Subsequently on the morning of 21 October it was to be in the area west of Walterkehmen, ready to advance to the west behind the 25th Guards Tank Brigade or to the north in the direction of Gumbinnen. The 26th Guards Tank Brigade was to cross the Rominte in the Samelucken or Drutischen area (3-4 kilometers north of Walterkehmen), arrive at the Nestonkehmen – Plicken line and prepare for an attack toward Gumbinnen. It was also to make contact with the 11th Guards Rifle Division, which had also received an order to arrive in this area, and work out all questions of collaboration for the attack toward Gumbinnen. The 4th Guards Tank Brigade was to cross the Rominte River in the Praβlauken area (4-6 kilometers southeast of Walterkehmen, and attacking to the northwest to the Plicken – Schulgen line, it was to be ready for an attack toward Gumbinnen. It was to establish contact with the 26th Guards Tank Brigade and 4th Guards Motorized Rifle Brigade on its right, which were moving out from the Walterkehmen area.

The operational command group moved to the area of the 4th Guards Motorized Rifle Brigade's dispositions. Back at daybreak, the brigades had reconnoitered the approaches to the Rominte River and had prepared the necessary means for readying the fords, and there, where there were bridges – for taking them. We had no information that the enemy had taken up an organized defense along the western bank of the Rominte, and the small screening detachments that were assembled primarily at the bridge locations couldn't offer serious resistance to us. We had to take advantage of this situation, while the enemy still hadn't brought up his reserves from the depth or hadn't shifted them from other sectors of the front. From the experience of past battles, we knew that the German soldiers weren't especially eager participants in nighttime battles and in these hours the resistance on their part sharply decreased. Moreover, a rapid advance by the troops of the 11th Guards Army, including of the tank corps, would cause the enemy great difficulties in organizing a firm defense in the operational zone. In either event, the decision was made not to waste the favorable situation for us, and we were not mistaken.

With the onset of darkness, the motorized battalions of the tank brigades moved up to the river and under the cover of the tanks that were ready to open fire at muzzle flashes from the western bank, crossed the river over the captured bridges and fords and seized a lodgment on its western bank (in the same fashion we had crossed the Berezina River in the June of 1944, although here the Rominte River didn't present a particularly large obstacle). Quickly the fords were reinforced and the tanks with submachine gunners aboard crossed to the western bank. The brigade commanders – Colonels V.K. Shashin, S.M. Bulygin and O.A. Losik – personally directed the fighting to establish a bridgehead on the western bank. Rifle and machine-gun fire and the exchange of fire between tanks was going on across the entire 8-10-kilometer front. Despite all their desire, the enemy proved unable to withstand our attack.

The start of the attack went most successfully for the 25th Guards Tank Brigade. The brigade arrived in its objective area sooner; indeed, given the great assistance rendered to if by the 4th Guards Motorized Rifle Brigade that was accompanying, it had a greater possibility to do so. By midnight the tank brigade was already on the western bank and hurried off toward its objective – the Nemmersdorf area. Having covered 10-12 kilometers, by 0800 21 October the brigade was approaching the Angerapp River at the location of a railroad bridge (the bridge served as a fine guidepost). The 2nd Tank Battalion under the command of Major K.V. Marchenko was moving at the head of the column, with tank riders mounted on the tanks. In the fog, the enemy's bridge security couldn't figure out whose tanks were approaching, and the railroad bridge was captured without any particular difficulty. Having assessed the situation, the battalion commander maintained his composure, pressed quickly on with his tanks and tank riders, and captured confused German soldiers that were cowering in their shelters and bunkers.

The fog began lifting, which accelerated the destruction of the enemy in this area. The panicked fear of the residents and garrison in the small village of Nemmersdorf also eased our task here. The old saying "Nothing ventured, nothing gained" is correct. Here the brigade destroyed up to 10 75mm guns in their positions, captured several bunkers, killed up to 100-150 resisting Nazis, and took 35 fascists prisoner. For the next two and a half days the brigade and the 4th Guards Motorized Rifle Brigade's motorized rifle battalion kept possession of this bridgehead that was so important for us. The enemy brought up reserves (a regiment of a Fallschirmjäger division) and throughout this period of time sought to eliminate our bridgehead, but all his efforts were in vain. The enemy air force in particular did its utmost; it was constantly "looming" over the brigade. The brigade commander Colonel S.M. Bulygin received a concussion, while the commander of the 1st Tank Battalion Major I.V. Zhukov and many other Guardsmen were wounded, but the men of El'nia didn't waver.

In the following days – the 21, 22 and first half of 23 October – the brigade not only repulsed all of the foe's attacks, but also having expanded the staging area, occupied the Wilken – Nemmersdorf – Budweitschen line. All the remaining brigades of the corps successfully crossed the Rominte River. Overcoming the resistance of strongpoints and enemy units that were moving up to the Rominte, in the afternoon and evening of 21 October the brigades reached their indicated phase lines.

Now it was necessary to pause and look into the situation. The corps and brigades sent out reconnaissance patrols and tried to reveal the German defenses of Gumbinnen. In addition, we were hoping for the rapid arrival of the rifle forces. With my headquarters staff, we spent a long time wondering where the 11th and 31st Guards Rifle Divisions were. Already at day's end, I managed to get in touch with the commander of the 11th Guards Rifle Division General N.G. Tsyganov, who informed me that the division had spent several days being shifted from one sector of the front to another, had taken heavy casualties, and was now on the march to the designated area – to the western bank, and would only be able to arrive no sooner than tomorrow (22 October), no earlier than 1000-1200. General N.G. Tsyganov himself and his headquarters operational group could arrive today and he asked to indicate a place of meeting. I set the place of meeting in Samelucken with the commander of the 26th Tank Brigade Lieutenant Colonel V.K. Shashin. I had no prior opportunity to meet personally with this quite remarkable commander. Up to this point in the offensive, I also hadn't managed to meet with the commander of the 16th Guards Rifle Corps General S.S. Gur'ev either. He, apparently, had made no effort to seek such a meeting, because back on 20 October he had received a new order and was preoccupied with it.

Throughout the latter half of 21 October, and over the night and morning of 22 October, our reconnaissance had spotted enemy artillery, tanks and infantry. An attempt to break into the city with the forward battalions on the evening of 21 October had no success and resulted in unjustified losses. The army commander was persistently demanding to take the city. My reports that I had no artillery at all in order to suppress the enemy's defenses in the city and that tanks in a city like Gumbinnen were helpless without infantry were brushed aside, pointing to the fact that I'd been given operational control of the 11th Guards Rifle Division.

From the memoirs of the commander of the 11th Guards Army General G.N. Galitsky:

The German command was urgently shifting fresh units and formations to the Walterkehmen area from other sectors of the front. On the night of 20-21 October, the 2nd Parachute-Panzergrenadier Division of the *Hermann Göring* unloaded from trains in the Gumbinnen area. The regiments, without waiting to assemble completely, received separate orders and immediately headed toward defensive positions. In particular, Panzergrenadier Regiment 3, reinforced with Flak Battalion 802, deployed in order to defend Gumbinnen from the southwest. It was supposed to prevent a breakthrough toward Gumbinnen on this direction. In addition, the 5th Panzer Division was shifted from the sector of the 1st Baltic Front to here, at first by railroad, then by its own march. It was in position to threaten the exposed flanks of the 11th Guards Army's shock grouping.

The foe's Stallupönen grouping was also prompting concern. Units of Volksgrenadier Division 561 and the arriving Panzer Brigade 102 and 1st Parachute-Panzer Division *Hermann Göring*, which were defending on the breakthrough's right flank in the direction of Groß Trakehnen, were putting up stubborn resistance to the 26th, 1st and 11th Guards Rifle Divisions. Indeed, this was completely understandable. Having deployed with a front facing the northwest and north in the direction of Groß Trakehnen, the divisions with a successful advance might contribute to expanding the breach made by the 2nd Guards Tank Corps and 31st Guards Rifle Division to the north, and accordingly, to the arrival of the 8th Corps on the flank of the Stallupönen grouping. This prospect greatly concerned the Nazis, and they were fighting bitterly, incessantly counterattacking, and striving to get into the rear of the units of the 2nd Guards Tank Corps and 16th Guards Rifle Corps.

When the tankers arrived on the line of the Rominte River, General Burdeinyi reported to me that he had decided for force a crossing that night, without waiting for the assembly of all the units, in the 8-kilometer-wide Nestonkehmen – Praßlauken sector. "I want to secure a bridgehead on the western bank," he continued, "and create favorable conditions for an attack toward Gumbinnen from the morning of 21 October." In addition, Aleksei Semenovich decided to break through that night toward Nemmersdorf with an attack to the west by the forces of the 25th Guards Tank Brigade and to take a bridge across the Angerapp River. "I request, Comrade Commander, to hasten the arrival of the 11th Division in the Walterkehmen area," he concluded.

"A bold decision," I thought, "and unquestionably a correct one." Of course, General Burdeinyi knew that his tankers were tired, that they had covered approximately 20 kilometers with heavy fighting and needed at least a short rest. However, as a commander with broad operational and tactical vision and as a strong-willed and decisive man, he also knew something else: to stop and let slip an opportunity to exploit the success was intolerable. There was the need to drive the enemy back from the line of the Rominte River before he could organize a strong defense along it. Giving the assignment to the brigade commanders, General Burdeinyi explained: "If we don't do this now, such a delay will cost the troops dearly tomorrow." Indeed, this was correct. There is nothing worse in combat than to miss a propitious moment. When the enemy resistance weakens, when his stubbornness on the defensive is waning, active operations give the attacker the best chance for a decisive success. The corps commander understood this, having decided to continue the offensive even at night.

In the army headquarters, we were closely monitoring the tankers' nighttime offensive. Indeed, not only we – the Front headquarters was constantly pestering us, demanding to be constantly updated on the situation. With the onset of darkness, the right-flank 26th Guards Tank Brigade fought its way across the river and arrived in the area west of Drutischken. The nighttime gloom and heavy fog, as well as the enemy's organized antitank artillery fire and counterattacks from the north forced the brigade commander to dig in temporarily in this area.

The 25th Guards Tank Brigade scored a particular success. Engaged in stubborn fighting in the Walterkehmen area, before midnight it captured a bridge across the Rominte and moved on further to the west. Over the night the brigade covered 12 km and by 0600 21 October was approaching the village of Budweitschen (9 km southwest of Gumbinnen), where it ran into stiff resistance. Meanwhile the 4th Guards Tank Brigade, launching an attack to the southwest, forced a crossing of the Rominte in the Praßlauken area and by morning reached the crossroads 3 kilometers northwest of this village. The 4th Guards Motorized Rifle Brigade was crossing the Rominte in trail behind the 25th Guards Tank Brigade in the Walterkehmen area.

It must be said that the night of 20-21 October was very unsettling. From General Burmakov a message arrived, saying that German tanks were counterattacking his 31st Guards Rifle Division. Then suddenly there was a break in communications. We also lost contact with the 1st and 84th Guards Rifle Divisions. The radio sets of the tank corps commander were also stubbornly silent. The army's chief of staff General Semenov was noticeably nervous. Apparently, the officers of the Operations Department were even more worried because of this. One after another they were sending liaison officers to the front, in order to find out what was happening. Only in the early morning hours of 21 October did we manage to pinpoint the location of the units and restore communications.

The introduction of the 2nd Guards Tank Corps into the breakthrough was successfully conducted. The tankers, acting boldly, decisively and aggressively, fulfilled their assigned tasks for the first day of the offensive with honor. Units of the tank corps and the 31st Guards Rifle Division in the course of 20 October inflicted significant losses on the foe. The tankers alone captured 20 pieces of artillery and mortars, and almost just as many machine guns; knocked out 14 tanks; and destroyed 49 guns and mortars. Unquestionably the corps also suffered losses – even significant ones, since the fighting was very bitter. Over 19 and 20 October it lost up to 40 tanks. Our attention was focused on the center, where units of the 2nd Guards Tank Corps and of the 11th Guards Rifle Division were operating. General Burdeinyi reported that on the morning of 21 October, the 11th Division, in cooperation with the 26th Guards Tank Brigade, was attacking out of the Walterkehmen area in the northwest direction toward Gumbinnen, while the forces of the 4th Guards Tank Brigade and 4th Guards Motorized Rifle Brigade were launching an attack along the Buylien – Kuttkuhnen direction and further on towards the southwestern outskirts of Gumbinnen. The 25th Guards Tank Brigade, having captured Nemmersdorf, was screening the tank corps' operations from the west on the line of the Angerapp River.

Initially the offensive went according to plan. The first to initiate combat actions was the 25th Guards Tank Brigade. Having destroyed the enemy's units in the Budweitschen area, it, in cooperation with the arriving battalion of the 4th Guards Motorized Rifle Brigade, from the march attacked the garrison in Nemmersdorf from the east and took a totally intact reinforced concrete bridge across the Angerapp River that had length of 45 meters. Corps pioneers that were mounted on the brigade's tanks, made passages across an antitank ditch, which enabled the brigade by 0930 to take the major strongpoint of Nemmersdorf, which was located on the western bank of the Angerapp River, deep in the enemy's rear. Simultaneously the brigade's 3rd Tank Battalion, pursuing the enemy that was retreating toward Gumbinnen, closed on the settlement of Wilken (5-6 kilometers south of Gumbinnen), where it was halted by the organized fire of enemy artillery and tanks. Meanwhile the remaining units of the 2nd Guards Tank Corps and 11th Guards Rifle Division initiated combat operations.

However, then General Burdeinyi made certain changes to his original plan, which soon had undesirable consequences. The point is that the 31st Guards Rifle Division that was attacking further south ran into strong opposition 3 kilometers west of the Rominte. The pace of its advance sharply slowed, and the threat arose that it would be unable to carry out its orders. Plainly concerned for his left flank, the commander of the 2nd Guards Tank Corps set the 4th Guards Tank Brigade and 4th Guards Motorized Rifle Brigade in motion to the southwest, having given them the task to take Pillkallen and Jucknischken, to smash the German units opposite the front of the 31st Guards Rifle Division, and to block the path of retreat for those of them that remained intact. Such a decision in the given case guaranteed the attacking forces of striking the enemy in the flank, but it prevented the possibility of defeating the foe in the Gumbinnen area on this day and from realizing the general plan of the army's operation.

When changing the brigades' tasks, General Burdeinyi dispersed the corps' strength and diverted the tankers from the main axis to a secondary, auxiliary axis. This weakened the strength of the attack toward Gumbinnen and led to the loss of surprise and time, which enabled the German command to organize a defense of Gumbinnen. When this decision became known to the army headquarters, the tank corps commander was ordered to pull the concerned brigades out of combat and direct them to carry out their previous assignments. However, the brigades had already become enmeshed in combat – one (the 4th Guards Tank Brigade) in the Pillkallen area, the other (the 4th Guards Motorized Rifle Brigade) in the Buylien area.

Meanwhile time was passing. I had to travel urgently to the tank corps. At its command post in Matzutkehmen, the corps chief of staff Colonel A.F. Karavan greeted me and briefed me in detail about the actions of the tankers and about the situation on the 31st Guards Rifle Division's front. The brigades had completely smashed the enemy in this area. Up to 800 Germans had killed or captured, and 7 tanks, 11 guns and 18 machine guns were destroyed. Colonel Karavan informed me that the corps commander's decision was prompted not only by the desire to help the 31st Division, but also to secure his left flank and rear from the direction of Maygunischken and Pillkallen, which was totally worrying him.

This worry was understandable to me, and I even gave thought whether or not to subordinate the 31st Guards Rifle Division to General Burdeinyi, which would give him the possibility of securing the corps' flank and rear. However, I didn't do this, concerned that such a re-subordination would burden the corps and divert its commander's attention from the main task – an attack toward Gumbinnen. Therefore, I made a different decision: to place responsibility for securing the tankers' left flank and rear on the commander of the 16th Guards Rifle Corps, and to focus all of the efforts of General A.S. Burdeinyi and the 11th Division that had been attached to him toward taking Gumbinnen. "Inform General Burdeinyi of this decision quickly," I ordered Colonel Karavan, before traveling to the command post of the 16th Guards Rifle Corps, where I gave the corresponding orders to General Gur'ev.

At 1200 on 22 October 1944, according to aerial reconnaissance reports, enemy tanks and motorized infantry had been spotted moving southward along a road from Jodzuhnen toward Walterkehmen. By this time the forward units of this German column were approaching Schmulken, where they encountered and destroyed a portion of the 2nd Guards Tank Corps' tanks. In the area of Nemmersdorf, the enemy was continuously attacking the 25th Guards Tank Brigade with tanks and panzergrenadiers, aiming to drive our units back from the western bank of the Angerapp River.

By end of day 22 October 1944 enemy mobile groups, operating from the northeast and south, reached the eastern bank of the Rominte River and fully re-captured the bridges and fords in the Walterkehmen, Samelucken and Praßlauken areas. Ten to fifteen German tanks crossed to the eastern bank of the Angerapp River in the Nemmersdorf area, and to the western bank of the Rominte River near Samelucken. The *Führer-Grenadier* Brigade, which belonged to the *Grossdeutschland* Panzer Corps, was moving to the north out of the Goldap area.

Thus, on 22 October 1944 the enemy had nearly encircled the corps' units in the area south of Gumbinnen. At 1900 on 22 October, the 2nd Guards Tank Corps adopted a strong all-round defense.

Here is how the day unfolded:

25th Guards Tank Brigade: Throughout the day and into the night of 22-23 October, the brigade's units were holding a line of defense: 3rd Tank Battalion – Wilken; 2nd Tank Battalion and motorized rifle battalion – Nemmersdorf and the bridge across the Angerapp; 1st Tank Battalion – Budweitschen with a front to the north and south, repulsing repeated enemy counterattacks made by tanks, artillery and infantry. The Germans in groups of 10-15 aircraft were bombing the brigade's combat formations repeatedly, supporting the actions of their ground units.

The enemy with infantry, supported by tanks and concentrated artillery fire repeatedly attacked the combat positions of the 2nd Tank Battalion and motorized rifle battalion, striving to drive the brigade's units out of the bridgehead on the western bank of the Angerapp River in the Nemmersdorf area. All of the German counterattacks were repulsed.

When repelling the enemy attacks on 22 October in the Nemmersdorf area, the brigade destroyed 2 German tanks, 4 guns, and killed up to 200 soldiers and officers. It also suppressed the fire of four mortar batteries. Over this same period the brigade lost one tank knocked-out; and 11 men killed and 36 wounded.

On the night of 22-23 October, on the basis of a received order, the 2nd Tank Battalion and motorized rifle battalion fell back across the Angerapp River to its eastern bank in the Nemmersdorf area, where they took up a defense in the Hill 68.5, Tutteln sector, tasked with preventing the enemy from crossing the river and to be ready to repel possible enemy attacks.

26th Guards Tank Brigade: At 1100 on 22 October, at a signal from the corps headquarters, the brigade launched an attack toward Gumbinnen with the objective of seizing the town's southern and southeastern outskirts. Overcoming stubborn fire resistance from enemy tanks and Flak artillery, the brigade pushed forward and by 1230 took Wilkoschen, and an hour later captured the patches of woods lying just 800 meters south of Gumbinnen, where it dug in on the achieved line and held it until darkness fell, driving back two enemy counterattacks.

As a result of the fighting, the brigade killed up to 150 German soldiers and officers, and destroyed four self-propelled guns, two tanks, 12 guns of various calibers, three automatic cannons, and up to 10 vehicles. Over this same period, the brigade lost 39 killed and 42 wounded; 11 T-34/85 tanks (9 destroyed and 2 knocked out), two antitank guns, four wheeled vehicles and one halftrack. By end of day 22 October 1944, the brigade had 20 combat-ready T-34/85 tanks, which were fully topped up with fuel and ammunition.

On the basis of an order from the corps commander, the brigade at 2000 on 22 October 1944 was removed from the line it occupied and by 2400 had taken up a defense on the line: isolated cottages 1 km south of Hill 52.8, Kailen, railroad 800 meters south of Wilkoschen. Over the night of 22-23 October, the brigade's men dug in their tanks and dug slit trenches for themselves.

4th Guards Tank Brigade: At 0900 on 22 October the brigade's battalion in cooperation with the 4th Guards Motorized Rifle Brigade launched an attack toward the southwestern and western sections of Gumbinnen: 2nd Tank Battalion in the direction of an isolated estate west of Hill 68.7 and Bernen; 3rd Tank Battalion in the direction of Thuren and Stannaitschen; 401st Guards Self-propelled Artillery Regiment as a pinning group on the right flank with fire from fixed positions was supporting the attacks of the tank battalions and motorized infantry.

By this time the enemy had taken up an organized defense on the southwestern outskirts of Gumbinnen, along the railroad and highway running to the west, and also had strongpoints consisting of tanks, assault guns and field artillery in the Kulligkehmen, brick factory, Wilkoschen, Thuren and Kampischkehmen areas. With a total number of up to 50-60 tanks and self-propelled guns, up to three battalions of field and anti-aircraft artillery, and up to two regiments of infantry, the Germans were putting up strong fire resistance from the front and right flank and blocking the advance of the attacking units.

The tanks of the 2nd and 3rd Tank Battalions with a methodical attack, bounding from cover to cover, kept pushing forward in the face of strong German fire, and by 1200 on 22 October took the brick factory in the Wilkoschen area, Thuren and Bernen. One company of the 2nd Tank Battalion with an impetuous attack, having brushed aside enemy covering detachments in the vicinity of the railroad station platform, cut the railroad and highway north of Bernen, where it was halted by intense enemy antitank artillery and tank fire while suffering heavy losses.

In the course of the afternoon and evening of 22 October, the 2nd and 3rd Tank Battalions, together with the motorized rifle battalion and units of the 4th Guards Motorized Rifle Brigade, held their occupied lines against incessant enemy attacks by tanks and self-propelled guns. By the end of day, the enemy, having brought up antitank reserves and tanks to the flanks of the brigade's units that had penetrated to the area of the woods west of Gumbinnen and Sabadszuhnen, intensified the attacks, supporting the counterattacks with airstrikes on the battalions' combat positions. Despite the enemy's numerical superiority in manpower and armor, the men of the 3rd Tank Battalion, 2nd Tank Battalion and motorized rifle battalion were courageously and skillfully repulsing the enemy counterattacks. In the fighting on the approaches to Gumbinnen, 12 enemy tanks and self-propelled guns were destroyed or knocked out by the tanks of the 2nd and 3rd Tank Battalions, as well as 6 anti-aircraft guns, up to two artillery batteries, and up to a battalion of infantry. Over this same time the battalions lost 8 T-34/85 tanks destroyed, one tank stuck in a swamp north of Thuren, and company commander Guards Senior Lieutenant Metel'sky's T-34/85 tank, which had deeply penetrated into the enemy's defenses and didn't return; the fate of the tank and crew is unknown.

The 1st Tank Battalion numbering 13 T-34/85 tanks and one submachine gun company (50 men), at an order from the corps commander, was sent southeastward to the Samelucken area with the task to hold the crossing sites on the Rominte River and to prevent the enemy from expanding to the west and into the rear of the 2nd Guards Tank Corps; by 1400 on 22 October, it seized the bridge across the Rominte River in the Samelucken area and held it until the end of 23 October, repulsing incessant, numerous attacks by enemy tanks, self-propelled guns and infantry supported by up to two battalions of artillery. The Germans committed 25-30 tanks, including heavy tanks, to retake the crossing site. The tankers of the 1st Tank Battalion under the command of the brigade's deputy commander Guards Major Mastashev, demonstrated exceptional heroism and courage, successfully fighting off superior enemy forces in order to retain possession of Samelucken and the crossing site there. The fighting was exceptionally bitter, going over to close-range tank combat at a distance of 150-200 meters.

In the fighting on the approaches to Gumbinnen, the tankers of the 4th Guards Tank Brigade's 2nd and 3rd Tank Battalions also distinguished themselves. Guards Senior Lieutenant Popov, having received an order to cut the highway and railroad west of Gumbinnen, made an impetuous attack while conducting concentrated fire from the tanks, and carried out his order. He himself, engaging in combat from his tank, by his personal example, led the tankers of the remaining tanks in his tank company into the battle with superior enemy forces. Popov's tank company destroyed 5 self-propelled guns, one tank, up to two batteries of artillery and two anti-aircraft guns, while killing up to 200 Nazis. Having penetrated deeply into the enemy's defenses, Guards Senior Lieutenant Popov's tank wound up encircled by German submachine gunners, but in spite of this Popov continued to direct the company and to destroy enemy manpower and weapons.

Platoon commander Guards Lieutenant Smyk of the 2nd Tank Battalion, having surged ahead, cut the highway and railroad west of Gumbinnen and led his platoon deeply into the depth of the enemy's defenses, engaging in combat on the immediate approaches to Gumbinnen. Despite the fact that the tanks of his platoon were encircled by enemy tanks from every direction, Smyk and his platoon continued to fight; after receiving an order to pull out of the battle, he managed to bring his tanks out of the encirclement, having properly organized covering fire. Wounded, he continued stay in command and direct the fighting.

Company commander Senior Lieutenant Saprykin of the 3rd Tank Battalion when taking the settlement of Skarpudchen, personally broke into this fortified knot of German resistance with his tank, destroying the enemy with fire and tracks. By his personal example Saprykin inspired the company's tankers, and thanks to the tankers audacious actions, the enemy strongpoint in the Skarpudchen area was destroyed. In this action Saprykin's company destroyed 3 enemy tanks, an anti-aircraft battery and up to a company of enemy infantry. The elimination of this strongpoint allowed the brigade's units to execute a further advance, since Sarpudchen was located on the flank and hindering a successful advance with strong flanking fire coming from that direction.

By the end of day on 22 October the enemy, with strong mobile groups of panzergrenadiers, tanks and self-propelled guns and attacks from the northeast encircled the units of the 2nd Guards Tank Corps, having cut-off the combat formations from their rear services, and was aiming to destroy the corps' units that were operating south of Gumbinnen with attacks from the west and northeast. The enemy's main panzer grouping was concentrated in the area east of Samelucken, operating to the west in the effort to seize the crossing site on the Rominte River and to emerge in the flank of the tank brigades. The 4th Guards Tank Brigade and 401st Guards Self-propelled Artillery Regiment, according to a combat order from the corps commander, with the onset of darkness on 22 October 1944 were pulled out of combat in the Wilkoschen – Thuren – Bernen area and by 2400 had taken up a defense on the Samelucken – Szameitschen line. Throughout the night of 22-23 October, the 4th Guards Tank Brigade's units fought with enemy tanks, self-propelled guns and infantry that were attacking from the northeast and east. In the sector of the 1st Tank Battalion in the Samelucken area, the enemy undertook four attacks in strength of up to 10-15 tanks and self-propelled guns and up to a battalion of infantry, supported by heavy artillery fire, striving to take the crossing site and emerge in the brigade's flank and rear. With the decisive actions of the 1st Tank Battalion's tankers and thanks to their tenacity, all of the enemy's counter-attacks were thrown back with heavy losses for the Germans.

4th Guards Motorized Rifle Brigade: From 1100 on 22 October, the brigade's 1st and 3rd Battalions launched an attack together with the tanks of the 4th Guards Tank Brigade, in the direction of the western outskirts of Gumbinnen. Overcoming stubborn enemy resistance with fire, by 1300 2200 October they reached the following line: 3rd Battalion – its 9th Company had taken the brick factory and cut the Gumbinnen – Darkehmen railroad, having seized in the process three guns; its 7th Company meanwhile was fighting in the area of the Kulligkehmen estate, where it destroyed up to two platoons of German infantry and cut up one battery. The 1st Battalion with its left flank reached the railroad at a checkpoint, engaging in intense fighting and repulsing numerous enemy attacks. Guards Lieutenant Iadykin's platoon of the 3rd Battalion was the first to break into the enemy's firing positions in the vicinity of the brick factory, wiped out an entire crew and blew up three cannons. Guards Private Lavrik stealthily crawled up to an enemy heavy machine gun and tossed grenades at it – and destroyed the machine gun and killed its crew.

The 2nd Battalion up until 1500 22 October was firmly holding its occupied line at Nemmersdorf. Over this time the enemy undertook six attacks with tanks and infantry, supported by artillery and mortar fire. The fighting was savage, at times switching over to hand-to-hand combat. At 0700 the enemy in strength of up to a regiment of infantry and 20 tanks with supporting artillery fire went on the attack. The battalion's men accepted the unequal battle and not only withstood the enemy's overwhelming forces, but also inflicted painful losses to him in personnel and tanks. The 4th Company particularly stood out while being supported by Guards Lieutenant Tupkalo's machine-gun company, which gunned down the attacking German infantry at close range. When the ammunition was exhausted, the men switched to using hand grenades. The antitank rifle company was also successfully frustrating the enemy's tank attacks. Guards Private Akhtiamov, who with his antitank rifle knocked out three tanks, three self-propelled guns and two vehicles, particularly distinguished himself. In order to reinforce the hard-pressed 2nd Battalion, a battery of the 273rd Mortar Regiment was sent to the Eszerischken area at 1300. In this fighting the enemy lost 300 soldiers and officers, three self-propelled guns, three tanks, two vehicles and 1 cannon. The battalion suffered 25 men killed and 61 wounded.

On the morning of 22 October, the enemy with tanks and infantry and an attack from the north cut our lines of communication in the area of Walterkehmen Station, thereby preventing the possibility of delivering ammunition, food and fuel and lubricants to the combat units and evacuating the wounded. All of the brigade's elements were issued strict orders to economize on fuel and placed on a very tight regimen for the expenditure of ammunition. At 1900 on 22 October, according to a combat directive from the corps headquarters, the brigade went over to a defense.

The enemy on the Point 58.4, brick factory, Thuren, Kampischkehmen, Nemmersdorf line and further to the south in the course of 22 October conducted heavy rifle and machine-gun fire, as well as artillery and mortar fire, at the combat formations of our battalions, often going over to counterattacks with tanks, self-propelled guns and infantry. The Luftwaffe in the latter half of the day was supporting the counterattacks and bombing the combat positions of the brigade. As a result of extremely bitter fighting and repulsing the enemy counterattacks, over 22 October the brigade had the following casualties: 57 men (including 3 officers) killed, and 200 men (including 9 officers) wounded. One 57mm gun, 2 heavy machine guns, 3 RPD machine guns, 18 rifles and 25 submachine guns were destroyed. At 1600 on 22 October, according to a verbal order, the 1st Battalion was removed from it occupied line in the Kuttkuschen – Stulgen area and re-assembled in the wooded area south of Plicken, in readiness aboard vehicles to operate in any direction; however, it was subsequently returned to its defensive area with the aim of forestalling an enemy attack to the south with infantry and tanks. At 2030 the 1st Battalion was occupying a defense and had dug in, ready to repulse the enemy attack.

The **401st Guards Self-propelled Artillery Regiment** from 0600 22 October, together with the attached battalion from the 4th Guards Motorized Rifle Brigade, took up firing positions in the Kattkuhnen – Wilken area, with the assignment from the start of the Soviet attacks to cover the boundary between the 26th Guards Tank Brigade and 4th Guards Tank Brigade, while simultaneously attacking toward the southern outskirts of Gumbinnen. On the evening of 22 October, the regiment, pursuant to a verbal order from the commander of the 4th Guards Tank Brigade, took up a defense in the sector of an intersection of paved roads and a dirt road 200 meters west of Nestoskehmen – Augstupönen, having the task to prevent the enemy from crossing the Rominte River. In the fighting near Gumbinnen, two of the regiment's SU-85 self-propelled guns were knocked out, but they were put back into service by the regiment's own men the very next day.

The **1500th Self-propelled Artillery Regiment** from the morning of 22 October was occupying firing positions on the northern outskirts of Stulgen; together with one battalion of the 4th Guards Motorized Rifle Brigade and taking advantage of the poor visibility (the dense fog), by 1000 it had reached the area north of Thuren, where it took up positions in readiness to operate to the northeast, securing the right flank of the 4th Guards Motorized Brigade's 1st Battalion that was attacking toward the southwestern outskirts of Gumbinnen, and to cooperate with the 4th Guards Motorized Rifle Brigade's 3rd Battalion, that was attacking toward the southern outskirts of Gumbinnen. In this fighting the self-propelled gun crew under the command of Junior Lieutenant Andrianov distinguished itself; having arrived in the area north of the cemetery in Thuren and under the heavy direct fire of guns and rifle and machine gun fire, in these difficult conditions it superbly maneuvered on the battlefield and with the fire of their gun destroyed two German anti-aircraft guns, one antitank gun, one machine gun and killed up to 30 Nazis. Being wounded and without his gunner, Lieutenant Andrianov continued to fire, and only after being severely wounded was he extracted from his burning self-propelled gun and carried off the battlefield under heavy enemy fire. The regiment's deputy political commander Major Bogoliubov, deputy combat commander Captain Dakhno and assistant chief of staff Senior Lieutenant Shchukin all distinguished themselves; they were located up among the batteries' combat positions and were directly organizing the combat. The 3rd Battery commander Captain Bushuev and 4th Battery commander Senior Lieutenant Zhikharev also stood out in the fighting. In difficult conditions and at the tensest moment of the battle, under heavy artillery and mortar fire, they calmly by their own example encouraged the men to do their duties, properly organized reconnaissance, and took direct part in it.

Over the day of fighting on 22 October 1944, the enemy had the following losses: 26 tanks, 3 self-propelled guns, 6 halftracks, 4 mortar batteries, and 2 artillery batteries destroyed, and more than 1,000 soldiers and officers killed. In return, the corps' losses amounted to 13 T-34/85 tanks destroyed, 3 knocked out and 4 stuck in a swamp; and 1 SU-76 and 2 SU-85 knocked out. Casualties were 40 men killed and 110 wounded.

By the end of day 22 October, the 2nd Guards Tank Corps had 98 T-34/85 tanks operational (27 in the 4th Guards Tank Brigade; 40 in the 25th Guards Tank Brigade; and 19 in the 26th Guards Tank Brigade). The 401st Guards Self-propelled Artillery Regiment had 17 operational SU-85, while the 1500th Self-propelled Artillery Regiment had 13 SU-76. The corps' supply situation was 0.7 refills of fuel and lubricants, 1 day of a standard combat load, 3 days' worth of rations.

Table 2.11: Status of the armored fighting vehicles of the German Fourth Army on 22 October 1944

Formations and units	Combat materiel				Knocked-out materiel			Total
	StuG	Tanks	Sf	sPak mot Z	Short-term	Long-term	Destroyed	
LV Armee Korps								
28.Jäger Division	-	-	-	7	-	-	-	7
Panzerjäger Kp. 1028	9	-	-	-	1	-	-	10
StuG Brigade 259	39	-	-	-	1	3	-	43
562.Volksgrenadier Division	-	-	-	9	-	-	-	9
Fest. Pak Kp. 10	-	-	-	(5)	-	-	-	(5)
Fest. Pak Kp. 17	-	-	-	(12)	-	-	-	(12)
Total for LV Korps:	48	-	-	16 (17)	2	3	-	69 (17)
VI Armee Korps								
203 Sicherungs Division	-	-	-	5	-	-	-	5
3 Kp./Panzer Abt. 118	8	-	-	-	1	-	-	9
50.Infanterie Division	-	-	-	15	1	-	-	16
Panzerjäger Kp. 1150	9	-	-	-	1	-	-	10
4 Bat., StuG Lehr Brigade 920	8	-	-	-	-	1	-	9
Kampfgruppe "Hannibal"	-	-	-	1	1	-	-	2
3 Kp./Jagdpanzer Abt. 69	7	-	-	-	2	-	-	9
Fest. Pak Kp.	-	-	-	(12)	(2)	-	-	(14)
Total for VI Korps:	32	-	-	21 (12)	6 (2)	1	-	60 (14)
XXXXI Panzer Korps								
Kavallerie Brigade 4 (mot.)	-	-	-	6	-	-	-	6
Jagdpz. Abt. 69 (- 2 and 3 Kp.)	4	-	-	-	3	7	-	14
StuG Abt. 1558	3	-	-	-	-	-	-	3
170.Infanterie Division	-	-	-	9	2	3	-	14

Formations and units	Combat materiel				Knocked-out materiel			Total
	StuG	Tanks	Sf	sPak mot Z	Short-term	Long-term	Destroyed	
Panzerjäger Kp. 1240	6	-	-	-	-	-	-	6
sPanzerjäger Abt. 1057	-	-	-	6	3	4	-	13
131.Infanterie Division	-	-	-	15	1	-	-	16
Panzerjäger Kp. 1131	4	-	-	-	2	2	-	8
367.Infanterie Division	-	-	-	15	1	-	-	16
Panzerjäger Kp. 1367	6	-	-	-	1	-	-	7
Fest. Pak Kp.	-	-	-	(12)	-	-	-	(12)
Total for XXXXI Panzer Korps:	23	-	-	51 (12)	13	16	-	103 (12)
XXVI Armee Korps								
561.Volksgrenadier Division	-	-	-	2	-	-	-	2
Jagdpanzer Abt. 170	9	-	-	-	-	-	-	9
Panzer Brigade 102	4	2 (V)	-	-	-	-	-	6
Panzer Brigade 103	5	2 (V)	-	-	-	-	-	7
549.Volksgrenadier Division	-	-	-	5	-	-	-	5
StuG Abt. 1549	2	-	-	-	2	3	-	7
1 Kp., sJagdpanzer Abt. 665	-	-	-	3 (88)	-	-	-	3
3 Bat., StuG Abt. 203	6	-	-	-	2	-	-	8
Panzerjäger Kp. 1349	10	-	-	-	-	-	-	10
Panzer Abt. 118 (- 3 Kp.)	12	-	-	-	10	11	-	33
Panzerjäger Kp. 1156	2	-	-	-	2	3	-	7
StuG Brigade 276	8	-	-	-	6	8	-	22
sPanzerjäger Abt. 1065	-	-	-	6	1	-	-	7
Jagdpanzer Abt. 92	6	-	-	-	10	4	-	20
4 Kp., Panzer Abt. 21	-	10 (IV)	-	-	1	3	-	14
sPanzer Abt. 302	17	-	-	-	5	8	-	30
Panzer Abt. 2101, Panzer Brigade 101	-	10 (V)	-	-	1	-	-	11
Panzerjäger Kp. 42	-	-	10	-	4	-	-	14
1.Infanterie Division	-	-	-	2	1	1	-	4
Aufklär. Abt., 1.Infanterie Div.	-	-	-	1	1	-	?	2
Panzerjäger Kp. 1001	5	-	-	-	5	-	-	10
StuG Brigade 277	17	-	-	-	2	10	-	29
56.Infanterie Division	-	-	-	11	3	-	-	14
Panzerjäger Kp. 1349	-	-	-	6	1	-	-	7
Pionier Kp. 2, 644 Bn.	-	-	-	3	-	-	-	3
Panzerjäger Kp. 1156	3	-	-	-	-	-	-	3
Fest. Pak Kp. 6	-	-	-	(2)	-	-	1	(2)
Fest. Pak Kp. 11	-	-	-	(10)	-	-	-	(10)
Fest. Pak Kp. 5	-	-	-	(9)	-	(1)	-	(9)
Fest. Pak Kp. 9	-	-	-	(7)	-	-	-	(7)
Total for the XXVI Korps:	106	24	11	38 (28)	56	52	3	287 (29)
XXVII Army Corps								
StuG Abt. 1547	3	-	-	-	-	-	-	3

Formations and units	Combat materiel				Knocked-out materiel			Total
	StuG	Tanks	Sf	sPak mot Z	Short-term	Long-term	Destroyed	
StuG Brigade 279	10	-	-	-	4	5	14	19
Panzer Brigade *Führer Grenadier*	-	32 (V)	-	-	5	-	-	37
	-	5 (IV)	-	-	-	-	-	5
	12	-	-	-	-	-	-	12
	-	-	-	4	-	-	-	4
Korps *Hermann Göring*	-	-	-	24	-	-	-	24
	-	20 (IV)	-	-	-	-	-	20
	-	47 (V)	-	-	-	9	-	56
Panzerjäger Kp. 1023	10	-	-	-	-	-	-	10
Total for the XXVII Korps:	35	104	-	28	9	14	14	190
Total for the Fourth Army:	244	128	11	154 (69)	86	86 (1)	17	709 (70)

Note: The parenthesized numbers represent captured Soviet 76mm guns. The "sPak mot Z" means schwere Panzerabwehrkanone motorisiert mit Zugmaschine, or Heavy Anti-tank Gun with motorized tow.

Table 2.12: Report on the status and losses of tanks, assault and self-propelled guns in the units and formations of the German Fourth Army over the period from 16 October to 23 October 1944

Formations	Combat-ready on 15 October 1944		Combat-ready on 23 October 1944		Losses over 21-23 October 1944				Irrecoverable losses between 15 and 23 October 1944	
	StuG	Tanks	StuG	Tanks	StuG In repair	StuG Irrecoverably lost	Tanks In repair	Tanks Irrecoverably lost	StuG	Tanks
LV AK	56	-	47	-	6	-	-	-	-	-
VI AK	25	-	33	-	4	-	-	-	6	-
XXXXI PzK	60	-	25	-	17	-	-	-	6	-
XXVII AK	112	49	23	32	15	-	5	-	24	1
Korps *HG*	-	-	34	40	3	-	-	-	-	-
XXVI AK	59	-	111	22	105	-	8	-	9	-
Total:	312	49	273	94	150	-	13	-	48	1

From the memoirs of Colonel General of Tank Forces A.S. Burdeinyi:

Carrying out these persistent demands [from the commander of the 11th Guards Army], I decided with the main forces – two brigades – to outflank the town to the west and from there to launch an attack from west to east, while with one brigade (the 26th Guards Tank Brigade) and the approaching units of the 11th Guards Rifle Division to launch an attack from the east. The brigades were given the following tasks: 26th Guards Tank Brigade and the arriving units of the 11th Guards Rifle Division were to attack toward the eastern outskirts of Gumbinnen and take it. The 4th Guards Tank Brigade and 4th Guards Motorized Rifle Brigade were to outflank Gumbinnen from the west, cut the railroad and highway to the west of the town, and take the town's western outskirts. The corps' artillery units (the 28th Guards Mortar Battalion and the approaching artillery of the 11th Guards Rifle Division) would support the brigades' attack. The arriving rifle units and elements of this division would take part in the attack. The attack was set for 1000 after a 15-minute artillery barrage. I asked the army headquarters to launch a powerful attack by bomber aircraft in the period between 0930 and 1000 on 22 October.

At the designated time, the corps' units went on the attack. We watched from an observation post (a nameless hill north of Panken) as the tank brigades entered combat with tank riders aboard toward the eastern and western outskirts of Gumbinnen. The 26th Guards Tank Brigade together with rifle elements of the 11th Guards Rifle Division attacked the enemy's outer ring of defensive works around Gumbinnen, destroyed the enemy defending here, and neared the eastern outskirts of the town. Here they ran into heavy antitank fire, as a result of which several tanks were lost and the attack came to a stop. At this moment the enemy launched a counterattack, but it in turn was halted by the tankers of the 26th Guards Tank Brigade. Tanks from one side and the other were burning, and movement came to a stop. Later it turned out that the brigade had encountered arriving units of the *Hermann Göring* Panzer Division, which had reached the Gumbinnen area not long before this.

A tank duel went on over the entire day of 22 October on this axis, with no progress made by either side. The Guardsmen of the 26th Tank Brigade burned with the desire to break into the town of Gumbinnen and were showing both courage and tenacity. The evening before, operating as part of the lead battalion, which was being temporarily commanded by Captain D.S. Sysoev (Major I.F. Lolenko had received his next wound), a tank platoon commander of the 2nd Tank Battalion Junior Lieutenant Iu.N. Malakhov broke into the enemy's forward edge of defense southeast of Gumbinnen and wound up in midst of hostile tanks. With the first shots, two Panther tanks were set ablaze by Malakhov. The other two tanks of his platoon were also engaging the enemy tanks. At the very height of the battle, an enemy shell struck the tank of the valiant commander and set it ablaze. Malakhov and his crew refused to abandon the tank, and they fired more intensively at the enemy tanks. Malakhov set another enemy tank ablaze. A second German shell, apparently, struck the ammunition compartment of Malakhov's tank – it blew up, together with the crew. Closely around Iuria Malakhov's tank were three burned-out enemy tanks, two smashed antitank guns and a large number of fascist dead.

That is how heroes fought in the war years. Demonstrating heroism, they didn't even think that this was heroism, and went into battle and died not for high honors and decorations, about which they would no longer be able to find out about. They went into battle for duty and at the call of their Motherland, in the name of victory over the foe, dedicated to its honor and freedom. The people will remember and honor their names forever. Guards Junior Lieutenant Iurii Nikolaevich Malakhov was awarded the Motherland's highest honor – Hero of the Soviet Union (posthumously), and the members of his crew were posthumously decorated with Orders. In the brigade, one of the tanks acquired the honorific title "Iurii Malakhov", and it was entrusted to the brigade's top crew.

No less heavy fighting went on as well in the sector of the 4th Guards Tank Brigade and 4th Guards Motorized Rifle Brigade. Outflanking Gumbinnen to the west through Thuren and Bernen (3-5 kilometers southwest and west of the town), the 4th Guards Tank Brigade by 1200 on 22 October had cut the highway and railroad west of Gumbinnen. Here on the approaches to Gumbinnen, the brigade destroyed up to 15 enemy tanks, several enemy antitank batteries, and killed a large number of soldiers and officers. It was impossible to suppress the enemy fire, coming from the stone buildings, with machine-gun fire from the tanks and the fire of one artillery battalion. Having assembled a large group of tanks, infantry and artillery here, the enemy was putting up stiff resistance to us, and having lost approximate ten tanks here, the brigade was forced to stop the attack. Later it became clear that units of *Hermann Göring* and the 5th Panzer Division had arrived in this area on this day from the north and northeast.

At the peak of the fighting for Gumbinnen, it became known to me that the enemy in strength of more than 100 tanks with accompanying panzergrenadiers, supported by active operations of the Luftwaffe, had launched an attack against the right flank of the 11th Guards Army's units out of the Sadweitschen area (5-7 kilometers east of Gumbinnen) and was exploiting the attack along the eastern bank of the Rominte River in the direction of Walterkehmen. Our supplies of fuel, ammunition and food, and the evacuation of wounded, ran through this village. In my reserve there was only a single tank battalion (the 1st Tank Battalion) of the 4th Guards Tank Brigade, which was being temporarily commanded by Major I.V. Mastashev in place of the tank battalion's regular commander Major T.P. Davydov, who'd been killed the evening before. The battalion and a submachine gun platoon had halted the evening before (21 October) in the vicinity of the bridge near Walterkehmen with the task to guard the bridge from possible enemy saboteurs until being relieved by approaching rifle troops. On the approach to Walterkehmen the enemy tanks fired at our rear elements, set several trucks ablaze, and our line of communications with the rear was closed. The tankers of the 1st Tank Battalion, having spotted the enemy tanks that were approaching from the north and northeast along the eastern bank of the Rominte River, engaged them and set ablaze several enemy tanks. The enemy was on the eastern bank of the river, and we were on the opposite bank. The corps' troops wound up in the interval of land between the Rominte and Angerapp Rivers, isolated from the forces of the 11th Guards Army. In the course of 22 and 23 October, the tankers repulsed all of the enemy's attacks and didn't allow the enemy to split the corps into pieces, but suffered heavy losses, primarily from constant airstrikes. In one of the aerial attacks, the deputy commander of the 4th Guards Tank Brigade Major N.V. Mastashov was mortally wounded. Having learned of the battalion's heavy losses, the commander of the 4th Guards Tank Brigade Colonel O.A. Losik urgently sent a reinforced tank detachment to the area of the 1st Tank Battalion's fighting, which enabled the bridge in the Walterkehmen area to be held until 23 October.

The difficult situation in which the tank corps was located was being reported to the headquarters of the 11th Guards Army and the headquarters of the Front's armored and mechanized forces. Requests went out to hasten the movement of rifle forces into the area between the Rominte and Angerapp Rivers, but for some totally incomprehensible reasons the army headquarters kept doubting that the tank corps was engaged in combat in the Gumbinnen area for a long time, and often asked where I and my operational command group was, and where the brigades were. Possibly, this is explained by the fact that the 31st Guards Division, having received a new order, marched away to the southwest and lost contact with us, while the units of the 8th Guards Rifle Corps that were approaching the Rominte River bumped into the enemy, which had penetrated to the Walterkehmen from the north, in the vicinity of this village, and of course reported what they had seen, namely: "The enemy is located on the eastern bank of the Rominte River, and there are none of our tanks here whatsoever." Whether everything happened this way or not, in the war anything took place, especially when command and control over the troops was disrupted even for a short period.

During the period of our actions west of the Rominte, the Front's deputy commander of the armored and mechanized forces Major General G.N. Utkin was always located in the operational command group of the corps headquarters. He was confirming our messages, and the Front headquarters knew the situation on our axis, at a time when neither the commander of the 16th Guards Rifle Corps nor any of his representatives were with us. Apparently, this was the reason why the army headquarters had little knowledge of the situation in our offensive sector. On this day the enemy intensified the attacks from every direction. Apparently, he'd been given the objective of encircling our forces between the Rominte and Angerapp Rivers and to restore the situation at least along the Rominte River. In order to achieve this objective, the Germans committed significant forces into the fighting: Parachute-Panzer Corps *Hermann Göring*'s 1st and

2nd Parachute-Panzergrenadier Regiments and 1st Panzer Division, the 5th Panzer Division, the *Führer* Panzer Brigade, and other units, which had been transferred to our offensive sector from other sectors of the front. The fighting flared up with renewed strength. Making use of the terrain, the tank and motorized rifle brigades, maneuvering with fire and shifts in position, were repulsing the enemy attacks. We were simply not in the condition to prepare or take up some specific line of defense, much less to dig the tanks and infantry into the earth. Moreover, the task before remained active – on the morning of 23 October to resume the offensive and to take Gumbinnen.

The 25th Guards Tank Brigade was engaged in very heavy fighting in the Nemmersdorf area. Having brought up significant forces, the enemy again attempted to drive the brigade out of its bridgehead on the Angerapp River and to regain his positions in the Nemmersdorf area, but the tankers, artillerymen and motorized rifle elements demonstrated their high level of training and tenacity, and each time inflicted heavy losses on the enemy and fought off the attacks. The Luftwaffe was particularly bothering us during operational hours, but even it was unable to do anything with the stubbornness and tenacity of our troops. The tankers, and especially the Guardsmen of the motorized rifle companies, took advantage of the foe's prepared defensive positions that had been seized by us, ducked into shelters during bombing runs, and then returned to their fighting positions as soon as the enemy aircraft flew away.

I will cite the example of an antitank rifle man of the 4th Guards Motorized Rifle Brigade's 2nd Motorized Rifle Battalion Guards Private Sabir Akhtiamov as a model of the courage and high combat discipline of the defenders. Early on the morning of 23 October, the enemy again went on the offensive against our defenses. Two tanks and up to a platoon of infantry that had materialized out of the fog were advancing directly toward Sabir. Having allowed them to approach to close range, the valiant Guardsman with an accurate shot from his antitank rifle set an enemy tank ablaze, but the second tank kept coming. Not a single muscle of the brave antitank rifleman quivered. Having reloaded the weapon, with his following two shots he set the second tank on fire. The crew that leaped out of the tank was immediately shot down by submachine gunners. Over the two and a half days in fighting in the bridgehead, he destroyed 2 tanks, 3 self-propelled guns, 2 halftracks and several vehicles.

From the recollections of Hero of the Soviet Union Sabir Akhtiamov:

With the start of the Great Patriotic War, my father was called up to the front. He left me, a 15-year-old adolescent and the oldest of eight children, as the senior blacksmith. In the fall of 1943, we received word about my father's heroic death near Smolensk. I swore to take revenge for my father against the fascist aggressors, as well as for several other of my fellow townsmen, whose lives had been pitilessly interrupted by the war.

At the beginning of November 1943, I was already in the ranks of the Red Army. So, I had swapped my blacksmith's tools for an antitank rifle.

With the passage of time I became an accurate marksman with the antitank rifle, serving in the 4th Guards Motorized Rifle Brigade of the 2nd Guards Tank Corps. As part of this brigade, which was in the 3rd Belorussian Front, I traveled a long combat path from Smolensk (where my father had been killed) all the way to Königsberg. I took part in the liberation of Belorussia, the Baltic republics, and in the fighting in East Prussia.

In October 1944 we reached the village of Nemmersdorf. Our 2nd Battalion received an order to take this point from the march together with the tanks, and to hold our occupied positions until receipt of a special order. A strong enemy firing position was checking our advance. Together with my No. 2, Junior Sergeant Lukovkin, we received an order to destroy this firing position. Under a hurricane of enemy fire, we approached to within 50-70 meters of the target at a crawl, and realized that we would fail in our mission if we resorted only to grenades. It was impossible to get any closer to the enemy and remain concealed.

My gaze stopped on an object, which looked like a fuel tank, that was sitting on the edge of the position. With several shots I managed to set it ablaze. The burning fuel penetrated into a self-propelled gun that had been dug into the ground. Its on-board shells began to explode. Our soldiers with the cry "Ura-a-a!" rushed the enemy's positions. That night this village switched to our possession.

Soon an enemy infantry company launched a reconnaissance-in-force. Our team destroyed two more self-propelled guns. At sunrise, a swarm of enemy tanks and infantry launched a counterattack. When 150-200 meters was left between our position and the enemy tanks, we opened fire. I managed to damage a tank on the left flank. Then we damaged the tracks on a second tank, and with several more shots, the machine burst into flames. A third tank rolled right up to trench parapet; we crept to a position right behind it and shot it at point-blank range.

Our artillerymen destroyed many more tanks. The machine gunners and riflemen cut the infantry off from the tanks. The attack ceased. The fascists retreated. Two days of fighting ended in complete victory for the Guardsmen. For this action I was in fact awarded the title Hero of the Soviet Union – at 18 years of age. They decorated my combat comrade Lukovkin posthumously; he was killed in one of the subsequent battles.

During the second offensive into East Prussia, I managed to destroy two heavy tanks – Panthers – and for this I was awarded with the Order of the Red Banner. I fought right up to the end of the war. I was wounded. On 24 June 1945 I took part in the Victory Parade. On the following day the country's leadership received the parade's participants in the Kremlin.

The commendation for Sabir Akhtiamov's Hero of the Soviet Union title reads:

SABIR AKHTIAMOV – an antitank rifleman of the 4th Guards Motorized Rifle Brigade, a Guards private. In the fighting in East Prussia in October 1944, during the assault on the strongly fortified point of Nemmersdorf he knocked out one tank, three self-propelled guns, two halftracks and two trucks loaded with shells from his anti-tank rifle. For the model fulfillment of the command's combat tasks, awarded the title Hero of the Soviet Union.

Hero of the Soviet Union Sabir Akhtiamov in a firing position. East Prussia, October 1944.

From the memoirs of the commander of the 11th Guards Army General K.N. Galitsky:

On the morning of 22 October, the cloudy weather and fog were restricting visibility. Aircraft could not operate. At first it seemed sensible to postpone the offensive; the weather forecasters were promising better weather later that day, no earlier than 1300. Such a delay with the attack was plainly not in our favor, because it would exclude one of the main conditions that would ensure success – the element of surprise. After a short thought I made the decision to resume the attack toward Gumbinnen at 0900, as was foreseen by the plan.

A totally short artillery preparation preceded the attack toward Gumbinnen, which was counting on the element of surprise. We assumed that the element of surprise and decisive and impetuous actions by the units of the 2nd Guards Tank Corps, which had 158 tanks and 39 self-propelled guns, and by the units of the 11th Guards Rifle Division would demoralize the enemy and secure success for the Guardsmen.

The 16th Guards Rifle Corps initiated the attack in two directions. Its 31st Guards Rifle Division, securing the actions of General Burdeinyi's tankers from the south, was attacking to the west, having the mission to force a crossing of the Angerapp River and dig in on its left bank (south of Nemmersdorf). The 1st and 16th Guards Rifle Divisions, which jumped off on the attack from the Schwiegseln – Gaidzen line (a front of 14-16 kilometers) in the general direction of Groß Trakehnen, were covering the army's right flank in the event of possible German counterattacks by infantry and tanks from the north. It was indicated to the corps commander to pay particular attention to antitank defense.

When taking this decision, we anticipated that the fighting would be quite intense, and moreover on certain directions the possibility of meeting engagements could not be excluded. It was necessary to be ready for any surprises. In connection with the fact that the 2nd Guards Tank Corps' frontal attack on the day before hadn't brought about any positive results, General Burdeinyi decided to outflank Gumbinnen from the west and thereby deprive the enemy of the possibility to bring reserves up to the town, and then to take Gumbinnen with a simultaneous attack from the west and southeast. With this aim he ordered the 4th Guards Tank and 4th Guards Motorized Rifle Brigades to cut the railroad and highway in the Bernen and Stannaitschen areas first, and subsequently, developing the attack in the eastern direction, to take the western section of Gumbinnen. The 26th Guards Tank Brigade, in cooperation with the 11th Guards Rifle Division, attacking to the northwest, was to take the eastern portion of Gumbinnen, while the 25th Guards Tank Brigade was to keep a tight grip on the line on the western bank of the Angerapp River in the Nemmersdorf area.

Air support for the combat operations of the 2nd Guards Tank Corps rested on two bomber aviation divisions (the 6th and 276th) and one ground attack aviation division (the 1st). They were to launch airstrikes in two phases – during the preparation for the attack and at the moment of the direct assault on the town. Thus, the success of the attack toward Gumbinnen would be achieved by the unexpectedness of the attack without a lengthy artillery preparation. All of this depended on suppressing the enemy's defenses with aircraft and the rapidly unfolding combat operations of the tank brigades and of the 11th Guards Division.

By 22 October the enemy had fully taken up the defensive fortifications with arriving units of *Hermann Göring*'s 2nd Parachute-Panzergrenadier Division. The first attacks of our units were met by intense artillery and mortar fire from out of Guminnen's fortified positions. The attempts by the 11th Guards Division and 26th Guards Tank Brigade to advance had no success. Repulsing the attack, the German units launched counterattacks, striving to drive the Guardsmen from the line they occupied. In the center of the 2nd Guards Tank Corps's formation, the 4th Guards Tank and 4th Guards Motorized Rifle Brigades, supported by artillery and mortar fire, advanced to the southwestern outskirts of Gumbinnen in bitter fighting. Meanwhile, to the east the right-flank divisions of the 16th Guards Rifle Corps (the 1st and 16th Guards Rifle Divisions) with stubborn fighting made an advance of just 800 – 1,500 meters toward Groß Trakehnen.

Starting from this time, the situation on the front of the 11th Guards Army sharply deteriorated. The German command, assembling two shock groupings on the flanks of the army's central grouping, launched a powerful counterblow, striving to reach the line of the Rominte

River at Walterkehmen in order to isolate the divisions of the 11th Guards Army and brigades of the 2nd Guards Tank Corps and then to destroy them, thereby liquidating the salient reaching toward Gumbinnen. These shock groupings were created out of *Hermann Göring*'s 2nd Parachute-Panzergrenadier Division, the 5th Panzer Division, the 61st Infantry Division, and the *Führer* Panzergrenadier Brigade. The grouping, assembled east of Gumbinnen consisted of more than 40 tanks and was supposed to launch an attack from the north at the boundary between the 11th Guards and 16th Guards Divisions in the general direction of Walterkehmen, while the grouping in the area north of Goldap, which had 60-80 tanks, attacked from south to north.

The grouping of the *Hermann Göring* 1st Parachute-Panzer Division and Panzer Brigade 102, which was assembled in the Groß Trakehnen area in order to reinforce the German Stallupönen grouping, essentially comprised a third shock grouping. It had 60 tanks. In order to support the ground forces, the German command assembled a lot of air strength on the nearest airfields to Gumbinnen. Just the designations of the German formations speak to their combat qualities. The *Führer* Brigade, according to prisoner testimony, had been formed out of units of Panzer Division *Grossdeutschland*. The 5th Panzer Division had a lot of combat experience.

Unquestionably realizing that the Nazis would resist furiously and even counterattack our troops in order to retain possession of Gumbinnen, I considered it necessary to reinforce the 2nd Guards Tank Corps with one more rifle division and to focus its main efforts toward assaulting Gumbinnen. The decision of the Front commander-in-chief, in our view, fully corresponded to the situation as it existed at the front at that time. The capture of Gumbinnen would place the adversary's Stallupönen grouping in an extremely precarious situation – the forces of the 5th and 28th Armies might encircle and destroy it.

Did we really have the possibility to implement the designated plan? Yes, unquestionably so. At this time, the 2nd Guards Tank Corps and 11th [Guards Rifle] Division, as has been already stated, were fighting on the outskirts of Gumbinnen and had been directed to take it. The thrust of the enemy's two panzer groupings from the north and the south in the direction of Walterkehmen could not interfere with the capture of Gumbinnen. Accordingly, the army's objective – to take Gumbinnen – was fully realistic. By this time the 28th Army possessed even more significant forces, and if necessary it could reinforce the attack of the 11th Guards Army's central grouping at the expense of its formations.

As a result of the defeat that the Nazis suffered at the outset of the operation, especially by 22 October their strength had been significantly weakened, and their morale had been totally undermined. In contrast, the troops of our army, despite the difficult and bitter fighting, had preserved their combat capabilities. The army had an adequate number of tanks, self-propelled guns and artillery. It was being actively supported by the 1st Air Army and a number of artillery units that had been attached to us as reinforcements. In order to destroy the German tanks and panzergrenadiers that had surged forward on the army's flanks, it wasn't necessary to bring the army's offensive operations to a halt.

Having issued the orders to the corps, I remained in army's observation post in Kaszelehken. It was necessary to put the final touches to the organization of the troops' combat actions and the cooperation of the tank corps with the air force and infantry. One more question arose that was totally unexpected: Keeping the 2nd Guards Tank Corps supplied with ammunition. Between the eighth and ninth hours of the evening, General Burdeinyi reported that according to his information, the enemy, having taken Walterkehmen, had cut his line of communications and he was short on ammunition. Thus, he requested that aircraft deliver ammunition. Such a situation, of course, couldn't help but alarm a corps commander. Apparently, General Burdeinyi didn't know that our 83rd Rifle Division was in fact holding our line of communications in the Walterkehmen area.

At 2200 a new message arrived: "To the commander of the 11th Guards Army. The units' situation is difficult. The enemy has taken Samelucken and Walterkehmen and is attacking me in the rear. I request that you hasten the movement of field units to the indicated area and to protect my right flank. I am with my operational command group in Dauginten. BURDEINYI." Since prior to this message I'd received no alarming information with respect to this, I was surprised, and immediately wrote down on a blank message form: "To the Army Chief of Staff: Ask Burdeinyi why this message was sent only at 20.20, since prior to this time there'd been no messages about this. GALITSKY, 22 October, 22.10." Then I immediately directed the Army's operations chief to check the disposition of the forces in this area.

The additional check indicated that the situation remained unchanged in the Walterkehmen area. The 83rd Division was not only holding its occupied positions, but according to report from its chief of staff Colonel I.P. Kosenko, with a portion of its strength it was continuing to attack to the north. The 11th Division was securely holding its positions in the Samelucken area. What had prompted this, at first glance, premature reaction by the commander of the 2nd Guards Tank Corps regarding the existing situation? Obviously, the complexity of the situation could not help but raise the concern of even such a strong-willed commander as General Burdeinyi.

Around 22.30 on 22 October, my chief of staff General I.I. Semenov, who was located with the rest of the headquarters staff at the army's command post in Martischken, reported that a preliminary directive from the Front's chief of staff had arrived about going over to the defensive and about withdrawing the central grouping out of the Gumbinnen area to the eastern bank of the Rominte River. He also announced that the Front commander-in-chief was on his way to visit us. "The Commander-in-Chief requests," said Semenov, "that you be present upon his arrival at the command post."

Wasting no time, I drove to Martischken. Soon the Front commander-in-chief General of the Army I.D. Cherniakhovsky and Front Military Council member Lieutenant General V.E. Makarov arrived. Having heard my short briefing on the situation, Cherniakhovsky expressed the opinion that plainly the 11th Guards Army would have to go over to a defense. This decision of his flowed out of the overall situation that now existed in the sector of the 3rd Belorussian Front, and especially from the fact that the left-flank forces of the 1st Baltic Front (2nd Guards Army), after mopping up the northern bank of the Nieman River of the enemy, had no further success.

The events arising from the German breakthrough in the direction of Walterkehmen drew General Cherniakhovsky's particular attention. Having pulled out a map and having indicated the directions of the enemy's tank attacks that were marked on it, he said: "The Germans, according to our information, have brought up one tank and two infantry divisions to the Gumbinnen area, and one tank division to the area east of Darkehmen. Up to 200 tanks and assault guns took part in the counterattacks from the Gumbinnen – Groβ Trakehnen – Stallupönen line, and up to 100 tanks and assault guns from the areas northeast of Darkehmen and Goldap, for a total of 300 armored fighting vehicles with infantry. On the other hand, Burdeinyi has 98 tanks and 30 self-propelled guns. The correlation is plainly disadvantageous.

Apparently, the Front's intelligence had reported exaggerated information on the enemy's numbers to General Cherniakhovsky. According to our information, which was immediately presented to the commander-in-chief, the Germans had no more than 180-200 armored fighting vehicles, of which more than 90 had been knocked out or destroyed in the course of the present day. Of course, the process of gathering intelligence and revealing the enemy's grouping is complex. However here, according to my deep conviction, mistakes had been made in assessing the enemy's strength.

Possibly, Ivan Danilovich was somewhat overrating the enemy's progress and the fact itself of his breakthrough in the direction of Walterkehmen. Therefore, having heard him out, I remarked that the actions undertaken by the Germans were, in my view, their last attempt to thwart our offensive into the interior of East Prussia, and that after the losses the Germans had taken and the exhaustion of reserves, they hardly had adequate strength and means in order to encircle and destroy our central grouping. After all it was no coincidence that our neighbors were making certain progress: the 28th Army – with one corps (3rd Guards Corps) about 5 kilometers, and the 31st Army – up to 4 kilometers.

"We are deeply convinced," I reported to the Front commander-in-chief, "that in the next day or two the situation on the army's front will be restored, and the enemy that has broken through will be partially destroyed, and partially hurled back. This task can be resolved simultaneously with the main task standing before the army – the seizure of Gumbinnen and the arrival on the Angerapp River. Moreover, the tactical situation of these German groupings is quite unfavorable for the enemy; they themselves have wound up isolated and are located, essentially, in semi-encirclement."

Member of the army's Military Council General P.N. Kulikov and the chief of staff General I.I. Semenov were supporting me. For a certain time, General I.D. Cherniakhovsky remained unyielding, but then, considering our persistent request, agreed with continuation of the offensive on the army's flanks, but ordered to go over to a defense on the sector of the 2nd Guards Tank Corps in the Gumbinnen area.

"You are asking to leave the units of the 2nd Guards Tank Corps and the army's rifle divisions in the Gumbinnen area and on the line of the Angerapp River, but to attack with the divisions of the 16th and 36th Rifle Corps on the army's flanks," Military Council member General Makarov said to General Kulikov; "This might create a complex situation. The men might not understand it. Doubts might arise. Therefore, send members of the army's Political Department to the tank corps' units and to the rifle divisions – the 11th, 31st and 16th Rifle Divisions. The operational situation that has arisen must be explained."

At midnight we parted from the Front commander-in-chief and set to working out the new plan for 23 October. It foresaw an active offensive on the army's flanks with the task to smash the German 5th Panzer Division north of Walterkehmen and the *Führer* Panzergrenadier Brigade south of there. In the center it was proposed to take Darkehmen and the line of the Angerapp River. On the Gumbinnen direction, the 2nd Guards Tank Corps and 11th Guards Divisons were to go over to a defense. In accordance with this decision, the army's chief of staff issued preliminary orders to the corps commanders, so that they could initiate and in the course of the night complete the regrouping of their troops.

By morning, all of the heavy weapons (tanks, self-propelled guns and artillery) in the 2nd Guards Tank Corps had been dug in, and slit trenches had been dug for the men. The divisions of the rifle corps, having regrouped, prepared to resume the offensive, which was supposed to kick-off early that morning. The enemy in the course of the night showed no activity on the front of the tank corps.

The Front commander-in-chief's decision and the situation that had arisen in connection with it could not but trouble me. Despite the enemy's fierce counterattacks and partial success, Walterkehmen and Goldap remained in our possession. We had reached the approaches to Darkehmen and Gumbinnen. However, early that morning an order arrived to go over to the defense …

Yes, in war it happens that all kinds of unforeseen "however" intrude into combat life, and then everything abruptly changes. Such is what happened this time as well. At 0615 on 23 October, when the divisions of the 11th Guards and 28th Armies had conducted the regrouping and were poised to start an attack in the assigned directions, the Front commander-in-chief, pursuant to directives of the General Staff, gave the 11th Guards Army a fresh task: "To the commander of the 11th Guards Army. In connection with the situation as it stands, I am ordering: 11th Guards Army is to go over to the defense on the Mattischkehmen (5 km west of Groß Trakehnen) – Neuhof – Walterkehmen – Rominte River – Kiauten – Warkallen – Goldaper Lake line. Withdraw the force grouping consisting of the 2nd Guards Tank Corps and the 11th, 31st and 26th Guards Rifle Divisions in the course of 23 October to the eastern bank of the Rominte River."

Thus, the previously assigned task to take Gumbinnen and to reach the Angerapp River had been totally cancelled. This meant the stifling of the army's offensive operations, at a time when it had managed to penetrate 55-70 kilometers into the enemy's defenses, to seize a large area between the Rominte and Angerapp Rivers, and to breach a strongly-fortified enemy line on the Angerapp River, which created the possibility for the army's formations to fight their way right up to the outskirts of Gumbinnen and Darkehmen. Now it meant withdrawing 15-18 kilometers to the line of the Rominte River.

I tried to understand the reason for the Front commander-in-chief's change of mind. It seemed to me that it could be explained by the complexity of the overall operational situation that had arisen at the front.

On the morning of 23 October, the Front commander-in-chief sent a staff officer Lieutenant Colonel V.T. Lazutin in an airplane to the 2nd Guards Tank Corps, who was supposed to relay the order in person to General Burdeinyi about withdrawing the tanks out of the Gumbinnen area to a line behind the Rominte River. In the latter half of the day of 23 October, the organized withdrawal of the 11th Guards Army's forces to the indicated line began on almost every sector of the front. In the north the withdrawal of the main grouping was secured by attacks made by the 16th Corps' 16th and 83rd Divisions, and in the south – the joint actions of the 36th Corps' 5th and 84th Divisions. The enemy showed no activity. Under no enemy pressure, the 31st Division fell back to Groß Tellitzkehmen. At 18.30 the withdrawal of the main forces of the 26th Division began, which by the end of the day reached the eastern bank of the Rominte River in an organized fashion, without any losses in men or equipment.

However, our movement had been plainly figured out by the German command by evening; an order sent out in open text over the radio to its troops testifies to this: "An order from higher headquarters has just arrived – to defend your present positions with every means. All the previous orders about a withdrawal are no longer in effect. Quickly make contact to the right and to the left and continue to defend." Accordingly, the enemy that was intending to withdraw in the present circumstances decided to hold their occupied lines firmly.

Reporting to the Front commander-in-chief between 1000 and 1100 on 23 October about the course of combat operations in the army's sector and about the execution of his directive, I once again expressed an opinion about the senselessness of the withdrawal of the forces of the central grouping to the Rominte River and requested that they be left in their occupied positions. I explained, "By this, we will secure the necessary staging area for the organization of a subsequent offensive into East Prussia's interior."

At 14.30 a message arrived above the signature of the Front's commander-in-chief and of a Military Council member, which instructed the commander of the 2nd Guards Tank Corps: "Follow the orders, relayed to you through Lazutin. I confirm the order to leave a covering detachment in the Nemmersdorf area and to withdraw the 25th Guards Tank Brigade to the area of the assembly of the corps' main forces in order to reach the direction that has been indicated to you." This meant that General Burdeinyi was supposed to continue the corps' withdrawal to the assembly area that had been designated for it.

By the morning of 24 October, the army's central grouping and the 2nd Guards Tank Corps completed the withdrawal to the eastern bank of the Rominte. By this time the corps had 98 operational T-34/85 tanks and 27 operational self-propelled guns, for a total of 125 armored fighting vehicles, and one standard combat load of ammunition. As General Burdeinyi reported, the withdrawal proceeded in an organized manner, "having insignificant losses in the process." The enemy on the other hand, which attempted to attack the Guardsmen, took painful losses. The units that were operating in the Walterkehmen area against the German panzer grouping that had made the penetration alone destroyed 22 tanks, 18 assault guns and 26 field guns, 22 mortars, 10 vehicles and 4 halftracks.

In the latter half of the day of 23 October, in accordance with the order from the Front commander-in-chief, I directed the 11th Guards Army to go over to a defense. It foresaw the organization of a deeply-echeloned defense on a front of 32.5 kilometers with the use of a bridgehead on the western bank of the Rominte River and a reliable reserve. The 2nd Guards Tank Corps was withdrawn to the rear at the direction of the Front commander-in-chief.

The organization and withdrawal of the 2nd Guards Tank Corps out of the encirclement south of Gumbinnen

Throughout the night of 22-23 October and morning of 23 October, the units of the 2nd Guards Tank Corps were firmly holding its occupied area, repulsing incessant enemy attacks with infantry and tanks. At 0900 23 October, the arriving chief of staff of the 3rd Belorussian Front's armored and mechanized forces Guards Lieutenant Colonel Lazutin verbally passed along the order of the Front commander-in-chief to withdraw the corps from encirclement on the basis of which "with an attack in the Praßlauken – Kaszemeken direction, the corps together with the 11th Guards Rifle Division and 317th Guards Mortar Regiment is to break out of the ring of encirclement in the Praßlauken – Dakehnen sector and to emerge in the Elluschönen – Raudohnen – Kaszemeken area, in readiness to repulse enemy attacks from the northwest and west. Initiate the breakout at 1200 on 23 October 1944." The 25th Guards and 26th Guards Tank Brigades, the 401st Guards Self-propelled Artillery Regiment, the 317th Guards Mortar Regiment, the 1311th Light Artillery Regiment and the 28th Separate Flamethrower Battalion were to create the breach for the withdrawal of the rest of the 2nd Guards Tank Corps and rifle divisions from the pocket. The 4th Guards Tank Brigade and 4th Guards Motorized Rifle Brigade were to remain behind to serve as a rearguard and secure the withdrawal from the northwest and eastern directions.

At 1200 on 23 October, the 2nd Guards Tank Corps began to withdraw from the pocket. By 1300 the brigades had reached the following areas: 25th Guards Tank Brigade – Jodszen; 26th Guards Tank Brigade – Maygunischken, Emilienhof; 28th Separate Flamethrower Battalion and 317th Guards Mortar Regiment – Pillkallen; 1311th Light Artillery Regiment and one battalion of the 4th Guards Motorized Rifle Brigade – Jodszen, Schestoken, Gross Tellitzkehmen. The 4th Guards Tank Brigade and the 4th Guards Motorized Rifle Brigade (minus one battalion) were continuing to hold the enemy on their previously occupied line: Samelucken, Augstupönen, Stulgen. With the arrival at the Jodszen, Schestoken, Point 108.9 line, the 25th Guards Tank Brigade encountered enemy opposition. The 26th Guards Tank Brigade conducted a reconnaissance-in-force in order to clarify the situation. By this time the enemy was holding a line 500 meters west of the Tellitzkehmen – Dakehnen line. On this line the corps encountered opposition from the separate *Führer* Panzer Brigade and a kampfgruppe that had 20 Pz.Kpfw. IV tanks and 20 Pz.Kpfw. V tanks.

Message on the personnel losses of the units and formations of the Fallschirm.-Panzer Corps *Hermann Göring* over the day of 23 October 1944, and the damage done to the enemy

a) Over the day of 23 October, the corps destroyed 43 tanks, 7 SU-76, 1 self-propelled gun, 49 heavy anti-tank guns, 14 machine guns and killed more than 400 enemy soldiers and officers.
b) Over this same period the corps lost 1 officer, 20 junior officers and 72 enlisted men killed, and 1 officer, 33 junior officers and 196 enlisted men wounded; missing in action – 2 officers and 34 enlisted men.

Table 2.13: Casualties of the *Fsch. Panzerkorps Hermann Göring* for 23 October 1944: *Fsch. Gren. Div. 1 HG, Fsch. Gren. Div. 2 HG*

Casualties	Officers	Non-commissioned officers	Rank and File	Total
Killed	1	20	72	93
Wounded	1	33	196	230
Missing in action	-	2	34	36
Total:	2	55	302	359

Thus, over the period between 16 October and 23 October 1944, the irrecoverable losses amounted to 49 tanks and assault guns. Another 163 tanks and assault guns had been knocked out and were located under repair.

Table 2.14: Casualties of the 5.Panzer Division for 23 October 1944

Casualties	Officers	Non-commissioned officers	Rank and file	Total
Killed	2	3	16	21
Wounded	5	49	43	97
Total:	7	52	59	118

Casualties of the units and formations of the German Fourth Army over the period between 16 and 23 October 1944

a) Officers:
   547 Volksgrenadier Division (16-20 October): 23 killed, 50 wounded, 7 missing in action;
   3 Cavalry Brigade (20-22 October): 7 killed, 5 wounded;
   170 Infantry Division: 1 wounded
   558 Volksgrenadier Division (22-23 Oct): 2 killed, 11 wounded, 1 missing in action;
   Total losses in officers: 32 killed, 67 wounded, 8 missing in action
b) Junior officers and enlisted men: 609 killed, 1,369 wounded, 882 missing in action. These losses were distributed among the army's units in the following manner:
c) 547 Volksgrenadier Division: 550 killed, 1,140 wounded, 720 missing in action;
   3 Cavalry Brigade: 22 killed, 76 wounded, 111 missing in action;
   170 Infantry Division: 15 killed, 62 wounded, 2 missing in action;
   558 Volksgrenadier Division: 17 killed, 56 wounded, 19 missing in action;
   367 Infantry Division: 5 killed, 2 wounded.

The total casualties over the period 16-23 October 1944 for the above indicated units of the German Fourth Army: 3,649 men, of which 641 killed, 1,436 wounded, 859 missing in action, and 60 sick.

At 1800 on 23 October 1944, the 25th and 26th Guards Tank Brigades went on the attack with the task to destroy the enemy on the western bank of the Rominte River and secure the tank corps' crossing. The 25th Guards Tank Brigade as a result of heavy fighting against enemy tanks and artillery broke out of the pocket and reached a bridge in the Langkischken area, where it linked up with friendly units. Meanwhile, the 4th Guards Tank Brigade and 4th Guards Motorized Rifle Brigade that were covering the withdrawal of the corps' units were engaged in heavy fighting against the enemy's superior force of tanks, artillery and panzergrenadiers: the 4th Guards Tank Brigade in the Samelucken – Augstupönen area; the 4th Guards Motorized Rifle Brigade in the area between the railroad on the right and Stulgen on the left. On this line the 4th Guards Motorized Rifle Brigade was attacked out of the Nestonkehmen area by a force of up to 10 tanks from the *Hermann Göring* Division, and 50 tanks and a regiment of infantry from the north. One battalion of the 4th Guards Motorized Rifle Brigade at 1730 on 23 October was surrounded by the enemy in the Stulgen area, but it broke out of the pocket and continued to carry out orders as part of the brigade.

At 1830 23 October, at a signal from the corps commander, the 4th Guards Tank and 4th Guards Motorized Rifle Brigades, covering the rest of the corps, began to fall back to the following line: Nestonkehmen, Szamaitschen, Kailen. At 1800, the 11th, 31st and 26th Guards Rifle Divisions had begun to cross the Rominte River. By this time the 25th and 26th Guards Tank Brigades had taken up positions to cover their crossing.

At 1900 on 23 October, units of the 2nd Guards Tank Corps began crossing to the eastern bank of the Rominte across two bridges. The 4th Guards Tank and 4th Guards Motorized Rifle Brigades began their crossing of the river at midnight, and by 0600 24 October the corps had completed the withdrawal across the river. By 0900 on the following morning, the 2nd Guards Tank Corps was assembled in the following area: 4th Guards Motorized Rifle Brigade – Budszedszen; 4th Guards Tank Brigade – Kubillehnen; 25th Guards Tank Brigade – south of Karszamupchen; 26th Guards Tank Brigade – south of Warschlegen, southern outskirts of Schwiegseln. The corps headquarters was in Raudohnen.

The **4th Guards Tank Brigade:** from the morning of 23 October, according to an order from the corps commander, had the task to keep in check the enemy that was attacking from the northeast and to cover the withdrawal of the corps' units to the east from out of the pocket. The 401st Guards Self-propelled Regiment was taken out of its defensive positions and passed to the operational control of the 25th Guards Tank Brigade. The 2nd Tank Battalion was pulled back in order to take over its sector of defense between Gertschen and Szamaitschen; the motorized rifle battalion was allocated by company to the tank brigades. All of the brigade's firing means, including anti-aircraft, were employed as antitank and anti-infantry weapons against the enemy.

At 1730 on 23 October the brigade's units were still holding their line, engaged in heavy fighting against the enemy's superior forces of tanks, self-propelled artillery and infantry, which launched repeated attacks. In the morning the enemy had concentrated its main efforts in the sector of the 1st Tank Battalion in the direction of the bridge at Samelucken; in the course of the day, 6 attacks were launched in strength of up to 15-20 tanks and self-propelled guns and up to a battalion of infantry, each time supported by two-three artillery battalions, but despite the enemy's superiority in force, the tankers of the 1st Tank Battalion under the command of the brigade's deputy combat commander Major Mastashev drove back all of the German attacks. Having no success in taking the bridge, the enemy shifted some of his strength to the Szamaitschen axis on the brigade's left flank.

At 1300 up to a battalion of enemy infantry and 10 self-propelled guns, supported by strong artillery fire, went on the attack in the direction of the 2nd Tank Battalion, but this attack also failed. Four self-propelled guns and up to a company of infantry were destroyed by the 2nd Tank Battalion. The attack was foiled and the Germans were thrown back. Simultaneously up to 15 enemy tanks and a battalion of infantry attacked the 3rd Tank Battalion's positions in the center of the brigade's defensive line, but they were driven back by the fire of the 3rd Tank Battalion's tanks; in the process, the Nazis lost 1 tank destroyed, two tanks knocked out, and up to two platoons of infantry.

From midday on 23 October, the enemy again began to bring up tanks and infantry toward the bridge in the Samelucken area, placing heavy artillery fire on the 1st Tank Battalion's area of dispositions. By this time the 1st Tank Battalion had just two tanks left, which were engaged in an unequal struggle to hold the bridge against superior enemy forces. Two platoons of the 2nd Tank Battalion were sent to the area of the 1st Tank Battalion in order to strengthen the defense's right flank; having taken up an echeloned defense with the remaining two tanks of the 1st Tank

Battalion, they continued to fight off the enemy's incessant attacks by infantry and tanks, securing first the regrouping, and then the corps' and rifle divisions' withdrawal from encirclement.

At 1730 on 23 October, a signal was received for the brigade's units to fall back to the following line: Samelucken, Girnen, Hill 111.5. Up until 2200 the brigade's tank battalions and motorized rifle battalion, keeping in check the Nazi's attack with superior forces, fell back to the second line while echeloning the combat formations and organizing a mobile defense. After the withdrawal of the brigade's battalions to the second line, the enemy's onslaught began to weaken in connection with the falling darkness and the proper handling of the fighting withdrawal.

At 2200 23 October at a signal, the brigade's units began to pull back from the second line of defense, covering their withdrawal with rearguard detachments, and having gained separation from the pursuing enemy, they reached the bridge across the Rominte River in the Matzutkehmen area. Having crossed the river and bringing itself back to order, the brigade by 0700 24 October was assembled in the Budszedszen area and to the southeast of there.

In the defensive fighting and the combat to secure the withdrawal of the corps' units from out of the pocket, the 4th Guards Tank Brigade destroyed or knocked out 26 enemy tanks and self-propelled guns, three artillery batteries, 17 vehicles loaded with infantry, two halftracks, four motorcycles and up to two battalions of infantry. In return the brigade lost 9 T-34/85 tanks (destroyed by the fire of enemy tanks and antitank guns), and had 25 killed, 33 wounded and 18 men missing in action.

In the defensive fighting, the tankers of the 1st Tank Battalion under the command of Guards Major Mastashev particularly distinguished themselves. Major Mastashev personally directed the tanks' fighting and by his courage and heroism led the men into bitter fighting against the enemy. Mastashev, left with just two tanks against 20 enemy tanks and self-propelled guns and a large amount of infantry, continued to direct the fighting, properly deploying the tanks and inflicting heavy damage to the enemy. Being wounded, Mastashev refused to leave the battlefield and carried out his duties until the fighting ended, holding the line of defense and preventing the German tanks and infantry from breaking through.

The crew of Guards Junior Lieutenant Orel's tank (1stTank Battalion, 4th Guards Tank Brigade), positioned on the eastern bank of the Rominte River in the Samelucken area, engaged three enemy tanks and destroyed one of them, while also knocking out two anti-tank guns and putting up to 50 Nazis out of action. The rest of the enemy's tanks fled.

Tank company commander of the 1st Tank Battalion Senior Lieutenant Trushnikov on 22 October was the first to break through to the eastern bank of the Rominte River in the Samelucken area with four tanks, and repulsed a counterattack by 12 German tanks, setting ablaze two tanks and wiping out up to 20 Nazis in the process.

The T-34/85 tank commander of the same company Guards Junior Lieutenant Artem'ev, operating as part of the four tanks on the eastern bank of the Rominte in the Samelucken area, knocked out two enemy tanks while repulsing the German attack. His tank was knocked out and set on fire by the enemy. Artem'ev put out the flames and in his damaged tank continued to fight throughout the day of 23 October – positioned at the bridge across the Rominte, repulsing German attacks and knocking out one more German tank.

Tank platoon commander Guards Lieutenant Gavrikov of the 1st Tank Battalion throughout the night of 22-23 October, left with just one operational T-34/85 tank, engaged in combat with German assault guns that closed to within a range of 150-200 meters. In this action he destroyed one self-propelled gun and killed up to 15 Nazis. Despite the fact that four enemy assault guns attacked his tank, Gavrikov fought off the enemy attack and kept possession of the bridge.

Tank platoon commander of the 3rd Tank Battalion Guards Lieutenant Grishaev, positioned on the defense in the Perkallen area, with his skillful actions out of ambush positions, repulsed an enemy attack of four self-propelled guns, destroying two of them in the process.

The **25th Guards Tank Brigade** with its 1st and 3rd Tank Battalions on the morning of 23 October 1944 was withdrawn from its line of defense in the Budweitschen area and by 0900 on that day it was assembled in the area of the Wilken estates as the corps commander's reserve. At 1300 23 October the brigade's units on the basis of an order from the corps commander set out from the Wilken estates, Point 68.5, Tutteln area with the mission to breach the enemy's ring of encirclement with an attack [to the southeast] in the Rodszen, Jodszen, Dakehnen direction and to reach the ford 1 km south of Matzutkehmen, where it was to link up with units of the 84th Guards Rifle Division and 2nd Assault Engineer Brigade. Afterward it was to take up a defense with a front to the south, southwest and west in order to secure the evacuation of the corps' trucks and units of the 31st Guards Rifle Division.

At 1310 October 23, the brigade's units arrayed in a combat formation launched a decisive attack out of the Rodszen in the direction of Jodszen, Dakehnen and Matzutkehmen, and as a result of energetic action, the enemy in these areas was destroyed and the brigade's units arrived on the eastern bank of the Rominte River in the Langkischken area, where it linked up with the 84th Guards Rifle Division and 2nd Assault Engineer Brigade, after which it took up a defense with a front to the south and southwest in the area 500 meters north of Gelleszuhnen.

When breaking out of the pocket, the brigade's units destroyed 8 tanks and self-propelled guns, two mortar batteries and killed up to 60 Germans.

In the fighting the brigade lost 18 T-34/85 tanks destroyed and 3 tanks knocked out. Casualties were 30 men killed and 56 wounded. The brigade commander Guards Colonel Bulygin received a severe concussion.

At 0500 on 24 October, the brigade's units were removed from the occupied line of defense, conducted a march along the Matzutkehmen, Budszedszen, Sodehnen route, and by 0900 24 October took up a defense with a front to the north in the direction of Karszamupchen, in readiness to operate to the north and northwest directions.

The **26th Guards Tank Brigade** at 1100 on 23 October received an assignment from the corps commander to advance in the direction of Szameitschen, the Marienthal farm, Girnen and Emilienhof and with an attack in the direction of Praßlauken to cut the highway and capture the bridge across the Rominte River in the Praßlauken area. Then it was to assume a defense with a front to the north with the mission to secure the withdrawal of the corps' units from out of the pocket.

Carrying out the order of the corps commander, at 1300 on 23 October the brigade arrived in the Emilienhof area, where it ran into strong enemy fire resistance from tanks and artillery out of the areas of Hill 103.9 and the isolated cottages to the north of the hill. Having left behind a screening detachment in the Emilienhof area, the brigade bypassed Hill 103.9 to the south and at 1400 fought its way across the Schestoken – Tellitzkehmen road in the vicinity of an isolated cottage 1 km to the north of Schestoken, having destroyed 2 enemy tanks and six vehicles in the process.

The enemy with tanks and artillery increased the resistance from the Jockeln, Hill 98.2 area. With a decisive attack the 26th Guards Tank Brigade broke the German resistance in the Jockeln area and to the south, and at 1500 cut the Gumbinnen – Goldap highway, having destroyed in the process 4 enemy tanks and self-propelled guns, 8 vehicles, 4 antitank guns and having killed up to 70 enemy soldiers and officers.

By 0300 on 24 October, all of the 2nd Guards Tank Corps' units had fully emerged from the pocket, and pursuant to a verbal order from the corps commander, the 26th Guards Tank Brigade was removed from its defensive positions and by 0500 on 24 October was assembled in the Meldienen area, before moving on to the area of the northern outskirts of Budszedszen and Schwiegseln, where it had the task to block enemy counterattacks from the north and northwest.

In the course of 24 October, the brigade's men spent the day servicing their tanks and topping up with fuel and ammunition. The brigade headquarters was establishing communications with the forward units and reconnoitering the enemy.

As of 25 October, the 26th Guards Tank Brigade had 14 combat-ready T-34/85 tanks. The tanks were fully supplied with fuel, lubricants and ammunition. On 25 October, at an order from the corps commander the brigade turned over its operational tanks to the 4th Guards Tank Brigade and 25th Guards Tank Brigade, and was withdrawn to the Podszohnen area in order to reform.

In the recent fighting, the following units and men particularly stood out: Guards Lieutenant Starostin's tank platoon, with the tank crews of Goncharov, Tututbalen, Malakhov and Scherbakov; Guards Lieutenant Ibetulov's mortar platoon; and Guards Lieutenant Shestakov's and Guards Lieutenant Iakhin's submachine gun platoon.

The **4th Guards Motorized Rifle Brigade**'s 1st Battalion at 1200 on 23 October had to defend against an enemy attack in strength of up to a battalion of infantry and 9 self-propelled guns and several tanks. The 1st Battalion met the enemy with the organized fire of all types of weapons and with the fire of antitank artillery batteries and batteries of the 1500th Self-propelled Artillery Regiment. Quickly two German self-propelled guns were knocked out, and the German infantry was dispersed and partially destroyed. A second German attack also failed.

At 0300 on 24 October, the brigade fully and successfully crossed the Rominte River in the Matzutkehmen area, and by 0400 was occupying a defense: 3rd Battalion – in the area 2 kilometers northwest of Waldauladel Station, with positions facing toward the northwest across the railroad bed; 1st Battalion – in the area west of Meldienen with a front to the west; 2nd Battalion – positioned between the 1st and 3rd Battalions.

As a result of the rearguard fighting on 23 October, the brigade inflicted the following damage to the enemy: 3 self-propelled guns and 3 halftracks knocked out; and up to 4 firing positions and 200 Germans eliminated. Over this time the brigade had 264 casualties, with 61 men killed and 263 men wounded.

At 0800 on 24 October the 4th Guards Motorized Rifle Brigade was removed from its occupied positions at an order from the corps commander, and by 1030 on the same day was assembled in the area north of Kubillen, where it took up a defense in readiness to repulse enemy tank and infantry attacks.

By 0700 on 25 October, the brigade's 3rd Battalion had transferred its remaining men and sergeants to the 1st and 2nd Battalions, while the command staff and the battalion train moved to the brigades' rear area – the Kroscheln farmstead.

In the stubborn fighting in encirclement and to break out of the pocket, the brigade inflicted the following losses on the Germans: 22 tanks, 18 self-propelled guns, 26 guns, 56 machine guns, 22 mortars and 2 halftracks; up to 1,000 enemy soldiers and officers were killed. The brigade also captured 10 vehicles, 6 mortars and 6 guns of various calibers.

Without any particular losses, all of the units of the corps and of the 31st Guards, 11th Guards and 26th Guards Rifle Divisions of the 11th Guards Army came fully out of pocket out of the area south of Gumbinnen. Only the rearguard units, the 4th Guards Tank and 4th Guards Motorized Rifle Brigades, suffered losses.

Our air force was supporting the corps and rifle divisions as they came out of encirclement. Because of the murky situation, sometimes the air force struck friendly units as they were coming out of the pocket.

Table 2.15: Status of the German Fourth Army's (AOK 4) tanks and assault guns on 24 October 1944

Formations and units	Types of tanks and assault guns	Combat ready	In repair Short-term	In repair Long-term
Panzerjäger Kp. 1028	StuG	9	1	-
StuG Brigade 259	StuG	36	4	3
3 Kp./ Panzer Abt. 118	StuG	8	1	-
Panzerjäger Kp. 1150	StuG	9	1	1
4 Bat./StuG Brigade 920	StuG	8	-	1
3 Kp./Jagdpanzer Abt. 69	StuG	8	1	-
StuG Abt. 1558	StuG	5	-	4
Panzerjäger Kp. 1240	StuG	5	1	2
StuG Brigade 209	StuG	25	-	4
Panzerjäger Kp. 1367	StuG	5	1	2
Panzerjäger Kp. 1131	StuG	1	3	2
Jagdpanzer. Abt. 69 (- 3 Kp.)	StuG	6	9	15
StuG Abt. 1547	StuG	2	-	-
StuG Brigade 279	StuG	16	-	5
Panzerjäger Kp. 1006	StuG	10	-	-
Panzer Brigade *Führer Grenadier*	Pz V	33	1	3
	Pz IV	7	-	2
	StuG	28	1	2
Total for the above formations and units of the Fourth Army	Tanks and StuG	221	24	45
Korps *Hermann Göring*				
1 Division, *Hermann Göring*	Pz IV	5	32	
	Pz V	20	20	
	StuG	6	22	
2 Division, *Hermann Göring*	StuG	9	26	
5.Panzer Division	Pz IV	1	19	
	Pz V	5	27	
	StuG	7	16	
sPanzer Abt. 505	Pz VI	3	31	
Total for Korps *Hermann Göring*	Tanks and SP Guns	56	193	
Total for Fourth Army	Tanks and SP Guns	277	262	

Table 2.16: Casualties of the German *Fsch.* Panzer Korps *Hermann Göring's Fsch.* – Panzergrenadier Regiments 1 and 2 for 24 October 1944[1]

Casualties	Officers	Non-commissioned officers	Rank and file	Total
Killed	6	9	47	62
Wounded	20	31	162	213
Missing in action	2	5	53	60
Total:	28	45	262	335

Note
Over this same period, the corps reported the destruction of 15 tanks, 15 anti-tank guns and 3 aircraft of the Red Army.

Table 2.17: Status of the German Fourth Army's tanks and self-propelled guns on 24 October 1944

Formations and units	Combat materiel				Knocked-out			Total
	StuG	Tanks	Sf	sPak mot Z	In short-term repair	In long-term repair	Destroyed	
1	2	3	4	5	6	7	8	9
LV Armee Korps								
28.Jäger Division	-	-	-	7	-	-	-	7
Panzerjäger Kp. 1028	9	-	-	-	1	-	-	10
StuG Brigade 259	36	-	-	-	4	3	-	43
562.Volksgrenadier Div.	-	-	-	9	-	-	-	9
Fest. Pak Kp. 10	-	-	-	(5)	-	-	-	(5)
Fest. Pak Kp. 17	-	-	-	(12)	-	-	-	(12)
Total for LV Korps	45	-	-	16 (17)	5	3	-	69 (17)
VI Armee Korps								
203.Sicherungs Division	-	-	-	5	-	-	-	5
3 Kp., Panzer Abt. 118	8	-	-	-	1	-	-	9
50.Infanterie Division	-	-	-	17	1	-	-	18
Panzerjäger Kp. 1150	9	-	-	-	1	-	-	10
4 Kp., StuG Brigade 920	8	-	-	-	-	1	-	9
Kampgruppe "Hannibal"	-	-	-	1	1	-	-	2
3 Kp., Jagdpanzer Abt. 69	8	-	-	-	1	-	-	9
Fest. Pak Kp.	-	-	-	(13)	-	(1)	-	(14)
Total for VI Korps	33	-	-	23 (13)	5	1 (1)	-	62 (14)
XXXXI Panzer Korps								
131.Infanterie Division	-	-	-	11	1	-	-	12
Panzerjäger Kp. 1131	1	-	-	-	3	2	-	6
Jagdpanzer Abt. 69 (- 3 Kp.)	6	-	-	-	9	15	-	30
StuG Abt. 1547	2	-	-	-	-	-	-	2
StuG Brigade 279	16	-	-	-	-	5	-	21
Panzer Brigade *Führer Grenadier*	-	33 (V)	-	-	1	3	-	37
	-	2 (IV)	-	-	-	-	-	2
	-	5 (IV)	-	-	-	-	-	5
	24	-	-	-	1	1	-	26
sJagdpanzer Abt. 665	-	-	-	14	-	1	-	15
Total for XXXXI Panzer Korps	63	40	-	25	15	30	-	173
Fallschirm.-Panzer Korps *Hermann Göring*								
1 Fallschirm.-Panzer Division *Hermann Göring*	6	-	-	-	22	-	-	28
	-	5 (IV)	-	-	32	-	-	37
	-	20 (V)	-	-	20	-	-	40
	-	-	2	8	5	-	-	15
2 Fallschirm.-Panzer Division *Hermann Göring*	9	-	-	-	26	-	-	35
	-	-	-	6	3	-	-	9
StuG Abt., Korps *Hermann Göring*	-	-	-	4	1	-	-	5

Formations and units	Combat materiel				Knocked-out			Total
	StuG	Tanks	Sf	sPak mot Z	In short-term repair	In long-term repair	Destroyed	
1	2	3	4	5	6	7	8	9
5.Panzer Division	-	1 (IV)	-	-	19		-	20
	-	5 (V)	-	-	27		-	32
	7	-	-	-	16		-	23
	-	-	4	8	4		-	16
sPanzer Abt. 505	-	3 (VI)	-	-	31		5	34
Total for Korps *Hermann Göring*	22	34	6	26	206		5	294
Total for the Fourth Army	203	74	6	124 (12)	28	253 (1)	5	688 (43)

The numbers in the parentheses indicate captured Soviet 76-mm guns.

The casualties of the German Fourth Army's units over the period from 20 October to 24 October 1944

a) Officer casualties:
   Fallschirm. – Panzer Corps *Hermann Göring* (23-24 October): 10 killed, 12 wounded, 2 missing in action;
   5 Panzer Division (23-24 October): 1 killed, 12 wounded, 3 missing in action;
   170 Infantry Division (24 October): 1 wounded;
   558 Volksgrenadier Division (21-24 October): 6 wounded, 1 missing in action;
   Total losses in officers (20-24 October): 32 killed, 67 wounded, 8 missing in action.

b) Non-commissioned officers and enlisted men: A total of 214 killed, 621 wounded and 87 missing in action; 17 were out of action due to illnesses. These casualties were distributed among the army's units in the following manner:
   Fallschirm. – Panzer Corps *Hermann Göring*: 112 killed, 152 wounded, 26 missing in action;
   5 Panzer Division: 26 killed, 150 wounded, 23 missing in action;
   50 Infantry Division: 3 wounded, 14 out of action due to illness;
   203 Security Division: 5 killed, 5 wounded, 3 out of action due to illnesses;
   367 Infantry Division: 1 killed, 1 wounded;
   170 Infantry Division: 7 killed, 13 wounded, 2 missing in action;
   4 Cavalry Brigade: 7 killed, 54 wounded;
   558 Volksgrenadier Division: 4 killed, 48 wounded, 4 missing in action;
   Other units and elements of the Fourth Army: 52 killed, 195 wounded, 32 missing in action;
   The total casualties of the German Fourth Army's above-indicated over the period between 16 and 23 October 1944, the course of the Soviet offensive: 3,649 men, of which 641 were killed, 1,436 were wounded, 859 went missing in action, and 60 men were sick.

Conclusions of the 2nd Guards Tank Corps' command on the conducted operation:

The corps on the western bank of the Pissa River broke through the enemy's defense in cooperation with the 16th Guards Rifle Corps. Successfully developing the offensive, it overcame two previously-prepared defensive belts that were still not completely occupied by enemy troops, and by the morning of 21 October had emerged in the area south of Gumbinnen, having overcome three river barriers in the process. On the Rominte River in the Walterkehmen, Perkallen area, the enemy hurled a strong group of 25-30 tanks and self-propelled guns and Infantry Regiment 78 into the battle with the mission to keep in check the tank corps' advance toward Gumbinnen. This combat group was almost completely destroyed by the corps by an attack from three directions. Having reserves in the town of Gumbinnen, the Germans moved into prepared lines of defense and offered strong resistance on the approaches to the town. Subsequently the enemy reinforced his defense by moving up operational reserves: the 5th Panzer Division, the Parachute-Panzer Division *Hermannn Göring*, the Führer Grenadier Brigade and other units.

The low density of our forces in between the Pissa and Rominte Rivers enabled the enemy with counterattacks to the south to isolate the corps from our forces, and to encircle the corps and rifle divisions west of the Rominte with reserve units out of the Goldap area. Having received an order to withdraw, the corps broke out of the pocket, bringing out three rifle divisions together with it, and emerged almost fully intact, suffering only insignificant losses in the process. The corps' main losses, mainly in tanks, were suffered in the fighting for Gumbinnen, when overcoming strongly fortified defensive lines on the immediate approaches to the town.

Commander of the 2nd Guards Tatsinskaia Tank Corps Guards
Lieutenant General of Tank Forces A.S. BURDEINYI
Corps chief of staff
Guards Colonel KARAVAN

Conclusions of the corps' brigade and regiment commanders regarding the operation and the condition of the corps' units upon wrapping up combat operations:

4th Guards Tank Brigade: Over the period of fighting from 15 to 24 October 1944, on the territory of East Prussia the brigade destroyed 49 tanks and self-propelled guns, up to 8 batteries of field guns of various calibers, 57 vehicles with various loads, 2 halftracks, 4 motorcycles, and more than three battalions of infantry. The brigade captured 2 heavy guns, a fuel dump, and a stockpile of ammunition.

Over this same period the 4th Guards Tank Brigade lost 98 men killed, 104 wounded, 44 missing in action and 1 man taken prisoner. Among the dead are the commander of the 1st Tank Battalion Guards Lieutenant Colonel Davydov, the deputy commander of the 1st Tank Battalion for political affairs Guards Major Polezhaev, the senior adjutant of the 1st Tank Battalion Senior Lieutenant Krutchinsky, and the deputy chief of the Political Department Guards Captain Kovalenko. The deputy combat commander of the motorized rifle battalion Guards Captain Antonets was severely wounded; the brigade's deputy combat commander Guards Major Mastashev was lightly wounded.

Tank losses: 32 T-34/85 destroyed and 12 T-34/85 knocked out. Of the number of disabled tanks, 6 were evacuated from the battlefield, while the rest were left on the battlefield because of the impossibility of evacuating them. Of the number of the 6 evacuated disabled tanks turned over for repair, 3 will require return to the factory for repair, and 3 will require moderate repairs.

The brigade's condition upon the completion of combat operation on 24 October 1944: 21 operational T-34/85 tanks, 3 T-34/85 tanks needing moderate repairs, 3 T-34/85 tanks needing factory repairs, and 141 operational trucks and cars; manpower – 219 officers and 1008 sergeants and privates.

Conclusion: The men were sufficiently trained in the period of preparation for the battle, with the main focus on engaging in combat with an enemy in strong fortifications, as well as with enemy that has recently gone over to the defense. In addition, the men were prepared for engaging in combat on East Prussian territory. In the fighting, which had a bitter nature, when the enemy was stubbornly resisting, striving to hold each meter of native soil, the tankers demonstrated exceptional heroism and courage, as well as the ability to destroy enemy manpower and equipment while in the process suffering relatively small losses.

The officer staff correctly assessed the situation in complex combat conditions and reached timely decisions, which ensured combat success.

The particularities of combat operations on East Prussian territory consisted in a numerically superior enemy having a large number of strongly fortified knots of resistance on the one hand, and the presence of a well-developed network of railroads and roads on the other, which demanded from the men the ability to recognize the enemy's intentions and to regroup forces to key sectors in a timely manner.

As a result of the sufficient tactical training and the high morale, the brigade's men were able to handle the given task – both in the period of offensive operations and in the defensive fighting. The combat mission, given by the corps commander, was carried out by the brigade.

Commander of the 4th Guards Tank Brigade
Guards Colonel LOSIK

25th Guards Tank Brigade: Over the period of combat between 15 and 24 October 1944, the brigade destroyed 16 enemy tanks and self-propelled guns, 39 guns of various calibers, 27 mortars, 4 prime movers, 1 ammo dump, 24 trucks loaded with munitions, 1 wagon loaded with munitions, 1 railroad train, and up to 660 enemy soldiers and officers; 68 prisoners were taken.

Over this same period of time, the brigade lost 25 T-34/85 tanks, 7 vehicles, and 3 76mm guns, and had 78 men killed, 191 wounded and 5 missing in action.

Conclusion: In the period of combat operations, the brigade's units dealt with their mission. In battle it was revealed that the officer staff was weakly prepared in a tactical respect and poor in topography; incompetently direct their units over the radio; and the commander of the platoon, company, battalion – poorly orient themselves with respect to the terrain.

Commander of the 25th Guards Tank Brigade
Guards Colonel Bulygin

26th Guards Tank Brigade: The brigade's condition at the completion of the combat operations on 26 October 1944 was 6 operational T-34/85 tanks, 3 tanks needing moderate repairs, 2 tanks needing to be returned to the factory for repair; 169 vehicles; 3 37mm anti-aircraft guns, 1 76mm anti-tank gun; 6 mortars; 8 DShK heavy machine guns, 4 DP machine guns and 4 Maksim heavy machine guns; and 207 officers, 398 sergeants and 474 enlisted men reporting for duty.

Conclusion: Throughout the operation, despite the stubborn enemy resistance, the brigade's men fought self-sacrificingly and decisively. The brigade operated in the lead on an exposed flank and was repeatedly subjected to the counterattacks of enemy tanks and infantry. The brigade had no artillery means of reinforcement. The corps' supporting artillery didn't fulfill a single brigade request for fire, because it was moving behind the corps' left column. It is necessary to reinforce the lead brigades with artillery, especially when operating on an exposed flank.

The brigade in the recent operation suffered large losses in tanks, because it was engaged in constant combat with enemy tanks and self-propelled guns positioned in ambush positions. In addition, the commanders of the platoons, companies and even battalions didn't always properly organize the combat with enemy tanks, made poor use of the terrain, and fired inaccurately. Reconnaissance and observation over the battlefield are being poorly organized. All this led to at times to needless tank losses.

It is necessary when putting combat teamwork together in the units to pay especial attention to the organization of combatting enemy tanks, the correct use of the ground when on the offensive, and combining fire and movement in the platoon, company and battalion, as well as good observation over the battlefield and conducting accurate fire.

In the preceding operation there was a case when the lead echelon of the brigade's rear services, which was located at a distance of 8 kilometers from the forward units, became cut off from the brigade's combat units. Thus during operations in the operational depth, the lead echelon of the brigade's rear must be kept at a distance of not more than 3 kilometers from the forward units. The rear services must be secured with escorting means.

Commander of the 26th Guards Tank Brigade
Guards Colonel SHANIN

4th Guards Motorized Rifle Brigade: Over the period of combat from 15 to 25 October 1944, the brigade eliminated 720 enemy soldiers and officers (including 1 general, 2 colonels and 1 major); destroyed 1 aircraft, 5 tanks, 8 self-propelled guns, 14 halftracks, 42 vehicles, 6 mortars, 2 prime movers, 6 75mm guns, 28 heavy and light machine guns, 65 supply wagons, 11 firing positions, 1 88mm battery, 14 guns of various calibers, and partially destroyed and dispersed up to a battalion of enemy infantry. The brigade captured 77 prisoners, 2 food stockpiles, 3 vehicles, 12 horses, and 4 machine guns. Nineteen enemy counterattacks were repulsed.

Over this same period, the brigade lost 173 men killed and 398 wounded. The casualties included 14 officers killed and 33 wounded, 39 NCOs killed and 75 wounded, and 120 enlisted men killed and 290 wounded. In equipment and weapons, the brigade lost 4 57mm guns, 1 76mm gun, 8 heavy machine guns, 12 light machine guns, 14 vehicles (of which 7 have returned to service after being repaired), 1 armored personnel carrier and 1 radio.

The brigade's condition at the completion of combat operations on 25 October 1944:

- Manpower: 296 officers, 1008 NCOs and 1428 enlisted men reporting for duty. The brigade is short 36 officers, 373 NCOs and 483 privates;
- Weapons: 11 76mm guns, 5 57mm guns, 13 82mm mortars, 11 120mm mortars, 26 antitank rifles, 11 heavy machine guns, 14 light machine guns, 864 rifles and carbines, 882 submachine guns, 8 DShK heavy machine guns;
- Motorized transport: 179 combat vehicles, 19 specialized vehicles, 6 light vehicles, 2 motorcycles;
- Combat vehicles: 5 halftracks, 4 armored cars, 29 radios.

Conclusion: In the conducted fighting, in the difficult conditions of struggle with the enemy on East Prussian territory while overcoming a long-term and deeply-echeloned defense, the brigade's men once again demonstrated valor, bravery and Russian endurance. The brigade's officer staff capably handled their troops in battle, even in the hard circumstances of encirclement. As a result of the fierce fighting and in a relatively short period of time, the brigade inflicted significant damage to the enemy in equipment and troops, which pointed to good training and proper use of all of the brigade's firepower. The lack of an adequate amount of motorized transport reduces the maneuverability and mobility in combat operations. Instead of the authorized 262 combat vehicles, the brigade has only 174. The brigade is combat effective and is ready to carry out a combat mission.

Commander of the 4th Guards Motorized Rifle Brigade
Guards Lieutenant Colonel ANTIPIN

401st Guards Self-propelled Artillery Regiment: Over the period of combat between 15 and 24 October 1944, the regiment destroyed 3 enemy tanks, 2 self-propelled guns, 25 guns of various caliber, 10 trucks with their loads, 5 anti-aircraft mounts, 2 heavy machine guns, 4 mortars, 7 halftracks, and killed 380 enemy soldiers and officers. In addition, it knocked out 1 tank, 1 self-propelled gun, and 4 vehicles. Two motorcycles were captured. The brigade expended 859 shells.

Over this same period the regiment had the following losses:

Casualties: 23 killed, 36 wounded, for a total of 59 men.
Armored fighting vehicles: 3 SU-85 and one vehicle mounting a ZIS-5 were left behind in enemy-occupied territory.
The brigade's condition at the completion of combat operations on 24 October 1944:
  18 SU-85, of which 7 require moderate repair, and 6 require light repairs
  Motorized transport: 27 trucks, 8 specialized vehicles, 2 light vehicles
  Men: 52 officers, 109 sergeants, 100 enlisted men.

Conclusion: In view of the worn out self-propelled guns that arrived in the regiment from the repair shops, there were cases when combat machines could not keep up with the regiment's column, as a result of which the regiment had losses in combat material not due to combat, but as a consequence of mechanical breakdowns and their capture by the enemy. Primarily the men over the period of forming up gained the complete knowledge and ability to conduct combat with the adversary, with the exception of the submachine gun companies, the men of which arrived just a day before the start of the fighting. As a result of this, there were high casualties in the submachine gun companies.

With the establishment number of BA-64 armored cars and three motorcycles, the regiment lacked the mobile means in order to conduct reconnaissance or regulate traffic, in connection with which the regiment needs to be supplemented with mobile means. It is also necessary to replenish the regiment with officers, in particular, self-propelled gun commanders.

Commander of the 401st Guards Self-propelled Artillery Regiment
Guards Major KOTLIAROV

1500th Self-propelled Artillery Regiment: Over the period of fighting between 19 and 24 October 1944, the regiment destroyed 4 enemy tanks, 1 self-propelled gun, 2 halftracks, 9 guns of various calibers, 8 vehicles, 1 prime mover, 1 motorcycle, 21 machine guns, 8 earth and timber bunkers, and killed up to 600 enemy soldiers and officers.

Over this same period the regiment had losses:

In manpower: 8 killed and 26 wounded. Total casualties: 34 men;
In self-propelled guns: 6 SU-76 destroyed and 1 SU-76 knocked out (and in repair);

Th regiment's condition on 25 October 1944:

- Self-propelled guns: 6 combat-ready SU-76, 9 SU-76 under repair (of which 8 required repair of the running gear and engine, while 1 SU-76 is at a field repair base);
- Personnel: the SU-76 are fully staffed with crews according to the available men.

Conclusion: The regiment was properly used tactically in accordance with the given missions. The arriving self-propelled guns for the regiment before the operation differed in their mechanical condition: 10 SU-76 were new, but 11 SU-76 came from factory overhauls. The latter had and continue to have bad running gear, which delayed the regiment from carrying out its given orders. Smoke candles were used effectively in the conducted operation; they yielded positive results in the aims of concealing the self-propelled guns during enemy airstrikes, and while on the march and while moving into their firing positions. In the course of the operation, the regiment didn't have adequate information about the situation. The regiment didn't have its own inherent reconnaissance means. The regiment is ready to carry out a combat assignment within the limits of its available self-propelled guns and men.

Commander of the 1500th Self-propelled Artillery Regiment
Major LOGINOV

Results of the corps' combat between 18 and 25 October 1944:

a) Damage inflicted on the enemy: 5,500 soldiers and officers, 82 tanks and self-propelled guns, 142 guns of various calibers, 3 aircraft, 81 mortars, 250 machine guns, 181 vehicles, 14 halftracks, 760 submachine guns and 1 ammo dump eliminated. Enemy soldiers and officers captured: 450.

b) Casualties of the 2nd Guards Tank Corps:

	Officers	Sergeants	Privates	Total
Killed	79	197	195	471
Wounded	127	327	682	1136
Missing in action	10	30	23	63
Taken prisoner	1	5	-	6
Total	**217**	**559**	**900**	**1676**

c) Losses in armored fighting vehicles:
92 T-34/85 destroyed by artillery fire and 34 T-34/85 knocked out; 3 SU-85 destroyed and 3 knocked out; 6 SU-76 destroyed and 7 knocked out. In addition, another 15 tanks were destroyed or knocked out by enemy airstrikes, and 2 more T-34/85 tanks blew up on mines. One more SU-76 was destroyed by enemy aircraft fire.
The irrevocable loss in armored fighting vehicles: 108 T-34/85, 3 SU-85, 6 SU-76, for a total of 117.

In the period from 18 to 30 October 1944, 46 tanks and self-propelled guns were evacuated from the battlefield by recovery units and the corps. By 31 October, the repair of all of the evacuated tanks and self-propelled guns had basically been completed.

The thorough preparation of the crews and tanks for combat operations ensured the continuous and accident-free work of the tanks in the conducted operation. The corps' evacuation means and repair means successfully handled the tasks of evacuating and putting tanks and self-propelled guns back into service.

Men of the 2nd Guards Tatsinskaia Tank Corps, who distinguished themselves in the fighting of October 1944

Left to right: Nikolai Eremin, Stepan Nesterov and Sabir Akhtiamov.

Guards Lieutenant Iurii Malakhov – a T-34/85 tank platoon commander. On 20 October 1944, operating in the spearhead, broke into the adversary's positions, destroyed a German Tiger tank, and with his tank's tracks crushed two antitank guns, which enabled the deployment and successful advance of the entire tank battalion on the western bank of the Pissa River.

Continuing the further offensive, Malakhov's platoon on 21 October with a daring attack captured a bridge across the Rominte River. Then, having overcome stubborn enemy resistance, it burst into the depth of the enemy's defenses and became tied up in an unequal combat with six tanks. Having set two of the tanks ablaze, with his tank's tracks he crushed an anti-aircraft mount, but his tank was also set ablaze. Malakhov directed his smoking machine in the direction of the enemy's artillery positions. The explosion of the tank's on-board munitions destroyed the battery and opened the path for a further advance for the other tanks. For his exemplary fulfillment of the command's assignments, Malakhov was posthumously awarded the title Hero of the Soviet Union

Guards Major Nikolai Mastashev – deputy combat commander of the 4th Guards Tank Brigade. In the fighting south of Gumbinnen he demonstrated exceptional courage and ability to lead the tanks in a most difficult combat situation. On 22 October in the fighting in the Girnen area, the commander of the 1st Tank Battalion Lieutenant Colonel Davydov fell bravely in battle; Mastashev assumed command of the battalion and in the course of three days of constant fighting led its actions. In the course of 36 hours the battalion engaged superior enemy forces, secured the brigade's and corps' right flank, and held a bridge across the Rominte River in the Samelucken area. Fifteen enemy tanks and self-propelled guns and up to a battalion of infantry was destroyed by the battalion in the Samelucken area. In this battle Mastashev personally wiped out a group of German submachine gunners that had broken through, and tossed grenades at the crossing tanks. The battalion played an exceptional role in securing the actions of the brigade and corps. Mastashev was awarded the Order of the Red Banner.

Guards Junior Lieutenant Sergei Lazarev – a T-34 tank platoon commander with the 4th Guards Tank Brigade's 2nd Tank Battalion. During the offensive in East Prussia, in the area of Kuttkuhnen with a swift attack he was the first to break into the village together with his platoon and destroyed 4 enemy guns, 2 self-propelled guns and killed up to 10 Nazis. In the fighting for the railroad in the Bermen area, Lazarev destroyed two guns that were hindering the advance of the two other platoons of the tank company and with his fire covered their flanks. He timely spotted enemy firing positions and over the radio timely kept the company commander informed about them. He was awarded the Order of the Red Banner.

Guards Lieutenant Aleksei Pichugin – a T-34 tank platoon commander with the 25th Guards Tank Brigade's 2nd Tank Battalion. In the fighting in East Prussia he proved himself to be a bold and enterprising officer. His platoon throughout the entire period of combat operations was located out in front as the point platoon. Despite the enemy's heavy artillery fire and aerial bombing, the platoon fought off enemy counterattacks in the Kassuben area. When the tank company commander was wounded, Pichugin assumed command of the company; his company served as the battalion's point company, and with its actions ensured the battalion's success and from the march it captured a bridge in the Schmulken area. When the battalion reached the Nemmersdorf area and took up a defense on its western outskirts, Pichugin together with his company in the course of 21 October 1944 repulsed enemy counterattacks. In this action he was severely wounded, but refused to leave the battlefield and continued to command the company; only after the counterattack was repelled did he relinquish command at the order from the battalion commander and go to a hospital. Over the period of fighting his company destroyed 6 enemy tanks and self-propelled guns, a battalion of guns, 12 vehicles, and killed up to 300 Nazis. Pichugin himself destroyed 2 self-propelled guns, 5 vehicles, and eliminated 40 soldiers and officers. He was ordered the Order of the Red Banner.

Guards Lieutenant Pavel Ivanov – a T-34 tank platoon commander with the 25th Guards Tank Brigade's 2nd Tank Battalion. Positioned with his platoon in the Nemmersdorf area, in the course of two days (21-22 October 1944) he held the bridge across the Angerapp River against charging German submachine gunners, thereby giving the possibility of delivering ammunition and food to our infantry that were occupying the defense on the western outskirts of Nemmersdorf. Ivanov was wounded in the leg, but continued to command the platoon and in the course of 21 October repulsed 4 counterattacks of enemy tanks and infantry. When the situation became increasingly difficult, his battalion was supposed to break through the enemy's ring of encirclement; until the final minute Ivanov was located in his tank and only after taking a bridge was he sent to the hospital. His crew destroyed 2 self-propelled guns, 4 machine guns, 2 150mm howitzers, 5 vehicles and eliminated up to 50 Nazis. He was awarded the Order of the Red Banner.

Guards Senior Lieutenant Mikhail Popov – a T-34 tank company commander with the 4th Guards Tank Brigade's 2nd Tank Battalion. In the fighting on East Prussian territory, he showed himself to be a brave and strong-willed officer. During the offensive against Kuttkuhnen, he led his company through concealing terrain and launched a surprise attack against the enemy, as a result of which his company killed up to 120 Nazis and captured a self-propelled gun. Operating out of concealed positions in this area, the company knocked out 4 enemy batteries, 4 self-propelled guns and an anti-aircraft battery. In the vicinity of a checkpoint, with a rapid attack the company killed up to 300 Nazis and destroyed 2 self-propelled guns, 3 antitank batteries and an anti-aircraft battery. Thanks to keen observation, Popov commanded the company well and pointed out to the platoons enemy firing positions, which were quickly put out of action. Popov personally from his tank destroyed one antitank gun battery and killed up to 20 Germans. He was awarded the Order of the Red Banner.

Guards Lieutenant Stepan Smyk – a T-34 platoon commander with the 4th Guards Tank Brigade's 2nd Tank Battalion. In the fighting on East Prussian territory on 22 October 1944, in the combat action for possession of the checkpoint he operated boldly and decisively – he was the first to cross the railroad running between Gumbinnen and Insterburg and held it, repulsing furious counterattacks by enemy tanks and infantry. In this fighting he destroyed 1 tank, 2 anti-tank guns, 1 anti-aircraft cannon, 1 mortar battery, and killed up to 50 Germans. For his capable command of the platoon and the valor he demonstrated, Smyk was awarded the Order of the Patriotic War 1st Class.

Guards Captain Andrei Taldykin – the commander of a tank-riding company of the 4th Guards Motorized Rifle Brigade. In the battle in the area of the Plinken estates on 21 October 1944 his company received an attack order, and Taldykin led his soldiers toward the foe. The enemy opened up heavy machine-gun fire, and German snipers didn't allow and forward movement. The company's 1st Platoon had run into an enemy strongpoint. The soldiers of the company became engaged in close-combat and drove the Germans out of the strongpoint. In this action up to 30 Nazis were killed. On 20 October one platoon that was operating as tank riders in the Girgen area found itself in an enemy ambush. Dismounting and engaging the enemy, the soldiers forced the Germans to flee, having killed more than 30 of them. During this action, Taldykin's company saved 7 T-34/85 tanks, which successfully came out of the ambush area. In the fighting in the Thuren area on 22 October, the enemy launched a counterattack. The company, under heavy artillery and mortar fire, engaged in combat and held its line of defense, having wiped out up to 20 German soldiers and a heavy machine gun in the process. Taldykin personally killed 2 Nazis and blew up the heavy machine gun with a grenade. In this action he fell bravely on the battlefield, struck by a shell fragment. Taldykin was posthumously awarded the Order of the Patriotic War 1st Class.

Guards Senior Lieutenant Aleksandr Shekhonin – a T-34 tank company commander with the 4th Guards Tank Brigade's 1st Tank Battalion. As the commander of the point company in the battalion, he was the first to take up a defense in the Sweinen area on 19 October 1944 and throughout the night of 19-20 October he drove back German tank and infantry counterattacks. In the process, his company destroyed up to 5 enemy tanks. On 21 October Shekhonin together with two tanks captured the bridge in the Walterkehmen area and subsequently straddled the road and held the bridge until the arrival of the battalion's main forces. In the battle for the bridge across the Rominte River at the village of Samelucken Shekhonin, commanding the remaining tanks of two companies, drove back strong Nazi counterattacks. He personally destroyed 2 Panther tanks. When only two tanks were left in the company, Shekhonin decided in one tank to move toward the enemy and ram a German tank. When his tank was emerging from its cover, it was set ablaze and Shekhonin was killed. For his courage, valor and disdain for death, he was posthumously awarded the Order of the Patriotic War 1st Class.

Guards Captain Nikolai Eremin – the deputy chief of staff of the 401st Guards Self-propelled Artillery Regiment. He showed himself to be a competent and energetic officer. He was always located up among the regiment's combat formation. He frequently led the defense of the command post and carried out combat assignments. For example, near Wiłkowyszki he organized the repulse of enemy counterattacks that closed within 100 meters of the command post. On the Gumbinnen direction, located together with the batteries and having run into the enemy on the morning of 21 October 1944, he shot up 4 enemy batteries at point-blank range and killed up to 80 Nazis. When coming out of encirclement, he remained behind with the regiment's chief of staff and directed the defense to screen the left flank as the corps came out of the pocket, where he was in fact killed at his combat post. He was posthumously awarded the Order of the Patriotic War 1st Class.

Guards Senior Lieutenant Mikhail Prozorov – the chief of the 401st Guards Self-propelled Artillery's chemical service. In the Gumbinnen operation, located directly up among the batteries' combat positions, he directed the placement of smoke screens during the river crossings and carried out combat assignments. In the difficult combat situation on 23 October 1944, when the corps was coming out of the pocket, the commander of the self-propelled gun in which Prozorov was located was killed. He assumed command and courageously led it in combat in order to break out of the enemy encirclement. With his self-propelled gun's tracks and fire, he destroyed an enemy antitank gun together with its crew, and personally killed up to 15 Germans with a submachine gun. In this combat he fell bravely on the battlefield. Prozorov was posthumously awarded the Order of the Patriotic War 1st Class.

Information about the enemy from the 3rd Belorussian Front's intelligence headquarters

A prisoner from the 644th Fortress Battalion Unteroffizier Johann Nagel testified that the battalion had become subordinate to the 1st (East Prussia) Infantry Division and consisted of three companies of 93 men each. It was armed with 24 machine guns, 4 Panzerfausts, 8 Panzerschrecks and 160 grenades. The company was occupying 8 bunkers, which were spaced 800 to 2,500 meters apart from each other.

A soldier of the 9th Squadron of the 13th Cavalry Brigade who was taken prisoner testified that on 16 October the brigade was transferred from the Loma area to the Woidoty area and was thrown into combat from the march. It suffered significant losses.

Prisoners of the 4th Company of the 20th Panzer Division's Panzergrenadier Regiment 112 testified that one battalion from this regiment had arrived in the Eydtkuhnen area. The prisoners supposedly didn't know where the rest of the division's units were located at this time, but according to information from the Red Army's Main Intelligence Command, the division at this time was forming up in Upper Silesia.

Prisoners of Panzer Brigade 101 testified that the brigade had arrived in the Eydtkuhnen area from Latvia. The brigade had four companies each with 10 tanks, 16 armored halftracks, and 5 self-propelled guns.

A prisoner of Separate Panzer Regiment 112 testified that the regiment had 800 men and 29 tanks, and had arrived in the area of fighting on 18 October 1944 from Carpathia.

According to the information of a soldier of a panzer regiment taken prisoner in the area northwest of Wisztyniec, it was established that on 19 October the Parachute-Panzer Division *Hermann Göring* had arrived from Germany, where it had been refitting. The division had one panzer regiment, the 1st and 2nd Panzergrenadier Regiments, an antitank battalion, a pioneer battalion and a signals battalion. The panzer regiment consisted of two battalions: the 1st Battalion had four companies with a combined 68 Panther tanks; the 2nd Battalion had four companies with a combined 68 Pz.Kpfw. IV tanks.

Due to the heavy casualties, the numerical strength of the enemy's units had been significantly reduced by the end of the operation. For example, a prisoner taken from the 12th Company of the 1st (East Prussia) Infantry Division's Infantry Regiment 45 testified that on 27 October only 20-45 men remained in the regiment's companies and the division, and in view of the heavy casualties had to be pulled out of combat for reforming.

A prisoner of Panzer Abteilung 1 of the Parachute-Panzer Division *Hermann Göring* testified that the battalion, which had 48 Panther tanks, had lost 18 tanks by 27 October. A prisoner of a motorized transport company of the 561st Volksgrenadier Division testified that the division was awaiting replenishments from the Volkssturm.

In connection with the heavy losses and the unsuccessful course of the fighting, according to the information from the 3rd Belorussian Front's Intelligence Department, the commander of the 131st Infantry Division Lieutenant General Weber was dismissed from his post. Over the period of combat operations, the Germans also suffered casualties among its generals. For example, a German Ju-52 transport aircraft was shot down in the Stulgen area (4 kilometers southwest of Gumbinnen), and in the wreckage the body of the commander of the German XVII Korps General of Infantry Priess was found. Documents were found on his body: an ID card, a pass to Führer Headquarters, a bundle of photographs, etc.

Here it makes sense to talk about the falsifications of history to which the former German generals resort when describing combat operations on the Soviet – German front after the war, in particular those in the Gumbinnen area.

Take, for example, K. Tippelskirch, who writes:

> By 22 October the Russians, exploiting the breakthrough, had reached Nemmersdorf on the Angerapp River and had created a threat of enveloping Gumbinnen from the south and southwest. In the center they had taken Goldap. In the south their offensive was managed to be stopped only after the loss of Filipów, Suwalki and Augustów. Having brought up its reserves, the Fourth Army under the command of General Hoßbach managed at the last moment to deprive the Russians of the possibility to enter operational space north of the Rominter Heide. With counterattacks from the flanks against the salient that had forced, by 27 October a significant portion of the enemy forces that had penetrated as far as the Angerapp River had been destroyed, and the breach that had been created here had been closed ….
>
> Between the Neman River and Augustów, the Russians committed five armies into the offensive, which had a total number of around 40 rifle divisions and a large number of tank formations. They left behind on the battlefield approximately 1,000 destroyed tanks and more than 300 guns.

The former Nazi Major General Horst Freiherr Treusch von Buttlar-Brandenfels in his memoirs also asserts: "… the troops of the Fourth Army managed by way of counterattacks against the exposed flanks of the Russian penetration to cut off a significant portion of the enemy forces that had reached the Angerapp River and to destroy them…. In these battles approximately 1,000 tanks and 300 guns of the enemy were destroyed."

So, both generals write one and the same thing, although they undoubtedly knew that this was far-fetched. There was at the start of the operation a total of only 688 tanks in all of the 3rd Belorussian Front's five armies and its other formations and units, about which the German former generals write. The Front received no replenishment with tanks in the course of the operation. The question raises itself: From just where could the 3rd Belorussian Front lose "approximately 1,000 tanks"?

In the course of the intense fighting between 19 and 24 October 1944, the opponents of the 2nd Guards Tank Corps were the 1st Parachute-Panzer Division *Hermann Göring*, the 5th Panzer Division and the Führer Grenadier Brigade. Let's take a look at Franz Kurowski's book *The History of the Fallschirm Panzerkorp* Hermannn Göring (Winnipeg: J.J. Fedorowicz Publishing, 1995) and turn to the chapter dedicated to the corps' fighting in East Prussia in October 1944. From this book, which pretends to be the corps' combat chronicle, it is impossible to figure out the corps' strength and composition with which it entered the fighting, how many combat-ready tanks and self-propelled guns were in the corps and its divisions, and what was the enemy's real, not alleged, strength. Instead of laying out the facts, Kurowski cites a wartime article in his book written by military correspondent Becker, who was supposedly an eyewitness of the fighting. The text reads: "Never before had Soviet units and formations been committed into a battle in such quantity and quality. Under the pitiless eye of the Kremlin, the *Stavka* directed an offensive toward Königsberg. In accordance with Stalin's order, all of East Prussia was to be taken within 10 days …."

This propagandistic text in the spirit of Doctor Göbbels cannot hold up to any criticism. In the first place, on the Soviet side in the Gumbinnen operation, five armies (among which was only one Guards army – the 11th Guards Army) of the 3rd Belorussian Front took part. The 3rd Belorussian Front didn't have a single tank army, and had just one tank corps (the 2nd Guards Tank Corps), five separate tank brigades and nine separate tank regiments. It is sufficient to compare this grouping with, for example, the Voronezh Front's grouping during the Battle of Kursk, or with the grouping of Soviet forces in the course of Operation Bagration and the L'vov-Sandomierz operation, in order to convince oneself that correspondent Becker's assertion in Kurowski's retelling doesn't correspond to reality.

A question to Kurowski: Did he himself see the text of the order, supposedly signed by Stalin, that all of East Prussia was to be taken within 10 days? Where is it possible to become acquainted with this order?

Speaking seriously, the fact is evident that on 22 October 1944 the 1st Parachute-Panzer Division *Hermann Göring* had 47 Panthers, 20 Pz.kpfw. IV and 34 StuG in formation. Already after two days of combat, this division now had only 20 Panthers, 5 Pz.kpfw. IV and 15 StuG still operational.

The dry facts speak to the intensity of the fighting. In the course of it, the commander of the 1st Panzer Abteilung of Parachute-Panzer Regiment *Hermann Göring* Joachim Renz was killed; his Panther was destroyed in the fighting on 23 October 1944. On this same day in a different battle, the commander of Führer Grenadier Brigade's panzer battalion Major von Uslar-Gleichen was killed when his Panther was also destroyed. It is sufficient to say that already on 25 October 1944, the Parachute-Panzer Corps *Hermann Göring*, according to the operational summary of the German Fourth Army, had only a total of 56 serviceable tanks and assault guns in its 1st and 2nd Parachute-Panzer Divisions, the 5th Panzer Division and Schwere Panzer Abteilung 505, at a time when it had 193 machines in various states of repair. Here once again we are dealing with concealed irrevocable losses, which were often written off at a later date.

What about the Führer Grenadier Brigade? If to judge from the summaries of the Fourth Panzer Army, then the parachute-panzer divisions of *Hermann Göring,* the 5th Panzer Division and the Führer Grenadier Brigade didn't lose a single tank irrevocably. Yet as has already been mentioned above, in the fighting, for example, the Panthers of the two panzer battalion commanders were destroyed, in which they had perished together with their crew members, but for some reason their destroyed tanks were included in the table "Tanks under short-term and long-term repair"). Altogether according to official German data, between 16 and 23 October 1944 the Fourth Army irrevocably lost 1 panzer and 48 assault guns. Over four days of fighting alone, Parachute-Panzergrenadier Divisions 1 and 2 *Hermann Göring* lost 1,192 men (215 killed, 815 wounded, 162 missing in action); the 5th Panzer Division over two days of fighting (22-24 October 1944) lost 411 men (69 killed, 316 wounded and 26 missing in action); the 549th Volksgrenadier Division lost more than 2,000 men killed and missing in action; the 547th Volksgrenadier Division lost 2,490 men (573 killed, 1,190 wounded, 727 missing in action); the 561st Volksgrenadier Division lost 2,180 men (1,115 killed, 1,065 wounded); the 131st Infantry Division lost 628 men (119 killed, 462 wounded, 47 missing); and so on and so forth.

The conclusion of the 3rd Belorussian Front's command regarding the conducted operation

In the course of 10 days of savage fighting on the defensive lines of East Prussia, the Front's troops didn't fully carry out the task that had been given to them. The 31st Army had the greatest success; over 6 days of fighting (from 17 to 22 October 1944), its units advanced 48 km, which means an average pace of advance of 8 km a day. This is explained by the enemy's weak resistance; between the areas of Goldap and Suwalki, the enemy was unable to keep the army's advance in check. On the Gumbinnen direction, the operation (after 10 days) ended with the capture of our troops of Stallupönen (Ebenrode), which was an objective for the 3rd day of the operation. On the Angerburg direction, we captured Goldap (a task for the 5th day of the operation). Thus, of all the armies only the 31st Army fully carried out its task (with a delay of 24 hours).

By the breakthrough of the enemy's defense on the indicated directions, the German system of defenses was revealed, as well as the nature of their resistance and their possibilities. It should be noted that one of the reasons for the failure to carry out the tasks according to phase lines and timetables was the unsatisfactory handling of the troops on the part of corps headquarters (36th Rifle Corps and 5th Guards Rifle Corps) and the poor command over the units and formations (the 352nd Rifle Division of this same corps). The troops were experiencing certain difficulties with respect to the kicking-off of the offensive. The morning fog in connection with the arriving drop in temperatures didn't allow them to start the offensive early in the morning. Targets were scarcely visible, so on separate sectors there was the need to increase the amount of artillery, in particular guns capable of laying direct fire. In separate cases the quantity of these guns approached 50 percent of all the available artillery (39th Army).

The maneuvering of the means by the army commanders in the course of the operation, although going as planned, didn't always have a substantial influence on the course of the fighting. If the 2nd Guards Tank Corps served as the fist that ensured the infantry's relatively rapid arrival in the area southeast of Gumbinnen, then the focus of the artillery and armor on the right flank of the 45th Rifle Corps 5th Army), for example on 22 October 1944 during its right flank's offensive toward Schilleningken, didn't yield any particular results.

All types of troops without exception performed as a rule well in the conducted operation. Having encountered the enemy's permanent fortifications for the first time, the infantry, in cooperation with the tanks and artillery, in relatively short periods of time overcame the German resistance and made an advance.

The 2nd Guards Tatsinskaia Tank Corps, operating on the axis of the most apparent success (south of Gumbinnen) quickly lunged ahead, but under the pressure of enemy counterattacks was forced to abandon the lines it had attained, despite the close contact with the infantry formations that were operating on this direction (11th Guards Army).

The air force demonstrated good examples of work both on the first and on subsequent days of the operations, having complete superiority in the air. The artillery rendered great assistance to the infantry throughout the operation.

The tragedy at Nemmersdorf

In conclusion, it is impossible not to discuss the tragedy at Nemmersdorf, which later provoked a lot of attention. First, the chronology of events. Nemmersdorf was one of the first villages in East Prussia to be occupied by Soviet forces. The village had approximately 600 residents; however, by the morning of 21 October 1944 the majority of its citizens had been evacuated. Nemmersdorf was on the left bank of the Angerapp River and presented a German strongpoint with well-furnished bunkers, fieldworks, barbed wire obstacles and an anti-tank ditch. A 45-meter-long reinforced concrete bridge led into the village. Because of the rapid advance by the Soviet forces, some of the German baggage trains intermingled with German refugees didn't have time to cross to the opposite bank before the bridge was captured. On this same day, the Luftwaffe began bombing the village, and a group of German residents took cover in a bomb shelter. According to the testimony of the eyewitness Gerda Meczulat, there were 11 people in the bunker. After the start of the aerial bombing, several Red Army soldiers descended into the shelter. In the evening a Red Army officer arrived, who ordered the residents to leave the shelter, after which they were supposedly shot. The eyewitness Gerda Meczulat somehow remained alive.

Soon, units of the elite Parachute Panzerkorp *Hermann Göring* were brought up to the Nemmersdorf area. On 22 October units of the Panzergrenadier Battalion 413 and Volkssturm launched several attacks. In the difficult situation that had developed by that time, at an order from the commander-in-chief of the 3rd Belorussian Front General of the Army Cherniakhovsky, the Soviet tankers on 23 October fell back across the Angerapp River 10-15 kilometers, and already on 24-25 October, the first members of a German commission appeared in Nemmersdorf, consisting of representatives of the German National Socialist Party, the SS, the Ministry of Propaganda and military reporters.

Two reports were put together on 25 and 26 October. The first report contained information regarding Nemmersdorf and Tutteln. On 27 October, an article appeared in Göbbel's newspaper *Völkischer Beobachter* which contained a detailed description of the mass atrocities supposedly perpetrated against the civilian population by Red Army soldiers in Nemmersdorf and its surroundings. According to this information, 62 German women were raped, sometimes repeatedly, before being shot.

Another commission was created, this time an "international" commission under the direction of the recently unemployed leader of the Estonian "self-government", the nationalist Hjalmar Mäe, whom even in the 1990s the present Estonian leadership, albeit reluctantly, had to acknowledge as one of the main guilty parties of Nazi crimes on Estonian land. On 31 October 1944, several eyewitnesses addressed this commission at a conference. It is understandable that this commission's conclusions were fully in line with the official German version of the events. Shocking photographs with raped and dead women widely circulated. True, the "eyewitnesses" were constantly confused in their testimonies. As purported, German Volkssturm troops had buried their fellow townsmen and relatives just as they found them, with torn, hiked-up skirts and lowered underpants. In any event, it was in just this appearance that the bodies were exhumed for the "international commission". The numbers of victims also diverge, and no one ever saw the several dozen French military prisoners, who'd supposedly been executed "in the heat of the moment" by the Red Army soldiers together with the German civilians, even though information about them began to light up the air waves and print media in the West only after the war ended. One of the conclusions of the commission was that "almost all of the young women were subjected to rape." The commission came to the conclusion that the "actions of the Bolsheviks violate the norms of waging war." The execution of the civilians in Nemmersdorf was widely used by Nazi propaganda. Materials dedicated to the given events featured in newspapers, radio transmissions and movie theaters, which led to a panic among the German people. In Great Britain in November 1944, the German communiques regarding Nemmersdorf were labeled as a lie.

After the war, Bernhard Fisch, who took part in the fighting for Nemmersdorf, and who subsequently published several books and articles on the subject, doesn't exclude the possibility of a provocation on the German side. In his book *Nemmersdorf 1944 – was in Ostpreussen tatsächlich geschah* [*Nemmersdorf 1944: What actually happened in East Prussia*], he states that he saw a different scene in Nemmersdorf that strongly differed from the film footage shown in the *Wochenschau* [the German cinema news series]. After discovering the bodies, not a single effort was made on the German side to identify them. Bernhard Fisch also concluded that the bodies of the dead from several villages in East Prussia were shown in the film. In an article on the website for the German *ZDF* channel (from 2001) it states that possibly there were no rapes, but the killings were used by the Nazi press in order to generate fear of the Soviet troops among the population.

According to the testimony of one eyewitness – the former Werhmacht soldier Helmut Hoffman, who served as a Feldwebel in Panzergrenadier Battalion 413 and was one of the first to arrive at the place of the events, the German propaganda was fiction: "Not one of the women had been raped. As they were lying when they were filmed – this was done after I saw them. Their clothing had been hiked up or pulled down." Hoffman also declared that some of the victims, possibly, had been killed from a great distance. Several days had passed from the moment German troops re-entered the village – adequate time in order to make the cruel reality even more shocking. The Russian researcher of this tragedy Igor' Petrov considers it improbable that after two days of fierce fighting in and around the village, which was repeatedly bombed and shelled by howitzers and mortars, not a single civilian had been harmed according to German information – all of the dead had instead supposedly been "tortured to death by the Russians".

Now let's return once again to October 1944. When Soviet forces had broken through the forward German positions and began to advance swiftly toward Gumbinnen, the chaos on the roads intensified. The retreating German troops, the German refugees and the Soviet troops on the Gumbinnen direction all had to cross the Angerapp River, and this was possible to do only across the single bridge at Nemmersdorf. Of course, this could not have gone by without civilian casualties. Moreover, some of the civilians took up arms in the effort to offer some sort of resistance to the attacking Soviet troops.

Nemmersdorf proved to be the first village and exceptionally important bridgehead taken by the Red Army in the course of the fighting, and it was later abandoned. The village, situated on a high bank of the Angerapp River and its reinforced concrete was useful for an offensive or to the defense, depending on who it belonged to at the time. The capture of Nemmersdorf was so unexpected for the German command, that it didn't have time to evacuate the civilian population in the area, and it also suffered in the course of the fighting.

The given circumstance was later used by Göbbel's propaganda in order to accuse the Russian soldiers of genocide with respect to the civilian population, the mutilation of the bodies, and so forth. Let's take a look at a German summary from 23 October 1944: "The Bolsheviks succeeded in making a deep penetration into our defenses between Szudden and Goldap. After heavy street fighting, Goldap fell into the hands of the enemy. In the rear of the Russians that had broken through, south of Gumbinnen, infantrymen cut the main supply artery. The attempt by the Bolsheviks to break through along both sides of Ebenrode bogged down in blood. By this time, in this zone of combat operations in the course of seven days of fighting, 616 enemy tanks have been knocked out or captured."

On 16 October the commander of the 25th Guards Tank Brigade Colonel Bulygin had received a combat mission: operating in the first echelon of the 2nd Guards Tank Corps' left-hand column, with the arrival of the rifle units on the Stanajcie, Eydtkuhnen, Klein Wisztyniec line, to enter the breakthrough and operate in two directions. The first through Kattenau, Brakupönen and further on toward Gumbinnen, in order to seize the eastern portion of the town and take up a defense with a front toward the south and southeast; the second – to break through to the Walterkehmen, take the bridge across the Rominte River there, and to attack further along the route Maygunischken, Budweitschen in order to capture the bridge across the Angerapp and to take Nemmersdorf. The capture of this strategically important point on the western bank of the Angerapp River rested specifically on the 2nd Tank Battalion, in cooperation with a mechanized battalion of submachine gunners.

In the written account of the tankers' combat operations from 11 to 25 October 1944, the brigade commander Guards Colonel Bulygin reported on this subject: "The 2nd Tank Battalion, in cooperation with the mechanized battalion, with fighting took Nemmersdorf and the bridge across the Angerapp River at 0903, having killed up to 60 enemy soldiers and officers and having destroyed a supply train carrying ammunition.… Having mopped up Nemmersdorf of enemy infantry and the civilian population, the units took up an all-round defense in readiness to repulse possible enemy counterattacks."

The phrase about "mopping up Nemmersdorf" of the civilian population, as written in the report agitated several contemporary German historians. In particular, Dr. B. Fisch saw in this a confirmation of possible Soviet repressions by Soviet soldiers with respect to the village's civilians, and in order to establish the truth proposed an archeological excavation of the combat area. In actual fact the brigade commander's words in the report was a commonly-used expression in the war years. It meant actions connected with the evacuation of civilians who'd been caught in a zone of particularly bitter fighting. In such cases the population was warned about the mortal danger to their lives and was ordered to leave the zone of danger. The circumstance that under the guise of civilians, German scouts and saboteurs might wind up in the Soviet rear, was also not insignificant.

For two days, in the course of which the Soviet tankers and infantry managed to keep hold of Nemmersdorf, the village actually represented a seething cauldron of fire. The ground shook from the explosions of shells and bombs, dropped on the defensive positions of the Soviet units. The Luftwaffe in wave after wave of 10-15 bombers flew over the battalions' combat positions, scattering death and destruction. Throughout the night of 21-22 October, the Germans attacked Nemmersdorf five times, but all the attacks were repulsed. At 0800 on 22 October, after a short pause, German tanks and infantry again moved out on the attack and were once again thrown back by the defenders. At 1030, 20 enemy tanks with artillery support repeated the attack. This time a portion of the accompanying German infantry infiltrated into the village. At 1240 there followed a third powerful enemy attack. At the end of the day, the 2nd Tank Battalion and mechanized submachine gun battalion received an order to abandon Nemmersdorf, cross to the eastern bank of the Angerapp River, and take up a defense in the Hill 68.5 area and await new orders. Other of the brigade's tank units also fell back under enemy pressure.

In a report from the 25th Guards Tank Brigade's Chief of the Political Department A. Slepov to the Political Department of the 2nd Guards Tank Corps dated 25 October 1944 it is indicated that during the offensive, including the battle for Nemmersdorf, "no instances of immoral conduct or extraordinary occurrences among the officers and soldiers were noted."

So, what happened in Nemmersdorf in October 1944? Was there really acts of mass murder perpetrated against civilians by Red Army troops, as German sources report? At present, one can only state with certainty that at this time there was fierce fighting taking place in the Nemmersdorf area, in the center of which there was a significant number of civilians, many of which, undoubtedly, perished. This is a fact.

It is also possible to assert that there were no violent acts on the part of Soviet soldiers with respect to the German civilian population? No, there were such cases. Of course, the German command was waiting for just such a case, in order to use it for propaganda purposes, which happened in the case with Nemmersdorf.

Nevertheless, there is still insufficient documentary basis for how German historians treat what happened. Here there are more emotions and propaganda, and one must give credit to Göbbel's apparatus – in the case of Nemmersdorf, it worked masterfully: to the present day, these events agitate Germans.

As the scholar Igor' Petrov noted in his research, on 21-22 October 1944, 26 local residents and refugees perished in Nemmersdorf. In the fighting for Nemmersdorf in October 1944 and in January 1945, more than 300 soldiers and officers of the Red Army were killed.

3

The Kielce – Łysów Tank Battle

The largest tank battle of 1945 took place in the area of Kielce, Poland between 13 and 15 January 1945. Here, the main forces of the General Walther Nehring's XXIV Panzer Corps, consisting of the 16th and 17th Panzer Divisions, Heavy Panzer Battalion 424 and the 20th Panzergrenadier Division attempted to cut off and destroy the forward detachments of the 10th Guards Tank Corps and 6th Guards Mechanized Corps of General D.D. Leliushenko's 4th Tank Army [Guards Tank Army in March 1945]. The Soviet tankers entered into a difficult meeting battle involving armored forces.

From the recollections of Hero of the Soviet Union General of the Army A.I. Radzievsky:

In the course of developing offensive operations, one of the main tasks that the tank armies had to resolve in cooperation with the air force and other service branches was the struggle against the enemy's operational reserves. To a decisive extent, the course and outcome of an offensive by the tank armies on the whole depended on how successfully this particular problem was handled.

One of the means of resolving it was the enemy's defeat in a meeting engagement. Meeting battles involving tank armies in the years of the Great Patriotic War arose as a rule on the directions of the *fronts'* main attacks, at the most criticial moments of the operations and in various phases of conducting them: at the outset of the operation, in the course of it as it unfolded, and in the concluding stage. At the outset of an operation, meeting battles took place as the tank armies were breaking through the enemy's tactical zone of defense or immediately after breaching it, when the enemy sought to regain the initial positions by introducing the nearest operational reserves.

General of the Army A.I. Radzievsky, a postwar photograph.

One of the most characteristic examples of a meeting battle that arose in such conditions was the battle involving the 4th Tank Army and the enemy's XXIV Panzer Corps in the Kielce area in January 1945. This panzer corps, which included the 16th and 17th Panzer Divisions and the 20th Panzergrenadier Division (with approximately 360 tanks altogether) and was located in the operational reserve of Army Group "A", received orders on the morning of 13 January 1945 (the second day of the operation) to launch a counterattack, destroy the grouping of the 1st Ukrainian Front that had broken through, and regain the previously occupied positions. On the night of 12-13 January, the panzer corps' divisions began moving up to the line of deployment. Meanwhile the forward detachments of the 4th Tank Army's corps, having entered the enemy's second defensive belt, were from the march breaking through it. At sunrise on 13 January, they collided with the forward detachments of the XXIV Panzer Corps, which were in the process of moving up in order to launch the counterattack. A meeting clash erupted in the area south of Kielce.

The forward detachments of the corps of the first echelon – the 16th Mechanized Corps and 63rd Guards Tank Brigade, operating in an unclear situation, detached part of their strength to hold the Germans in place, while the main forces maneuvered and attacked the enemy in the flank and rear. With the bold and decisive actions, they disrupted the enemy divisions' organized movement into their designated jumping-off positions. The enemy was forced to join battle with their main forces not simultaneously, but in sequence.

The commander of the 4th Tank Army General D.D. Leliushenko, having assessed the situation, decided to screen the front with two brigades and to conduct a double envelopment of the 17th Panzer Division that had surged ahead, and in cooperation with the 3rd Guards Tank Army's 6th Guards Tank Corps to launch simultaneous attacks against both of its flanks. Executing the maneuver, the Guardsmen of the 10th Tank and 6th Mechanized Corps struck the enemy's 17th Panzer Division from both flanks; after savage fighting, the German panzer division was shattered by the end of 13 January. With the approach of the 16th Panzer Division to the battlefield area, it was pinned in place by the 49th Mechanized Brigade in the Radomicze area. Meanwhile the main forces of the 4th Tank Army on 14 January launched an attack against its right flank. On the following day the remnants of the XXIV Panzer Corps was encircled and destroyed in the area south of Kielce.

Thus, in the course of a fierce armor meeting battle, which lasted for approximately two and a half days, the enemy's counterattack grouping consisting of three divisions was smashed. The Germans lost up to 180 tanks and assault guns, while the 4th Tank Army lost approximately 130 tanks and self-propelled guns.

The defeat of such a major enemy grouping in a relatively short period of time to a great extent helped the troops of the 1st Ukrainian Front's left wing, which successfully developed an offensive on the Krakow axis, and especially the troops of the 1st Belorussian Front, which on 14 January, at the very height of the meeting battle, unleashed a powerful attack against the enemy from out of the Magnuszewski and Pulaw bridgeheads. In order to attempt to stop the offensive by both Soviet *fronts*, the German command was forced to commit its remaining reserves and was unable to render any sort of assistance to its counterattack grouping that was operating in the Kielce area. General Tippelskirch, looking back on the events of those days, later wrote: "The attack was so strong that it not only rolled over the divisions of the first echelon, but also the rather large mobile reserves …. The Fourth Panzer Army's front was torn apart into pieces … enemy formations of armor … launched an outflanking maneuver toward Kielce."

The meeting battle near Kielce arose when completing the breakthrough of the enemy's tactical zone of defense in the circumstances when both sides were striving to resolve their assigned tasks with an attack. The battle ensued with actions of the forward detachments with the subsequent entry of main forces. The commander of the 4th Tank Army made the decision within a relatively limited amount of time and in the conditions of an insufficiently clear situation. The rapidity of the deployment of the tank army's main forces, the pre-empting of the enemy's actions and the broad maneuvering of forces and means decided the outcome of the meeting battle. The enemy's counterattack grouping was defeated in detail, with the launching of flank attacks against it while it was pinned down from the front by part of the tank army's strength. Such a method of operation led to the separation of the enemy's divisions and to their encirclement and destruction in isolated areas.

The operational-tactical situation

The German forces in the course of the L'vov – Sandomierz operation of 1944 were driven back from the western bank of the Vistula River south of the town of Sandomierz, and fell back to the Łagów, Szydłów, Stopnica sector, where after unsuccessful counterattacks with the aim of eliminating the Soviet bridgehead on the western bank of the Vistula, went over to the defensive in the first half of September 1944. For the next four months, they rushed to complete the process of fortifying the sector, expanding it in depth, and conducted reconnaissance probes. By 12 January 1945, the enemy's defense presented two to three lines of full-profile trenches, connected by communication trenches, with machine-gun nests. There were positions for heavy weapons (mortars, antitank guns) behind the second line of trenches. The commanding heights and built-up areas were adapted for a defense as strongpoints and centers of resistance. The second defensive belt ran along the Skrzelczyce, Pierzchnica, Chmielnik, Śladków Maly line and consisted of two lines of full-profile trenches, as well as communication trenches and cleared areas for machine guns. Switch positions had been prepared in the Chmielnik – Raczyce sector. The strongpoints of Szydłów, Chmielnik, Mały Gość and Szczekociny had been prepared for an all-round defense, with a large number of bunkers and cleared areas for machine guns, as well as equipped artillery positions; brick buildings had all been converted into firing positions. Reckoning on our offensive, the enemy had created a number of intermediary and main defensive lines, exploiting commanding terrain and water obstacles. In addition, a number of anti-tank and anti-personnel obstacles had been put in place.

Lacking an adequate number of troops to man the forward edge, the Germans strengthened their defense with weapons, particular antitank weapons, and ensured the proper centralized direction of artillery fire, hoping this would be sufficient to repulse the Soviet offensive. Opposite the designated breakthrough sector, the enemy had the specialized units of the 68th and 168th Infantry Divisions in tactical reserve, as well as units of reinforcement: the 255th Security Battalion; the 733rd, 14th and 749th Pioneer Battalions; the 16th Mortar Regiment; and a brigade of assault guns (with up to 30 assault guns). The enemy had General Nehring's XXIV Panzer Corps in operational reserve. It consisted of the 20th Panzergrenadier Division (in the Beczków-Zaskale area, east of Kielce), the 16th Panzer Division (in the area of Wierzbnik), Heavy Panzer Battalion 424 in the Busko-Zdrój area, the 17th Panzer Division (in the Miechów, Skalbmierz area); a kampfgruppe of the Kalmykian Cavalry Corps (in the Końskie area); and a number of units of reinforcement, including the North Ukraine Regiment (in the Krajno, Wola Jachowa area – east of Kielce.) Thus, by the start of the combat operations of General D.D. Leliushenko's 4th Guards Tank Army, the enemy had arranged his operational reserves directly within the tactical zone of his defense.

By the end of 11 January 1945, the 4th Guards Tank Army's 10th Guards Tank Corps had taken up a jumping-off position in the woods northeast of Wola Osowa (7 km northwest of Staszów), from where it was supposed to enter a breakthrough in the sector of the 6th and 112th Rifle Divisions of the 13th Army's 27th Rifle Corps. On the right, the 4th Guards Tank Army's 6th Mechanized Corps was occupying its jumping-off position in the woods north and east of Chańcza. On the left, the 3rd Guards Tank Army had moved up into the sector of the 52nd Army.

The general nature of the terrain

In the sector of the army's forthcoming combat operations, the terrain presented a plain that was cut by a large number of swampy ravines and rivers, which presented difficult areas for the movement of tanks. Up to 40 percent of the terrain was covered by woods, which contributed to movements that were concealed from aerial and ground observation. The roads in the direction of the

4th Tank Army's actions were either dirt or paved, passable for all types of transport and combat machines, which facilitated the rapid advance of the formations and units into the operational depth of the enemy's defenses.

Tankers of the 62nd Guards Tank Brigade of the 10th Guards Tank Corps. The brigade commander is standing in front of the formation.

An assembly of the tanks of the 10th Guards Tank Corps.

A tactical exercise involving officers of the 61st Guards Tank Brigade, winter of 1945.

The command of the 1st Ukrainian Front and the 4th Tank Army, January 1945

Left to right: I.S. Konev, V.D. Sokolovsky, K.V. Krainiukov, N.A. Novikov.

Left to right: D.D. Leliushenko, K.I. Upman, V.G. Guliaev, S.S. Mariakhin.

left to right: V.F. Orlov, E.E. Belov, N.D. Chuprov, M.G. Fomichev.

Left to right: B.V. Kurtsev, V.I. Zaitsev, S.V. Privezentsev, V.E. Ryvzh.

4th Tank Army

Left to right: V.I. Koretsky (Chief of Staff), I.S. Vaganov, A.G. Skriago, V.I. Sokolovsky (Artillery commander).

Left to right: S.A. Denisov (62nd Guards Tank Brigade commander), N.G. Zhukov (61st Guards Tank Brigade commander), A.I. Efimov (29th Guards Motorized Rifle Brigade commander), I.I. Proshin (62nd Guards Tank Brigade).

Left to right: M.I. Malevanny (62nd Guards Tank Brigade), A.I. Akrusha (Chief of Staff), G.M. Shcherbak (16th Mechanized Brigade), P.N. Turkin (49th Mechanized Brigade).

Left to right: N.Ia. Selivanchik (56th Tank Regiment), N.E. Shcherbakov (17th Guards Mechanized Brigade), L.D. Churilov (17th Mechanized Brigade commander).

Command staff of the 4th Guards Tank Army, 12 January 1945

Field command of the army
Army commander – Guards Colonel General of Tank Forces D.D. Leliushenko
Military Council member – Guards Major General of Tank Forces V.G. Guliaev
Army deputy commander – Guards Lieutenant General of Tank Forces E.E. Belov
Chief of staff – Guards Major General of Tank Forces K.I. Upman
Chief of operations – Guards Colonel S.S. Mariakhin
Chief of intelligence – Guards Lieutenant Colonel N.V. Bzyrin
Chief of the Political Department – Guards Colonel N.G. Kladovoi
Artillery commander – Guards Major General N.F. Mentiukov
Assistant commander for technical matters – Guards Engineer-Colonel V.M. Liapishev
Chief of engineers – Guards Colonel M.A. Poluektov
Chief of rear services – Guards Colonel A.K. Iarkov
Chief of communications – Guards Colonel A.Ia. Ostrenko
Chief of Sanitary-Medical Department – Colonel of Medical Service V.S. Vasil'ev

Army Formations

10th Guards Volunteer Tank Corps
Corps commander – Guards Colonel N.D. Chuprov
Chief of staff – Guards Colonel K.T. Khmylov
Chief of the Political Department – Guards Colonel I.F. Zakharchenko
61st Guards Tank Brigade – Guards Colonel N.G. Zhukov (KIA 13 January 1945); replaced by Guards Lieutenant Colonel V.I. Zaitsev
62nd Guards Tank Brigade – Guards Colonel S.A. Denisov
63rd Guards Tank Brigade – Guards Colonel M.G. Fomichev
29th Guards Motorized Rifle Brigade – Guards Colonel A.I. Efimov
72nd Guards Heavy Tank Regiment – Guards Lieutenant Colonel M.D. Kostin
356th Guards Self-propelled Artillery Regiment – Guards Colonel F.D. Parkhomenko

6th Guards Mechanized Corps
Corps commander – Guards Colonel V.F. Orlov
Chief of staff – Guards Colonel V.I. Koretsky
Chief of the Political Department – Guards Colonel G.I. Potapov
16th Guards Mechanized Brigade – Guards Colonel V.E. Ryvzh; replaced by Guards Lieutenant Colonel Makhno
17th Guards Mechanized Brigade – Guards Lieutenant Colonel L.D. Churilov
49th Mechanized Brigade – Guards Colonel P.N. Turkin
28th Guards Heavy Tank Regiment – Guards Lieutenant Colonel Chikhin
1st Guards Self-propelled Artillery Regiment – Guards Lieutenant Colonel V.F. Gaidash; 1433rd Self-propelled Artillery Regiment – Major G.M. Korolev; 29th Tank Regiment – Major Grachev; 56th Tank Regiment – Guards Colonel Selivanchik; 240th Mortar Regiment – Lieutenant Colonel Nabiev

Units subordinate to the army
51st Motorcycle Regiment – Lieutenant Colonel Stepanov
93rd Tank Brigade – Major A.A. Dement'ev

The combat strength of the 4th Guards Tank Army by the start of the operation (11 January 1945)

By the start of the operation, the 4th Guards Tank Army had been brought back up to authorized strength with personnel and equipment. By the start of the operation, the 4th Guards Tank Army had 482 T-34, 63 IS-122, and 113 SU-76 and SU-85, for a total of 685 tanks and self-propelled guns. In addition, the army had 61 SU-57 light self-propelled guns. With the exception of 30 tanks, fresh T-34 with the 85mm gun had been received, as well as factory-new self-propelled guns. The subordinate corps each received one regiment of heavy IS-2 tanks. Well-trained crews were seated in all the tanks. Eighty to ninety percent of the crews during gunnery training achieved the following results: in the course of 1 to 2 minutes, they were able to hit an enemy tank or gun with their first or second shot. The tankers were also well-prepared for night combat operations.

The command positions were fully staffed, primarily through cultivating cadres within the army. The tank army's artillery consisted of 348 guns and 261 mortars of various calibers, and it had 965 machine guns (not including the DShK anti-aircraft machine guns). The 4th Guard Tank Army's supply situation was fine: 3.5 standard combat loads of ammunition and 3.4 refills of fuel and lubricants.

Table 3.1: The correlation of forces on 12 January 1945 at the moment of the 4th Guards Tank Army's introduction into the breakthrough in the Komórki, Skrzelczyce, Maleszowa sector[1]

	German forces	Soviet forces	Correlation
Total personnel	23920	42875	1:1.7
Active bayonets	17800	29281	1:1.6
Tanks and self-propelled guns	325	620	1:1.9
SU-57 and armored transports	90	61	1.5:1
Guns	216	351	1:1.6
Mortars	142	261	1:1.8
Machine guns	645	965 (not including A-A guns)	1:1.5

1 The German forces include the XXIV Panzer Corps, which consisted of the 16th and 17th Panzer Divisions, the 20th Panzergrenadier Division, the Heavy Panzer Battalion 424, the 68th and 168th Infantry Divisions, and a kampfgruppe of the Kalmyck Cavalry Corps.

The officers and men had ample time to prepare for the operation. The process started in the latter half of December 1944.

By 1 January 1945, the preparations were in full swing. In tactical training, the primary attention was focused on readying the elements and units for nighttime operations: the ability to take strongpoints in the enemy's defenses and hold them until the arrival of the main forces. The units and formations trained to conduct swift nighttime march-maneuvers, to capture bridges, to make forced crossings of water obstacles with the assistance of whatever means at hand, to consolidate bridgeheads and to destroy approaching enemy reserves in a meeting battle.

The army commander personally checked the gunnery training of the tankers and artillerymen of one crew from each platoon and one gun of each battery. The training of the other crewmen and gun crews was checked by the corps commanders. Two large target ranges were set up in Klimantów and in the woods 6 km southwest of Iwaniski, where real targets were displayed for the tankers and artillery: knocked-out enemy King Tigers, Panthers and Pz.kpfw. IV tanks. The tankers and artillerymen who demonstrated outstanding results received honors: watches, cigar boxes, or expressions of gratitude from the army and from the corps.

Five to seven training exercises were conducted with the commanders and officer staffs of the battalions and companies. Each exercise focused on an offensive with regard for the conditions of the upcoming operations. On the eve of the operation, the objective was made known to all the personnel.

Between 2 and 5 January 1945, thorough reconnoitering of the jumping-off position and the forward edge and tactical depth of the enemy's defenses was conducted, and questions of the infantry's cooperation with the artillery, air force, engineers both within the army and with the 13th Army and 2nd Air Army were worked out and reconciled. On 6 January, the army commander, corps commanders and brigade commanders met with their counterparts in the 3rd Guards Tank Army to settle questions of cooperation. The course of the events demonstrated that such gunnery training of the artillery men and tankers and the preliminary training for the operation completely justified themselves.

From the recollections of the commander of the 63rd Guards Tank Brigade Twice Hero of the Soviet Union M.G. Fomichev:

We never before had such training as we had in the Vistula bridgehead. This is explained by a number of reasons. First of all, we had a lot of time. In addition, this time was avaible after already receiving the tanks and self-propelled guns. A decisive offensive was being prepared from the Vistula to Berlin. Therefore, time was given for the preparations. This is the one circumstance that was decisive. The second circumstance was the fact that there was no need for us to hurry. Therefore, we were preparing for a classic, decisive operation. We were now fully equipped with engineering equipment. Why then ruin the roads? It was better to wait two weeks or a month and play it safe. That's what happened. As we readied for the operation, we could sense our power. Time was on our side, and who knew this better than Iosif Vissarionovich (Stalin)? So, then it was interesting to take a look at how things were going for the Allies. This [when to start the offensive] was a deep question, one difficult to resolve. Konev kept saying when we were at the training exercises that we should begin as soon as possible. The question was who would take Berlin, and not just Berlin itself as a city with a transportation hub and line of defense, but instead the capital of Germany itself. Here, this would have an important political effect – who would be first to capture the capital of Germany and put a decisive and effective end to this war? It would also strongly influence the future diplomacy connected with the post-war future of Germany. There was the same question about Prague. The Americans and British were closer than us to Prague. Whether or not we entered [the city] first, everything about the Czech problem had already been decided. In the period of training we placed top priority on gunnery. Secondly, everything was based around detachment exercises with regard for the fact that we foresaw that the combats would be exceptionally mobile, as well as the fact that such elements as a platoon would represent a detachment that might be able to fight independently. Sometimes, even a single tank with the tank riders mounted on it might decide the fate of some town or the capture of some bridge. For example, Przemyśl, Warta or Chinzyny. If the Germans were organizing a defense there, I'd never go there, because when you were approaching it, you'd see the town was standing in a hollow, and we'd knock out two Tigers and the Germans would flee in panic. Thus, we worked with the platoon, the company and the battalion. The unit exercises ran at night. We used up quite a lot of shells, but this justified itself. The main emphasis was on gunnery. On the battlefield, fire is primarily decisive. We achieved a level of training where the first or second shell fired would hit the target.[1]

---

1   Editor's note: Fomichev in his recollections expressed himself very clumsily and unclearly, so there was some bit of conjecture about what he really meant to say. I consulted with several native Russians about the translation of this passage, and we arrived at the final translation you see in this book.

The German command of Army Group A and of the XXIV Panzer Corps, 12 January 1945

Left to right: Josef Harpe; Heinz Guderian; Walter Nehring, commander of the XXIV Panzer Corps.

Left to right: Dietrich von Müller, commander of the 16th Panzer Division; Georg Scholze, commander of the 20th Panzergrenadier Division; Albert Brux, commander of the 17th Panzer Division.

The commander of XXIV Panzer Corps Walter Nehring on the eve of the Soviet offensive in January 1945.

The availability of tanks and self-propelled guns in the German formations and units in the Kielce area by the start of the operation

The combat strength of the 16th Panzer Division on 30 December 1944

The 16th Panzer Division had 13 operational Pz.Kpfw. IV tanks (with 1 more tank under repair and 2 on the way); 57 operational Pz.Kpfw. V tanks (with another tank under repair and 4 on the way); Panzerbefehlswagen III command tanks – 2 (both serviceable); Artillerie-Panzerbeobachtungswagen III artillery observation tanks – 7 (all operational); 24 operational StuG III assault guns (with one assault gun under repair and 7 more on the way) Berge Pz.Kpfw. V armored recovery vehicles – 5 operational (with another 2 on the way); 13 Wespe self-propelled howitzers (all operational); 6 Hummel self-propelled howitzers (with 1 more on the way); 5 Grille self-propelled guns [mounting the 150mm sIG 33 infantry gun] operational (with 1 under repair); 3 light halftracks armed with MG machine guns (all operational); 2 light halftracks armed with a 20mm cannon (both operational); 2 operational heavy halftracks armed with a 20mm cannon (with one more under repair); 2 heavy halftracks armed with a 75mm cannon (both operational); 1 operational artillery observation armored car (with 1 more under repair); 53 operational Sd.Kfz. 250 light halftracks (with another 5 under repair); and 117 operational Sd.Kfz. 251 medium halftracks (with another 5 under repair). Thus, the 16th Panzer Division had operational 70 tanks, 14 specialized tanks, 24 assault guns, and 24 self-propelled guns for a total of 132 combat machines, with another 16 tanks and self-propelled guns that were on the way on 30 December 1944 and were to arrive by the start of combat operations.

Combat strength of the 17th Panzer Division on 30 December 1944

The 17th Panzer Division had 53 operational Pz.Kpfw. IV L/48 tanks (with another 5 tanks under repair); 33 operational Pz.Kpfw. IV L/70 tanks (with another 4 under repair and 21 on the way); Panzerbefehlswagen III command tanks – 4 (all operational); one operational Artillerie-Panzerbeobachtungswagen III artillery observation tank; one operational Berge Pz.Kpfw. V armored recovery vehicle; one Marder II 75mm self-propelled gun (under repair); one operational Marder II 76mm self-propelled gun; 6 operational Marder III 75mm self-propelled guns (with one under repair); 13 Wespe self-propelled howitzers (all operational); 7 Hummel self-propelled howitzers (all operational); one operational light halftrack armed with a machine gun; 9 light halftracks armed with a 20mm cannon (all operational); 1 operational heavy halftrack armed with a 75mm cannon; 1 operational artillery observation armored car; 4 Sd.Kfz 250 halftracks (all operational); 16 Sd.Kfz. 251 halftracks (with 3 more under repair).

Thus, the 17th Panzer Division had operational 86 tanks and 6 specialized tanks, and 32 self-propelled guns, for a total of 124 combat machines plus another 21 tanks that were on their way on 30 December 1944 and were to arrive by the start of combat operations.

The combat strength of the 20th Panzergrenadier Division on 30 December 1944

The 20th Panzergrenadier Division had 46 operational StuG III assault guns (plus one gun under repair); 16 operational Marder II 75mm self-propelled guns (plus one more on the way); 2 Marder II 76mm self-propelled guns (both en route); 7 Marder III 76mm self-propelled guns; 1 operational light halftrack armed with an MG machine gun; 9 operational light halftracks armed with a 20mm cannon (all operational); 1 operational heavy halftrack armed with a 75mm gun; 1

artilllery observation armored car; 4 Sd.Kfz. 250 halftracks (all operational); and 16 operational Sd.Kfz. 251 halftracks (plus 3 more under repair). Thus, the 20th Panzergrenadier Division had a total of 69 operational self-propelled guns, plus 3 more that were on the way on 20 December 1944 and were to arrive by the start of combat operations.

From north to south along the front in the Kielce area, the Germans had the following infantry divisions in position: the 214th Infantry Division, the 342nd Infantry Division, the 72nd Infantry Division, the 88th Infantry Division, the 291st Infantry Division, the 168th Infantry Division, the 68th Infantry Division, the 304th Infantry Division, the 371st Infantry Divison, the 359th Infantry Division, and the 544th Volksgrenadier Division.

The former Chief of the German OKH (Oberkommando des Heeres) recalls that the German reserves were positioned as follows: the 17th Panzer Division in the Pinczow area; the 16th Panzer Division, south of Kielce; and the 20th Panzergrenadier Division between Vierzonik and Ostrowicz.

The German infantry divisions in the Kielce area had the following assault guns and self-propelled guns on 30 December 1944:

214th Infantry Division had 8 StuG III assault guns (all operational), 2 StuH 42 assault guns (both operational), and 1 operational Berge T-34.
342nd Infantry Division had 9 operational StuG III assault guns, plus one undergoing light repairs, and 1 operational Berge Pz.Kpfw. III.
72nd Infantry Division had 9 operational StuG III assault guns, plus one undergoing light repairs, and 1 operational Berge Pz.Kpfw. III.
88th Infantry Division had 10 StuG IV assault guns (all operational), and 1 operational Berge Pz.Kpfw. III.
291st Infantry Division had 10 StuG IV assault guns (all operational), and 1 operational Berge Pz.Kpfw. III.
168th Infantry Division had 12 operational StuG IV assault guns, plus 2 undergoing light repairs, and 1 Berge Pz.Kpfw. III.
68th Infantry Division had 12 operational Marder 75mm self-propelled guns (plus 2 undergoing light repairs), and one operational Berge Hetzer.
304th Infantry Division had 10 operational Hetzer self-propelled guns (plus another 4 undergoing light repairs), and 1 operational Berge Hetzer.
371st Infantry Division (on 15 January 1944) had 8 operational StuG III assault guns (plus 2 more undergoing light repairs).

Information on the presence of assault guns and self-propelled guns in the 359th Infantry Division and 544th Volksgrenadier Division is lacking.

In addition, the following units were equipped with assault guns:

201st Assault Gun Brigade on 30 December 1944 had 23 StuG III (all operational) and 13 StuH 42 assault guns (all operational).
210th Assault Gun Brigade on 30 December 1944 had 19 operational StuG III (plus 2 more undergoing light repairs).
322nd Assault Gun Brigade on 30 December 1944 had 19 StuG III (all operational) and 15 StuH 42 assault guns (all operational), plus 4 Sd.Kfz. 251 halftracks (all operational).

Finally, the Fourth Panzer Army had the following units operationally subordinate to it:

A separate battalion of assault guns (**StuG Rgt Pz AOK 4**), which on 30 December 1944 had 12 StuG IV assault guns (all operational);

Heavy Panzer Battalion 424 (sPz Abt 424), which on 30 December 1944 had 1 operational Berge Pz.Kpfw. V, 4 artillery observation armored cars (all operational), 3 Sd.Kfz. 250 halftracks (all operational). 3 Sd.Kfz. 251 halftracks (all operational), 28 Tiger II (King Tiger) and 22 Tiger I tanks (with another 4 undergoing light repairs). The presence of Tigers above the authorized table strength is explained by the fact that in September and December 1944, Heavy Panzer Battalion 424 received approximately 11 Tigers from Heavy Panzer Battalion 509;

Heavy Panzer Jäger Battalion 653 (Pz Jg Abt 653), which on 30 December had 5 operational Elefant self-propelled guns (plus 2 more undergoing light repairs).

Situation of the German formations and units on the eve of the operation

The XXIV Panzer Corps was positioned between the Hubertus Stellung in the first line of defense and the A-1 Stellung of the main defensive line, along the Kielce – Busko-Zdrój road. The 17th Panzer Division's headquarters was located in the Chmielnik area, together with Heavy Panzer Battalion 424. The headquarters of the 16th Panzer Division was positioned further to the north, between the northern outskirts of Chmielnik and an area 10 km from Kielce. The 20th Panzergrenadier Division was located in the Kielce area not far from the 16th Panzer Division's assembly area.

Table 3.2: Information on the combat losses of tanks and self-propelled guns of the 4th Tank Army over the period from 12 to 15 January 1945

Type	Engaged in combat	Knocked out of action	Of those machines knocked out of action:			
			Due to artillery fire	Due to mines	Due to air strikes/ bogged down in swamps	Due to mechanical breakdowns
T-34/85	272	79	59/34[1]	16	-	4
T-34/76	22	3	-	3	-	-
SU-122	63	9	7/4	2	-	-
SU-85	58	3	2/2	1	-	-
IS-122	19	12	4/2	2	-	6
SU-57	64	2	-	1	-	-
SU-76	48	1	-	1	-	-

1 Although there was no explanation in the report for the numbers split by the forward slash, the author considers it likely that the number to the left gives the total number of machines knocked out by any sort of artillery fire, including anti-tank artillery fire, while the number to the right gives the number knocked out by the fire from German panzers and self-propelled guns.

Deputy commander of the 4th Tank Army for Technical Affairs Guards Engineer-Colonel
LIAPISHEV
Chief of the 4th Tank Army's Department of Recovery and Evacuation Service Guards
Engineer-Major KOSTIANOY

The Breakthrough of the Enemy's Defenses

On the morning of 12 January 1945, following a powerful artillery preparation, the units of the 13th Army stepped off on the offensive. In the Raków, Szydłów area, immediately after the infantry took the enemy's second line of trenches, two forward detachments of the 4th Guards Tank Army were introduced into the fighting: the 16th Mechanized Brigade and the 63rd Tank Brigade, as well as the 150th Tank Brigade from the 13th Army. As a result of the fighting it was confirmed that the Germans had pulled back the forward edge of their defense somewhat into the depth.

Combat operations of the 10th Guards Tank Corps on 12 January 1945

The 10th Guards Tank Corps, advancing in the wake of the infantry with forward brigades, by 1800 on 12 January caught up with the infantry of the 27th Rifle Corps' 6th and 112th Rifle Divisions on the Rudki, Brzeziny, Podlesie line and began to develop the offensive in the general direction of Maleszowa, Dębska Wola and Chęciny [15 km southwest of Kielce] in two echelons.

The corps had the task on the first day of the offensive (12 January 1945) to take and hold the road hub of Chęciny with forward detachments by the end of the day. The main forces were to reach the Hill 250.7 (2 km northwest of Morawica), Chałupki, Lisów, Górki, Morawica area. On the second day of the operation (13 January 1945) it was to continue the offensive with its main forces in the Chęciny, Rykoszyn, Promnik direction, and by the end of the day take the Strawczyn, Łosień, Rykoszyn, Piecaszów, Piekoszów area. The forward detachments were to take Radoszyce and Łopuszno. The corps' forward brigade reached Pierzchnica by 2400 on 12 January, where it ran into heavy enemy fire.

The **61st Guards Tank Brigade** had a combat strength of 65 T-34 tanks; 3 76mm guns; 5 82mm mortars; 9 DShK machine guns; 3 heavy machine guns; 13 light machine guns; and 1391 men, of which 312 men were active combatants. The personnel were fully prepared for the forthcoming combat operations. Particular attention had been paid to work with the brigade's technical staff: the driver-mechanics of the tanks and the motor vehicle drivers.

Having received an order from the commander of the 10th Guards Tank Corps, the brigade by 0930 on 11 January had conducted a march with its 1st, 2nd and 3rd Tank Battalions, its motorized rifle battalion, its anti-aircraft machine-gun company and its radio center and assembled in the Duży Kurozwęki Woods, where the crews began to camouflage their tanks and to scout the routes leading to their jumping-off area near the crossing sites [on the Czarna River] and the forward edge of the enemy's defenses. Over the two days prior to the breakthrough, the 13th Army's reconnaissance units managed to drive back the enemy's outposts, which allowed the rapid construction of a bridge across the river in the Jasien – Korytnica area [northwest of Staszów]. At 0800 on 12 January the brigade received a supplemental order from corps headquarters: together with the attached two battalions of the 359th Anti-aircraft Regiment and a company of the 72nd Guards Separate Heavy Tank Regiment, to enter the breakthrough behind the 63rd Guards Tank Brigade in the corps' first combat echelon on the Życiny – Point 252.0 line, in readiness to overtake the 63rd Guards Tank Brigade and carry out an independent task to reach the Promnik area by the end of day on 12 January 1945. The enemy, screening his withdrawal with small groups of fragmented units of the 168th Infantry Division, the 17th Panzer Division and elements of the Heavy Panzer Battalion 424, throughout the day and first half of the night was retreating to the west. The brigade had no combat in the tactical zone of the enemy's defenses.

On 12 January 1945, the artillery of the 13th Army's 12th Rifle Corps began an artillery preparation, which continued for 1 hour and 47 minutes, after which units of the 6th Rifle Division, some of which waded across the Czarna River at fords, while the others attacked across hasty footbridges, and broke into the enemy's first line of trenches, where they became tied up in combat.

The **63rd Guards Tank Brigade** entered the battle with 65 T-34 tanks; 83 vehicles; 4 76mm guns; 6 82mm mortars; 4 heavy machine guns; 20 light machine guns; 422 submachine guns; 260 rifles; and 300 active bayonets. It had a strength of 1,307 men, of which 254 were officers, 683 were NCOs, and 370 were enlisted men.

On 12 January the brigade entered a breakthrough in the Kotuszów – Korytnica sector as the corps' forward detachment, and bypassing enemy centers of resistance, continued a rapid advance. In the course of the attack to penetrate the enemy's forward edge of defense, the Germans were using a new tactic of declining combat in the tactical zone of defense with the aim of conserving men and equipment.

In view of the brigade's rapid advance, the enemy didn't have the time to dig in on intermediary defensive lines and was forced to abandon equipment while suffering heavy losses. The brigade at 2100 on 12 January when approaching Maleszówa was counterattacked by 15 enemy tanks and a battalion of infantry from the direction of Hill 288.7. Hard fighting broke out for possession of Maleszówa. The brigade commanders decided to screen the eastern direction with one tank battalion, while the main forces would envelop Maleszówa from the northeast and launch an attack against it from the north. By 23.30 on 12 January, after stubborn fighting the brigade broke the enemy resistance, having destroyed 10 tanks, 13 halftracks and 12 guns, and captured Maleszówa. The losses of the 63rd Guards Tank Brigade in the fighting amounted to 7 T-34 tanks destroyed. Over the first day of fighting, the brigade made an advance of 24 km.

The **62nd Guards Tank Brigade** by 0700 on 12 January assembled in its jumping-off area with 65 T-34 tanks, having the assignment to be ready to enter the breakthrough in the Kortuszów sector (the corps' left-hand route of advance), and having caught up with the infantry on the Rudki – Bokszyca [Bokrzyska] line, by the end of the first day of the operation with energetic operations it was able to take the Maleszówa, Lisów, Dębska Wola area. A reinforced tank battalion of the 63rd Guards Tank Brigade was operating out in front as the corps' forward detachment. In the jumping-off area, a sapper company from the 131st Guards Sapper Battalion and the 2nd Battery of the 1999th Anti-aircraft Artillery Regiment became operationally subordinate to the brigade.

In order to introduce the brigade into the breakthrough, the brigade commander made the following decision: The brigade would operate in two combat echelons along one route, having a strong forward detachment at the point of the main forces. A tank platoon of the 1st Tank Battalion, a reconnaissance platoon of the motorized rifle battalion, and a squad of engineers from the 131st Guards Sapper Battalion's platoon would serve as the advance party of the forward detachment. One tank company with two platoons of tank riders from the motorized rifle battalion would comprise the core of the forward detachment. The first combat echelon would consist of the 2nd Tank Battalion, a motorized rifle company, one battery of the 1999th Anti-aircraft Artillery Regiment, an operational group with reconnaissance assets, a reconnaissance platoon of the signals battalion and the reconnaissance platoon of the 3rd Tank Battalion, with an antitank reserve moving behind the first combat echelon. The second combat echelon would consist of the 3rd Tank Battalion (minus two platoons), the 2nd Company of the motorized rifle battalion, and a sapper platoon of the 131st Guards Sapper Battalion. The 356th Self-propelled Artillery Regiment would serve as the brigade commander's reserve and march between the first and second echelons. The brigade's rear services and the rearguard detachment (a tank platoon of the 3rd Tank Battalion) would bring up the brigade's rear.

By 1400 on 12 January the brigade formed up into a column together with its attached and supporting units in readiness to enter the breakthrough at corps commander's signal. At 1600 of this same day, the signal to move out along the route was received, and the reinforced brigade began to roll out of its jumping-off area. The march was well-organized and went normally in nighttime conditions. There were no hitches or lagging behind on the march.

On the right, the 6th Mechanized Corps was attacking in the Szczecno, Dyminy direction, having the assignment on the first day to reach the Mojcza [6 km southeast of Kielce], Leśniówka area and with part of its force to take Zagrody [7 km southwest of Kielce]. On the second day of the operation it was to seize the Kostomłoty, Wyręba, Selęgur area and with part of its force to launch an attack toward Kielce from the northwest, in order to cooperate with the 3rd Guards Army and 13th Army in taking the city.

A T-34 tank of the 10th Guards Tank Corps crosses a river.

The 4th Guards Tank Army in the January 1945 fighting

Officers of the 10th Guards Tank Corps interrupt their meal to pose for a photograph. In the center is the deputy corps commander Guards Colonel P.D. Belov. Behind him on his left is the commander of the 61st Guards Tank Brigade Lieutenant Colonel N.G. Zhukov. Behind him on his right is the corps' chief of staff Guards Lieutenant Colonel M.G. Fomichev. They are flanked by delegates from Sverdlovsk, L.G. Sulimov on the right and I.F. Il'in on the left.

Mortarmen of the 10th Guards Urals Volunteer Tank Corps. From left to right: Guards Sergeant Anisimov, Guards Lieutenant Semykin, and Guards Private Sturov.

Guards Captain A.A. Kasovitsky, the commander of the 10th Guards Tank Corps' separate signals battalion, emerges from his vehicle.

Officers of the 10th Guards Tank Corps' sapper battalion. From left to right: Guards Captain V.I. Semenov, Guards Captain F.P. Gubin, Guards Senior Lieutenant V.A. Medvedev and Guards Senior Lieutenant I.M. Briukhanov.

A decorated tank crew stands together with the captain of the 2nd Tank Battalion. From left to right: Tank commander A.V. Dodonov, gunner Sergeant Major Aleksandr Marchenko, gun layer Sergeant I.I. Mel'nichenko, the commander of the 2nd Tank Battalion Captain P. Chirkov, and Hero of the Soviet Union driver-mechanic Sergeant Major Fedor Surikov.

A tank crew of the 63rd Guards Cheliabinsk Tank Brigade's 1st Tank Battalion. Tank commander Lieutenant Burianov leans out of the driver's hatch.

A tank crew of the 63rd Guards Cheliabinsk Tank Brigade's 3rd Tank Battalion.

Another tank crew of the 63rd Guards Cheliabinsk Tank Brigade's 3rd Tank Battalion.

A tank crew of the 2nd Tank Company of the 63rd Guards Tank Brigade's 1st Tank Battalion. Company commander Senior Lieutenant N.N. Shilov is on the left.

A tank crew of the 63rd Guards Tank Brigade's 3rd Tank Battalion listens to the Komsomol organizer of the 3rd Tank Battalion.

A tank crew of the 63rd Guards Tank Brigade's 2nd Tank Battalion. The emblem on the front of the tank says, "With victory over Berlin."

Tank commander Guards Junior Lieutenant Semenov stands (on the left) in front of his tank together with his driver-mechanic Senior Sergeant A.S. Basinsky.

Chronology of the events: the German view 12 January 1945

1.35   The Russian artillery begins an artillery preparation.
1.00   The headquarters of the 17th Panzer Division's Panzer Regiment 40 comes under a Russian artillery attack.
10.00   The beginning of the Soviets' second wave of the artillery preparation.
10.30 – 12.00   Disruption of telephone communications in the area of the 16th Panzer Division.
12.00 – 13.30   16th Panzer Division sent out reconnaissance patrols, which established contact with Soviet units that are attacking the positions of XXIV Panzer Corps. Reconnaissance informed the headquarters of the 16th Panzer Division that Soviet forces had managed to break through the first line of defense.
12.00   The first defensive belt has been taken by the Soviets (by the 13th Army in the area of the 16th Panzer Division and 20th Panzergrenadier Division, and by the 52nd Army in the area of the 17th Panzer Division and Heavy Panzer Battalion 424.
14.00   The Russians' 4th Tank Army is introduced into a breakthrough in the sector of the 13th Army, and units of the 10th Guards Tank Corps' 63rd and 61st Guards Tank Brigades and of the 6th Mechanized Corps' 16th Guards Mechanized Brigade are located in the forward detachments.
15.00   The headquarters of II/Panzergrenadier Regiment 64 in Szczecno has been attacked by Russian tanks. Several of the battalion's halftracks have been destroyed. The Russians' 4th Tank Army is reporting about the first encounters with German panzer units.
17.00 – 18.00   Units of the 16th Panzer Division are joining combat with the Soviets and suffering heavy losses.
18.00   The 16th Panzer Division receives its first order about preparing a counterattack.
22.00 – 24.00   General Nehring's XXIV Panzer Corps receives an order about launching a counterattack against the Soviet forces that have broken through and to reach the Kielce area.
On the night of 12-13 January 1945, the field command and headquarters of the 17th Panzer Division while on the march were attacked by enemy tanks. The division commander was wounded and captured by the Russians.

Combat operations of the 6th Mechanized Corps on 12 January 1945

At 0600 on 12 January 1945, the corps commander together with the headquarters' operational group drove out to an observation post on Hill 263.9, which lies 2 km north of Chańcza. Simultaneously, the corps' chief of intelligence Guards Lieutenant Colonel Iarovsky and the assistant chief of operations Guards Major Goroshko drove to the headquarters of the 102nd Rifle Corps with the task to inform the corps' chief of staff Guards Colonel Koretsky about the advance of the field forces.

At 0800 12 January the artillery of the 13th Army initiated the artillery preparation, which continued for two hours. The artillery fire blanketed the entire tactical depth of the enemy's defenses. Meanwhile, because of the poor weather conditions, our air force was unable to work over the enemy's defenses as had been planned.

At 1000 the units of the 172nd Rifle Regiment and 117th Rifle Regiment (102nd Rifle Corps), supported by tanks of the 150th Tank Brigade, rose onto the attack, and without meeting strong enemy resistance, swiftly moved ahead. At 1200 the corps commander issued an order to the commander of the 16th Mechanized Brigade to move out a reconnaissance group along both routes directly behind the combat formations of the 102nd Rifle Corps' units. Meanwhile, the rest of the 6th Mechanized Corps began moving out of their jumping-off areas.

At 1300 on 12 January, over the telephone via the corps' chief of staff, the corps commander, who was at his observation post, received the signal from the commander of the 4th Tank Army Colonel General of Tank Forces D.D. Leliushenko to introduce the mechanized corps into the breakthrough. At 1320, at the order of the corps commander, the 16th Mechanized Brigade set out from its jumping-off position and began advancing along the previously indicated routes. By this time the 16th Mechanized Brigade's Reconnaissance Group No. 1 had reached the northwestern fringe of the woods north of Życiny. Its Reconnaissance Group No. 2 had reached the southwestern fringe of the same woods. The 17th Mechanized Brigade moved out from its staging area to its jumping-off area in the Duży Kurozwęki Woods. The 49th Mechanized Brigade together with its attached units of reinforcement was located in its jumping-off area, in the woods 1 km southeast of Rakówki.

By 1500 12 January units of the 102nd Rifle Corps reached the Księża Niwa, Potok line. By this time units of the 16th Mechanized Brigade were approaching this line. According to the operation's plan, the 16th Mechanized Brigade was supposed to operate along two routes of advance, but because of the dense minefields emplaced by the enemy, as well as limited quantity of roads, both columns of the 16th Mechanized Brigade linked up in the Księża Niwa area and subsequently operated along the same route. Its forward detachment included the 28th Tank Regiment (minus one company), the 3rd Motorized Rifle Battalion, a company of IS-122 heavy tanks from the 28th Guards Heavy Tank Regiment, and an artillery battalion. The remaining elements came together as the brigade's main forces.

The 16th Mechanized Brigade's forward detachment also included a company of tanks and minesweeping vehicles, which moved at the head of the forward detachment's column and detonated mines. Upon reaching the fringe of woods 500 meters north of Księża Niwa, two of the minesweeping vehicles and one tank blew up on mines. Up until 1800, combat engineers of the 16th Mechanized Brigade and a company of the 22nd Separate Guards Sapper Battalion worked to clear a 500-meter-wide minefield, after which the forward detachment caught up with infantry's combat formations and began rapidly advancing along its own route while bypassing enemy knots of resistance.

By 2030 12 January the 6th Mechanized Corps had reached the following line: 16th Mechanized Brigade – had reached Podwale with its main forces; the 49th Mechanized Brigade had reached Księża Niwa; the 17th Mechanized Brigade (minus the 3rd Motorized Rifle Battalion) together with two companies of heavy IS-122 tanks from the 28th Guards Heavy Tank Regiment, two batteries of the 396th Anti-aircraft Artillery Regiment and a sapper company from the 22nd Guards Separate Sapper Battalion had arrived in the Potok area. The corps commander's reserve, the 56th Tank Regiment and the 2nd Battalion of the 258th Light Artillery Regiment had reached the northern fringe of the woods lying 1 km west of Fafara. The 29th Tank Regiment, 1st Self-propelled Artillery Regiment, 13th Guards Heavy Tank Regiment and the 95th Separate Motorcycle Battalion had arrived in Życiny.

The headquarters was in the woods 0.5 km southwest of Batuga. Its operational group was moving directly behind the 16th Mechanized Brigade's forward detachment.

At 0700 on 13 January 1945, the headquarters of the 4th Tank Army sent Combat Report No. 6 to the chief of staff of the 1st Ukrainian Front with an update on the situation: "Forces of the 4th Tank Army throughout the night continued to operate with forward detachments and by 0100 13 January reached: forward detachment of the 10th Guards Tank Corps (63rd Guards Tank Brigade) – Zaogrodwie; the 62nd Guards Tank Brigade – Zakarczmie. The location of the 6th Mechanized Corps' forward detachment – the 16th Mechanized Brigade – is being ascertained."

Combat operations on 13 January 1945

The enemy, committing his tactical reserves into battle, with fire and counterattacks by tanks and infantry, began to put up resistance to the corps' attacking units from the Skrzelczyce, Pierzchnica, Maleszówa line, with the task to hold the second defensive line until the approach of the operational reserves, with which it was planned to launch a counterattack in order to restore the situation.

Attacking throughout the night of 12-13 January 1945, the forward detachments of the 4th Tank Army cut the main road running from Daleszyce to Chmielnik. The forward detachment of the 6th Guards Mechanized Corps – the 16th Guards Mechanized Brigade – took Skrzelczyce and by 0700 on 1300 captured Lipa; the forward detachment of the 10th Guards tank Corps – the 63rd Guards Tank Brigade – was in the area 1 km east of Maleszowa. The corps' main forces had reached the following line: 6th Guards Mechanized Corps – by 0800 on 13 January 1945 was in the Klamka, Podstoła, Głuchów area with the 17th Guards Mechanized Brigade; the 10th Guards Tank Corps – Zakarczmie.

The main forces of the 10th Guards Tank Corps were approaching Wierzba, without running into any enemy resistance. The corps' forward detachment by sunrise on 13 January had reached Piotrkowice with its point units, where they were met by enemy tank and artillery fire.

On 13 January the 4th Tank Army joined combat with the enemy's 17th and 16th Panzer Divisions on the Komórki, Skrzelczyce, Maleszowa line, 25 km in the rear of the enemy's forward defensive edge. At 0530 on 13 January, the 10th Guards Tank Corps' 63rd Guards Tank Brigade joined combat with the forward units of the 17th Panzer Division in the Maleszowa area. The 17th Panzer Division's main forces were still 5 to 10 km south and southwest of Maleszowa.

The 16th Guards Mechanized Brigade, the forward detachment of the 16th Guards Mechanized Corps, bypassing populated places and destroying small enemy groups in its path, by 1800 on 13 January forced a crossing of the Czarna Nida River in the Bieleskie-Mlyny area and cut the main road running from Kielce to Pińczów in the Bilcza Podgóze area, having sent out strong reconnaissance groups along the road toward Zagrody and Kielce, while the main forces moved out toward Kowala.

This generated panic in the enemy rear. The commander of the 6th Guards Mechanized Corps Guards Colonel Orlov was located with the 16th Guards Mechanized Brigade.

To the south, at 1630 on 13 January the enemy in strength of 15-20 tanks and self-propelled guns, escorted by infantry, drove the 63rd Guards Tank Brigade's reconnaissance group out of Maleszowa and took the village. The commander of the 63rd Guards Tank Brigade deployed a screening group outside of Maleszowa, and bypassing the village to the south, began moving toward Piotrkowice. Following the 63rd Guards Tank Brigade were the 61st Guards Tank Brigade and the 72nd Guards Heavy Tank Regiment. The 61st Guards Tank Brigade when advancing behind the forward detachment (the 63rd Guards Tank Brigade) encountered heavy resistance from enemy tanks as it was approaching the Gumienice, Maleszowa, Brody line. At an order from the corps commander that had been transmitted over the radio, the commander of the 61st Guards Tank Brigade was instructed to leave behind one tank battalion as a screen, and without getting tied up in combat with its main forces, to bypass the Maleszowa strongpoint, and operating in the direction of Piotrkowice, Lisów and Zalesie to emerge on the route taken by the forward detachment and to continue to carry out its task.

Breaking away from the column and bypassing Piotrkowice to the north, the 61st Guards Tank Brigade rapidly advanced in the direction south of Lisów, Chałupki and Ostrów while brushing aside small enemy groups, by 0600 on 14 January reached Tokarnia, while sending out a strong reconnaissance group in the direction of Chęciny. The rapid actions of the forward detachment (the 63rd Guards Tank Brigade) secured a passage for the 61st Guards Tank Brigade through the enemy's second line of defenses from the march and the emergence in the rear of the enemy's operational reserves.

The enemy was hastily bringing up his operational reserves to the point of the breakthrough: units of the 17th Panzer Division from the south and of the 16th Panzer Division from the north, striving to cut off the forward detachment of the 10th Guards Tank Corps from the main forces and to link up on the Kielce, Chmielnik line.

From the account of the 10th Guards Tank Corps' 61st Guards Tank Brigade:

The enemy, covered by small groups of the shattered units of the 168th Infantry Division, 17th Panzer Division and elements of Heavy Panzer Battalion 501, throughout the day and the first half of the night of 12 January 1945 was retreating to the west. The brigade had no combat in the tactical zone of the German defenses. The 63rd Guards Tank Brigade, bypassing centers of resistance, continued to advance swiftly and only at 0200 on 13 January encountered strong enemy resistance on the Gumienice, Maleszowa, Brody line.

The 61st Guards Tank Brigade by 0200 on 13 January was approaching Point 262.6 with its forward detachment, the 1st Tank Battalion. By this time the 63rd Guards Tank Brigade was locked in combat for Maleszowa. The commander of the 61st Guards Tank Brigade Guards Colonel Zhukov decided, without getting bogged down in combat with its main forces (the 2nd and 3rd Tank Battalions) and leaving behind the 1st Tank Battalion as a screen, to bypass Maleszowa and to reach its own route of advance by moving in the direction of Piotrkowice, Lisów and Zalesie. A reconnaissance sent out in the direction of Piotrkowice at 0500 on 13 January reached the town center, where it encountered an enemy reconnaissance group that had been moving toward Piotrkowice from the direction of Włoszczowice. Having destroyed a halftrack and having captured one of its crew, the commander of the reconnaissance platoon reported that 60 tanks of the 17th Panzer Division were moving toward Piotrkowice from Włoszczowice. Having received this report, the brigade commander decided to bypass Piotrkowice on its eastern side, having reached the Lisów area, to continue to carry out its previous decision.

At 0900 on 13 January 1945, the 61st Guards Tank Brigade consisting of the 1st and 2nd Tank Battalions and two companies of the motorized rifle battalion broke into Lisów from the march.

The enemy wasn't expecting the appearance of our units. Submachine gunners of the motorized rifle battalion that had been mounted on the tanks and didn't have time to dismount, fired at the Nazis that were fleeing in panic at point-blank range from the tanks. The shattered and partially destroyed enemy fled from Lisów in panic, leaving behind a large number of vehicles and stockpiles of ammunition and uniforms. In addition, the tankers captured 2 50mm guns and 40 Germans, including the commander of the 168th Infantry Division's Artillery Regiment 248.

At 0930 on 13 January the enemy launched his first counterattack with up to a battalion of infantry from the 168th Infantry Division supported by 20 tanks of the 17th Panzer Division. Fifteen minutes later, three 10-tubed Nebelwerfers opened fire at Lisów, which subsequently placed methodical fire throughout the day of 13 January.

Our tanks, maneuvering among the burning buildings, nimbly crushed the counterattacking enemy. Our submachine gunners, despite the storm of fire from enemy tanks and the Nebelwerfers, drove back fierce counterattacks. The Germans launched 12 counterattacks throughout the day of 13 January 1945. Approximately 60 enemy tanks and more than a battalion of infantry, with the support of three Nebelwerfers and a battalion of artillery, was attempting to drive the Guardsmen out of Lisów. Despite the superiority in force and the density of fire, the Germans had no success. When repelling one of the attacks, the commander of the 61st Guards Tank Brigade Guards Colonel Nikolai Grigor'evich Zhukov died heroically.

At 2000 on 13 January the enemy ceased his counterattacks. Meanwhile, the 1st Tank Battalion, located in the brigade commander's reserve in Piotrkowice, was counterattacked by the enemy and throughout the day repulsed three counterattacks from the north and southwest.

The fighting in Lisów was an armored clash in which a large number of tanks from both sides took part. The enemy here had 60 Panthers and Tigers, 50 halftracks and 15 self-propelled guns that were being supported by up to a battalion of artillery, three Nebewerfers and up to a regiment of infantry. On the Russians' side were 40 T-34/85 tanks and two companies of submachine gunners from the 61st Guards Tank Brigade.

Over the day of fighting on 13 January 1945, the 61st Guards Tank Brigade lost 4 T-34/85 tanks destroyed and 10 T-34/85 tanks knocked-out. Its casualties consisted of 18 killed and 37 wounded. In return, it destroyed 5 King Tiger tanks, 7 Tigers, 5 Panthers and 2 self-propelled guns. Throughout the night of 13-14 January 1945, the brigade's men worked to make light repairs to their tanks and refuel them, and buried their dead.

The 29th Guards Motorized Rifle Brigade by 0900 on 13 January took Pierzchnica, and in order to screen the corps' right flank took up a defense on the northwestern outskirts of Pierzchnica while repulsing counterattacks by units of the 16th Panzer Division out of the woods east of Skrzelczyce.

From the account of the 10th Guards Tank Corps' 29th Guards Motorized Rifle Brigade:

On 12 January 1945, the brigade had assembled in its jumping-off area in preparation for entering the breakthrough, having diligently camouflaged its men and vehicles. At 14.00 of this same day, the brigade was introduced into the breakthrough in the Kasztelany – Szydłów sector along the right-hand route of the 10th Guards Tank Corps behind the 61st Guards Tank Brigade. Having caught up with the units of the 27th Rifle Corps on the Rudki, Bokrszyce line, the brigade, having made no contact with the enemy, reached Pierzchinica on 13 January, where it met stubborn German resistance and entered combat from the march. The enemy, having converted Pierzchnica into a strongpoint, strove to check the further advance of our units. The brigade's 3rd Motorized Rifle Battalion and a battalion of SU-122, with the support of the artillery battalion from the northwest, in cooperation with units of the 6th Rifle Division from the northeast, took Pierzchnica after bitter fighting and inflicted serious damage to the enemy. The enemy, having lost three heavy tanks, two Panthers, four halftracks and 150 soldiers and officers, retreated to the previously-prepared Górki, Lisów line. From this line the Germans went over to counterattacks 4 times with the aim of regaining Pierzchnica and to prevent the brigade from reaching its own route of advance and to check its further progress. The brigade went over to a defense on this line. Having bled the enemy white and having successfully repulsed all of his attacks while inflicting heavy losses to them (up to 12 tanks and up to a company of infantry were destroyed), it forced the enemy to abandon his occupied line. The Nazis, taking advantage of the darkness and covered by a mobile blocking detachment, fell back and dug in on the commanding heights east of Lisów.

On the night of 13-14 January 1945, the 29th Guards Motorized Rifle Brigade, in cooperation with elements of the 112th Rifle Division, destroyed the German strongpoing in Górki. On the night of 14-15 January, the brigade conducted a bold nighttime maneuver without any combat, and without any losses passed through the enemy's combat positions in the Lisów area despite strong enemy fire. Reaching its assigned route, by the morning of 15 January the 29th Guards Motorized Rifle Brigade was assembled in Chęciny, where it took up an all-round defense and conducted reconnaissance in every direction. On the afternoon of 15 January, the brigade set out along the Chęciny, Gałęzice route, and at the end of the day encountered an enemy column on the northern outskirts of Rykoszyn that was retreating from Kielce. Having deployed from the march and making an outflanking maneuver with one motorized rifle battalion from the left, it smashed the enemy column. Thanks to the proper arrangement of the combat formation on the march, the brigade preempted the enemy in deploying, which ensured its destruction with only a few losses in our elements (5 wounded), while inflicting heavy damage to the enemy: 1 tank and 50 trucks carrying ammunition were knocked out, and up to 100 enemy soldiers were killed. In the course of 16 January, the brigade conducted a march, and without making any enemy contact, by 1700 was assembled in Radoszyce, where it took up an all-round defense and conducted reconnaissance to the east and west.

The 62nd Guards Tank Brigade, having met stubborn enemy resistance, and having approached and dug in on the German second line of defense, deployed on the following line: 1st Tank Battalion – Pierzchnica; 2nd Tank Battalion – western outskirts of Gumienice; 3rd Tank Battalion – western outskirts of Podlesie.

From the account of the 10th Guards Tank Corps' 62nd Guards Tank Brigade:

The brigade's units at 16.00 on 12 January 1945 received the signal to begin movement along the route from its jumping-off area. The march was well-organized and went normally, even though it was in the conditions of nighttime. There were no hitches or lagging behind on the march. The brigade's units by 0900 on 13 January were occupying the following positions: 1st Tank Battalion – Pierzchnica; 2nd Tank Battalion – western outskirts of Gumienice; 3rd Tank Battalion – western outskirts of Podlesie. The brigade's command post was in Podlesie. The situation by 0900 13 January was as follows: the enemy had shifted the 17th Panzer Division against the units that had entered the breakthrough and which had made the breach. By 0900 units of the 17th Panzer Division, which had appeared from the southwest numbering 50 tanks, took up the Maleszowa – Ługi area, having an assembly of tanks in the woods west of Ługi, and went on the counterattack in the direction of Pierzchnica, Gumienice and Podlesie. Throughout the day of 17 January, the enemy launched seven counterattacks. All of the German counterattacks had no success and were fought off with heavy losses for them. Throughout the day the 62nd Guards Tank Brigade was locked in combat with the pressing enemy, and by the end of the day, together with units of the 3rd Guards Tank Army, drove the enemy from his occupied lines and under the cover of darkness began moving along its assigned route.

Over the day of fighting on 13 January 1945, the enemy took the following losses: 11 tanks and 2 self-propelled guns destroyed, and 159 soldiers and officers killed. A stockpile with ammunition and military gear was captured. The 62nd Guards Tank Brigade lost 3 T-34/85 tanks destroyed, and suffered 16 casualties, 9 killed and 7 wounded.

Conclusion: In the period from 12 to 15 January 1945, the 62nd Guards Tank Brigade together with other units of the 10th Guards Tank Corps fought against the enemy's operational reserves consisting of two tank divisions (the 16th and 17th Panzer Divisions), which were striving to separate the army's and corps' forward detachments from the main forces and to plug the gap created in their lines. The results of the tank fighting demonstrated the growing military and gunnery skills of our tankers, and the heightened competence of the officer staff in organizing a battle and in defeating an enemy that was superior in strength. As a result of the fighting in the period between 13 and 15 January, the brigade basically destroyed the 16th Panzer Division and cleared a path for a successful advance to the west for the units of the corps and of the army.

From the account of the 72nd Guards Heavy Tank Regiment:

The breakthrough of the enemy's tactical zone of defense was made by rifle divisions (the 13th Army's 6th and 112th Rifle Divisions). On 12 January 1945, after an hour-long artillery preparation, our infantry went on the attack. Without encountering strong resistance, the infantry swiftly drove in the combat outposts, and having overcome the enemy's forward defensive fieldworks with a decisive lunge, reached the forward edge, penetrated the enemy's defense, and reached the proximate line where our tanks would overtake the infantry. The tanks, advancing directly behind the infantry's combat formations, entered the breakthrough on the Rudki Mały – Bokrzycka line. The tanks with an impetuous and daring dash began to advance into the enemy's operational depth. The 72nd Guards Heavy Tank Regiment was operating together with the 63rd Guards Tank Brigade in the corps' forward detachment, having the task to offer direct support to the medium tanks and to destroy enemy heavy tanks, operating out of ambush positions, with their anti-tank fire. From the moment of the commitment of the corps' forward detachment into the breakthrough, the tanks encountered no enemy whatsoever as far as the Zagrodzie, Podlesie line in the operational depth of the German defenses.

Conclusion. As a result of the offensive breakthrough made by our units and the impetuous actions in the depth, the enemy, with the forces of the 68th Infantry Division, the 20th Panzergrenadier Division and the 17th Panzer Division resorted to a new tactic on this axis. He refrained from holding the tactical belt of defenses and withdrew his units into cover (woods, impassable places) against our mechanized forces, and allowed our main forces to pass by, with the aim of destroying our rear areas and severing our main lines of communication. However, we got wind of this enemy tactic, and all the troop rear units were escorted by tanks and armored personnel carriers, which didn't allow the enemy the possibility of severing our rear services from the units that were operating up ahead. The Germans strove to conserve their forces and to withdraw them to an advantageous natural line of defense. The 72nd Guards Heavy Tank Regiment took no direct part in the destruction of the enemy's Kielce – Radom grouping, since the 10th Guards Tank Corps, to which it was subordinate, was operating farther south in the direction of Chęciny, and thereby contributing to the encirclement of the Kielce – Radom grouping and blocking the path of retreat to the west and southwest

The 10th Guards Tank Corps wound up in a precarious situation. Its forces were split up into three pieces that were separated from each other by the enemy. The neighbor on the right, the 6th

Guards Mechanized Corps, was tied up in stubborn offensive fighting in the Skrzelczyce area and in the woods to the north. The neighbor on the left, the 3rd Guards Tank Army's 6th Guards Tank Corps, was continuing to fight south of Chmielnik.

The 10th Guards Tank Corps had made an advance and its flanks remained exposed, since the infantry of the 13th Army was lagging behind. The main task of the corps' main forces consisted in not allowing the possibility for the units of the German 16th Panzer Division, which was attacking from the north toward Pierzchnica, and the 17th Panzer Division, which was attacking from the southwest toward Lisów together with the Heavy Panzer Battalion 424, from linking up.

The main burden of this battle fell on the 61st Guards Tank Brigade, which was occupying a defense in Lisów, and on the 29th Guards Motorized Rifle Brigade, which was occupying a defense on the northwestern outskirts of Pierzchnica. The outcome of the battle depended on the resolve of the men and on the bravery and skill to direct the fighting shown by their commanders.

Having assessed the existing situation, the corps commander decided in order to eliminate the enemy's attempts to link up the units of the 16th Panzer and 17th Panzer Division to keep hold of the Pierzchnica and with the 29th Guards Motorized Brigade and the Lisów area with the 61st Guards Tank Brigade and to sap the enemy's strength, while simultaneously bringing up the main forces of the 62nd Guards Tank Brigade and the corps' artillery to the Pierzchnica area. Then with the arrival of the forward units of the 27th Rifle Corps to the Pierzchnica area, with the main forces of the 62nd Guards Tank Brigade in cooperation with the 29th Motorized Rifle Brigade and the support of the corps' artillery grouping to launch an attack in the Skrzelczyce, Zoborze direction in order to link up the corps' main forces with the corps' forward detachment – the 63rd Guards Tank Brigade. Subsequently the forward detachment was to capture a bridge across the Czarna Nida River in the Tokarnia area.

On the morning of 13 January 1945, the enemy attacked the 61st Guards Tank Brigade out of the Grabowiec area with up to 50 tanks. At 0930, after a strong artillery barrage, the enemy simultaneously launched counterattacks from three directions: out of the Zaborze area with 15 tanks and up to a battalion of infantry; out of the woods west of Lisów with 9 tanks and up to two companies of infantry; and out of Piotrkowicze with 15 tanks and up to a battalion of infantry. The tank and infantry counterattacks were being supported by heavy artillery and mortar fire. The enemy also committed up to 15 tanks and self-propelled guns, 7 halfracks and up to a battalion of infantry into a counterattack toward Pierzchnica. Finally, 8 tanks, 4 self-propelled guns and up to six companies of infantry attacked Gumienice from the direction of Maleszowa. Intense tank combat erupted. The enemy had committed a large number of tanks and self-propelled guns, among which Tiger tanks comprised up to 20% of the total figure. The Germans arranged their combat formations in echelons, with Tiger tanks leading, while light and medium tanks operated from behind the flanks of the heavy tanks. In certain places the German tanks closed to within 100-150 meters to the 10th Guards Tank Corps' combat positions, but thanks to the excellent gunnery training and the tenacity of the tankers and artillerymen, the enemy tanks were being knocked out at pointblank range, and the Nazis proved unable to drive the corps' units from their occupied line.

Throughout the day of 13 January, the enemy undertook 12 unsuccessful counterattacks, while suffering heavy losses in men and armored vehicles. The 61st Guards Tank Brigade was engaged in exceptionally heavy fighting in the Lisów area. According to information from the 4th Guards Tank Army's journal of combat operations, the enemy here had 60 tanks, 50 halftracks, 15 self-propelled guns, up to a battalion of artillery and up to a regiment of infantry, while in return the 61st Guards Tank Brigade was operating with 40 T-34/85 tanks and two submachine gun companies. An analysis of German sources, however, doesn't support the operations of self-propelled guns and such a large number of halftracks in the Lisów area. However, they do support the fact that the full-strength Heavy Panzer Battalion 424 (previously Heavy Panzer Battalion 501) was committed into the fighting in this area with approximately 50 operational Tiger tanks. Despite the plain superiority in force (approximately 50 heavy Tiger and King Tiger tanks against approximately 40 medium T-34/85 tanks), the enemy had no success here. The tanks of the 61st Guards Tank Brigade, maneuvering among the burning buildings, with accurate fire were destroying the enemy's counterattacking tanks and infantry; repulsing one attack after another together with the submachine gunners, they destroyed up to 35 tanks, while in the process losing 15 tanks either knocked-out or destroyed. While repelling one of the fiercest counterattacks, the commander of the 61st Guards Tank Brigade Colonel Zhukov was killed while heroically directing the combat.

The Chronology of Events: The German view

13 January 1945: Early on the morning of 13 January 1945, Heavy Panzer Battalion 424 attempts to go to the help of the 17th Panzer Division and counterattacks. First half of the day: The Tigers of the Heavy Panzer Battalion 424 make a second attempt to breakthrough to the headquarters of the 17th Panzer Division. This attempt also ends in failure. [According to the information of Wolfgang Schneider (a German historian and former Colonel of the Bundeswehr), in these counterattacks Heavy Panzer Battalion 424 destroyed 27 enemy tanks without losing a single Tiger in return.] Then the battalion begins movement in the direction of Kielce through Lisów. Several Tigers bog down in the mud and can't be evacuated. When entering Lisów, Heavy Panzer Battalion 424 falls into an enemy ambush. As a result of the fighting, the majority of the battalion is destroyed. On the Soviet side, T-34 tanks of the 4th Tank Army's 61st Guards Tank Brigade take part. Second half of the day: The remnants of several infantry divisions retreat to Kielce and become operationally subordinate to XXIV Panzer Corps. The 16th Panzer Division and 17th Panzer Division cover their retreat.

Later we'll return again to an analysis of the events that took place on 13 January 1945 in the Lisów area. This will include a critical analysis of the version of events put forward by Western scholars of this fighting.

From the Combat Path of the 4th Guards Tank Army:

On 13 January 1945 the enemy launched a powerful counterattack with forces of the 16th Panzer and 20th Panzergrenadier Divisions (up to 200 tanks and self-propelled guns) and the 17th Panzer Division (more than 100 tanks and self-propelled guns) in converging directions. The enemy panzer pincers were supposed to close shut in the Lisów area. The Nazi command was anticipating to cut off our forward units and to encircle and destroy them. The 17th Panzer Division became tied up in fighting with the 63rd Guards Tank Brigade's reconnaissance group in Maleszowa and captured the village. The brigade, having deployed a blocking force, assembled in the woods east of Piotrkowice. In connection with the situation, the commander of the 4th Tank Army ordered to halt the further advance of the forward units, to leave blocking detachments on the achieved lines, and with their main forces to launch an attack in the general direction of Lisów. Meanwhile, all the other units and formations were to attack to the west and encircle the enemy from the east, north and south. Colonel N.G. Zhukov's 61st Guards Tank Brigade was moving in the direction of Lisów. Its tank reconnaissance platoon under the command of Lieutenant M.V. Pobedinsky was moving in the vanguard. After midnight on 13 January he spotted a German column numbering more than 70 Tigers and Panthers. Pobedinsky reported about this to the brigade commander, and having received an order to avoid combat, he continued marching along the indicated route.

At sunrise on 13 January, the forward detachment of the 61st Guards Tank Brigade – Guards Major V.N. Novikov's tank battalion – burst in to Lisów and smashed a column of vehicles that was towing cannons. At 0800 the enemy attacked Lisów with 50 tanks, a large number of halftracks and submachine gunners. The first attack was driven back. After the passage of a certain amount of time, the Nazis launched another counterattack.

Zhukov's tankers on this day repulsed several attacks. However, the fighting became increasingly bitter. Fires broke out in the town. A heavy shell struck the casualty collection station where our wounded were located. An armor-piercing slug fired by a German tank hit the brigade commander's tank, directly striking the ammunition load. A powerful explosion followed. Guards Colonel N.G. Zhukov was killed. The chief of staff Guards Lieutenant Colonel V.I. Zaitsev assumed command of the brigade. The fighting continued until the onset of darkness.

The enemy proved unable to take Lisów. He lost 35 tanks either knocked-out or left burned-out. The brigade also suffered significant losses – 15 tanks.

Former Guards Lieutenant Colonel V.I. Zaitsev recalls those days:

One can say that never before had the brigade been so fully equipped with combat gear and weapons, as it was on the eve of the forthcoming operation. The tank battalions received new T-34 tanks armed with an 85mm cannon in place of the 76mm cannon, and now it was possible to engage in single combat with Tigers. The brigade was brought up to its authorized strength in personnel. Veterans of the brigade returned from hospitals. In order to transfer our combat experience to the raw recruits and to foster teamwork among the elements, training exercises were conducted in situations that were as close as possible to real combat. The soldiers greeted the new, 1945 year in high spirits and faith in a soon victory. On 10 January the brigade received an order: with the start of the offensive, to move at the head of the corps' main forces behind its forward detachment – the 63rd Guards Tank Brigade – in readiness to expoit the forward detachment's success and on the first day seize the road hub of Chęciny. On the night of 10-11 January, the brigade formed up into battalion columns in the following order: 1st Tank Battalion, brigade headquarters, 2nd and 3rd Tank Battalions, and the motorized rifle battalion's artillery battery and mortar company. The 1st and 2nd Motorized Rifle Companies and a company of submachine gunners were mounted on the tanks. Considering the frigid weather, we set up a cubicle in our staff Dodge truck in order to ease the work of the officers of the headquarters' operational group, which was always located in the brigade's combat formations. The brigade arrived in the jumping-off area for the introduction into the breakthrough on the night of 11-12 January.

Guards Lieutenant Colonel V.I. Zaitsev.

On 12 January the artillery preparation began at 1000. Although we were located rather distant from the firing positions, the powerful roar of the guns, which was shaking the earth, made an impression like nothing other of the all-destroying power of the "God of war", as the artillery was called back then. The fact that many enemy soldiers and officers who had been rendered senseless by fear came back to themselves only in captivity speaks to the effectiveness of our artillery fire. Soon after noontime, our rifle units captured the enemy's first and second line of trenches, and at 1400 there followed the signal to commit the main forces of the 10th Guards Tank Corps into the breakthrough. Just several minutes before the start of the offensive, brigade commander Guards Colonel N.G. Zhukov walked up to our staff Dodge and told me, "Vasilii Ivanovich, I'm not feeling well, I have the chills, and therefore I'm asking you: Lead the column in a Willys, and I will travel in the staff truck." This was my final conversation with the brigade commander. I left with a signals officer to go to the head of the 1st Tank Battalion's column, where the Willys of the brigade commander was standing with its fearless driver Guards Sergeant Vania Poplavsky. I gave

Enemy tanks, destroyed or disabled by the tankers of the 4th Tank Army in the Kielce – Lisów area, January 1945

Detroyed King Tigers of Heavy Panzer Battalion 424 in Lisów, January 1945.

Knocked out and captured Tigers and King Tigers of Heavy Panzer Battalion 424 in the Kielce – Lisów area, January 1945.

More photographs of knocked out or disabled Tigers and King Tigers. The above photograph also shows the wreckage of a German supply column.

notice to the commander of the 1st Tank Battalion Guards Captain V.G. Skrin'ko that he and his battalion would be unflaggingly following behind the Willys. We marched as far as the enemy's forward edge in daylight hours. On the right and left of the road that had been compacted by treads stood signs with the label "Mines!" Out in front of us, a tank exploded on a mine. Everyone went around it to the right. At a turn, the combat formation of the leading 63rd Guards Tank Brigade was clearly visible, and just behind us was the column of our brigade's 1st Tank Battalion. The remaining elements weren't visible, but I had no concern about them, because even in the arriving twilight gloom, there was no way they could become separated from the lead battalion. At 1800 it became completely dark, the pace of march decreased; the tanks were moving without lights, guided by rear lamps in order not to fall behind or to collide with a tank that was moving in front. Around midnight, we caught the sound of frequent shots from tank guns, the hollow chatter of machine guns and the rattle of submachine guns out in front of us. The 63rd Guards Tank Brigade's column came to a stop. Having ordered battalion commander Skrin'ko to hold in place, I drove up to the head of the column, where I saw the commander of the 63rd Guards Tank Brigade Colonel N.G. Fomichev. He was observing how the combat was going for his lead battalion, which was being commanded by Guards Captain M.F. Korotaev. I asked the brigade commander if he needed any sort of help from our brigade. He replied that Korotaev could deal with enemy's small force by himself.

At this time the corps commander Guards Colonel N.D. Chuprov drove up and came to a stop. M.G. Fomichev briefed him on the situation, and I presented myself. "Where is your brigade commander?" N.D. Chuprov asked. I reported that he was following behind the 1st Tank Battalion. The corps commander ordered, "Summon him." A liaison officer that I sent soon returned and reported to me that he hadn't found anyone behind the column of the 1st Tank Battalion. In turn, I reported about this to the corps commander. He ordered me to move together with the 1st Tank Battalion behind the corps headquarters and simultaneously take steps to search for the brigade's main forces. At approximately 0400, a group of enemy tanks approached the corps headquarters and opened fire. At an order from the corps commander, the 1st Tank Battalion repulsed the attack of the enemy tanks, after which we followed behind the corps headquarters to the village of Piotrkowice. Throughout the night I and Guards Captain Skrin'ko kept trying to make contact over the radio with the brigade, but without success.

On the morning of 13 January, we intercepted a radio message, which reported that the brigade was engaged in heavy combat with superior enemy tank forces in the village of Lisów. I reported about this to the corps commander and requested permission to move out with the 1st Tank Battalion to the brigade's relief, but I received a refusal. At mid-day the brigade's chief of chemical services Guards Captain A.Ia. Klimovich arrived with a message from Guards Lieutenant Colonel I.I. Skop. Our deputy political commander was reporting that brigade commander Guards Colonel N.G. Zhukov had been killed, and asked that I immediately arrive at the brigade. I reported the contents of the message to the corps commander. Disturbed by this, Guards Colonel N.D. Chuprov authorized me to set out to the brigade, but left the 1st Tank Battalion subordinate to him as a combat screen for the corps headquarters. Accompanied by Guards Captain Klimovich and two scouts, I headed off to Lisów. In the village of Lisów, a sad sight appeared before us. In place of the former homes and outbuildings were smoking charred ruins. Everywhere you could see the burned-out carcasses of tanks. The sole surviving building was serving simultaneously to house the wounded and the brigade's command post. Having exchanged greetings with Guards Lieutenant Colonel I.I. Skop and the staff officers, I assumed command of the brigade. Having sent scouts out to search for the body of Guards Colonel N.G. Zhukov, I listened to reports from tank battalion commanders Guards Major Nikonov and Guards Major Ankudinov, and from the commander of the submachine gun battalion Guards Major Bendrikov about the condition of their units. The tank battalions had lost 11 T-34 tanks destroyed, and just as many which had taken serious damage. On the battlefield stood the hulks of 35 burned out and semi-demolished enemy tanks. The Germans had the time to evacuate even more of their knocked-out tanks.

According to the story of I.I. Skop and the reports of the battalion commanders and staff officers, the events that took place in the brigade after it lost sight of the lead 1st Tank Battalion developed as follows: Brigade commander Guards Colonel N.G. Zhukov, having convinced himself that the lead machine being commanded by the brigade's deputy chief of staff Guards Major Dolgopolov had lagged behind, assumed control. He sent a reconnaissance patrol headed by tank platoon commander Guards Lieutenant M.V. Pobedinsky up ahead, in the direction of Lisów. Moving without lights at night, Pobedinsky noticed a column of fascist tanks that were approaching from the west. Taking cover in a hut near the road, the scouts counted up to 70 tanks, which they reported over the radio to the brigade commander. Located in the combat formations of the 2nd Tank Battalion, Guards Colonel N.G. Zhukov ordered to let the German tanks pass. Having reached the village of Lisów and rolling to its center, the scout tanks came right up to column of German vehicles that were towing artillery guns. Soldiers, who had obviously taken Pobedinsky's tanks as friendly, were warming themselves around small fires on the side of the road, as if nothing had happened. At the order of Guards Captain V.A. Markov, who was riding in Pobedinsky's tank, the platoon opened fire with their main guns and machine guns; the Germans scattered in every direction, and many of them were captured, including the commander of the 17th Panzer Division's panzer artillery regiment. From a report from Guards Lieutenant Pobedinsky and the prisoner interrogations, it became clear to Guards Colonel N.G. Zhukov that 17th Panzer Division headquarters had received word about the action in Lisów, and was poised to launch an attack with its main forces toward the village. Zhukov issued an order to the elements to repulse the enemy attack. The company of Guards Captain Markov took up key positions at the church and in the cemetery.

Not even an hour had passed, when the Germans opened up a storm of artillery and mortar fire, and fascist tanks appeared on the approach to the village. Fires had started in the village, and women and children were rushing about in confusion. Considering that the village in the next 10-15 minutes would become the arena of fierce tank combat, the commander of the 3rd Tank Battalion Guards Major Andikulov instructed the battalion's Komsomol organizer Guards Sergeant Ryzhov and the driver-mechanic of his tank Guards Sergeant Muzychenko to evacuate the village's residents as quickly as possible to a safe place. Most of the residents obediently followed Ryzhov and Muzychenko. Carrying out the order of the battalion commander, the tankers took their positions in their tanks. At this time the fascist tanks entered the village and the main attack struck the positions of Guards Major Nikonov's 2nd Tank Battalion, especially Markov's company. Seventeen Tigers rolled toward the tanks of Lieutenants Pobedinsky, Kuznetsov, Abuzgaliev and Marinin. Markov reported on the situation to Guards Colonel N.G. Zhukov. The brigade commander ordered, "Not one step back from Lisów!"

Having deployed their tanks so as to do maximum damage to the fascists and simultaneously striving to safeguard his tanks and men, Markov ordered to allow the enemy machines to approach as closely as possible, and then to make sure to target their most vulnerable places. When the enemy tanks had closed to within 150 meters, he issued the command to open fire. Four Tigers, which had been accurately hit by the crews of Guards Junior Lieutenant Labuz and Guards Lieutenants Abuzgaliev and Pobedinsky, became immobilized and began to smoke. Firing at the German tanks, Markov and his feisty tankers who knew no fear knocked out several more machines and kept possession of their occupied position. The tank "sniper" Tikhon Agafonov of Pobedinsky's crew and the 18-year-old loader Volodia Anfalov of Trofimov's crew particularly distinguished themselves. The enemy began to withdraw, leaving behind 13 burned-out Tigers and Panthers around the church and cemetery. The tank company under Guards Senior Lieutenant M.N. Vertiletsky also courageously routed the enemy. It destroyed 10 tanks. The company commander was severely wounded, losing his sight, but continued to remain on duty until the end of the battle.

Brigade commander N.G. Zhukov showed exceptional valor and fearlessness. He personally destroyed seven enemy tanks. His tragic death painfully affected the hearts of the brigade's troops, who loved their commander for his courage, just insistence on high standards, and his fatherly concern for his subordinates. Together with the battalion commanders and staff officers, the loss of our leader and combat comrade who had taught us so much hit me hard. His skillfull and prudent direction of battle, first of all his artful use of maneuver and speed; his tactic of combining tank ambushes with actions of a shock group; his constant concern over constant reconnaissance; his ability to coordinate the actions of the tanks with the motorized infantry and artillery; and particularly his desire to inflict as much damage to the enemy while minimizing his own losses – all this enriched us with precious combat experience, which we strove to increase in every way possible in the future.

Already in the first stage of the battle for Lisów, the brigade achieved success, but also suffered more than a few losses. Guards Lieutenant Marinin was killed by a shell that struck his tank's turret and his loader was severely wounded; the signals chief of the 2nd Tank Battalion Guards Senior Lieutenant G. Neroslavsky and the battalion adjutant Guards Lieutenant V. Chekirov were killed by the direct hit of a shell while shifting position across open ground. The critically wounded Guards Lieutenant Toropchin died in the embrace of Guards Lieutenant Lebedinsky.

After a brief rest, the battle resumed in new intensity. Yes, the "Sverdolvsk – L'vov" tank brigade was justly proud of such tankers, such faithful defenders of the Motherland as Vladimir Aleksandrovich Markov and Mikhail Vasil'evich Pobedinsky and their combat associates of the 2nd Tank Battalion. A veteran of the brigade, volunteer Valentin Chesnokov said, "I've been fighting since 1941 and been engaged in 46 tank combats, but not once have I been involved in one like today."

After this remarkable battle, the first full Cavaliers of the Order of Glory appeared in our brigade. These were the Sverdlovsk volunteers, the tank machine gunners Aleksandr Demidovich Kataev and Evgenii Parfenovich Samodurov, who had four destoyed tanks, five halftracks and up to a company of enemy infantry on their combat score. The combat actions of the brigade and of the 10th Guards Tank Corps as a whole were worthily assessed by the commander of the 4th Tank Army General D.D. Leliushenko. He noted that in the Lisów area, "the adversary suffered a major defeat; more than 180 tanks that belonged to the 16th and 17th Panzer Divisions were left smoking on the battlefield …." Our 61st Guards "Sverdlovsk" Tank Brigade under the command of Colonel N.G. Zhukov, chiefly Major V.N. Nikonov's 2nd Tank Battalion showed exceptional heroism in the night combat.

As noted above in Zaitsev's recollections, one of the key participants in this nighttime combat in the Lisów area was M.V. Pobedinsky. He left behind his own memories of this action:

Thirty-five years have passed since the Great Victory Day, and the savage fighting for the Polish village of Lisów holds a dominant place in my memory. After the Sverdlovsk tank brigade was introduced into the breakthrough on 12 January 1945, my tank reconnaissance platoon advanced as the vanguard of the brigade's column. One night we spotted a column of facist tanks that were moving from the west toward our place of breakthrough. Having turned off the main road into a tiny hamlet and having counted more than 70 Tigers[2] and Panthers, we switched on the illuminated indicators in the optical sights for night combat, and set the sights for direct fire. However, our guns remained silent. Advised beforehand over the radio, the commander of the "Sverdlovsk" tank brigade Guards Colonel Nikolai Grigor'evich Zhukov (who was located in the combat formations of the lead battalion) ordered to allow the German tanks to pass.

---

2 Many of which were King Tigers.

At dawn the platoon at high speed flew into Lisów. The lead tank had passed a gully, a whitestone church on a hill and a building in the center of the town, when I and the battalion's deputy commander Guards Senior Lieutenant Vladimir Markov (we were sitting on the front armor) caught sight of a column of German vehicles that were towing cannons. German soldiers were sitting on the roadside and warming themselves by small fires. The sound of our machines didn't shake the Germans out of their hypnotic state. They probably thought that it was their own tanks that were retreating.

A long burst from a submachine gun stirred up the Germans. Two of them fell, while the rest scattered into buildings. At Markov's order, I rushed together with a group of submachine gunners to drive the enemy soldiers out of their shelters. Meanwhile, the lead tank, as well as the tanks of Lieutenant Fedor Onischenko and Junior Lieutenant Marinin sliced through the German motorized column on the road. The machines of Vladimir Toropchin's and Aleksandr Kuznetsov's tank platoons hurried to follow. The German column was completely destroyed. Surviving Germans fled.

Lisów was now in our hands. For about 30 minutes things were quiet, and then the Germans opened up a furious mortar and artillery barrage. Explosions shot upward with a white, cold flame like an electric-arc welder. Fires broke out. We caught the sound of wailing children and the cries of frightened women. Suddenly, a warning shout rang out: "Attention, German tanks!"

The Tigers and Panthers, which had passed by us to the east in the night, had been hastily pulled back to Lisów; possibly, the Germans had called back their own tanks after the destruction of their rear support units and headquarters in Lisów. The first Tigers appeared on the crest of a hill, and having turned their long, jointed 88mm barrels with "knobs", as we called their muzzle brake compensators, cumbersomely began rolling toward us, lumbering from side to side like behemoth tortoises. Some of them were firing from short halts.

Seventeen Tigers were attacking the flank, where the machines of my platoon and Kuznetsov's, Abuzgaliev's and Labuz's tanks were positioned. Markov ran off to brief Colonel Zhukov on the situation.

"Not one step back from Lisów" – the brigade commander ordered.

Returning to us, Markov gave thought to how best to deploy the tanks so as to inflict the greatest possible damage to the Germans while conserving our own tanks and men. He placed my tanks and Abuzgaliev's tank in the cemetery, behind the stone wall of the church, and positioned Kuznetsov's and Labuz's tanks on the hill.

Halftracks carrying submachine gunners were advancing behind the Tigers. They leaped out of their machines and formed into lines. Markov ordered us not to reveal our positions until the last possible moment. If the German submachine gunners charged, then the tank commanders, driver-mechanics and radio-machine gunners would remove the machine guns from the tanks and together with the tank riders drive back the infantry attack with machine-gun fire, submachine gun fire and grenades. The loaders and gunners would remain in their tanks.

"Fire at the vulnerable locations – at the flanks and rears of the hulls!"

Two Tigers, having descended the slope, were heading toward the opposite hill, on the crest of which Junior Lieutenant Labuz's tank was concealed behind a burning building. One hundred meters was left to the lead tank, when Markov jumped on to the T-34's armor and shouted to gunner Anatolii Borzenkov through the open hatch: "Now! It's showing its flank! Fire!"

Radio-machine gunner Sasha Vostretsov just in time had replaced the wounded loader. A shell had already been loaded. The gun's breechblock wedge briefly clanked. Borzenkov took aim, pressed the trigger, and couldn't believe his own eyes: He had hit the barrel of the gun right on the Tiger's muzzle brake. A minute later I heard in my headset the exultant voice of Lieutenant Abuzgaliev: "I'm bronze, I'm bronze – I've set ablaze a Tiger!"

Meawhile eight Tigers were encircling the horseshoe formation of my platoon. The gunner Tikhon Agafonov, the well-known tank "sniper", nestled up to the ocular sight, was shouting as if the Germans could hear him: "Akh, vermin! It's fired a round from its bitch of a cannon … Aha! You don't see me; you've presented your flank – now I'll give you a wallop!"

Tikhon's shell struck its target. The Tiger gave a jerk and impotently dropped its barrel until its brake muzzle was buried in the snow-powdered ground. A bluish white flame rose out from under its turret.

The armored beasts with their black-and-white crosses on their fronts and turrets never ceased clambering toward us. Tikhon Agafanov had been forged in battle, but even he was nervous in these minutes. I could see sweaty neck and his tense back. What could be said about Volodia Anfalov – a whiskerless youth, who was taking part in his first tank battle on this day, and who had only just rescued his commander Trofimov from out of his tank, which had been set ablaze by an enemy shell? After Volodia had leaped out of the fire like a madman, with a burned face, scorched hair and blistered hands, I asked him to replace my concussed gunner, and he acted according to the unwritten rule of the tankers: he could have gone to seek treatment for his burns; he had every justification, but he joined my crew and continued to fight ….

A shot rang from our gun. I stuck my head out of the turret hatch. The steel colossus of a Tiger is spinning in one place – the broad ribbon of its track is slipping onto the ground from its right side with a clatter. Having left behind more than 10 crippled and burned-out tanks after the first attack, the Nazis began backing away, spitting fire from their guns. The German infantry was rolling back to the west. A multitude of enemy dead were darkening the gray-colored snow.

We also took losses. A solid shot penetrated the turret of Junior Lieutenant Marinin's tank, killing him and wounding his loader. The battalion's signals chief Senior Lieutenant Georgii Neroslavsky and the acting senior adjutant of the battalion headquarters Lieutenant Vasilii Chekirov were killed by the direct hit of shell while running across a wasteland.

The death of my two close friends and the severe wounding of a combat comrade, Lieutenant Volodia Toropchin, shook me … Volodia died in my arms and was buried by me.

A short rest, like a deep breath, and then the Germans renewed their artillery and mortar barrage. This time it was more intense; fires multiplied around the entire village, and the fiery air was melting the remnants of snow. I was standing in my turret, viewing the eastern outskirts, and I see a large building with shattered windows, to which our wounded tankers and submachine gunners were being carried. Above the building, a white flag with a bright red cross in the middle of it is flapping. Then just in front of my eyes, a German heavy-caliber shell penetrated the roof and blew up everyone inside. The white flag seemingly flew into the sky, before fluttering down into the flames. At this moment it seemed to me like a white dove, which had soared into the sky one last time, and the red cross on the panel of material – like a bloody wound on white plumage.

Once again, observers shout, "Attention, tanks!"

The Tigers and Panthers are moving cautiously, slowly swinging their long barrels from side to side, coming to frequent halts and belching flames from their gun barrels. Behind them halftracks are rolling, firing from heavy and light machine guns. Above us are green and yellow streaks of tracer rounds. Explosive bullets are striking the fences and walls of the buildings with a staccato popping sound, and back then it seemed as if someone had gotten behind you and was firing at you from close range. The distance from the Germans to us was around 600 meters, but it was inexorably closing rapidly.

The gunners were seemingly glued to their sights. The loaders with enflamed faces barely had time to open the breech mechanisms of the cannons and jam the heavy and long, cylindrical brass shells into the gun breeches. The breechblock wedges would give a clang. The guns would roar. Then once again, the sound of an empty shell casing in the canvas shell catcher. The acrid smoke of their own salvoes and from the flames that had enveloped all of Lisów began to fill the tanks and enter our mouths and nostrils, causing coughing and choking. The turret ventilators are whirring violently, but they're unable to purge the gases and smoke from the machines. If we could close the hatches … but that's forbidden! If you interrupt observation for just a minute, the German tanks would get behind you, and then ….

We often had to change positions, to get away from burning buildings. I climb out and show the driver-mechanic Zhora Ukhanov where best to get away from a conflagration, and I see a Panther speeding toward me. I leap back into the hatch. Afaganov is sitting on his little stool behind the gunsight, his arms and head lowered. He was nauseous, overcome by the noxious gases.

I shove him off the little stool onto the floor of the turret, take his place at the gunsight, but I've barely had time to set the crosshairs of the two floating lines, when the Panther rushes past. I pivot the turret to the left. In my sight, I see the abruptly bobtailed rear of the Panther. It is highballing it across the burial mounds of the cemetary, crushing the crosses, headstones and grave enclosures. Just a bit longer, and it will disappear from the field of vision. The sight's crosshairs catch its bouncing black-and-white cross. I press the pedal of the foot-operated trigger, and the Panther, its gun barrel taking a bite out of burial mind, became enveloped in smoke. Immediately, as if to replace the Panther, a Tiger appears. It is bulling its way forward, having become separated from the machines following behind it. With his last discarding sabot shell, Sasha Kuznetsov accurately hit the imprudent fellow.

Attacks … attacks … We lost count of them! During one of them, a fascist armor-piercing round struck the brigade commander's T-34, right in the ammo load. The sound of a seeming double explosion carried to us. In front of the eyes of the Guardsmen, their beloved commander Colonel Zhukov was killed. On the right flank, confusion arose among the tankers of a different battalion of our brigade; the nerves gave out of some of them, and the Germans had the opportunity to attack Vladimir Markov's group from a different direction, this time from the rear. He gathered all the machines that he had left in the cemetery and told us simply and honorably: "It is possible that we won't get out of this alive, – let's say our farewells." He then exchanged kisses with me, with Kuznetsov, with Abuzgaliev, and with each of the tankers. We decided to die, but not to give Lisów up to the Germans. In fact, we didn't! We repulsed 12 fearful tank attacks, setting Tigers and Panthers ablaze.

The evening twilight crept over the semi-demolished town, shrouding it like a mourning crepe. The first timid stars began to twinkle in the somber sky. Was it really nighttime? Did we really withstand this hell since the predawn hour? Staggering, we came together in a circle. Volodia Markov took a seat on stacked pair of automobile tires. Pale, with dried blood on his face, in a torn one-piece tanker's suit that was burned in several places, he looked utterly exhausted, but at the same time he eyes sparkled with care for us, and with pride for his tankers. What about us? Our lips were scaly and encrusted. A few of the men dropped to the ground, grabbed handfuls of filthy slush from the snow, and were spastically swallowing it. The still burning pockets of fire were dying down. A light, humid breeze was trying to stir them back up, and from time to time revealed glowing eyes in the piles of ashes – burning embers. We were sitting together in a tight circle and were silent, deafened, poisoned by noxious fumes, and worn out. Some of the men were greedily inhaling tobacco smoke; others, their heads hanging, were dozing. A silver-headed Roman Catholic Jan Banach priest came out of the church. It turned out that he had been watching from the church as we fought with the German tanks from sunrise to sundown. He joined our silent circle, tenderly embraced the bloody, bandaged head of Tolia Borzenkov and whispered like a prayer: *Wszystko widzialem … Wszystko …* [*I witnessed everything … everything …*] The old priest had seen a lot in his time, but he never could imagine that there were such men on this earth as Soviet tankers.

When it became completely dark, we count the sound of the rumble of diesel engines, the clear clattering and squeaking of tracks, and spotted an endless procession of headlamps that was approaching us from the east. It was the [10th Guards] "Urals" Tank Corps that was coming up. We greeted our friends in exultant, soaring spirits.

The enemy ceased the counterattacks at 2000 on 13 January. Meanwhile, the 61st Guards Tank Brigade's 1st Tank Battalion, which was located in the reserve of the corps commander in Piotrkowice, was counterattacked by the enemy and throughout the day fought off three counterattacks from the north and southwest.

The units of the 63rd Guards Tank Brigade by 0900 on 13 January were occupying the following positions: 1st Tank Battalion – Pierzchnica; the 2nd Tank Battalion – western outskirts of Gumienice; the 3rd Tank Battalion – western outskirts of Podlesie. The situation by this time was as follows: the enemy had moved the 17th Panzer Division to counter the units that had entered the breakthrough, and by 0900 approximately 50 tanks and self-propelled guns had appeared from the southwest and taken up position in the area of Maleszowa and Ługi, before launching a counterattack in the direction of Pierzchnica, Gumienice and Podlesie with the tanks and self-propelled guns from out of the woods west of Ługi. Throughout the day of 13 January in this sector, the Germans launched seven counterattacks, but had no success and each attack was driven back with heavy losses for them. While the 63rd Guards Tank Brigade and 72nd Guards Heavy Tank Regiment were engaged in combat with the enemy that was pressing them from out of Maleszowa and Ługi, the 62nd Guards Tank Brigade which had arrived from the east began to advance toward Maleszowa. By noontime on 13 January, the enemy was driven out of Maleszowa and began to retreat to the northwest toward Górki and Zaborze. Six enemy tanks that had pulled out of Maleszowa in retreat to the northwest became bogged down one by one in a swampy area of low ground in the vicinity of Brody.

The 63rd Guards Tank Brigade then moved out to relieve the 61st Guards Tank Brigade, which was engaged in bitter fighting in Lisów. The 63rd Guards Tank Brigade's advance into the enemy flank at the Wygwizdów estate decisively decided the outcome of the fighting in Lisów in favor of the Soviet forces.

The brigade made wide use of the infantry as on-foot reconnaissance, which allowed the detection of the enemy without revealing itself. On 13 January the infantry scouted the settlement of Podlesie; approaching silently, they discovered there three Tiger tanks and six Panthers and passed on this important information to higher command for making a decision.

The 63rd Guards Tank Brigade moved out with attached assets: three companies of heavy IS-122 tanks were operating in the combat formations of the tank battalions. Facing them were enemy Tiger and King Tiger tanks. So, in the Maleszowa area the IS-122 heavy tanks played a major role in destroying German tanks that were firing from long ranges. Over the day of fighting on 13 January 1945, the 63rd Guards Tank Brigade destroyed 11 enemy tanks, 2 self-propelled guns and killed approximately 160 enemy soldiers and officers. In return, the brigade lost 3 T-34/85 tanks destroyed, and 16 casualties (9 killed and 7 wounded).

From the recollections of the commander of the 63rd Guards Tank Brigade Twice Hero of the Soviet Union Lieutenant General of Tank Forces M.G. Fomichev:

The combat at Maleszowa was blind fighting. Of course, one could expect the enemy in any town or village there, but it was impossible to anticipate such enemy strength was actually in Maleszowa. It was clear that the German 16th Panzer Division stood north of our axis of advance, and the 17th Panzer Division to the south, but the 3rd Guards Tank Army was advancing south of us, and to the north – our 6th Guards Mechanized Corps. I was assuming that most likely we wouldn't have to deal with the German 16th Panzer Division. In any case I wasn't expecting it on the first night, and regarding the 17th Panzer Division – I had no suspicion that it would pop up in the way it did. The 16th Panzer Division began moving out of Melnik, and they reached the route of our tank corps in my rear. If I had been informed, I never would have become tied up in fighting in Maleszowa. I was already standing on one of its streets, when it seemed the Germans woke up, and it turned out that they had tanks there. It was their 16th Panzer Division that had come up. So, then we took fire, as it turned out from the Germans. One must take into account that at the time we were exhausted and hadn't had a bite to eat, and the brain can no longer think straight. Also, I hadn't been expecting the 17th Panzer Division at all. As we approached Maleszowa, there wasn't a single airplane in the air. Obviously, there was no timely intelligence of any kind on our part. Perhaps the Front informed somebody, but that person was at the army level. However, before this information reached us, we had already lost 5 tanks in vain. Sometimes one can sacrifice even a brigade if something is being accomplished, but in this case the enemy delayed us.

Lieutenant General of Tank Forces M.G. Fomichev.

The enemy's 17th Panzer Division with its attached Heavy Panzer Battalion 424 was badly battered by the forces of the 10th Guards Tank Corps in the Maleszowa, Ługi, Piotrkowice, Lisów, Brudzów-Duży area and thrown back to the Dębska Wola, Obice, Włoszczowice line.

Over the day of fighting in this sector, in the assessment of the 4th Tank Army's Intelligence Department, the German 17th Panzer Division and Heavy Panzer Battalion 424 lost 68 tanks either knocked out or destroyed, including 7 Tiger Ausf. A tanks, 19 Panthers, 5 Tiger Ausf. B tanks, 2 halftracks and 18 infantry-loaded vehicles, and killed up to 450 soldiers and officers; in addition, 4 German halftracks and 80 soldiers were captured.

The losses of the 10th Guards Tank Corps over the day of 13 January amounted to 26 T-34/85 tanks (19 knocked out and 7 destroyed), and 5 SU-122 destroyed. Its casualties amounted to 32 killed and 61 wounded. The 61st Guards Tank Brigade lost 4 T-34/85 tanks destroyed and 10 T-34/85 knocked out, and 18 men killed and 37 wounded. The losses of the 62nd Guards Tank Brigade amounted to 4 T-34/85 tanks destroyed, 4 T-34/85 tanks knocked out, and 2 T-34/85 tanks damaged; its casualties were 7 men killed and 16 wounded.

The enemy, having had no success in the Lisów area, by 2000 on 13 January ceased the counterattacks and began to try to bypass the corps' units from the east in the Maleszowa – Ługi direction. This attempt also had no success. On the night of 13-14 January, the main forces of the 10th Guards Tank Corps remained on their occupied lines, put themselves back into order, replenished supplies, did light repair work on the tanks, refueled the machines, and buried their dead.

The combat operations of the 6th Mechanized Corps on 13 January 1945

Continuing to carry out its previous assignment, the forward detachment of the 16th Mechanized Brigade at 0500 on 13 January bypassed the enemy strongpoint of Pierzchnica to the north and by 0600 approached Skrzelczyce, where it encountered forward units of the enemy's 16th Panzer Division that had arrived on this line from the Mechów area and retreating groups of the 168th Infantry Division. The Germans were trying to hold the road hub of Skrzelczyce, in order to secure the approach of the main forces of the 16th Panzer Division to the given line. The forward detachment of the 16th Guards Mechanized Brigade, reconnoitering under the cover of darkness, impetuously attacked the enemy that was defending Skrzelczyce. In the process it destroyed up to a company of enemy infantry, 10 vehicles, 1 tank and 1 halftrack. Exploiting the success, by 0700 on 13 January it seized Lipa, where it destroyed the headquarters of the German Artillery Regiment 248.

By this time the main forces of the 16th Guards Mechanized Brigade were located in the area of the northern outskirts of Osiny. With the arrival in the vicinity of Lipa, the forward detachment sent out a special reconnoitering party of engineers along the Zagóze, Marzysz Kiełków, Marzysz route, with the task to find a ford in order to cross the units across the Czarna Nida River, since it was impossible to cross the ford 2 km southeast of Bilcza Zastawie because of the large, swampy basin of the river. The party of engineers found a frozen ford in the vicinity of Kuby-Młyny which after a little reinforcement would allow wheeled vehicles to cross the ice, while the tanks could cross it directly.

At 0800 on 13 January 1945 the forward detachment of the 16th Guards Mechanized Brigade under the cover of darkness began the process of crossing the Czarna Nida, and by 0900 it had fully crossed, without encountering organized enemy resistance. The German operational reserves hadn't had time to take up the prepared defensive line along the northwestern bank of the Czarna Nida River and weren't expecting that the Soviet units would be able to reach this line so quickly.

At 1000 the forward detachment of the 16th Guards Mechanized Corps reached the woods east of Bilcza Ciołów, where the corps commander received reconnaissance information that a large aggregation of enemy infantry, artillery and motorized transport had been observed in Bilcza Ciołów and Bilcza Podgórze. The commander of the 6th Guards Mechanized Corps ordered the commander of the forward detachment to attack the enemy quickly and to take the indicated villages and cut the Kielce – Morawica road.

At 1100 the forward detachment of the 16th Guards Mechanized Corps deployed into a combat formation and attacked the enemy via Hill 260.3 toward Bilcza Podgórze. After an hour-long combat the forward detachment seized the village of Bilcza Podgórze, where it destroyed 40 vehicles and 4 halftracks that belonged to the 20th Panzergrenadier Division and killed up to 50 Germans. The enemy's remaining elements fled in disorder into the woods and fled in a fragmented manner along the main road to the north in the direction of Kielce.

The 16th Guards Mechanized Brigade's forward detachment upon taking Bilcza Podgórze was saddling the Kielce – Morawica road and with a strong blocking detachment took Bilcza Jawornia, while organizing reconnaissance toward Zagrody and along the main road to the north in the direction of Kielce. One artillery battery of the artillery battalion and two tanks of the 28th Tank Regiment together with the operational group from the corps headquarters, because of the large traffic jam involving the motorized transport of the 16th Guards Mechanized Brigade's main forces and the field artillery, and the lack of alternative routes due to the dense German mining, were lagging somewhat behind the forward detachment of the 16th Guards Mechanized Brigade and arrived in Skrzelczyce only at 0730.

By this time the main forces of the German 16th Panzer Division had arrived in this sector; consisting of the tanks of Panzer Regiment 2 and panzergrenadiers of Panzergrenadier Regiment 64, they had the task of linking up with the 17th Panzer Division's tanks in Maleszowa. The German armor was moving toward Skrzelczyce and Maleszowa, and ran into the main forces of the 6th Guards Mechanized Corps on the Komórki – Skrzelczyce line and 2 km southeast of this point as they were following the 16th Guards Mechanized Brigade. Here, a fierce battle erupted. With their panzers, the Germans were firmly blocking the roads leading out of Skrzelczyce to the north and northwest, and by 1200 on 13 January cut off the 16th Guards Mechanized Brigade's forward detachment from the rest of the brigade. At this time the 49th Mechanized Brigade had reached the fringe of the woods 2.5 km southeast of Szczecno, while the 150th Tank Brigade was fighting for that village.

The 6th Guards Rifle Division and the main forces of the 16th Guards Mechanized Brigade reached the Zaborze line, while 5 T-34/76 tanks of the 150th Tank Brigade, which were attached to the 6th Guards Rifle Division, entered Skrzelczyce. At 1800 on 13 January, with the appearance of the artillery batteries of the 16th Guards Mechanized Brigade and the operational group of the corps headquarters that were moving toward Lipa from the western outskirts of Skrzelczyce, enemy tanks opened up heavy fire out of the Zastawie and destroyed two vehicles of the 16th

Guards Mechanized Brigade and the guns they were towing; simultaneously, from the area of the woods 2 km northwest of Zastawie and Podchojnie, the German opened up heavy artillery fire on Skrzelczyce and the combat formations of the 6th Guards Rifle Division in the Piekło, Zahebdzie area.

At 1400 of this same day, the Germans brought up 20 tanks and up to a regiment of infantry to the Podchojnie and Hill 296.4 area, and at 1430, after a powerful artillery barrage, launched a counterattack from two directions: a) in strength of up to 10 Pz.Kpfw. V tanks and up to two battalions of infantry from a line 500 meters southeast of Podchojnie toward the northeastern outskirts of Skrzelczyce; and b) in strength of up to a battalion of infantry and 6 Pz.Kpfw. V tanks from Hill 296.4 toward Piekło.

The units of the 6th Guards Rifle Division, which were located on the Piekło line, were unable to organize a repulse of the enemy's counterattacks and began to retreat in disorder to the east. The 16th Guards Mechanized Brigade's 2nd Motorized Rifle Battalion and a company of tanks of the 28th Tank Regiment, as well as the tanks that were with the operational command group, from out of Skrzelczyce opened up a concentrated fire at the enemy and at 1500 on 13 January stopped the enemy counterattack while destroying 4 Pz.Kpfw. V tanks, 2 Pz.Kpfw. IV tanks and killing up to 80 enemy soldiers and officers. The fleeing infantry of the 6th Guards Rifle Division were stopped by officers of the 16th Guards Mechanized Brigade on a line 1.5 km west of Pierzchnica and was returned to their jumping-off position.

By this time (around 1430 on 13 January 1945), the now isolated forward detachment of the 16th Guards Mechanized Brigade with one tank company carrying tank riders took the village of Zagrody, where it smashed an enemy column of motorized transport and artillery that was in the process of moving from Chęciny toward Kielce, and in the process destroyed 18 vehicles, 6 guns, 2 motorcycles and killed up to 30 enemy soldiers.

Continuing to press forward rapidly, at 1600 on 13 January the forward detachment of the 16th Guards Mechanized Brigade broke into Białogon, where it destroyed up to 30 enemy vehicles loaded with infantry and military cargo. In the Białogon, Zagrody area the forward detachment captured 6 enemy stockpiles of military gear and weapons. With the arrival in the Białogon area, the forward detachment was now blocking the Kielce – Chęciny and Kielce – Kruków roads, thereby depriving the enemy of the possibility of shifting reserves from the Kielce area to the south and southwest and of linking up the Germans' Radom grouping with the retreating Kielce grouping. Meanwhile the main forces of the 16th Guards Mechanized Brigade continued to remain in the Bilcza-Jaworznia area and the woods to the north.

As a consequence of the fact that the commander of the 6th Guards Mechanized Corps was located with the forward detachment of the 16th Guards Mechanized Brigade, while the corps' main forces had been cut off and were fighting on a line running from the fringe of woods east of Szczecno to Piekło and the corps commander was unable to command them, the commander of the 4th Guards Tank Army General Leliushenko placed command of the main forces on the corps' chief of staff Guards Colonel Koretsky, and at 1500 on 13 January issued a verbal order to him: to destroy the enemy on the Szczecno, Skrzelczyce line with the corps' main forces, to force a crossing of the Czarna Nida River, to link up with the forward detachment of the 16th Guards Mechanized Brigade, and to reach the second day's objective area.

In connection with this, Guards Colonel Koretsky at 1600 on 13 January issued the following tasks to his subordinate units with a combat order: the 16th Guards Mechanized Brigade with its former assets was to continue to carry out the second day's tasks; the 2nd Motorized Rifle Battalion, with 8 tanks of the 28th Tank Regiment, in cooperation with the 17th Guards Mechanized Brigade and the 49th Mechanized Brigade, is to attack in the direction of Skrzelczyce and with the arrival on the Morawica line is to occupy the road hub on the Hill 250.7 – Morawica line. The brigade headquarters – along the axis of the brigade's movement. The 17th Guards Mechanized

Brigade and the 29th Tank Regiment and 56th Tank Regiment, together with two companies of the 28th Guards Heavy Tank Regiment and two batteries of the 396th Anti-aircraft Artillery Regiment, from the line 500 meters southeast of Skrzelczyce was to bypass this strongpoint from the south, and in cooperation with the 16th Guards Mechanized Brigade's 2nd Motorized Rifle Battalion and 49th Mechanized Brigade, to drive the enemy from the heights south and southwest of Skrzelczyce; subsequently is was to attack impetuously in the overall direction of Hill 268.8, Bilcza-Podgórze and Zagrody. With the arrival on the Zagrody line, it was to deploy a combat screen facing the west on the Slówik, Markowiczna line. It was then to detach tank companies of the 126th Tank Regiment and a company of IS-122, the motorized rifle battalion and the artillery battalion for a night-time operation [to the west of Kielce] in the direction of Piekoszów, Promnik, Chelmce, Mnów, Miedżeta; by the morning of 14 January it was to reach the Sielpia, Miedzieża area with its main forces, having a forward detachment on the Stąporków, Hucisko line and the reinforced 56th Tank Regiment on the Końskie line. The 49th Mechanized Brigade, together with the 1433rd Self-propelled Artillery Regiment, the 2nd Battalion of the 240th Mortar Regiment (minus two batteries), two batteries of the 1995th Anti-aircraft Artillery Regiment and a battery of the 504th Cannon Artillery Regiment, from a jumping-off area northwest of Pierzchnica, was to take Komórki in cooperation with the 17th Guards Mechanized Brigade, and subsequently to attack in the Marzysz, Białogon direction, covered by a screen along the Hill 258.8, nameless hill west of Marzysz, Suków, Leśniówka, Dyminy, Białogon line.

The main forces by the morning of 14 January are to reach the Tumlin, Kamien, Kostomłoty line. Conduct reconnaissance in the direction of Januszów. The reserve: 1st Guards Self-propelled Artillery Regiment, 1st Battalion of the 258th Light Artillery Regiment, the 95th Separate Motorcycle Battalion, two batteries of the 1433rd Self-propelled Artillery Regiment, and two companies of the 22nd Guards Sapper Battalion. The task: by 0700 on 14 January to assemble in Skrzelczyce, and subsequently to advance along Route No. 2 in readiness to support the actions of the 17th Guards Mechanized Brigade and 49th Mechanized Brigade.

At 1700 on 13 January the 49th Mechanized Brigade and main forces of the 16th Guards Mechanized Brigade continued to be located on their former lines and were exchanging fire with the enemy. The 17th Guards Mechanized Brigade was deploying on the line 500 meters southeast of Skrzelczyce. The corps headquarters had arrived in Pierzchnica.

At 1730 on 13 January units of the 49th and 17th Mechanized Brigades and the 2nd Motorized Rifle Battalion of the 16th Guards Mechanized Brigade, with their attached assets, after working out questions of cooperation, went on the attack. At 2100 of this same day after stubborn combat the 16th Guards Mechanized Brigade's 2nd Motorized Rifle Battalion, in cooperation with the 17th Guards Mechanized Brigade, seized Skrzelczyce, Podchojnie, Zastawie and Hill 296.4 and had reached the western outskirts of Podchojnie, southwestern fringe of the woods southeast of Lipa line together with a company of tanks from the 28th Tank Regiment and an IS-122 platoon from the 28th Guards Heavy Tank Regiment. The 17th Guards Mechanized Brigade on the southern outskirts of Zastawie, Lipie line ran into heavy fire from enemy infantry and tanks on the Radomice-Lipa, Radomice-Kaczeniec line.

At 2000 on 13 January the 153rd Tank Brigade took Szczecno; the 49th Mechanized Brigade bypassed Szczecno to the south and became tied up in combat with the enemy for possession of Komórki. The 16th Guards Mechanized Brigade's forward detachment by the end of 13 January was located in its previous areas and was engaged in combat with the enemy, which was trying to break through from the north in the southwestern direction. By the end of the day, the enemy resistance was broken and the 49th Mechanized Brigade took Marzysz; the 17th Guards Mechanized Brigade had occupied Lipa and reached the Czarna Nida River.

The enemy's 16th Panzer Division over the day of fighting on 13 January 1945 lost 38 tanks. The 6th Guards Mechanized Corps lost 18 tanks. By 2000 on 13 January, the German 16th Panzer

Division had been defeated in a meeting battle and had been pushed back to the Czarna Nida River to the Marzysz, Morawica line by the forces of the 6th Guards Mechanized Corps.

From the Combat Path of the 4th Guards Tank Army:

Meanwhile on 13 January 1945, the 63rd Guards Tank Brigade and 72nd Guards Heavy Tank Regiment were engaged in stubborn fighting with enemy tanks and infantry that were attacking out of Maleszowa. The 62nd Guards Tank Brigade arrived from the east and launched an attack toward Maleszowa. By 1200 it had driven the enemy out of the town. The Germans began to retreat to the northwest. This allowed the directing of the 63rd Guards Tank Brigade to go to the relief of the 61st Guards Tank Brigade, which was engaged in heavy fighting in Lisów. The 63rd Guards Tank Brigade arrived on the enemy's flank. This decided the outcome of the battle in our favor.

The forward detachment of the mechanized corps at 0500 on 13 January took Skrzelczyce. At 1300, a meeting engagement began between the 6th Guards Mechanized Corps' 49th and 17th Mechanized Brigades and the German 16th Panzer Division's Panzer Regiment 2 and Panzergrenadier Regiment 64. Fighting went on for possession of each line. It was only by the end of the day that the enemy was defeated, having lost 33 tanks either knocked out or destroyed and a large quanity of infantry. Our units reached the Czarna Nida River. The 16th Mechanized Brigade by 1800 had forced a crossing of the Czarna Nida and had cut the Kielce – Pińczów railroad. The German 17th Panzer Division had suffered heavy losses – 68 knocked out or burned out tanks and assault guns.

The tank formations of our army had achieved a major success. By the end of day 13 January, the 6th Mechanized Corps had reached the Czarna Nida River, while the 10th Guards Tank Corps had reached the Lisów, Piotrkowice area.

That evening at 2100 on 13 January 1945, the headquarters of the 4th Tank Army issued Combat Report No. 8 to the commander-in-chief of the 1st Ukrainian Front Marshal of the Soviet Union Konev:

1. The forces of the 4th Tank Army in the course of 13 January 1945 developed the offensive in the Gluchów, Pierzchnica, Morawica, Chęciny direction, and having overcome the resistance of the enemy's 168th Infantry Division and 17th Panzer Division, reinforced with unidentified tank units [the Heavy Panzer Battalion 424], from 1630 with the forward units was engaged in heavy fighting on the following line: 16th Guards Mechanized Brigade – eastern outskirts of Kowala; 63rd Guards Tank Brigade – eastern outskirts of Brzeziny (both places 7-8 kilometers southwest of Kielce); 61st Guards Tank Brigade – was engaged in fighting with the counterattacking units of the 17th Panzer Division [and its attached Heavy Panzer Battalion 424] 1 km south of Radomice-Kaczeniec, Brudzów-Duży line. The enemy with units of the 168th Infantry Division, 17th Panzer Division and the Separate Panzer Battalion 501 [the former designation of Heavy Panzer Battalion 424] in the second half of the day repeatedly counterattacked from the Zalesie, Górki, Maleszowa line, and with forces of 20-30 tanks (of the 17th Panzer Division) and infantry from the Chmielnik, Maleszowa line, and at 1800 captured Skrzelczyce, thereby isolating the 16th Guards Mechanized Brigade and the 63rd and 61st Tank Brigades from the army's main forces.

2. The 6th Guards Mechanized Corps and the 17th Guards Mechanized Brigade at 2000 were engaged in fighting for Skrzelczyce. The 10th Guards Tank Corps: 29th Guards Motorized

Rifle Brigade throughout the day repulsed three enemy counterattacks in strength of up to a battalion of infantry and 12 tanks from the Maleszowa, Górki direction, before attacking behind the 49th Mechanized Brigade and 17th Guards Mechanized Brigade in the Skrzelczyce direction; the 62nd Guards Tank Brigade is defending the Podlesie, Zagrody, Strojnów line; the 93rd Separate Tank Brigade is in Gumienice; the 22nd Sapper Brigade is assembled in the wooded area 0.5 km northwest of Drugnia-Rzadowa. The losses inflicted on the enemy: 17 tanks, 6 assault guns and 5 halftracks knocked out or destroyed; 4 halftracks have been seized; and up to 400 enemy soldiers and officers have been eliminated. Our losses: 5 tanks destroyed, and 20 tanks that were either disabled or blown up on mines over 12 and 13 January 1945.

3. The army commander has decided: the 93rd Separate Tank Brigade and 62nd Guards Tank Brigade are to screen [along the line of hills] 1 km west of the Gumienice, Podlesie, Strojnów line; and with units of the 49th Mechanized Brigade, 17th Guards Mechanized Brigade and 29th Guards Motorized Rifle Brigade to destroy the enemy in the Skrzelczyce area and to continue to carry out the day's mission. The army commander is located at his command post.

Chief of staff of the 4th Tank Army Guards Major General of Tank Forces UPMAN

By the end of day on 13 January, the 6th Guards Mechanized Corps had reached the Marzysz – Łabędziów line with its main forces, having the assignment over the night to cross the Czarna Nida River and to developed the offensive toward Zagrody and Białogon. The forward 16th Guards Mechanized Brigade was engaged in combat with the enemy in the woods 2 km north of Kowala and Zagrody.

The 10th Guards Tank Corps by the end of day on 13 January with its main forces had reached the wooded area 1 km west of Duże, Lisów and Piotrkowice, with the assignment over the night to develop the offensive toward Chęciny. The 63rd Guards Tank Brigade was in movement toward Tokarnia.

The combat operations of the 6th Guards Mechanized Corps on 14 January 1945

By midnight on 13 January, the enemy with remnants of the 168th Infantry Division, 68th Infantry Division and the 16th Panzer Division, totaling up to two infantry regiments and 50 tanks supported by three battalions of artillery, was continuing to hold the Komórki, Łipa, Radomice, Radomice-Kaczeniec, Brudzów-Duży line, putting up strong resistance with fire against the corps' attacking units, while simultaneously striving to destroy the forward detachment of the 16th Guards Mechanized Brigade in the Bilcza Jaworznia area with units of the 20th Panzergrenadier Division and panzers of the 17th Panzer Division.

Continuing the offensive, at 2000 on 13 January the 49th Mechanized Brigade together with its previously attached assets had taken Komórki, where up until 0400 on 14 January it repulsed three enemy counterattacks from out of the woods west of Komórki in strength of up to a battalion of infantry and 10 tanks, while in the process destroying 8 enemy tanks and eliminating up to 200 Germans.

The 17th Guards Mechanized Brigade at 0200 on 14 January took Radomice-Kaczeniec, where it captured 6 prisoners that belonged to the 16th Panzer Division; through interrogation they revealed that the 16th Panzer Division had 63 operational Pz.Kpfw. V and Pz.Kpfw. IV tanks. Exploiting this success, the 17th Guards Mechanized Brigade at 0800 on 14 January took Łabędziów with one motorized rifle battalion and two tank compies from the 126th Tank Regiment and reached the Czarna Nida River in the area south of Bieleckie-Młyny.

The forward detachment of the 16th Guards Mechanized Brigade, with which the corps commander was located, on the night of 13-14 January became tied up in fighting for the southwestern outskirts of Kielce, while simultaneously blocking the Kielce – Morawica road in the Bilcza-Jaworznia area with one tank company mounting tank riders from the 3rd Motorized Rifle Battalion and defending Białogon with one rifle company and two tank platoons. By holding this latter position, it was blocking the Kielce – Chęciny road, thereby depriving the enemy of the possibility of withdrawing the Kielce grouping to the southwest or south, while simultaneously blocking the enemy Radkowice grouping's path of retreat to the north and northwest.

At 1000 on 14 January the 49th Mechanized Brigade took Marzysz after a short combat and reached the Czarna Nida River. In the fighting for Marzysz, it killed up to 200 enemy soldiers and officers and destroyed 8 tanks (including 1 Tiger), 10 vehicles, 3 guns and 10 machine guns, and captured 6 tanks, 2 halftracks and one self-propelled gun.

The 16th Guards Motorized Rifle Brigade's 1st and 2nd Motorized Rifle Battalions, together with a company of tanks from the 28th Tank Regiment, a platoon of IS-122 tanks from the 28th Guards Heavy Tank Regiment and the 52nd Separate Guards Mortar Battalion under the command of the deputy combat commander of the 16th Guards Motorized Rifle Brigade Hero of the Soviet Union Guards Major Fedor Spekhov, operating in close cooperation with the 17th Guards Mechanized Brigade, captured Radomice and Łipa at 0400 on 14 January, where it was counterattacked out of the Zagórze area by up to a battalion of infantry and 10 tanks. With the concentrated fire from the tanks of the 28th Tank Regiment and the rifle and machine-gun fire of the 16th Guards Motorized Rifle Brigade's 2nd Motorized Rifle Battalion, 6 German tanks were destroyed and up to 100 enemy soldiers and officers were killed.

At 0430 the enemy remnants retreated into the woods west of Zagórze. Meanwhile the 16th Guards Motorized Rifle Brigade's 2nd Motorized Rifle Battalion and 6 tanks of the 28th Tank Regiment captured Zagórze and with part of its force reached an isolated home 1 km northwest of Zagórze, thereby in close cooperation with the 17th Guards Mechanized Brigade encircling the enemy grouping in the woods east of Łabędziów consisting of 17 tanks and up to two infantry companies. With the arrival of the 17th Guards Mechanized Brigade and 49th Mechanized Brigade to the Czarna Nida River, the enemy from the northwestern bank of this river opened up intense rifle and machine-gun fire, as well as artillery fire from tanks at the Soviet troops.

At 1900 on 14 January, sappers of the 17th Guards Mechanized Brigade under the cover of darkness began work building a bridge across the river in the Bieleckie-Młyny area. The enemy with the aim of frustrating the completion of the bridge maintained constant fire at the worksite from the flanks, because two companies of the 17th Guards Mechanized Brigade's 1st Motorized Rifle Battalion, which had crossed to the northwestern bank, were covering the sapper's work from the front from the direction of Bieleckie-Młyny. At 0900 the enemy with up to a company of infantry and 5 Tiger tanks attacked the 17th Guards Mechanized Brigade's small bridgehead on the northwestern bank of the river from out of the area 2 km east of Bieleckie-Młyny, striving to throw the elements of the mechanized brigade back across the river. However, the attack was beaten back with the fire of the tanks of the 126th Tank Regiment and the IS-122 tanks of the 28th Guards Heavy Tank Regiment from the southeastern bank of the river. In the attack, the Germans lost 20 soldiers and 2 Tiger tanks.

At 0930 the enemy again counterattacked the small bridgehead of the 17th Guards Mechanized Brigade on the northwestern bank of the river, this time with up to two companies of infantry and 4 tanks from out of the Bieleckie-Młyny area, but again the Germans had no success. At 0940, German Nebelwerfers opened heavy fire on the Łabędziów area from out of the area of Wola-Morawicka, and at 1000 up to a battalion of infantry with 10 tanks and 10 halftracks launched a counterattack out of the Wola-Morawicka area in the direction of the woods east of Łabędziów with the aim of linking up with the panzers that were encircled in the woods.

Elements of the 6th Guards Rifle Division and a portion of the tanks of the 29th Tank Regiment that had been located over the night on the Łabędziów, Radomice-Kaczeniec line over the night fell back in the direction of Skrzelczyce. The enemy attack managed to reach the southwestern fringe of the woods south of Łabędziów.

The commander of the 17th Guards Mechanized Brigade Guards Lieutenant Colonel Churilov ordered the commander of the 52nd Separate Guards Mortar Battalion to fire a salvo from one rocket artillery battery on the area of Wola-Morawicka and to silence the Nebelwerfers there. Simultaneously he shifted 3 IS-122 tanks and 10 T-34/85 tanks of the 126th Tank Regiment from the northern outskirts of Łabędziów to the southern outskirts of the village, and ordered them to open artillery and machine-gun fire at the exposed flank of the counterattacking infantry. Then, together with the 2nd Battalion of the 17th Guards Mechanized Brigade and the 1st Motorized Rifle Battalion of the 16th Guards Motorized Rifle Brigade, they launched an attack and threw the enemy back beyond the Morawka River (a tributary of the Czarna Nida River), while in the process killing 125 enemy soldiers and officers and destroying 7 tanks and 5 halftracks. In return, the Soviets lost 2 T-34 tanks destroyed and 2 tanks knocked out.

The rocket artillery salvo from the 52nd Separate Guards Mortar Battalion in the Wola Morawicka area destroyed 2 Nebelwerfer batteries. At 0900 the corps headquarters moved to Skrzelczyce. At 1100 the corps' chief of staff arrived at the command post of the commander of the 49th Mechanized Brigade.

At 1230 on 14 January, the enemy with 5 tanks counterattacked in the direction of Marzysz from out of the woods southwest of there; the commander of the 49th Mechanized Brigade in order to repulse the enemy's counterattack sent two tanks to the threatened sector. As a result of a fleeting battle, the enemy and the 49th Mechanized Brigade each lost one tank destroyed. The enemy's remaining tanks withdrew back into the woods.

Also at 1230 the corps' chief of staff issued an order to the commander of the 49th Mechanized Brigade to begin crossing the river in the Kuby-Młyny area and to continue to carry out the second day's mission. By 1400 a company of sappers of the 22nd Separate Guards Sapper Battalion and sappers of the 49th Mechanized Brigade had improved a ford in order to cross the tanks in the Kuby-Młyny area, and built a bridge for the wheeled vehicles; their work was being covered by infantry of the 49th Mechanized Brigade's 1st Battalion, which had crossed to the northwestern bank of the river at 1300.

At 1400 on 14 January 1945, the main forces of the 49th Mechanized Brigade began crossing the Czarna Nida River, and by 1700 they had finished the process of crossing. The corps' chief of staff Guards Colonel Koretsky personally directed the river crossing.

The 17th Guards Mechanized Brigade, together with Major Spekhov's group, was counterattacked at 1200 by up to 20 tanks and 15 halftracks of the German 17th Panzer Division (as later established through prisoner interrogation) out of the Morawica area along the river. In order to counter it, the commander of the 17th Guards Mechanized Brigade committed two IS-122 tanks of the 28th Guards Heavy Tank Regiment, 12 tanks of the 126th Tank Regiment, and 5 tanks of the 29th Tank Regiment into the battle, and with fire from out of ambush positions on the northeastern outskirts of Łabędziów and from a hill 300 meters north of there, they destroyed 9 tanks and 8 halftracks. The enemy's remaining panzers and halftracks fell back in the direction of Morawica. By this time the sappers had finished the bridge, but since their work was being done under enemy fire, the bridge's load-bearing capacity allowed only vehicles up to 4 metric tons to cross.

At 1200 on 14 January the tanks of the 16th Guards Mechanized Brigade, which were located together with the main forces, began crossing by a ford 500 meters west of Hill 231.0, but as a result of the absence of a preliminary check by engineers, one IS-122 tank and one T-34 tank immediately bogged down in the river, and the crossing in this sector of the river was halted.

Through reconnoitering conducted by the 17th Guards Mechanized Brigade it was established that it was impossible to get the tanks across the river by fording in the Beleckie-Młyny – Kuby Młyny, which the commander of the 17th Guards Mechanized Brigade reported to the corps' chief of staff at 1230. Based on this information, the corps' chief of staff at 1300 issued an order to the commander of the 17th Guards Mechanized Brigade to pivot the brigade to the 49th Mechanized Brigade's crossing site. At 1500, the brigade began moving in the direction of the 49th Mechanized Brigade's crossing location in piecemeal fashion, while the remaining elements, together with the main forces of the 16th Guards Mechanized Brigade, continued to fight to destroy the enemy's encircled grouping in the woods east of Łabędziów, where by this time there were only 8 German tanks left, while 9 tanks had already been destroyed by the fire from the 16th and 17th Guards Mechanized Brigade's tanks and artillery. At 1530 on 14 January, the 4th Tank Army's chief of operations Colonel Moriakhin arrived to see the commander of the 17th Guards Mechanized Brigade, and relayed an order from the army commander General Leliushenko to return the brigade to its own route and to force a crossing of the river in the Beleckie-Młyny area and to resume carrying out the second day's task.

In connection with this order, the brigade turned around and headed back to its own axis of advance, and initiated work to reinforce the bridge that had been previously built for the wheeled vehicles, while scouts went in search for a ford to get the tanks across.

As soon as the tanks of the 49th Mechanized Brigade crossed the river and emerged on the northern outskirts of Kuby-Młyny, up to 14 enemy tanks opened fire at them from the southern fringe of the woods north of Kuby-Młyny. The commander of the 49th Mechanized Brigade deployed the 127th Tank Regiment and one IS-122 company that had arrived by this time under his subordination from the 13th Guards Heavy Tank Regiment. As a result of the battle, 3 of the enemy tanks were destroyed, and the rest withdrew to the north into the woods. Having left behind a screen – one motorized rifle battalion with 8 tanks on a hill northeast of Kuby-Młyny – in order to secure the right flank, the brigade's main forces began an attack along a village road toward Suków-Babie and by 1800 on 14 January reached the fringe of woods south of this point, where it took fire from enemy tanks. The brigade commander withdrew the brigade from the fringe of the woods back into the woods. By 1900 the 56th Tank Regiment that had been advancing in the wake of the brigade arrived in this area. Simultaneously the 117th Rifle Division reached the Czarna Nida River east of Kuby-Młyny and was crossing the river. In connection with this, the corps' chief of staff issued an order to the commander of the 49th Mechanized Brigade to remove the covering screen in the Kuby-Młyny area and to continue to implement the second day's task with the entire brigade. This was promply done by the commander of the 49th Mechanized Brigade. In order to cover the bridge, the corps' chief of staff positioned a sapper company of the 22nd Separate Guards Sapper Battalion together with 3 tanks of the 95th Separate Motorcycle Battalion and one IS-122 heavy tank of the 28th Guards Heavy Tank Regiment in defensive positions on the hills south of Kuby-Młyny.

By 2300 on 14 January the 49th Mechanized Brigade reached the wooded area 1 km south of Dyminy. The main forces of the 16th Guards Mechanized Brigade by this time had completed mopping up the enemy in the woods east of Łabędziów and was preparing a ford 1.5 km east of Beleckie-Młyny in order to get the tanks across. The forward detachment of the 16th Guards Mechanized Brigade by this time was located in the Białogon area, and was engaged in combat on the southwestern outskirts of Kielce with part of its strength.

In the course of the day of 14 January, units of the 6th Guards Mechanized Corps eliminated up to 650 enemy soldiers and officers, and destroyed 53 tanks (including 7 Tiger tanks), 13 halftracks, 8 guns, 6 rocket launchers, and 15 vehicles. They also captured 50 prisoners, 8 tanks, 5 halftracks and one self-propelled gun.

The 10th Guards Tank Corps' actions to destroy the enemy's Kielce – Radom grouping

The situation on 14 January 1945

The enemy with units of the 168th Infantry Division fell back to the Skrzelchyce, Górki, Maleszowa, Ługi line. With units of the 16th Panzer Division, the Germans were pinning down the 6th Guards Mechanized Corps east of Kielce, while also counterattacking the corps' units from the north in the Pierzchnica area. The German 17th Panzer Division with the arrival of Panzer Regiment 39 and Panzergrenadier Regiment 40 on the Szczecno, Skrzelchyce, Maleszowa, Suchowola line was striving in the Zalesie, Lisów, Piotrkowice area to cut off the units of the 63rd and 61st Guards Tank Brigades that had broken through.

Inflicting heavy losses on the enemy in manpower and equipment, the commander of the 10th Guards Tank Corps Guards Colonel Orlov decided on the morning of 14 July to go over to a decisive attack with the forces of the 62nd Guards Tank Brigade and 29th Guards Motorized Rifle Brigade, with orders to destroy the opposing enemy, to link up with the 61st Guards Tank Brigade in the Lisów area, and then to continue the offensive toward Chęciny together with all the forces. The corps, screening to the north with artillery and one tank battalion of the 62nd Guards Tank Brigade (the 1st Tank Battalion), with the rest of the 62nd Guards Tank Brigade and the 1222nd Light Self-propelled Artillery Regiment, in close cooperation with the 29th Guards Motorized Rifle Brigade, was supposed to link up with the forward operating brigades in the Zalesie area and in the area 4 km outside of Piotrkowice, before proceeding on to capture the Piekoszów railroad station and the town of Chęciny.

At 1130 on 14 January, the 63rd Guards Tank Brigade went on the attack along the Tokarnia – Chęciny route. At 1200 the brigade broke into the town with a rapid dash of the 1st Tank Battalion from the south and became tied up in street fighting. The enemy, equipped with anti-tank artillery and strong fortifications, was putting up heavy resistance with fire.

Owing to the decisive actions of the tanks, the skillful handling on the part of the brigade command and the combat experience in conducting street fighting in large towns and cities, by 1400 on 14 January 1945 the town of Chęciny fell into Soviet hands and was completely mopped up of the enemy. The town of Chęciny represented a major enemy strongpoint on the western bank of the Czarna Nida River. The town's defenses included strong fortifications; anti-tank ditches, abatis, and several rows of trenches with pillboxes and bunkers encircled the town. All of the town's streets were barricaded. Brick buildings had been adapted for defense. Up to two regiments of infantry were defending the town together with tanks and up to 30 halftracks.

In the fighting for the town, the enemy lost 13 tanks (including 1 King Tiger), 3 halftracks, 2 guns, 150 vehicles and up to 200 soldiers and officers. The brigade also captured 3 halftracks, 70 vehicles and 4 guns, and took 44 German prisoners. In return, the 63rd Guards Tank Brigade lost 3 tanks that were knocked out and had 27 casualties (9 dead and 18 wounded). In the fighting for Chęciny, the commander of the 1st Tank Battalion Guards Captain Egorov, tank company commander of the 1st Tank Battalion Guards Senior Lieutenant Iakovlev, and tank platoon commander Guards Lieutenant Tsyganov all distinguished themselves.

After capturing Chęciny, the 63rd Guards Tank Brigade took up an all-round defense of the town. At 1700 on 14 January, it was joined by the commander of the 10th Guards Tank Corps Guards Colonel Orlov and his operational command group.

From the recollections of the commander of the 63rd Guards Tank Brigade twice Hero of the Soviet Union Lieutenant General of Tank Forces M.G. Fomichev:

The exploitation of nighttime operations was characteristic in the raid toward Chęciny. If we hadn't been operating in the night, but in the daytime, the Germans would have gotten their act together. The 61st Tank Brigade set off on the left, and the enemy was checking its advance. I took advantage of this and reached Chęciny itself without battle; there was one combat action for a bridge, but it was small. The Germans didn't even have time to spread the warning that the Russians were coming. So, we took advantage of the night and the cooperation with the 61st Guards Tank Brigade, which tied down the enemy. That's how we were operating: wherever the enemy was pressing, we moved to counter him. If there hadn't been such impetuousity of actions, Chęciny wouldn't have fallen so easily. Chęciny was important for the fact that it was a railroad hub, and from there it was possible to take Kielce. The 61st Guards Tank Brigade moved out strictly to the north, but I – to the west. The enemy would see that we were emerging in his rear, and would have to give up Kielce unwillingly, but why would he have to give it up, if he could defend the Kielce – Chęciny line? To Chęciny it was 60 km as the crow flies, but then approximately another 70 km beyond Chęciny as the crow flies, and we would now emerge in operational space. The Germans had only the battered 16th and 17th Panzer Divisions, nothing more. The Volkssturm was now already unable to do anything substantial. Egorov's 1st Tank Battalion, Egorov himself, and Baranov and I were the first to enter Chęciny. The Germans began to throw up barricades, but we smashed through them. A German tank emerged and we knocked it out, just as we did with a second enemy tank that appeared. The Polish residents said that more than 20 German tanks were on their way to here from Kielce. They refused battle and departed to the north. If we had waited just a bit, the 20 tanks wouldn't have gotten away from here.

The 61st Guards Tank Brigade, having rendered assistance to the 62nd Guards Tank Brigade in the destruction of the enemy in the Zaborze, Brudzów area, at 0900 on 14 January went on the attack along the Lisów, Zalesie, Poręba Morawicka, Dębska-Wola route, bypassing eney strongpoints and destroying remnants of the shattered units of the enemy's 16th and 17th Panzer Divisions. The brigade was unable to reach its assigned route of advance in the Morawica area, because a reconnaissance patrol that had been sent out in the direction of Morawica at 1300 spotted up to 60 enemy tanks and halftracks in the woods northwest of Point 233.3. The brigade commander Guards Lieutenant Colonel Zaitsev decided to avoid the enemy without getting tied up in combat, and to bypass to the left of the enemy-held woods along the Dębska-Wola, Zbrza, Ostrów, Wolica, Tokarnia, Chęciny, Zelejowa, Szewce, Łaziska route and to arrive at Piekoszów. Moving along the route, the brigade, having caught up with units of the 63rd Guards Tank Brigade in Chęciny and having destroyed a section of the railroad between Lesica and Szczukowice, by 2100 on 14 January 1945 reached Piekoszów, where it took up a hedgehog defense while sending one tank company as a forward detachment to the Promnik area. The commander of the forward detachment Guards Senior Lieutenant Markov decided to bypass Micigózd. At 0300 on 15 January, the forward detachment reached Promnik, thereby cutting off the final path of retreat available to the German Kielce grouping.

As a result of the fighting that ensued with the German Promnik garrison, the forward detachment forced the enemy to withdraw to a distillery on its northeastern outskirts. In this clash, the commander of the forward detachment Guards Senior Lieutenant Markov fell wounded. At 0400 the enemy, having brought up tanks and infantry, launched a counterattack, having orders to drive Markov's tanks out of Promnik. The commander of the 2nd Tank Battalion, who had hurried to the assistance of the forward detachment, repulsed the counterattack together with Markov's tank company and restored the situation.

At 1230 on January 1945, the headquarters of the 4th Tank Army sent its Combat Report No. 10 to the chief of staff of the 1st Ukrainian Front:

1. The 4th Tank Army continues to be engaged in heavy fighting with units of the enemy's 16th and 17th Panzer Divisions and the 168th Infantry Division on the Marzysz, Kuby-Młyny, Piaseczna-Górki line and in the Kowala, Brzeziny, Tokarnia area.
2. The 6th Guards Mechanized Corps together with forces of the 16th Guards Mechanized Brigade (the forward detachment) continues to engage in combat with the 16th Panzer Division in order to force a crossing of the Bobrza River in the Kowala area. The 49th Mechanized Brigade, attacking in the direction of Suków-Babie, continues to struggle for Marzysz and with part of its strength for Kuby-Młyny. Since the morning three enemy counterattacks (by the 16th Panzer Division and 168th Infantry Division) have been repulsed, and one self-propelled gun has been captured. The 17th Guards Mechanized Brigade is engaged in fighting with counterattacking units of the 16th Panzer Division in the Piaseczna-Górki, Beleckie-Młyny area. The 10th Guards Tank Corps' 63rd Guards Tank Brigade, having overcome strong enemy resistance, has fully crossed the Czarna Nida River and continued to develop the offensive toward Lipowice and Chęciny. The 61st Guards Tank Brigade and the 29th Guards Motorized Rifle Brigade by 0700 reached Morawica and are in the process of crossing the Czarna Nida River. The 62nd Guards Tank Brigade is advancing behind the 29th Guards Motorized Rifle Brigade.
3. According to adjusted data, over 13 January 1945 the enemy lost up to 60 tanks and 200 vehicles either destroyed or knocked out, and up to 500 soldiers and officers killed or wounded; 17 guns have been destroyed, and 4 ammunition and fuel stockpiles have been captured. Our own losses: 29 tanks. Casualties are being ascertained.

Chief of staff of the 4th Tank Army Guards General Major of Tank Forces UPMAN
4th Tank Army's chief of operations Guards Colonel Mariakhin

The 62nd Guards Tank Brigade together with the 1222nd Light Self-propelled Artillery Regiment at 0300 14 January from the Gumienice area set out along the Gumienice, Pierzchnica, Górki Maleszowka, Lisów, Zalesie, Morawica route. At dawn the 1st and 2nd Tank Battalions became tied up in combat with units of the German 16th Panzer Division in the Zaborze area. By 1100 of the same day, the enemy had been driven out of Zaborze and Brudzów and had begun to withdrawn in the direction of Morawica. The brigade's units, pursuing the enemy, by 1450 reached the wooded area 200 meters south of Wola-Morawicka, having the orders to to reach Piekoszów area by the end of the day. The brigade's further advance was cancelled in view of an order from the commander of the 4th Tank Army to remain in the Morawica area with the task to assist the units of the 6th Guards Mechanized Corps with capturing Kielce.

As a result of the fighting for Zaborze and Brudzów, the enemy suffered the destruction of 2 King Tigers, 5 Tigers, 7 Panthers, 4 Pz.Kpfw. IV tanks, 3 self-propelled guns and 10 vehicles, while losing 480 soldiers and officers. The Soviets captured 4 halftracks, 4 vehicles, 10 machine guns, and 12 men. In return, the brigade lost 8 tanks (4 destroyed and 4 knocked out) and 23 men (7 killed and 16 wounded).

The 29th Guards Motorized Rifle Brigade on the morning of 14 January moved out behind the 62nd Guards Tank Brigade in the direction of Zalesie and reached the 61st Guards Tank Brigade's route of advance while destroying small, shattered enemy groups that it met along the way. By 1900 on this same day, the brigade reached Chęciny with its forward units, and spent the rest of the night bringing itself back to order and allowing the remaining units to come up.

At 1900 on 14 January the corps commander issued a directive to the commander of the 63rd Guards Tank Brigade to remove the 2nd Tank Battalion from the defense of Chęciny and to take

Rykoszyn by 2100. At 2000 the 2nd Tank Battalion set out along the Szewce, Zawada, Galęzica route, and without encountering any enemy resistance, reached the vicinity of a lineman's hut in Rykoszyn, thereby cutting the Kielce – Małogoszcz railroad. It then took up a hedgehog defense in the Rykoszyn area.

From the memoirs of the former Chief of the General Staff General H. Guderian:

Army Group A had sent its reserves for a counter-thrust. A direct order from Hitler had resulted in these forces being stationed closer to the front than Colonel General Harpe had originally intended. The result of this interference was that they were shelled by the strong Russian artillery and suffered heavy casualties before they ever reached the battle area. The Russians succeeded in partially encircling these forces. Now under command of General Nehring, they had to be withdrawn westwards, fighting their way back and out of the Russians' mobile encirclement as they did so; this most difficult maneuver was successfully carried out thanks to the stalwart behavior of the troops, a highly credible performance. A number of infantry formations became involved in this mobile encirclement battle and slowed down our armored forces.

From the Combat Path of the 4th Guards Tank Army:

Over the night and day of 14 January, bitter fighting went on, in which up to 1,000 tanks from both sides took part. The 6th Mechanized Corps had fluctuating success in the struggle with the enemy tanks. A number of villages changed hands repeatedly. On the afternoon of 14 January, the enemy managed to capture Morawica. As a result, the forward detachment of the 17th Guards Mechanized Brigade, which was located on the northern bank of the Czarna Nida River, wound up isolated from its main forces. Toward evening the 49th Mechanized Brigade, in cooperation with the 17th Guards Mechanized Brigade, launched an attack into the enemy's flank, forcing him to retreat. This enabled the crossing of the Czarna Nida River to resume.

The 10th Guards Tank Corps' 63rd Guards Tank Brigade was attacking toward Chęciny. Reconnaissance reported that the bridges across the Czarna Nida River had been blown up, the riverbanks were mined, the town had been converted into a strongpoint belted by an anti-tank ditch, and the streets had been blocked by barricades. At 1400 the advance guard patrol consisting of Guards Junior Lieutenant P.I. Tsyganov's tank platoon was closing on Chęciny; it forced a crossing of the river and burst into the town. Guards Senior Lieutenant Ivan Liubived' tank company crossed the river obstacle in the wake of it. The enemy opened fire from heavy guns and tanks. Simultaneously a group of enemy aircraft appeared. The Germans set one tank ablaze, but the remaining machines were already moving into the town. Tsyganov's tank in the street fighting rammed through three barricades and knocked out a King Tiger, but then was set ablaze by an enemy shell and Tsyganov was wounded. The crew had no success in putting out the fire, so encircled by Germans, fought their way out with submachine gun fire and grenades. Tsyganov was wounded a second time. Ammunition was running low. At a most critical moment, Guards Junior Lieutenant Biriukov's tank arrived to bail them out of their predicament. For his demonstrated courage, P.I. Tsyganov was deemed worth of the title "Hero of the Soviet Union".

The 61st Guards Tank Brigade and 29th Guards Motorized Rifle Brigade by the end of day on 14 January had closed on Chęciny. The 62nd Guards Tank Brigade was engaged in combat in the Morawica area. It had inflicted significant detachment on the enemy: 21 tanks knocked out, including 2 King Tigers, and had killed or captured approximately 500 soldiers and officers. In return, the 62nd Guards Tank Brigade lost 10 tanks.

On 14 January a German panzer regiment had penetrated the gap between the army's forward detachments and its main forces, and on the march attacked the 2007th Anti-aircraft Artillery Regiment at the village of Kaczemiec, which was in the process of moving up to the Czarna Nida River in order to cover the crossing sites at Morawica. The regiment was equipped with 85mm anti-aircraft guns. It required a matter of minutes to deploy them. The fortuitous position of its column on the road allowed it to arrange its guns so they encircled the village. The enemy nevertheless got the jump on the anti-aircraft gunners in opening fire. A direct hit by a shell killed several soldiers. The batteries opened return fire. With their first shots, they knocked out three tanks and inflicted casualties on the submachine gunners that were following behind them. The anti-aircraft gunners repulsed three attacks. The third attack, which was conducted under nighttime conditions, results in particularly heavy fighting. The enemy fire was so intense that it seemed impossible to raise a head. The Germans managed to set ablaze the mobile artillery repair shop. However, the anti-aircraft gunners were able to find a proper response. Squad leader Senior Sergeant A.O. Shamaev and master armorer Sergeant M.P. Popov knocked out an enemy tank with grenades. In this action, Shamaev fell heroically in battle; Sergeant Popov was wounded, but remained on duty. Soon thereafter a truck loaded with boxes of shells erupted in flames. The chief of artillery supply Captain M.I. Vorob'ev and several soldiers of the ammunition train rushed to it and put out the flames.

The batteries of Senior Lieutenant I.P. Emel'ianenko and Captain I.Ia. Kravchenko wound up in a difficult situation during the battle. German panzers and halftracks attacked their firing positions. The enemy knocked out a gun of the 1st Battery, but using antitank grenades, its crew continued to fight to repulse the attack. The situation became critical near the end of the battle. German tanks had almost approached right up to the firing positions. Many guns were firing at pointblank range. The barrels became overheated. However, the gunnery didn't weaken. Sergeant A.N. Tsybin's crew knocked out a tank and a halftrack, while Sergeant A.V. Galushkin destroyed two tanks. Wounded men refused to leave their posts. For example, gunner Sergeant V.S. Iastrebov, being wounded, didn't leave his combat post. His gun knocked out two halftracks and a tank. Private S.E. Vashkarin, ignoring his wound, until the end of the battle continued to fight while taking on two roles as fuze setter and gun loader. Sergeants M.M. Fokin, Iu.G. Varabin and Privates A.A. Merkulov, F.A. Lazarev and others fought heroically. In this battle the anti-aircraft gunners knocked out or set ablaze 9 tanks and 14 halftracks, and captured two tanks and four halftracks in good working order. The enemy suffered heavy losses. Several of the Nazi soldiers were taken prisoner, including an officer carrying important operational documents.

Gunner Sergeant N.V. Andriushok, positioned in ambush, opened sudden fire at the enemy machines. He managed to destroy two tanks and to eliminate dozens of attacking enemy soldiers. He was deemed worth of the title "Hero of the Soviet Union". Tank company commander Guards Captain Bocharov spotted German tanks on the move in the Łabędziów area. They were presenting a threat to the flanks of the 16th and 17th Mechanized Brigades and a crossing site on the Czarna Nida River. Bocharov opened fire and then attacked. The tank company drove back the enemy and compressed the Germans against a swamp. In this action, Bocharov's tank company destroyed 4 tanks and 7 halftracks, and captured 2 more German tanks in good working order.

By the end of 14 January 1945, the formations and units of the 4th Tank Army had shattered the German 16th and 17th Panzer Divisions and the 20th Panzergrenadier Division. Over just two days of fighting, 117 enemy tanks and self-propelled guns were destroyed. Forces of the 3rd Guards Tank Army and 13th Army also took active part in the destruction of the enemy's operational reserves. Over this same period (13-14 January 1945), the losses of the 4th Tank Army amounted to 59 tanks.

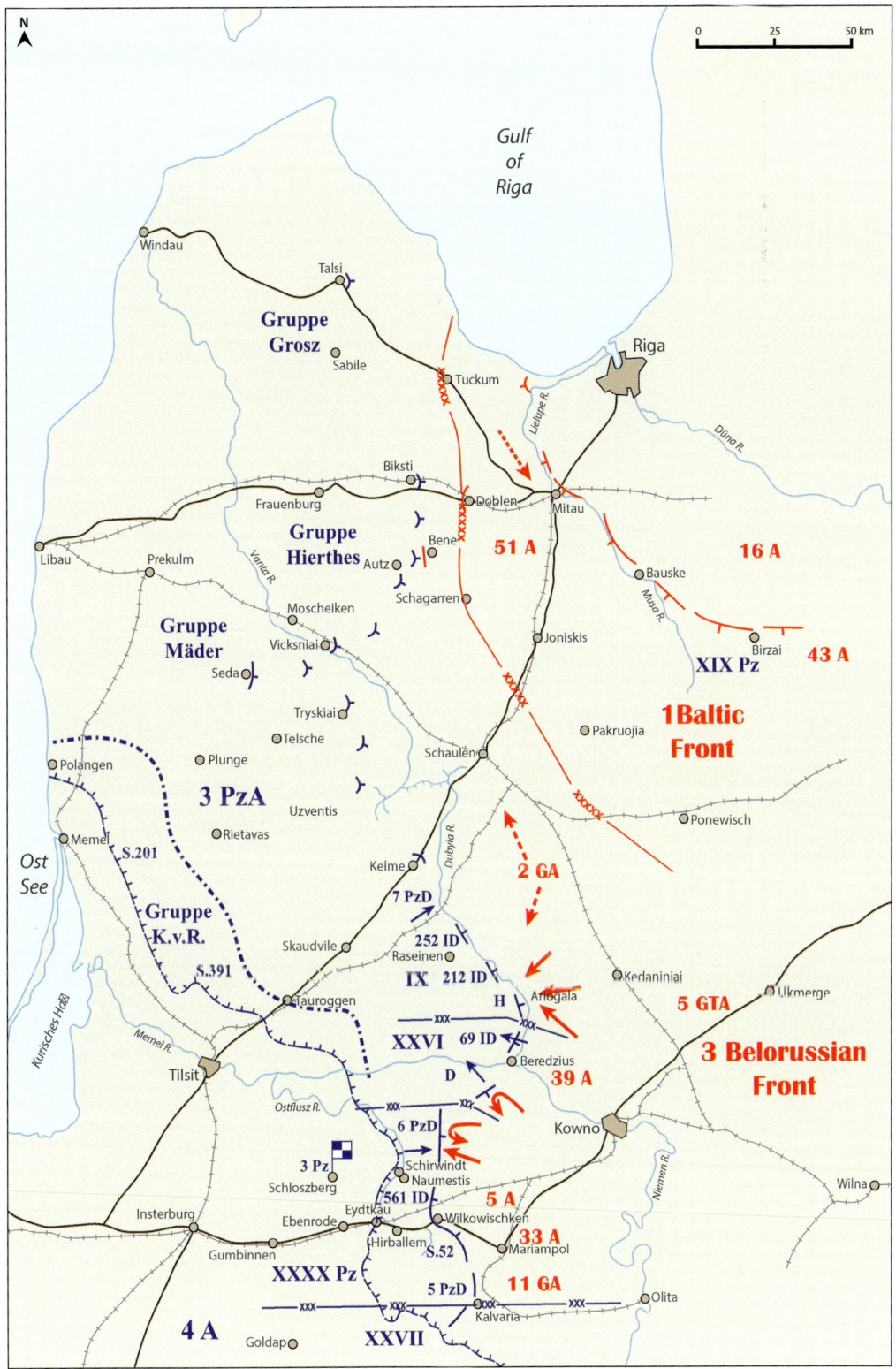

Map 1 Operational map of the German Third Panzer Army as of evening, 3 August 1944.

i

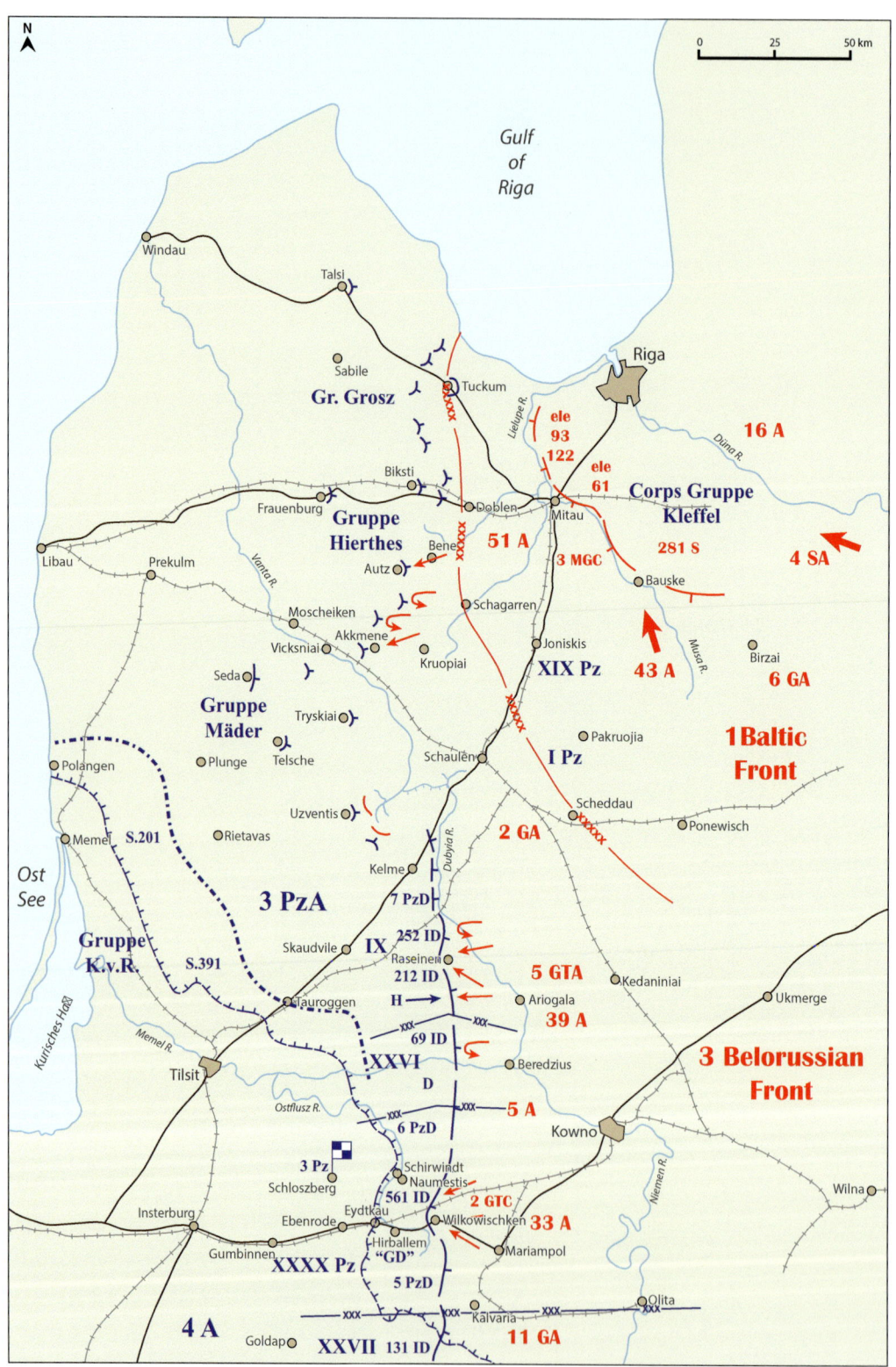

Map 2 Operational map of the German Third Panzer Army as of evening, 9 August 1944.

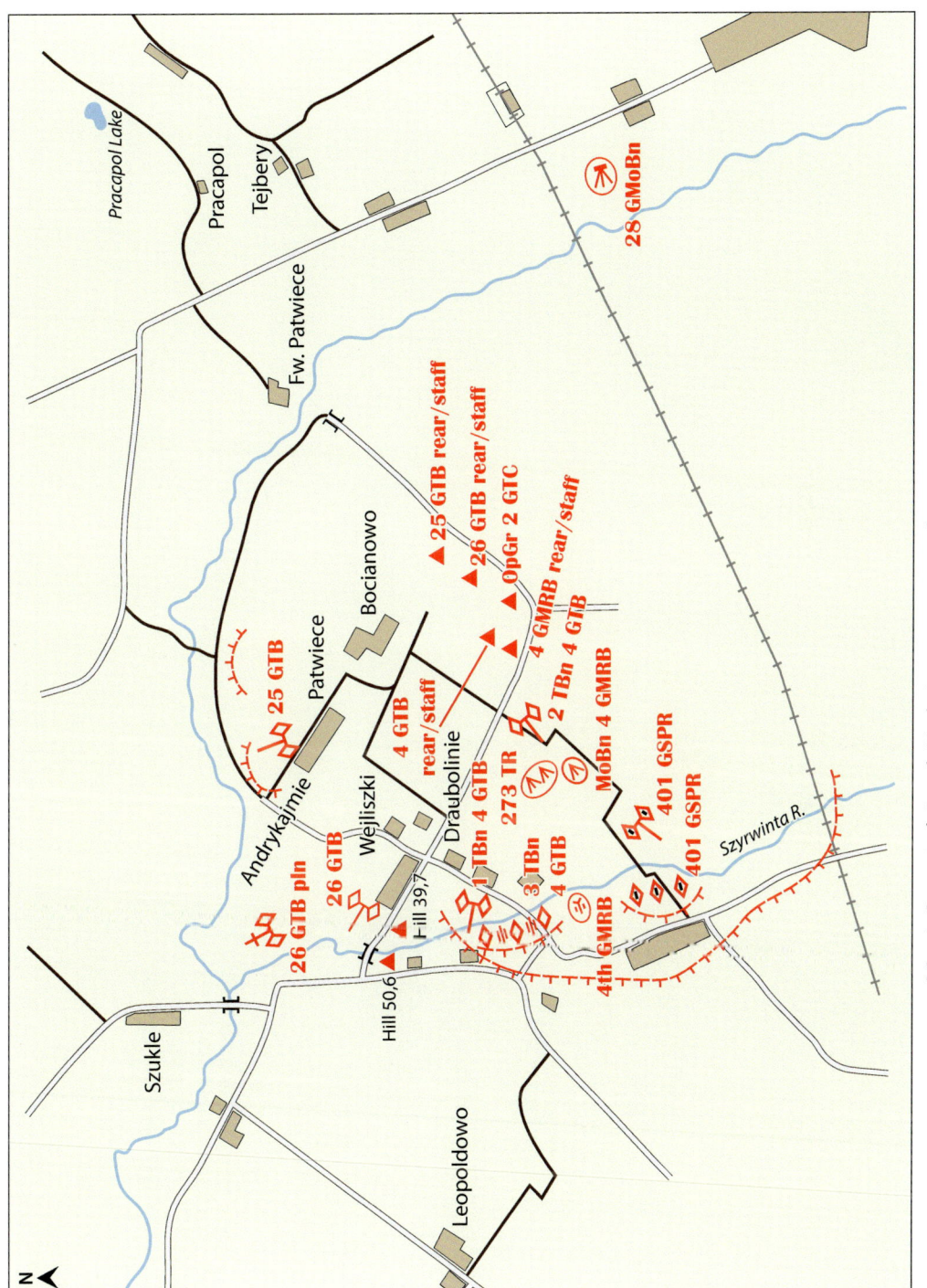

Map 3 Soviet 2nd Guards Tank Corps position as of 12.00, 6 August 1944.

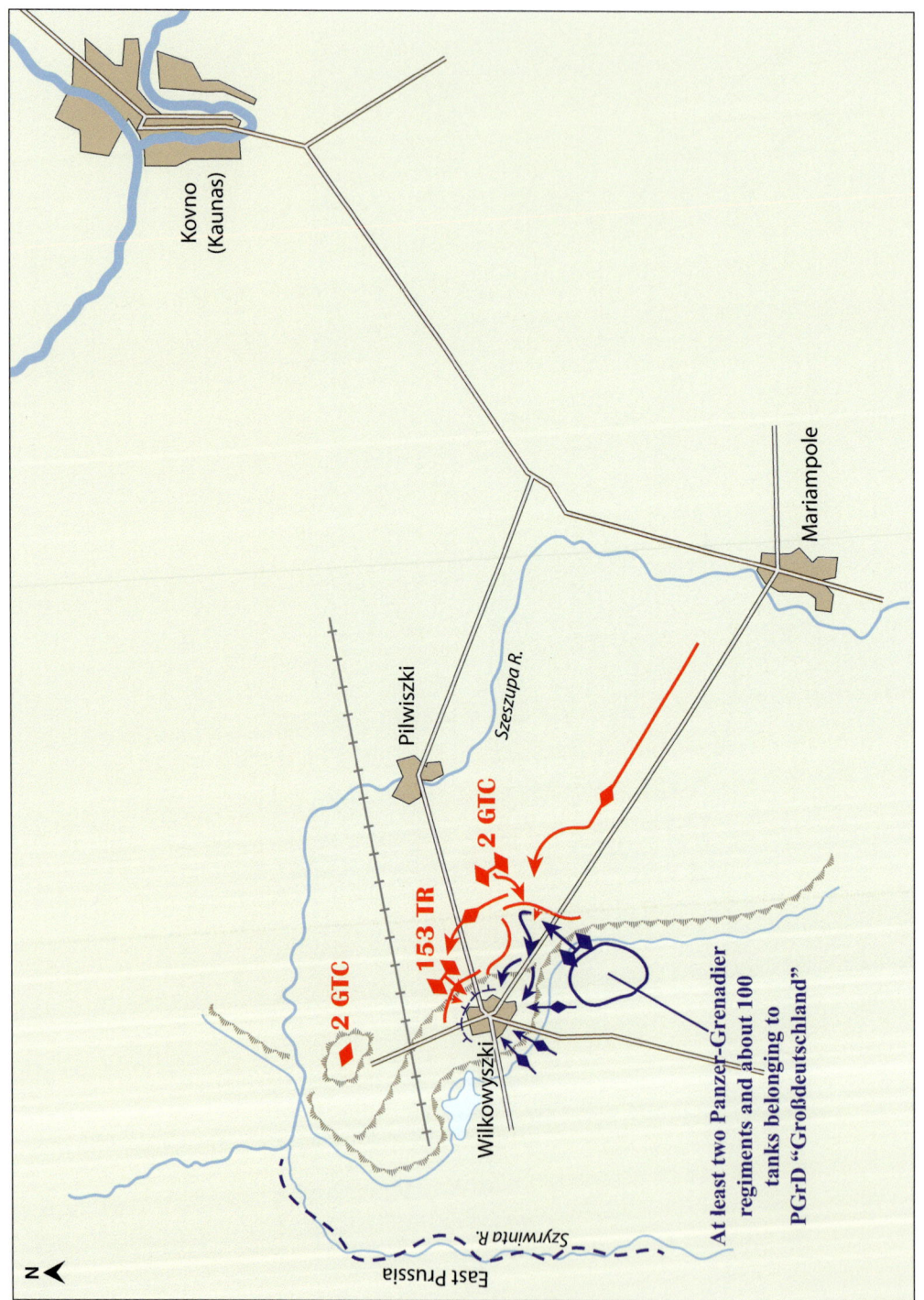

Map 4 Battle for Wiłkowyszki, 9 August 1944 – Soviet operational map.

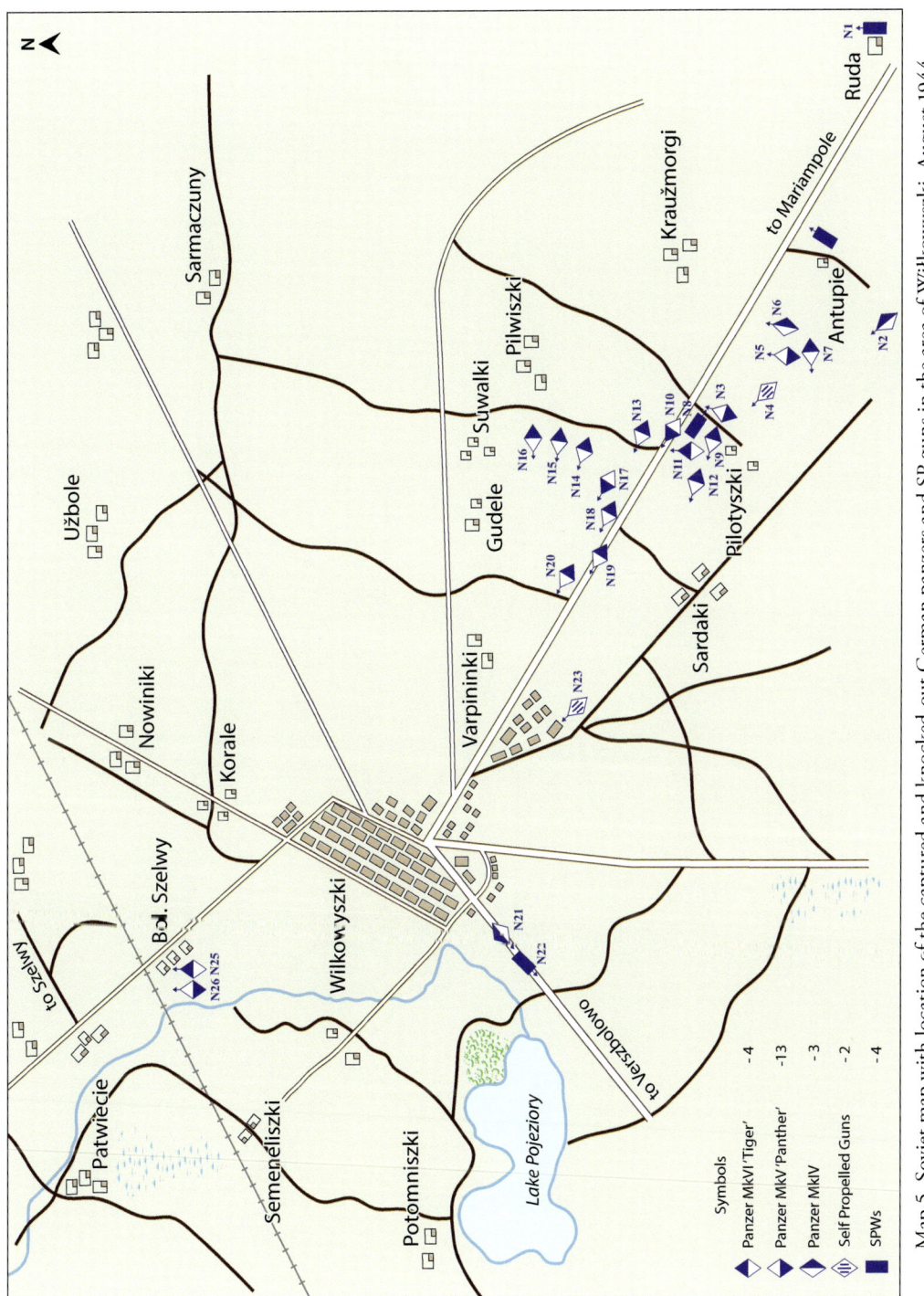

Map 5 Soviet map with location of the captured and knocked-out German panzers and SP guns in the area of Wiłkowyszki, August 1944.

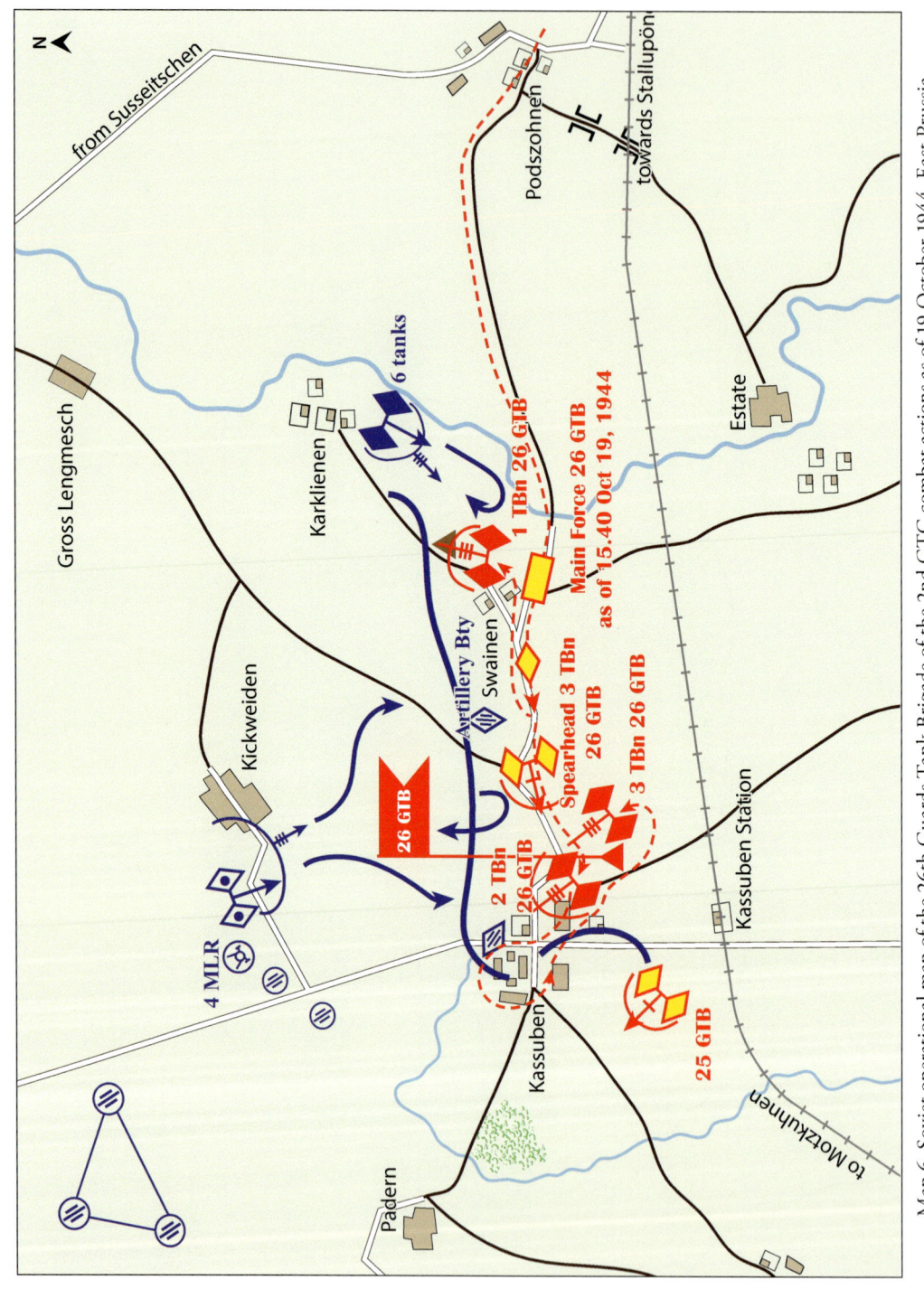

Map 6 Soviet operational map of the 26th Guards Tank Brigade of the 2nd GTC combat actions as of 19 October 1944, East Prussia.

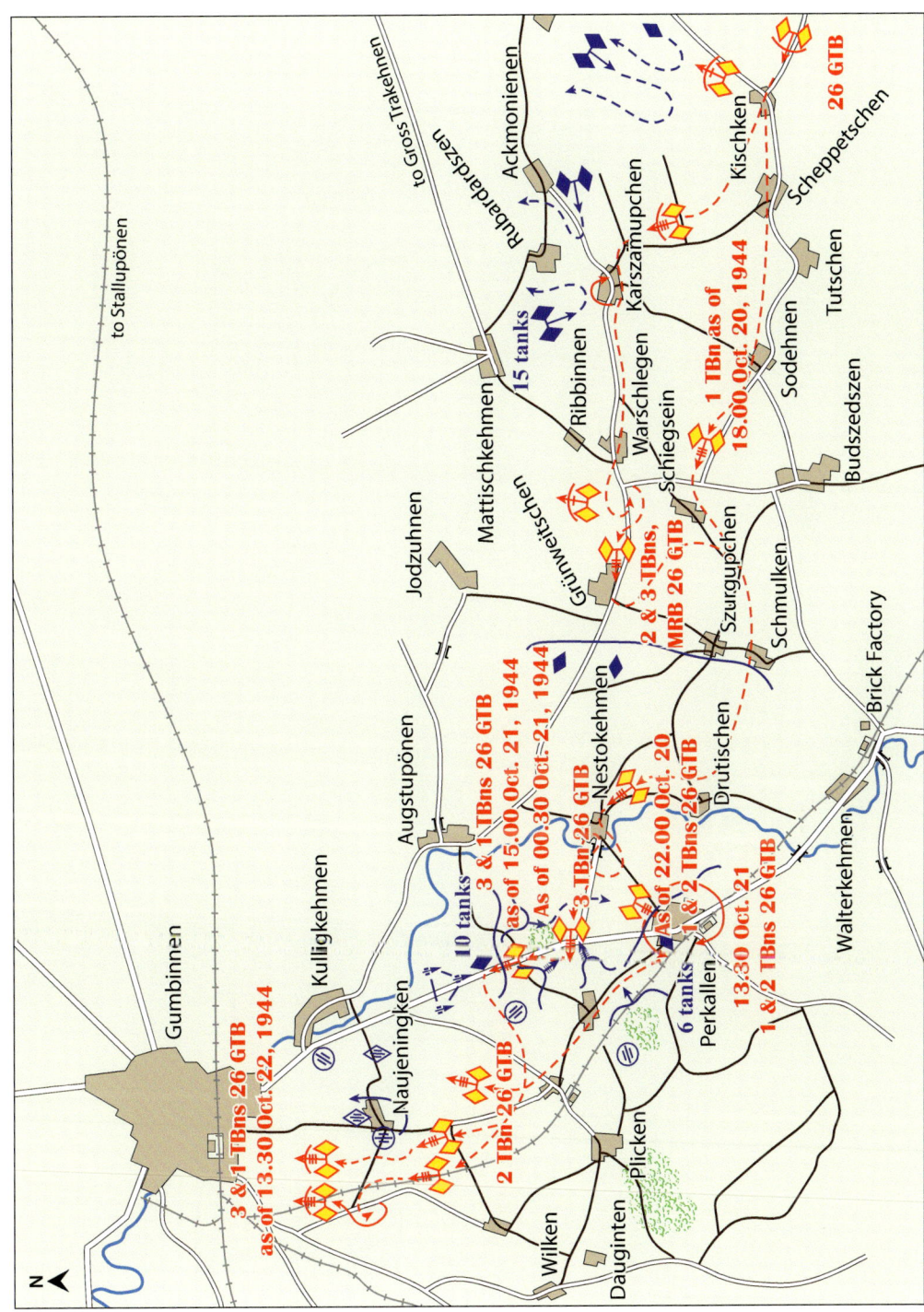

Map 7 Soviet operational map of the 26th Guards Tank Brigade's combat actions as of 20 October 1944, East Prussia.

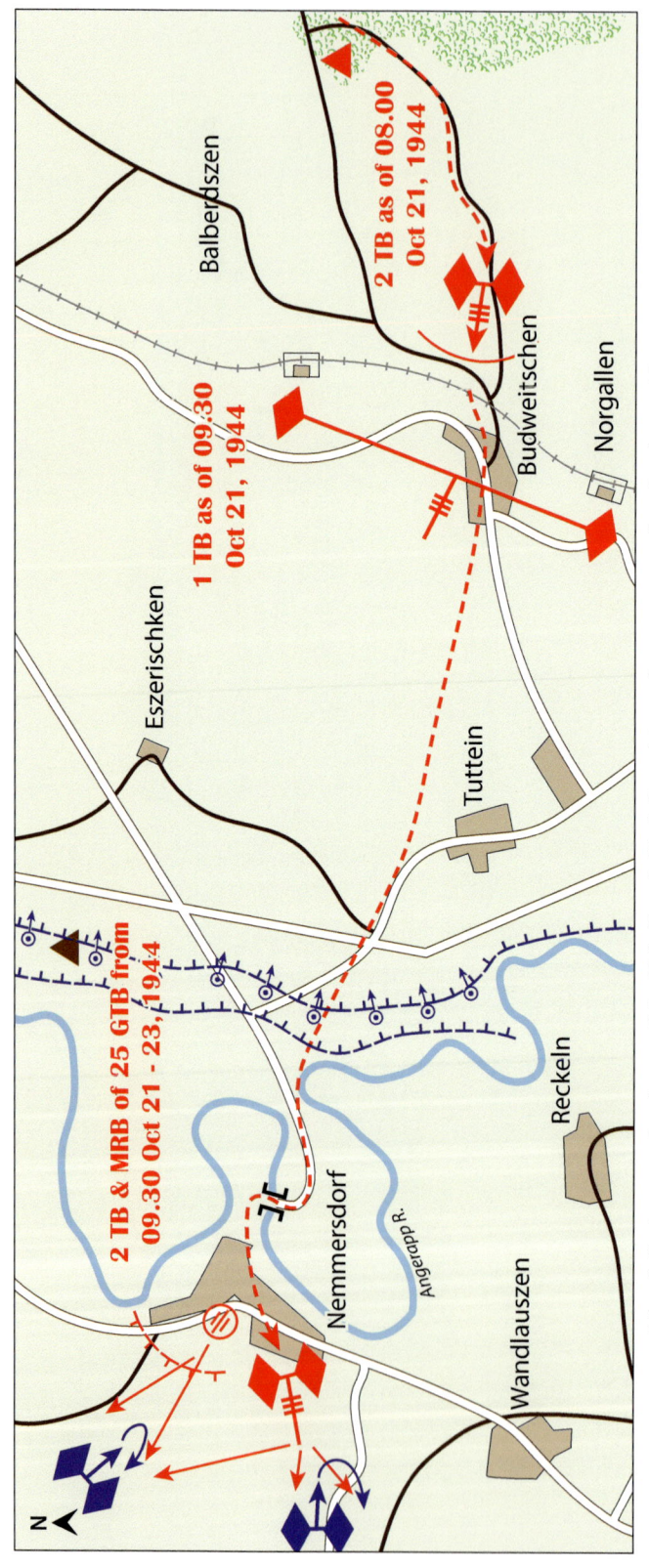

Map 8 Soviet operational map of the 25th Guards Tank Brigade's combat actions as of 21 October 1944, East Prussia.

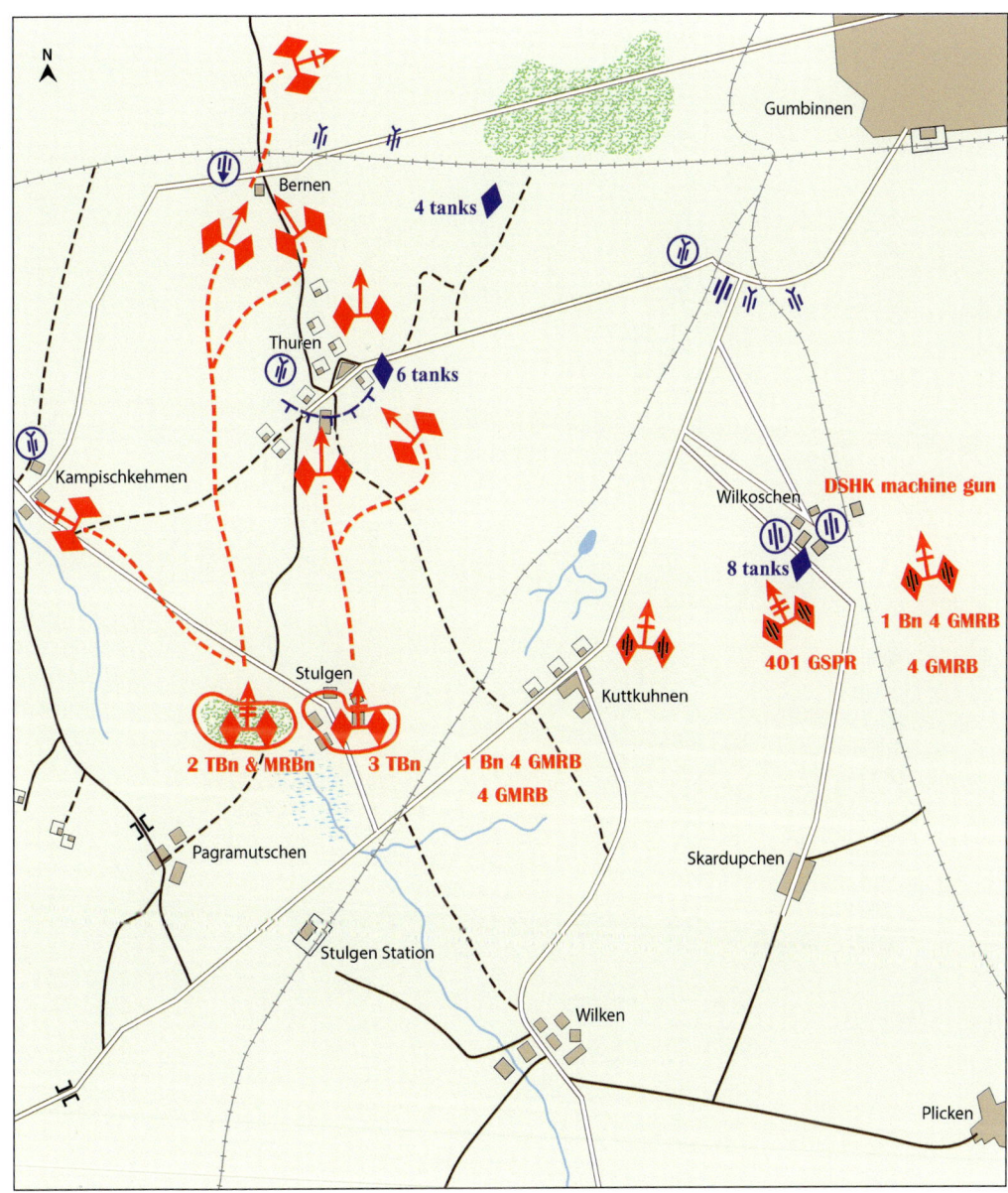

Map 9 Soviet operational map of the 4th Guards Tank Brigade's combat actions as of 22 October 1944, East Prussia.

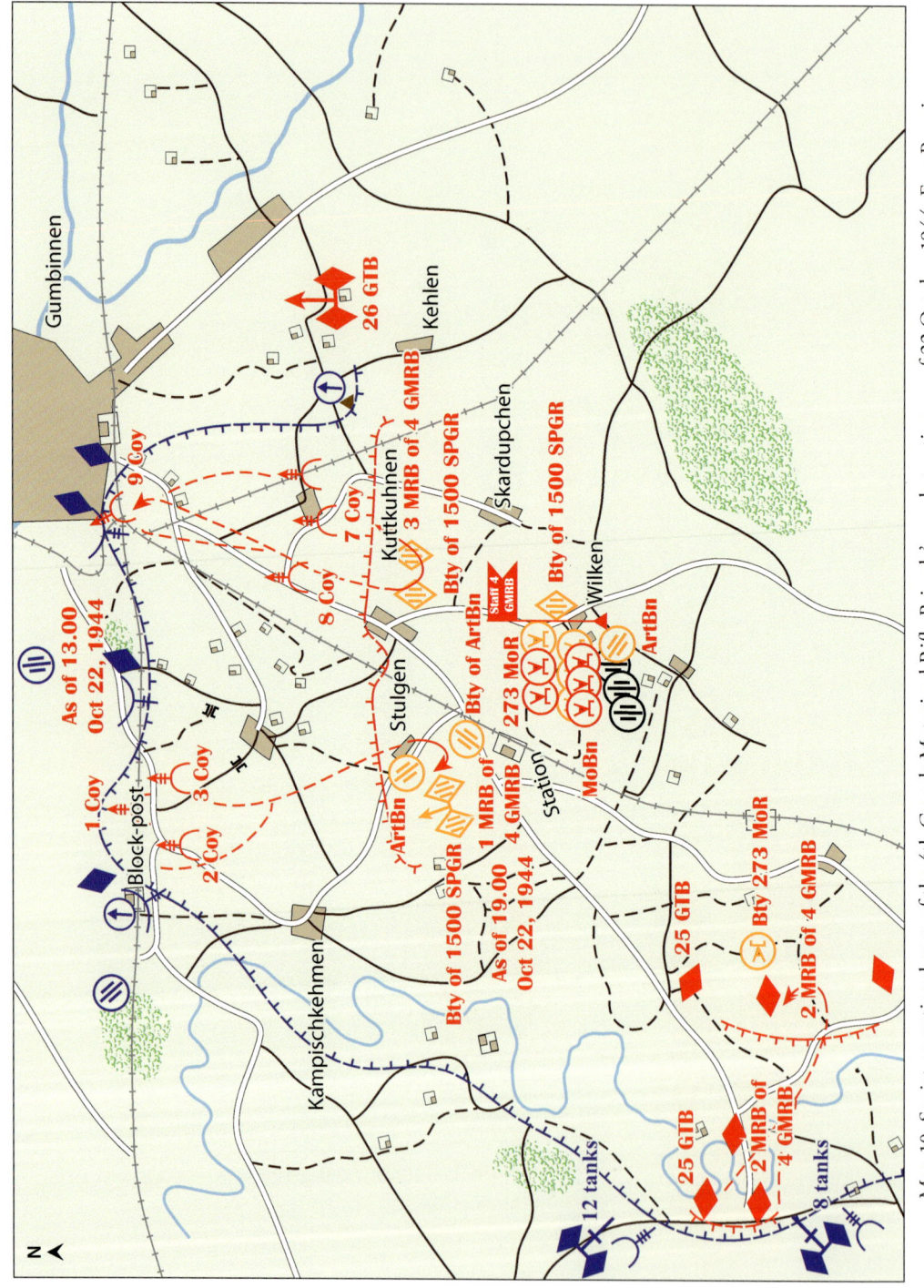

Map 10 Soviet operational map of the 4th Guards Motorized Rifle Brigade's combat actions as of 22 October 1944, East Prussia.

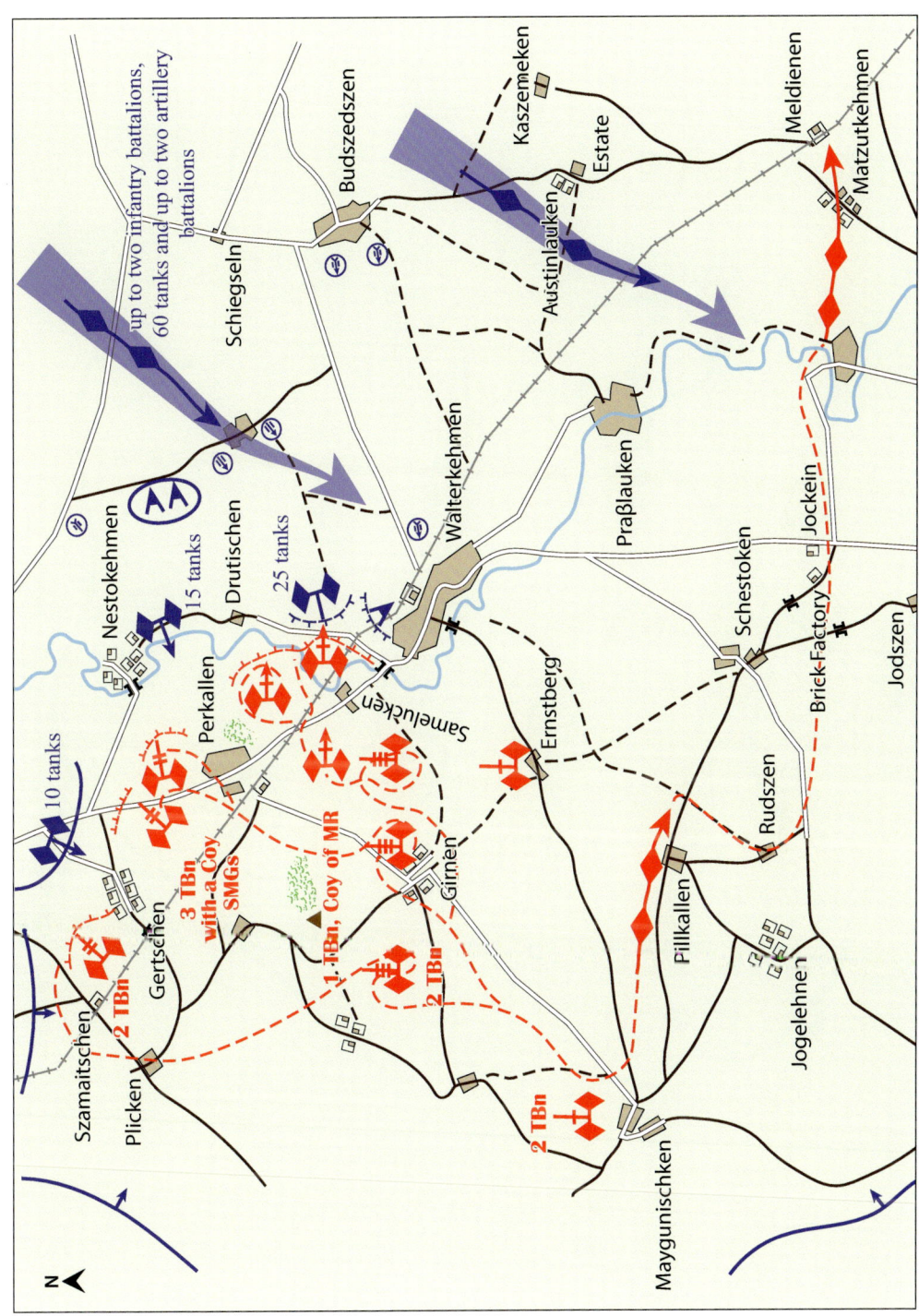

Map 11 Soviet operational map of the 4th Guards Tank Brigade's combat actions as of 23 October 1944, East Prussia.

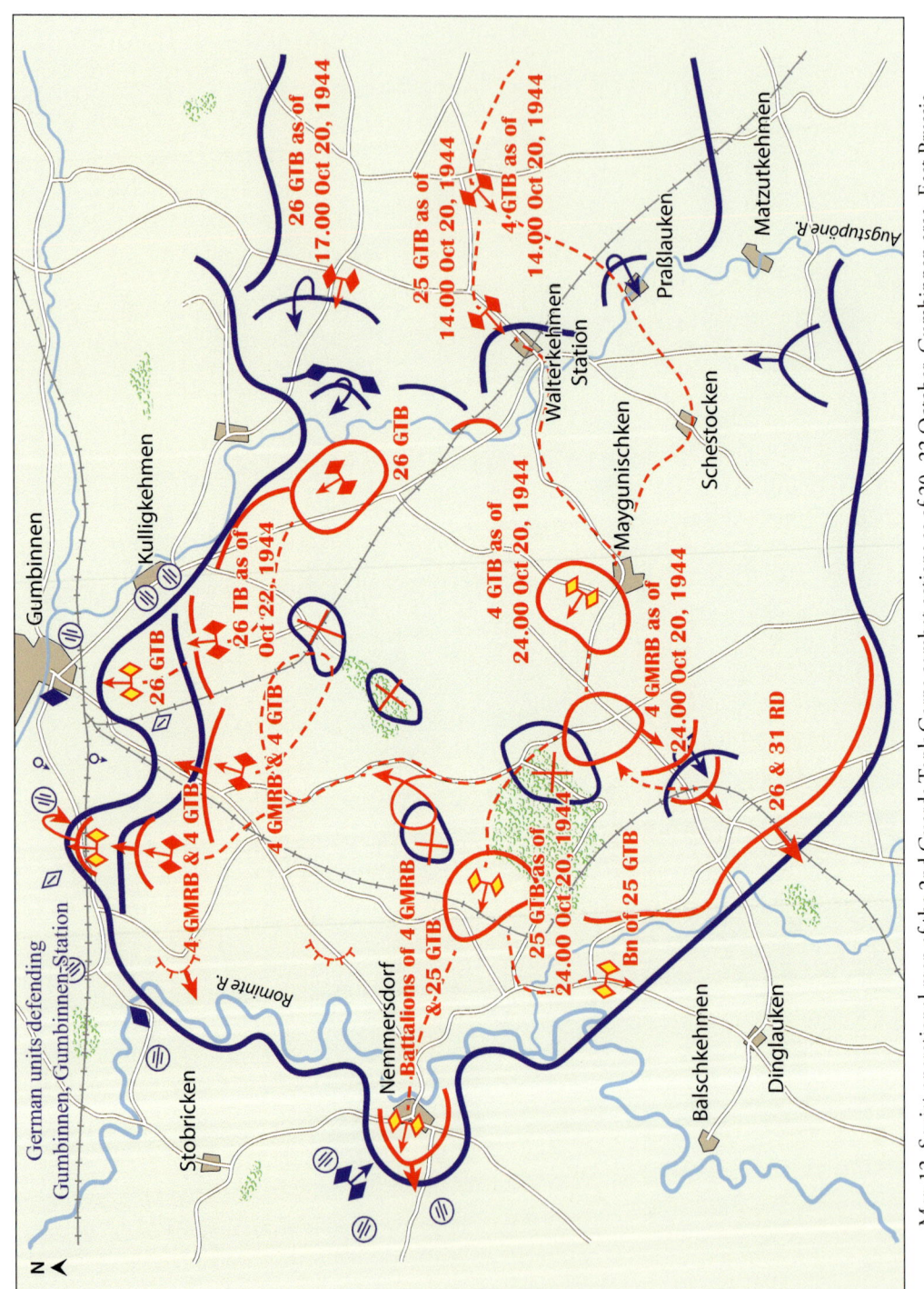

Map 12 Soviet operational map of the 2nd Guards Tank Corps combat actions as of 20–22 October, Gumbinnen area, East Prussia.

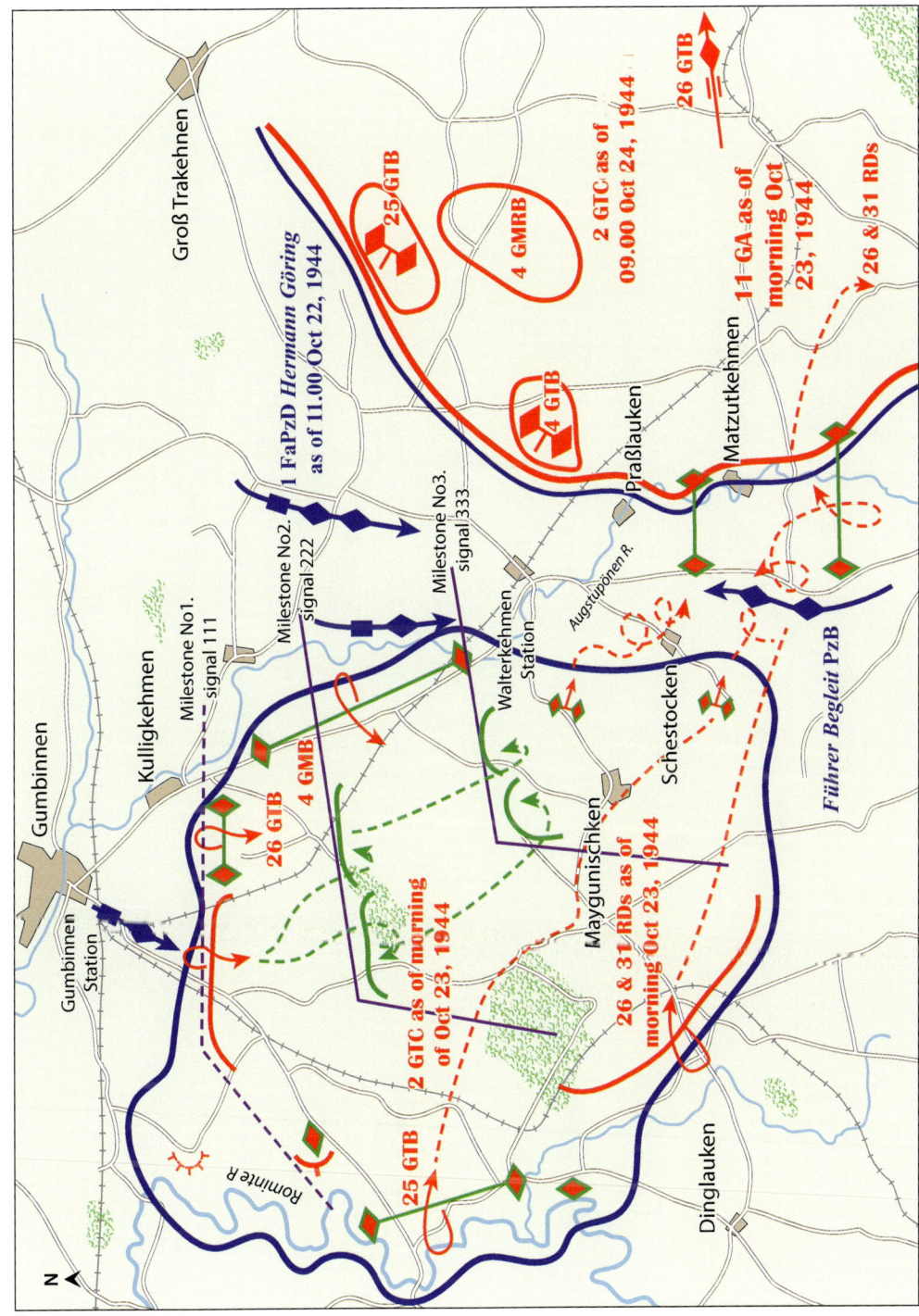

Map 13 Soviet operational map of the 2nd Guards Tank Corps combat actions as of 23–25 October, Tanennberg area, East Prussia.

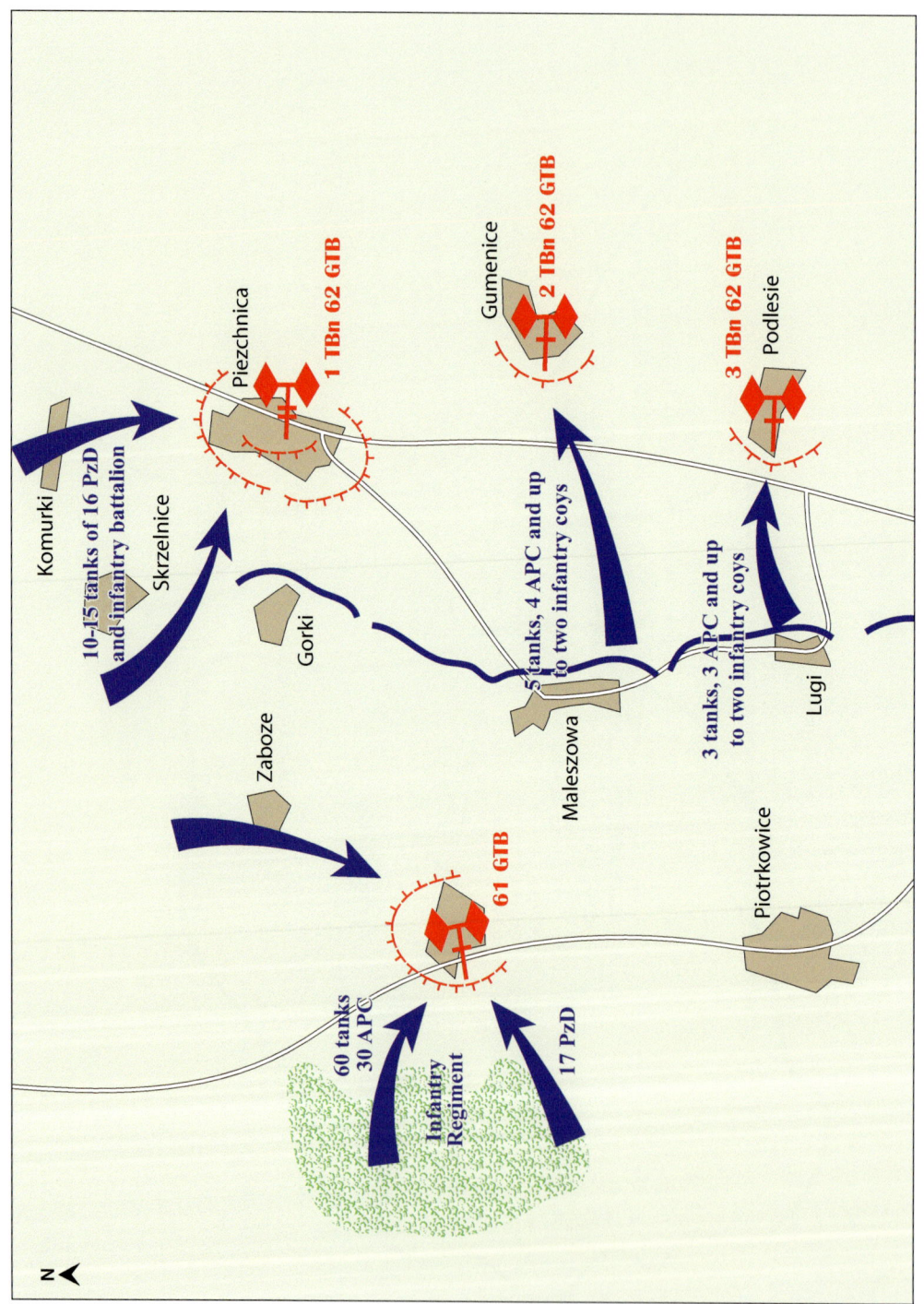

Map 14 Soviet operational map of the 10th Guards Tank Corps as of morning of 13 January 1945.

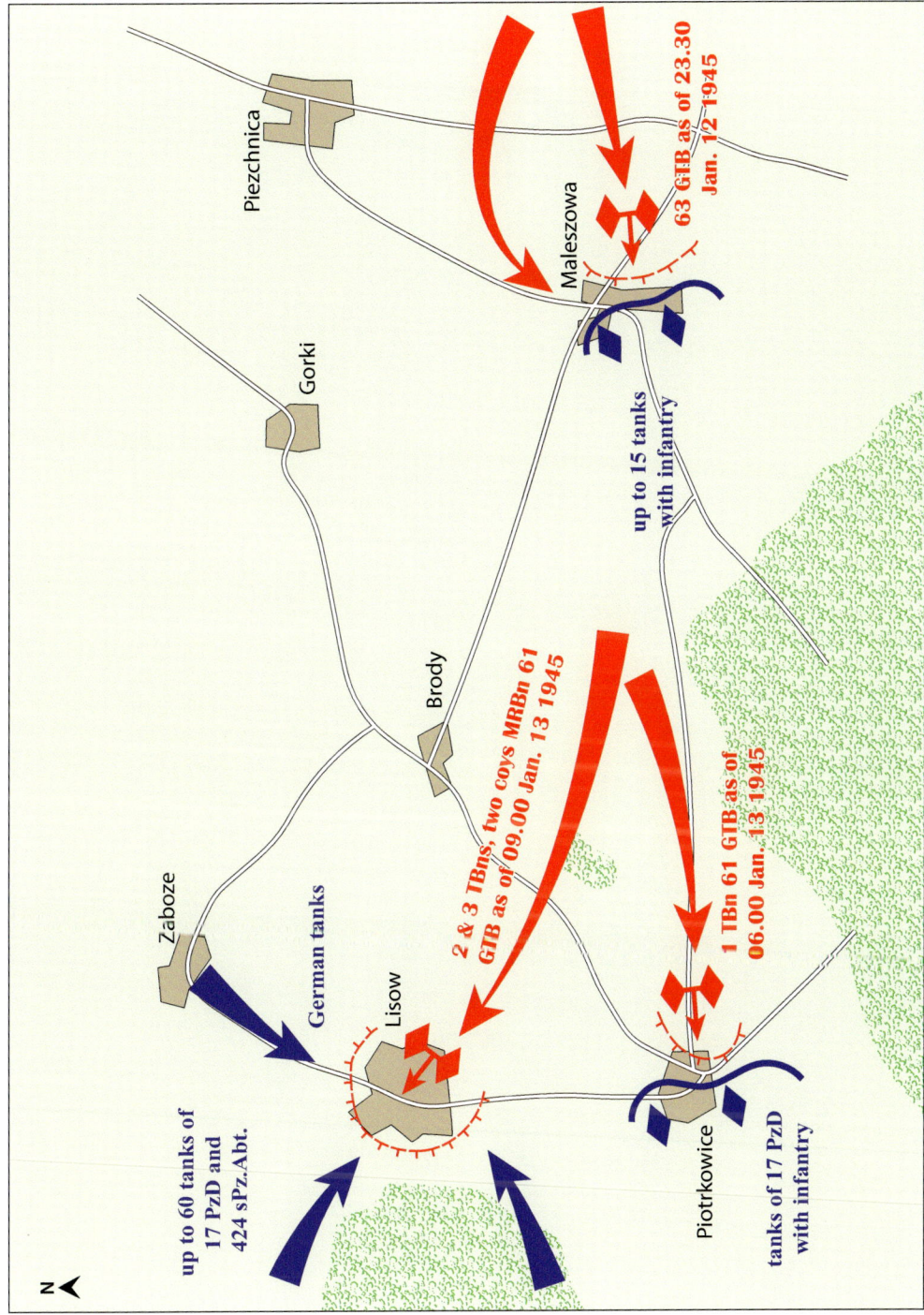

Map 15 Soviet operational map of the 10th Guards Tank Corps combat actions as of evening of 13 January 1945, Battle for Lisow.

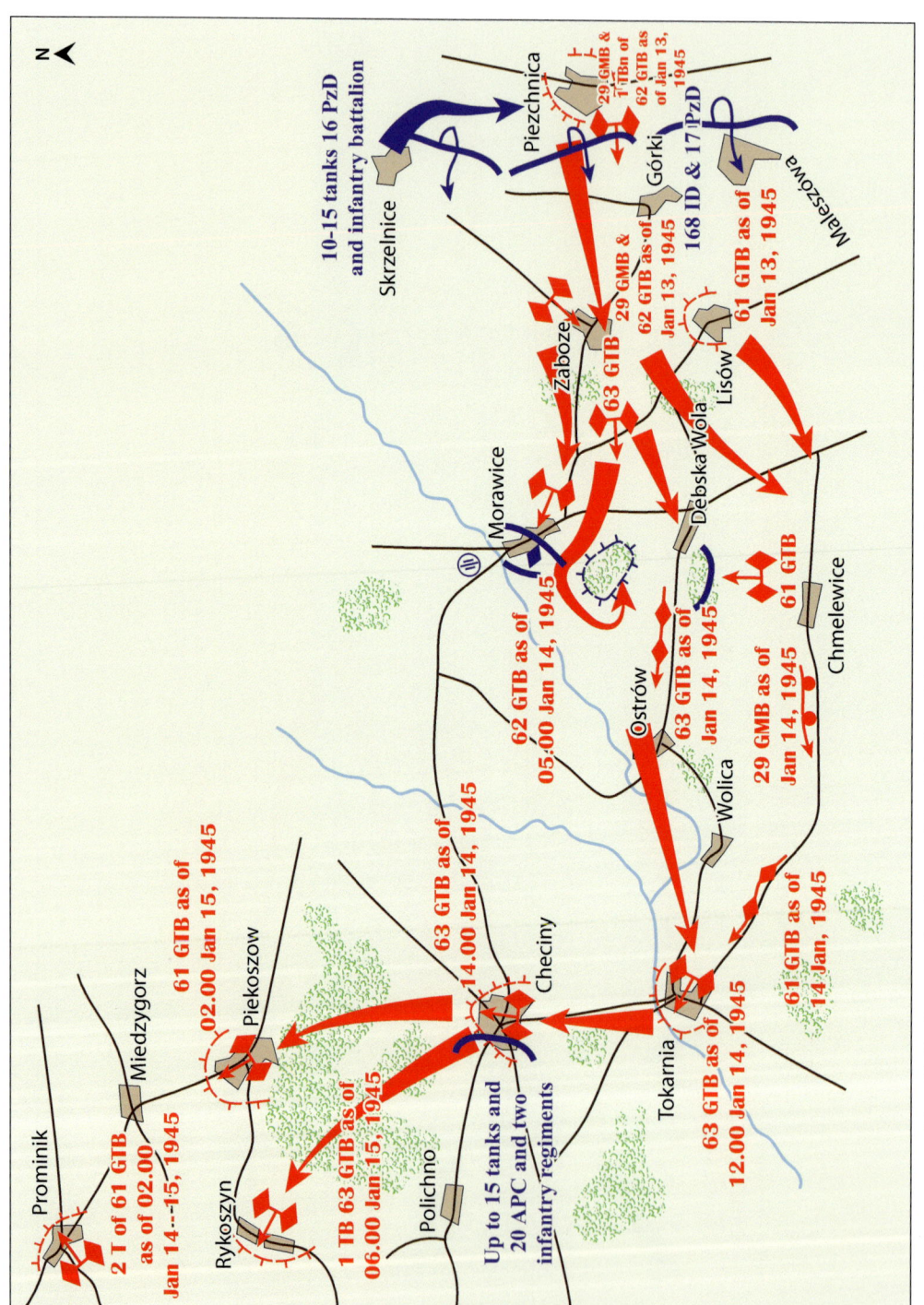

Map 16 Soviet operational map of the 10th Guards Tank Corps combat actions as of 14–15 January 1945.

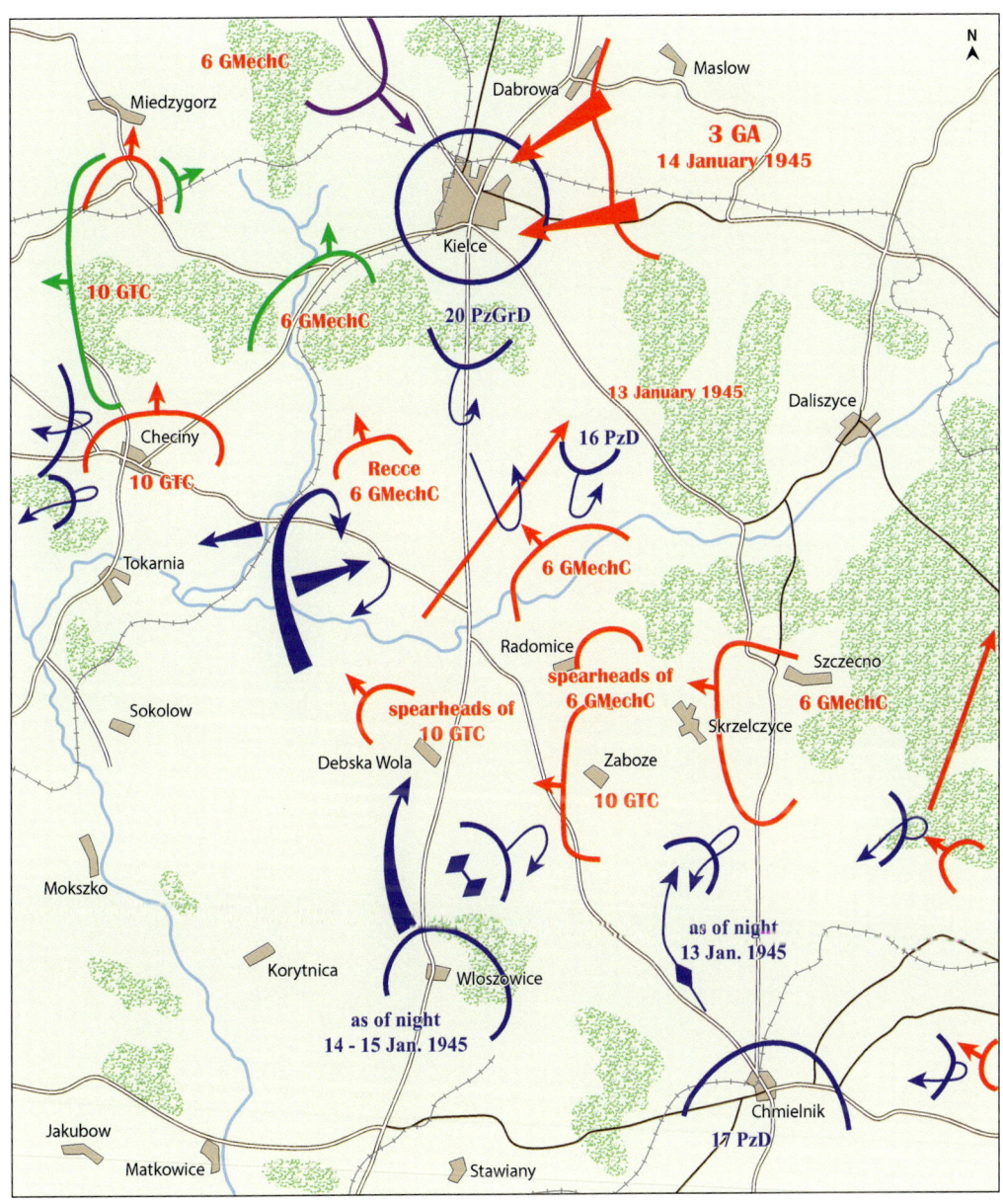

Map 17 Soviet operational map of the 4th Tank Army in the area of Kielce, Lisow, 13–15 January 1945.

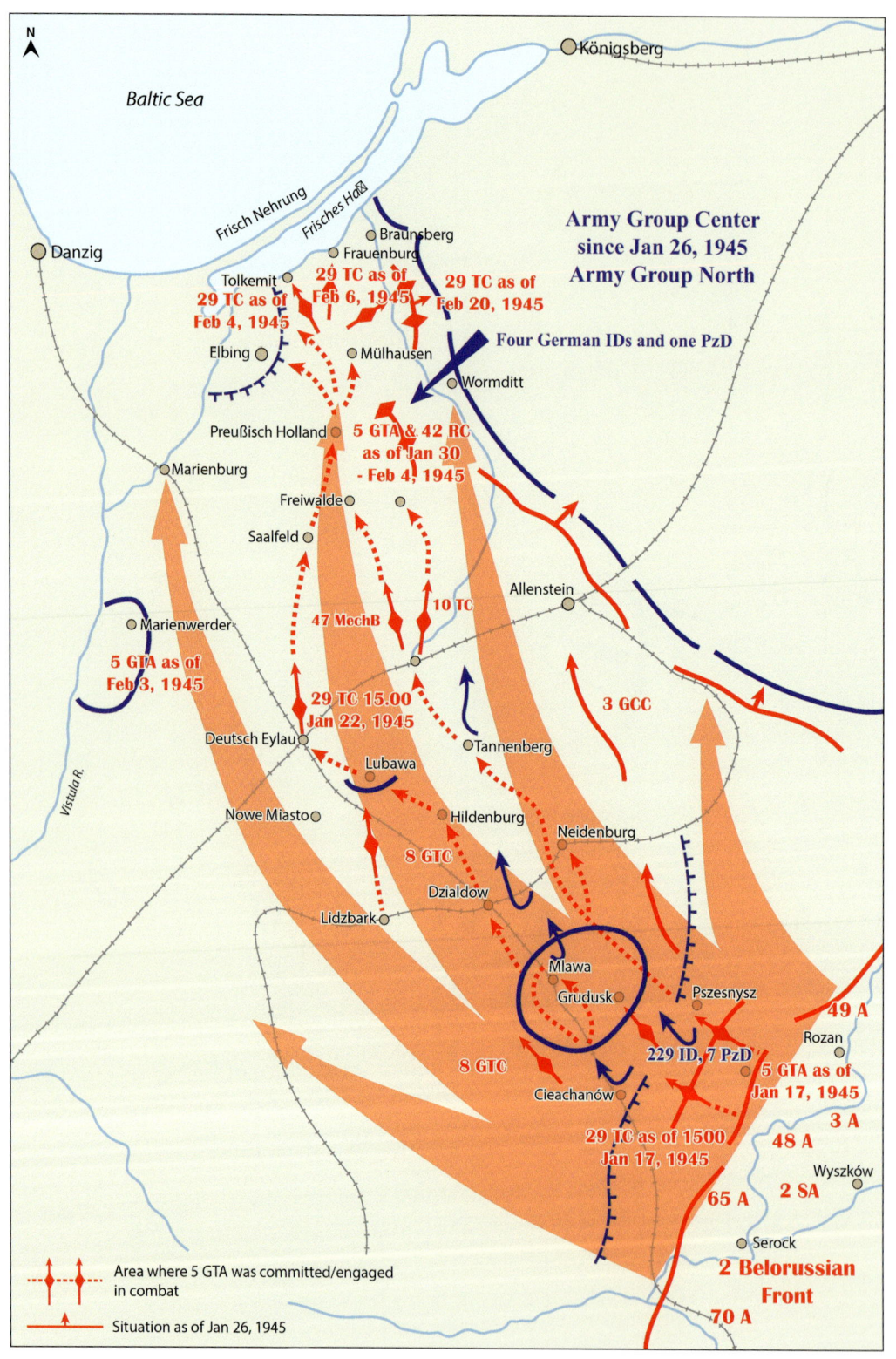

Map 18 Combat actions of the Soviet 5th Guards Tank Army in East Prussia, January–February 1945.

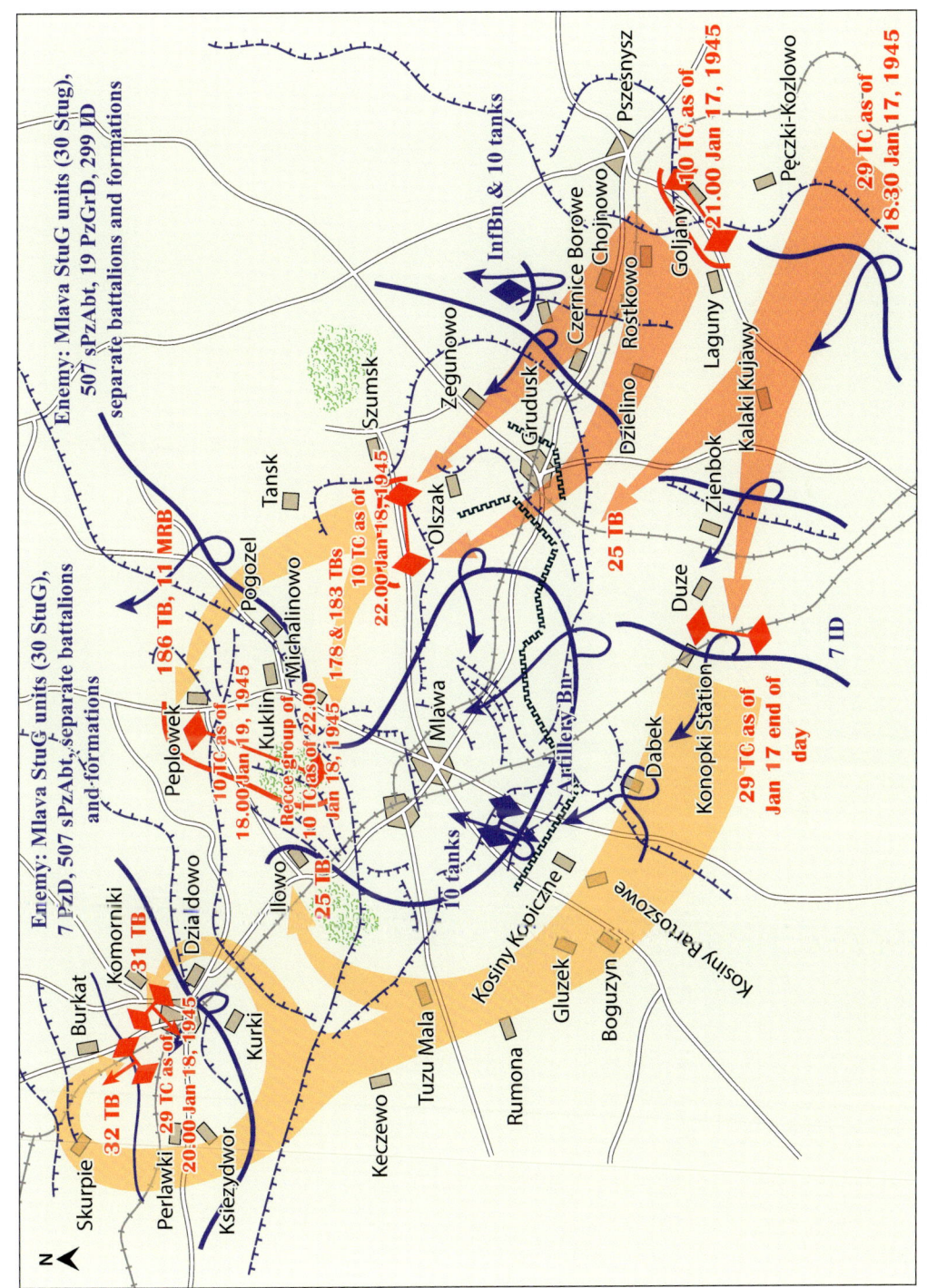

Map 19 Soviet operational map of the 5th Guards Tank Army as of 18–19 January 1945.

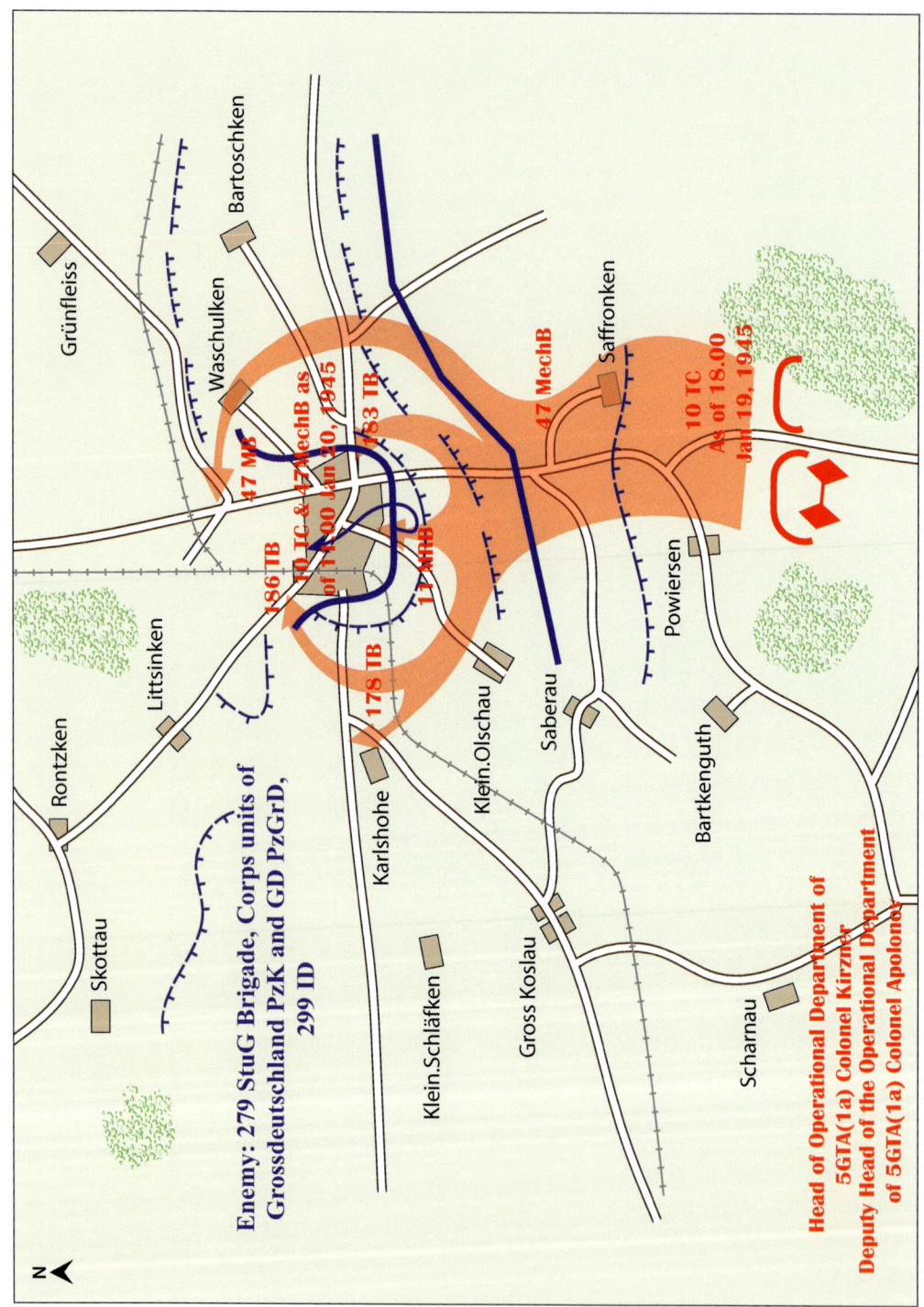

Map 20 Soviet operational map of the 5th Guards Tank Army as of 20 January 1945.

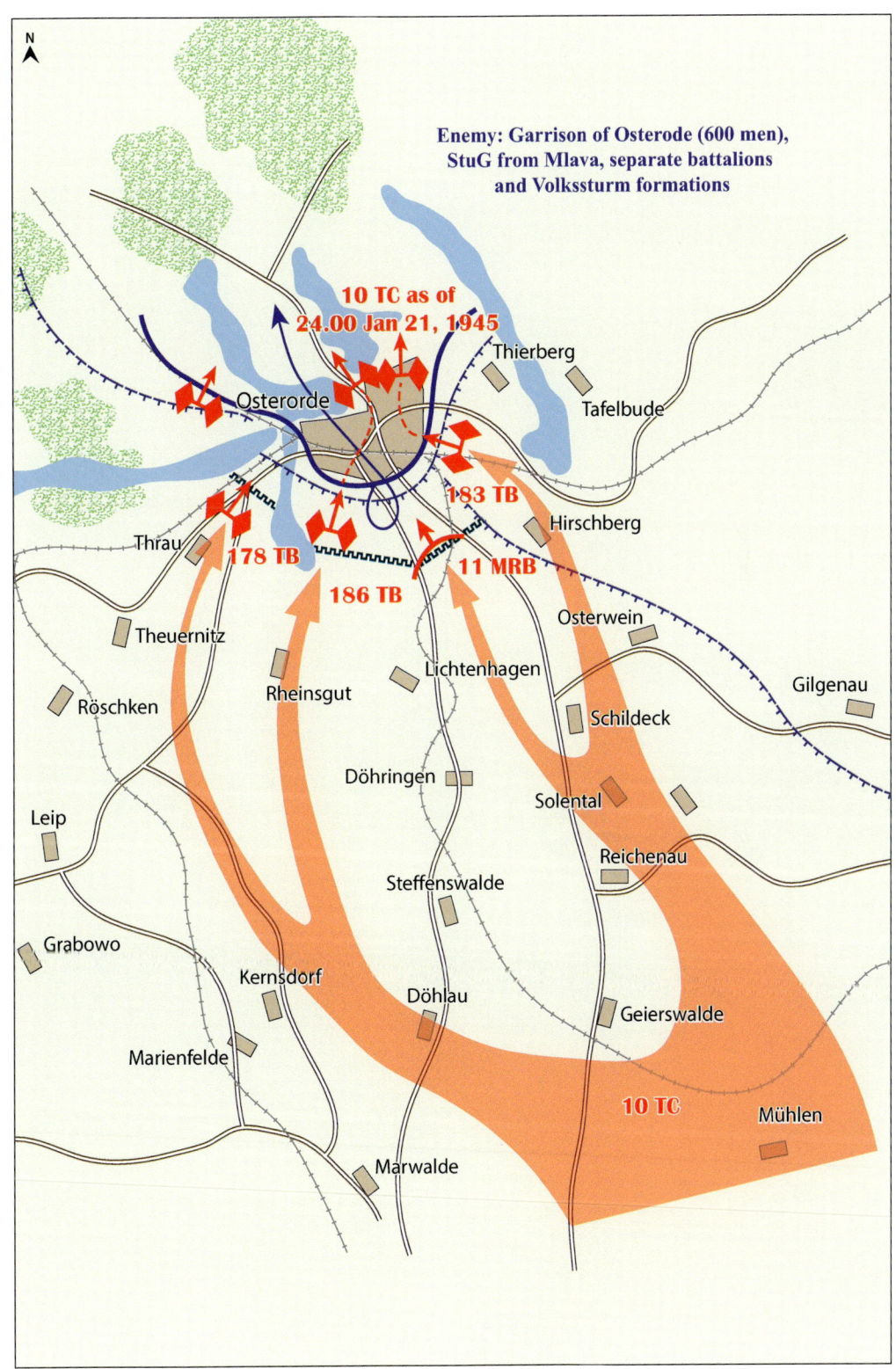

Map 21 Soviet operational map of the 5th Guards Tank Army as of 22 January 1945.

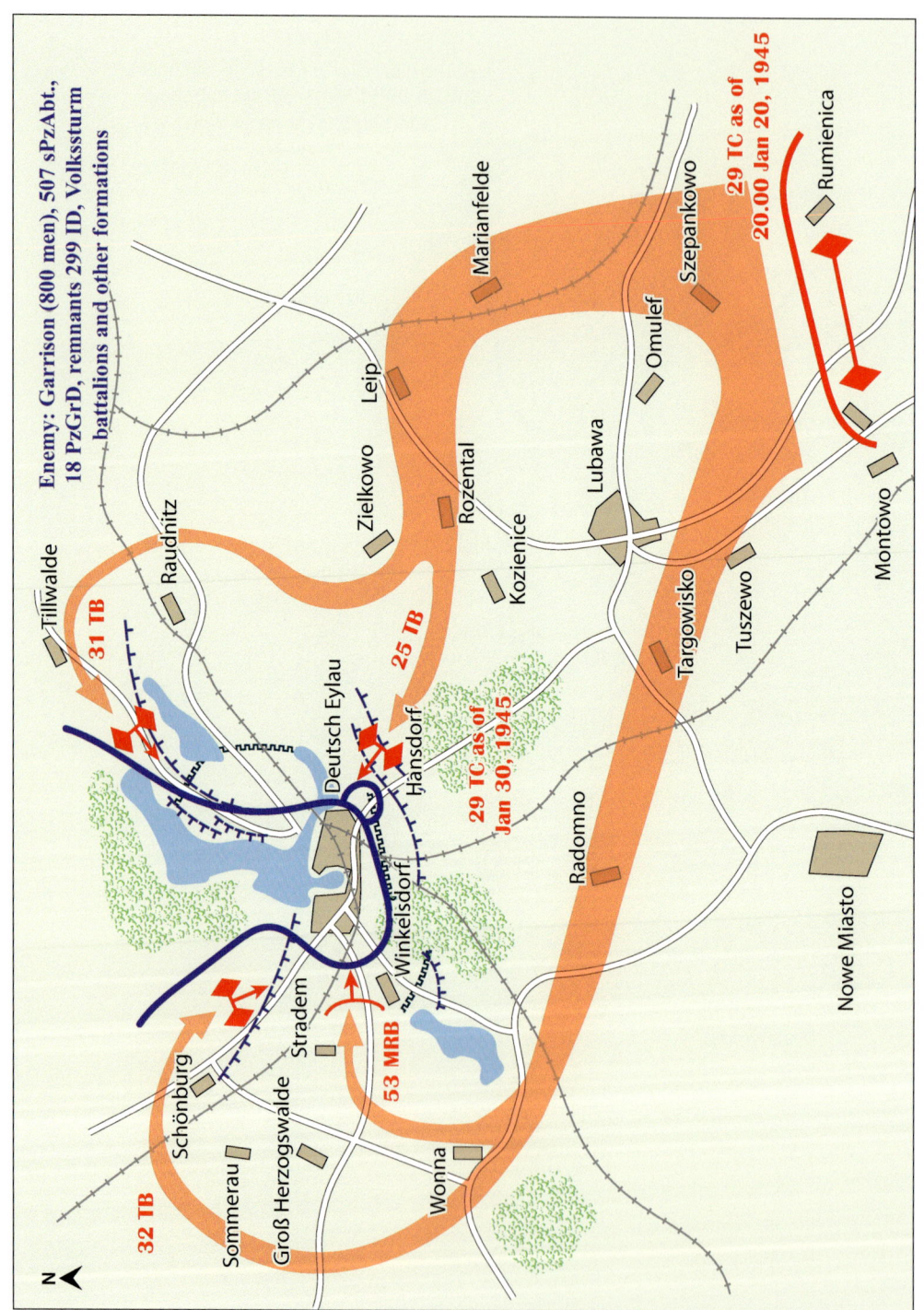

Map 22 Soviet operational map of the 5th Guards Tank Army as of 21 January 1945.

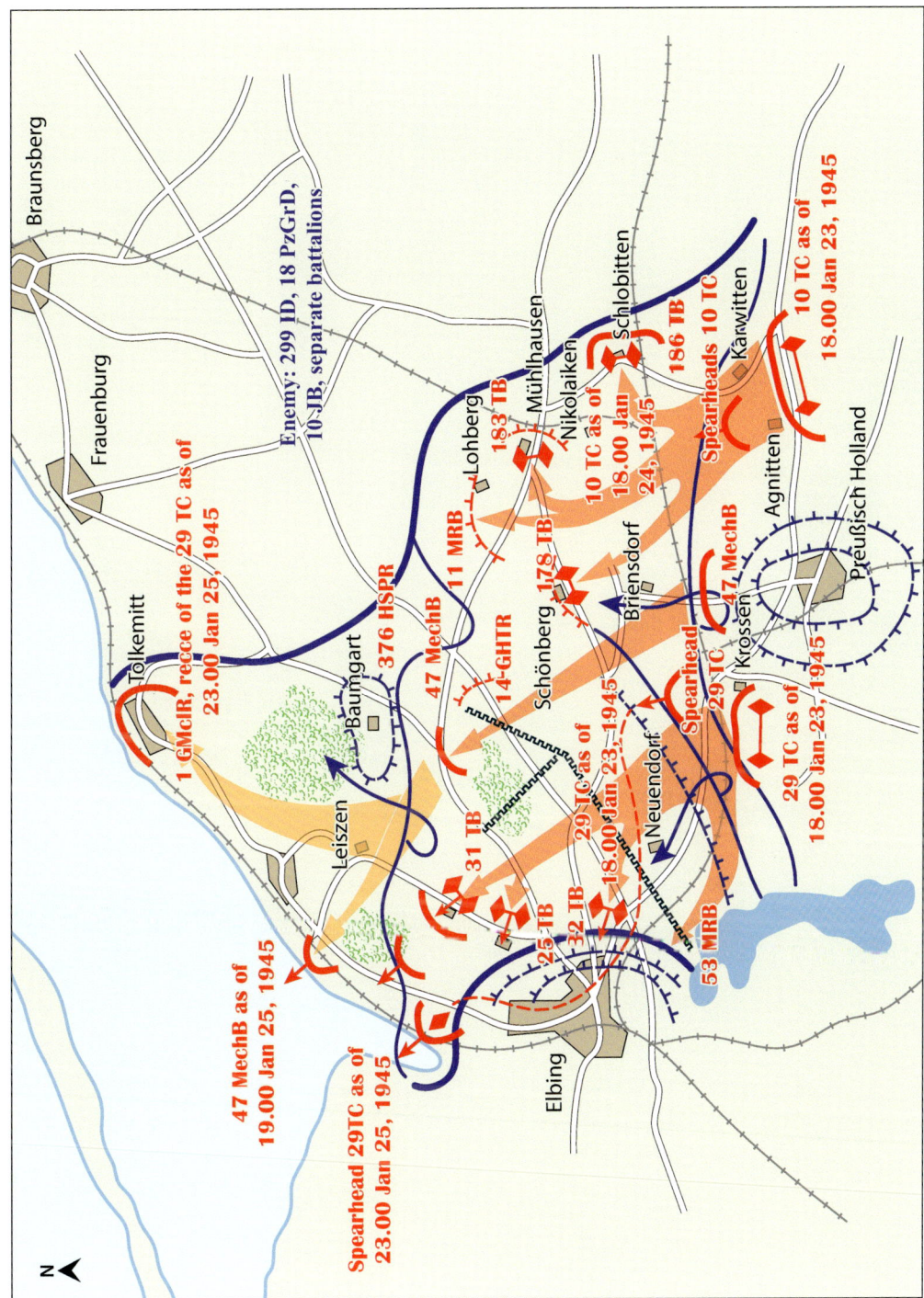

Map 23 Soviet operational map of the 5th Guards Tank Army as of 23–25 January 1945, Elbing area, East Prussia.

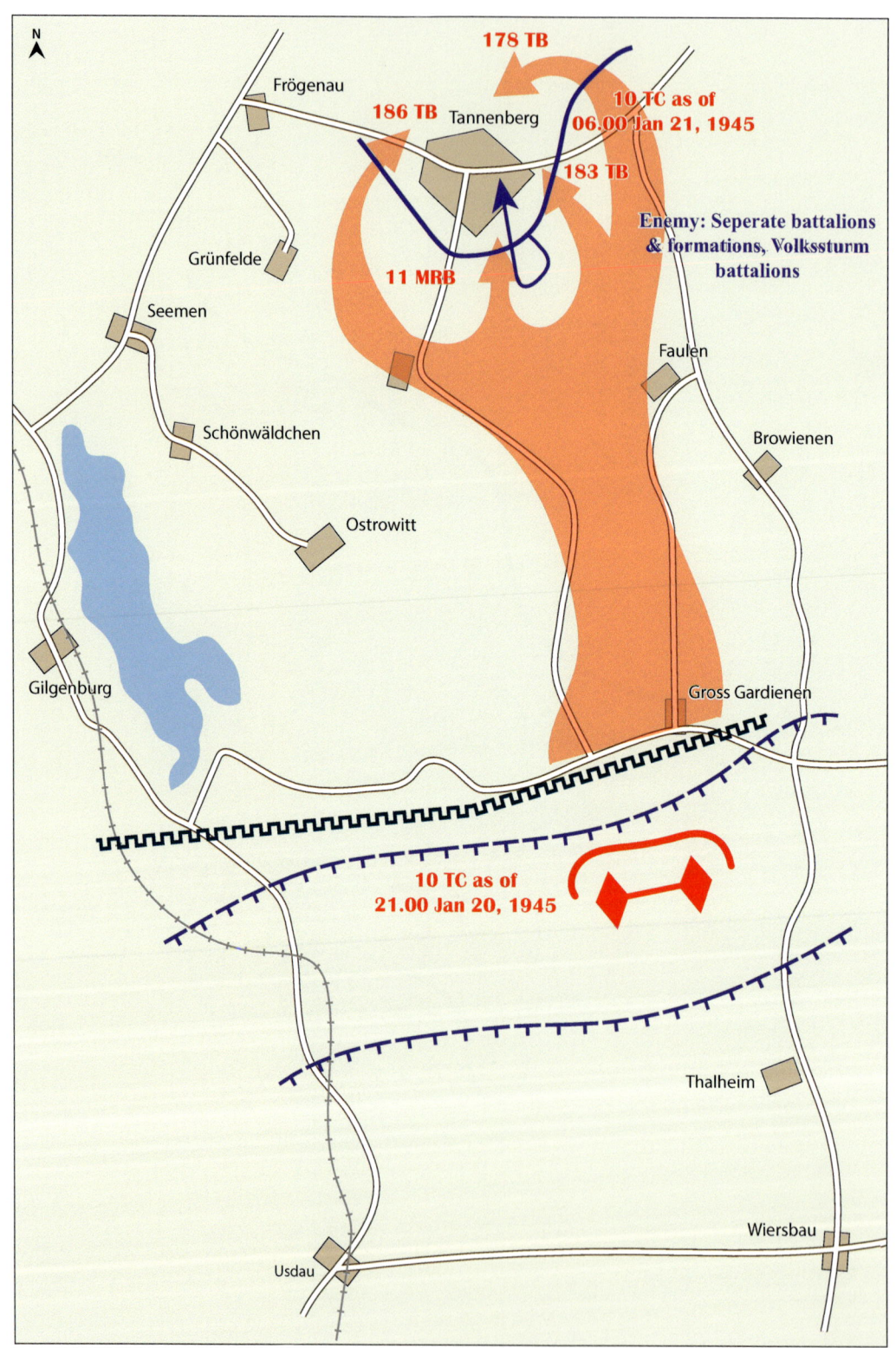

Map 24 Soviet operational map of the 5th Guards Tank Army as of 21 January 1945, Tannenberg area, East Prussia.

Excerpt from the "Account of the activity and status of the 4th Tank Army's combat reconnaissance in the Vistula – Oder operation:

With the start of the breakthrough, the enemy became disorganized; in view of the rapid advance by our mobile units, the enemy's attempt to withdraw in an organized fashion and to offer resistance on an intermediary line came to failure. Introducing units of the 17th Panzer Division into battle on the night of 12-13 January, the enemy undertook counterattacks in the following directions: a) in strength of 30 tanks from out of Maleszowa toward Podlesie; b) 20 tanks from Suchowola and 5 tanks and 9 halftracks from Lisów to the northeast and north; and c) with an infantry battalion and 14 tanks from out of Maleszowa toward Pierzchnica.

The objective of the counterattacks was to crush our forward units that had broken through with a flank attack, and to cut them off from the army's main forces. Due to the skillful maneuver of our units and the timely revelation of the enemy's intentions by reconnaissance, his attempts had no success and he was forced to retreat with heavy losses. A captured *Obergefreitor* Norbert of the 17th Panzer Division's Panzer Regiment 39 testified to this: in the first hours of combat with Russian tanks, the enemy's losses in tanks amounted to 16 combat vehicles.

Making widespread use of Panzerfausts in the struggle with our tanks, the enemy, by means of organizing ambushes and creeping up to our tanks in the nighttime in wooded areas, sought to inflict substantial damage to our units; in isolated cases such actions were successful and required urgent countermeasures to prevent the enemy's actions. On 13 January 1945 German soldiers, equipped with Panzerfausts, were silently moving from the Ługi area in the direction of low ground between Ługi and Maleszowa, with the aim of destroying tanks of the 10th Guards Tank Corps that were located in this area; however, they were detected and dispersed. On this same day a group of tank hunters armed with Panzerfausts that was concealed in ambush on the banks of the Morawka River set two of our tanks ablaze. In the majority, the set-up ambushes with Panzerfaust-equipped soldiers were revealed by our reconnaissance; the combing through of wooded areas or villages was organized, during which these groups were destroyed or captured. On the matter of the German command's large attention to the mass introduction of Panzerfausts in the troops and the formation of tank hunting elements, German prisoners revealed the following. Soldier Sigfried Weissweder, who belonged to the Panzerjäger battalion of the *Grossdeutchland* reserve-training battalion, reported: "The battalion in the majority moved on motorcycles, with two Panzerfausts per each motorcycle." Soldier Paul Eckardt from Kampfgruppe Meyer testified: "A group consists of three tank hunting companies, armed with 1944 machine pistols; the soldiers ride bicycles, each equipped with two Panzerfausts." It should be mentioned that despite the large equipping of the infantry units with Panzerfausts, the enemy had no adequate success in view of the poor training of the Volkstürm soldiers, the absence among the latter of suitable combat qualities, and their short period of training. The enemy often put into practice tank ambushes, both in woods and in populated places, on the path of advance of the army's forces. On 14 January 1945, 3-5 enemy tanks organized an ambush in the vicinity of a road fork west of Waltersdorf, and up to 20 tanks that stealthy emerged out of woods south of Mahrsdorf. As a result of the organized ambush, they destroyed one of our tanks, one self-propelled gun and several vehicles, and kept possession of the forest road leading toward Sohrau. The enemy's attempts to compensate for the shortage of men and tanks through successful maneuvers are confirmed by the following statements made by prisoners – the headquarters commandant of the 16th Panzer Division and a radio operator of this same division, who were captured in Lisów: the 16th and 17th Panzer Divisions had the task of allowing our forces into the depth of the German defenses, then to encircle and destroy them. In particular, the 16th Panzer Division, which was positioned in woods, had the assignment of launching a surprise attack into the rear of our penetrating units. The armor clashes that followed in the Pierzchnica, Lisów, Ługi area confirm this information.

Subsequently in the fighting for the bridgehead on the Oder River, the enemy, undertaking a number of counterattacks in various directions, was rapidly maneuvering with the very same tanks, shifting them along the front. The enemy in a number of cases made wide use of radio direction finding and made attempts to use provocations over the radio. Between 1500 on 13 January and 1100 on 14 January, the radio of the commander of the 10th Guards Tank Corps was located in the yard of a Roman Catholic priest's home. Throughout the entire period of its operation there, German radio sets were interfering with it. At 2400 on 13 January a German radio openly broadcast in Russian, "Report to me where my chief of staff is located". At this time, the commander of the 10th Guards Tank Corps had contact with his chief of staff only over by radio. At 0530 on 14 January a German radio transmitted a message in the name of Zaitsev (the chief of staff of the 61st Guards Tank Brigade) to move out, at a time when Zaitsev wasn't moving. At 0700 on 14 January, our radio received a message: "Deputy corps commander, report your coordinates." All of the above-cited examples had no success, in view of the fact that all the radio messages to the troops were transmitted only in an enciphered and codified form.

After an artillery preparation, under the influence of our units' actions, the enemy fled in disorder, unsuccessfully trying to offer resistance to the advance of our army. On 13 January 1945 the enemy hastily committed the 17th Panzer Division into the fighting from out of the Chmielnik area, and the Heavy Panzer Battalion 501 [sic] from out of the Szczecno area, and with repeated counterattacks to the south in strength of a battalion to a regiment of infantry with 20-30 tanks from the Maleszowa – Podlesie line, and from the Komórki – Szczecno line, striving to cut off our forward units and to prevent the advance of our forces to the west. On 14 January the enemy introduced units of the 16th Panzer Division from out of the Kowala – Brzeziny area and southwest of Morawica, striving to stop our offensive. On 15 January 1945, having reinforced his operating grouping in the Kielce area with the newly-committed Fusilier Regiment 79, Reserve Regiment 61 and Artillery Regiment 20 of the 20th Panzergrenadier Division, the enemy was putting up stubborn resistance to the army's advance in the areas south of Chałupki, Dębska-Wola, Morawica, Bilcza-Podgórze and Brzeziny, but by the end of the day was shattered and hastily withdrawing to the west and northwest. The smashed units of the XXIV Panzer Corps' 16th Panzer Division, 17th Panzer Division, Heavy Panzer Battalion 501 [sic], 168th Infantry Division, 68th Infantry Division and its Pioneer Battalion 424, as well as the East Prussian Security Regiment, Mortar Regiment 15 and Panzerjäger Regiment 71 along with separate reserve groups throughout 16 January were hastily retreating, unable to offer organized resistance.

The nature and tactics of the enemy's actions

During the breakthrough of the tactical zone of the defenses of the 68th Infantry Division's Infantry Regiment 188 and the 168th Infantry Division's Infantry Regiment 442, suffering significant losses, the German troops began a disorderly retreat in the western direction. Tactical reserves introduced into the fighting – Infantry Regiment 417 and a fusilier battalion of the 168th Infantry Division – were unable to put up serious resistance and were also retreating to the west. By end of day on 12 January 1945 the enemy, striving to delay the units of the Red Army that had broken through his lines, introduced the 17th Panzer Division's Panzer Regiment 39 and Panzergrenadier Regiment 40 out of the Mechów, Chmielnik area; Panzer Regiment 2 and Panzergrenadier Regiment 64 of the 16th Panzer Division out of the Kielce area; and XXIV Panzer Corps' Fusilier Regiment 79 on the Pierzchnica – Chmielnik line, which having had no time to deploy into combat formations, were unable in columns to hold our advancing units. By the end of the second day the enemy deployed units of the 16th and 17th Panzer Divisions, and with counterattacks in strength of up to 60 tanks and up to a regiment of infantry sought to isolate our units that had broken through in the area southeast of Morawica. Suffering heavy losses, the enemy managed to link up in the area west of Pierzchnica and to seal off the lines of communication to the forward units. After stubborn fighting west of Pierzchnica the enemy, having lost the majority of his men and tanks, began a disorderly withdrawal to the west, offering resistance in isolated areas, and striving to withdraw the remnants of units out of encirclement. In the period from 14 to 16 January 1945 the enemy with remnants of the 68th Infantry Division, 16th Panzer Division, 17th Panzer Division, 20th Panzergrenadier Division, XXIV Panzer Corps' Fusilier Regiment 79, Pioneer Battalions 215 and 916, and Mortar Regiment 52 sought to break out of the pocket. At the same time, units of the Kalmyck Cavalry Corps were committed into the fighting; however, suffering significant losses, the enemy's units began a disorderly retreat to the west and north. Between 16 and 20 January the enemy continued a fighting withdrawal to the west, while striving to withdraw the remnants of units that had suffered heavy losses beyond the Warta River.

Conclusion: The enemy introduced his operational reserves, which for the most part were shattered and partially captured, into battle on the first day of the operation. Having lost command and control over the formation and units, the Germans throughout the entire operation were unable to put up organized resistance.

Description of characteristic actions of the 4th Tank Army's reconnaissance and intelligence organs

Episode 1: On 13 January 1945 the reconnaissance patrol, consisting of a tank platoon and two squads of submachine gunners from the 61st Guards Tank Brigade, led by Guards Lieutenant Pobedinsky, was operating in the direction of Lisów. The commander of the reconnaissance patrol arranged his combat formation in the following manner: one T-34 tank was deployed out in front, followed at a distance of 2 km by the 2 other tanks of the platoon with mounted tank riders. The lead tank at 1600 on 13 January reached the fringe of the woods west of Lisów, while the following tanks had reached the western outskirts of Lisów. At this time the commander of the lead tank reported over the radio: "An enemy column consisting of two tanks, 8 vehicles and up to two companies of infantry is moving from Chałupki toward Zalesie; the head of the column has entered the woods west of Zalesie." The patrol commander decided to delay the enemy column west of Zalesie with his submachine gunners, and to attack the column in the flank with two tanks along the road running from the Wygwizdów estate to Zalesie, while the lead tank simultaneously attacked the column from the rear.

At 1700 13 January the enemy column ran into the screening force north of Lisów and was stopped by the machine-gun fire and submachine-gun fire. At this time the two tanks attacked the column in the woods west of Zalesie, while the lead tank quickly arrived on the tail of the column and attacked. As a result of the combat, up to 50 Germans were killed, and 5 soldiers that belonged to the 168th Infantry Division, 16th Panzer Division or Heavy Panzer Battalion 501 [sic] were captured.

Conclusion: As a result of the correct decision by the reconnaissance patrol commander, the proper use of the terrain and the arising situation, and the decisive actions of the men, the enemy column was partially destroyed and scattered, without any losses for the reconnaissance patrol.

Episode 2: On 13 January 1945 a reconnaissance patrol consisting of 7 men of the 29th Guards Motorized Rifle Brigade, led by Guards Lieutenant Fadeev, had the task to infiltrate through the enemy's combat positions on the Pierznchica – Maleszowa line, establish the enemy's presence in

Górki, and capture a prisoner for identification purposes. For 2 hours the patrol kept watch in the Pierzchnica area with the aim of identifying a place for passing through the German combat positions, which they managed to do. With the onset of darkness, the patrol infiltrated in the area south of Pierzchnica and approached the southern outskirts of Górki. It was established that a large number of infantry and vehicles were in Górki. The movement of vehicles from Skrzelczyce to Górki was spotted. The patrol leader decided to attempt to snatch a prisoner, taking advantage of the poor security around Górki. The patrol silently approached an outlying home. Having checked that no one was at home, they organized an ambush. A short time later a German soldier approached the home, who was jumped and captured. The testimony of the prisoner under interrogation established that the 16th Panzer Division was moving out to the Pierzchnica – Chmielnik line.

Conclusion: The decisive actions of the reconnaissance patrol allowed them to implement their order. A small patrol has a great superiority when conducting reconnaissance in the enemy rear.

Episode 3: On 14 January 1945 a reconnaissance patrol consisting of four halftracks and five armored cars from the 7th Guards Separate Motorcycle Battalion, led by Guards Captain Kontsevoi, had the assignment to scout in the direction of Chałupki and to establish the enemy strength in the village. Having reached the western fringe of the woods east of Chałupki, the reconnaissance patrol was attacked by a battalion of enemy infantry and halftracks. There was no time to avoid combat, because the forest road didn't allow them to turn around. The patrol leader, having deployed the halftracks and armored cars, accepted battle, taking advantage of the wooded terrain. As a result of active operations, the enemy lost up to 100 soldiers and officers killed, and 120 captured.

Conclusion: The successful actions of the reconnaissance patrol is explained by the decisive actions of its men. Upon meeting a superior enemy force and having no way to get away without accepting battle, rapid and decisive actions are necessary, which the reconnaissance patrol in fact implemented.

Episode 4: On 15 January 1945, a reconnaissance patrol consisting of 18 men of the 29th Guards Motorized Rifle Brigade, led by Senior Lieutenant Belik, had the assignment to scout along the Chęciny, Korzecko, Jedlinica, Podpolichno route and to establish whether or not the enemy was present in the villages along the way, determine the strength, and to capture prisoners. Moving along the route, the patrol, without meeting the enemy, reached the area south of Podpolichno, where through observation it established that up to 30 enemy soldiers were present in this village. The patrol leader decided to wait until nightfall and with a surprise attack drive the enemy out of Podpolichno and capture prisoners. Having left behind observers, the reconnaissance patrol, without revealing itself, disappeared into the woods. With the setting of the sun, the reconnaissance patrol, having split into two groups (one group operating along the road from Bolmin, the other along the road from Jedlinica) silently approached the village from two directions and with a sudden charge caught the enemy by surprise. As a result of a fleeting combat action, the enemy lost 20 men killed; 1 prisoner was taken who belonged to the 168th Infantry Division's Infantry Regiment 442. The patrol had no casualties.

Conclusion: Characteristic in the actions of the patrol was the accurate assessment of the enemy's strength and the element of surprise, thanks to which it carried out its mission.

Episode 5: On 16 January 1945 a forward reconnaissance patrol consisting of 2 T-34 tanks and 20 tank riders from the 62nd Guards Tank Brigade had the task to scout out of Końskie along the Modliszewice, Pomorzany route and further along the road to the west. In the Pomorzany area, the reconnaissance patrol bumped into the enemy. The road east of Pomorzany had been mined.

Through observation the presence of an enemy garrison in strength of up to two companies of infantry was in Pomorzany. The patrol, without accepting combat, bypassed Pomorzany on its southern side and resumed its advance on its assigned route. It discovered that the enemy had deployed a minefield in the Kopaniny area, which the patrol bypassed; by 1700 16 January it had reached Soczówki area, where it was fired upon by the enemy from the woods northwest of that point. Having decided to establish the enemy's strength in the woods, the patrol leader issued an order to open fire from the tanks and feigned an attack toward the woods. As a result, the enemy was forced to open fire from all his weapons and to move tanks up to the eastern fringe of the woods. With observation the reconnaissance had established that 15 enemy tanks and infantry were in the woods northwest of Soczówki. The mission had been carried out.

Conclusion: Characteristic in the reconnaissance patrol's actions was refusing combat while on reconnaissance by means of bypassing and infiltration, which grants the possibility of carrying out the assignment within the prescribed period of time without losses.

Episode 6: On 16 January 1945 a reconnaissance patrol consisting of 2 halftracks from the 29th Guards Motorized Rifle Brigade, led by Guards Lieutenant Limbersky, had the mission to conduct reconnaissance in the direction of Gałęzice and Rykoszyn. When approaching Rykoszyn, the patrol spotted a column of enemy vehicles being covered by 5 tanks and a halftrack, which was heading out of Rykoszyn to the west. The patrol leader ordered to open fire at the column; the column came to a stop and the tanks opened fire at the reconnaissance patrol. As a result of this action, the enemy lost 2 vehicles. The reconnaissance patrol lost 2 halftracks, and 2 men killed and 5 wounded.

Conclusion: The reconnaissance patrol encountered a superior enemy force; the patrol leader didn't assess the situation and accepted combat, instead of withdrawing the patrol back into cover and conducting observation. Characteristic are the adverse effects of the patrol leader's decision, who decided not to follow the precepts of Army regulations, as a result of which the order was not carried out.

Episode 7: On 16 January 1945 a reconnaissance patrol consisting of 3 tanks and 3 submachine gun squads from the 61st Guards Tank Brigade, led by Guards Lieutenant Saprykin, had the orders to conduct reconnaissance along the Aldenau, Kaczurien, Glijenicy, Nabyszyce, Łąkoncin route. Having set out toward Aldenau, the separate reconnaissance patrol by 1400 on 16 January reached the woods north of Kaczurien, where it ran into small groups of the enemy. Having dispersed them with fire, the separate reconnaissance patrol continued to carry out its orders. By 1430 the patrol reached Nabyszyce. There, it sent out 1 tank toward Wierzbno, which by 1500 reached the northern outskirts of Wierzbno, where with observation it established that up to a platoon of enemy infantry was approaching Wierzbno from the north. Having assessed the situation, the patrol leader decided that this was an advance detachment. The leader opted to continue reconnaissance toward Dianiszin and to reach Łąkoncin, where he calculated that they would meet the enemy's main forces. By 1600 on 16 January the separate reconnaissance patrol reached an area 1 km east of Dianiszin. At this time, up to a battalion of enemy infantry and 40 trucks were moving through Łąkoncin toward Wierzbno. The separate reconnaissance patrol in full strength decided to attack the column at the intersection of the roads south of Łąkoncin. As a result of the patrol's sudden and impetuous attack, the enemy lost up to a company killed and 35 trucks. Twenty-five prisoners from the 25th Panzer Division and 136th Infantry Division were captured. The Nazi remnants disorderly retreated into the woods east of Lonkocin. The reconnaissance patrol had no losses.

Conclusion: In the separate reconnaissance patrol's successful actions, primarily the correct assessment of the situation and the decision by the patrol leader were significant. It is necessary when on patrol to always strive to find the enemy's main forces. If it had become tied up in combat with the enemy vanguard in the Wierbzno area, then the battalion of infantry, following behind, would have deployed and taken up a defense, thereby preventing the fulfillment of the given assignment in full.

Episode 8: With the arrival of the army's forces to the Czarna Nida River, a reconnaissance patrol from the 88th Engineer Battalion received the assignment to reconnoiter the river. When moving toward a bridge in the Kuby-Młyny area, it bumped into a group of Germans. The scouts boldly joined combat, partially destroyed and scattered the enemy group, reconnoitered the river, and timely brought back information that contributed to resolving the question about where to lay bridges across the river. On 17 January 1945 Lieutenant Boiko's sapper platoon, which had been sent to check out the bridge in the village of Rogyzno, encountered a German demolition team which was hurrying toward the bridge in order to blow it up. Having allowed the Germans to approach to within close range, the scouts opened fire at them, killed several of them, and captured several more.

The reconnaissance troops of Colonel General of Tank Forces D.D. Leliushenko's 4th Tank Army throughout the entire operation captured 970 enemy soldiers and officers:

a) Rudki, Jasen – 4 prisoners of the 168th Infantry Division's Infantry Regiment 442;
b) 13 January, Maleszowa – 3 prisoners of the 17th Panzer Division's Panzer Regiment 39 and 2 prisoners of the 17th Panzer Division's Panzergrenadier Regiment 40;
c) 14 January, Radoszyce – 2 prisoners of Panzer Regiment 2 and 3 prisoners of 16th Panzer Division's Panzergrenadier Regiment 64;
d) 15 January, Zalesie – 95 prisoners from the 17th Panzer Division's Panzergrenadier Regiment 40, the 86th Infantry Division's Infantry Regiment 188, the XXIV Panzer Corps' Fusilier Regiment 79, and Flak Battalion 297.
e) 16 January, Polichno – Rykoszyn area – 21 prisoners from the 17th Panzer Division's Panzergrenadier Regiment 40, the 16th Panzer Division's Pioneer Battalion 16, a reconnaissance squad of the 16th Panzer Division, Pioeneer Battalion 215, the XXIV Panzer Corps' Fusilier Regiment 70, Pioneer Battalion 916, the 68th Infantry Division's Infantry Regiment 52 and the 20th Panzergrenadier Division's Panzergrenadier Regiment 90.
f) 17 January, Końskie – 130 prisoners: 19 from the 16th Panzer Division's Panzergrenadier Regiment 64; 5 from the 17th Panzer Division's Pioneer Battalion 27; 10 from Fusilier Battalion 342 and Pioneer Battalion 342 of the 342nd Infantry Division; 9 from the 17th Flak Division; 15 from elements of the 4th Tank Army; 7 from the XXIV Panzer Corps' Fusilier Regiment 79; 4 from the 68th Infantry Division's Infantry Regiment 169; and 61 from separate battalions.
g) 18 January, Paradyż area – 133 prisoners: 5 from the 16th Panzer Division's Panzergrenadier Regiment 64; 6 from the 17th Panzer Division's Panzergrenadier Regiment 40; 4 from the 19th Panzer Division; 3 from rear units of the 25th Panzer Division; 14 from the 17th Infantry Division; 6 from the 17th Flak Division; 10 from the 20th Panzergrenadier Division's Panzergrenadier Regiment 90; 3 from the 10th Panzergrenadier Division's Panzergrenadier Regiment 20; 8 from the 72nd Infantry Division; 4 from the 342nd Infantry Division's Fusilier Battalion 342; 8 from the 45th Infantry Division; 10 from Pioneer Battalion 107; 2 from Artillery Regiment 71; 1 from Security Battalion 353; 5 from the Mortar Regiment 52; and 44 from the 817th Azerbaidzhanian Battalion.

Combat Report No. 12 from the headquarters of the 4th Tank Army, 14 January 1945

To the commander-in-chief of the 1st Ukrainian Front Marshal of the Soviet Union I.S. Konev

1. The enemy with units of the 16th and 17th Panzer Divisions, the 168th Infantry Division and Heavy Panzer Battalion 501 [sic] throughout the night of 13-14 January and day of 14 January 1945, with fire and counterattacks in strength of 10-30 tanks with infantry and artillery, put up stubborn resistance to the actions of the 6th Guards Mechanized Corps in the Marzysz, Kuby-Młyny, Bilcza-Ciołkow sector, and to the 10th Guards Tank Corps on the Morawica – Dębska-Wola line and in the Chęciny – Tokarnia area.
2. The forces of the 4th Tank Army on 14 January 1945 continued to develop the offensive in the directions: 6th Guards Mechanized Corps – Radomice-Kaczeniec, Bilcza-Ciołkow; 10th Guards Tank Corps – Wola-Morawicka, Ostrów, Chęciny.
3. **6th Guards Mechanized Corps**: 49th Mechanized Brigade with the 1433rd Self-propelled Artillery Regiment from the morning repulsed three counterattacks by tanks of the 16th Panzer Division's Panzer Regiment 2. At 1030 it fought off a counterattack by 35 enemy tanks from the Kuby-Młyny area. The enemy lost 11 tanks, 10 vehicles and 200 soldiers and officers. Having thrown back the counterattacking enemy, it took Marzysz and by 1500 forced a crossing of the Czarna Nida River with a reinforced battalion; it is engaged in combat to expand the bridgehead on the river's western bank and is completing the crossing of the brigade's remaining forces. The 17th Guards Mechanized Brigade with the 29th Tank Regiment since 1300 has been engaged in combat with enemy tanks north of Bilcza-Ciołkow. The 16th Guards Mechanized Brigade is located in the area of the western outskirts of Kowala and is repulsing counterattacks by enemy tanks. The 56th Tank Regiment is moving behind the 49th Mechanized Brigade. The **10th Guards Tank Brigade**: 63rd Guards Tank Brigade by 1300 was crossing the Czarna Nida River north of Tokarnia, rapidly developing the offensive along the road to the north, and by 1500 it took Chęciny and is continuing to attack toward Rykoszyn. The 61st Guards Tank Brigade by 1600 was crossing the Czarna Nida River in the Tokarnia area and moving behind the 63rd Guards Tank Brigade. The 62nd Guards Tank Brigade is in the area of Brzeziny. The 29th Guards Motorized Rifle Brigade is moving behind the 61st Guards Tank Brigade. The 93rd Separate Tank Brigade is following behind the 29th Guards Motorized Rifle Brigade. At 1700 it passed through Radomice-Kaczeniec. The 22nd Sapper Brigade with one battalion is in Łipa, while the rest of the brigade is in its former area; the 51st Separate Motorcycle Regiment is in Pierzchnica.
4. The losses inflicted on the enemy over 14 January 1945: up to 20 tanks, 6 halftracks, and up to 30 vehicles knocked-out or destroyed; more than 250 men killed or wounded. Our own losses are being ascertained. The deputy commander of the 17th Mechanized Brigade Lieutenant Colonel Cherniak has been killed.
5. The army commander has decided: From the morning of 15 January 1945 to continue to attack in the Piekoszów, Oblęgór, Miedzierza direction with the order by the end of the day to reach the following area with the main forces: 6th Guards Mechanized Corps – Wyręba, Oblęgór, Kostomłoty; its forward detachment is to reach the Sielpia, Miedzierza, Wólka Smolana area, having reinforced detachments in Stąporków and Końskie. 10th Guards Tank Corps – Promnik, Łosien, Rykoszyn, Micigózd; to take Radoszyce with a forward detachment. The 93rd Separate Tank Brigade by the end of the day is to take Łopuszno. The army commander is located at his observation post.

Member of the Military Council of the 4th Tank Army Guards
Major General of Tank Forces GULIAEV, Chief of staff Guards
Major General of Tank Forces UPMAN

By the end of 14 January and on the night of 14-15 January 1945 there was no clear information about the location of the forward detachments of the 6th Guards Mechanized Corps; the army commander was assuming that they were 6-10 km west and northwest of Kielce. The 10th Guards Tank Corps had occupied Chęciny, which had been reported to the commander-in-chief of the 1st Ukrainian Front Marshal I.S. Konev, and on this basis, he issued an order to the commander of the 4th Tank Army General D.D. Leliushenko: The 10th Guards Tank Corps was to take Końskie. Having received this order, the commander of the 4th Tank Army issued a combat order on the morning of 15 January, where he assigned the task to take Konckie to the 10th Guards Tank Corps. It was also to send out strong reconnaissance groups toward Milkowiec and Ruski Bród. The commander of the 6th Guards Mechanized Corps by the end of 15 January 1945 was to take the Radoszyce, Słupia, Szestaki area; the 16th Guards Mechanized Brigade was to prevent enemy movement from Kielce toward Piekoszów and Chęciny. The forward detachment was to take a bridge across the Pilica River in the Ochotniki area. The 93rd Separate Tank Brigade by the end of 15 January 1945 was to take Łopuszno.

Końskie already fell to the Soviets on the night of 14-15 January 1945. It was taken by the 56th Tank Regiment and the 6th Guards Mechanized Corps' 1st Guards Self-propelled Artillery Regiment.

The combat operations of the 6th Guards Mechanized Corps on 15 January 1945

The enemy with remnants of the 168th Infantry Division, the 16th and 17th Panzer Divisions, and the 20th Panzergrenadier Division was offering strong resistance with fire to the corps' units on a previously prepared line that ran from Suków-Babie through Dyminy, Bilcza-Podsukowie, Bilcza-Spólnice, the patch of woods northwest of Kuby-Młyny, Bilcza-Zastawie, Bieleskie-Młyny to Morawica, while simultaneously withdrawing its rear service units and some of its elements to the north and west. With the aim of delaying the Soviet units that had crossed to the northwestern bank of the Czarna Nida River and to destroy the bridges built by the units of the 17th Guards Mechanized Brigade and 49th Mechanized Brigade, throughout the night the enemy counterattacked the sapper company of the 22nd Separate Guards Sapper Battalion and the tanks of the 95th Separate Motorcycle Battalion that were protecting the bridge in the Kuby-Młyny area. Three times, the Germans attacked in strength of up to a company of infantry and 5 tanks from out of the woods northwest of Kluby-Młyny.

All of the enemy counterattacks were driven back by the sapper company of the 22nd Separate Guards Sapper Battalion and the 3 tanks of the 95th Separate Motorcycle Battalion. In the process 80 enemy soldiers and officers were killed, and two enemy tanks were knocked out. The losses of our units were 1 T-34 tank destroyed, 4 men killed and 6 wounded. The corps' chief of staff Guards Colonel Koretsky, who was located directly near the bridge, personally directed the fighting. A signals officer of the corps' command Guards Captain Krasachenko and the commander of the tank company from the 95th Separate Motorcycle Battalion Senior Lieutenant Rusetsky both distinguished themselves in the combat.

During the enemy's first counterattack, the 117th Rifle Division's 337th Rifle Regiment, which was positioned in the Kuby-Młyny, began to flee in disorder in the direction of Marzysz; the corps' chief of staff Guards Colonel Koretsky personally brought the fleeing men to stop at the threat of using his weapon and restored order among them. At that point, the signals officer Captain Krasachenko personally led the infantry of the 337th Rifle Regiment on the attack. This attack was being supported by the tank company commander of the 95th Separate Motorcycle Battalion Guards Senior Lieutenant Rusetsky, who from his tank knocked out two enemy tanks, and the remaining enemy tanks withdrew from the battle. In this action, Senior Lieutenant Rusetsky's tank was set ablaze.

At 0245 on 15 January an enciphered order arrived from the commander of the 4th Tank Army General D.D. Leliushenko: by the morning of 15 January, to gather the corps into a fist in the Zagroda Sitkówka – Wola Murawska area and with energetic operations in the Piekoszów, Promnik direction to take Kobylanka, Wżymanków and Promnik by the end of the day. A forward detachment was to take Miedzierza. The corps was also to scout in the direction of Stąporków and Końskie. With the force of one brigade and an attack from the west, it was to take Kielce in cooperation with units of the 13th Army, while having a blocking screen on the Dyminy line to prevent a breakout by enemy forces to the south. Pursuant to this order, the corps' chief of staff over the telephone issued an order to the commanders of the 17th Guards Mechanized Brigade and 49th Mechanized Brigade: with energetic actions throughout the night to carry out the task that was assigned in Leliushenko's order.

The 49th Mechanized Brigade, continuing to push forward throughout the night, by 0800 on 15 January took Posłowice after a short battle. The 17th Guards Mechanized Brigade at 0800 began crossing its tanks at a ford 1.5 km east of Beleskie-Młyny and by 1000 the tanks of the 126th Tank Regiment, 29th Tank Regiment and 10 IS-122 heavy tanks of the 28th Guards Heavy Tank Brigade had crossed the Czarna Nida River. The motorized rifle battalions had also crossed the river, with the exception of the wheeled vehicles and the brigade's second echelon.

At 1100 the 17th Guards Mechanized Brigade reached the eastern outskirts of Bilcza-Zastawie, where the brigade was counterattacked by a total of 20 tanks and self-propelled guns, 10 halftracks and up to a battalion of infantry from three directions. The 1st and 3rd Tank Companies of the 126th Tank Regiment together with their tank riders and the guns of the artillery battalion took up a defense on the eastern outskirts of Bilcza-Zastawie and opened fire at the enemy, while the 2nd Tank Company of the 126th Tank Regiment and heavy tanks with tank riders aboard with a maneuver to the south bypassed the action at Bilcza-Zastawie and reached the southeastern outskirts of Bilcza-Ciołków where they took up a defense with a front facing the northwest. By 1200 the enemy counterattack had been repulsed and all organized resistance by the enemy had collapsed. In return, the composite force of the 17th Guards Mechanized Brigade and tank regiments lost 5 tanks, of which 2 were destroyed and 3 knocked-out.

After this the 17th Guards Mechanized Brigade with its attached assets began a rapid advance along its assigned route and at 1400 burst into the Sitkówka railroad station, where it killed up to 80 enemy soldiers and officers and destroyed 30 vehicles and 15 halftracks. In addition, it captured 40 prisoners, 5 halftracks, 20 vehicles, a large quantity of cargo and a stockpile of bicycles.

In this combat action the men of the 17th Guards Mechanized Brigade demonstrated exceptional valor and courage. For example, Guards Lieutenant Iurchin's tank was sent out to reconnoiter the southern outskirts of Pszonka, where it ran into an ambush set by three enemy Tiger tanks. Lieutenant Iurchin with the fire from his tank knocked out two of the German tanks, but then the third Tiger set his tank ablaze.

The 49th Mechanized Brigade together with the 56th Tank Regiment and attached artillery assets initially began moving out of the Poslowice area directly toward Białogon along a local road through the woods, but at an order from the corps' chief of staff via a liaison officer, the brigade was turned back to its own assigned route. At the Słowik railroad station the brigade destroyed 18 enemy vehicles after a swift attack. At 1400 on 15 January the brigade linked up with the forward detachment of the 16th Guards Mechanized Brigade in the Białogon area and continued to carry out its assignment along the Szczukowice, Brynica, Bugaj, Porzecze route, brushing aside small groups of infantry and smashing retreating German columns of vehicles. By 1900 of this same day, the brigade was assembled in the Bobrza-Przyjma, Bobrza area. By 2000 the commander of the 49th Mechanized Brigade had organized a defense facing the east and north on the Tumlin-Rurarna, Tumlin line with 7 tanks and two platoons of infantry. The 6th Guards Mechanized Corps' commander Guards Colonel Orlov personally accompanied the 49th Mechanized Brigade on its march from the Białogon area.

The 17th Guards Mechanized Brigade was continuing a rapid advance along the Białogon, Janów, Jaworznia, Piekoszów, Micigózd, Promnik route. Destroying isolated groups of enemy infantry and vehicles along the route, the forward detachment of the 17th Guards Mechanized Brigade at 1900 took Widoma. The brigade's remaining units were in movement along the route behind the forward detachment, destroying separate enemy groups that were fleeing in disorder to the west. The 16th Guards Mechanized Brigade was following behind the 17th Guards Mechanized Brigade and by 2400 on 15 January linked up with its forward detachment in the Białogon area, which by this time was struggling for possession of Kielce with part of its force.

The corps headquarters between 1500 and 1900 was located in Marzysz, together with the 95th Separate Motorcycle Battalion, 22nd Separate Guards Sapper Battalion and 33rd Separate Guards Signals Battalion. After 2000, it was located in Posłowice.

At 1900 on 15 January, as the 49th Mechanized Brigade's rear units together with a battery of the 1995 Anti-aircraft Regiment and a battery of SU-76 self-propelled guns from the 1433rd Self-propelled Artillery Regiment were rolling through Posłowice, they were suddenly attacked by up to 15 tanks from out of the woods north of Posłowice, which destroyed 10 vehicles. Then the fire of the anti-aircraft battery and SU-76 battery knocked out 7 of the enemy tanks, and the rest pulled back into the woods.

Over the period of fighting between 12 and 15 January 1945, the 16th Guards Mechanized Brigade lost 99 men killed, including 8 officers; 214 wounded; and 13 tanks (5 destroyed and 8 knocked-out). The other units of the 6th Guards Mechanized Corps over the day of 15 January lost 5 T-34/85 tanks and 4 ZIS trucks.

At 2115 on 15 January, and order was received from the commander of the 4th Tank Army in cipher:

> The enemy's Ostrów – Opatów grouping has began to retreat to the west. The commander of the 6th Guards Mechanized Corps is to continue a rapid advance in the Kowala, Rykoszyn, Łopuszno direction and is to take Radoszyce, Slupie and Szestaki by the end of the day. The 16th Guards Mechanized Brigade is to prevent an enemy withdrawal from Kielce toward Piekoszów and Chęciny. The 10th Guards Tank Corps is attacking on the left with the task to take Konskie by the end of the day.

Pursuant to this order, the commander of the 6th Guards Mechanized Corps at 2130 issued a verbal order to the commander of the 56th Tank Regiment: "The regiment together with two motorized rifle companies, a battery of the 258th Light Artillery Regiment, two batteries of SU-85 and a company of IS-122 tanks is to operate as the corps' forward detachment along the Mniów, Królewiec, Sielpa-Wielka route and by the morning of 16 January is to take Konskie, where it is to dig in and hold the city until the arrival of the main forces."

At 2200 on 15 January the commander of the 6th Guards Mechanized Corps issued an order to the commander of the 29th Tank Regiment: "The regiment together with a company of the 17th Guards Mechanized Brigade's 3rd Battalion is to operate as a forward detachment of the corps along the Piaski, Stachura, Skoki, Borki, Mniów, Krasna, Hucisko route and is to capture Stąporków and to prevent an enemy retreat from the east and in the western direction." Until midnight on 15 January, the 29th and 56th Tank Regiments worked to clarify their assignments and prepared for nighttime operations.

The combat operations of the 10th Guards Tank Corps on 15 January 1945

With a combat directive from the 10th Guards Tank Corps' commander Colonel N.D. Chuprov, an assignment was given to the commander of the 63rd Guards Tank Brigade to keep firm possession of Chęciny up until 0600 on 15 January 1945, and then by 0620 to turn the sector of defense over to the commander of the 29th Guards Motorized Rifle Brigade. The commander of the 4th Tank Army General D.D. Leliushenko issued an order to the corps to reach the Przedbórz area by the end of 15 January.

The corps commander, to carry out this order, decided to move the corps out along a single route, having a reinforced tank brigade out in front as a forward detachment. The corps' main forces would move out in two combat echelons, with a tank brigade in the first echelon, and the motorized rifle brigade and artillery group in the second echelon. The 10th Guards Tank Corps would be operating to the left of the 6th Guards Mechanized Corps.

Pursuant to this, the corps' formations and units were given combat directives. At 1100 on 15 January the corps' forward detachment – the 63rd Guards Tank Brigade and two companies of IS-122 tanks from the 72nd Guards Heavy Tank Regiment – set out from Chęciny along the Chęciny – Łopuszno – Mnin – Wólka – Ruda Pilczyska – Przedbórz route with the assignment to take Przedbórz and hold it until the arrival of the corps' main forces.

At 1500 of the same day, the 3rd Tank Battalion, moving as the point unit of the 63rd Guards Tank Brigade, arrived in Łopuszno and took up a hedgehog defense, cutting all the roads leading to Łopuszno and securing the arrival of the brigade's main forces.

At 1930 the 1st Tank Battalion, having caught up with the 3rd Tank Battalion in Łopuszno, moved out along the route and in the Jasien area encountered an enemy supply train and destroyed it from the march. By 2100 it was approaching Mnin.

The 61st Guards Tank Brigade throughout the day of 15 January was conducting an active defense in the Piekoszów area. At 1730 outposts of the motorized rifle battalion of submachine gunners, which were positioned on the western outskirts of Piekoszów, spotted the movement of a large number of vehicles being guarded by 3 Pz.Kpfw V tanks from the Zręby direction toward Micigózd. The column was moving cross-country across a field. The brigade commander moved out two tank platoons of the 1st Tank Battalion with the order to destroy the enemy column. With the appearance of our tanks, the enemy Panthers that were guarding the column hastily began to retreat toward the woods northwest of Zręby. One Panther was knocked out, 50 vehicles were completely destroyed, and more than 150 vehicles were left abandoned on the battlefield. More than 100 enemy soldiers and officers surrendered.

The former commander of the 61st Guards Tank Brigade Guards Lieutenant Colonel V.I. Zaitsev left behind his recollections of this operation:

> In connection with the fact that the situation was developing in our favor, the Front Commander-in-Chief Marshal of the Soviet Union I.S. Konev, wasting no time, issued an order for the 4th Tank Army while on the march to bypass to the southwest of Kielce in order to block the arrival of fresh enemy reserves in this area. In order to carry out this new combat assignment, we were in need of at least 24 hours of rest in order to recover our strength to be in full combat readiness. I appealed to the corps commander to grant us this time, and also to return the 1st Tank Battalion to the brigade. He granted this request. By the end of 13 January, the 1st Tank Battalion returned to rejoin us.
>
> Throughout the night of 13-14 January repair teams worked together with the crews to restore disabled and broken-down tanks to service, and they successfully completed this work by the morning of 14 January. The fact that we once again had more than 50 combat-ready tanks speaks to the great merits of the Chief of Technical Services Guards Lieutenant Colone

E.N. Shiriaev. "Whiskers", as he was respectfully called in the brigade, had extraordinary engineering and organizational capabilities, and demonstrated creativity and persistence when carrying out this assignment. He never grabbed even a moment of shut-eye until all of the damaged combat machines were put back into service.

In the middle of the day the brigade received the task to reach the Piekoszów – Promnik area and to block the enemy's path of retreat from Kielce to the northwest. Before moving out to execute this order, we gave our final respects to the remains of the dead brigade commander N.G. Zhukov, and sent the coffin containing his body to be buried in L'vov, where even today his bones lay in rest on the Hill of Glory. We gave our remaining fallen comrade-tankers a ceremonial burial in Lisów.

When moving out toward the Piekoszów – Promnik area, I was marching at the head of the main forces, with a vanguard party and reconnaissance out in front. The conduct of General E.E. Belov in a number of preceding battles served as an example for me; he preferred to be located directly up among the combat forces, in order to receive first-hand information about changes in the situation and to direct a battle efficiently. That is also how the deceased brigade commander N.G. Zhukov always behaved.

Guards Lieutenant M.V. Pobedinsky, the hero of the fighting in Lisów, was heading the reconnaissance group out in front. Having spotted an aggregation of enemy tanks out in front along the brigade's route of march, he began to pinpoint their dispositions on the spot, and ignoring the danger, stuck his head up out of the turret hatch. A burst of fire from a heavy machine gun rang out, and the brave commander fell back into the tank with a bleeding head. The wound was serious, and in order to strive to save the life of the hero, we sent him back to a hospital in a halftrack. Escorting the unconscious Pobedinsky to the rear, we were all in grief over the fact that a real man and valiant soldier had been seriously wounded, who was honestly loved throughout the brigade for his combat prowess and cheerful nature. Fortunately, thanks to the skill of the doctors and his own outstanding physical condition, Misha Pobedinsky survived, and throughout the rest of his life he maintained an affectional attachment to his former combat comrades.

By the end of the day we had taken Piekoszów rather easily, but the enemy was putting up tough resistance in Promnik to our 2nd Tank Battalion, which had been reinforced with a submachine gun company. Here, the fighting reached the point of hand-to-hand combat, but in the end, we took the town and thereby blocked the path of retreat of the enemy's Kielce grouping to the northwest.

In the fighting for Promnik, one of the brigade's bravest commanders, Vladimir Markov was wounded. We also lost a courageous scout, the volunteer Guards Sergeant Folin.

In the middle of the day 15 January, large enemy columns began to appear, moving in our direction along the main road, dirt roads and cross-country. It was the encircled enemy Kielce grouping trying to break out to the northwest. Our tank cannons spoke up, and their fire destroyed several enemy self-propelled guns, halftracks and wheeled vehicles. Abandoning vehicles and equipment, the German units were striving to break out of the pocket, avoiding the roads. Several tank platoons of the 1st and 3rd Tank Battalions were detached with the assignment to pursue and destroy them. All of the enemy's attempts to break out through Promnik and Piekoszów were repulsed.

Thus, the brigade took an active part in the encirclement and destruction of the enemy's Kielce grouping. However, the 62nd Guards "Perm" Tank Brigade, which received the honorific title of "Kielce", made the main contribution in taking the city of Kielce.

At 2300 on 15 January the 61st Guards Tank Brigade received a verbal order from the corps' deputy commander to move out from its occupied area. It was to reach the Radoszyce area by the end of 16 January.

The 29th Guards Motorized Rifle Brigade, having turned over the defense of the town to the 359th Anti-aircraft Artillery Regiment at 1400, set off along the route behind the 63rd Guards Tank Brigade. Engaging in combat with retreating enemy columns, by 2400 on 15 January 1945 it had arrived in the area of Okrajki with its forward units, continuing to carry out its assignment.

The 62nd Guards Tank Brigade and the 1222nd Light Self-propelled Artillery Regiment, which was operationally subordinate to the 4th Tank Army's commander, were engaged in fighting to destroy the enemy's encircled grouping in the Morawica area. At 0845 on 15 January, following a 30-minute artillery preparation, in which the 299th Mortar Regiment took part, the brigade went on the attack toward Morawica and seized a bridge across the Czarna Nida River. Simultaneously its 2nd Tank Battalion was engaged in combat to destroy the remnants of the enemy that were retreating from Morawica in the wooded area northeast of Zbrza.

In the fighting for Morawica, the 62nd Guards Tank Brigade destroyed 17 tanks, 10 self-propelled guns, 50 vehicles, and eliminated up to 500 enemy soldiers and officers. In addition, it knocked out another 10 tanks, 7 self-propelled guns and 95 vehicles. Finally, it captured 4 halftracks, 8 vehicles, a stockpile of ammunition, and 57 enemy soldiers and officers. In return, the brigade lost 3 tanks destroyed, 3 tanks knocked out, 13 men killed, and 35 men wounded.

At 1430 on 15 January 1945 the commander of the 62nd Guards Tank Brigade received an order from the commander of the 4th Tank Army General D.D. Leliushenko to destroy the retreating enemy in the Zbrza area, while simultaneously blocking the enemy's path of retreat to the bridge in the Morawica area. At 1500 the 62nd Guards Tank Brigade set out to implement this order and up until 2000 the brigade was fighting to mop up the remnants of disorganized enemy groups from the 16th Panzer Division and the XXIV Panzer Corps' Regiment 97 in the wooded area northeast of Zbrza, where it destroyed 4 Tiger tanks, 1 Panther tank, 3 Pz.Kpfw. IV tanks, 12 guns, 9 halftracks, 3 anti-aircraft guns and 19 vehicles. The brigade's casualties amounted to 4 killed and 8 wounded. By 2115 the brigade was assembled in the wooded area 1 km south of Wola Majkowska, where it began putting its tanks and equipment back into order.

The 6th Guards Mechanized Corps was operating on the left of the 10th Guards Tank Corps. In cooperation with units of the 3rd Army, by the end of 15 January it had taken the major road hub and enemy strongpoint of Kielce.

From the account of the 10th Guards Tank Corps' 62nd Guards Tank Brigade:

At 0330 on 14 January 1945, the brigade set out along the route: Gumienice, Pierzchnica, Górki-Maleszowskie, Górki, Lisów, Zalesie, Morawica. With the sunrise, the 1st and 3rd Tank Battalions entered combat with units of the 16th Panzer Division in the Zaborze area and by 1100 on 14 January the enemy had been driven out of Zaborze and Brudzów. The brigade's units emerged on the highway and began to pursue the enemy in the direction of Morawica. Over the day of fighting on 14 January 1945, the 62nd Guards Tank Brigade inflicted the following damage on the enemy: Destroyed – 2 King Tigers, 5 Tigers, 2 Panthers, 3 self-propelled guns, 5 vehicles, 10 horse-drawn wagons. It also killed 480 enemy soldiers and officers. In return, the brigade lost 4 T-34/85 tanks destroyed and 2 damaged. Casualties amounted to 7 killed and 16 wounded.

The enemy with units of the 16th Panzer Division and the XXIV Panzer Corps' Separate Infantry Regiment 79, defending the Morawica area, repeatedly tried to attack our units from out of the Chałupki area: at 2330 on 14 January and at 0300 on 15 January in the direction of Wola Morawicka with the order to cross the highway and breakout to the west in order to link up with the Kielce grouping. All of the enemy counterattacks were driven back with heavy losses for the attackers. The enemy left behind a large amount of combat gear and equipment on the battlefield.

From the morning of 15 January, the brigade launched a decisive attack toward Morawica. After a 30-minute artillery preparation, at 0845 on 15 January the 62nd Guards Tank Brigade, in cooperation with the attached units of the 290th Mortar Regiment and the 1222nd Self-propelled Artillery Regiment attacked the enemy in the Morawica area and captured a bridge across the Czarna Nida River with the forces of the 1st and 3rd Tank Battalions. Simultaneously the 2nd Tank Battalion fought to destroy the enemy remnants retreating out of Morawica in the wooded area northeast of Zrbza.

As a result of the fighting, the following damage was done to the enemy: 17 Tigers, 8 Panthers, 10 self-propelled guns and 50 vehicles destroyed, and 500 soldiers and officers killed. It knocked out another 5 Tigers, 5 Panthers, 7 self-propelled guns and 95 vehicles, and captured 4 halftracks, 8 vehicles, 1 ammo dump, and 57 soldiers and officers. The brigade in return lost 3 T-34/85 tanks destroyed and 3 knocked-out, and 50 casualties, including 15 killed and 35 wounded. In the fighting for Morawica, the commander of the 1st Tank Battalion Guards Major Mikhail Boikov fell bravely in battle.

Up until 2000 on 15 January the brigade was mopping up the remnants of the disorganized enemy groups from the 16th Panzer Division and the XXIV Panzer Corps' Infantry Regiment 79 in the woods northeast of Zrbza. By 2115 on 15 January it was assembled in the woods 200 meters south of Wola Morawicka, servicing its tanks. During the elimination of the enemy grouping in the woods northeast of Zrbza, 200 enemy soldiers and officers were killed, and 4 Tiger tanks, 1 Panther, 3 Pz.Kpfw. IV, 12 guns, 9 halftracks, 3 anti-aircraft guns, and 19 vehicles were destroyed. The brigade lost 4 killed and 2 wounded. When eliminating the enemy remnants, the brigade's assistant chief of staff for intelligence Guards Captain Khristofor Nekrasov was killed.

From the account of the 72nd Guards Heavy Tank Regiment:

At 1330 on 14 January 1945 the 72nd Guards Separate Heavy Tank Regiment, together with the 63rd Guards Tank Brigade, took Chęciny, where it took up a defense on the western and northwestern outskirts of this point, thereby securing the flank of the 6th Guards Tank Corps (of the 3rd Guards Tank Army), cutting the path of retreat to the west and isolating the approach of the enemy units that were trying to break through to the encircled grouping. On the morning of 15 January, the regiment was removed from the defense and received an assignment to conduct a march along the Chęciny, Galęzice, Łopuszno route, where the tanks took up ambush positions on the Kielce – Łopuszno, Łopuszno – Malogosz and Łopuszno – Mnin roads.

The 1st Tank Company, which was operating with the 63rd Guards Tank Brigade, was pursuing the retreating enemy along the Łopuszno, Mnin, Wólka Pilczyska, Ruda Pilczyska, Niwki-Piskorzeniec, Przedbórz route and ran into organized enemy resistance along the eastern fringe of the woods west of Wojciechów. In this area the enemy had previously-prepared antitank ditches, minefields, barbed wire obstacles and had deployed several heavy tanks in ambush positions. With the arrival of the 63rd Guards Tank Brigade's 3rd Tank Battalion and 5 IS-122 tanks, having maneuvered and thrown the enemy into confusion, the 1st Tank Company pivoted strictly to the north in the direction of Końskie.

Conclusion: The rapid maneuvering of the corps' units, with which the regiment was cooperating, ensured the defeat and destruction of the enemy's Kielce – Radom grouping. The screening of the flank of the 6th Guards Tank Corps by units of the 72nd Guards Separate Tank Regiment ensured the encirclement and destruction of the enemy group that was trying to break through to the encircled grouping.

Table 3.3: Breakdown of the tank losses in the 4th Tank Army in the period between 12 and 18 January 1945

Period (1945)	Total damaged	Including due to:				Bogged down	Mechanical breakdown	Total irrecoverable losses
		Artillery fire	Mines	Air strikes	Panzerfausts			
12-18 January	217	159	28	-	-	15	15	98

At 2130 on 15 January 1945, the headquarters of the 4th Tank Army issued Combat Report No. 16 to the commander-in-chief of the 1st Ukrainian Front Marshal of the Soviet Union S.I. Konev:

1. The enemy with units of the 17th Panzer Division and the XXIV Panzer Corps' Fusilier Regiment 79 throughout the night attempted to break out to the north from out of the Obice area and the woods west of Piotrkowice, and by 0600 linked up in the Morawica area with units of the 16th Panzer Division that was operating out of the woods north of Kuby-Młyny toward Piaseczna-Górki. In the course of the day of 15 January, the battered units of the enemy's 16th and 17th Panzer Divisions, Fusilier Regiment 79 and Reserve Regiment 61 with fire and counterattacks put up tough resistance to the actions of our units in the Bilcza-Podgórze, Kowala, Brzeziny, Morawica and Dębska Wola areas, but by the end of the day suffered defeats in these areas.
2. The 4th Tank Army on 15 January continued to develop the offensive with the forces of the 6th Guards Mechanized Corps in the Dyminy, Zagrody, Białogon direction, and of the 10th Guards Tank Corps in the Chęciny, Promnik, Miedzierza direction, and by the end of the day was occupying the following lines: 6th Guards Mechanized Corps – 16th Guards Mechanized Brigade was occupying the Zagrody, Białogon line; the 49th Mechanized Brigade had reached the Zagrody area, where it linked up with the 16th Guards Mechanized Brigade; 17th Guards Mechanized Brigade – throughout the day was engaged in bitter fighting with enemy tanks that retreating from Brzeziny toward Kielce in the Kowala area. The 10th Guards Tank Corps at 0430 from the Piekoszów, Rykoszyn line was continuing to reach the Końskie area. The units' positions will be reported separately. The 93rd Separate Tank Brigade at 1800 passed through Polichno.
3. I have decided: to continue to develop a rapid offensive in the Gzymalków, Końskie direction and with the main forces to take Końskie with the 10th Guards Tank Corps with the assignment to prevent the withdrawal of the enemy's Ostrów – Opatów grouping to the west. I will conduct reconnaissance toward Szydłowiec and Ruski Bród. The 6th Guards Mechanized Corps is to screen in the direction of Stąporków with the 16th Guards Mechanized Corps and with its main forces is to take the Radoszyce, Słubia, Szestaki area. A forward detachment is to seize bridges across the river in the Skotniki area. The 93rd Separate Tank Brigade is to reach the Łopuszno area. The operational group of the army's headquarters is in Polichno.

Commander of the 4th Tank Army Guards Colonel General of Tank Forces LELIUSHENKO
Military Council member Guards Major General of Tank Forces GULIAEV
Chief of staff Guards Major General of Tank Forces UPMAN

The combat operations of the 6th Guards Mechanized Corps on 16 January 1945

The enemy opposite the corps' front was putting up no organized resistance. Only small, disorganized groups of the shattered units of the 20th Panzergrenadier Division, 168th Infantry Division, and 16th and 17th Panzer Divisions were operating in the area of the units' dispositions.

At 0100 on 16 January the 29th Tank Regiment and 56th Tank Regiment moved out to carry out their assigments. Throughout the night, swiftly advancing along their indicated routes and destroying small groups of enemy and enemy supply trains, at 0300 on 1600 the 56th Tank Regiment broke into Sielpia-Wielki, and as a result of a 30-minute battle, this village had been completely mopped up of the enemy.

The commander of the 56th Tank Regiment in Sielpia-Wielki left behind a blocking detachment of 5 T-34/85 tanks, 2 SU-85 and a battery of 76mm guns with the assignment to organize a hedgehog defense and to hold this road hub until the arrival of the corps' main forces. Meanwhile, the rest of the regiment continued to implement its orders. The 29th Tank Regiment by 0300 on 16 January, after a brief clash with enemy infantry, captured Hucisko. At 0400 the 56th Tank Regiment, after a 5-minute artillery barrage, attacked Końskie from the southwest and after a 2-hour combat fully mopped up the town.

From prisoner testimony and captured documents, it was established that the town of Końskie had been defended by a battalion of the 20th Panzergrenadier Division, 8 Panther tanks and two batteries of 75mm guns. In addition, the rear services of the German Fourth Panzer Army and a kampfgruppe of the Kalmyck Cavalry Corps were located in the town.

In the course of the 3 hours of fighting for Sielpia-Wielki and Końskie, the 56th Tank Regiment eliminated 800 enemy soldiers and officers, and destroyed 3 tanks, 3 Nebelwerfers, 7 guns and 45 vehicles. It also captured 105 vehicles, 3 stockpiles of food, a stockpile of engineering equipment, an ammunition dump, 14 76mm guns in good working order, 38 wagons and 2 steam engines. The regiment in return had no tank losses and had only 3 men wounded.

The 29th Tank Regiment's battle for Stąporków

Having reached the Mniów – Stąporków highway, the regiment at 0200 on 16 January 1945 became tied up in combat for the village of Krasna, where it knocked out 1 self-propelled gun and killed up to 50 Germans. At 0300 the regiment burst into Hucisko, where it killed another 300 enemy soldiers and officers, 3 Pz.Kpfw. IV tanks and up to 350 vehicles. At 0330 the regiment resumed the advance toward Stąporków, reached the southeastern outskirts of Wołów, overran a column of vehicles, and impetuously broke into the eastern outskirts of Stąporków, where it became tied up in combat to clear it of its defenders. By 0500 on 16 January 1945, Stąporków had been fully mopped up of the enemy. The regiment went over to a defense of the town on the Grzybów, Koprusa, Wołów, Mostki line, having set up ambushes with tanks and infantry.

With the fall of Stąporków, the regiment captured or destroyed 1 fuel train, 1 ammunition stockpile, 1 clothing depot; destroyed 2 Tiger tanks, 6 Panthers, up to 100 vehicles carrying military gear, 3 prime movers and 12 halftracks. It also captured 1 Tiger tank in good working order, 1 heavy assault gun, up to 300 vehicles, and 100 enemy soldiers and officers.

From 0900 to 1900 on 16 January the enemy undertook three attacks from the direction of Gołób and out of the woods northeast of Stąporków in strength of up to a battalion of infantry with the support of 8 tanks. When repulsing the attacks, the enemy lost up to 300 soldiers and officers killed or wounded, 2 tanks, 1 self-propelled gun and 8 halftracks. After a new enemy attack, the regiment adopted a mobile defense and at 1900 reached the woods 1 km northwest of

Stąporków, where it was once again attacked by the enemy at 2030 from the direction of Sadykierz in strength of up to a battalion of infantry and 5 tanks. The enemy counterattack by tanks and infantry was repelled. In the course of the battle, 1 enemy tank and up to a company of infantry were destroyed.

The 17th Guards Mechanized Brigade, on the basis of an order from the corps commander, at 0830 began to operate in the direction of Końskie. By 1200 the brigade's first combat echelon reached the Młyny Dziebałtowskie area. One tank platoon had been left behind in an ambush position in Sielpia-Wielki, but with the arrival of the 17th Guards Mechanized Brigade, the responsibility for guarding the town had been lifted from the 56th Tank Regiment's platoon, and it left to rejoin the regiment's main forces.

The 49th Mechanized Brigade's battle in the Bobrza – Bobrza-Przyjmo area

The 49th Mechanized Brigade together with a battalion of the 240th Mortar Regiment, the 1433rd Self-propelled Artillery Regiment and the 13th Guards Heavy Tank Regiment by 0300 on 16 January 1945 was occupying the following combat positions: A company of the 1st Motorized Rifle Battalion and a battery of its artillery battalion and 7 tanks of the 127th Tank Regiment were holding the road hub of Mniów, strongly blocking the roads leading to the northwest and east. Two platoons of the 1st Motorized Rifle Battalion together with a self-propelled gun battery of the 1433rd Self-propelled Artillery Regiment, an anti-tank rifle squad and a platoon of heavy machine guns was defending Borbza-Przyjmo, strongly blocking the roads leading to the northwest. Two platoons of the 1st Motorized Rifle Battalion, a tank platoon and a battery of the artillery battalion were defending Hill 327.1, blocking the roads leading to the east and south. A platoon of heavy machine guns and a battery of self-propelled guns were in defensive positions on the southern outskirts of Borbza. A company of infantry from the 3rd Motorized Rifle Battalion, a battery of the 504th Cannon Artillery Regiment and a platoon of heavy machine guns were holding Hill 320.2 and the eastern outskirts of Borbza. The 2nd Motorized Rifle Battalion, a battery of the artillery battalion and 5 tanks of the 127th Tank Regiment remained in the brigade commander's reserve together with the brigade's specialized elements, and were positioned in Borbza.

At 0330 on 16 January, the retreating remnants of the units of the 16th and 17th Panzer Divisions and the 20th Panzergrenadier Division brushed aside the 49th Mechanized Brigade's blocking detachment on the southern outskirts of Borbza and continued on to the north into the village of Borbza, where the brigade commander's reserve and the headquarters of the 49th Mechanized Brigade and the 240th Mortar Regiment were located. As a consequence of the poor security in the village of Borbza, when the fighting broke out, the elements of the 49th Mechanized Brigade that were located there were thrown into confusion; the elements didn't know the direction from which the Germans had come and fired wildly, which gave the enemy the opportunity to inflict casualties on the elements of the 49th Mechanized Brigade. In this action the commander of the 240th Mortar Regiment Guards Lieutenant Colonel Eshagin and his political deputy Major Bibe were killed. Through the efforts of the commander and headquarters staff of the 49th Mechanized Brigade, order was restored among the defenders and they prepared to launch a counterattack. Next at 0600 on 16 January, through the actions of the brigade commander's reserve, the enemy was driven out of the southern outskirts and thrown back to the south.

At 1100 retreating enemy units from the east counterattacked the 49th Mechanized Brigade out of the Kobylany area with major forces of infantry supported by tanks and artillery. The German attacked the northern outskirts of Borbza, trying to take possession of the Jakoszów – Mniów road; with the concentrated fire of infantry, artillery, mortars and tanks of the 49th Mechanized Brigade, the enemy counterattack was repulsed. Subsequently throughout the day the enemy undertook one counterattack after another from this direction and from the south, but they were all repelled. The brigade commander's reserved played the main role in defeating them. By the evening of 16 January, the Nazis, having incurred heavy losses and having achieved no success, in small groups began to withdraw into the woods north of Borbza.

Throughout the day of 16 January, the brigade together with its attached assets destroyed 15 tanks, 5 self-propelled guns, 150 vehicles, 10 halftracks, 6 Nebelwerfers and 6 guns, and killed up to 400 enemy soldiers and officers. It also captured 60 prisoners, 8 vehicles, 10 halftracks, 3 Nebelwerfers and a large quantity of rifles and submachine guns. In return the 49th Mechanized Brigade lost 79 killed and 231 wounded, with 9 men missing-in-action; it also lost 3 tanks destroyed, 2 armored cars and 2 halftracks; and 2 76mm guns, 1 57mm gun, 6 82mm mortars and 2 120mm mortars that were demolished.

Back on the day of 15 January a coded telegram had been received from the Military Council of the 4th Tank Army, which had announced that the commander-in-chief of the 1st Ukrainian Front Marshal of the Soviet Union S.I. Konev had expressed his personal gratitude to the 6th Guards Mechanized Corps for the successful destruction of the 16th Panzer Division, 17th Panzer Division and 20th Panzergrenadier Division; this news had been made known to all of the corps' men. On that same day, a second coded telegram had arrived from Major General of Tank Forces Guliaev, a member of the 4th Tank Army's Military Council, which passed along the gratitude of the Supreme Commander-in-Chief Marshal of the Soviet Union I.S. Stalin to all of the corps' men.

The combat operations of the 10th Guards Tank Corps on 16 January 1945

The corps' forward detachment (the 63rd Guards Tank Brigade) was advancing along the corps' assigned route. Its forward units of the 1st Tank Battalion at 0200 on 16 January was stopped by strong enemy fire on the Stanisławów Wielki – Borowa line. The further advance of the corps' forward detachment was brought to a halt. According to intelligence information, prisoner testimony and interviews with local residents, the enemy had a fixed defense on the Przedbórz line, equipped with strong fortifications. The defense had two rows of full-profile trenches; antitank ditches that were full of water; and dense minefields and barbed wire obstacles. The line was being defended by up to a regiment of infantry with 25 halftracks.

As a result of the fighting on 16 January 1945 along the corps' route and on the Wojciechów line, the following damage was done to the enemy: 1 tank, 3 antitank guns, 5 mortars, 2 halftracks, 20 vehicles and 7 machine guns were destroyed. Up to 100 German soldiers and officers were killed, and 12 were taken prisoner. War booty was taken: 3 large-caliber guns, 5 supply wagons with their loads, 10 horses, and 6 various stockpiles.

The 61st Guards Tank Brigade, advancing along the corps' route behind the 63rd Guards Tank Brigade, by 1900 on 16 January was assembled in Radoszyce, where it took up a defense in readiness to repulse enemy counterattacks from the east and west. Throughout the subsequent night the tanks were topped up with fuel and underwent inspections.

The 29th Guards Motorized Rifle Brigade together with the corps' artillery group by the end of the day was fully assembled in Mnin. After the difficult night march that included combat actions along the route, the men were given four hours of rest.

The 62nd Guards Tank Brigade and the 1222nd Light Self-propelled Artillery Regiment were under the operational control of the 4th Tank Army's commander, and having received an order from the army headquarters, at 0900 on 16 January set out from the wooded area 800 meters south of Wola Morawicka and conducted a march along the Wola Morawicka, Gałęzice, Kolodiec-Ruda, Michala Góra route and by 1400 on 16 January had re-assembled in Łopuszno.

At 1500 the brigade commander received a supplementary order from the commander of the 4th Tank Army General D.D. Leliushenko to move out along the Łopuszno, Mnin, Czerwona Wola, Pijanów, Jakimowice route and to take up a defense in Radoszyce. The brigade, carrying out this order, by 2300 on 16 January was fully assembled in Radoszyce and had taken up a defense there, while reconnoitering in the Końskie direction.

Overall conclusions of the 10th Guards Tank Corps' command

The enemy's defense [at the outset of the operation] was deeply-echeloned and antitank, with an elaborate system of fortifications (fieldworks, communication trenches, bunkers and obstacles, minefields, barbed wire obstacles, and in places antitank ditches that were 6 meters wide and 4 meters deep). All of the defensive fortifications and obstacles were well-camouflaged. The enemy had sufficient strength and means for firmly holding the defensive belt, while possessing major tactical reserves; with their occupation of the second defensive line, they would give the enemy the possibility of offering serious resistance to our units' advance. A new enemy tactic was declining to have his main forces drawn into holding the defense's tactical belt with the aim of preserving manpower and equipment and to inflict a defeat on the attacking Soviet units on an advantageous line. However, it was implemented in a disorganized manner and had no success. The corps' rapid advance to the west yielded its results. The enemy didn't have time to occupy the defenses on the Kielce – Chmielnik line with his operational reserves. The arrival of the corps' units in the Lisów – Chałupki area split the enemy's operational reserves that were positioned in the Kielce area (16th Panzer Division) and southwest of Chmielnik (17th Panzer Division), which gave the opportunity of defeating the enemy in piecemeal fashion. The arrival of the 10th Guards Tank Corps' units in the Chęciny area created a deep wedge, which split apart the enemy's operational reserves and thereby deprived him of unified command and control. The breakthrough of the second defensive line by our units in the Maleszowa, Pierzchnica sector demoralized the foe. Suffering heavy losses, the Nazis were forced to retreat, abandoning weapons and equipment.

The 10th Guards Tank Corps was introduced into the breach as part of a powerful echelon for exploiting the breakthrough, occupying the central position in it. Its neighbor on the right was the 6th Guards Mechanized Corps and its neighbor on the left was the 3rd Guards Tank Army's 6th Guards Tank Corps. It would seem that the corps' position in the combat formation was advantageous, since its flanks were covered by strong armored formations. In reality it turned out to the opposite. Already on the third day of the operation the corps, engaging in combat with the enemy's operational reserves, reached the Chęciny area. The 6th Guards Mechanized Corps was locked in heavy fighting on the approaches to Kielce. The 3rd Guards Tank Army's 6th Guards Tank Corps was fighting south of Chmielnik. Thus, the corps' flanks turned out to be exposed, which unquestionably was exploited by the enemy. By the end of day of 13 January, at the cost of heavy losses the Nazis were able to threaten the corps' line of communications west of Pierzchnica.

Thanks to the exceptionally meticulous preparations for the operation, which anticipated enemy counterattacks, the corps was prepared to repulse them. The corps' combat formation was arranged with the calculation of conducting combat with each combat echelon in case of its isolation from the corps' other units. For this purpose, each combat echelon was given an adequate number of assets. The availability of an artillery group under the centralized control of the corps' artillery commander allowed him to influence the course of the brigades' fighting.

On 14 January with an attack by the 62nd Guards Tank Brigade with the 29th Guards Motorized Rifle Brigade, the 1222nd Light Self-propelled Artillery Regiment and the 290th Mortar Regiment from Pierzchnica toward Zaborze, the enemy was driven out of his occupied line, and the corps' main forces linked up with the units that were operating out in front. The enemy's desire to cut the lines of communication had no success. The corps organized antitank firing positions with its artillery at road hubs, deployed mobile blocking detachments of tanks with motorized infantry on likely directions of counterattacks, and always anticipated the enemy's intentions.

Command and control over the corps' formations and units during the operation was implemented over the radio, through liaison officers, and by face-to-face communications among the commanders. Wire communications was a backup means of communication. The operational command group of the corps' headquarters was moving behind the corps' forward detachment, and consisted of the chief of operations, the artillery commander, the chief of intelligence, and the assistance chief of communications, and had means of communication, a reconnaissance group, and the corps' chief engineer with a group of sappers. The corps' headquarters forward echelon advanced behind the first echelon, and was supporting the corps commander's command and control over the corps' formations and units by maintaining constant communication between them and the army headquarters. During the fighting the corps commander, located in the operational command group, had the opportunity to influence the course of the fighting personally, making maximum use of radios and driving out to the units' combat positions. Face-to-face contact between the corps commander and the brigade commanders, which took place rather often, played a major role in maintaining command and control. There was no direct contact with the neighbors on the left or right throughout 13 and 14 January. The mutual exchange of information took place through the army headquarters.

As the tank versus tank fighting in a variety of conditions demonstrated, the battle would be won by that side that would use a rapid maneuver to take up a line suitable for meeting the enemy, or by first declining battle, then appearing from a direction that the enemy wasn't expecting. Examples: the bypassing maneuver of the 61st Guards Tank Brigade in the Piotrkowice area and its movement toward Lisów. In such cases, a large responsibility falls on the forward detachment. The results of the conducted tank battles demonstrated the higher military skill of our tankers and the higher proficiency of the officers' staff to shape a battle and to defeat the enemy that has a superiority in strength.

The main shortcomings are the insufficient ability of the tank battalion commanders to command a battle from a tank, which leads to unnecessary losses, as well as the insufficient use of the T-34 tank's high speed in order to take an important objective or line. Delay at times led to excessive losses in tanks, men and time.

The enemy is using a tactic of declining to defend the tactical zone with the aim of conserving manpower and equipment, and to offer resistance on a new line later. Having in mind the significant distance of the brigades from the army's supply dumps, it is necessary to keep the necessary amount of ammunition, fuel and lubricants, calculated for the operation, in the rears of the brigades and battalions and to keep the supplies moving along with it.

The IS-122 tank companies that were attached to the brigades (three companies of heavy IS-122 tanks had been attached to the 63rd Guards Tank Brigade) played a substantial role in the fighting; they were used to used to counter the heavy enemy tanks of the Tiger and Panther types. It makes sense to add one company of heavy IS-122 tanks to the table of organization of the tank brigades.

Excerpt from the 28th Guards Heavy Tank Regiment's journal of combat operations:

The status of the regiment's tanks and vehicles on 10 January 1945 on the eve of the offensive: Operational 21 IS-122 tanks, 1 KV-T prime mover, 3 M3A1 halftracks, 1 BA-64, 6 GAZ-AA trucks, 20 ZIS-5 trucks, 8 Studebaker trucks, 2 Ford trucks, 1 Dodge truck, 1 GAZ-55 ambulance, 2 ZIS-5 fuel trucks, and 1 Studebaker; 1 Type "A" repair vehicle, 1 Type "B" repair vehicle and 1 mobile charging station; and 2 M-72 motorcycles and 1 Indian motorcycle. Situation with supplies: 3 refills of diesel fuel; 2 refills of petrol; ammunition – 3 standard combat loads; food – 10 days of rations.

At 2000 on 11 January a combat order was received, pursuant to which the regiment by sunrise on 12 January was to assemble in a jumping-off position: 1st and 3rd Tank Companies – in the area of the 17th Guards Mechanized Brigade in the woods 1.5 km east of Hańga; the 2nd and 4th Tank Companies with the 16th Guards Mechanized Brigade in the woods 500 meters northeast of Hańga. The 1st and 3rd Tank Companies moved out to their jumping-off positions at 2200, the 2nd and 4th Tank Companies moved out at 2300; and the headquarters and rear elements – at 0700 on 12 January.

On 12 January the regiment was introduced into the breakthrough in three groups: the 1st and 3rd Tank Companies together with the 126th Tank Regiment and the main forces of the 17th Guards Mechanized Brigade along route No. 2; the 4th Tank Company and two tanks of the 2nd Tank Company along route No. 2; three tanks of the 2nd Tank Company – along Route No. 1 together with the 28th Tank Regiment in the forward detachment of the 16th Guards Mechanized Brigade. The unexpectedness of the offensive played a decisive role in the units' rapid advance. The enemy offered no resistance whatsoever on the forward edge and on the first intermediary line, retreating and abandoning military gear and equipment. Up until the first intermediary line, particular attention was paid to passage through the dense minefields that were positioned alongside the roads and in populated places. By 2400 on 12 January the regiment had reached the Smyków – Klamka line. The regiment had no losses in men or tanks, with the exception of IS-122 No. 112, which became disabled by mines in the Klamka area. Within two days this tank had been repaired and restored to service.

On 13 January the 4th Tank Company and the 2nd Platoon of the 2nd Tank Company, as part of the 16th Guards Mechanized Brigade's forward detachment, conducting a march in anticipation of a meeting battle, by 0800 captured a bridge across the Bobrza River in the Zagorody area. The enemy, caught by surprise, fled without combat, leaving behind an intact bridge and equipment.

The commander of the 6th Guards Mechanized Corps, leaving behind a group of tanks from the 28th Tank Regiment, including 1 IS-122 tank of the 4th Tank Company, moved out toward the Białogon area with the main forces of the forward detachment, and by 1200 13 January they had captured it, having left three IS-122 tanks (2nd Platoon of the 2nd Tank Company and IS-122 No. 412 of the 4th Tank Company) and three T-34 tanks in ambush positions on the Kielce – Chmielnik road, 6 km south of Kielce. By the end of day on 13 January, the 4th Tank Company minus the one tank was located on the defense in Białogon, repulsing numerous attacks by enemy tanks and infantry that were trying to escape from Kielce. As a result of the combat, it destroyed 2 Tiger tanks, 1 Panther, 2 self-propelled guns, 30 vehicles and 1 halftrack, while killing or wounding up to 50 Germans.

The tanks that were positioned in ambush between 1400 and the end of the day on 13 January were engaged in fighting with the enemy, which in strength of up to 40 tanks and a regiment of infantry, was trying to move along the road in the direction of Chmielnik. Changing firing positions (upon the enemy's detection of the original positions), as a result of a 6-hour battle up to a company of infantry and 4 tanks, 10 vehicles and 6 halftracks were destroyed. The enemy column was scattered.

The 1st and 3rd Tank Companies together with the main forces of the 17th Guards Mechanized Brigade and two tanks of the 2nd Tank Company were conducting a march along Route No. 1 in anticipation of a meeting battle. At 1200 they reached Route No. 2. A change in the direction of movement depended on the strength of enemy resistance. Wherever the enemy resistance was less, that's were the movement of the column was directed with the aim of falling on the enemy's line of communications deep in the rear. At 1700 on 13 January enemy resistance was encountered on the direction of movement of the 1st and 3rd Tank Companies in Pierzchnica area, and on the direction of movement of the 2nd Tank Company's tanks in the Skrzelczyce area. The 1st and 3rd Tank Companies in the area of Pierzchnica and the 2nd Tank Company in the Skrzelczyce area engaged in combat to repulse the enemy's counterattacks of tanks and infantry. Taking advantage of the crest of hills as an advantageous line of defense, the enemy was preventing the possibility of advancing the medium tanks. Having selected firing positions, with the fire from fixed positions the enemy resistance was broken. In the course of the fighting, 6 tanks and 3 guns were destroyed, and up to 60 enemy soldiers and officers killed. The losses of the 28th Guards Heavy Tank Regiment: in the 1st Tank Company IS-122 No. 122 was set ablaze by enemy antitank fire, and one IS tank was knocked out; in the 2nd Tank Company, two IS tanks were knocked out. Losses in personnel: Driver-mechanic Guards Senior Technician-Lieutenant Olontsev perished in the burning tank; three more men of this crew (the tank commander, gunner and loader) received burns and were evacuated to a hospital. The commander of the 2nd Tank Company Guards Captain Shershnev and the commander of an IS tank platoon Guards Senior Lieutenant Popov were both wounded.

In the fighting on 13 January, Guards Captain Shershnev and Guards Senior Lieutenant Popov both distinguished themselves. Being severely wounded, they both remained at their posts until their assignment had been carried out. Until the end of the day on 13 January, the 1st and 3rd Tank Companies and one platoon of the 2nd Tank Company conducted a march along the Pierzchnica, Lipa, Radzymiód route, and lagered in Radzymiód up until 0500 on 14 January.

On 14 January the 4th Tank Company continued to remain in the Białogon area, repulsing enemy counterattacks from the direction of Kielce and stubbornly holding their defensive area. The 2nd Platoon of the 2nd Tank Company was stubbornly holding a sector of the highway in the Bilcza-Jaworznia area. At 0200 on 14 January an enemy column of up to 100 vehicles, escorted by 5 tanks, tried to break out from the direction of Kielce. With fire from ambush positions, the column was almost completely destroyed, and two of the enemy tanks were destroyed in the process.

The 1st and 3rd Tank Companies and two tanks of the 2nd Tank Company moved out from Radomice along the route toward Łabędziów. Upon reaching the fringe of the woods 800 meters west of Radomice, they were counterattacked by the enemy from the southwest. As a result of an hour-long battle, the attack was repelled. Two enemy tanks and one rocket launcher were destroyed.

At 0600 on 14 January the 1st and 3rd Tank Companies were assembled, together with the 17th Guards Mechanized Brigade, along the western fringe of the woods lying east of Morawica in expectation of crossing the Czarna Nida River in the area of Beleskie-Młyny. At 0630 of this same day, enemy remnants in strength of 8 tanks and infantry from the northern portion of the woods (the assembly area of our tanks) at slow speed approached right up to the location of the regiment's and brigade's rear elements, which were located in a clearing in the area of the tanks' location and set ablaze some of the vehicles, and then counterattacked the tanks. As a result of the combat action, 1 Tiger tank was set ablaze by the 1st Tank Company. Our own losses: a staff vehicle with all of the documents of the headquarters, a radio truck carrying signals equipment, the mobile charging station, a Studebaker fuel truck, an M3A1 halftrack, a truck carrying food supplies and a vehicle of the technical service unit were all left burned out. Casualties: the chief of the regiment's chemical service Guards Captain Popov and the regiment's chief of artillery supplies Guards Senior Lieutenant Voronin were both killed; a platoon commander of the 2nd Tank Company who happened to be in the vehicle of the technical service Guards Senior Lieutenant Popov was wounded, as well as 6 non-commissioned officers and a private. At the decision of the commander of the 17th Guards Mechanized Brigade, the 3rd Tank Company was moved out to the Łabędziów in order to screen the construction of a bridge. At 1800 on 14 January, the enemy in strength of up to 8 tanks and 5 halftracks with infantry aboard, trying to break out of encirclement and link up with friendly forces, were moving in a column along the left bank of the Czarna River toward the bridge. Having allowed the Nazis to within extreme range, the 3rd Tank Company, which was guarding the bridging site, opened fire; 1 halftrack was knocked out, and another halftrack was captured in good working order. In this action the company had no losses in tanks or men. By the end of 14 January, the enemy was showing no active operations, and the regiment was located in the former place.

Conclusion: The enemy, having been unable to put up organized resistance, was retreating in disorder. Disorganized enemy groups that remained, especially in the woods, having lost all sense of direction and striving to get back to friendly lines, kept emerging in the positions of our forces and being destroyed. The regiment, despite the difficulty of command and control over its subordinate units in view of their scattering, carried out all of its assignments.

On 15 January 1945 the 4th Tank Company as part of the 16th Guards Mechanized Brigade's forward detachment was positioned on the defense in the Białogod area (one tank in Zagrody and one tank as part of an ambush on the highway in the Bilcza Jaworznia area. According to an order from the brigade commander, 2 IS-122 tanks of the 28th Guards Tank Regiment with attached infantry had received the task by the end of the day to take the major road hub of Stąporków. As a result of a forced march by 0800 on 16 January the task was carried out. The enemy, caught by surprise, was unable to put any resistance and fled.

In order to repulse the enemy's intensifying counterattacks from the direction of Kielce, one IS-122 tank from out of the Białogon area was moved up to the eastern outskirts of Kielce to the vicinity of a brick factory. The 2nd Platoon of the 2nd Tank Company with one tank from the 4th Tank Company was located in ambush positions. At 1200 the enemy, in strength of up to 10 tanks with the support of infantry attempted to break through to Kielce. Having allowed the enemy to close within short range, three IS-122 tanks that were deployed in ambush opened fire. As a result of the battle, 5 German tanks and up to a company of infantry were destroyed.

The 1st and 3rd Tank Companies, 2 tanks of the 2nd Tank Company, together with the 17th Guards Mechanized Brigade, at 0800 on 15 January after the laying down of a bridge across the Czarna Nida River in the area 2 km east of Beleckie-Młyny, set out from the wooded area east of Łabędziów. In order to screen the crossing of the tanks of the 17th Guards Mechanized Brigade, three IS-122 tanks of the 1st Tank Company were set up in ambush positions. After the regiment's tanks crossed the river together with the 17th Guards Mechanized Brigade, they re-assembled in the woods west of Kuby-Młyny.

The enemy, pursued by our units, turned to put up resistance on the Bilcza-Ciołków line. As a result of the following, this village was taken. The retreating enemy forces left behind an ambush in Bilcza Podgórze in order to cover the withdrawal. The Soviet tanks with fire from fixed positions destroyed 1 tank and 1 self-propelled gun, and entered this village. The 1st Tank Company, together with the 17th Guards Mechanized Brigade, next captured Kowala. Having taken the Bilcza-Ciołków, Bilcza Podgórze and Kowala lines of resistance, the regiment, together with the 17th Guards Mechanized Brigade, cut the Kielce – Chmielnik road and reached the eastern bank of the Bobrza River, thereby linking up with the forward detachment of the 16th Guards Mechanized Brigade and the 4th Tank Company, which were located in the Białogon area; from the march, they forced a crossing of the Bobrza River and continued to pursue the enemy.

Over the day of combat operations on 15 January, the 1st and 3rd Tank Companies destroyed 3 tanks, 1 mortar, 2 guns, and killed up to 35 Germans; the 2nd and 4th Tank Companies destroyed 4 tanks, 3 self-propelled guns, 4 guns of various calibers, 5 vehicles, and killed up to 50 Germans. Our own losses: a) in tanks – 1 tank was left burned-out on the fringe of the woods west of [indecipherable] due to enemy anti-tank artillery fire; 1 more tank was lost in the area of the fringe of woods north of Bilcza Jaworznia and 1 tank in Stąporków; b) in men – 1 officer, 1 non-commissioned officer and 1 private were killed; 4 men were wounded. In the fighting, Guards Junior Lieutenant Zhuzhukin's tank crew distinguished itself. Zhuzhukin himself refused to leave his combat post, until the enemy counterattack was defeated.

Analysis of tank losses

The losses of tanks in the 4th Tank Army over the first stage of the Vistula – Oder operation are shown in the following two tables:

Table 3.4: Armored losses of the 4th Tank Army by date in the period between 12 and 18 January 1945

Date (1945)	Irrecoverable losses	Repairable	Total knocked-out or destroyed	Due to mechanical breakdown	Total
12 January	5	20	25	-	-
13 January	16	29	45	-	-
14 January	21	36	57	-	-
15 January	Information not compiled				
16 January	23	68	91	-	-
17 January	10	22	32	-	-
18 January	2	5	7	-	-
Total:	77	180	257	15	272

Table 3.5: Date of the appearance of the enemy's acting formations and units

Unit	Date of introduction and in which sector	When and how the information was confirmed
17th Panzer Division	In the Maleszowa area on 13 January 1945	In the same area, by the capture of prisoners on 13 January 1945
16th Panzer Division	On the night of 13-14 January 1945 in the Komórki area	The capture of prisoners on 14 January 1945 in Komórki
20th Panzergrenadier Division	On the night of 13-14 January 1945 south of Komórki	The capture of prisoners on 14 January 1945 in Komórki
Heavy Panzer Battalion 501 (424)	On 13 January 1945 in the Szczytno area	The capture of prisoners on 13 January 1945 in the Szcytno area

Details of the Enemy's Tactics

In the conducted operation, the characteristic details in the enemy's tactics were: a) from the first days of the operation, the employment of major groups of tanks (15-30) in the conducted counterattacks; b) the widespread deployment of tank and anti-tank ambushes on the paths of movement of our forces; c) the increased commitment of infantry units armed with Panzerfausts and the introduction of special tank-hunting battalions into the fighting; d) the concentration of assault tank groupings with the aim of flank attacks against our units; e) attempts to cut off our forward operating units with the aim of encircling them and attempts to capture bridges; f) the organization of acts of sabotage on the routes of our troop movements; g) attempts to compensate for the lack of troops and tanks by maneuvers in the necessary directions; and h) the increased use of radio direction finding and radio provocations.

The enemy was disorganized from the outset of the operation. The attempt to withdraw the men and tanks in an organized manner and to put up resistance on the intermediary line, because of the rapid advance of our mobile units, came to failure. Introducing units of the 17th Panzer

Division into battle on the night of 12-13 January 1945, the enemy launched counterattacks in the following directions: a) with up to 30 tanks out of Maleszowa toward Podlesie; b) with 20 tanks out of Suków Wola and 5 tanks and 9 halftracks out of Lipa in the north and northeast directions; c) with an infantry battalion and 14 tanks from out of Maleszowa toward Pierzchnica. The objective of the counterattacks was to destroy our penetrating forward units with a flank attack and to cut them off from the army's main forces. Thanks to the capable maneuvering of our units and the timely revealing of the enemy's intentions through reconnaissance, his attempts were frustrated and he was forced to retreat, suffering heavy losses.

One of the key participating German units in the counterattacks against the 4th Tank Army was Heavy Panzer Battalion 424. It is worth taking a closer look at this heavy panzer unit, its role in the fighting, and what happened to it as a result. Heavy Panzer Battalion 424 had been formed in December 1944 on the basis of Heavy Panzer Battalion 501; the battalion adopted its new numerical designation on 21 December 1944. The commander was Major Saemisch. Tiger tanks from Heavy Panzer Battalioin 501 were transferred into the battalion, and in addition it received 11 new Tiger I tanks from Heavy Panzer Battalion 509. On 30 December 1944, Heavy Panzer Battalion 424 had 28 Tiger II tanks (all operational) and 22 Tiger I tanks (with another 4 under repair).

The battalon was operationally subordinate to the XXIV Panzer Corps and took part in the counterattack on 13 January 1945 against units of the 10th Guards Tank Corps' 61st Guards Tank Brigade of the 4th Tank Army in the Lisów area. According to German information found in Wolfgang Schneider's book *Tigers in Combat I*, the Soviet 1st Ukrainian Front under the command of Marshal Konev, which had gone on the offensive on 12 January from the Baranów bridgehead, broke through the German defenses, and General Leliushenko's 4th Tank Army was introduced into the breach. German operational reserves consisting of Heavy Panzer Battalion 424 and units of the 168th Infantry Division were quickly committed into the fighting in order to localize the Russian penetration. Already on the following day of 13 January, the German XXIV Panzer Corps counterattacked in the Lisów area with the forces of Heavy Panzer Battalion 424. By this time this village had already been captured by the 61st Guards Tank Brigade, which according to German intelligence had 65 T-34 tanks, as well as several heavy IS-2 tanks from the 72nd Guards Heavy Tank Regiment and several anti-tank guns.

When the panzers of Heavy Panzer Battalion 424 entered Lisów, according to German information, they ran into numerous, well-prepared antitank positions and heavy IS-2 tanks, which opened fire at them and inflicted heavy losses to them. As a result of the attack, the majority of Heavy Panzer Battalion 424's Tigers were either destroyed, or lost due to mechanical breakdowns on ground that was difficult for the tanks to cross.

As a result of the meeting battle in the Lisów – Kielce area, over two days of fighting, 13 and 14 January, Heavy Panzer Battalion 424 virtually ceased to exist. On 1 February 1945, Heavy Panzer Battalion 424 was deactivated. This, doubtlessly, is one of the heaviest defeats of a German heavy panzer battalion of Tiger tanks in the course of the Second World War.

Schneider's book is just one of several books by Western authors who have written about the January 1945 Soviet offensive from out of the Vistula River bridgeheads.

Earl Ziemke, the well-known American military historian in his book *Stalingrad to Berlin: The German Defeat in the East*, presents another Western view of the fighting in the Lisów – Kielce area:

> Before dawn the massed Soviet artillery, estimated at 420 pieces per mile, laid a barrage on the northern two-thirds (approximately twenty miles) of XXXXVIII Panzer Corps' front. After three hours the fire shifted to a strip pattern and the infantry moved out into the openings. The Germans were caught forward of the main battle line; they had expected the Russians

to wait for better weather. During the morning the Russian infantry drove in deep; by noon it had opened gaps wide enough for the armor to come through. XXXXVIII Panzer Corps' three divisions were cut up and destroyed. XXIV Panzer Corps had orders to counterattack, but its two divisions west of the bridgehead were overrun in their assembly areas.

On the 13th *Fourth Tank Army* wheeled northwest toward Chęciny, and *Fifty-Second Army* and *Third Guards Tank Army* pushed due west past Chmielnik. During the night some of the tank spearheads had reached the [Czarna] Nida River. Across the [Czarna] Nida River a 40-mile-wide path to Upper Silesia and the Oder was open. On the north flank XXIV Panzer Corps, what was left of it, dug in around Kielce.

...

During the day [of 15 January] *Thirteenth*, *Fourth Tank*, and *Third Guards Tank Armies* pushed the XXIV Panzer Corps out of Kielce, thereby removing that not very significant threat to *First Ukrainian Front*'s flank.

Reading the version of the fighting in the Lisów as presented by Wolgang Schneider in his book *Tigers in Combat*, as well as the versions presented by other Western historians such as Christian Wilbeck in his book *Sledgehammers: Strengths and Flaws of Tiger Tank Battalions in World War II* and Norbert Bączyk in his book *Kielce 1945* a number of points arise that merit discussion:

1. It is worth noting that Heavy Panzer Battalion 424 had an unusual number of Tigers and was equipped with them above the authorized table strength of 45 Tigers due to the heavy tanks it received from Heavy Panzer Battalion 509 (11 Tigers). On 12 January 1945, the battalion had 51 combat-ready Tigers.
2. It isn't clear how Christoper Wilbeck comes to a conclusion based on which sources that in the course of the two unsuccessful attempts to break through to the headquarters of the 17th Panzer Division on the night and early morning of 13 January, Heavy Panzer Battalion 424 supposedly destroyed 27 Russian tanks without losing a single tank in return. If he bases this conclusion on the reports from Heavy Panzer Battalion 424 itself, then it is necessary to check these figures against the information on the Soviet side. As one can see from the Soviet archival records of the 4th Tank Army, over the entire day of 12 January it lost 5 tanks irrecoverably. Over the day of 13 January, the 4th Tank Army irrecoverably lost 16 tanks. Most of the losses on 13 January stem from the meeting battle in Lisów. Thus it is obvious that the information that Heavy Panzer Battalion 424 destroyed 27 Russian tanks in the course of the attempts to relieve the headquarters of the 17th Panzer Division, even prior to the start of the fighting in Lisów, is incorrect.
3. The fact that Heavy Panzer Battalion 424 didn't conduct the necessary reconnoitering of the terrain and the enemy is obvious. An analogous episode with this same battalion (which was designated Heavy Panzer Battalion 501 at the time) took place in August 1944 in the Oględów area, when the King Tigers that had just arrived to arm this battalion fell into an ambush set by the T-34/85 tanks of the 3rd Guards Tank Army's 53rd Guards Tank Brigade and the 71st Guards Heavy Tank Regiment, as a result of which the Soviet side inflicted heavy losses on the battalion and captured three King Tigers, which at that time were the latest tankers in the German arsenal. In the West, many consider that the German tanks were better trained and tactically superior to their Soviet counterparts. On the basis of Heavy Panzer Battalion 424's (501's) service record, one can conclude that by the summer of 1944, this wasn't always so.
4. Wolfgang Scheider reports that Tiger 111 in the course of one day of fighting on 13 January 1945 destroyed 20 Russian tanks. If you momentarily reflect on this assertion, then all of the other tanks of Heavy Panzer Battalion 424 togther could only have knocked out a few Russian tanks. This assertion sounds more like Goebbel's propaganda, if one considers that

according to the combat report from the commander of the 61st Guards Tank Brigade Guards Lieutenant Colonel Zaitsev, the brigade's losses in the fighting for Lisów amounted to 4 T-34/85 tanks destroyed and 10 T-34/85 tanks knocked-out.

5. Schneider informs his readers that in the fighting in Lisów, the Tigers of Heavy Panzer Battalion 424 destroyed 50-60 Russian tanks. Now let's try to picture this situation. A war was going on. Both sides meet in a battle. One side suffers a defeat; its tanks were almost fully destroyed, and that side abandons the battlefield. That side is not even able to check how many of its tanks were destroyed or simply disabled, because it can't evacuate them from the battlefield; but somehow at the same time it knows that the losses on the other side (the Soviet side) amounted to 50-60 tanks in this battle. As already noted above, the losses of Soviet side in the Lisów area didn't exceed 20 tanks that were knocked out or left burned out, and Schneider's information regarding 50-60 destroyed Soviet tanks isn't confirmed by any evidence. It is also necessary to mention that Schneider, Wilbeck and the Polish military historian Norbert Bączyk all write that the Tigers of Heavy Panzer Battalion 424 were caught in an ambush set by IS-2 tanks, which Bączyk assigns to the 13th Heavy Tank Regiment. The analysis of documents from the 4th Tank Army's Operations Department, as well as the accounts and operational summaries of its subordinate regiments, brigades and corps, allow one to conclude without any doubt that the Joseph Stalin tanks of the 13th Guards Heavy Tank Regiment took no part in the fighting for Lisów. On this day Heavy Panzer Battalion 424's adversary was the 10th Guards Tank Corps' 61st Guards Tank Brigade, which didn't have any heavy tanks, and fought only with T-34/85 tanks.

After reading this text, a number of additional questions arise. In the first place, Kleine and Kühn, just like Schneider and Wilbeck previously, don't cite any evidence of the 20 Russian tanks supposedly destroyed by the German tank in the morning fighting on 13 January 1945, but they do give an interesting detail. It turns out the *Oberleutnant* Oberbracht destroyed 12 tanks on the morning of 13 July, and in the action in Lisów on this same day, Oberbracht destroyed only 7 Russian tanks, and not 20, as Scheider and Wilbeck separately reported. As already indicated above, the archival documents from the Russian Ministry of Defense's Central Archives fully refute this version presented by the German authors. There is one more interesting detail. Kleine and Kühn don't write anything about the destruction in Lisów of 50-60 Russian tanks, as Schneider claimed in his book.

Then finally, the main point: The source of the original information about the Tigers of Heavy Panzer Battalion 424 that had fallen into an ambush and had been shot up in Lisów from close range by Soviet heavy IS tanks has been found. This was Leutnant Bähr and another leutnant from *2./schwere Panzer-Abteilung 424* who had somehow escaped from their burning tanks and survived. They, obviously, must have been the eyewitnesses of the Leutnant Oberbacht's exploits. As the reader already knows, there were no IS tanks in the Lisów area; there were only the T-34/85 tanks of the 61st Guards Tank Brigade. That's how myths arose, which were snatched up by Goebbel's propaganda during the war, in order to try to justify the destruction of a full-strength Tiger battalion in a matter of a day or two. After the war, this version was picked up by many Western historians during a wave of anti-Sovietism, who pounded into the heads of their readers the notion of the tactical superiority of the Wehrmacht's tankers. It was convenient for the defeated German generals,

A Red Army gun crew in their firing position; winter of 1945.

like, for example, Heinz Guderian and Walther Nehring, to avoid the subject of the complete destruction of Heavy Panzer Battalion 424 in January 1945, since they had no desire to write about their own defeats. At the same time during the Cold War, there was an Iron Curtain operating on the Soviet side; all of the archival documents were strictly classified and were inaccessible to scholars. Thus, in Soviet times, historians of the Second World War had no way to refute these legends on the basis of Soviet documents. Only now, thanks to the possibility of working with previously classified documents that has appeared, the historical truth about these battles is being salvaged, and the long-standing myths in the West are being dispelled. Victory in the meeting tank battle of January 1945 between Colonel-General D.D. Leliushenko's 4th Tank Army and General Walther Nehring's XXIV Panzer Corps in the Kielce area can unquestionably be credited to the Soviet tankers.

Major Boris Kurtsev – commander of the 28th Tank Regiment of the 6th Guards Mechanized Corps' 16th Guards Mechanized Brigade. He skillfully organized the regiment's actions during the breakthrough of the enemy's defenses and when raiding through the enemy's rear areas. Operating as part of the corps' forward detachment, the tank regiment on 12 January 1945, having cut the major Kielce – Kraków railroad, captured the large villages of Zabrody and Bialogon, and two days later was the first to enter the city of Kielce and took it. Developing the further offensive, on 17 January the regiment was the first to force a crossing of the Pilica River and captured the towns of Piotrków and Tuszino on its western bank. Despite being wounded, Major Kurtsev continued to command the regiment and on 19 January was the first to break into the southern outskirts of Łódz. For his model fulfillment of command orders and the courage and heroism he displayed, awarded the title Hero of the Soviet Union.

Captain Vasilii Filatenkov – battalion commander with the 380th Light Artillery Regiment of the 4th Tank Army's 200th Light Artillery Brigade. On 12 January 1945 in the Sandomir bridgehead, his artillerymen supported the breakthrough of the enemy's defenses in the vicinity of Korytnica. For his exemplary fulfillment of the command's combat assignments and the courage and heroism he demonstrated in the process, awarded the title Hero of the Soviet Union.

Heroes of the Soviet Union and distinguished combatants of the 4th Guards Tank Army, January 1945

P.I. Labuz, tank commander in the 61st Guards Tank Brigade's 2nd Tank Battalion and Hero of the Soviet Union; V.S. Petrov, radio operator – machine gunner in the 61st Guards Tank Brigade's 2nd Tank Battalion; M.V. Pobedinsky, platoon commander of T-34/85 tanks of the 61st Guards Tank Brigade's 2nd Tank Battalion; I.V. Sobovlev, reconnaissance scout of the 61st Guards Tank Brigade.

Heroes of the Soviet Union of the 4th Guards Tank Army, January 1945

Left to right: G.A. Nazar'ev, M. Verteletsky, F.Ia. Spekhov and V.A. Makarov.

Left to right: P.I. Tsyganov, N.V. Andriushok, V.G. Ryzhov and L.T. Bykov.

Left to right: B.V. Kurtsev, V.F. Filatenkov, M.V. Remizov and K.A. Savel'ev.

Left to right: I.S. Naborsky, I.P. Gusev, V.S. Tereshchenko and I.F. Zhuzhukin.

Senior Lieutenant Mikhail Remizov – battery commander with the 258th Light Artillery Regiment of the 4th Tank Army's 200th Light Artillery Brigade. Between 12 and 16 January 1945 when breaking through the enemy's deeply-echeloned defenses northwest of Sandomir in Poland, his battery inflicted damage to the enemy in manpower, [thereby] helping the tank and infantry to liberate the town of Kon'ske and to force a crossing of the Oder River in the vicinity of the city of Steinau (present-day Ścinawa in Poland). For his exemplary command of the battery and the personal courage and heroism demonstrated in the process, awarded the title Hero of the Soviet Union.

Senior Sergeant Konstantin Savel'ev – tank gunner of the 28th Tank Regiment of the 6th Guards Mechanized Corps' 16th Guards Mechanized Brigade. On 13 January 1945 in fighting on the approaches to the town of Kielce, the T-34 tank crew of which Senior Sergeant Savel'ev was a member knocked out a Panther tank; destroyed 7 vehicles, 3 halftracks and 2 guns; and eliminated more than 20 enemy soldiers. Between 13 and 15 January, repulsing enemy counterattacks, the tankers set 3 enemy tanks, 3 halftracks and 9 loaded trucks ablaze and killed more than 30 Nazis. Awarded the title Hero of the Soviet Union.

Senior Lieutenant Ivan Naborsky – tank company commander in the 4th Tank Army's 93rd Separate Tank Brigade. In the fighting between 12 and 30 January 1945, when conducting a 600-kilometer raid that included fighting, he demonstrated exceptional daring and ability to command the company in combat. On 17 January, having received an order to capture the town of Sulejów, an important German strongpoint and communications hub, his tank company was the first to enter the town and held it until the approach of our units. In this action he destroyed 2 tanks, 15 armored cars, 10 guns, 20 machine guns, and eliminated 140 enemy soldiers and officers. Awarded the title Hero of the Soviet Union.

Senior Lieutenant Ivan Gusev – tank platoon commander with the 28th Tank Regiment of the 6th Guards Mechanized Corps' 16th Guards Mechanized Brigade. On 13 January 1945 Gusev together with his elements cut both the Kielce – Kraków highway and railroad and seized the Zagrody railroad station. In this combat dozens of Nazis were killed, and 15 vehicles, 7 halftracks and one tank were knocked out or set ablaze. In the course of two days, the platoon held the station, destroying another 5 tanks, 6 halftracks and 15 vehicles, and eliminating a large quantity of enemy personnel. Awarded the title Hero of the Soviet Union.

Guards Lieutenant Leonid Bykov – tank commander with the 28th Tank Regiment of the 6th Guards Mechanized Corps' 16th Guards Mechanized Brigade. In mid-January 1945, the tank platoon that included Bykov's machine was ordered to make an 80-km advance toward the city of Kielce, to conduct reconnaissance, and to spread panic among the retreating Nazis. Of the platoon's 5 tanks, 2 blew up on mines. However, the remaining 3 tanks drove into the depth of the German defenses. Having forded the Czarna Nida River, the 3 tanks approached the Kraków – Kielce highway and spotted an enemy column. Having spread out to create the illusion of a breakthrough by major forces, the 3 tanks opened fire at the column while on the move. Fires began to blaze on the highway – vehicles were burning. At mid-day the reconnaissance group neared the town of Kielce. The mission had been carried out. Soon, the tank regiment came up as well. However, the main forces were still far behind, and the regiment wound up encircled, having taken up a hedgehog defense. The regiment commander handed Bykov a dispatch and ordered him to break out back to the corps and to deliver the dispatch to the commander. When breaking through, Bykov's T-34 crushed 2 enemy anti-tank guns and destroyed 1 tank. Successfully taking advantage of the nighttime darkness, the tank at full speed disappeared from the sight of its pursuers. Soon the sparing words from the dispatch took the form of a route marked out on a map. It was along this route that the avalanche of armor of the corps' main forces set out. Awarded the title Hero of the Soviet Union.

Junior Lieutenant Vasilii Tereshchenko – platoon commander of the 127th Separate Tank Regiment of the 6th Guards Mechanized Corps' 49th Mechanized Brigade. On 15 January 1945 in the fighting north of the village of Poslowice, Kielce area, his tank crew destroyed 4 enemy guns together with their crews, 12 vehicles and killed 40 Nazis. On 16 January 1945 his platoon was the first to break into Samsonów, where in the course of the tank he rammed 2 enemy tanks and set 2 self-propelled guns ablaze. On the northern outskirts of the village his platoon destroyed 60 vehicles together with their military gear and loads, 40 horse-drawn wagons, 3 guns, 3 halftracks and eliminated more than 150 enemy soldiers and officers. When one of his platoon's tanks was knocked out by enemy artillery fire, he evacuated it from the battlefield with his tank and in the course of several hours together with its crew repaired the disabled tank and restored it to service. Awarded the title Hero of the Soviet Union.

Guards Junior Lieutenant Ivan Zhuzhukin – tank commander in the 28th Guards Heavy Tank Regiment of the 4th Tank Army's 6th Guards Mechanized Corps. On 13-14 January 1945 I.F. Zhuzhukin, separate from his regiment, repulsed six counterattacks in the Kielce area, knocked out 7 tanks and destroyed more than 2 enemy platoons. For two days his crew held a line on the Kielce – Chmielnik road in Poland until the approach of the rest of the regiment. He was wounded in action, but continued fighting. For his exemplary fulfillment of combat orders and for the courage and heroism he demonstrated in the process, awarded the title Hero of the Soviet Union.

Guards Junior Lieutenant Petr Tsyganov – tank platoon commander with the 1st Tank Battalion of the 10th Guards Tank Corps' 63rd Guards Tank Brigade. On 15 January 1945, operating in the advanced point, Tsyganov forded the Czarna Nida River in the Morawica area (south of the town of Kielce). His platoon was one of the first to break into the town of Chęciny, destroying in the process an enemy rocket launcher. In the street fighting his crew destroyed two more enemy tanks. When their T-34 was knocked out, the tankers, having bailed out of their machine, engaged enemy infantry in combat. Cut off from friendly tanks, the Guardsmen headed by the wounded Tsyganov experienced an improbably difficult close combat action until they were rescued by the tanks of their comrades-in-arms that had hurried to the scene. For the exemplary fulfillment of combat orders and for the courage demonstrated, awarded the title Hero of the Soviet Union.

Guards Sergeant Georgii Nazar'ev – a submachine gun squad leader with the 6th Guards Mechanized Corps' 17th Guards Mechanized Brigade. For the courage and heroism demonstrated in the fighting, awarded the title Hero of the Soviet Union.

Guards Sergeant Vasilii Isakov – squad leader in the 10th Guards Tank Corps' 29th Guards Motorized Rifle Brigade. Posthumously awarded the title Hero of the Soviet Union.

Guards Sergeant Major Ivan Nikonov – commander of a squadron of halftracks of the reconnaissance platoon of the headquarters company of the 10th Guards Tank Corps' 62nd Guards Tank Brigade. On 13 January 1945 together with the soldiers assigned to him, the platoon broke through to a bridge across the Czarna Nida River in the area of the settlement of Morawica, located 13 km south of the town of Kielce, and conducted combat reconnaissance until the next day. The enemy managed to surround the bravehearts. Nikonov, having climbed into a German Tiger heavy tank together with soldiers of his squadron, drove back furious counterattacks until the arrival of the tank brigade. In the unequal struggle, the reconnaissance men killed more than 100 Nazis. Awarded the title Hero of the Soviet Union. Nikonov eventually took part in the Victory Parade on Red Square in Moscow in June 1945.

Sergeant Nikolai Andriushok – gunner with the 1995th Anti-aircraft Artillery Regiment of the 4th Tank Army's 68th Anti-aircraft Artillery Division. In the vicinity of the village of Poslowice, located 6 km southwest of the town of Kielce, on 15 January 1945 his battery was subjected to an attack by two infantry battalions and tanks. Using his anti-aircraft cannon to fire at ground targets, the fearless gunner personally destroyed a tank and wiped out a lot of Nazis. For the exemplary fulfillment of combat orders and for the heroism and courage demonstrated in the process, awarded the title Hero of the Soviet Union.

Guards Major Vladimir Ryzhov – commander of the 3rd Motorized Rifle Battalion of the 6th Guards Mechanized Corps' 16th Guards Mechanized Brigade. On 13 January 1945, the battalion entrusted to Ryzhov broke through the enemy defenses in the vicinity of the town of Kielce, and having cut the Kielce – Kraków highway and railroad, skillfully maneuvering, destroyed 13 enemy tanks, 8 halftracks, 17 guns, 36 vehicles and killed up to 200 Nazi soldiers and officers. For the exemplary fulfillment of combat orders and for the courage and heroism demonstrated in the process, awarded the title Hero of the Soviet Union.

Guards Colonel Nikolai Zhukov – commander of the 10th Guards Tank Corps' 61st Guards Tank Brigade. Commanding the brigade during combat operations, he showed himself to be a bold officer. Over the time of the corps' combat operations, from 12 January 1945 he was always located up in the brigade's combat formations, skillfully handling the brigade's fighting and doing great damage to the enemy. On 13 January he fell bravely in battle. During the lastest fighting in the Lisów area, the brigade destroyed 5 Tiger tanks, 3 self-propelled guns and killed up to 200 enemy soldiers and officers. Posthumously awarded the Order of the Patriotic War 1st Class.

Guards Senior Lieutenant Mikhail Verteletsky – commander of a company of T-34 tanks with the 2nd tank Battalion of the 10th Guards Tank Corps' 61st Guards Tank Brigade. Skillfully commanding the company and taking good advantage of the terrain, in the fighting for the village of Lisów on 13 January 1945 his company destroyed 6 Tiger tanks, 1 King Tiger, 3 halftracks, up to 25 vehicles and killed more than 150 enemy soldiers and officers, with insignificant losses in personnel and equipment of their own. Awarded the Order of the Patriotic War 1st Class.

Guards Senior Lieutenant Mikhail Pobedinsky – commander of a platoon of T-34 tanks in the 2nd Tank Battalion of the 10th Guards Tank Corps' 61st Guards Tank Brigade. In the fighting for the village of Lisów on 13 January 1945, together with his crew he destroyed 1 Tiger tank, 1 King Tiger, 2 halftracks, up to 25 vehicles, 2 antitank guns and killed up to 70 Nazis. Pobedinsky through his personal valor and courage served as an example in the battle for the remaining soldiers. Having broken into Lisów first, he personally killed 18 enemy soldiers and officers. Worthy of being awarded the Order of the Red Banner. Awarded the Order of the Patriotic War 1st Class.

Guards Senior Lieutenant Vladimir Markov – deputy commander of the 2nd Tank Battalion of the 10th Guards Tank Corps' 61st Guards Tank Brigade. From the initiation of combat operations on 12 January 1945, he was always located with the reconnaissance group of tanks. On 13 January 1945 Markov and 3 T-34 tanks reached the settlement of Lisów, having the mission to occupy its northern outskirts and to repulse possible enemy counterattacks. On this same day, the enemy in strength of 17 tanks, 10 halftracks and up to a battalion of infantry went on the counterattack, striving to take Lisów and the crossroads. Markov appealed over the radio to the tank crews: "Comrade Guardsmen, we will stand to the death, but shall not let the enemy pass!" In the course of the attack by superior enemy forces and a fierce artillery barrage, some of the crewmen showed a lack of resolve, but Markov through his personal example and skillful handling of the battle held these machines in their positions. Running from tank to tank and conducting accurate fire from the cannons, he inspired the tankers to an unprecedented level of tenacity. Twelve enemy attacks were repulsed. The road hub was held until the arrival of the brigade's main forces, which ensured the successful advance of the army's remaining units. In this combat the enemy lost 10 Tiger tanks, 3 King Tiger tanks, 8 halftracks, 4 antitank guns, 30 vehicles and up to two companies of infantry. On the night of 14-15 January 1945 Markov and 7 tanks with a sudden attack from the flank seized the important road hub of Promnik, which cut the German Kielce grouping's path of retreat. The Germans in this action lost 2 Tigers, 6 Panthers, 4 Pz.Kpfw. IV, 70 vehicles and up to 1400 soldiers and officers. Simultaneously commanding the tank riders, whose officer was knocked out of action, Markov personally killed up to 70 Nazis. In this combat action he was wounded, but refused to leave the battlefield and continued to carry out his combat orders. Put up for the title Hero of the Soviet Union. Awarded the Order of the Red Banner.

Guards Sergeant Aron Kokaev – gun loader of a T-34 tank of the 2nd Tank Battalion of the 10th Guards Tank Corps' 61st Guards Tank Brigade. In the fighting for the village of Lisów on 13 January 1945 as part of his crew he destroyed 1 tank, 2 halftracks, and killed up to 30 Nazis. In the combat for the village of Promnik on 15 January 1945 as part of his crew he destroyed 4 tanks and up to 20 vehicles, 2 halftracks, and killed up to 100 Nazis. He was killed in action in this battle. Posthumously awarded the Order of the Patriotic War 1st Class.

Guards Junior Lieutenant Nikolai Kliuev – commander of a T-34/85 tank with the 3rd Tank Battalion of the 10th Guards Tank Corps' 61st Guards Tank Brigade. On 13 January 1945 during the defense of the village of Lisów (Poland) he courageously fought against numerically superior enemy tanks, but took no step back, destroying 1 Tiger tank. He bravely perished in this battle together with his crew. Posthumously awarded the Order of the Patriotic War 1st Class.

Guards Lieutenant Fedor Strausov – commander of a T-34/85 tank of the 61st Guards Tank Brigade's 2nd Tank Battalion. In the fighting for the village of Lisów on 13 January 1945, as part of his crew he destroyed 1 tank and wiped out more than 20 Nazis. On 17 January 1945 while on reconnaissance, in the vicinity of the village of Stąporków, together with his crew he destroyed 2 antitank guns, 1 mortar and a number of Nazis. Through his energetic and capable conducting of reconnaissance, he ensured the enemy's rapid defeat. Awarded the Order of the Patriotic War 1st Class.

Guards Lieutenant Spandiiarov – commander of a T-34/85 tank with the 2nd Tank Battalion of the 10th Guards Tank Corps' 61st Guards Tank Brigade. In the combat for Lisów on 13 January 1945, together with is crew he destroyed 2 tanks, 3 vehicles and eliminated 35 Nazis. On 15 January 1945 in the fighting for the village of Promnik, together with his crew he destroyed 1 tank, 10 vehicles, and killed 125 enemy soldiers and officers. Awarded the Order of the Patriotic War 1st Class.

Guards Major Mikhail Grachev – commander of the 29th Separate Tank Regiment of the 6th Guards Mechanized Corps. On 13 January 1945, the 29th Separate Tank Regiment was introduced into a breakthrough in the Zaguże area as a regiment of support and to develop the success of the 17th Guards Mechanized Brigade. Thanks to the capable and hard-charging leadership of the regiment on the part of Grachev, the regiment on 14 January 1945, having made a deep penetration into the enemy's combat ranks, was the first to arrive in the Zaguże (Poland) area, where it repulsed two enemy counterattacks in strength of up to a battalion of infantry with the support of 12 tanks and 8 halftracks. Continuing the offensive, advancing well ahead of the corps' main forces and in the absence of infantry and artillery, thanks to impetuous actions the regiment captured a major enemy strongpoint of resistance in Stąporków, and in the course of the next two days drove back enemy counterattacks with numerically superior forces, and maintained possession of Stąporków while screening the corps' and army's right flank. Over the period of combat operations the regiment destroyed 6 Tiger tanks, 10 Panthers, 4 Pz.Kpfw. IV tanks, 23 halftracks, 4 self-propelled guns, more than 600 vehicles, and eliminated up to 1200 enemy soldiers and officers. Grachev was bold and decisive in combat, and in difficult moments of the fighting inspired all the men with his personal example. For his skillful leadership of the regiment and the personal bravery demonstrated, he was nominated for the Order of Suvorov 3rd Class. Awarded the Order of the Red Banner.

Guards Major Il'ia Slutsky – commander of the 10th Guards Tank Corps' 1222nd Self-propelled Artillery Regiment. During the regiment's combat operations since 12 January 1945, he showed himself to be a bold, decisive and tactically literate officer. On 13 January 1945 in the Maleszowa area the regiment repulsed three counterattacks made by enemy infantry and tanks, while inflicting heavy losses in manpower and tanks. The regiment, going over to the attack, broke the enemy resistance and in cooperation with the 61st Guards Tank Brigade took up to 100 villages. In the vicinity of Wola Morawiczka, an enemy column of up to 60 vehicles carrying infantry and equipment was destroyed by the regiment. Over the period of combat the regiment destroyed 3 artillery batteries, 2 Tiger tanks together with their crews, and killed up to 300 Nazis. Nominated for the Order of Suvorov 3rd Class. Awarded with the Order of the Red Banner.

Guards Lieutenant Colonel Vasilii Zaitsev – commander of the 10th Guards Tank Corps' 61st Guards Tank Brigade. From the start of combat operations on 12 January 1945, while still serving as the brigade's chief of staff, he managed to work out properly the plan of the brigade's introduction into the breakthrough and ensured the timely delivery of the order to the units and elements. On 13 January 1945, when the brigade commander was killed in action in the village of Lisów, he assumed command of the brigade. Always located up among the combat formations, he skillfully directed the fighting, and boldly led the brigade in the combat. The brigade inflicted the following losses to the enemy: more than 1,000 soldiers and officers, up to 35 machine-gun nests, 47 tanks, 50 halftracks, 25 armored cars, up to 450 vehicles, while suppressing the fire of up to 60 artillery batteries. For his exemplary carrying out of the command's orders and for the demonstrated courage and heroism, awarded the title Hero of the Soviet Union.

Guards Junior Lieutenant Il'ia Marinin – commander of a T-34/85 tank with the 2nd Tank Battalion of the 10th Guards Tank Corps' 61st Guards Tank Brigade. In the fighting for the village of Lisów on 13 January 1945, he destroyed 1 Panther, 1 Pz.Kpfw. IV tank, 2 halftracks, 7 vehicles, and eliminated up to 30 enemy soldiers and officers. He behaved daringly, with no regard for his own life, in order to achieve victory over the foe. While bravely directing his tank, he was killed in this battle. Posthumously awarded the Order of the Patriotic War 1st Class.

Conclusions regarding the conducted operation

1. The 4th Tank Army's rapid advance to the west yielded its fruits. The enemy didn't have time to take up defensive fortificationa on the Kielce – Chmielnik line with his operational reserves.
2. The direction of the army's operations was properly chosen, which played a large role in the success. The arrival of the army's formations and units in the Lisów – Chałupki area split the enemy's operational reserves that were positioned on this axis.
3. Facing the fact of a breakthrough of the defenses, as a result of the powerful artillery preparation, the rapid advance made by our forces, and the heavy casualties suffered by the enemy'frontline units, the enemy was unable to make an organized withdrawal to the second line of defense.
4. The commitment of the operational reserves consisting of the XXIV Panzer Corps had no success. Having previously-prepared intermediate defensive lines, the enemy, in view of the unavailability of troops to hold these lines, couldn't organize a defense and prevent our forces from advancing. Putting up strong resistance in prepared major strongpoints that had been adapted for an all-round defense, and being bypassed and isolated from friendly forces, the enemy was unable to hold these strongpoints for an extended period of time and ended up destroyed. Lacking adequate operational reserves and committing hastily-assembled various training, reserve and security battalions, as well as Volksturm battalion, into battle in a piecemeal fashion, the enemy was unable to organize proper resistance, and his designated elements were destroyed from the march by our forces.

4

Combat operations of the 5th Guards Tank Army in East Prussia (14 January–28 February 1945)

The overall situation at the front

Northeast of Warsaw, the front lines by 10 January 1945 ran along the Narew River; in the areas north and south of Pułtusk, the forces of the 2nd Belorussian Front were holding two previously established bridgeheads. The ground between the southern border of East Prussia and the Vistula River, by both the nature of the terrain and by the flanking locations of the border fortifications of Poland and East Prussia presented a natural corridor for the effective maneuvering of large tank and mechanized formations in a direction to the west toward Thorn (Toruń), and to the northwest in the direction of Mława and Marienburg. For the last several months, the front along the Narew River was stable. The enemy, awaiting an offensive by the 2nd Belorussian Front, used the time to improve the old and recently-constructed defensive lines and strongpoints, in particular by converting all the town and a majority of the larger villages into local strongpoints adapted for an all-round defense, with strong fortifications (trenches, antitank ditches, and barriers). As a result of this work, by the start of the January 1945 operation, the enemy had created a deeply-echeloned system of defenses, which extended for more than 200 km along the entire northern part of Poland and East Prussia, which consisted of seven developed and completed defensive lines and several switch positions, and included a multitude of knots of resistance and local strongpoints.

East Prussia and the northern part of Poland were being covered by the forces of the German Fourth, Second and Third Panzer Armies, which were all subordinate to Army Group Center. They had the overall task of a rigid defense, with the assignment to prevent at any cost a breakthrough by the Russian forces between East Prussia and the northern part of Poland to the lower reaches of the Vistula River. The commander-in-chief of Army Group Center Colonel General Rheinhardt and his headquarters were located in Ortelsburg (Szczytno).

On the axis bordered on the north by the border of East Prussia and on the left by the lower course of the Vistula River, Army Group Center was defending with a strong grouping consisting of the Fourth Army's LV Army Corps, which was holding defensive positions north of Ostrołęka; and the Second Army's XX, XXIII and XXVII Army Corps, which were in positions that extended for 94 km from Ostrołęka to the southwest as far as the Vistula. The defending Germans had an average operational density of one infantry division per 11 kilometers of the front.

The XX Army Corps included the 14th, 292nd and 129th Infantry Divisions; the XXIII Army Corps commanded the 299th and 7th Infantry Divisions and the 5th Jäger Division; the XXVII Army Corps included the 35th, 252nd and 541nd Infantry Divisions. The commander of the Second Army was Colonel General Weiß. His headquarters was in Szreńsk.

The enemy's operational and strategic reserves

In the latter half of December 1944, the Germans had four panzer divisions (the 6th, 3rd, 3rd SS and 5th SS Panzer Divisions) and up to six infantry divisions in reserve on this operational axis. Given the presence of such a powerful panzer grouping and the deeply-echeloned system of defenses, the enemy had the possibility with active defensive operations to defend the territory of northern Poland stubbornly. However, the successful offensive by the forces of the 2nd and 3rd Ukrainian Fronts in Hungary forced the German high command to regroup its operational and strategic reserves. Confident in the strength of their elaborate fortified lines in East Prussia and northern Poland and the possibility of successfully holding them with fewer forces, the German command considered it possible to remove the four above-indicated panzer divisions from northern Poland and the 20th Panzer Division from East Prussia, as well as one cavalry brigade and two infantry divisions (the 211th and 708th Infantry Divisions), and shift them hastily to Hungary.

This was one of the major blunders by the German high command, which eventually cost it dearly. At the same time, it must be acknowledged that this enemy mistake significantly eased the conditions for the forces of the 2nd Belorussian Front in carrying out their orders as part of the January offensive, especially for the 5th Guards Tank Army.

Immediately prior to the January offensive launched by the 2nd Belorussian Front, in place of the divisions that had been sent to Hungary, the command of Army Group Center as part of an internal regrouping shifted the 7th Panzer Division from East Prussia to the vicinity of Ciechanów in northern Poland into the reserve of the Second Army; a portion of the Panzergrenadier Division *Grossdeutschland* to the area of Krasnosielc; and the fusilier regiment from Panzer Corps *Grossdeutschland* to the Przasnysz area. Units of the 18th Panzergrenadier Division were in the process of shifting from East Prussia to the Mława area. The 7th Panzer Division and the Panzergrenadier Division *Grossdeutschland* had been sent from the Königsberg area before completing the process of re-equipping and replenishing after the fighting on the Memel axis.

Other German reserves that might have an influence on the actions of the 5th Guards Tank Army in the depth of the enemy's defenses, were assembled: a) in the Mława area – a training center for self-propelled artillery that had up to 70 self-propelled guns and tanks, a storm regiment of the Second Army, and Panzerjäger Abteilung 474; b) in the Gołmin Stary area – Heavy Panzer Abteilung 507; in the Szrensk area – up to 8,000 men that were forming up; d) in Deutsh Eylau – the 461st Reserve Division; and e) in the Mewe area (Gniew, 40 km north of Graudenz [Grudziądz] – an infantry division.

The enemy grouping directly opposite the sector where the 5th Guards Tank Army was introduced into the breach

Three German infantry divisions were defending the sector where the 5th Guards Tank Army was introduced into the breakthrough and on its closest flanks, in the Dąbrówka, Maków, Pultusk sector that extended for 33 kilometers:

a) in the Dąbrówka, Orzyc River sector that extended for 10 kilometers – the 299th Infantry Division and Pioneer Battalion 475, reinforced by StuG Brigade 209, the 1st Artillery Regiment, two artillery battalions, and elements of Mortar Regiment 57;
b) in the Orzyc River, Glodowo sector that extended for 11 kilometers – the 7th Infantry Division and Construction Battalion 80, reinforced with StuG Brigade 185, Artillery Regiment 63, one battalion of Artillery Regiment 109, two battalions of an unidentified artillery regiment, and elements of Mortar Regiment 57;

c) in the Glodow, Pultusk sector that extended for 12 kilometers – the 5th Jäger Division and Pioneer-Construction Battalion 745, reinforced with one battalion of Artillery Regiment 47, Artillery Battalions 316 and 603; and elements of Mortar Regiment 57.

Altogether on a front of 33 kilometers, the enemy had 24 infantry battalions and 8 specialized battalions. On the forward edge of the defense, of the total number of 32 battalions, the enemy had 16 battalions, supported by 24 battalions of artillery. In the regimental and divisional reserves, of the total number of 32 battalions, the enemy had 16 battalions (or 50% of the total); as means of reinforcements, the Germans in this sector of the front had two assault gun brigades and 36 self-propelled artillery vehicles.

On average, each infantry battalion was occupying a frontage of 2.1 kilometers. For each kilometer of the front (including divisional reserves), the enemy had between 440 and 550 men, or 500 combat troops on average; between 44 and 67 heavy and light machine guns, or 55 machine guns on average; and 6 to 8 mortars.

The density of artillery (including antitank guns, field artillery and self-propelled artillery, but not including Flak artillery) varied between 14 guns per kilometer of front to 23 guns per kilometer of front, and together with mortars – between 20 to 30 guns and mortars per kilometer of front. The defenses were strongest surrounding the bridgehead north of Pultusk, in the sectors being held by the 299th and 7th Infantry Divisions. The defenses were weakest on the flanks of the bridgehead, which were protected by a water obstacle, the Narew River.

Of the operational reserves of the enemy's Second Army, which might offer serious resistance to the 5th Guards Tank Army during its introduction into the breach and its subsequent actions in the depth of the enemy's defenses, these included: a) unts of the Panzergrenadier Division *Grossdeutschland*, which were positioned in the Krasnosielc and Przasnysz areas and had up to 70 panzers and self-propelled guns; b) the 7th Panzer Division, positioned in the Ciechanów area, which had 80 panzers and 40 self-propelled guns available; c) the Mława training grounds for self-propelled artillery, which had up to 70 armored fighting vehicles; and d) Heavy Panzer Battalion 507, which was positioned in Gołmin Stary and had 32 Tigers.

From the materials of the 2nd Belorussian Front's intelligence command and the Intelligence Department of the 5th Guards Tank Army's headquarters cited above, it was possible to come to the conclusion that the command of the enemy's Army Group Center and the Second Army, which lacked sufficiently strong operational reserves, had based their plans on a rigid defense of the occupied front, counting upon the strength of the combat formations of the frontline divisions (by bringing them up to a strength of 8,000 to 10,000 men and attaching powerful assets to them). At the same time, they were overestimating the significance of their deeply-echeloned system of elaborate defensive lines, switch positions and strongpoints. The latter might be a serious obstacle in the path of our forces' advance only in the event of their timely occupation by significant forces moved out of the reserves up to the front. This fact doesn't speak to any ingenious arrangement of the combat positions of their forces by the German command to offer a stiff defense against the contemporary means of an offensive, but suggests the tactics of a positional defense of 1915-1918 in the First World War.

General characteristics of the terrain

The ground on the territory of northern Poland, north of the Vistula River, presents a flat plain with low undulations, cut by the valleys of rivers and streams that flow primarily in a southern direction. The most elevated and hilly terrain is on the territory adjacent to East Prussia and in the southwestern portion of East Prussia – in the Deutsch Eylau and Osterode area. Not more than 10 to 20 percent of the land is covered by woods, primarily coniferous.

On the approaches to the southern border of East Prussia on the Chorzele, Mława, Sierpc line there was a stretch of extremely swampy moors that was up to 40 kilometers wide. Small rivers from 3 to 10 meters wide flowing across the axis of the 5th Guards Tank Army's pending offensive, such as the Sonia, the Łydynia, the Dzialdowka and others in wintry conditions didn't present particularly serious obstacles for tanks.

A distinguishing feature of the land of western East Prussia and northern Poland is the presence of a large number of lakes, big and small, into which numerous small streams with boggy banks flow. Some of these streams have been directed into land-reclamation canals, which by their form and dimensions are similar to antitank ditches, with a width of 3 to 5 meters, a depth of 1.5 to 2 meters, and slopes of 70°. These do present a serious obstacle for the movement of tanks. The area has a well-developed road network. The main roads and bridges were in good condition.

In general, the terrain in northern Poland, with the exception of the Mława area with its swamps and moors, was rated as suitable for mechanized forces. The terrain in western East Prussia right up to the coastline of the Baltic Sea (as a consequence of the large number of lakes and the narrow defiles between them, as well as the multitude of narrow streams with boggy banks and the drainage canals) is amenable for the actions of small elements of mechanized forces, but creates great difficulties for the deployment of large tank forces and constrain their broad maneuvering, while at the same time is convenient for organizing ambushes with tanks and anti-tank artillery, and for defending with small forces.

The enemy's system of defensive lines

In the northern part of Poland and the southwestern part of East Prussia, by 10 January 1945 the enemy had created a deeply-echeloned system of defenses that extended for more than 200 kilometers, and consisted of highly developed fortified defensive lines, switch positions and strongpoints. The overwhelming majority of these lines had been built within the previous 18 months. The local Polish population and the labour from other occupied countries that had been forcibly removed to Germany were widely used on the defensive works. The defensive lines were as follows:

1. The first defensive line ran along the western bank of the Narew River and was most strongly developed opposite our bridgeheads north and south of Pultusk. This line was of the field type. It consisted of 2-4 trenchlines (depending on the sectors of terrain) with an elaborate system of communication trenches and numerous bunkers and dugouts, with up to 20 machine-gun positions per kilometer of front. This line was developed with a depth of 4-6 km, had antitank ditches in separate sectors, and was protected by minefields and 3-4 rows of barbed wire.
2. The second defensive line ran at a distance of 8-15 km from the first line along the Itaka, Kadzidlo, Krasnosielc, 4 km west of Maków, Gołmyn Stary, east of Nasielsk line, and was anchored on the Narew River west of Dębe. This line was also of the field type, consisting of two lines of full-profile trenches with machine-gun nests, bunkers and communication trenches. In separate sectors it had minefields and barbed wire obstacles. On the Przasnysz axis, the line was strengthened by a water obstacle – the Orzysza River. The first and second defensive lines were linked along their entire extent by switch positions, consisting of trenches, earth-and-timber bunkers, and antitank ditches.
3. The third defensive line ran along the line: Budki (4 km southeast of Chorzele), Mchowo, 3 km west of Przasnysz, 10 km east of Ciechanów, Nowe Miasto, and further along to the Vistula River. This line was also of the field type, consisted of 2-4 trenches linked by communication trenches, and was furnished with bunkers and machine-gun positions. From Cieachanów to as far as the Dziazdowa River (a distance of approximately 50 km), there was a continuous

antitank ditch. There were small intermediate lines and switch positions between the send and third defensive lines, which primarily consisted of one or two lines of trenches.

A characteristic detail of the construction of all of the numerous switch positions that were present between the first, second and third defensives lines was the fact that as a rule they presented the defending German troops the possibility of creating tactical traps, in which the attacking tanks would come under flanking fire from antitank artillery, and the accompanying infantry would be exposed to attacks from the flanks.

The cities of Przasnysz and Ciechanów, like all the other towns, had been adapted for an all-round defense ringed by three to five continuous trenches and an antitank ditch that encircled the entire town. The third defensive line was in essence the rear line of the tactical zone of defense, but this time the enemy didn't limit himself to these three lines and in the operational depth created an entire array of lines and defensive positions.

4. The fourth defensive line ran from Janowo through the heavily-fortified Mława strongpoint to Strzegowo and Plonsk. The construction of this line began in August 1944, and it was less developed in comparison with the first three defensive lines.

   The city of Mława represented a powerful strongpoint, which had the task of blocking the immediate approaches to East Prussia from the south. It combined the old Polish border permanent works, which the Germans had reversed in the southeastern direction with supplementary fortifications of the field type built in 1944. The Mława strongpoint consisted of four rings of trenches. The outer ring had been thrown up with a 20-km salient to the southeast. On the northern and western sides of the town, the outer ring of trenches lay 8 km outside the city. The trenches were linked by communication trenches and had a large quantity of bunkers, gunports, and machine-gun and artillery positions. Between the trenches, two antitank ditches had been dug with a width of 3.5 meters and a depth of 2.5 meters.

5. The fifth defensive line ran along the southern border of East Prussia on the line: Neidenburg (Nidzica), Neide River, Działdowka River to Liubowidze, Skrwilno, Sierpc, Plock. This was a line of a field type with the use of a water obstacle, and consisted of three lines of trenches. There was an antitank ditch that was 5-meters wide in the Sierps – Plock sector.

6. The sixth line of defense ran along the Marienburg, Jablonowo, Brodnica, northwestern bank of the Drwęca River as far as Thorn. This line had three lines of trenches and had pillboxes in separate sectors.

7. The seventh defensive line ran along the western bank of the Vistula River from Danzig to Thorn.

The 5th Guards Tank Army didn't have to make the effort to overcome the sixth and seventh lines of defenses, since from the Neidenburg, Działdowo line its combat path pivoted to the north, into western East Prussia.

In addition to these primary defensive lines and switch positions, the enemy created numerous powerful centers of resistance in both northern Poland and in East Prussia, having converted all the towns into local strongpoints with extensive all-round defensive fortifications: Przasnysz, Ciechanów, Grudusk, Mława, Napierki (15 km north of Mława), Neidenburg, Działdowo, Hilgenberg, Lubawa (Lübau), Osterode, Deutsch Eylau, Libem, Liebemühl, Saalfeld, Mohrungen, Preußisch Holland, Elbing, and Frauenburg. Before the start of the operation, not all of the above listed defensive lines and strongpoints were known by the Red Army command; many of them were revealed by reconnaissance and fighting in the course of the operation itself and were checked by a special commission sent out by the headquarters of the 5th Guards Tank Army at the end of the operation, which made up to 60 photographs.

The status of the 5th Guards Tank Army at the start of the operation

By the start of the operation, on 14 January 1945 the 5th Guards Tank Army had the following armaments and manpower:

Table 4.1: Armaments and manpower of the 5th Guards Tank Army on 14 January 1945

Armaments	29th Tank Corps	10th Tank Corps	47th Mechanized Brigade	Units directly subordinate to Army HQ	21st Motorized Engineer Brigade	Total
T-34	128	107	-	5	-	240
Mk-IX	2	-	-	-	-	2
M4A2	19	10	35	10	-	74
IS-122	-	-	-	29	-	29
SU-152	42	-	-	24	-	66
SU-122	-	-	-	20	-	20
SU-100	-	42	-	-	-	42
SU-85	25	21	-	1	-	47
SU-76	44	21	-	-	-	65
100-mm guns	-	-	-	18	-	18
76-mm guns	33	30	11	47	-	121
57-mm guns	21	20	12	31	-	84
85-mm A-A guns	-	-	-	18	-	18
37-mm A-A guns	6	15	-	72	-	93
DShK/large caliber MGs	29/68	28/52	9/16	48/22	3/0	117/158
M-13 rocket launchers	9	8	-	32	-	49
120-mm mortars	25	28	6	-	-	59
82-mm mortars	36	32	26	9	-	103
Anti-tank rifles	24	89	44	54	6	217
Heavy MGs	26	32	34	11	3	106
Light MGs	64	91	62	63	29	309
Submachine guns	2638	3232	1141	1967	332	9310
Rifles	2591	3754	954	2775	353	10427
Motorcycles	-	-	-	171	-	171
Vehicles	756	1015	338	697	131	2937
Manpower						
Officers	1790	1694	385	1003	111	4983
Non-commissioned officers	2916	3531	1278	2836	236	11297
Rank and file	5722	6126	1882	4883	851	18854
Total:	11428	11351	3545	7622	1199	35144

The command staff of the 5th Guards Tank Army at that time included:

The field command of the army
Commander – Colonel General of Tank Forces V.T. Vol'sky
Military Council member – Major General of Tank Forces P.G. Grishin
Deputy commander – Lieutenant General of Tank Forces M.D. Sinenko
Second deputy commander – Lieutenant General of Tank Forces D.T. Zaev

Chief of staff – Major General of Tank Forces G.S. Sidorovich
Operations chief – Guards Colonel Fedorov
Intelligence chief – Colonel S.I. Fridman
Chief of the Political Department – Colonel A.M. Kostylev
Artillery commander – Major General I.V. Vladimirov
Assistant commander for technical matters – Engineer Colonel F.I. Galkin
Chief of rear services – Major General S.S. Potapov

The 5th Guards Tank Army's formations
10th Tank Corps
Corps commander – Major General of Tank Forces M.G. Sakhno
Chief of staff – Colonel O.M. Omiulisty
Chief of the Political Department – Colonel N.P. Storozhenko
178th Tank Brigade – Colonel I.V. Polukarov
183rd Tank Brigade – Colonel N.S. Grishin
186th Tank Brigade – Colonel D.A. Gnezdilov
11th Motorized Rifle Brigade – Colonel I.A. Shimanovsky
381st Guards Self-propelled Artillery Regiment (SU-100) – Guards Lieutenant Colonel F.P. Shiriaev
1450th Self-propelled Artillery Regiment (SU-85) – Lieutenant Colonel L.M. Lebedev
1207th Self-propelled Artillery Regiment (SU-100) – Captain S.G. Kursukov
727th Self-propelled Artillery Regiment (SU-76) – Major A.V. Belykh
Also, the 705th Light Artillery Regiment, the 287th Mortar Regiment, the 1693rd Anti-aircraft Artillery Regiment, the 128th Separate Guards Mortar Battalion and the 77th Separate Motorcycle Battalion.

29th Tank Corps
Commander – Major General of Tank Forces K.M. Malakhov
Chief of staff – Colonel V.I. Smirnov
Chief of the Political Department – Lieutenant Colonel D.G. Gromov
25th Tank Brigade – Colonel I.O. Stanislavsky
31st Tank Brigade – Lieutenant Colonel A.I. Pokolov
32nd Tank Brigade – Lieutenant Colonel S.G. Kolesnikov (KIA 1 February 1945)
53rd Motorized Rifle Brigade – Lieutenant Colonel N.A. Safonov
332nd Guards Heavy Self-propelled Artillery Regiment (SU-152) – Guards Lieutenant Colonel I.V. Utkin
365th Guards Heavy Self-propelled Artillery Regiment (SU-152) – Guards Lieutenant Colonel Ia.G. Larochkin
1446th Self-propelled Artillery Regiment (SU-85) – Lieutenant Colonel I.M. Lutsenko
1223rd Self-propelled Artillery Regiment (SU-76) – Lieutenant Colonel A.S. Shchevaev
Also, the 165th Light Artillery Regiment, the 271st Mortar Regiment, the 409th Separate Guards Mortar Battalion and the 75th Separate Motorcycle Battalion

Units directly subordinate to the Army
47th Mechanized Brigade – Lieutenant Colonel N.M. Chernyshov
21st Motorized Engineer Brigade – Lieutenant Colonel V.A. Troitsky
Also, the 1st Separate Guards Motorcycle Regiment, the 201st Separate Light Artillery Brigade (651st Cannon Artillery Regiment, 1315th and 1619th Light Artillery Regiments), the 376th Heavy Self-propelled Artillery Regiment, the 14th Guards Heavy Tank Regiment, the 689th Destroyer Anti-tank Artillery Regiment, the 76th Guards Mortar Regiment, the 6th Anti-aircraft Artillery Division, and the 249th Reserve Battalion.

Command staff of the 2nd Belorussian Front and the 5th Guards Tank Army, January 1945]

Left to right: K.K. Rokossovsky, A.N. Bogoliubov, N.E. Subbotin and M.L. Cherniavsky.

Left to right: V.T. Vol'sky, M.D. Sinenko, General P.G. Grishin and Head of Polical Department of the 5th Guards Tank Army A.M. Kostylev

Left to right: D.I. Zaev, G.S. Sidorovich, M.G. Sakhno, K.M. Malakhov.

Left to right: A.I. Pokolov, S.G. Kolesnikov, K.S. Kolganov, F.I. Galkin.

5th Guards Tank Army in the East Prussian operation, 1945

In the headquarters of the 5th Guards Tank Army. Army commander V.T. Vol'sky is in the center. (TsAMO)

The commander of the 5th Guards Tank Army Colonel General of Tank Forces V.T. Vol'sky takes a phone call at his desk. (TsAMO)

Before the start of the operation, the 5th Guards Tank Army had 585 tanks and self-propelled guns in formation. The amount of service hours remaining on the engines in the combat machines was: from 0 to 30 hours – 6 machines; from 30 to 50 hours – 10 machines; from 50 to 75 hours – 65 machines; from 75 to 100 hours – 170 machines; from 100 to 160 hours: 269 machines; from 160 to 200 hours: 65 machines. Altogether 251 machines had less than 100 service hours left on their engines, or 43 percent of all the available combat machines. The average lifetime left on an engine was equal to 145 service hours.

The correlation of forces in the offensive sector of the 5th Guards Tank Army prior to its commitment into the breakthrough on 14 January 1945

The 5th Guards Tank Army was introduced into the breakthrough at the boundary between the attacking 48th Army and 2nd Shock Army on the offensive's fourth day. The table below gives the correlation of the armored forces between the 5th Guards Tank Army and the enemy's formations and units in the sector of the 5th Guards Tank Army's offensive:

Table 4.2: The comparative strength in tanks and self-propelled guns between the 5th Guards Tank Army and the defending enemy units

5th Guards Tank Army Formations and units	Tanks	S-P guns	Total	German forces Formations and units	Tanks	S-P guns	Total
29th Tank Corps	149	111	260	299.Infanterie Division (Pz. Jg. Abt.)	-	12	12
10th Tank Corps	117	84	201	StuG Brigade 209	-	32	32
47 Separate Mechanized Brigade	35	-	35	7.Infanterie Division (Pz. Jg. Abt.)	-	12	12
14 Guards Heavy Tank Regiment	29	-	29	StuG Brigade 185	-	33	33
376 Heavy Self-propelled Artillery Regiment	-	24	24	5.Jäger Division (Pz.Jg. Abt.)	-	12	12

5th Guards Tank Army Formations and units	Tanks	S-P guns	Total	German forces Formations and units	Tanks	S-P guns	Total
326 Heavy Self-propelled Artillery Regiment	-	20	20	7.Panzer Division	80	40	120
1 Guards Separate Motorcycle Regiment	10	-	10	Panzer Division *Grossdeutschland*	70	20	90
Army headquarters	5	1	6	Mława training ctr.	20	50	70
				sPanzer Abt. 507	32	-	32
Total:	345	240	585	Total:	202	146	413

From the table it is obvious that in the sector of the 5th Guards Tank Army's offensive, its advantage in the number of armored fighting vehicles over the enemy was not large. It had only 1.4 times the number of tanks and self-propelled guns than the enemy had. However, the enemy's armored forces were not used simultaneously and in full against the 5th Guards Tank Army, since some of them were tied up in fighting with the neighboring formations during their own successful offensive, especially in the combat for possession of Przasnysz and Ciechanów, and later they were diverted to screen the retreat of their infantry from these towns.

From the combat journal of the 10th Guards Tank Corps

Between 25 December 1944 and 12 January 1945, the corps was receiving replenishments with tanks and self-propelled guns. It also assumed command of the 381st Guards and 1207th Self-propelled Artillery Regiments (with 21 SU-100 in each). By the start of combat operations, the corps numbered 11,343 men, 117 tanks (107 T-34/85 and 10 M4A2) and 104 self-propelled guns (20 ISU-122, 42 SU-100, 21 SU-85 and 21 SU-76).

Because of the shortage of tanks in the tank brigades, each brigade had only two tank battalions. In place of the third battalion, the corps commander attached a self-propelled artillery regiment to each of them. The 178th Tank Brigade received the 381st Guards, the 183rd Tank Brigade received the 1450th, and the 186th Tank Brigade received the 1207th Self-propelled Artillery Regiment.

The SU-100 self-propelled guns, the production of which began in the autumn of 1944, were armed with a 100mm cannon. Its armor-piercing shell was capable of penetrating the armor of any enemy tank. The M4A2, supplied to the USSR through Lend-Lease, had inadequate combat qualities and were unsuitable for combat against the enemy's Tigers and Panthers.

Earl Ziemke in his classic study *Stalingrad to Berlin: The German Defeat in the East*, describes the composition of Army Group Center prior to the 5th Guards Tank Army's offensive:

> At the beginning of December 1944 Army Group Center had 33 infantry divisions and 12 panzer or panzer grenadier divisions. Of the latter 3 were at the front, 9 in reserve. The army group held a 360-mile front, roughly ten miles of frontage per division, about as good a ratio as the Germans were accustomed to at that stage of the war. To the rear, in East Prussia, it had an extensive system of field fortifications and on the border of East Prussia and around Koenigsberg some concrete emplacements; the latter had been built before the war and would have been more valuable if in the meantime the guns and barbed wire had not been removed and installed elsewhere, in the Atlantic Wall, for instance.
>
> In early December Army Group Center could have faced an attack confidently; by the turn of the year it no longer could; in the interval it had lost 5 panzer divisions and 2 cavalry brigades by transfers.

The command staff of the German Army Group Center, January–February 1945 (from 26 January 1945, Army Group North)

Left to right: Georg Reinhardt, Freidrich Hoßbach, Walter Weiß, Deitrich von Saucken.

Left to right: Lothar Rendulic, Wilhelm Müller, Erhard Raus.

A German half-tracked prime mover tows a heavy gun along a city street.

...

On 12 January, in an attempt to mislead the Germans and tie down their reserves, the Russians attacked Fourth Army north and south of the Rominrener Heide. The next day, opening the offensive in earnest, *Third Belorussian Front* hit Third Panzer Army at Stallupönen and Pilkallen. On the 14th *Second Belorussian Front* attacked the Second Army out of the Serock and Rozan bridgeheads. Both armies held up well in the first two days, went into the main battle lien, and patched the holes. Fog prevented the Russians from bringing their air power and armor into play. Unfortunately for the army group, this momentary success – especially in comparison with what Army Group A was experiencing, looked almost like a defensive victory. On the 14th, when Guderian reported to Hitler that apparently Army Group Center could prevent an operational breakthrough on the Narew and into East Prussia, Hitler ordered Panzer Corps *Grossdeutschland* and its two panzer divisions transferred to Army Group A.

The strength in panzers and self-propelled guns of the panzer and panzergrenadier divisions and separate units of Army Group Center on 12 January 1945 (according to German archival data)

5th Panzer Division (on 31 December 1944): 33 Pz IV (32 operational), 47 Pz V (40), 32 Jg Pz IV and Jg Pz IV/70 (25), 6 StuG (6).

7th Panzer Division (31 December 1944): 28 Pz IV (27), 5 Bef Pz V (5), 32 Pz V. On 3 January 1945 the division additionally received 10 Jg Pz IV/70 (A), and on 8 January 1945 Pz Jg Abt 42 was transferred out of the area of Mielau in East Prussia and made subordinate to the division with 21 Jg Pz IV/70.

1st Parachute-Panzer Division *Hermann Göring* (31 December 1944): 4 Pz III (2), 35 Pz IV (29), 42 Pz V (33).

2nd Parachute-Panzer Division *Hermann Göring* (5 January 1944): 32 StuG III. Korps Pz Jg Abt HG (30 December 1944) was operationally subordinate to the division with 17 StuG.

18th Panzergrenadier Division (12 January 1945): 44 StuG III (under the 118th Panzer Battalion).

Panzergrenadier Division *Grossdeutschland* (30 December 1944): 4 Pz IV (2), 61 Pz V (56), 1 Bef Pz III (1), 22 Aufkl Pz 38(t) (16), 19 Pz VI (15), and StuG Pz Kp 218 z.b.V – 10 StuG IV. The division with its attached units, but excluding the Panzerjäger Abteilung *Grossdeutschland*, on 10 January 1945 had 126 tanks and assault guns, including 60 Pz V, 19 Pz VI, 21 Jg Pz IV/70, 26 StuG, 22 Aufkl Pz 38(t), 36 leSPW, and 189 mSPW.

Panzergrenadier Division *Brandenburg* (8 January 1945): 21 StuG IV (Pz Jg Abt BR) and 32 StuG III + 8 StuH (StuG Br GD). The latter unit on 16 January 1945 was loaded on trains in Mielau and arrived on the same day as part of the division.

Heavy Panzer Battalion 505 on 30 December 1944 had 37 Tigers (34 operational).

Heavy Panzer Battalion 507 on 30 December 1944 had 55 Tigers (51 operational).

Heavy Panzer Battalion 511 on 30 December 1944 had 20 Tigers.

The composition of the separate assault gun brigades (5 January 1945)

Assault Gun Brigade 185: 28 StuG; Assault Gun Brigade 190: 33 StuG; Assault Gun Brigade 201: 31 StuG; Assault Gun Brigade 209: 29 StuG; Assault Gun Brigade 232: 29 StuG; Assault Gun Brigade 249: 23 StuG; Assault Gun Brigade 259: 43 StuG; Assault Gun Brigade 276: 25 StuG; Assault Gun Brigade 277: 24 StuG; Assault Gun Brigade 278: 42 StuG; Assault Gun Brigade 279: 18 StuG; Assault Gun Brigade 901: 31 StuG; Assault Gun Brigade 909: 30 StuG. On 5 January 1945 Colonel General Heinz Guderian reported that Army Group Center additionally had 301 StuG that belonged to 28 separate panzerjäger companies.

Thus, on the eve of the Russians' offensive on 12 January 1945 Army Group Center had approximately 1380 tanks and self-propelled guns (Pz II, Pz III L/60, Pz IV, Panther, Tiger, StuG III, StuG IV, Jagdpanzer IV Nashorn, Marder III, T-34, Hetzer, Wespe, Hummel and Grille). In addition, the troops had approximately 950 halftracks and specialized machines (SPW/Pz Spah Wg RFA). Some units, for example the 5th Jäger Division, had T-34 tanks. The 542nd Volksgrenadier Division had Pz III L/60 tanks. The 35th Infantry Division had Marder III equipped with 76.2mm guns.

The operation's plan and the 5th Guards Tank Army's mission

The January 1945 offensive operation was planned by the command of the 2nd Belorussian Front as a deep operation (to a depth of 250 – 300 km) with decisive objectives, and with the active participation of all of the Front's forces. In this Front operation, the 5th Guards Tank Army was given one of the decisive and responsible roles, which consisted in exploiting a success by the Front's shock grouping (48th Army and 2nd Shock Army) in the northwestern direction toward Mława, Lidzbark, Deutsch Eylau, Marienburg, coastline of Danzig Bay, with the ultimate objective of cutting off the enemy's East Prussian grouping from the rest of Germany.

The commander of the 5th Guards Tank Army Colonel General of Tank Forces V.T. Vol'sky and his chief of staff Major General of Tank Forces G.S. Sidorovich became familiar with the Front's plan for the operation and the overall mission given to the 5th Tank Army in this operation when, in the aim of maintaining secrecy, they were summoned to the Front headquarters on 10 January 1945. According to the 2nd Belorussian Front's plan, the 5th Guards Tank Army would take no direct part in penetrating the enemy's forward edge and tactical zone of defense, but would remain in full readiness for combat operations as the reserve of the Front commander-in-chief, and would be moved up to the frontlines behind the advancing divisions of the 48th Army and 2nd Shock Army and introduced into the breach at the boundary of these two armies once their forward units reached the Przasnysz – Ciechanów line. This would require them to make an advance of 20-25 kilometers into the depth of the enemy's defenses.

In the course of the offensive, the 2nd Belorussian Front headquarters strictly stuck to this plan. The 5th Tank Army received its own concrete assignment only on the morning of 17 January 1945, directly with its introduction into the breakthrough. In connection with this the 5th Guards Tank Army didn't work out its own plan, with the exception of preliminary drafts of several possible alternatives of the army's commitment depending on the situation.

Preparations for the offensive

Upon returning from the Front headquarters, the commander of the 5th Guards Tank Army General V.T. Vol'sky held a limited meeting with the formation commanders, their deputies, and the chiefs of various service categories on 11 January, in which he informed them of the upcoming offensive and the army's general task in the operation, and ordered them to initiate intensive preparations for the operation, while keeping the designated time schedule, direction and objective of the upcoming operations by the 5th Guards Tank Army and the 2nd Belorussian Front in strict secrecy.

The preparation for the offensive was expressed in the following manner:

a) By accelerating the repair of the combat machines and in preparing all the equipment for a lengthy march and a deep operation;

b) By increasing the pace of the combat preparations of the units and formations, with working out the most important themes and questions relating to the tasks of the upcoming operation;
c) By working out the questions of cooperation with the 48th Army and 2nd Shock Army and all questions of supply by the army headquarters and the chiefs of various types of troops and services;
d) By accelerating the work of the rear services to keep the troops supplied with the established norms of ammunition, fuel and lubricants, and food;
e) By preparing means of communication and command for uninterrupted work in the conditions of the forthcoming rapid and deep operation;
f) By reconnoitering and preparing the routes of the army's movement from its assembly area to its staging and jumping-off areas, and in preparing engineering support for the army's actions in the depth of the enemy's defenses.

From the "Combat Path of the 10th Guards Tank Army":

Trains carrying combat equipment and weapons were arriving in the army in a constant flow. In fact, of course, the headquarters of the corps, the brigades and the battalions had a lot of work to do in order to receive and distribute the arriving 372 tanks and self-propelled artillery vehicles.

On 1 January 1945 Military Council member General P.G. Grishin conducted a conference with the chiefs of the Political Departments of the corps and brigades, and with the deputy political commanders of the army's units. At the conference, the tasks of the political organs to prepare the personnel for the forthcoming offensive fighting were discussed, as were the forms and methods for readying the soldiers and officers for operations beyond the borders of their own homeland. Emphasis was placed on the fact that the commanders and political workers were paying attention to nurturing feelings of Soviet patriotism and national pride in the troops. Broad explanation of the significance of the forthcoming operation was going on in the regiments, battalions and companies. Particularly large attention was paid to work among the incoming replacements. The young soldiers were made familiar with the traditions of the units and the exploits of heroes. Ceremenies were held to bestow Orders and medals upon soldiers who had distinguished themselves in preceding battles, and combat arms to new soldiers. At technical conferences driver-mechanics and chauffeurs exchanged their experience with taking care of their vehicles and unsing them in wintry conditions.

At the end of the first ten days of the month, the Political Department held a meeting of Cavaliers of the Order of Glory. Six hundred and forty-seven honored masters of conducting combat came together. This was the flower of the army. Many of them had been awarded several government Orders and medals. The assistant commander of the sapper platoon of the 25th Tank Brigade Sergeant Major D.I. Novikov, a gunner of the 1446th Self-propelled Artillery Regiment Senior Sergeant V.F. Gashin, a submachine gunner of the 53rd Motorized Rifle Brigade's 2nd Motorized Rifle Battalion Sergeant M.E. Gerasimov, the foreman for the repair of SU-85s of the 1436th Self-propelled Artillery Regiment Senior Sergeant P.P. Porfir'ev, a submachine gunner of a motorcycle battalion of the 1st Guards Motorcycle Regiment Private Ia.V. Kurdiumov, heavy machine gunner of the 2nd Company of a motorized rifle battalion of the 53rd Motorized Rifle Brigade Sergeant F.I. Kurochkin and many others held the Order of Glory 2nd Class and 3rd Class. The army's commander Colonel General of Tank Forces V.T. Vol'sky, Military Council member Major General of Tank Forces P.G. Grishin, and Military Council member for rear services Colonel I.K. Syromolotnyi arrived at the meeting.

In a brief introductory statement, the chief of the Political Department Colonel A.M. Kostylev reported on the aims of the conference. General Grishin presented a report on the combat path of the 5th Guards Tank Army and the tasks of the Cavaliers of the Order of Glory in the upcoming fighting. The veteran Order-bearers listened raptly to the story of the achievements of their combat comrades, who mercilessly crushed the fascist aggressors at Prokhorovka, on the right bank of the Dnepr River, in Belorussia and in Lithuania. Then the army commander gave a speech to those in attendance. He discussed the possible nature of the upcoming fighting and the role of the Cavaliers of the Order of Glory when carrying out assignments. The army commander paid particular attention to the need to increase combat skills, to strengthen discipline and organization in the combat elements. The honored tankers, motorized riflemen, reconnaissance scouts, antitank artillerymen and mortarmen shared their rich combat experience, and assured the command that they would fight like Guardsmen in the future battles.

On 10 January 1945 the army's commander and chief of staff were briefed on the Front's plan. The 5th Guards Tank Army was designated for commitment into the breakthrough in the sector of the 48th Army, and was to advance in the direction of Mława and Lidzbark.

The First Stage of the Operation
The movement of the 5th Guards Tank Army into its staging and jumping-off areas

The general offensive of the 2nd Belorussian Front kicked-off on 14 January 1945. The troops of the 48th Army and 2nd Shock Army in the course of the day fought their way through the enemy's first defensive line and, having made an advance of 4-6 km into the depth of the enemy's defenses, were engaged in combat in the switch positions and intermediate lines between the first and second defensive belts for possession of Malków and Pułtusk.

Pursuant to an order from the commander-in-chief of the 2nd Belorussian Front Marshal of the Soviet Union K.K. Rokossovsky, the troops of the 5th Guards Tank Army in the course of 14 and 15 January conducted a 145-kilometer march observing strict camouflage measures along three routes out of their assembly area, and by the end of 15 January had reassembled in the Łudzin, Jażąbka, Żąśnik, Szarłat, Gródek, Nowe Wielątki, Leszczydól-Nowiny, Brańszczyk area. Each formation conducted the march along one route: 10th Tank Corps – Route 1; 47th Mechanized Brigade – Route 2; 29th Tank Corps – Route 3.

The details of the organization of the march, with the aims of camouflage and deception, consisted in the following:

a) The echelons of the wheeled vehicles moved separately from the tracked vehicles and set out in small groups before the latter. For example, the wheeled transport of the 29th Tank Corps moved out at 0100 on 14 January, while the tracked machines didn't set out until 1600 of the same day. The wheeled transport of the 10th Tank Corps moved out at 0200 on 14 January, followed by the tracked machines at 1600. The wheeled transport of the 47th Mechanized Brigade began moving at 0900 on 14 January, while its tanks moved out at 1500;
b) Approximately midway along the route, both the wheeled and tracked machines were given a day's rest that lasted 13 to 20 hours for the separate echelons;
c) The tracked machines moved out from the assembly area and from the area of the halt in the evening and assembled in area of the halt and the staging area at night;
d) The tracked machines were forbidden from marching through the city of Ostrów Mazowiecka and Wyszków;
e) In the event of weather that grounded aircraft, the tanks and self-propelled guns were allowed to end the rest halts and to continue the march in daylight hours, but marches during the night were only done with masked lights.

Such an organization of the march pursued the aim of concealing the approach to the front of such a large formation as a tank army from the enemy, and given the impossibility of full concealment – to confuse the enemy and cause the enemy to underestimate the number of machines that were approaching the front. As became clear later, these measures fully justified themselves, and the introduction of the 5th Guards Tank Army came as a surprise to the enemy.

The good roads, the absence of a deep snow cover and the temperatures of -8 to -10 C. made for good conditions for such a lengthy march. En route on the march, of the total number of 428 combat machines moving with caterpillar drives, 25 fell behind, primarily those that had been received from factories following major repairs. The heavy regiments of tanks and self-propelled guns – the 14th Guards Heavy Tank Regiment, the 376th, 326th and 365th Heavy Self-propelled Artillery Regiments, and the 1207th and 381st Self-propelled Artillery Regiments, totaling a number of 157 combat machines, with the aim of preventing wear and tear on their engines, were transported during this same time period by railroad to the staging area, having been loaded at the Belsk railroad station and having unloaded at the Dalekie railroad station. The 5th Guards Tank Army, including the combat machines that were transported by rail, had fully reassembled in the staging area by 1000 on 16 January.

The troops of the 48th Army and 2nd Shock Army in the course of 15 and 16 January took full possession of Malków and Pułtusk, broke through the enemy's second defensive belt, and by the end of 16 January reached the Dąbrówka, Łukowo, Burkaty, Gąsocin line, continuing to drive the enemy back to the third defensive belt, which ran along the Przasnysz – Ciechanów line. With Combat Order No. 0034/OP, communicated by code on the afternoon of 16 January, the Commander-in-Chief of the 2nd Belorussian Front issued a task to the 5th Guards Tank Army: "By the morning of 17 January 1945, assemble in the area: Maków, Karniewo, Pienkowo, Białowieża, Gnojno, Cieplewo. Be in readiness from the Ciechanów line to enter the breach in the direction of Mława and Lidzbark."

Lacking sufficient time to inspect the tanks and self-propelled guns after the 145-kilometer march, the troops of the 5th Guards Tank Army at 2000 on 16 January began moving out under the cover of darkness to the designated area. Having completed the march, which for the formations varied between 40 km and 70 km, and having crossed bridges over the Narew and Orzyc Rivers, by the morning of 17 January the tank army had fully assembled in its designated jumping-off area. This area up until 15 January had been occupied by the enemy, as a result of which a lot of prior work had to be done hastily by engineers in order to clear mines and obstacles, and backfill antitank ditches and shell craters before occupying it. Despite the measures taken, one tank and two wheeled vehicles were blown up in uncleared minefields when taking up this area.

The immediate task of the 5th Guards Tank Army and General Vol'sky's decision

With Directive No. 1055 from 0030 on 17 January 1945, the commander-in-chief of the 2nd Belorussian Front Marshal of the Soviet Union K.K. Rokossovsky ordered: "The 5th Guards Tank Army at 1200 on 17 January enters the breach in the Maków – Karniewo sector in the general direction toward Grudusk, Mława and Lidzbark. The army's immediate task: by the morning of 18 January 1945, reach the Mława line, and by the morning of 19 January, take Neidenburg and Działdowo."

Having assessed the situation, General Vol'sky issued the following orders:

> When entering the breakthrough, the army's forces are to deploy in the Maków, Karniewo, Golmyn Stary sector (with a width of 16 km), with the main grouping on the right flank. Have the tank corps on a single line: 10th Tank Corps on the right flank, 29th Tank Corps

echeloned to the left. Each corps is to operate along two routes. The 47th Mechanized Brigade is to advance in the second echelon behind the 10th Tank Corps along both of its routes. The 201st Light Artillery Brigade, the 14th Guards Heavy Tank Regiment and the 76th Guards Mortar Regiment are to follow the 29th Tank Corps, with both regiments along its right-hand route. The 201st Light Artillery Brigade – along its left-hand route. Use the army's assets as reinforcements: 10th Tank Corps – 326th Heavy Self-propelled Artillery Regiment, 689th Destroyer Anti-tank Artillery Regiment, and one sapper battalion of the 21st Motorized Engineer Brigade; 29th Tank Corps – 651st Cannon Artillery Regiment of the 201st Light Artillery Brigade, the 366th Anti-aircraft Artillery Regiment, and one sapper battalion of the 21st Motorized Engineer Brigade; 47th Mechanized Brigade – 376th Heavy Self-propelled Artillery Regiment.

Instructions regarding reconnaissance: 10th Tank Corps, 29th Tank Corps and the 47th Mechanized Brigade are to conduct strong combat and tactical reconnaissance along the directions of their actions and on their outer flanks. The 1st Separate Guards Motorcyle Regiment is to conduct reconnaissance in the directions: a) Przasnysz, Dzierzgowo, Nowa Wieś, Neidenburg; b) Paluki, Regimin, Szreńsk, Zielona.

Engineers: Support the passage of the army's formations through the corridors in our minefields and the German minefields. With scouting by engineers, reveal the enemy's artificial and antitank obstacles. Ensure the timely creation of passages through the minefields and antitank obstacles in the depth of the enemy's defenses, as well as the passage of the army's tanks, artillery and motorized transport through them.

The army's introduction into the breakthrough and combat operations, 17-19 January 1945

At 1200 on 17 January 1945, the 5th Guards Tank Army entered the breakthrough in the Maków, Karniewo, Golmyn Stary sector, having a combat formation according to the scheme presented below. The corps' lead brigades (the 186th and 178th Tank Brigades of the 10th Tank Corps and the 25th and 31st Tank Brigades of the 29th Tank Corps had strong forward detachments out in front of them consisting of not less than one tank battalion, one self-propelled gun battery, a submachine gun company, a sapper company, and anti-aircraft means to provide air cover.

The forward detachments, having combat reconnaissance patrols out in front, moved out in approach march formations. Such an arrangement was prompted by the army's need to penetrate the enemy's third defensive belt on a frontage of 13-14 km and to be ready to repulse possible counterattacks by enemy tanks from the flanks. Counterattacks by the German Panzergrenadier Division *Grossdeutschland* from the direction of Przasnysz and the 7th Panzer Division from the direction of Ciechanów were expected. In addition, such a combat formation enabled the timely receipt of information about the enemy, the timely coping with encountered artificial obstacles, the rapid deployment of the units and their subsequent maneuvering toward the flanks, and good command and control over the units.

At 1500 on 17 January the forces of the 5th Guards Tank Army, after briefly working out questions of cooperation at the level of the of the tank brigade commanders with the commanders of the rifle divisions, passed through the combat formations of the 48th Army's 53rd Rifle Corps on the Zalesie – Mosaki – Kołaczkow – Pałuki line, and from the march attacked the opposing units of the 299th Infantry Division and 7th Panzer Division, which were occupying switch positions between the second and third defensive lines on the army's right flank, and the third defensive line itself on the left flank, in strength of up to two regiments of infantry supported by 15-20 self-propelled guns and up to 10 batteries of artillery and mortars.

The enemy was putting up the most stubborn resistance to the actions of the 10th Tank Corps on the army's right flank, against which up to a regiment of infantry and up to 10-12 self-propelled guns supported by 5-6 artillery batteries were defending. The enemy was attempting not only hold in check the 10th Tank Corps' advance, but twice went over to the counterattack from the Krasne and Kozin directions.

The commander of the 10th Tank Corps Major General of Tank Forces Sakhno was forced to deploy his two lead brigades (the 186th and 178th Tank Brigades) and introduce them into the combat. Having pinned down the enemy from the front with part of his strength, with his main forces he launched an attack toward Krasne from the east and toward Kozin from the west. After two hours of stubborn fighting, the 186th and 178th Tank Brigades crushed the enemy in the Zalesie, Krasne, Kozin area and in Mosaki, and resumed the offensive in the designated northwestern direction.

By 2100 17 January, the lead brigades of the 10th Tank Corps, fighting their way forward, cut the Przasnysz – Ciechanów highway and reached the following points: 186th Tank Brigade – in Golany; 178th Tank Brigade – in Łaguny; 183rd Tank Brigade – in Pęczki-Kozłowo; and the 11th Mechanized Brigade – in Nowy.

5th Guards Tank Army in the East Prussia Operation, 1945

Soviet artillery firing at the enemy; East Prussia, January 1945. (TsAMO)

Artillery of the 5th Guards Tank Army on the march; East Prussia, January 1945. (TsAMO)

The 29th Tank Corps, after catching up with the infantry, encountered less organized enemy resistance (than did the 10th Tank Corps) on the Kołaczkow, Bogucin line, and subsequently on the Pokojewo, Opinogóra Górna line. It was being opposed by up to two battalions of enemy infantry with the support of 4 self-propelled guns and up to three artillery batteries. As a result of the fighting, the lead brigades of the 29th Tank Corps (the 25th and 31st Tank Brigades) only with their forward detachments, without deploying their main forces, from the march attacked and penetrated the enemy's third line of defenses.

By 1830 on 17 January, the units of the 29th Tank Corps were cutting the Przasnysz – Ciechanów highway and had captured: 25th Tank Brigade – Sosnowo; 31st Tank Brigade – the road hub in the vicinity of Dzbonie; 32nd Tank Brigade, following behind the 31st Tank Brigade, had reached Czernice with its forward elements; 53rd Motorized Rifle Brigade (trailing behind the 25th Tank Brigade) with its forward elements had reached Rembowo.

Without pausing on the attained line, units of the 29th Tank Corps continued to carry out their given orders with nighttime actions. The 25th Tank Brigade, brushing aside the enemy's weak rear-guard detachments, by the end of 17 January reached the outer of fortifications surrounding the

Mława center of resistance in the vicinity of the Kozły railroad station and Mierzanowo, 4 km southwest of Grudusk. On this line, the enemy offered tough resistance to the brigade with up to two battalions of infantry and the support of up to three artillery batteries. By 0300 on 18 January, the brigade took the Kozły railroad station after a sharp combat action. At the order of the corps commander, the 25th Tank Brigade was halted on this line with the task to screen the corps' right flank temporarily.

The 31st Tank Brigade, advancing in the lead on the corps' left-hand route, attacked and routed weak enemy forces that were occupying switch positions on the Przybyszewo – Regimin line, and by the end of 17 January captured Żmijewo-Ponki. In the area of Konopki Station, the enemy put up more stubborn resistance to the brigade, using shattered units of the 7th Infantry Division and Panzerjäger Battalion 511, reinforced with artillery. After a short barrage of fire, the brigade attacked and captured Konopki Station. The 32nd Tank Brigade, advancing in the wake of the 31st Tank Brigade, by the end of 17 January reached the Zeńbok, Jarluty Duże area, where it spent the night refueling the machines and preparing for actions as the corps' forward detachment in the direction of Dzialdowo, bypassing Mława on its southern and western sides.

The 53rd Motorized Rifle Brigade, advancing behind the 25th Tank Brigade, by the end of 17 January arrived in the area of Kołaki-Kwasy (9 km northwest of Ciechanów). The 47th Mechanized Brigade, moving in the second echelon behind the 10th Tank Corps, by the end of the day reached the Mosaki, Kozin area.

From the memoirs of F.I. Galkin:

Having returned to my headquarters, I issued an order to prepare for a march. Indeed, I wasn't mistaken. On the night of 13-14 January, the army was alerted and moved out along three routes for a 145-km march. It was to assemble in a staging area by 15 January, which was several kilometers northwest of the Polish town of Wyszków. All of the engineers, technicians and repair teams set out first, in the event of a need to provide technical assistance. The corps and evacuation companies then went on the march. Irklei, Pustil'nikov and I also set out behind the tanks in our Willys jeeps, which struggled to make their way through the sludge. Not a single broken-down machine could be left unnoticed. On the first half of the route, 11 machines stopped due to mechanical problems. They were all repaired en route and arrived in the area of the day's halt for rest. On the second half of the route, 13 more machines broke down. Two required new parts, while the rest needed only minor repairs.

By the end of 15 January, the main forces of our army were assembled in the Urżyn, Jażąbki, Nowe Wielątki area. The heavy [tank] regiments, sent by rail, arrived the next morning, and 12 machines were left for repairs in the Briansk area.

The situation at the front was as follows: Northeast of Warsaw, the enemy's defenses ran along the Narew River. Making use of the front's temporary stability, the enemy worked to improve his fortifications and created a deeply-echeloned defense. He was covering East Prussia and northern Poland with Army Group Center. Colonel General Reinhardt commanded the army group.

The troops of the 2nd Belorussian Front were occupying two previously secured bridgeheads on the western bank of the Narew, north and south of Pultusk. Our army was to exploit a success by the Front's shock grouping in the general direction of Mława, Lidzbark and the coastline of the Danzig harbor.

The army's ultimate task was to isolate the Nazi's East Prussia grouping from the rest of Germany. It was intended to introduce the tanks in the breakthrough at the boundary between the 48th Army and 2nd Shock Army on the Przasnysz – Ciechanów line. According to intelligence information, three German infantry divisions, reinforced with assault guns, sapper-bridging elements and other units, were defending in front of our army and on its flanks.

The 2nd Belorussian Front's offensive got underway on 14 January 1945. Having run into a dense network of fighting positions and stubborn German resistance, our troops over the first day made an advance of only 5-6 kilometers. However, on the following two days, the units of the 48th and 2nd Shock Armies captured the towns of Maków and Pultusk, broke through the second defensive line, and by the evening of 16 January were continuing to drive the enemy back toward the third defensive belt.

The 5th Guards Tank Army received the order to assemble in the Maków – Białowieża – Ciepelow area and to be ready to enter the breakthrough in order to exploit the success. The tankers had just completed a 145-kilometer march. Now they faced making approximately another 70-kilometer march that night. There was no time for doing maintenance work on the tanks. It was time to move out!

So once again the tracks were throwing up swirls of powdery snow, churning the frozen layers of autumnal tillage, and thundering across the bridges over the Narew and Orzyc Rivers. The next morning, just as dawn was breaking, the tanks were concealed in their jumping-off area. No matter how much care we took, nevertheless one tank and two vehicles blew up on mines. The driver-mechanics used the final hours and minutes in order to check their "property": Was the steering in good working order? Were there any fuel or lubricant leaks? Was the retaining pin set in proper position?

One more detail leaped to the eye, which suggested that combat was nigh. The tankers were exchanging the addresses of their families – just in case. Others were writing letters on small pieces of paper. Soon these precious triangles of paper would wind up in the hands of the field post office workers and begin their journey to the rear …

Colonel General Vol'sky, trim and focused, was listening to short reports from staff officers in his bunker, and was issuing final orders together with the Chief of Staff Sidorovich. Both of Vol'sky's deputies – Sinenko and Zaev – were already up among the troops. The former was "patronizing" General Sakhno's tank corps, and the latter – General Malakhov's tank corps. When I entered, Vasilii Timofeevich, striving to show no concern, asked: "Well, supreme technician, will the machines let us down?"

"They shouldn't, Comrade General. To be sure, the commander of the 25th Brigade Stanislavsky is unsettled. He received some of his machines straight from the repair factories on the eve before moving out, and they haven't had time to even check the machines like they should. Indeed, a few of them broke down on the march …."

"Does that mean he has grounds to be worried?"

"Yes, he has cause. However, we've already had time to eliminate the majority of defects. Factory experts that I've summoned have already arrived in response to our complaints. Yet they've not had time to do any work on the machines that arrived aboard the last train."

Having answered all of Vol'sky's questions, I headed to see the driver-mechanics, in order to go over once again the task assigned by the command. It amounted to the following: The army's forces were to deploy on the Maków – Korniewo – Gołmyn line (which extended for 16 kilometers), having its main grouping on the right flank. Sakhno's tank corps would be operating here, while Malakhov's tank corps would comprise the left flank. The 47th Mechanized Brigade – the second echelon – would advance behind Sakhno's corps, which having bypassed Mława, was supposed to take Neidenburg by the morning of 19 January. Meanwhile, Malakhov's tank corps, also bypassing Mława, was to capture Dzialdowo.

One matter concerned the Military Council: Would we be able to implement a "clean" breakthrough, through which the armor would pour through like a broken dam, or would we have to finish the breakthrough and ram our way through the cracked, but still active German defenses?

The answer to this important question could only be obtained in battle. The army's corps, brigades, regiments and battalions were ready. The repair teams – the trustworthy friends and peers of the tankers – were also ready.

However, any period of waiting comes to an end at some time. The command arrived at the moment when tensions in troops were at their highest. The tanks moved out. The forward detachments of the lead tank brigades began slowly to advance, as if feeling out the roads. The machines receded in clouds of snow and became invisible, while the increased snowfall quickly covered over the tracks they left behind in the snow.

The 183rd and 178th [Tank] Brigades set out in the first echelon of General Sakhno's corps, while the 25th and 31st [Tank] Brigades comprised the first echelon of General Makhalov's corps. Vol'sky briefly, but expressively described their role:

"Today they face clashing with the forces of the German Second Army. The adversary is serious – the old and experienced fascist wolf *Generaloberst* Weiß."

Sidorovich continued his thought: "The main point is that the Nazis will defend East Prussia at any cost. Unquestionably, we will encounter many surprises. Hitler and his generals understand that to lose East Prussia means to open a path to Berlin."

We all already understood this and were seemingly sensing a dual responsibility – a military and a political responsibility.

By 3:00 that afternoon, the forces of our tank army had passed through the combat formations of the 48th Army's 53rd Rifle Corps and from the march attacked the enemy on the Zalesie – Kołaczkowo – Poluki line. Malakhov's corps had already driven back the Nazi's disorganized infantry and had already begun to advance in the direction of Dzialdowo.

The 10th Tank Corps met fierce resistance. However, General Sakhno accepted the initial difficulties that threatened to disrupt all of the planning calmly, which even surprised me somewhat.

I recall that as soon as the attack started, I arrived by car at the corps commander's command post – it was located on the edge of a hamlet, in a small, two-room cottage, the walls of which were covered with old newspapers and pictures from journals. Staff officers and telephone operators were huddled together in the first room, and in the second room, Generals Sinenko and Sakhno were leaning over a map that had been spread out across a small folding table. They were attentively listening to a radio operator, who was giving a report from the commander of the 183rd [Tank] Brigade that the Germans were counterattacking with major forces from the direction of the villages of Krasne and Kozin. Unrattled, Sakhno listened to the full report, consulted with Sinenko, and then slowly and calmly told the radio operator: "Give the brigade commander the order to deploy the self-propelled artillery regiment."

Reports were coming in incessantly over the radio, and from them one realized that the bitterness of the fighting was increasing with each passing minute. Striving to give a check to the progress of our tanks, the German infantry was being thrown into counterattacks together with tanks and assault guns, but each time they fell back, suffering losses.

After two hours of fighting, the enemy resistance was broken; the Germans began to retreat, covered by strong rearguard detachments. However, Sakhno's tankers were brushing them aside and kept stubbornly advancing toward Mława. The fighting was going on around the clock.

The combat operations of 18 January

Continuing a ceaseless advance on the night of 17-18 January and over the day of 18 January, the forces of the 5th Guards Tank Army, destroying rearguard enemy detachments, and by the morning reached the outer ring of Mława's fortifications: the 29th Tank Corps by 0300 on 18 January was located in the vicinity of the Kosily railroad station, while the 10th Tank Corps by 0800 of this same day was located in the vicinity of the Wiśniewo to Mlawa railroad station. Having run into heavy fire from the positions of the outer ring of fortifications, the army's forces enveloped Mława from the east and southwest and by 2200 completed the encirclement of the

Mława center of resistance, having severed all of the enemy's primary routes of retreat out of Mława, and having captured the major railroad and road hub of Działdowo.

The 10th Tank Corps by 0800 on 18 January had fought its way through the third defensive belt in the Rostkowo, Łaguny sector; by 1000 it reached and cut the Przasnysz – Mława road, and had captured Chojnowo, Czernice Borowe and the Wisniewo to Mława railroad station. Tough fighting developed in the vicinity of the latter place.

The enemy, in strength of up to a battalion of infantry supported by 10 self-propelled guns and several artillery batteries launched a counterattack from out of the woods north of Czernice Borowe against the combat formations of the 178th Tank Brigade in the direction of Dzielin (1.5 km southeast of Czernice Borowe). The counterattack was driven back with heavy losses for the enemy (up to 200 men killed, and 40 men captured and 5 75mm guns captured).

Having allowed the tanks of the 178th Tank Brigade to pass in the direction of the Wisniewo to Mława railroad station, the enemy launched a second counterattack toward Dzielin from out of these same woods, reached the headquarters and rear services of the 178th Tank Brigade, and captured Dzielin. Continuing their advance to the south, this enemy group reached the headquarters of the 10th Tank Corps in the Jędrzejki, where it was met by pointblank fire from the nearby 1693rd Anti-aircraft Artillery Regiment and the 128th Separate Guards Mortar Battalion. Hurled back to the east, this group was attacked by the 11th Motorized Rifle Brigade in the Górki area and annihilated, having lost 7 self-propelled guns destroyed, up to 100 men killed, and 130 men captured.

The 186th Tank Brigade, attacking to the north toward Chojnowo (6 km west of Przasnysz) and beyond, upon approaching Węgra encountered a motorized enemy column of the 18th Panzergrenadier Division's Panzergrenadier Regiment 30 that was transporting artillery. Without allowing the enemy time to deploy, the brigade with a swift pincer attack attacked the enemy from both flanks and smashed it, having destroyed more than 100 vehicles, 20 guns, 5 self-propelled guns and having eliminated up to 250 enemy soldiers and officers.

Continuing to develop the offensive and knocking aside enemy blocking detachments, the corps' units by 1900 on 18 January arrived on the following line: 186th Tank Brigade – Rzęgnowo (5 km northeast of Grudusk); 11th Motorized Rifle Brigade – advancing behind the 186th Tank Brigade had reached Pawłówko. The 178th Tank Brigade, together with the 183rd Tank Brigade which had been introduced into the battle from the second echelon, with tough fighting had broken through the outer ring of the Mława fortifications (which included an antitank ditch), and had taken Grudusk. By 2200 on 18 January, the forward units of the 10th Tank Corps captured Kitki and Budy Garlińskie (approximately 13 km east of Mława), thereby cutting the Szumsk – Mława road. The 77th Motorcycle Battalion, comprising the corps' reconnaissance group, reached the Kuklin area on the highway leading north out of Mława toward the East Prussian town of Hohenstein [present day Olsztynek]. Continuing to envelop the main fortifications of the Mława center of resistance from the northeast, the 10th Tank Corps' units passed through a roadless area of peat bogs that was up to 8-10 kilometers wide.

By 0200 on 19 January, the 178th Tank Brigade captured Michalinowo (2 km south of the Kuklin road hub), thereby cutting the Mława – Neidenburg road. The remaining units of the 10th Tank Corps by 0600 on 19 January fought their way forward to the following line: 183rd Tank Brigade – Hill 185.0 (1 km east of Michalinowo); 186th Tank Brigade – the estates 1 km northeast of Pogorzel; the 11th Motorized Rifle Brigade – 1 km east of of Kuklin. The 77th Motorcycle Regiment (the corps' reconnaissance group) by 0600 on 19 January, bypassing Kuklin, from the march broke into and seized Peplowo (4 km north of Kuklin). Thus, the 10th Tank Corps, bypassing Mława on its eastern side, in the course of the day of 18 January cut all of the paths of retreat from Mława to the east, northeast and north.

The 29th Tank Corps on the night of 17-18 January and over the day of 18 January continued a rapid advance, bypassing the Mława center of resistance from the south and southwest. The

31st Tank Brigade, brushing aside the enemy's small mobile detachments that consisted of 3-6 tanks and self-propelled guns each, operating out of ambush positions, by 1100 on 18 January took Dąbek, followed by the capture of Stare Kosiny at 1300, when it was counterattacked by the enemy with 10 tanks supported by 2-3 batteries of artillery from the direction of Wiśniewo.

The 22nd Tank Brigade, which up to this point had been following in the second echelon, received an order from the corps commander: It was to deploy from behind the left flank of the 31st Tank Brigade, and without getting tied up in the 31st Tank Brigade's combat, with a rapid dash forward it was to arrive west of Dzialdowo and cut the enemy's path of retreat to the west.

From the "Combat path of the 5th Guards Tank Army":

In the course of 18 January, the forces of the 5th Guards Tank Army continued to be engaged in combat on the approaches to Mława's defensive zone. The 10th Tank Corps repulsed several strong Nazi counterattacks. The Germans were throwing cadets from the Mława military academy into the fighting. The brigades of the 29th Tank Corps, repulsing the enemy's counterattacks and bypassing his blocking detachmentsm were stubbornly advancing toward Dzialdowo.

The 32nd [Tank] Brigade, having from the march forced a crossing of the Dziadowka River, two hours later reached the northwestern outskirts of Dzialdowo and cut the enemy's path of retreat from the town to the west and northwest. The 3rd Tank Battalion was operating in the brigade's forward detachment, which was being commanded by Hero of the Soviet Union Guards Captain A.A. Chepurenko. A company of this battalion, headed by Lieutenant P.V. Ivanov, crushed a lot of vehicles, up to 70 wagons, and eliminated more than 100 Nazis. Altogether with fire and tracks, Chepurenko's battalion destroyed 7 halftracks, 160 vehicles, 7 guns of various caliber, and killed up to 150 enemy soldiers and officers on the outskirts of Dzialdowo.

By evening the 31st [Tank] Brigade arrived on the northeastern outskirts of Dzialdowo. The enemy greeted it with heavy artillery and mortar fire: the Nazis realized that the loss of Dzialdowo would decide the fate of the entire Mława fortified area. Having struck the enemy simultaneously, the 31st and 32nd Tank Brigades crushed the garrison's main forces and took the railroad station. In the process a company of the 31st Tank Brigade, commanded by Senior Lieutenant A.I. Rukhliad'ev, an experienced officer who had previously been awarded the Order of the Red Banner, distinguished itself. The events unfolded in the following manner:

Pursuing the enemy's disorganized groups, Rukhdliad'ev and his combat comrades wound up in front of a high railroad embankment. A train carrying tanks, cannons and ammunition was standing on the tracks. An armored train was standing somewhat off to the side, which was intensively firing at the attackers. There was no way to bypass the train, and time was very short. Then Rukliad'ev decided to breakthrough to the embankment, to unlink the railcars, and to pull them apart with the help of a tank. While Rukhdial'ev's tank, maneuvering under enemy fire, moved out toward the train, our artillery set several of the railcars containing ammunition ablaze. The flames grew, and from minute to minute an explosion might occur. However, Rukhdial'ev stuck to his decision. He leaped out of his tank and under heavy enemy fire crawled up to the railway. Bullets, striking the rails, were ricocheting off them with a buzz, knocking chips out of the wooden walls of the burning railcars. Having covered the remaining distance with a dash, the stoutheart unlinked the railcars, then gave a signal to his driver-mechanic Senior Sergeant X. Faizrakhmanov. He drove the tank up to the train's flat bed cars and pulled them apart in opposite directions. The road was clear. The battalion drove across the embankment and the tanks burst into the station.

On the evening of 18 January, the results of the offensives were being summed up in the army's headquarters. The Mława fortified area was completely encircled and was totally blockaded.

From the memoirs of F.I. Galkin:

By the morning of 18 January, the corps reached the outer ring of the Mława fortifications. The garrison was fighting back. Then Vol'sky ordered to envelop the city from the east and west and to cut all the roads leading into it. The armored pincers encircled Mława. At the same time Malakhov's tank corps reached Dzialdowo and took the town after a short battle.

That evening Sidorovich at the army headquarters reported the initial results of the operation with a feeling of satisfaction. The main point was that all of the enemy's paths of retreat out of Mława had been cut, and the garrison was completely isolated. Glancing at a map, Vol'sky observed with plain contentment: "Beautiful pincers! Another two to three such envelopments, and we will be at the gates of Tolkemit … Where is the infantry now?"

"Approaching the outer ring," Sidorovich replied. "Sinenko is already setting up cooperation to ensure the success of the nighttime assault."

"Good, the infantry needs help."

On the night of 18-19 January General Sinenko, tired, but contented, excitedly reported to the army commander:

"The German Mława garrison has been defending desperately. It's hard to say how many counterattacks there have been. However, our tankers and infantrymen broke into the city from several directions. Now there is street fighting going on in the center of Mława. In the morning, troops of the 48th Army, supported by the tankers of Sakhno's corps, fully mopped up the town of fascists. A portion of the enemy garrison was destroyed, and another portion of it fled in different directions under the cover of the night; many have surrendered."

After the capture of Mława, I immediately drove out to the visit the repair elements that were positioned south of the town. Combat clashes were continuing, erupting in one place or another. I became an eyewitness of an artillery duel with a fascist battery of self-propelled assault guns.

Our artillery battalion was already about to leave their firing positions, when in the nearest woodlot there was the sudden sound of tank engines. The commander of the flank battery standing by the road took notice and ordered to deploy in the direction of the woods. The crews had barely had time to carry out this order, when four self-propelled guns showed up. Gathering speed and firing on the move, they charged the battery. The self-propelled guns needed not more than 90 seconds to reach the firing positions. However, our artillery crews needed even less time to take aim at the enemy. Two shots merged into one. The lead German machine came to a stop, clouds of smoke rose from its hulk, a plume of fire shot up from it, and a powerful explosion shook the air. The second self-propelled gun, having traced an odd turn, rammed into the hulk of the first self-propelled gun that had been overturned by the explosion, and also burst into flames. The Nazis leaped out of the remaining two: seeing that there was no way for the machines to get away from the Soviet gunners, the crews attempted to make use of a deep roadside ditch and escape into the woods. I waited, until the bursts of automatic weapons' fire died down, then drove out to take a look at the fascist machines. The two lead machines were already burned out, but the other two proved to be completely serviceable and had a full load of ammunition and nearly full tanks of fuel. Lushnikov hastened to top up the Willys with fuel, and artillerymen who had come up by that time began to examine the captured trophies. The dead Nazis in their black cotton uniforms bearing cadet shoulder straps and a swastika sharply stood out against the snow. I remembered Vol'sky's words before the offensive: "Remember, Galkin, the Nazis have a self-propelled gun training school in Mława. Don't forget to check it out. There might be something useful there." Then I immediately ordered Lushnikov: "Into Mława!"

The ancient Polish town was in ruins. An endless column of Soviet troops was moving along the streets to the northwest. I found the German self-propelled gun training school without any trouble and immediately drove across the grounds of it. More than two dozen bays with concrete floors and entrances had been broken wide open. Opposite, on the other side of a broad yard lined with little paving blocks stretched a row of warehouses. They were jammed with all kinds of materiel, instruments and spare parts. More than 1,000 20-liter canisters containing anti-freeze were in one of the warehouses – a mixture that wouldn't freeze, necessary for refilling the radiators of the machines given low temperaures. Everything had been sorted and stored with purely German tidiness. Particularly valuable were the shaped steel of various designs, shapes and dimensions, as well as the dozens of metric tons of sheet steel. The metalworking and machining tools proved beneficial.

Having returned, I ordered for the repair department to house the headquarters of the 83rd Battalion in the former school, together with a company of specialized workers and the administrative platoon, and to send logistics officers to the field stockpile of armored vehicle support material.

About three days later, I drove by the school to check on how the repair workers were utilizing the captured goods. At the entrance to a warehouse, a sergeant major, the supervisor of the repository, greeted me and reported that all of the parts and materials had been inventoried.

"Are the sizes what we need, Sergeant Major?"

"As if by order, Comrade Guards Colonel."

"And have you figured out the stamps?"

"There was nothing to figure out with them. The markings were all ours. The Fritzes, you see, had taken the steel from our own iron and steel stockpiles."

The materials captured in the school's warehouses were sufficient to keep us supplied for the entire operation.

Success encourages one and gives one strength; the proximity of an objective beckons to you. In front of us was the German – Polish border.

The 5th Guards Tank Army in the East Prussia operation, 1945

German obstacles on the third defensive line north of Ciechanów. The forces of the 5th Guards Tank Army overcame them on the same day it was introduced into the breakthrough on 17 January 1945. (TsA MO)

'Scorched earth' in East Prussia, February 1945. (TsA MO)

Soviet Infantry on the streets of Tolkemit, East Prussia, winter 1945. (TsA MO)

Soviet M4A2 tank, Tolkemit, East Prussia, winter 1945. (TsA MO)

Carrying out its mission, the 32nd Tank Brigade successively captured the villages of Bogurzyn, Rumoka, Lipowiec-Kościelny, Kęczewo and Rywociny, before making a forced crossing of the Dzialdowka River 2 km west of Dzialdowo. Having broken through a defensive line that was occupied by weak enemy forces, the tank brigade by 1600 on 18 January reached the western outskirts of Dzialdowo with its forward detachments, where it was met by heavy enemy anti-tank artillery fire. The commander of the 32nd Tank Brigade made the correct decision: while distracting the enemy's attention with the forward detachment, the brigade's main forces would envelop Dzialdowo from the west and northwest. Implementing this maneuver, the 32nd Tank Brigade by 1800 on 18 January had taken the Burkat – Skupie – Pierławki area, thereby severing the enemy's path of retreat to the west and northwest.

The commander of the 31st Tank Brigade, having repulsed an enemy counterattack at 1400 on 18 January in the Stare Kosiny area (south of Mława) also made the correct decision: until the 25th Tank Brigade (which was operating on the right, but lagging somewhat behind) reached this area, to screen his right flank with the artillery battalion, while with his main forces to continue to advance rapidly behind the 32nd Tank Brigade in the Dzialdowo direction. By 1800 the brigade reached Kurki, having been tied up in combat with the enemy in the Kosiny area. The enemy had been crushed and the German remnants had fled in disorder toward Dzialdowo. The enemy retreat was so hasty that he didn't have time to blow up the bridges across the Dzialdowka River. On the heels of the retreating enemy, the brigade rolled across the bridges and broke into the southeastern outskirts of Dzialdowo. With an enveloping maneuver along the eastern outskirts, the brigade reached the town's northeastern outskirts and cut the Dzialdowo – Neidenburg highway. By 2000 on 18 January the 32nd and 31st Tank Brigades, operating in cooperation with each other, had smashed the main forces of the Dzialdowo garrison and captured the Dzialdowo railroad station, and by the next morning, together with the arriving 53rd Motorized Rifle Brigade and a portion of the 25th Tank Brigade, they had fully mopped up the town of the small remaining pockets of enemy troops.

The 25th Tank Brigade and 53rd Motorized Rifle Brigade, attacking along the corps' right-hand route, at an order from the corps commander, with the break of day on 18 January had continued to advance to the west along their route while bypassing to the south of the Mława fortifications. In the areas of Wiśniewo and Podkrajewo, the brigades were twice counterattacked by the enemy from the direction of Mława in strength of up to 1 to 2 battalions of infantry and 7-10 tanks, which tried to intercept the 29th Tank Corps' advance to the west. Having repulsed the enemy counterattacks and having deployed strong blocking detachments of artillery on the Wiśniewo – Podkrajewo line, the 25th Tank Brigade and 53rd Motorized Rifle Brigade with their main forces had resumed their advance along the route toward Dzialdowo.

The forward detachment of the 25th Tank Brigade, having detected a weakly-defended sector of the outer ring of Mława's fortifications in the Turza Mala area, broke through it and by 2000 on 18 January reached the Iłowo area, thereby cutting the railroad running between Mława and Dzialdowo. By end of day on 18 January, the 25th Tank Brigade and 53rd Motorized Rifle Brigade reached the southeastern outskirts of Dzialdowo, and together with the 31st and 32nd Tank Brigades fully mopped up the town of the small remaining enemy pockets. By the morning of 19 January, they had reached the Komorniki, Kolgartowo area 1.5 km north of Dzialdowo.

Major trophies had been captured by the 29th Tank Corps in Dzialdowo: 4 railroad trains, 14 steam engines, 8 operational tanks that had been loaded on platform cars, and in the town itself approximately 150 vehicles, 20 guns of various caliber, 2 stockpiles of fuel and lubricants, and a lot of other military gear. Altogether more than 20 trains (of which two were carrying vehicles), 34 steam engines, 8 railway inspection cars and 13 military stockpiles wound up cut-off and were later captured on the sector of railroad between Dzialdowo and Mława. In addition, more than 15,000 Russian military prisoners and Russian civilians that had been forcibly taken to Germany for slave labor were liberated in Dzialdowo.

As a result of the combat operations of the 5th Guards Tank Army over 18 January 1945, the powerful Mława defensive strongpoint had been isolated; its outer ring of fortifications had been ruptured in several places; all of the main paths of retreat from Mława had been cut; and the important road and railroad hub and German strongpoint of Dzialdowo (18 km northwest of Mława) had been captured, its garrison crushed by the sudden and decisive attacks of tanks. By the end of day on 18 January, disarray and a hasty regrouping of forces was observable in the German Mława garrison. The fire resistance and activity of the defenders of this defensive strongpoint had sharply fallen in its southeastern, southern and southwestern sectors.

By the units of the 48th Army that had arrived by the evening of 18 January and the decisive cooperation of the forces of the 5th Guards Tank Army that were encircling Mława from every direction, on the night of 18-19 the town of Mława and the entire Mława fortified area was mopped up of the enemy. The fall of this powerful Mława strongpoint with all its numerous, costly and strong fortifications in the matter of just one day must be recognized as one of the brightest examples of the proper use of armored formations and the proper cooperation between the tank and infantry units when capturing centers of resistance and strongpoints. The primary role of the tanks is to use maneuvering actions to encircle the garrison of the strongpoint or center of resistance, disperse his forces and attention in every direction, and by this weaken and partially demoralize him, while the infantry with the support of artillery and if necessary the tanks attacks the weakest places cracks the defenses and captures the town, having destroyed or captured its garrison.

From the "Combat Path of the 29th Tank Corps":

From the morning of 15 January 1945, the forces of the shock groupings resumed the offensive. On 17 January 1945 the forward detachments of the 29th Tank Corps under the command of Major General of Tank Forces K.M. Malakhov caught up with the forward infantry formations of the 48th Army's first echelon and became tied up in combat with the enemy. A new stage of the 29th Tank Corps' glorious combat path began on this day. Its first assignment was to capture the Polish town of Dzialdowo, which was located not far from the border with East Prussia.

The Front's successful combat operations secured the 5th Guards Tank Army's rapid advance. Without encountering serious resistance, the 29th Tank Corps conducted an offensive along its designated direction. The enemy was defending opposite the front of Colonel I.O. Stanislavsky's tank brigade in strength of up to an infantry battalion, which was being supported by four tanks and two artillery batteries. Facing Colonel A.I. Pokolov's brigade, the enemy strength was approximately the same. With the actions of the brigade's forward detachments, the enemy was driven from the occupied line, and the brigades in a night action on 18 January 1945 captured the Kosily railroad station – Żmijewo – Konopki line.

In the vicinity of the Konopki railroad station, the enemy was offering resistance with the shattered units of the 7th Infantry Division and Panzerjäger Battalion 511. After a short preparatory fire, the 31st Tank Brigade from the march attacked the enemy and at midnight on 18 January 1945 captured the Konopki railroad station.

In the course of this attack, the first to break into station was a company of the 1st Tank Battalion under the command of Lieutenant I.N. Grudinkin. Having opened fire at a train that was loaded with ammunition and explosives and was ready for departure, the tankers set several of the railcars ablaze. From the detonation of shells, an explosion of terrible force occurred, which wiped out everything out to radius of 200 meters. Not even a trace was left of the station's buildings. The blast ripped the turret from Lieutenant Grudinkin's tank and its crew was killed. Lieutenant Grudinkin had been sitting on the tank's armor, and he was found 300 meters away from the tank in critical condition. The failure of the turret occurred because the tank hatches were open. This was the reason for the death of the crew.

In the course of the fighting that developed in the vicinity of the Mława center of resistance, it became clear that the enemy had decided to stop the Soviet advance at whatever the cost, in order to gain time and, if successful, to grind down our units on the approaches to East Prussia. However, the enemy's plans were frustrated. The Front's forces broke through the enemy's defenses on the outer ring of Mława's fortifications, enveloped the town on two sides, and exploited the offensive in the northwestern direction. The 29th Tank Corps bypassed the town of Mława from the south and launched an attack toward Dzialdowo. In order to cover the corps' right flank, Major General of Tank Forces K.M. Malakhov decided to halt Colonel I.O. Stanislavsky's tank brigade in the Kosily area. Throughout the night of 17-18 January and the day of 18 January 1945, the corps conducted successful combat operations. Its 31st Tank Brigade captured Dąbek and took Kosiny-Stary, where it was counterattacked by enemy tanks. The brigade, having deployed its main forces, joined combat with them.

The corps commander decided to exploit the success of the offensive by introducing Lieutenant Colonel S.G. Kolesnikov's 32nd Tank Brigade into the fighting, having given it an order to deploy from behind the left flank of Colonel A.I. Pokolov's brigade, and without getting bogged down in extended fighting, to reach the Dzialdowo area with a dash and to cut the enemy's path of retreat. Carrying out its orders, the brigade with its main forces at mid-day captured Księży Dwor, while its forward detachment reached the western outskirts of Dzialdowo, where it became tied up in fighting with a strong enemy rearguard. Lieutenant Colonel S.G. Kolesnikov decided to continue to divert the enemy's attention with the forward detachment, and to push around the town to an area northwest of it. Implementing this maneuver, his units took the Burkat, Skupie, Pierlawki area, thereby cutting the enemy's path of retreat to the west. Colonel A.I. Pokolov's brigade, having repulsed an enemy counterattack to the south of the Mława strongpoint, continued the offensive in the Glużek, Kęczewo, Kurki direction.

The 31st Tank Brigade reached the approaches to Dzialdowo from the southeast. In the vicinity of Kisiny, the enemy's covering screen was driving back in a short combat action, and on his bootheels the 31st Tank Brigade broke into the town. Major N.D. Tuz's battalion was the first to enter it.

Senior Lieutenant A.I. Rukhliad'ev's tank company attacked the railroad station on 18 January 1945. A burning train loaded with ammunition was blocking the tanker's path. Ignoring the fire of the resisting Germans and the exploding ammunition, the company under the command of Senior Lieutenant A.I. Rukhliad'ev captured the station with an impetuous attack, in the process capturing three trains carrying tanks and another loaded with combat equipment. Pursuing the retreating enemy, the tankers were one of the first to break into the town of Elbing and reach the coastline of the Baltic Sea. On 1 February 1945, Senior Lieutenant Aleksandr Ignat'evich Rukhliad'ev fell bravely in battle. He was posthumously awarded the title Hero of the Soviet Union.

> One of the companies of Major Tuz's battalion, entering the town, took the entire fascist attack on itself. Slugs, shells and bullets flew toward it from every direction. However, the company, led by its commander, continued to attack. Soon, gloomy barracks surrounded by barbed wire materialized in front of the tankers. Quickly, the posts and observation towers were knocked over and crushed by the tanks' tracks, and the camp guards were slaughtered. Approximately 15,000 Russian and Polish citizens in striped prisoner garb were standing in front of the tankers. There were prisoners of war among them. Emaciated, haggard, many of them could barely stand on their feet, but their faces were lit up by joyous smiles. Embracing their liberators, they expressed their gratitude for freeing them.
>
> On the night of 18-19 January 1945, the town of Dzialdowo was completely mopped up of the remaining enemy by the corps' second echelon. The armored pincers enveloped Mława.
>
> In the fighting for Dzialdowo, Lieutenant L.D. Mitiat'ko's mortar crews, Captain G.F. Panchenko's artillerymen and especially the crews of Senior Sergeant E.P. Krylov and Sergeant G.T. Akulov demonstrated great skill and fearlessness. A lot of knocked out guns, tanks and dead Nazis went to their credit.

On the morning of 19 January 1945, the forces of the 5th Guards Tank Army continued the offensive in the general direction of Neidenburg and in the middle of the day reached and crossed the Polish-German border south and west of Neidenburg. On its old border on the approaches to Neidenburg, using strong fortifications in the Kuklin and Napierken area, the enemy offered fierce resistance with the forces of up to two infantry regiments, 30-40 tanks and self-propelled guns, and up to two battalions of infantry.

The 10th Tank Corps undertook an attempt to take this area from the march on the morning of 19 January, but had no success. Throughout the day of 19 January, the enemy, with the support of heavy artillery and mortar fire, itself repeatedly launched counterattacks in strength of 20 to 30 tanks and self-propelled guns and one to three battalions of infantry, against both the 10th Tank Corps and in the direction of Dzialdowo against the 29th Tank Corps. All of the enemy counterattacks were thrown back. In the tough fighting, both sides suffered heavy losses in men and armor.

At 1700 on 19 January, having finally ground down the enemy, the troops of the 5th Guards Tank Army launched a decisive attack. The 47th Separate Mechanized Brigade, which up to this point had been operating in the second echelon, was committed into the fighting from behind the 10th Tank Corps' right flank. By 1800 on 19 January, the 5th Guards Tank Army, having broken the enemy's stubborn resistance, reached the following line: 47th Separate Mechanized Brigade and 10th Tank Corps – had taken the road hub of Napierken and were fighting on the Powiersen (Powierz) – Krokau (Krokowo) line; 29th Tank Corps, while topping up its machines with fuel and replenishing ammunition, with its forward detachment had taken Uzdowo and Wiersbau, thereby blocking the enemy's path of retreat from Neidenburg to the west.

The availability of tanks and self-propelled guns in the formations and units of the 5th Guards Tank Army at 2000 on 19 January 1945

10th Tank Corps: The corps has in service 80 T-34, 39 SU-100, 19 SU-85, 21 ISU-122 and 6 M4A2. Available supplies: 1.0 refills of diesel fuel, 1.0 refills of gasoline; 1.8 combat loads of ammunition, and 8 days of food.

29th Tank Corps: The corps has in service 80 T-34, 23 SU-152, 18 SU-85, 23 SU-76. Available supplies: 0.7 refills of diesel fuel, 1.0 refills of gasoline; 1.5 combat loads of ammunition, and 3 days of food.

47th Mechanized Brigade: The brigade has in service 38 M4A2 and 1 Mk-IX. Available supplies: 0.5 refills of diesel fuel, 0.5 refills of gasoline; 1.5 combat loads of ammunition, and 3 days of food.

14th Guards Heavy Tank Regiment: The regiment had in service 14 IS-122 tanks.

376th Guards Heavy Self-propelled Artillery Regiment: The regiment had in service 19 ISU-152.

76th Guards Mortar Regiment: The regiment had in service 32 BM-13 rocket launchers.

Total: 357 armored fighting vehicles in service.

Chief of staff of the 5th Guards Tank Army
Major General of Tank Forces SIDOROVICH

Continuing the offensive, on the night of 19-20 January 1945 the 10th Tank Corps, in cooperation with the 47th Separate Mechanized Brigade, drove the enemy out of the fortifications south of Kandien and by 0700 on 20 January had taken the Kandien – Wasienen line and reached the approaches to Neidenburg. The town of Neidenburg was located in the zone of the enemy's fifth defensive belt and represented a heavily-fortified strongpoint. Three lines of trenches with bunkers, pillboxes, barbed wire and an antitank ditch ran just in front of the town. Some of the buildings on the town's outskirts had been adapted for defense.

The commander of the 10th Tank Corps Major General of Tank Forces Sakhno, assessing the situation, made the proper decision and issued the following orders to his units: 183rd Tank Brigade in cooperation with the 47th Separate Mechanized Brigade was to bypass the eastern side of the city in order to cut the roads in the Robertshof area and take the road fork 2 km north of Neidenburg; 186th Tank Brigade was to envelop the town from the west and cut the road running to the northwest in the Littfinken area; 178th Tank Brigade, operating on the 186th Tank Brigade's left, was to cut the road in the Karlshohe area and to block any enemy counterattack from the west; 11th Motorized Rifle Brigade with a frontal assault in cooperation with the 47th Separate Mechanized Brigade, which was to launch an attack from the east, was to clear the city of enemy troops and reach the line of the brick factories 2 km north and northwest of Neidenburg. After a 15-minute barrage with all types of guns, the corps' units at 0900 on 19 January moved out to storm the town of Neidenburg.

Having overcome the enemy resistance, the corps' units by 1000 had closed the ring of encirclement and had cut off all the paths of retreat from out of Neidenburg: 178th Tank Brigade had reached the Karlshohe area; 186th Tank Brigade had reached the Littfinken area; 183rd Tank Brigade had taken the road fork 2 km north of Neidenburg; 47th Separate Mechanized Brigade had captured Robertshof and had broken into the city's eastern outskirts; 11th Motorized Rifle Brigade was assaulting the city from the south. By 1100 on 20 January, the city of Neidenburg was completely mopped up by the enemy through the joint operations of the 47th Separate Mechanized Brigade and 11th Motorized Rifle Brigade, with the cooperation of the tank brigades. In the fighting for the town of Neidenburg, the 10th Tank Corps killed more than 500 enemy soldiers and officers, destroyed 12 self-propelled guns and up to 200 vehicles, and captured around 300 men, several military stockpiles, and up to 300 vehicles.

With the capture of the towns of Dzialdowo and Neidenburg, the 5th Guards Tank Army had carried out its immediate task; moreover, the Dzialdowo area had been occupied ahead of schedule by 2000 on 18 January, and not on the morning of 19 January as had been planned. The taking of the city of Neidenburg was delayed until 1100 on 20 January, because the enemy was taking advantage of the strong border defenses here and was putting up tough resistance with significant forces, including units of the 18th Panzergrenadier Division and elements of Panzergrenadier Division *Grossdeutschland*. On the whole, the immediate task set before the 5th Guards Tank Army had been carried out on time and with fine results.

From the recollections of V.P. Gud:

One can say that we crawled into East Prussian on our belly. The Germans were resisting there particularly fiercely. Here, in East Prussia, something struck me. There was a lot of cattle in each village and at each farm. Each household might have had 10 to 15 cows. You see, all of the precious cows had been driven to here from all of the Soviet Union. From all of the occupied territory. Our own people were working in the factories. They'd been forcibly brought here. Our adolescent girls, 15 to 17 years of age. From our Russian oblasts, Belorussia, Ukraine. They were enslaved. There were no men present in the households. Plainly, they'd all been called up into the army, and they were all fighting.

I recall how we entered East Prussia. We went into the breakthrough in a dense fog. There was almost no way to employ the heavy weapons. All of our aircraft were grounded and sitting on their airfields. The tanks, the armored halftracks and the Katiushas were all advancing behind us. We would make an advance of a kilometer or two, and they would be a kilometer or two in our rear. They were never committed into the fighting. But later, when we had broken through the defenses to the entire depth, the tanks entered this breakthrough like a compact avalanche. At night, with switched on head lights. In the fog. They had been rolling through the night for around five or six hours in order to overtake us. Virtually all-night long. We looked at this thundering horde and thought, "Well, the juggernaut has been set in motion, now nothing will stop us." In the morning we moved out after them. That's how East Prussia was cut off from Central Germany.

We took the first village – there were just two old women there, as old as the hills or just about. We were asking them, "Where are all the people?" And they answered us: "Everyone left. We were being told that the Russians were coming, with horns on their heads, and that they were going to kill or hang everyone. Get away. So, everyone left. But we're old; we aren't afraid of death. Now you've arrived. You've made contact with us, and we're convinced: you aren't devils, you don't have horns."

Further on, more Germans began to appear. We even saw young babes soon. But we had nothing to do with them – nothing at all. True, we were soon provided with condoms. Just in case. Just like the gas masks at the start of the war. After all, we were young guys back then and ready to have sex with any (even German) females.

But one time ... We were standing around somewhere, lighting campfires. The Germans were far off. An accordion started up. The guys immediately called, "Join hands and hop to it!" A circular dance got going! We were all young! Bright-eyed and bushy-tailed! Wearing medals! Some had even two each!

The Germans, the civilians, they were hiding. But there were Polish hamlets there, in East Prussia. They were audacious. As soon as we arrived, they were going around, doing business. They were selling various trifles so as to buy something. There was one Polish woman who kept coming around us. Noone was buying anything from her. She grew irritated, walked up, and gave me a little shove: "*Ty pierdolony żołnierzu!*" This is something like, "You, you're one fucked up soldier!"

On the spot I spoke up and replied, "*Co trzeba pierdolona dupo, twoja matka tez byla zasraną kurwa!* [What do you want, you fucking whore? Your mother was also a shitty whore.]" Her eyes opened wide in astonishment – and how she scrambled to run away! The guys asked me, "Where did you learn your Polish?" I told them that before the war in the hamlets around Kaluga we spoke four languages: Russian, Ukrainian, Belorussian and Polish.

I was assigned to a reconnaissance platoon, as a sniper. We were taking a rest. A lieutenant walks up, the commander of the reconnaissance platoon, and asks, "Who knows the Polish language?" I replied, "I know a little." He simply said, "Let's go." We walked into the hamlet. There, some Pole had set up a tent and was selling home brew, pouring it with a small dipper. The lieutenant tells me: "Ask, what money is he accepting – ours or Polish?" I asked the Pole, "*Jakie pan bierze pieniądze?*" – He replied in crude Russian, "Huh, what's the difference?" Aha, we could see the Pole was an amiable fellow, and that we could strike a deal with him about anything. The platoon leader gulped down the homebrew. You could see that he liked it. Then the lieutenant told me: "Tell him that we need two wenches." I translated, "*Panie potrzebne będą dwie dziewczyzy. – "A co ja będę mieć?* [*What will I get in exchange?*]" – "*Pieniądze* [*Money*]" – "*Dobrze. Wszystko będzie* [OK. It will be taken care of]." Then the lieutenant prompted me: "Tell him to make sure that the wenches are "safe". You know, so they don't spread any infections. I'm asking because the Germans were here before us …" I passed that along to the Pole. He burst out laughing: "*Dobrze, dobrze panie oficerze.* [*Fine, very well Sir Officers*]" I arrive back at the platoon. The word was already spreading. Reconnaissance!! Then all the guys forgot my last name and began to call me, "*Pan* Kalinowski! *Pan* Kalinowski!"[1] That's what they called me, until I got wounded on that damned sandbar.

From the memoirs of N.E. Udik:

After breaking through the German defenses, we stopped in some rather large village, the name of which I no longer recall. Back then the Prussians were living not badly. The homes were of good quality; they had good furniture and lovely dishware. Well-fed cows, pigs and chickens were wandering around in the farmsteads. The Germans didn't have time to evacuate all this in their hasty departure. In Lithuania the situation was completely different. Here, the people lived impoverished lives. It was hard to forage for supplies at the expense of the local population. Yet here, in the households of the German burghers of East Prussia, our commissary officers had no problems replenishing their supplies.

We spent the night in this German village. For dinner we received some alcohol that had been found in this village. It had been sent to us by Sergeant Major Popov of a 120mm mortar battery. We also had the clerk Mashevsky who know how to organize such things quickly. He himself was quite fond of drinking and therefore kept constant contact with the commanders and commissary officers of the battalion's platoons and of other units. When we poured out the spirit into drinking glasses and diluted it with water, a whitish fluid, almost like milk, formed in the glasses. I tested this fluid with my tongue and had no wish to drink it. The assistant chief of staff Paegle and Mashevsky himself, as well as the clerks Semen Ivanovich Tishkin, Nikolai Zhirnov and Petr Sidorkevich also gave it a try and didn't want to drink it. However, our driver drank up his portion and consumed the portions of several comrades, saying, "OK, to me, an old man, it tastes just fine!"

---

1 This is a reference to Marcin Kalinowski, a Polish nobleman back in the 17th Century famous for his campaigns against the Cossacks and Tatars until he was killed at the Battle of Batoh after his army was surprised by a combined Cossack-Tatar army.

That night I was on duty at the headquarters. When I tried to wake up Il'in for his shift, he couldn't even stand on his feet – he was drunk. I had to give his shift to a different comrade.

When we were approaching the borders of East Prussia, two soldiers were assigned to guard the headquarters; in addition to them we had two staff cars and two drivers. These men were submachine gunners Petr Sidorkevich and Vladimir Sova, and drivers Il'in and Trizna Emel'ian. Sergeant Sidorkevich also was used as a clerk. It was these comrades, who in addition to their direct responsibilities, also carried out service to guard the headquarters.

We spent a second day in this village. Our Il'in was suffering after his bout of drinking. He would drink water and again become intoxicated. He began to suffer by evening, and it was obvious that he was feeling badly. From the evening of our second day in East Prussia, there was a lengthy march that continued all night: we were being shifted to a different sector. Il'in was unable to walk on his own, and he rode in a vehicle. When we arrived in our new positions, they sent Il'in to the medical company, and there he passed away. In the same condition soldiers of the 120mm battery, of the signals company, the chemical defense platoon and others also arrived at the medical company – altogether more than 10 men. Almost all of them died. Several of the men became blind and were sent on to a hospital. Among the deceased from the chemical defense platoon was driver Sorokin. Almost all of the poisoned men were old soldiers, who had been mobilized back in Novosibirsk when the division departed for the front.

As became clear, the soldiers of the mortar battery, having discovered the spirits, shared it with friends and acquaintances. They themselves perished, and they accidentally killed their friends. The spirits proved not to be consumable, but wood alcohol (methanol), and methanol is a strong poison. By this time an order had gone out that banned the consumption of any fluid found in the liberated cities and villages without prior checking. However, obviously not everyone observed these orders, and especially those who were not against drinking alcohol.

Our units in East Prussia advanced with heavy fighting. The civilian population was fleeing together with the retreating units. Almost none of the local population remained in the hamlets. Upon occupying a town with our troops, as a rule, no major violations of discipline took place, but homes were igniting after being occupied by our soldiers. Obviously, the Germans were leaving behind self-igniting devices. In addition, our soldiers didn't spare buildings in captured cities, and didn't always observe the proper rules of handling fire. There were cases when our soldiers for no particular reason triggered automatic burst of weapon fire at mirrors, cupboards containing expensive china, and so forth and so on. Our Russian soldier was full of malice toward fascism and sometimes dealt with this in some absurd manner. Moreover, at the time no one knew that these places and property would eventually become part of the Soviet Union. I no longer recall the name of a town that was captured in a night assault; the Germans had fled almost in their underpants. The city was taken almost intact, but indeed after several days it had turned into ruins ....

From the recollections of L. Rabichev:

On 19 January 1945 I received an order over the radio to dismiss the sentries, relocate the platoon, and wait for further orders. The sappers filled ditches, disassembled five lines of barbed wire obstacles, and eliminated one more ditch or embankment. In this fashion, a gap around 15-meters wide appeared in the obstacles, through which ran a country lane from Poland into East Prussia. A paved road began about 100 meters away, with woods on either side of it, and several kilometers away, a road to the Gollubinen estate.

This was a two-story manor, covered with a red tile roof, encircled by all kinds of service buildings. Inside, the walls were decorated with tapestries and wall hangings from the XVII Century. In one of the room there was a Rokotov painting on the wall, and next to it (and around the entire house) was a multitude of family photographs – Daguerrotypes from the start of the century – of generals and officers encircled by well-dressed ladies and children; then – officers in helmets with shakoes, who had returned from the First World War, and completely recent photographs: young boys wearing arm bands with swastikas and their sisters, plainly students, and finally, photographs of young SS *Oberleutnants*, who had gone missing on the Russian front – the last generation of this traditional family of the military aristocracy. Family portraits of Prussian barons were hanging among the photographs, and then suddenly two more paintings, one by Rokotov, the other by Borovikovsky, that were captured portraits of Russian generals and their wives and children.

Our infantrymen and tankers who had been in this "museum" before us didn't remain indifferent to the hunting lodge of the Prussian royalty: all of the mirrors encased in gilded frames had been smashed by them, all of the feather bedding and pillows had been torn apart, and all of the furniture and floors were covered by a layer of down and feathers. In the hallway there was a tapestry that reproduced Rubens' famous painting *Aphrodite Rising from the Sea*. Someone, taking his revenge on the aggressors by scrawling a three-letter word across the painting with black oil paint. The 1.5-meter-long tapestry, scrawled with the three letters, reminded me of my pre-war interest in art back in Moscow. I rolled it up and placed it in a captured German satchel, which had already been serving as my pillow for the past three months.

I took a look out the window. The estate, which consisted of a secondary palace and brick service buildings, was encircled by a wrought-iron fence, and on the other side of the fence, and on the green meadows that stretched as far as the eye could see was an unbelievable number of enormous black and white pure-bred cows, wandering, mooing and crying. Already a week had passed since the Germans – both the troops and the civilians – had departed without offering battle. No one had milked the cows. Their swollen udders were painful and they were calling for relief. Two of my female telephone operators, who had once lived in villages, filled several buckets of milk, but it was bitter, and we refused to drink it.

Then a wild disturbance outside caught my attention. One of the signalers had found a chicken coop among the brick buildings, opened its gates, and hundreds of hungry, pure-bred chickens came running out into the yard. My soldiers were literally stunned. Like madmen, they were chasing the chickens, running and leaping, and when they caught one, they ripped off its head. Then they found an enormous kettle. They gutted the chickens and plucked them. There were already more than 100 chickens in the kettle, and only 45 individuals in my platoon. We made boiled chicken with broth, and then stuffed ourselves until everyone dropped where they were and fell fast asleep. This was the evening of our first day in East Prussia. About two hours later the entire platoon got sick. We woke up, jumped to our feet, and went running for the henhouse ….

Several kilometers from the border, and as it seems, from our positions was a wealthy East Prussian city. The day before our units had encircled it, but there were no citizens or German soldiers in the city, and when our regiments and divisions entered it, the generals and officers completely lost control over them. The infantrymen and tankers rampaged through the apartment complexes and shops. All the contents of the shops went flying out the shop windows onto the sidewalks. Thousands of pairs of shoes, dishware, radios, dinnerware sets, all kinds of household and pharmacy goods and wares – all jumbled up together. Clothing, underwear, pillows, bedding, blankets, paintings, gramophones and musical instruments came flying out apartment windows. Barricades were being formed in the streets.

It was just then that German artillery and mortars started up. Several reserve German divisions threw our demoralized units out of the city with almost lightning speed. However, at the demand of the Front headquarters, the capture of the first German city had already been reported. So, we had to take once again. However, the Germans again drove our guys out of it, but this time did not occupy it. So the city became no-man's land.

…

Outside two soldiers from the separate anti-aircraft artillery brigade were saying that the city had already changed hands three times, but since this morning had again become no-man's land, but the road leading into it was being shelled. But my God! To see the ancient German city with your own eyes!

I climbed into a truck with Corporal Starikov, who had been a driver back in civilian life. Faster, faster! We sped down the road, while shells were dropping to our right and left. Just in case I ducked down, but we were quickly through the zone of fire. Out in front of us, looking just like the scenes on captured German postcards, were cottages with gabled, red tile roofs and weather vanes, among which were marble fountains and monuments at the street intersections. We stopped in the center of the almost empty city. Europe! It was all so interesting! However, this journey was also an absence without leave, and we had to return quickly to the unit.

All of the doors to the apartments were open, and on the beds – real beds – were pillows in pillow cases and blankets in duvet covers; in the kitchens were colorful tubes containing aromatic condiments. In the pantry were cans of home-made preserves, soups, and a variety of side dishes, as well as something about which we only dreamed – the freshest dairy cream in sealed half-liter containers (what kind of technology was this without heating?). There were proprietary wines, liqueurs, flavor infusions, Italian vermouths and cognacs. Hanging in the wardrobes were brand new civilian suits and vests of various sizes.

We had ten more minutes. We couldn't resist and changed into the suits, and then twirled around in front of mirros just like a damoiselles. Lord, how handsome we looked! But the time! We quickly changed back into our uniforms, and threw pillows, blankets, matresses, toys and cigarette lighters out the windows.

The memories of this gnaw at my mind. I recalled this moment, when several weeks later I arrived in Moscow for five days. The shop shelves were barren, and everything was being rationed. How happy my mother was for my supplementary officer's rations – a can of vegetable lard and two cans of American Spam, as well as for each dinner, which I was receiving according to my 10-days' away mission allotment card somewhere in an officers' mess hall in Syromiatniki, and bringing back home. Meanwhile, my neighbors were going hungry.

Why did I get this benefit? Here's why: We, half-starved and weary, were victorious, while the well-fed Germans who had no need for anything lost the war. I was thinking about this as Starikov and I were loading the back of the truck with pillows, mattresses and blankets, intending to distribute them to our soldiers, so that for at least three nights they could sleep like humans. Some hadn't seen a pillow for three years, while a few others hadn't seen one for the full six years of the war [obviously, soldiers who had participated in the operations against Poland in 1939 and in the Winter War against Finland].

We were not alone in the city. Several dozen other soldiers and officers from other combat units of our army were doing the same thing we were doing, collecting spoils of war, and loading them onto trucks of various sizes, from one-and-a-half ton trucks to Studebakkers and Willys jeeps – there were 30 to 40 of them.

Then suddenly a German Focke-Wolf appeared in the sky above the city – a nimble and highly maneuverable German reconnaissance plane – and just ten minutes later German batteries began working over the city. We quickly get on our way. Shells are exploding in front of us and behind us, and we were getting lost in a maze of streets and intersections. However, I had a compass; we set a course to the east, and ultimately, speeding past burning, abandoned trucks of the Red Army, we reached the highway over which we had entered the city, where we again came under German shelling. However, we were lucky, and toward evening we were arriving back at the headquarters of our company.

From the recollections of F.I. Galkin regarding the work of the recovery and repair services during the operation:

The fighting still hadn't ended for Mława before the forward brigades of Sakhno's tank corps set out toward Neidenburg. The driver-mechanics, grilling their steering levers until their fingers ached, drove their tanks onward. Many of them went into the attack with open hatches. This wasn't a senseless stunt: it was easier to see the enemy. The hatred for the fascists, which seethed in the soldiers' hearts, was seemingly increasing their strength, willpower and resolve ten-fold …

From Mława and Dzialdowo, having again left the infantry behind, the tank army's forces kept advancing to the northwest, and at mid-day on 19 January, they fought their way across the Germany – Poland border south and west of Neidenburg. The cradle of German fascism – East Prussia – was hearing the menacing rumble of our tanks. Neidenburg was part of the Germans' fifth defensive belt, and the Nazis were retreating toward it.

Rising, Vol'sky told me, "Here they've decided to give battle, making use of the fortifications and strong garrison. I will drive to see Malakhov, and you, Georgii Stepanovich, are to send another radio message to Sakhno to make sure he doesn't slacken the pace."

Several minutes after the commander-in-chief's departure, the phone rang – it was a call from the 10th Tank Corps' chief of staff Colonel Omeliusty. He reported to General Sidorovich, "The enemy in strength of up to two infantry regiments and up to fifty tanks and self-propelled guns supported by artillery has counterattacked out of the Kandien area. The counterattack was repulsed. We have losses. Five enemy tanks have been knocked out."

A minute later Sidorovich again answered the phone. The chief of staff of the 29th Tank Corps Colonel Smirnov was reporting: "The enemy in strength of two infantry battalions and up to twenty tanks is counterattacking from the direction of Napierken …."

Without waiting for the end of the report, I drove to Sakhno's tank corps in order to check on the organization of technical support. On the way to the 186th Tank Brigade, I stopped near two knocked-out T-34s, that were hidden behind a hill in a balka. A mobile repair shop was there, and repairmen were bustling about. The deputy chief of staff of the 171st Mobile Tank Repair Shop Engineer-Captain Nechaev was with them.

"Where is the deputy brigade commander?"

"Major Abramenko is up ahead, with the prime movers."

The Germans were counterattacking for the third time. There were several more knocked-out tanks. We climbed the hill. Up ahead, about 1.5-2 kilometers, the brigade was engaged in combat. The tanks, maneuvering, were slowly advancing, discharging shell after shell. Out in front of the machines, black sheafs of fire were now and then throwing up the frozen soil: enemy artillery was firing from out of the fortifications in the Kandien area. It was distinctly obvious that a group of our machines, having separated from the combat formations, were crawling into the enemy rear. About five minutes later, we detached two armored prime movers that were hitched together in tandem: they towed back a T-34 and quickly took cover in the low ground. Only a short time passed, when both prime movers reappeared, now without the tank, and head back again to where the battle was continuing.

"That's Major Abramenko who is running things," explained Engineer Nechaev. "The ground is suitable; they have a small balka, so they're evacuating knocked-out machines into cover. The repair teams are working on them in that balka."

"Excellent! Good man!" – I couldn't refrain from praising Abramenko.

"It's all well and good, but the brigade doesn't have any prime movers. These are the army's that have come up, he's temporarily using them …."

I returned to the corps command post that evening. General Sakhno was readying a night attack against Neidenburg. Sinenko had issued an order to the commander of the 47th Separate

Mechanized Brigade Colonel Mikhailov and was in the process of briefing him on the last details. Catching sight of me, Maksim Denisovich greeted me with a barely discernible nod of the head before leaning back in his chair. After three days, he was exhausted: his voice was hoarse, his eyes were reddened, and his face was ashen.

"The German doesn't want to give up Neidenburg; we must storm it," he said quietly to no one in particular. Then, plainly addressing me, he announced: "I've decided to commit our reserve into combat – Mikhailov's brigade from behind the tank corps' right flank. With an outflanking maneuver it is to strike the fortified area south of Kandien and help the corps take the city."

No one slept throughout the night. The generals and staff officers never separated from their operational maps and telephones; radio operators were constantly passing along reports, and the signalmen were hurrying to carry out all orders. On the night of 19-20 January, the forces of our tank army reached the approaches to Neidenburg. The assault on the city began at dawn. Neidenburg was taken by a simultaneous attack from the north, west and northwest. The attempt of the Nazis to protect the border of East Prussia fell apart under the rapid onslaught of the Soviet tankers. Vol'sky had every justification to "sum up the results" of the offensive toward Neidenburg with the following words: "Maksim Denisovich Sinenko and Mikhail Gordeevich Sakhno played out this attack note by note!"

With the invasion of East Prussia and the capture of Neidenburg, the first stage of the 5th Guards Tank Army's operation was over. Over four days of intense combat, the army commander only once was able to get a briefing on the condition of the tanks and self-propelled guns. He was continuously up at the front among the troops. However, now Vasilii Timofeevch was taking an interest in everything: "What are Sakhno's and Malakhov's losses? How is the work to put them back into service going? How well are the foreign tanks managing the snow and slush?"

As for myself, I was anxious to report about this. On the right flank, not only the enemy, but our own units as well had suffered significant losses. It had been costly to drive the tanks at high speeds, and on many of them the rubber rims of the roller wheels had peeled off. The fuel pump in some of the tanks were working poorly, and this was causing the motors to conk out. For this reason alone, around ten of the tanks had been left behind on the routes of advance. Several more tanks were knocked out when taking the Iłowo railroad station.

"It is clear," Vol'sky summarized after hearing my detailed report; "The problems are ordinary. However, get those tanks repaired!"

On the routes taken by the 25th Tank Brigade, south of Iłowo, I stopped at a group of tanks that were clustered not far from the road. The bare rims of the roller wheels leaped to the eye. One of the tanks was completely lacking rubber rims, while others had only pieces of rubber. Engineer Major Pavlov drove up in some captured hybrid vehicle – a combination of an armored halftrack and a tankette. For the first time in over four months, his typical smile wasn't on Boris Grigor'evich's face. He looked completely fatigued. Over all this time, Pavlov had been driving back and forth along the routes of advance, organizing the search and repair of damaged machines.

Approaching an immobilized tank, he muttered, "The men must fight, but now we must pray for forgiveness of our sins, stop, and patch things up."

Then he was summoned over to Skvortsov, where he spent a long time explaining things to him and pointing to a map.

I interjected: "You, Boris Grigor'evich, have you found any stockpiles of roller wheels?"

He replied, "No stockpile yet, but we're collecting one-and-a half dozen roller wheels."

"Where are you gathering such a harvest?"

"Southwest of Mława there are two knocked-out tanks. The roller wheels on both are intact."

"Whose tanks? Do they have turret numbers?"

"I didn't notice; I was paying more attention to the roller wheels. I'm only certain they aren't from our army."

"But you can't take them from the neighbor without asking."

"We'll deal with that if the owner is found," Pavlov replied, cracking a sly smile.

While we were talking, Skvortsov and the repair brigade, having loaded two hydraulic jacks on the mobile repair vehicle, drove off toward Mława. Of course, I reported the losses in Stanislavsky's tank brigade to the army commander.

"What's going on, are all the tanks being delivered from the repair factories in this condition?", he asked with irritation.

"No, but it happens sometimes. It takes place because they have a shortage of spare parts … but the front needs tanks. So sometimes they produce something that is low quality."

"Does that mean we were the "lucky" ones? Nevertheless, you must file complaints about all the tanks with defects. Let them know …."

Sakno's tank corps had begun to lose machines as soon as it entered the breakthrough. However, it suffered the greatest losses on the approaches to Neidenburg. The 178th and 186th Tank Brigades were deprived of more than half of their tanks and retained their combat effectiveness only through the work of the repair teams.

On the very first day of the offensive, it became clear to me and the deputy corps commander D.M. Kozyrev that the corps couldn't handle the recovery and repair of knocked out tanks through its own efforts. Therefore, on the evening of 17 January a repair company of the 83rd Army Recovery and Repair Battalion arrived on the routes of advance being followed by the 10th Tank Corps and organized a collecting point for disabled machines in the area of the fighting for the third defensive line. On the next day, a second field collecting point for disabled machines was created northeast of Mława.

In order to accelerate the return of machines to service, Kozyrev promptly reassigned all of the skilled technicians of the Technical-Repair Service and the corps' depot with the least amount of work to the repair of tanks. Meanwhile, machines that required light overhauls were temporarily left behind. This significantly hastened the process of replenishing the units. Having met with Kozyrev at the corps command post, I told him about the actions of Major Abramenko, which I had observed at Kandien.

"No prime movers; if only all of our guys had them available," he observed regretfully. "So, it is clear what comes of this: we do the recovery with combat machines. … During an enemy counterattack, I was with the 178th Tank Brigade. What's the point? The deputy commander for technical matters Engineer-Major Kabanov himself was recovering knocked out machines with a tank. It prevented it from finishing off a single enemy tank!"

"Was his own tank knocked out?"

"No. One shell, to be sure, struck the front of his tank, but it ricocheted away."

"Even so, Dmitrii Mikhailovich, keep the deputy commander for technical matters out of the way of enemy fire. Their duty is to organize work."

Kozyrev's report about the lack of prime movers in the corps simply disheartened me. "How did we overlook this?" – I thought, jolting along in the Willys. We'd become accustomed to the fact that the corps themselves obtain prime movers for themselves, both according to the table of organization and equipment and above the authorized number, but we overlooked the newly arriving tank corps. We'd have to assign it two or three prime movers from the army's evacuation companies. This was little, of course, but we couldn't gather more.

Several days later, I learned from Kozyrev that Engineer-Major Kabanov had been killed.

"Did he once again go out under enemy fire?"

"That's what happened, but wasn't the cause. He snuck out time after time, and everything went well, but they got him behind our lines …"

"In our rear area? How?"

"He was on his way to the Osterode area, in order to hasten the repairs. There, some Nazis that were lurking in some woods attacked him. He was a marvelous fellow …."

It was always dangerous in the rear, when the tank army was operating in the operational depth and separated from the infantry. Time and again our repair teams had to repulse enemy soldiers that were attacking from the rear! I told Kozyrev about coming upon four self-propelled guns near Mława and once again reminded him about the need to take care of the men.

...

I found the deputy commander of the 47th Mechanized Brigade for technical matters Protasov at a knocked-out machine on the outskirts of Neidenburg. He was walking around the tank and growling at the repair workers: "Two hours you've been messing around with the running gear, and this should not take you longer than ninety minutes."

However, Protasov didn't know how to swear. His comments were more like entreaties. The soldiers listened to him and didn't take his grumbling serious; smiling, they were exchanging side glances. "In the presence of a superior officer, he suddenly gets strict."

"What's troubling you, Sergei Stepanovich?" I asked, having exchanged greetings with him. Are the losses high?"

"One burned out, and four have minor damage. By evening, I think, all four will be returned to service."

"How are the American Sherman tanks handling the slippery surfaces?"

"Like cows. They go and go, and then suddenly one will topple over into a roadside ditch. Or one will suddenly pivot crossways on the road. We have to forge metal cleats for the American tracks."

"You're kidding – forge. How many studs will you have to weld onto each?"

"Not less than thirty, if on both sides of the track."

"That means sixty for each machine? If it takes two minutes for each stud, then it will take two hours for each tank. You have one welder, and it will take him a week for this hassle. Yet we're supposed to reach the Baltic Sea within three or four days."

That evening M.I. Pustil'nikov reported that more than ten tanks had become bogged down in a peat bog east of Mława. Captain Denisov had already led a recovery team to the location.

We calculated that over four days of fighting, the repair teams and evacuation companies had returned more than 250 tanks and self-propelled guns to service. That wasn't so bad.

The 5th Guards Tank Army in the East Prussia operation, 1945

Supply vehicles of the 5th Guards Tank Army, East Prussia, 1945. (TsA MO)

T-34 (commander - Sr. Lieutenant Pimen Byn'kov) of the 186th Tank Brigade of the 10th Tank Corps, East Prussia, February 1945. (TsA MO)

COMBAT OPERATIONS OF THE 5TH GUARDS TANK ARMY 339

T-34 of the 5th Guards Tank Army, Frauenburg, East Prussia, February 1945.

Tankers and tank riders of the 5th Guards Tank Army roll down a street in Neidenburg after the battle. (TsA MO)

A devastated German self-propelled gun on the approaches to Neidenburg, destroyed in the tank battle on 20 January 1945. (TsA MO)

A burning building on one of Neidenburg's streets during the street fighting, January 1945. (RGAKFD)

Another shot of the burning and shattered buildings on one of the streets of Neidenburg during the street fighting, January 1945. (RGAKFD)

One of the streets of Neidenburg, which was taken by forces of the 2nd Belorussian Front, 1945. (RGAKFD)

Riders on an SU-76M self-propelled gun of the 5th Guards Tank Army's 10th Tank Corps enter Mühlhausen, East Prussia on 24 January 1945. (TsA MO)

The Second Stage of the Operation

Combat operations of the 5th Guards Tank Army in the period between 20 and 22 January 1945

The commander-in-chief of the 2nd Belorussian Front Marshal of the Soviet Union K.K. Rokossovsky by the end of day on 19 January through Directive No. 1307 issued an assignment to the 5th Guards Tank Army: "From the morning of 20 January 1945 from the Neidenburg, Dzialdowo line continue an offensive in the Hildenburg, Osterode direction. The immediate task: On 21 January 1945 take the Osterode, Deutsch Eylau area. In the future keep in mind the army's actions in the direction of Liebemühl and Elbing."

The situation by the start of the second stage of the operation

The German forces that were crushed in the Mława, Neidenburg, Dzialdowo area (the 18th Panzergrenadier Division; the fusilier and artillery regiments of the incompletely formed Panzer Corps *Großdeutschland*; separate units of the Panzergrenadier Division *Großdeutschland*; the Mława training center for self-propelled and anti-tank artillery; the Heavy Panzer Battalion 507; remnants of the 299th and 7th Infantry Division, which were hastily replenished with various reserve, training and specialized battalions; 6 to 8 various separate battalions [engineer, construction, transport, Landwehr, and others], as well as Assault Gun Battalion 279 that had just been moved up out of the reserve) were in retreat to the north and northwest to previously prepared, strong switch positions with an antitank ditch, running from Jablonken (15 km northeast of Neidenburg) to Thurau, Gilgenburg (Dabrówno) and Neumark (Nowe Miasto). The 5th Guards Tank Army noted no other fresh German formations in front of it, other than Assault Gun Battalion 279.

By the end of 19 January, the forward rifle units of the 48th Army had reached the Kuklin – Dzialdowo line, while units of the 2nd Shock Army were on the Dzialdowo – Jabłonowo (12 km southwest of Dzialdowo) – Żuromin (25 km southwest of Dzialdowo) – Bieżun line. This means they were keeping pace behind the 5th Guards Tank Army.

The commander of the 5th Guards Tank Army Colonel General of Tank Troops V.T. Vol'sky, having received a fresh task, decided to make maximum use of the successfully developing situation and through Directive No. 004/OP from 0400 on 20 January 1945 issued the following orders to the army's formations:

> 10th Tank Corps – by 1100 20 January 1945 is to take Karlshohe, while cooperating with the 47th Separate Mechanized Brigade with part of its strength to capture Neidenburg. Subsequently with energetic actions to the northwest through the Reinshof estate, Seewalde (2 km east of Tannenberg), Geierswalde and Osterode. Take Osterode on 21 January 1945; 29th Tank Corps [operating on the 10th Tank Corps' left] – by 1100 on 20 January 1945 with its main forces is to reach the Uzdowo, Gralewo railroad station area, and with an attack in the general direction of Gilgenburg, Marianfelde and Leip, is to take Deutsch Eylau on 21 January 1945. The 47th Separate Mechanized Brigade and the 376th Heavy Self-propelled Artillery Regiment – with energetic actions to the north are to take Neidenburg by 1100 on 20 January 1945, and subsequently as my reserve, are to advance along the route: Neidenburg, Wiesenfeld estates (13 km west of Neidenburg), Oschekau, Tannenberg, Steffenswalde.

The combat operations between 20-22 January 1945 and the 5th Guards Tank Army's arrival on the Osterode – Deutsch Eylau line

The forces of the 5th Guards Tank Army set out on the morning of 20 January in order to carry out their assignments. The 10th Tank Corps, after the fall of Neidenburg, at 1100 on 20 January began topping up its machine with fuel and replenishing ammunition. At 1500 20 January, it resumed its offensive along two routes following its designated path of advance with its combat formation arranged as previously in two combat echelons, with the following changes: the 186th Tank Brigade remained in the first echelon, but was now directed along the left-hand route; the 11th Motorized Rifle Brigade was in the second echelon behind it; and the 178th Tank Brigade had been withdrawn from the first echelon into the second echelon behind the 186th Tank Brigade. These changes in the corps' combat formation were prompted by the prudence of having less fatigued and stronger units in the first echelon, and especially on the corps' more critical right flank.

Brushing aside and destroying the enemy's rearguard detachments, the forward brigades of the 10th Tank Corps at 2100 on 20 January, upon reaching the Thurau – Groß Gardienen line, encountered an antitank ditch in its path that was 6 meters wide and 3 meters deep. Through reconnaissance it was established that beyond the ditch the enemy had up to three artillery battalions and up to two battalions of infantry in the Thurowken, Browienen, Oschekau area.

The corps commander decided to employ sappers and motorized infantry to create three passages across this broad antitank ditch, using whatever means were available: in the Thurau area, north of Groß Gardienen, and with the forces of the 186th Tank Brigade, in the area south of Oschekau. The passage north of Groß Gardienen was finished first by 0400 on 21 January, and the 178th Tank Brigade, moving in the second echelon behind the 186th Tank Brigade, moved out to cross the antitank ditch. An enemy antitank artillery battalion that was positioned in firing positions in the area of Hill 215.0 that was 2 km north of Groß Gardienen, mistook the 178th Tank Brigade that was approaching the passage with lit headlights as a retreating German column. This enemy antitank artillery battalion didn't open fire until the moment that the brigade's tanks approached right up to the firing positions, and was captured fully intact with all of its guns and men.

During the attempt by the 183rd Tank Brigade to cross the ditch in the Thurau area, the brigade ran into heavy fire from up to two battalions of antitank artillery. At an order from the corps commander, the 183rd Tank Brigade was re-directed to the passage in the Groß Gardienen area and was to cross the ditch behind the 178th Tank Brigade.

Once the 178th and 183rd Tank Brigade's tanks that had crossed reached the area 1 km south of Faulen, the 11th Motorized Rifle Brigade with a swift attack overcame the ditch near Thurau, and having driven back the enemy that was located in the Thurowken, Browienen area, reached its own axis behind the 183rd Tank Brigade.

The 186th Tank Brigade together with accompanying sappers created a passage across the antitank ditch in the area south of Oschekau, over which it had crossed by 0500 on 21 January, and by 0700 reached Frögenau, just northwest of Tanneberg, where it was met by the fire from up to two batteries of artillery and up to 6 tanks and self-propelled guns. There it was temporarily halted in order to scout the enemy's positions.

The 183rd Tank Brigade, having caught up with the 178th Tank Brigade in Faulen, by 0600 on 21 January reached the approaches to a point that twice became well-known in history – the town of Tannenberg, which became famous a) in the war of the Slavic peoples against the Germans in 1410, in which the Teutons were routed by a composite force of Slavic troops (Russians, Poles, Lithuanians and Czechs) in the Grunwald – Tannenberg area; and b) for the German victory in August 1914 over the Russian army under General Samsonov during the opening days of the First World War.

On the approaches to Tannenberg, the forward detachment of the 183rd Tank Brigade was met by enemy machine-gun, artillery and mortar fire. The 183rd Tank Brigade was halted on the approaches to the town in order to reconnoiter the terrain and the enemy's strength and dispositions. The reconnaissance patrols established that no less than two regiments of infantry, 8-10 self-propelled guns and no less than two artillery regiments were defending Tannenberg.

The commander of the 10th Tank Corps Major General of Tank Troops Sakhno made the bold decision to bring up the corps' artillery, including a rocket launching battalion, and with its support to assault Tannenberg in the pre-dawn hours. The assault would count upon the unexpected, concentrated fire, the dense early morning fog, and the clatter of the tanks to shake the German defenders.

The corps' brigades were given the following assignments: the 183rd Tank Brigade was to attack the town from the front and from the east; the 11th Motorized Rifle Brigade was to envelop the city from the right and attack it from the north; and the 178th Tank Brigade was to cooperate with the 183rd Tank Brigade and 11th Motorized Rifle Brigade by launching an attack from the south and southwest. The 186th Tank Brigade, remaining in the Frögenau area, was to assist the other brigades in capturing Tannenberg.

At 0730 on 21 January, after a short, but powerful artillery barrage, the units of the 10th Tank Corps moved out on the attack against Tannenberg. The 183rd Tank Brigade with an energetic attack broke into the town, and in cooperation with the 11th Motorized Rifle Brigade and the 178th Tank Brigade, which were assaulting it from the north and southwest, broke the resistance of the stunned enemy at 0830 on 21 January and took full possession of the town of Tannenberg while inflicting heavy losses to its garrison.

At the end of the assault on Tannenberg by units of the 10th Tank Corps, the enemy in strength of 10 self-propelled guns and a battalion of infantry counterattacked the corps' units from the rear from the direction of Mühlen and reached Seewalde. The corps' chief of staff, who at the time was located with the headquarters south of Seewalde, took steps to repulse the counterattack, and the Germans were driven back by the reserve 376th Heavy Self-propelled Artillery Regiment and the arriving lead battalion of the 47th Mechanized Brigade.

The competently organized and decisive fighting by the 10th Tank Corps when taking Tannenberg and the crushing of its large garrison in less than three hours was one more clear example of the Soviet army's successful combat in East Prussia, which did heavy damage to the morale and prestige of the entire German Army, the invincibility and strength of which had been glorified and propagandized by the Germans ever since their victory over General Samsonov's 2nd Army in the Battle of Tannenberg back in August 1914.

With the fall of Tannenberg, the units of the 10th Tank Corps continued in the same combat formation a rapid pursuit of the enemy units that were retreating to the north. On the Geierswalde – Steffenswalde line, the enemy attempted to check the corps' advance. By 1200 on 21 January, after two hours of combat, the 183rd and 186th Tank Brigades broke the enem resistance on this line and took the Geierswalde and Steffenswalde railroad stations, having in the process killed up to 150 enemy soldiers and officers and destroyed up to six artillery guns.

Continuing the offensive and brushing aside the enemy's weak rearguard detachments, the lead 183rd and 186th Tank Brigades by 1700 on 21 January reached the outer fortifications of the city of Osterode, where they ran into heavy, organized enemy artillery fire. The attempts by both tank brigades to break into the city's southern outskirts from the march proved unsuccessful. Time was required to analyze thoroughly both the terrain and the enemy's system of defense and dispositions.

Osterode was an important railroad and road hub and a powerful strongpoint in the East Prussian system of border fortifications. The Osterode area was characterized by numerous narrow

5th Guards Tank Army in the East Prussia operation, 1945

The antitank ditch that stretched along the Jablonken – Seythen – Thurau – Groß Gardienen – Gilgenburg – Nowe Miasto line. The 5th Guards Tank Army fought its way across this ditch on the night of 20-21 January 1945. (TsA MO)

An isolated German pillbox 2 km west of Gilgenburg, January 1945. (TsA MO)

The streets of Tannenberg after its occupation by the 5th Guards Tank Army, January 1945. (TsA MO)

An East Prussian town now occupied by the 5th Guards Tank Army after the fighting ended. (TsA MO)

lakes that surrounded the town, with narrow defiles between them, which made the ground unsuitable for the broad maneuvering of tanks.

Osterode's fortifications consisted of three continuous trench lines and an antitank ditch that was 3.5 meters wide and 2.5 meters deep. The ditch blocked the narrow defiles between the lakes and its flanks were anchored on lakes. Some of the city's stone buildings had been adapted for a defense. Defending the Osterode area were remnants of the Mława training center for self-propelled and antitank artillery, which numbered 15 tanks and self-propelled guns; the Fortress Regiment 6; a local garrison of 600 men; and a number of separate battalions such as Machine Gun Battalions "Vistula" and "Preghel", Machine Gun Battalion 63, Fortress Battalion 75, the "Gneisenau" Battalion, Reserve Battalions 1 and 53, and Reserve Artillery Regiment 37.

Having received reconnaissance information about the enemy's dispositions, the commander of the 10th Tank Corps General Sakhno decided to take Osterode with a night assault. First, however, he would bring up all the artillery and cut all of the main roads leading into the city.

In accordance with this, the brigade's were given their combat orders: the 183rd Tank Brigade was to envelop the town from the east in the direction of Hirschberg, Lubainen and the northern outskirts of the town and to prevent an enemy retreat to the northeast and north; the 178th Tank Brigade was to envelop Osterode from the west in the direction of Thurau and the woods north of Mörlen in order to take the narrow defile between the Drewen-See and Mörlen-See lakes and to prevent an enemy retreat to the west; the 11th Motorized Rifle Brigade with a portion of the 186th Tank Brigade and 326th Heavy Tank Regiment was to capture Osterode with a night assault from the south and southeast.

At 2100 on 21 January 1945, the corps' units set out to carry out their given assignments. After a massed, but brief artillery preparation, the assault on the city of Osterode began. At 2300 21 January, the 183rd Tank Brigade, having penetrated the enemy fortifications on its path of advance, reached the northern outskirts and broke into the city from the north. Meanwhile, the 11th Motorized Rifle Brigade with its attached units penetrated the city from the south. By 0200 on 22 January, the enemy's resistance had completely collapsed and the units of the 10th Tank Corps had taken complete control of Osterode.

In this night action the corps' units killed 600 enemy soldiers and officers, and destroyed 19 guns, 7 self-propelled guns and up to 150 vehicles. In addition, they captured 400 prisoners, approximately 1,000 vehicles, and several stockpiles of military gear and food. A large number of Russian prisoners-of-war and Soviet civilians that had been forcibly removed from their villages for slave labor in Germany were liberated.

Excerpt from a preliminary report on the losses of the 5th Guards Tank Army as of 2400 on 21 January 1945:

10th Tank Corps: 17 T-34 tanks and 4 SU-100 destroyed; 7 T-34 tanks and 2 SU-100 knocked-out.
29th Tank Corps: 14 T-34 tanks burned out and 1 blown-up by mines; 7 T-34 tanks knocked-out.
47th Mechanized Brigade: 9 M4A2 tanks burned out and 1 M4A2 knocked-out; 13 killed and 19 wounded.
Note: No information on the losses of the 29th Tank Corps has arrived, with the exception of messages from the army's deputy commander General Zaev.
Army's senior assistant chief of operations Guards Lieutenant Colonel NIKITIN

The commander of the 29th Tank Corps Major General of Tank Troops K.M. Malakhov, having received the task to attack out of the Uzdowo area toward Gilgenburg, Marienfelde and Leip, and to take Deutsch Eylau by 21 January, decided to bypass Gilgenburg, which was positioned in a narrow corridor between two lakes, on its western side with the corps' main forces, and to advance in the same combat formation along two routes, in two combat echelons, but with the following changes: Along the right-hand route in the direction of Groß Grieben, Szczupliny, Elgenau, Marienfelde, Leip, the Damerau estate, Raudnitz and Tillwalde, the 31st Tank Brigade would take the lead with the task to take Leip by the end of 20 January, and subsequently on 21 January to take the Frödenau, Tillwalde, Raudnitz area, in readiness with the brigade's main forces to operate toward Deutsch Eylau; the 25th Tank Brigade was to advance in the second echelon behind the 31st Tank Brigade with the task by the end of 20 January to capture Rozental and Kazanice, and subsequently on 21 January to take Hansdorf (5 km east of Deutsch Eylau), in readiness with its main forces to take Deutsch Eylau; the corps' forward detachment (the reinforced 32nd Tank Brigade) would take the lead with the task by the end of 20 January to take Lubawa, and subsequently on 21 January 1945 to capture Deutsch Eylau.

The 53rd Motorized Rifle Brigade would advance in the second echelon behind the 32nd Tank Brigade with the task by the end of 20 January to take Lubawa together with the 32nd Tank Brigade. Subsequently on 21 January, advancing in the direction of Klein Heyde and Klein Sehren, it was to help take Deutsch Eylau in cooperation with the 32nd Tank Brigade.

Units of the 29th Tank Corps moved out from the Uzdowo, Gralewo railroad station area precisely at the designated time to carry out their assignments. At 1100 on 20 January, the corps was approaching an area with a multitude of lakes with strong German fortifications between them. The corps ran into the enemy's intermediate line of defense, which was being defended by relatively weak forces, on the Gilgenburg, Szczupliny, Tuczki, Grabacz line that also ran between the Groß Damerau-See, Rumian and Wehr lakes. The corps broke through it from the march and by 1400 on 21 January was approaching the strong switch positions with an antitank ditch that was up to 5-6 meters wide and 3 meters deep, which ran from Gilgenburg through Lehwalde, Groszki and Hartowiec to Nowe Miasto. This line was being strongly defended by significant enemy infantry forces supported by tanks and artillery.

After tough fighting, the units of the 29th Tank Corps broke the enemy resistance by 2000 on 20 January and immediately set about making passages across the antitank ditch with the efforts of sappers and motorized infantry. Having crossed the ditch, they broke through the strong switch positions and reached the Elgenau – Rumienica – Zwiniarz line.

On the morning of 21 January the corps resumed its offensive, and having broken the opposing enemy's resistance, the lead 31st Tank Brigade reached Marienfelde by 0800 on 21 January, while the 32nd Tank Brigade was approaching the outer trenches of the fortifications of Lubawa from the east. Simultaneously, units of the 8th Tank Corps, which the day before had been operating in the Lidzbark area and the orders of which were unknown to command of the 29th Tank Corps or the headquarters of the 5th Guards Tank Army, unexpectedly arrived from the south.

The 5th Guards Tank Army in the East Prussia operation, 1945

A Soviet soldier examines the German antitank ditch in the Osterode area, 1945. (TsA MO)

A captured German officer's bunker in the trenches on the approaches to Osterode, January 1945. (TsA MO)

A German pillbox destroyed by the fire from an SU-152, January 1945. (TsA MO)

In cooperation with the brigades of the 8th Tank Corps, the units of the 29th Tank Corps by 1000 on 21 January took possession of the German strongpoint of Lubawa. The commander of the 29th Tank Corps, already having received information from reconnaissance patrols that the approaches to Deutsch Eylau from the southeast and south were obstructed by dense forests and strong enemy fortifications, decided to alter the direction of the brigades following the left-hand route and issued an assignment to the 32nd Tank Brigade and 53rd Motorized Rifle Brigade to advance in the direction of Radomno, Wonna, Groß Herzogswalde, Sommerau and Schönburg, to cut off the enemy's path of retreat out of Deutsch Eylau to the west, and closely cooperating together, to take Deutsch Eylau with an attack from the northwest and west.

Pursuing the hastily retreating enemy units and brushing aside his weak rearguard screens, the corps' units by 1730 on 21 January took the following towns and villages with fighting: 31st Tank Brigade – Frödenau and Tillwalde; 25th Tank Brigade – Hansdorf and Groß Sehren; 32nd Tank Brigade – Sommerau and Schönburg; and the 53rd Motorized Rifle Brigade – Stradem and Winkelsdorf. Thereby, they had severed all of the main paths of enemy retreat from Deutsch Eylau.

At the end of the assault on Tannenberg by units of the 10th Tank Corps, the enemy in strength of up to a battalion of infantry and 10 self-propelled guns counterattacked the corps' units from the rear from the direction of Mühlen, and reached Seewalde, just east of Tannenberg. The corps' chief of staff, who was located at this time at the headquarters in the area south of Seewalde organized a counterattack with the forces of the reserve 376th Heavy Self-propelled Artillery Regiment and the arriving lead battalion of the 47th Mechanized Brigade. The German attack was repulsed.

On the morning of 21 January, the corps resumed the offensive, having broken the resistance of the opposing enemy, and by 0800 21 January the forward 31st Tank Brigade reached Marienfelde, while the 32nd Tank Brigade was closing on the outer trenches of Lubawa's fortifications from the east. Simultaneously, units of the 8th Tank Corps, which had been operating in the Lidzbark area the day before, unexpectedly showed up from the south. Neither the command of the 29th Tank Corps nor the headquarters of the 5th Guards Tank Army knew anything about the 8th Tank Corps' orders.

In cooperation with the brigades of the 8th Tank Corps, units of the 29th Tank Corps by 1000 on 21 January captured the German strongpoint of Lubawa. The commander of the 29th Tank Corps, having already received information from reconnaissance patrols that the approaches to Deutsch Eylau from the southeast and south were hindered by dense woods and strong enemy fortifications, decided to alter the direction of the brigades' advance on the left-hand route, and issued an order to the 32nd Tank Brigade and 53rd Motorized Rifle Brigade to attack in the Radomno, Wonna, Gross Herzogswalde, Sommerau, Schönberg direction, to sever the enemy paths of retreat to the west out of Deutsch Eylau, and cooperating closely together, to take Deutsch Eylau with an attack from the northwest and west.

Pursuing the hastily retreating enemy units and brushing aside weak rearguard covering screens, the corps' units by 1730 on 21 January had taken the following villages with fighting: 31st Tank Brigade – Frödenau and Tillwalde; 25th Tank Brigade – Hansdorf and Gross Sehren; 32nd Tank Brigade – Sommerau and Schönberg; and the 53rd Motorized Rifle Brigade – Stradem and Winkelsdorf. The 29th Tank Corps had thus cut all of the enemy's paths of retreat out of Deutsch Eylau.

From the memoirs of F.I. Galkin:

The army's troops couldn't linger in Neidenburg. The situation demanded an immediate attack toward Tannenberg, Osterode and Deutsch Eylau. Each passing minute was costly. So even though the tankers were still engaged in street fighting in Neidenburg, General Sakhno dispatched a strong forward detachment toward Tannenberg. Colonel Omeliustyi hadn't even had time to finish his report that Neidenburg had been mopped up of the enemy, when General Sidorovich was already issuing orders for the corps' main forces to move out toward Tannenberg.

"The pace must be picked up. Don't linger on petty objectives; bypass them and leave them behind. They'll collapse of their own accord …."

Soon Colonel Omeliustyi again reported: "The corps, brushing aside weak rearguard detachments, is approaching Gross Gardienen. The forward detachment is tied up in fighting on the Thurau – Gross Gardienen line. It is foggy, and the visibility is poor."

Further events, as soon became apparent, unfolded as follows. During the foggy night, the 183rd Tank Brigade, which was under the command of Colonel Grishin, came to a stop on the approaches to Gross Gardienen. A deep and wide antitank ditch was blocking the way.

Enemy artillery gunners and submachine gunners, concealed behind the ditch, began to illuminate the ground with flares and to fire at our tanks. Grishin's brigade, under the enemy fire, began to lay down passages across the ditch. At this time, a multitude of lights began to appear on the right flank. Headlights, penetrating the fog, were projecting yellowish beams of light on the dirty snow. It was Colonel Petrov's 178th Tank Brigade that was approaching, and the Germans weren't firing a single shot at it.

Why? Prisoners later answered this question: they had taken the 178th Tank Brigade's column as one of their own. As a result, an entire German artillery battalion fell into Petrov's hands. The path was now clear for the 183rd Tank Brigade. It advanced across the ditch in the wake of the 178th Tank Brigade and overtook it at Faulen.

By dawn the fog was heavy and blanketed the fields, lakes and woods that stretched in front of Tannenberg. However, the 183rd Tank Brigade had already neared the town, and after a massed artillery barrage, took full possession of Tannenberg. Excitement reigned at the army's command post.

"That's how a third Tannenberg was fashioned!" Georgii Stepanovich Sidorovich exclaimed.

"A lot of Slavic blood has been spilled on this ground."

"Yeah, and they were dreaming about Tannenberg's new glory. But it didn't turn out that way," Vasilii said.

Vol'sky was constantly demanding not to let the enemy gain separation, and to stay right on his bootheels … The tankers were almost getting no sleep. They ate on the move. They refilled the machine's fuel tanks in haste.

On 21 January General Sakhno reported that the corps was approaching Osterode and preparing a nighttime assault. The frontline veterans know how difficult street fighting is, especially with only tanks, without infantry. It is twice as difficult to fight at night. The tank cannons were firing down the streets. They were breaking down barricades with their tracks. However, the upper floors of the stone buildings remained intact, and panzerfaust-equipped troops and antitank grenadiers were lurking there. General Sakhno's tankers ran into all these difficulties, but nevertheless on the night of 21-22 January they mopped up Osterode of the enemy.

In the evening, when I was reporting on the status of the tanks, Vol'sky said: "The 178th was unlucky. A fine brigade, combative men … however, go figure …."

"What happened?"

"They had a rough day today … the deputy commander was killed, and the brigade commander Polukarov was severely wounded. The chief of staff and the deputy political commander were almost killed. It is painful to lose men …." Vol'sky was silent for a short time, then unexpectedly asked, "By the way, Sakhno, it seems, is putting up two tankers for the title Hero of the Soviet Union. Have you heard about this?"

"I've heard something about it. The talk, apparently, is about crewmen of a tank from the reconnaissance group …"

"Go on …" – Vol'sky brightened up.

"The guys were breaking into a small town not far from Osterode, which was still being held by the Germans, and blocked a street intersection. When the Nazis began pressing, the turret gunner Sergeant Krasnov destroyed two antitank guns and one self-propelled gun. Next, he set ablaze several vehicles and a halftrack. However, then our tank took a hit; it burst into flames. Two men of the crew perished in the machine, but Krasnov and the radio operator had time to emerge from it with machine guns. They made their way into the nearest building and ensconced themselves in the cellar. There they held out for more than two hours, until our guys arrived. They say that the intersection where the burned-out T-34 is standing is piled up with corpses. When the Germans began to retreat, Krasnov and Shabel'sky once again saw them off with machine-gun fire. Kostylev, probably, already knows all about this. The political staff quickly reports to him about such cases."

"Ozhogin!" – the General shouted. "Call the Political Department, ask about Krasnov and Shebel'sky."

…

The left flank was advancing no less rapidly. The units of Malakhov's corps, attacking out of the Uzdau area, captured the strongpoint of Lubawa on the morning of 21 January. Here the corps commander received information that the next objective – the road and railroad hub of Deutsch Eylau – was strongly fortified. An elaborate system of irrigation ditches and a multitude of large and small lakes, linked by antitank ditches, were fringing the town on its northern, eastern and southern sides. The garrison numbered up to 800 regular soldiers. In addition, Volkssturm were also located there, which were being met for the first time on the path of our army.

Two experienced generals, D.I. Zaev and K.M. Malakhov, were exchanging opinions and forming a plan to isolate Deutsch Eylau. The Military Council approved their decision …

Deutsch Eylau was another important road and railroad hub and a powerful strongpoint in the system of East Prussia's main border defensive belt of fortifications. The Deutsch Eylau area is also characterized by the presence of a large number of lakes, and the town stands on the banks of one of the largest lakes. In addition, there are wooded areas to the south, west and north of the town. Deutsch Eylau's fortifications consisted of two continuous lines of trenches with an antitank ditch between them that was 3.5 meters wide and 2.5 meters deep. The flanks of the antitank ditch rested on natural obstacles: lakes and dense woods. The enemy had thrown up numerous antitank barriers on all of the roads leading into the town. The barriers were 2 to 2.5 meters high and had been filled with stones and dirt. Some of the stone buildings on the city's outskirts had been adapted to an all-round defense.

The garrison of Deutsch Eylau that had been encircled by units of the 29th Tank Corps consisted of remnants of the 18th Panzergrenadier Division, the 299th Infantry Division, Heavy Panzer Battalion 507, the 1224th Fortress Battalion, several battalions of Volkssturm and one armored train. Caught in pincers from every direction, the Deutsch Eylau garrison was resisting desperately. In the course of the night and on the morning of 22 January, it undertook four unsuccessful counterattacks with the aim of breaking out to the west.

On the morning of 22 January, units of the 29th Tank Corps launched a decisive attack toward Deutsch Eylau. The 32nd Tank Brigade and 53rd Motorized Rifle Brigade launched the main attack from the northwest and west; the 25th Tank Brigade attacked from the east and southeast; the 31st Tank Brigade with a part of its force cooperated with the 25th Tank Brigade's attack from the northeast.

The encircled garrison of Deutsch Eylau had to fight in exceptionally unfavorable, cramped conditions, under the murderous crossfire of the units of the 29th Tank Corps that were closing in on the town. At 1300 on 22 January with a decisive attack by the 32nd Tank Brigade and the 53rd Motorized Rifle Brigade, the enemy resistance was broken on the approaches to the town, and these brigades broke into the northwestern and western outskirts of Deutsch Eylau with their main forces. After tenacious two hours of street fighting, the city's garrison was crushed, and at 1500 on 22 January the units of the 29th Tank Corps took full possession of Deutsch Eylau. The enemy losses in the town in killed alone amounted to 1500 soldiers and officers. A large amount of loot was seized: equipment, stockpiles of military gear, and up to 300 prisoners.

Earl Ziemke, in his fundamental work *Stalingrad to Berlin: The German Defeat in the East*, describes these heady days for the Red Army in East Prussia:

> The offensive picked up speed on 21 January. Against Second Army, *Second Belorussian Front* went as far as Deutsch Eylau and turned a force north toward Allenstein. *Third Belorussian Front* took Gumbinnen, removing that obstacle on the route to Koenigsberg along the Pregel. The thrust to the coast to cut off the army group was developing; Second Army reported that it might delay but could not prevent it. More alarming, the attacks south of the Pregel and toward Allenstein seemed to presage an attempt to force the whole army group away from the coast and into an encirclement in the interior of East Prussia. Fourth Army was already lying in the bottom of a lopsided sack 130 miles from the coast.
>
> After Reinhardt reported that all the lower commands were pressing for relief and that a complete loss of confidence in the higher leadership was impending, Hitler finally agreed to let Fourth Army withdraw to the eastern edge of the Masurian Lakes. This was something, but far from enough.

The 47th Mechanized Brigade, upon capturing Neidenburg, in the middle of the day of 20 January was withdrawn into the army commander's reserve with the task to advance behind the 10th Tank Corps along the Neidenburg, Gross Lauben, Seewalde, Geierswalde, Schildeck route, and to be in readiness to exploit a success by the 10th Tank Corps and to repulse possible enemy counterattacks from the east, northeast and north.

At 1900 on 20 January the 47th Mechanized Brigade moved out from Neidenburg along the designated route. On the march the brigade's forward units skirmished with disorganized enemy groups, which were left behind or were retreating after the passage of the units of the 10th Tank Corps that was attacking out in front. By the end of day on 20 January, the 47th Mechanized Brigade reached the Geierswalde, Steffenswalde, Döhlau area, where it took up a hedgehog defense.

Thus, the task to take the Osterode, Deutsch Eylau and Leip area on 21 January had been carried out by the 5th Guards Tank Army on schedule. The towns of Osterode and Deutsch Eylau, which had been converted by the enemy into powerful strongpoints, had been fully encircled and taken by assault by 2100 on 21 January. Moreover, Osterode was being occupied by units of the 10th Tank Corps by 0200 on 22 January, and Deutsch Eylau by units of the 29th Tank Corps by 1500 on 22 January.

Red Army veteran V. Zalgaller remembers the spoils of war available in Deutsch Eylau, and how useful they later proved to be to Russian citizens after the war:

> We had taken Deutsch Eylau. The city with the famous name proved to be a small one. There were blocks left untouched by the war. No people were around. I entered a department store that had the owner's apartment above it. I grabbed a suit that was hanging on the bed's footboard and sent it home (at the time, it was permissible to send packages home). I later graduated from a university in this suit. Under the window, a truck carrying female traffic controllers came to a stop. I opened a closet, grabbed a few dresses, and threw them into the truck. I sent one dress home to Maia, and gave a white coat to Aletvina. She would wear it on trips to Leningrad when she was around 25 years old.

The 5th Guards Tank Army in the East Prussia operation, 1945

The antitank ditch on the approaches to Deutsch Eylau, 1945. (TsA MO)

A destroyed German prime mover that had been towing a 75mm gun; East Prussia, 1945. (TsA MO)

Motorized submachine gunners and riflemen of the 5th Guards Tank Army, East Prussia, January–February 1945. (TsA MO)

Self-propelled guns and tanks of the 5th Guards Tank Army rolling into one of the villages of East Prussia, January–February 1945. (TsA MO)

Self-propelled guns of the 5th Guards Tank Army entering one of the towns in East Prussia, January–February 1945. (TsA MO)

One of the hotspots of the battlefield on the western outskirts of Deutsch Eylau. German dead and a knocked-out StuG III self-propelled gun resulting from the attack by the 32nd Tank Brigade and 53rd Motorized Rifle Brigade of the 29th Tank Corps, January 1945. (TsA MO)

More spoils of war for the men of the 5th Guards Tank Army, January 1945. Over the period between 17 January and 10 February 1945, the 5th Guards Tank Army gathered 15,000 head of cattle, 5,900 head of sheep, and 3,200 pigs, a significant amount of which was transferred to the rifle formations. (TsA MO)

A column of German prisoners, both military and civilians, captured by the units of the 5th Guards Tank Army. The men show a mixture of relief, apprehension and dejection over their fates. East Prussia, January 1945. (TsA MO)

A column of German prisoners, captured by the 5th Guards Tank Army; January 1945. (TsA MO)

From the "Combat Path of the 29th Tank Corps":

In Lubawa the commander of the 29th Tank Corps Major General of Tank Forces K.M. Malkhalov received information that the town of Deutsch Eylau was strongly fortified. The canals and lakes were linked by antitank ditches and skirted the city in a semi-circle on its eastern side. The garrison numbered up to 800 cadre soldiers. There were also Volkssturm there, which the corps hadn't yet encountered in battle. It was decided to isolate Deutsch Eylau from three directions. The army's Military Council approved this decision.

Having broken through the enemy's defenses, the Red Army on 21 January 1945 crossed the border between Poland and Germany and entered the boundaries of East Prussia. The corps' entry into enemy territory was marked by three volleys of all types of weapons in the enemy's direction. This momentous event inspired all of the troops to new achievements. The foe was still strong. With the transfer of combat operations onto his territory, his tenaciousness redoubled. However, by now nothing could save the Nazis. Their fate had been pre-determined. Our tanks advanced like a whirlwind to the west.

Pursuing the enemy's hastily retreating units and brushing aside rearguard detachments, the 29th Tank Corps on the same day reached Frödenau and Tillwalde with Colonel A.I. Pokolov's brigade, having cut the routes to the northeast out of Deutsch Eylau, while Colonel I.O. Stanislavsky's brigade had captured Hansdorf and Sehren on the approaches to Deutsch Eylau from the southeast. Lieutenant Colonel S.G. Kolesnikov's brigade had neared Deutsch Eylau from the west and taken the villages of Sommerau and Schönberg. Colonel D.N. Dolganov's brigade to the south had taken Sradem. With the arrival of the brigades on the indicated lines, all of the enemy's Deutsch Eylau grouping's paths of retreat were severed. The encircled garrison consisted of remnants of the 18th Motorized [sic], 299th Infantry and 114th Gebirgsjäger Divisions, reinforced by the artillery and tanks of the shattered 16th Panzer Division and the 507th Battalion of Tiger tanks.

The town of Deutsch Eylau was the first East Prussian city for which the tankers of the 29th Tank Corps fought. The combat for possession of the town began with the onset of twilight. The city couldn't be taken in the nighttime fighting. The battle flared up with new intensity on the morning of 21 January 1945 and didn't cease until late that night, but little progress was made. The adversary was putting up stubborn resistance. Fired on from every direction by Soviet artillery and tanks, the enemy garrison was suffering heavy losses. Our corps had also taken losses. In Colonel S.G. Kolesnikov's brigade, the commander of the 3rd Tank Battalion Captain A.A. Chepurenko, the chief of staff Senior Lieutenant I.N. Gatilov and a number of other commanders were killed.

The decisive assault on the city began at dawn on 22 January 1945. With a simultaneous attack from three directions, the corps finally managed to tighten the noose around the town. The corps' brigades after the lengthy siege finally broke into the western and northwestern outskirts of the city. The troops of the corp's units were driving the enemy back, house by house, block by block. After stubborn, bloody street fighting, the enemy resistance finally collapsed and the garrison surrendered. The foe lost 1500 soldiers and officers in killed alone, and around 7,000 were taken prisoner. The fall of Deutsch Eylau to the 29th Tank Corps saved the lives of many hundreds of people, who had been languishing here in a concentration camp. At 1500 on 22 January 1945, the corps' chief of staff Colonel V.I. Smirnov reported to the army headquarters that the enemy garrison had been destroyed, and the town of Deutsch Eylau was in our possession.

Even as the fighting for Deutsch Eylau had been still continuing, the commander of the 5th Guards Tank Army Colonel General of Tank Forces T.P. Vol'sky directed the commander of the 29th Tank Corps Major General of Tank Forces K.M. Malakhov to turn the direction of the offensive sharply to the north in the direction of the Bay of Danzig, which lay 100 km away.

The town of Saalfeld lay on the way; it was taken by the tankers from the march by the end of the first day of fighting. The German people, who had blindly trusted in the strength of the Führer's army, were so stunned that at first, they took the Soviet tanks that were entering the town as their own friendly tanks. After the situation became clear, the Germans began to flee in panic in every direction. By 0500 in the morning, the corps had fully assembled in Saalfeld, and began to refuel their machines and replenish ammunition.

The combat operations over 22-24 January 1945 and the 5th Guards Tank Army's arrival on the coast of the Baltic Sea

The commander-in-chief of the 2nd Belorussian Front Marshal of the Soviet Union K.K. Rokossovsky through Directive No. 1472 from 0335 on 22 January 1945 issued the following task to the 5th Guards Tank Army: "Upon taking the Osterode, Deutsch Eylau area, continue the offensive to the north. Mission: in the course of 22 January 1945, capture the Morungen, Saalfeld line; by the morning of 24 January 1945, take the Elbing, Preussisch-Holland, Mühlhausen area and sever the enemy's path of retreat to the west."

The situation after the 5th Guards Tank Army's capture of the strongpoints of Osterode and Deutsch Eylau

The enemy units that had been defeated in the areas of Osterode and Deutsch Eylau were in retreat to the northeast, north and northwest. Opposite the army's front, no fresh formations from out of the enemy's reserve had been identified, with the exception of the following small combat elements: Fortress Regiment 6; Machine-gun Battalions "Vistula" and "Pregel"; 63rd Machine-gun Battalion; Battalion "Gneisenau"; the 75th Fortress Battalion; the 201st and 713th Landwehr Battalions; the 1st, 53rd, 400th and 1444th Reserve Battalions; the 37th Reserve Artillery Battalion; the 31st Reserve Flak Battalion; a battalion of the "Todt" construction organization; and Volkssturm battalions. Regarding the remnants of the 18th Panzergrenadier Division, the 299th Infantry Division and Assault Gun Brigade 279, their viability can be explained by their constant replenishment with various training and reserve units.

The forward rifle units of the 48th Army and 2nd Shock Army by the end of 21 January had reached the Jablonken, Mühlen, Tanneberg, Gilgenburg, Nowo Miasto line. This means they were successfully advancing in the wake of the 5th Guards Tank Army, about 35-50 kilometers behind it.

The commander of the 5th Guards Tank Army Colonel General of Tank Forces V.T. Vol'sky at 0700 on 22 January issued the following tasks to the army's formations and units:

a) To the 10th Tank Corps: Upon taking Osterode, continue the offensive in the northern direction and take Mohrungen by the end of 22 January 1945;
b) To the 29th Tank Corps: Upon taking Deutsch Eylau, continue the offensive in the northern direction and take Saalfeld by the end of 22 January 1945;
c) To the 47th Mechanized Brigade: From the Stenkendorf jumping-off area (10 km southwest of Osterode), with an attack in the direction of Bogunschöwen, Nickelshagen, Freiwalde direction, take the latter point by the end of 22 January 1945.

The **10th Tank Corps** set out along two routes to carry out its assigned task at 1100 on 22 January in the same combat formation, in two combat echelons with the following changes: The 11th Motorized Rifle Brigade, 727th Self-propelled Artillery Regiment and 287th Mortar Regiment were moved up into the first echelon along the right-hand route with the task to attack in the direction of Rotskrug, Tharden, Paradies and Simonetti (1 km northwest of Mohrungen), and take Simonetti by 1800. The 183rd Tank Brigade was withdrawn from the first echelon into the second echelon behind the 11th Motorized Rifle Brigade with the task to move out from behind the 11th Motorized Rifle Brigade's right flank in the Himmelforth area, and operating in the direction of Döringshof and Schertingswalde, to take Pfarrsfeldchen (1 km northeast of Mohrungen) by 1800 on 22 January. The 186th Tank Brigade was also withdrawn into the second echelon behind the 178th Tank Brigade with the task to reach the Paradies area by 1800.

Up to the Sonnenborn, Reußen line, the enemy offered no serious resistance to the 10th Tank Corps' advance. However, on this line up to a regiment of infantry supported by a battalion of artillery and 6-8 tanks and self-propelled guns put up strong resistance. Having whipped the opposing enemy in the Reußen, Sonnenborn area, the corps' units by 1800 22 January were approaching the fortifications surrounding the town of Mohrungen, which consisted of two to three rings of full profile trenches. All of the main roads leading into the city had been mined. The upper stories of buildings had been converted into firing positions for machine guns and submachine gunners.

In the fortifications of Mohrungen, the enemy put up bitter resistance and repeatedly launched counterattacks, which were repulsed by the corps' units with heavy losses for the Germans. The fierce fighting continued throughout the evening of 22 January and the night of 22-23 January.

By 0600 on 23 January, the 183rd Tank Brigade had enveloped the town from the east and had captured Pfarrsfeldchen, while the 178th Tank Brigade had enveloped the city from the west and had taken Simonetti. The 11th Motorized Rifle Brigade, in cooperation with the 186th Tank Brigade, broke into Mohrungen's southern outskirts and by 1100 23 January had fully mopped up the town of its remaining defenders.

Once the **29th Tank Corps** had taken complete control of Deutsch Eylau, at 1300 on 22 January the corps commander, anticipating difficulties that faced the corps when trying to advance through the narrow corridors between the lakes north of Deutsch Eylau, ordered the 31st Tank Brigade that was operating north of the town to attack in the direction of Frödenau, Kallitken, Sallewen, Bienau, Groß Altenhagen, Saalfeld (all east of the lakes) and to take Saalfeld from the march by the end of 22 January. At 1500 on 22 January, the brigade encountered an enemy column of up to 50 trucks that were transporting infantry and combat supplies, belatedly hastening to the assistance of the Deutsch Eylau garrison. The 31st Tank Brigade from the march attacked and destroyed this column. In the Groß Altenhagen area the 31st Tank Brigade also from the march made a decisive charge, and exploiting the element of surprise of their appearance, smashed through the artificial obstacles of East Prussia's primary border defensive belt, which was being held in this sector only by weak forces of Volkssturm battalions. Then the brigade pivoted sharply to the west and continued its rapid pursuit of the enemy in the direction of Saalfeld.

At 1900 on 22 January the 31st Tank Brigade was closing in on Saalfeld's defensive fortifications from the northeast. After a short combat, the brigade penetrated the town, and having eliminated its weak garrison, took complete control of Saalfeld, having captured more than 40 vehicles in it.

At 1600 on 22 January, after taking Deutsch Eylau, the 25th Tank Brigade, having received a fresh set of orders from the corps commander, launched an attack toward Saalfeld from the south through a corridor between two lakes that ran through Sumpf and Auer. In the area north of Auer, the brigade from the march attacked a fortified line that ran between the lakes, which was being defended by weak infantry forces, and broke through the line. By 0200 on 23 January, the 25th Tank Brigade reached Saalfeld.

The 32nd Tank Brigade and 53rd Motorized Rifle Brigade at 1730 on 22 January, having refueled their tanks and vehicles, set out from Deutsch Eylau along the route taken by the 25th Tank Brigade. By 0500 on 23 January, all of the brigades of the 29th Tank Corps had fully assembled in the Saalfeld area in readiness for future combat operations.

The 47th Mechanized Brigade at 1300 on 22 January moved out from the area it was occupying near Steffenswalde and at 1400, having taken up a combat formation in the woods south of Bogunschöwen, attacked the enemy fortifications on the approaches to Bogunschöwen after a short artillery barrage. After an hour-long battle the brigade drove the opposing enemy units back, the rearguard detachments of which were offering light resistance with fire. By 1700 on 22 January the 47th Mechanized Brigade reached Sallewen, and at 1900 of the same day took possession of Liebemühl.

Without pausing in Liebemühl, the brigade's men climbed back into their vehicles and went in pursuit of the enemy in the direction of Freiwalde, leaving behind the 2nd Motorized Rifle Battalion behind to mop up the remaining pockets of enemy in Liebemühl. By 2300 on 22 January the brigade's reconnaissance groups and the 1st Motorized Rifle Battalion broke into the southern outskirts of Freiwalde in their vehicles and became tied up in street fighting. The 18th

Tank Regiment and the 3rd Motorized Rifle Battalion attacked the town from the west and from the march seized the railroad station.

The enemy, consisting of a battalion of Assault Regiment 2, one reserve battalion, one labor battalion and other separate units, caught by surprise by the midnight appearance of our tanks and motorized infantry in the town's area, offered weak resistance and quickly retreated, some into the woods east of Freiwalde, the rest along the highway to the north.

By midnight on 22 January, the town of Freiwalde had been completely mopped up of the enemy, and the 47th Mechanized Brigade took up an all-round defense of the town. The brigade captured 125 prisoners in Freiwalde. Thus, all of the 5th Guards Tank Army's formations and units had achieved the objectives set for 22 January 1945 on schedule.

From the recollections of F.I. Galkin:

In the evening the corps' chief of staff Colonel Smirnov reported to the army headquarters: "Pokolov's brigade, bypassing the town [Deutsch Eylau] on its eastern side, has passed through the settlement of Zielkowo and is continuing to push quickly to the north. Stanislawsky's brigade is approaching the town from the southeast, brushing aside weak detachments. The 32nd Tank and 53rd Motorized Rifle Brigades are bypassing to the west of the lakes."

On Sidorovich's map, once again enormous pincers appeared, just like they had before around Neidenburg. Vol'sky studied this map for a long time and in full concentration, then straightened up and said to no one in particular: "Malakhov has a chance to untie a knot no worse than Neidenburg's. It is a pity that all aircraft are grounded by the weather; it would be great to support them in the morning with a bombing attack." Then turning to me, he asked "How many serviceable tanks does Malakhov have?" I briefed the army commander on the mechanical condition of the combat machines.

"Where did Stanislavsky get his tanks?

"He assembled and repaired all the tanks that had been left behind."

Vasilii Timofeevich carefully examined the figures in the briefing papers' table, marked something on the cells, and placed it down on the chief of staff's table.

"It is still possible to fight with such a number of machines, Georgii Stepanovich."

Sidorovich nodded in agreement.

After midnight the pincers on the map had almost fully closed around Deutsch Eylau. Colonel Smirnov reported that the brigades had reached their designated areas. When dawn broke on 22 January, he reported again: "The tankers and motorized infantry have entered the town and are tied up in street fighting."

By 1500 on 22 January Deutsch Eylau was completely liberated. Several hours later the mechanized brigade also took the town of Freiwalde.

The advance of Malakhov's tankers was so rapid, that the residents of some towns, who wholeheartedly believed in the invincibility of the Führer's army, didn't even imagine that Soviet forces were already nearby. Peaceful life was going on under the sharply-pitched tile roofs of the homes that hugged the road, until the Soviet tanks appeared on the streets.

The same thing happened on the evening of 22 January. When the Major Tuz's 1st Tank Battalion of Colonel Pokolov's brigade burst into Saalfeld, everywhere electrical lamps were burning under colored lampshades, and the pubs and beer halls were open. Residents were peacefully strolling along the sidewalks. The appearance of the tanks with stars on their flanks was so unexpected, that the panic that instantly erupted enveloped the entire town. "Russian panzers!" – the Germans were shouting as they rushed from home to home and gathered in deep stone cellars.

Our offensive was accelerating on almost every axis of advance. The brigades were making daily advances of many kilometers and were rolling forward unchecked. However, rumors about the

Russians' approach nevertheless outpaced the brigades' advance and gave rise to fear in the local garrisons and terrified burghers of the inevitable retribution.

News that the Reds had broken through the border and were advancing into the depth of Germany spread throughout Prussia like lightning. Goebbel's propaganda, which until recently had been extolling the successes of the Nazi troops, began now to draw terrible pictures of the Communists' atrocities. All of the civilians were ordered urgently to prepare for evacuation.

The tankers had been fighting for six days without interruption, in order to reach Freiwalde. The tanks and self-propelled guns by this time had already advanced up to 400 kilometers, having expended 60 to 80 operating hours on the engines, and were in need of required inspection.

On 23 January we checked all of the machines in turn in both of the tank corps. We even managed to give the crews a short rest, without ceasing combat operations.

Our success was inspiring not only the combat commanders, but also the mechanics. They didn't lag behind the combat units and sought to put knocked-out tanks and self-propelled guns back into service as quickly as possible. They tackled small repair jobs as the first order of business. A repair stock, as the troops called those machines that required lengthier repairs, remained behind. The units kept advancing, while the repair stock stretched for many kilometers to the rear.

Pustilnikov was the first to get alarmed. Constantly adjusting his eyeglasses, he spoke nervously, in agitation: "Machines in need of moderate repairs are piling up and piling up. The corps' repair assets have fully switched to maintenance and light repairs, while leaving machines needing longer repair jobs behind."

"What in your opinion, Maer Izrailevich, needs to be done to the contrary? First and foremost, patch up machines that need a large amount of work, and put a hold on those with minor damage?"

"God forbid! I'm only reporting that we don't have the strength to offset the daily losses. The repair stock is lengthening and is stretching along all the routes. Bogachin is still sitting around near Mława."

"Yes, he's been left somewhat far behind. But right now, a different thing is troubling me: There are still a lot of machines, the locations of which are unknown to Bogachin. How do we search for them in the swamps and canals? Even Denisov, most likely, doesn't know where they are."

Pustil'nikov dug into a pile of papers.

"According to Denisov's information, he knows the location of eight machines, which have become badly stuck in swamps."

"Yet according to the information of the corps and army's units – there are fourteen. That means, six have become lost. Add as well those, that are unknown to Bogachin ...."

"It is the same old story," Putil'nikov sighed bitterly; "Once again we have no means of command and control. Once again, the repair workers are driving around the places of fighting and are themselves searching for machines, wasting time. Yet after all, we wrote about this in the last report ...."

"And we'll keep writing about this. We'll keep writing until our command in Moscow grasps this!"

"The recovery teams and repair workers, who have left around knocked-out machines, are losing contact not only with the fighting troops, but also with the technical service unit. Where to find someone? How and where to reach them? Not by choice, they are sending out vehicles "in a general direction". The accompanying officer or sergeant often doesn't even have a map. So now repaired tanks and self-propelled guns wander along the roads in search of their units."

"Just like at Memel, we'll have to organize the retrieval and movement of these machines," I advised; "This will at least ease the situation a little. Yesterday I myself became convinced that you are absolutely correct ... Yesterday evening I came across such "nomads". I was driving through some village. There wasn't a soul on the streets. I see three T-34 tanks standing in the village square. The crews have gathered at the lead machine. One, having slapped a tanker's headset on his

The 5th Guards Tank Army in the East Prussia operation, 1945

A self-propelled gun crewmember of the 5th Guards Tank Army holds a paper in his hands entitled "My personal score of vengeance against the enemy" in the jumping-off positions near Mohrungen, 22 January 1945. (TsA MO)

The commander of the 5th Guards Tank Army Colonel General V.T. Vol'sky (on the left) at the East Prussian border. (TsA MO)

An enemy column of 50 vehicles that was transporting soldiers and military gear, destroyed by the 29th Tank Corps' 31st Tank Brigade in the Bienau area 3 kilometers west of Liebemühl; January 1945. (TsA MO)

head, is saying something and gesticulating wildly, while the others are laughing. Having noticed me, the tanker wearing the headset took a step to meet me …."

Colonel Irklei interrupted our conversation.

"I've just come back from Malakhov's tank corps," Mikhail Fedorovich said, greeting us. "I met with Belianchev, and spent time at Gusev's depot. Their work is running briskly, but they have one complaint: a lot of tanks are wandering around somewhere, searching for their units.

"I was just talking about this with Pustil'nikov. We have no radios … what can be done? In addition, this is foreign soil. On our own land the people might have helped us, but here, there are no roadsigns and no people. The fascists have driven them all away. We've decided to organize a drive-around of all the routes, but this is a lengthy undertaking. Take a seat here for now, while I try to arrange for an airplane. Think of which of the officers it is best to send. It is necessary to fly around the entire "corridor", land next to each spotted tank, examine it, and mark its location down on a map."

I couldn't catch the commander in his headquarters; he had just left to drive out to see the troops. The Military Council member initially regarded my proposal skeptically, but then all the same directed to assign an airplane to me. Early the next morning, the senior assistant chief of the Department of Repairs Engineer-Major Pavel Fedorovich Ovcharenko, equipped with a map of the area of fighting and a list of the machines' turret numbers, flew off in search of them.

Simultaneously, a group of officers set out from the corps in various directions in vehicles with the same instructions.

Ovcharenko's flight proved difficult, but fruitful.

Later he told me, "I couldn't land the airplane next to each machine. At a glance you could see that the tank had bogged down in a peat swamp up to its turret. You had to find some hillock nearby. You had to land a kilometer or two away, directly on a road or a forest clearing, and then walk there and back again on your own two feet."

The tall, slightly stooped Ovcharenko usually seemed gloomy and wasn't fond of excessive talk. However, this time he looked cheerful and was telling me the story of his flight in some detail.

"In some of the machines, only one or two men were left. They'd been sitting there for several days. They ate up their rations, and somehow kept themselves fed with scavenged food. They greeted me just like the Cheliuskin crew members greeted their rescuers. However, I arrived without any kitchen and didn't bring along any tobacco – I don't smoke … In one place I landed in a puny forest clearing, and my landing gear was scrapiing the tree tops. Well, I was thinking we'd nose over. However, somehow this was avoided …."

"How many tanks did you find?"

"Over two days – 23. I've transmitted all the coordinates to Bogachin's headquarters, and of course, to Captain Denisov …"

Over a week of fighting, the recovery teams and mechanics had returned approximately 400 tanks and self-propelled guns to service. This amounted to almost two-thirds of the number that the army had before the start of the offensive. However, machines that were in need of repair or recovery from swamps and canals still remained on the battlefield.

It was particularly difficult to evacuate the heavy tanks. Their maneuverability was rather high, and the tankers had boldly rolled across peaty, soft sectors of ground. However, falling into a bog, the 46-tonne leviathan began to lose traction and would sink into the muck up to their turrets. Ordinary evacuation means had no use in these situations – heavy tackle, prime movers and dozens of cubic meters of wood were required. Captain Denisov had this gear, but he couldn't be everywhere at once and soon lagged behind.

Once I drove to the Osterode area – and saw a group of men and tractors on a railway embankment: Denisov and his prime movers were hauling out a heavy tank that had sunk into a quagmire. Winch cables were slowly pulling the machine, and it, pushing an entire heap of muck out in front of it, was moving toward the embankment. A deep channel, filled with filthy, agitated water was being left behind by the hull. The exit from the quagmire had been furbished with thick pine skids.

"Where did you get the skids?" I asked Denisov.

"We got them from a sawmill," he replied, pointing at a settlement about a kilometer away.

"Was there someone really there?"

"Nope, nobody."

"With whom are you planning to settle the account?"

"With Hitler in Berlin, if he doesn't kill himself before then. They'd be useful for a coffin."

"The best coffin for him is our best tank. How many badly mired tanks have you evacuated?"

"This is our twelfth," Denisov said, after exhaling loudly. "Almost all of them are in good working order …."

Belenev's and Lobzhenidze's companies had also recovered more than 150 machines. The majority of them after inspection and small adjustments immediately returned to their units. This unnoticed, but difficult work helped our army retain its combat effectiveness even after a week of bitter fighting. Meanwhile the offensive was rolling forward constantly. Having crossed the southern border of East Prussia, our forces, without stopping, kept advancing.

The commander of the 5th Guards Tank Army Colonel General of Tank Forces V.T. Vol'sky with combat orders from 1.55 on 23 January 1945 issued the following objectives to the army's formations and units for 23-24 January 1945:

- 10th Tank Corps: After taking possession of Mohrungen, with an energetic attack in the direction of Kohlau, Schönau and Mühlhausen, was to capture Mühlhausen by 2400 on 23 January 1945, take up all-round defense of the town, and prevent an enemy retreat from East Prussia to the west.
- 29th Tank Corps: Out of the Saalfeld area, with a rapid advance in the direction of Groß Arnsdorf, Hirschfeld, the Güldenboden railroad station and Elbing, take Elbing by 2400 on 23 January 1945, cut all the lines of communication in the Elbing area, sent out a forward detachment to the coastline of the bay in the Herrenpfeil area. There it was to take up an all-round defense and prevent an enemy retreat from East Prussia to the west.
- 47th Mechanized Brigade: After taking possession of Freiwald, was to make a rapid advance in the direction of Grünhagen and Preußisch Holland and capture the latter town. From there it was to send out a forward detachment to sever the railroad while taking up an all-round defense in order to block an enemy retreat from East Prussia to the west.

The 10th Tank Corps set out to carry out its assignments at 1200 on 23 January in its previous combat formation. After the corps captured Mohrungen, the enemy in front of the tank corps went in hasty retreat in the direction of Mühlhausen. On the Bordehnen, Behlenhof, Karwitten line, and subsequently on the Breunken, Schlobitten line, the enemy attempted to delay the corps' advance by the fire of significant forces.

As a result of the fighting, the 10th Tank Corps drove the enemy back from the lines indicated above, and by 2000 on 23 January took Bordehnen and the road hub 1.5 kilometers west of Behlenhof, and by the end of 23 January captured Schlobitten. Continuing to pursue the retreating enemy, the 10th Tank Corps by the morning of 24 January reached the Mühlhausen area, where it became tied up in street fighting. By 1300 24 January the 10th Tank Corps had suppressed the enemy's resistance and had fully eliminated the remaining pockets of resistance in the town of Mühlhausen – a key junction of six primary roads. By 1900 on 24 January, the corps' units had organized an all-round defense of this junction and were occupying the following positions: 186th Tank Brigade – woods 1 km west of Schlobitten; 183rd Tank Brigade – Herrndorf; 11th Motorized Rifle Brigade – Gardienen, Lohberg and Greulsberg; 178th Tank Brigade – Schönberg. The corp's reconnaissance group was scouting in the direction of Tolkemit.

The 47th Mechanized Brigade moved out to carry out its mission at 1000 on 23 January. At 1100 on 23 January, the brigade, having broken the enemy's fire resistance, took Grünhagen. Continuing the advance, by 1200 on 23 January the brigade reached the defensive fortifications protecting Preußisch Holland (2 km south of the of the town), which consisted of two lines of trenches. The stone buildings on the city's outskirts had been adapted for defense, with loopholes for machine guns and submachine guns. The attempt by the brigade's forward detachment to break into the town from the march had no success. The enemy with well-organized fire repulsed the attack of the brigade's forward detachment. Up to three battalions of infantry, supported by an artillery battalion and 10 tanks and self-propelled guns were defending in Preußisch Holland.

On the night of 22-23 January 1945, the 5th Guards Tank Army received the task to accelerate the rapid advance and to take Mühlhausen and Elbing with its main forces. Meanwhile the corps' forward detachments were to reach the Frisches Haff and to isolate the enemy's East Prussia grouping from the rest of the German forces that were operating on the Eastern Front. Once there, the 5th Guards Tank Army was supposed to go over to the defense and to block an enemy breakout attempt to the west.

The commander of the 5th Guards Tank Army General V.T. Vol'sky decided to continue the advance through the night. The 10th Tank Corps broke the enemy resistance in the Mohrungen area, and continuing an energetic advance, captured Mühlhausen on 24 January. On the approaches to the town, the men of Captain F.A. Rudskoi's tank battalion demonstrated heroism and courage. North of Mühlhausen, the tankers destroyed a large enemy column on the Königsberg – Elbing highway, in the process killing up to 500 Nazis and destroyed 100 vehicles, while capturing approximately 150 vehicles and up to 70 loaded wagons. The enemy attempted to drive the battalion back from the highway with continuous counterattacks, but with no success. The battalion's men withstood the German onslaught until the arrival of the brigade's main forces. For his skillful command, heroism and courage, Captain F.A. Rudskoi earned the title Hero of the Soviet Union, while his combat subordinates received Orders and medals.

Heroes of the 5th Guards Tank Army, January–February 1945

Guards Lieutenant Colonel Semen Kolesnikov – commander of the 29th Tank Corps' 32nd Tank Brigade: Distinguished in the period of offensive fighting from 17 to 31 January 1945. Always located up in the brigade's combat formations, he skillfully oversaw the destruction of the enemy grouping that was defending the approaches to East Prussia. The combat for Deutsch Eylau was especially successful, where the 32nd Tank Brigade unexpectedly arrived from the west in the enemy's rear at night, and from the march broke into Deutsch Eylau, where it smashed the enemy's 114th Mechanized Division [sic], capturing a lot of prisoners and loot. Swiftly advancing to the west in night marches, the brigade arrived significantly to the west of the city of Elbing and cut off the enemy's path of retreat. Heavy fighting went on for three days. The Germans were throwing tanks and motorized infantry into the fighting, but out tankers refused to take one step back. Over these days the 32nd Tank Brigade under the command of S.G. Kolesnikov destroyed 10 tanks, 36 guns, 3 aircraft, 9 stockpiles, 8 trains, 1,200 vehicles, and a lot of enemy manpower, while capturing 5 operational tanks, 8 guns, 700 vehicles and 300 men. On 1 February 1945 after heavy fighting, the unit stopped in front of a small village. It was risky to proceed. Guards Lieutenant Colonel S.G. Kolesnikov unfolded a map. It was possible to bypass the village, but a swamp lay in front of it. There was no other way forward. The machines exited the woods and headed toward the swamp. The commander clambered out of the tank, in order to check how the work of the sappers was going, who were preparing a passage for the tank column. However, just at this moment there was the sound of an incoming shell, which having exploded, sprayed fragments. Guards Lieutenant Colonel Semen Kolesnikov was killed on the spot. For his leadership in the destruction of the enemy's 114th Mechanized Division [sic], the capture of an important road hub, and his ensuring that the Front's tasks were fullfiled even at the cost of his own life, as well as for the courage and heroism he showed in the process, Kolesnikov was posthumously awarded the title Hero of the Soviet Union.

Senior Lieutenant Aleksandr Rukhliad'ev –tank company commander in the 29th Tank Corps' 31st Tank Brigade: On 18 January 1945 the tank company under the command of Senior Lieutenant Rukhliad'ev with a surprise attack seized the Soldau [Dzialdowo, Poland] railroad station and three trains carrying enemy tanks and vehicles. Pursuing the retreating enemy, it was the first to penetrate into the town of Elbing and reach the Baltic Sea. In this fighting the company commander knocked out several enemy tanks and halftracks. Continuing the successful offensive, the tank brigade together with other formations on 21 January breached the strongly-fortified German defenses on the southern border of East Prussia and invaded its territory. On 1 February

1945 in the fighting for the town of Preußisch Holland, company commander Rukhliad'ev made a bold decision – to emerge in the Germans' rear with his tanks and to break into the town from the west. Rukhliad'ev's crew alone destroyed 12 halftracks, 10 vehicles, 2 heavy guns and a bunker, and eliminated more than 50 Nazis. The tanks from the march rolled into the city. The commander's tank was in the lead. The tank took a direct hit from a shell that penetrated the armor, and Rukhliad'ev was mortally wounded and passed away. For his exemplary fulfillment of command assignments and for the courage and heroism he demonstrated, Rukhliad'ev was posthumously awarded the title of Hero of the Soviet Union.

Senior Lieutenant Mikhail Vaniushkin – commander of a tank platoon in the 47th Mechanized Brigade's 18th Tank Regiment. On 19 January 1945 when the regiment was introduced into the breakthrough, operating in the forward detachment, his platoon was first to cross the East Prussia border, thereby blocking the enemy's path of retreat out of Neidenburg. Repulsing enemy counterattacks in the area of Napierken, it destroyed 2 Tigers, 1 self-propelled gun and killed more than 100 enemy soldiers and officers. Pursuing the retreating enemy, it broke into Neidenburg, where it engaged in street fighting for 8 hours, thereby securing the approach of the brigade's main forces. On 7 February when assaulting the town of Frauenburg [on the coast of the Frisches Haff], Senior Lieutenant Vaniushkin's tank was set ablaze. Being wounded, in the burning tank he attacked the enemy, and destroyed 2 antitank guns, 4 mortars, 6 machine-gun nests and killed more than 30 soldiers and officers. This ensured the infantry's advance and the capture of the town. On 8 February in the fighting for a bridge across the Baude River, he was again badly wounded, and his tank was knocked out. Ignoring the pain, he fought to repulse the pressing enemy, and having allowed 2 enemy tanks carrying submachine gunners onto the bridge, he blew it up together with the enemy. He himself perished heroically on the battlefield. For his exemplary fulfillment of the command's orders and for the demonstrated courage and heroism, Vaniushkin was posthumously awarded the title Hero of the Soviet Union.

Lieutenant Mikhail Tratnikov – a tank commander in the 2nd Tank Battalion of the 10th Tank Corps' 178th Tank Brigade. In the area of Trunz on 26 January 1945 he repulsed repeated attacks of the enemy, which was trying with all its might to break through our defenses. Having taken the initiative into his own hands, Tratnikov demonstrated exceptional heroism; launching an attack, with targeted fire from his cannon he brewed up 2 enemy tanks and 3 self-propelled guns. Entering operational space in the enemy rear, with his tank's tracks and fire he destroyed 3 antitank guns, 8 field guns, 12 mortars, 60 vehicles and killed up to 75 enemy soldiers and officers. On 1 February 1945 in the area of Karwitten, repulsing an enemy counterattack, he set ablaze 1 tank and 2 self-propelled guns. On 6 February 1945 in an attack toward the village of Barden, his tank overran 2 cannons and rammed three prime movers. Put forward for the title Hero of the Soviet Union. He was awarded the Order of the Red Star.

Sergeant Major Pavel Porfir'ev – commander of a reconnaissance squad of the headquarters company (of the 29th Tank Corps' 25th Tank Brigade); sergeant major at the moment he was recommended for being awarded the Order of Glory 1st Class. During the East Prussia offensive, the squad's halftracks, led by Sergeant Major Porfir'ev, operated as a rule in the enemy's rear. In January 1945 on the approaches to Deutsch Eylau, having conducted a 70-kilometer dash through the enemy's rear, the squad of halftracks together with a tank unexpectedly at night burst into a railroad station. The reconnaissance men captured military trains that were standing at the station, and having taken up an all-round defense, repulsed four enemy attacks until the brigade's main forces arrived. On 23 January 1945 the sergeant major with a group of soldiers blew up the railroad tracks in the enemy rear in the vicinity of Polwitten railroad station (town of Osterode).

When returning, the scouts accepted combat with superior enemy forces. In the fighting Porfir'ev personally killed up to 10 soldiers, and took quite a few prisoners. On 24 January 1945 the squad in its halftracks under the command of Porfir'ev took possession of an important road junction in the city of Elbing and captured a bridge. Fighting off enemy counterattacks, the scouts destroyed 15 vehicles and wiped out approximately 50 Nazis. Porfir'ev ended the war as an officer. For the courage, heroism and valor, he was awarded the Order of Glory 1st Class. He became a full Cavalier of the Order of Glory. On 24 June 1945 in the Victory Parade, Guards Junior Lieutenant Porfir'ev marched across Red Square in a column of the 2nd Belorussian Front's best soldiers and officers.

Sergeant Major Ivan Shchabel'sky – a radio operator-machine gunner with a tank of the 10th Tank Corps' 186th Tank Brigade. Shchabel'sky particularly stood out in the fighting for the town of Osterode on 21 January 1945. Having destroyed an enemy antitank gun, the crew of the T-34 tank burst into the town. Carrying out the assignment to block the enemy's paths of retreat, the tankers captured an important road junction, scattered an enemy column, and became tied up in combat. In the fighting, the crew destroyed 2 antitank guns, 3 self-propelled guns, a halftrack, 18 vehicles, and approximately a company of soldiers. The Soviet tank was knocked out from a hit by an enemy shell and the tank commander and driver-mechanic were both killed, while Shchabel'sky and tank gunner Sergeant Krasnov were wounded. Ignoring the pain, the wounded tankers continued to conduct fire from the main gun and machine gun, killing up to 20 Nazis. When Shchabel'sky's tank erupted in flames from a second shell hit, the surviving tankers moved into a nearby building and engaged in an unequal combat for three hours, until the arrival of our units. Shchabel'sky was awarded the title Hero of the Soviet Union.

Sergeant Viktor Krasnov – tank gunner with the 1st Tank Battalion of the 10th Tank Corps' 186th Tank Brigade. In the fighting on the approaches to the border of East Prussia, the tank crew, in which Krasnov served as the tank gunner, repeatedly distinguished itself. Located all the time in a forward reconnaissance patrol, the tank's tankers were the first in the brigade to cross the border of Germany and enter the territory of Poland. On 21 January 1945 the tankers reached the town of Osterode and at full speed broke through to the town center, where they grabbed an intersection of two streets. In this action Krasnov with shots from his cannon destroyed 3 enemy self-propelled guns, 4 halftracks, 18 vehicles and approximately a company of soldiers. Krasnov's tank was knocked out by the hit of an enemy shell, the commander and driver-mechanic were killed, while Krasnov and a fourth crew member were wounded. Neglecting the pain, the wounded tankers contined to fire the main gun and machine gun, killing up to 60 Nazis. Krasnov didn't cease fighting until his tank was set ablaze. Removing the machine gun, wounded and burned, he took up a position in the cellar of the nearest building and continued to wipe out Nazis with accurate machine-gun fire. When Sergeant Major Shchabel'sky joined up with Krasnov, the two of them together for the next three hours fired at Nazis on the nearby streets. Not knowing the number of Soviet soldiers in the building, the Germans committed 19 vehicles and 3 towed guns into the fighting. The two tankers held the town center until the arrival of our main units. For the courage and valor demonstrated in the fighting for the town of Osterode, the sergeant was awarded the title Hero of the Soviet Union.

Guards Captain Gennadii D'iachenko – tank battalion commander of the 31st Tank Brigade. Over the period of combat operations from 16 to 31 January 1945, he proved himself to be a capable commander. The battalion advanced 500 kilometers with combat. Located in the forward detachment, he skillfully directed the battalion, bypassing enemy centers of resistance, especially when crossing the border of East Prussia and in the area of Dzialdowo, where two antitank ditches and four lines of German defenses were overcome. Reaching the enemy rear, he penetrated 80 kilometers, destroying enemy supply trains in the process. Through his bold and decisive actions, his battalion advanced 70 kilometers over a half-day and by the evening of 23 January 1945 unexpectedly to the enemy entered Elbing, where it rolled along the streets from east to west and south to north, killing in the process up to 1,000 enemy soldiers and officers and up to 500 vehicles with the tanks' fire and tracks. The brigade also destroyed a railroad train and up to 20 cannons. His tank battalion arrived at the Baltic Sea, thereby having cut road junctions and railroad lines, as well as a water canal that linked Elbing with the Baltic Sea, and in the process, sank 6 barges and 3 steamships. Holding a road junction, he was separated from the rest of our units, having contact only over the radio. Over these two days his detachment repulsed up to 8 enemy attacks. His name was submitted for the title Hero of the Soviet Union. The submission was supported by the commander of the 29th Tank Corps and the Military Council of the 5th Guards Tank Army. The commander of the 2nd Belorussian Front's Armored and Mechanized Forces rejected the submission. Awarded instead the Order of the Red Banner.

Major Nikolai Tuz – tank battalion commander of the 29th Tank Corps' 31st Tank Brigade. Over the period of combat operations from 16 to 31 January 1945 on the territory of Poland and East Prussia, he showed himself to be a bold and hard-charging commander. His tank battalion advanced more than 400 kilometers with fighting. On 20 January 1945, pursuant to a combat order, the battalion under his command unexpectedly to the enemy burst into Dzialdowo and captured a train carrying tanks and vehicles. In the town he captured a bridge across the river,

The 5th Guards Tank Army in the East Prussia operation, 1945

Tanks and self-propelled guns of the 5th Guards Tank Army with tank riders aboard roll through the streets of Mühlhausen after the fighting on the morning of 24 January 1945. (TsA MO)

A column of T-34 tanks of the 5th Guards Tank Army on the march; East Prussia, January 1945. (TsA MO)

A T-34 tank of the 5th Guards Tank Army on the attack, followed by its dismounted submachine gunners. (TsA MO)

Motorized infantry of the 10th Tank Corps pass a burning German restaurant, 24 January 1945, on their way out of Mühlhausen in order to carry out their next assignment. (TsA MO)

T-34 tanks of the 5th Guards Tank Army on the march, crossing an antitank ditch; East Prussia, January 1945. (TsA MO)

An officer of the 5th Guards Tank Army reads a letter from home to his combat comrades during a break in the fighting; East Prussia, February 1945. (TsA MO)

Self-propelled guns and tanks of the 5th Guards Tank Army marching; East Prussia, January 1945. (TsA MO)

On the coast of the Baltic Sea; East Prussia, February 1945. (TsA MO)

A soldier of the 5th Guards Tank Army who wears the Order of Glory stands on a jetty on the Baltic Sea coastline; East Prussia, 1945. (TsA MO)

thereby ensuring the passage of the entire brigade. Through his bold and decisive actions on 22 January 1945, he broke into the town of Saalfeld unexpectedly with meager forces, and having crushed the enemy garrison, captured the town. Subsequently he captured a road junction east of Elbing and devastated a motorized column of the German Third Panzer Army's Artillery Regiment 3, which was attempting to break through to Elbing. In the process up to 300 vehicles and up to 25 field and anti-aircraft guns were destroyed, and up to 400 Nazis were killed. In the course of two days he held the road hub and fought off 6 enemy counterattacks. For his capable leadership of the tank battalion, D'iachenko was awarded the Order of Lenin.

The commander of the 47th Mechanized Brigade decided to bring up all of his forces, and after a 15-minute artillery barrage from guns of all calibers, including the tanks and self-propelled guns (a total of 90 barrels in the brigade), to take Preußisch Holland with an assault. At 1300, after the concentrated 15-minute artillery preparation, the brigade moved out to storm the town. With a decisive charge in the wake of the tanks, the motorized infantry broke into the town from the south and encircled it from the east and west. The brigade's tanks rolled onto a square in the center of the town, and fired down the streets leading to the north and northwest, preventing the enemy from launching counterattacks. The enemy was putting up especially bitter resistance on the streets in the northern and northwestern outskirts of the town, where the defenders were ensconced in all the stone buildings. The enemy was driven out of these city outskirts only with the arrival of our tanks and with the help of their fire. Ten enemy tanks and self-propelled guns, which prior to the start of the assault were positioned in a patch of woods 1 km north of the town, took no part in the street fighting, and their attempt to render help to the garrison of Preußisch Holland from outside of the town proved late.

By 1800 the city garrison's resistance was finally broken, and its remnants together with 9 tanks and self-propelled guns began to withdraw to the north toward Mühlhausen. At 1900 on 23 January the city of Preußisch Holland was fully mopped up of the enemy. By 2000 on 23 January, the 47th Mechanized Brigade had taken up a defense around Preußisch Holland with a front facing to the east, northeast, north and northwest, having set out a combat post on the railroad 5 km north of the town. On the night of 23-24 January, the enemy from the direction of Kaymen (4 km northeast of Preußisch Holland) launched several counterattacks toward the town. The brigade successfully drove back all of the counterattacks. In the fighting for Preußisch Holland, the enemy lost 300 soldiers and officers killed, and more than 200 men captured, while two self-propelled guns and one cannon were destroyed.

From an interview with Lieutenant Colonel M.A. Bykadorov

I completed the 2nd Khar'kov Tank School for Self-propelled Artillery as a member of the top class in October 1944. Having arrived in Mytishchi at the where the formation was forming up, I was directed into the 1st Separate Battalion and given a post of commander of a SU-76 self-propelled gun in the fully-manned 153rd March Battery, in place of an officer who had departed the day before. My first crew consisted of driver-mechanic Sergeant Ivan Zviaglov, gunlayer Senior Sergeant Pavel Maiorov, and loader Senior Sergeant Ivan Cherenkov. On our journey to the front, we traveled through Moscow, Mozhaisk, Gzhatsk, Viaz'ma, Smolensk, Orsha, Borisov, Minsk, Baranovichy and

Lieutenant Colonel M.A. Bykardov, a post-war photograph.

Volkovyshki. In Berestovets we crossed the national boundary, and then passed through Białystok. We unloaded in Belsk somewhere around evening. It finally became clear that we had arrived at the 2nd Belorussian Front.

We received a warm welcome in the brigade. The 31st Tank Brigade had taken up quarters in the assembly area in some woods east of the Narew bridgehead. On 12 January 1945 an assembly took place in the brigade, at which Generals Malakhov and Zaitsev bestowed the Order of the Red Banner to the brigade for its past combat operations.

Also, on 12 January, we learned that the 1st Ukrainian Front had gone on the offensive. On 13 January we were informed that our neighbor on the right, the 3rd Belorussian Front, had kicked off an offensive.

Night arrived, the final night before the offensive. Around 0900 the next morning on 14 January, it was made clear to us that the 1st and 2nd Belorussian Fronts were going on the offensive today. At 1000, located in the assembly area of the 5th Guards Tank Army, we heard the loud thunder of an artillery cannonade, signaling that it had started. An artillery preparation started that shook the ground for dozens of kilometers. All other sounds were swallowed up by the din of the artillery barrage. The offensive of the 2nd Belorussian Front had started. The formations and units of the forward armies had moved out to break open the enemy's deeply-echeloned defenses. The Mława – Elbing operation had begun. Our combat spirits rose sharply upon entering the territory of East Prussia. The cry, "Forward, to Berlin!" was the most popular in those days.

My brother Vasilii was also traveling on the frontal roads of East Prussia. He fought in the 289th Guards Destroyer Antitank Artillery Brigade of the Supreme Command Reserve from February 1944 to the end of the war. Even before the January offensive, we had found out through letters that we were located somewhere not far from each other. Letters were arriving rapidly, but we couldn't find out exactly where each other was located, and there was no time for a reunion. Later it became clear that at one point, we were moving along the very same road, but at the end of January, our paths separated: I headed to the north toward Elbing, but Vasilii headed to the northwest.

On 22 January our brigade, in cooperation with other units, took the town of Deutsch Eylau with an assault. This was a major railroad hub. We, the tankers, weren't taking German soldiers and officers prisoner. We never had anything to do with them. We simply sent them on to our rear. Where they ever actually reached the prisoner collection points, I can't say. I simply don't know, but I suppose that some portion of them made it there, while others probably simply got away from us. From where else could all sorts of "wandering groups" of them have appeared?

On the night of 23-24 January, I received a personal order from the commander of the 31st Tank Brigade – to remain in ambush with the task to prevent a breakout of the Germans toward Elbing across a bridge on a road about 200-250 meters away from us. Our self-propelled gun took up a combat position in a swale; having concealed it behind piled up snow, we readied for combat. The commander of the 31st Tank Brigade Colonel Pokolov was located not far from us together with his operational command group. I was warned once again that a German withdrawal was possible along this road to Elbing.

It was a moonlit night. On the right and left of us, the approaches to the bridge were screened by folds in the terrain; our field of vision amounted to around 250-300 meters. The crew of the self-propelled gun, taking advantage of the pause in operations, grabbed some rest, if you can call it such. One crewmember took the watch. Around 0200, machines began to creep across the bridge. We opened fire from our gun. The first shots didn't yield any results. At that time, we had no night vision equipment in our army. Then I gave an order to gunner P.M. Maiorov to aim the gun at the bridge at its lowest setting. We were successful! With the next shot we set a machine ablaze. It stopped, lighting up the area around it. Now it was easier for us to aim the gun. With our next shot, we knocked out another machine. The Germans began to hurry across the bridge, and opened fire from submachine guns and light mortars in our directing, trying to suppress the fire of our self-propelled gun. The German fire was inaccurate. They simply couldn't see us. With our following shots, we brewed up three more machines and knocked out two others at various distances from the bridge and on the bridge itself. The movement of the German machines that had come to a stop resumed. We fired several more shots at the Germans, who were conducting automatic weapons fire at us. They still couldn't spot us! Our self-propelled gun was covered with white paint. Now only separate "bravehearts" decided to try to make it across the bridge under these conditions. We set two more machines ablaze and knocked out another one.

The road across the bridge was full of knocked-out and burning machines. The movement stopped. The fire from the submachine guns and mortars also ceased. It again became silent. The fighting had lasted approximately 90 minutes. The crew was satisfied with the results. In this combat action the gunner P.M. Maiorov didn't let us down and fully justified our trust in him. The next morning, we counted up the score from the nighttime action. There were 6 burned-out machines and 4 knocked-out machines. Three of the machines had been towing anti-aircraft guns. Approximately 150 vehicles of the German column were abandoned by the Germans. Many of them had anti-aircraft guns hitched to them. The Germans had fled in different directions, fearing captivity.

From the memoirs of Hero of the Soviet Union General of the Army I.F. Ivanovsky:

The offensive continued. We were making energetic, unexpected maneuvers. On the night of 17-18 January 1945, the tank and mechanized formations of the 2nd Belorussian Front undertook a maneuver in broad operational space with the aim of encircling the Mława fortified area, which guarded the approaches to East Prussia from the south. The Nazi command, as it later turned out, had its own plan: to draw our attacking troops into prolonged fighting and to attempt to split them in two. The enemy's calculations remained on paper – our tankers preempted it and didn't allow them to assemble an adequate amount of force in the Mława area. The double envelopment maneuver by the formations of the 5th Guards Tank Army encircled the Mława fortified area.

Our corps, screening the 5th Guards Tank Army's left flank, broke up an attack by approaching enemy reserves. In this fighting Senior Lieutenant A. Alimov particularly distinguished himself. Moving in the lead tank, he ensured timely and reliable reconnaissance. The battalion's columns and the entire brigade was following behind it. Alimov's tank crushed two enemy guns beneath its tracks, destroyed a Panther with its fire, and eliminated dozens of Nazis that wound up in its path.

General of the Army I.F. Ivanovsky, a post-war photograph.

On 19 January we arrived at the border of East Prussia and were the first of the 2nd Belorussian Front's troops to cross it. The Front Commander-in-Chief Marshal of the Soviet Union K.K. Rokossovsky sent the Guardsmen a congratulatory telegram in connection with this combat success. The Political Departments released a flash leaflet. It stated, "We've reached the boundary of Germany. Forward, Guardsmen! Don't allow the foe a rest!" The leaflet passed from hand to hand.

Both day and night the tanks were advancing along snow-covered roads past cottages with steeply-pitched tiled roofs, firing on the move at the retreating Nazis. They were leading the infantry and artillery; units and elements were moving behind them. The neat German villages were bristling with stone ruins, and isolated farmsteads were burning. It was precisely from here, from East Prussia, as well as from Poland, Czechoslovakia and other European countries subjugated by the Nazis that the divisions of the Fascist aggressors pounced on us. It was precisely it, East Prussia, that was always the nest of rabid German imperialism … I was not the only one consumed by these thoughts. I was watching as my combat comrades swiftly advanced with such fervor, and how they hurled themselves at the foe, disdaining danger and even death itself.

Yellow road signs went flashing past: "Lautenburg", "Deutsch Eylau", "Osterode". We would have to take these and other settlements with combat, at times fleeting, but very fierce …. Over a week of the ceaseless offensive, the corps' units advanced more than 200 kilometers with fighting. Hundreds of enemy tanks and self-propelled guns and a multitude of vehicles, guns, armored cars and wagons were destroyed or captured by us. A large number of soldiers and officers were taken prisoner. The Nazi high command's strictest orders to hold defensive lines and struggle to the last drop of blood were no longer being carried out as zealously as before. The German soldiers were beginning to see the hopelessness of resisting and were surrendering.

Nevertheless, on those days when our ring of encirclement was constricting around the German troops who had at their backs the shores of the Baltic Sea, the fighting acquired a bitter character. Concentrating forces on separate sectors, the Nazis were throwing themselves into counterattacks. The enemy was striving at any cost to hold the town and railroad hub of Dutch Eylau. On the approaches to it, the Germans had set up a tight belt of defenses, which the retreating units and the reserve formations formed according to total mobilization were occupying.

The corps' units launched an attack from two directions. Our regiment was attacking from the southeast. In cooperation with the tankers of the 58th Guards Tank Brigade, we overcame the enemy resistance in a sector of his "invulnerable" defenses and broke into the town. The taking of Deutsch Eylau and the settlement of Saalfeld had no little significance in the course of the East Prussia offensive operation. On 23 January an artillery salute was fired in Moscow in honor of the troops that had distinguished themselves in the fighting for Deutsch Eylau and Saalfeld. In addition, an order of the Supreme Commander expressed gratitude to our tankers. In the course of the operation to compress and encircle the enemy grouping on the Baltic coastline, the army and the tank corps with forced marches advanced into the depth of the enemy's defenses, cutting lines of communication and catching enemy formations in pincers. These model expressions from the military lexicon, incidentally, reflect the operations with almost photographic accuracy. When the encirclement was completed and the Nazis found themselves in a pocket, the all-arms formations were required to keep a firm grip on the adversary's grouping and complete its destruction.

At 1500 on 23 January 1945 the 47th Mechanized Brigade, pursuant to an order from the army commander, set out along the Preußisch Holland, Pomehrendorf, Trunz, Dörbeck, Wogenap route with the task by 1800 on 24 January to cut the highway and railroad in an area 4 km north of Elbing and to cooperate with the 29th Tank Corps' attack against Elbing. One battalion was to remain behind to protect Preußisch Holland.

By 0200 the brigade loaded in its machines reached Groß Stoboy. In view of the strong snowstorm and snow drifts, the further movement of the wheeled vehicles proved to be impossible. The motorized infantry dismounted and was forced to continue the march on foot. The brigade had no contact with the enemy as far as the Dörbeck area, with the exception of small, disorganized groups, which were easily destroyed or captured by the brigade's forward units. At 1400 the brigade reached the woods that lay 2 km northwest of Dörbeck, where it ran into heavy enemy fire. After two hours of fighting, the enemy was driven back, and the 47th Mechanized Brigade reached the sea's coastline in the Groß Röbern area, where it took up a blocking position on the railroad and highway in this area and organized a hedgehog defense. The tanks of the 31st Tank Brigade had already left this area by this time. The brigade occupied a defense in the Wogenap – Groß

Röbern area until 1600 on 25 January, and then took part in the 29th Tank Corps' attack toward Elbing in the direction of the town's northern outskirts.

The 29th Tank Corps set out in its previous combar formation at 1130 on 23 January in order to carry out its assignment, moving out along two routes in two combat echelons. The 31st Tank Brigade was moving along the right-hand route in the first echelon, with the task by the end of 23 January to take the Groß and Klein Stoboy estates (4 km northeast of Elbing); the 25th Tank Brigade was in the second echelon as the corps commander's reserve, with the task to reach the Stagnitten area by the end of 23 January. The 32nd Tank Brigade was moving along the lefthand route in the first echelon, with the task to take Elbing together with the 53rd Motorized Rifle Brigade and to reach the western banks of the Fischau River by the end of 23 January. The 53rd Guards Motorized Rifle Brigade in the second echelon behind the 32nd Tank Brigade had the task to take Elbing by the end of 23 January in cooperation with the 32nd Tank Brigade.

The 31st Tank Brigade advanced along its route, and without meeting any serious enemy resistance with the exception of disorganized German groups that were destroyed by the brigade's forward detachment, at 1400 on 23 January closed within firing range of the western outskirts of Preußisch Holland and took part in the crushing of the enemy garrison in this town in cooperation with the 47th Mechanized Brigade. At 1600 the brigade, without delaying in Preußisch Holland, continued the offensive and by 2100 on 23 January the brigade's forward detachment reached the outer fortifications of Elbing from the east. Taking no enemy fire, the chief of the forward detachment – the commander of the 3rd Tank Battalion Captain D'iachenko – decided to break into the eastern outskirts of Elbing unexpectedly, without firing. This battalion managed to do.

The garrison and residents of Elbing, plainly not expecting such a rapid appearance of our forces in this area, were caught totally by surprise. Having entered the town, the forward detachment found that Elbing was living the normal life of a city in the rear. Soldiers and cadets of the tank school were taking evening strolls along the streets, singing as they walked. Officers and residents were emerging from a movie theater. Electrical lights were on in the city, and the streetcars were operating. At the most opportune moment, Captain D'iachenko gave the signal to move out. The tanks with fire and tracks destroyed a column of soldiers out for a walk, several dozen vehicles, and a lot of wagons. Panic erupted in the city.

Carrying out its assignment, the forward detachment, having silenced the random fire of several antitank guns, exited the city through its northern quarter. By 2300 the forward detachment reached the coastline of the sea in the Groß Röbern area and cut the coastal railroad and highway.

Earl Ziemke, in his study *Stalingrad to Berlin: The German Defeat in the East*, describes the scene in Elbing:

> By nightfall on 23 January *Second Belorussian Front* had cut all the roads and railroads crossing the Vistula except the coast road through Elbing. After dark, the *Fifth Guards Tank Army*'s lead tank detachment approached the city. Finding that it had not been alerted – the streetcars were running and on one street German soldiers from a local armored school were marching in formation – the Russian crews turned on the headlights of their tanks and rolled through the main streets firing as they went. By daylight, when the next wave of Soviet tanks arrived, the Germans in Elbing had recovered enough to fight them off and force them to detour east around the city. In the meantime, however, the Russian lead detachment reached the coast, and Army Group Center was isolated.

The main forces of the 31st Tank Brigade, which were lagging somewhat behind the forward detachment, ran into the organized resistance of up to two battalions of antitank artillery and 8-10 tanks in the area of the Dambitzen estates on the eastern outskirts of Elbing. This speaks to the fact that the enemy had time to recover from the chaos that had erupted in the city after the appearance of the forward detachment, had come to his senses and had managed to prepare for a defense. After two hours of fighting, suffering losses, the main forces of the 31st Tank Brigade had made no progress and had adopted a defense in the vicinity of the Dambitzen estates.

The 25th Tank Brigade by midnight on 23 January had reached the Wolsdorf Höhe area, and its forward detachment – in Stagmitten, where it was counterattacked by up to a battalion of infantry with the support of two batteries of artillery and two self-propelled guns. After two hours of tough fighting, the 25th Tank Brigade broke the enemy resistance and by 0400 on 24 January reached the Klein Stoboy area, where it took up an all-round defense. The 376th Heavy Self-propelled Artillery Regiment had by this time reached the Neu Schönwalde estates, having cut the Lenzen – Elbing highway.

The 32nd Tank Brigade by 2300 on 23 January reached the road fork on the southeastern outskirts of Grunau, where it was met by heavy enemy fire and adopted a defense. The 53rd Motorized Rifle Brigade, advancing in the wake of the 32nd Tank Brigade, by the morning of 24 January reached the western outskirts of Grunau, where it also ran into heavy enemy fire and took up a defense.

The commander of the 29th Tank Corps Major General of Tank Forces K.M. Malakhov, in preparation for an attack toward Elbing, on the morning of 25 January 1945 conducted the following regrouping: the 31st Tank Brigade – by 1400 on 24 January reached the estates in the Koggenhofen area, where it linked up with its 3rd Tank Battalion under the command of Captain D'iachenko; the 376th Heavy Self-propelled Artillery Regiment continued to occupy a defense in the area of the estates in the Neu Schönwalde area (2 km south of Dörbeck), having cut the highway; the 32nd Tank Brigade by 2200 on 24 January had reached the Damerau area; the 25th Tank Brigade continued to hold a defense in the Klein Stoboy area; and the 53rd Motorized Rifle Brigade was defending a line between the Dambitzen estates and Grunau with a front facing toward the southeastern outskirts of Elbing.

The strong reconnaissance group of the 29th Tank Corps, in cooperation with the army's 1st Motorcycle Regiment, was operating along the coastline and by the end of 24 January had reached the approaches to Tolkemit. The sector of the Frisches Haff coastline now being held by troops of the 5th Guards Tank Army extended up to 15-20 kilometers.

Thus, the troops of the 5th Guards Tank Army had achieved their objectives – to cut the enemy East Prussian grouping's path of retreat to the west on land with their arrival to the Baltic Sea in a sector of 15-20 kilometers; and to firmly isolate the city of Elbing from the northeast, east and southeast. They had carried out the operation's objectives within a span of just seven days from their introduction into the breakthrough.

From the "Combat Path of the 5th Guards Tank Army":

By the morning of 23 January, the army was ready to launch the decisive blow. Meetings had taken place in the units and elements, at which the Military Council's address to the troops was read to those in attendance. At 1000 on 23 January, the units of the 47th Mechanized Brigade set out to carry out their assignments. An hour later, the 29th Tank Corps moved out, followed later by formations of the 10th Tank Corps. By midday the 47th Mechanized Brigade reached Preußisch Holland. At a critical point in the fighting, T-34 tanks unexpectedly appeared on the western outskirts of the town. As became clear later, Lieutenant Colonel A.I. Pokolov, the commander of the 31st Tank Brigade, which was attacking toward Elbing, had decided to lend a hand to the 47th Mechanized Brigade. With their combined efforts, the enemy resistance collapsed.

The tankers then moved on toward Elbing, while the motorized infantry cleared the enemy from the final streets. The fighting moved so quickly that the fascists didn't have time to employ tanks and self-propelled guns, which were positioned north of the town, in the street fighting. The Germans lost more than 300 men killed. Around 200 more soldiers and officers surrendered.

The 31st Tank Brigade's forward detachment, headed by the commander of the 3rd Tank Battalion Captain G.L. D'iachenko, was the first to reach Elbing. He had the task to bypass to the east of Elbing and to cut the highway and railroad in the vicinity of Groβ Röbern, which was situated 4 km north of Elbing on the banks of the Frisches Haff.

Carrying out his orders, Captain D'iachenko demonstrated boldness, initiative and resourcefulness. Having studied the route, along which he was supposed to bypass Elbing, the battalion commander decided that it offered difficult going for the tanks. So G.L. D'iachenko decided to bypass the city along its beltway. However, even here they couldn't push through – a destroyed bridge was blocking the path.

Evening was falling. Having consulted with his subordinate officers, D'iachenko decided to force their way through to the objective directly through the city. The plan was based on the attack's element of surprise and a rapid advance. It was a risky step to take. The tankers didn't have any detailed information about the layout of the defenses or the enemy's available strength and means. Moreover, they would have to operate in a city of ancient construction, where it would be easily to get confused in the labyrinth of narrow streets. Emitting a bluish gray smoke, the detachment's machines moved out on a broad highway. Along both of its sides, fruit trees covered with hoarfrost stretched like a fluffy white belt. They left behind them crushed machines and wagons. The sharply-pitched roofs of the suburban homes came into sight in the evening twilight.

The residents of Elbing calmy observed the menacing machines that were passing by them. Possibly, they took D'iachenko's tank column to be the elements of the tank school returning from an exercise, or perhaps as reinforcements sent from the Fatherland. In any case, the appearance of the Soviet tanks in the very center of the city came as a complete surprise for everyone. Upon emerging on the main square, the lead tank abruptly came to a stop. Confusion rose among the German officers standing on the sidewalks: it is possible that they realized that these were Soviet tanks standing in front of them. There was no time to delay. Captain D'iachenko's command – "Do what I do!" – rang out in the tankers' headsets.

The commander's tank surged forward, and throwing up sparks on the bridge with its tracks, sped across it at full speed. The rest of the tanks followed it. The loud chatter of bursts of machine-gun fire shattered the evening calm. A panic ensued. The lights went out, and the city fell into darkness. "Turn on the headlights!" – D'iachenko's command came in over the airwaves. However, now the Germans were coming back to their senses, and they began to deploy antitank guns on some of the street intersections. The Nazis managed to knock out the commander's tank. Having made his way across to a different tank, the battalion led the column forward, to the city's northern outskirts.

The forward detachment reached its objective around midnight, took up blocking positions on the highway and railroad, and organized an all-round defense. Enemy attacks began at dawn. The forward detachment engaged in combat for several hours. Riddled steam engines stood motionless on the railroad tracks, and vehicles were burning on the highway and in the roadside ditches. The tankers also sank two steamships and a barge, which were just offshore.

The main forces of the 31st Tank Brigade were advancing toward Elbing in the wake of its forward detachment; however, by the time they were approaching the city, the German defenders had woken up and met the tanks with heavy fire. Tough street fighting ensued. It was impossible to break through the defenses. Then the brigade moved to bypass Elbing on its eastern side and on the afternoon of 24 January reached the forward detachment's area of defense north of Elbing. The reconnaissance groups of the 29th Tank Corps and the 1st Guards Motorcycle Regiment that were advancing along the coastline neared Tolkemit on the evening of the same day.

The 25th Tank Brigade was advancing behind the 31st Tank Brigade. Its commander I.O. Stanislavsky sent several reconnaissance groups up ahead in order to take important road junctions and to disorganize the withdrawal of the enemy units. Sergeant Major P.P. Porfir'ev, a Cavalier of the Order of Glory and the commander of an element of halftracks of the reconnaissance platoon, was heading one such reconnaissance group. His halftracks, which had stealthily moved forward, set up an ambush in the indicated place on the highway. Triggering the ambush, more than 50 enemy corpses were left here, and the scouts took 20 enemy soldiers prisoner. For his skillful actions, individual daring and courage, Sergeant Major Pavel Porfir'evich Porfir'ev was awarded the Order of Glory 1st Class.

F.I. Galkin recalls:

The Front Commander-in-Chief Marshal Rokossovsky issued an order to the army: having captured Osterode and Deutsch Eylau, to continue the offensive to the north and to take Elbing, Preußisch Holland and Mühlhausen by the morning of 24 January. Carrying out the Marshal's order, Vol'sky moved Mikhailov's mechanized brigade out to the left flank, which on the afternoon of 23 January attackd Preußisch Holland. The fascists resisted. Very heavy fighting flared up. Things would have been difficult for Mikhailov, if Pokolov's brigade hadn't pivoted toward the sounds of fighting and helped to take the town.

The fate of Mühlhausen was also decided. General Sakhno's tank corps, pursuing the retreating Germans, on the morning of 24 January approached this Prussian town. Here, six highways came together. They connected East Prussia with Pomerania, Danzig and Königsberg, and joined the Königsberg – Elbing coastal thoroughfare. To cut this road hub meant to paralyze the maneuver of the German reserves. Therefore, the Military Council was hurrying Sakhno.

Lean, with an upright military bearing, Sakhno had inexhaustible energy and passed it down to his subordinates. The staff officers and runners didn't walk away from the general – they flew away to carry out his instructions. Picking up the phone, he would issue orders calmly and concisely, without stopping to make notes on his weatherbeaten map.

The attack against Mühlhausen went successfully. The town had been completely mopped up of the enemy by midday. Malakhov's tank corps, after conclusively liberating the Deutsch Eylau area from the enemy, swung by Saalfeld in order to refuel the tanks. The brigade commanders were hoping to give the men a short rest here, but that didn't happen: Malakhov and Zaev told the men to mount up and led the units on toward Elbing – the second largest city in East Prussia.

During this rapid march – with fighting and maneuvers – Captain D'iachenko, a battalion commander in Pokolov's tank brigade, distinguished himself. Having received an order to cut the coastal highway north of Elbing in the Groß Röbern area, D'iachenko demonstrated exceptional audacity, resourcefulness and sensible initiative. The previously designated route that bypassed far to the east of Elbing proved difficult and impassable for the tanks. So D'iachenko then changed the route, thinking that he would bypass Elbing along its beltway, and set a course directly toward the city. The battalion approached the outer fortifications of Elbing at high speeds, but found that swampy fields lay to the east, and canals and lakes lay to the west, which would prevent it from getting around the city. Time was passing. So the captain made the only correct decision: to breakthrough from the east to the north directly through the city: a large, unfamiliar enemy city! Dangerous? Yes. Risky? Unquestionably so! However, it is possible to reduce both danger and risk to a minimum, if you operate sensibly, and not throw caution to the winds.

From the seven tanks of his detachment D'iachenko assigned his three best crews to a reconnaissance patrol. He designated Junior Lieutenant Beregovoi to lead the group, and gave him Semenov's, Isaev's and Aleinikov's tanks. Senior Sergeant Kamenev took a seat behind the driver's levers of the lead machine. The three T-34s went on up ahead. The sun began to set. The reconnaissance patrol unexpectedly broke into the suburbs of Elbing, having first destroyed two supply trains that were in their path, and shot up an airfield where 18 Messerschmitts were standing. Not a single one of them was able to make it into the air.

Somewhat later, the remaining tanks of D'iachenko's battalion linked up with the reconnaissance patrol. Then the Soviet machines, their tracks throwing up sparks from the bridges, raced through the streets of Elbing. The city was slumbering peacefully. Electric lights covered by shades were lit up on the squares and in the entrances of the buildings. The doors of pubs and restaurants, opening and closing every minute, were allowing leisurely visitors to enter or exit. The gaudy names of film hits glowed on the billboards. The lead machine sharply came to a stop upon emerging out onto a large central square. Here, a dense crowd of cadets of a German tank school were strolling along, under the watchful eye of unteroffiziers. D'iachenko issued the order, "Do what I do!" and sped his tank toward the crowd of cadets and soldiers. Bursts of machine-gun fire split the air and echoed in the lanes and alleys. One tank crushed a supply train that appeared beneath its tracks. A second tank smashed a cannon before it managed to fire. A third tank rammed the door of a restaurant, toward which the overfrightened Nazi officers had rushed …

An alarm was raised, machine pistols and submachine guns began to chatter … Only now did the fascists figure out what had happened. It was too late, though … On the square and in the narrow labyrinth of back streets, the cannons of the Soviet tanks thundered, and the shattered fragments of window panes tinkled on the pavement. The Germans attempted to deploy antitank guns on some intersections, but not all of them managed to fire a shot before they fell under the tracks of Soviet tanks. One more side street, one more alley, and then finally the desolate northern outskirts of Elbing appeared. Thus, having broken through the hostile town, D'iachenko had reached his designated objective, and quickly saddled the highway and railroad. Disorganized enemy groups, retreating in panic, were striving to break out to the west, but D'iachenko's tankers dispersed them and stoutly blocked their path.

D'iachenko together with his small group held onto this area for more than 24 hours, until at last the main forces of Pokolov's tank brigade arrived, having widely bypassed Elbing. It was carrying out the role as the corps' forward detachment. Malakhov's tank corps, having encountered tough resistance, on 24 January conducted a regrouping and prepared an attack toward Elbing. Meanwhile its forward detachment, operating along the coastline, broke into Tolkemit together with scouts of the 1st Guards Motorcycle Regiment. Tolkemit was another large city on the shore of the Baltic Sea. Thus, the sea had been reached a second time. It was heavier than the first occasion, back in October 1944. Select Nazi units were stubbornly defending Tolkemit. In order to break their resistance, a lot of effort, military skill, heroism and self-sacrificing solidarity was required.

From the "Combat Path of the 29th Tank Corps":

In the final stage of the offensive actions of the troops of the 2nd Belorussian Front, a task was laid on the 5th Guards Tank Army: to reach the Frisches Haff in the area of Elbing and to cut all of the German East Prussia grouping's lines of communication on land. The 29th Tank Corps under the command of Major General of Tank Forces K.M. Malakhov was supposed to deliver a swift attack out of the Saalfeld area in the direction of Groß Arnsdorf, the Gildenboden railroad station and Elbing and to take the area northeast of Elbing by the end of day on 23 January 1945. There, it was to send a forward detachment to the coastline of the Frisches Haff in the Herrenpfiel area, take up an all-round defense, and prevent an enemy retreat to the west.

Colonel A.I. Pokolov's brigade was directed to reach the area of the Groß and Klein Stoboy farms east of Elbing, and thereby cut all of the main roads running from Elbing to the northeast.

Lieutenant Colonel S.G. Kolesnikov's brigade, in cooperation with Colonel D.N. Dolganov's brigade, was supposed to launch an attack toward Elbing and take the city. Colonel I.O. Stanislavsky's brigade would remain in reserve.

The 5th Guards Tank Army's Military Council issued an appeal to its tankers. In particular, the appeal stated: "Comrades! You were the first to cross the southern boundary of East Prussia; behind you is the breakthrough of the southern fortified line, the main strongpoints of Neidenburg, Tannenburg, Lubawa, Deutsch Eylau, Osterode, Saalfeld, and hundreds of other villages. For this, the Supreme Commander has announced his gratitude to you. Combat friends! Reach the Baltic Sea! In the name of the glory of Russian arms, in the name of our holy vengeance, only onward and onward!"

On the evening of 23 January 1945, the corps moved out to carry out its mission. Colonel A.I. Pokolov's brigade attacked to the north, and without encountering any serious opposition on the enemy's part, soon reached the town of Preußisch Holland. The tank army's 47th Mechanized Brigade closed on the same place. The town was attacked from the march. Having crushed the garrison and an enemy supply train that was passing through there, the brigades captured Preußisch Holland. Without delaying in it, they continued the offensive. Overcoming the enemy's resistance, destroying his strongpoints and blocking detachments, the Soviet soldiers drove deeper into his dispositions. The adversary kept introducing more fresh reserves into the fighting. However, he didn't have enough strength that might have stopped the tanker-heroes.

The enemy began to adopt new tactical methods. If before his tank ambushes, supported by self-propelled guns and infantry cover, opened fire from a range of 1,200 meters before falling back, now these ambushes, carefully camouflaged, allowed our tankers and submachine gunners to close within 100-200 meters, in order to fire at pointblank range. Having figured out this enemy tactic, the Soviet units strengthened their reconnaissance, and having detected an ambush, engaged it with fire. The rifle elements would bypass these ambushes to one side, while the tankers, without waiting for the outcome of the clash, would break through in those places where reconnaissance had identified a lightly defended sector. The Germans after this would have to either surrender, or else attempt to break out back to their own lines.

Only several dozen kilometers were left to reach the sea. To cover them meant to put the enemy in a hopeless situation and to predetermine his complete and rapid destruction. It was necessary to reach the coastline as quickly as possible. This important task rested on on the 31st Tank Brigade's 3rd Tank Battalion under the command of Captain G.A. D'iachenko, which was assigned to operated in the forward detachment. Captain G.A. D'iachenko decided upon a daring step – to drive to the sea through the city of Elbing. Reconnaissance patrols were moving out in front of the battalion. Along the route, they came upon an airbase with 18 Messerschmitts standing on it. The tank turrets quickly turned, and having fired 23 shells and bursts of machine-gun fire at them, they set all of the German fighters ablaze.

Rapidly advancing, the battalion entered the city. To the surprise of the Soviet tankers, the city was living the typical life of a city in the rear. Captain D'iachenko led the battalion further into the city, and fighting his way forward, approached the bridge and crossed it. The Germans overcame their shock and began to organize opposition. They brought up guns and several tanks, and opened fire. One of the German shells struck the battalion commander's tank. Seeing that it was impossible to save the machine, Captain G.L. D'iachenko took a seat in a different tank and led his battalion to a different street. On the northern outskirts of the city, grenades and shells flew at the Soviet tankers. However, it was already too late. The battalion emerged from the city and within several minutes was at the coast. The tankers noticed two barges being towed by a cutter. They opened fire at them and sank them. The battalion had reached the endpoint of their raid – the village of Groß Röbern. There was no where to go any further – ahead lay the sea, and ammunition and fuel were running low. They had to be conserved for the future. Captain G.L. D'iachenko believed that the units following him would consolidate the achieved successes and soon come up. However, the main forces of Colonel A.I. Pokolov's tank brigade, and later the tank corps as well, were unable to take Elbing from the march. They were unable to take it in the following two days either. Captain G.L. D'iachenko's forward detachment remained isolated. It took up an all-round defense. A firing position and a sector of observation and fire were determined for each tank. The submachine gunners took up defensive positions somewhat out in front of the tanks.

One tank had become stuck in a swamp and couldn't be recovered. Only 8 combat machines remained in the detachment, ammunition and fuel were almost at an end, and the only available food were dry rations sufficient for one day. However, there was no sense of dismay among the tankers. They believed in their commander and in the rapid arrival of the main forces. However, they had become separated so distant from the main forces, that they couldn't even make radio contact with them.

The Nazi command realized that breakthrough of Soviet tanks to the sea presented a mortal danger, and already the next morning hurled major forces and antitank artillery into the fighting in order to destroy the Soviet tanks that had broken through to the sea. However, the adversary's attacks ran into an organized defense and suffered a defeat. On the second day, Captain G.L. D'iachenko finally made radio contact with the corps commander Major General of Tank Forces K.M. Malakhov. The general thanked the tankers for their heroic actions and ordered them to hold out until the arrival of the main forces. They indeed held out. They held out and trusted that help was on the way. For the daring and valor demonstrated, Captain G.L. D'iachenko and his combat comrades were decorated with Orders and medals.

When the main forces of the 31st Tank Brigade, which was being commanded by Lieutenant Colonel A.I. Pokolov, approached the city, it found the enemy ready behind strong defenses and ran into stubborn resistance. Then the brigade changed course and bypassed Elbing on its eastern side, and on the morning of 24 January reached the Frisches Haff, where it linked up with its forward detachment. Thus, the enemy's East Prussia grouping wound up cut off from the German forces that were retreating beyond the Vistula.

That evening a telegram from the Commander-in-Chief of the 2nd Belorussian Front was read out in the units and elements. The message read: "To the commander of the 5th Guards Tank Army: I congratulate the honorable Guardsmen-tankers, artillerymen and motorized infantry for their glittering achievements. I wish you further successes in crushing the foe. ROKOSSOVSKY, BOGOLIUBOV."

From the "Combat Path of the 29th Tank Corps":

Meanwhile the corps was unsuccessfully attacking Elbing. The 31st Tank Brigade, trying to break-though east of the city to it forward detachment, had no success. Up to two artillery battalions and 10 enemy tanks were standing in its path. An exchange of fire continued for more than 2 hours, and during an attempt to attack the enemy, the tankers suffered heavy losses. The brigade was forced to go over to a defense.

The city of Elbing was a powerful center of defense. The Germans had assembled major forces in it. Elbing's garrison had under command units of the German 7th Panzer Division, an assault gun brigade, two regiments of naval infantry, and one fortress and three tank battalions. The city was being protected by defensive fortifications that ran along the Tolkemit – Groß Stoboy – Kunersdorf line and along the southeastern outskirts of the city. Major General of Tank Forces K.M. Malakhov decided to conduct a regrouping in order to take the city. Colonel A.I. Pokolov's brigade and Lieutenant Colonel S.G. Kolesnikov's brigade were to assemble northeast of the city, in order to launch the main attack toward Elbing out of the Röbern and Damerau area against its northeastern outskirts. It was decided to isolate the garrison from the southeast with Colonel D.N. Dolganov's motorized rifle brigade. The corps commander decided to position the 31st Tank Brigade on the right flank, so that it could assist its cut-off 3rd Tank Battalion. The corps' reconnaissance group, consisting of the 7th Motorcycle Battalion, was penetrating toward Tolkemit together with the army's reconnaissance group.

On the morning of 25 January, the corps launched a second attack toward Elbing, and once again the attack was thrown back. The army commander decided to reinforce the attack against the city. For this purpose, he removed the 47th Mechanized Brigade from the coastline and sent it for joint operations with the 29th Tank Corps. On 26 January, the tank corps, in cooperation with the 47th Mechanized Brigade, made one more attempt to break the enemy's resistance and take the city. The 47th Mechanized Brigade, reinforced with the 14th Guards Heavy Tank Regiment, attacked form the north, while the corps' tank brigades attacked from the northeast and east.

The assault got underway after a 30-minute artillery preparation. The attack from the east by the 29th Tank Corps' units was repulsed by the enemy. During the attack from the north, the mechanized brigade's 2nd Motorized Rifle Battalion, with the support of the heavy tanks, broke into the northern outskirts of Elbing and there became tied up in street fighting, which continued throughout the night of 26-27 January. Repeated attempts by the enemy to drive the battalion out of its occupied positions had no success. The 47th Mechanized Brigade dug in and kept a grip on the city's northern quarters.

Colonel A.I. Pokolov's tankers had to endure heavy trials. Fuel and ammunition had been nearly exhausted. The Germans were keeping all of the paths to the city under targeted fire. It was almost impossible to bring up fuel and shells. The deputy technical commander of the 1st Tank Battalion Senior Technician-Lieutenant Kh.Kh. Gubaidullin made three trips in a prime mover through the dangerous zone of fire and delivered cases of shells and drums of fuel to the tankers. Each arrival of the valiant officer was met by joyful shouts of the tankers. On the third day, Captain G.L. D'iachenko's detachment spotted a large group of soldiers with artillery and mortars approaching their positions from the direction of Mileewo. Junior Lieutenant Isaev went out to meet them in order to find out who these people were. They were motorized riflemen of the 31st Tank Brigade. Joy of the link-up seized the men, who exchanged hugs and kisses. The three-day siege had come to an end.

An issue of the frontline newspaper was dedicated to the heroic deeds of Captain G.L. D'iachenko's tankers. It laid out on its pages how the breakthrough to the sea had been executed. The lead article ended with the words: "Glory to Captain D'iachenko's Suvorov-tankers, who embued our Red Combat Banner with an immortal achievement! Glory to the heroes of the Great Patriotic War!" The Motherland highly regarded the exploit of their faithful sons, having decorated Captain Gennadii L'vovich D'iachenko, Senior Lieutenants Modest Firsovich Kononenko and Gavril Gavrilovich Suvalov, Junior Lieutenants Andrei Zakharovich Aleinikov and Pavel Ivanovich Isaev, and Senior Sergeant Andrei Denisovich Kamenev with Orders of the Red Banner. Junior Lieutenant Pavel Iakovlevich Beregov and Sergeant Viktor Ivanovich Milofanov were decorated with Orders of the Patriotic War 2nd Class. Somewhat later, Captain Aleksandr Silaevich Piliaev received the Order of Lenin for his combat deeds in East Prussia.

The Third Stage of the Operation

The 5th Guards Tank Army's combat operations to expand the gap separating the enemy's East Prussia grouping from the rest of Germany, and its arrival at the Passarge River

The situation by the start of the third stage

Upon reaching the sea on a frontage of 15-20 kilometers and the isolation of Elbing from the northeast, east and southeast, the forces of the 5th Guards Tank Army on 24 January 1945 had completed the full encirclement of the enemy's East Prussia grouping on land. Trapped inside the pocket were the remnants of divisions of the German Fourth Army and Third Panzer Army, as well as half of the Second Army. The latter army with the rapid advance of the 5th Guards Tank Army had been split into two parts: all of the divisions belonging to the XX Army Corps and the 299th Infantry Division of the XXIII Army Corps had been thrown back to the east into a pocket, while the remaining divisions of the XXIII Corps and the entire XXVII Corps had been thrown back to the west.

The city of Elbing, the second largest city in East Prussia after the city of Königsberg, with a population of more than 100,000 people, was an important hub of railways and roads and a powerful enemy strongpoint. By 24 January, at the moment of the approach of the 5th Guards Tank Army to Elbing, its garrison consisted of the Elbing tank school, units of the 7th Panzer Division, Stug Battalion 277, the 1st and 3rd Regiments of the 1st Naval Infantry Brigade, a regiment of the *Felderrhalle* Division, the 1424th Fortress Battalion, the 5th and 10th Reserve (Lehr) Panzer Battalions, the 662nd and 286th Training Battalions, several battalions of Volkssturm, the 251st Flak Battalion, and disorganized groups from the remnants of shattered enemy units that had previously been operating in front of the 5th Guards Tank Army.

Elbing had been converted by the enemy into a strong center of resistance. Its fortifications, which protected the approaches from the north, east and south, consisted of three defensive lines with two antitank ditches, barriers and dragon's teeth on the tank-vulnerable directions. All three lines had full-profile trenches, linked by communication trenches, and protected by 3-4 lines of coiled barbed wire. Minefields had been laid on all the roads and likely directions of tank actions. The stone buildings on the outskirts of the city had been adapted for defense. The conditions of the approaches to the city from the west, because of the swampy terrain that contained a dense network of irrigation ditches that were filled with water and served as natural antitank ditches, prevented the possibility of using a maneuver of the tanks to bypass the city from the west. Armor operations on the ground from Elbing to the west as far as the Vistula River were possible only along paved roads, which might easily be blocked by obstacles and mines.

The attempts by the 29th Tank Corps and 47th Mechanized Brigade to take Elbing from the march on the night of 23-24 January and in the course of 24-25 January had no success. The Elbing garrison was responding to the attacks with heavy fire. There was no possibility to use any of the 10th Tank Corps' strength to aid the 29th Tank Corps, because of the direct threat of an enemy attack toward Elbing from the east, with the aim of relieving the defenders and reestablishing a line of communications with the rest of Germany to the west.

The 10th Tank Corps and additional elements of the army were occupying a defense in the course of 24-26 January in the Mühlhausen, Neu Münsterberg, Preußisch Holland area with a front to the east and northeast. They were in full readiness to repulse any such attempts by the enemy while waiting for the arrival of the 48th Army's rifle divisions.

It proved impossible to capture such a large city, as Elbing, given the presence of a major garrison and powerful fortifications around the city, with the forces of the 29th Tank Corps and one mechanized brigade alone. Moreover, these forces had been weakened by the continuous combat operations over the last seven days since 17 January.

On 25 January 1945 the 5th Guards Tank Army's formations had the following number of operational tanks and self-propelled guns: 10th Tank Corps – 64; 29th Tank Corps – 72; 47th Mechanized Brigade – 33; for a total of 169 tanks and self-propelled guns of the 496 tanks and self-propelled guns that these formations had ready at the start of the operation on 17 January. Supplies were also running low. There were only 0.7 to 1 refuels with diesel remaining and only 0.5 to 1 standard combat load of ammunition remaining. All of the tanks and self-propelled guns, after 10 days of continuous heavy work, were in need of technical inspections and service. The casualties over the period from 17 to 24 January inclusively amounted to more than 1,500 killed and wounded.

The forward rifle units of the 48th Army and 2nd Shock Army, which were advancing behind the 5th Guards Tank Army, by the end of 23 January had reached the Allenstein, Liebemühl, Saalfeld, Freistadt line. This meant they were lagging behind the 5th Guards Tank Army by 60 to 70 kilometers.

The combat operations of the 5th Guards Tank Army from 25 January to 10 February 1945

The 10th Tank Corps throughout the day of 25 January was stubbornly defending the Mühlhausen area and the vital junction of six roads. By 1800 the corps' units were occupying the following positions: 186th Tank Brigade and attached assets – the Karwinden, Breunken line; the 183rd Tank Brigade – the Herrndorf, Gardienen line; 11th Motorized Rifle Brigade and attached assets – Gardienen, Lohberg; 178th Tank Brigade and attached assets – Falkhorst, Schönberg; the 376th Heavy Self-propelled Artillery Regiment – the Trunz, Baumgart area; the 14th Guards Heavy Tank Regiment – the Groß Stoboy area. Both of these regiments were in readiness to repulse enemy attacks from the east and northeast.

The 47th Mechanized Brigade was defending the important road hub and city of Preußisch Holland with one reinforced battalion. With its main forces, by 1900 it had reached the coastline in the Groß Röbern area.

The 29th Tank Corps, conducting a regrouping of its units, by the evening of 24 January was occupying the following position: 31st Tank Brigade – in the Dörbeck area; 25th Tank Brigade – the Klein Bieland area; 32nd Tank Brigade – the Damerau area; and the 53rd Motorized Rifle Brigade – in the area of the Dambitzen estates.

On the morning of 25 January, the 29th Tank Corps launched an attack against Elbing's fortifications along concentric, converging lines toward the city. Elbing's garrison put up strong, organized resistance. The tank corps' attack failed. In turn, the enemy garrison over the day of 25 January counterattacked six times with tanks and infantry in the eastern direction with the aim of breaking through to the encircled grouping and to restore its ground communications to the west.

F.I. Galkin remembers:

On 25 January Colonel Mikhailov's mechanized brigade also reached the coastline of the Baltic Sea in the Groß Röbern area. The soldiers were moving on foot: that night such a storm occurred that the vehicles became stuck and had to be left behind. From the time of our army's introduction into the breakthrough, eight days had passed. The objective had been reached: we were cutting off the East Prussia grouping's path of retreat to the west and were firmly blocking all approaches to the city from the east. Now a 20-km corridor separated East Prussia from the rest of Germany. The tankers had advanced at a rate of 60 to 70 kilometers a day. The infantry, naturally, was lagging behind. The repair teams were also struggling to keep up. However, their work output managed to adapt to the offensive pace of the combat units: over these eight days, they had returned 525 tanks and self-propelled guns to service.

With each passing day, it became increasingly difficult to implement command and control over the repair-recovery elements. They were now stretched from Mława to the sea's coastline in an area that covered 4,000 square kilometers. Information about the location of the units was reaching the rear on occasion, or through officers of the technical service that had driven out to the repair shops. The number of machines in service, as a rule, didn't comport with the figures in the summaries of the machines "in working order", which prompted confusion and bewilderment among the command staff. On 24 January, when K.M. Makhalov was preparing the corps' troops for an attack against Elbing, Senior Lieutenant Ozhogin phoned me:

"The commander is requesting information about the status of the tanks and self-propelled guns."

I found Vol'sky walking around the room, his hands placed behind his back, and dictating something to Sidorovich, who was sitting at a map with pencils in his hands. A shadow of fatigue lay on the faces of both generals. Vasilii Timofeevish had spent all night up among the troops of the first echelon. Meanwhile Georgii Stepanovich hadn't left the map and communications equipment for many hours: subordinates were reporting and making requests.

When I entered, Vol'sky stopped, fixed me with a searching gaze and asked: "Which one of you is confusing things?"

"I ask that you clarify, Comrade; I don't understand."

"And I don't understand a thing, so that's why I've summoned you. How many tanks does Malakhov have?"

"According to the latest information, 72 tanks and self-propelled guns."

"Are all of them in working order?"

"I am indeed reporting about those that are in working order. Belianchev doesn't provide unchecked figures."

"And how many are there according to your information, Georgii Stapovhich?"

The chief of staff glanced at an operational summary and gave a figure that was half as large.

"So, who is giving you this information? Probably, these are also checked figures?"

"Unquestionably. The corps headquarters sums up the reports from the units, and they are giving accurate information about the number of operational tanks."

"There now, take a look: You have "operational", and Galkin has "in working order". Both of you are correct. So where are the rest?"

I assured him: "Vasilii Timofeevich, I am vouching for the accuracy of my information. There can only be one of two explanations: either the headquarters are holding back machines for their own security, or they are doing nothing to take in those machines that are coming out of repairs. They are now in working order, but haven't yet rejoined the combat formations."

"What do you propose?"

"Allow me to leave immediately and check each machine. I can send my deputy – Colonel Irklei."

"Dispatch your deputy, and you, Georgii Stepanovich," he said as he turned to Sidorovich, "I request that you get in touch with Makhalov and double-check these figures."

"I've just got off the phone with Makhalov, and he is confirming his headquarters' numbers."

"I guess we're lucky, then. But where are the tanks?"

"The majority in the brigades, but some are guarding the headquarters, and others are carrying out some other task. In general, more than 15 are at the disposal of the corps headquarters, and just as many are loafing around on the roads. They've been repaired and have been included in the records, but no one is concerned about bringing them up.

"Are they now still wandering around?"

"No. Beliachev has dispatched officers of the brigades. Now, most likely, they've already been brought up."

That evening I consulted with Sidorovich, and we decided to compel the brigades and corps to provide all the summaries regarding the availability and condition of the tanks and self-propelled guns over two signatures – the chief of staff and the deputy chief for technical matters. We also stipulated to show separately the number of machines "operational" and the number "in working order" (and such a condition was preserved until the end of the fighting). Meanwhile the corps received instructions to keep a signals officer on duty with the materiel and maintenance unit.

People continued to work around the clock, although the number of machines that required light overhauls kept increasing. On 25 January, when the tank army reached the Baltic Sea, more than 50 machines had accumulated at the collection points for disabled machines, which stretched back from Elbing almost as far as Mława. Only 25 of them were being repaired. In addition, an additional 21 machines had to be recovered from canals and swampy areas.

Just as before, the chief of the Logistics Department Engineer-Lieutenant Colonel Ivanov and his assistant Engineer-Major Timchenko were working intensively together with Captain Piliugin. Thanks to their attention, the mobile supply dump was regularly replenished with parts and components, which then went immediately to the repair teams.

A sea breeze was ruffling the waters of the Frisches Haff lagoon; low waves, slightly warmed by the sun, were breaking the thin ice up that covered the southwestern portion of the lagoon. Columns of vehicles, infantry and wagons carrying civilians were moving along the narrow strip of sand that stretched from Pillau to Danzig, which separated the Bay of Danzig from the lagoon. These were fleeing Germans from the Baltic republics and Nazi troops that had not been annihilated at Memel, all seeking safety. At a respectful distance from the shore, large and small ships loaded with military gear and the remnants of fascist units were zig zagging along. Occasionally our 100mm guns fired at them, but the shells couldn't reach the targets. After D'iachenko's detachment, after emerging on the coastal road, had sunk two steamships and a barge, the German sailors became more cautious and were keeping their distance from the shoreline.

On 25 January 1945, the operations chief of the 42nd Rifle Corps Guards Colonel Fedorov issued a report on the combat strength of its units on that date:

> Manpower: 1567 officers, 2,494 non-commissioned officers, and 7,736 enlisted men, for a total of 11,142 men. Altogether, 2,449 horses, 6,156 rifles of all types, 2,816 submachine guns, 373 light machine guns, 101 heavy machine guns, and 36 anti-aircraft machine guns; 120mm mortars – 36, 82mm mortars – 92, 50mm mortars – 36. Guns: 120mm and 150mm – 23, 76mm – 23, 45mm – 54. Antitank rifles – 149. Vehicles of all types – 378.

The 29th Tank Corps, in cooperation with the 47th Mechanized Brigade, on 26 January undertook one more attempt to break the resistance of the Elbing garrison and break into the city. The 47th Mechanized Brigade, reinforced with the 14th Guards Heavy Tank Regiment, attacked out of area of Groß Röbern toward the northern outskirts of Elbing. Units of the 29th Tank Corps attacked from the northeast and southeast.

After a 30-minute artillery preparation, units of the 29th Tank Corps and the 47th Mechanized Brigade went on the attack at 1630 on 26 January. The enemy repulsed the attack by the 29th Tank Corps, but two motorized rifle battalions, with the support of heavy IS-122 tanks of the 14th Guards Heavy Tank Regiment, penetrated Elbing's northern outskirts, where they became tied up in heavy street fighting. The enemy was putting up particularly fierce resistance from out of the buildings of the tank school. The Germans in this area had few antitank guns. The Soviet tanks closed to within pointblank range of the buildings and poured fire into the enemy's firing positions; the motorized infantry would then move in and mop up these buildings from any surviving enemy groups.

The fighting in the northern quarter of the city continued throughout the night of 26-27 January. The 47th Mechanized Brigade and the 14th Guards Heavy Tank Regiment took the buildings of the tank school, the brewery, five city blocks and a ship wharf. The enemy's resistance with fire intensified. Lacking adequate strength to continue the advance, the units of the 47th Mechanized Brigade went over to a defense. Repeated enemy counterattacks to drive our units out of the northern quarter of the city failed. The 47th Mechanized Brigade and 14th Guards Heavy Tank Regiment kept a grip on their limited gains in the northern portion of Elbing until 29 January. In connection with the altered situation, the units of the 47th Mechanized Brigade, at an order from the army commander, were withdrawn from the northern outskirts of Elbing at 1200 on 29 January 1945 and received a new task.

On its part, the Elbing garrison throughout the day of 26 January undertook four counterattacks with tanks and infantry from various outskirts of the city, which were all repulsed by the units of the 29th Tank Corps. The 10th Tank Corps throughout the day of 26 January had been stubbornly defending the Mühlhausen area. The situation of its units remained unchanged. The attempts by small enemy groups to break out of the encirclement to the west were repulsed by the tank corps.

By the end of 26 January, the 48th Army's 42nd Rifle Corps consisting of the 137th, 170th and 399th Rifle Divisions had come up to the area occupied by the troops of the 5th Guards Tank Army. They took up a defense on a broad front that extended up to 30 kilometers on the Schlobitten, Fürstenau, Borchertsdorf, Tiedmannsdorf, Groß Rautenberg line, but on 29 January the 42nd Rifle Corps' front was extended to the left as far as Kreuzdorf and Tolkemit. Having a deficit of troops and such a large front on 26 January, the 42nd Rifle Corps was forced to take up a defense with isolated strongpoints, and not a continuous front. Small groups of its units were blocking the roads, and occupying large villages, hilltops and other more or less important locations.

Table 4.3: Status of the materiel of the German Fourth Army (Lage der panzerbrechenden Waffen – AOK 4) by the end of 25 January 1945]

Units	Armored vehicles and anti-tank guns					Under repair and not yet written off			Total
	StuG	Tanks	SP guns	sPak 76.2 mm	sPak 75-mm	Short-term	Long-term	Irrecoverable	
1	2	3	4	5	6	7	8	9	10
XX Armee Korps									
562.Volksgrenadier Division	-	-	-	-	11	-	2	-	13
Pz.Jg. Kp. 1562	5	-	-	-	-	-	-	-	5
14.Infanterie Division	-	-	-	-	12	-	-	-	12
Pz.Jg. Kp. 1102	4	-	-	-	-	-	-	-	4
292.Infanterie Division	-	-	-	-	10	-	-	-	10
Pz.Jg. Kp. 1292	1	-	-	-	-	-	-	-	1
StuG Brigade 185	5	-	-	-	-	-	-	-	5
StuG Brigade 209	11	-	-	-	-	-	-	-	11
129.Infanterie Division	-	-	-	-	6	-	-	-	6
Pz.Kp. 1014	5	-	-	-	-	-	-	-	5

Units	Armored vehicles and anti-tank guns					Under repair and not yet written off			Total
	StuG	Tanks	SP guns	sPak 76.2 mm	sPak 75-mm	Short-term	Long-term	Irrecoverable	
1	2	3	4	5	6	7	8	9	10
StuG Brigade 909	6	-	-	-	-	-	-	-	6
	9	-	-	-	-	-	-	-	9
Total for XX Korps	46	-	-	-	39	-	2	-	87
LV Armee Korps									
Kampfgruppe Hauser	-	-	-	-	63	-	-	-	63
88-mm guns	-	-	-	-	12	-	-	-	12
76.2-mm guns	-	-	-	18	-	-	-	-	18
Gruppe "Hannibal"	-	-	-	-	2	-	-	-	2
541.Volksgrenadier Division	-	-	-	-	12	1	-	-	13
102.Infanterie Division	-	-	-	-	13	-	-	-	13
Pz.Jg. Kp. 1541	12	-	-	-	-	-	2	-	14
203.Infanterie Division	-	-	-	-	12	-	-	-	12
547.Volksgrenadier Division	-	-	-	-	12	-	-	-	12
StuG Brigade 920 (4th Batterie)	3	-	-	-	-	2	-	-	5
Fest. Pak-Kp. 10/I	-	-	-	9	-	-	-	-	9
	-	-	-	-	10	-	-	-	10
Fest. Pak-Kp. 17/I	-	-	-	12	-	-	-	-	12
Total for LV Korps	15	-	-	39	136	3	2	-	195
VII Panzer Korps									
PGD Grossdeutschland	-	5	-	-	-	2	-	-	7
Pz IV	-	1	-	-	-	10	20	-	31
Pz V	-	5	-	-	-	3	8	1	16
Pz VI	4	-	-	-	-	-	-	-	4
24.Panzer Division Pz VI	-	6	-	-	-	-	-	-	6
(from Division Grossdeutschland)	2	-	-	-	-	-	2	-	4
18.Panzergrenadier Division 75-mm SPW	-	-	5	-	-	-	-	-	5
Panzer Abt. 118	4	-	-	-	-	-	-	-	4
sPz.Jg. Abt. 563 88-mm	13	-	-	-	-	-	-	-	13
Pz V	-	8	-	-	-	-	-	-	8
StuG Brigade 249	7	-	-	-	-	-	-	-	7
sPz.Jg. Abt. 664 88-mm	-	-	-	-	5	-	-	-	5
Panzer Abt. 302 Pz IV	-	5	-	-	-	-	31	3	36
	7	-	-	-	-	-	13	1	20
Sturm Kp. 218 Pz IV	-	7	-	-	-	-	-	-	7
299.Infanterie Division	-	-	-	-	4	-	-	-	4
	-	-	3	-	-	-	-	-	3
Pz.Jg. Kp. 1299	3	-	-	-	-	-	-	-	3
Pz.Jg. Kp. 16	-	-	-	4	-	-	-	-	4

Units	Armored vehicles and anti-tank guns					Under repair and not yet written off			Total
	StuG	Tanks	SP guns	sPak 76.2 mm	sPak 75-mm	Short-term	Long-term	Irrecoverable	
1	2	3	4	5	6	7	8	9	10
Total for VII Panzer Korps	40	37	8	4	9	15	74	5	187
VI Armee Korps									
131.Infanterie Division	-	-	-	-	13	-	-	-	13
Pz.Jg. Kp. 1131	5	-	-	-	-	4	-	-	9
I/AOK StuG Abt. 4	-	-	-	-	2	-	-	-	2
170.Infanterie Division	-	-	-	-	10	1	1	-	12
Pz.Jg. Kp. 1240	4	-	-	-	-	-	-	-	4
558.Volksgrenadier Division	-	-	-	-	10	-	2	-	12
Pz.Jg. Kp. 1558	5	-	-	-	-	2	1	-	8
Stab Treptow	-	-	-	-	33	-	-	-	33
Fest. Pak Kp.	-	-	-	-	4	-	-	-	4
Total for VI Korps	14	-	-	-	72	7	4	-	97
XXVI Armee Korps									
28.Jäger Division	-	-	-	-	4	-	-	-	4
Pz.Jg. Kp. 1028	7	-	-	-	-	-	-	-	7
Auflkl. Lehr-Abt.	-	-	-	-	4	-	-	-	4
Panzer Kp. 10 38(t)	2	-	-	-	-	-	-	-	2
Pz IV	-	1	-	-	-	-	-	-	1
T-34	-	1	-	-	-	-	-	-	1
StuG Brigade 277	10	-	-	-	-	-	-	-	10
Total for XXVI Korps	19	2	-	-	8	-	-	-	29
Total for the Fourth Army	134	39	8	43	264	25	82	5	595

On 25 January 1945, the VII Panzer Corps reported having the following number of tanks and self-propelled guns:

18th Panzergrenadier Division – Panzer Battalion 118: 4 StuG assault guns; Heavy Panzerjäger Battalion 563: 13 Jg Pz. IV, 8 Pz. V; Assault Gun Brigade 249 – 7 StuG; Heavy Panzerjäger Battalion 464 – 5 heavy 88mm self-propelled guns.
24th Panzer Division – 6 Pz. VI and 4 StuG (from Panzergrenadier Division *Grossdeutschland*).
299th Infantry Division – Panzerjäger Company 1299: 3 StuG.
Panzergrenadier Division *Grossdeutschland*: 4 Pz. VI, 6 Pz. V, 8 StuG.
367th Infantry Division – Panzerjäger Company 1367: 6 StuG.

An operational summary from the German Fourth Army on 26 January 1945 discusses the movement and reshuffling of the available tanks and self-propelled guns among its subordinate divisions in the attempt to retain their combat effectiveness:

At 0015 on 26 January 1945, transferred to the VII Panzer Corps' formations and units:

a) 24 January 1945 available in the 18th Panzergrenadier Division, 24th Panzer Division, 299th Infantry Division, the *Grossdeutschland* Division, the Heavy Panzerjäger Battalion 563 and the Assault Gun Brigade 249: 5 Pz. VI, 8 Pz. V, 18 StuG IV, 5 Pz. IV, 3 StuG III, 17 Pz. IV and 12 Pz. V. Altogether, 68 AFVs;
b) 25 January 1945 transferred to the VI Army Corps' 299th Infantry Division: 3 StuG III, 13 Pz. IV and 18 Pz. V;
c) 26 January 1945, located on the march to the Guttstadt area at 15.30: 4 Pz. V, 4 Pz. IV and 7 StuG IV (three of which require repairs);
d) On 26 January 1945, available and also transferred to the corps' subordination: 4 StuG IV (for 18th Panzergrenadier Division), 7 StuG III (for the 558th Volksgrenadier Division) and 1 Pz. V (for the *Grossdeutschland* Division);

This materiel is located on the march from the Wiesenthal area, and its arrival in Guttstadt is expected no earlier than 1900 26 January 1945.

Table 4.4: Status of the materiel of the German Fourth Army (Lage der panzerbrechenden Waffen – AOK 4) by the end of 26 January 1945

Units	Armored vehicles and anti-tank guns					Under repair and not yet written off		Irrecoverable	Total
	StuG	Tanks	SP guns	sPak 76.2 mm	sPak 75-mm	Short-term	Long-term		
1	2	3	4	5	6	7	8	9	10
1	2	3	4	5	6	7	8	9	10
XX Armee Korps									
562.Volksgrenadier Division	-	-	-	-	11	-	2	-	13
Pz.Jg. Kp. 1562	5	-	-	-	-	-	-	-	5
14.Infanterie Division	-	-	-	-	12	-	-	-	12
Pz.Jg. Kp. 1102	4	-	-	-	-	-	-	-	4
292.Infanterie Division	-	-	-	-	12	3	1	-	16
Pz.Jg. Kp. 1292	2	-	-	-	-	3	1	2	6
StuG Brigade 185	10	-	-	-	-	-	-	-	10
StuG Brigade 209	8	-	-	-	-	-	-	-	8
129.Infanterie Division	-	-	-	-	6	-	-	-	6
Pz.Jg. Kp. 1014	3	-	-	-	-	-	-	-	3
StuG Brigade 909	8	-	-	-	-	-	-	-	8
Total for XX Korps	40	-	-	-	41	6	4	2	91
LV Armee Korps									
Kampgruppe Hauser	-	-	-	-	47	-	-	-	47
88 and 76.2-mm guns	-	-	-	-	-	-	-	-	-
Captured Soviet 76-mm guns	-	-	-	13	-	-	-	-	13
Gruppe "Hannibal"	-	-	-	-	2	-	-	-	2
541.Volksgrenadier Division	-	-	-	-	12	1	-	-	13
102.Infanterie Division	-	-	-	-	13	-	-	-	13
Pz.Jg. Kp. 1541	12	-	-	-	-	-	2	-	14
203.Infanterie Division	-	-	-	-	12	-	-	-	12

Units	Armored vehicles and anti-tank guns					Under repair and not yet written off		Irrecoverable	Total
	StuG	Tanks	SP guns	sPak 76.2 mm	sPak 75-mm	Short-term	Long-term		
1	2	3	4	5	6	7	8	9	10
Fest. Pak Kp. 10	-	-	-	9	-	-	-	-	9
	-	-	-	-	10	-	-	-	10
Fest. Pak Kp. 17	-	-	-	12	-	-	-	-	12
Total for LV Corps	12	-	-	34	96	1	2	-	145
VII Panzer Korps									
PGD *Grossdeutschland*	-	3	-	-	-	2	2	-	7
Pz IV	-	5	-	-	-	8	18	-	31
Pz V	-	5	-	-	-	3	8	-	16
Pz VI	4	-	-	-	-	-	-	-	4
	-	-	-	-	9	-	-	-	9
	-	-	5	-	-	-	-	-	5
75-mm SPW	-	-	-	4	-	-	-	-	4
Panzer Abt. 302	-	5	-	-	-	-	31	-	36
	7	-	-	-	-	-	13	-	20
Sturm Kp. 218 Pz IV	-	5	-	-	-	2	-	-	7
24.Panzer Division	-	-	-	-	7	-	-	2	7
(from Division *Grossdeutschland*)	0	-	-	-	-	-	-	4	0
Pz VI	-	6	-	-	-	-	-	-	6
Pz V	-	1	-	-	-	-	-	-	1
Fest. Pak Verb VII 75-mm	-	-	-	-	10	-	-	-	10
88-mm	-	-	-	-	5	-	-	-	5
18.Panzergrenadier Division 75mm SPW	4	-	-	-	-	3	-	-	7
sPz.Jg. Abt. 563 88-mm	4	-	-	-	-	-	-	-	4
Pz V	-	4	-	-	-	-	-	-	4
StuG Brigade 249	3	-	-	-	-	4	-	-	7
558.Volksgrenadier Division	-	-	-	-	6	-	-	-	6
Pz.Jg. Kp. 1558	7	-	-	-	-	-	-	-	7
Total for VII Panzer Korps	29	34	5	4	37	22	72	6	203
VI Armee Korps									
131.Infanterie Division	-	-	-	-	6	-	-	-	6
Pz.Jg. Kp. 1131	4	-	-	-	-	-	-	-	4
3.Kp., sPz.Jg. Abt. 563	3	-	-	-	-	-	-	-	3
299.Infanterie Division	-	-	-	-	3	-	-	-	3
88-mm	-	-	-	-	6	-	-	-	6
170.Infanterie Division	-	-	-	-	17	-	-	-	17
Pz.Jg. Kp. 1240	4	-	-	-	-	-	-	-	4
StuG Brigade 904	16	-	-	-	-	-	-	-	16
Stab Treptow	-	-	-	-	33	-	-	-	33

Units	Armored vehicles and anti-tank guns					Under repair and not yet written off		Irrecoverable	Total
	StuG	Tanks	SP guns	sPak 76.2 mm	sPak 75-mm	Short-term	Long-term		
1	2	3	4	5	6	7	8	9	10
Fest. Pak Kp.	-	-	-	-	4	-	-	-	4
Kampgruppe von Einem: Pz IV and Pz V tanks	-	25	-	-	-	-	-	-	25
Total for VI Korps	34	25	-	-	71	-	-	-	130
XXVI Armee Korps									
28.Jäger Division	-	-	-	-	15	-	-	-	15
Pz.Jg. Kp. 1028	7	-	-	-	-	-	4	-	11
Pz V	-	2	-	-	-	-	-	-	2
Pz IV	-	0	-	-	-	3	-	-	3
T-34	-	6	-	-	-	5	-	-	11
StuG Brigade 277	12	-	-	-	-	6	-	-	18
Panzer Kp. Lt. Lutschki Pz III	-	2	-	-	-	-	-	-	2
Pz IV	-	1	-	-	-	-	-	-	1
10 Panzer Kp. (38t)	3	-	-	-	-	-	-	-	3
T-34	-	1	-	-	-	-	-	-	1
Total for XXVI Korps	22	12	-	-	15	14	4	-	67
Total for the Fourth Army	137	71	5	38	260	43	82	8	636

The "Combat Path of the 10th Tank Corps" provides the Soviet view of this German effort to free the East Prussian grouping:

> In order to hurl back the troops of the 2nd Belorussian Front that had reached the Frisches Haff lagoon and to restore the ground communications of the grouping that had been compressed to the sea with the Wehrmacht's main forces, the German command decided to launch a strong counterblow in the directions of Liebstadt and Elbing. For this, it had assembled 4 infantry, 2 motorized and one panzer division, as well as a brigade of assault guns, between the Frisches Haff lagoon and Wormditt.
>
> On the night of 26-27 January 1945, these forces suddenly went on the attack and broke through the defense of the 48th Army's divisions in a narrow sector. On the morning of 27 January, the Nazis neared Schlobitten, where the 186th Tank Brigade was defending. The tankers met them with intense fire. Having suffered a defeat in the frontal attack, the enemy decided to envelop the brigade from the south, through Behlenhof. Two batteries of the 689th Artillery Regiment that were standing there kept the enemy onslaught in check for approximately two hours, and after all eight cannons were knocked out of action, the artillery crews continued to fight using grenades and personal weapons.
>
> In order to restore the position in this sector, the corps commander General Sakhno shifted the 178th Tank Brigade to Behlenhof, having reinforced it with a motorized rifle battalion and a battery of heavy self-propelled guns. The enemy was thrown back with a decisive counterattack.

The enemy, having brought up major forces of the 131st Infantry Division, the 170th Infantry Division, the 28th Jäger Division, the 10th Mountain-Jäger Brigade, the 18th Panzergrenadier

Division's Panzergrenadier Regiment 51, the Assault Gun Brigade 209, and up to panzer battalion from the *Grossdeutschland* Panzer Division from other sectors of East Prussia, as well as the completely-equipped 24th Panzer Division in the reserve of this grouping in order to exploit any success, on the morning of 27 January 1945 launched a fierce counterattack with the aim of eliminating the encirclement and freeing the communications of the East Prussian grouping to the west. The main forces of this grouping launched an attack from Wormditt toward Preußisch Holland and Marienburg. The rest of the grouping attacked out of Braunsberg along the highway toward Groß Rautenberg, Trunz and Elbing, with the envelopment of Mühlhausen and Groß Stoboy with the left wing.

As a result of the combat on the morning of 27 January, the enemy on the 5th Guards Tank Army's right flank drove back the divisions of the 124th Rifle Corps, which had been advancing on the right of the 42nd Rifle Corps, from their occupied line, as well as a portion of the right flank units of the 42nd Rifle Corps' 399th Rifle Division, and continued to advance in the direction of Preußisch Holland. Having pushed back the divisions of the 124th Rifle Corps and the 42nd Rifle Corps' 399th Rifle Division, in separate sectors the Germans had made an advance of 10 to 20 kilometers. The enemy managed to seize the Mäken (5 km southeast of Preußisch Holland) – Weinings – Schönau – Karwinden – Behlenhof – Fürstenau line.

The northern part of the German grouping, which was attacking along the Königsberg – Elbing highway, drove back units of the 42nd Rifle Corps' 137th Rifle Division and reached the Parlack – Kurau – Bludau – Neu Münsterberg – Maibaum – Karschau – Heinrichsdorf – Bethkendorf line. With the entry of the 5th Guards Tank Army's tank units into the fighting, at 1300 on 27 January the enemy's further advance was brought to a halt. On the afternoon of 27 January, the troops of the 5th Guards Tank Army repulsed eight savage enemy attacks in strength of 20 to 50 tanks and self-propelled guns and 1 to 3 regiments of infantry, with the support of heavy artillery and mortar fire.

Table 4.5: Status of the materiel of the German Fourth Army (Lage der panzerbrechenden Waffen – AOK 4) by the end of 27 January 1945

Units	Armored vehicles and anti-tank guns					Under repair and not yet written off		Irrecoverable	Total
	StuG	Tanks	SP guns	sPak 76.2 mm	sPak 75-mm	Short-term	Long-term		
1	2	3	4	5	6	7	8	9	10
XX Armee Korps									
14.Infanterie Division	-	-	-	-	11	1	-	-	12
Pz.Jg. Kp. 1102	4	-	-	-	-	-	-	-	4
3 Bat., StuG Brigade 185	5	-	-	-	-	-	-	-	5
292.Infanterie Division	-	-	-	-	10	3	3	-	16
1 Bat., StuG Brigade 209	8	-	-	-	-	2	-	-	10
129.Infanterie Division	-	-	-	-	8	-	-	-	8
Pz.Jg. Kp. 1014	3	-	-	-	-	-	-	-	3
StuG Brigade 909	8	-	-	-	-	1	-	-	9
Pz.Jg. Kp. 1292	3	-	-	-	-	3	1	-	7
Total for XX Korps	31	-	-	-	29	10	4	-	74
LV Armee Korps									

Units	Armored vehicles and anti-tank guns					Under repair and not yet written off		Irrecoverable	Total
	StuG	Tanks	SP guns	sPak 76.2 mm	sPak 75-mm	Short-term	Long-term		
1	2	3	4	5	6	7	8	9	10
Kampgruppe Hauser	-	-	-	-	31	-	-	-	31
88-mm and 76.2-mm guns	-	-	-	-	7	-	-	-	7
Captured Soviet 76-mm guns	-	-	-	11	-	-	-	-	11
StuG Kp. 500	2	-	-	-	-	-	2	-	4
Gruppe "Hannibal"	-	-	-	-	2	-	-	-	2
541.Volksgrenadier Division	-	-	-	-	12	1	-	-	13
102.Infanterie Division	-	-	-	-	13	1	-	-	14
Pz.Jg. Kp. 1541	12	-	-	-	-	1	1	-	14
203.Infanterie Division	-	-	-	-	12	-	-	-	12
4 Bat., StuG Brigade 909	5	-	-	-	-	3	-	-	8
Fest. Pak Verb I	-	-	-	-	6	-	-	-	6
	-	-	-	19	-	-	-	-	19
Total for LV Korps	19	-	-	30	83	6	3	-	141
VII Panzer Korps									
24.Panzer Division	-	-	-	-	7	-	-	-	7
Fest. Pak Verb VII 75-mm	-	-	-	10	-	-	-	-	10
88-mm	-	-	-	-	5	-	-	-	5
18.Panzergrenadier Division	6	-	-	-	-	3	-	-	9
558.Volksgrenadier Division	-	-	-	-	6	-	-	-	6
Pz.Jg. Kp. 1558	5	-	-	-	-	1	1	-	7
Total for VII Panzer Korps	11	-	-	10	18	4	1	-	44
VI Armee Korps									
131.Infanterie Division	-	-	-	-	12	-	-	-	12
Pz.Jg. Kp. 1131	6	-	-	-	-	-	-	-	6
sPz.Jg. Abt. 563	8	-	-	-	-	3	-	-	11
Pz V	-	5	-	-	-	-	-	-	5
299.Infanterie Division	-	-	-	-	5	-	-	-	5
Pz.Jg. Kp. 1299	2	-	-	-	-	1	-	-	3
1 co. of StuG Brigade 299	3	-	-	-	-	-	-	-	3
I/AOK StuG Abt. 4	-	-	-	-	2	-	-	-	2
170.Infanterie Division	-	-	-	-	21	1	1	-	23
Pz.Jg. Kp. 1240	4	-	-	-	-	3	-	-	7
StuG Brigade 904	13	-	-	-	-	5	5	-	23
Stab Treptow	-	-	-	-	33	-	-	-	33
Fest. Pak Kp.	-	-	-	-	4	-	-	-	4
Total for VI Korps	36	5	-	-	71	13	6	-	137
XXVI Armee Korps									

Units	Armored vehicles and anti-tank guns					Under repair and not yet written off		Irrecoverable	Total
	StuG	Tanks	SP guns	sPak 76.2 mm	sPak 75-mm	Short-term	Long-term		
1	2	3	4	5	6	7	8	9	10
28 Jäger Division	-	-	-	-	15	-	-	-	15
1028 Pz.Jg. Kp.	5	-	-	-	-	-	1	-	6
Panzer Kp.	5	-	-	-	-	-	-	-	5
Pz. Kp. Lt. Lutschki Pz III	-	2	-	-	-	-	-	-	2
Pz IV	-	1	-	-	-	-	-	-	1
10. Panzer Kp. 38(t)	-	2	-	-	-	-	-	-	2
T-34	-	1	-	-	-	6	-	-	7
	1	-	-	-	-	-	-	-	1
Kampfgruppe von Einem	-	-	-	-	7	-	-	-	7
2 Bat., StuG Brigade 185	3	-	-	-	-	-	3	-	6
Pz.Rgt. 24 (10+11) Pz IV	-	12	-	-	-	-	7	-	19
1 Bat., Jg.Pz. Abt. 40	4	-	-	-	-	-	2	-	6
StuG Brigade 277	12	-	-	-	-	-	6	-	18
Pz VI	-	6	-	-	-	-	3	-	9
Pz V	-	2	-	-	-	-	-	-	2
T-34	-	5	-	-	-	-	6	-	11
Total for XXVI Korps	30	31	-	-	22	6	28	-	117
Pz.Jg. Kp. 1367	7	-	-	-	-	-	-	-	7
Total for the Fourth Army	134	36	-	40	229	39	42	-	520

Altogether over the day of 27 January 1945, the activity of up to 80 tanks and self-propelled guns were noted on the army's front (from the east). All of the enemy attacks were driven back by the troops of the 5th Guards Tank Army with heavy losses for him. On several sectors, the enemy soldiers were intoxicated and tried to attack at full height, making so-called "berserker attacks". By the end of the day of 27 January, intensive fighting was continuing on the line of the aforementioned points.

The 10th Tank Corps throughout the day of 27 January was subjected to repeated ferocious attacks from the direction of Karwinden toward Schlobitten, and from Bludau toward Mühlhausen. The position of the corps' units remained without changes.

One episode of the combat actions of the artillerymen of the 5th Guards Tank Army on this day merits attention. During the attack toward Schlobitten, the enemy collided with the strong defense of the 186th Tank Brigade. Suffering large losses and having suffered a check in the attempt to break out towards Schlobitten, the enemy went further to the south and on the afternoon of 27 January attacked in a strength of 20-25 tanks and self-propelled guns, supported by a battalion of infantry, two batteries of the 689th Destroyer Antitank Artillery Regiment, which was in firing positions at a road intersection 2 km west of Behlenhof. The gun crews of these two batteries of the 689th Destroyer Antitank Artillery Regiment endured 90 minutes of combat against superior enemy forces, and despite the loss of all eight guns that were knocked out in turn, kept possession of the occupied line until the arrival of tanks of the 178th Tank Brigade. The latter, together with the 2nd Battalion of the 11th Motorized Rifle Brigade and an SU-122 battery of the 326th Heavy Self-propelled Artillery Regiment, had been sent at 1500 on 27 January out of their positions in the Schönberg area to the aid of the artillerymen of the 689th Destroyer Antitank Artillery Regiment to the area west of Behlenhof, relieved the latter, and prevented the enemy from breaking through in the direction of Preußisch Holland.

The 29th Tank Corps, in connection with the enemy's offensive from the east, spent the day of 27 January conducting a regrouping of its units at an order from the army commander Colonel General of Tank Forces V.T. Vol'sky. The 32nd Tank Brigade had been sent from the Damerau area on the morning of 27 January to the southeastern and eastern outskirts of Preußisch Holland, with the task to defend the town with a front facing to the southeast, east and northeast, and in cooperation with the 10th Tank Corps, to prevent the enemy from breaking out in the southwestern direction. The 53rd Motorized Rifle Brigade together with the 1223rd Light Self-propelled Artillery Regiment, 165th Light Artillery Regiment and 271st Mortar Regiment on the morning of 27 January received an order to occupy a defense with one battalion on the Judendorf – Schönberg – Pomehrendorf line; to defend Koppeln (6 km east of Preußisch Holland) – Luxethen line with one battalion in cooperation with the 32nd Tank Brigade; and with one battalion to defend Grunau (4 km southeast of Elbing), covering the rest of the corps' units from the direction of Elbing. The 31st Tank Brigade received the assignment to occupy a defense on the Groß Stoboy – Trunz – Baumgart line and to prevent an enemy breakout from the east in the direction of Elbing. By 1000 all three brigades were occupying a defense on their indicated lines. On the night of 27-28 January, the 25th Tank Brigade was sent from the area of the Klein Bieland estates (3 km northeast of Elbing) to the southeastern outskirts of Preußisch Holland, in order to reinforce the defense being occupied there by the 32nd Tank Brigade and a battalion of the 47th Mechanized Brigade. On the afternoon of 27 January, the units of the 29th Tank Corps in their occupied areas of defense repulsed four enemy counterattacks in strength of 20 to 50 tanks and infantry, supported by heavy artillery and mortar fire.

The 47th Mechanized Brigade in the course of 27 January fought on the line it had achieved as a result of its actions on the night of 26-27 January, repulsing enemy counterattacks, which were attempting to drive it out of the northern section of Elbing. All of the enemy counterattacks were beaten back by the brigade.

Excerpt from Operational Summary No. 014 from the headquarters of the 5th Guards Tank Army, 27 January 1945, 2400:

In the course of 27 January 1945, the enemy from the Wormditt, Passarge River line in the sector of the Kagenau estates and Tiedmansdorf and out of the areas north and northwest of Mühlhausen with units of the withdrawing East Prussian grouping in strength of up to 80 tanks and self-propelled guns, three regiments of infantry and artillery, undertook an attempt to break out of the encirclement in the Preußisch Holland – Elbing direction and the Groß Stoboy – Elbing direction. By 1800 on 27 January 1945, the enemy was continuing to fight in the areas of the Behlenhof estates, east of Schlobitten, and north of Groß Stoboy.

The forces of the 5th Guards Tank Army in the course of 27 January 1945 repulsed enemy counterattacks from the east and northeast, and having repelled 8 counterattacks by enemy tanks and artillery in strength of 20 to 50 tanks, conducted a regrouping of forces, while simultaneously fighting to capture Elbing. Lieutenant General Kolganov's 42nd Rifle Corps, according to a verbal order from the Front's deputy commander Lieutenant General Trubnikov, at 1800 on 27 January 1945 passed to the operational control of the 5th Guards Tank Army.

The 10th Tank Corps throughout the day of 27 January 1945 conducted active operations to defend the road hub of Mühlhausen, and repulsed four enemy attacks in strength of 10 to 30 tanks supported by infantry and artillery from the directions of the Kagenau estates and Groß Rautenberg. The corps' units, repulsing enemy counterattacks, by 1900 on 27 January were occupying the following positions: 186th Tank Brigade – Karwinden, Breunken; 183rd Tank Brigade – Herrndorf, Gardienen; 11th Motorized Rifle Brigade with the 727th Self-propelled Artillery Regiment and the 287th Mortar Regiment – Gardienen, Lohberg; the 178th Tank Brigade had moved to the area of the crossroads 1 km west of the Behlenhof estates.

Altogether, the 10th Tank Corps has in service: 41 T-34, 15 SU-100, 13 SU-85, 12 SU-76 and 15 SU-152. On the way to the corps' area are 23 T-34, 7 SU-100 and 3 SU-85. In repair: 45 armored vehicles. Losses: 2 SU-100 destroyed, 1 SU-100 knocked out; 8 destroyed 57mm guns; 39 men dead and 129 men wounded. Supplies: Fuel and lubricants – 2.2 refills of diesel; 0.5 refills of gasoline; ammunition – 2 standard combat loads; food – for 7 days.

The 47th Mechanized Brigade and the 14th Guards Heavy Tank Regiment up until 1800 on 27 January 1945 was engaged in heavy fighting to take Elbing. At 1800 on 27 January 1945 it neared the center of Elbing. From 1900 27 January 1945 it has the task to defend the northern outskirts of Elbing and the road fork 5 km north of Elbing with one battalion, and artillery battalion and 6 tanks, having blocking detachments in Lenzen and the Schönwalde estates. The 3rd Battalion, together with the 14th Guards Heavy Tank Regiment, 1315th Light Artillery Regiment and the 201st Light Artillery Brigade are to assemble in the Dörbeck area, from where it is to operate in the direction of Groß Stoboy with the assignment to mop up the Groß Stoboy area and strongly dig in there. Damage, inflicted on the enemy: 3 Panther tanks and 15 guns of various calibers destroyed, and up to 200 soldiers and officers killed. Information about the brigade's losses and supply status haven't been received.

The 29th Tank Corps throughout the day of 27 January 1945 conducted a regrouping; with part of its force, it continued to destroy the enemy on the northeastern outskirts of Elbing, and with part of its force was occupying a defense in the Preußisch Holland area; it drove back four enemy counterattacks in strength of 20 to 50 tanks from the directions of Bordehnen and the Hensels property. At 1900 on 27 January 1945, the corps' units are occupying the following positions: 32nd Tank Brigade and a motorized rifle battalion of the 47th Mechanized Brigade are occupying a defense on the Quellnau – Robitten line, having combat outposts on the Schönau estates – crossroads 1 km west of the Behlenhof estates line; 25th Tank Brigade in the first half of the day of 27 January 1945 was fighting for possession of Elbing, before moving out in the direction of Preußisch Holland that afternoon. By 2100 on 27 January 1945 the head of the column had reached Szambor. The 53rd Motorized Rifle Brigade was fighting on the southeastern outskirts of Elbing.

Having left behind one battalion and an artillery battalion on the eastern outskirts of Elbing, it is moving into the line running between the estates 4 km northeast of Groß Stoboy and Schönberg with two battalions and attached assets, the 31st Tank Brigade, in cooperation with the 47th Mechanized Brigade, up until 1800 on 27 January 1945 was fighting for possession of Elbing, and by 2100 on 27 January 1945 it has reached the Königshagen area, having forward detachments in the Trunz and Baumgart areas.

Information on losses, supplies and damage done to the enemy is being ascertained.

Chief of Staff of the 5th Guards Tank Army Major General of Tank Forces Sidorovich
Chief of Operations Colonel Fedorov

From the "Combat Path of the 5th Guards Tank Army":

Despite the build-up of Soviet forces in the corridor, the German command wasn't losing hopes in restoring the lines of communications leading to the west, and to keep them intact as long as the struggle for the East Prussian bridgehead was possible and necessary. With this aim the enemy assembled four infantry and one tank division in the area north of Wormditt and on the morning of 27 January launched a counterattack in the Preußisch Holland, Marienburg direction, striving to restore the communications from East Prussia to the west. Simultaneously up to 2 infantry divisions accompanied by tanks attacked the positions of our troops northeast of Mühlhausen, attempting to break through to Elbing. In the very first hours the Nazis managed to shove back our rifle units and to make an advance of 10-20 kilometers in separate directions. The 10th Tank Corps, which was located in the Mühlhausen area, quickly joined combat. It repulsed several attacks, in which up to 80 enemy tanks took part.

At any minute the Nazis might have launched an attack from the direction of Elbing as well in order to link up with this grouping. In order to repel the adversary's attacks launched out of the Wormditt area, the commander of the 5th Guards Tank Army was forced to send elements of the 29th Tank Corps to assist the 10th Tank Corps. In order to keep the Elbing garrison pinned in place, the 47th Mechanized Brigade and 14th Guards Heavy Tank Regiment enlivened their actions on the city's outskirts. Heavy fighting continued all day.

On the evening of 27 January, the commander-in-chief of the 2nd Belorussian Front subordinated the 42nd Rifle Corps to the 5th Guards Tank Army. The 8th Mechanized Corps, which was located in the Saalfeld area, received the mission to move out to the area northeast of Freiwalde and launch an attack in the direction of Wormditt into the flank of the enemy grouping that was attempting to break out. Divisions of the 2nd Shock Army were also being brought up to the corridor. The 321st Rifle Division of this army already on the following day reached Elbing and took up blocking positions on its southern, eastern and northern sides. This allowed for the 47th Mechanized Brigade and 53rd Motorized Rifle Brigade to be withdrawn from the city's northern outskirts.

With the arrival of the 2nd Shock Army's units to the Elbing area, and the 8th Mechanized Corps north of Freiwalde, the situation of the 5th Guards Tank Army significantly eased: it now had the opportunity to use all of its forces in the eastern direction.

Having conducted a regrouping of its main forces to the area east of Preußisch Holland, the 5th Guards Tank Army together with the 42nd Rifle Corps on the morning of 30 January launched an attack in the general direction of Wormditt with the assignment to destroy the enemy forces that were trying to break out. In many of the sectors, the offensive actions took on the nature of bitter meeting battles, which went with alternating success. The troops had to fight in difficult weather conditions – a blizzard, deep snow cover and heavy snowfall. An especially difficult situation developed on the 31st Tank Brigade's axis of advance. The enemy committed major forces of tanks and infantry against it. Counterattacks followed one after another throughout the entire day. When repulsing one of the counterattacks, tank company commander Senior Lieutenant A.I. Rukhliad'ev was severely wounded. His combat comrades immediately rendered first aid to the commander, but he passed away from the loss of blood. A.I. Rukhliad'ev was buried with military honors near the village of Liebenau, 8 km east of Preußisch Holland. For the resolve, courage and valor he demonstrated in the fighting, Aleksandr Ignat'evich Rukhliad'ev was awarded the title of Hero of the Soviet Union.

In the course of several days, the formations of the 5th Guards Tank Army and 42nd Rifle Corps were engaged in heavy fighting. Although they were unable fully to destroy the enemy grouping, the German penetration was localized and the fighting became prolonged.

Table 4.6: The combat strength of the German Fourth Army on 28 January 1945

		Combat personnel	Units of Artillery
XXVI Armee Korps	28.Jäger Division	3066	44
	Radfahr-Jäger Brigade 10	1058	-
VI Armee Korps	170.Infanterie Division	3250	32
	131.Infanterie Division	2047	28
	299.Infanterie Division	535	
VII Panzer Korps	24.Panzer Division	2359	21
	18.Panzergrenadier Division	16988	21
	Panzergrenadier Division *Grossdeutchland*	2401	-
	Kampfgruppe Groche	413	-
	558.Volksgrenadier Division	a	a
LV Armee Korps	102.Infanterie Division	1302	45
	203.Infanterie Division	3450	38
	541.Volksgrenadier Division	3104	48
	Gruppe "Hannibal"	1478	26
	Gruppe Hauser	1000	59
XX Armee Korps	14.Infanterie Division	1466	41
	292.Infanterie Division	1057	38
	129.Infanterie Division	a	a

a No data given.

Table 4.7: Status of the materiel of the German Fourth Army (Lage der panzerbrechenden Waffen – AOK 4) by the end of 28 January 1945

Units	Armored vehicles and anti-tank guns					Under repair and not yet written off		Irrecoverable	Total
	StuG	Tanks	SP guns	sPak 76.2 mm	sPak 75-mm	Short-term	Long-term		
1	2	3	4	5	6	7	8	9	10
XX Armee Korps									
14.Infanterie Division	-	-	-	-	10	1	1	-	12
Pz.Jg. Kp. 1102	4	-	-	-	-	-	-	-	4
3 Bat., StuG Brigade 185	4	-	-	-	-	3	1	-	8
24.Panzer Division	-	-	-	-	7	-	-	-	7
Fest. Pak Verb VII 75-mm	-	-	-	10	-	-	-	-	10
88-mm	-	-	-	-	5	-	-	-	5
292.Infanterie Division	-	-	-	-	12	1	3	-	16
StuG Brigade 209	8	-	-	-	-	17	-	-	25
129.Infanterie Division	-	-	-	-	8	-	-	-	8
Pz.Jg. Kp. 1014	1	-	-	-	-	9	2	-	12
StuG Brigade 909	10	-	-	-	-	10	9	-	29
Pz.Jg. Kp. 1299	3	-	-	-	-	4	1	-	8
Total for XX Korps	30	-	-	10	42	45	17	-	144
LV Armee Korps									
102.Infanterie Division	-	-	-	-	13	-	-	-	13
Pz.Jg. Kp. 1541	12	-	-	-	-	1	1	-	14

Units	Armored vehicles and anti-tank guns					Under repair and not yet written off		Irrecoverable	Total
	StuG	Tanks	SP guns	sPak 76.2 mm	sPak 75-mm	Short-term	Long-term		
1	2	3	4	5	6	7	8	9	10
203.Infanterie Division	-	-	-	-	12	-	-	-	12
4 Bat., StuG Brigade 920	3	-	-	-	-	1	1	-	5
Fest. Pak Verb 17/I	-	-	-	9	-	-	3	-	12
541.Volksgrenadier Division	-	-	-	-	8	-	1	-	9
Fest. Pak Kp.	-	-	-	7	-	-	-	-	7
	-	-	-	-	9	-	-	-	9
Gruppe "Hannibal"	-	-	-	-	2	-	-	-	2
Kampfgruppe Hauser	-	-	-	-	30	-	-	-	30
StuG Kp. 500	1	-	-	-	-	1	2	-	4
Total for LV Korps	16	-	-	16	74	3	8	-	117
VII Panzer Korps									
18.Pzgrenadier Division	2	-	-	-	-	1	2	4	5
558.Volksgrenadier Division	-	-	-	-	6	-	-	-	6
Pz.Jg. Kp. 1558	4	-	-	-	-	1	2	-	7
Total for VII Panzer Korps	6	-	-	-	6	2	4	4	18
VI Armee Korps									
131.Infanterie Division	-	-	-	-	8	2	2	-	12
Pz.Jg. Kp. 1131	2	-	-	-	6	-	-	-	6
sPz.Jg. Abt. 563	8	-	-	-	-	3	-	-	11
Pz V									
88-mm	-	3	-	-	-	-	2	-	5
					6				6
299.Infanterie Division	-	-	-	-	4	1	-	-	5
Pz.Jg. Kp. 1299	2	-	-	-	-	1	-	-	3
1 co. of StuG Brigade 299	2	-	-	-	-	-	1	-	3
I/AOK StuG Abt. 4	-	-	-	-	2	-	-	-	2
170.Infanterie Division	-	-	-	-	21	1	1	-	23
Pz.Jg. Kp. 1240	4	-	-	-	-	3	-	-	7
StuG Brigade 904	15	-	-	-	-	5	3	-	23
Total for VI Korps	33	3	-	-	41	17	12	-	106
XXVI Armee Korps									
28.Jäger Division	-	-	-	-	15	-	-	-	15
Pz.Jg. Kp. 1028	5	-	-	-	-	5	-	-	10
Panzer Kp. Pz IV	-	1	-	-	-	-	-	-	1
Pz Kp. Lt. Lutschki Pz III	-	2	-	-	-	1	-	1	3
	1	-	-	-	-	-	-	-	1
Panzer Kp. 10 38(t)	-	0	-	-	-	2	-	-	2
T-34	-	1	-	-	-	6	-	-	7
	1	-	-	-	-	-	-	-	1
StuG Kp. 1006	4	-	-	-	-	-	-	-	4

Units	Armored vehicles and anti-tank guns					Under repair and not yet written off		Irrecoverable	Total
	StuG	Tanks	SP guns	sPak 76.2 mm	sPak 75-mm	Short-term	Long-term		
1	2	3	4	5	6	7	8	9	10
Kampfgruppe von Einem	-	-	-	-	7	-	-	-	7
2 Bat./StuG Brigade 185	3	-	-	-	-	3	-	-	6
Pz.Rgt. 24 (10+11) Pz IV	-	12	-	-	-	7	-	-	19
1 Bat., Jg.Pz. Abt. 40									
StuG Brigade 277	4	-	-	-	-	2	-	-	6
T-34	12	-	-	-	-	1	5	-	18
Radfahr-Jäger Brigade 10	-	2	-	-	-	6	3	-	11
	-	-	-	-	6	1	-	-	7
Total for XXVI Korps	30	18	-	-	28	34	8	1	118
Pz.Jg. Kp. 1367	7	-	-	-	-	-	-	-	7
Total for the Fourth Army	122	21	-	26	191	101	49	5	510

The forces of the 5th Guards Tank Army in the course of 28 and 29 January 1945 continued to occupy their previous lines and conducted an active defense, wearing down the enemy that was attempting to break out in a western direction. Over the day of 28 January, up to 10 enemy attacks were driven back, and over the day of 29 January, the 5th Guards Tank Army and attached 42nd Rifle Corps repulsed 8 more attacks from the directions of the woods southwest of Schönau, Bordehnen, the woods southeast of Schlobitten, and out of Karschau toward Trunz.

On 28 January the 321st Rifle Division arrived in the area east of Elbing, and there took up a defence facing toward the west, toward Elbing. This allowed the removal of the blocking detachments that were screening the army's actions from the west, from the direction of Elbing: the 47th Mechanized Brigade from the area north and northeast of Elbing, and the blocking detachments of the 29th Tank Corps that had been positioned on the lines it had reached east and southeast of Elbing.

The 47th Mechanized Brigade, consisting of its 3rd Motorized Rifle Battalion, the mechanized battalion and the 14th Guards Heavy Tank Regiment and 1619th Light Artillery Regiment that were attached to it, on 28 January after the arrival of the 321st Rifle Division east of Elbing moved out to the vicinity of Groß Stoboy with the assignment to prevent an enemy breakthrough from the east in the direction toward Trunz and Elbing.

Meanwhile, its 1st Motorized Rifle Battalion continued to defend Preußisch Holland. The 2nd Motorized Rifle Battalion and the 18th Tank Regiment were continuing to hold on stubbornly to the northern portion of Elbing, but at an order from the army commander they were withdrawn from there to the Groß Stoboy area to rejoin the 47th Mechanized Brigade's main forces, only by the end of 29 January, on the eve of the 5th Guards Tank Army's attack to the east.

The reinforced 1st Motorized Rifle Battalion of the 29th Tank Corps' 53rd Motorized Rifle Brigade, which had been removed from the Grunau area, by the end of 28 January had assembled in the 32nd Tank Brigade's sector northwest of Preußisch Holland, while corps' other small blocking detachments rejoined their own units.

The 42nd Rifle Corps, which had been attached to the 5th Guards Tank Army at an order from the commander-in-chief of the 2nd Belorussian Front Marshal of the Soviet Union K.K. Rokossovsky, remained operationally subordinate to it until 1000 on 10 February 1945. The position of the 5th Guards Tank Army with its arrival to the sea on 24 January on a front that was 15-20 kilometers wide, was in a precarious situation between 24 and 26 January until the arrival of the 42nd Rifle Corps. While waiting for the approach of the 48th Army's infantry units, it had to fight simultaneously to the west and the east only with its own forces. On 27 January, with the enemy grouping's launching of a fierce offensive from the east in the Elbing direction and the Preußisch Holland, Marienburg direction, and the retreat of the units of the 124th and 42nd Rifle Corps to a depth of 10 to 20 kilometers, the situation of the 5th Guards Tank Army's troops became even more problematic, because not less than 85% of its strength had to committed to counter this major German grouping. Its task was to stop its progress and prevent a German breakthrough toward Preußisch Holland and Elbing, while with its limited strength it had to screen the western direction with relatively weak forces, to prevent a possible breakout of the Elbing garrison.

In the course of 24-26 January, Elbing's garrison had suffered heavy losses while struggling against the forces of the 29th Tank Corps and 47th Mechanized Brigade. Clearly, only this and the actions of the elements of the 47th Mechanized Brigade and 14th Guards Heavy Tank Regiment, which had occupied and held the northern section of Elbing throughout 27 and 28 January, can explain the garrison's passivity and the absence of its attack throughout 27 and 28 January to the east to meet the enemy grouping that was attempting to break out to the west. With the arrival of the 321st Rifle Division to a line east of Elbing and its occupation of a defense facing the west toward Elbing, the situation of the 5th Guards Tank Army significantly eased, and it had the possibility only after the expiration of five days (24 to 28 January 1945) to pivot all of its forces strictly to the east.

An excerpt from Operational Summary No. 014 from the headquarters of the 5th Guards Tank Army at midnight on 28 January 1945 offers a viewpoint of the events from the Soviet side:

The enemy, with units of the 28th Jäger Division, the 18th Panzergrenadier Division and a bicycle jäger brigade, reinforced with tanks and self-propelled artillery, is striving to break out in the Preußisch Holland – Elbing direction and the Mühlhausen – Elbing direction. At the same time retreating units of the East Prussian grouping are coming up to the front. In the course of 28 January, the Germans repeatedly attacked the combat positions of our units in company to battalion strength, supported by self-propelled artillery and tanks.

The 5th Guards Tank Army throughout the day of 28 January 1945 with its main forces conducted an active defense on the line: Neuendorf, Preußisch Holland, Schlobitten, Breunken, Fürstenau, Borchertsdorf, Tiedmannsdorf, Groß Rautenberg, Heinrichsdorf. With separate units, it fought to mop up Elbing and clear the enemy from the Groß Stoboy, Maibaum, Hütte, Baumgart, Trunz area; the forces repulsed 10 enemy counterattacks, wiped out up to two battalions of enemy soldiers and officers, and destroyed 15 guns and 6 tanks; they also captured up to 150 soldiers and officers.

The 10th Tank Corps is occupying a defense on the line: Warnikam, Schlobitten, Mühlhausen. In the course of the day of 28 January 1945 it repulsed 6 enemy counterattacks from the wooded area northeast of Karwitten and Karwinden. By 1900 on 28 January 1945, the corps' units were occupying the following positions: 178th Tank Brigade – crossroads and woods southeast of the Warnikam railroad station; 186th Tank Brigade with the 727th Self-propelled Artillery Regiment and 2/689th Destroyer Antitank Artillery Regiment – Schlobitten; 183rd Tank Brigade with 1/689th Destroyer Antitank Artillery Regiment – Herrndorf; 11th Motorized Rifle Brigade – Gardienen, Lohberg; the 326th Heavy Self-propelled Artillery Regiment and the 705th Light Artillery Regiment – were in corps' reserve in the Nikolaiken area. Altogether the corps has in service 59 T-34 tanks, 13 SU-100, 13 SU-85, 15 ISU-122, 12 SU-76 and 2 M4A2. Supplies: diesel fuel – 1.2 refills, gasoline – 0.6 refills; ammunition – 2.0 combat loads; food – 6 days. According to preliminary information, the damage done to the enemy: Up to 200 soldiers and officers killed;

2 T-34 tanks and 2 SU-100 destroyed. Casualties: 5 killed, 42 wounded. The corps headquarters is in Nikolaiken.

The 29th Tank Corps in the course of 28 January 1945 repulsed four enemy counterattacks out of the Kwittainen area and the woods west of there. By 1900 28 January 1945 the corps' units were occupying the following positions: 32nd Tank Brigade – defending Preußisch Holland from the southeast and east, with combat outposts on the line 1.5 km southeast of Rogehnen, Koppeln; 25th Tank Brigade – is defending Preußisch Holland from the southeast and northeast; 31st Tank Brigade with the 14th Guards Heavy Tank Regiment and the 1st Battalion of the 47th Guards Mechanized Brigade is continuing to mop up the Groß Stoboy, Maibaum, Baumgart, Trunz area of the enemy. Its main forces are in the Königshagen area. In the course of 28 January 1945 up to a battalion of enemy infantry was destroyed by the brigade, and up to 50 enemy soldiers and officers were taken prisoner. The 53rd Motorized Rifle Brigade is defending the Hill 115.3, Judendorf, Schönmoor, Pomehrendorf line with a string of separate positions. The 165th Light Artillery Regiment, 271st Mortar Regiment and the 1223rd Self-propelled Artillery Regiment are supporting the brigade.

29th Tank Corps has in service 33 T-34 tanks, 10 SU-152, 5 SU-85, and 20 SU-76. Supplies: diesel fuel – 1.0 refill; gasoline – 0.5 refills; ammunition – 1.0 standard combat load; food – 3 days. The corps headquarters is in Marienfelde.

The 47th Mechanized Brigade (minus two battalions), in cooperation with the 321st Rifle Division, in the course of the day of 28 January 1945 was engaged in bitter fighting to take Elbing. By 1900 28 January 1945 it had reached the city center. Information about losses and supplies haven't come in from the brigade.

The army's artillery throughout the day of 28 January 1945 was repulsing enemy counterattacks of tanks and infantry. As a result of the artillery fire, 9 guns of various calibers and 7 heavy machine guns were destroyed, and 3 self-propelled guns were knocked out; up to two battalions of enemy infantry were dispersed and partially destroyed.

The 42nd Rifle Corps, operationally subordinate to the commander of the 5th Guards Tank Army, is occupying a defense on a broad front of more than 60 kilometers on the Schlobitten, Borchertsdorf, Tiedmannsdorf, Groß Rautenberg line. In the course of the day of 28 January 1945 the corps was repulsing enemy counterattacks from the east and northeast. By 1900 the corps' units were occupying the following positions: 399th Rifle Division – Muttersegen farm, Point 68.4. The division had 54 men killed, 145 wounded and 199 men missing-in-action for 27 January 1945. The 137th Rifle Division – Tiedmannsdorf. The division's casualties for 27 January 1945: 80 killed, 132 wounded and 233 missing-in-action. The 170th Rifle Division – Tiedmannsdorf, Schafsberg. The division's losses for 27 January 1945: 2 killed, 9 wounded and 11 men missing-in-action. The corps is experiencing great difficulties with the resupply of fuel and ammunition. Corps headquarters – in Herrndorf.

Chief of staff of the 5th Guards Tank Army Major General of Tank Forces SIDOROVICH
Chief of operations Colonel Fedorov

Over the day of 28 January 110 prisoners belonging to the 533rd Naval Artillery Battalion, the 311th Naval Battalion, Infantry Regiment 62, the 7th Panzer Division, Artillery Regiment 23 and the 23rd Infantry Division were taken in the Groß Mausdorf and Marienburg areas. The prisoners indicated that the 533rd Naval Artillery Battalion on the night of 26-27 January had been sent aboard vehicles to the Neutach area. The battalion numbered 500 to 600 men and was operating as an infantry unit. An Unterofizier from the headquarters of the 23rd Infantry Division testified that the 23rd Infantry Division consisting of Infantry Regiments 9, 67 and 68 was retreating toward Mewe. The headquarters had lost contact with the regiments. On the path of retreat, the division headquarters was forming separate detachments out of disorganized elements and units.

Excerpt from Combat Report No. 016 from the headquarters of the 5th Guards Tank Army at 2030 on 29 January 1945:

The enemy, having brought up remnants of units of the 24th Panzer Division, the 170th Infantry Division, the 18th Panzergrenadier Division and the 209th Assault Gun Brigade to the wooded area east and southeast of Preußisch Holland and Mühlhausen, throughout the day of 29 January 1945 repeatedly counterattacked our units in the directions of Preußisch Holland and Mühlhausen, striving to break out of encirclement in the directions of Elbing and Marienburg. Following the unsuccessful attempts to take Preußisch Holland, suffering heavy losses, the enemy with small groups infiltrated through the woods and ravines to the southwest in the direction of Neuendorf, where the groups were destroyed by units of the 29th Tank Corps and 8th Mechanized Corps.

The troops of the 5th Guards Tank Army throughout the day of 29 January 1945 was repulsing enemy counterattacks from the directions of the woods southwest of Schönau and Bardehnen, and the woods northeast of Schlobitten; by the end of the day, having inflicted heavy losses on the enemy, they were holding their previous lines.

The 29th Tank Corps's units and formations were stubbornly holding their occupied area. Between 0300 and 1000 29 January 1945, they were constantly fighting off enemy counterattacks. The corps destroyed 4 tanks, 6 self-propelled guns, 20 vehicles and 11 guns; and killed or wounded 200 enemy soldiers and officers while taking 80 men prisoner. By 1900 on 29 January 1945 the corps' units were occupying the following positions: the 32nd Tank Brigade – is occupying a defense southeast and east of Preußisch Holland on the Rogehnen –Koppeln line. Throughout the day it repulsed four enemy counterattacks, losing one T-34 tank in the process; the 25th Tank Brigade – in the course of the day strongly defended a line on the southeastern outskirts of Preußisch Holland, together with units of the 8th Mechanized Corps destroying small groups of the enemy that were trying to make their way out in the direction of Neuendorf. It lost 1 T-34 tank that blew up on a mine. The 31st Tank Brigade is defending the Groß Stoboy, Maibaum, Trunz, Königshagen area. Throughout the night it was repulsing the attacks of enemy infantry and tanks. The 53rd Motorized Rifle Brigade together with the 165th Light Artillery Regiment and the 1223rd Light Self-propelled Artillery Regiment is holding a defensive on the lines: 1st Motorized Rifle Battalion – in the sector of the 32nd Tank Brigade west of Preußisch Holland; 2nd Motorized Rifle Battalion – Koppeln, Luxethen; 3rd Motorized Rifle Battalion – Judendorf, Schönberg, Pomehrendorf. Losses: 2 SU-57, 3 76mm guns; 7 men killed and 33 wounded. Corps headquarters – Marienfelde.

In the course of the night and day of 29 January 1945 10th Tank Corps drove back enemy attacks and stubbornly held its occupied line; it repulsed 6 enemy attacks from the direction of the woods 4 km northeast of Schlobitten. Damage, inflicted on the enemy: 10 guns of various calibers, 3 mortars, 3 machine guns destroyed, and 6 tanks and 2 self-propelled guns knocked out. Captured: 5 machine guns, 4 mortars and 3 disabled self-propelled guns. It killed up to 600 enemy soldiers and officers and captured 120 more. By 1900 29 January 1945 the corps' units are occupying the following line: 178th Tank Brigade and 1/287th Mortar Regiment – crossroads and woods east of the Warnikom farmstead; 11th Motorized Rifle Brigade and 727th Self-propelled Artillery Regiment – 300 meters west of the Behlenhof estates and the fringe of the woods 1 km northwest of Herrndorf; 186th Tank Brigade – the road hub of Schlobitten; 183rd Tank Brigade – Herrndorf, Gardienen. The corps' artillery was supporting the actions of the corps' units when repulsing the enemy attacks. Losses of the 10th Tank Corps: 1 T-34 destroyed, 1 T-34 and 2 SU-100 knocked out; 14 men killed and 70 wounded. The corps headquarters – Nikolaiken.

The 47th Mechanized Brigade with its main forces was occupying a defense on the Pomehrendorf, Groß Stoboy line. With one battalion, together with units of the 29th Tank Corps, it was repulsing enemy counterattacks in the Preußisch Holland area. The damage, inflicted on the enemy over the period between 26 and 29 January 1945: 4 tanks, 12 guns and 80 vehicles destroyed; 380 enemy soldiers and officers killed or wounded, and 240 taken prisoner. In the fighting for Elbing, the brigade lost 57 killed and 165 wounded, as well as 9 tanks, 14 vehicles, 1 radio and 6 guns. The brigade headquarters – Königshagen.

The 42nd Rifle Corps is occupying a defense on the line: 399th Rifle Division (1343rd, 1345th and 1348th Rifle Regiments) – Muttersegen farmstead, Fürstenau; 137th Rifle Division (409th, 624th and 771st Rifle Regiments) – Fürstenau, Borchertsdorf, Tiedmannsdorf, Groß Rautenberg, Schafsberg; 170th Rifle Division – is in the second echelon: 117th Rifle Regiment – Fürstenau, Point 43.0; 422nd Rifle Regiment – Mühlhausen; 391st Rifle Regiment – Karschau. Corps headquarters – Herrndorf.

Commander of the 5th Guards Tank Army Colonel General of Tank Forces VOL'SKY
Military Council member Guards Major General of Tank Forces GRISHIN
Chief of staff Guards Major General of Tank Forces SIDOROVICH

From the "Combat Path of the 10th Tank Corps":

On the night of 28-29 January, a difficult situation developed in the Karwitten area. Taking advantage of an ongoing snowstorm, units of the 28th Jäger Division and elements of the 10th Bicycle Jäger Brigade penetrated into the depth of the corps' defenses. They managed to take Karwitten and to cut off the 178th Tank Brigade from the rest of the corps. In the middle of this difficult night, the commander of the 178th Tank Brigade Lieutenant Colonel M.E. Zhukov called the corps chief of staff Colonel N.M. Omeliusty. He reported that the enemy was incessantly attack with major forces, trying to break out through Karwitten to the northwest toward the highway. German detachments had entered the village and were approaching the brigade's headquarters. "I'm leaving to direct the repulse of the foe's attack!" – Zhukov said before dropping the telephone. With this, contact with the brigade was interrupted.

Omeliusty quickly reported about what had happened to the corps commander General Sakhno. He ordered to dispatch the reserve to Karwitten – the 326th Guards Heavy Self-propelled Artillery Regiment and a portion of the 11th Motorized Rifle Brigade under the command of his deputy Colonel S.S. Sergienko. Meanwhile, bitter fighting was going on in Karwitten. Enemy infantry encircled the building holding the brigade headquarters. Submachine gunners of the security and all of the staff officers, having taken up an all-round defense, repulsed the enemy's attacks until sunrise. The arriving corps reserve drove the enemy out of the village and restored the situation in the sector of the 178th Tank Brigade.

However, two Nazi groups (300 submachine gunners in one and around 500 in the other) had broken through to the corps' rear, to its headquarters, which was located south of Mühlhausen, and to the firing positions of the 705th Artillery Regiment. It was approximately 0200. Intense work was going on in the headquarters: General M.G. Sakhno, the deputy commander of the 5th Guards Tank Army General M.D. Sinenko and Colonel Omeliusty were working on a report to the army headquarters about the results of the corps' combat operations over the day. Suddenly, the sounds of heavy fire erupted almost simultaneously from every direction. A submachine gunner ran into room and shouted: "Fascists!" Approximately 300 enemy submachine gunners charged into the hamlet. Shots thundered out next to the building that held the headquarters. It was the tanks of the corps commander and chief of staff that were engaging two enemy assault guns. The officers and soldiers immediately ran out into the street and took up a defense. General Sakhno formed several groups out of the headquarters personnel and assigned each one a specific sector of defense. The corps' chief of operations Lieutenant Colonel N.S. Nazarov took charge of several armored halftracks, which enveloped the Nazis that were attacking the hamlet and struck them in the flank. The enemy fell back under the heavy fire from machine guns and submachine guns. However, soon the Germans undertook another attack and drove the defenders out of the hamlet.

The second group of submachine gunners that had broken through to the corps' rear fell upon the 705th Artillery Regiment's nearby headquarters. The deputy political commander of the regiment Lieutenant Colonel M.P. Makarov took charge of the headquarters' defense. He had a total of approximately 40 men under his command. They met the enemy with organized rifle and machine-gun fire, and with the fire of submachine guns. The Nazis had already gone on the attack for the tenth time. Bitter, close-range fighting flared up. Captain S.A. Blinov fought courageously. Commanding a group of soldiers, he rose them several times onto a counterattack and kept throwing back the enemy submachine gunners. Encircled by Nazis, he fired off his last cartridge, then charged them with a grenade in his hand. An explosion rang out. Captain Blinov was killed, but with his grenade's explosion, he killed several Nazis.

The defenders' ammunition was running low. Then the artillery regiment's chief of staff Major Popov issued an order over the radio: "To all the artillery battalions – drop fire on me!" Dozens of shells poured down on the hamlet. Two females of the signals team remained in an intact building: Senior Sergeant G. Tsapkina and Corporal V. Korneeva, who were maintaining constant contact with the artillery battalions and the corps headquarters. The Nazis captured the building. Two of them climbed into the attic, and making threatening gestures with their weapons, forced the brave women to come down. At this moment a shell struck the building and collapsed one of the corners of it. The collapsing logs crushed the enemy soldiers. Tsapkina and Korneeva ran out of the building and crawled off into some bushes. The friendly artillery fire became even heavier – two battalions were now conducting it. The German submachine gunners hit the earth, and then, having abandonded their dead, made off into the woods. Soon the signalers took up their combat post once again and reported to the corps headquarters about the situation that had developed. A short time later a composite detachment of artillerymen equipped with rifles and submachine guns arrived at the headquarters. They stopped the Nazis and threw them back. This action had lasted for three hours. The enemy lost up to 100 dead in the fighting. Our soldiers captured 10 wagons loaded with ammunition and food. Later it became known that the artillerymen had clashed with two battalions of the 28th Jäger Division.

The stubborn defense of the 178th Tank Brigade and 705th Artillery Regiment, and of the corps' rear echelon and headquarters staff prevented the foe from breaking out to the west. Soon, the enemy was thrown back to the east by a counterattack of the 11th Motorized Rifle Brigade and 326th Guards Heavy Self-propelled Regiment.

Over the day of 29 January 100 prisoners were taken in the Marienburg area by units of the 2nd Shock Army. They belonged to the 493rd Training Reserve Battalion, the 7th Infantry Division's Infantry Regiment 62, elements of the 3rd Naval Infantry Regiment, Machine-Gun Battalions "Vistula" and "Pregel", the 3036th and 3037th Fortress Batteries, and the 561st Volksgrenadier Division's Regiment 1142. According to prisoner testimony, the 7th Infantry Division's Infantry Regiment 62, which had suffered heavy losses in Poland, had been merged into a single battalion and sent to the Marienburg area. The battalion numbered 350 men. The 3036th and 3037th Fortress Howitzer Batteries had formed up in December 1944 in Elbing out of Volkssturm militia members. On 26 January the batteries had hastily taken up firing positions in the area southwest of Elbing, and on 27 January they'd been overrun. Before the fighting, the batteries had numbered 50-60 men each. Each battery had been equipped with 4 150mm howitzers.

On 29 January 1945, the chief of the Fourth Army's Operations Department issued a report on the casualties suffered by the army's formations and units between 21 and 28 January 1945:

Losses in personnel over the period from 21 to 28 January 1945: 432 men killed, 1,031 men wounded and 139 men missing-in-action. Of which:
  14th Infantry Division (24-28 January): 27 killed, 62 wounded and 21 missing;
  102nd Infantry Division (26-27 January): 16 killed, 39 wounded and 10 missing;
  292nd Infantry Division (24-25 January): 34 killed, 231 wounded and 16 missing;
  203rd Infantry Division (27-28 January): 11 killed, 21 wounded and 1 missing;
  129th Infantry Division (22 January): 7 killed and 27 wounded;
  Group "Hannibal" (26-27 January): 22 killed, 22 wounded and 2 missing;
  562nd Volksgrenadier Division (24 January): 2 killed, 5 wounded and 1 missing;
  131st Infantry Division (21-26 January): 57 killed, 107 wounded and 3 missing;
  170th Infantry Division (25 January): 48 killed, 62 wounded and 5 missing;
  28th Jäger Division (26-28 January): 37 killed, 101 wounded and 13 missing;
  558th Volksgrenadier Division (24-27 January): 32 killed, 61 wounded and 9 missing;
  18th Panzergrenadier Division (26-27 January): 48 killed, 82 wounded and 12 missing;
  541st Volksgrenadier Division (25-27 January): 91 killed, 211 wounded and 36 missing;
  Thus, the total losses in personnel of the Fourth Army over the period 21-28 January amounted to:
   a) officers – 121 men (31 killed, 82 wounded and 8 missing-in-action)
   b Non-commissioned officers and enlisted men – 5,269 (1,186 killed, 3,421 wounded, and 742 missing-in-action).

Armee-Oberkommando Der Chef des Generalstabes I.A.

Table 4.8: Status of the materiel of the German Fourth Army (Lage der panzerbrechenden Waffen – AOK 4) by the end of 29 January 1945

Units	Armored vehicles and anti-tank guns					Under repair and not yet written off		Irrecoverable	Total
	StuG	Tanks	SP guns	sPak 76.2 mm	sPak 75-mm	Short-term	Long-term		
1	2	3	4	5	6	7	8	9	10
XX Armee Korps									
14.Infanterie Division	-	-	-	-	10	1	1	-	12
Pz.Jg. Kp. 1102	4	-	-	-	-	-	-	-	4
3 Bat., StuG Brigade 185	4	-	-	-	-	3	1	-	8
24.Panzer Division	-	-	-	-	7	-	-	-	7
Fest. Pak Verb VII 75-mm	-	-	-	7	-	-	-	-	7
88-mm	-	-	-	-	8	-	-	-	8
292.Infanterie Division	-	-	-	-	10	2	4	-	16
Pz.Jg. Kp. 1292	2	-	-	-	-	3	7	-	12
StuG Brigade 209	8	-	-	-	-	17	-	-	25
129.Infanterie Division	-	-	-	-	8	-	-	-	8
Pz.Jg. Kp. 1014	3	-	-	-	-	5	4	-	12
StuG Brigade 909	6	-	-	-	-	12	11	-	29
Total for XX Korps	27	-	-	7	43	43	28	-	148
LV Armee Korps									
102.Infanterie Division	-	-	-	-	13	-	-	-	13
Pz.Jg. Kp. 1541	13	-	-	-	-	-	1	-	14
203.Infanterie Division	-	-	-	-	12	-	-	-	12

Units	Armored vehicles and anti-tank guns					Under repair and not yet written off		Irrecoverable	Total
	StuG	Tanks	SP guns	sPak 76.2 mm	sPak 75-mm	Short-term	Long-term		
1	2	3	4	5	6	7	8	9	10
Fest. Pak Verb 17/I	-	-	-	9	-	-	3	-	12
541.Volksgrenadier Division	-	-	-	-	8	-	1	-	9
4 Bat., StuG Brigade 920	3	-	-	-	-	1	1	-	5
Fest. Pak Kp.	-	-	-	7	-	-	-	-	7
	-	-	-	-	9	-	-	-	9
Kampfgruppe Hauser	-	-	-	-	30	-	-	-	30
StuG Kp. 500	1	-	-	-	-	1	2	-	4
Total for LV Corps	17	-	-	16	72	2	8	-	115
VII Panzer Korps									
558.Volksgrenadier Division	-	-	-	-	6	-	-	-	6
Pz.Jg. Kp. 1558	5	-	-	-	-	-	2	-	7
18.Panzergrenadier Division	-	-	-	-	3	-	-	-	3
Panzer Abt. 118	3	-	-	-	-	-	1	1	4
Total for VII Panzer Korps	8	-	-	-	9	-	3	1	20
VI Armee Korps									
131.Infanterie Division	-	-	-	-	8	2	2	-	12
Pz.Jg. Kp. 1131	2	-	-	-	-	1	3	-	6
sPz.Jg. Abt. 563	8	-	-	-	-	3	-	-	11
Pz V	-	3	-	-	-	-	2	-	5
88-mm	-	-	-	-	6	-	-	-	6
299.Infanterie Division	-	-	-	-	4	1	-	-	5
Pz.Jg. Kp. 1299	2	-	-	-	-	1	-	-	3
1 co. of StuG Brigade 299	2	-	-	-	-	-	1	-	3
I/AOK StuG Abt. 4	-	-	-	-	2	-	-	-	2
170.Infanterie Division	-	-	-	-	21	1	1	-	23
Pz.Jg. Kp. 1240	4	-	-	-	-	3	-	-	7
StuG Brigade 904	15	-	-	-	-	5	3	-	23
Total for VI Korps	33	3	-	-	41	17	12	-	106
XXVI Armee Korps									
28.Jaeger Division	-	-	-	-	15	-	-	-	15
Pz.Jg. Kp. 1028	6	-	-	-	-	-	4	-	10
Panzer Kp. Lt. Groetzki	3	-	-	-	-	-	-	-	3
Pz III	-	1	-	-	-	-	1	-	2
Pz IV	-	2	-	-	-	-	-	-	2
Panzer Kp. 10 38(t)	-	2	-	-	-	-	-	-	2
T-34	-	0	-	-	-	-	6	1	6
	0	-	-	-	-	-	-	1	0
Radfahr-Jäger Brigade 10	-	-	-	-	4	1	2	-	7

Units	Armored vehicles and anti-tank guns					Under repair and not yet written off		Irrecoverable	Total
	StuG	Tanks	SP guns	sPak 76.2 mm	sPak 75-mm	Short-term	Long-term		
1	2	3	4	5	6	7	8	9	10
Kampfgruppe von Einem	-	-	-	-	7	-	-	-	7
2 Bat./StuG Brigade 185	4	-	-	-	-	2	-	-	6
Pz.Rgt. 24 (10+11) Pz IV	-	10	-	-	-	8	-	-	18
1 Bat., Jg.Pz. Abt. 40	3	-	-	-	-	3	-	-	6
Höhe-Arko 302	3	-	-	-	-	5	8	-	16
StuG Brigade 277	3	-	-	-	-	-	-	-	3
StuG Kp. 1006 Pz IV	-	3	-	-	-	-	-	-	3
T-34	-	5	-	-	-	6	-	-	11
Total for XXVI Korps	19	23	-	-	26	25	21	6	114
Pz.Jg. Kp. 1367	7	-	-	-	-	-	-	-	7
Total for the Fourth Army	111	26	-	23	191	87	72	7	510

According to German archival records, in the attempt to breakout on 29 and 30 January 1945 in the area of Wormditt, the following German formations and units (from north to south) took part:

VI AK
10 Bicycle Jäger Brigade
28 Jäger Division
Kampfgruppe "von Einem" (24 Panzer Division)
170 Infantry Division
131 Infantry Division
VII PzK
18 Panzergrenadier Division + 1 infantry regiment of the 299 Infantry Division
209 and 904 StuG Brigades
Pz Aufkl Abt GD (Panzer reconnaissance battalion of Panzer Grenadier Division *Grossdeutschland*

The strength of the German grouping in armored fighting vehicles on 29-30 January 1945 (from south to north):

18 PzGD – 3 StuG assault guns;
131 ID – 2 StuG assault guns (with the attached sPz Jg Abt 563 – 8 StuG, 3 Jagdpanthers);
299 ID – 2 StuG assault guns (with the attached StuG Kompanie 249 – 2 StuG assault guns);
170 ID – 4 StuG (with the attached StuG Brigade 904 – 15 StuG assault guns);
28 JgD – 6 StuG assault guns (attached: Pz Ko Groetezki – 3 StuG, 1 Pz III, 2 Pz IV; and Pz Ko 10 – 2 Pz 38t tanks);
KG von Einem (24 PzD) – 7 StuG, 10 Pz IV;
Arko [Artillery corps] 302 (attached: StuG Brigade 277 – 3 StuG, 3 Pz IV and 5 T-34)

From the "Combat Path of the 10th Tank Corps":

In the course of 28-30 January 1945, the enemy again undertook several attacks, trying to break out to the west. The Germans launched the main attack against the 178th Tank Brigade, which was defending in the Behlenhof, Karwitten area. Daily repulsing 6 to 8 desperate enemy attacks, the brigade's men fought tenaciously and bravely. In the fighting, Lieutenant M.M. Tratnikov's crew distinguished itself. The tank was standing in ambush on the outskirts of a village, near a road fork. The position offered clear observation of all the approaches. A ravine was located not far away, in which, as reconnaissance reported, enemy tanks and infantry were accumulating for an attack. The tankers kept careful watch in that direction. When an assault gun clambered out of the ravine, Senior Sergeant P.I. Ivanenko quickly loaded an armor-piercing shell, and the gunner Sergeant P.D. Kondakov took careful aim before firing. The enemy self-propelled gun burst into flames. Tratnikov immediately ordered the driver-mechanic Senior Sergeant A.S. Aleksandrov to switch to an alternate position. Two German tanks emerged from the ravine; they opened intensive fire at the stone building, behind which Tratnikov's tank had stood in ambush just several minutes ago. However, it was no longer there: the crew from the new position kept watch over the closing enemy.

"Don't fire without an order!" – Tratnikov ordered.

Having selected the right moment, when the enemy tanks had exposed their flanks, Tratnikov issued the order to open fire. Using four shells, Kondakov knocked out both machines, and their crews were killed by bursts of machine-gun fire. Changing firing positions from time to time, the Soviet tank continued to engage the German infantry that was accompanying an assault gun, which it soon managed to set ablaze. Deprived of the support of tanks and assault guns, the enemy infantry retreated.

Table 4.9: Status of the materiel of the German Fourth Army (Lage der panzerbrechenden Waffen – AOK 4) by the end of 30 January 1945

Units	Armored vehicles and anti-tank guns					Under repair and not yet written off		Irrecoverable	Total
	StuG	Tanks	SP guns	sPak 76.2 mm	sPak 75-mm	Short-term	Long-term		
1	2	3	4	5	6	7	8	9	10
XXVI Armee Korps									
Gruppe "Wagner"									
StuG Brigade 277	3	-	-	-	-	5	8	-	16
Pz IV	-	3	-	-	-	-	-	-	3
T-34	-	2	-	-	-	9	-	-	11
461.Infanterie Division	-	-	-	-	3	-	-	-	3
Panzer Kp. 10 38(t)	-	2	-	-	-	-	-	-	2
Radfahr-Jäger Brigade 10	-	-	-	-	4	-	-	-	4
28.Jäger Division	-	-	-	-	13	2	-	-	15
Pz.Jg. Kp. 1028	5	-	-	-	-	3	2	-	10
Panzer Kp. Lt. Groetzki	4	-	-	-	-	-	-	-	4
Pz III	-	1	-	-	-	-	1	-	2
Pz IV	-	1	-	-	-	-	-	-	1
Kampfgruppe von Einem	-	-	-	-	7	-	-	-	7
2 Bat., StuG Brigade 185	3	-	-	-	-	3	-	-	6
Pz.Rgt. 24 (10+11) Pz IV	-	11	-	-	-	7	-	-	18
1 Bat., Jg.Pz. Abt. 40	3	-	-	-	-	3	-	-	6
StuG Brigade 209	10	-	-	-	-	14	-	1	24
Total for XXVI Korps	28	20	-	-	27	46	11	1	132
VI Armee Korps									

COMBAT OPERATIONS OF THE 5TH GUARDS TANK ARMY 405

Units	Armored vehicles and anti-tank guns					Under repair and not yet written off		Irrecoverable	Total
	StuG	Tanks	SP guns	sPak 76.2 mm	sPak 75-mm	Short-term	Long-term		
1	2	3	4	5	6	7	8	9	10
Report about the status of the formations and units not received.									
VII Panzer Korps									
558.Volksgrenadier Division	-	-	-	-	6	-	-	-	6
Pz.Jg. Kp. 1558	4	-	-	-	-	2	1	-	7
18.Panzergrenadier Division	-	-	-	-	3	-	-	-	3
Panzer Abt. 118	5	-	-	-	-	-	-	-	5
14.Infanterie Division	-	-	-	-	10	1	1	-	12
Pz.Jg. Kp. 1014	3	-	-	-	-	5	4	-	12
131.Infanterie Division	-	-	-	-	8	2	2	-	12
Pz.Jg. Kp. 1131	2	-	-	-	-	1	3	-	6
Total for VII Panzer Korps	14	-	-	-	27	11	11	-	63
XX Armee Korps									
102.Infanterie Division	-	-	-	-	12	1	-	-	13
Pz.Jg. Kp. 1102	5	-	-	-	-	-	-	-	5
Fest. Pak-Kp. 17/1	-	-	-	-	5	3	1	-	9
24.Panzer Division	-	-	-	-	7	-	-	-	7
3 Bat., StuG Brigade 185	3	-	-	-	-	3	2	-	8
129.Infanterie Division	-	-	-	-	5	1	2	-	8
StuG Brigade 909	6	-	-	-	-	12	11	-	29
292.Infanterie Division	-	-	-	-	8	4	4	-	16
Pz.Jg. Kp. 1292	0	-	-	-	-	3	7	2	10
Total for the XX Korps	14	-	-	-	37	27	27	2	105
LV Armee Korps									
203.Infanterie Division	-	-	-	-	2	1	2	7	5
Fest. Pak Verb 17/I	-	-	-	5	-	-	-	7	5
541.Volksgrenadier Division	-	-	-	-	8	-	1	-	9
4 Bat., StuG Brigade 920	2	-	-	-	-	1	2	-	5
Fest. Pak Kp.	-	-	-	7	-	-	-	-	7
	-	-	-	-	5	-	4	-	9
Pz.Jg. Kp. 1541	8	-	-	-	-	2	4	-	14
Kampfgruppe Hauser	-	-	-	-	20	5	5	-	30
StuG Kp. 500	1	-	-	-	-	1	2	-	4
Total for the LV Korps	11	-	-	12	35	10	20	14	88
XXXXI Panzer Korps									
Gruppe "Hannibal"	-	-	-	-	2	-	-	-	2
21.Infanterie Division	-	-	-	-	19	1	-	1	20
StuG Brigade 259	14	-	-	-	-	22	2	-	38
50.Infanterie Division	-	-	-	-	11	-	-	-	11

Units	Armored vehicles and anti-tank guns					Under repair and not yet written off		Irrecoverable	Total
	StuG	Tanks	SP guns	sPak 76.2 mm	sPak 75-mm	Short-term	Long-term		
1	2	3	4	5	6	7	8	9	10
Pz.Jg. Kp. 1150	-	2	-	-	-	-	1	-	3
	2	-	-	-	-	2	3	-	7
Gruppe "Blaurock" with StuG companies 1156, 1139 and 1549 and elements of StuG Brigade 209	-	-	-	-	8	3	3	-	14
	12	-	-	-	-	21	3	-	36
Fest. Pak Kp. 7 and 8/VII	-	-	-	17	-	-	-	-	17
61.Infanterie Division	-	-	-	-	5	-	-	-	5
Total for XXXXI Panzer Korps	29	2	-	17	45	49	13	1	155
1	2	3	4	5	6	7	8	9	10
Panzer Korps *Hermann Göring*									
2.Division *Hermann Göring*	6	-	-	-	-	7	9	-	22
Stug Brigade 279	3	-	-	-	-	2	3	-	8
547.Volksgrenadier Division	-	-	-	-	4	-	-	3	4
1st Bat., StuG Brigade 185	5	-	-	-	-	1	-	-	6
Division *Grossdeutschland*	-	-	4	-	10	-	-	-	14
StuG	-	-	-	4	-	-	-	-	4
Pz IV	3	-	-	-	-	6	13	1	22
Pz V	-	1	-	-	-	3	1	1	5
Pz VI	-	11	-	-	-	6	19	1	36
	-	2	-	-	-	4	5	-	11
562.Volksgrenadier Division	-	-	-	-	6	-	-	-	6
Pz.Jg. Kp. 1562	2	-	-	-	-	3	-	-	5
Total for Panzer Korps HG	19	14	4	4	20	32	50	6	143
Pz.Jg. Kp. 1367	7	-	-	-	-	-	-	-	7
Total for Fourth Army	122	34	6	33	191	175	132	24	693

On 31 January 1945, the Fourth Army's chief of operations issued another report on its casualties:

Losses in personnel over the period from 21 to 29 January 1945: Killed – 2,126 men, wounded – 6,112 men, missing-in-action – 1,575 men. Of which:

> 21 Infantry Division (21-29 January): 314 killed, 973 wounded and 447 missing;
> 50 Infantry Division (21-29 January): 161 killed, 1,154 wounded and 363 missing;
> 61 Infantry Division (21-29 January): 225 killed, 922 wounded and 254 missing;
> 349 Volksgrenadier Division (21-29 January): 176 killed, 802 wounded and 124 missing;
> Pz Division *Herman Göring* (20-21 January): 64 killed, 161 wounded and 89 missing;
> Pz Division *Herman Göring* (22-29 January): 285 killed, 693 wounded and 201 missing;

56 Infantry Division (28-29 January): 12 killed, 32 wounded and 2 missing;
14 Infantry Division (29 January): 41 killed, 49 wounded and 1 missing;
129 Infantry Division (27-29 January): 478 killed, 868 wounded and 61 missing;
292 Infantry Division (28 January): 32 killed, 79 wounded and 3 missing;
102 Infantry Division (29 January): 19 killed, 42 wounded and 2 missing;
131 Infantry Division (26-28 January): 162 killed, 211 wounded and 18 missing;
28 Jäger Division (28-29 January): 83 killed, 102 wounded and 3 missing;
24 Panzer Division (28-29 January): 17 killed, 80 wounded and 0 missing;
547 Volksgrenadier Division (28 January): 18 killed, 31 wounded and 1 missing;
203 Infantry Division (28-29 January): 3 killed, 11 wounded and 0 missing;
18 Panzergrenadier Division (28-29 January): 36 killed, 102 wounded and 7 missing.

Thus, the total losses of the Fourth Army in personnel over the period from 12 to 29 January amounted to:
a) officers – 542 men (131 killed, 381 wounded and 30 missing-in-action);
b) non-commissioned officers and enlisted men – 21,865 men (4,726 killed, 12,879 wounded and 4,260 missing-in-action).

Armee-Oberkommando Der Chef des Generalstabes I.A.

Excerpt from Operational Summary No. 017 from the headquarters of the 5th Guards Tank Army at 2030 on 30 January:

The enemy with units of the 170th Infantry Division, the 28th Jäger Division, a bicycle jäger brigade, the 18th Panzergrenadier Division and separate battalions, reinforced with tanks and self-propelled guns of the 24th Panzer Division, presumably the 5th Panzer Division, and the 209th Assault Gun Brigade, strove to break out in the Mühlhausen – Elbing and Preußisch Holland – Marienberg directions, in order to withdraw the troops of the East Prussian grouping.

Forces of the 5th Guards Tank Army at 1100 on 30 January 1945 went on the offensive in the 1) Behlenhof estates – Krickehnen – Wormditt; and 2) Karwinden – Hensels farmstead – Schlodien directions with the assignment to destroy the enemy group that was attempting to break out and to reach the Wormditt – Deutschendorf line by the end of 30 January.

The 29th Tank Corps, with the 376th Heavy Self-propelled Artillery Regiment, 14th Guards Heavy Tank Regiment, 651st Cannon Artillery Regiment, 366th Anti-aircraft Artillery Regiment and 377th Separate Motorized Engineer Battalion went on the offensive at 1100 30 January 1945 from their Behlenhof estates, Warnikam farmstead, Koppeln start line in the direction of Bordehnen, Krickehnen and Wormditt, with the task by the end of the day to take Wormditt, Wagten and Basien. Subsequently, they were to have in view actions toward Mehlsack. By 1600 on 30 January, the corps' units were occupying the following positions: 32nd Tank Brigade with the 376th Heavy Self-propelled Artillery Regiment and one battalion of the 53rd Motorized Rifle Brigade and the support of the 651st Cannon Artillery Regiment and 271st Mortar Regiment are attacking in the first echelon; the 25th Tank Brigade with the 14th Guards Heavy Tank Regiment and one battalion of the 53rd Motorized Rifle Brigade supported by the 165th Light Artillery Regiment, are attacking in the direction of Bordehnen. Having encountered an antitank ditch, minefields, and full-profile trenches occupied by enemy infantry running between Plehnen and the woods 0.5 km southeast of Liebenau, they are in the process of bypassing them: the 32nd Tank Brigade in the direction of Plehnen and Schmauch, the 25th Tank Brigade in the direction of Hermsdorf. One battalion of the 53rd Motorized Rifle Brigade, the 409th Separate Guards Mortar Battalion and the 1223rd Self-propelled

Artillery Regiment are in their area of jumping-off positions – the woods 0.5 km southeast of Warnikam. The 31st Tank Brigade is on the approach to its jumping-off area as the corps commander's reserve.

The damage, inflicted on the enemy by the corps' units over the day of 29 January: 6 self-propelled guns, 4 tanks, 8 guns of various caliber and 20 vehicles destroyed, and up to 1000 soldiers and officers killed. Captured: 3 guns of various caliber, 3 mortars, and 48 enemy soldiers and officers. The losses of the 29th Tank Corps: 1 T-34 tank knocked-out and 1 T-34 tank disabled by a mine; 11 killed and 33 wounded.

Altogether, the 29th Tank Corps has in service: 31 T-34 tanks, 14 SU-152, 10 SU-85 and 17 SU-76. Supplies: diesel fuel – 1.0 refill, gasoline – 0.4 refill; ammunition – 0.75 of a standard combat load; food – 3 days. The corps' command post is in the woods in the area of the road fork 1 km southeast of Warnikam.

The 10th Tank Corps, with the 689th Destroyer Antitank Artillery Regiment, the 326th Heavy Self-propelled Artillery Regiment, the 41st Cannon Artillery Regiment and the 65th Separate Motorized Engineer Battalion from its jumping-off position of the Muttersegen farmstead, Schlobitten station, Karwinden area at 1100 on 30 January 1945 went on the offensive in the direction of the Hensels farmstead and Schlodien with the task by the end of the day of 30 January to capture the Klein Damerau, Deutschendorf, Spanden area. Subsequently it was to have in view operating in the direction of Braunsberg. By 1600 30 January the corps' units were occupying the following positions: 183rd Tank Brigade – had captured Deutschendorf; 186th Tank Brigade and a battalion of the 11th Motorized Rifle Brigade – were engaged in combat for the railroad station 0.5 km west of the Hensels farmstead; the 178th Tank Brigade with a portion of the 11th Motorized Rifle Brigade's strength was engaged in combat to destroy an enemy force of up to 500 soldiers supported by 13 self-propelled guns in the area 1 km northwest of Herrndorf.

Altogether the 10th Tank Corps has in service: 31 T-34 tanks, 11 SU-100, 13 SU-85, 18 SU-76, 14 ISU-122 and 2 M4A2. In the course of the day of 29 January 1945, the corps had the following losses: 1 T-34 tank burned-out, and 1 T-34 and 2 SU-100 knocked-out. Casualties included 14 men killed and 70 wounded. The corps headquarters – Nikolaiken.

The 47th Mechanized Brigade with the 146th Anti-aircraft Artillery Regiment, the 201st Light Artillery Brigade and the 76th Guards Mortar Regiment – the army commander's reserve – are in the area of Briensdorf and the woods to the southwest. By 1600 30 January 1945 it is occupying the following positions: the 1st Battalion of the 47th Mechanized Brigade continues to defend the southeastern outskirts of Preuβisch Holland; the 2nd Battalion is in the Briensdorf area; one battalion is fighting in the Trunz area. Up until 1600 30 January, 170 enemy soldiers and officers had been taken prisoner by the battalion. The brigade's condition and the damage inflicted on the enemy are being ascertained. The 201st Light Artillery Brigade and the 76th Guards Mortar Regiment are in the Briensdorf area in readiness to carry out assignments.

The 1st Separate Guards Motorcycle Regiment is occupying a defense on the northeastern outskirts of Prueβisch Holland. According to supplementary information, the army's artillery units have destroyed 5 tanks, 9 self-propelled guns, 1 105mm gun, 2 vehicles, 1 prime mover, 32 wagons and 60 horses, and have killed up to 250 enemy soldiers and officers. They've knocked out 2 tanks and 2 self-propelled guns, and scattered and partially destroyed enemy units of up to 800 soldiers and officers. One 75mm gun, 1 prime mover and 12 light machine guns have been captured. The weather is cloudy with snow showers. Because of snowdrifts, the roads are almost impassable for motorized transport.

Chief of staff of the 5th Guards Tank Army Major General of Tank Forces SIDOROVICH
Chief of operations of the 5th Guards Tank Army Fedorov

Over the day of 30 January, 200 prisoners were captured by the formations and units of the 2nd Shock Army: in the area 7 to 10 kilometers southwest of Preußisch Holland – from Infantry Regiment 391, Infantry Regiment 399, Artillery Regiment 244, and the engineer and fusilier battalions of the 170th Infantry Division, Artillery Regiment 83 of the 28th Jäger Division, the 131st Infantry Division and the 299th Infantry Division; in the area of Nogatau (west of Elbing) – from the 7th Panzer Division's Panzergrenadier Regiment 7; in the Marienburg area – from the 5th Police Battalion and the Gdynsk naval school; and in the area west of Marienwerder – from a separate construction battalion.

A captured senior doctor from Infantry Regiment 399 of the 170th Infantry Division revealed that by 27 January, the 170th Infantry Division had assembled in the Guttstadt, Arnsdorf area. The 28th Jäger Division had arrived in the same area, as well as another infantry division, which the doctor couldn't identify. The divisions were given a task to break through the front of the Soviet forces and to link up with German units on the Vistula. The route of Infantry Regiment

A column of tanks of the 5th Guards Tank Army's 10th Tank Corps; East Prussia, January–February 1945. (TsA MO)

Tanks of the 5th Guards Tank Army; East Prussia, January–February 1945. (TsA MO)

Tank riders aboard a tank of the 5th Guards Tank Army on a street of one of East Prussia's cities. (TsA MO)

Soviet submachine gunners keep a watchful eye over the outskirts of Elbing; January–February 1945. (TsA MO)

One of the central streets of Elbing after the fighting ended; January–February 1945. (TsA MO)

A building of the railroad terminal in Elbing, destroyed by the retreating Germans; 1945. (RGAKFD)

A view of the city of Elbing overlooking the Elbing River during the combat for the city; 1945. (RGAKFD)

Soviet tanks on the move through a forest toward combat positions; East Prussia. (RGAKFD)

A Soviet soldier on one of Elbing's rubbled streets after the fighting; 1945. (RGAKFD)

A knocked-out German gun, abandoned on one of Elbing's streets; 1945. (RGAKFD)

Knocked-out German assault guns; East Prussia, February 1945. (RGAKFD)

This German column of vehicles in East Prussia was caught by Soviet tankers.

Another German column of vehicles destroyed in East Prussia, 1945.

A German prime mover knocked-out on a road in East Prussia, February–March 1945.

A destroyed German vehicle; East Prussia, February–March 1945.

A knocked-out and abandoned German Pz IV tank; East Prussia, February–March 1945.

The wreckage of German trains in East Prussia; January–February 1945.

A burned-out freight car of a German train caught by Soviet tankers on a railroad in East Prussia; January–February 1945.

Another shot of the wreckage of German trains in East Prussia; January–February 1945.

A knocked-out and captured German assault gun with the Saukopf gun mantlet; East Prussia, winter of 1945. (TsA MO)

399: Arnsdorf, Sommerfeld, Schönau, Rogehnen, Neuendorf, Schönfeld, Hohendorf (south of the Drausen See). The regiment was supposed to reach the latter point on 29 January and there receive further instruction from the division commander. A prisoner from the headquarters of the 170th Infantry Division testified that units of the 170th and 131st Infantry Divisions were assembled in the Schönau area (8 km southeast of Preußisch Holland). Twenty self-propelled guns had been attached to the 170th Infantry Division. Their orders had been to attack in the southwestern direction. After the unsuccessful attack toward Preußisch Holland, the decision had been taken to break out in the direction of Leischten (10 km southwest of Preußisch Holland). A prisoner from the 7th Panzer Division's Panzergrenadier Regiment 7 indicated that the regiment had been shifted to the area west of Elbing with orders to dig in behind the Nogat River and to prevent the Russians from reaching the sea.

The combat operations of the 5th Guards Tank Army from 31 January to 6 February 1945

The front lines became stabilized and continued to remain without significant changes for the next six days, up until 5 February 1945 inclusively. The enemy, having reinforced his grouping, was trying to break out to the west with units of the 23rd Infantry Division, the 14th Infantry Division and a motley assortment of other attached reinforcements, such as Kampfgruppen "Nehrung", "Wolf", "Büchner" and "Herzenberg" (numbering 200-800 men each, which had been formed out of the remnanats of shattered units), as well as training tank battalions, assault guns and a complete array of specialized battalions. The Germans were offering stubborn resistance to the advance of the 5th Guards Tank Army, both with fire and numerous counterattacks.

The troops of the 5th Guards Tank Army daily repulsed fierce enemy counterattacks while inflicted heavy losses to the Germans. For example, on 2 February the army repelled 17 counterattacks, and on 3 February – 10 more enemy counterattacks.

The enemy, apparently convinced of the futitily of their attempts to breakout towards Elbing through Preußisch Holland and Mühlhausen, altered the direction of their attack and undertook an attempt to break through to Elbing along the coastline from Frauenburg towards Tolkemit. With this goal, the Germans launched an attack towards Tolkemit with up to a regiment of infantry supported by 10-15 tanks and self-propelled guns from the Frauenburg direction and across the ice from the Frische Nehrung spit with up to a regiment of infantry. By 1400 on 3 February, the Germans, having a superiority in strength, captured Tolkemit, having driven the 170th Rifle Division's 391st Rifle Regiment out of the town. In connection with this, the threat arose of an enemy breakthrough towards Elbing along the coastline.

In response, the commander of the 5th Guards Tank Army at 1500 on 3 February 1945 issued an order to the 29th Tank Corps: with the arrival of the 8th Mechanized Corps on the Plehnen – Liebenau line, it was to move to the Neukirch-Höhe area and take Tolkemit on 4 February. Once that was accomplished, it was to block all of the roads leading to the west, and in cooperation with the 42nd Rifle Corps, stubbornly hold the Tolkemit area, having one battalion deployed on the spit of the Frische Nehrung. Simultaneous with this, at an order from the commander-in-chief of the 2nd Belorussian Front Marshal of the Soviet Union K.K. Rokossovsky, the 32nd Tank Brigade, the 29th Tank Corps' 1223rd Self-propelled Artillery Regiment, the 14th Guards Heavy Tank Regiment and the 376th Heavy Self-propelled Artillery Regiment were made operationally subordinate to the 124th Rifle Corps' commander.

By 1100 on 4 February the 29th Tank Corps (minus the 32nd Tank Brigade and 1223rd Self-propelled Artillery Regiment) was assembled in the Neukirch-Höhe area and the Neuendorf, Hütte, Rückenau area. The 25th Tank Brigade, comprising the tank corps' forward detachment, had arrived in the assembly area before the corps' other units. There, on the morning of 4 February, it had proceeded to attack Tolkemit together with one battalion of the 391st Rifle Regiment, the 72nd Guards Special-purpose Naval Infantry Battalion and the 1st Separate Guards Motorcycle Regiment. By 0900 fighting was underway for passion of Tolkemit, and by 1900 Tolkemit was once again in Soviet possession. The Soviet attackers moved on and reached a line 1 km northeast of the town.

The 29th Tank Corps was given a new order on the night of 4-5 February: in cooperation with the 170th Rifle Division, it was to launch a night attack towards Frauenburg and take that objective by the morning of 5 February. Carrying out this order, by 1000 on 5 February the corps' units had reached a line stretching from Narz to the northern fringe of woods 3 km east of Tolkemit. On the approaches to Frauenburg, the units of the 29th Tank Corps encountered an antitank ditch and minefields. Meanwhile, the enemy was placing heavy fire on the attackers with up to two battalions of artillery and four self-propelled guns. The attack at that point bogged down and the corps' units made no further advance.

A reconnaissance group from the 72nd Separate Guards Special-purpose Naval Infantry Battalion [Marines] was conducting reconnaissance on 5 February across the ice towards the Schmergrube woods on the Frische Nehrung. When approaching the southern coast of the spit of land, the reconnaissance group was hit by intense mortar and machine-gun fire, after which it fell back to the coastline. The reconnaissance group was given a fresh task: on the night of 5-6 February, to conduct reconnaissance in the direction of Kahlberg on the Frische Nehrung.

Units of the 10th Tank Corps, in cooperation with the 47th Mechanized Brigade, having worn down the enemy, went on the offensive on 6 February and by 1900 had thrown the Nazi's back to the eastern banks of the Passarge River in the Schlodien – Berchertsdorf sector, which extended for 10 kilometers, and were fighting to gain footholds across the river. Meanwhile, the 29th Tank Corps, having run into bitter resistance, was continuing to fight for possession of Frauenburg.

Excerpt from Operational Summary No. 017 from the headquarters of the 5th Guards Tank Army at 2400 on 31 January 1945:

The enemy, with units of the 170th Infantry Division, the 24th Panzer Division, the 28th Jäger Division, a bicycle jäger brigade, and presumably of the 5th Panzer Division and Assault Gun Brigade 209, was offering tough resistance to our forces' advance on the Rogehnen – Schönau – Plehnen – Bordehnen – Hermsdorf – Spitzen – eastern outskirts of Deutschendorf – Seepothen line. Simultaneously, with the support of tanks and artillery, the enemy continued the attempts to fight their way out of the pocket in the western direction out of the Quittainen, Schönau, Pergusen and Karwitten areas, as well as out of the woods to the northeast. The Luftwaffe in groups of 10 to 25 aircraft were bombing our combat positions in the Preußisch Holland and Schlobitten areas.

The 5th Guards Tank Army, having resumed the offensive on the morning of 31 January 1945, is engaged in heavy fighting with enemy infantry, artillery and tanks on the line:

29th Tank Corps, with the 376th Heavy Self-propelled Artillery Regiment, the 14th Guards Heavy Tank Regiment, the 651st Cannon Artillery Regiment, the 366th Anti-aircraft Artillery Regiment and the 377th Separate Motorized Engineer Battalion, attacking in the direction of Bordehnen, Krickehnen and Wormditt, ran into heavy enemy resistance in strength of up to two regiments of the 28th Jäger Division, supported by two artillery battalions, two battalions of heavy and medium mortars, separate antitank guns and 8-10 tanks on the Nauten, Bordehnen, Hermsdorf line. Overcoming stubborn enemy resistance, by 1800 on 31 January 1945, the tank corps is fighting on the following line:

25th Tank Brigade – 1 km west of Bordehnen. Losses: 2 T-34 tanks destroyed, 4 T-34 knocked-out. The brigade has in service: 2 T-34 tanks and 3 SU-152; and 170 submachine gunners.

32nd Tank Brigade – southwestern outskirts of the Behlenhof estate. Losses: 2 T-34 tanks, 1 SU-85, 1 SU-76 destroyed. Wounded: the commander of the motorized rifle battalion Major Rudenko and tank battalion commander Captain Maliutin. The brigade has in service: 6 T-34 tanks, 9 SU-85, 6 SU-76; the brigade has 46 submachine gunners.

31st Tank Brigade – on the northeastern fringe of the woods lying 2 km north of the Teschenwalde estate. The brigade has in service 8 T-34 tanks, 7 SU-152 and 3 SU-76; and 55 submachine gunners.

53rd Motorized Rifle Brigade – is engaged in combat together with the tank brigades 1 km northeast and southeast of the Behlenhof estate. Losses – 25 killed, 35 wounded. It has in service: 3 76mm guns, 2 SU-57, 25 mortars and 185 active bayonets.

165th Light Artillery Regiment – in firing positions on the eastern fringe of the woods 2 km east of Koppeln. It has in formation 11 76mm guns. 271st Mortar Regiment is in firing positions northeast of Koppeln. It has 21 operational 120mm mortars. 376th Heavy Self-propelled Artillery Regiment is occupying firing positions in the Koppeln area. It has 5 operational ISU-152 and 7 disabled ISU-152. The 366th Anti-aircraft Artillery Regiment is in firing positions on the Warnikom farmstead and the Teschenwalde estate.

The 651st Cannon Artillery Regiment is supporting the actions of the tank brigades. It has 14 operational 100mm guns. The 1223rd Self-propelled Artillery Regiment and 409th Separate Guards Mortar Battalion are in the corps commander's reserve in the woods 0.5 kilometers east of Koppeln, with 7 operational SU-76 and 6 M-13 rocket launchers. The corps headquarters has 3 operational T-34 tanks. The 75th Separate Motorcycle Battalion has 3 operational M4A2 tanks.

The total losses of the 29th Tank Corps are 4 T-34, 1 SU-85 and 1 SU-76 destroyed, and 5 T-34 and 1 SU-76 knocked-out. The damage inflicted on the enemy: 4 tanks, 2 self-propelled guns and 8 antitank guns destroyed, and up to 200 soldiers and officers killed. Altogether, the corps has in service: 19 T-34 tanks, 10 SU-152, 9 SU-85 and 16 SU-76. Altogether for the corps: 56 armored fighting vehicles and 446 men reporting for duty. Supplies: diesel fuel – 0.8 refills, gasoline – 0.7 refills; ammunition – 0.8 of a standard combat load; food – 3 days. The corps headquarters is in Koppeln.

The **10th Tank Corps** with the 689th Destroyer Antitank Artillery Regiment, the 326th Self-propelled Artillery Regiment, the 41st Cannon Artillery Regiment, and the 65th Separate Motorized Engineer Battalion throughout the day of 31 January 1945 repulsed enemy counterattacks from the directions of Karwitten and Hermsdorf, in strength of up to two companies of infantry supported by 4 self-propelled guns. The enemy attacks were repulsed.

Overcoming tough enemy resistance and destroying his personnel and equipment, the corps' units are now in combat:

The 178th Tank Brigade and the 1st Battalion of the 11th Motorized Rifle Brigade attacked Karwitten. When the brigade reached the Hill 58.3 – southern outskirts of Karwitten line, it was counterattacked by the enemy out of the Scharnitt Woods in strength of up to a battalion of infantry supported by 2 tanks and 3 self-propelled guns. Simultaneously, it came under fire from an antitank battery and three self-propelled guns in Karwitten. The brigade dug in on the Hill 58.3 – northern fringe of the woods 1 km south of Karwitten line. It has in service: 4 T-34 tanks and 2 SU-100; and 105 men reporting for duty. Losses: 2 T-34 and 2 SU-100 knocked-out.

The 186th Tank Brigade and the 3rd Battalion of the 11th Motorized Rifle Brigade was counterattacked from the direction of Hermsdorf by up to two companies of infantry supported by artillery and 3 self-propelled guns. The attack was repulsed. The brigade reached the intersection of the railroad and highway 1 km east of a railroad station (1 km north of Breitfeld). It has in service 5 T-34 tanks and 3 SU-100; reporting for duty – 64 men.

The 183rd Tank Brigade's 1st Tank Battalion has taken Fürstenau and reached the road fork 500 meters east of this point, where it is engaged in combat. The 2nd Tank Battalion is on the western outskirs of Deutschendorf. The brigade has in service 6 T-34 tanks and 10 SU-85, with 110 men reporting for duty. Losses: 4 T-34 tanks and 1 SU-85 destroyed.

The 11th Motorized Rifle Brigade has functional 10 76mm guns and 26 82mm and 120mm mortars. Reporting for duty: 592 men.

The combat and numerical strength of the attached assets:

727th Self-propelled Artillery Regiment: 12 operational SU-76. The corps headquarters has 3 operational T-34 tanks.

77th Separate Motorcycle Battalion and 1 operational M4A2 and 116 men reporting for duty.

705th Light Artillery Regiment has 22 76mm guns in service. The 287th Mortar Regiment has 19 serviceable 120mm mortars. The 128th Separate Guards Mortar Battalion has 8 serviceable M-13 rocket launchers. The 1693rd Anti-aircraft Artillery Regiment has 13 serviceable 37mm guns. The 326th Heavy Self-propelled Artillery Regiment in the Schlobitten – Warnikam farmstead area has been attached to the 10th Tank Corps. It has 12 operational ISU-122. The 14th Guards Heavy Tank Regiment has been attached to the 29th Tank Corps. It is in firing positions in the Nikolaiken area with 6 operational IS-122 tanks. The 689th Destroyer Antitank Artillery Regiment has 14 serviceable 57mm guns.

The 41st Cannon Artillery Regiment is in firing positions 1 km south of Mühlhausen. It has in service 8 122mm howitzers.

The 10th Tank Corps has the following losses: a) in materiel – 4 T-34 tanks and 1 SU-85 destroyed; 2 T-34 tanks, 2 SU-100, 1 SU-85, 1 armored car, 1 halftrack and 4 vehicles knockedout; b) in personnel – 28 killed and 101 wounded. Damage inflicted on the enemy: Up to 400 soldiers and officers, and 1 tank, 4 self-propelled guns, 6 guns of various caliber, 4 heavy machine guns, 5 mortars and 13 vehicles knocked-out. Three heavy guns in good working order have been captured. Altogether, the 10th Tank Corp has in service: 18 T-34, 8 IS-122, 12 ISU-122, 5 SU-100, 10 SU-85, 12 SU-76 and 1 M4A2, for a total of 46 tanks and self-propelled guns; and 987 men reporting for duty. Supplies: diesel fuel – 0.8 of a refill, gasoline – 0.4 of a refill; ammunition – 0.9 of a standard combat load; food – 3 days. The corps headquarters is in Nikolaiken.

The **47th Mechanized Brigade** by 1800 on 31 January 1945 was assembled with two motorized rifle battalions in the Briensdorf – Hasselbusch area and the woods 1 kilometer to the north. One motorized rifle battalion is occupying a defensive line east of Preußisch Holland on the Rehnau – Koppinen line. The brigade has 11 operational M4A2 tanks, 2,822 men, 84 machine guns of all types, 29 mortars, 4 76mm guns, 9 57mm guns, and 4 anti-aircraft guns. Supplies: diesel fuel – 1.0 refill, gasoline – 1.0 refill; ammunition – 0.8 of a standard combat load; food – 2 days. At 1900 on 31 January 1945 the brigade was on the march to the Schlobitten jumping-off area, having the task in cooperation with the 10th Tank Corps to attack in the direction of Hermsdorf and to take the railroad station 1 km west of the Hensels estate; and to cooperate with the 29th Tank Corps in capturing Hermsdorf and by the morning of 1 February 1945 to assemble in the Döbern area.

Army-level units. The 1st Separate Guards Motorcycle Regiment is assembled in the Krossen area. The men are bringing their materiel back into order and setting up an all-round defense of the Krossen area. The regiment has 93 men reporting for duty, and 2 M4A2, 3 SU-57 and 3 BA-64 armored cars all operational.

The damage done to the enemy between 20 and 31 January 1945: 6 antitank guns, 4 heavy machine guns, 18 light machine guns, 80 vehicles, 12 prime movers and halftracks, 8 mortars, and 4 tanks destroyed. It has killed up to 800 enemy soldiers and officers and taken 99 Germans prisoner.

Over this same period, the regiment's losses amounted to 9 killed and 29 wounded; it has had 1 M4A2 knocked-out and 15 M-72 motorcycles and 1 vehicle destroyed; 3 76mm guns have been wrecked.

The 6th Anti-aircraft Artillery Division: the 146th Anti-aircraft Artillery Regiment is covering the 47th Mechanized Brigade's combat formations; the 366th Anti-aircraft Artillery Regiment is covering the 29th Tank Corps; and the 516th Anti-aircraft Artillery Regiment is covering the army headquarters in the Weeskenhof (Rzeczna) area. The 1062nd Anti-aircraft Artillery Regiment is covering Preußisch Holland. The division has in service 63 37mm guns and 17 85mm guns.

The 201st Light Artillery Brigade (minus the 651st Cannon Artillery Regiment) is moving together with the 47th Mechanized Brigade to the Schlobitten area. It has 23 serviceable 76mm guns. The 76th Guards Mortar Regiment is in the reserve of the army's artillery commander. It is in firing positions in the Weeskenhof, northern outskirts of Preußisch Holland and Wickerau areas. It has 32 serviceable M-13 rocket launchers.

The army headquarters has 5 operational T-34 tanks.

Altogether the 5th Guards Tank Army has in service 6 IS-122, 41 T-34, 17 M4A2, 15 SU-152, 12 SU-122, 5 SU-100, 19 SU-85 and 28 SU-76, **for a total of 143 operational armored fighting vehicles**.

The 42nd Rifle Corps throughout the course of the day was stubbornly holding its occupied line and repulsing enemy counterattacks from the direction of the Lauck estate. By 1800 on 31 January 1945 it was occupying the following positions: 399th Rifle Division – Breunken, western outskirts of Deutschendorf, eastern outskirts of Fürstenau. The division has casualties: 18 killed and 43 wounded. The 137th Rifle Division – Fürstenau, Tiedmannsdorf, Schafsberg. It has casualties: 4 killed and 16 wounded. The 170th Rifle Division is occupying a defense in separate strongpoints. The division has casualties: 6 killed and 18 wounded. The damage done to the enemy by the 42nd Rifle Corps: up to 800 enemy soldiers and officers killed; 16 vehicles destroyed and 2 self-propelled guns knocked-out; and 6 105mm howitzers captured. Corps headquarters is in Herrndorf.

Chief of staff of the 5th Guards Tank Army Major General of Tank Forces SIDOROVICH
Chief of operations Guards Colonel Fedorov

Table 4.10: Information on the losses of materiel, weapons and personnel in the forces of the 5th Guards Tank Army over the period of combat operations between 17 and 31 January 1945

Losses in materiel and weapons:	Destroyed	Knocked out	Blown up on mines	Total
10th Tank Corps				
T-34 tanks	36	26	2	64
M4A2 tanks	2	-	1	3
SU-100	12	19	-	31
SU-85	5	9	-	14
SU-76	6	2	1	9
Armored cars	3	1	-	4
Armored transporters	-	2	2	4
Vehicles	21	23	-	44
76-mm guns	1	3	-	4
120-mm mortars	1	-	-	1
57-mm guns	-	14	-	14
M-13 rocket launchers	-	1	-	1
82-mm mortars	-	7	-	7
Losses in personnel	**Killed**	**Wounded**	**Sick**	**Total**
	243	679	12	934
29th Tank Corps				
Losses in materiel and weapons				
T-34 tanks	32	28	-	60

COMBAT OPERATIONS OF THE 5TH GUARDS TANK ARMY

Losses in materiel and weapons:	Destroyed	Knocked out	Blown up on mines	Total
M4A2 tanks	1	-	-	1
SU-152	3	3	1	7
SU-85	3	7	-	10
SU-76	4	2	-	6
SU-57	2	-	-	2
Armored cars	2	-	-	2
Armored transporters	5	-	-	5
		Broken		
Vehicles	-	18	-	18
76-mm guns	-	11	-	11
57-mm guns	-	1	-	1
M-13 rocket launchers	-	2	-	2
Heavy machine guns	-	7	-	7
Light machine guns	-	2	-	2
82-mm mortars	-	4	-	4
Radio sets	-	2	-	2
Losses in personnel	**Killed**	**Wounded**	**Sick**	**Total**
	366	1249	-	1615

47th Mechanized Brigade
Losses in materiel and weapons

	Destroyed	Knocked out	Blown up on mines	Total
M4A2 tanks	21	7	-	28
Armored cars	3	-	-	3
Armored transporters	1	3	-	4
Vehicles	-	32	-	32
76-mm guns	-	8	-	8
57-mm guns	-	1	-	1
Anti-tank rifles	-	12	-	12
Heavy machine guns	-	14	-	14
Light machine guns	-	21	-	21
PPSh submachine guns	-	92	-	92
Rifles	-	175	-	175
Radio sets	-	5	-	5
Telephone sets	-	32	-	32
Telephone cable	47 km	-	-	-
Losses in personnel	**Killed**	**Wounded**	**Sick**	**Total**
	254	652	-	906

Units directly subordinate to Army Headquarters
Losses in materiel and weapons

	Destroyed	Knocked out	Blown up on mines	Total
M4A2 tanks	4	3	-	7
IS-122 tanks	2	1	-	3
SU-152	2	7	-	9
SU-122	-	4	-	4
		Badly damaged		
76-mm guns	-	8	-	8
57-mm guns	-	10	-	10
37-mm guns	-	4	-	4

Losses in materiel and weapons:	Destroyed	Knocked out	Blown up on mines	Total
Vehicles	1	23	-	24
M-72 motorcycles	-	15	-	15
PO-2 aircraft	-	2	-	2
Losses in personnel	**Killed**	**Wounded**	**Sick**	**Total**

Total Losses of the 5th Guards Tank Army between 17 and 31 January 1945

Losses in materiel and weapons

	Destroyed	Knocked out	Blown up on mines	Total
T-34 tanks	68	64	2	124
M4A2 tanks	28	9	1	38
IS-122 tanks	2	1	-	3
SU-152	5	10	-	15
SU-122	-	4	-	4
SU-100	12	19	-	31
SU-85	8	16	-	24
SU-76	10	4	1	15
SU-57	2	-	-	2
Armored cars	8	1	-	9
Armored transporters	6	5	2	13
	Destroyed	**Badly damaged**	-	**Total**
Vehicles	22	96	-	118
76-mm guns	1	30	-	31
57-mm guns	-	28	-	28
37-mm guns	-	4	-	4
M-13 rocket launchers	-	3	-	3
120-mm mortars	1	-	-	1
82-mm mortars	-	12	-	12
Heavy machine guns	-	21	-	21
Light machine guns	-	23	-	23
Radio sets	-	7	-	7
Motorcycles	-	15	-	15
Anti-tank rifles	-	12	-	12
PPSh submachine guns	-	23	-	23
Rifles	-	175	-	175
Telephone sets	-	32	-	32
PO-2 aircraft	-	2	-	2
Telephone cable	47 km	-	-	47 km
Total losses in personnel	**Killed**	**Wounded**	**Sick**	**Total**
	955	2786	12	3,753

42nd Rifle Corps

Losses in personnel and materiel over the period between 20 and 31 January 1945	170th Rifle Division	137th Rifle Division	399th Rifle Division	Total
Rifles	15	13	21	49
Heavy machine guns	6	6	9	21
45-mm guns	4	5	5	14
76-mm anti-tank guns	1	1	4	6
76-mm divisional guns	3	4	7	14

Losses in materiel and weapons:	Destroyed	Knocked out	Blown up on mines	Total
122-mm howitzers	-	-	3	3
82-mm mortars	-	-	11	11
120-mm mortars	-	-	7	7
Vehicles	-	5	13	18
Losses in horses and personnel	**Killed**	**Wounded**	**Sick**	**Total**
Horses	50	65	-	115
Personnel	428	1503	48	1,979

Chief of staff of the 5th Guards Tank Army Guards Major General of Tank Forces
SIDOROVICH
Chief of the Operations Department Guards Colonel FEDOROV

Table 4.11: Status of the materiel of the German Fourth Army (Lage der panzerbrechenden Waffen – AOK 4) by the end of 31 January 1945

Units	Armored vehicles and anti-tank guns					Under repair and not yet written off		Irrecoverable	Total
	StuG	Tanks	SP guns	sPak 76.2 mm	sPak 75-mm	Short-term	Long-term		
1	2	3	4	5	6	7	8	9	10
XXVI Armee Korps									
Gruppe "Wagner"									
StuG Brigade 277	5	-	-	-	-	-	11	-	16
38(t)	-	1	-	-	-	-	4	-	5
Pz IV	-	1	-	-	-	-	3	-	4
Pz V	-	0	-	-	-	-	2	-	2
T-34	-	4	-	-	-	-	5	-	9
From Lt. Groetzki's company	3	-	-	-	-	-	-	-	3
461.Infanterie Division	-	-	-	-	-	-	-	-	-
Panzer Kp. 10 38(t)	-	1	-	-	-	-	1	-	2
Radfahr-Jäger Brigade 10	-	-	-	4	-	-	-	-	4
28.Jäger Division	-	-	-	-	11	2	2	-	15
Pz.Jg. Kp. 1028	6	-	-	-	-	2	2	-	10
Panzer Kp. Lt. Groetzki	1	-	-	-	-	-	-	-	1
Pz III	-	1	-	-	-	-	1	-	2
Pz IV	-	1	-	-	-	-	-	-	1
Kampfgruppe von Einem	-	-	-	-	-	-	-	-	-
2 Bat., StuG Brigade 185	4	-	-	-	-	2	-	-	6
Pz.Rgt. 24 (10+11) Pz IV	-	10	-	-	-	5	3	-	18
1 Bat., Jg.Pz. Abt. 40	1	-	-	-	-	3	2	-	6
StuG Brigade 209	10	-	-	-	-	14	-	-	24
Total for XXVI Korps	30	19	-	-	15	28	11	-	128
VI Armee Korps									
170.Infanterie Division	-	-	-	-	-	-	-	-	-
Pz.Jg. Kp. 120	-	-	-	-	11	-	2	-	13
StuG Brigade 904	9	-	-	-	-	3	1	-	13
Total for VI Korps	9	-	-	-	11	3	3	-	26

Units	Armored vehicles and anti-tank guns					Under repair and not yet written off		Irrecoverable	Total
	StuG	Tanks	SP guns	sPak 76.2 mm	sPak 75-mm	Short-term	Long-term		
1	2	3	4	5	6	7	8	9	10
VII Panzer Korps									
558.Volksgrenadier Division	-	-	-	-	6	-	-	-	6
Pz.Jg. Kp. 1558	4	-	-	-	-	2	1	-	7
18.Panzergrenadier Division	-	-	-	-	3	-	-	-	3
Panzer Abt. 118	7	-	-	-	-	-	-	-	7
14.Infanterie Division	-	-	-	-	8	1	3	-	12
Pz.Jg. Kp. 1014	3	-	-	-	-	5	4	-	12
131.Infanterie Division	-	-	-	-	3	-	3	-	6
Pz.Jg. Kp. 1131	4	-	-	-	-	-	-	-	4
299.Infanterie Division						Report hasn't yet arrived			
sPz.Jg. Abt. 563 Pz V	-	3	-	-	-	-	-	-	3
Total for VII Panzer Korps	18	3	-	-	20	8	11	-	60
XX Armee Korps									
102.Infanterie Division	-	-	-	-	12	1	-	-	13
Pz.Jg. Kp. 1102	5	-	-	-	-	-	-	-	5
Fest. Pak-Kp. 17/1	-	-	-	-	5	3	1	-	9
129.Infanterie Division	-	-	-	-	5	1	2	-	8
StuG Brigade 909	6	-	-	-	-	12	11	-	29
292.Infanterie Division	-	-	-	-	8	4	4	-	16
Pz.Jg. Kp. 1292	0	-	-	-	-	3	7	-	10
24.Panzer Division	-	-	-	-	7	-	-	-	7
3 Bat., StuG Brigade 185	3	-	-	-	-	3	2	-	8
Total for the XX Korps	14	-	-	-	37	27	27	-	105
LV Armee Korps									
203.Infanterie Division	-	-	-	-	2	1	2	-	5
Fest. Pak Verb 17/I	-	-	-	5	-	-	-	-	5
541.Volksgrenadier Division	-	-	-	-	8	-	1	-	9
4 Bat., StuG Brigade 920	2	-	-	-	-	1	2	-	5
Fest. Pak Kp.	-	-	-	7	-	-	-	-	7
	-	-	-	-	5	-	4	-	9
Pz.Jg. Kp. 1541	8	-	-	-	-	2	4	-	14
Kampfgruppe Hauser	-	-	-	-	32	-	-	-	32
StuG Kp. 500	6	-	-	-	-	-	3	-	9
Total for the LV Korps	16	-	-	12	47	4	16	-	95
XXXXI Panzer Korps									
Gruppe "Hannibal"	-	-	-	-	2	-	-	-	2
21.Infanterie Division	-	-	-	-	17	3	-	-	20
	1	-	-	-	-	-	1	-	3
StuG Brigade 259	20	-	-	-	-	9	2	-	31

Units	Armored vehicles and anti-tank guns					Under repair and not yet written off		Irrecoverable	Total
	StuG	Tanks	SP guns	sPak 76.2 mm	sPak 75-mm	Short-term	Long-term		
1	2	3	4	5	6	7	8	9	10
50.Infanterie Division	-	-	-	-	11	-	-	-	11
Pz.Jg. Kp. 1150	-	2	-	-	-	-	1	-	3
	2	-	-	-	-	2	3	-	7
Gruppe "Blaurock"	-	-	-	-	13	1	-	-	14
Pz.Jg. Kp. 1156	5	-	-	-	-	4	1	-	10
Pz.Jg. Kp. 1349	6	-	-	-	-	5	1	-	12
StuG Brigade 203	8	-	-	-	-	10	-	-	18
Fest. Pak Kp. 7 and 8/VII	-	-	-	13	-	2	2	-	17
61.Infanterie Division	-	-	-	-	4	1	-	-	5
2 Bat., StuG Brigade 203	5	-	-	-	-	-	-	-	5
Total for XXXXI Panzer Korps	47	2	-	13	47	37	11	-	157
Panzer Korps *Hermann Göring*									
2.Division *Hermann Göring*	5	-	-	-	-	10	9	-	24
	-	-	-	-	5	4	-	-	9
StuG Abt. *Hermann Göring*	-	-	0	-	-	1	-	-	1
Pz.Jg. Abt. *Hermann Göring*	1	-	-	-	-	6	-	-	7
StuG Brigade 279	11	-	-	-	-	2	2	-	15
547.Volksgrenadier Division	-	-	-	-	2	4	-	-	6
1st Bat., StuG Brigade 185	5	-	-	-	-	1	-	-	6
Division *Grossdeutschland*	-	-	-	-	11	-	-	-	11
	-	-	2	-	-	1	1	-	4
	-	-	-	2	-	2	-	-	4
StuG									
Pz IV	3	-	-	-	-	6	13	-	22
Pz V	-	3	-	-	-	2	1	-	6
Pz VI	-	6	-	-	-	9	21	-	36
	-	2	-	-	-	4	5	-	11
562.Volksgrenadier Division	-	-	-	-	8	-	-	-	8
Pz.Jg. Kp. 1562	2	-	-	-	-	2	1	-	5
Total for Panzer Korps HG	27	11	2	2	26	54	53	-	175
Pz.Jg. Kp. 1367	7	-	-	-	-	-	-	-	7
Total for Fourth Army	168	33	4	27	203	161	129	-	753

Over the day of 31 January 1945, 20 prisoners were captured by the 2nd Shock Army: in the vicinity of Rogau (10 km east of Elbing) from the 170th Infantry Division's Infantry Regiment 391; in the Hagenau area (12 km east of Preußisch Holland) from the Machine-gun Battalion "Pregel" and the 400th Reserve Battalion; in the Marienburg area from the 1233rd Separate Panzer Company; in the area 5-10 kilometers southeast of Preußisch Holland from the 28th Jäger

Division's Infantry Regiments 83 and 49; from the 170th Infantry Division's Infantry Regiments 401 and 391, Artillery Regiment 240, and the fusilier, pioneer and field reserve battalions; from the 18th Panzergrenadier Division's Panzergrenadier Regiment 30; from Infantry Regiments 529 and 299; from I/Reserve Regiment 5; from the 1142nd Fortress Construction Battalion, and army military school, and the 1113th and 1142nd Reserve Infantry Battalions. A captured Oberleutnant – the commander of the 10th Company of the 28th Jäger Division's Infantry Regiment 83 – testified that on 22 January 1945 the division had begun to retreat to the west from the Goldapp area and reassembled in the Mehlsack area on 26 January. Infantry Regiment 83 on 26 January then began movement from Mehlsack in the western direction through Preußisch Holland with the task to link up with German units that were operating in the Marienburg area. In the Karwitten area, Infantry Regiment 83 ran into our units, and suffering heavy losses, fell back into the woods, where it abandoned or partially destroyed its heavy weapons and motorized transport. When approaching Schlobitten, the regiment's remnants fell into encirclement. Here an order had been issued to abandon the horses and personal items and to break out in the northwestern direction in small groups of 15-20 men each.

Excerpt from Operational Summary No. 019 from the headquarters of the 5th Guards Tank Army at midnight on 1 February 1945:

The enemy in the course of 1 February 1945 offered tough resistance to our units' offensive and strove to throw them back in the western direction with heavy artillery and mortar fire, groups of tank destroyers, and counterattacks by infantry supported by tanks and self-propelled guns from out of the strongpoints of Bordehnen, Liebenau, the Hensels estate and Deutschendorf. Altogether opposite the front of the 5th Guards Tank Army, the activity of up to 40 tanks and self-propelled guns and two artillery regiments belonging to the 170th Infantry Division, 28th Jäger Division, the 24th Panzer Division and presumably the 5th Panzer Division and Assault Gun Brigade 209.

The forces of the 5th Guards Tank Army throughout the day of 1 February 1945 were engaged in heavy offensive fighting against major forces of enemy infantry, artillery and tanks on the Plehnen, Bordehnen, Liebenau, Hensels estate, Deutschendorf, Seepothen line, while fighting off enemy counterattacks from out of the Plehnen – Bordehnen area in strength of up to an infantry regiment, 5 self-propelled guns and 6 tanks; from out of Liebenau and the woods to the north in strength of up to an infantry battalion, 6 self-propelled guns and 3 tanks; and from out of the Hensels estate and woods to the north in strength of up to an infantry battalion, 12 self-propelled guns and an artillery battalion. All of the enemy's attacks were driven back with heavy losses for him.

The **29th Tank Corps** with the 376th Heavy Self-propelled Artillery Regiment, 651st Cannon Artillery Regiment, 1619th Light Artillery Regiment, 366th Anti-aircraft Artillery Regiment, and the 377th Separate Motorized Engineer Battalion was engaged in heavy fighting on the Behlenhof, Liebenau line and in the woods to the northwest. Simultaneously the corps repulsed 6 enemy counterattacks from the Bordehnen, Liebenau area and the woods to the northwest. By 1900 on 1 February 1945 the corps' units were engaged in combat: 31st Tank Brigade – had taken Alt Teschen, and has operational 10 T-34, 7 SU-152 and 5 SU-76; 53rd Motorized Rifle Brigade – on the eastern outskirts of Behlenhof, having 90 active bayonets; 25th Tank Brigade – on the northeastern outskirts of Behlenhof, having operational 1 T-34 and 1 SU-152; 32nd Tank Brigade – is fighting for possession of Liebenau with 5 T-34 and 8 SU-85 still operational. Altogether, the 29th Tank Corps has in service: 18 T-34, 8 SU-152, 8 SU-85 and 5 SU-76. Supplies: diesel fuel – 0.7 of a refill, gasoline – 0.8 of a refill; ammunition – 0.5 of a standard combat load; food – 3 days.

As a result of the fighting on 1 February 1945, the 29th Tank Corps has the following losses: 2 T-34 and 2 SU-152 destroyed; 2 T-34 tanks knocked-out. Casualties consist of 42 men killed, including the commander of the 32nd Tank Brigade Lieutenant Colonel Kolesnikov, and 86 wounded. Damage inflicted on the enemy: 3 tanks, 2 self-propelled guns, 11 mortars, 4 guns of various caliber, 8 machine guns and 11 bunkers destroyed; up to 300 enemy soldiers and officers killed or wounded. The corps headquarters is in Angnitten.

The **10th Tank Corps** with the 689th Destroyer Antitank Artillery Regiment, the 14th Heavy Tank Regiment, the 326th Heavy Self-propelled Artillery Regiment and the 65th Separate Motorized Engineer Battalion in the course of 1 February 1945 was engaged in combat on the Karwitten, Point 48.9, 500 meters west of Deutschendorf line. It was repulsing enemy counterattacks from out of the Hensels estate and Deutschendorf areas and destroying an encircled enemy grouping in the Scharnitt Woods, north of Karwitten. By 1900 on 1 February 1945, the corps' units were in the following positions: The 178th Tank Brigade together with the 11th Motorized Rifle Brigade, the 14th Guards Heavy Tank Regiment and a battery of the 326th Self-propelled Artillery Regiment with a striked from the north and south had attacked Karwitten, driven the enemy out of this point, and had taken up a defense on its southeastern outskirts; the brigade has 5 T-34 and 2 SU-100 operational; the 11th Motorized Rifle Brigade has 312 active bayonets. The 186th Tank Brigade is occupying a line stretching from the northern fringe of the woods 500 meters south of the Karwinden estate to the Muttersegen farmstead, and has 4 T-34 and 6 SU-100 still operational. The 183rd Tank Brigade is in the area of the woods 1 km west of Deutschendorf, while defending Fürstenau with one battalion; the brigade has 11 T-34 and 11 SU-85 still operational.

The combat strength of the corps' attached assets: 14th Guards Heavy Tank Regiment has 8 operational IS-122 in the Lenzeten area; the 326th Heavy Self-propelled Artillery Regiment has 11 ISU-122 and 1 IS-122 in firing positions 1 km northeast of Nikolaiken. The 689th Destroyer Antitank Artillery Regiment has 14 serviceable 57mm antitank guns in firing positions in the Schlobitten area; the 727th Self-propelled Artillery Regiment had 8 operational SU-76; the 77th Separate Motorcycle Battalion has 1 operational M4A2; the 705th Light Artillery Regiment has 22 serviceable 76mm guns; the 287th Mortar Regiment has 19 120mm mortars in service; the 41st Cannon Artillery Regiment, which is supporting the corps units from firing positions in the area 2 km south of Mühlhausen, has 8 functioning 122mm howitzers.

Altogether the 10th Tank Corps has in service: 23 T-34 tanks (of which 3 are with the corps' headquarters), 9 IS-122, 11 SU-122, 8 SU-100, 11 SU-85 and 8 SU-76. Supplies: diesel fuel – 1.0 refill, gasoline – 0.7 of a refill; ammunition – 1.0 standard combat load; food – 4 days.

In the course of 1 February 1945, the corps took the following losses: 1 SU-76 destroyed; 1 T-34, 1 SU-76, 5 vehicles, 1 76mm gun, 1 82mm mortar knocked-out. Casualties: 25 killed and 93 wounded. The damage, inflicted on the enemy: 4 self-propelled guns destroyed; 3 self-propelled guns, 1 tank and 16 vehicles knocked-out. Fifteen enemy soldiers were taken prisoner. Up to 200 enemy soldiers and officers were eliminated. The corps headquarters is in Nikolaiken.

The **47th Mechanized Brigade** and the 146th Anti-aircraft Artillery Regiment throughout the day of 1 February 1945 was engaged in heavy fighting for possession of the Karwinden estate and had taken it by 1900 on 1 February 1945. Simultaneously the brigade was repulsing enemy counterattacks out of the Louisenwalde area. The 47th Mechanized Brigade's 1st Battalion turned over its defense on the southeastern outskirts of Preußisch Holland to units of the 8th Mechanized Corps and from 1900 1 February 1945 was on the march to the brigade's area. The brigade has 7 operational M4A2 tanks. Supplies: diesel fuel – 0.5 of a refill, gasoline – 0.9 of a refill; ammunition – 1.0 standard combat load; food – 2 days. The losses of the 47th Mechanized Brigade over the day of 1 February 1945: 2 M4A2 tanks destroyed and 2 M4A2 knocked-out. Casualties: 30 killed and 70 wounded. Damage done to the enemy: 4 guns and 10 machine guns destroyed, and up to 250 enemy soldiers and officers killed or wounded. Brigade headquarters – Schlobitten.

The army's artillery was supporting the corps' actions. The 376th Heavy Self-propelled Artillery Regiment was attached to the 29th Tank Corps and is in the area 500 meters west of Behlenhof. The regiment has 4 operational SU-152.

The 42nd Rifle Corps throughout the day of 1 February 1945 was holding its previously-occupied line and repulsing enemy counterattacks from the Frauenburg direction. By 1900 on 1 February 1945 it is occupying the following positions: 399th Rifle Division – Breunken, 1 km west of Deutschendorf, Fürstenau; 137th Rifle Division – Fürstenau, Borchertsdorf, Tiedmannsdorf, Groß Rautenberg, Schafsberg. 170th Rifle Division – was fighting on the approaches to Frauenburg, while part of its force reached the coastline 2 km southwest of Frauenburg, and another portion of its force is defending Karschau, Neukirch Höhe, Neuendorf and Tolkemit. The corps has taken casualties: 15 killed and 41 wounded. The damage done to the enemy: 4 guns and 5 vehicles destroyed; and up to 450 enemy soldiers and officers eliminated. The corps headquarters is in Herrndorf.

The weather is cloudy with snow showers. The roads are almost impassable for motorized transport.

Chief of staff of the 5th Guards Tank Army Major General of Tank Forces SIDOROVICH
Chief of operations Guards Colonel Fedorov

Earl Ziemke in his book *Stalingrad to Berlin* describes the actions of the day of 1 February 1945 and their denouement on the German side in the following passage:

On 1 February Fourth Army made a last attempt to break through to Elbing. It ran into a strong counterattack and was stopped dead in its tracks …. Rendulic [who now commanded Army Group North which included the Fourth Army], in the few months left in the war, was setting out to carve a niche in history next to Schoerner. One characteristic remarked on by all of his former superiors had been his absolute nervelessness. For him, keeping the army group in East Prussia raised no questions other than how it could best be accomplished. In one order he made the battalion and regimental commanders responsible for "every foot of ground" voluntarily given up and appended the example of a captain he had ordered shot the day before for taking his battalion back a mile after it had been broken through. In another, he ordered "flying courts-martial" created to scour the rear areas. Every soldier not wounded, picked up outside his unit area, was to be tried and shot on the spot.

From the "Combat path of the 10th Tank Corps":

Up until 2 February 1945, the enemy made several more attempts to break out to the northwest, toward the highway, but the brigades successfully repulsed all of his attacks. The corps' units were tenaciously defending Karwitten and the crossroads that were located 600 meters southeast of the Schlobitten railroad station. In this fighting alone, the 178th Tank Brigade destroyed 10 tanks and self-propelled guns and eliminated more than 500 enemy soldiers and officers. A battalion of the 11th Motorized Rifle Brigade was holding the defenses at the crossroads and nearby elevations. On the night of 31 January – 1 February 1945, the Nazis launched their next attack. Up to a battalion of infantry attacked the motorized riflemen's front together with four assault guns, while up to two companies attempted to envelop their left flank. Reconnaissance timely detected the enemy maneuver, which was trying to get in the motorized riflemen's rear. Battalion commander V.S. Sizonenko quickly shifted Lieutenant I.F. German's company to the left flank, having first reinforced it with machine guns. The company settled down into ambush positions near the railroad embankment. The Germans were moving in a column. Having allowed their forward patrol to pass by in the darkness, the company opened heavy machine-gun and submachine-gun fire at almost pointblank range. Dozens of enemy soldiers fell heavily into the snow, while those remaining alive turned and fled. In the course of this action, the commander of the machine-gun platoon Junior Lieutenant I.P. Lunev personally killed up to 20 Nazis.

Over 1 February 1945 25 prisoners were captured by the units and formations of the 2nd Shock Army: in the Grunau area from the 8th March Company; 3 km west of Elbing – from the 7th Panzer Division's Panzergrenadier Regiment 7, the Machine Gun Battalion "Vistula" and naval infantry from Naval Infantry Regiment 3's 311th Battalion; in Rogau – from the 37th Naval Infantry Battalion; in Schönau – from the 170th Infantry Division's Artillery Regiment 240. The prisoners indicated that up to 2,000 naval infantry soldiers arrived in Marienburg on 23 January 1945 from Wilhelmshafen. Naval Infantry Battalion 311 was moved from Marienburg to Elbing with the task to check the Russians' offensive. Elbing is being defended by a garrison that numbers up to 4,000 men.

Table 4.12: Status of the materiel of the German Fourth Army (Lage der panzerbrechenden Waffen – AOK 4) by the end of 1 February 1945

Units	Armored vehicles and anti-tank guns					Under repair and not yet written off		Irrecoverable	Total
	StuG	Tanks	SP guns	sPak 76.2 mm	sPak 75-mm	Short-term	Long-term		
1	2	3	4	5	6	7	8	9	10
XXVI Armee Korps									
Gruppe "Wagner"									
StuG Brigade 277	9	-	-	-	-	7	-	-	16
38(t)	-	1	-	-	-	4	-	-	5
Pz IV	-	1	-	-	-	3	-	-	4
Pz V	-	0	-	-	-	2	-	-	2
T-34	-	2	-	-	-	5	-	2	7
461.Infanterie Division	-	-	-	-	-	-	-	-	-
Panzer Kp. 10	2	-	-	-	-	-	-	-	2
38(t)	-	1	-	-	-	-	1	-	2
Radfahr-Jäger Brigade 10	-	-	-	-	4	-	-	-	4
28.Jäger Division	-	-	-	-	9	1	-	2	10
Pz.Jg. Kp. 1028	5	-	-	-	-	2	-	3	7
Panzer Kp. Lt. Groetzki	1	-	-	-	-	-	-	-	1
Pz III	-	1	-	-	-	-	1	-	2
Pz IV	-	1	-	-	-	-	-	-	1
Kampfgruppe von Einem	-	-	-	-	5	-	-	-	5
2 Bat., StuG Brigade 185	1	-	-	-	-	2	1	2	4
Pz.Rgt. 24 (10+11) Pz IV	-	14	-	-	-	5	1	-	20
1 Bat., Jg.Pz. Abt. 40	9	-	-	-	-	-	-	-	9
Total for XXVI Korps	27	23	-	-	18	31	4	9	103
VI Armee Korps									
170.Infanterie Division	-	-	-	-	11	-	-	2	11
Pz.Jg. Kp. 120	3	-	-	-	-	-	-	-	3
StuG Brigade 904	11	-	-	-	-	2	1	-	14

426 TANK BATTLES IN EAST PRUSSIA AND POLAND, 1944-1945

Units	Armored vehicles and anti-tank guns					Under repair and not yet written off		Irrecoverable	Total
	StuG	Tanks	SP guns	sPak 76.2 mm	sPak 75-mm	Short-term	Long-term		
1	2	3	4	5	6	7	8	9	10
Total for VI Korps	14	-	-	-	11	2	1	2	28
VII Panzer Korps									
558.Volksgrenadier Division	-	-	-	-	6	-	-	-	6
Pz.Jg. Kp. 1558	2	-	-	-	-	2	3	-	7
18.Panzergrenadier Division	-	-	-	-	3	-	-	-	3
Panzer Abt. 118	5	-	-	-	-	-	2	-	7
14.Infanterie Division	-	-	-	-	8	1	-	3	9
Pz.Jg. Kp. 1014	3	-	-	-	-	5	1	3	9
131.Infanterie Division	-	-	-	-	6	-	-	-	6
Pz.Jg. Kp. 1131	2	-	-	-	-	1	-	1	3
StuG Brigade 901	4	-	-	-	-	-	-	-	4
sPz.Jg. Abt. 563 Pz IV	-	1	-	-	-	-	-	-	1
Pz V	-	4	-	-	-	-	-	-	4
Total for VII Panzer Korps	16	5	-	-	23	9	6	7	59
XX Armee Korps									
102.Infanterie Division	-	-	-	-	12	1	-	-	13
Pz.Jg. Kp. 1102	5	-	-	-	-	-	-	-	5
Fest. Pak-Kp. 17/1	-	-	-	-	5	3	1	-	9
129.Infanterie Division	-	-	-	-	5	1	2	-	8
StuG Brigade 909	3	-	-	-	-	12	14	-	29
292.Infanterie Division	-	-	-	-	8	4	4	-	16
Pz.Jg. Kp. 1292	0	-	-	-	-	3	7	-	10
24.Panzer Division	-	-	-	-	7	-	-	-	7
3 Bat., StuG Brigade 185	2	-	-	-	-	3	2	1	7
StuG Brigade 209	3					14	2	3	19
Total for the XX Korps	13	-	-	-	37	41	32	4	123
LV Armee Korps									
203.Infanterie Division	-	-	-	-	2	1	2	-	5
Fest. Pak Verb 17/I	-	-	-	5	-	-	-	-	5
541.Volksgrenadier Division	-	-	-	-	3	1	1	4	5
4 Bat., StuG Brigade 920	2	-	-	-	-	1	2	-	5
Pz.Jg. Kp. 1541	1	-	-	-	-	1	-	12	2
Fest. Pak Kp.	-	-	-	7	-	-	-	-	7
	-	-	-	-	5	-	4	-	9
Kampfgruppe Hauser	-	-	-	-	22	3	7	-	32
StuG Kp. 500	3	-	-	-	-	-	5	1	8
Gruppe "Hannibal"	-	-	-	-	2	-	-	-	2
Total for the LV Korps	6	-	-	12	34	7	21	17	80
XXXXI Panzer Korps									

COMBAT OPERATIONS OF THE 5TH GUARDS TANK ARMY

Units	Armored vehicles and anti-tank guns					Under repair and not yet written off		Irrecoverable	Total
	StuG	Tanks	SP guns	sPak 76.2 mm	sPak 75-mm	Short-term	Long-term		
1	2	3	4	5	6	7	8	9	10
21.Infanterie Division	-	-	-	-	17	3	-	-	20
	1	-	-	-	-	-	1	-	2
StuG Brigade 259	15	-	-	-	-	9	7	-	31
50.Infanterie Division	-	-	-	-	11	-	-	-	11
Pz.Jg. Kp. 1150	-	2	-	-	-	-	1	-	3
	1	-	-	-	-	2	2	2	5
Gruppe "Blaurock"	-	-	-	-	13	1	-	-	14
Pz.Jg. Kp. 1156	5	-	-	-	-	4	1	-	10
Pz.Jg. Kp. 1349	5	-	-	-	-	5	2	-	12
StuG Brigade 203	7	-	-	-	-	10	1	-	18
Fest. Pak Kp. 7 and 8/VII	-	-	-	13	-	2	2	-	17
61.Infanterie Division	-	-	-	-	7	1	-	-	8
2 Bat., StuG Brigade 203	2	-	-	-	-	1	1	1	4
Total for XXXXI Panzer Korps	36	2	-	13	48	38	18	3	155
Panzer Korps *Hermann Göring*									
2.Division *Hermann Göring*	5	-	-	-	-	10	9	-	24
	-	-	-	-	5	4	-	-	9
StuG Abt. *Hermann Göring*	-	-	0	-	-	1	-	-	1
Pz.Jg. Abt. *Hermann Göring*	2	-	-	-	-	2	2	1	6
StuG Brigade 279	15	-	-	-	-	-	1	-	16
547.Volksgrenadier Division	-	-	-	-	8	-	-	-	8
1st Bat., StuG Brigade 185	0	-	-	-	-	3	3	-	6
Panzer Abt. 302	4	-	-	-	-	2	13	-	19
Division *Grossdeutschland*	-	-	-	-	7	2	2	-	11
	-	-	2	-	-	1	-	1	3
	-	-	-	4	--	-	-	-	4
StuG	2	-	-	-	-	6	13	1	22
Pz IV	-	0	-	-	-	-	6	-	6
Pz V	-	6	-	-	-	11	6	7	23
Pz VI	-	1	-	-	-	6	1	3	8
562.Volksgrenadier Division	-	-	-	-	7	1	-	-	8
Pz.Jg. Kp. 1562	2	-	-	-	-	2	1	-	5
Total for Panzer Korps HG	30	7	2	4	27	51	67	13	188
Total for Fourth Army	142	35	4	29	198	158	149	55	736

Excerpt from Combat Report No. 020 from the headquarters of the 5th Guards Tank Army at 20.45 on 2 February 1945:

The enemy on the Zallenfelde, Deutschendorf, north of Tiedmannsdorf, north of Tolkemit line was putting up stubborn resistance with fire to the actions of our units with units of the 170th Infantry Division, 28th Jäger Division, the 10th Motorized Brigade of the Panzergrenadier Division *Grossdeutschland*, the 24th Panzer Division, presumably Assault Gun Brigade 209, the 451st Reserve Regiment and the remnants of shattered, separate battalions, and with repeated counterattacks from Bordehnen, the Hensels estate, Lindwald and north of Tolkemit directions in strength of a battalion or regiment of infantry and 7-10 tanks attempted to throw our units back and breakthrough in the western and southwestern directions.

The forces of the 5th Guards Tank Army throughout the day of 2 February 1945 firmly held their occupied line and repulsed the enemy attacks of infantry, artillery and tanks that were striving to break out of the encirclement in the Elbing, Marienburg direction. In the course of the day, the troops fought off 17 enemy attacks.

The 29th Tank Corps (minus the 32nd Tank Brigade and 1223rd Light Self-propelled Artillery Regiment) is stubbornly defending its occupied line running from 500 meters east of Behlenhof to the western fringe of the woods 800 meters east of Karwitten; it repulsed 5 enemy attacks from out of the areas of Grossainen and Einhöfen in strength of an infantry regiment supported by 4-6 tanks and artillery. The damage done to the enemy: 3 guns destroyed and up to 200 enemy soldiers and officers. By 1900 on 2 February 1945, the corps' units were occupying the following position: 53rd Motorized Rifle Brigade – the Behlenhof, Karwitten line; the 31st Tank Brigade – in the first half of the day drove back enemy attacks from the Neu Teschen and Einhöfen areas, and since 1400 2 February 1945 has been in the Karwitten, Schlobitten railroad station area; the 25th Tank Brigade – is in the Angnitten area minus its tanks; the 32nd Tank Brigade and 1223rd Light Self-propelled Artillery Regiment are operationally subordinate to the 124th Rifle Corps. The corps' losses over 2 February 1945: 1 T-34 tank left burned out. The corps headquarters is in Angnitten.

The 47th Mechanized Brigade – at 1400 on 2 February 1945 was attacked by up to a battalion of enemy infantry and 3 self-propelled guns and fell back to the western outskirts of Karwinden. The casualties of the 47th Mechanized Brigade over the day of fighting: 40 killed and 30 wounded. Over this same period of time, 4 enemy guns, 13 machine guns and up to 350 enemy soldiers and officers were eliminated by the brigade. The brigade headquarters is in Schlobitten.

The 10th Tank Corps is occupying a defense on the Karwitten, fringe of woods 1 km south of Karwinden, fringe of woods 1 km west of Deutschendorf, Fürstenau line. In the course of the day of 2 February 1945, the corps fought off enemy attacks from out of the Hensels estate and Deutschendorf areas in strength of up to an infantry regiment supported by 5 tanks, 2 self-propelled guns, up to a regiment of artillery, and teams equipped with Panzerfausts. All of the attacks were repulsed. The damage done to the enemy: 1 tank and 1 self-propelled gun knocked out, 2 machine guns and 2 mortars destroyed, and up to 150 enemy soldiers and officers killed or wounded. The corps' losses: 1 T-34 tank knocked out, and 1 man killed and 2 men wounded. By 1900 on 2 February 1945, the corps' units are occupying the following positions: 178th Tank Brigade and the 1st Battalion of the 11th Motorized Rifle Brigade – in the Karwitten area in the corps commander's reserve; the 186th Tank Brigade – is holding a defense running from the northern fringe of woods 1 km south of Karwinden to Breunken; together with the 47th Mechanized Brigade, it was repulsing enemy attacks from out of the Hensels estate area; 183rd Tank Brigade – fringe of woods 1 km west of Deutschendorf to Fürstenau; 11th Motorized Rifle Brigade and the 326th Heavy Self-propelled Artillery Regiment and 287th Mortar Regiment – woods southwest of Fürstenau. The corps headquarters is in Nikolaiken.

The 42nd Rifle Corps in the course of the day was stubbornly holding its occupied lines, conducting reinforced reconnaissance probes, and repulsing fierce enemy attacks in strength of up to 800 soldiers supported by tanks and self-propelled guns. At 0700 on 2 February 1945 the enemy attacked the 137th Rifle Division with a force of up to 800 men supported by 7 tanks from the directions of the Lindwald estate and the woods 2 km east of Klein Rautenberg. The fighting continued until 1300. The enemy, having lost up to 400 men killed or wounded, fell back to their jumping-off position. In the Tolkemit area on the morning of 2 February 1945, the enemy repeatedly attacked elements of the 170th Rifle Division and at 1700 combat was continuing on the northeastern outskirts of Tolkemit.

Observers spotted an aggregation of up to two regiments of enemy infantry and 13 tanks in the Deutschendorf – Lauck area. Simultaneously this group attempted to break out to the west, but it was thrown back to its jumping-off position. By 1900 on 2 February 1945, the corps' formations were occupying the following positions: 399th Rifle Division – Muttersegen farmstead, eastern fringe of the woods 1 km west of Deutschendorf, Fürstenau; 137th Rifle Division – Fürstenau, Borchertswald, Tiedmannsdorf, Groß Rautenberg, Schafsberg; 170th Rifle Division – with one regiment is defending the Rahnenfeld, Kreuzdorf line; with a second regiment in the course of the day of 2 February 1945 was repulsing enemy attacks on the northeastern outskirts of Tolkemit, Neuendorf line; with a third regiment, is in the Mühlhausen area. Casualties: 399th Rifle Division – 2 killed, 9 wounded; 137th Rifle Division – 12 killed, 19 wounded; 170th Rifle Division – 4 killed, 10 wounded. Losses inflicted on the enemy: up to 600 soldiers and officers killed; 6 tanks left burned-out; and up to 12 soldiers taken prisoner. The corps headquarters is in Herrndorf.

Commander of the 5th Guards Tank Army Guards Major General of Tank Forces V.T VOL'SKY
Military Council Member Guards Major General of Tank Forces GRISHIN
Chief of staff of the 5th Guards Tank Army Guards Major General of Tank Forces SIDOROVICH

During the day of 2 February 1945 the 2nd Shock Army captured 150 prisoners in the following areas: north of Elbing – from the East Prussian 1st Infantry Division's reconnaissance battalion; 3 km northwest of Elbing – from the 311th Naval Infantry Battalion; 4 km west of Elbing – from the 7th Panzer Division's Artillery Regiment 78; south of Elbing – from the 170th Infantry Division's 240th Reserve Training Battalion; in the Grunau area (southeast of Elbing) – from the 7th Panzer Division's Panzergrenadier Regiment 6 and the 170th Infantry Division's Infantry Regiment 391.

In the rear of our forces in the area 10 km southwest of Preußisch Holland, the commander of the 170th Infantry Division's Infantry Regiment 391 Oberstleutnant Hans Klausen was taken prisoner; under interrogation, he revealed that on 21 January all of the 170th Infantry Division's regiments had been assembled in the area east of Armsdorf. The division received the assignment to attack in the western direction with the aim of creating a corridor for a link-up with German units at the Vistula River. The 131st Infantry Division and 28th Jäger Division were operating with a similar assignment. In the prisoner's opinion, the reason for the failure was the lengthy march and the absence of reserves. Infantry Regiment 391 had been advancing in the division's vanguard and was completely destroyed. The reasons for this: the poor weather conditions, the soldiers' exhaustion, and the Russians' constant flanking attacks. The regiment commander, in view of the hopelessness of the situation, made the decision to give his subordinates the right to break out independently to the west, or to the east toward the 170th Infantry Division's other units.

The captured commander of the 311th Naval Infantry Battalion Major Richard Rost testified that the 311th Naval Infantry Battalion was part of Naval Infantry Regiment 3 (and the latter was part of Naval Infantry Brigade "Nord"). Naval Infantry Regiment 3 included the 309th, 311th and 315th Naval Infantry Battalions. The 312th Naval Infantry Battalion was operating in the Elbing area. The 310th Naval Infantry Battalion is located in the Wilhelmshafen area. Naval Infantry Brigade "Nord" includes Naval Infantry Regiments 1, 2, 3 and 4. Regiments 1, 2 and 4 are located in Germany and are being employed for coastal protection. At present Naval Infantry Regiment 3 is subordinate to the 7th Panzer Division. Up until 26 January the elements of Naval Infantry Regiment 3 were occupying a defense along the Nogat River in the Groß Mausdorf – Marienburg sector. On 26 January, the 309th and 311th Naval Infantry Battalions were replaced by elements of the 7th Panzer Division and sent to the Einlage area (7 km northwest of Elbing). The 311th Battalion consists of three companies with a total strength of up to 200 men. The 531st Naval Artillery Battalion is operating in the Lindenowo area (11 km northeast of Marienburg). Prisoners of II/Panzergrenadier Regiment 6 of the 7th Panzer Division revealed that the regiment had been shifted on 30 January from Dirschau to the area southeast of Elbing with the task to counterattack the Russian units in the eastern direction. On 1 February II/Panzergrenadier Regiment 6 together with the 7th Panzer Division's reconnaissance battalion is defending on the southeastern outskirts of Elbing. Panzergrenadier Regiment 7 since 27 January has been operating west of Elbing. Panzergrenadier Regiment 6 consists of two battalions. The II Battalion has a total strength of up to 400 men. Units of the 7th Panzer Division, remnants of the 170th Infantry Division's Infantry Regiment 391, the 312th Naval Infantry Battalion, naval batteries, airfield service units and an artillery battalion (four batteries of 105mm and 150mm howitzers) are defending in the Elbing area. Buildings on the city's outskirts have been adapted for a defense. Prisoners from Infantry Regiment 391's 1st, 2nd, 3rd and 5th Companies and the 170th Infantry Division's 240th Training Reserve Battalion indicated that separate groups from shattered units of the 170th Infantry Division were breaking through to Elbing from the east and had been destroyed in the process.

Hero of the Soviet Union General of the Army I.F. Ivanovsky recalls:

> On the morning of 2 February 1945 when it was still dark, we reached a line 1300 meters northwest of Stollen. Having spotted our tanks, the Germans opened fire out of ambush positions. One of the IS tanks burst into flames. Having encountered heavy artillery and machine-gun fire, our motorized riflemen were also unable to advance. The infantry was pinned down. The tanks, in order not to become separated from them, stopped and opened fire from fixed positions. The situation was murky. It was necessary to organize close reconnaissance. I made contact over the radio with the commander of a company of heavy tanks Captain Tishchenko and issued him orders to carry out this task. He implemented the order not only efficiently, but also creatively. A man of few words, by appearance somewhat phlegmatic, Iakim Tishchenko was in fact a highly aggressive officer. I only suggested to him in one phrase: "Draw upon the neighbors", and he, having taken the advice, made a sensible decision. Together with the commander of the rifle battalion, with whom he was cooperating, Captain Tishchenko organized three reconnaissance groups for the close reconnaissance. Just 30-40 minutes later they had already returned with reliable information about the strength and positions of the enemy blocking detachments. The heavy tanks opened direct fire at the targets. Several tanks moved up along a ravine. Their fire from close range was even more effective.

Table 4.13: Manpower of the German Fourth Army (AOK 4) on 2 February 1945

		Combat Infanterie	Total personnel
XXVI Armee Korps	Arko 302	2690	3360
	Radfahr-Jäger Brigade 10	1535	3531
	Regiment Stahblak	1962	2217
	Kampfgruppe von Einem	1070	2411
VI Armee Korps	28.Jäger Division	3092	10590
	170.Infanterie Division	1370	6400
VII Panzer Korps	14.Infanterie Division	1510	4068
	131.Infanterie Division	1389	7396
	18.Panzergrenadier Division	2257	2963
	558.Volksgrenadier Division	2651	No data
	StuG Abt. AOK 4	343	456
XX Armee Korps	24.Panzer Division	1700	No data
	129.Infanterie Division	450	No data
	102.Infanterie Division	1902	No data
	292.Infanterie Division	737	No data
XXXXI Panzer Korps	21.Infanterie Division	3761	12044
	50.Infanterie Division	3354	10733
	61.Infanterie Division	2184	7898
	Gruppe Blaurock	3864	12400
LV Armee Korps	203.Infanterie Division	1629	No data
	541.Volksgrenadier Division	2986	No data
	Kampfgruppe Hauser	2120	No data

Table 4.14: Status of the materiel of the German Fourth Army (Lage der panzerbrechenden Waffen – AOK 4) by the end of 2 February 1945

Units	Armored vehicles and anti-tank guns					Under repair and not yet written off		Irrecoverable	Total
	StuG	Tanks	SP guns	sPak 76.2 mm	sPak 75-mm	Short-term	Long-term		
1	2	3	4	5	6	7	8	9	10
XXVI Armee Korps									
Gruppe "Wagner"									
StuG Brigade 277	10	-	-	-	-	3	-	3	13
38(t)	-	1	-	-	-	4	-	-	5
T-34	-	1	-	-	-	3	1	2	5
461.Infanterie Division	-	-	-	-	-	-	-	-	-
Panzer Kp. 10	2	-	-	-	-	-	-	-	2
38(t)	-	2	-	-	-	-	-	-	2
Pz IV	-	-	-	-	-	-	1	-	1
Pz V	-	-	-	-	-	-	1	-	1
T-34	-	1	-	-	-	-	-	-	1
Radfahr-Jäger Brigade 10	-	-	-	-	4	-	-	-	4
38(t)	-	1	-	-	-	-	1	1	2
Total for XXVI Korps	12	6	-	-	4	10	4	6	36
VI Armee Korps									

432 TANK BATTLES IN EAST PRUSSIA AND POLAND, 1944-1945

Units	Armored vehicles and anti-tank guns					Under repair and not yet written off		Irrecoverable	Total
	StuG	Tanks	SP guns	sPak 76.2 mm	sPak 75-mm	Short-term	Long-term		
1	2	3	4	5	6	7	8	9	10
28.Jäger Division	-	-	-	-	9	1	-	-	10
Pz.Jg. Kp. 1028	4	-	-	-	-	2	1	-	7
Panzer Kp. Lt. Groetzki	-	-	-	-	-	1	-	-	1
Pz III	-	1	-	-	-	-	1	-	2
Pz IV	-	1	-	-	-	-	-	-	1
Kampfgruppe von Einem	-	-	-	-	5	-	-	-	5
2 Bat., StuG Brigade 185	1	-	-	-	-	2	1	-	4
Pz.Rgt. 24 (10+11) Pz IV	-	16	-	-	-	3	1	-	20
1 Bat., Jg.Pz. Abt. 40	9	-	-	-	-	-	-	-	9
170.Infanterie Division	-	-	-	-	9	-	-	-	9
Pz.Jg. Kp. 120	3	-	-	-	-	-	-	-	3
StuG Brigade 904	10	-	-	-	-	2	2	-	14
Total for VI Korps	27	18	-	-	23	11	6	-	85
VII Panzer Korps									
558.Volksgrenadier Division	-	-	-	-	6	-	-	-	6
Pz.Jg. Kp. 1558	2	-	-	-	-	2	3	-	7
18.Panzergrenadier Division	-	-	-	-	3	-	-	-	3
Panzer Abt. 118	4	-	-	-	-	1	1	1	6
14.Infanterie Division	-	-	-	-	8	1	-	-	9
Pz.Jg. Kp. 1014	3	-	-	-	-	5	1	-	9
131.Infanterie Division	-	-	-	-	6	-	-	-	6
Pz.Jg. Kp. 1131	2	-	-	-	-	1	-	-	3
StuG Brigade 901	4	-	-	-	-	-	-	-	4
sPz.Jg. Abt. 563 Pz IV	-	1	-	-	-	-	-	-	1
Pz V	-	4	-	-	-	-	-	-	4
Total for VII Panzer Korps	15	5	-	-	23	10	5	1	58
XX Armee Korps									
102.Infanterie Division	-	-	-	-	12	1	-	-	13
Pz.Jg. Kp. 1102	4	-	-	-	-	-	1	-	5
Fest. Pak-Kp. 17/1	-	-	-	-	1	3	1	4	5
129.Infanterie Division	-	-	-	-	5	1	2	2	8
StuG Brigade 909	7	-	-	-	-	8	14	-	29
292.Infanterie Division	-	-	-	-	8	4	4	6	16
Pz.Jg. Kp. 1292	0	-	-	-	-	-	-	10	0
24.Panzer Division	-	-	-	-	7	-	-	-	7
88-mm	-	-	-	-	4	-	-	-	4
	-	-	-	7	-	-	-	-	7
3 Bat., StuG Brigade 185	1	-	-	-	-	1	-	5	2

Units	Armored vehicles and anti-tank guns					Under repair and not yet written off		Irrecoverable	Total
	StuG	Tanks	SP guns	sPak 76.2 mm	sPak 75-mm	Short-term	Long-term		
1	2	3	4	5	6	7	8	9	10
StuG Brigade 209	7	-	-	-	-	5	5	2	17
Total for the XX Korps	19	-	-	7	37	23	27	29	113
LV Armee Korps									
203.Infanterie Division	-	-	-	-	2	1	2	-	5
Fest. Pak Verb 17/I	-	-	-	5	-	-	-	-	5
541.Volksgrenadier Division	-	-	-	-	3	1	1	-	5
	2	-	-	-	-	1	2	-	5
4 Bat., StuG Brigade 920 Pz.Jg. Kp. 1541	1	-	-	-	-	1	-	-	2
Fest. Pak Kp.	-	-	-	7	-	-	-	-	7
	-	-	-	-	5	-	4	-	9
Kampgruppe Hauser	-	-	-	-	22	3	7	-	32
StuG Kp. 500	3	-	-	-	-	-	5	-	8
Gruppe "Hannibal"	-	-	-	-	2	-	-	-	2
Total for the LV Korps	6	-	-	12	34	7	21	-	80
XXXXI Panzer Korps									
21.Infanterie Division	-	-	-	-	17	3	-	-	20
	1	-	-	-	-	-	1	-	2
StuG Brigade 259	20	-	-	-	-	10	1	-	31
50.Infanterie Division	-	-	-	-	9	2	-	-	11
Pz.Jg. Kp. 1150	-	-	2	-	-	-	1	-	3
	2	-	-	-	-	1	4	-	7
Gruppe "Blaurock"	-	-	-	-	13	1	-	-	14
Pz.Jg. Kp. 1156	5	-	-	-	-	4	1	-	10
Pz.Jg. Kp. 1349	5	-	-	-	-	5	2	-	12
StuG Brigade 203	9	-	-	-	-	8	1	-	18
Fest. Pak Kp. 7 and 8/VII	-	-	-	13	-	2	2	-	17
61 Infanterie Division	-	-	-	-	7	1	-	-	8
2 Bat., StuG Brigade 203	2	-	-	-	-	1	1	-	4
Total for XXXXI Panzer Korps	44	-	2	13	46	38	14	-	157
Panzer Korps *Hermann Göring*									
Division *Grossdeutschland*	-	-	-	-	-	-	-	-	-
	-	-	-	-	3	4	4	-	11
	-	-	2	-	-	1	-	-	3
StuG	2	-	-	-	-	6	13	-	21
Pz IV	-	1	-	-	-	-	2	3	3
Pz V	-	6	-	-	-	-	8	11	14
Pz VI	-	1	-	-	-	7	-	-	8

Units	Armored vehicles and anti-tank guns					Under repair and not yet written off		Irrecoverable	Total
	StuG	Tanks	SP guns	sPak 76.2 mm	sPak 75-mm	Short-term	Long-term		
1	2	3	4	5	6	7	8	9	10
2.Division *Hermann Göring*	7	-	-	-	-	10	17	-	34
	-	-	-	-	6	3	-	-	9
	-	-	0	-	-	-	1	-	1
Pz.Jg. Abt. *Hermann Göring*	3	-	-	-	-	1	2	-	6
StuG Brigade 279	5	-	-	-	-	3	8	-	16
StuG Abt. *Hermann Göring*	0	-	-	-	-	1	-	-	1
547.Volksgrenadier Division	-	-	-	-	8	-	-	-	8
1st Bat., StuG Brigade 185	4	-	-	-	-	2	-	-	6
562.Volksgrenadier Division	-	-	-	-	9	-	-	-	9
	-	-	-	4	-	-	-	-	4
Pz.Jg. Kp. 1562	3	-	-	-	-	1	1	-	5
Panzer Abt. 302	3	-	-	-	-	4	-	14	7
Total for Panzer Korps HG	27	8	2	4	26	52	47	28	166
Total for Fourth Army	150	37	4	36	193	144	124	64	695

Excerpt from Combat Report No. 021 from the headquarters of the 5th Guards Tank Army at 2045 on 3 February 1945:

The enemy in the areas northeast of Preußisch Holland throughout the day of 3 February 1945 was putting up tough resistance to our units' offensive with heavy artillery and mortar fire and counterattacks by infantry and tanks, and was continuing to hold the occupied line. On the coastline of the Frisches Haff the enemy, having reinforced the sector south of Frauenburg and Tolkemit with unidentified units, was fighting for possession of Tolkemit with infantry and tanks, striving to break out to the south.

The forces of the 5th Guards Tank Army in the course of the day of 3 February 1945 were engaged in heavy offensive fighting against enemy infantry, tanks and artillery, while simultaneously repulsing the counterattacks of the enemy that was striving to break out in the western direction. By 1900 on 3 February 1945, the corps' units were occupying the following positions: 25th Tank Brigade – from 1300 on 3 February 1945 was occupying a defense in the area 500 meters west of the Behlenhof estate; at 1800 on 3 February it moved out from its occupied area to the Neukirch-Höhe area for actions in a northern direction; the 31st Tank Brigade was defending the area 1 km east of Karwitten and Stopen; the 53rd Motorized Rifle Brigade is defending a line running from a point west of Behlenhof to the cemetery 2 km north of Behlenhof; the 32nd Tank Brigade with the 1223rd Self-propelled Artillery Regiment, the 14th Guards Heavy Tank Regiment and the 376th Heavy Self-propelled Artillery Regiment are operationally subordinate to the commander of the 124th Rifle Corps. The corps headquarters is in Angnitten.

The 10th Tank Corps since 1000 on 3 February 1945 following an artillery preparation attacked the enemy in the direction of Deutschendorf, while simultaneously counterattacked by the enemy from the area south of Deutschendorf in a force of 600 infantry soldiers and 12 self-propelled guns and tanks, and throughout the entire day was repulsing the enemy counterattacks, inflicted heavy losses to the Germans. At 1900 on 3 February 1945 the corps' units are occupying the following positions: the 178th Tank Brigade spent the night turning over its area of defense to the 29th Tank Corps' 31st Tank Brigade and by 1900 3 February 1945 was assembled in the woods 300 meters east of Schönfeld; the 186th Tank Brigade is occupying a defense on the Karwitten – Schlobitten railroad station line; the 183rd Tank Brigade with two batteries of the 689th Destroyer Antitank Artillery Regiment was repulsing enemy counterattacks from the Deutschendorf area on a line stretching from 1 km west of Deutschendorf to the eastern outskirts of Fürstenau; the 11th Motorized Rifle Brigade with the 326th Heavy Self-propelled Artillery Regiment and the 287th Mortar Regiment was stubbornly their occupied line from the woods 1 km west of Deutschendorf to Fürstenau.

As a result of the fighting on 3 February 1945, the 10th Tank Corps lost 2 SU-85 destroyed and 1 SU-85 knocked out; and 1 man killed and 12 wounded. The damage done to the enemy: up to 200 soldiers and officers killed or wounded; 2 self-propelled guns destroyed; 2 vehicles and 3 heavy machine guns knocked-out. The corps headquarters is in Nikolaiken.

The 47th Mechanized Brigade in the course of 3 February 1945 was repulsing frenzied enemy counterattacks from out of the Karwinden area and killed up to 150 enemy soldiers and officers while destroying 2 tanks. Its own losses are being ascertained. The brigade is occupying a line extending from the northern fringe of woods 1 km south of Karwinden to 500 meters west of Karwinden.

The 42nd Rifle Corps in the course of 3 February 1945 was holding its previous line; its units and formations were conducting increased observation over the enemy's actions, repulsing violent attacks by the Germans, who were trying to break out of encirclement in the western direction. On 3 February 1945 the enemy out of the Deutschendorf and Lauck area twice counterattacked the 1345th Rifle Regiment and units of the 10th Tank Corps in strength of up to 600 infantry soldiers supported by 12 tanks and self-propelled guns. The enemy's attacks were driven back. In the Tolkemit area, for two straight days the enemy launched incessant attacks against the 331st Rifle Regiment in strength from a battalion to a regiment of infantry supported by self-propelled guns. Having a superiority in force, by 1500 on 3 February 1945 the Germans captured the northern portion of Tolkemit.

Throughout the day, observers spotted an aggregation of enemy infantry and tanks in the Deutschendorf, Lauck, Braunsburg and Luisenthal areas. By 1900 on 3 February 1945 the corps' units were occupying the following positions: 399th Rifle Division – Muttersegen, eastern fringe of the woods 1 km west of Deutschendorf, Fürstenau; 137th Rifle Division – Fürstenau, Borchertsdorfwald, Tiedmannsdorf, Groß Rautenburg; 170th Rifle Division – with one regiment in the Mühlhausen area, with two regiments in the course of two days of incessant fighting and repeated enemy attacks in strength from a battalion to a regiment of infantry supported by tanks and self-propelled guns, yielded the northern portion of Tolkemit; since 1800 on 3 February it has been fighting to regain the positions. The corps' casualties: 14 killed and 52 wounded. Equipment losses: 1 heavy machinegun and 2 radio sets. Damage done to the enemy: up to 1,000 enemy soldiers and officers killed or wounded; 5 self-propelled guns, 3 machine guns and up to 30 wagons knocked-out. The corps headquarters is in Herrndorf.

The units directly subordinate to the army headquarters: the 651st Cannon Artillery Regiment is supporting the 53rd Motorized Rifle Brigade from firing positions in the Angnitten area and 3 km east of there; the 1619th Light Artillery Regiment and 31st Tank Brigade are in firing positions at the crossroads 1 km southeast of the Schlobitten railroad station; the 1315th Light Artillery Regiment and 47th Mechanized Brigade are in firing positions in the Schlobitten area; the 76th Guards Mortar Regiment is in the wooded area 800 meters south of Koppeln; the 14th

Guards Heavy Tank Regiment and 376th Heavy Self-propelled Artillery Regiment with the 32nd Tank Brigade are operationally subordinate to the 124th Rifle Corps; the 326th Heavy Self-propelled Artillery Regiment is in firing positions in the wooded area 1.5 km southeast of Neumark; the 6th Anti-aircraft Artillery Division: 146th Anti-aircraft Artillery Regiment is covering the 47th Mechanized Brigade with firing positions in the Schlobitten area; 366th Anti-aircraft Artillery Regiment is covering the 29th Tank Corps with firing positions in the Warnikam, Teschenwalde area; 516th Anti-aircraft Artillery Regiment is covering the army's command post in the Weeskenhof area; the 1062nd Anti-aircraft Artillery Regiment is in firing positions in the Preußisch Holland area. The 72nd Guards Special Purpose Naval Battalion – with the arrival of the 29th Tank Corps' units in the Tolkemit area is passing to the operational control of the corps commander. By 1700 on 3 February 1945 it was assembled in the Neukirch-Höhe area. The 41st Cannon Artillery Regiment by 1700 on 3 February 1945 was assembled in the Neukirch-Höhe area. The army headquarters' operational command group is in Weeskenhof.

Commander of the 5th Guards Tank Army Guards Major General of Tank Forces V.T. VOL'SKY
Military Council Member Guards Major General of Tank Forces GRISHIN
Chief of staff of the 5th Guards Tank Army Guards Major General of Tank Forces SIDOROVICH

From the "Combat Path of the 5th Guards Tank Army":

Convinced in the hopelessness of the attempts to break through in the direction of Marienburg, the German command on 3 February launched an attack along the coastline of the Frisches Haff toward Tolkemit. Simultaneously up to a regiment of infantry, which had crossed the spit of the Frische Nehrung, also undertook at attack toward Tolkemit. Enjoying a superiority in strength and means, the hostile forces shoved back our rifle units, took Tolkemit, and began to advance along the coastline to the southwest. The threat of an enemy breakthrough to Elbing had arisen.

The army commander moved up the 29th Tank Corps and 42nd Rifle Corps to meet the attacking enemy grouping. The 25th Tank Brigade was the first to close on Tolkemit and it attacked the enemy from the march. By evening the town had been liberated. Continuing to throw the Nazis back to the northeast, the 29th Tank Corps on 5 February approached Frauenburg. A day later the 10th Tank Corps, together with the 47th Mechanized Brigade and formations of the 48th Army, having worn down the enemy and having moved out in the direction of Preußisch Holland, threw the Germans back to the right bank of the Passarge River.

To the Commander-in-Chief of the 2nd Belorussian Front by Coded Telegram No. 2550 from 3 February 1945:

I am reporting that as of 3 February 1945, the army has the following combat strength:

Designation of formations and units	Officers	Non-commissioned officers	Rank and file	Total	Tanks	Self-propelled guns
29th Tank Corps						
25th Tank Brigade	188	548	346	1122	6	-
31st Tank Brigade	222	416	444	1082	6	8
32nd Tank Brigade	236	556	463	1255	8	10
53rd Motorized Rifle Brigade	255	657	867	1779	-	8
Total for the corps, including the brigades	1640	3505	4298	9443	28	46

Designation of formations and units	Officers	Non-commissioned officers	Rank and file	Total	Tanks	Self-propelled guns
10th Tank Corps						
178th Tank Brigade	215	370	400	985	10	-
183rd Tank Brigade	196	375	457	1029	10	-
186th Tank Brigade	215	272	502	1089	-	-
11th Motorized Rifle Brigade	230	595	1291	2116	-	-
Total for the corps, including the brigades	1496	2888	5098	9482	27	43
Units directly subordinate to Army Headquarters						
47th Mechanized Brigade	335	945	1404	2384	7	-
Total for the army-level units, including the brigade	1066	3208	5539	9813	30	4
Total for the 5th Tank Army	4202	9601	14935	28738	85	93

Personnel losses (killed, wounded and missing-in-action)

	Officers	Non-commissioned officers	Rank and file	Total
29th Tank Corps	161	572	1220	1953
10th Tank Corps	179	466	854	1499
47th Mechanized Brigade	60	341	644	1045
Total for the 5th Tank Army	461	1495	2926	4881

Losses of tanks and self-propelled guns

	Irrecoverable losses		Needing repair					
			Factory repair		Light overhaul		Minor repair	
	Tanks	Self-propelled guns	Tanks	Self-propelled guns	Tanks	Self-propelled guns	Tanks	Self-propelled guns
29th Tank Corps	40	17	26	5	30	27	11	12
10th Tank Corps	41	29	12	10	13	16	24	7
47th Mechanized Brigade	26	-	1	-	4	-	6	-
Total for the army, including units directly subordinate to headquarters	114	49	42	16	55	51	44	26

Commander of the 5th Guards Tank Army Guards Major General of Tank Forces V.T. VOL'SKY
Military Council Member Guards Major General of Tank Forces GRISHIN
Chief of staff of the 5th Guards Tank Army Guards Major General of Tank Forces SIDOROVICH

Table 4.16: Status of the materiel of the German Fourth Army (Lage der panzerbrechenden Waffen – AOK 4) by the end of 3 February 1945

Units	Armored vehicles and anti-tank guns					Under repair and not yet written off		Irrecoverable	Total
	StuG	Tanks	SP guns	sPak 76.2 mm	sPak 75-mm	Short-term	Long-term		
1	2	3	4	5	6	7	8	9	10
XXVI Armee Korps									
Gruppe "Wagner"									
StuG Brigade 277	10	-	-	-	-	3	-	-	13
38(t)	-	1	-	-	-	4	-	-	5
T-34	-	1	-	-	-	3	1	-	5
Panzer Kp. 10	2	-	-	-	-	-	-	-	2
38(t)	-	2	-	-	-	-	-	-	2
Pz IV	-	0	-	-	-	-	1	-	1
Pz V	-	0	-	-	-	-	1	-	1
T-34	-	1	-	-	-	-	-	-	1
Radfahr-Jäger Brigade 10	-	-	-	-	4	-	-	-	4
Pz-IV	-	0	-	-	-	1	-	-	1
38(t)	-	0	-	-	-	2	-	-	2
Total for XXVI Korps	12	5	-	-	4	13	3	-	37
VI Armee Korps									
28.Jäger Division	-	-	-	-	9	1	-	-	10
Pz.Jg. Kp. 1028	4	-	-	-	-	2	1	-	7
Panzer Kp. Lt. Groetzki									
Pz III	-	-	-	-	-	1	-	-	1
Pz IV	-	1	-	-	-	-	1	-	2
	-	1	-	-	-	-	-	-	1
Kampfgruppe von Einem	-	-	-	-	5	-	-	-	5
2 Bat., StuG Brigade 185	1	-	-	-	-	2	1	-	4
Pz.Rgt. 24 (10+11) Pz IV	-	17	-	-	-	3	-	-	20
1 Bat., Jg.Pz. Abt. 40	-	2	-	-	-	-	-	-	2
	5	-	-	-	-	1	3	-	9
170.Infanterie Division	-	-	-	-	-	-	-	-	-
Pz.Jg. Kp. 120	-	-	-	-	2	-	-	7	2
StuG Brigade 904	9	-	-	-	-	-	-	-	9
Total for VI Korps	19	21	-	-	16	10	6	7	72
VII Panzer Korps									
558.Volksgrenadier Division	-	-	-	-	3	1	-	2	4
Pz.Jg. Kp. 1558	4	-	-	-	-	1	1	1	6
18.Panzergrenadier Division	-	-	-	-	2	-	-	1	2
Panzer Abt. 118	5	-	-	-	-	1	-	-	6
14.Infanterie Division	-	-	-	-	8	1	-	-	9
Pz.Jg. Kp. 1014	6	-	-	-	-	-	-	-	6

COMBAT OPERATIONS OF THE 5TH GUARDS TANK ARMY

Units	Armored vehicles and anti-tank guns					Under repair and not yet written off		Irrecoverable	Total
	StuG	Tanks	SP guns	sPak 76.2 mm	sPak 75-mm	Short-term	Long-term		
1	2	3	4	5	6	7	8	9	10
131.Infanterie Division	-	-	-	-	6	-	-	-	6
Pz V	-	1	-	-	-	-	-	-	1
Pz.Jg. Kp. 1131	2	-	-	-	-	1	-	-	3
StuG Brigade 901	0	-	-	-	-	4	-	-	4
sPz.Jg. Abt. 563 Pz IV	-	0	-	-	-	2	-	-	2
Pz V	-	3	-	-	-	2	-	-	5
Total for VII Panzer Korps	17	4	-	-	22	13	1	4	57
XX Armee Korps									
102.Infanterie Division	-	-	-	-	12	1	-	-	13
Pz.Jg. Kp. 1102	4	-	-	-	-	-	1	-	5
Fest. Pak-Kp. 17/1	-	-	-	-	1	3	1	4	5
129.Infanterie Division	-	-	-	-	5	1	2	2	8
StuG Brigade 909	6	-	-	-	-	4	-	-	10
292.Infanterie Division	-	-	-	-	8	4	4	-	16
Pz.Jg. Kp. 1292	0	-	-	-	-	-	-	10	0
StuG Brigade 209	7	-	-	-	-	10	-	-	17
24.Panzer Division	-	-	-	-	7	-	-	-	7
88-mm	-	-	-	-	4	-	-	-	4
	-	-	-	7	-	-	-	-	7
3rd Bat., StuG Brigade 185	1	-	-	-	-	1	-	5	2
Total for the XX Korps	18	-	-	7	37	24	8	-	94
LV Armee Korps									
203 Infanterie Division	-	-	-	-	2	1	2	-	5
Fest. Pak Verb 17/I	-	-	-	5	-	-	-	-	5
541 Volksgrenadier Division	-	-	-	-	3	1	1	-	5
4 Bat., StuG Brigade 920	2	-	-	-	-	1	2	-	5
Pz.Jg. Kp. 1541	1	-	-	-	-	1	-	-	2
Fest. Pak Kp.	-	-	-	7	-	-	-	-	7
	-	-	-	-	5	-	4	-	9
Kampgruppe Hauser	-	-	-	-	22	3	7	-	32
StuG Kp. 500	3	-	-	-	-	-	5	-	8
Gruppe "Hannibal"	-	-	-	-	2	-	-	-	2
Total for the LV Army Corps	6	-	-	12	34	7	21	-	80
XXXXI Panzer Corps									
21 Infanterie Division	-	-	-	-	17	3	-	-	20
	1	-	-	-	-	-	1	-	2

Units	Armored vehicles and anti-tank guns					Under repair and not yet written off		Irrecoverable	Total
	StuG	Tanks	SP guns	sPak 76.2 mm	sPak 75-mm	Short-term	Long-term		
1	2	3	4	5	6	7	8	9	10
StuG Brigade 259	20	-	-	-	-	10	1	-	31
50 Infanterie Division	-	-	-	-	9	2	-	-	11
Pz.Jg. Kp. 1150	-	-	2	-	-	-	1	-	3
	2	-	-	-	-	1	4	-	7
Group "Blaurock"	-	-	-	-	14	-	-	-	14
Pz.Jg. Kp. 1156	17	-	-	-	-	-	-	-	17
Pz.Jg. Kp. 1349									
StuG Brigade 203									
Fest. Pak Kp. 7 and 8/VII	-	-	-	13	-	-	-	-	17
61 Infanterie Division	-	-	-	-	7	1	-	-	8
	-	-	3	-	-	-	-	-	3
2 Bat., StuG Brigade 203	4	-	-	-	-	-	-	-	4
Total for XXXXI Panzer Corps	44	-	5	13	47	17	7	-	133
Panzer Corps *Hermann Göring*									
Division *Grossdeutschland*	-	-	-	-	-	-	-	-	-
	-	-	-	-	3	4	4	-	11
	-	-	2	-	-	1	-	-	3
StuG	2	-	-	-	-	6	13	-	21
Pz IV	-	1	-	-	-	1	2	-	4
Pz V	-	5	-	-	-	-	10	-	15
Pz VI	-	1	-	-	-	7	-	-	8
2 Division *Hermann Göring*	5	-	-	-	-	12	17	-	34
Pz.Jg. Abt. *Hermann Göring*	-	-	-	-	6	3	-	-	9
	-	-	0	-	-	-	1	-	1
StuG Brigade 279	3	-	-	-	-	2	2	-	7
StuG Abt. *Hermann Göring*	7	-	-	-	-	5	2	2	14
	0	-	-	-	-	1	-	-	1
547 Volksgrenadier Division	-	-	-	-	8	-	-	-	8
1st Bat., StuG Brigade 185	5	-	-	-	-	1	-	-	6
562 Volksgrendadier Division	-	-	-	-	9	-	-	-	9
Pz.Jg. Kp. 1562	2	-	-	-	-	2	1	-	5
Fest. Pak Kp. 16/1	-	-	-	4	-	-	-	-	4
Panzer Abt. 302	2	-	-	-	-	5	-	-	7
Total for Panzer Corps HG	26	7	2	4	26	50	51	2	166
Total for Fourth Army	142	37	7	36	186	134	97	13	639

On 3 February 1945 45 prisoners were taken in the following areas: 3 km southeast of Preußisch Holland from I/Infantry Regiment 399 of the 170th Infantry Division; the western outskirts of Elbing – from the 1561st Pioneer Battalion; northwest of Elbing – from the 561st Volksgrenadier Division's Regiment 1142; Hoppenau (10 km southwest of Elbing) – from Machine Gun Battalion "Pregel"; and on the northwestern outskirts of Marienburg – from the 2nd Luftwaffe Training Battalion.

A captured adjutant of the 170th Infantry Division's I/Infantry Regiment 399 testified that his regiment was advancing in the 170th Infantry Division's second echelon; the 170th Infantry Division's fusilier battalion was operating on the right, but their left flank was hanging in the air. On 31 January 1945 I/Infantry Regiment 399 went over to a defense and spent the next two days defending Greißings (3 km southeast of Preußisch Holland). The battalion number up to 350 men.

A prisoner from the 1561st Pioneer Battalion indicated that his battalion had arrived on 21 January from Königsberg with the task to defend Elbing.

A prisoner from the 2nd Luftwaffe Training Battalion "Ramme" testified that the battalion had been formed up in December 1944 from Luftwaffe recruits. The battalion numbered up to 300 men and went through infantry training. It arrived in Marienburg on 1 February 1945 and was made surbordinate to the fortress commandant. The fortress' garrison number up to 500 men.

Lieutenant Colonel M.A. Bykadorov recalls:

> On 1 February the snow began to melt under a bright sun. The scent of springtime was in the air. The SU-76 battery was supporting our troops' offensive on a line 12-14 km east of Preußisch Holland, attacking with a front to the east. This was 40-50 km east of Elbing. We made little progress. The Germans were putting up desperate resistance and conducting intense artillery and mortar fire. On 3 and 4 February our battery, now part of a new unit, engaged in heavy fighting for Schmauch (15 km east of Preußisch Holland). We suffered casualties and assault gun losses.

Excerpt from Operational Summary No. 022 from the headquarters of the 5th Guards Tank Army at 2400 on 4 February 1945:

In the area southeast of Mühlhausen, the enemy throughout the day of 4 February 1945 put up resistance with heavy artillery and mortar fire to the actions of our units and was continuing to hold the Hensels estate, Deutschendorf and Lauck. Southwest of Frauenburg, elements of the 28th Jäger Division, supported by self-propelled guns, fought to hold on to Tolkemit and were eventually thrown back to the coast line of the Frisches Haff lagoon. Separate groups of infantry attempted to break out in the southwestern direction. Solitary enemy aircraft conducted reconnaissance over the combat formations of our forces.

The 5th Guards Tank Army in the course of 4 February 1945 with its main forces continued to hold its occupied lines firmly, while conducting a regrouping with part of its force and launching offensive actions: on the right flank they captured Karwinden and Deutschendorf, while on the left flank they fought to retake Tolkemit; by 1700 on 4 February 1945, they had fully mopped up Tolkemit of its remaining pockets of defenders.

The 10th Tank Corps together with the 689th Destroyer Antitank Artillery Regiment, the 1st Battery of the 76th Guards Mortar Regiment and the 326th Heavy Self-propelled Artillery Regiment kept a firm grip on its occupied lines in readiness to attack in the Deutschendorf, Packhausen direction. By 1900 on 4 February 1945 the corps' units are occupying the following positions: 186th Tank Brigade together with the 1st Battalion of the 11th Motorized Rifle Brigade, the 705th Light Artillery Regiment and the 689th Destroyer Antitank Artillery Regiment (minus two batteries) is occupying a defense on the northeastern fringe of the woods 1 km east of Karwinden, Schlobitten line; the 183rd Tank Brigade together with two batteries of the 689th Destroyer Antitank Artillery Regiment is occupying a defense on the eastern fringe of the woods west of Deutschendorf and on the eastern outskirts of Fürstenau. the 178th Tank Brigade is in the wooded area east of Schönfeld. In the course of the night and day of 4 February 1945, the corps suffered the following losses: 2 SU-76 destroyed, and 3 men killed and 8 wounded. Damage done to the enemy: up to 100 soldiers and officers and 2 heavy machine guns eliminated; 1 self-propelled gun knocked-out; and two wagons carrying ammunition captured.

Altogether the 10th Tank Corps has in service: 34 T-34, 1 M4A2, 11 SU-122, 12 SU-100, 8 SU-85 and 7 SU-76. Supplies: diesel fuel – 1.4 refills, gasoline – 0.3 of a refill; ammunition – 1.0 standard combat load; food – 9 days.

The 47th Mechanized Brigade and the 146th Anti-aircraft Artillery Regiment in the course of 4 February 1945 launched an attack and by 1200 on 4 February captured Karwinden. By 1800 on 4 February they took Deutschendorf and are now occupying a defense on the northern and eastern outskirts of Deutschendorf. The brigade has 6 M4A2 tanks operational and 394 active bayonets, of which 158 are newly-arrived replacements. Damaged done to the enemy: 180 soldiers and officers killed or wounded, and 7 antitank guns, 8 75mm guns, 14 heavy machine guns and 45 vehicles knocked-out. Losses are being ascertained. The brigade headquarters is in Schlobitten.

The 29th Tank Corps together with the 651st Cannon Artillery Regiment and the 366th Anti-aircraft Artillery Regiment throughout the night and day of 4 February 1945 was on the march to the Neukirch-Höhe area. A portion of its force remained in Tolkemit in order to mop the town up of its remaining defenders and drove back enemy counterattacks from the Frauenburg direction. By 1900 on 4 February 1945 the corps' units were occupying the following positions: 25th Tank Brigade together with one battalion of the 391st Self-propelled Artillery Regiment, the 72nd Separate Guards Special-purpose Naval Infantry Battalion and the 1st Guards Separate Motorcycle Regiment from the morning of 4 February 1945 were engaged in combat for possession of Tolkemit. At 1900 on 4 February 1945 they captured Tolkemit and were engaged in combat northeast of the town; the 31st Tank Brigade by 1030 on 4 February 1945 was assembled in the Neukirch-Höhe area and since 1800 is attacking in the Frauenburg direction together with units of the 170th Rifle Division, with the task to take Frauenburg by the end of the day. The 53rd Motorized Rifle Brigade from 1830 4 February 1945 was conducting a march and by 1900 had assembled in the Neuendorf area. It has the task to mop up the enemy from the woods north of Neuendorf. The 32nd Tank Brigade with the 14th Guards Heavy Tank Regiment and the 1223rd Self-propelled Artillery Regiment at 1700 on 4 February 1945 was engaged in combat at the crossroads 1 km north of the Spanden estate. Altogether the 29th Tank Corps has 19 T-34 and 16 SU-152 operational. The condition of the 32nd Tank Brigade and its assets is being ascertained. Supplies: diesel fuel – 0.75 of a refill, gasoline – 0.4 of a refill; ammunition – 1.0 standard combat load; food – 3 days. Damage done to the enemy and our own losses are being ascertained. The corps headquarters is in Rutenau.

The 42nd Rifle Corps in the course of the day of 4 February 1945 held its previous line, repulsing enemy attacks from the Frauenburg direction and together with units of the 29th Tank Corps, fighting for possession of Tolkemit. By 1900 on 4 February 1945, the corps' units were occupying the following positions: 399th Rifle Division – the Muttersegen farmstead, Deutschendorf, Fürstenau; the 137th Rifle Division – Fürstenau, Borchertsdorfwald, Tiedmannsdorf, Groß Rautenberg; 170th Rifle Division – with one regiment in the Herrndorf, Mühlhausen area; two regiments, together with units of the 29th Tank Corps, the 72nd Separate Guards Special-purpose Naval Infantry Battalion were fighting for possession of Tolkemit and driving back German attacking groups of 200-300 men each from the direction of Frauenburg on the Grundhof, Neuhof line and the highway to the left. The corps' losses and the damage done to the enemy are being ascertained. The corps headquarters is in Herrndorf.

The 72nd Separate Guards Special-purpose Naval Battalion, together with units of the 29th Tank Corps and the 170th Rifle Division, was fighting for possession of Tolkemit; it was also controlling the coastline of the Frisches Haff with the task to block the spit and cut off the enemy's path of retreat to the west.

The 33rd Separate Motorized Engineer Brigade is fulfilling the task of deploying antitank mines and electrified obstacles in the following areas: Parlack, 1 km northeast of Groß Rautenberg, north of Klakendorf, Neukirch-Höhe, 1 km north of Neuendorf, Point 121.3, and 1 km southwest of Tolkemit.

The 41st Cannon Artillery Regiment is operationally subordinate to the commander of the 29th Tank Corps. The 1315th and 1619th Light Artillery Regiments are supporting the 47th Mechanized Brigade from firing positions in the Schlobitten area. They have in service 28 76mm guns. The 76th Guards Mortar Regiment is supporting the 10th Tank Corps with one battalion, while two battalions are in the corps commander's reserve. Firing positions – in the Nikolaiken area. It has 32 operational M-13 rocket launchers. The 659th Destroyer Antitank Artillery Regiment has been attached to the 10th Tank Corps. It has in service 14 57mm guns.

The 376th Heavy Self-propelled Artillery Regiment is supporting the actions of the 47th Mechanized Brigade in the Karwitten area. It has 8 operational SU-152. The 326th Heavy Self-propelled Artillery Regiment has been attached to the 10th Tank Corps. It has 11 operational SU-122.

The 6th Anti-aircraft Artillery Division: the 146th Anti-aircraft Artillery Regiment is covering the combat formations of the 47th Mechanized Brigade from out of the Schlobitten area; the 366th Anti-aircraft Artillery Regiment is covering the 29th Tank Corps in the Neukirch-Höhe area; the 516th Anti-aircraft Artillery Regiment is covering the army headquarters' operational command group in the Weeskenhof area; the 1062nd Anti-aircraft Artillery Regiment is in the Preußisch Holland area.

The weather is clear and the roads are passable.

Chief of staff of the 5th Guards Tank Army Guards Major General of Tank Forces SIDOROVICH
Chief of operations Guards Colonel FEDOROV

On 4 February 1945, 50 prisoners were taken in the following areas: Behlenhof – from I/Infantry Regiment 401 of the 170th Infantry Division; Hensels railroad station – from the 28th Jäger Division's Infantry Regiments 49 and 83; southeast of Elbing – from 7th Panzer Division's Panzergrenadier Regiment 6; in Elbing – from training elements of the Division *Feldhernhalle*, 561st Volksgrenadier Division's Volksgrenadier Regiment 1142, and the 312th Naval Infantry Battalion; 7 km west of Elbing – from an assault regiment of the Second Army.

Prisoners revealed that the Division *Feldhernhalle* is operating on the Western Front. The division's training elements (the reserve panzer battalion without its tanks, the reserve antitank company, the reserve motorized battalion, the reserve pioneer company and artillery battalion) are defending Elbing. The prisoner taken from the Second Army indicated that remnants of his assault regiment (200 men) were located in the area west of Dirschau, where they were bringing themselves back to order. On 1 February a kampfgruppe comprised of the regiment's remnants was shifted to the Eingal area (7 km west of Elbing) with the task to attack and link up with the Elbing garrison, but failed to carry out this task. A lieutenant, the commander of the 7th Company of II/Panzergrenadier Regiment 6 of the 7th Panzer Division, who was captured on 2 February in the area southeast of Elbing, revealed that on 31 January Panzergrenadier Regiment 6 and the 7th Panzer Division's reconnaissance battalion, reinforced with 8 150mm howitzers and 2 assault guns, had undertaken an attack out of the Grunau area in the southeastern direction with the mission to establish contact with General Hoßbach's group, which was trying to break through from the east. In the area northeast of Preußisch Holland Panzergrenadier Regiment 6 lost a lot of halftracks in a battle and on the night of 31 January – 1 February received an order to withdraw in the direction of Elbing. Between 15 and 25 January Panzergrenadier Regiment 6 lost up to 250 men killed or wounded. Panzer Regiment 25 over this same period lost 30 tanks, and in addition, on 22 January its remaining 13 tanks had been blown up in the Freistadt area because of the lack of fuel. Panzer Regiment 25 on 2 February numbered no more than 300 men and 2 assault guns.

F.I. Galkin remembers those days:

On 26 and 27 January units of the 42nd Rifle Corps approached the coastline along the corridor that had been laid down by the tank army and took up a defense on a broad front, which extended up to 30 kilometers. The army was preparing to storm Elbing by moving up Kolesnikov's and Pokolov's brigades toward Groß Röbern, as well as Kartashov's heavy tank and self-propelled artillery regiment. However, the attack of the combined forces never took place. Kartashov's regiment was forced to take up a defense of the large and important road hub of Thorn. Meanwhile, Kolesnikov's and Pokolov's brigades were taken from the march and sent to repulse enemy counterattacks, which had unexpectedly grown in activity in several places simultaneously. There remained only Mikhailov's mechanized brigade. By itself, it attacked Elbing with the support of the heavy tank and self-propelled artillery regiment, broke into its northern outskirts, and became tied up in street fighting.

The fighting didn't subside all night. By morning our troops had mopped up the enemy from five city blocks, the shipyard, a building of the tank school and the brewery, but they were unable to make any further progress.

Now, when the combined-arms formations had also reached the coastline of the Baltic Sea, a task was given to the tank army to expand the breakthrough sector and to reach the Passarge River. By the evening of 27 January – already how many times over the recent days! – a snowstorm descended on us. The roads became covered. Only tanks could break through the snow drifts; the trucks that were bringing up fuel, ammunition and reserve units became stuck in the wind-blown piles of snow. Nevertheless, the tank army was regrouping. Malakhov's corps, having pivoted to the west, was supposed to launch an attack against besieged Elbing; the 10th Tank Corps, having pivoted to the east, was to repulse a concentrated attack of the enemy, which was striving to break through to Elbing from the east. Having recovered from the initital shock, the Nazis began fighting for the sector along the sea: they needed the Königsberg – Elbing highway. Having brought together three infantry divisions, panzer units and assault brigades, they launched an attack with two strong groups. The attacks were delivered toward Preußisch Holland and along the Königsberg – Elbing highway.

That evening Vol'sky and Sidorovich were seated over a map, lost in deep thought. In order to hold back the enemy that was being used for the breakthrough, it was necessary not to fragment the army's forces, but to concentrate them. Also, not to stand in place, repulsing counterattacks, but to seize the initiative and attack themselves. The commander and his chief of staff understood this full well. However, the army's strength had been scattered; Mikhailov's brigade and its attached heavy tank and self-propelled artillery regiment were tied up in Elbing. No matter how regretful it was to abandon the gains made in the city, the commander decided nevertheless to do so.

On 29 January Mikhailov's brigade headed out of Elbing. On this same day the Nazi troops resumed the attack in the direction of Preußisch Holland with the aim of breaking out to the west. Having repulsed several attacks and having exhausted the enemy, on the morning of 30 January our forces once again went on the offensive toward the east. Sakhno's tank corps, with the active support of army-level units, captured the town of Deutschendorf. Malakhov's corps was attacking the Germans in the Elbing area, but made no progress.

In the first days of February, having lost hope in breaking out in the direction of Preußisch Holland, the Nazis reinforced their pressure on the coastline and broke into Tolkemit. From here they planned to reach Elbing. However, this attempt also failed. On 4 February Stanislavsky's tank brigade recaptured Tolkemit with an impetuous attack. Bitter fighting had now continued incessantly for 15 days. The frigid temperatures were being replaced by thaws. It became difficult not only for the vehicles to move along the roads, but also for the tanks.

In a sector of the Succase – Elbing road, almost all of the Sherman tanks that were on the march to a new line wound up in a ditch (we hadn't succeeded in "shoeing" them) [Ed. note: Adding metal cleats to the tracks to provide better traction].

"How did you contrive to pile up so many machines in the ditch?" – I asked the major who'd been leading the column.

"Don't even ask", he replied with despair. "For what sins are we paying for these lame machines? All you can do in them is parade across asphalt. But here …" He shook his head sadly, "Our allies really fixed us up."

"Yep, a real kettle of fish … there's only one way out: chop up the ice in front of the tracks and feed some tow cables beneath them. Otherwise you won't get them out without prime movers."

No sooner had I driven off, when cannons spoke up somewhere near by, and burst of automatic weapon fire began to chatter. Later it became clear that a group of fascist submachine gunners and two self-propelled guns, which had penetrated our defenses, had attacked the tanks that were stuck in the ditches.

Encounters with wandering groups of Nazis now became a not so seldom incident. Having brought up fresh units from the depths of East Prussia, the Germans were increasing their pressure against our positions. Simultaneously the enemy began to use a new tactic: infiltration in small groups of men. Elements of enemy infantry were sometimes making their way into the depth of our combat positions and even making it as far as the headquarters of formations.

There was a case when an entire company of Germans unexpectedly emerged right next to the hamlet in which the army's command post was situated. The chief of staff Sidorovich tore himself away from the map, and having picked up a field telephone, ordered the headquarters' commandant: "Take two halftracks of the security company and a platoon of soldiers, and destroy these univited guests."

Fifteen minutes later, having driven out to the highway, I saw how our two halftracks and two self-propelled guns had shot up the enemy infantry. Attempting to save themselves, the Nazis fled into the nearest settlement. However, our motorcyclists were located there. They didn't miss with their shots.

Toward evening Kozlov reported: "Just as you drove away, Fritz submachine gunners approached almost right up to the hut, and behind them, from out of the patch of woods, came more and more … They were pushing forward directly toward the commander's cottage."

"Did you have a scuffle?"

"No, but Major Salo's security company responded to an alarm four times."

Meanwhile, all the while, armored fighting vehicles were hurrying through the hamlet. The headquarters, of course, might have moved to a safer place. However, General Sidorovich made no attempt to do this. He was calmly directing the actions of the troops, using every possible means of communication. He was directing them even when the glowing tracers from machine guns and submachine guns were flying past the windows of his cottage and striking the tiled roofs of the structures. To retreat meant to raise doubt and a lack of confidence in the minds of the commanders. So, they fought almost side by side.

Table 4.17: Status of the materiel of the German Fourth Army (Lage der panzerbrechenden Waffen – AOK 4) by the end of 4 February 1945

Units	Armored vehicles and anti-tank guns					Under repair and not yet written off		Irrecoverable	Total
	StuG	Tanks	SP guns	sPak 76.2 mm	sPak 75-mm	Short-term	Long-term		
1	2	3	4	5	6	7	8	9	10
XXVI Armee Korps									
Gruppe "Wagner"									
StuG Brigade 277	8	-	-	-	-	6	-	-	14
Pz III	-	1	-	-	-	-	-	-	1
Pz IV	-	1	-	-	-	-	-	-	1
38(t)	-	1	-	-	-	4	-	-	5
T-34	-	0	-	-	-	4	1	-	5
Panzer Kp. 10	0	-	-	-	-	2	-	-	2
38(t)	-	2	-	-	-	-	-	-	2
Pz IV	-	0	-	-	-	-	1	-	1
Pz V	-	1	-	-	-	-	-	-	1
T-34	-	1	-	-	-	1	-	-	2
Gruppe Wolf	-	-	-	-	5	-	-	-	5
299.Infanterie Division	-	-	-	-	2	-	-	-	2
Radfahr-Jäger Brigade 10	-	-	-	-	5	1	-	-	6
Total for XXVI Korps	8	7	-	-	12	12	8	-	47
VI Armee Korps									
28.Jäger Division	-	-	-	-	15	-	-	-	15
Pz.Jg. Kp. 1028	5	-	-	-	-	1	2	-	8
2 Bat., StuG Brigade 185	1	-	-	-	-	2	3	-	6
Panzer Kp. Lt. Groetzki	-	-	-	-	-	1	-	-	1
Pz III	-	1	-	-	-	-	1	-	2
Pz IV	-	1	-	-	-	-	-	-	1
Kampfgruppe von Einem	-	-	-	-	5	-	-	-	5
Pz.Rgt. 24 (10+11) Pz IV	-	17	-	-	-	3	-	-	20
1 Bat., Jg.Pz. Abt. 40	-	2	-	-	-	-	-	-	2
	5	-	-	-	-	1	3	-	9
170.Infanterie Division	-	-	-	-	0	-	-	2	-
Pz.Jg. Kp. 1240	-	-	-	-	0	-	-	3	-
StuG Brigade 904	5	-	-	-	-	3	1	-	9
Total for VI Korps	16	21	-	-	20	11	10	5	78
VII Panzer Korps									
18.Panzergrenadier Division	-	-	-	-	2	-	-	-	2
Panzer Abt. 118	3	-	-	-	-	1	2	-	6
sPak Abt. 664 88-mm	-	-	-	-	3	-	-	-	3
14.Infanterie Division	-	-	-	-	13	-	-	-	13
Pz.Jg. Kp. 1014	7	-	-	-	-	-	-	-	7
Fest. Pak Kp. 21/VII	-	-	-	-	2	-	-	-	2

COMBAT OPERATIONS OF THE 5TH GUARDS TANK ARMY

Units	Armored vehicles and anti-tank guns					Under repair and not yet written off		Irrecoverable	Total
	StuG	Tanks	SP guns	sPak 76.2 mm	sPak 75-mm	Short-term	Long-term		
1	2	3	4	5	6	7	8	9	10
131.Infanterie Division	-	-	-	-	6	-	-	-	6
Pz.Jg. Kp. 1131 Pz V	-	1	-	-	-	-	3	-	4
StuG Brigade 901	0	-	-	-	-	4	-	-	4
sPz.Jg. Abt. 563 Pz IV	-	1	-	-	-	1	-	-	2
Pz V	-	5	-	-	-	-	-	-	5
Total for VII Panzer Corps	10	7	-	-	26	6	5	-	54
XX Armee Korps									
102.Infanterie Division	-	-	-	-	11	1	1	-	13
Pz.Jg. Kp. 1102	2	-	-	-	-	3	-	-	5
Fest. Pak-Kp. 21/VII	-	-	-	-	1	1	1	-	3
129.Infanterie Division	-	-	-	-	4	2	2	-	8
StuG Brigade 909	3	-	-	-	-	2	5	-	10
292.Infanterie Division	-	-	-	-	18	1	2	-	21
StuG Brigade 209	5	-	-	-	-	1	2	-	8
24.Panzer Division	-	-	-	-	7	-	-	-	7
88-mm	-	-	-	-	2	-	-	-	2
	-	-	-	6	-	-	-	-	6
3 Bat., StuG Brigade 185	3	-	-	-	-	1	-	-	4
Total for the XX Korps	13	-	-	6	43	12	13	-	87
XXXXI Panzer Korps									
203.Infanterie Division	-	-	-	-	2	1	2	-	5
Fest. Pak Verb 17/I	-	-	-	5	-	-	-	-	5
541.Volksgrenadier Division	-	-	-	-	1	1	1	-	3
4 Bat., StuG Brigade 920	2	-	-	-	-	1	2	-	5
Pz.Jg. Kp. 1541	1	-	-	-	-	1	-	-	2
Fest. Pak Kp.	-	-	-	7	-	-	-	-	7
	-	-	-	5	-	-	4	-	9
Kampgruppe Hauser	-	-	-	-	32	-	2	-	34
with Gruppe Hannibal and StuG Kp. 500	2	-	-	-	-	5	1	-	8
21.Infanterie Division	-	-	-	-	18	2	-	-	20
	1	-	-	-	-	-	1	-	2
StuG Brigade 259	20	-	-	-	-	8	2	1	30
50.Infanterie Division Pz.Jg. Kp. 1150	-	-	-	-	6	5	-	-	11
	3	-	-	-	-	1	3	-	7
	-	-	2	-	-	-	1	-	3
Gruppe "Blaurock"	-	-	-	-	14	-	-	-	14
Pz.Jg. Kp. 1156 Pz.Jg. Kp. 1349 StuG Brigade 203	16	-	-	-	-	7	-	-	23

Units	Armored vehicles and anti-tank guns					Under repair and not yet written off		Irrecoverable	Total
	StuG	Tanks	SP guns	sPak 76.2 mm	sPak 75-mm	Short-term	Long-term		
1	2	3	4	5	6	7	8	9	10
Fest. Pak Kp. 7 and 8/VII	-	-	-	13	-	-	-	-	17
61.Infanterie Division	-	-	-	-	7	1	-	-	8
	-	-	3	-	-	-	-	-	3
2 Bat., StuG Brigade 203	4	-	-	-	-	-	-	-	4
Total for XXXXI Panzer Korps	50	-	5	25	85	33	13	1	211
Panzer Korps *Hermann Göring*									
Division *Grossdeutschland*	-	-	-	-	-	-	-	-	-
	-	-	-	-	7	4	-	-	11
	-	-	-	-	3	-	-	-	3
StuG	2	-	-	-	-	6	13	-	21
Pz IV	-	1	-	-	-	1	2	-	4
Pz V	-	6	-	-	-	9	1	-	16
Pz VI	-	1	-	-	-	6	1	-	8
2.Division *Hermann Göring*	-	-	-	-	5	3	-	-	8
Pz.Jg. Abt. *Hermann Göring*	5	-	-	-	-	13	16	-	34
StuG Abt. *Hermann Göring*	0	-	-	-	-	-	6	-	6
	-	-	0	-	-	1	-	-	1
StuG Brigade 279	7	-	-	-	-	3	4	-	14
547.Volksgrenadier Division	-	-	-	-	12	-	-	-	12
1 Bat., StuG Brigade 185	3	-	-	-	-	1	-	2	4
562.Volksgrenadier Division	-	-	-	-	9	-	-	-	9
Pz.Jg. Kp. 1562	4	-	-	-	-	1	-	-	5
Fest. Pak Kp. 16/1	-	-	-	3	-	-	-	-	3
Panzer Abt. 302	3	-	-	-	-	4	-	-	7
Total for Panzer Korps HG	24	8	-	3	36	52	43	2	166
Total for Fourth Army	121	43	5	34	222	126	92	8	643

Report on the German Fourth Army's casualties, 5 February 1945

Casualties over the period from 28 January to 5 February 1945: 416 killed, 1,636 wounded and 426 missing-in-action, of which:

> 292nd Infantry Division (1-4 February): 27 killed, 83 wounded and 35 missing;
> 102nd Infantry Division (29 January to 2 February): 32 killed, 107 wounded and 17 missing;
> Kampfgruppe Hannibal: 14 killed, 59 wounded and 24 missing;
> 24th Panzer Division (2-4 February): 25 killed, 148 wounded and 11 missing;

170th Infantry Division (2-5 February): 63 killed, 230 wounded and 75 missing;
28th Jäger Division (4 February): 5 killed, 13 wounded;
Units directly subordinate to VI Corps (29 January – 4 February): 6 killed, 19 wounded and 27 missing;
129th Infantry Division (28 January to 4 February): 40 killed, 139 wounded and 76 missing;
1436th Infantry Battalion (31 January): 13 wounded;
420th Battalion: 7 wounded;
Division "Herman Göring" (4-5 February): 43 killed, 256 wounded and 90 missing;
562nd Volksgrenadier Division (4-5 February): 78 killed, 253 wounded and 51 missing;
547th Volksgrenadier Division (4-5 February): 30 killed, 75 wounded and 19 missing;
Panzergrenadier Division *Grossdeutschland* (4-5 February): 53 killed, 234 wounded and 1 missing.

Armee-Oberkommando Der Chef des Generalstabes I.A.
(Army's chief of operations)

Excerpt from Operational Summary No. 023 from the headquarters of the 5th Guards Tank Army at 2400 on 5 February 1945:

The enemy on the Schlodien, Tiedmannsdorf, Tolkemit front throughout the day of 5 February 1945 conducted containing combat, putting up stubborn resistance to our units' offensive with fire and counterattacks of a company to a battalion of infantry, while simultaneously withdrawing troops along the Frische Nehrung spit. The Luftwaffe in groups of 4-7 aircraft were covering their troops and reconnoitering the combat formations of our units.

The 5th Guards Tank Army in the course of 5 February 1945 conducted offensive combat in the directions of: a) Deutschendorf, Kagenau estate; b) Fürstenau, Lauck; and c) Narz, Frauenburg, while simultaneously repulsing enemy counterattacks from the Kagenau estate, Lauck and Frauenburg directions and mopping up the coastline of the Frisches Haff lagoon in the Narz, Tolkemit sector. The 47th Mechanized Brigade with the 1315th Light Artillery Regiment, 376th Guards Heavy Self-propelled Artillery Regiment and the 146th Anti-aircraft Artillery Regiment, attacking in the Wusen direction, was engaged in bitter fighting against enemy tanks and self-propelled guns. By 1700 on 5 February 1945 the brigade had captured the road fork at Point 63.9, 1.5 kilometers northeast of Deutschendorf. In the course of the day it drove back in strength of up to two companies from the directions of Baarden and Seepothen. According to preliminary information, the damage inflicted on the enemy amounts to 2 self-propelled guns destroyed and up to 60 enemy soldiers and officers killed or wounded. The brigade's own losses in the course of 5 February 1945 are being ascertained. The brigade has in service 4 M4A2 tanks, and by the morning of 6 February 1945 4 more tanks will be put back in service. Supplies: diesel fuel – 1.0 of a refill, gasoline – 1.0 of a refill; ammunition – 1.0 standard combat load; food – 3 days. The brigade headquarters is in Schlobitten.

The 10th Tank Corps together with the 326th Heavy Self-propelled Artillery Regiment, the 689th Destroyer Antitank Artillery Regiment, and the 2nd Battalion of the 76th Guards Mortar Regiment since 1000 on 5 February 1945 has been attacking in the Fürstenau, Lauck, Langwalde direction, having driven back 5 enemy counterattacks from the directions of Baarden and the Kagenau estate; at 2100 on 5 February 1945 is engaged in combat on the following line: 186th Tank Brigade in cooperation with the 47th Mechanized Brigade has captured the road fork at Point 63.9 (1.5 kilometers east of Deutschendorf); the brigade has in service 8 T-34 and 7 SU-100; the 11th Motorized Rifle Brigade and the 326th Heavy Self-propelled Artillery Regiment are engaged in combat on the western outskirts of Seepothen. In the course of the day of 5 February it repulsed 5 enemy counterattacks from the direction of Seepothen in strength of up to two infantry battalions supported by 8-10 self-propelled guns. The brigade has in service 371 active bayonets, 8 76mm guns, and 25 82mm and 120mm mortars; the 183rd Tank Brigade in cooperation with the 409th Rifle Regiment has taken the Lauck estate; the brigade has 13 tanks and 6 SU-85 still operational; the 178th Tank Brigade set out from the wooded area east of Schönfeld at 2200 on 5 February 1945, and by midnight had reassembled in the woods 0.5 kilometers northeast of the Hensels estate, with the task to attack in the direction of Schlodien on the morning of 6 February 1945. The brigade has in service 8 T-34 and 5 SU-100. The corps headquarters has 3 T-34 tanks.

The status of the 10th Tank Corps' attached assets: the 727th Self-propelled Artillery Regiment has 7 operational SU-76; the 77th Motorcycle Battalion has one operational M4A2 tank and 123 active bayonets; the 705th Light Artillery Regiment has 21 76mm guns in service; the 287th Mortar Regiment has 14 120mm mortars; the 1693rd Anti-aircraft Artillery Regiment has 12 serviceable 37mm guns; the 128th Guards Mortar Battalion has 8 M-13 rocket launchers; the 326th Guards Heavy Self-propelled Artillery Regiment has 8 operational SU-122 and 1 operational IS-122 tank; the 689th Destroyer Antitank Artillery Regiment has 14 57mm guns in service; the 2nd Battalion of the 76th Guards Mortar Regiment has in service 12 M-13 rocket launchers. Altogether, the corps' attached assets have in service 32 T-34, 1 IS-122 and 1 M4A2 tanks, 8 SU-122, 12 SU-100, 6 SU-85 and 7 SU-76; and 783 active bayonets.

In the course of the day of 5 February 1945 the 10th Tank Corps took the following losses: 4 T-34, 2 SU-122 and 1 SU-85 destroyed; 1 T-34 and 2 SU-122 knocked-out; and 13 killed and 49 wounded.

The following losses were inflicted on the enemy by the 10th Tank Corps: 5 enemy tanks and self-propelled guns, 16 guns of various caliber, 10 vehicles, and up to 300 soldiers and officers. Five guns of various caliber and 34 prisoners have been captured. The corps headquarters is in Neumark.

The 29th Tank Corps (minus the 32nd Tank Brigade and 1223rd Self-propelled Artillery Regiment) with the 41st Cannon Artillery Regiment, the 366th Anti-aircraft Artilery Regiment and the 1619th Light Artillery Regiment, in cooperation with units of the 170th Rifle Division, was attacking in the direction of Frauenburg, mopping up the coastline northeast of Tolkemit, and simultaneously repulsing enemy counterattacks from the Frauenburg direction. By 1900 on 5 February 1945 the corps' units were occupying the following position: the 31st Tank Brigade together with units of the 170th Rifle Division were engaged in combat 1 km southwest of Frauenburg. Throughout the day of 5 February 1945, the brigade repelled two enemy counterattacks from the direction of Frauenburg in strength of up to two companies of infantry and the support of tanks and self-propelled guns. The brigade has in service 10 T-34 tanks, 10 SU-152 and 90 submachine gunners. The 53rd Motorized Rifle Brigade (minus one battalion) was mopping up the woods in the area 3 km northeast of Tolkemit and engaged in combat for the Louisenthal railroad station. The brigade has in service 115 active bayonets, 4 76mm guns, and 28 82mm and 120mm mortars. The 25th Tank Brigade is defending Tolkemit together with one battalion of the 53rd Motorized Rifle Brigade. The brigade has in service 2 T-34, 2 SU-152 and 59 submachine gunners. The 32nd Tank Brigade, the 14th Guards Heavy Tank Regiment and the 1223rd Self-propelled Artillery Regiment are operationally subordinate to the commander of the 124th Rifle Corps. By 1500 on 5 February 1945 it was engaged in combat in the area 2 km northeast of the Spanden estate. The condition of the brigade and attached assets is being ascertained.

The status of the corps' attached assets: the 271st Mortar Regiment is in firing positions in the vicinity of Hill 107.6 with 17 serviceable 120mm mortars; the 165th Light Artillery Regiment is in firing positions in the Tolkemit area with 15 serviceable 76mm guns; the 409th Separate Guards Mortar Battalion has 5 operational M-13 rocket launchers; the 651st Cannon Artillery Regiment is in firing positions 1.2 km west of Heinrichsdorf with 13 servicable 100mm guns; the 1619th

Light Artillery Regiment is in firing positions 1.2 km west of Heinrichsdorf and 1 km southeast of Vierzighuben.

Altogether the 29th Tank Corps has in service (minus the 32nd Tank Brigade and 1223rd Self-propelled Artillery Regiment) 15 T-34 tanks (with 3 in the corps headquarters' possession) and 12 SU-152, and 264 active bayonets. Supplies: diesel fuel – 1.0 of a refill, gasoline – 0.4 of a refill; ammunition – 1.0 standard combat load; food – 3 days. Losses: 2 T-34 tanks destroyed, 4 SU-152 knocked-out, and 12 killed and 22 wounded.

Losses inflicted on the enemy over 4 and 5 February 1945: 7 tanks, 12 guns of various caliber, 3 mortars, up to 40 vehicles, 13 motorcycles, 150 wagons carrying military gear, and up to 500 soldiers and officers. The corps headquarters is in Rückenau.

The 42nd Rifle Corps throughout the day of 5 February 1945 stubbornly held its occupied line, while part of its forces in cooperation with the 10th Tank Corps and 29th Tank Corps attacked in the directions: 399th Rifle Division – Fürstenau, Lauck. By 2100 on 5 February 1945 it was fighting on the western outskirts of Seepothen after taking full possession of Lauck. The 137th Rifle Division was stubbornly holding its occupied line: Point 63.4, Borchertswald, Tiedmannsdorf, Groß Rautenberg, Schafsberg. By 2100 on 5 February 1945 it was fighing on the line: Point 46.5, 1 km north of Narz. The corps' losses: 9 killed and 32 wounded. Casualties inflicted on the enemy: up to 400 soldiers and officers killed or wounded. The corps headquarters is in Blüdau.

The 33rd Motorized Engineer Brigade is doing work to set up artificial obstacles. The 72nd Separate Guards Special-purpose Naval Infantry Battalion throughout the day of 5 February 1945, in cooperation with units of the 29th Tank Corps, was mopping up the coastline of the Frishes Haff lagoon northeast of Tolkemit of remaining pockets of enemy; while reconnoitering the Frische Nehrung spit, it ran into organized resistance along the southeastern shore of the spit – the fire of heavy and light machine guns and mortars. In separate sectors the ice had been mined and then blown up. The battalion on the night of 5-6 February 1945 has the assignment to conduct reconnaissance in the Kahlberg, Liep direction. The battalion's condition and the losses inflicted on the enemy are being ascertained.

The 1st Separate Guards Motorcycle Regiment at 1400 on 5 February 1945 was assembled in the Blumenau area. The regiment's men were servicing their machines and weapons. In the fighting for Tolkemit on 4 February 1945, the regiment lost 2 M4A2 and 1 SU-57 destroyed, 1 SU-57 knocked out and 51 casualties, including 18 killed and 33 wounded. Damage inflicted on the enemy: 2 Pz 38(t) tanks, 2 self-propelled guns, 1 halftrack, 2 antitank guns, 3 heavy machines guns, 4 light machine guns, 15 vehicles destroyed, and up to 200 soldiers and officers eliminated. The regiment has in service 85 active bayonets, 2 M4A2 tanks, and 4 SU-57 self-propelled guns.

Chief of staff of the 5th Guards Tank Army Guards Major General of Tank Forces SIDOROVICH
Chief of operations Guards Colonel Fedorov

Table 4.18: Status of the materiel of the German Fourth Army (Lage der panzerbrechenden Waffen – AOK 4) by the end of 5 February 1945

Units	Armored vehicles and anti-tank guns					Under repair and not yet written off		Irrecoverable	Total
	StuG	Tanks	SP guns	sPak 76.2 mm	sPak 75-mm	Short-term	Long-term		
1	2	3	4	5	6	7	8	9	10
XXVI Armee Korps									
Gruppe "Wagner"									
StuG Brigade 277	7	-	-	-	-	2	7	-	16
Pz III	-	1	-	-	-	-	-	-	1
38(t)	-	1	-	-	-	-	-	-	1
T-34	-	2	-	-	-	1	2	-	5
Panzer Kp. 10	-	-	-	-	-	-	-	-	2
38(t)	-	0	-	-	-	-	-	2	0
Pz IV	-	0	-	-	-	-	-	1	0
T-34	-	0	-	-	-	-	1	-	1
Fest. Pak Kp Verb 7/VII	-	-	-	5	-	-	-	-	5
88-mm	-	-	-	-	2	-	-	-	2
Gruppe "Reichert"	-	-	-	-	7	-	-	-	7
Radfahr-Jäger Brigade 10	-	-	-	-	2	1	2	1	5
Pz III	-	1	-	-	-	-	-	-	1
Pz IV	-	1	-	-	-	-	-	-	1
38 (t)	-	4	-	-	-	-	-	-	4
Total for XXVI Korps	7	10	-	5	11	4	12	4	47
VI Armee Korps									
28.Jäger Division	-	-	-	-	10	1	-	-	11
Pz.Jg. Kp. 1028	6	-	-	-	-	-	2	-	8
2nd Bat., StuG Brigade 185	0	-	-	-	-	2	3	1	5
Panzer Kp. Lt. Groetzki	-	0	-	-	-	1	-	-	1
Pz III	-	1	-	-	-	-	1	-	2
Pz IV	-	1	-	-	-	-	-	-	1
170.Infanterie Division	-	-	-	-	4	-	-	-	4
StuG Brigade 904	6	-	-	-	-	2	2	-	10
Total for VI Korps	12	8	-	-	14	6	8	1	42
VII Panzer Korps									
18.Panzergrenadier Division	-	-	-	-	2	-	-	-	2
Panzer Abt. 118	6	-	-	-	-	-	-	-	6
sPak Abt. 664 88-mm	-	-	-	-	2	-	1	-	3
14.Infanterie Division	-	-	-	-	13	-	-	-	13
Pz.Jg. Kp. 1014	7	-	-	-	-	-	-	-	7
Fest. Pak Kp. 21/VII	-	-	-	-	2	-	-	-	2
131.Infanterie Division	-	-	-	-	5	1	-	-	6
Pz.Jg. Kp. 1131	0	-	-	-	-	-	3	-	3

COMBAT OPERATIONS OF THE 5TH GUARDS TANK ARMY

Units	Armored vehicles and anti-tank guns					Under repair and not yet written off		Irrecoverable	Total
	StuG	Tanks	SP guns	sPak 76.2 mm	sPak 75-mm	Short-term	Long-term		
1	2	3	4	5	6	7	8	9	10
sPz.Jg. Abt. 563 Pz V	-	1	-	-	-	-	-	-	1
Pz IV	-	1	-	-	-	1	-	-	2
Pz V	-	3	-	-	-	1	1	-	5
Total for VII Panzer Korps	13	5	-	-	24	3	5	-	50
XX Armee Korps									
102.Infanterie Division	-	-	-	-	12	-	1	-	13
Pz.Jg. Kp. 1102	2	-	-	-	-	2	1	-	5
Elements of Fest. Pak-Kp. 21/VII	-	-	-	-	1	-	-	-	1
Elements of StuG Brigade 909	3	-	-	-	-	1	1	-	5
129.Infanterie Division	-	-	-	-	4	2	-	-	6
Portion of StuG Brigade 909	2	-	-	-	-	-	-	-	2
292.Infanterie Division	-	-	-	-	18	1	1	-	20
StuG Brigade 209	7	-	-	-	-	2	2	-	11
24.Panzer Division	-	-	-	-	7	-	-	-	7
88-mm	-	-	-	-	2	-	-	-	2
	-	-	-	6	-	-	-	-	6
3rd Bat., StuG Brigade 185	3	-	-	-	-	1	-	-	4
Total for the XX Korps	17	-	-	6	44	9	6	-	82
XXXXI Panzer Korps									
541.Volksgrenadier Division	-	-	-	-	2	-	1	-	3
4 Bat., StuG Brigade 920	2	-	-	-	-	1	1	-	4
Pz.Jg. Kp. 1541	2	-	-	-	1	-	-	-	3
Fest. Pak Kp.	-	-	-	-	2	-	2	-	4
	-	-	-	2	-	-	1	-	3
Kampfgruppe Hauser	-	-	-	-	30	-	2	-	32
With Gruppe "Hannibal" and StuG Kp. 500	2	-	-	-	-	-	5	-	7
21.Infanterie Division	-	-	-	-	16	3	1	-	20
	1	-	-	-	-	-	1	-	2
StuG Brigade 259	19	-	-	-	-	4	7	-	30
50.Infanterie Division	-	-	-	-	6	-	-	-	6
Pz.Jg. Kp. 1150	2	-	-	-	-	1	2	2	5
	-	-	2	-	-	-	1	-	3
56.Infanterie Division	-	-	-	-	12	2	-	-	14
Pz.Jg. Kp. 1156	13	-	-	-	-	13	7	-	33
Pz.Jg. Kp. 1349									
StuG Brigade 203									

Units	Armored vehicles and anti-tank guns					Under repair and not yet written off		Irrecoverable	Total
	StuG	Tanks	SP guns	sPak 76.2 mm	sPak 75-mm	Short-term	Long-term		
1	2	3	4	5	6	7	8	9	10
Fest. Pak Kp. 7 and 8/VII	-	-	-	9	-	5	-	-	14
558.Volksgrenadier Division	-	-	-	-	5	-	-	-	5
Pz.Jg. Kp. 1558	4	-	-	-	-	-	-	-	4
Kampfgruppe von Einem	-	-	-	-	5	-	-	-	5
Elements of StuG Brigade 209	7	-	-	-	-	-	-	-	7
Panzer Rgt. 24 (10+11) Pz IV	-	17	-	-	-	3	-	-	20
Bef.	-	2	-	-	-	-	-	-	2
1 Bat., Jg.Pz. Abt. 40	5	-	-	-	-	1	3	-	9
61.Infanterie Division	-	-	-	-	8	1	2	-	11
	-	-	3	-	-	-	-	-	3
2 Bat., StuG Brigade 203	4	-	-	-	-	-	-	-	4
Fest. Pak Kp. 17/1	-	-	-	3	-	-	-	-	3
Total for XXXXI Panzer Korps	61	19	5	14	86	36	35	2	256
Panzer Korps Hermann Göring									
Division Grossdeutschland	-	-	-	-	10	10	3	-	23
	-	-	-	-	4	-	-	-	4
	-	-	3	-	-	2	-	-	5
StuG	2	-	-	-	-	6	13	-	21
Pz IV	-	0	-	-	-	2	2	-	4
Pz V	-	5	-	-	-	10	1	-	16
Pz VI	-	4	-	-	-	4	1	-	9
2.Division Hermann Göring	-	-	-	-	8	1	-	-	9
Pz.Jg. Abt. Hermann Göring	5	-	-	-	-	13	16	-	34
StuG Abt. Hermann Göring	0	-	-	-	-	-	6	-	6
	-	-	0	-	-	1	-	-	1
StuG Brigade 279	6	-	-	-	-	3	5	-	14
547.Volksgrenadier Division	-	-	-	-	12	-	-	-	12
1st Bat., StuG Brigade 185	2	-	-	-	-	1	1	-	4
562.Volksgrenadier Division	-	-	-	-	9	-	-	-	9
Pz.Jg. Kp. 1562	4	-	-	-	-	1	-	-	5
Fest. Pak Kp. 16/1	-	-	-	3	-	-	-	-	3
Panzer Abt. 302	3	-	-	-	-	4	-	-	7
Total for Panzer Korps HG	22	9	3	3	43	58	48	-	186
Total for Fourth Army	126	51	8	28	222	116	114	7	665

On 6 February 1945 the Chief of Operations of the German Fourth Army issued an updated report on the casualties suffered by the army:

> Losses in personnel over the period between 12 January and 5 February 1945 amounted to a) 1,224 officers (286 killed, 835 wounded and 102 missing); b) and 41,001 non-commissioned officers and enlisted men (8,816 killed, 25,149 wounded and 7,036 missing).
> *Armee-Oberkommando Der Chef des Generalstabes I.A.*

Excerpt from Operational Summary No. 024 from the headquarters of the 5th Guards Tank Army at 2400 on 6 February 1945:

The enemy in the areas southwest of Mehlsack and Frauenburg in the course of 6 February 1945 offered tough resistance to our troops' offensive with units of the 28th Jäger Division, 10th Bicycle Jäger Brigade, 24th Panzer Division, Regiment "Stabliag", elements of the 966th Security Battalion, the 44th Reserve Battalion, the 37th Heavy Artillery Battalion, the 10th Training Panzer Battalion and the fire of field artillery, anti-aircraft artillery and antitank artillery. By 1600 on 6 February 1945 he was thrown back to the line of the Passarge River in the Wusen, Bortchersdorf sector and was continuing to hold Frauenberg.

The 5th Guards Tank Army in the course of the day of 6 February 1945 conducted offensive actions in the Langwalde, Packhausen direction and Narz, Frauenburg direction.

By the end of 6 February 1945 the army's units and formations had thrown back the enemy to the eastern bank of the Passarge River in the sector 1 km east of Schlodien, 1 km east of the Kagenau estate, Borchertsdorfwald, and to the northwest to Tiedmannsdorf; had fully mopped up the western bank of the Passarge River; and was fighting to force a crossing of the river in the sectors 2 km east of Schlodien, 2 km east of Kagenau, and 1 km east of Hopfenbruch. In the sector 1 km southwest of Frauenburg, the army's troops ran into heavy enemy fire from the southwestern outskirts of Frauenburg, as well as an antitank ditch and a minefield. The fire was coming from two heavy artillery batteries, two anti-aircraft batteries, one mortar battery, and heavy machine guns. The units and formations of the 5th Guards Tank Army, bypassing the obstacles to the right and left of them, fought their way forward to carry out their orders to take Frauenburg. Several reconnaissance groups were prepared for actions that night to probe across the Frisches Haff lagoon.

The 10th Tank Corps with the 326th Heavy Self-propelled Artillery Regiment, the 689th Destroyer Antitank Artillery Regiment and the support of a battalion of the 76th Guards Mortar Regiment in the course of 6 February 1945 attacked in the direction of Packhausen against heavy enemy fire from the 10th Bicycle Jägers Brigade, the 28th Jäger Division and an unidentified assault gun battalion. The enemy here had 8 antitank guns, 6-10 self-propelled guns and tanks, an artillery battery and up to a regiment of infantry in the Klingenberg area; up to a battalion of heavy artillery in the Wusen, Langwalde area; and up to two mortar batteries in the area southeast of Klingenberg. The approaches to a bridge across the Passarge River 1.5 km southwest of Klingenberg had been mined, and the bridge had been demolished. By 2100 on 6 February 1945 the corps' units had reached the line of the western bank of the Passarge River.

The 178th Tank Brigade together with units of the 47th Mechanized Brigade had take Schlodien, mopped up the woods east of there, and reached the western bank of the Passarge, where they were fighting to force their way across it. The brigade has 8 T-34, 6 SU-100 and 133 active bayonets.

The 186th Tank Brigade had captured Baarden and was fighting for a crossing site 1.5 km southeast of Klingenberg. The brigade has in service 4 T-34, 4 SU-100 and 79 active bayonets.

The 11th Motorized Rifle Brigade at 0200 on 6 February 1945 took Seepothen, and by 1900 had mopped up enemy from the Kagenau estate and the patch of woods to the north. The brigade has in service 242 active bayonets, 8 76mm guns and 25 82mm and 120mm mortars.

The 183rd Tank Brigade, having run into heavy enemy fire in the Lauck area, by 1600 on 6 February 1945 had broken the resistance and thrown the enemy back to the eastern bank of the Passarge River, arrived at the western bank, and was fighting for crossing sites on it. The brigade has in service 15 T-34, 6 SU-85 and 114 active bayonets.

The status of the units directly subordinate to the corps and attached assets: 727th Self-propelled Artillery Regiment has 5 operational SU-76; the 77th Separate Motorcycle Battalion has 1 operational M4A2 tank; the 287th Mortar Regiment has 16 120mm mortars in service; the 1693rd Anti-aircraft Artillery Regiment has 12 37mm guns in service; the 128th Separate Guards Mortar Battalion has 8 M-13 rocket launchers in service; 3 operational T-34 tanks are located at corps headquarters; the 326th Guards Heavy Self-propelled Artillery Regiment has operational 7 SU-122 and 1 IS-122; the 689th Destroyer Antitank Artillery Regiment has in service 14 57mm guns; the 2nd Battalion of the 76th Guards Mortar Regiment has in service 12 M-13 rocket launchers.

Altogether the 10th Tank Corps has in service: 30 T-34, 1 M4A2 and 1 IS-122 tanks; 7 SU-122, 10 SU-100, 6 SU-85, and 5 SU-76 self-propelled guns.

In the course of 6 February 1945, the corps took the following losses: 2 T-34 destroyed, and 1 T-34, 1 SU-100 and 2 SU-76 knocked-out; 1 T-34 and 1 SU-100 disabled by mines; and 9 killed and 24 wounded. Losses inflicted on the enemy: 16 guns of various caliber, 4 vehicles, 10 loaded wagons, 6 mortars, 10 machine guns and up to 500 soldiers and officers. Captured: 11 guns of various caliber, 4 205mm howitzers together with their prime movers, 26 Panzerfausts, and 96 prisoners. Supplies: diesel fuel – 1.2 refills, gasoline – 0.7 of a refill; ammunition – 1.1 standard combat loads; food – 6 days. The corps headquarters is in Neumark.

The 47th Mechanized Brigade, together with the 376th Heavy Self-propelled Artillery Regiment, the 1315th Light Artillery Regiment and the support of the 1st Battalion of the 76th Guards Mortar Regiment, in cooperation with units of the 10th Tank Corps, overcoming strong enemy resistance, captured Schlodien and reached the western bank of the Passarge River in the area northeast of a patch of woods lying east of this point, where it is fighting for a crossing site on the Passarge. The brigade has in service: 7 M4A2 tanks and 228 active bayonets.

As a result of the fighting, the brigade had casualties: 5 killed and 16 wounded. Losses inflicted on the enemy: 2 antitank guns, 3 75mm guns, 11 heavy and light machine guns and 20 vehicles, as well as 85 soldiers and officers killed and 20 taken prisoner. The brigade headquarters is in Schlobitten.

The 29th Tank Corps together with the 41st Cannon Artillery Regiment, the 366th Anti-aircraft Artillery Regiment, and the 201st Light Artillery Brigade (minus the 1315th Light Artillery Regiment), supported by a battalion of the 76th Guards Mortar Regiment, is stubbornly holding the Neukirch-Höhe, Tolkemit area; a portion of its forces, in cooperation with units of the 170th Rifle Division, is fighting to take Frauenburg and encountering heavy enemy fire; the town is being defended by the 299th Infantry Division, the 1444th Separate Infantry Battalion, the 23rd Training Machine Gun Battalion, the 10th Training Panzer Battalion, and presumably the 24th Panzer Division and Assault Gun Brigade 277. Along the southern outskirts of Frauenburg the Germans have prepared an antitank ditch, full-profile trenches, minefields and other artificial obstacles. By 2100 on 6 February 1945, the corps' units were engaged in combat: the 31st Tank Brigade in cooperation with units of the 170th Rifle Division are attacking toward Frauenburg; they have encountered an antitank ditch, a minefield and the fire of artillery and mortar batteries. By 1600 6 February 1945 they were fighting in the wooded area 1 km southwest of Frauenburg. The brigade has in service 11 T-34, 7 SU-152, 3 SU-76 and 80 active bayonets.

The 53rd Motorized Rifle Brigade in the course of the day of 6 February 1945 was fighting to wipe out the enemy in the wooded area 1 km northeast of Conradswalde and by 2100 is occupying a defense on the coastline of the Frisches Haff in the sector between the East Prussian boundary and Tolkemit, screening the sea and preventing an enemy breakout in the southwestern direction. The brigade has in service 6 76mm guns, 18 82mm and 120mm mortars, and 110 active bayonets.

The 25th Tank Brigade and the 1st Motorized Rifle Battalion of the 53rd Motorized Rifle Brigade are occupying a defense in Tolkemit and guarding the coastline of the Frisches Haff southwest of Tolkemit.

The 32nd Tank Brigade with the 14th Guards Heavy Tank Regiment and 1223rd Self-propelled Artillery Regiment are operationally subordinate to the commander of the 124th Rifle Corps. The condition and supply levels of the brigade and attached assets are being ascertained.

The 165th Light Artillery Regiment is in firing positions on the eastern and southeastern outskirts of Tolkemit with 14 serviceable 76mm guns; the 271st Mortar Regiment is in firing positions in the vicinity of Hill 107.6 with 17 serviceable 120 mortars.

The 409th Separate Guards Mortar Battalion is in Vierzighuben with 9 serviceable M-13 rocket launchers. The 75th Separate Motorcycle Battalion is conducting reconnaissance in the corps' operational sector. It has operational 5 M4A2 tanks and 2 halftracks. The corps commander's reserve consists of 2 T-34 tanks and 7 SU-85 from the 32nd Tank Brigade, and is in Rückenau. The corps headquarters has 2 operational T-34 tanks. Altogether, the corps (minus the 32nd Tank Brigade and 1223rd Self-propelled Artillery Regiment) has in service: 18 T-34, 5 M4A2, 10 SU-152, 7 SU-85, 3 SU-76 and 247 active bayonets.

The losses of the 29th Tank Corps over the day of 6 February 1945: 1 T-34 and 1 SU-152 destroyed; 2 SU-152 knocked-out; and 30 killed and 85 wounded. Losses inflicted on the enemy: 1 tank, 2 anti-aircraft guns, 8 antitank guns, 12 heavy and light machine guns, 8 vehicles, 17 loaded wagons, and up to 250 soldiers and officers. Captured: 2 motorcycles, 1 supply stockpile, and 10 prisoners. Supplies: diesel fuel – 1.0 refill, gasoline – 0.5 of a refill; ammunition – 1.2 standard combat loads; food – 3 days. The corps headquarters is in Rükenau.

The 42nd Rifle Corps in cooperation with units of the 10th and 29th Tank Corps attacked in the Kagenau estate, Langwalde direction and the Narz, Frauenburg direction, and ran into heavy enemy fire from the eastern bank of the Passarge River and the western outskirts of Frauenburg. By 2100 on 6 February it was engaged in combat:

-- 399th Rifle Division: The 1345th Rifle Regiment, in cooperation with the 47th Mechanized Brigade, took Schlodien and mopped up the enemy from the woods east of there, before arriving at the Passarge River in the sector 1 km southeast of the Schlodien woods; the 1343rd Rifle Regiment took the woods in the Schlodien area and cut the paved road running between the Kagenau estate and Klingenberg; the 1348th Rifle Regiment assisted in cutting the Kagenau – Klingenberg road and cleared the enemy from the woods along the western bank of the Passarge River as far as Hopfenbruch. The division has 3,840 men reporting for duty.

-- the 137th Rifle Division: is stubbornly holding its occupied line of defense in the Hopfenbruch – Borchertsdorfwald – Tiedmannsdorf – Groß Rautenberg – Schafsberg sector. In the course of the day of 6 February, the division repulsed two enemy counterattacks in strength of 100-150 men, with the support of artillery and self-propelled guns. The division has 4,833 men reporting for duty.

-- the 170th Rifle Division: in cooperation with the 29th Tank Corps is attacking toward Frauenburg. By 2100 on 6 February 1945, it is fighting on the Schafsberg, Neufeld, Rahnenfeld, coastline of the Frisches Haff 1 km southwest of Frauenburg line. The division has 4,183 men reporting for duty.

The losses of the 42nd Rifle Corps for the day of 6 February 1945: 24 killed and 53 wounded. Losses, inflicted on the enemy: up to 450 soldiers and officers killed or wounded, and 13 taken prisoner. The corps headquarters is in Blüdau.

The 72nd Separate Guards Special-purpose Naval Infantry Battalion is occupying a defense in the Tolkemit area. Throughout the day it was monitoring the coastline of the Frisches Haff lagoon southwest of Tolkemit and conducting reconnaissance on the spit of the Frische Nehrung, where it encountered heavy enemy fire from heavy machine guns, mortars and artillery, as well as mined sectors on the ice.

The 41st Cannon Artillery Regiment is in firing positions in the Neukirch-Höhe area with 16 serviceable 122mm howitzers.

The 1st Separate Guards Motorcycle Regiment is assembled in the Blumenau area. Throughout the day, it was servicing its machines and weapons. One reconnaissance group reconnoitered the spit of the Frische Nehrung. The regiment has in service 85 active bayonets, 2 M4A2 tanks and 4 SU-57.

The army's artillery throughout the day of 6 February 1945 was supporting the army's attacking troops. The weather is cloudy, the roads are passable.

The army headquarters' operational command group is in Schönberg.

Chief of staff of the 5th Guards Tank Army Guards Major General of Tank Forces SIDOROVICH
Chief of operations Guards Colonel FEDOROV

Table 4.19: Status of the materiel of the German Fourth Army (Lage der panzerbrechenden Waffen – AOK 4) by the end of 6 February 1945

Units	Armored vehicles and anti-tank guns					Under repair and not yet written off		Irrecoverable	Total
	StuG	Tanks	SP guns	sPak 76.2 mm	sPak 75-mm	Short-term	Long-term		
1	2	3	4	5	6	7	8	9	10
XXVI Armee Korps									
Gruppe "Wagner"									
StuG Brigade 277	10	-	-	-	-	2	4	-	16
Pz III	-	0	-	-	-	-	-	1	0
38(t)	-	1	-	-	-	-	-	-	1
T-34	-	2	-	-	-	6	5	-	13
Panzer Kp. 10 T-34	-	0	-	-	-	-	-	1	0
Pz V	-	1	-	-	-	-	-	-	1
Fest. Pak Kp Verb 7/VII									
88-mm	-	-	-	5	-	-	-	-	5
	-	-	-	-	2	-	-	-	2
Gruppe "Reichert"	-	-	-	-	7	-	-	-	7
Radfahr-Jäger Brigade 10	-	-	-	-	2	1	2	-	5
Pz III	-	0	-	-	-	-	1	-	1
Pz IV	-	0	-	-	-	-	-	1	0
38 (t)	-	4	-	-	-	-	-	-	4
Total for XXVI Korps	10	8	-	5	11	9	12	3	55
VI Armee Korps									
28.Jäger Division	-	-	-	-	13	-	2	-	15
Pz.Jg. Kp. 1028	3	-	-	-	-	2	3	-	8
2nd Bat., StuG Brigade 185	0	-	-	-	-	2	3	-	5

COMBAT OPERATIONS OF THE 5TH GUARDS TANK ARMY

Units	Armored vehicles and anti-tank guns					Under repair and not yet written off		Irrecoverable	Total
	StuG	Tanks	SP guns	sPak 76.2 mm	sPak 75-mm	Short-term	Long-term		
1	2	3	4	5	6	7	8	9	10
170.Infanterie Division	-	-	-	-	4	-	-	-	4
StuG Brigade 904	4	-	-	-	-	3	3	-	10
Total for VI Korps	7	-	-	-	17	7	11	-	42
VII Panzer Korps									
18.Panzergrenadier Division	-	-	-	-	1	-	-	-	1
Aufklär. Abt. *Grossdeutschland*	-	-	-	-	2	-	-	-	2
Panzer Abt. 118	6	-	-	-	-	-	-	-	6
1 Abt. sPak Abt. 664 88-mm	-	-	-	-	2	-	1	-	3
14.Infanterie Division	-	-	-	-	12	1	1	-	14
Pz.Jg. Kp. 1014	8	-	-	-	-	-	-	-	8
Fest. Pak Kp. 21/VII	-	-	-	-	2	-	-	-	2
131.Infanterie Division	-	-	-	-	5	-	-	-	5
Pz.Jg. Kp. 1131	1	-	-	-	-	2	1	-	4
sPz.Jg. Abt. 563 Pz IV	-	1	-	-	-	1	-	-	2
Pz V	-	4	-	-	-	1	-	-	5
Total for VII Panzer Korps	15	5	-	-	24	5	4	-	53
XX Armee Corps									
102.Infanterie Division	-	-	-	-	12	-	1	-	13
Pz.Jg. Kp. 1102	3	-	-	-	-	-	2	-	5
Elements of StuG Brigade 909	4	-	-	-	-	5	4	1	13
129.Infanterie Division	-	-	-	-	4	2	-	-	6
Elements of StuG Brigade 909	2	-	-	-	-	-	1	-	3
292.Infanterie Division	-	-	-	-	18	1	1	-	20
StuG Brigade 209	6	-	-	-	-	7	1	-	13
24.Panzer Division	-	-	-	-	7	-	-	-	7
88-mm	-	-	-	-	2	-	-	-	2
	-	-	-	6	-	-	-	-	6
3rd Bat., StuG Brigade 185	3	-	-	-	-	1	-	-	4
Kampfgruppe von Einem	-	-	-	-	5	-	-	-	5
Elements of StuG Brigade 209	4	-	-	-	-	-	-	-	4
Panzer Rgt. 24 (10+11) Pz IV	-	17	-	-	-	3	-	-	20
Bef.	-	2	-	-	-	-	-	-	2
1 Bat., Jg.Pz. Abt. 40	5	-	-	-	-	1	3	-	9
Total for the XX Korps	27	19	-	6	48	22	11	1	133

Units	Armored vehicles and anti-tank guns					Under repair and not yet written off		Irrecoverable	Total
	StuG	Tanks	SP guns	sPak 76.2 mm	sPak 75-mm	Short-term	Long-term		
1	2	3	4	5	6	7	8	9	10
XXXXI Panzer Korps									
541.Volksgrenadier Division	-	-	-	-	2	-	1	-	3
Pz.Jg. Kp. 1541	2	-	-	-	-	1	-	-	3
4 Bat., StuG Brigade 920	2	-	-	-	-	1	1	-	4
21.Infanterie Division	-	-	-	-	19	1	-	-	20
StuG Brigade 259	17	-	-	-	-	7	5	-	29
Kampfgruppe Hauser 88-mm	-	-	-	-	4	-	-	-	4
Fest. Pak Kp. 22-28/VII	-	-	-	-	17	-	-	-	17
	-	-	-	8	-	-	-	-	8
StuG Kp. 500	2	-	-	-	-	1	2	2	5
50.Infanterie Division	-	-	-	-	7	-	-	-	7
Pz.Jg. Kp. 1150	2	-	-	-	-	1	2	-	5
	-	-	2	-	-	-	1	-	3
56.Infanterie Division	-	-	-	-	15	-	-	-	15
Pz.Jg. Kp. 1156 Pz.Jg. Kp. 1349 StuG Brigade 203	12	-	-	-	-	19	2	-	33
Fest. Pak Kp. 7 and 8/VII	-	-	-	9	-	5	-	-	14
558.Volksgrenadier Division	-	-	-	-	6	-	-	-	6
Pz.Jg. Kp. 1558	3	-	-	-	-	3	-	-	6
61.Infanterie Division	-	-	-	-	6	2	3	-	11
2 Bat., StuG Brigade 203	2	-	-	-	-	2	-	-	4
Fest. Pak Kp. 17/1	-	-	-	3	-	-	-	-	3
Total for XXXXI Panzer Korps	42	-	2	20	76	41	17	2	200
Panzer Korps *Hermann Göring*									
Division *Grossdeutschland*	-	-	-	-	21	4	3	2	28
	-	-	-	-	4	-	-	-	4
	-	-	1	-	-	1	-	-	2
StuG	2	-	-	-	-	6	13	-	21
Pz IV	-	1	-	-	-	1	2	-	4
Pz V	-	5	-	-	-	10	1	-	16
Pz VI	-	3	-	-	-	4	2	-	9
2.Division *Hermann Göring*	-	-	-	-	8	1	-	-	9
	8	-	-	-	-	10	16	-	34
StuG Abt. *Hermann Göring*	2	-	-	-	-	2	2	-	6
Pz.Jg. Abt. *Hermann Göring*									

Units	Armored vehicles and anti-tank guns					Under repair and not yet written off		Irrecoverable	Total
	StuG	Tanks	SP guns	sPak 76.2 mm	sPak 75-mm	Short-term	Long-term		
1	2	3	4	5	6	7	8	9	10
StuG Brigade 279	-	-	1	-	-	-	-	-	1
	7	-	-	-	-	2	4	1	13
547.Volksgrenadier Division	-	-	-	-	12	-	-	-	12
1st Bat., StuG Brigade 185	3	-	-	-	-	-	1	-	4
562.Volksgrenadier Division	-	-	-	-	9	-	-	-	9
	4	-	-	-	-	1	-	-	5
Pz.Jg. Kp. 1562 Fest. Pak Kp. 16/1	-	-	-	3	-	-	-	-	3
Panzer Abt. 302	3	-	-	-	-	3	-	1	6
Total for Panzer Korps HG	29	9	2	3	54	45	44	4	186
Total for Fourth Army	130	41	4	34	230	129	99	10	669

On 7 February 1945 the Chief of Staff of the German Fourth Army issued an updated report on the casualties suffered by its subordinate formations and units:

Kampfgruppe Göbbel – 299th Infantry Division (6 February): 18 killed, 86 wounded, 33 missing;
Division *Hermann Göring* and 2nd Infantry Division, units directly subordinate to the headquarters (6 February): 26 killed, 123 wounded and 19 missing;
Panzergrenadier Division *Grossdeutschland* (6 February): 43 killed, 239 wounded and 29 missing;
662nd Volksgrenadier Division (4 and 6 February): 23 killed, 103 wounded and 6 missing;
547th Volksgrenadier Division (6 February): 104 killed, 332 wounded and 84 missing;
14th Infantry Division (5-6 February): 39 killed, 187 wounded and 21 missing;
18th Panzergrenadier Division (5-6 February): 23 killed, 198 wounded and 119 missing;
131st Infantry Division (5-6 February): 57 killed, 185 wounded and 2 missing;
170th Infantry Division (4-6 February): 113 killed, 534 wounded and 207 missing;
28th Jäger Division (5-6 February): 49 killed, 146 wounded and 115 missing;
24th Panzer Division (4-6 February) and (23-31 January): 337 killed, 1143 wounded and 164 missing;
129th Infantry Division (4-5 February): 25 killed, 117 wounded and 18 missing;
292nd Infantry Division (30 January – 5 February): 85 killed, 328 wounded and 80 missing;
VI Army Corps' directly subordinate units (28-31 January): 4 killed, 26 wounded and 48 missing;
21st Infantry Division (5 February and 28 January – 4 January): 59 killed, 222 wounded and 9 missing;
VII Panzer Corps' directly subordinate units (2 and 4 February): 1 killed, 6 wounded;
558th Volksgrenadier Division (5 February): 18 killed, 74 wounded;
541st Volksgrenadier Division (5 February): 25 killed, 115 wounded and 2 missing;
Kampfgruppe Hauser (5 February): 26 killed, 198 wounded;
203rd Infantry Division (5 February): 5 killed, 29 wounded;
102nd Infantry Division (30-31 January): 10 killed, 4 wounded;

50th Infantry Division (4 February): 25 killed, 111 wounded and 30 missing;
61st Infantry Division (4 February): 8 killed, 47 wounded and 10 missing;
Kampgruppe Blaurock (4 February): 46 killed, 161 missing;
Total casualties of the German Fourth Army over the period from 12 January to 6 February: a) in officers – 1,342 (310 killed, 928 wounded and 104 missing); b) in non-commissioned officers and enlisted men – 47,880 (9,985 killed, 29,863 wounded and 8,032 missing).

Armee-Oberkommando Der Chef des Generalstabes I.A.

The combat operations of the 5th Guards Tank Army from 7 to 10 February 1945

The forces of the 5th Guards Tank Army in the course of 7 February 1945 were engaged in heavy fighting in order to force a crossing of the Passarge River in the Baarden – Hopfenbruch sector. On the right flank, at 1350 on this day motorized infantry seized a bridgehead on the eastern banks of the Passarge River in the area of isolated cottages 1 km southwest of Klingenberg and the woods to the northwest. Under heavy German artillery and mortar fire, a bridge was quickly constructed in order to cross the tanks and self-propelled guns. On the left flank, motorized infantry was fighting for possession of Frauenburg.

Units of the 10th Tank Corps together with the 326th Heavy Self-propelled Artillery Regiment and the 689th Destroyer Antitank Artillery Regiment, and the 399th Rifle Division, throughout the day of 7 February were fighting in order to establish a bridgehead across the Passarge River against heavy enemy fire out of the Rawusen and Langwalde areas consisting of 4 heavy artillery batteries and 2 mortar batteries; and on the eastern outskirts of Klingenberg consisting of 6 antitank guns and up to a regiment of infantry, as well as the 10th Bicycle Jäger Brigade and up to a battalion of assault guns. The corps' units, overcoming the enemy's heavy fire, at 1750 on 7 February were forcing a crossing of the Passarge River and seized a bridgehead on the eastern bank in the area west of Klingenberg, where under enemy fire they constructed two bridges for the tanks and self-propelled guns.

By 2100 on 7 February 1945, the 186th Tank Brigade was fighting to cross the Passarge River at a point 500 meters west of Stigehnen, running into heavy enemy fire from out of the Luben area consisting of up of to a battalion of infantry, 3 artillery and mortar batteries, and 4-5 guns that were laying direct fire on the attackers. The 186th Tank Brigade had in service: 3 T-34, 4 SU-100 and 42 active bayonets.

The 11th Motorized Rifle Brigade at 1350 on 7 February 1945 was forcing a crossing of the Passarge River in the sector west of Klingenberg and was engaged in combat 500 meters west of that point while covering the construction of two bridges across the Passarge River. Throughout the day it fought off two counterattacks from the Klingenberg and Langwalde directions in strength of up to a battalion of infantry supported by 10 tanks and artillery. The brigade had in service: 196 active bayonets, 8 76mm guns, and 25 82mm and 120mm mortars.

The 183rd Tank Brigade was fighting to establish a bridgehead across the Passarge River 1 km east of Hopfenbruch with a battalion of submachine gunners, fighting in the woods 2 km northwest of Klingenberg, and covering the construction of the bridges for the tanks and self-propelled guns. The brigade had in service: 18 T-34, 5 SU-85 and 32 active bayonets.

The 178th Tank Brigade was 1 km northwest of Baarden as the corps commander's reserve. The brigade had in service: 8 T-34, 5 SU-100 and 99 active bayonets.

The 326th Heavy Self-propelled Artillery Regiment was in firing positions in the area of the Kagenau estate. The regiment had 5 operational ISU-122. The 727th Self-propelled Artillery

Regiment had 6 operational SU-76. The 689th Destroyer Antitank Artillery Regiment was in firing positions in the Hopfenbruch, Baarden area and had 14 serviceable 57mm guns.

Altogether the 10th Tank Corps and its attached assets had in service 32 T-34, 5 SU-122, 2 M4A2, 9 SU-100, 5 SU-85 and 6 SU-76; and 487 active bayonets. Over the day of fighting on 7 February the corps lost 1 T-34 destroyed, 2 SU-122 disabled by mines, and 1 SU-100 stuck in a swamp. Its casualties consisted of 14 killed and 96 wounded. According to preliminary information, the losses inflicted on the enemy included 4 antitank guns and 2 anti-aircraft guns destroyed, and 4 vehicles, 13 wagons and 3 mortars knocked-out. It killed or wounded up to 450 enemy soldiers and officers and took 16 prisoners. The corps headquarters was in Neumark.

On the 5th Tank Army's left flank, the 29th Tank Corps, together with the 366th Anti-aircraft Artillery Regiment, the 41st Cannon Artillery Regiment and the 201st Light Artillery Brigade (minus the 1315th Light Artillery Regiment), in cooperation with the 170th Rifle Division and 47th Mechanized Brigade, was engaged in heavy fighting to take the town of Frauenburg, having encountered strong enemy resistance on the town's southern outskirts (an antitank ditch and elaborate trenches, covered by the fire of tanks, antitank guns and anti-aircraft guns). At 2100 on 7 February the corps' units were engaged in combat:

The 31st Tank Brigade in cooperation with units of the 170th Rifle Division and the 47th Mechanized Brigade went on the attack at 1130 on 7 February with the mission to take Frauenburg. Having run into intense enemy fire from a city park and Hill 46.5, it is engaged in fighting on the line of the highway and railroad 800 meters west of Hill 46.5. The brigade has in service: 10 T-34, 7 SU-152, 3 SU-76 and 50 active bayonets.

The 53rd Motorized Rifle Brigade (minus one battalion) is holding a brick factory with one battalion, an artillery battalion and a mortar battalion, screening the shoreline of the sea and preventing an enemy breakout in the southwestern direction, while continuing to mop up fully the woods in the area of the Louisenthal Station and southwest of there of enemy infantry. One motorized rifle battalion is assembled in Conradswalde in the corps commander's reserve. The brigade had in service: 113 active bayonets, 6 76mm guns, and 18 82mm and 120mm mortars.

The 25th Tank Brigade and one battalion of the 53rd Motorized Rifle Brigade are occupying a hedgehog defense in Tolkemit and scouting in the northeastern and southwestern directions. The brigade had in service: 5 T-34, 4 SU-152, and 57 active bayonets.

The 32nd Tank Brigade with the 1223rd Light Self-propelled Artillery Regiment and the 14th Guards Heavy Tank Regiment were operationally subordinate to the 124th Rifle Corps. At 1100 on 7 February they were fighting in the area northeast of the Schaden.

The 75th Separate Motorcycle Regiment is reconnoitering in the corps' operational sector. It had 5 operational M4A2 tanks and 2 halftracks.

The reserve of the corps commander from the 32nd Tank Brigade was assembled in Rückenau with 2 T-34 and 7 SU-85 operational. The corps headquarters had 2 operational T-34 tanks.

The 47th Mechanized Brigade together with the 146th Anti-aircraft Artillery Regiment, the 1315th Light Artillery Brigade and the 376th Heavy Self-propelled Artillery Regiment on the night of 6-7 February 1945 conducted a march and by 0900 on 7 February was in assembled in the Narz area (3 km southwest of Frauenburg). At 1100 on 7 February it became operationally subordinate to the commander of the 29th Tank Corps. In cooperation with the 31st Tank Brigade and units of the 170th Rifle Division, at 1130 it went on the attack with the objective of capturing Frauenburg. By 2100 on 7 February it was engaged in combat 800 meters southwest of this town. The brigade had in service: 3 M4A2 tanks, 4 SU-152 and 280 active bayonets.

The 1315th Light Artillery Regiment was in firing positions 2 km north of Kreuzdorf with 13 serviceable 76mm guns. The 376th Heavy Self-propelled Artillery Regiment was up among the brigade's combat formations.

The 41st Cannon Artillery Regiment was in firing positions northeast of Neukirch-Höhe, supporting the 31st Tank Brigade and 47th Mechanized Brigade. It had 16 serviceable 122mm howitzers. The 1619th Light Artillery Regiment was in firing positions 2 km north of Kreuzdorf with 14 serviceable 76mm guns. The 651st Cannon Artillery Regiment was in firing positions in the Klakendorf area with 14 serviceable 100mm guns.

Altogether, the 29th Tank Corps (minus the 32nd Tank Brigade and 1223rd Self-propelled Artillery Regiment) with its attached assets had in service 19 T-34, 8 M4A2, 15 SU-152, 7 SU-85 and 3 SU-76; and 836 active bayonets. Over the day of 7 February 1945, the corps lost 1 T-34 and 2 SU-152 that were knocked out; 1 M4A2 tank destroyed; and 31 men killed or wounded. The damage inflicted on the enemy: 5 guns of various caliber, 1 antiaircraft gun, 3 mortars and [?] tanks destroyed, and up to 150 soldiers and officers eliminated. The corps headquarters was in Rückenau.

The 42nd Rifle Corps, in cooperation with the 10th and 29th Tank Corps, spent the day of 7 February fighting to force a crossing of the Passarge River in the Baarden, Hopfenbruch sector, and to take the town of Frauenburg.

The 72nd Guards Special-purpose Naval Infantry Battalion was operationally subordinate to the 29th Tank Corps. Throughout the night of 6-7 February 1945 it conducted reconnaissance toward the Frische Nehrung while its main forces were assembled in the Tolkemit area. On the southern bank of the spit in the Schmergrube and Kahlberg – Liep directions it ran into intense fire from heavy machine guns and submachine guns, as well as mined sectors of the ice. On the night of 7-8 February, it was in readiness to operate in full strength with the task to straddle the Frische Nehrung spit and to prevent an enemy withdrawal in the western direction. The battalion had 100 Ford amphibious jeeps and 331 men reporting for duty.

The 1st Guards Separate Motorcycle Regiment was in the Blumenau area. It had formed a reconnaissance detachment consisting of 5 reconnaissance groups (a total of 141 men with light weapons: 2 mortars and 6 heavy machine guns on sleds), which on the night of 7-8 February reached the Frische Nehrung and took up a defense in the Kahlberg – Liep, Langhagen, Schellmühl and Schottland areas, with the missions to prevent an enemy retreat in the western direction, to mine the roads, and to form obstructions on the roads from fallen trees and debris. The lagoon's ice was suitable only to cross infantry with light weapons. The regiment had in service: 2 M4A2, 4 SU-57, 120 motorcycles and 78 active bayonets.

From the recollections of L. Rabichev:

February 1945. East Prussia. It was precisely then that a strange occurance arose, information about which I've never seen either in memoirs or fictional literature. As a result of bloody, uncompromising and incessant fighting, both our units and the German units had lost more than half their men, and had begun to lose their combat effectiveness from extreme, incomparable exhaustion. Cherniakhovsky kept ordering to attack, and the generals – the army commanders, corps commanders and division commanders were repeating these orders. The *Stavka* was getting carried away, and all the regiments, separate brigades, battalions and companies were making no headway. So as if to force the units that had become worn out by the fighting to advance, the Front headquarters had moved to within a disconcertingly close distance of the front, the headquarters of the armies were situated almost right next the corps headquarters, and the division headquarters were side by side with the regiment headquarters. The generals were seeking to give a prod to the battalions and companies, but nothing came of this.

So then the days arrived when both our soldiers and the German soldiers were in the grip of insurmountable depression. The Germans had fallen back about 3 kilometers, but we were coming to a stop. Sunny, spring-like days arrived, no one was firing, and there was the impression that the war was ending, but the command had seeminly lost its senses. Plainly striving to curry favor with his superiors, my commander Tarasov ordered me and a portion of the platoon to relocate closer to the front with a new American radio set that had an operational range of up to 100 kilometers. The broadcast tower was ensuring superb performance. In this stage of the offensive, no one was bothering to use codes or Morse telegraphs. All the orders were going out in open text, and the radio waves were full of finely layered, hoarse swearing of unprecedented exertion, yet the soldiers slept, and it was impossible to rouse them to action. They would wake up, and swap stories about their pre-war shenanigans and about the German women that hadn't been able to evacuate. Kotlov was astonished: You could enter a home, and without saying a word, the German woman would drop her trousers, hike up her skirt, lie down on a bed, and spread her legs. Then once again the radio operator would deliver the order about an attack. We would have to ensure communications with an anti-aircraft artillery brigade.

In February 1945 I spent 48 hours at an order from the deputy artillery commander keeping contact with an anti-aircraft artillery brigade, which was being used in a ground role to fire at German tanks. When we reached the shores of the Frisches-Haff, out in front of us was the sea, and on the horizon was the Danzig – Pillau spit. The entire coastline was strewn with German helmets, submachine guns, unexploded grenades, cans of food, packages of cigarettes, and cigarette lighters. Along the shore, two-story cottages were standing approximately 200 meters from each other, in which wounded, diehard Fritzes were lying either on beds or on the floors. Some remotely, others indifferently, were silently looking at us. Neither fear nor hatred, but an apathetic indifference was showing on their faces; any one of us could raise our submachine guns and massacre them. However, nothing remained of the seething hatred that had recently been still been roiling in us. Consciously or unconsciously, they were demonstrating their vulnerability and emptiness inside.

At this moment the thought occurred not only to me, but also to many thousands of soldiers and officers of my army, that the war had ended on our axis of advance, and from some improbable coincidence, and everyone who was able and who had some sort of weapon began firing into the air. Submachine guns, pistols, mortars, tanks, and self-propelled guns. Thousands of pyrotechnics and tracer rounds soared into the air, and the laughter and commotion lasted around fifteen minutes. This was our first, free, happy victory salute in our lives. Then flasks and bottles of liquor appeared. We were laughing, crying, drinking and remembered. No one was hurrying us to go anywhere.

Several days later I received an order over the radio to gather my platoon and at our own march, which is to say on our horse-drawn transport on eight wagons and horseback, to return along the road we had recently traveled to the town of Siethen, which was standing on a railroad line. With surprise we looked at absolutely empty villages and towns, which just two weeks before had been full of women, old men and children. It was a dead land.

Table 4.20: Status of the materiel of the German Fourth Army (Lage der panzerbrechenden Waffen – AOK 4) by the end of 7 February 1945

Units	Armored vehicles and anti-tank guns					Under repair and not yet written off		Irrecoverable	Total
	StuG	Tanks	SP guns	sPak 76.2 mm	sPak 75-mm	Short-term	Long-term		
1	2	3	4	5	6	7	8	9	10
XXVI Armee Korps									
Gruppe "Wagner"									
StuG Brigade 277	12	-	-	-	-	9	-	-	21
38(t)	-	2	-	-	-	-	-	-	2
T-34	-	3	-	-	-	6	-	-	9
T-34	-	3	-	-	-	-	-	-	3
Gruppe "Reichert"	2	-	-	-	-	-	-	-	2
	-	-	1	-	-	-	-	-	1
	-	-	-	-	2	-	-	-	2
Gruppe "Wulf"	-	-	-	-	5	-	-	-	5
Fest. Pak Kp Verb 7/VII	-	-	-	5	-	-	-	-	5
88-mm	-	-	-	-	2	-	-	-	2
Total for XXVI Korps	14	8	1	5	9	15	-	-	52
VI Armee Korps									
28.Jäger Division	-	-	-	-	13	-	-	-	13
Pz.Jg. Kp. 1028	5	-	-	-	-	2	-	-	7
2nd Bat., StuG Brigade 185	0	-	-	-	-	2	3	-	5
Radfahr-Jäger Brigade 10	-	-	-	-	2	1	2	-	5
	2	-	-	-	-	-	-	-	2
38 (t)	-	4	-	-	-	-	-	-	4
170.Infanterie Division	-	-	-	-	4	-	-	-	4
StuG Brigade 904	4	-	-	-	-	2	1	-	7
Total for VI Korps	11	4	-	-	19	7	6	-	47
VII Panzer Korps									
18.Panzergrenadier Division	-	-	-	-	1	-	-	-	1
Aufklär. Abt. GD	-	-	-	-	2	-	-	-	2
Panzer Abt. 118	6	-	-	-	-	-	-	-	6
1 Abt. sPak Abt. 664 88-mm	-	-	-	-	2	-	1	-	3
14.Infanterie Division	-	-	-	-	12	1	1	-	14
Pz.Jg. Kp. 1014	8	-	-	-	-	-	-	-	8
Fest. Pak Kp. 21/VII	-	-	-	-	5	-	-	-	5
131.Infanterie Division	-	-	-	-	2	-	-	-	2
Pz.Jg. Kp. 1131	1	-	-	-	-	2	1	-	4
sPz.Jg. Abt. 563 Pz IV Pz V	-	1	-	-	-	1	-	-	2
	-	4	-	-	-	1	1	-	6
Total for VII Panzer Korps	15	5	-	-	24	5	4	-	53
XX Armee Korps									

Units	Armored vehicles and anti-tank guns					Under repair and not yet written off		Irrecoverable	Total
	StuG	Tanks	SP guns	sPak 76.2 mm	sPak 75-mm	Short-term	Long-term		
1	2	3	4	5	6	7	8	9	10
102.Infanterie Division	-	-	-	-	12	-	1	-	13
Pz.Jg. Kp. 1102	3	-	-	-	-	2	-	-	5
Elements of StuG Brigade 909	4	-	-	-	-	5	4	-	13
129.Infanterie Division	-	-	-	-	5	1	-	-	6
Elements of StuG Brigade 909	3	-	-	-	-	-	1	-	3
292.Infanterie Division	-	-	-	-	18	1	1	-	20
StuG Brigade 209	6	-	-	-	-	5	3	-	14
24.Panzer Division	-	-	-	-	9	-	-	2	9
1 Bat., Jg.Pz. Abt. 40	4	-	-	-	-	1	3	-	8
Pz.Rgt. 24 (10+11) Pz IV	-	9	-	-	-	8	2	1	19
Bef.	-	2	-	-	-	-	-	-	2
3rd Bat., StuG Brigade 185	2	-	-	-	-	2	-	-	4
Elements of StuG Brigade 209	4	-	-	-	-	-	-	-	4
sPak Kp. 88-mm	-	-	-	-	2	-	-	-	2
Separate Pak Kp.	-	-	-	4	-	-	-	-	4
558.Volksgrenadier Division	-	-	-	-	6	-	-	-	6
Pz.Jg. Kp. 1558	3	-	-	-	-	1	-	-	4
Fest. Pak Kp. 21/VII	-	-	-	-	1	-	-	-	1
Total for the XX Korps	29	11	-	4	54	26	14	3	137
XXXXI Panzer Korps									
541.Volksgrenadier Division	-	-	-	-	2	-	1	-	3
Pz.Jg. Kp. 1541	2	-	-	-	-	1	-	-	3
4 Bat., StuG Brigade 920	2	-	-	-	-	1	1	-	4
21.Infanterie Division	-	-	-	-	20	-	-	-	20
StuG Brigade 259	17	-	-	-	-	7	5	-	29
Kampfgruppe Hauser 88-mm	-	-	-	-	4	-	-	-	4
Fest. Pak Kp. 22-28/VII	-	-	-	-	17	-	-	-	17
	-	-	-	8	-	-	-	-	8
StuG Kp. 500	2	-	-	-	-	1	-	-	3
50.Infanterie Division	-	-	-	-	7	-	-	-	7
Pz.Jg. Kp. 1150	2	-	-	-	-	1	2	-	5
	-	-	1	-	-	1	1	-	3
56.Infanterie Division	-	-	-	-	16	-	-	-	16
Pz.Jg. Kp. 1156	5	-	-	-	-	5	-	-	10
Pz.Jg. Kp. 1349	6	-	-	-	-	4	-	-	10
Fest. Pak Kp. 7 and 8/VII	-	-	-	-	9	-	-	-	9

Units	Armored vehicles and anti-tank guns					Under repair and not yet written off		Irrecoverable	Total
	StuG	Tanks	SP guns	sPak 76.2 mm	sPak 75-mm	Short-term	Long-term		
1	2	3	4	5	6	7	8	9	10
61.Infanterie Division	-	-	-	-	6	2	3	-	11
2 Bat., StuG Brigade 203	2	-	-	-	-	2	-	-	4
Fest. Pak Kp. 17/1	-	-	-	3	-	-	-	-	3
Total for XXXXI Panzer Korps	43	-	1	20	72	30	18	-	184
Panzer Korps *Hermann Göring*									
Division *Grossdeutschland*	-	-	-	-	21	4	3	-	28
	-	-	-	-	4	-	-	-	4
	-	-	1	-	-	1	-	-	2
StuG	2	-	-	-	-	6	13	-	21
Pz IV	-	1	-	-	-	1	2	-	4
Pz V	-	5	-	-	-	10	1	-	16
Pz VI	-	3	-	-	-	4	2	-	9
2.Division *Hermann Göring*	-	-	-	-	8	1	-	-	9
	8	-	-	-	-	10	16	-	34
StuG Abt. *Hermann Göring*	2	-	-	-	-	2	2	-	6
Pz.Jg. Abt. *Hermann Göring*									
StuG Brigade 279	-	-	1	-	-	-	-	-	1
	7	-	-	-	-	2	4	-	13
547.Volksgrenadier Division	-	-	-	-	12	-	-	-	12
1st Bat., StuG Brigade 185	3	-	-	-	-	-	1	-	4
562.Volksgrenadier Division	-	-	-	-	9	-	-	-	9
Pz.Jg. Kp. 1562	4	-	-	-	-	1	-	-	5
Fest. Pak Kp. 16/1	-	-	-	3	-	-	-	-	3
Panzer Abt. 302	3	-	-	-	-	3	-	-	6
Total for Panzer Korps HG	29	9	2	3	54	45	44	-	186
Total for Fourth Army	141	37	4	32	231	128	86	3	659

Table 4.21: Available artillery in the formations and units of the German Fourth Army (Lage der panzerbrechenden Waffen – AOK 4) by end of 7 February 1945

	Machine guns	88-mm guns	120-mm guns	Light field guns	Heavy field guns	Light howitzers	Heavy howitzers	100-mm cannon K	210mm mortars
XXVI Armee Korps	44	162	24	43	21	38	63	-	17
VI Armee Korps	48	189	6	33	2	29	43	44	-
VII Panzer Korps	44	49	11	21	9	15	26	5	-
XX Armee Korps	21	73	3	14	13	14	36	11	-
XXXXI Panzer Korps	30	72	9	21	8	24	48	33	-
Panzer Korps HG	18	51	3	9	3	23	37	21	8

On 8 February 1945, the Chief of Staff of the Fourth Army issued another report on the army's casualties:

> Losses in men: 818 killed, 2,749 wounded and 441 missing-in-action. Of which:
> 28th Jäger Division (4-7 February): 78 killed, 179 wounded and 29 missing;
> 14th Infantry Division (3-6 February): 78 killed, 377 wounded and 11 missing;
> 18th Panzergrenadier Division (3-6 February): 89 killed, 536 wounded and 147 missing;
> 131st Infantry Division (3-6 February): 132 killed, 334 wounded and 24 missing;
> 170th Infantry Division (2-7 February): 17 killed and 114 wounded;
> 102nd Infantry Division (31 January – 4 February): 74 killed, 197 wounded and 28 missing;
> Kampfgruppe Wagner (3-5 February): 43 killed, 211 wounded and 72 missing;
> Kampgruppe Göbbel (3-5 February): 167 killed, 376 wounded and 95 missing;
> 1st (East Prussian) Infantry Division (20 January – 7 February): 140 killed, 425 wounded and 35 missing.
> **Total casualties of the German Fourth Army over the period from 12 January to 7 February 1945 amounted to:** a) officers – 1,146 (336 killed, 992 wounded and 118 missing); b) non-commissioned officers and enlisted men: 51,888 (10,803 killed, 32,612 wounded and 8,473 missing).
>
> Armee-Oberkommando Der Chef des Generalstabes I.A.

In his memoirs, Hero of the Soviet Union General of the Army I.F. Ivanovsky described the Soviet tactics employed during this offensive:

The town of Liebstadt was a powerful center of resistance of the Nazis. A rather large grouping of enemy forces was defending here. The task of the units and heavy tank crews was to drive a gap into the enemy's system of defenses, and then energetically advance, without allowing the Nazis to consolidate on an advantageous line and brushing aside their rearguard detachments and ambushes. A short artillery preparation or artillery barrage normally preceded the tank attack. Here there was no need for a lengthy preparation with artillery fire. The arrangement of the tanks' combat formation took into account the details of the enemy's defenses.

The T-34 tanks, deployed into combat line, initiated the attack, and behind them, on the flanks and the boundaries of the units' elements, the heavy tanks advanced. In the depth of the combat formation was the self-propelled artillery. Such an arrangement, as we'd become convinced, ensured the reliable collaboration of the units and elements, and an effective impact on the enemy. Putting it more simply, nothing could hold back this tidal wave of armor. At the moment of the breaching the enemy's defense, the heavy tanks with their powerful fire facilitated the advance of the T-34s, fought the enemy artillery, and repulsed the adversary's counterattacks. Our crews also took on counterattacking Nazi groups consisting of elements of tanks, self-propelled guns and submachine gunners, which in truth sometimes presented a serious danger. It such a group that was penetrating into the depth of our combat formations wasn't stopped or destroyed, it was capable of inflicting heavy losses on the attackers.

Whenever issuing the next mission, I would emphasize to the commanders of the elements about the need for more energetic maneuvering. The tank after all isn't a gun, but a combat machine. The crew must not limit itself to conducting fire from an advantageous position – it must make full use of the tank's ability to move.

The breakthrough of the enemy's positions in the Liebstadt area, because of the fact that the enemy had hastily gone over to a defense, was organized according to just this scheme. The artillery conducted a short, but powerful artillery barrage on the enemy's fortifications and gun positions. It should be noted that our artillerymen, who possessed accurate intelligence information and who had high degree of skill with their artillery pieces, knew how to place each shell on target. Indeed, on this occasion after their work the enemy's defense was sufficiently suppressed and compromised. After the artillery barrage, not wasting a minute, our crews, together with the units of the 60th Tank Brigade, advanced swiftly along the ravines and through the woodlots, bypassing Liebstadt on its western outskirst.

I made the decision to straddle two important roads in order to cut off the enemy's path of retreat. Indeed, subsequently this decision proved correct. In the ensuing battle the Nazis from the first minutes took significant losses from the fire of our 122mm guns. Even so, they resisted stubbornly, and brought up their tanks and self-propelled guns in separate sectors, trying to stop our advance. Guards Captain M. Ponomarev's and Guards Captain Ia. Tishchenko's heavy tank companies focused their efforts on the fascist strongpoints – destroying them with accurate fire and killing the Nazis who were abandoning cover. They stopped an enemy attempt to organize a counterattack at the very outset, in the process destroying two fascist tanks. Other tank elements at this time were probing weakpoints in the enemy's defenses and penetrated ever deeper into the town. In the wake of them, the rifle units broke into the outskirts, and then then into the town's center.

One of the companies, as a rule, I kept in my reserve. Given a clear turning point in the situation, I was always able to augment the force and to impact the enemy there, wherever this was particularly acutely necessary. During the breakthrough of the enemy's defenses in the Liebstadt area, Guards Captain S. Andrievsky's tank company was in my reserve. In this combat action we were cooperating with "little brothers" – the tankers of Guards Colonel Turenkov's T-34 brigade. Our commander's tanks per usual were moving not far from each other. We were keeping contact not only by radio. When necessary it was possible, having opened the hatch and stood up, to make an explanation with gestures.

On the axis of the T-34s' attack, German Tiger tanks appeared, which presented a serious danger.

"Falcon! Falcon! Your guys aren't seeing the Tigers!" – Turenkov shouted with frustration over the radio. "Your guys aren't helping us!"

We were both standing in the hatches of our tanks up to our chests. It was clear to me how brigade commander Turenkov was gesturing with his arms – hey, he needed the support of the heavy tanks right now! I summoned the commander of the reserve tank company Guards Captain Andrievsky, and when he came running up, I leaped down onto the ground. It was best of all at that critical moment to issue the orders directly on the spot, without turning to a map. Given the noise of the tank engines, I had to shout.

"Andrievsky, so you see that corner of the woods and the low hill next to it?"

"I see them, Comrade Colonel."

"Take that line and go on the attack from it."

"Understood."

"There, on the eastern slopes, Tigers are moving out. Strike them as necessary."

"Understood, yes sir!"

The company commander rushed back to his tank. On the run, he gave a circular motion with his arm: "Start them up!" The reserve tank company moved out to intercept the Tigers, attacked them, and prevented them from attacking the "little brothers". I hear the voice of brigade commander Turenkov in my headset: "Thanks, Falcon, thanks!"

Abstracting somewhat from the dynamics of this battle at Liebstadt, I will say that even now, at training maneuvers, I counsel the commanders always to have a reserve, so that by this they can have an effect on the situation, if necessary. Moreover, it is necessary to give the reserve commander his orders personally on the ground. His actions must be active right away. How might it happen otherwise? Over the radio, directions are given to increase speed, to reach a line by a certain time.

"I'm fast-tracking your departure" – this certifies that commander that someone is very much counting on his rapid arrival. Time passes, and there is no sign that the troops are moving out. Just when the moment of impact on the enemy has been ultimately thrown away, they appear … on the outskirts of the maneuver area.

The grouping of enemy forces in Liebstadt was crushed, and this had it effect on the subsequent course of events. Under the onslaught of our units the enemy was retreating in the northwestern direction. On certain lines, chiefly on the flanks, the Nazis were leaving behind blocking detachments in the form of mobile ambushes of two to three tanks or self-propelled guns each. The ambush positions were reinforced by groups of submachine gunners, who conducted close-range patrols and kept their command informed about the movement of our forcs. The 62nd Guards Tank Regiment, in cooperation with the 60th Guards Tank Brigade, was pursuing the enemy.

The enemy, relying on Frauenburg's previously prepared, elaborate antitank defenses, in the course of 8 February 1945 was putting up stubborn resistance with the fire of artillery, tanks, anti-aircraft guns and infantry, but was being pushed back to the north.

On the spit of the Frische Nehrung, the enemy brought up unidentified units to the Kahlberg – Liep area, drove some of our detachments off the spit, and blocked the movement of our units across the Frisches-Haff. The Germans were shelling the Tolkemit area from beyond the spit with naval guns. The Luftwaffe in groups of FW-190 fighter-bombers were bombing our troops and conducting reconnaissance over the coastline of the Frisches-Haff.

Throughout the night and day of 8 February 1945 the troops of the 5th Guards Tank Army conducting a regrouping with part of its strength, while continuing to hold their occupied line firmly with its main forces and also conducting offensive actions to take possession of Frauenburg. The fighting established that the enemy, with units of the 1444th Fortress Battalion, the 10th Naval Junkers School and tanks of the 24th Panzer Division, was fiercely defending Frauenburg, having an antitank ditch, full-profile trenches, six artillery batteries, two Flak batteries and four Panther tanks on the southwestern outskirts. After three days of bitter fighting, the Soviet motorized infantry, with the support of artillery and tanks, overcame the fierce resistance and broke into the city at 1700 on 8 February; by 1800 fighting was going on in the center of the town. Simultaneously, the Soviet troops were repulsing enemy counterattacks in strength of a battalion of infantry supported by tanks from the northeastern outskirts of Frauenburg. By 1900, the city was completely mopped up of the enemy.

The 10th Tank Corps, having turned over its occupied sector to the 29th Rifle Corps at 0200 on 8 February, by 0900 of the same day had assembled in the Heinrichsdorf, Dittersdorf, Vierzighuben area. The tank corps was given the order to set out on the morning of 9 February and with the forces of the 183rd Tank Brigade and 11th Motorized Rifle Brigade to sweep the western bank of the Baude River clear of the enemy in cooperation with the 29th Tank Corps' 47th Mechanized Brigade and 31st Tank Brigade. The 10th Tank Corps' 178th Tank Brigade, remaining in Dittersdorf, and the 186th Tank Bank Brigade – in the woods 2 km north of Bludau, were to be in full readiness to repulse enemy counterattacks from the east and northeast.

By 2100 on 8 February the 10th Tank Corps' units were occupying the following positions: 186th Tank Brigade – had assembled in the wooded area 1.5 km southeast of Vierzighuben with 5 T-34 tanks and 5 SU-100 still operational; the 178th Tank Brigade was in the Dittersdorf area with 8 T-34 tanks and 7 SU-100 in service; the 183rd Tank Brigade was assembled in Heinrichsdorf up until 2000 on 8 February, but at 2000 it set out on the march to the Rothhof, Narz, Neuhof area and had assembled in this area by 2400; the 11th Motorized Rifle Brigade by 0900 on 8 February had assembled in the wooded area 1 km east of Vierizhuben, but at 2000 it also set out to a new area and by midnight, together with the 183rd Tank Brigade, it had assembled in the Rothhof, Narz, Neuhof area in readiness to operate in the direction of Frauenburg. The brigade had 196 men reporting for duty, together with 8 76mm guns and 21 82mm mortars. By midnight the 727th Self-propelled Artillery Regiment had joined the 183rd Tank Brigade and 11th Motorized Rifle Brigade in the indicated area with 6 operational SU-76. The 705th Light Artillery Regiment was in an area 200 meters west of Vierzighuben with 21 serviceable 76mm guns. The 77th Separate Motorcycle Battalion was in a wooded area 300 meters west of Vierzighuben with 4 operational M4A2 tanks. The 326th Heavy Self-propelled Artillery Regiment by midnight on 8 February had assembled in the 183rd Tank Brigade's operational area with 8 serviceable SU-122.

Altogether, the 10th Tank Corps had in service 33 T-34, 4 M4A2 and 1 ISU-122 tanks; 12 SU-00, 8 SU-122 and 6 SU-76 assault guns; 7 SU-85 tank destroyers; and 513 active bayonets. Supply status: diesel fuel – 1.5 refills; gasoline – 0.4 of a refill; ammunition – 1.5 standard combat loads; and 5 days worth of food. The corps headquarters was in Vierzighuben.

The 29th Tank Corps together with its attached assets was firmly holding the Neukirch-Höhe, Tolkemit area, while fighting for possession of Frauenburg with part of its force in cooperation with the 47th Mechanized Brigade and units of the 170th Rifle Division. After three days of savage fighting, they broke the Frauenburg garrison's resistance and broke into the southwestern outskirts of the town at 1700 on 8 February. By 1900 they had fully mopped up Frauenburg of the enemy in street fighting. In the combat for Frauenburg, the Germans lost more than 2,000 men killed alone.

By 2100 on 8 February the corps' units were occupying the following positions: 31st Tank Brigade – by 1030 on 8 February, together with the 47th Mechanized Brigade and in cooperation with units of the 170th Rifle Division and the 72nd Separate Special-Purpose Naval Infantry Battalion, in pursuit of its previously assigned orders, had gone on the offensive with the objective of capturing Frauenburg. After three days of fire combat, having broken the enemy's stubborn resistance, together with its cooperating and attached units, it broke into the southwestern outskirts of Frauenburg and had taken full possession of the town by 1930 on 8 February. The brigade had in service 3 T-34 tanks, 5 SU-152 and 3 SU-76, and 48 active bayonets.

The 53rd Motorized Rifle Brigade with one motorized rifle battalion, an artillery battalion and a mortar battalion was screening the coastline, preventing an enemy breakout in the southwestern direction. Throughout the day of 8 February, it fought to mop up the woods in the vicinity of the Louisenthal railroad station. One motorized rifle battalion was holding the defense in Tolkemit, operationally subordinate to the commander of the 25th Tank Brigade. The remaining motorized rifle battalion was in the Conradswalde area in the corps commander's reserve. The brigade had in service 11 76mm guns, 24 82mm and 120mm mortars, and 134 active bayonets. The 53rd Motorized Rifle Brigade's 5th Tank Battalion and the 1st Motorized Rifle Battalion were occupying an all-round defense in Tolkemit. At 1400 on 8 February it was engaging in combat with an enemy group of 300 men supported by 4 self-propelled guns in the wooded area 1 km southeast of Kickelhof. In the combat, it wiped out up to 150 enemy soldiers and officers and destroyed one self-propelled gun. It captured the other three self-propelled guns in good working order. The brigade had in service 4 T-34 tanks, 5 SU-152 and 57 active bayonets.

The 32nd Tank Brigade with the 1223rd Light Self-propelled Artillery Regiment and 14th Guards Heavy Tank Regiment was operationally subordinate to the commander of the 124th Rifle Corps and occupying a hedgehog defense in the area of the Spanden estate with 5 T-34 tanks, 2 SU-152, 2 SU-85 and 18 SU-76 still operational, and 45 active bayonets. The brigade had lost 2 T-34 tanks destroyed and 3 T-34 tanks knocked-out, as well as 1 SU-85 destroyed and 2 SU-85 knocked-out. The 1223rd Light Self-propelled Artillery Regiment had lost 2 SU-76 destroyed and 1 SU-76 knocked-out. The 14th Guards Heavy Tank Regiment had just 1 ISU-122 tank still in service. Three ISU-122 tanks had been destroyed, and 6 ISU-122 tanks had been knocked-out. The 165th Light Artillery Regiment was in firing positions in the area of the eastern and southeastern outskirts of Tolkemit with 14 serviceable 76mm guns. The 271st Mortar Regiment was in firing positions in the vicinity of Hill 107.6 supporting the operations of the 47th Mechanized Brigade with 19 serviceable 120mm mortars. The 75th Separate Motorcycle Battalion was conducting reconnaissance in the corps' operational sector; it had 5 operational M4A2 tanks and 2 halftracks. The corps commander's reserve, consisting in 2 T-34 tanks and 7 SU-85 tank destroyers from the 32nd Tank Brigade, was in the Rückenau area.

Altogether the 29th Tank Corps had operational 15 T-34 tanks and 5 M4A2 tanks, 10 SU-152 and 18 SU-76 assault guns, and 9 SU-85 tank destroyers; and 284 active bayonets. Its casualties consisted of 4 killed and 8 wounded, and it had lost 3 T-34 tanks destroyed and 1 T-34 knocked-out. The losses inflicted on the enemy were 3 Panther tanks, 3 assault guns, 2 self-propelled guns, 2 artillery batteries and 2 machine guns destroyed; and up to 650 enemy officers and soldiers killed or wounded. It also captured 1 mortar battery and 3 self-propelled guns. Supply status: diesel fuel – 1.5 refills; gasoline – 0.5 of a refill; ammunition – 1.5 standard combat loads; and 3 days worth of food. The corps headquarters was in Rückenau.

The 47th Mechanized Brigade in cooperation with the 31st Tank Brigade and the 170th Rifle Division's 422nd Rifle Regiment had captured Frauenburg by 1900 on 8 February, and by 2000 had reached the western bank of the Baude River in the sector 1 km northeast of Willenberg and was saddling the highway and railroad. As a result of the fighting the brigade had the following losses: 39 killed and 11 wounded, as well as 2 M4A2 tanks destroyed, and 2 M4A2 tanks, 3 76mm guns and 1 57mm gun knocked-out. The damage done to the enemy: 7 guns of various calibers and 21 machine guns destroyed, and up to 1,000 enemy soldiers and officers killed or wounded. In addition, it knocked out 4 tanks and took 98 enemy soldiers prisoner. The brigade has in service 5 M4A2 tanks and 547 active bayonets.

The 42nd Rifle Corps in the course of 8 February was firmly holding its occupied line, while the 170th Rifle Division's 422nd Rifle Regiment, in cooperation with the 29th Tank Corps, was attacking toward Frauenburg. Over the day of 8 February, the corps lost 20 men killed and 68 wounded. The damage done to the enemy: Up to 350 enemy soldiers and officers killed or wounded, and another 32 soldiers captured, as well as 2 tanks destroyed, 2 tanks captured, and 2 antitank guns. The 41st Cannon Artillery Regiment was in firing positions on the northeastern outskirts of Neukirch-Höhe, supporting the reconnaissance groups that were operating on the spit of the Frische Nehrung with its fire. The regiment had 16 serviceable 122mm guns. The 72nd Separate Special-Purpose Naval Infantry Battalion from the morning of 8 February was fighting for possession of Hill 45.5 and had taken it by 1240. By 2000 it was fighting on the western bank of the Baude River. The 376th Heavy Self-propelled Artillery Regiment was supporting the operations of the 47th Mechanized Brigade with 6 operational SU-152.

The 1st Separate Guards Motorcycle Regiment was assembled in the Blumenau area while its men were servicing the tanks and weapons. A reconnaissance detachment of it consisting of 141 men, 2 82mm mortars on sleds, 6 heavy machine guns on sleds, 6 light machine guns, 2 antitank rifles, 95 submachine guns, 22 carbines, and 1 RSB radio and 3 RBM radios was operating toward the Frische Nehrung spit, and on the night of 7-8 February the reconnaissance detachment had taken up defensive positions on the spit with five groups.

In the course of the day of 8 February, the enemy repeatedly attacked the reconnaissance groups with infantry supported by tanks from the direction of the Kamelrücken ridge near Kahlberg. By 1800 of the same day the Germans had driven three of the reconnaissance groups back onto the ice 800 southeast of the Frische Nehrung spit. The other two reconnaissance groups were tenaciously holding their positions on the Frische Nehrung, repulsing enemy attacks in the Lunghaken – Schellmühl area. The reconnaissance groups that had been thrown back onto the ice, having linked up into a single detachment, had the task in the course of the night to regain their position on the spit.

The enemy, with units of the 23rd Infantry Division, 28th Jäger Division, 24th Panzer Division, Flak Regiment 18, the 428th Fortress Battalion and the 10th Training Panzer Battalion throughout the day of 9 February was offering stubborn resistance to our units' offensive, repeatedly launching counterattacks out of the Drewsdorf, Bethkendorf and Stangendorf areas in strength of between a battalion and regiment of infantry, supported by 10-12 tanks, and tried to restore their positions and drive our units out of Frauenburg. In the area of the Frische Nehrung spit, a force of up to 200 German submachine gunners, supported by tanks and artillery, drove the reconnaissance detachment out of the Kahlberg-Liep, Schellmühl area.

5th Guards Tank Army in the East Prussian Operation, 1945

The commander of the 5th Guards Tank Army Colonel General of Tank Forces V.T. Vol'sky (in the center) with a group of subordinate staff officers; East Prussia, February 1945. (TsA MO)

The commander of the 5th Guards Tank Army Colonel General of Tank Forces V.T. Vol'sky shares a laugh with a group of staff officers. The heady advance made by the tank army is reflected on their faces; East Prussia, 1945. (TsA MO)

The deputy commander of the 5th Guards Tank Army Major General of Tank Forces Maksim Sinenko (on the right); East Prussia, February 1945. (TsA MO)

The commander of the 5th Guards Tank Army Colonel General of Tank Forces V.T. Vol'sky stands with a group of staff officers on a rubbled street in Frauenburg; February 1945. (TsA MO)

Colonel General V.T. Vol'sky in a moment of relaxation; East Prussia, February 1945. (TsA MO)

The commander of the 5th Guards Tank Army Colonel General of Tank Forces V.T. Vol'sky amid the rubble of a devastated East Prussian town. (TsA MO)

The commander of the 5th Guards Tank Army Colonel General of Tank Forces V.T. Vol'sky poses amid the rubble of a devastated East Prussian town. (TsA MO)

Tanks of the 5th Guards Tank Army roll into Tolkemit, East Prussia. (TsA MO)

A political instructor leads motorized infantry of the 5th Guards Tank Army in a cheer in the Tolkemit area; East Prussia, 1945. (TsA MO)

Units of the 5th Guards Tank Army in the Tolkemit area; East Prussia, 1945. (TsA MO)

Capture German tanks, self-propelled guns and self-propelled artillery; East Prussia, 1945. (TsA MO)

Captured German Tiger tanks; East Prussia, 1945. (TsA MO)

Tank riders are mounted on these two IS-2 tanks of the 14th Guards Heavy Tank Regiment, which are standing on the streets of an East Prussian city; February 1945. (TsA MO)

Residents of an East Prussian town warily greet the tankers of the 5th Guards Tank Army; February 1945. (TsA MO)

A column of IS-2 tanks of the 5th Guards Tank Army's 14th Guards Heavy Tank Regiment on the streets of Tolkemit. This section of the city seems untouched by the fighting. (TsA MO)

Soviet soldiers march through one of East Prussia's towns, led by a military band; 1945. (TsA MO)

Another shot of IS-2 tanks of the 14th Guards Heavy Tank Regiment rolling through Tolkemit in 1945. (TsA MO)

Monument to Kaiser Wilhelm II in East Prussia. (TsA MO)

From the Combat Path of the 5th Guards Tank Army:

At this time the task to cut the Germans' path of retreat on the Frische-Nehrung spit was carried out. On the night of 7-8 February, a reconnaissance detachment from the 1st Guards Motorcycle Regiment, consisting of 141 men with 2 mortars and 6 heavy machine guns that were mounted on sleds, silently crossed the lagoon's ice and by morning had cut all of the roads leading to the west. The scouts took up an advantageous line, mined the approaches to it, and threw up obstructions on the roads. Mopping up the coastline of enemy troops, the 29th Tank Corps together with arriving elements of the 47th Mechanized Brigade and the 48th Army's 170th Rifle Division broke the enemy resistance and rolled into Frauenburg, having killed or wounded more than 2,000 Nazi soldiers and officers in the process.

On the city's outskirts, Senior Lieutenant M.S. Vaniushkin's tank was set ablaze by an enemy shell – he was commander of a tank platoon of the 47th Mechanized Brigade's 18th Tank Regiment. However, the crew remained in the burning tank and continued to crush the enemy. The tankers destroyed 2 antitank cannons, 4 mortars, 6 machine guns, and killed more than 30 enemy soldiers and officers. Impetuously advancing, the crew reached a bridge across the Baude River. All night long, the valiant men held the bridge. In the morning, fresh enemy attacks began. On the afternoon of 8 February, the tank was knocked out, and Vaniushkin was severely wounded. For his exemplary courage and valor, Mikhail Stepanovich Vaniushkin was awarded the title Hero of the Soviet Union.

On 9 February 1945, the troops of the 5th Guards Tank Army stubbornly defended their occupied lines, repulsing repeated enemy counterattacks. The 10th Tank Corps, consisting of the 183rd Tank Brigade and 11th Motorized Rifle Brigade, as well as the operationally subordinate 47th Mechanized Brigade and 31st Tank Brigade from the 29th Tank Corps, went on the attack at 1200 on 9 February following a strong artillery and mortar barrage with the task to hurl the enemy back to the eastern bank of the Baude River. Having overcome the enemy's resistance in heavy fighting, the 10th Tank Corps by 2200 on 9 February had driven the Germans back from the western bank of the Baude River. On the eastern bank, the corps encountered a prepared enemy line of defense, consisting of 3-4 lines of full-profile trenches with machine-gun nests and pillboxes.

By the end of 9 February, the corps' units were occupying the following positions: 11th Motorized Rifle Brigade – was saddling the highway and railroad 1 km west of the Baude River with 183 active bayonets, 8 76mm guns and 25 82mm and 120mm mortars; the 183rd Tank Brigade, together with 11th Motorized Rifle Brigade, was saddling the highway and railroad 1 km northwest of the Sonnenberg estate, having in service 16 T-34 tanks and 7 SU-85, along with 27 active bayonets; the 186th Tank Brigade was in the area 1.5 km north of Blüdau in readiness to repulse enemy counterattacks from the directions of Bludau and Groß Rautenberg, having in service 5 T-34, 5 SU-100 and 67 active bayonets; the 178th Tank Brigade – in the Dittersdorf area in readiness to repulse enemy counterattacks from the Heinrichsdorf, Schafsberg and Bethkendorf directions, having in service 7 T-34, 5 SU-100 and 129 active bayonets. Attached units: 326th Heavy Self-propelled Artillery Regiment – in the area 1 km north of Neuhof with 6 SU-122 and 1 IS-122, all operational; the 689th Destroyer Antitank Artillery Regiment – in the Vierzighuben area with 14 57mm guns. The corps headquarters has 3 operational T-34 tanks. The 77th Motorcycle Battalion has 4 operational M4A2 tanks and 115 active bayonets. The 727th Self-propelled Artillery Regiment has 6 operational SU-76 assault guns.

The corps' losses over the day of 9 February are being ascertained. The damage inflicted on the enemy: Up to 200 soldiers and officers killed or wounded, and 2 tanks and 3 guns knocked-out. Altogether, the tank corps had in service 31 T-34, 1 IS-122, 4 M4A2, 10 SU-100, 7 SU-85, 6 SU-76 and 6 SU-122. Supply status: diesel fuel – 1.0 refill; gasoline – 0.4 of a refill; ammunition – 1.2 standard combat loads; and 4 days worth of food. The corps headquarters was in Narz.

The 29th Tank Corps (minus the 31st and 32nd Tank Brigades) in the course of 9 February was defending the occupied Frauenburg – Tolkemit – Succase line. The corps' reserve consisting of 2 T-34 and 7 SU-85 from the 32nd Tank Brigade was in Rückenau. The corps headquarters had 2 operational T-34 tanks. The 75th Motorcycle Battalion throughout the night of 8-9 February was conducting reconnaissance on the Frische-Nehrung spit. At 0300 it reached the northeastern outskirts of Kahlberg-Liep, where it ran into strong artillery and automatic weapons' fire. Suffering losses, the battalion withdrew across the ice to Tolkemit. It has in service 5 M4A2 and 2 halftracks. Altogether the 29th Tank Corps on 9 February had in service, including the 32nd Tank Brigade: 12 T-34, 5 M4A2, 10 SU-152, 8 SU-85, 14 SU-76 and 2 IS-122. Supply status: diesel fuel – 1.5 refills; gasoline – 0.8 of a refill; ammunition – 1.3 standard combat loads; and food – 3 days worth. The corps headquarters was in Rückenau.

The 47th Mechanized Brigade, consisting of the 1st, 2nd and 3rd Motorized Rifle Battalions, the 18th Tank Regiment, its artillery battalion and mortar battalion, together with the attached 376th Heavy Self-propelled Artillery Regiment, the 146th Anti-aircraft Artillery Regiment and the support of tanks from the 31st Tank Brigade had thrown the enemy back to an area 2 km east of Frauenburg, and had fought its way to a line along the western bank of the Baude River between the railroad and the coastline of the Frisches-Haff lagoon. The 376th Heavy Self-propelled Artillery Regiment was in the area of the eastern outskirts of Frauenburg, supporting the 47th Mechanized Brigade's attack. The regiment had 5 SU-152 heavy self-propelled guns.

The 42nd Rifle Corps was continuing to hold its occupied lines firmly and driving back repeated enemy counterattacks. The corps headquarters was in Bludau.

The army-level units: The 1st Guards Separate Motorcycle Regiment was in the Blumenau area. Reconnaissance groups detached from the regiment were operating on the Frische-Nehrung spit in the direction of Kahlberg-Liep and Langhaken. By 0700 on 9 February one reconnaissance group was assembled on the northern outskirts of Tolkemit, where it was replenishing its ammunition, servicing the weapons and preparing to resume carrying out combat orders. Since the group was fighting on the ice of the Frisches-Haff lagoon, which was covered by water, among the group's members, 73 (7 officers and 66 men) had been rendered combat-ineffective because of trench foot, fungal infections and other issues. The regiment had in service 2 M4A2 tanks and 122 active bayonets. The 201st Light Artillery Brigade's 651st Cannon Artillery Regiment was in firing positions in the area 200 meters southwest of Frauenburg with 13 100mm guns; the 1315th Light Artillery Regiment – in firing positions on the eastern outskirts of Frauenburg with 13 76mm guns; the 1619th Light Artillery Regiment – in firing positions in the area 2 km southwest of Frauenburg, 1km north of Kreuzdorf with 14 76mm guns. The 41st Corps Artillery Regiment, subordinate to the army commander, was occupying firing positions in the area 500 meters southwest of Narz and Neukirch-Höhe. The 33rd Motorized Engineer Brigade, subordinate to the army commander, was located by battalion in the Kurau, Bludau and Hütte areas. The 72nd Special-purpose Naval Infantry Battalion on 10 February 1945 was withdrawn from its operational subordination to the commander of the 5th Guards Tank Army and became subordinate to the commander of the 2nd Shock Army.

Lieutenant Colonel M.A. Bykadorov recalls an episode of the hard fighting in his memoirs:

Around 0900 on 9 February 1945, without an artillery preparation, the infantry went on the attack from the edge of some woods; our three self-propelled guns moved out to escort it. Once we crossed the low ground and had emerged on a rise, the Germans detected the infantry. They opened heavy machine-gun and automatic weapons' fire at it. A mortar barrage began to fall. We were firing from our self-propelled gun's main gun. The infantry was pinned down. At this time, I saw the self-propelled gun that was moving about 40-50 meters behind me and to the left burst into flames. Just a moment later, our own self-propelled gun caught fire from a direct hit. I ordered the crew to abandon the machine.

I had been anticipating this calamity. After all, men and machines had been consumed in the fighting in front of our very eyes for many days now. Now it was our turn. As we found out somewhat later, a German Tiger tank, which had pounced on us from the right flank, had set our two self-propelled guns ablaze. The crew of my self-propelled gun survived; the shell had entered the right side and had penetrated the engine and fuel tanks, which were filled with KB-70 aviation fuel. The fuel ignited and set our machine ablaze. Two men of the other crew were killed, while the commander was badly burned and hospitalized; he didn't return to the unit until after the war ended. Several minutes after what had happened to our self-propelled gun, shells began to explode nearby. Ominous columns of black smoke rose above our machines. The attack bogged down. The infantry, having suffered numerous casualties, fell back to the jumping-off position.

This unhappy event took place on 9 February 1945. The crew was left with painful memories of the tragedy. I kept recalling this combat action for my entire lifetime. On a map, which I have kept in my archive to the present day, I've marked the place of the self-propelled gun's destruction with the symbol of a self-propelled gun, drawn in black pencil. This place is located 9 km west of Wormditt or 13 km southwest of the town of Mehlsack.

On 10 February 1945 the enemy, refusing to accept the loss of Frauenburg, urgently shifted the 14th Infantry Division from the Wormditt area, brought up a regiment-sized group of artillery and up to two regiments of Nebelwerfers, and with the support of 10 to 15 tanks and self-propelled guns went on the attack in the morning with the aim of driving our troops out of Frauenburg. The troops of the 5th Guards Tank Army throughout the day of 10 February tenaciously clung to their occupied lines, conducted a regrouping, and fought off enemy attacks in strength of a battalion to a regiment of infantry supported by 8 to 10 tanks and artillery from out of the Willenberg, Stangendorf and Kalberhaus areas. Altogether over the course of the day, they repulsed 6 German counterattacks.

The 10th Tank Corps, together with the 326th Guards Heavy Self-propelled Regiment, the 689th Destroyer Antitank Artillery Regiment and a battalion of the 76th Guards Mortar Regiment stubbornly defended Frauenburg throughout the day of 10 February, while simultaneously repulsing enemy counterattacks from the Willenberg, Stangendorf and Kalberhaus directions. By 2100 on 10 February the corps' units were occupying the following positions:

- The 183rd Tank Brigade was stubbornly occupying a defense on the eastern slopes of a hill 1.8 km southeast of Frauenburg with 14 T-34 tanks and 5 SU-85 tank destroyers, as well as 136 active bayonets, and repelling enemy counterattacks from the direction of Willenberg;
- The 11th Motorized Rifle Brigade was holding a defense along the western bank of the Baude River on the line of the Sonnenberg --- Frauenburg highway and further along to the north as far as the patch of woods 2 km east of Frauenburg; throughout the day it was fighting off enemy attacks from the direction of Stangendorf, with 190 active bayonets, 8 76mm guns and 24 82mm and 120mm mortars in service;
- The 178th Tank Brigade from the Vierzighuben area conducted a march and by 1600 had reassembled and was occupying a defense on the eastern outskirts of Frauenburg, in readiness to repulse enemy counterattacks from the east and southeast; the brigade had in service 9 T-34, 8 SU-100 and 120 active bayonets;

- The 186th Tank Brigade from the Bludau area conducted a march and reassembled in the Narz area and the woods to the southwest; the brigade had in service 12 T-34, 6 SU-100 and 112 active bayonets;
- The 287th Mortar Regiment with 16 120mm mortars was occupying a combat position in the center of Frauenburg;
- The 705th Light Artillery Regiment was in firing positions 1.5 km southeast of Narz with 22 76mm guns;
- the 1693rd Anti-aircraft Artillery Regiment was covering the Narz area with two batteries, and the Rahnenfeld area with its other two batteries; altogether, it had 12 serviceable 37mm guns;
- the 727th Self-propelled Artillery Regiment had 6 operational SU-76 self-propellled guns;
- The 77th Separate Motorcycle Battalion had 4 M4A2 tanks and 105 active bayonets;

The corps headquarters had 3 operational T-34 tanks. The 326th Heavy Self-propelled Artillery Regiment was in the area 1 km north of Neuhof with 9 operational SU-122 heavy self-propelled guns and 1 IS-122 tank. The 689th Destroyer Antitank Artillery Regiment had two batteries in firing positions 800 meters north of Bludau, and two batteries in the Baudehof area. Altogether it had 14 serviceable 57mm guns.

In the course of 10 February, the corps lost 1 T-34 tank and 1 SU-85 tank destroyer, both destroyed, and had 15 men killed and 38 wounded. Back on 1 February, a batch of 185 replacements for the tank corps had arrived. In return, the enemy lost 2 tanks and 1 self-propelled guns destroyed, and 5 tanks and 2 self-propelled guns knocked-out. It also destroyed 4 guns and 3 heavy machine guns and killed or wounded up to 340 soldiers and officers.

Altogether, the 10th Tank Corps together with its attached assets had serviceable 33 T-34, 4 M4A2, 1 IS-122, 9 SU-122, 14 SU-100, 5 SU-85 and 6 SU-76, as well as 663 active bayonets. Supply status: diesel fuel – 1.2 refills; gasoline – 0.5 of a refill; ammunition – 1.3 standard combat loads; and 6 days of food. The corps headquarters was in Narz.

The 47th Mechanized Brigade and 376th Heavy Self-propelled Artillery Regiment were both operationally subordinate to the commander of the 10th Tank Corps. Throughout the night and day, they had fought off enemy attacks in strength of a company to two battalions of infantry, supported by 5 tanks and 6 self-propelled guns from the directions of Stangenberg and Kahlberhaus. All of the enemy attacks were driven back with heavy losses for the Germans. By 2200 on 10 February the 47th Mechanized Brigade was occupying a defense on a line northwest of the woods 2 km east of Frauenberg. The enemy was subjecting Frauenburg to heavy artillery and mortar firing, while simultaneously conducting methodical artillery fir from ships on the Neukirch-Höhe area; a direct hit destroyed the building that the headquarters of the 18th Tank Regiment was occupying, wounding the chief of staff Guards Major Merzliakov, the assistant commander for logistics Senior Lieutenant Chalyi, the regiment's signals chief Senior Lieutenant Tur'ev, and the commander of the 3rd Motorized Rifle Battalion Captain Semenov. Altogether on 10 February, the 47th Mechanized Brigade had 35 men killed or wounded. In return, the brigade destroyed 15 heavy and light machine guns and knocked out 5 guns, while killing up to 90 enemy soldiers and officers. The brigade had in service 6 M4A2 tanks, 64 active bayonets, 5 76mm guns, and 21 82mm and 120mm mortars.

At an order from the corps commander, the 178th Tank Brigade had been shifted from the Dittersdorf area to the Frauenburg area, and the 186th Tank Brigade to the area of the northern fringe of the woods near Kreuzdorf, with the task to be ready to counterattack the enemy in the eastern and northeastern directions.

On the night of 10-11 February, the enemy managed to make a penetration at the boundary between the 183rd Tank Brigade and 11th Motorized Rifle Brigade. Separate groups of Germans reached the southeastern outskirts of Frauenburg.

The 29th Tank Corps throughout the day of 10 February was firmly defending the coastline of the Frische-Haff lagoon in the Frauenburg – Tolkemit – Succase sector, while simultaneously mopping up separate shattered enemy groups from the woods southwest of Tolkemit. By 2100 on 10 February, the corps' units were occupying the following positions:

The 53rd Motorized Rifle Brigade with one reinforced motorized rifle battalion was defending the coastline of the Frische-Haff in separate strongpoints in the Frauenburg – Tolkemit sector; one motorized rifle battalion together with the 25th Tank Brigade was mopping up the woods southwest of Tolkemit. The third motorized rifle battalion was in the Conradswalde area, serving as the corps commander's reserve. The brigade had in service 480 active bayonets, 18 halftracks, 3 SU-57 and 24 82mm and 120mm mortars.

The 25th Tank Brigade with the 165th Light Artillery Regiment and one battalion of the 53rd Motorized Rifle Brigade was defending the coastline of the Frische-Haff between Tolkemit and Succase. By 1700, it had fully cleared the enemy from out of the woods southwest of Tolkemit. The brigade had in service 5 T-34, 6 SU-152 and 129 active bayonets.

The 31st Tank Brigade had been removed from the operational subordination to the commander of the 10th Tank Corps and by 1000 on 10 February was occupying a defense on the northeastern outskirts of Neukirch-Höhe. The brigade had in service 2 T-34, 2 SU-152, 3 SU-76 and 50 active bayonets.

The 32nd Tank Brigade and the 1223rd Light Artillery Regiment had been removed from the operational subordination to the commander of the 124th Rifle Corps. The brigade conducted a march from the Spanden estate area to an assembly area in Trunz. By 2200 on 10 February, 9 T-34 tanks had arrived in the assembly area. The brigade had in service 11 T-34, 2 SU-152, 1 SU-85, 13 SU-76 and 70 active bayonets.

The 271st Mortar Regiment was in firing positions in the woods west of Neuendorf. The 75th Motorcycle Battalion throughout the night of 9-10 February had conducted reconnaissance with groups on the Frische Nehrung spit. It had 5 operational M4A2 tanks. The reserve of the corps commander – from the 32nd Tank Brigade – was assembled in Rückenau with 2 T-34 tanks and 7 SU-85 in service. The corps headquarters had 2 operational T-34 tanks.

Altogether the 29th Tank Corps had in service 22 T-34, 5 M4A2, 10 SU-152, 8 SU-85, 16 SU-76 and 729 active bayonets. Supply status: diesel fuel – 1.5 refills; gasoline – 0.8 of a refill; ammunition – 1.1 standard combat loads; and 2 days of food.

Over 10 February, the corps' units had no losses. In return, over the day of 9 February the corps destroyed 7 guns of various calibers, 2 mortars, and kill or wounded up to 250 soldiers and officers. In addition, according to confirmed information, more than 50 loaded barges and steamships were captured in the Tolkemit area, and up to 30 barges in the Frauenburg area that were loaded with a variety of combat gear and industrial equipment.

Of the units directly subordinate to the 5th Guards Tank Army headquarters, the 1st Guards Separate Motorcycle Regiment was in the Blümenau area. The regiment had detached a reconnaissance group that was located in Tolkemit. The regiment had in service 2 M4A2 tanks, 111 motorcycles and 201 active bayonets. The 376th Heavy Self-propelled Artillery Regiment was in the area of the eastern outskirts of Frauenburg, supporting the 47th Mechanized Brigade with 5 operational SU-152. The 14th Guards Heavy Tank Regiment had been removed from operational subordination to the commander of the 124th Rifle Corps and was on the march to the Mühlhausen area. As for the artillery, the 201st Light Artillery Brigade's 651st Cannon Artillery Regiment was in firing positions in the area 200 meters southwest of Frauenburg, shelling the enemy's counterattacking infantry and tanks. As a result of the combat, it had knocked out 1 tank, 1 gun and 4 machine guns. It had 12 serviceable 100mm guns. The 1315th Light Artillery Regiment was in firing positions on the eastern outskirts of Frauenburg, placing fire on the counterattacking enemy with 13 76mm guns. The 1619th Light Artillery Regiment was in firing positions 2 km southwest of Frauenburg with 14 serviceable 76mm guns.

On 10 February the 5th Guards Tank Army passed to the operational control of the commander-in-chief of the 3rd Belorussian Front. The 42nd Rifle Corps at 1000 on 10 February was withdrawn from operational subordination to the commander of the 5th Guards Tank Army.

By the end of 10 February, at the moment the army passed to the operational control of the 3rd Belorussian Front, the 5th Guards Tank Army had the following in service: 10th Tank Corps – 67 tanks and self-propelled guns and 663 active bayonets; 29th Tank Corps – 61 tanks and self-propelled guns and 729 active bayonets; 47th Mechanized Brigade – 6 tanks and self-propelled guns and 64 active bayonets; the units directly subordinate to the army headquarters – 21 tanks and self-propelled guns. In total, the 5th Guards Tank Army at this moment had 155 operational tanks and self-propelled guns, and 1,456 active bayonets.

The operating lifetimes of the engine in the overwhelming majority of the available combat machines were either nearing the end or had exceeded that limit, because as a result of the developing situation, the army had been conducting ceaseless, active combat operations for almost a month since 14 January, with no time for mechanical servicing or repairs. This fact to a significant extent restricted the army's effective use in the upcoming fighting.

On the morning of 11 February, the units of the 10th Tank Corps went on the offensive and by 1600 had restored the situation and cleared the enemy from the western bank of the Baude River. The 29th Tank Corps (minus the 31st and 32nd Tank Brigades) and the 42nd Rifle Corps in the course of 10 and 11 February kept firm possession of their occupied lines. The latter corps in the course of the two days repulsed five enemy counterattacks.

F.I. Galkin remembers:

Our troops were not restricting themselves to keeping the enemy in check alone, but periodically launched short, but powerful attacks. The Nazis' strength began to dwindle. That was when the order was given to storm Elbing. Rifle divisions broke into the city. This was on 10 February.

I arrived in Elbing two days after it fell. The scent of gunpowder and cinders lingered in the narrow streets that were squeezed between the gray hulks of the old stone buildings. Several knocked-out tanks, left behind by Mikhailov's brigade after the initial attacks, still remained on one of the squares. I began to inspect them. At this time General Sinenko drove up. His face was ashen, his eyes were swollen and irritated, but his customary energy hadn't diminished. He adroitly leaped out of the Willys and walked up to me.

"Help them," Mikhail Denisovich said, pointing at the knocked-out machines; "Do it as soon as possible. Since yesterday evening we've passed to the control of the 3rd Belorussian Front and together with the 47th Army will be finishing off the isolated enemy grouping. So the tanks will be very useful to Mikhailov."

"All will be in order. The mobile repair shops are already here, and Bogachin's repair teams are on the approach. Tomorrow, some of the machines will be returned to service."

"Now you're talking … but I'm in a hurry. I need to head to the western outskirts to see what is going on there…."

Protasov was already tinkering on one of the tanks.

"Just look, the damned men, they were in a hurry," he muttered; "They damaged the turret hatch. Were they being fired on from above?"

"And what did you expect, Sergei Stepanovich, that you'd be spared such a treat? Panzerfausts were being fired at your tanks from the balconies."

"Of course, they were … It's just that we really need these tanks."

"Then put them back into service all the sooner. There are still parts in good working order in the burned-out tanks, make use of them!"

A mobile repair shop was deploying at another tank, and a jib crane was being set up by it. In essence a collecting point for disabled machines was being created here, in the center of the city.

During the recent fighting, when the army was no longer advancing 30-50 kilometers a day, like before, the repair crews were catching up with their units. Not rarely, they were forced to work within the range of enemy shells. Such was the case, for example, on 4 February, which Stanislavsky's brigade had driven the Germans out of Tolkemit for the second time. The Germans hadn't abandoned the thought of breaking through to Elbing along the coastline, which is why they were putting constant pressure on the Frauenburg – Tolkemit line and were keeping these points under artillery fire.

Engineer-Major Popov towed the damaged tanks and self-propelled guns to the city's outskirts, concealed them as far as possible behind buildings, and organized their repair on the spot. Almost an entire technical service company had already gathered here. Company commander Captain Tsikulov was already making arrangements for accommodating his working group; repair crews had already begun to settle down in the nearby buildings, even though now and then shells and mortar rounds, whistling in the air, were passing over the steeply-pitched roofs of the homes. Sometimes they exploded quite nearby and flinging fragments of the red tiling about.

Boris Grigor'evich Pavlov and Engineer-Captain Gringerg were examing a machine.

"Isn't it dangerous here?", I asked.

"Not at all. The shells are being intercepted by the roofs, and Kochetkov has protected against fragments by a rug," Pavlov jokingly replied, pointing at the senior sergeant, who was trying to make some sort of tent out of a German rug.

The short, very agile Kochetkov with abrupt tosses of his head was tossing aside the light brown curls of hair that had escaped out from under his cap with ear flaps, and kept repeating a rhyme: "We'll survive, so we don't die, and soon Fritz will run helter-skelter away from our little shelter. Our Ivan is peeved, which means he'll soon stoutly cleave."

Smiling, I exchanged glances with Pavlov.

"What are the losses around Tolkemit?" I asked.

"Four tanks and a self-propelled gun. We're putting the tanks back into service, but the self-propelled gun needs a factory overhaul."

"How many remain in service?"

"It's slim pickings. Around ten in the brigade."

The situation in the 32nd Tank Brigade was even more difficult. Attacking Elbing from the east, it came under the targeted fire of German self-propelled guns and in addition had found itself enmeshed in a convoluted system of irrigation ditches. Some of the machines became bogged down in ditches, while a few more were disabled by German antitank fire. The deputy commander of the brigade Engineer-Major Ageev had to gather all the prime movers and the repairmen of the technical maintenance service and introduce them directly up among the combat formations. The evacuation teams were making their way up to the bogged machines and extracting them from the ditches, even as nearby, the tankers were maneuvering and exchanging fire with the enemy. When the next counterattack faltered and the Germans rolled back, the platoon commander Technician-Lieutenant Eremchenko led the repair crews right up to the machines that had just been knocked out. There was a reason why four Orders and two medals decorated Eremchenko's chest.

Despite all the efforts of the repair teams, in the 10th Tank Corps as well, the tank brigades numbered just 8-10 tanks each. Just the day before, the 186th and 178th Tank Brigades, engaged in heavy fighting in a comparatively small space, left behind 15 knocked-out tanks on the battlefield.

"What are you thinking to do with such a number?" I asked D.M. Kozyrev.

"We'll repair them. Major Abramenko has already brought up the men right up to the battlefield. While it was still light, they set out on foot with their tool boxes, because the Germans are always keeping the tanks under fire, but in the evening the mobile repair shops will come up."

Indeed, by the next morning 11 tanks returned to service. Deputy Chief of the Mobile Tank Repair Base Captain Nechaev said:

"While the mechanics and repairmen were fixing the damage, in some tanks the gunner and loader were at their posts. After all the Germans might have attacked at any moment. I'm not even mentioning the mortar rounds and shells. No one was paying any attention to them. Never!"

Now it was possible to sum up some results. Pustil'nikov was coming up with the figures, striving not to overlook a single machine. Having checked the figures again and again, he reported:

"On the roads from Mława as far as Neidenburg and Osterode, we ended up with ten tanks, and from Osterode to the current combat positions, approximately another thirty tanks have been collected. In addition, the evacuation of 15 badly stuck machines is expected, of which two self-propelled guns are under enemy fire. Engineer-Captain Denisov more than once attempted to make his way up to them but was unsuccessful."

Over the two recent weeks of fighting, our army lost more than 300 tanks and self-propelled guns. However, 284 machines have returned from repairs. Altogether since the start of combat operations, which is to say between 14 January and 10 February 1945, 809 tanks and self-propelled guns have been repaired and returned to service. This is significantly more than the army had prior to the offensive.

In a small village, situated southwest of Tiedmannsdorf, a moonless night had fallen. Making my way with difficulty through the darkness, I walked to Vol'sky's hut, I held a silent conversation with myself:

"How have the tanks behaved? Not at all bad. Over 28 days of constant fighting, the mechanics rarely stopped the engines. Some were operating 15 to 20 hours a day. It isn't surprising that the motors began losing power and with increased loads were leaving behind the hull plumes of bluish-gray smoke. To be sure, some of the engines were replaced during repair, but even these had already exhausted their operating lifetimes. The rolling assembly was worn out. Close inspection and realignment were necessary. What to ask the commander? I will insist on a second complete maintenance work and technical servicing, otherwise the machines will come to a stop. There is no other choice."

Sinenko, Zaev and the Chief of Staff Sidorovich had assembled at Vol'sky's headquarters. They had just familiarized themselves with a directive from the Commander-in-Chief of the 3rd Belorussian Front General of the Army I.D. Cherniakhovsky, to whom we were now subordinate.

"Talk of the devil" Vol'sky responded to my greetings. "Now the technical god will accurately say what we have today and what we'll have tomorrow."

"We only have a few odds and ends regarding spare parts and tools, and 155 operational tanks and self-propelled guns. As for tomorrow …"

Vol'sky grew worried: "What about tomorrow?"

"Tomorrow it is extremely necessary to work on all the tanks and self-propelled guns, otherwise they'll grind to a halt."

"All that and come to a standstill?"

"If in fact we don't take a break, the engines will die and we won't be able to restart them."

"Well, then, Galkin, as you please," the army commander said after a short pause. "The 11th and the first half of the 12th are yours. Organize everything as is necessary. We will leave all the units where they are for two days, but on the 13th they will move to the Tiedmannsdorf and Groß Rautenberg area. On the 14th we'll begin to finish off the Germans. Only don't forget to get Mikhailov's tanks ready."

The army commander's health was continuing to deteriorate. In the days of fighting, when the situation demanded inhuman exertion with all your strength, this wasn't noticeable, but today it seemed as if he had succumbed to the pressures. His face was guant. There were slight bags under his eyes. Bright, crimson blemishes stood out sharply on his cheeks.

"What's up with the army commander?" I asked Ozhogin, entering his room. "He's unrecognizable. Has it been awhile since a doctor has visited?"

"Doctors are coming by every day if he's in his headquarters. If he isn't, how can you catch him? Today both a doctor and a professor dropped by, and they consulted about something for quite a while. They didn't tell me anything, but it is clear the situation is bad."

Vol'sky's health alarmed both Sinenko and Sidorovich. Maksim Denisovich consulted with the doctors. As a result, a "secret pact" came together: as soon as the army began finishing off the encircled enemy grouping, Vol'sky would be persuaded to travel to Moscow for a consultation.

Irklei and Pustil'nikov were already waiting for me. I told them of my conversation with the army commander.

Pustil'nikov observed with satisfaction, "A lot can be done over 36 hours."

"Splendid!" Irklei said cheerfully.

"Mikhail Fedorovich, I'll ask you to go now to Sakhno's corps and help Kozyrev begin work in the morning. Send one of your officers to Malakhov's corps. Beliachev will cope. But where is Ovcharenko?"

"Ovcharenko drove off to Pokolov's brigade. An order has been signed about appointing him as the deputy commander for technical matters."

Even though I myself had recommended Ovcharenko for the position, although it was hard for me to part with such an officer, and that couldn't be helped. The man had deservedly been promoted. Indeed, it was behooving to strengthen the brigade.

Pustil'nikov, without waiting for instructions about where he should go, asked, "Permit me to go to Protasov? In addition to servicing the machines, we have to get on with the process of welding cleats to the Shermans' tracks."

"No. Dispatch officers, but you remain here. We have sufficient machines for a week, not longer. Take a seat with Ivanov and tally up everything you need to revamp all the tanks and self-propelled guns over ten days."

Irklei and Pustil'nikov drove off when day began to break. The engineers, techicians and mechanics once again arrived to help the crews. They were checking and adjusting all the mechanisms, replacing the worn-out parts, and applying fresh grease … Precisely at the designated time, by midday of 12 February, all of the tanks and self-propelled guns were in full working order.

That evening I dropped by the chief of staff with a summary on the condition of the tanks and self-propelled guns.

"That's why I need you, Fedor Ivanovich," General Sidorovich said. "You remembered the time limit?"

"I remembered, Georgii Stepanovich. Time was pressing."

"That's right. On the defense, as the soldiers say, grub is the most important thing. However, that's not the case here. I will now issue an order to Malakhov – to assemble in the Tiedmannsdorf area by morning, and to Sakhno – to assemble at Groß Rautenberg. Are the machines ready?"

"We dealt with everything, and the men have even managed to get a little rest."

"Excellent."

"Are you leaving out Mikhailov's brigade? Fortunately, over these two days with him we "shoed" almost all the machines. Now they may not even slip on the ice."

The army commander decided to leave Mikhailov in Tolkemit, so that the enemy didn't break out to Pomerania along the coast. The correct decision! As soon as we began to apply pressure from here, the Nazis would begin to thrash around more than ever, and of course attempt to slip away along the highway."

On 12 February 1945 the bulk of the 5th Guards Tank Army stubbornly defended the occupied lines, but the 10th Tank Corps conducted offensive actions. Together with the 376th Heavy Self-propelled Artillery Regiment and the 689th Destroyer Antitank Artillery Regiment and in cooperation with the 170th Rifle Division, it attacked and by 1700 had captured Klein Rautenburg and Drewsdorf, meeting strong enemy resistance with fire from the direction of Bethkendorf.

On 12 February the 5th Guards Tank Army received an order from the Front Commander-in-Chief: "In cooperation with units of the 48th Army, launch an attack in the general direction of Steffenshöh, Schillgehnen, south of Braunsberg and Heiligenbeil with the mission to destroy the opposing enemy and to act together with the combined-arms armies in the final destruction of the enemy's East Prussian grouping."

In pursuit of this order, the 29th Tank Corps at 0900 on 13 February set off on a 25-kilometer march from its occupied area to a new assembly area: Tiedmannsdorf, Parlack and the woods southwest of Tiedmannsdorf. By 1600 on 13 February, the tank corps had reassembled in the designated area.

The 47th Mechanized Brigade, having turned over its sector of defense along the Baude River from the highway 2 km east of Frauenburg to the coastline to the 399th Rifle Division, by 2000 on 13 February had shifted to the Tolkemit area with the new task of strongly defending the coastline of the Frische-Haff together with the attached 249th Reserve Battalion, 727th Self-propelled Artillery Regiment and 146th Anti-aircraft Artillery Regiment in the Louisenthal Station – Tolkemit – Succase – Groß Röbern – Eichfelde – Lenzen – Dörbeck – Neuendorf – Conradswalde sector.

From the "Combat Path of the 29th Tank Corps":

On 12 February 1945 the corps was given the task to conduct active combat operations: on the morning of 14 February, jointly with the combined-arms formations, to go over to a decisive offensive, having the immediate objective of mopping up the enemy from the western bank of the Passarge River between Pettelkau and the highway and to seize crossing sites from the march. Subsequently it was to develop the offensive toward Vogelsang, Damerau and Heiligenbeil. The Tiedmannsdorf, Parunz [sic – Parlack] area and the woods to the southwest were designated as the jumping-off area.

The corps conducted a march that extended for 25 kilometers and reassembled in the jumping-off area at the designated time, where it remained until the attack and spent the time preparing for it. The 31st and 32nd Tank Brigades also arrived here; they had been temporarily withdrawn from subordination to the corps. At the appointed time, the brigades went on the attack. The enemy defended ferociously and launched counterattacks. The deeply-echeloned fire from machine guns and cannons pinned the brigades' motorized rifle elements to the ground. Tank company commander Senior Lieutenant P.A. Rukhliad'ev climbed out of his tank and raised the attached infantry on the attack.

Grinding forward meter by meter, the brigades approached the town of Pettelkau. One more lunge, and the tanks would be in the town. However, the charge didn't bring the expected result. The enemy launched a counterattack from Pettelkau under the cover of artillery fire. The motorized riflemen accompanying the tanks again became pinned down, while the tankers opened intense cannon and machine-gun fire from fixed positions at the counterattacking enemy. The foe couldn't withstand the fire and began to fall back. The tankers decided to break into Pettelkau on the bootheels of the retreating enemy, but the infantry, pinned down by dense enemy fire, refused to rise onto the attack.

For the fourth time that day, Senior Lieutenant Rukhliad'ev left his tank in order to inspire the infantry with his personal example and raise it on the attack. The infantry got up and attacked, while Rukhliad'ev ran back to his tank. Just several meters from it, the officer fell when struck by fragments from an exploding nearby enemy shell. A large fragment struck his leg, severing an artery. The medical first aid rendered on the battlefield proved ineffective. He died on the way to the brigade's medical platoon from the loss of blood.

In the face of the enemy's resistance, the tankers took the town of Pettelkau. The situation at the front was fluid and abruptly changing. The tank brigades attempted to force a crossing of the Passarge River from the march, but the attempt failed. The enemy's heavy artillery and mortar fire forced the corps command to reject making a river crossing here. The corps, suffering losses, went on the attack along the river's western bank and neared Fehlau before sunset. A further advance was stopped by concentrated enemy fire.

Heavy fighting went on for the next two days in the Fehlau area. The enemy, stubbornly defending the town of Fehlau and the bridge there, inflicted significant losses on the attackers, knocking a lot of tanks and men out of action. In this fighting, the commander of the 53rd Motorized Rifle Brigade Colonel Dmitrii Nikiforovich Dolganov was killed. The commander of the 25th Tank Brigade Colonel Ivan Onufrievich Stanislavsky received a severe wound to his right arm, which had to be amputated. Chief of staff Lieutenant Colonel N.A. Safonov assumed command of the 53rd Motorized Rifle Brigade, while Colonel T.E. Kartashov was appointed to command the 25th Tank Brigade from out of the reserve command pool.

The formations of the 5th Guards Tank Army had the following tasks for 14 February 1945:

- The 29th Tank Corps from the morning of 14 February, together with the 29th Rifle Corps, was to launch a decisive attack with the immediate objective of clearing the western bank of the Passarge River of the remaining enemy in the sector between Pettelkau and the highway, and to seize bridges from the march. Subsequently on 15 February it was to cross its main forces to the eastern bank of the Passarge River and develop the offensive in the Volgelsang, Dömerau, Heiligenbeil direction;
- The 10th Tank Corps from the morning of 14 February, together with units of the 42nd Rifle Corps, was to launch a decisive attack in the Steffenshöh, Schillgehnen, Kleine Anitsmühle direction, having the immediate objective of mopping up the enemy from the western bank of the Passarge River in the Zagern sector and to seize bridges across the river from the march, before attacking in the Kleine Anitsmühle, Heiligenbeil direction, bypassing Braunsberg on

its eastern side; meanwhile, the 186th Tank Brigade was to operate in the direction of Hill 35.5, Hermannsdorf and the Obertor railroad station, and capture Braunsberg in cooperation with units of the 42nd Rifle Corps.

The forces of the 5th Guards Tank Army in cooperation with the 29th and 42nd Rifle Corps went on the offensive at 1200 on 14 February. The 29th Tank Corps with its attached assets and in concert with the 29th Rifle Corps went on the attack in the Pettelkau, Grunenberg direction, captured Pettelkau after a short combat action, and by 1900 was exchanging fire while attempting to force a crossing of the Passarge River.

The 10th Tank Corps with its attached assets and in cooperation with the 42nd Rifle Corps went on the attack in the Steffenshöh, Fehlau, Lindwald estate direction, but ran into the fierce resistance of major enemy forces, which on their part counterattacked the 10th Corps six times. After stubborn combat against superior enemy forces, at 1300 it abandoned the Lindwald estate and made no further advance before the end of the day.

The 47th Mechanized Brigade with its attached assets by 1700 on 14 February had taken up a defense in isolated strongpoints on the coastline of the Frische-Haff lagoon in the Louisenthal Station – Tolkemit – Succase – Groß Röbern sector, securing the boundary with the 2nd Shock Army.

The troops of the 5th Guards Tank Army together with units of the 48th Army were locked in heavy offensive fighting against major forces of enemy tanks and artillery in the area south of Zagern and the woods to the west. The enemy repeatedly launched counterattacks with up to a regiment of infantry and 15 tanks, which were supported by the concentrated fire of artillery and mortars. The attempt by the 29th Tank Corps to force a crossing of the Passarge River in the Pettelkau area had no success due to the enemy's intense artillery and machine-gun fire from the eastern bank of the river. Unable to cross the river, the 29th Tank Corps received the order to attack at 1600 on 15 February and take Zagern by the end of the day together with the 10th Tank Corps and 29th Rifle Corps.

Attacking in the direction of Zagern along the western bank of the Passarge River, the 29th Tank Corps fought its way into Fehlau, but having run into concentrated artillery fire and the fire of tanks from out of ambush positions, made no further advance. There in the Fehlau area, it dug in.

In the course of 16 and 17 February the troops of the 5th Guards Tank Army were engaged in heavy fighting with the enemy on the Fehlau, Knorrwald, Lindwald line. Attacks by the army and counterattacks by the enemy alternated in turn. Both sides suffered heavy losses in materiel and men. There were no substantial changes in the front lines over these two days.

Finally, on the night of 17-18 February, one 60-metric-ton bridge for the tanks was erected in the area northeast of Pettelkau, and units of the 29th Tank Corps rolled across it. Having crossed the 32nd Tank Brigade and 53rd Motorized Rifle Brigade, the Soviet forces attacked in the Grunenberg and Lunau directions, captured Grunenberg by 1400 on 18 February, and reached and cut the main road between Schalmey and Böhmenhöfen. On this line the brigades encountered the strong resistance of enemy artillery and 15 tanks and self-propelled guns from the direction of the woods 1 km south of Schillgehnen.

At 1900 on 18 February the enemy managed to destroy the bridge for the tanks northeast of Pettelkau with heavy artillery fire. The 10th Tank Corps, in close cooperation with the 53rd Rifle Corps, fought off six enemy counterattacks over the day of 18 February from the direction of Zagern and the woods to the west, but made no progress over the day. The bridge across the Passarge River that had been destroyed by enemy artillery fire was rebuilt by the morning of 19 February.

The 29th Tank Corps over 19 February crossed the Passarge River with all of its brigades. The 32nd Tank Brigade and 53rd Motorized Rifle Brigade, attacking in the Schalmey, Anticken direction, took Schalmey and were engaged in fighting 1 km east of Schalmey by 1400 on 19 February.

Having crossed the bridge, the 31st Tank Brigade also arrived in the Schalmey area. The 25th Tank Brigade – the reserve of the corps commander – was in the area of the northeastern outskirts of Grunenberg, in readiness to repulse enemy counterattacks from the southeast, east and north.

The situation of the 10th Tank Corps and 47th Mechanized Brigade remained unchanged on 19 February. The 10th Tank Corps continued exchanging fire with the opposing enemy.

The 29th Tank corps in cooperation with the 290th Rifle Corps throughout the day of 20 February 1945 was engaged in heavy offensive fighting in the Anticken direction. Simultaneously, it was repulsing enemy counterattacks from the directions of Knoblach, Groß Maulen and Anticken in strength of up to a regiment of infantry and 10-25 tanks, with the support of massed artillery and mortar fire. Altogether over the day, eight enemy counterattacks were repelled. Through the fighting it was established that up to two regiments of infantry, 30 tanks and self-propelled guns, and up to 10 artillery and mortar batteries were operating opposite the corps' front. By the end of 20 February, units of the 29th Tank Corps and 29th Rifle Corps had made an advance of just 0.5 to 1 kilometer from Schalmei in the direction of Anticken over the previous 24 hours.

The 10th Tank Corps on the night of 19-20 February was pulled out of the front lines and by 0900 on 20 February it had reassembled in the Steffenshöh area, where the tankers did maintenance and repair work on their tanks and weapons. The 47th Mechanized Brigade was holding a defense on its previous line.

The 29th Tank Corps in the course of the night of 20-21 February drove back repeated counterattacks by German infantry supported by 5-8 tanks and artillery from the directions of Knobloch and Anticken. At 1400, in cooperation with units of the 29th Rifle Corps, it resumed the attack in the direction of Anticken and Mertensdorf. Overcoming stubborn enemy resistance, at 1530 on 21 February it broke into the western outskirts of Anticken; by 2100 of the same day, it had finished mopping up the remaining enemy defenders from the town.

In the course of 22-24 February, the 29th Tank Corps and the 29th Rifle Corps continued to be engaged in heavy offensive fighting toward the north, toward Mertensdorf and Lindenau, while continuing to defend Anticken with part of their strength. The enemy was putting up strong resistance with artillery fire and the fire of small groups of 5-10 tanks and self-propelled guns from out of ambush positions, while going over to counterattacks 3 to 6 times a day both from the flanks and the front in strength of one to three battalions of infantry and 5-12 tanks, supported by strong artillery and mortar fire. Over the three days of fighting, the units of the 29th Tank Corps were able to advance just 1 kilometer in the direction of Mertensdorf. Meanwhile, the 10th Tank Corps and 47th Mechanized Brigades in the course of 21 to 24 February were still located in their occupied areas and continuing to carry out their previous orders.

The troops of the 5th Guards Tank Army on 23 February 1945 received a fresh order from the Front Commander-in-Chief, which demanded that it leave two brigades (the 32nd Tank Brigade and 183rd Tank Brigade) in their former areas in full readiness to support the troops of the 48th Army with active operations, while the rest of the tank army was to relocate to the area southeast of Tolkemit with the task to take up a defense and to prevent the enemy from expanding in the western and southwestern directions in the event of a breakthrough of our units' combat positions and an enemy penetration from the Frische-Nehrung spit to the coastline. In fulfillment of this order, the 10th Tank Corps (minus the 183rd Tank Brigade) on 24 February conducted a march and reassembled in the Groß Rautenberg, Vierzighuben, Bludau area with the task to prevent an enemy breakout from the Braunsberg direction.

The 29th Tank Corps (minus the 32nd Tank Brigade and 165th Light Artillery Regiment) on the night of 24-25 February marched to the Kreuzdorf, Conradswalde, Neukirch-Höhe area with the task to prevent an enemy breakout from the Passarge, Frauenburg direction. The 47th Mechanized Brigade continued to defend the coastline of the Frische-Haff lagoon in the Louisenthal Station – Tolkemit – Succase – Groß Röbern sector.

The 5th Guards Tank Army's formations (minus the 32nd and 183rd Tank Brigades and the 165th Light Artillery Regiment) remained in the indicated areas until 1 March 1945. Their task remained prevented an enemy breakout from encirclement.

From the "Combat Path of the 29th Tank Corps":

On the night of 17-18 February 1945, sappers laid down a bridge for the tanks in the Pettelkau area. The forward 32nd Tank Brigade and 53rd Motorized Rifle Brigade on the same night crossed the river, captured the village of Grunenberg, and cut the Schalmey – Böhmenhöfen road. As they made an attempt to make a further advance, the fire of enemy tanks and artillery blocked their path. The Germans, having deployed all of their available forces opposite the attacking troops, opened fire with such an intensity that the entire battlefield solid sea of raging fire and metal. The homes, trees, and stacks of hay and straw were on fire. A black and acrid smoke enveloped everything around, so that nothing was visible. The corps' artillery that had come up opened fire on the enemy and silenced his fire for some time. Taking advantage of this pause, the tankers again charged ahead. In this fighting the repair crews particularly stood out; under enemy fire, they worked to repair combat machines directly on the field of battle.

Reaching the Anticken area, the corps was subjected to a counterattack by up to a regiment of infantry supported by tanks and concentrated artillery fire. Throughout the day the tankers repulsed seven attacks by the hard-pressing Germans and stubbornly continued to advance. On 21 February 1945 the corps, after bitter fighting, took Anticken and continued offensive fighting in the northeastern direction toward Mertensdorf and Lindenau. Here, the pace of advance was slow and amounted to 1.5 to 5 kilometers a day. The attackers were very short of armored vehicles and manpower, whereas the enemy had assembled significant forces in a narrow sector that had an elaborate system of fortifications available to them.

In connection with the threat of an enemy penetration from the Frische-Nehrung spit and the activization of his troops in the coastal area, the Front Commander-in-Chief shifted the 5th Guards Tank Army to the area southeast of Tolkemit, placed it on the defensive, and gave it the mission to prevent an enemy expansion in the western and southwestern directions. Lieutenant Colonel S.I. Morozov's 32nd Tank Brigade was left behind in the previous area for joint operations with the 48th Army; in order to increase its strength in tanks, it received tanks from Colonel A.I. Pokolov's brigade.

The corps continued to fight in this new area until 2 March 1945 and was then transferred to the 2nd Belorussian Front. Having conducted several movements, the corps reassembled in the Brendau area and was located there until 22 March 1945, preparing for the forthcoming fighting. This pause was dictated by the need to give rest to the fatigued troops, replenish its brigades with men and combat equipment, and bring up ammunition.

The forces of the 2nd Belorussian Front were conducting a successful offensive to the northwest. They cut off Eastern Pomerania from Western Pomerania and reached the Baltic Sea for the third time.

F.I. Galkin resumes the narrative in his memoirs:

After dinner I went to see Vol'sky. When time allowed, Vasilii Timofeevich usually scrupulously analyzed each coded message containing information about the status of the tanks and self-propelled guns. However, this time he absent-mindedly skimmed through the summary and then immediately returned it to me.

"I have a question, Vasilii Timofeevich," I asked.

"Spit it out."

"The machines are at their service limits. We've squeezed everything we can out of the engines. Now the transmission and rolling assembly are falling apart. In sum, we've no more than a week left …"

"So, after a week we'll fold our hands and take a seat around a warm stove?"

"No, but we'll have to make repairs again. Apparently, they're not sending you new tanks?"

Vol'sky gave a nod of his head.

"Then we'll be sending our remaining serviceable machines back into battle and be repairing knocked-out tanks once again."

"Get busy."

"Who, though, will supply us with spare parts? We've left the 2nd Belorussian Front but have wound up in the 3rd Belorussion Front only temporarily. Like hell they're going to give us any!"

"True enough. What do you suggest?"

"Perhaps you can travel to Moscow and obtain requisitions from the central subordinate depot that is closest to the front."

"You mean, I'll go to Moscow for spare parts in the role of a supply clerk, but you'll be fighting? Thanks, Comrade Colonel!"

Vol'sky quickly grabbed a telegram notepad.

"Here, take a seat and write out a request for parts," he ordered. "Later I'll call Moscow. If we don't receive the necessary response within two days, you will go to the capital yourself. Right now, we'll get by even without you!"

My ploy backfired; I really wanted Vol'sky to get treatment from Moscow doctors.

"You're a wretched negotiator," I thought to myself cheerlessly as I walked back to my hut. "You couldn't think up any better than to send an army commander for spare parts!"

Over three days, while the army's forces in essence stood pat, the repair crews of Bogachin, Gusev and Daneliuk, together with the evacuation teams, put another 20 tanks and self-propelled guns back into service. On 14 February I was able to report to the chief of staff that we now had 175 operational tanks and self-propelled guns.

"That's a fine number, Fedor Ivanovich; we've kicked off our attack with it."

"What, now?"

"Yes, now. An hour ago, in cooperation with the rifle corps, Makharov attacked toward Pettelkau, while Sakhno attacked toward Steffenshöh. The initial reports are comforting: after getting some rest, the tankers are putting up a good show."

Sidorovich asked me to take a seat at the telephones because the officer from the Operations Department had gone somewhere, and he left to see the army commander.

Georgii Stepanovich had worked out his own method of managing a battle. Staff officers weren't bustling about, phone operators weren't shouting with hoarsened voices, and it wasn't always possible even to catch sight of an adjutant. The chief of staff normally calmly worked over a map, either alone or with an officer of the Operations Department. He himself kept the map updated and marked it with particular precision. He maintained contact with the troops through two field telephones and a radio set and kept in contact with higher headquarters via a high frequency circuit. General Sidorovich would patiently listen to reports from the subordinate formations and units, calmly issue corresponding orders, and just as calmly report on the situation to the Front headquarters.

Over the entire time of combat operations in the Baltics and East Prussia, only once did I see Sidorovich's nerves nearly give out. This happened on the outskirts of Mława. Totally exhausted after working through the night, Georgii Stepanovich in the morning reported the operational situation to the Front chief of staff Colonel General Bogoliubov over the high frequency circuit. For some reason Bogoliubov doubted the veracity of the report and undeservedly insulted Sidorovich, accusing him of lacking sufficient knowledge of the situation, and even suggested that his nerves were giving out. How Georgii Stepanovich flushed in response! His face became scarlet and his eyes flashed with pain and anger. His hand that was gripping the telephone turned blue from the way he was squeezing it. It seemed as if he would explode in another second, and disrespectfully respond to the insults. However, this didn't happen. Drawing a deep breath, he promptly repeated the report, before hanging up the phone. Then, having thought for a minute, he picked it up again and called the Front Commander-in-Chief Marshal of the Soviet Union Rokossovsky. Sidorovich calmly reported to the Marshal about his chief of staff's short temper, attentively listened to Rokossovsky's reply, and then left the room, plainly satisfied.

Now, having taken a seat at the chief of staff's desk, where even the neatly arranged colored pencils suggested an organized nature and orderliness, I involuntarily recalled that episode. Several minutes later, the field telephone began to ring.

"Comrade Three," I heard in the receiver, "103 is reporting."

In the table of codes, the code name "103" meant the chief of staff of the 29th Tank Corps Colonel Smirnov.

"No, Vladimir Ivanovich, this isn't Number Three; its just Galkin speaking."

"Glad to hear it, Fedor Ivanovich. Accept my greetings. Pettelkau has been taken. Stanislavsky's brigade is mopping it up, while Pokolov has already proceeded onward."

"Wait just a second, Vladimir Ivanovich," I said, grabbing a red pencil. "I've marked the map with a red pencil. Now everything is in order. Is that all?"

"That's all, Fedor Ivanovich. I wish you success."

"How are the machines running?"

"Fine. Pokolov has no losses. Stanislavksy's brigade has left one behind on the approaches to Pettelkau."

Sidorovich returned and entered the room, and I handed him the phone. He asked several questions, and then ordered one of the switchboard operators to call Colonel Omeliusty. About two minutes later, Omeliusty reported that the tank corps was fighting on the approaches to Steffenshöh but was making slow progress due to the stubborn enemy resistance. Only toward evening did Sakhno's tankers take Steffenshöh together with rifle units, before moving on, striving to reach the banks of the Passarge River.

On 16 February the army was engaged in heavy fighting on the Fehlau – Knorrwald line. I was already intending to head to the repair teams when I was summoned to appear before the army commander.

"General Sosenkov called. Leave for Moscow tomorrow, and if necessary, go see Iakov Nikolaevich Fedorenko. They aren't giving us new machines, and the ones we have will soon come to a stop."

… Over the time of my short absence from the army, it reached the Passarge River and forced a crossing of it, after which it captured the towns of Grutenberg and Anticken and approached Mertensdorf. On 25 February, however, it moved to the area southeast of Tolkemit and took up a defense there with the orders to prevent an enemy breakout at the coastline and to hinder the Germans from escaping to the west across the Frische-Nehrung spit.

Having searched out my unit, I first of all asked Irklei to tell me about everything in detail.

"The Germans were fighting very stubbornly. Attacks and counterattacks – one after the other. Malakhov and Sakhno were barely able to withstand the onslaught. They forced a crossing of the Passarge River after tough combat."

"Which brigades crossed?"

"Kolesnikov's 32nd Tank Brigade and the 53rd Motorized Rifle Brigade. The tankers experienced a great tragedy: Colonel Kolesnikov was killed and the commander of the 25th Tank Brigade Stanislavsky was wounded."

For several seconds we both remained silent.

"War," Irklei said with a sigh, before switching the conversation to a different subject. "The tanks are no longer running, but crawling. For one and a half months, as they say, they've been in the harness. Approximately 130 machines are operational. The majority require urgent repair and maintenance …"

On 28 February a directive arrived: our army, minus the 10th Tank Corps, was again being transferred to the 2nd Belorussian Front. This mean that we again had to make a 125-kilometer march, but the machines were completely worn out. It seemed only a miracle would keep them running. Yet this miracle took place.

The army carried out the order and assembled in the Marienwerder area at the designated time. To be sure, the 32nd Tank Brigade remained in combat. It appeared back under the corps' command only on 3 March, having just 5 machines still running. Mikhailov's mechanized brigade also remained temporarily subordinate to the 48th Army. Now our army had a strength of 76 tanks and self-propelled gun. They all needed either light overhauls or factory overhauls.

One more battle conducted by the 5th Guards Tank Army ended glitteringly. On 12 March a meeting of the army's Military Council took place with the cavaliers of the Order of Glory. The army commander and Military Council member warmly congratulated them and called upon them to act just as courageously in the future and to strike the foe decisively. Then on 14 March, the command officers of the formations and units gathered in a large city club in order to mark the second anniversary of the army's glorious combat path. General Grishin in his presentation summed up the result of this path. Over two years of fighting, our Guards army had traveled 7,400 kilometers, all the way from the village of Prokhorovka to the German city of Marienwerder; liberated a thousand towns and villages; and had trained and developed thousands of brave, experienced, selfless combatants. Many of them were worthy of the highest government honor – the title Hero of the Soviet Union.

The army commander's health was deteriorating with each day. A fatal illness broke this powerful man. We saw that Vasilii Timofeevich could stand on his feet only with difficulty. However, he never had the thought of giving up his post. Entreaties didn't help. We understood his stubbornness. He had fought for three and a half years. He had experienced both the bitterness of defeats and the joy of victories. Two major operations had just ended … and suddenly, when the final blow against the enemy was being prepared, he would find himself discharged from the army. Indeed, how could he part from his harmonious combat collective?

"Fine. I will go." We at last heard Vol'sky's decision. "Only for a few days. Meanwhile, maintain and service all the machines, and there …"

Now Vasilii Timofeevich brought in one after another of his deputies and assistants. Having wrapped up his official business, he had heartfelt conversations with people about what was close and dear to his heart. I realized that tomorrow the army would again go into battle and that everything had to be done so that Vol'sky departed before this moment.

On the morning of 19 March Vasilii Timofeevich set off for Moscow in a covered car accompanied by a jeep. At his farewell, he said to General Sinenko, who was acting as the temporary commander, "I hope, Maksim Denisovich, that we will still have everything ready in time …."

He sincerely believed that he would return in a few days. No one who was accompanying had a thought either that we were parting forever with our combat friend and chief, together with whom we had passed through the harsh years of the war; with a man of great heart and an exacting commander. Vasilii Timofeevich Vol'sky in fact never returned to his combat post.

In December I visited him in the Kremlin hospital heard the words that were full of hopes: "We will still do a little work together …."

However, medicine proved to be ineffective. Our famous army commander was buried in Moscow …

The gratitude received by the 5th Guards Tank Army for successfully conducted combat operations in the period between 14 January and 5 March 1945

1. Gratitude of the Supreme Commander-in-Chief for the capture of the cities of Mława and Dzialdowo, announced by an order from 19 January 1945;
2. Gratitude of the Supreme Commander-in-Chief for the capture of the cities of Naidenburg and Tannenburg, announced by an order from 21 January 1945;
3. Gratitude of the Supreme Commander-in-Chief for the capture of the cities of Osterode and Deutsch-Eylau, announced by an order from 22 January 1945;
4. Gratitude of the Supreme Commander-in-Chief for the capture of the cities of Mohrungen and Saalfeld, announced by an order from 23 January 1945;
5. Gratitude of the Supreme Commander-in-Chief for the capture of the city of Mühlhausen, reaching the sea, and completing the encirclement of the enemy's East Prussia grouping, announced by an order from 26 January 1945;
6. Congratulations to the Commander-in-Chief of the 2nd Belorussian Front from 24 January 1945 under Order No. 393: "To the commander of the 5th Guards Tank Army. I congratulate the valiant Guardsmen tankers, artillerymen and motorized infantry for their glittering achievements. I wish future successes in the adversary's destruction. ROKOSSOVSKY, BOGOLIUBOV."
7. Gratitude of the Commander-in-Chief of the 3rd Belorussian Front from 5 March 1945 (on the day of the 5th Guards Tank Army's departure from the 3rd Belorussian Front): "Comrade Vol'sky, I am expressing my sincere gratitude to you and all the personnel of the 5th Guards Tank Army that you represent for those glorious achievements, which were accomplished by you on the lands of the Baltic republics and East Prussia. I am parting with you with great regret and pain. From my heart I wish you more successes on the new axis of advance – I have no doubt in them. VASILEVSKY."

Il'ia Ehrenburg's article "Retribution" describes the terrible scenes as the Red Army advanced through East Prussia. Ehrenburg, if you will, was the most famous Soviet war correspondent, and a writer much loved by the soldiers and officers of the Red Army, which had been demonized by Göbbel's propaganda. He left behind very interesting recollections about his time in East Prussia in January–February 1945, like the one below:

I spent two weeks in Germany, which was enveloped by burning and smoking horror. German men and women are shuffling along lengthy roads in the snow or mud. The roads are heaped with piles of furniture, utensils and junk. Towns are burning. Feral pigs wander into empty town halls. The wind is fluttering the town banners bearing eagles, lions and stags.

We could have said, "What goes around comes around;" but we are above rejoicing at the misfortune of others. A different feeling is inspiring us: we see the triumph of justice. Speaking about retribution, many were thinking only about the articles of the future treaty. I don't know what the verdict of the diplomats will be. Undoubtedly, fascist bigotry will find its defenders, those devotees of "balance", balance between the light and dark. No matter how we might imagine the future peace, one thing is clear: retribution has already begun, and Germany has found out what war means. So, who knows, perhaps the Germans will recall these weeks and months of war on German soil much more than all the obligations of peace treaties?

Street fighting went on in Elbing for several days. When the fighting ended, though, I caught sight of a rather picturesque scene: Germans were standing at the gates of a prison – a long line of them. Noone had chased them there. However, the prison seemed to these "supermen" to be a tranquil and even cozy place ….

They are desperately resisting, they are firing from each and every building, and they appear to be implacable. However, once the officer is killed or the ammunition is running out, even the "implacable" quickly snap to attention, salute our wagon drivers and even our horses, and begin to try to show their lack of participation in world conquest. Not only the Fritzes – Oberst Weinshenck changes right in front of your eyes. At first, he repeats through inertia: "Germany is invincible!", but then, just as if the clock has run out, he adds in a different voice: "How could I be a Nazi? I was married to a Jewish woman …."

The population is attempting to flee. Thousands and thousands of carts and wagons are streaming to the west. These wagons are simply carrying all sorts of things – trunks, featherbeds, furniture, girdles, mustache trainers – and (under the straw) several Italian carbines and knives, distributed by the Kreisleiters with the inscription "All for Germany" or "Blood and honor": the German men and women are supposed to kill Russians with these knives.

However, the Red Army is blocking their path here. Not only armchairs have been abandoned here, but even the mustache trainers. Tens of thousands of featherbeds are lying about (the Germans bed down on featherbeds); the down from all the geese from the time of Bismarck to our present day is being blown about by the East and West Prussian winds. As for the German men and women, once caught by us, they try to rid themselves of not only the knives, but also from their own past: "I'm a Frenchman … I have non-Aryan blood … My mother is Dutch … I'm half-Pole and half-Lithuanian …." They hastily wring their caps. The young women lewdly and ingratiatingly gaze at our passing soldiers, as if they aren't the daughters of burghers, but waitresses in a night cabaret. The Germans know all of the orders of our commandants by heart; they piously repeat: "This is the order of Sir Russian Commandant!"

I saw a lot of woods; they were empty …. Germans, who were just recently hurrying to the west and swearing to kill Russians, are now fervently marching to the east and bowing and scraping before the Russians. The further we advance to the west, the more we encounter the German population: they have no where to run.

In Western Prussia I saw the residents of the eastern areas. There was a lot of them: hundreds of thousands. They are snitching on each other: "The butcher here – is an active Nazi … Herr Müller beat Russian girls … Willy's stableman shot a Polish woman … Frau Schmidt received the gratitude of the Gauleiter himself …." They are all attempting to show their innocence. One produced a certificate: eleven years ago, he had been held by the Nazis in prison for a month. Another presents a testimonial signed by yesterday's slave – a Belgian prisoner of war. A third somewhere dug up the membership card of a Social Democratic club dating back to 1928.

Here a German woman in trousers is climbing the façade of a building in order to remove the swastika emblem. No one has ordered her to do this; she is perspiring and excited – it seems to her as if she has been rehabilitated in front of history. Don't even think to ask her how she scorned and mistreated her Russian servant Galia.

There a German is moving the clock hour two hours forward and triumphantly announcing: "Now it is exactly 3:20 according to Moscow time." He is beaming: he is ready to live not only according to Moscow time, but also to Vladvostok time; just don't question him about how four French women were working for him from dawn to dusk.

A dignified doctor says: "How could I be a Nazi? After all, I'm a doctor, and that means a humanist, but a Nazi – is a beast."

An archdeacon, rubbing his hands, babbles: "The Catholic church had always condemned Hitler; of course, I couldn't denounce him out loud, but I condemned him to myself. But the evangelical church …." However, a Lutheran pastor on his part swears: "We also denounced the ungodly regime …."

An engineer in Elbing reports, "As a man of progress, I am against Hitler," – and cleverly smiling, adds: "I can work for the Russians." A worker confirms, "Who counts me as a Nazi? My father was a genuine Social Democrat. I myself once voted for the Communist list of candidates. Of course, I can't speak up against the regime because this was strictly forbidden. However, I am now agreeable to speak out even against Hitler."

You can't trust a single one of them. They seem now like sheep, but they were wolves, and remain as them. They are tossing away the carbines and knives; but who knows what will happen a month later? The German doesn't know how to fight at his own initiative; he waits for an order. Among the bewildered, frightened crowd, there are people who've been instructed to organize diversions and putsches. Now they are concealed: the fear of their compatriots is too great; it is necessary to gather one's breath. However, if you allow them to catch their breath, if you don't whip them into shape, if you don't check them out and don't shine a light on each one of them, soon the most docile, those who shout "Rot Front!" and trample the Führer's image, will once again begin to be delirious with dreams of Greater Germany, and falling in line as a camouflaged *Oberleutnant* or *Rotenführer*, will take up their rifles, bombs and knives. After all, I didn't find genuine repentance in any one of the Germans: only fear and feigning.

If it is possible to pity anyone on the German roads, then it is only the tiny, totally uncomprehending children; the maddened, unmilked cows; and the abandoned dogs and cats. Only they are not implicated in acts of atrocity ….

War did not mean devastation and ruin for the Germans, but bounty; and when the war was raging on the Seine River or Volga River, it seemed pleasing to them. They had both sufficient living space and goods.

Here is the home of a wealthier Prussian peasant. Spacious rooms with tiled stoves, and on the walls – clocks, oleographs, and mounted antlers without fail. Dozens of captured Dutch cows, pigs and geese. His domain suffered little from the war: The Fritzes were eating imported beef and destroying the huts on foreign lands.

I visited dozens of German towns and cities. Over a month before the Red Army's arrival, the burghers were still reveling in their lawlessness. In Rastenburg, one German bought a hotel. In Guttstadt, a 42-year-old landlady with "dark chestnut hair who has kept her figure" (as the newspaper ad states), was looking for a suitor. In Deutch Eylau, a furniture shop was building a luxurious cabinet for some Dömke. In the townhouses were the apartments of the burgomeisters, splendidly appointed, with portraits of the Führer and green bottles for Rhein wine. There were beerhalls and little tables with flags "for customers".

One can add that the Germans spent the majority of their income on decorating their apartments; in peacetime, they didn't splurge on divertissements and dressed modestly, but their apartments were full of divans and armchairs, vases and pillows, cupboards with dinnerware, and various "souvenirs". Over the years of the war, they brought back to their homes various goods, utensils and trifles from Paris, Rotterdam, Florence, Warsaw and Kiev. Their apartments are consignment shops, and one soldier joking said about them, "It is possible to live in such a hovel." However, all this wasn't enough for them. They had slaves working for them. In the small, provincial town of Rastenburg, not only the rich, but also the families of workers had a Russian domestic servant – after all, they didn't have to pay her.

The German workers and farmhands looked with respect at the Prussian landlords; they were not dreaming about the Prussian estates, but about plots of arable land in Ukraine – after all, Erich Koch was promising each Prussian a fine plot of Russian soil. The German workers believed that if their masters seized Russian manganese and French bauxite, then they, the German workers, would also have a scrap come their way ….

In a saddler's linen closet were twelve German bedsheets, and Ukrainian bedsheets – "a gift from the son". Why did he need these two? Re-read the phrase in quotation marks. Here you can read it as "The gift – is your luxury", or as "Something useful in daylight hours, a pleasant sleep at night", and finally as "You can't have too many". It seems that it didn't hurt the saddler to have these two sheets; but it turned out quite the contrary: the son was killed at the Dniester River, and the saddler himself lost his shop, his bed and twelve German bedsheets ...

One can move the hands on a clock; one can tear down the street signs that read "Hitlerstrasse"; but it is impossible the evidence – it is everywhere. Next to the frightened slaveowner, you see, we are everywhere seeing the radiant slaves that had just been liberated. There are so many French, Polish, Czech, Belgian and Dutch people here! So many young women from Ukraine, from Belorussia, who are crying their eyes out! By some miracle, surviving Soviet prisoners of war. A Frenchman, a military doctor told me:

> "Of course, the Bosche abused us as well, but we lived like gods in comparison with the Russians. We sought to share our food with them, but the Germans sent us away to the Graudenz penal camp, saying: 'If you help the Bolsheviks, you are betraying the idea of a new Europe.' The Russian prison camp was rife with typhus. Every morning they carted away the corpses. The Germans would shout: 'Drag these as well!' I saw with my own eyes laid down the living with the dead, and the living men would be moaning, but the Germans would bury them alive ..."

No, the matter of Germany's crimes won't end with the shifting of the hour hand of a clock!

The world now knows that the Germans killed six million Jews. They killed all the Jews – from breastfeeding infants to old men. Until recently, the Germans were keeping the last thousand living Jews near Elbing: they were prolonging the sadists' enjoyment. Here there were Parisian architects, a composer from Amsterdam, doctors from Kaunas, a Belgrade professor. They placed them naked on stools and poured icy water over them – this in subfreezing temperatures. Then they killed them. Is it really enough to remove an awkward street sign in order to make sure that such evil is forgotten?

They are entering and bowing: "We know nothing. We're innocent ...." The evidence is at hand. They were fleeing so hastily that they were abandoning not only street signs, but also the printed material and archives of the police; they were even abandoning their personal papers. Here are the notes of Erich von Bremen. He isn't an ardent young man – he's 57 years old. Having familiarized myself with his autobiography, I found out that he was married to Ursula von Ramm and that two of his sons took part in the conquering of the world. The highbred German when fleeing left behind two internal reports. One was dedicated to the colonization of the Baltic republics, the other – to the acquisition of the Caucasus region. I will cite an excerpt from the latter: "We must take possession of the Caucasus, since we need the Groznyi and Baku oil in order to invigorate our economy. By this we will free ourselves from America. The North Caucasus grain will supply the Transcaucasus; we can't transport it in addition to the oil, lumber, fruit, canned goods, wine and tobacco. Thus, the Caucasus will become a German colony." I assume that somewhere in Stettin, the Red Army will find Erich von Bremen; the author of this internal report about the Caucasus will undoubtedly say, "I oppose Hitler and am shifting the clock to Moscow time."

Alongside the prosperity, everywhere we see consumption running wild. In any apartment – a library. What price the marvelous book bindings! Only don't open the books – the cannibal's *Mein Kampf*; collected works dedicated to Himmler: *Campaign against Poland*, *Racial Genetics*, *The Jewish Pestilence*, *The Russian Subhumans*, *Our True Prussia* ... squalor and spiritual poverty. Incidentally, it is clear that few read these books; the volumes were decorations, like the vases and porcelain cats. In vain I searched for city libraries in Lötzen, in Rastenburg, or in Tilsit: there weren't any. I found only one museum – in Bartenstein. What was on display in it? Portraits of Hildenburg and the epaulettes of an officer of the Tsarist Army with the caption: "Won at Tannenburg". The uniform of a Polish officer and photographs of devastated Warsaw: "Campaign against Poland". Skeletons of apes, and no less than a hundred portraits of Hitler; a beer mug from the time of Bismarck; miniature barracks and photographs of a city philanthropist. That was the entire museum. In Heilsberg, there was a club of the Nazi Party; this was a booze joint, a counter where they poured the beer, and several bloodthirsty, trashy books. Everywhere were enormous police buildings: here the Germans thought, composed, fantasized and confessed. Maps of the world with discolored paper flaglets, still sticking out of El Barani and Maikop …

The retribution has begun. It will be carried through to the end. Nothing more can save the gangster Germany. The first words of that treaty, which can be called a peace treaty, has been written in the blood of Russia. Germany is now hearing these words. As for me – for a Soviet citizen, a Russian writer, and a man who has seen Madrid, Paris, Orel and Smolensk; for me the greatest happiness is to tread on this ground of the villains and know that it wasn't coincidence, it wasn't fortune, and it wasn't speech or articles that save the world from fascism, but our people, our army, our heart, our Stalin.

1 March 1945

As was customary in the Red Army by this time, once the operation to isolate the German East Prussia grouping came to its successful conclusion and the process began of reducing the pocket, the Military Council of the 5th Guards Tank Army produced a report that summarized the results of the operation and drew lessons and recommendations for future operations from the experience:

Results of the operation and general conclusions

1. One detail of the conducted operation was the fact that it was planned as an operation with totally decisive objectives and depth, extending up to 300 km. The shock grouping of the 2nd Belorussian Front, consisting of the 48th Army, 2nd Shock Army and 5th Guards Tank Army were given tasks that amounted to the following: Attacking out of the bridgeheads north and south of Pultusk, to break through the enemy's strong defenses and advancing as rapidly as possible to the northeast, to reach the Danzig harbor of the Baltic Sea in the shortest amount of time and to cut off the enemy's East Prussia grouping from the rest of Germany. The conducted operation, by its planning and the results of its implementation, was crowned by a complete and glittering success.
2. In the conducted operation, the question of properly employing tanks in full accordance with our main regulations regarding the use of armored and mechanized forces merits particular attention. The 8th Guards Tank Corps and 8th Mechanized Corps, as smaller formations, were committed into the battle before the 5th Guards Tank Army and took part in grinding through the tactical zone of the enemy's defenses together with the infantry. The strength of the 5th Guards Tank Army was fully preserved, and it was introduced into the fighting only on 17 January 1945, on the fourth day of the operation once the regular infantry units had advanced 20-25 km into the depth of the enemy's defenses. The principle of systematically enhancing the force of the blow by attacking out of the depth was skillfully and completely followed in the conducted operation.
3. In the task of "cutting off the enemy's East Prussia grouping from Germany", the 5th Guards Tank Army received the leading and most decisive role, which judging from results and the time required to carry it out, it handled completely successfully.
4. According to the interrogation of prisoners and an entire array of other indicators, it is clear that the appearance of the 5th Guards Tank Army in the indicated area came as a complete surprise to the enemy command, which speaks to the fact that the 5th Guards Tank Army's movement and assembly in the staging and jumping-off areas went unnoticed by the enemy, and that complete operational surprise was achieved when using it in this sector of the front.

5. Having conducted a 145-kilometer march from its assembly area to the staging area and a 50-kilometer march (on average) to the jumping-off area, the 5th Guards Tank Army on the morning of 24 January 1945 reached the sea with its main forces and isolated Elbing from three directions (from the north, the east and the south), thereby having carried out its main task in a period of time of less than seven days. Altogether over the course of the conducted operation up until the moment of its arrival at the sea, the 5th Guards Tank Army with its march covered 500 km.
6. The average daily rate of combat advance equaled 43 kilometers. Considering that the terrain in the army's combat path had an abundant number of lakes, swamps, peat bogs and small streams with boggy banks, as well as irrigation canals full of water (which by their nature and width in many cases were equivalent to antitank ditches), but also had seven previously-prepared fortified lines with an elaborate system of artificial obstacles (like antitank ditchs, minefields, and barriers up to 2 meters high) – the average daily rate of the tanks' advance of 43 km is unquestionably a rapid tempo. This pace was achieved by the ceaseless, impetuous offensive of the 5th Guards Tank Army's forces with the exertion of all its strength.
7. During the conducted operation the 5th Guards Tank Army captured the following 21 towns and cities: Grudusk, Mława, Dzialdowo (Soldau), Neidenburg, Uzdau, Tannenberg, Hilgenburg, Geierswalde, Lubawa, Osterode, Deutsch-Eylau, Liebemühl, Saalfeld, Mohrungen, Freiwalde, Grünhagen, Preußisch Holland, Mühlhausen, Tolkemit, Deutschendorf, Frauenburg and more than 1,000 other populated places.
8. Reaching the sea north of Elbing with its main forces by the morning of 24 January 1945 and having isolated Elbing from north, east and south, the garrison of which not only put up fierce resistance but also launched repeated counterattacks with an attempt to break through to the east and link up with the encircled grouping – the troops of the 5th Guards Tank Army spent three days (24-26 January 1945) firmly defending and holding its occupied Mühlhausen – Tolkemit – Elbing – Preußisch Holland area while waiting for the infantry to come up, and prevented a single enemy machine, wagon or soldier of the encircled enemy grouping from escaping to the west.
9. With the arrival of the 42nd Rifle Corps to the area of the 5th Guards Tank Army's dispositions, starting on 27 January 1945 and on following days, when the enemy had brought up major forces opposite the front of the 5th Guards Tank Army from other sectors of East Prussia, including the 131st Infantry Division, 170th Infantry Division, 28th Jäger Division, 10th Bicycle-Jäger Brigade, 18th Panzergrenadier Division's Panzergrenadier Regiment 51, the 24th Panzer Division, Assault Gun Brigade 279 and up to a battalion of tanks from the Panzergrenadier Division *Großdeutschland* and launched a ferocious counteroffensive with the aim of breaking through, eliminating the encirclement, and freeing the East Prussia grouping's lines of communication to Elbing and Marienburg, the troops of the 5th Guards Tank Army comprised the hard nut of an active defense, upon which all of the enemy's vain attempts to break out to the west were shattered. Having made contact with the forces of the 5th Guards Tank Army, the enemy was stopped and then as a result of bitter and heavy fighting thrown back beyond the Passarge River 35-40 km away from Elbing.
10. The army's combat operations over the period from 27 January to 25 February 1945, by their character, as a result of the gradual compression of the ring of encirclement and the growing density of the enemy's combat formations with their plentiful availability of all kinds of equipment and ammunition, can be compared to prolonged defensive fighting or to actions of a group of direct support to the infantry when grinding through the enemy's organized and deep defenses, but continuous over the course of an entire month. Such operations are very difficult for major tank formations, costly in all respects, and at the same time insufficiently effective in the sense of the full exploitation of the tank's main qualities. When aggregating

the experience of fighting over this period, it is necessary once again to acknowledge that it would be more sensible to withdraw tank armies and corps after 8-10 days of intense combat work in turn from the frontlines and give them not less than 5-7 days in order to service their tanks and put them back into good working order, and then use them in mass on a narrow front in order to split the encircled grouping into pieces.

11. From the analysis of the experience of the conducted operation, and in particular, the situation on the army's front upon reaching the sea and in the course of the following three days (24-26 January 1945) flows the conclusion regarding the inadequate authorized number of motorized infantry in the tank armies (only one mechanized brigade in the 5th Guards Tank Army, and just one motorized rifle brigade each in the two tank corps). This shortcoming could be offset by assigning the Front's trucks to bring up 1-2 rifle divisions behind the tank army, at the very least in echelons consisting of 1-2 regiments. The arrival of 1-2 rifle divisions in the Elbing area on 24 January 1945 or on the morning of 25 January would have created the possibility of a successful advance by the 5th Guards Tank Army further to the northeast in the direction of Braunsberg agains the enemy's rear communications.

12. The experience of fighting in the conducted operation demonstrated the possibility and advantageousness of nighttime operations by the tank units and motorized infantry in the depth of the defenses. An entire number of towns, which had been converted by the enemy into powerful strongpoints (Neidenburg, Dzialdowo, Tannenberg, Osterode and Freiwalde) were taken by the troops of the 5th Guards Tank Army from the march or through a nighttime assault – after a sudden, concentrated, but short (10-15 minutes) artillery barrage.

13. The conducted operation, as in preceding operations, demonstrated the unsuitability of introducing the tank army into a breakthrough in the afternoon, as a result of which it overtakes the infantry and its first encounter with the enemy and his defenses takes place toward evening, and this puts a brake on the initial momentum in the tanks' actions. It is sensible to commit the tank armies and corps into the breach either in the morning, no later than 1200, or at night, when the overtaking of the infantry and fighting with the enemy in his tactical zone will take place in daylight hours.

14. The arrangement of the combat formation of the army's tank corps along two routes of advance, in two combat echelons, with the assignment of strong forward detachments on each route, consisting of no less than one tank battalion, one self-propelled gun battery, a submachine gun company, a sapper company and antiaircraft weapons from the brigades of the first echelon, completely justified itself. The forward detachments set out from the jumping-off areas in partially deployed formations. Out in front of themselves, the forward detachments sent out reconnaissance patrols consisting of a platoon of tanks, a platoon of submachine gunners, a sapper squad, a halftrack, and motorcycles for communications. The corps commanders together with their operational command group moved in the first echelon's combat formations. The corps headquarters headed by the chiefs of staff and the corps' reserves advanced behind the second echelons. An artillery-tank reserve was present in both corps. No less than a company of reserves were in the brigades. Army-level reserves moved along the routes taken by the tank corps, with the main forces advancing along outer routes. The army headquarters made bounding advances in the zone of the army-level reserves at a distance of 10-25 km from the corps headquarters. The army commander and senior officers of the Operations Department periodically drove out to visit the corps' combat formations. The deputy army commanders were assigned to each direction and in the mobile period of the operation were located in the corps' combat formations up to 95% of the time, personally directing the troops and putting the army commander's will and decisions into practice. The role of the deputy commanders of all levels significantly rose in questions regarding the command of the troops. Such a combat formation secured the

timely receipt of information about the enemy, the roads and the terrain lying ahead; the timely overcoming of encountered artificial obstacles; the rapid deployment of the units; the possibility of maneuvering the units in the direction of the flanks; and good command over the troops. However, it must be noted that in several forward detachments and in the combat reconnaissance patrols sent out by them, major miscalculations in the sense of tardiness and indecisive actions were present. The pace of advance of the brigade, the corps and the army depends on their work. Their operations must be daring, rapid and bold. In connection with this, the preparation of the men for actions in a forward detachment and in combat reconnaissance, in particular right before an operation, as well as the choice of the commanders for the forward detachment and combat reconnaissance must be given more attention as exceptionally important questions.

15. The experience of the conducted operation demonstrated that in order to maintain the pace of advance, it is necessary periodically to replace the brigades moving in the first echelons with brigades from the second echelons, since the stress, which means as well the fatigue of the men in the first echelon is significantly higher than the men of the second echelon have.

16. The rich experience of liquidating a large number of enemy strongpoints gained by the troops of the 5th Guards Tank Army in the conducted operation leads to the conclusion that the main role of the tank units and formations is to make enveloping maneuvers to encircle the strongpoint's (town's) garrison or a knot of resistance, to disperse his forces and attention in every direction, and by this to weaken and partially demoralize him, while the infantry's role is to break the enemy's defenses through an attack– with the support of artillery and if necessary a small number of self-propelled guns or tanks (as a group of direct infantry support) – at the most vulnerable locations, penetrate into a strongpoint (town) and take it. In the conducted operation, the clearest and most instructive example of the tactical cooperation between the tank and infantry formations when eliminating knots of resistance and strongpoints should be considered the taking of the powerful Mława center of resistance, with its major garrison and numerous and strong fortifications, within a period of time of less than a day from the moment the tanks approached the outer ring of fortifications.

17. The army's artillery in the conducted operation handled its assigned tasks in a generally successful fashion. In defensive fighting, the artillery operated well in the overwhelming majority of cases. On the offensive and during marches, the artillery didn't lag behind the tank and motorized rifle units and moved, as a rule, in their combat formations and supported their operations with fire. However, there still substantial shortcomings in the use of artillery, particularly in the use of the self-propelled artillery. Questions of escorting the tanks with artillery fire haven't yet been worked out concisely. There are many shortcomings in the issuing of fire mission on the part of commanders of the units and elements to the artillery that is attached to them. There is still confusion regarding the conceptual understanding and roles of the tanks and self-propelled guns; many don't see any difference between them. The experience of the fighting in the conducted operation showed that the tank remains the primary maneuvering and shock force, while the self-propelled gun is a means for supporting their operations. Using the artillery to eliminate tank ambushes with direct fire, as practiced by certain tank commanders, leads to heavy losses in artillerymen and guns. According to the experience of the conducted fighting, the heavy self-propelled artillery and self-propelled artillery regiments must be considered as the main and primary means for the struggle against tank ambushes. The primary shortcomings of the self-propelled gun are its slow rate of fire and poor maneuverability; attention should be paid to eliminating them. Bad command and control can be found in the majority of the self-propelled artillery regiments, and in the heavy self-propelled artillery regiments, poor maneuvering as well. The practice of attaching one heavy self-propelled artillery regiment each to the tank brigades for the conducted operation

didn't justify itself. It is more sensible to have the heavy self-propelled gun regiments in the corps' reserves.
18. The primary forms of communication in the maneuvering period of the operation were radios and mobile means (the Willys jeep, the armored car, and the PO-2 airplane). The mobile means of communication worked well throughout the operation. Radio communications, which had a heavy burden in the course of the operation, performed fully satisfactorily in the daytime, but in the nighttime, as a rule, performed poorly because of frequent interference. There were cases of the interruptions in radio contact throughout the command network for 4 to 6 hours (in the 29th Tank Corps because of the loss of radio sets when moving the corps headquarters). Wire communications in the maneuvering period of the operation performed with large interruptions because the laying of the lines lagged behind, but in general worked satisfactorily.
19. Despite the large stretching of the rear services, the rapid advance of the combat units, and the lack of motorized transport, the rear services and technical support services successfully dealt with their tasks in the conducted operation.

Commander of the 5th Guards Tank Army Guards Colonel General of Tank Forces VOL'SKY
Military Council Member Guards Major General of Tank Forces GRISHIN
Army Chief of Staff Guards Major General of Tank Forces SIDOROVICH

At the same time, the 5th Guards Tank Army's deputy chief of operations Guards Colonel Appalonov issued a report on the army's losses in manpower, tanks and self-propelled guns:

Losses of the 5th Guards Tank Army over the period from 17 January to 1 March 1945

1. Manpower losses

Table 4.22 (Numbered as "1" and contained within the report; also title given in text)

	Killed	Wounded	Missing-in-action	Total
29th Tank Corps	891	2740	41	3672
10th Tank Corps	779	2747	51	3577
47th Mechanized Brigade	399	1431	1	1831
Units directly subordinate to army headquarters	101	310	10	421
Total:	2170	7228	103	9501

2. Losses of tanks and self-propelled guns

Table 4.23 (numbered as "2" and contained within the report; title is already given in the text)

Units and formations	Type of machine	Total losses	Of which, irrecoverable
29th Tank Corps	T-34	133	66
	M4A2	1	-
	SU-76	22	12
	SU-85	31	22
	SU-152	47	19
Total:		234	119

Units and formations	Type of machine	Total losses	Of which, irrecoverable
10th Tank Corps	T-34	110	80
	M4A2	3	3
	SU-76	12	5
	SU-85	15	10
	SU-100	51	23
	SU-122	15	3
Total:		206	124
47th Mechanized Brigade	M4A2	29	16
14th Guards Heavy Tank Regiment	IS-122	6	1
376th Heavy Self-Propelled Artillery Regiment	SU-152	4	2
Total for the 5th Guards Tank Army:		479	262

The losses inflicted on the enemy by the 5th Guards Tank Army over the period from 17 January to 1 March 1945, and the captured booty

Smashed: 299th Infantry Division, 18th Panzergrenadier Division; 28th Jäger Division's Infantry Regiment 83, 170th Infantry Division's Infantry Regiment 391, 24th Panzer Division's Panzergrenadier Regiment 21; the Second Army's assault regiment; Heavy Panzer Battalion 507; the 118th Assault Gun Battalion and 474th Panzerjäger Battalion; the Mława training and forming center of self-propelled artillery; Assault Gun Brigades 277, 185 and 209; the 10th Training Reserve Battalion; Machine-gun Battalions "Vistula" and "Pregel"; the 75th Fortress Battalion; the 201st and 713th Landwehr Battalions; the 353rd and 583rd Transport Battalions; Flak-Assault Regiment 5; the 662nd and 286th Training Battalions; the 1st and 53rd Reserve Battalions, the 31st Flak Battalion; the 37th Reserve Artillery Battalion; the 1444th Fortress Battalion; the 5th and 10th Training Panzer Battalions; and Combat Groups "Herzig", "Nehrung", "Wolf" and "Hannibal" that were created from the remnants of previously shattered enemy units.

Heavy losses were inflicted on: units of the 24th Panzer Division; Assault Gun Brigade 279 and the *Großdeutschland* Division's assault gun brigade; the 7th Infantry Division; the 28th Jäger Division's Infantry Regiments 49 and 28; 170th Infantry Division's Infantry Regiments 398 and 401; the 14th Infantry Division; the Bicycle-Jäger Brigade 10; the Engineer-Assault Brigade 627; the 37th Naval Infantry Battalion; and the Regiment *Feldernhalle*.

Over the period of the operation, the enemy lost a total of 453 tanks and self-propelled guns; 749 guns of various calibers; 85 halftracks; 385 mortars; 1,294 machine guns and 6,800 rifles and submachine guns; 9 aircraft; 87 various supply dumps; 35 steam engines; 16 railroad trains and 233 railroad wagons and platform cars; 23 railroad cisterns; 4,597 trucks and cars; 340 motorcycles; 5,645 wagons carrying military items; 24 steamships, cutters and barges; 22 prime movers and tractors, and 40,000 officers and soldiers killed or wounded, as well as 6,200 taken prisoner.

According to an account from Army Group North to the German General Staff (Org Abt I OKH) on 8 March 1945, the army group's losses in personnel over the period of January and February 1945 amounted to 213,000 men (30,000 killed, 126,000 wounded and 57,000 missing-in-action). In the account it is noted that this is the minimal estimate of losses, which will be corrected by supplementary reports in the direction of increases.

These figures don't include the casualties of the *Volksturm* and various police formations. The losses of Army Group North over January–February 1945, according to this account, amounted to one-third of all the German Army's casualties on the Eastern Front.

According to a combat report from 8 February 1945, the German Fourth Army over the period from 12 January to 7 February 1945 alone lost 53,034 men, including 1,146 officers (336 killed,

992 wounded and 118 missing), and 51,888 non-commissioned officers and men (10,803 killed, 32,612 wounded and 8,473 missing).

On 15 January 1945, the 7th Panzer Division was introduced into the fighting with the aim of plugging the breach made by the Russian forces north of Warsaw. The attack by the division's panzer regiment (which had 102 operational tanks and self-propelled guns on the morning of 15 January 1945) ran into the tank ambushes set by 2nd Belorussian Front's 2nd Shock Army, and in a brief action west of Ostenburg (Pultusk), which lasted around 20 minutes, the division irrecoverably lost 40 tanks. The panzer division had to retreat and abandon all of its knocked-out tanks on the battlefield. On the evening of 15 January, it had only around 40 tanks still in service.

Joachim Huber, a participant in this combat from V./Panzer Regiment 25, recalled: "A counterattack on the morning of 15 January was launched by the 7th Panzer Division's Panzer Regiment 25 with the strength of around 70 panzers and 10 self-propelled guns. My company irrecoverably lost 5 of the 13 Pz IV L/48 literally in the course of several minutes after lunch on 15 January, when Panzer Regiment 25's attack ran into Russian tank ambushes. Still, my company was lucky, since it was advancing closer to the center of the attacking group of panzers. Other companies, attacking on the flanks, were less fortunate and they suffered much heavier losses."

On 1 February 1945 the 7th Panzer Division had 0 Pz Bef Wg III, 1 Pz III (50mm L/60), 2 Flak Pz IV (37mm), 8 (0) Pz IV (75mm L/48), 19 (2) Pz V, 4 Pz IV/70 (V) and Pz IV/70 (A), for a total of 57 (+6) panzers and assault guns in Panzer Regiment 25 and Panzerjäger Regiment 42. Panzerjäger Regiment 42 also had 7 Marder III (75mm) and 1 Marder III (76mm) for a total of 8 (7) self-propelled guns in its I Battalion. A total of 35 of the surviving knocked-out tanks and assault guns and 3 self-propelled guns were undergoing short-term repairs (up to 14 days), while the remaining machines were undergoing long-term repairs (longer than 14 days).

The *Großdeutschland* Division over 10 days of fighting in January 1945 lost more than 100 panzers and assault guns. Moreover, in Mława it lost 21 panzerjägers that belonged to the Division *Großdeutschland*'s panzerjäger battalion (Pz Jg Abt GD).

The irrecoverable losses of the 7th Panzer Division over the second half of January 1945, the majority of which were lost on the single day of 15 January, amounted to 1 Pz Bef Wg III, 21 Pz IV (75mm L/48), 18 Pz V, 4 Pz IV/70 (V) and Pz IV/70 (A), for a total of 44 panzers and assault guns, plus 6 Marder III self-propelled guns. Only 6 operational panzers remained in the division on 1 February 1945, while more than 50 panzers and self-propelled guns were under repair.

Heavy Panzer Battalion 507 when retreating around 26 January 1945 blew up 22 Tigers due to the reason of the impossibility of getting them across the Vistula River. The bridge across the river had already been blown.

Heroes of the 5th Guards Tank Army, January–February 1945

Junior Lieutenant PAVEL ISAEV – a T-34 tank commander of the 3rd Tank Battalion of the 29th Tank Corps' 31st Tank Brigade. From the moment his battalion entered the breakthrough to its arrival at the sea, it spent all of its time on combat reconnaissance. When located in the Dzialdowo area, he spotted the movement of an enemy column. Having set up his tank in an ambush position, from its cannon he destroyed shot up 8 tanks and up to 20 vehicles. The path of retreat for the enemy columns had been cut. His further path ran to the area of a bridge, where as part of reconnaissance, with a bold dash in nighttime conditions, he cut the path of retreat of the German elements that were defending the bridge, as a result of which 35 Nazis were killed by him. Located on combat reconnaissance along the Dzialdowo – Reishof route, Isaev intercepted a column of retreating German wagons carrying military loads and crushed up to 27 wagons while killing up to 30 Germans. While conducting the 60-kilometer march to the Saalfeld area, located on combat reconnaissance, he spotted the movement of a column of German vehicles. Making use of an outflanking maneuver, he reached the head of the column and with his tracks crushed 6 enemy vehicles. Bursting into the streets of the town, Isaev detected a large column of retreating enemy vehicles and wagons. At high speed he sliced into the enemy column, and with the tank's cannon fire and tracks killed up 33 German soldiers and officers. As a result of the bold and skillful maneuver, the town was taken without a single loss on our side. Having received the assignment to move out toward the city of Elbing on reconnaissance, throughout the lengthy march he operated boldly, in accordance with the situation. He destroyed up to 20 wagons with their loads and provisions and killed up to 25 Nazis. Upon reaching Elbing, Isaev spotted a large movement of vehicles. Charging into the column, with tank's tracks and cannon and machine-gun fire he destroyed up to 50 vehicles, 2 trolleys, 2 anti-aircraft mounts, 5 halftracks and killed up to 150 soldiers and officers. When the alarm rang out in the city, the Germans attempted to destroy our reconnaissance with the forces of up to 150 soldiers and officers armed with Panzerfausts. Isaev continued to carry out his orders, despite the difficult combat conditions. He reached the coastline of the sea and with a shot from his cannon sank an enemy barge loaded with cargo and men. Through his decisive actions, he contributed to the rapidest fulfillment of his battalion's missions. Put up for the title Hero of the Soviet Union; recipient of the Order of the Red Banner.

Guards Major GEORGII MALINOVSKY – commander of the 2nd Battalion of the 1619th Light Artillery Regiment of the 5th Guards Tank Army's 201st Separate Light Artillery Brigade. In the fighting for the village of Kondi and the town of Neidenburg, he was located with his battalion in the forward detachment and supported the tanks of the 10th Tank Corps' 186th Tank Brigade and the tanks and motorized infantry of the 47th Mechanized Brigade. Over the entire time of combat from 18 to 21 January 1945, the regiment's battalion was operating together with the tanks, never lagged behind them, and was the first to arrive at a point 2 km northwest of Neidenburg and the first to join combat with enemy submachine gunners and tanks, which had the assignment to allow our tanks to pass and to cut them off from the main forces; however, thanks to the actions of the 2nd Battalion, this enemy attempt was thwarted and the enemy was shoved back several kilometers. With the battalion's fire, then Captain Malinovsky in the area of Kondi destroyed 7 100mm guns and 9 vehicles; set one Tiger tank ablaze; and knocked out one self-propelled gun while killing 120 enemy soldiers and officers and seizing 1 75mm artillery battery, 4 vehicles and 20 enemy soldiers. He knocked out 2 halftracks. In the combat for Neidenburg on 20 January 1945, with the battalion's fire Captain Malinovsky knocked out 4 anti-tank guns, 2 trucks loaded with ammunition, killed 65 enemy soldiers and officers, and captured 2 prime movers and 2 cars. Awarded the Order of the Red Banner.

Senior Lieutenant VLADIMIR SEREGIN – commander of a machine-gun company of the 1st Motorized Rifle Battalion of the 10th Tank Corps' 11th Motorized Rifle Brigade. On 21 January 1945 in the fighting for Osterode he showed bravery, courage and skill in directing his company. When approaching Osterode, his company with the fire from heavy machine guns killed 80 Nazis thanks to the proper deployment of the machine guns. The company was the first to enter the city. When combing through the city, it killed 69 more Germans and took 36 prisoners. Seregin personally killed 9 Germans. For his personal valor and skillful leadership, he was awarded the Order of the Patriotic War, 1st Class.

Lieutenant VASILII VITKOVSKY – a T-34 tank commander with the 1st Tank Battalion of the 10th Tank Corps' 186th Tank Brigade. In the fighting when crossing the border of East Prussia and on the approaches to the border, he demonstrated exceptional courage and valor. His tank was always located in the forward detachment, and skillfully using folds in the terrain, he kept appearing where the enemy wasn't expecting him. His tank in the fighting destroyed 17 vehicles, 3 antitank guns, 2 self-propelled guns and up to a company of Germans. In his last battle Vitkovskii was badly wounded. Nevertheless, he refused to abandon his post and leave the battlefield, until the village was taken; only after this was he evacuated to a hospital. Awarded the Order of the Patriotic War, 1st Class.

Lieutenant ANDREI GONCHAROV – a T-34 tank commander with the 2nd Tank Battalion of the 10th Tank Corps' 186th Tank Brigade. During the combat operations, he demonstrated model examples of how to command a tank capably on the battlefield. In the fighting for the villages of Mosaki and Żbiki, he demonstrated heroism, courage and valor. In the battle for Mosaki, the advance of his company prevented an ambush set by a medium tank and 2 antitank guns. Having spotted the location of the medium tank and 2 antitank guns, with accurate shots he personal destroyed them, thereby securing the advance of the company. He killed 30 Nazis with the fire from his cannon and machine guns. In the combat for Żbiki Goncharov destroyed a self-propelled gun and 2 halftracks and killed 20 Germans. For the demonstrated courage and ability in commanding a tank on the battlefield, the personal initiative and his excellent mastery of his weaponry, awarded the Order of the Patriotic War, 1st Class.

Junior Lieutenant IVAN KHOROVODOV – a T-34 tank commander with the 1st Tank Battalion of the 10th Tank Corps' 186th Tank Brigade. On the battalion's entire combat path, he was located in its forward detachment. Artfully bypassing focal points of enemy resistance, he would appear with his tank there, where the enemy wasn't expecting it. Through his mastery of conducting combat, he was securing the success of the entire brigade. With personal fire from his tank, he destroyed 3 artillery batteries, 20 loaded wagons; ensured the capture of 12 populated places; suppressed 7 machine-gun nests; and killed up to 150 Nazis and took 37 German soldiers prisoner. Worthy of the Order of the Red Banner. Recipient of the Order of the Patriotic War, 1st Class.

Bibliography

Archival Sources

TsAMO

Operativnye svodki, boevye doneseniia chastei i soedinenii 33-i armii o boevykh deistviiakh za period s 1 po 13 Avgusta 1944 [Operational summaries and combat reports of the 33rd Army's formations and units on the combat operations over the period from 1 to 13 August 1944].

Operativnye svodki, boevye doneseniia chastei i soedinenii 5-i gvardeiskoi tankovoi armii o boevykh deistviiakh za period s 17 ianvaria po 1 marta 1945 [Operational summaries, combat reports of the units and formations of the 5th Guards Tank Army about the combat operations from 17 January to 1 March 1945].

Operativnye svodki, boevye doneseniia chastei i soedinennii 4-i tankovoi armii o boevykh deistviiakh za period s 12 po 19 ianvaria 1945 [Operational summaries and combat reports from the units and formations of the 4th Tank Army regarding the combat operations over the period from 12 to 19 January 1945].

Otchet 3-i nemetskoi tankovoi armii za avgust 1944 [Account of the German Third Panzer Army for August 1944], F. 500, Op. 12462, D. 286.

Otchet 4-i tankovoi armii o deistviiakh armii v Vislo – Oderskoi operatsii, ianvar' 1945 [4th Tank Army's account about the army's actions in the Vistula – Oder operation, January 1945].

Otchet 5-i gvardeiskoi tankovoi armii o deistviiakh armii v Vostochno-Prusskoi operatsii, 14 ianvaria – 01 marta 1945 [Account of the 5th Guards Tank Army about the army's operations in the East Prussia operation, 14 January – 01 March 1945].

Otchet chastei 2-go gvardeiskogo tankovogo korpusa o boevykh deistviiakh [Accounts of the units of the 2nd Guards Tank Corps' combat operations], F.3400, Op.1, D.51

Otchet o boevykh deistviiakh shtaba 2-go gvardeiskogo tankovogo korpusa [Account of the combat operations from the 2nd Guards Tank Corps' headquarters], F.3400, Op.1, D.37.

Otchet o boevykh deistviiakh shtaba 2-go gvardeiskogo tankovogo korpusa [The 2nd Guards Tank Corps headquarters' account of combat operations], F. 3400, Op. 1, D. 37.

Otchet shtaba artillerii 33-i armii o boe s tankami protivnika v raione goroda Vilkavishkis, 9 August 1944 [Account of the 33rd Army's artillery headquarters on the battle with enemy tanks in the area of the city of Wiłkowyszki, 9 August 1944].

Otchety chastei 2-go gvardeiskogo tankovogo korpusa o boevykh deistviiakh [Accounts of the units of the 2nd Guards Tank Corps about combat operations], F. 3400, Op. 1, D. 51.

Zhurnal boevykh deistvii 10-go gvardeiskogo tankovogo korpusa za ianvar' 1945 [Combat Journal of the 10th Guards Tank Corps for January 1945].

Zhurnal boevykh deistvii 10-go tankovogo korpusa za ianvar'-fevral' 1945 [Journal of combat operations of the 10th Tank Corps for January-February 1945].

Zhurnal boevykh deistvii 1-go Ukrainskogo fronta za ianvar' 1945 [Combat Journal of the 1st Ukrainian Front for January 1945].

Zhurnal boevykh deistvii 29-go tankovogo korpusa za ianvar' 1945 [Journal of combat operations of the 29th Tank Corps for January 1945].
Zhurnal boevykh deistvii 2-go Belorusskogo fronta za ianvar'-fevral' 1945 [Journal of combat operations of the 2nd Belorussian Front for January-February 1945].
Zhurnal boevykh deistvii 2-go gvardeiskogo tankovogo korpusa [Journal of the 2nd Guards Tank Corps' combat operations], F.3400, Op.1, D.72.
Zhurnal boevykh deistvii 2-go gvardeiskoi tankovogo korpusa [Journal of combat operations of the 2nd Guards Tank Corps], F. 3400, Op. 1, D. 72.
Zhurnal boevykh deistvii 33-i armii [Journal of combat operations of the 33rd Army].
Zhurnal boevykh deistvii 3-go Belorusskogo fronta [Journal of combat operations of the 3rd Belorussian Front].
Zhurnal boevykh deistvii 3-go Belorusskogo fronta [Journal of the 3rd Belorussian Front's combat operations].
Zhurnal boevykh deistvii 4-i tankovoi armii za ianvar' 1945 [Combat Journal of the 4th Tank Army for January 1945].
Zhurnal boevykh deistvii 5-i gvardeiskoi tankovoi armii za ianvar'-fevral' 1945 [Journal of combat operaions of the 5th Guards Tank Army for January-February 1945].
Zhurnal boevykh deistvii 6-go gvardeiskogo mekhanizirovannogo korpusa za ianvar' 1945 [Combat Journal of the 6th Guards Mechanized Corps for January 1945].

National Archives, Washington DC

Electronic archives of the National Archives (AOK 4 section), T. 312, R 253, R. 260, R. 261 and R. 262.
Electronic archives of the National Archives, T. 312, R. 262, Frame 00059.

Other

Author's correspondence with Martin Blok (Germany), Ron Klages (USA), Kamen Nevenkin (Bulgaria), Aleksandr Tomzov (Russia).
Burdeinyi, A.S. "V boiiakh za Rodinu", 1985 rukopis' [In the fighting for the Motherland, 1985 manuscript.]

Photographs

Photographs are from the following sources:
Fotografii Rossiiskogo gosudarstvennogo arkhiva kinofotodocumentov (RGAKFD) [The Russian State Archive of Film and Photo Documents].
Fotosnimki k dokladu o boevykh deistviiakh 5-i gvardeiskoi tankovoi armii za period s 14 ianvaria po 01 marta 1945. Operatsiia po okruzhenniiu Vostochno-Prusskoi gruppirovki nemtsev: Al'bom [Photographs for the report about the combat operations of the 5th Guards Tank Army over the period from 14 January to 01 March 1945. Operation to encircle the German East Prussian grouping: Album.] (TsAMO, F. 332, op. 4948, d. 343).
The website "Voennyi al'bom" ["War album"], School Museum of the Combat Glory of the 2nd Guards Tatsinsky Tank Corps and a number of open sources.

Printed Sources

Bączyk, N., *Kielce 1945* (Warsaw: Wydawnistwo Militaria, 2003).

Burkov, V.V., Kravchenko, I.M., *Desiatyi tankovyi Dneprovskii* [*10th Dnepr Tank Corps*] (Moscow: Voenizdat, 1986).

Buttar, P., *Battleground Prussia: The Assault on Germany's Eastern Front 1944-1945* (Oxford: Osprey Publishing, 2010).

Buttlar, E. von, *Voina v Rossii // Vtoraia mirovaia voina na sushe: Prichiny porazheniia sukhoputnykh voisk Germanii* [*War in Russia // Second World War on the Ground: The reasons for the defeat of Germany's ground forces*] (Moscow: Tsentrpoligraf, 2011).

Dieckert, K. and Grossman, H., *Der Kampf um Ostpruessen: Der umfassende Dokumentarbericht über das Kriegschehen in Ostpreussen* (Stuttgart: Motorbuch Verlag, 1998).

Dobrovol'tsy Urala: Ocherki, vosponinaniia [*Urals volunteers: Essays, recollections*], compiled and edited by Ia.L. Reznik. Sverdlovsk: Sredne-Ural'skoe knizhnoe izdatel'stvo, 1972.

Duffy, C., *Red Storm on the Reich: The Soviet March on Germany, 1945* (New York: Da Capo Press, 1993).

Egorov, P.Ia., Ivlev, I.K., Krivoborsky, I.V. and Rogalevich, A.I., *Dorogami pobed: Boevoi put' 5-i gvardeiskoi tankovoi armii* [*Along the roads of victory: The combat path of the 5th Guards Tank Army*] (Moscow: Voenizdat, 1969).

Ehrenburg, I.G., *Voina: 1941-1945* [*War: 1941-1945*] (Moscow: Olimp, AST, Astrel', 2004).

Galitsky, K.N., *V boiakh za Vostochnuyu Prussiiu: Zapiski komandueshchego 11-i gvardeiskoi armii* [*In the fighting for East Prussia: Notes of the commander of the 11th Guards Army*] (Moscow: Nauka, 1970).

Galkin, F.I., *Snova k moriu: Tanki vozvrashchaiutsia v boi* [*Once again to the sea: Tanks are returning to combat*] (Moscow: Voenizdat, 1964).

Guderian, *Vospominaniia soldata* [*Remembrances of a soldier*] (Smolensk: Rusich, 1998). This is the Russian-language edition of Guderian's memoirs, published in English under the title *Panzer Leader*.

Ivanovsky, E.F., *Ataku nachinali tankisty* [*Tankers started the attack*] (Moscow: Voenizdat, 1984).

Jentz, T. (ed.), *Panzer Truppen: 1942-1945*, Vol. 2: *The Complete Guide to the Creation and Combat Employment of Germany's Tank Force* (Shiffer Publishing, 1996).

Jung, H-J, *The History of Panzerregiment Grossdeutschland* (Winnipeg: J.J. Fedorowicz Publishing, 2008).

Kleine, E. and Kühn, V., *Tiger: The History of the Legendary Weapon, 1942-1945* (Winnipeg: J.J. Fedorowicz Publishing, 2008).

Krupchenko (ed.), *Sovetskie tankovye voiska 1941-1945: Voenno-istoricheskii ocherk* [*Soviet tank forces 1941-1945: Military-historical compendium*] (Moscow: Voenizdat, 1973).

Kurowski, F., *The History of the Fallschirmpanzerkorps Hermann Göring: Soldiers of the Reichsmarschall* (Winnipeg: J.J. Fedorowicz Publishing, 1995)

Leliushenko, D.D., *Moskva – Stalingrad – Berlin – Praga: Zapiski komandarma* [*Moscow – Stalingrad – Berlin – Prague: Notes of an army commander*] (Moscow: Nauka, 1987).

Mikheenkov, S.E., *V doneseniiakh ne soobshchalos ... Zhizn' i smert' soldata Velikoi Otechestvennoi, 1941-1945* [*It isn't announced in reports ... Life and death of a soldier of the Great Patriotic War, 1941-1945*] (Moscow: Tsentropoligraf, 2011).

Nehring, W., *Nemetskie bronetankovye voiska. Razvitie voennoi tekhniki i istoriia boevykh operatsii, 1916-1945* [*German panzer troops. Development of military equipment and the history of combat operations, 1916-1945*] (Moscow: Tsentrpoligraf, 2016).

Nemmersdorf: mezhdu pravdoi i propagandoi. Issledovanie I. Petrov [Nemmersdorf: between truth and propaganda. Research of I. Petrov] in A. Diukov [ed.], *Velikaia obolgannaia voina: Sbornik* [*Great Maligned War: Collected Works*] (Moscow: Iauza, Eksmo, 2008)

Nevenkin, K., *Fire Brigades: The Panzer Divisions 1943-1945* (Winnipeg, CA: J.J. Fedorowicz Publishing, 2008).

Niepold, Gerd, *Panzer-Operationen "Doppelkopf" und "Cäsar" Sommer 1944* (Herford, Bonn: E.S. Mittler & Sohn, 1987)

Radzievsky, A.I., *Tankovyi udar* [*Tank attack*] (Moscow: Voenizdat, 1977).

Refeld, H.H. *V ad s "Velikoi Germaniei": Frontovoi dnevnik veterana tankovogo korpusa "Gross Doichland"* [*Into hell with Grossdeutschland: Frontline diary of a veteran of Panzer-[grenadier] Corps Grossdeutschland*] (Moscow: Iauza-Press, 2010).

Schneider, W., *Tigers in Combat* (Winnipeg: J.J. Fedorowicz Publishing, 2000).

Spaeter, H., *The History of the Panzerkorps Grossdeutschland*, Vol. 2 (Winnipeg: J.J. Fedorowicz Publishing, 1995).

Tatsintsy – boevoi put' 2-go gvardeiskogo tankovogo korpusa [*Tatsintsy – Combat path of the 2nd Guards Tank Corps*] (Leningrad, 1957).

Tippelskirch, K. von, *Istoriia Vtoroi mirovoi voiny* [*History of the Second World War*] (Moscow: AST, 1999)

Wilbeck, Ch. W., *Sledgehammers: Strengths and Flaws of Tiger Tank Battalions in World War II* (The Aberjona Press, 2004).

Zaitsev, V.I., *Gvardeiskaia tankovaia* [*Guards tank army*] (Sverdlovsk: Sredne-Ural'skoe knizhnoe izdatel'stvo, 1989).

Ziemke, E. F., *Stalingrad to Berlin: The German Defeat in the East* (Washington DC: United States Army Center of Military History, 2011).

Websites

Bykadorov, M.A. "Boevoi put': Bessmertnyi polk" [Combat path: Immortal regiment]. Available at http://moypolk.ru/soldiers/bykadorov-mihail-artemevich/story

Kulan, I.N., "Snova k Baltike" ["Once again to the Baltic"] and "70 let na sluzhbe Otechestvu: Istoriia i boevoi put' 29-go Znamenskogo ordena Lenina Krasnoznamennogo ordena Suvorova II stepeni tankovogo korpusa" ["70 years in service to the Fatherland: History and combat path of the 29th Znamensk Order of Lenin Red Banner Order of Suvorov 2nd Class Tank Corps"]. Available at http://nasledie-sluck.by/ru/sluchina/114/3543/3631/

Memorial, available at http://www.obd-memorial.ru

Online archive of documents "Pamiat' naroda v Velikoi Otechestvennoi voine 1941-1945" [People's memory in the Great Patriotic War 1941-1945]. Available at: http://pamyatnaroda.ru/

Onlive archive of documents "Podvig naroda v Velikoi Otechestvennoi voine 1941-1945." [People's achievement in the Great Patriotic War 1941-1945]. Available at: http://podvignaroda.mil.ru/

"Podzemel'ia Kenigsberga: istoriia Vostochnoi Prussii i Kaliningradskoi oblasti" ["Underground Königsberg: history of East Prussia and Kaliningrad Oblast"] [website: URL: www.forum-kenig.ru]

Udikov, N.E., "Kak ia umiral na fronte; Vostochnaia Prussiia: pervye boi na nemetskoi zemle" ["How I was dying at the front; East Prussia: Initial fighting on German soil"]. Available at http://udikov.livejournal.com/1644824.html

"Zhivoi zhurnal" Alekseia Karpycheva ["Live journal" of Aleksei Karpychev] at http://altyn73.livejournal.com/ and http://warhistory.livejournal.com/2561439.html

Index

Index of People

Akhtiamov, Guards Private Sabir 19, 26, 179, 185-186, 206

Burdeinyi, Major General A.S 10-12, 16-18, 20, 26, 29, 36, 43, 50, 65-66, 70-71, 104, 112, 116, 118-119, 121, 125, 132, 139-140, 143-144, 149-151, 160, 162-164, 168, 170, 173-175, 182, 187-189, 191, 201, 508

Cherniakhovsky, General of the Army I.D. 10, 25, 35, 52, 113, 121, 124-125, 142-144, 189-190, 213, 464, 484
Chuprov, Guards Colonel N.D 220, 222, 244, 275

D'iachenko, Captain G.L. 30, 362, 365, 369-376, 380
Davydov, Major T. P 29, 117, 184, 201, 206

Fedorov, Guards Colonel 306, 380, 391, 397, 408, 416, 419, 424, 443, 451, 458

Galitsky, General K.N. 137, 140-142, 150, 162, 186
Grishin, Major General of Tank Forces P.G. 305-307, 313, 347, 399, 429, 436-437, 493, 502
Guderian General Heinz 105, 122, 225, 263, 292, 311, 509
Guliaev, Major General of Tank Forces 271, 279, 282

Hitler, Adolf 20, 123, 263, 311, 320, 349, 358, 495-497
Hoßbach, General Friedrich W. 137, 210, 310, 443

Iablochkin, Colonel 28, 53, 59, 85, 87, 99
Ivanovsky, General of the Army I.F. 367, 430, 469, 509

Karavan, Colonel A.F. 140, 142, 175
Kolesnikov, Lieutenant Colonel S.G. 306-307, 327, 352, 360, 374-375, 423, 444, 492
Konev, Marshal of the Soviet Union S.I. Konev 220, 224, 255, 271-272, 275, 279, 282, 289
Kostylev, Colonel A.M. 306-307, 313, 348
Kuz' mich, Stepan 118, 161, 163

Leliushenko, General D.D. vii, 216-218, 220, 222, 234, 246, 253, 259, 270, 272-273, 275, 277, 279, 283, 289, 292, 509
Losik, Colonel O. A 17, 26, 29, 67-68, 110-113, 117, 119, 127, 162-163, 171, 184, 202

Makarov, Lieutenant General V.E. 125, 138, 189
Makhalov, Major General of Tank Forces K.M. 306-307, 320, 326-327, 344, 348, 351-352, 370, 373, 375, 379
Malakhov, General K.M. 319-320, 323, 326-327, 335-336, 344, 348, 352, 355, 357, 366, 370, 372-373, 375, 379, 444-445, 485-486, 492

Malakhov, Junior Lieutenant Iu.N. 28, 30, 183, 197, 206
Manteuffel, General Hasso von 42, 73
Mastashev, Guards Major 166, 177, 184, 194-195, 201, 206
Metel'sky, Guards Senior Lieutenant 140, 166, 177
Mikhailov, Colonel D. 336, 372, 378, 444, 482, 485-486, 493
Morozov, Lieutenant General 35, 61, 98

Nehring, General Walter vii, 216, 218, 225, 233, 263, 292, 509
Nesterov, Colonel S.K. 67, 118, 161, 163

Orlov, Guards Colonel 235, 260, 274

Pokolov, Colonel A.I. 306-307, 327, 351, 355, 366, 370, 372-376, 444, 485, 490, 492

Reinhardt 40, 137, 310, 318, 349
Rodin, Colonel General A.G. 25, 70, 93, 113, 125, 141-143
Rokossovsky, Marshal of the Soviet Union K.K. 307, 314-315, 340, 352, 367, 372, 375, 395, 412, 492, 494

Sakhno, Major General of Tank Forces 306-307, 317, 319-320, 323, 329, 335-336, 342-343, 346-347, 372, 386, 399, 444, 485-486, 491-492
Semenov, General I.I 144, 174, 189-190, 231, 233, 372, 480
Sidorovich, Major General of Tank Forces G.S. 306-307, 312, 319-320, 323, 329, 335, 347, 355, 379-380, 391, 397, 399, 408, 416, 419, 424, 429, 436-437, 443-445, 451, 458, 484-485, 491-492, 502
Sinenko, Lieutenant General of Tank Forces M.D. 305, 307, 335, 399
Stanislavsky, Colonel I.O. 306, 319, 327, 337, 352, 355, 372, 374, 445, 483, 487, 492

Timofeevich, Vasilii 319, 355, 379, 490-491, 493

Vol'sky, Colonel General of Tank Forces V.T. 305, 307-308, 312-313, 315, 319-320, 323, 335-336, 340, 347-348, 352-353, 355, 357, 359-360, 372, 379, 390, 399, 429, 436-437, 444, 474-475, 484-485, 490-491, 493-494, 502

Zaev, Lieutenant General of Tank Forces D.T. 305, 307, 319, 344, 348, 372, 484
Zaitsev, Guards Lieutenant Colonel 53, 59, 87, 99, 220, 222, 242, 246, 261, 266, 275, 291, 298, 366, 510
Zhukov, Guards Colonel N.G. 221-222, 231, 236-237, 241-242, 244-247, 249, 276, 296, 399

Index of Places

Anderskehmen 151, 153, 162-163
Angerapp River vii, 122-123, 130, 132, 134, 137, 139-145, 151, 154, 164, 167, 170-176, 184-185, 187, 190-191, 207, 210, 213-215
Antupie 54-56, 58, 63, 69-71, 73, 86, 97
Arnsdorf 359, 373, 409, 412
Augstupönen 154, 179, 192-193

Baarden 449, 455, 462-464
Babie 259, 262, 272
Baltic Republics 122, 185, 380, 494, 497
Baltic Sea 122, 130, 137, 303, 328, 338, 352, 360, 363-364, 368, 370, 373-374, 378, 380, 444, 490, 498
Bardowskie 55, 58, 69, 77, 84
Baude River 361, 471, 473, 477-479, 482, 486
Baumgart 378, 390-391, 396-397
Behlenhof 359, 386-387, 389-391, 398, 403, 407, 414, 422, 424, 428, 434, 443
Beleckie-Młyny 259, 262, 287
Belorussia 110-111, 114, 117, 121, 160, 185, 314, 330, 497
Berezina River 103, 110, 171
Berlin 121, 137, 224, 233, 289, 309, 320, 349, 358, 366, 369, 424, 509-510
Bernen 176-178, 183, 187
Bethkendorf 387, 474, 477, 486
Białogon 253-254, 256-257, 259, 273-274, 279, 285-287
Bilcza 235, 252-254, 256-257, 266, 271-273, 279, 286-287
Bilcza-Jaworznia 253, 257, 286
Bilcza-Podgórze 254, 266, 279
Bludau 387, 389, 451, 458, 471, 477-478, 480, 489
Blumenau 451, 458, 464, 473, 478
Bobławka 23, 32-33, 35, 38, 40-43, 82, 132, 138
Bobrowszczyzna 58, 65, 70, 85-86
Bobrza River 262, 285, 287
Bobrza 262, 273, 281, 285, 287
Bocianowo 33, 46, 53
Bogoliubov 30, 180, 307, 375, 491-492, 494
Borchertsdorf 381, 396-397, 399, 424
Bordehnen 359, 391, 395, 407, 413, 422, 428
Braunsberg 387, 408, 486-489, 500
Breunken 359, 378, 391, 396, 416, 424, 428
Brudzów 251, 255-256, 261-262, 277
Brudzów-Duży 251, 255-256
Brzeziny 229, 255, 262, 266, 271, 279
Budjeziory 55, 71, 85, 132
Budszedszen 132, 139, 151-154, 194-196
Budweitschen 46, 71, 92, 149, 154-155, 172, 174, 176, 196, 214
Budziszki 33, 46-47, 49, 53, 59, 98
Buylien 153-155, 165-166, 174-175

Chałupki 229, 236, 266-268, 277, 283, 299
Chęciny 229, 236, 238-239, 242, 253, 255-257, 260-263, 268, 271-272, 274-275, 278-279, 283, 290, 295
Chmielnik 218, 228, 235-236, 240, 255, 266, 268, 283, 285, 287, 290, 295, 299
Ciechanów 301-304, 309, 312, 315-318, 324
Conradswalde 457, 463, 472, 481, 486, 489
Czarna Nida River 235, 240, 252-260, 262-264, 270-273, 277-278, 286-287, 294-295

Damerau 344-345, 370, 375, 378, 390, 408, 486
Danzig 304, 312, 318, 352, 372, 380, 465, 498

Darkehmen 122-123, 130, 137, 170, 178, 189-191
Darzeniki 83-84, 87, 95
Dębska Wola 229-230, 251,261, 266, 271, 279
Deutsch Eylau 302, 304, 312, 340-341, 344, 346, 348-355, 360-361, 366, 368, 372, 374
Deutschendorf 407-408, 413, 415-416, 422-424, 428-429, 434-435, 441-442, 445, 449, 499
Dittersdorf 471, 477, 480
Dörbeck 368, 370, 378, 391, 486
Drebulinė 35, 38-39, 41, 43, 133
Dydwiże 16, 18, 21, 23, 33
Dyminy 230, 254, 259, 272-273, 279
Działdowo 318-323, 325-328, 330, 335, 338, 340, 360, 362-363, 494, 499-500, 504

Ebenrode 40, 54, 157, 212, 214
Egglenischken 139, 143, 149
El'nia 29, 119, 161, 172
Elbing 304, 328, 340, 353, 359-360, 362-363, 365-366, 368-381, 386-387, 390-392, 395-400, 407, 409-410, 412, 421, 424-425, 428-430, 436, 441, 443-445, 482-483, 494-495, 497, 499-500, 505
Eydtkuhnen 23-24, 31, 40, 139, 209, 214

Frauenburg vii, 304, 339, 361, 412-413, 424, 434, 436, 441-442, 449-450, 455-457, 462-464, 471-474, 477-483, 486, 489, 499
Freiwalde 353-356, 392, 499-500
Frische Nehrung 412-413, 436, 449, 451, 458, 464, 471, 473-474, 477-478, 481, 489-490, 492
Frisches Haff 123, 359, 361, 370-371, 373, 375, 380, 386, 434, 436, 441, 443, 449, 455, 457-458, 465, 471, 478
Frödenau 344, 346, 351, 354
Fürstenau 381, 387, 396, 399, 414, 416, 423-424, 428-429, 435, 442, 449, 451

Gałakausze 18, 85, 93, 99
Gałęzice 238, 269, 282
Gallkehmen 139, 141, 143
Gardienen 341, 343, 347, 359, 378, 391, 396, 398
Garszwinie 82, 85-86, 93-94, 98
Geierswalde 340, 342, 349, 499
Gertschen 164-166, 194
Giedriai 16, 18, 21, 86, 92-93, 95, 132
Gilgenburg 340, 343-345, 353
Girnen 164, 166, 195-196, 206
Goldap 83, 122-123, 130, 137, 175, 188-190, 196, 201, 210, 212, 214
Górki 229, 238, 250, 255-256, 260, 262, 268, 277, 279, 321
Grenszej 33, 82, 98
Groß Rautenberg 381, 387, 390, 396-397, 399, 424, 429, 442-443, 451, 457, 477, 485-486, 489
Groß Röbern 368-369, 371-372, 374, 378, 380, 444, 486, 488-489
Groß Sodehnen 139-140, 144, 149
Groß Stoboy 368, 375, 378, 387, 390-391, 395-398
Groß Trakehnen 163, 170, 173, 187-190
Grudusk 304, 315, 318, 321, 324, 499
Grunau 370, 390, 395, 425, 429, 443
Gudele 32, 53, 65, 70, 80, 84-85, 91, 97-98, 108
Gumbinnen vii, 40, 46, 49, 64-65, 79, 93, 122-123, 130, 132-134, 137, 140-145, 151, 154, 163-168, 170-179, 182-185, 187-192, 196-197, 201, 206, 208-212, 214, 349

INDEX   513

Gumienice 236, 238, 240, 250, 256, 262, 277

Hansdorf 344, 346, 352
Heinrichsdorf 387, 396, 450-451, 471, 477
Herrndorf 359, 378, 391, 396-399, 408, 416, 424, 429, 435, 442-443
Hill 50.6 32, 35, 37, 43-44, 47, 51
Hopfenbruch 455, 457, 462-464

Insterburg 24, 69, 83, 112, 122-123, 130, 133, 137, 208
Irklei 318, 357, 379, 485, 492-493
Iszkarty 40, 46-47, 49, 71, 79-80, 97-98

Jablonken 340, 343, 353
Jelekcie 69, 79, 93, 133
Jodzuhnen 133, 151, 175

Kaczeniec 254-256, 258, 271
Kagenau 390, 449, 455-457, 462
Kahlberg 413, 451, 464, 471, 473-474, 478
Kailen 164-165, 176, 194
Kallnen 164, 166, 168
Karklienen 141, 143, 149-151, 154
Karszamupchen 151-152, 194, 196
Karwinden 378, 387, 389, 391, 396, 407-408, 423, 428, 435, 441-442
Karwitten 359, 361, 396, 399, 403, 413-414, 422-424, 428, 434-435, 443
Kassuben 132-133, 143-144, 148-152, 161-162, 207
Kaunas 11-16, 20, 42, 112, 161, 497
Kibarty 21, 35, 139
Kielce iii, vii, 216-218, 226-230, 233, 235-236, 238-239, 241, 243, 252-255, 257, 259-263, 266, 272-279, 283, 285-287, 289-290, 292, 294-297, 299, 509
Kischken 132-133, 139, 151
Klein Stoboy 369-370, 373
Klingenberg 455, 457, 462
Komórki 223, 252, 254, 256, 266, 288
Königsberg 112-114, 123, 130, 132-133, 137, 185, 211, 301, 360, 372, 377, 387, 441, 444, 510
Königshagen 391, 397-399
Końskie 218, 254, 268, 270-273, 278-281, 283
Koppeln 390, 397-398, 407, 414, 435
Korale 33, 80, 82, 84, 92-95, 99
Kostromłoty 230, 254, 271
Kowala 235, 255-256, 262, 266, 271, 274, 279, 287
Kozłowa Ruda 11, 13-15, 114-117, 121
Kraków 292, 294, 296
Kraużmorgi 59, 86, 91
Kreuzdorf 381, 429, 463-464, 478, 480, 489
Kuby-Młyny 252, 258-259, 262, 270-272, 279, 287
Kuklin 321, 328, 340
Kuttkuhnen 166-167, 174, 206-207

L'vov 211, 218, 246, 276
łabędziów 256-259, 264, 286-287
Langwalde 449, 455, 457, 462
Lauck 416, 429, 435, 441, 449-451, 456
Leip 340, 344, 349
Lenzen 370, 391, 486
Leopoldowo 32, 35-36, 40, 43, 46-47, 49
Lidzbark 312, 314-315, 318, 345-346
Liebemühl 304, 340, 354, 357, 378, 499
Liebenau 392, 407, 412, 422
Liep 451, 464, 471, 474, 478

Lipa 235, 251-252, 254, 286, 289
Lisów 229-230, 236-238, 240-251, 255-256, 260-262, 265, 267, 276-277, 283-284, 289-291, 296-299
Lithuania vii, 16, 74-76, 112, 114, 117, 314, 331
Lohberg 359, 378, 391, 396
Łopuszno 229, 271-272, 274-275, 278-279, 282-283
Lötzen 123, 133, 497
Louisenthal 450, 463, 472, 486, 488-489
Lubawa 304, 344-346, 348, 351, 374, 499

Mackobudzie 46, 58, 69
Maków 301, 303, 315-316, 319
Maldehne 32, 49, 85, 138
Maleszowa 223, 229, 235-236, 238, 240-241, 250-252, 255-256, 260, 265-267, 270, 283, 288-289, 298
Mariampol 40-42, 52, 54, 58, 105
Marienburg 300, 304, 312, 387, 392, 396-398, 400, 409, 421-422, 425, 428, 430, 436, 441, 499
Marienfelde 344-346, 397-398
Marienthal 133, 165-166, 196
Marijampolė 11-17, 60, 69-72, 75-76, 79-80, 87
Martischken 152, 154, 189
Marzysz 252, 254-258, 262, 271-272, 274
Mattischkehmen 152, 190
Matuliszki 48, 70-72, 79-82, 84, 86, 92-94, 97
Maygunischken 154, 164, 175, 192, 214
Mehlsack 407, 422, 455, 479
Memel 114, 301, 356, 380
Mercze 40-41, 46, 65, 83, 85, 93, 99, 133
Micigózd 261, 271, 274-275
Miedzierza 271, 273, 279
Minsk 44, 67, 110-111, 125, 161, 365
Mława 300-304, 309, 312, 314-315, 318-328, 335-338, 340, 343, 356, 366-367, 379-380, 484, 491, 494, 499, 501, 503-504
Młyny 252, 256-259, 262, 270-273, 279, 281, 286-287
Mnin 275, 278, 282-283
Mohrungen 304, 353-354, 357, 359-360, 494, 499
Morawica 229, 252-253, 255, 257-258, 261-264, 266-267, 271-272, 277-279, 286, 295
Morawicka 257-258, 261-262, 271, 277-278, 282
Moscow 20, 111, 149, 296, 333-334, 356, 365, 368, 485, 491-493, 495, 497, 509-510
Motzkuhnen 152-153, 162
Mühlen 342, 346, 353
Mühlhausen 339, 353, 359-360, 363-365, 372, 377 378, 381, 387, 389-390, 392, 396, 398-399, 407, 412, 415, 423, 429, 435, 441-442, 481, 494, 499
Muttersegen 397, 399, 408, 423, 429, 435, 442

Narew River 114, 300, 302-303, 311, 315, 318-319, 366
Narz 413, 449, 451, 455, 457, 463, 471, 477-478, 480
Naszyszki 23, 33, 85, 93
Neidenburg 304, 315-316, 319, 321, 325, 328-330, 335-341, 346-347, 349, 355, 361, 374, 484, 499-500, 505
Neman River 10-11, 17, 22, 38, 62, 90, 114, 138, 210
Nemmersdorf vii, 132-133, 139-140, 142, 154, 164-165, 167, 170-176, 178-179, 185-187, 191, 207, 210, 212-215, 510
Nesterov 26, 29, 67, 102, 118-119, 155, 161, 163, 206
Nestonkehmen 152, 154, 164, 171, 173, 193-194
Neuendorf 396, 398, 412, 424, 429, 442-443, 481, 486
Neuhof 190, 442, 471, 477, 480
Neukirch 412, 424, 434, 436, 442-443, 456, 458, 464, 472-473, 478, 480-481, 489

Neumark 340, 436, 450, 456, 463
Nida River 235, 240, 252-260, 262-264, 270-273, 277-278, 286-287, 290, 294-295
Nikolaiken 396-398, 408, 415, 423, 428, 435, 443
Nowe Miasto 303, 340, 343, 345
Nowiniki 17, 23, 80, 84, 93, 95, 97

Oder River 265-266, 288, 290, 294, 507
Olksniany 16, 18, 71
Olwita 46-47, 49, 85, 88, 90
Osterode 302, 304, 337, 340-349, 352-353, 358, 361-362, 368, 372, 374, 484, 494, 499-500, 505
Ostrów 236, 261, 271, 274, 279, 314

Parlack 387, 443, 486
Passarge River 377, 390, 413, 436, 444, 455-457, 462, 464, 486-488, 492, 499
Patwiecie 32, 35, 37, 40, 43, 47, 49, 72, 93
Perkallen 154-155, 164-166, 195, 201
Pettelkau 486-488, 490-492
Piekoszów 229, 254, 260-262, 271-276, 279
Pierzchnica 218, 229, 235, 237-238, 240, 250-251, 253-255, 260, 262, 265-268, 271, 277, 283, 286, 289
Pillupönen 133, 139, 142, 144-145, 148-150
Piłotyszki 69, 71, 80, 107
Pilwiszki 13-15, 17, 20, 22, 71, 79, 84, 116
Piotrkowice 235-237, 241, 244, 250-251, 255-256, 260, 279, 284
Pissa River 134, 139, 141-145, 148-151, 153, 162, 170, 201, 206
Plicken 164, 166-167, 171, 179
Pobedinsky 241, 245-246, 267, 276, 292, 296
Podlesie 229, 238-239, 250, 256, 265-266, 289
Podsohnen 139, 148, 197
Pogramdyszki 48, 70, 80, 85-87, 93-94
Pojeziory, Lake 55, 83-84, 105, 132-133, 138
Poland i, vii, 54, 216, 294-295, 297-298, 300-304, 318, 332, 334-335, 351, 360, 362-363, 368, 400, 497
Pomerania 372, 486, 490
Pracapol 18, 40, 86, 95, 97
Praßlauken 153, 155, 162-163, 165, 171, 173-175, 192, 196
Pregel 349, 353, 400, 421, 441, 503
Preußisch Holland 304, 359, 361, 365, 368-370, 372, 374, 377-378, 387, 390-392, 395-398, 407-409, 412-413, 415-416, 421-423, 429, 434, 436, 441, 443-445, 499
Prokhorovka 161, 314, 493
Promnik 229, 254, 261, 271, 273-274, 276, 279, 297
Przasnysz 301-304, 309, 312, 315-318, 321
Przedbórz 275, 278, 282
Pultusk 301-303, 318-319, 498, 504
Pustil'nikov 318, 338, 356-357, 484-485

Radom 239, 253, 260, 278
Radomice 254-258, 271, 286
Radoszyce 229, 238, 270-272, 274, 276, 279, 282-283
Rahnenfeld 429, 457, 480
Rastenburg 123, 496-497
Röbern 368-369, 371-372, 374-375, 378, 380, 444, 486, 488-489
Romantyszki 21, 53, 84, 86, 94
Rominte River 140-143, 145, 148, 152-155, 162-164, 170-173, 175, 177-179, 184, 187, 189-197, 201, 206, 208, 214
Rotkirch 24, 34, 39, 90
Rückenau 412, 451, 457, 463-464, 473, 478, 481

Ruda 11, 13-15, 56, 58, 71-73, 82, 114-117, 121, 132, 138, 275, 278, 282
Rudki 229-230, 237, 239, 270
Rykoszyn 229, 238, 263, 269-271, 274, 279
Ryzhov 245, 293, 296

Saalfeld 304, 352-355, 359, 365, 368, 372-374, 378, 392, 494, 499, 504
Sabadszuhnen 132, 170, 177
Samarczuny 69, 83, 138
Samelucken 154, 164, 171-172, 175, 177-178, 188-189, 192-195, 206, 208
Sandomierz 211, 218
Schafsberg 397, 399, 416, 424, 429, 451, 457, 477
Schestoken 153, 192, 196
Schirwindt 15-16, 21, 40, 84, 92, 133, 139
Schlobitten 359, 381, 386, 389-390, 395-398, 408, 413, 415-416, 422-424, 428, 435-436, 442-443, 449, 456
Schlodien 407-408, 413, 449-450, 455-457
Schmulken 152-153, 175, 207
Schönau 359, 387, 391, 395, 398, 412-413, 425
Schönberg 346, 352, 359, 378, 389-391, 398, 458
Schönfeld 412, 435, 442, 450
Schwiegseln 163, 187, 194, 196
Seepothen 413, 422, 449-451, 456
Seewalde 340, 342, 346, 349
Semeneliszki 21, 23, 32-33, 38, 47, 49, 53, 56, 70, 72, 81
Sielpia 254, 271, 280-281
Sinenko 305, 307, 319-320, 323, 335-336, 399, 474, 482, 484-485, 493
Skordupiany 35-36, 40, 46-47, 49, 85
Skrzelczyce 218, 223, 235, 237, 240, 251-256, 258, 268, 286
Smolensk 30, 119, 161, 185, 365, 498, 509
Sodehnen 132, 139-140, 144, 149, 153, 196
Soginten 139, 153, 162
Spanden estate 442, 450, 472, 481
Stalingrad 161, 289, 309, 349, 369, 424, 509-510
Stallupönen 122-123, 143, 157, 161, 173, 188-189, 212, 311
Stanajcie 23, 31, 139, 214
Stannaitschen 167, 176, 187
Stąporków 254, 271, 273-274, 279-281, 287, 297-298
Steffenshöh 486-489, 491-492
Steffenswalde 340, 342, 349, 354
Sterniszki 48, 53, 70-71, 85, 99, 132-133, 138
Stulgen 164, 166-168, 179, 192-194, 210
Succase 445, 478, 481, 486, 488-489
Sudawa 18, 21, 48, 60, 86, 95
Suków 254, 259, 262, 272, 289
Suwalki 53, 85, 95, 210, 212
Szameitschen 166, 178, 196
Szczecno 230, 233, 252, 253-254, 260, 266
Szejmena River 17, 19, 33, 46, 71, 79-81, 90
Szelwy 16-17, 19, 21, 23, 33, 79-82, 84-87, 91-95, 97, 99, 105
Szestaki 272, 274, 279
Szeszupa River 13, 20, 91, 133-134
Szukle 32, 35, 37-38, 41, 43, 46, 49, 85
Szyrwinta River 32, 35-39, 41, 43-44, 47

Tannenberg 340-343, 346-347, 374, 497, 499-500
Tauroggen 77, 90, 114
Tejbery 80, 86, 92-95
Tellitzkehmen 153, 191-192, 196

Thurau 340-341, 343, 347
Thuren 167-168, 176-179, 183, 208
Tiedmannsdorf 381, 396-397, 399, 416, 424, 428-429, 435, 442, 449, 451, 455, 457, 484-486
Tillwalde 344, 346, 351
Tilsit 18, 22, 69, 83, 132, 137, 145, 497
Tokarnia 236, 240, 256, 260-262, 271
Tolkemit 323, 359, 370-371, 373, 375-376, 381, 412-413, 424, 428-429, 434-436, 441-443, 445, 449-451, 456-458, 463-464, 471-472, 475-476, 478, 481, 483, 486, 488-490, 492, 499
Trakehnen 132, 163, 170, 173, 187-190
Trunz 361, 368, 378, 387, 390-391, 395-398, 408, 481
Tutteln 154, 176, 196, 213

Ukraine 161, 218, 330, 496-497
Uzdowo 328, 340, 344

Vasilevsky 98, 138, 494
Vierzighuben 451, 457, 471-472, 477, 479, 489
Virbalis 34, 38, 49, 71, 105
Vistula River 218, 289, 300, 302-304, 377, 429, 504
Vistula Region 218, 224, 265, 288-289, 300, 302-304, 343, 353, 369, 375, 377, 400, 409, 425, 429, 503-504, 507

Walterkehmen 140-144, 152-154, 162-164, 170-171, 173-175, 179, 184, 188-191, 201, 208, 214

Warnikam 396, 407-408, 415, 436
Warsaw 300, 318, 496-497, 504, 509
Weeskenhof 416, 436, 443
Wilken 164-168, 172, 174, 176, 179, 196
Wiłkowyszki iii, 9-10, 15-24, 31, 33-34, 38, 40-42, 46, 48-49, 51, 53-58, 60-65, 69-74, 77-95, 97-100, 103-109, 132, 137-138, 208, 507
Wirballen 34, 40, 54, 71, 84, 92, 110
Wiśniewo 320, 322, 325-326
Wisztyniec 139, 209, 214
Wiżajdy 55-57, 69, 79-80
Wokiszkiele 71, 80, 93
Wola-Morawicka 257-258, 262, 271, 277-278, 282
Wólka 271, 275, 278
Wormditt vii, 386-387, 390, 392, 403, 407, 413, 479
Wyszczokajmie 17, 21, 33, 81

Zaborze 240, 250, 252, 261-262, 277, 283
Zagrody 230, 235, 252-254, 256, 279, 287, 294
Zalesie 46-47, 49, 79-80, 84, 93, 97, 236, 255, 260-262, 267, 270, 277, 316-317, 320
Zastawie 252-254, 272-273
Zielonka 31-32, 40-41, 46-50, 65, 70, 72, 79-80, 83-85, 87, 93, 95, 97, 99, 133
Znaczki 56-59, 65, 69-70, 73, 79, 107
Žvangučiai 33, 41, 70
Żynie 40, 46-47, 71, 80, 94, 97-98

Index of Military Formations

German Armed Forces

Luftwaffe 55, 133, 179, 184-185, 213, 215, 413, 441, 449, 471

Army Groups:
Army Group A 225, 263, 311
Army Group Center 20, 22-23, 34, 38, 48, 50, 77, 87, 90, 99, 105, 137, 145, 300-302, 309-312, 318, 369
Army Group North 40, 106, 137, 310, 424, 503

Armies:
Second Panzer Army vii, 44, 87, 133, 135-137, 145, 147-148, 159, 169, 180, 182, 193, 198-200, 210-211, 217, 227, 280, 290, 300-302, 304, 308, 311, 320, 349, 362, 377, 381, 383-384, 386-387, 389, 393, 395, 400-401, 403-404, 406-407, 419, 421, 424-425, 427, 431, 434, 438, 440, 443, 446, 448, 452, 454-455, 458, 461-462, 466, 468-469, 487, 498, 503

Third Panzer Army vii, 20, 22-24, 34, 38-39, 44-45, 48, 50, 73, 77-79, 87-91, 99, 106, 110, 133, 135-137, 145, 147-148, 159, 169, 180, 182, 193, 198-200, 210-211, 217, 227, 280, 290, 300, 304, 308, 311, 349, 362, 365, 377, 381, 383-384, 386-387, 389, 393, 395, 400-401, 403-404, 406-407, 419, 421, 424-425, 427, 431, 434, 438, 440, 446, 448, 452, 454-455, 458, 461-462, 466, 468-469, 487, 498, 503, 507
Fourth Panzer Army vii, 44, 87, 133, 135-137, 145, 147-148, 159, 169, 180, 182, 193, 198-200, 210-211, 217, 227, 280, 290, 300, 304, 308, 311, 349, 362, 377, 381, 383-384, 386-387, 389, 393, 395, 400-401, 403-404, 406-407, 419, 421, 424-425, 427, 431, 434, 438, 440, 446, 448, 452, 454-455, 458, 461-462, 466, 468-469, 487, 498, 503
Fourth Army 133, 135-137, 145, 147-148, 159, 169, 180, 182, 193, 198-200, 210-211, 300, 311, 349, 377, 381, 383-384, 386-387, 389, 393, 395, 400-401, 403-404, 406-407, 419, 421, 424-425, 427, 431, 434, 438, 440, 446, 448, 452, 454-455, 458, 461-462, 466, 468-469, 503

Corps:
VII Panzer Corps 383, 447, 461
XX Army Corps 300, 377, 381-382, 384, 387, 393, 401, 405, 420, 426, 431-433, 439, 447, 453, 459, 466-468
XXIII Army Corps 300, 377, 381-382, 384, 387, 393, 401, 405, 420, 426, 431-433, 439, 447, 453, 459, 466-468
XXIV Panzer Corps 216-218, 223, 225, 228, 233, 241, 266-267, 270, 277-279, 289-290, 292, 299
XXVI Korps 133, 136, 146-147, 160, 181, 383, 386, 389, 395, 403-404, 419, 425, 431, 438, 446, 452, 458, 466
XXVII Korps 133, 136, 146-147, 182, 300, 377, 381-382, 384, 387, 393, 401, 405, 420, 426, 431-433, 439, 447, 453, 459, 466-468
XXX Panzer Corps 24, 34, 39, 50, 77-78, 87, 89-91, 99
XXXX Panzer Corps 24, 34, 39, 50, 77-78, 87, 89-91, 99
Parachute-Panzer Corps Hermann Göring 133, 137, 145, 184, 192-193, 200, 211, 440

Divisions:
2nd Parachute-Panzergrenadier Division 173, 187-188
5th Jäger Division 300, 302, 312
5th Panzer Division vii, 24, 34, 39, 45, 48, 69, 78, 84, 87-88, 90-92, 99, 145, 173, 183, 185, 188, 190, 193, 200-201, 210-211, 311, 407, 413, 422
6th Panzer Division 12, 17, 20, 22-24, 34, 38-39, 45, 48, 78, 84, 88-89, 92, 99, 106, 154, 163
7th Infantry Division 301, 318, 327, 340, 400, 503
7th Panzer Division 24, 34, 45, 48, 78, 88, 301-302, 309, 311, 316, 375, 377, 397, 409, 412, 425, 429-430, 443, 504
14th Infantry Division 401, 412, 461, 469, 479, 503
16th Panzer Division 217-218, 225-228, 233, 236-237, 239-241, 250-252, 254-256, 260, 262, 265-268, 270-271, 277-279, 282-283, 288, 352
17th Panzer Division 217-218, 225-229, 233, 235-241, 245, 250-252, 255-256, 258, 260, 265-267, 270, 279, 282-283, 288, 290
18th Panzergrenadier Division vii, 301, 311, 321, 330, 340, 348, 353, 383-384, 386, 396, 398, 401, 407, 422, 461, 469, 499, 503
20th Panzer Division 137, 209, 301
20th Panzergrenadier Division vii, 216, 218, 223, 225-228, 233, 239, 252, 256, 264, 266-267, 270, 272, 280-282, 288
23rd Infantry Division 397, 412, 473
24th Panzer Division vii, 383-384, 387, 398, 407, 413, 422, 428, 448, 455-456, 461, 471, 473, 499, 503
28th Jäger Division 386, 396, 399-401, 407, 409, 413, 421-422, 428-429, 441, 443, 449, 455, 461, 469, 473, 499, 503
61st Infantry Division 137, 188, 462
68th Infantry Division 227, 239, 256, 266-267, 270
102nd Infantry Division 401, 448, 461, 469
129th Infantry Division 401, 449, 461
131st Infantry Division 134, 148, 210-211, 386, 401, 409, 429, 461, 469, 499
168th Infantry Division 227, 229, 236-237, 251, 255-256, 260, 262, 266-268, 270-272, 280, 289
170th Infantry Division 386, 398, 401, 407, 409, 412-413, 421-422, 425, 428-430, 441, 443, 449, 461, 469, 499, 503
292nd Infantry Division 401, 448, 461
299th Infantry Division 301, 316, 348, 352-353, 377, 383-384, 409, 456, 461, 503
541st Volksgrenadier Division 148, 401, 461

547th Volksgrenadier Division 211, 449, 461
549th Volksgrenadier Division 91, 148, 211
558th Volksgrenadier Division 134, 384, 401, 461
561st Volksgrenadier Division 20, 22, 24, 38, 50, 77, 88-91, 99, 209, 211, 400, 441, 443
Hermann Göring Panzer Division 154, 163-164, 183
Panzer Division Grossdeutschland vii, 60, 69-70, 82, 84, 91-92, 95, 188, 309
Panzergrenadier Division Grossdeutschland vii, 24, 34, 38-40, 42, 45, 48, 50-51, 54-55, 64, 69, 71, 74, 76-79, 87-91, 99, 103, 105-110, 301-302, 311, 316, 330, 338, 340, 383-384, 428, 449, 461

Brigades, Battlegroups and other formations:
10th Bicycle Jäger Brigade 399, 455, 462
Führer Grenadier Brigade vii, 160, 201, 210-211
Kampfgruppe Hauser 382, 394, 402, 405, 420, 426, 431, 453, 460, 467
Panzer Brigade 101 160, 181, 209
Panzer Brigade 102 141, 146, 148, 163, 173, 181, 188
StuG Brigade 185 301, 308, 381, 384, 387, 389, 393, 395, 401, 403-406, 419-421, 425-427, 432, 434, 438-440, 446-448, 452-454, 458-459, 461, 466-468
StuG Brigade 203 24, 34, 39, 45, 48, 78, 88, 136, 146-147, 159, 169, 421, 427, 433, 440, 447-448, 453-454, 460, 468
StuG Brigade 209 198, 301, 308, 311, 381, 384, 387, 393, 401, 404, 406, 413, 419, 422, 426, 428, 433, 439, 447, 453-454, 459, 467
StuG Brigade 232 24, 34, 39, 45, 48, 78, 88
StuG Brigade 277 24, 34, 39, 48, 78, 88, 90, 136, 146, 148, 160, 169, 181, 383, 386, 389, 395, 403-404, 419, 425, 431, 438, 446, 452, 458, 466
StuG Brigade 279 145-147, 169, 182, 198-199, 279, 311, 353, 406, 421, 427, 434, 440, 448, 454, 461, 468, 499, 503

Regiments
Fusilier Regiment 79 266-267, 270, 279
Infantry Regiment 391 409, 421, 429-430, 503
Infantry Regiment 442 266, 268, 270
Panzer Regiment 2 252, 255, 266, 270-271
Panzer Regiment 39 260, 265-266, 270
Panzer Regiment Grossdeutschland 34, 39, 48, 78, 88
Panzergrenadier Regiment 6 429-430, 443-444
Panzergrenadier Regiment 7 409, 412, 425, 430
Panzergrenadier Regiment 40 260, 266, 270
Panzergrenadier Regiment 64 233, 252, 255, 266, 270

Other:
Heavy Panzer Battalion 424 216, 218, 223, 228-229, 233, 240-241, 243, 251, 255, 289-292
Heavy Panzer Battalion 501 236, 240, 266-267, 271, 288-290
Heavy Panzer Battalion 507 302, 311, 340, 348, 503-504
Heavy Panzer Battalion 509 228, 289-290
Heavy Panzer Battalion 510 510 34, 39, 45, 48, 78, 88
Heavy Panzerjäger Battalion 519 34, 39, 45, 48, 78, 88
Heavy Panzerjäger Battalion 731 34, 39, 45, 48, 78, 88
Volkssturm 123, 209, 213, 299, 353-354, 377, 400, 503

Soviet forces

Stavka 137-138, 211, 464

INDEX   517

Fronts:
1st Baltic Front 114, 137, 173, 189
2nd Belorussian Front 114, 137, 300-302, 307, 312, 314-315, 318-319, 339-340, 352, 362-363, 366-367, 373, 375, 386, 392, 395, 412, 436, 490-491, 493-494, 498, 504, 508
3rd Belorussian Front 9-10, 17, 20, 25, 35, 40, 46, 49-51, 54, 65, 70, 75, 79, 82-84, 91-93, 98, 102-105, 110, 112, 114, 116, 121, 123-125, 132, 134, 137-142, 144, 185, 189, 192, 209-213, 366, 482, 484, 494, 508
1st Ukrainian Front 216-217, 220, 235, 255, 262, 271-272, 279, 282, 289, 366, 507

Armies:
1st Air Army 69, 83, 143-144, 188
2nd Shock Army 308, 312-315, 318, 340, 353, 378, 392, 400, 409, 421, 425, 429, 478, 488, 498, 504
3rd Guards Tank Army 217-218, 224, 238, 240, 250, 264, 278, 283, 290
4th Guards Tank Army 218, 222-223, 228, 231, 240-241, 253, 255, 263, 292-293
4th Tank Army vii, 216-217, 219-221, 228, 233-235, 241, 243, 246, 251, 255-256, 259, 262, 264-265, 267, 270-275, 277, 279, 282-283, 288-292, 294-296, 299, 507-508
5th Army 103, 105-106, 122-123, 130, 132, 134, 138-140, 143, 212
5th Guards Tank Army iii, vii, 300-309, 312, 314-317, 319-320, 322, 324-330, 336, 338-341, 343-346, 349-353, 355, 357, 359-360, 363-364, 366-367, 370, 373-375, 377-378, 381, 387, 389-392, 395-399, 407-409, 412-413, 416, 418-419, 422, 424, 428-429, 434, 436-437, 441, 443, 449, 451, 455, 458, 462, 471, 474-479, 481-482, 486-490, 493-494, 498-505, 507-509
11th Guards Army 123, 130, 132, 134, 137-142, 144-145, 150-151, 162, 170-173, 182-184, 186-192, 197, 211-212, 509
13th Army 218, 224, 228-230, 233-234, 239-240, 264, 273
28th Army 130, 137, 170, 188, 190
33rd Army vii, 10-11, 17, 22-23, 25, 28, 31-32, 35, 40-41, 46-47, 49-61, 63, 65, 69-70, 78-80, 83-85, 87, 91-93, 95, 97-99, 106, 507-508
39th Army 114, 134, 138, 212
48th Army 308, 312-316, 318, 320, 323, 326, 340, 353, 377-378, 381, 386, 395, 436, 477, 486, 488-490, 493, 498

Corps:
2nd Guards "Tatsinskaia" Tank Corps vii, 10-12, 14, 16, 18-23, 25, 29, 31-32, 35-36, 39-43, 46-47, 49, 51, 58, 63, 65-71, 73, 79-83, 90-95, 97, 99-100, 102, 104, 106, 110, 112, 114, 116, 118-126, 129-130, 132, 138-145, 148, 150-151, 155, 161, 163-165, 168, 170, 173-178, 180, 185, 187-192, 194, 196, 201, 205-206, 210-212, 214-215, 507-508, 510
6th Guards Mechanized Corps 216, 222, 235, 239, 250, 252-256, 259-260, 262, 271-272, 274-275, 277, 279-280, 282-283, 285, 292, 294-297, 508
6th Guards Tank Corps 217, 240, 278, 283
6th Mechanized Corps 217-218, 230, 233-235, 251, 255, 263
8th Mechanized Corps vii, 392, 398, 412, 423, 498
10th Guards Tank Corps 216, 218-219, 229, 231, 233, 235-240, 242, 246, 251, 255-256, 260, 262-263, 265-266, 271-272, 274-275, 277, 279, 282-283, 289, 291, 295-298, 309, 507
10th Tank Corps 217, 305-306, 308, 314-318, 320-322, 325, 328-329, 335, 337, 339-344, 346, 349, 353, 359-362, 364, 370, 377-378, 381, 386, 389-392, 396, 398-399, 403, 408-409, 413-416, 423-424, 428, 434-437, 441-444, 449-451, 455-456, 462-463, 471-472, 477, 479-482, 484, 486-489, 493, 502-503, 505-507
16th Guards Mechanized Corps 235, 252, 279
16th Guards Rifle Corps 140-145, 150-151, 162, 164, 170, 172-173, 175, 184, 187, 201
19th Rifle Corps 22, 28, 41, 46, 69, 80, 87, 91, 93
27th Rifle Corps 218, 229, 237, 240
29th Tank Corps 305-306, 308, 314-317, 320-322, 325-329, 335, 340, 344-346, 348-354, 357, 359-361, 363, 368-371, 373, 375-378, 380-381, 390-392, 395-398, 407-408, 412-416, 422, 424, 428, 435-437, 442-443, 450-451, 456-457, 463-464, 471-473, 477-478, 481-482, 486-490, 492, 502, 504, 508
42nd Rifle Corps 380-381, 387, 390, 392, 395-397, 399, 412, 416, 418, 424, 429, 435-436, 442, 444, 451, 457-458, 464, 473, 478, 482, 487-488, 499
53rd Rifle Corps 316, 320, 488
62nd Rifle Corps 28, 41, 46, 59, 65, 69, 84, 87, 91, 93, 95
124th Rifle Corps 387, 412, 428, 434, 436, 450, 457, 463, 472, 481

Divisions:
6th Anti-aircraft Artillery Division 306, 416, 436, 443
11th Guards Rifle Division 141, 144, 164, 170-174, 182-183, 187, 192
11th Rifle Division 39, 49, 54, 80, 123, 130, 132, 134, 137-142, 144-145, 150-151, 162, 164-165, 170-175, 182-184, 186-192, 194, 197, 211-212, 306, 317, 321, 329, 341-342, 344, 353-354, 359, 378, 389, 391, 396, 398-400, 408, 414-415, 423-424, 428, 435, 437, 441, 449, 456, 462, 471-472, 477, 479, 481, 485, 505, 509
16th Rifle Division 39, 49, 54, 80, 123, 130, 132, 134, 137-142, 144-145, 150-151, 162, 164-165, 170-175, 182-184, 186-192, 194, 197, 211-212, 306, 317, 321, 329, 341-342, 344, 353-354, 359, 378, 389, 391, 396, 398-400, 408, 414-415, 423-424, 428, 435, 437, 441, 449, 456, 462, 471-472, 477, 479, 481, 485, 505, 509
31st Guards Rifle Division 39, 49, 54, 80, 123, 130, 132, 134, 137-145, 149-152, 160, 162-165, 170-175, 182-184, 186-192, 194, 196-197, 211-212, 306, 317, 321, 329, 341-342, 344, 353-354, 359, 378, 389, 391, 396, 398-400, 408, 414-415, 423-424, 428, 435, 437, 441, 449, 456, 462, 471-472, 477, 479, 481, 485, 505, 509
32nd Rifle Division 28, 58, 69-70, 86, 93
49th Rifle Division 28, 37, 49, 80, 85-86, 93-94, 97
70th Rifle Division 28, 41, 47, 49, 80, 83-84, 86-87, 93, 97
137th Rifle Division 387, 397, 399, 416, 418, 424, 429, 435, 442, 451, 457
157th Rifle Division 56, 63, 65, 70, 80, 83, 86, 91, 93-94, 97
170th Rifle Division 397, 399, 412-413, 416, 418, 424, 429, 435, 442-443, 450, 456-457, 463, 472-473, 477, 486
222nd Rifle Division 29, 56, 70, 80-81, 86, 91, 93
277th Rifle Division 80-81, 84-86, 93-95, 103
321st Rifle Division 392, 395-397
344th Rifle Division 28, 41, 47, 70, 80, 83-84, 86, 93, 95
362nd Rifle Division 29, 69, 80, 86, 93
399th Rifle Division 387, 397, 399, 416, 418, 424, 429, 435, 442, 451, 457, 462, 486

Brigades:

4th Guards Motorized Rifle Brigade 10-14, 16-17, 19, 31-32, 35-36, 39, 41-44, 47, 49-50, 55-56, 58, 63, 69-70, 72, 79-82, 91, 93-95, 116, 132, 139, 155, 162, 164, 167-168, 171-172, 174-179, 182-183, 185-186, 192-194, 197, 203-204, 208

4th Guards Tank Brigade 10-15, 17-18, 21, 23, 29, 31-33, 35-37, 39, 43-44, 46, 49-50, 55, 68, 70, 72-73, 79-82, 91-95, 101-102, 110-112, 115, 117, 119, 125, 127, 132, 139, 151, 153, 155, 162-168, 171, 174-180, 182-184, 192-195, 197, 201-202, 206-208

11th Motorized Rifle Brigade 306, 321, 329, 341-342, 344, 353-354, 359, 378, 389, 391, 396, 398-400, 408, 414-415, 423-424, 428, 435, 437, 441, 449, 456, 462, 471-472, 477, 479, 481, 505

16th Guards Mechanized Brigade 222, 233, 235, 251-259, 262, 271-274, 279, 285, 287, 292, 294, 296

16th Mechanized Brigade 221, 228, 234-235, 251, 255

17th Guards Mechanized Brigade 221-222, 235, 253-259, 262-263, 271-274, 279, 281, 285-287, 295, 298

17th Mechanized Brigade 221, 234, 271

25th Guards Tank Brigade 10-14, 16-19, 21-23, 31-33, 35, 37, 40, 43, 47, 49, 56, 65, 68-71, 79-80, 82, 91-95, 101, 112, 116, 139, 148-155, 161-165, 167-168, 170-176, 180, 185, 187, 191-194, 196-197, 202, 207, 214-215

25th Tank Brigade 306, 313, 317-318, 325-326, 336, 344, 346, 348, 354, 361, 369-370, 372, 378, 390-391, 397-398, 407, 412-413, 422, 428, 434, 436, 442, 450, 457, 463, 472, 481, 487, 489, 492

26th Guards "El'nia" Tank Brigade 10-16, 18-19, 21, 23, 29, 31-33, 35-37, 40, 43, 47, 49-50, 55, 58, 67, 69-71, 79-80, 82, 91-95, 100-102, 112, 116, 118-119, 132, 139-140, 142, 145, 148-152, 154-155, 161-165, 168, 171, 174, 176, 179-180, 182-183, 187, 190, 192-194, 196-197, 202-203

29th Guards Motorized Rifle Brigade 221-222, 237-238, 240, 255-256, 260, 262-263, 267-269, 271, 275, 277, 282-283, 295

31st Tank Brigade 306, 317-318, 322, 325, 327, 344-346, 348, 354, 357, 360, 362-363, 366, 368-372, 374-376, 378, 390-392, 397-398, 408, 414, 422, 428, 434-436, 442, 450, 456, 463-464, 471-473, 477-478, 481, 489, 504

32nd Tank Brigade 306, 317-318, 325, 327, 344-346, 348, 350, 354, 360, 369-370, 378, 390-391, 395, 397-398, 407, 412, 414, 422-423, 428, 434, 436, 442, 450-451, 457, 463-464, 472-473, 478, 481, 483, 488-490, 492-493

43rd Destroyer Antitank Artillery Brigade 29, 53, 55, 59-60, 85-86, 99

47th Destroyer Antitank Artillery Brigade 29, 53, 55-57, 59, 85-86

47th Mechanized Brigade 305-306, 314, 316, 318-319, 329, 338, 342, 344, 346, 349, 353-355, 359, 361, 365, 368-370, 374, 376-378, 380-381, 390-392, 395-398, 408, 413, 415-417, 423, 428, 435-437, 442-443, 449, 455-457, 463-464, 471-473, 477-478, 480-482, 486, 488-489, 502-503, 505

49th Mechanized Brigade 217, 221-222, 234, 252-254, 256-259, 262-263, 271-274, 279, 281-282, 295

53rd Motorized Rifle Brigade 306, 313, 317-318, 325-326, 344, 346, 348, 350, 354, 369-370, 378, 390-392, 395, 397-398, 407, 414, 422, 428, 434-436, 442, 450, 457, 463, 472, 481, 487-488, 490, 492

61st Guards Tank Brigade 219, 221-222, 229, 231, 236-237, 240-242, 250-251, 255, 260-263, 266-267, 269, 271, 275-276, 282, 284, 289, 291-292, 296-298

62nd Guards Tank Brigade 219, 221-222, 230, 235, 238-240, 250-251, 255-256, 260-263, 268, 271, 277-278, 282-283, 295

63rd Guards Tank Brigade 217, 222, 224, 229-230, 232-233, 235-236, 239-242, 244, 250, 255-256, 260-263, 271, 275, 277-278, 282, 284, 295

93rd Separate Tank Brigade 256, 271-272, 279, 294

142nd Cannon Artillery Brigade 53, 59, 85-86, 98

150th Tank Brigade 229, 234, 252

153rd Tank Brigade 52, 69-70, 80, 92-93, 97, 254

178th Tank Brigade 306, 309, 317, 321, 329, 337, 341-343, 347, 353-354, 359, 361, 378, 386, 389, 391, 396, 398-400, 403, 408, 414, 423-424, 428, 435, 437, 442, 450, 455, 462, 471, 477, 479-480

183rd Tank Brigade 306, 309, 317, 321, 329, 341-344, 347, 353-354, 359, 378, 391, 396, 398, 408, 414, 423, 428, 435, 437, 442, 450, 456, 462, 471-472, 477, 479, 481, 489

186th Tank Brigade 306, 309, 317, 321, 329, 335, 341-342, 344, 353-354, 359, 362, 378, 386, 389, 391, 396, 398, 408, 414, 423, 428, 435, 437, 441, 449, 455, 462, 471, 477, 480, 488, 505-506

201st Light Artillery Brigade 316, 391, 408, 416, 456, 463, 478, 481

Regiments:

1st Guards Motorcycle Regiment 313, 371, 373, 477

1st Guards Self-propelled Artillery Regiment 222, 254, 272

1st Guards Separate Motorcycle Regiment 442, 464, 478, 481

1st Separate Guards Motorcycle Regiment 306, 408, 413, 415, 451, 458, 473

6th Anti-aircraft Artillery Division 306, 416, 436, 443

13th Guards Heavy Tank Regiment 235, 259, 281, 291

14th Guards Heavy Tank Regiment 306, 315-316, 329, 376, 378, 380-381, 391-392, 395-397, 407, 412-413, 415, 423, 434-435, 442, 450, 457, 463, 472, 476, 481, 503

18th Tank Regiment 354, 361, 395, 477-478, 480

28th Guards Heavy Tank Regiment 222, 234-235, 254, 257-259, 284, 286, 295

28th Tank Regiment 234, 252-254, 257, 285, 292, 294

29th Tank Regiment 222, 235, 254, 258, 271, 273-274, 280

41st Cannon Artillery Regiment 408, 414-415, 423, 436, 443, 450, 456, 458, 463-464, 473

56th Tank Regiment 221-222, 235, 254, 259, 271-274, 280-281

57th Mortar Regiment 39, 301-302

72nd Guards Heavy Tank Regiment 222, 236, 239, 250, 255, 275, 278, 289

76th Guards Mortar Regiment 306, 316, 329, 408, 416, 435, 441, 443, 449-450, 455-456, 479

79th Motorcycle Regiment 70, 82, 112

83rd Guards Artillery Regiment 59, 84, 87, 99

126th Tank Regiment 254, 256-258, 273, 285

146th Anti-aircraft Artillery Regiment 408, 416, 423, 436, 442-443, 449, 463, 478, 486

165th Light Artillery Regiment 306, 390, 397-398, 407, 414, 450, 457, 472, 481, 489-490

240th Mortar Regiment 222, 254, 281

258th Light Artillery Regiment 235, 254, 274, 294

271st Mortar Regiment 306, 390, 397, 407, 414, 450, 457, 472, 481

273rd Mortar Regiment 11-12, 47, 51, 63, 72-73, 81-82, 94, 120, 139, 171, 179
287th Mortar Regiment 306, 353, 391, 398, 415, 423, 428, 435, 450, 456, 480
326th Guards Heavy Self-propelled Artillery Regiment 399, 450, 456
326th Guards Mortar Regiment 85, 87, 99
326th Heavy Self-propelled Artillery Regiment 316, 389, 396, 408, 415, 423, 428, 435-436, 441, 443, 449, 455, 462, 472, 477, 480
366th Anti-aircraft Artillery Regiment 316, 407, 413-414, 416, 422, 436, 442-443, 456, 463
376th Heavy Self-propelled Artillery Regiment 306, 316, 340, 342, 346, 370, 378, 407, 412-414, 422, 424, 434, 436, 443, 456, 463, 473, 478, 480-481, 486, 503
401st Guards Self-propelled Artillery Regiment 12, 14, 18, 21, 23, 32-33, 35-36, 38-39, 44, 47-48, 51, 73, 81-82, 101, 110, 132, 153, 155, 167-168, 176, 178-180, 192, 204, 208
516th Anti-aircraft Artillery Regiment 416, 436, 443
538th Mortar Regiment 59, 86, 98
578th Destroyer Antitank Artillery Regiment 55-57, 59, 98
651st Cannon Artillery Regiment 306, 316, 407, 413-414, 416, 422, 435, 442, 450, 464, 478, 481
689th Destroyer Antitank Artillery Regiment 389, 396, 408, 414-415, 423, 435, 441-442, 449-450, 455-456, 462-463, 477, 479-480, 486
705th Light Artillery Regiment 306, 396, 415, 423, 441, 450, 472, 480
727th Self-propelled Artillery Regiment 306, 353, 391, 396, 398, 415, 423, 450, 456, 462, 472, 477, 480, 486
1025th Self-propelled Artillery Regiment 53, 56, 58-59, 70, 98
1062nd Anti-aircraft Artillery Regiment 416, 436, 443
1222nd Light Self-propelled Artillery Regiment 260, 262, 277, 282-283
1223rd Light Self-propelled Artillery Regiment 390, 398, 428, 463, 472
1223rd Self-propelled Artillery Regiment 306, 397, 407, 412, 414, 434, 442, 450-451, 457, 464
1311th Light Artillery Regiment 120, 132, 139, 192
1315th Light Artillery Regiment 391, 435, 449, 456, 463, 478, 482
1433rd Self-propelled Artillery Regiment 222, 254, 271, 274, 281
1500th Self-propelled Artillery Regiment 11-12, 14, 21, 30, 38, 51, 73, 81-82, 120, 139, 153, 155, 167-168, 179-180, 197, 204-205
1619th Light Artillery Regiment 395, 422, 435, 450, 464, 478, 482, 505
1693rd Anti-aircraft Artillery Regiment 306, 321, 415, 450, 456, 480
1695th Anti-aircraft Artillery Regiment 11-12, 14, 30, 37, 47, 49-51, 71, 73, 82, 94, 120, 148
1964th Destroyer Antitank Artillery Regiment 60
1995th Anti-aircraft Artillery Regiment 254, 296

Index of Military Equipment

BA-64 Armored Car 16, 204, 284, 415

DShK machine gun 16, 19, 37, 47, 50-51, 73, 82, 94, 115, 202-203, 223, 229, 305

Hetzer Light Tank Destroyer 24, 34, 39, 45, 48, 78, 88, 227, 312
Hummel Self Propelled Gun 34, 39, 45, 48, 107, 226, 312

IS-122 Heavy Tank (variant) 223, 228, 234-235, 250, 254, 257-259, 273-275, 278, 284-287, 305, 329, 380, 415-418, 423, 450, 456, 477-478, 480, 503
IS-2 Heavy Tank 223, 289, 291, 476

JU-87 'Stuka' Dive Bomber 36, 64, 81, 149

King Tiger, Tiger II Heavy Tank 228, 237, 241, 250, 260, 263, 296-297

M4A2 Sherman Tank 305, 309, 329, 344, 396, 408, 414-418, 423, 442, 449-451, 456-458, 463-464, 472-473, 477-478, 480-481, 502-503
Marder Self Propelled Anti-Tank Gun 226-227, 312, 504

Nashorn Tank Destroyer 24, 39, 45, 48, 78, 88, 312
Nebelwerfer Rocket Mortar 149, 237, 257-258, 280, 282, 479

Panzerfaust, Anti-Tank Rocket 111, 209, 265, 279, 288, 347, 428, 450, 483, 505
Pz.kpfw. IV Tank 22, 24, 34, 39, 54, 70, 73, 96-97, 99, 105-106, 192, 209, 211, 223, 226, 253, 256, 262, 277-278, 280, 297-298, 438
Pz.Kpfw. IV Tank 22, 24, 54, 70, 99, 106, 192, 209, 211, 223, 226, 253, 256, 262, 277-278, 280, 297-298
Pz.kpfw. V Panther Tank 22, 24, 34, 39, 48, 54-55, 96-97, 104-108, 110-112, 117, 149, 183, 192, 208-209, 211, 226, 228, 249, 253, 256, 275, 277-278, 280, 284-285, 294, 298, 312, 338, 367, 391, 471, 473
Pz.kpfw. VI Tiger Tank vii, 18, 22, 24, 34, 39, 43-44, 54, 57-58, 62, 64, 70, 81, 104, 106-107, 109, 112, 117, 206, 228, 237, 240-241, 247-251, 257, 259-260, 263, 273, 277-278, 280, 284-286, 289-291, 295-298, 312, 338, 352, 470, 475, 479, 505, 509-510

StuG Assault Gun vi-vii, 22, 24, 34, 39, 45, 48, 51, 77-78, 88, 90, 97, 105-106, 108, 133, 135-136, 145-148, 159 160, 169, 180-182, 198-199, 211, 226-227, 301, 308, 311-312, 350, 377, 381-389, 393-395, 401-406, 419-421, 425-427, 431-434, 438-440, 446-448, 452-454, 458-461, 466-468
SU-57 Self Propelled Anti-Tank Gun 223, 228, 398, 414-415, 417-418, 451, 458, 464, 481
SU-76 Self Propelled Gun 11-12, 14, 21, 23, 32, 36, 38, 51, 70, 73, 78, 80, 82, 115, 144, 154-155, 168, 180, 192, 204-205, 223, 228, 274, 305-306, 309, 329, 365, 391, 396-397, 408, 414-418, 422-423, 441-442, 450, 456-457, 463-464, 472-473, 477-478, 480-481, 502-503
SU-85 Tank Destroyer 11-12, 14, 21, 23, 32-33, 36, 39, 44, 51, 70, 73, 78-80, 82, 93, 110, 115, 144, 155, 168, 179-180, 204-205, 223, 228, 274, 280, 305-306, 309, 329, 391, 396-397, 408, 414-418, 422-423, 435, 442, 450, 456-457, 462-464, 472-473, 477-481, 502-503
SU-100 Tank Destroyer 305-306, 309, 329, 338, 344, 391, 396-398, 408, 414-416, 418, 423, 442, 449-450, 455-456, 462-463, 471, 477, 479-480, 503

SU-122 Self Propelled Howitzer 228, 237, 251, 305, 389, 416-418, 423, 442-443, 450, 456, 463, 472, 477, 480, 503

SU-152 Self-Propelled Gun 131, 305-306, 329, 345, 391, 397, 408, 413-414, 416-418, 422, 424, 442-443, 450-451, 456-457, 463-464, 472-473, 478, 481, 502-503

T-34 Tanks 11-16, 18-19, 21-23, 31-33, 36-37, 39-40, 43-44, 46-47, 49-51, 67-68, 70-73, 78-82, 93-94, 110-112, 115-116, 129, 144, 149-150, 152-153, 155, 166, 168, 176-177, 180, 191, 195-197, 201-202, 205-208, 223, 227-231, 237, 239-242, 244, 247, 249-252, 258, 267-268, 272, 274, 277-278, 280, 284-285, 289-292, 294-298, 305, 309, 312, 329, 335, 339, 344, 348, 356, 362-364, 370, 383, 386, 389, 391, 394-398, 402-404, 408, 413-416, 418-419, 422-423, 425, 428, 431, 438, 442, 446, 449-452, 455-458, 462-464, 466, 469-473, 477-481, 502-506

Index of Miscellaneous & General Terms

Antitank ditches 9, 17-18, 42, 80-81, 174, 304, 321, 325, 329, 340-341, 343, 345, 347-348, 350, 364, 407, 413, 455-456, 463, 471

Antitank gun 16, 33, 37-38, 41, 57, 86, 94, 98, 179, 207, 209, 362

Artillery v, vii, 11-19, 21, 23-24, 28-40, 43-63, 65, 69-73, 75, 77, 79, 81-87, 89-101, 103-105, 110-111, 115-116, 119-120, 124, 128, 132-134, 136, 138-140, 142-144, 148-155, 157, 160, 162-168, 171-174, 176-180, 182-183, 187-188, 190, 192-197, 202, 204-209, 212, 215, 218, 221-224, 226, 228-230, 233-235, 237, 239-240, 242, 245-248, 251-254, 256-260, 262-264, 266, 270-275, 277-284, 286-287, 289, 292, 294-299, 301-304, 306, 308-309, 313, 315-318, 320-323, 325-329, 333-335, 340-347, 352-354, 359, 365-370, 375-376, 378, 380, 386-387, 389-391, 393, 395-400, 403, 407-409, 412-416, 422-425, 428-430, 434-436, 441-444, 449-451, 455-458, 462-465, 468-475, 477-483, 486-490, 500-501, 503, 505-507

Assault guns 22, 33-34, 39, 54, 62, 79, 99, 103, 106, 138, 145, 147, 150, 176, 189, 191, 193, 195, 198, 211, 217-218, 226-227, 255-256, 311, 318, 320, 323, 383, 386, 399, 403-404, 410, 412, 424, 443-444, 462, 472-473, 477, 504

Barbed wire 9, 133, 164, 213, 278, 282-283, 303, 309, 328-329, 332, 377

Cavalier of the Order of Glory Award 62-63, 246, 313-314, 362, 372, 493

First World War 123, 302, 333, 341

Halftracks 16, 21, 34, 39, 44, 47, 49, 51, 54, 60-62, 70, 72, 78-79, 86, 91, 103, 165, 167, 180, 185-186, 191, 195, 197, 201, 203-205, 209, 226-228, 230, 233, 237-238, 240, 242, 246-248, 251-252, 256-262, 264-265, 268-269, 271, 273, 276-278, 280, 282, 284-285, 287, 289, 294-298, 312, 322, 330, 360-362, 372, 399, 415, 444-445, 457, 463, 473, 478, 481, 503, 505-506

Hero of the Soviet Union Award 56, 61, 63-65, 67, 102, 110-113, 119, 127, 160-161, 163, 183, 185-186, 206, 216, 224, 232, 250, 257, 261, 263-264, 292, 294-298, 322, 328, 347, 360-363, 367, 392, 430, 469, 477, 493, 505

Military Council 28, 61, 98, 124-125, 138, 143, 189-191, 222, 271, 279, 282, 305, 313, 319, 348, 351, 357, 363, 370, 372, 374, 399, 429, 436-437, 493, 498, 502

Minefields 234, 269, 455-456

Mortars 11-12, 16, 18, 21, 24, 30, 32-33, 37, 39-41, 43-44, 46-47, 49-51, 53, 55, 57, 59, 63, 65, 69, 71-73, 77, 81-82, 84-87, 90-91, 93-94, 98-99, 115, 120, 132, 134, 139, 149-150, 153, 168, 171, 176, 178-180, 182, 187, 192, 196-197, 208, 218, 222, 240, 242, 245, 247-248, 254, 257-258, 266-267, 270, 277-278, 281, 283, 287, 297, 301-302, 306, 316, 321-322, 328-329, 331-332, 342, 353, 387, 390-391, 397-398, 407-408, 413-416, 422-423, 428, 434-435, 441, 443, 449-450, 455-457, 462-463, 472-473, 477-481, 483-484, 487, 489

Order of Glory 1st Class Award 63, 361-362, 372

Order of Lenin Award 365, 376, 510

Order of the Patriotic War 1st Class Award 41, 208-209, 296-298

Order of the Red Banner Award 41-42, 44, 46, 61, 63, 111, 118, 121, 124-126, 186, 206-207, 296-298, 322, 363, 366, 505-506

Panzergrenadiers 13, 164, 175, 178, 184, 188, 193, 252

Self-propelled Guns 11-12, 14, 16, 18-19, 21, 24, 31-41, 43, 45-46, 48, 51, 54-59, 61, 65, 69-71, 78-79, 81, 87-89, 91-92, 99, 104-106, 110, 114-115, 117, 135, 141, 145, 147-148, 150, 152-155, 161, 164-170, 176-180, 182, 185-191, 194-197, 199, 201-207, 209-210, 217, 223-224, 226-228, 236-237, 239-241, 250, 262, 264, 273-274, 276-278, 281-282, 285, 287, 295-296, 298, 301-302, 308-309, 311-312, 314-317, 321-323, 328-329, 335-336, 338, 341-344, 346, 350, 353, 356, 358-359, 361-365, 368, 370-371, 374, 378-380, 383, 386-387, 389-390, 397-398, 407-408, 412-416, 422-424, 428-429, 435-437, 441, 445, 449-451, 455-457, 462, 465, 469-473, 475, 478-480, 482-485, 488-491, 501-504, 506